1995–96
Accredited
Institutions of
Postsecondary
Education

1995–96 Accredited Institutions of Postsecondary Education

Programs
Candidates

A directory of accredited institutions, professionally accredited programs, and candidates for accreditation

Edited by Alison Anaya
Published for the Commission on Recognition
of Postsecondary Accreditation

American Council on Education
Washington, DC

Additional copies of this directory are available from:
The Oryx Press
4041 North Central Avenue
Phoenix, AZ 85012-3397
(800) 279-6799 or (602) 265-2651

American Council on Education
One Dupont Circle, NW
Washington, DC 20036

Printed in the United States of America

printing number
1 2 3 4 5 6 7 8 9 10

This publication was prepared on an Apple Macintosh Centris 610 computer, using QuarkXPress desktop publishing software, and was printed on an Apple LaserWriter Pro laser printer.

Library of Congress Cataloging in Publication Data

The Library of Congress has cataloged this serial as follows:

Accredited institutions of postsecondary education, programs,
    candidates / published by the American Council on Education,
    Washington, DC.

    v.; 24 cm.

    Annual
    Began with issue for 1976–77.
    A directory of accredited institutions, professionally accredited programs, and candidates for accreditation.
    Description based on: 1980–81.
    Spine title: Accredited Institutions of Postsecondary Education

    ISBN 0-89774-950-2
    ISSN 0270-1715 = Accredited institutions of postsecondary education, programs, candidates.

I. Education, Higher—United States—Directories   I. American Council on Education.
II. Title: Accredited Institutions of Postsecondary Education.
    [DNLM: L901 A172]

L901.A48   378.73   81-641495
                                                                                        AACR2   MARC-S

Table of Contents

About This Directory

Accredited Institutions of Postsecondary Education is published by the American Council on Education (ACE) for the Commission on Recognition of Postsecondary Accreditation (CORPA). Previous editions of the directory have been the joint effort of ACE and the Council on Postsecondary Accreditation (COPA). However, on December 31, 1993, COPA was dissolved and a new organization, CORPA, was created as a successor structure for the non-governmental recognition of accrediting bodies. There has been an orderly transition from COPA to CORPA, and those accrediting bodies previously recognized by COPA who wished to continue recognition were approved to do so by CORPA.

Neither CORPA nor ACE is an accrediting body; the listings in the directory are supplied by the national, regional, and specialized accrediting groups that have been evalua-ted by CORPA and recognized as meeting acceptable levels of quality and performance.

The institutions and programs listed, in turn, have been evaluated by the recognized accreditors and determined by their peers to meet acceptable levels of educational quality.

Those institutions designated as "candidates for accreditation" have achieved initial recognition from the appropriate accrediting commission or association. The designation "candidate" means that an institution is progressing toward accreditation but is not assured accredited status.

Most of the data contained in each entry have been provided by the individual accrediting bodies. They, in turn, have had an opportunity to verify the listings as late in the publication process as possible.

Institutional listings are split into two primary sections: Accredited Degree Granting Institutions and Accredited Non-Degree Granting Institutions. The reason for this is to provide the user with the opportunity to more easily identify those accredited institutions that grant degrees and those that do not.

Users of the directory should note that the entries show only accredited institutions and indicate professional programs within those institutions that have sought and attained specialized accreditation. *The listings do not include all curricula offered by an institution.* Also listed are institutions having one or more accredited programs. For example, curricula in anthropology, English, physics, and many other disciplines are not listed because no recognized specialized accreditation exists for those fields. The absence of a particular discipline or course of study in these listings does not necessarily mean that it is not offered at that institution, nor that it is not a quality program if it is offered.

Also, the user is reminded that the accreditation process is ongoing and that institutions and programs are accredited (or dropped from accredited status) throughout the year. Information about the accreditation status of a specific institution or program beyond what is given should be sought directly from the appropriate accrediting body. (Addresses, names, and telephone numbers of persons to contact begin on page 685.)

Please take time to review the section on how to use this directory and interpret the listings (page ix). For further clarification regarding entries in the directory, please contact the Commission on Recognition of Postsecondary Accreditation, One Dupont Circle, NW, Suite 305, Washington, DC 20036; (202) 452-1433.

How to Use This Directory

Initial entry into the directory should be through the index, which lists more than 5,500 accredited institutions alphabetically by institutional name, as well as numerous cross references.

The main body of the directory lists institutions alphabetically by state in two sections: Accredited Degree Granting Institutions and Accredited Non-Degree Granting Institutions.

Information for the individual listings is arranged as follows (not all categories are listed for each institution):

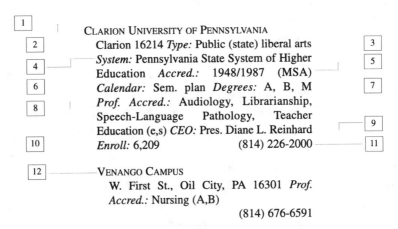

CLARION UNIVERSITY OF PENNSYLVANIA
Clarion 16214 *Type:* Public (state) liberal arts
System: Pennsylvania State System of Higher Education *Accred.:* 1948/1987 (MSA)
Calendar: Sem. plan *Degrees:* A, B, M
Prof. Accred.: Audiology, Librarianship, Speech-Language Pathology, Teacher Education (e,s) *CEO:* Pres. Diane L. Reinhard
Enroll: 6,209   (814) 226-2000

VENANGO CAMPUS
W. First St., Oil City, PA 16301 *Prof. Accred.:* Nursing (A,B)
(814) 676-6591

1. Name of the institution.

2. Address.

3. Brief description of *(a)* control (e.g., Public); *(b)* type of institution; and *(c)* type of student body (no indication means coeducational).

4. Indication of membership in a public/private system of higher educationor state coordinating board.

5. Dates of first accreditation (or of admission as a candidate) and of latest renewal or reaffirmation of this status, followed by accrediting body. (Consult the accrediting body for dates of interruption in or limitations on accreditation status.)

6. Type of academic calendar.

7. Level(s) of degrees offered.

8. Specialized accreditation by any of 36 professional accrediting agencies, including one umbrella organization representing 17 joint review committees.

9. Title and name of chief executive officer.

10. Latest enrollment figure. Figures are included to provide an indication of the relative size of the student body and indicate either the total number enrolled or full-time equivalent (FTE) calculated figures.

11. Telephone number.

12. Branch campus(es).

Abbreviations

3-3 ....academic year of three terms

4-1-4 ....academic year of two 4-month terms with a 1-month intersession

4-4-x ....academic year of two 4-month terms with one term of flexible length

A ....associate degree or equivalent

ABA ....American Bar Association

AMA ....American Medical Association

B ....bachelor's degree or equivalent

C ....certificate/diploma

D ....doctoral degree

FTE ....full-time equivalent (enrollment calculation)

M ....master's degree or equivalent

P ....first professional degree (e.g., those degrees such as J.D., M.D., or M.Div. requiring six or more years of post–high school education)

prelim. ....preliminary

Qtr. ....quarter (calendar year of four academic terms)

Sem. ....semester (calendar year of two academic terms)

Tri. ....trimester (calendar year of three 15-week terms, with students typically attending two of the three terms)

Key to Institutional Accrediting Bodies

AABC ....Accrediting Association of Bible Colleges

AARTS ....Association of Advanced Rabbinical and Talmudic Schools

ABHES ....Accrediting Bureau of Health Education Schools

ACCSCT ....Accrediting Commission for Career Schools/Colleges of Technology

ACICS ....Accrediting Council for Independent Colleges and Schools

ATS ....The Association of Theological Schools in the United States and Canada

COE ....Council on Occupational Education (formerly Southern Association of Colleges and Schools/Commission on Occupational Education Institutions (SACS/COEI)

DETC ....Distance Education and Training Council (formerly the National Home Study Council)

MSA ....Middle States Association of Colleges and Schools

NASC ....The Northwest Association of Schools and Colleges

NCA ....North Central Association of Colleges and Schools

NEASC-CIHE ....New England Association of Schools and Colleges, Inc./Commission on Institutions of Higher Education

NEASC-CTCI ....New England Association of Schools and Colleges, Inc./Commission on Technical and Career Institutions

SACS-CC ....Southern Association of Colleges and Schools/Commission on Colleges

WASC-Jr. ....Western Association of Schools and Colleges/Accrediting Commission for Community and Junior Colleges

WASC-Sr. ....Western Association of Schools and Colleges/Accrediting Commission for Senior Colleges and Universities

Key to Specialized Accrediting Bodies

Acupuncture ....National Accreditation Commission for Schools and
Colleges of Acupuncture and Oriental Medicine

Anesthesiologist Assisting ....Commission on Accreditation of Allied Health
Education Programs

Art ....National Association of Schools of Art and Design*

Athletic Training ....Commission on Accreditation of Allied Health
Education Programs

Audiology ....American Speech-Language-Hearing Association

Blood Bank Technology ....Commission on Accreditation of Allied Health
Education Programs

Cardiovascular Technology ....Commission on Accreditation of Allied Health
Education Programs

Chiropractic Education ....The Council on Chiropractic Education

Clinical Psychology ....American Psychological Association

Combined Maxillofacial
Prosthodontics ....American Dental Association

Combined Professional-Scientific
Psychology ....American Psychological Association

Combined Prosthodontics ....American Dental Association

Computer Science ....Computing Science Accreditation Board

Construction Education ....American Council for Construction Education

Counseling ....Council for Accreditation of Counseling
and Related Educational Programs

Counseling Psychology ....American Psychological Association

Cytotechnology ....Commission on Accreditation of Allied Health
Education Programs

Dance ....National Association of Schools of Dance*

Dental Assisting ....American Dental Association

Dental Hygiene ....American Dental Association

Dental Laboratory Technology ....American Dental Association

Dental Public Health ....American Dental Association

Dentistry ....American Dental Association

Diagnostic Medical Sonography ....American Medical Association

Dietetics ....The American Dietetic Association

Electroneurodiagnostic Technology ....Commission on Accreditation of Allied Health
Education Programs

EMT-Paramedic ....Commission on Accreditation of Allied Health
Education Programs

Endodontics ....American Dental Association

Engineering ....Accreditation Board for Engineering and Technology*

Engineering Technology ....Accreditation Board for Engineering and Technology*

Forestry ....Society of American Foresters

Funeral Service Education
(Mortuary Science) ....American Board of Funeral Service Education

General Dentistry ....American Dental Association

* Agency relinquished CORPA recognition, February 1996.

Key to Specialized Accrediting Bodies (continued)

General Practice Residency ....American Dental Association
Health Services Administration ....Accrediting Commission on Education for Health Services Administration
Home Economics ....American Association of Family and Consumer Sciences
Interior Design ....Foundation for Interior Design Education Research
Journalism ....Accrediting Council on Education in Journalism and Mass Communications
Landscape Architecture.........................American Society of Landscape Architects
Law ....Association of American Law Schools/ American Bar Association
Librarianship ....American Library Association
Marriage and Family Therapy ....American Association for Marriage and Family Therapy
Maxillofacial Prosthodontics ....American Dental Association
Medical Assisting..................................Accrediting Bureau of Health Education Schools
Medical Illustration...............................Commission on Accreditation of Allied Health Education Programs
Medical Laboratory Technology...........Accrediting Bureau of Health Education Schools
Medical Record Administration.............Commission on Accreditation of Allied Health Education Programs
Medical Record Technology ....Commission on Accreditation of Allied Health Education Programs
Music...National Association of Schools of Music*
Nuclear Medicine Technology...............Joint Review Committee on Educational Programs in Nuclear Medicine Technology
Nurse Anesthesia Education ....Council on Accreditation of Nurse Anesthesia Educational Programs
Nursing..National League for Nursing
Occupational Therapy............................American Occupational Therapy Association
Occupational Therapy Assisting............American Occupational Therapy Association
Ophthalmic Medical Technology...........Commission on Accreditation of Allied Health Education Programs
Optometric Residency............................American Optometric Association
Optometric Technician...........................American Optometric Association
Optometry ....American Optometric Association
Oral and Maxillofacial Surgery ....American Dental Association
Oral Pathology ....American Dental Association
Orthodontics..American Dental Association
Osteopathy ....American Osteopathic Association
Pediatric Dentistry ....American Dental Association
Perfusion ....Commission on Accreditation of Allied Health Education Programs
Periodontics...American Dental Association
Physical Therapy...................................American Physical Therapy Association
Physical Therapy Assisting...................American Physical Therapy Association
Physician Assisting ....Commission on Accreditation of Allied Health

* Agency relinquished CORPA recognition, February 1996.

Key to Specialized Accrediting Bodies (continued)

Physician Assisting ....Commission on Accreditation of Allied Health Education Programs
Planning ....Planning Accreditation Board
Podiatry...American Podiatric Medical Association
Practical Nursing....................................National League for Nursing
Psychology Internship............................American Psychological Association
Public Administration ....National Association of Schools of Public Affairs and Administration
Recreation and Leisure Services.............National Recreation and Park Association
Rehabilitation Counseling......................Council on Rehabilitation Education
Respiratory Therapy ....Commission on Accreditation of Allied Health Education Programs
Respiratory Therapy Technology...........Commission on Accreditation of Allied Health Education Programs
School Psychology..................................American Psychological Association
Social Work..Council on Social Work Education
Speech-Language Pathology...................American Speech-Language-Hearing Association
Surgeon Assisting ....Commission on Accreditation of Allied Health Education Programs
Surgical Technology ....Commission on Accreditation of Allied Health Education Programs
Teacher Education...................................National Council for Accreditation of Teacher Education
Theatre ....National Association of Schools of Theatre*
Veterinary Medicine...............................American Veterinary Medical Association
Veterinary Technology ....American Veterinary Medical Association

* Agency relinquished CORPA recognition, February 1996.

Accredited Degree Granting Institutions

ALABAMA

ALABAMA AGRICULTURAL AND MECHANICAL UNIVERSITY
4900 Meridian Ave., Normal 35762 *Type:* Public (state) liberal arts *System:* Alabama Commission on Higher Education *Accred.:* 1963/1994 (SACS-CC warning) *Calendar:* Sem. plan *Degrees:* A, B, M, D *Prof. Accred.:* Engineering Technology (civil/construction, electrical, mechanical, mechanical drafting/design), Home Economics, Planning (B,M), Social Work (B), Speech-Language Pathology, Teacher Education *CEO:* Interim Pres. Virginia Caples
FTE Enroll: 4,805   (205) 851-5000

ALABAMA AVIATION AND TECHNICAL COLLEGE
P.O. Box 1209, South Union Ave., Ozark 36361-1209 *Type:* Public (state) *System:* State of Alabama Department of Postsecondary Education *Accred.:* 1991 (SACS-CC) *Calendar:* Qtr. plan *Degrees:* A *CEO:* Pres. Shirley H. Woodie
FTE Enroll: 291   (205) 774-5113

ALABAMA SOUTHERN COMMUNITY COLLEGE
P.O. Box 2000, Monroeville 36461 *Type:* Public (state) *System:* State of Alabama Department of Postsecondary Education *Accred.:* 1992/1995 (SACS-CC) *Calendar:* Qtr. plan *Degrees:* A *CEO:* Pres. John A. Johnson
FTE Enroll: 1,595   (334) 575-3156

THOMASVILLE CAMPUS
Hwy. 43, S., Thomasville 36784
(205) 636-9642

ALABAMA STATE UNIVERSITY
915 S. Jackson St., Montgomery 36101-0271 *Type:* Public (state) liberal arts *System:* Alabama Commission on Higher Education *Accred.:* 1966/1990 (SACS-CC) *Calendar:* Sem. plan *Degrees:* A, B, M *Prof. Accred.:* Music, Social Work (B), Teacher Education *CEO:* Pres. William H. Harris
FTE Enroll: 5,221   (334) 293-4100

ATHENS STATE COLLEGE
300 N. Beaty St., Athens 35611 *Type:* Public (state) liberal arts *System:* State of Alabama Department of Postsecondary Education *Accred.:* 1955/1991 (SACS-CC) *Calendar:* Qtr. plan *Degrees:* B *CEO:* Pres. Jerry Bartlett
FTE Enroll: 2,387   (205) 233-8100

AUBURN UNIVERSITY
Auburn University 36849-5206 *Type:* Public (state) *System:* Auburn University System *Accred.:* 1922/1993 (SACS-CC) *Calendar:* Qtr. plan *Degrees:* B, M, D *Prof. Accred.:* Art, Audiology, Business (B,M), Clinical Psychology, Computer Science, Construction Education (B), Counseling, Counseling Psychology, Engineering Technology (textile), Engineering (aerospace, agricultural, chemical, civil, computer, electrical, forest, industrial, materials, mechanical), Forestry, Home Economics, Interior Design, Journalism, Landscape Architecture (B), Marriage and Family Therapy (M), Music, Nursing (B), Public Administration, Rehabilitation Counseling, Social Work (B), Speech-Language Pathology, Teacher Education, Theatre (A), Veterinary Medicine *CEO:* Pres. William V. Muse
FTE Enroll: 19,783   (334) 844-4000

AUBURN UNIVERSITY AT MONTGOMERY
7300 University Dr., Montgomery 36117-3596 *Type:* Public (state) *System:* Auburn University System *Accred.:* 1968/1988 (SACS-CC) *Calendar:* Qtr. plan *Degrees:* B, M *Prof. Accred.:* Business (B,M), Clinical Lab Scientist, Nursing (B), Public Administration, Teacher Education *CEO:* Chanc. Roy H. Saigo
FTE Enroll: 5,158   (334) 244-3000

BESSEMER STATE TECHNICAL COLLEGE
1100 9th Ave., N., Bessemer 35021 *Type:* Public (state) *System:* State of Alabama Department of Postsecondary Education *Accred.:* 1972/1992 (COE) *Calendar:* Qtr. plan *Degrees:* A *Prof. Accred.:* Dental Assisting *CEO:* Pres. W. Michael Bailey
FTE Enroll: 11,587   (205) 428-6391

BEVILL STATE COMMUNITY COLLEGE
P.O. Box 800, 101 State St., Sumiton 35148
Type: Public (state) *System:* State of
Alabama Department of Postsecondary Education *Accred.:* 1994 (SACS-CC) *Calendar:*
Qtr. plan *Degrees:* A *CEO:* Pres. Harold
Wade
FTE Enroll: 2,802   (205) 648-3271

BREWER CAMPUS
2631 Temple Ave. N., Fayette 35555
(205) 932-3221

BIRMINGHAM-SOUTHERN COLLEGE
900 Arkadelphia Rd., Birmingham 35254
Type: Private (United Methodist) liberal arts
Accred.: 1922/1994 (SACS-CC) *Calendar:* 4-
1-4 plan *Degrees:* B, M *Prof. Accred.:* Music,
Teacher Education *CEO:* Pres. Neal R. Berte
FTE Enroll: 1,673   (205) 226-4600

BISHOP STATE COMMUNITY COLLEGE
351 N. Broad St., Mobile 36603-5898 *Type:*
Public (state) *System:* State of Alabama
Department of Postsecondary Education
Accred.: 1992/1994 (SACS-CC) *Calendar:*
Qtr. plan *Degrees:* A *Prof. Accred.:* Funeral
Service Education (Mortuary Science), Medical Record Technology, Nursing (A), Physical Therapy Assisting *CEO:* Pres. Yvonne
Kennedy
FTE Enroll: 4,640   (334) 690-6416

BRANCH CAMPUS
414 Stanton St., Mobile 36617
(205) 473-8692

SOUTHWEST CAMPUS
925 Dauphin Island Pkwy., Mobile 36605-
3299
(205) 479-7476

CENTRAL ALABAMA COMMUNITY COLLEGE
908 Cherokee Rd., P.O. Box 699, Alexander
City 35010 *Type:* Public (state) *System:* State
of Alabama Department of Postsecondary
Education *Accred.:* 1969/1994 (SACS-CC)
Calendar: Qtr. plan *Degrees:* A *CEO:* Pres.
James H. Cornell
FTE Enroll: 1,755   (205) 234-6346

CHATTAHOOCHEE VALLEY STATE COMMUNITY
COLLEGE
2602 College Dr., Phenix City 36869 *Type:*
Public (state) *System:* State of Alabama
Department of Postsecondary Education
Accred.: 1976/1992 (SACS-CC) *Calendar:*
Qtr. plan *Degrees:* A *Prof. Accred.:* Nursing
(A) *CEO:* Pres. Richard J. Federinko
FTE Enroll: 1,723   (205) 291-4900

CHAUNCEY SPARKS STATE TECHNICAL COLLEGE
Hwy. 431, S., P.O. Drawer 580, Eufaula
36072-0580 *Type:* Public (state) *System:*
State of Alabama Department of Postsecondary Education *Accred.:* 1973/1993
(COE) *Calendar:* Qtr. plan *Degrees:* A *CEO:*
Pres. Linda C. Young
FTE Enroll: 518   (205) 687-3543

COMMUNITY COLLEGE OF THE AIR FORCE
130 W. Maxwell Blvd., Maxwell Air Force
Base 36112-6613 *Type:* Public (federal) technical *Accred.:* 1980/1986 (SACS-CC warning) *Degrees:* A *CEO:* Pres. Paul A. Reid
FTE Enroll: 42,675   (334) 953-7848

SCHOOL OF HEALTH SCIENCES CAMPUS
3790th MSTG, Sheppard Air Force Base,
TX 76311 *Prof. Accred.:* Clinical Lab
Technology (C), Physical Therapy Assisting, Physician Assisting/Surgeon Assisting, Radiography, Surgical Technology
(817) 676-2700

CONCORDIA COLLEGE
1804 Green St., P.O. Box 1329, Selma 36701
Type: Private (Lutheran) *Accred.:* 1983/1989
(SACS-CC) *Calendar:* Sem. plan *Degrees:*
A, B *CEO:* Pres. Julius Jenkins
FTE Enroll: 348   (205) 874-5700

DOUGLAS MACARTHUR STATE TECHNICAL
COLLEGE
Hwy. 331 N., P.O. Box 649, Opp 36467 *Type:*
Public (state) *System:* State of Alabama
Department of Postsecondary Education
Accred.: 1972/1992 (COE) *Calendar:* Qtr.
plan *Degrees:* A *CEO:* Pres. Raymond V.
Chisum
FTE Enroll: 544   (205) 493-3573

DRAUGHONS JUNIOR COLLEGE
122 Commerce St., Montgomery 36104
Type: Private Junior *Accred.:* 1954/1991
(ACICS) *Calendar:* Qtr. plan *Degrees:* A
Prof. Accred.: Medical Assisting (AMA)
CEO: Pres. Victor K. Biebighauser
(334) 263-1013

ENTERPRISE STATE JUNIOR COLLEGE
600 Plaza Dr., P.O. Box 1300, Enterprise
36331 *Type:* Public (state) *System:* State of
Alabama Department of Postsecondary Education *Accred.:* 1969/1994 (SACS-CC) *Calendar:* Qtr. plan *Degrees:* A *CEO:* Interim
Pres. Stafford L. Thompson
FTE Enroll: 1,492   (334) 347-2623

FAULKNER UNIVERSITY
5345 Atlanta Hwy., Montgomery 36109-
3378 *Type:* Private (Church of Christ) liberal
arts *Accred.:* 1971/1990 (SACS-CC) *Calendar:* Sem. plan *Degrees:* A, B, D *CEO:* Pres.
Billy D. Hilyer
FTE Enroll: 2,090   (205) 272-5820

GADSDEN STATE COMMUNITY COLLEGE
P.O. Box 227, Gadsden 35902-0227 *Type:*
Public (state) *System:* State of Alabama
Department of Postsecondary Education
Accred.: 1968/1992 (SACS-CC) *Calendar:*
Qtr. plan *Degrees:* A *Prof. Accred.:* Clinical
Lab Technology (A), EMT-Paramedic, Nurs-
ing (A), Radiography *CEO:* Pres. Victor B.
Ficker
FTE Enroll: 4,847   (205) 549-8200

GEORGE C. WALLACE STATE COMMUNITY
COLLEGE
Rte. 6, Box 62, Dothan 36303-9234 *Type:*
Public (state) *System:* State of Alabama
Department of Postsecondary Education
Accred.: 1969/1994 (SACS-CC) *Calendar:*
Qtr. plan *Degrees:* A *Prof. Accred.:* Clinical
Lab Technology (A), Diagnostic Medical
Sonography, EMT-Paramedic, Medical
Assisting (AMA), Medical Record Technol-
ogy, Nursing (A) Respiratory Therapy *CEO:*
Pres. Larry Beaty
FTE Enroll: 2,881   (334) 983-3521

GEORGE CORLEY WALLACE STATE COMMUNITY
COLLEGE
P.O. Drawer 1049, 3000 Range Line Rd.,
Selma 36702-1049 *Type:* Public (state) *Sys-
tem:* State of Alabama Department of Post-
secondary Education *Accred.:* 1974/1989
(SACS-CC) *Calendar:* Qtr. plan *Degrees:* A
Prof. Accred.: Nursing (A), Practical Nursing
CEO: Pres. Julius R. Brown
FTE Enroll: 1,599   (334) 875-2634

HARRY M. AYERS STATE TECHNICAL COLLEGE
1801 Coleman Rd., P.O. Box 1647, Anniston
36202-1647 *Type:* Public (state) *System:*
State of Alabama Department of Postsec-
ondary Education *Accred.:* 1972/1993
(COE) *Calendar:* Qtr. plan *Degrees:* A *CEO:*
Interim Pres. Don Jarrells
FTE Enroll: 371   (205) 835-5400

HERZING INSTITUTE
1218 S. 20th St., Birmingham 35205-3852
Type: Private *Accred.:* 1971/1993 (ACCSCT)
Degrees: A, C *CEO:* Dir. Donald Lewis
(205) 933-8536

HUNTINGDON COLLEGE
1500 E. Fairview Ave., Montgomery 36106-
2148 *Type:* Private (United Methodist) liberal
arts *Accred.:* 1928/1990 (SACS-CC) *Calendar:* Sem. plan *Degrees:* A, B *Prof. Accred.:*
Music *CEO:* Pres. Wanda D. Bigham
FTE Enroll: 681   (334) 265-0511

INGRAM STATE COMMUNITY COLLEGE
P.O. Box 209, 5375 Ingram Rd., Deatsville
36022 *Type:* Public (state) *System:* State of
Alabama Department of Postsecondary Edu-
cation *Accred.:* 1977/1992 (COE) *Calendar:*
Qtr. plan *Degrees:* A *CEO:* Interim Pres.
James Selman
FTE Enroll: 1,075   (334) 285-5177

INTERNATIONAL BIBLE COLLEGE
3625 Helton Dr., P.O. Box IBC, Florence
35630-6235 *Type:* Private (Churches of
Christ) *Accred.:* 1988/1994 (AABC) *Calendar:* Sem. plan *Degrees:* A, B *CEO:* Pres.
Dennis Jones
FTE Enroll: 87   (205) 766-6610

JACKSONVILLE STATE UNIVERSITY
700 N. Pelham Rd., Jacksonville 36265-9982 *Type:* Public (state) *System:* Alabama Commission on Higher Education *Accred.:* 1935/1993 (SACS-CC) *Calendar:* Sem. plan *Degrees:* B, M *Prof. Accred.:* Art (A), Music, Nursing (B), Social Work (B), Teacher Education, Theatre (A) *CEO:* Pres. Harold J. McGee
FTE Enroll: 6,089   (205) 782-5781

JAMES H. FAULKNER STATE COMMUNITY COLLEGE
1900 Hwy. 31 S., Bay Minette 36507 *Type:* Public (state) *System:* State of Alabama Department of Postsecondary Education *Accred.:* 1970/1995 (SACS-CC) *Calendar:* Qtr. plan *Degrees:* A *Prof. Accred.:* Dental Assisting *CEO:* Pres. Gary L. Branch
FTE Enroll: 3,418   (334) 580-2100

JEFFERSON DAVIS COMMUNITY COLLEGE
220 Alco Dr., Brewton 36426 *Type:* Public (state) *System:* State of Alabama Department of Postsecondary Education *Accred.:* 1978/1988 (COE); 1994 (SACS-CC) *Calendar:* Qtr. plan *Degrees:* A *Prof. Accred.:* Nursing (A) *CEO:* Pres. Sandra K. McLeod
FTE Enroll: 1,630   (334) 867-4832

JEFFERSON STATE COMMUNITY COLLEGE
2601 Carson Rd., Birmingham 35215-3098 *Type:* Public (state) *System:* State of Alabama Department of Postsecondary Education *Accred.:* 1968/1993 (SACS-CC) *Calendar:* Qtr. plan *Degrees:* A *Prof. Accred.:* Clinical Lab Technology (A), Engineering Technology (electrical), Funeral Service Education (Mortuary Science), Nursing (A), Radiography *CEO:* Pres. Judy M. Merritt
FTE Enroll: 4,883   (205) 856-1200

J.F. DRAKE STATE TECHNICAL COLLEGE
3421 Meridian St., N., Huntsville 35811 *Type:* Public (state) *System:* State of Alabama Department of Postsecondary Education *Accred.:* 1971/1991 (COE) *Calendar:* Qtr. plan *Degrees:* A *CEO:* Pres. Johnny L. Harris
FTE Enroll: 576   (205) 539-8161

JOHN C. CALHOUN STATE COMMUNITY COLLEGE
P.O. Box 2216, Decatur 35609-2216 *Type:* Public (state) *System:* State of Alabama Department of Postsecondary Education *Accred.:* 1968/1992 (SACS-CC) *Calendar:* Qtr. plan *Degrees:* A *Prof. Accred.:* Dental Assisting, Nursing (A), Practical Nursing *CEO:* Pres. Richard G. Carpenter
FTE Enroll: 6,134   (205) 306-2500

JOHN M. PATTERSON STATE TECHNICAL COLLEGE
3920 Troy Hwy., Montgomery 36116-2699 *Type:* Public (state) *System:* State of Alabama Department of Postsecondary Education *Accred.:* 1972/1993 (COE) *Calendar:* Qtr. plan *Degrees:* A *CEO:* Pres. J. Larry Taunton
FTE Enroll: 670   (205) 288-1080

JUDSON COLLEGE
P.O. Box 120, Marion 36756 *Type:* Private (Southern Baptist) liberal arts for women *Accred.:* 1925/1994 (SACS-CC) *Calendar:* Sem. plan *Degrees:* B *Prof. Accred.:* Music *CEO:* Pres. David E. Potts
FTE Enroll: 295   (205) 683-5100

LAWSON STATE COMMUNITY COLLEGE
3060 Wilson Rd., S.W., Birmingham 35221 *Type:* Public (state) *System:* State of Alabama Department of Postsecondary Education *Accred.:* 1968/1992 (SACS-CC) *Calendar:* Qtr. plan *Degrees:* A *Prof. Accred.:* Nursing (A) *CEO:* Pres. Perry W. Ward
FTE Enroll: 1,878   (205) 929-2515

LURLEEN B. WALLACE STATE JUNIOR COLLEGE
P.O. Drawer 1418, Andalusia 36420 *Type:* Public (state) *System:* State of Alabama Department of Postsecondary Education *Accred.:* 1972/1987 (SACS-CC) *Calendar:* Qtr. plan *Degrees:* A *CEO:* Pres. Seth Hammett
FTE Enroll: 996   (334) 222-6591

MARION MILITARY INSTITUTE
1101 Washington St., Marion 36756 *Type:* Private junior for men *Accred.:* 1926/1994 (SACS-CC) *Calendar:* Sem. plan *Degrees:* A *CEO:* Pres./CEO W. Thomas Adams
FTE Enroll: 217   (205) 683-2303

MILES COLLEGE
P.O. Box 3800, Birmingham 35208 *Type:* Private (Christian Methodist Episcopal) liberal arts *Accred.:* 1969/1993 (SACS-CC) *Calendar:* Sem. plan *Degrees:* A, B *CEO:* Pres. Albert J.H. Sloan, II
FTE Enroll: 1,043   (205) 923-2771

NORTHEAST ALABAMA STATE COMMUNITY COLLEGE
P.O. Box 159, Hwy. 35, Rainsville 35986 *Type:* Public (state) *System:* State of Alabama Department of Postsecondary Education *Accred.:* 1969/1994 (SACS-CC) *Calendar:* Qtr. plan *Degrees:* A *Prof. Accred.:* Nursing (A) *CEO:* Pres. Charles M. Pendley
FTE Enroll: 1,447   (205) 228-6001

NORTHWEST SHOALS COMMUNITY COLLEGE
P.O. Box 2545, George Wallace Blvd., Muscle Shoals 35662 *Type:* Public (state) *System:* State of Alabama Department of Postsecondary Education *Accred.:* 1994 (SACS-CC) *Calendar:* Qtr. plan *Degrees:* A *Prof. Accred.:* Nursing (A), Practical Nursing *CEO:* Pres. Larry McCoy
FTE Enroll: 2,534   (205) 331-5200

OAKWOOD COLLEGE
Oakwood Rd., N.W., Huntsville 35896 *Type:* Private (Seventh-Day Adventist) liberal arts *Accred.:* 1958/1991 (SACS-CC) *Calendar:* Qtr. plan *Degrees:* A, B *Prof. Accred.:* Social Work (B), Teacher Education *CEO:* Pres. Benjamin F. Reaves
FTE Enroll: 1,392   (205) 726-7000

REID STATE TECHNICAL COLLEGE
I-65 at Hwy. 83, P.O. Box 588, Evergreen 36401 *Type:* Public (state) *System:* State of Alabama Department of Postsecondary Education *Accred.:* 1972/1994 (COE) *Calendar:* Qtr. plan *Degrees:* A *CEO:* Pres. Ullysses McBride
FTE Enroll: 518   (205) 578-1313

SAMFORD UNIVERSITY
800 Lakeshore Dr., Birmingham 35229 *Type:* Private (Southern Baptist) *Accred.:* 1994 (ATS candidate); 1920/1986 (SACS-CC) *Calendar:* 4-1-4 plan *Degrees:* A, B, M, D *Prof. Accred.:* Law, Music, Nursing (A,B),

Teacher Education *CEO:* Pres. Thomas E. Corts
FTE Enroll: 4,443   (205) 870-22800

SELMA UNIVERSITY
1501 Lapsley St., Selma 36701 *Type:* Private (Baptist) liberal arts and teachers *Accred.:* 1991 (SACS-CC probational) *Calendar:* Sem. plan *Degrees:* A, B *CEO:* Pres. Willie L. Muse
FTE Enroll: 200   (334) 872-2533

SHELTON STATE COMMUNITY COLLEGE
202 Skyland Blvd., Tuscaloosa 35405 *Type:* Public (state) *System:* State of Alabama Department of Postsecondary Education *Accred.:* 1973/1988 (COE); 1994 (SACS-CC) *Calendar:* Sem. plan *Degrees:* A *Prof. Accred.:* EMT-Paramedic, Nursing (A) *CEO:* Pres. Thomas E. Umphrey
FTE Enroll: 6,123   (205) 759-1541

SNEAD STATE COMMUNITY COLLEGE
P.O. Drawer D, 220 N. Walnut Street, Boaz 35957 *Type:* Public (state) *System:* State of Alabama Department of Postsecondary Education *Accred.:* 1941/1993 (SACS-CC) *Calendar:* Qtr. plan *Degrees:* A *Prof. Accred.:* Veterinary Technology *CEO:* Pres. William H. Osborn
FTE Enroll: 1,451   (205) 593-5120

SOUTHEAST COLLEGE OF TECHNOLOGY
828 Downtowner Loop W., Mobile 36609-5404 *Type:* Private *Accred.:* 1986 (ACC-SCT) *Degrees:* A, B *CEO:* Pres. Mike Lanouette
                                       (205) 343-8200

SOUTHEASTERN BIBLE COLLEGE
3001 Hwy. 280 E., Birmingham 35094 *Type:* Private (nondenominational) *Accred.:* 1962/1994 (AABC) *Calendar:* Sem. plan *Degrees:* A, B *CEO:* Pres. John Talley, Jr.
FTE Enroll: 134   (205) 970-9200

SOUTHERN CHRISTIAN UNIVERSITY
1200 Taylor Rd., Montgomery 36124-0240 *Type:* Private professional *Accred.:* 1989/1994 (SACS-CC) *Calendar:* Qtr. plan *Degrees:* B, M, D *CEO:* Pres. Rex A. Turner, Jr.
FTE Enroll: 60   (334) 277-2277

SOUTHERN UNION STATE COMMUNITY COLLEGE
P.O. Box 1000, Roberts Street, Wadley
36276 *Type:* Public (state) *System:* State of
Alabama Department of Postsecondary Edu-
cation *Accred.:* 1971/1992 (COE); 1994
(SACS-CC) *Calendar:* Qtr. plan *Degrees:* A
Prof. Accred.: Nursing (A), Radiography
CEO: Pres. Roy W. Johnson
FTE Enroll: 3,813   (205) 395-2211

SPRING HILL COLLEGE
4000 Dauphin St., Mobile 36608-1791 *Type:*
Private (Roman Catholic) liberal arts
Accred.: 1922/1985 (SACS-CC) *Calendar:*
Sem. plan *Degrees:* B, M *CEO:* Pres.
William J. Rewak, S.J.
FTE Enroll: 1,094   (334) 380-4000

STILLMAN COLLEGE
P.O. Drawer 1430, Tuscaloosa 35403 *Type:*
Private (Presbyterian) liberal arts *Accred.:*
1953/1990 (SACS-CC) *Calendar:* Sem. plan
Degrees: B *CEO:* Pres. Cordell Wynn
FTE Enroll: 945   (205) 349-4240

TALLADEGA COLLEGE
627 W. Battle St., Talladega 35160 *Type:* Private liberal arts (Church of christ) *Accred.:*
1931/1989 (SACS-CC) *Calendar:* Sem. plan
Degrees: B *Prof. Accred.:* Social Work (B)
CEO: Pres. Joseph B. Johnson
FTE Enroll: 928   (205) 362-0206

TRENHOLM STATE TECHNICAL COLLEGE
1225 Air Base Blvd., P.O. Box 9039, Mont-
gomery 36108 *Type:* Public (state) *System:*
State of Alabama Department of Postsec-
ondary Education *Accred.:* 1972/1994
(COE) *Calendar:* Qtr. plan *Degrees:* A *Prof.
Accred.:* Dental Assisting, Dental Labora-
tory Technology, EMT-Paramedic, Medical
Assisting (AMA), Practical Nursing *CEO:*
Interim Pres. Leroy Bell, Jr.
FTE Enroll: 2,909   (205) 832-9000

TROY STATE UNIVERSITY
University Ave., Troy 36082 *Type:* Public
(state) liberal arts and teachers *System:* Troy
State University System *Accred.:* 1934/1994
(SACS-CC) *Calendar:* Qtr. plan *Degrees:* A,
B, M *Prof. Accred.:* Nursing (A,B,M), Social

Work (B), Teacher Education *CEO:* Chanc.
Jack Hawkins, Jr.
FTE Enroll: 9,199   (334) 670-3200

TROY STATE UNIVERSITY AT DOTHAN
P.O. Box 8368, 3601 U.S. Hwy. 231 N.,
Dothan 36304-0368 *Type:* Public (state) lib-
eral arts and teachers *System:* Troy State
University System *Accred.:* 1985/1990
(SACS-CC) *Calendar:* Qtr. plan *Degrees:* A,
B, M *Prof. Accred.:* Teacher Education
CEO: Interim Pres. Doug Patterson
FTE Enroll: 1,784   (334) 983-6556

TROY STATE UNIVERSITY IN MONTGOMERY
231 Montgomery St., P.O. Drawer 4419,
Montgomery 36103-4419 *Type:* Public
(state) liberal arts and teachers *System:* Troy
State University System *Accred.:* 1983/1989
(SACS-CC) *Calendar:* Qtr. plan *Degrees:* A,
B, M *CEO:* Pres. Glenda S. McGaha-Curry
FTE Enroll: 2,383   (334) 834-1400

TUSKEGEE UNIVERSITY
Tuskegee 36088 *Type:* Private *Accred.:*
1933/1988 (SACS-CC) *Calendar:* Sem. plan
Degrees: B, M, D *Prof. Accred.:* Clinical
Lab Scientist, Engineering (aerospace,
chemical, electrical, mechanical), Nursing
(B), Occupational Therapy, Social Work (B),
Teacher Education, Veterinary Medicine
CEO: Pres. Benjamin F. Payton
FTE Enroll: 3,147   (334) 727-8011

UNITED STATES SPORTS ACADEMY
One Academy Dr., Daphne 36526 *Type:* Pri-
vate professional *Accred.:* 1983/1988
(SACS-CC) *Calendar:* Qtr. plan *Degrees:*
M, D (candidate) *CEO:* Pres. Thomas P.
Rosandich
FTE Enroll: 213   (334) 626-3303

THE UNIVERSITY OF ALABAMA
P.O. Box 870166, Tuscaloosa 35487-0166
Type: Public (state) *System:* University of
Alabama System *Accred.:* 1897/1994
(SACS-CC) *Calendar:* Sem. plan *Degrees:*
B, M, D *Prof. Accred.:* Accounting (A,C),
Art, Audiology, Business (B,M), Clinical
Psychology, Computer Science, Counseling,
Dietetics (coordinated), Engineering (aero-
space, chemical, civil, electrical, industrial,

mechanical, metallurgical, mineral), Home Economics, Interior Design, Journalism (B,M), Law, Librarianship, Music, Nursing (B), Rehabilitation Counseling, Social Work (B,M) Teacher Education *CEO:* Pres. E. Roger Sayers
FTE Enroll: 16,963   (205) 348-6300

THE UNIVERSITY OF ALABAMA AT BIRMINGHAM
701 S. 20th St., Birmingham 35294-0111 *Type:* Public (state) *System:* University of Alabama System *Accred.:* 1970/1994 (SACS-CC) *Calendar:* Qtr. plan *Degrees:* B, M, D *Prof. Accred.:* Accounting (A,C), Art (A), Business (B,M), Clinical Lab Scientist, Clinical Lab Technology (A), Clinical Psychology, Combined Prosthodontics, Cytotechnology, Dental Assisting, Dental Hygiene, Dental Public Health, Dentistry, Dietetics (internship), EMT-Paramedic, Endodontics, Engineering Technology (industrial hygiene), Engineering (civil, electrical, materials, mechanical), General Dentistry, General Practice Residency, Health Services Administration, Maxillofacial Prosthodontics, Medical Record Administration, Medical Record Technology, Medicine, Music (A), Nuclear Medicine Technology, Nurse Anesthesia Education (M), Nursing (B,M), Occupational Therapy, Optometric Residency, Optometry, Oral Pathology, Oral and Maxillofacial Surgery, Orthodontics, Pediatric Dentistry, Periodontics, Physical Therapy, Psychology Internship, Public Administration, Radiation Therapy Technology, Radiography, Rehabilitation Counseling, Respiratory Therapy, Social Work (B), Teacher Education, *CEO:* Pres. J. Claude Bennett
FTE Enroll: 12,887   (205) 934-4011

UNIVERSITY OF ALABAMA BIRMINGHAM—
WALKER COLLEGE
1411 Indiana Ave., Jasper 35501 *Type:* Public *Accred.:* 1959/1990 (SACS-CC) *Calendar:* Sem. plan *Degrees:* A *Prof. Accred.:* Nursing (A) *CEO:* Interim Pres. David Rowland
FTE Enroll: 872   (205) 387-0511

THE UNIVERSITY OF ALABAMA IN HUNTSVILLE
301 Sparkman Dr., Huntsville 35899 *Type:* Public (state) *System:* University of Alabama System *Accred.:* 1970/1995 (SACS-CC) *Calendar:* Sem. plan *Degrees:* B, M, D *Prof. Accred.:* Business (B,M), Computer Science, EMT-Paramedic, Engineering (chemical, civil, computer, electrical, industrial, mechanical), Music (A), Nursing (B,M) *CEO:* Pres. Frank A. Franz
FTE Enroll: 4,696   (205) 895-6120

UNIVERSITY OF MOBILE
P.O. Box 13220, Mobile 36663-0220 *Type:* Private (Southern Baptist) liberal arts *Accred.:* 1968/1993 (SACS-CC) *Calendar:* Sem. plan *Degrees:* A, B, M *Prof. Accred.:* Music, Nursing (A,B) *CEO:* Pres. Michael A. Magnoli, Jr.
FTE Enroll: 1,865   (334) 675-5990

UNIVERSITY OF MONTEVALLO
Sta. 6001, Montevallo 35115-6001 *Type:* Public (state) liberal arts and professional *System:* Alabama Commission on Higher Education *Accred.:* 1925/1990 (SACS-CC) *Calendar:* Sem. plan *Degrees:* B, M *Prof. Accred.:* Art, Audiology, Business (B), Home Economics, Music, Social Work (B), Speech-Language Pathology, Teacher Education *CEO:* Pres. Robert M. McChesney
FTE Enroll: 3,053   (205) 665-6000

UNIVERSITY OF NORTH ALABAMA
601 N. Pine St., Florence 35632-0001 *Type:* Public (state) liberal arts and teachers *System:* Alabama Commission on Higher Education *Accred.:* 1934/1992 (SACS-CC) *Calendar:* Sem. plan *Degrees:* B, M *Prof. Accred.:* Art, Music, Nursing (B), Social Work (B), Teacher Education *CEO:* Pres. Robert L. Potts
FTE Enroll: 4,560   (205) 760-4100

UNIVERSITY OF SOUTH ALABAMA
307 University Blvd., Mobile 36688 *Type:* Public (state) liberal arts *System:* Alabama Commission on Higher Education *Accred.:* 1968/1993 (SACS-CC) *Calendar:* Qtr. plan *Degrees:* B, M, D *Prof. Accred.:* Audiology, Business (B,M), Clinical Lab Scientist,

Computer Science, EMT-Paramedic, Engineering (chemical, civil, electrical, mechanical), Medicine, Music, Nursing (B,M), Occupational Therapy, Physical Therapy, Radiography, Respiratory Therapy, Speech-Language Pathology, Teacher Education *CEO:* Pres. Frederick P. Whiddon
FTE Enroll: 10,791   (334) 460-6101

THE UNIVERSITY OF WEST ALABAMA
Station 4, Livingston 35470 *Type:* Public (state) liberal arts *System:* Alabama Commission on Higher Education *Accred.:* 1938/1992 (SACS-CC) *Calendar:* Qtr. plan *Degrees:* A, B, M *Prof. Accred.:* Nursing (A) *CEO:* Pres. Donald C. Hines
FTE Enroll: 1,985   (205) 652-3400

VIRGINIA COLLEGE
1900 28th Ave. S., Birmingham 35209 *Type:* Private junior *Accred.:* 1993 (ACICS) *Degrees:* A *CEO:* Pres. Kenneth C. Horne
                          (205) 802-1200

HUNTSVILLE CAMPUS
2800-A Bob Wallace Ave., Huntsville 35805 *Accred.:* 1993 (ACICS)
                          (205) 533-7387

SALEM CAMPUS
2163 Apperson Dr., Salem, VA 24153-7235 junior *Accred.:* 1990 (ACICS) *Calendar:* Qtr. plan
                          (540) 776-0755

WALLACE STATE COMMUNITY COLLEGE
801 Main St., N.W., P.O. Box 2000, Hanceville 35077-2000 *Type:* Public (state) *System:* State of Alabama Department of Postsecondary Education *Accred.:* 1978/1994 (SACS-CC) *Calendar:* Qtr. plan *Degrees:* A *Prof. Accred.:* Clinical Lab Technology (A), Dental Assisting, Diagnostic Medical Sonography, EMT-Paramedic, Medical Record Technology, Nursing (A), Occupational Therapy Assisting, Physical Therapy Assisting, Radiography, Respiratory Therapy *CEO:* Pres. James C. Bailey
FTE Enroll: 5,738   (205) 352-8000

ALASKA

ALASKA BIBLE COLLEGE
College Rd., Box 289, Glennallen 99588
Type: Private *Accred.:* 1982/1992 (AABC)
Calendar: Sem. plan *Degrees:* A, B, C *CEO:*
Pres. Gary J. Ridley, Sr.
FTE Enroll: 23 (907) 822-3201

ALASKA PACIFIC UNIVERSITY
4101 University Dr., Anchorage 99508-4672
Type: Private (Methodist) *Accred.:* 1981/1991
(NASC) *Calendar:* Tri. plan *Degrees:* A, B,
M *CEO:* Pres. Douglas M. North
Enroll: 1,546 (907) 564-8248

CHARTER COLLEGE
Ste. 120, 2221 E. Northern Lights Blvd.,
Anchorage 99508 *Type:* Private business
Accred.: 1988 (ACICS) *Degrees:* A, C *CEO:*
Pres. Milton Byrd
(907) 227-1000

PRINCE WILLIAM SOUND COMMUNITY COLLEGE
P.O. Box 97, Valdez 99686 *Type:* Public junior
System: University of Alaska System *Accred.:*
1989/1994 (NASC) *Calendar:* Sem. plan
Degrees: A *CEO:* Pres. Jo Ann C. McDowell
Enroll: 1,398 (907) 835-2421

SHELDON JACKSON COLLEGE
801 Lincoln, Sitka 99835 *Type:* Private (United Presbyterian) liberal arts *Accred.:*
1966/1994 (NASC) *Calendar:* 4-1-4 plan
Degrees: A, B *CEO:* Interim Pres. Kenneth
Cameron
Enroll: 269 (907) 747-5222

UNIVERSITY OF ALASKA ANCHORAGE
3211 Providence Dr., Anchorage 99508
Type: Public (state) *System:* University of
Alaska System *Accred.:* 1974/1995 (NASC)
Calendar: Sem. plan *Degrees:* A, B, M *Prof.
Accred.:* Art, Clinical Lab Technology (A),
Dental Assisting, Dental Hygiene (conditional), Engineering (civil), Journalism (B),
Medical Assisting (AMA), Nursing
(A,B,M), Social Work (B) *CEO:* Chanc.
Edward Lee Gorsuch
Enroll: 18,100 (907) 786-1437

KENAI PENINSULA COLLEGE
34820 College Dr., Soldotna 99669
(907) 262-5801

KODIAK COLLEGE
Kodiak 99615
(907) 486-4161

MATANUSKA-SUSITNA COLLEGE
Box 2889, Palmer 99645
(907) 745-9774

UNIVERSITY OF ALASKA FAIRBANKS
320 Signers' Hall, Fairbanks 99775 *Type:*
Public (state) *System:* University of Alaska
System *Accred.:* 1934/1995 (NASC) *Calendar:* Sem. plan *Degrees:* A, B, M, D *Prof.
Accred.:* Accounting (A), Business (B,M),
Computer Science, Engineering (civil, electrical, geological/geophysical, mechanical,
mining), Journalism (B), Music, Social Work
(B), Teacher Education *CEO:* Chanc. Joan
K. Wadlow
Enroll: 9,277 (907) 474-7112

CHUKCHI CAMPUS
P.O. Box 297, Kotzebue 99752
(907) 442-3400

KUSKOKWIM CAMPUS
Bethel 99559
(907) 543-4502

NORTHWEST CAMPUS
Pouch 400, Nome 99762
(907) 443-2201

UNIVERSITY OF ALASKA SOUTHEAST
11120 Glacier Hwy., Juneau 99801 *Type:*
Public (state) *System:* University of Alaska
System *Accred.:* 1983/1994 (NASC) *Calendar:* Sem. plan *Degrees:* A, B, M *CEO:*
Chanc. Marshall L. Lind
Enroll: 5,177 (907) 465-6509

KETCHIKAN CAMPUS
Ketchikan 99901
(907) 225-6177

SITKA CAMPUS
1332 Seward Ave., Sitka 99835
(907) 747-6653

AMERICAN SAMOA

AMERICAN SAMOA COMMUNITY COLLEGE
P.O. Box 2609, Pago Pago 96799 *Type:* Public (territorial) junior *Accred.:* 1976/1991 (WASC-Jr. probational) *Calendar:* Sem. plan *Degrees:* A *CEO:* Pres. Failautusi Avegalio *Enroll:* 1,235   (684) 699-9155

ARIZONA

ACADEMY OF BUSINESS COLLEGE
3320 W. Cheryl Dr., Ste. 115, Phoenix 85051-9576 *Type:* Private business *Accred.:* 1985/1996 (ACICS); 1993 (NCA candidate) *Degrees:* A, C *CEO:* Pres. Toby D. Jalowsky *Enroll:* 266   (602) 942-4141

AL COLLINS GRAPHIC DESIGN SCHOOL
1140 S. Priest Dr., Tempe 85281-5206 *Type:* Private *Accred.:* 1981/1987 (ACCSCT) *Calendar:* Qtr. plan *Degrees:* A, B *CEO:* Pres. Terrell Harrison
                                      (602) 966-3000

AMERICAN GRADUATE SCHOOL OF
INTERNATIONAL MANAGEMENT
15249 N. 59th Ave., Glendale 85306 *Type:* Private professional; graduate only *Accred.:* 1969/1996 (NCA) *Calendar:* Sem. plan *Degrees:* M *Prof. Accred.:* Business (M) *CEO:* Pres. Roy A. Herberger, Jr.
Enroll: 1,264   (602) 978-7250

AMERICAN INDIAN COLLEGE OF THE
ASSEMBLIES OF GOD
10020 N. 15th Ave., Phoenix 85021 *Type:* Private (Assemblies of God) *Accred.:* 1988/1993 (NCA) *Calendar:* Sem. plan *Degrees:* A, B *CEO:* Pres. W. Duane Collins *Enroll:* 116   (602) 944-3335

AMERICAN INSTITUTE
3443 N. Central Ave., Ste. 1800, Phoenix 85012 *Type:* Private business *Accred.:* 1981/1999 (ACICS) *Calendar:* Sem. plan *Degrees:* A, C *CEO:* Dir. Ann F. Kennedy
                                      (602) 252-4986

APOLLO COLLEGE—PHOENIX, INC.
8503 N. 27th Ave., Phoenix 85051 *Type:* Private *Accred.:* 1978/1992 (ABHES) *Degrees:* A, C *Prof. Accred.:* Medical Assisting, Occupational Therapy Assisting, Respiratory Therapy, Respiratory Therapy Technology *CEO:* Dir. Tom Sawyer
                                      (602) 864-1571

APOLLO COLLEGE—TRI-CITY, INC.
630 W. Southern Ave., Mesa 85210-5004 *Type:* Private *Accred.:* 1980/1992 (ABHES)

Degrees: A, C *Prof. Accred.:* Medical Assisting *CEO:* Dir. Robert Clements
                                      (602) 831-6585

APOLLO COLLEGE—TUCSON, INC.
3870 N. Oracle Rd., Tucson 85705-3227 *Type:* Private *Accred.:* 1987/1992 (ABHES) *Degrees:* A, C *Prof. Accred.:* Medical Assisting *CEO:* Dir. Elaine Cue
                                      (602) 888-5885

ARIZONA COLLEGE OF THE BIBLE
2045 W. Northern Ave., Phoenix 85021-5157 *Type:* Private (nondenominational) *Accred.:* 1981/1991 (AABC) *Calendar:* Sem. plan *Degrees:* A, B, C *CEO:* Pres. Robert W. Benton
FTE Enroll: 96   (602) 995-2670

ARIZONA INSTITUTE OF BUSINESS AND
TECHNOLOGY
6049 N. 43rd Ave., Phoenix 85019 *Type:* Private business *Accred.:* 1982/1988 (ACICS) *Degrees:* A, C *CEO:* Dir. Gordon Phillips
                                      (602) 242-6265

MESA CAMPUS
925 S. Gilbert Rd., Ste. 201, Mesa 85204 *Accred.:* 1991 (ACICS)
                                      (602) 545-8755

PHOENIX CAMPUS
4136 N. 75th Ave., Ste. 211, Phoenix 85033-3172 *Accred.:* 1988 (ACICS)
                                      (602) 849-8208

TUCSON CAMPUS
4023 E. Grant Rd., Ste. A, Tucson 85712-2508 *Accred.:* 1988 (ACICS)
                                      (520) 881-1541

ARIZONA STATE UNIVERSITY
Tempe 85287-2203 *Type:* Public (state) *System:* Arizona Board of Regents *Accred.:* 1931/1993 (NCA) *Calendar:* Sem. plan *Degrees:* B, M, P, D *Prof. Accred.:* Accounting (Type A,C), Audiology, Business (B,M), Clinical Lab Scientist, Clinical Psychology, Computer Science, Construction Education (B), Counseling Psychology, Dance, Engineering

Technology (aerospace, electrical, manufacturing), Engineering (aerospace, bioengineering, chemical, civil, computer, electrical, general, industrial, mechanical), Health Services Administration, Interior Design, Journalism (B,M), Law, Music, Nursing (B,M), Planning (M), Psychology Internship, Public Administration, Recreation and Leisure Services, School Psychology, Social Work (B,M), Speech-Language Pathology, Theatre, *CEO:* Pres. Lattie F. Coor

Enroll: 33,580   (602) 965-9011

ARIZONA STATE UNIVERSITY EAST
6001 S. Power Rd., Bldg. 314, Mesa 85206-0903 *Type:* Public *System:* Arizona Board of Regents *Accred.:* 1931/1993 (NCA) *Calendar:* Sem. plan *Degrees:* B, M, D *CEO:* Interim Pres. Ben R. Forsyth

(602) 965-3278

* Indirect NCA accreditation through Arizona
  State University

ARIZONA STATE UNIVERSITY WEST
4701 W. Thunderbird Rd., P.O. Box 37100, Phoenix 85069-7100 *Type:* Public (state) *System:* Arizona Board of Regents *Accred.:* 1992 (NCA) *Calendar:* Sem. plan *Degrees:* B, M, C *Prof. Accred.:* Accounting (A), Business (B,M), Recreation and Leisure Services, Social Work (B) *CEO:* Vice Pres. Ben R. Forsyth
Enroll: 2,581   (602) 543-5500

ARIZONA WESTERN COLLEGE
P.O. Box 929, Yuma 85366 *Type:* Public (district) junior *System:* State Board of Directors for Community Colleges of Arizona *Accred.:* 1968/1989 (NCA) *Calendar:* Sem. plan *Degrees:* A, C *Prof. Accred.:* Nursing (A) *CEO:* Pres. James Carruthers
Enroll: 2,987   (602) 726-1000

THE ART CENTER
2525 N. Country Club Rd., Tucson 85716 *Type:* Private *Accred.:* 1993 (ACCSCT) *Degrees:* A, C *CEO:* Pres. Sharmon R. Woods

(602) 325-0123

ALBUQUERQUE CAMPUS
2268 Wyoming Blvd., N.E., Albuquerque, NM 87112 *Accred.:* 1993 (ACCSCT)
(505) 298-1828

THE CAD INSTITUTE
E. Broadway Rd., Ste. 150, 4100 Phoenix 85040 *Type:* Private senior *Accred.:* 1993/1995 (ACICS) *Degrees:* A, B, C *CEO:* Pres. Dominic Pistillo

(602) 437-0405

CENTRAL ARIZONA COLLEGE
8470 N. Overfield Rd., Coolidge 85228 *Type:* Public (district) junior *System:* State Board of Directors for Community Colleges of Arizona *Accred.:* 1973/1993 (NCA) *Calendar:* Sem. plan *Degrees:* A, C *Prof. Accred.:* Nursing (A) *CEO:* Pres. John J. Klein
Enroll: 2,041   (602) 426-4444

CHANDLER-GILBERT COMMUNITY COLLEGE
2626 E. Pecos Rd., Chandler 85225-2499 *Type:* Public (district) junior *System:* Maricopa County Community College District *Accred.:* 1992 (NCA) *Calendar:* Sem. plan *Degrees:* A, C *CEO:* Chanc. Arnette S. Ward
Enroll: 3,303   (602) 732-7000

CHAPARRAL CAREER COLLEGE
4585 E. Speedway Blvd., Ste. 204, Tucson 85712 *Type:* Private junior *Accred.:* 1969/1987 (ACICS) *Calendar:* Qtr. plan *Degrees:* A *CEO:* Pres. Scott Rhude

(520) 327-6866

COCHISE COLLEGE
4190 W. Hwy. 80, Box 100, Douglas 85607 *Type:* Public (district) junior *System:* State Board of Directors for Community Colleges of Arizona *Accred.:* 1969/1996 (NCA) *Calendar:* Sem. plan *Degrees:* A, C *Prof. Accred.:* Nursing (A) *CEO:* Pres. Walter S. Patton
Enroll: 4,908   (800) 966-7943

DEVRY INSTITUTE OF TECHNOLOGY—PHOENIX
2149 W. Dunlap Ave., Phoenix 85021-2995 *Type:* Private *System:* DeVry Institutes *Accred.:* 1981/1992 (NCA) *Calendar:* Sem. plan *Degrees:* A, B *Prof. Accred.:* Engineer-

ing Technology (electrical) *CEO:* Pres. James A. Dugan

(602) 870-9222

* Indirect NCA accreditation through DeVry Institutes

EASTERN ARIZONA COLLEGE
600 Church St., Thatcher 85552-0769 *Type:* Public *System:* State Board of Directors for Community Colleges of Arizona *Accred.:* 1966/1996 (NCA) *Calendar:* Sem. plan *Degrees:* A, C *CEO:* Pres. Gherald L. Hoopes, Jr.
Enroll: 4,771   (602) 428-8233

FRANK LLOYD WRIGHT SCHOOL OF
ARCHITECTURE
Taliesin West, Scottsdale 85261-4430 *Type:* Private professional *Accred.:* 1987/1992 (NCA) *Calendar:* 12-mos. program *Degrees:* B, M *CEO:* Managing Trustee Richard Carney
Enroll: 24   (602) 860-2700

GATEWAY COMMUNITY COLLEGE
108 N. 40th St., Phoenix 85034 *Type:* Public (district) junior *System:* Maricopa County Community College District *Accred.:* 1971/1990 (NCA) *Calendar:* Sem. plan *Degrees:* A, C *Prof. Accred.:* Diagnostic Medical Sonography, Nuclear Medicine Technology, Nursing (A), Physical Therapy Assisting (candidate), Radiography, Respiratory Therapy, Respiratory Therapy Technology *CEO:* Pres. Phil D. Randolph
Enroll: 6,047   (602) 392-5000

GLENDALE COMMUNITY COLLEGE
6000 W. Olive Ave., Glendale 85302 *Type:* Public (district) junior *System:* Maricopa County Community College District *Accred.:* 1967/1992 (NCA) *Calendar:* Sem. plan *Degrees:* A, C *Prof. Accred.:* Engineering Technology (electrical), Nursing (A) *CEO:* Pres. Tessa Martinez Pollack
Enroll: 20,095   (602) 435-3000

GRAND CANYON UNIVERSITY
3300 W. Camelback Rd., Phoenix 85017 *Type:* Private (Southern Baptist) liberal arts and teachers *Accred.:* 1968/1987 (NCA) *Calen-*

dar: 4-1-4 plan *Degrees:* B, M *Prof. Accred.:* Nursing (B) *CEO:* Pres. Bill Williams
Enroll: 1,878   (602) 249-3300

HIGH-TECH INSTITUTE
1515 E. Indian School Rd., Phoenix 85014-4901 *Type:* Private *Accred.:* 1984/1989 (ACC-SCT) *Degrees:* A, C *CEO:* Dir. Marilyn Pobiak
(602) 279-9700

SACRAMENTO CAMPUS
1111 Howe Ave., Sacramento, CA 95825 *Accred.:* 1993 (ACCSCT) *Prof. Accred.:* Medical Assisting
(916) 988-0986

INTERSTATE CAREER COLLEGE
6367 E. Tanque Verde Rd., Ste. 100, Tucson 85715 *Type:* Private business *Accred.:* 1977/1995 (ACICS) *Calendar:* Qtr. plan *Degrees:* A, C *CEO:* Pres. Susan Jensen
(602) 327-6851

ITT TECHNICAL INSTITUTE
4837 E. McDowell Rd., Phoenix 85008-4292 *Type:* Private *Accred.:* 1977/1988 (ACCSCT) *Degrees:* A *CEO:* Dir. Michael M. Henry
(602) 231-0871

ITT TECHNICAL INSTITUTE
1840 E. Benson Hwy., Tucson 85714-1770 *Type:* Private *Accred.:* 1986 (ACCSCT) *Degrees:* A *CEO:* Dir. William Fennelly
(602) 294-2944

ALBUQUERQUE CAMPUS
5100 Masthead St., N.E., Albuquerque, NM 87109-4366 *Accred.:* 1991 (ACCSCT)
(505) 828-1114

LAMSON JUNIOR COLLEGE
1980 W. Main St., Ste. 250, Mesa 85201 *Type:* Private junior *Accred.:* 1981/1995 (ACICS) *Calendar:* Qtr. plan *Degrees:* A, C *CEO:* Pres. William D. Antonelli
(602) 898-7000

MESA COMMUNITY COLLEGE
1833 W. Southern Ave., Mesa 85202 *Type:* Public *System:* Maricopa County Community College District *Accred.:* 1967/1995

(NCA) *Calendar:* Sem. plan *Degrees:* A, C *Prof. Accred.:* Nursing (A) *CEO:* Pres. Larry K. Christiansen
Enroll: 21,454   (602) 461-7000

METROPOLITAN COLLEGE OF COURT REPORTING
4640 E. Elwood St., Phoenix 85040 *Type:* Private *Accred.:* 1992 (ACCSCT) *Degrees:* A, C *CEO:* Pres./Owner David L. Stephenson
(602) 955-5900

MOHAVE COMMUNITY COLLEGE
1971 Jagerson Ave., Kingman 86401 *Type:* Public (district) junior *System:* State Board of Directors for Community Colleges of Arizona *Accred.:* 1981/1993 (NCA) *Calendar:* Sem. plan *Degrees:* A, C *CEO:* Pres. Charles W. Hall
Enroll: 5,805   (520) 757-4331

NATIONAL EDUCATION CENTER—ARIZONA AUTOMOTIVE INSTITUTE
6829 N. 46th Ave., Glendale 85301-3597 *Type:* Private *Accred.:* 1972/1988 (ACCSCT) *Calendar:* Qtr. plan *Degrees:* A, C *CEO:* Dir. Ralph Vieau
(602) 934-7273

NAVAJO COMMUNITY COLLEGE
Tsaile 86556 *Type:* Public *Accred.:* 1976/1995 (NCA) *Calendar:* Sem. plan *Degrees:* A, C *CEO:* Pres. Tommy Lewis
Enroll: 1,276   (602) 724-3311

NORTHERN ARIZONA UNIVERSITY
Box 4092, Flagstaff 86011-4092 *Type:* Public (state) *System:* Arizona Board of Regents *Accred.:* 1930/1988 (NCA) *Calendar:* Sem. plan *Degrees:* B, M, D *Prof. Accred.:* Business (B,M), Dental Hygiene, Engineering Technology (civil/construction, electrical), Engineering (civil, computer, electrical, mechanical), Forestry, Music, Nursing (B), Physical Therapy, Social Work (B) *CEO:* Pres. Clara Lovett
Enroll: 19,242   (602) 523-3232

NORTHLAND PIONEER COLLEGE
103 First Ave. at Hopi Dr., P.O. Box 610, Holbrook 86025 *Type:* Public (district) junior *System:* State Board of Directors for Community Colleges of Arizona *Accred.:*

1980/1990 (NCA) *Calendar:* Sem. plan *Degrees:* A, C *CEO:* Pres. John H. Anderson
Enroll: 4,614   (602) 524-1993

PARADISE VALLEY COMMUNITY COLLEGE
18401 N. 32nd St., Phoenix 85032 *Type:* Public (district) junior *System:* Maricopa County Community College District *Accred.:* 1990/1995 (NCA) *Calendar:* Sem. plan *Degrees:* A, C *CEO:* Pres. Raul Cardenas
Enroll: 5,235   (602) 493-2600

PARALEGAL INSTITUTE, INC.
3602 W. Thomas Rd., Ste. 9, P.O. Drawer 11408, Phoenix 85061-1408 *Type:* Private home study *Accred.:* 1979/1993 (DETC) *Degrees:* A, C *CEO:* Pres. John W. Morrison
(602) 272-1855

PHOENIX COLLEGE
1202 W. Thomas Rd., Phoenix 85013 *Type:* Public (district) junior *System:* Maricopa County Community College District *Accred.:* 1928/1986 (NCA) *Calendar:* Sem. plan *Degrees:* A, C *Prof. Accred.:* Clinical Lab Technology (A), Dental Assisting, Dental Hygiene (conditional), Medical Assisting (AMA), Medical Record Technology, Nursing (A) *CEO:* Pres. Marie Pepicello
Enroll: 11,466   (602) 264-2492

PIMA COUNTY COMMUNITY COLLEGE DISTRICT
4905 E. Broadway Blvd., Tucson 85709-1010 *Type:* Public (district) junior *System:* State Board of Directors for Community Colleges of Arizona *Accred.:* 1975/1991 (NCA) *Calendar:* Sem. plan *Degrees:* A, C *Prof. Accred.:* Dental Assisting, Dental Hygiene, Dental Laboratory Technology, Nursing (A), Radiography, Respiratory Therapy *CEO:* Chanc. Robert D. Jensen
Enroll: 27,960   (520) 748-4666

PIMA MEDICAL INSTITUTE
3350 E. Grant Rd., Tucson 85716 *Type:* Private *Accred.:* 1982/1994 (ABHES) *Degrees:* A *Prof. Accred.:* Radiography, Respiratory Therapy, Respiratory Therapy Technology *CEO:* Pres. Richard L. Luebke, Sr.
(602) 326-1600

MESA CAMPUS
957 S. Dobson Rd., Mesa 85202 *Accred.:*
1986/1992 (ABHES) *Prof. Accred.:* Radiography, Respiratory Therapy, Respiratory Therapy Technology
(602) 345-7777

DENVER CAMPUS
1701 W. 72nd Ave., No. 130, Denver, CO
80221 *Accred.:* 1988 (ABHES) *Prof.
Accred.:* Radiography, Respiratory Therapy, Respiratory Therapy Technology
(303) 426-1800

ALBUQUERQUE CAMPUS
2201 San Pedro Dr., N.E., Bldg. 3, Ste.
100, Albuquerque, NM 87110 *Accred.:*
1985/1991 (ABHES) *Prof. Accred.:* Radiography
(505) 881-1234

SEATTLE CAMPUS
1627 Eastlake Ave. E., Seattle, WA 98102
Accred.: 1990 (ABHES) *Prof. Accred.:*
Clinical Lab Technology (A), Radiography, Respiratory Therapy, Respiratory
Therapy Technology
(206) 322-6100

PRESCOTT COLLEGE
220 Grove Ave., Prescott 86301 *Type:* Pri-
vate liberal arts *Accred.:* 1984/1990 (NCA)
Calendar: 4-1-4 plan *Degrees:* B, M *CEO:*
Co-Pres. Joe Hiller; Co-Pres. Lady Branham
Enroll: 870   (520) 778-2090

THE REFRIGERATION SCHOOL
4210 E. Washington St., Phoenix 85034-
1894 *Type:* Private *Accred.:* 1973/1990
(ACCSCT) *Degrees:* A, C *CEO:* Dir. Ola
Lee Loney
(602) 275-7133

RIO SALADO COMMUNITY COLLEGE
640 N. First Ave., Phoenix 85003 *Type:* Public (district) junior *System:* Maricopa County
Community College District *Accred.:* 1981/
1992 (NCA) *Calendar:* Sem. plan *Degrees:*
A, C *CEO:* Pres. Linda M. Thor
Enroll: 9,007   (602) 223-4000

SCOTTSDALE COMMUNITY COLLEGE
9000 E. Chaparral Rd., Scottsdale 85250-
2699 *Type:* Public (district) junior *System:*
Maricopa County Community College District *Accred.:* 1975/1987 (NCA) *Calendar:*
Sem. plan *Degrees:* A, C *Prof. Accred.:* Nursing (A) *CEO:* Pres. Arthur W. DeCabooter
Enroll: 9,821   (602) 423-6000

SCOTTSDALE CULINARY INSTITUTE
8100 E. Camelback Rd., Scottsdale 85251-
3940 *Type:* Private *Accred.:* 1989 (ACCSCT)
Degrees: A *CEO:* Pres. Elizabeth S. Leite
(602) 990-3773

SOUTH MOUNTAIN COMMUNITY COLLEGE
7050 S. 24th St., Phoenix 85040 *Type:* Public (district) junior *System:* Maricopa County
Community College District *Accred.:*
1984/1989 (NCA) *Calendar:* Sem. plan
Degrees: A, C *CEO:* Pres. John A. Cordova
Enroll: 2,491   (602) 243-8000

SOUTHWESTERN COLLEGE
2625 E. Cactus Rd., Phoenix 85032 *Type:*
Private (Conservative Baptist) *Accred.:*
1977/1987 (AABC); 1992 (NCA) *Calendar:*
Sem. plan *Degrees:* A, B, C *CEO:* Pres.
Brent Garrison
Enroll: 175   (602) 992-6101

UNIVERSAL TECHNICAL INSTITUTE
3121 W. Weldon Ave., Phoenix 85017-4599
Type: Private *Accred.:* 1968/1993 (ACCSCT)
Degrees: A, C *CEO:* Dir. Randall R. Smith
(602) 264-4164

GLENDALE HEIGHTS CAMPUS
601 Regency Dr., Glendale Heights, IL
60139-2208 *Accred.:* 1990 (ACCSCT)
(708) 529-2662

UNIVERSITY OF ARIZONA
712 Administration Bldg., Tucson 85721
Type: Public (state) *System:* Arizona Board of
Regents *Accred.:* 1917/1990 (NCA) *Calen-
dar:* Sem. plan *Degrees:* B, M, P, D *Prof.
Accred.:* Audiology, Business (B,M), Clinical
Lab Scientist, Clinical Psychology, Dance,
Dietetics (internship), Engineering (aero-
space, agricultural, chemical, civil, computer,
electrical, geological/geophysical, industrial,

materials, mechanical, mining, nuclear, systems), Journalism (B,M), Landscape Architecture (B), Law, Librarianship, Medicine, Music, Nursing (B,M), Perfusion, Psychology Internship, Public Administration, Rehabilitation Counseling, School Psychology, Speech-Language Pathology, Theatre, *CEO:* Pres. Manuel T. Pacheco
Enroll: 35,306   (602) 621-5511

SIERRA VISTA CAMPUS
1140 N. Colombo, Sierra Vista 85635 *Accred.:* 1995 (NCA)
(602) 629-0335

UNIVERSITY OF PHOENIX
4615 E. Elwood St., 4th Fl., Phoenix 85040 *Type:* Private professional *Accred.:* 1978/1992 (NCA) *Calendar:* Sem. plan *Degrees:* A, B, M *Prof. Accred.:* Nursing (B) *CEO:* Pres. William H. Gibbs
Enroll: 21,459   (602) 966-9577

LAS VEGAS CAMPUS
2975 South Rainbow, Las Vegas, NV 89102 *Degrees:* B, M
(702) 876-5004

ALBUQUERQUE, NEW MEXICO CAMPUS
7471 Pan American Fwy., N.E., Albuquerque, NM 87109
(505) 821-4800

CENTER FOR DISTANCE EDUCATION CAMPUS
4615 E. Elmwood St., P.O. Box 52069, Phoenix 85071-2069
(602) 921-8014

DENVER CAMPUS
7800 E. Dorado Pl., Englewood, CO 80111
(303) 755-9090

FOUNTAIN VALLEY CAMPUS
10540 Talbert Ave., Fountain Valley, CA 92708
(714) 968-2299

HAWAII MAIN CAMPUS
1585 Kapiolani Blvd., No. 722, Honolulu, HI 96814
(808) 949-0573

ONLINE CAMPUS
100 Spear St., San Francisco, CA 94107
(415) 541-0141

PHOENIX MAIN CAMPUS
4605 E. Elmwood St., P.O. Box 52076, Phoenix 85072-2076 *Prof. Accred.:* Counseling
(602) 966-7400

PUERTO RICO CAMPUS
P.O. Box 3870, R.D. 177 KM2, Guaynabo, PR 00970-3870
(809) 731-5400

SACRAMENTO CAMPUS
1485 Response Rd., Sacramento, CA 95815
(916) 923-2107

SALT LAKE CITY CAMPUS
5251 Green St., Salt Lake City, UT 84123
(801) 263-1444

SAN DIEGO CAMPUS
3890 Murphy Canyon Rd., San Diego, CA 92123
(619) 576-7392

SAN JOSE CAMPUS
3590 N. First St., San Jose, CA 95134
(408) 435-8500

TUCSON CAMPUS
5099 E. Grant Rd., Tucson 85712 *Prof. Accred.:* Counseling
(602) 881-6512

WESTERN INTERNATIONAL UNIVERSITY
9215 N. Black Canyon Hwy., Phoenix 85021 *Type:* Private *Accred.:* 1984/1992 (NCA) *Calendar:* Tri. plan *Degrees:* A, B, M, C *CEO:* Pres. Michael Seiden
Enroll: 1,499   (602) 943-2311

LONDON CAMPUS
3 Muirfield Crescent, Glengall Bridge W., Millharbour, London Great Britain E14 9SZ
[01] (071) 345-8277

YAVAPAI COLLEGE

1100 E. Sheldon St., Prescott 86301 *Type:* Public (district) junior *System:* State Board of Directors for Community Colleges of Arizona *Accred.:* 1975/1995 (NCA) *Calendar:* Sem. plan *Degrees:* A, C *Prof. Accred.:* Nursing (A) *CEO:* Pres. Doreen B. Dailey *Enroll:* 5,980   (520) 445-7300

ARKANSAS

ARKANSAS BAPTIST COLLEGE
Dr. Martin Luther King Jr. Dr., Little Rock
72202 *Type:* Private (Baptist) liberal arts
Accred.: 1987/1995 (NCA) *Calendar:* Sem.
plan *Degrees:* A, B, C *CEO:* Pres. W.
Thomas Keaton
Enroll: 225   (501) 372-6883

ARKANSAS STATE UNIVERSITY
P.O. Box 10, State University 72467 *Type:*
Public (state) *System:* Arkansas Department
of Higher Education *Accred.:* 1928/1993
(NCA) *Calendar:* Sem. plan *Degrees:* A, B,
M, P, C *Prof. Accred.:* Art (A), Business
(B,M), Clinical Lab Scientist, Clinical Lab
Technology (A), Computer Science, Engi-
neering (agricultural, general), Journalism
(B,M), Music, Nursing (A,B), Public
Administration, Radiography, Rehabilitation
Counseling, Social Work (B), Speech-Lan-
guage Pathology, Teacher Education *CEO:*
Pres. Leslie Wyatt, III
Enroll: 11,966   (501) 972-2100

BEEBE CAMPUS
P.O. Drawer H, Beebe 72012 *System:*
Arkansas Department of Higher Educa-
tion *Accred.:* 1981/1992 (NCA) *Calen-
dar:* Sem. plan *Degrees:* A, C
Enroll: 2,000   (501) 882-6452

MOUNTAIN HOME TECHNICAL COLLEGE
213 East 6th St., Montain Home 72653
System: Arkansas Department of Higher
Education *Accred.:* 1928/1993 (NCA)
Calendar: Sem. plan *Degrees:* A, C
Enroll: 1,500   (501) 425-3949

NEWPORT CAMPUS
7648 Victory Blvd., Newport 72112 *System:* Arkansas Department of Higher Education *Accred.:* 1981/1992 (NCA) *Calendar:* Sem. plan *Degrees:* A, C
Enroll: 459   (501) 523-8966

ARKANSAS TECH UNIVERSITY
Russellville 72801-2222 *Type:* Public (state)
liberal arts *System:* Arkansas Department of
Higher Education *Accred.:* 1930/1991
(NCA) *Calendar:* Sem. plan *Degrees:* A, B,

M *Prof. Accred.:* Engineering (general),
Medical Assisting (AMA), Medical Record
Administration, Music, Nursing (B), Teacher
Education *CEO:* Pres. Robert C. Brown
Enroll: 4,696   (501) 968-0389

BLACK RIVER TECHNICAL COLLEGE
Hwy. 304 E., P.O. Box 468, Pocahontas
72455 *Type:* Public technical *System:*
Arkansas Department of Higher Education
Accred.: 1993/1995 (NCA candidate) *Calen-
dar:* Sem. plan *Degrees:* A, C *Prof. Accred.:*
Respiratory Therapy Technology *CEO:* Dir.
Richard Gaines
Enroll: 985   (501) 892-4565

CENTRAL BAPTIST COLLEGE
1501 College Ave., Conway 72032 *Type:*
Private (Missionary Baptist Association)
Accred.: 1993 (NCA) *Calendar:* Sem. plan
Degrees: A, B, C *CEO:* Pres. Charles E.
Attebery
Enroll: 297   (501) 329-6872

EAST ARKANSAS COMMUNITY COLLEGE
Newcastle Rd., Forrest City 72335-9598
Type: Public (district) junior *System:*
Arkansas Department of Higher Education
Accred.: 1979/1989 (NCA) *Calendar:* Sem.
plan *Degrees:* A, C *CEO:* Pres. George
McCormick
Enroll: 1,303   (501) 633-4480

GARLAND COUNTY COMMUNITY COLLEGE
101 College Dr., Hot Springs 71913 *Type:*
Public (district) junior *System:* Arkansas
Department of Higher Education *Accred.:*
1981/1992 (NCA) *Calendar:* Sem. plan
Degrees: A, C *Prof. Accred.:* Clinical Lab
Technology (A), Medical Record Technol-
ogy (A), Nursing (A), Radiography *CEO:* Pres.
Tom Spencer
Enroll: 1,946   (501) 767-9371

HARDING UNIVERSITY
Box 2256, 900 E. Center Ave., Searcy
72149-0001 *Type:* Private (Churches of
Christ) liberal arts *Accred.:* 1954/1995
(NCA) *Calendar:* Sem. plan *Degrees:* A, B,
M *Prof. Accred.:* Music, Nursing (B), Social

Work (B), Teacher Education *CEO:* Pres. David B. Burks, Jr.
Enroll: 3,997   (501) 279-4274

HENDERSON STATE UNIVERSITY
1100 Henderson St., Arkadelphia 71999-0001 *Type:* Public (state) liberal arts and teachers *System:* Arkansas Department of Higher Education *Accred.:* 1934/1992 (NCA) *Calendar:* Sem. plan *Degrees:* A, B, M *Prof. Accred.:* Music, Nursing (B), Teacher Education *CEO:* Pres. Charles D. Dunn
Enroll: 4,034   (501) 230-5000

HENDRIX COLLEGE
1601 Harkrider St., Conway 72032-3080 *Type:* Private (United Methodist) liberal arts *Accred.:* 1924/1989 (NCA) *Calendar:* Sem. plan *Degrees:* B *Prof. Accred.:* Music, Teacher Education *CEO:* Pres. Ann H. Die
Enroll: 941   (501) 329-6811

JOHN BROWN UNIVERSITY
Siloam Springs 72761 *Type:* Private liberal arts *Accred.:* 1962/1992 (NCA) *Calendar:* Sem. plan *Degrees:* A, B *Prof. Accred.:* Teacher Education *CEO:* Pres. LeVon Balzer
Enroll: 1,209   (501) 524-9500

LYON COLLEGE
P.O. Box 2317, Batesville 72503 *Type:* Private (Presbyterian) *Accred.:* 1959/1992 (NCA) *Calendar:* 4-1-4 plan *Degrees:* B *Prof. Accred.:* Social Work (B), Teacher Education *CEO:* Pres. John V. Griffith
Enroll: 628   (501) 793-9813

MISSISSIPPI COUNTY COMMUNITY COLLEGE
P.O Drawer 1109, Blytheville 72316 *Type:* Public (district) junior *System:* Arkansas Department of Higher Education *Accred.:* 1980/1992 (NCA) *Calendar:* Sem. plan *Degrees:* A, C *Prof. Accred.:* Nursing (A) *CEO:* Pres. John P. Sullins
Enroll: 1,603   (501) 762-1020

NATIONAL EDUCATION CENTER—ARKANSAS COLLEGE OF TECHNOLOGY
9720 Rodney Parham Rd., Little Rock 72207-6288 *Type:* Private *Accred.:* 1972/1988 (ACCSCT) *Calendar:* Qtr. plan *Degrees:* A, C *CEO:* Exec. Dir. Byron Thompson
                    (501) 224-8200

NORTH ARKANSAS COMMUNITY/TECHNICAL COLLEGE
Pioneer Ridge, Harrison 72601 *Type:* Public (district) junior *System:* Arkansas Department of Higher Education *Accred.:* 1979/1991 (NCA) *Calendar:* Sem. plan *Degrees:* A, C *Prof. Accred.:* Nursing (A) *CEO:* Pres. William Bert Baker
Enroll: 1,584   (501) 743-3000

NORTHWEST ARKANSAS COMMUNITY COLLEGE
P.O. Box 1408, 1 College Dr., Bentonville 72712 *Type:* Public (district) junior *System:* Arkansas Department of Higher Education *Accred.:* 1993/1995 (NCA) *Calendar:* Sem. plan *Degrees:* A, C *Prof. Accred.:* Physical Therapy Assisting, Radiation Therapy Technology, Respiratory Therapy Technology *CEO:* Pres. Bob C. Burns
Enroll: 2,029   (501) 636-9222

OUACHITA BAPTIST UNIVERSITY
410 Ouachita, OBU Box 3753, Arkadelphia 71998 *Type:* Private (Southern Baptist) *Accred.:* 1927/1990 (NCA) *Calendar:* Sem. plan *Degrees:* B, M *Prof. Accred.:* Music, Teacher Education *CEO:* Pres. Ben Elrod
Enroll: 1,440   (501) 245-5000

PHILANDER SMITH COLLEGE
812 W. 13th St., Little Rock 72202 *Type:* Private (United Methodist) liberal arts *Accred.:* 1949/1990 (NCA) *Calendar:* Sem. plan *Degrees:* B *CEO:* Pres. Myer L. Titus
Enroll: 841   (501) 375-9845

PHILLIPS COUNTY COMMUNITY COLLEGE
Box 785, Helena 72342-0785 *Type:* Public (district) junior *System:* Arkansas Department of Higher Education *Accred.:* 1972/1995 (NCA) *Calendar:* Sem. plan *Degrees:* A, C *Prof. Accred.:* Clinical Lab Technology (A), Nursing (A) *CEO:* Pres. Steven W. Jones
Enroll: 1,520   (501) 338-6474

PULASKI TECHNICAL COLLEGE
3000 W. Scenic Rd., North Little Rock
72118-3399 *Type:* Public technical *System:*
Arkansas Department of Higher Education
Accred.: 1993/1995 (NCA candidate) *Calendar:* Sem. plan *Degrees:* A, C *Prof. Accred.:*
Dental Assisting, Respiratory Therapy Technology *CEO:* Pres. Benjamin Wyatt
Enroll: 1,176   (501) 771-1000

RED RIVER TECHNICAL COLLEGE
Hwy. 29 S., P.O. Box 140, Hope 71801 *Type:*
Private *System:* Arkansas Department of
Higher Education *Accred.:* 1994 (NCA candidate) *Degrees:* A, C *Prof. Accred.:* Respiratory Therapy Technology *CEO:* Dir.
Johnny Rapert
Enroll: 787   (501) 777-5722

RICH MOUNTAIN COMMUNITY COLLEGE
1100 Bush St., Mena 71953 *Type:* Public
(district) junior *System:* Arkansas Department of Higher Education *Accred.:* 1990/
1995 (NCA) *Calendar:* Sem. plan *Degrees:*
A, C *CEO:* Pres. Bill Abernathy
Enroll: 744   (501) 394-5012

SHORTER COLLEGE
604 Locust St., North Little Rock 72114 *Type:*
Private (African Methodist Episcopal) junior
Accred.: 1981/1992 (NCA) *Calendar:* Sem.
plan *Degrees:* A, C *CEO:* Pres. Katherine P.
Mitchell
Enroll: 309   (501) 374-6305

SOUTH ARKANSAS COMMUNITY COLLEGE
P.O. Box 7010, 300 S.W. Ave., El Dorado
71731-7010 *Type:* Public (district) junior
System: Arkansas Department of Higher
Education *Accred.:* 1983/1988 (NCA) *Calendar:* Sem. plan *Degrees:* A, C *Prof.
Accred.:* Clinical Lab Technology (A), Radiography *CEO:* Pres. Ben T. Whitfield
Enroll: 995   (501) 862-8131

SOUTHERN ARKANSAS UNIVERSITY
SAU Box 1402, Magnolia 71753 *Type:* Public (state) liberal arts and teachers *System:*
Arkansas Department of Higher Education
Accred.: 1929/1993 (NCA) *Calendar:* Sem.
plan *Degrees:* A, B, M, C *Prof. Accred.:*

Music, Nursing (A), Teacher Education
CEO: Pres. Steven G. Gamble
Enroll: 2,638   (501) 235-4001

TECH BRANCH CAMPUS
SAU Tech Sta., Camden 71701 (state) 2-
year *System:* Arkansas Department of
Higher Education *Accred.:* 1980/1990
(NCA) *Calendar:* Sem. plan *Degrees:* A, C
Enroll: 1,000   (501) 574-4500

UNIVERSITY OF ARKANSAS AT FAYETTEVILLE
Administration Bldg. 425, Fayetteville
72701 *Type:* Public (state) *System:* University of Arkansas System Administration
Accred.: 1924/1987 (NCA) *Calendar:* Sem.
plan *Degrees:* A, B, M, P, D *Prof. Accred.:*
Accounting (A,C), Business (B,M), Engineering (agricultural, chemical, civil, computer, electrical, industrial, mechanical),
Home Economics, Interior Design, Journalism (B,M), Landscape Architecture (B),
Law, Music, Nursing (A), Rehabilitation
Counseling, Social Work (B), Speech-Language Pathology, Teacher Education *CEO:*
Chanc. Daniel E. Ferritor
Enroll: 14,480   (501) 575-2000

UNIVERSITY OF ARKANSAS AT LITTLE ROCK
2801 S. University Ave., Little Rock 72204
Type: Public (state) *System:* University of
Arkansas System Administration *Accred.:*
1929/1990 (NCA) *Calendar:* Sem. plan
Degrees: A, B, M, P, D *Prof. Accred.:* Art
(A), Audiology, Business (B,M), Computer
Science, Engineering Technology (civil/construction, computer, electrical, manufacturing, mechanical), Health Services Administration, Journalism (B,M), Law, Music,
Nursing (A), Public Administration, Social
Work (M), Speech-Language Pathology,
Surgical Technology, Teacher Education,
Theatre *CEO:* Chanc. Charles E. Hathaway
Enroll: 11,509   (501) 569-3200

UNIVERSITY OF ARKANSAS AT MONTICELLO
P.O. Box 3596, Monticello 71655-3596
Type: Public (state) *System:* University of
Arkansas System Administration *Accred.:*
1928/1995 (NCA) *Calendar:* Sem. plan
Degrees: A, B, M, C *Prof. Accred.:* Forestry,

Music (A), Nursing (A), Teacher Education
CEO: Chanc. Fred J. Taylor
Enroll: 2,394   (501) 367-6811

UNIVERSITY OF ARKANSAS AT PINE BLUFF
1200 N. Univ. Dr., Pine Bluff 71601 *Type:*
Public (state) *System:* University of
Arkansas System Administration *Accred.:*
1950/1987 (NCA) *Calendar:* Sem. plan
Degrees: A, B, M *Prof. Accred.:* Home Eco-
nomics, Music, Nursing (B), Social Work
(B), Teacher Education *CEO:* Chanc.
Lawrence A. Davis, Jr
Enroll: 3,823   (501) 543-8000

UNIVERSITY OF ARKANSAS FOR MEDICAL
SCIENCES
4301 W. Markham St., Little Rock 72205
Type: Public (state) *System:* University of
Arkansas System Administration *Accred.:*
1987 (NCA) *Calendar:* Sem. plan *Degrees:*
A, B, M, D, C *Prof. Accred.:* Clinical Lab
Scientist, Clinical Psychology, Cytotechnol-
ogy, Dental Hygiene, Dietetics (internship),
Medicine, Nuclear Medicine Technology,
Nursing (B,M), Psychology Internship,
Radiography, Respiratory Therapy, Respira-
tory Therapy Technology *CEO:* Chanc.
Harry P. Ward
Enroll: 1,864   (501) 686-5000

UNIVERSITY OF CENTRAL ARKANSAS
Conway 72035-0001 *Type:* Public (state) lib-
eral arts and teachers *System:* Arkansas
Department of Higher Education *Accred.:*
1931/1990 (NCA) *Calendar:* Sem. plan
Degrees: A, B, M, P *Prof. Accred.:* Business
(B,M), Music, Nursing (B,M), Occupational
Therapy, Physical Therapy, Physical Ther-

apy Assisting, Speech-Language Pathology,
Teacher Education *CEO:* Pres. Winfred L.
Thompson
Enroll: 9,292   (501) 450-5000

UNIVERSITY OF THE OZARKS
415 College Ave., Clarksville 72830 *Type:*
Private (United Presbyterian) liberal arts
Accred.: 1931/1993 (NCA) *Calendar:* 4-1-4
plan *Degrees:* A, B, M *Prof. Accred.:*
Teacher Education *CEO:* Pres. Gene
Stephenson
Enroll: 577   (501) 979-1000

WESTARK COMMUNITY COLLEGE
P.O. Box 3649, Fort Smith 72913-3649
Type: Public (district) junior *System:*
Arkansas Department of Higher Education
Accred.: 1973/1995 (NCA) *Calendar:* Sem.
plan *Degrees:* A, C *Prof. Accred.:* Clinical
Lab Technology (A), Nursing (A), Surgical
Technology *CEO:* Pres. Joel Stubblefield
Enroll: 5,339   (501) 788-7000

WILLIAMS BAPTIST COLLEGE
Box 3667, 201 Fulbright Ave., Walnut Ridge
72476 *Type:* Private (Southern Baptist)
Accred.: 1963/1994 (NCA) *Calendar:* Sem.
plan *Degrees:* A, B, C *CEO:* Pres. Jerol
Swaim
Enroll: 607   (501) 886-6741

CALIFORNIA

ACADEMY OF ART COLLEGE
79 New Montgomery, San Francisco 94105-3893 *Type:* Private *Accred.:* 1973/1990 (ACCSCT) *Calendar:* Qtr. plan *Degrees:* B *Prof. Accred.:* Art (A), Interior Design *CEO:* Vice Pres. Jan Schroeder
                              (415) 274-2200

ACADEMY OF CHINESE CULTURE AND HEALTH SCIENCES
1601 Clay St., Oakland 94612 *Type:* Private professional *Calendar:* Tri. plan *Degrees:* M *Prof. Accred.:* Acupuncture (M) *CEO:* Pres. Wei Tsuei
FTE Enroll: 42   (510) 763-7787

THE ADVERTISING ARTS COLLEGE
10025 Mesa Rim Rd., San Diego 92121-2913 *Type:* Private *Accred.:* 1986 (ACCSCT) *Degrees:* A, B, C *CEO:* Pres. Gary R. Cantor
                              (619) 546-0602

ALLAN HANCOCK COLLEGE
800 S. College Dr., Santa Maria 93454-6399 *Type:* Public (district) junior *System:* Allan Hancock Joint Community College District *Accred.:* 1952/1992 (WASC-Jr.) *Calendar:* Sem. plan *Degrees:* A *CEO:* Pres. Ann Foxworthy Stephenson
Enroll: 9,610   (805) 922-6966

AMERICAN ACADEMY OF DRAMATIC ARTS WEST
2550 Paloma St., Pasadena 91107 *Type:* Private professional *Accred.:* 1981/1991 (WASC-Jr.) *Calendar:* Sem. plan *Degrees:* A *Prof. Accred.:* Theatre *CEO:* Pres. George C. Cuttingham
Enroll: 300   (818) 798-0777

AMERICAN BAPTIST SEMINARY OF THE WEST
2606 Dwight Way, Berkeley 94704-3029 *Type:* Private (Baptist) graduate only *Accred.:* 1938/1994 (ATS) *Calendar:* Sem. plan *Degrees:* M, D *CEO:* Pres. Theodore Keaton
Enroll: 81   (510) 841-1905

AMERICAN COLLEGE OF TRADITIONAL CHINESE MEDICINE
455 Arkansas St., San Francisco 94107-2813 *Type:* Private professional *Calendar:* Qtr. plan *Degrees:* M *Prof. Accred.:* Acupuncture *CEO:* Pres. Lixin Huang
FTE Enroll: 56   (415) 282-7600

AMERICAN COMMONWEALTH UNIVERSITY
2801 Camino Del Rio S., San Diego 92108-3801 *Type:* Private senior *Accred.:* 1995 (ACICS) *Calendar:* Tri. plan *Degrees:* B, M *CEO:* Pres. Henry W. Gaylor, Jr.
Enroll: 146   (619) 298-9040

AMERICAN CONSERVATORY THEATER
30 Grant Ave., San Francisco 94108-5800 *Type:* Private professional *Accred.:* 1984/1992 (WASC-Sr.) *Calendar:* Sem. plan *Degrees:* M *CEO:* Dir. Carey Perloff
FTE Enroll: 154   (415) 834-3350

THE AMERICAN FILM INSTITUTE CENTER FOR ADVANCED FILM AND TELEVISION STUDIES
2021 N. Western Ave., Los Angeles 90027 *Type:* Private professional; graduate only *Calendar:* 24-mos. program *Degrees:* M *Prof. Accred.:* Art *CEO:* Dir. Jean Firstenberg
Enroll: 160   (213) 856-7628

AMERICAN RIVER COLLEGE
4700 College Oak Dr., Sacramento 95841 *Type:* Public (district) junior *System:* Los Rios Community College District *Accred.:* 1959/1995 (WASC-Jr.) *Calendar:* Sem. plan *Degrees:* A *Prof. Accred.:* Respiratory Therapy *CEO:* Pres. Marie B. Smith
Enroll: 19,926   (916) 484-8011

ANTELOPE VALLEY COLLEGE
3041 W. Ave. K, Lancaster 93536 *Type:* Public (district) junior *System:* Antelope Valley Community College District *Accred.:* 1952/1993 (WASC-Jr.) *Calendar:* Sem. plan *Degrees:* A *CEO:* Pres. Allan W. Kurki
Enroll: 9,640   (805) 943-3241

ARMSTRONG UNIVERSITY
2222 Harold Way, Berkeley 94704 *Type:* Private senior *Accred.:* 1979/1997 (ACICS)

Calendar: Sem. plan *Degrees:* A, B, M
CEO: Pres. Ronald Hook
(510) 848-2500

ART CENTER COLLEGE OF DESIGN
1700 Lida St., P.O. Box 7197, Pasadena
91109 *Type:* Private professional *Accred.:*
1955/1988 (WASC-Sr.) *Calendar:* Tri. plan
Degrees: B, M *Prof. Accred.:* Art *CEO:* Pres.
David R. Brown
FTE Enroll: 1,318   (818) 584-5000

LA TOUR-DE-PELIZ CAMPUS
Chateau de Sully, Rte. de Chailly 144, La
Tour-de-Peliz Switzerland CH-1814 *Prof.
Accred.:* Art
[41] (21) 944-6464

ART INSTITUTE OF SOUTHERN CALIFORNIA
2222 Laguna Canyon Rd., Laguna Beach
92651 *Type:* Private *Accred.:* 1990 (WASC-
Sr. candidate) *Calendar:* Sem. plan *Degrees:*
B *Prof. Accred.:* Art *CEO:* Pres. John W.
Lottes
FTE Enroll: 126   (714) 497-3309

AZUSA PACIFIC UNIVERSITY
901 E. Alosta, P.O. Box 7000, Azusa 91702-
7000 *Type:* Private liberal arts *Accred.:* 1990
(ATS); 1964/1992 (WASC-Sr.) *Calendar:* 4-
4-x plan *Degrees:* A, B, M *Prof. Accred.:*
Nursing (B,M), Social Work (B) *CEO:* Pres.
Richard E. Felix
FTE Enroll: 3,429   (818) 969-3434

BAKERSFIELD COLLEGE
1801 Panorama Dr., Bakersfield 93305 *Type:*
Public (district) junior *System:* Kern Com-
munity College District *Accred.:* 1952/1995
(WASC-Jr.) *Calendar:* Sem. plan *Degrees:*
A *Prof. Accred.:* Radiography *CEO:* Pres.
Richard L. Wright
Enroll: 12,518   (805) 395-4011

BARSTOW COLLEGE
2700 Barstow Rd., Barstow 92311 *Type:*
Public (district) junior *System:* Barstow
Community College District *Accred.:*
1962/1994 (WASC-Jr.) *Calendar:* Sem. plan
Degrees: A *CEO:* Pres. Judith A. Strattan
Enroll: 1,709   (619) 252-2411

BETHANY COLLEGE OF THE ASSEMBLIES OF GOD
800 Bethany Dr., Scotts Valley 95066 *Type:*
Private (Assemblies of God) *Accred.:* 1966/
1985 (WASC-Sr.) *Calendar:* 4-1-4 plan
Degrees: A, B *CEO:* Pres. Tom L. Duncan
FTE Enroll: 550   (408) 438-3800

BIOLA UNIVERSITY
13800 Biola Ave., La Mirada 90639 *Type:*
Private liberal arts and professional *Accred.:*
1977/1988 (ATS); 1961/1995 (WASC-Sr.)
Calendar: 4-1-4 plan *Degrees:* B, M, P, D
Prof. Accred.: Clinical Psychology, Music,
Nursing (B) *CEO:* Pres. Clyde Cook
FTE Enroll: 2,698   (310) 903-6000

BROOKS COLLEGE
4825 E. Pacific Coast Hwy., Long Beach
90804 *Type:* Private 2-year *Accred.:* 1977/
1992 (WASC-Jr.) *Calendar:* Qtr. plan
Degrees: A *CEO:* Exec. Dir. Steven B.
Sotraidis
Enroll: 737   (310) 597-6611

BROOKS INSTITUTE OF PHOTOGRAPHY
801 Alston Rd., Santa Barbara 93108 *Type:*
Private senior *Accred.:* 1984/1996 (ACICS)
Calendar: Tri. plan *Degrees:* B, M, C *CEO:*
Pres. Ernest H. Brooks, II
(805) 966-3888

BUTTE COLLEGE
3536 Butte Campus Dr., Oroville 95965
Type: Public (district) junior *System:* Butte
Community College District *Accred.:*
1972/1991 (WASC-Jr.) *Calendar:* Sem. plan
Degrees: A *Prof. Accred.:* Respiratory Ther-
apy *CEO:* Pres. Betty M. Dean
Enroll: 10,258   (916) 895-2511

CABRILLO COLLEGE
6500 Soquel Dr., Aptos 95003 *Type:* Public
(district) junior *System:* Cabrillo Community
College District *Accred.:* 1961/1995
(WASC-Jr.) *Calendar:* Sem. plan *Degrees:*
A *Prof. Accred.:* Dental Hygiene, Radiogra-
phy *CEO:* Pres. John D. Hurd
Enroll: 13,529   (408) 479-6100

CALIFORNIA BAPTIST COLLEGE
8432 Magnolia Ave., Riverside 92504 *Type:* Private (Southern Baptist) liberal arts *Accred.:* 1961/1987 (WASC-Sr.) *Calendar:* Sem. plan *Degrees:* B, M *Prof. Accred.:* Music *CEO:* Pres. Ronald L. Ellis
FTE Enroll: 751   (909) 689-5771

CALIFORNIA COLLEGE FOR HEALTH SCIENCES
222 W. 24th St., National City 91950-9998 *Type:* Private professional and home study *Accred.:* 1980/1987 (ACCSCT); 1981/1992 (DETC) *Degrees:* A *Prof. Accred.:* Respiratory Therapy, Respiratory Therapy Technology *CEO:* Pres. Kenneth Scheiderman
(619) 477-4800

CALIFORNIA COLLEGE OF ARTS AND CRAFTS
5212 Broadway, Oakland 94618 *Type:* Private professional *Accred.:* 1954/1984 (WASC-Sr.) *Calendar:* Tri. plan *Degrees:* B, M *Prof. Accred.:* Art, Interior Design *CEO:* Pres. Lorne M. Buchman
FTE Enroll: 1,005   (510) 653-8118

CALIFORNIA COLLEGE OF PODIATRIC MEDICINE
1210 Scott St., San Francisco 94115 *Type:* Private professional *Accred.:* 1961/1983 (WASC-Sr.) *Calendar:* Sem. plan *Degrees:* B, M, P, D *Prof. Accred.:* Podiatry *CEO:* Pres. Leonard Levy
FTE Enroll: 413   (415) 563-8070

CALIFORNIA CULINARY ACADEMY
625 Polk St., San Francisco 94102-3368 *Type:* Private *Accred.:* 1982/1988 (ACCSCT) *Degrees:* A, C *CEO:* Pres. Alexander Hehmeyer
(415) 771-3536

CALIFORNIA DESIGN COLLEGE
3440 Wilshire Blvd., Los Angeles 90010 *Type:* Private business *Accred.:* 1995 (ACICS) *Calendar:* Qtr. plan *Degrees:* A, C *CEO:* Exec. Dir. Sabrina Kay
Enroll: 50   (213) 251-3636

CALIFORNIA INSTITUTE OF INTEGRAL STUDIES
765 Ashbury St., San Francisco 94117 *Type:* Private graduate only *Accred.:* 1981/1984

(WASC-Sr.) *Calendar:* Qtr. plan *Degrees:* B, M, D *CEO:* Pres. Robert McDermott
FTE Enroll: 820   (415) 753-6100

CALIFORNIA INSTITUTE OF TECHNOLOGY
1201 E California Blvd., Pasadena 91125-0001 *Type:* Private *Accred.:* 1949/1990 (WASC-Sr.) *Calendar:* Qtr. plan *Degrees:* B, M, D *Prof. Accred.:* Engineering (chemical, engineering physics/science) *CEO:* Pres. Thomas E. Everhart
FTE Enroll: 1,960   (818) 356-6811

CALIFORNIA INSTITUTE OF THE ARTS
24700 McBean Pkwy., Valencia 91355 *Type:* Private *Accred.:* 1955/1992 (WASC-Sr.) *Calendar:* Sem. plan *Degrees:* B, M *Prof. Accred.:* Art, Dance, Music *CEO:* Pres. Steven D. Lavine
FTE Enroll: 1,037   (805) 255-1050

CALIFORNIA LUTHERAN UNIVERSITY
60 Olsen Rd., Thousand Oaks 91360 *Type:* Private (Evangelical Lutheran Church) liberal arts *Accred.:* 1962/1989 (WASC-Sr.) *Calendar:* 4-1-4 plan *Degrees:* B, M *CEO:* Pres. Luther S. Luedtke
FTE Enroll: 2,098   (805) 492-2411

CALIFORNIA MARITIME ACADEMY
200 Maritime Academy Dr., P.O. Box 1392, Vallejo 94590-0644 *Type:* Public (state) *System:* California State University System *Accred.:* 1977/1992 (WASC-Sr.) *Calendar:* Tri. plan *Degrees:* B *Prof. Accred.:* Engineering Technology (naval architecture/marine) *CEO:* Pres. Mary E. Lyons
FTE Enroll: 498   (707) 648-4200

CALIFORNIA POLYTECHNIC STATE UNIVERSITY— SAN LUIS OBISPO
San Luis Obispo 93407 *Type:* Public (state) *System:* California State University System *Accred.:* 1951/1990 (WASC-Sr.) *Calendar:* Qtr. plan *Degrees:* B, M *Prof. Accred.:* Business (B,M), Computer Science, Construction Education (B), Engineering Technology (air conditioning), Engineering (aerospace, agricultural, architectural, civil, electrical, environmental/sanitary, industrial, materials, mechanical, metallurgical), Forestry Land-

scape Architecture (B) Recreation and Leisure Services (B) *CEO:* Pres. Warren J. Baker
FTE Enroll: 14,115 (805) 756-1111

CALIFORNIA SCHOOL OF PROFESSIONAL PSYCHOLOGY—ALMEDA
1005 Atlantic Ave., Alameda 94501 *Type:* Private professional *System:* California School of Professional Psychology *Accred.:* 1977/1989 (WASC-Sr.) *Calendar:* Sem. plan *Degrees:* M, D *Prof. Accred.:* Clinical Psychology *CEO:* Chanc. Katsuyuki Sakamoto
FTE Enroll: 490 (510) 523-2300

CALIFORNIA SCHOOL OF PROFESSIONAL PSYCHOLOGY—FRESNO
1350 M St., Fresno 93721 *Type:* Private professional *System:* California School of Professional Psychology *Accred.:* 1977/1989 (WASC-Sr.) *Calendar:* Sem. plan *Degrees:* M, D *Prof. Accred.:* Clinical Psychology *CEO:* Chanc. Mary Beth Kenkel
FTE Enroll: 324 (209) 486-8420

CALIFORNIA SCHOOL OF PROFESSIONAL PSYCHOLOGY—LOS ANGELES
1000 S. Fremont Ave., Alhambra 91803-1360 *Type:* Private professional *System:* California School of Professional Psychology *Accred.:* 1977/1989 (WASC-Sr.) *Calendar:* Sem. plan *Degrees:* M, D *Prof. Accred.:* Clinical Psychology *CEO:* Chanc. Lisa M. Porche-Burke
FTE Enroll: 554 (818) 284-2777

CALIFORNIA SCHOOL OF PROFESSIONAL PSYCHOLOGY—SAN DIEGO
6160 Cornerstone Ct. E., San Diego 92121-3275 *Type:* Private professional *System:* California School of Professional Psychology *Accred.:* 1977/1989 (WASC-Sr.) *Calendar:* Sem. plan *Degrees:* M, D *Prof. Accred.:* Clinical Psychology *CEO:* Chanc. Raymond J. Trybus
FTE Enroll: 630 (619) 452-1664

CALIFORNIA STATE POLYTECHNIC UNIVERSITY—POMONA
3801 W. Temple Ave., Pomona 91768 *Type:* Public (state) *System:* California State Uni-

versity System *Accred.:* 1970/1990 (WASC-Sr.) *Calendar:* Qtr. plan *Degrees:* B, M *Prof. Accred.:* Computer Science, Dietetics (internship), Engineering Technology (general), Engineering (aerospace, agricultural, chemical, civil, electrical, industrial, manufacturing, mechanical, surveying), Landscape Architecture (B,M), Planning (B,M) *CEO:* Pres. Bob H. Suzuki
FTE Enroll: 12,714 (909) 869-7659

CALIFORNIA STATE UNIVERSITY—BAKERSFIELD
9001 Stockdale Hwy., Bakersfield 93311-1099 *Type:* Public (state) *System:* California State University System *Accred.:* 1970/1990 (WASC-Sr.) *Calendar:* Qtr. plan *Degrees:* B, M *Prof. Accred.:* Business (B,M), Clinical Lab Scientist, Nursing (B,M), Public Administration, Teacher Education *CEO:* Pres. Tomas A. Arciniega
FTE Enroll: 4,172 (805) 664-2011

CALIFORNIA STATE UNIVERSITY—CHICO
First and Normal Sts., Chico 95929-0110 *Type:* Public (state) *System:* California State University System *Accred.:* 1949/1989 (WASC-Sr.) *Calendar:* Sem. plan *Degrees:* B, M *Prof. Accred.:* Art, Business (B,M), Computer Science, Construction Education (B), Engineering (civil, computer, electrical, mechanical), Music, Nursing (B), Recreation and Leisure Services (B), Social Work (B), Speech-Language Pathology *CEO:* Pres. Manuel A. Esteban
FTE Enroll: 12,628 (916) 898-6116

CALIFORNIA STATE UNIVERSITY—DOMINGUEZ HILLS
1000 E. Victoria St., Carson 90747 *Type:* Public (state) *System:* California State University System *Accred.:* 1965/1990 (WASC-Sr.) *Calendar:* Qtr. plan *Degrees:* B, M *Prof. Accred.:* Art, Clinical Lab Scientist, Music, Nuclear Medicine Technology, Nursing (B,M), Public Administration, Teacher Education *CEO:* Pres. Robert C. Detweiler
FTE Enroll: 7,711 (310) 516-3300

CALIFORNIA STATE UNIVERSITY—FRESNO
5241 N. Maple Ave., Fresno 93740-0054 *Type:* Public (state) *System:* California State

University System *Accred.:* 1949/1994 (WASC-Sr.) *Calendar:* Sem. plan *Degrees:* B, M *Prof. Accred.:* Audiology, Business (B,M), Construction Education (B), Counseling, Engineering (civil, electrical, industrial, mechanical, surveying), Interior Design, Journalism (B,M), Music, Nursing (B,M), Physical Therapy, Public Administration, Recreation and Leisure Services (B), Rehabilitation Counseling, Social Work (B,M), Speech-Language Pathology, Teacher Education, Theatre (A) *CEO:* Pres. John D. Welty
FTE Enroll: 14,594   (209) 278-4240

CALIFORNIA STATE UNIVERSITY—FULLERTON
800 N. State College Blvd., P.O. Box 34080, Fullerton 92634 *Type:* Public (state) *System:* California State University System *Accred.:* 1961/1991 (WASC-Sr.) *Calendar:* Sem. plan *Degrees:* B, M *Prof. Accred.:* Art, Business (B,M), Computer Science, Dance, Engineering (civil, electrical, mechanical), Journalism (B,M), Music, Nursing (B), Public Administration, Speech-Language Pathology, Teacher Education, Theatre *CEO:* Pres. Milton A. Gordon
FTE Enroll: 15,682   (714) 773-2011

CALIFORNIA STATE UNIVERSITY—HAYWARD
25800 Carlos Bee Blvd., Hayward 94542-3011 *Type:* Public (state) *System:* California State University System *Accred.:* 1961/1995 (WASC-Sr.) *Calendar:* Qtr. plan *Degrees:* B, M *Prof. Accred.:* Art, Business (B,M), Music, Nursing (B), Public Administration, Speech-Language Pathology, Teacher Education *CEO:* Pres. Norma S. Rees
FTE Enroll: 10,655   (510) 881-3000

CALIFORNIA STATE UNIVERSITY—LONG BEACH
1250 Bellflower Blvd., Long Beach 90840 *Type:* Public (state) *System:* California State University System *Accred.:* 1957/1992 (WASC-Sr.) *Calendar:* Sem. plan *Degrees:* B, M *Prof. Accred.:* Art, Audiology, Business (B,M), Construction Education (B), Dance, Engineering Technology (civil/construction, computer, electrical, industrial, manufacturing), Engineering (chemical, civil, computer, electrical, mechanical),

Home Economics, Journalism (B), Music, Nurse Anesthesia Education (M), Nursing (B,M), Physical Therapy, Public Administration, Radiation Therapy Technology, Recreation and Leisure Services (B), Social Work (B,M), Speech-Language Pathology, Theatre, *CEO:* Pres. Robert C. Maxson
FTE Enroll: 19,422   (310) 985-4111

CALIFORNIA STATE UNIVERSITY—LOS ANGELES
5151 State University Dr., Los Angeles 90032 *Type:* Public (state) *System:* California State University System *Accred.:* 1954/1990 (WASC-Sr.) *Calendar:* Qtr. plan *Degrees:* B, M *Prof. Accred.:* Art, Audiology, Business (B,M), Counseling, Dietetics (coordinated), Engineering (civil, electrical, mechanical), Music, Nursing (B,M), Public Administration, Rehabilitation Counseling, Social Work (B), Speech-Language Pathology, Teacher Education *CEO:* Pres. James M. Rosser
FTE Enroll: 12,589   (213) 343-3000

CALIFORNIA STATE UNIVERSITY—NORTHRIDGE
18111 Nordhoff St., Northridge 91330 *Type:* Public (state) *System:* California State University System *Accred.:* 1958/1991 (WASC-Sr.) *Calendar:* Sem. plan *Degrees:* B, M *Prof. Accred.:* Art, Audiology, Business (B,M), Computer Science, Counseling, Engineering (general), Home Economics, Journalism (B,M), Music, Physical Therapy, Radiography, Recreation and Leisure Services (B), Speech-Language Pathology, Teacher Education, Theatre (A), *CEO:* Pres. Blenda J. Wilson
FTE Enroll: 17,438   (818) 885-1200

CALIFORNIA STATE UNIVERSITY—SACRAMENTO
6000 J St., Sacramento 95819-2694 *Type:* Public (state) *System:* California State University System *Accred.:* 1951/1990 (WASC-Sr.) *Calendar:* Sem. plan *Degrees:* B, M *Prof. Accred.:* Art, Audiology, Business (B,M), Computer Science, Construction Education (B), Counseling, Engineering Technology (civil/construction, mechanical), Engineering (civil, computer, electrical, mechanical), Interior Design, Music, Nursing (B,M), Recreation and Leisure Services

(B), Rehabilitation Counseling, Social Work (B,M), Speech-Language Pathology *CEO:* Pres. Donald R. Gerth
FTE Enroll: 17,362   (916) 278-6011

CALIFORNIA STATE UNIVERSITY—SAN BERNARDINO
5500 State University Pkwy., San Bernardino 92407-2397 *Type:* Public (state) *System:* California State University System *Accred.:* 1965/1994 (WASC-Sr.) *Calendar:* Qtr. plan *Degrees:* B, M *Prof. Accred.:* Art, Business (B,M), Computer Science, Nursing (B), Public Administration, Rehabilitation Counseling, Social Work (M) *CEO:* Pres. Anthony H. Evans
FTE Enroll: 9,342   (909) 880-5000

CALIFORNIA STATE UNIVERSITY—SAN MARCOS
San Marcos 92096-0001 *Type:* Public (state) *System:* California State University System *Accred.:* 1993 (WASC-Sr.) *Calendar:* Sem. plan *Degrees:* B, M *CEO:* Pres. Bill W. Stacy
FTE Enroll: 1,995   (619) 750-4000

CALIFORNIA STATE UNIVERSITY—STANISLAUS
801 W. Monte Vista Ave., Turlock 95380 *Type:* Public (state) *System:* California State University System *Accred.:* 1963/1991 (WASC-Sr.) *Calendar:* 4-1-4 plan *Degrees:* B, M *Prof. Accred.:* Art, Computer Science, Music, Nursing (B), Public Administration, Teacher Education, Theatre *CEO:* Pres. Marvalene Hughes
FTE Enroll: 4,202   (209) 667-3122

CALIFORNIA WESTERN SCHOOL OF LAW
350 Cedar St., San Diego 92101 *Type:* Private professional *Calendar:* Sem. plan *Degrees:* P *Prof. Accred.:* Law *CEO:* Dean Michael H. Dessent
Enroll: 730   (619) 239-0391

CANADA COLLEGE
4200 Farm Hill Blvd., Redwood City 94061 *Type:* Public (district) junior *System:* San Mateo County Community College District *Accred.:* 1970/1995 (WASC-Jr.) *Calendar:*

Sem. plan *Degrees:* A *Prof. Accred.:* Radiography *CEO:* Pres. Marie E. Rosenwasser
Enroll: 5,714   (415) 306-3100

CENTURY BUSINESS COLLEGE
2665 Fifth Ave., San Diego 92103-6613 *Type:* Private *Accred.:* 1985/1990 (ACC-SCT) *Degrees:* A *CEO:* Vice Pres. Wayne G. Miletta
          (619) 233-0184

LOS ANGELES CAMPUS
3325 Wilshire Blvd., Los Angeles 90010-1703 *Accred.:* 1985/1990 (ACCSCT)
          (213) 383-1585

CENTURY SCHOOLS
3075 E. Flamingo Rd., Ste. 114, Las Vegas, NV 89121 *Accred.:* 1990 (ACC-SCT)
          (702) 451-6666

CERRITOS COLLEGE
11110 Alondra Blvd., Norwalk 90650 *Type:* Public (district) junior *System:* Cerritos Community College District *Accred.:* 1959/1990 (WASC-Jr.) *Calendar:* Sem. plan *Degrees:* A *Prof. Accred.:* Dental Assisting, Dental Hygiene, Nursing (A), Physical Therapy Assisting *CEO:* Pres. Fred Gaskin
Enroll: 19,030   (310) 860-2451

CERRO COSO COMMUNITY COLLEGE
3000 College Heights Blvd., Ridgecrest 93555 *Type:* Public (district) junior *System:* Kern Community College District *Accred.:* 1975/1995 (WASC-Jr.) *Calendar:* Sem. plan *Degrees:* A *CEO:* Pres. Raymond A. McCue
Enroll: 9,248   (619) 375-5001

CHABOT COLLEGE
25555 Hesperian Blvd., Hayward 94545-5001 *Type:* Public (district) junior *System:* Chabot-Las Positas Community College District *Accred.:* 1963/1991 (WASC-Jr.) *Calendar:* Qtr. plan *Degrees:* A *Prof. Accred.:* Dental Assisting (conditional), Dental Hygiene (conditional), Medical Assisting (AMA), Medical Record Technology *CEO:* Pres. Raul Cardoza
Enroll: 12,146   (510) 786-6600

CHAFFEY COLLEGE
5885 Haven Ave., Rancho Cucamonga 91701 *Type:* Public (district) junior *System:* Chaffey Community College District *Accred.:* 1952/1992 (WASC-Jr.) *Calendar:* Sem. plan *Degrees:* A *Prof. Accred.:* Dental Assisting, Nursing (A), Radiography *CEO:* Pres. Jerry W. Young
Enroll: 15,497   (909) 987-1737

CHAPMAN UNIVERSITY
333 N. Glassell St., Orange 92666 *Type:* Private (Disciples of Christ) liberal arts *Accred.:* 1956/1988 (WASC-Sr.) *Calendar:* 4-1-4 plan *Degrees:* A, B, M *Prof. Accred.:* Physical Therapy *CEO:* Pres. James L. Doti
FTE Enroll: 5,601   (714) 997-6815

CHARLES R. DREW UNIVERSITY OF MEDICINE AND SCIENCE
1621 E. 120th St., Los Angeles 90059 *Type:* Private *Accred.:* 1988/1995 (WASC-Sr.) *Calendar:* Sem. plan *Degrees:* A, B, M, D *Prof. Accred.:* Clinical Lab Scientist, Dietetics (coordinated), Medical Record Technology, Nuclear Medicine Technology, Physician Assisting/Surgeon Assisting, Radiography *CEO:* Pres. Reed V. Tuckson
FTE Enroll: 625   (213) 563-4800

CHRISTIAN HERITAGE COLLEGE
2100 Greenfield Dr., El Cajon 92019 *Type:* Private (Scott Memorial Baptist Church) liberal arts *Accred.:* 1984 (WASC-Sr.) *Calendar:* Sem. plan *Degrees:* B *CEO:* Pres. David P. Jeremiah
FTE Enroll: 439   (619) 441-2200

CHURCH DIVINITY SCHOOL OF THE PACIFIC
2451 Ridge Rd., Berkeley 94709-1211 *Type:* Private (Episcopal) professional; graduate only *Accred.:* 1954/1994 (ATS); 1978/1994 (WASC-Sr.) *Calendar:* Qtr. plan *Degrees:* M, P, D *CEO:* Pres. Donn F. Morgan
FTE Enroll: 81   (510) 204-0700

CITRUS COLLEGE
1000 W. Foothill Blvd., Glendora 91741-1899 *Type:* Public (district) junior *System:* Citrus Community College District *Accred.:* 1952/1992 (WASC-Jr.) *Calendar:* Sem. plan

Degrees: A *Prof. Accred.:* Dental Assisting *CEO:* Pres. Louis E. Zellers
Enroll: 10,489   (818) 963-0323

CITY COLLEGE OF SAN FRANCISCO
50 Phelan Ave., San Francisco 94112 *Type:* Public (district) junior *System:* San Francisco Community College District *Accred.:* 1952/1994 (WASC-Jr.) *Calendar:* Sem. plan *Degrees:* A *Prof. Accred.:* Dental Assisting, Dental Laboratory Technology, Medical Assisting (AMA) Radiation Therapy Technology *CEO:* Chanc. Del M. Anderson
                    (415) 239-3000

THE CLAREMONT GRADUATE SCHOOL
160 E. 10th St., Claremont 91711 *Type:* Private graduate only *System:* Claremont University Center *Accred.:* 1949/1993 (WASC-Sr.) *Calendar:* Sem. plan *Degrees:* M, D *Prof. Accred.:* Business (M) *CEO:* Pres. John D. Maguire
FTE Enroll: 1,038   (909) 621-8000

CLAREMONT MCKENNA COLLEGE
850 Columbia Ave., Claremont 91711 *Type:* Private liberal arts *System:* Claremont University Center *Accred.:* 1949/1991 (WASC-Sr.) *Calendar:* Sem. plan *Degrees:* B *CEO:* Pres. Jack L. Stark
FTE Enroll: 939   (909) 621-8111

CLEVELAND CHIROPRACTIC COLLEGE
590 N. Vermont Ave., Los Angeles 90004 *Type:* Private professional *Calendar:* Tri. plan *Degrees:* B, P *Prof. Accred.:* Chiropractic Education *CEO:* Pres. Carl S. Cleveland, III
FTE Enroll: 460   (213) 660-6166

COASTLINE COMMUNITY COLLEGE
11460 Warner Ave., Fountain Valley 92708 *Type:* Public (district) junior *System:* Coast Community College District *Accred.:* 1978/1994 (WASC-Jr.) *Calendar:* Sem. plan *Degrees:* A *CEO:* Pres. Leslie N. Purdy
Enroll: 13,433   (714) 546-7600

COGSWELL POLYTECHNICAL COLLEGE
1175 Bordeaux Dr., Sunnyvale 94089-1299 *Type:* Private technical *Accred.:* 1977/1982 (WASC-Sr. probational) *Calendar:* Tri. plan

Degrees: A, B *Prof. Accred.:* Engineering Technology (electrical, mechanical) *CEO:* Pres. James T. Thompson
FTE Enroll: 315   (408) 541-0100

COLEMAN COLLEGE
7380 Parkway Dr., La Mesa 91942-1532 *Type:* Private senior *Accred.:* 1967/1994 (ACICS) *Calendar:* Qtr. plan *Degrees:* A, B, M, C *CEO:* Acting CEO Michael Maier
                                     (619) 465-3990

SAN MARCOS CAMPUS
1284 W. San Marcos Blvd., San Marcos 92069 senior *Accred.:* 1967/1994 (ACICS) *Calendar:* Qtr. plan *Degrees:* A, C
Enroll: 130   (619) 747-3990

COLLEGE OF ALAMEDA
555 Atlantic Ave., Alameda 94501 *Type:* Public (district) junior *System:* Peralta Community College District *Accred.:* 1973/1993 (WASC-Jr.) *Calendar:* Qtr. plan *Degrees:* A *Prof. Accred.:* Dental Assisting *CEO:* Pres. George Herring
Enroll: 5,597   (510) 522-7221

COLLEGE OF MARIN
835 College Ave., Kentfield 94904 *Type:* Public (district) junior *System:* Marin Community College District *Accred.:* 1952/1993 (WASC-Jr.) *Calendar:* Sem. plan *Degrees:* A *Prof. Accred.:* Dental Assisting, Nursing (A) *CEO:* Pres. James E. Middleton
Enroll: 8,847   (415) 457-8811

COLLEGE OF NOTRE DAME
1500 Ralston Ave., Belmont 94002-9974 *Type:* Private (Roman Catholic) liberal arts *Accred.:* 1955/1991 (WASC-Sr.) *Calendar:* Sem. plan *Degrees:* B, M *Prof. Accred.:* Music *CEO:* Pres. Margaret A. Huber
FTE Enroll: 1,271   (415) 593-1601

COLLEGE OF OCEANEERING
Los Angeles Harbor, 272 S. Fries Ave., Wilmington 90744 *Type:* Private *Accred.:* 1982/1992 (WASC-Jr.) *Calendar:* 12-mos. program *Degrees:* A *CEO:* Exec. Dir. Ron Friedrich
Enroll: 400   (310) 834-2501

COLLEGE OF OSTEOPATHIC MEDICINE OF THE PACIFIC
309 E. College Plaza, Pomona 91766-1889 *Type:* Private *Accred.:* 1990 (WASC-Sr. candidate) *Calendar:* Sem. plan *Degrees:* B, M *Prof. Accred.:* Osteopathy, Physical Therapy, Physician Assisting/Surgeon Assisting *CEO:* Pres. Philip Pumerantz
FTE Enroll: 853   (909) 623-6116

COLLEGE OF SAN MATEO
1700 W. Hillsdale Blvd., San Mateo 94402 *Type:* Public (district) junior *System:* San Mateo County Community College District *Accred.:* 1952/1995 (WASC-Jr.) *Calendar:* Sem. plan *Degrees:* A *Prof. Accred.:* Dental Assisting *CEO:* Pres. Peter J. Landsberger
Enroll: 12,088   (415) 574-6161

COLLEGE OF THE CANYONS
26455 N. Rockwell Canyon Rd., Santa Clarita 91355 *Type:* Public (district) junior *System:* Santa Clarita Community College District *Accred.:* 1972/1990 (WASC-Jr.) *Calendar:* Sem. plan *Degrees:* A *CEO:* Pres. Dianne G. Van Hook
Enroll: 6,795   (805) 259-7800

COLLEGE OF THE DESERT
43-500 Monterey Ave., Palm Desert 92260 *Type:* Public (district) junior *System:* Desert Community College District *Accred.:* 1963/1993 (WASC-Jr.) *Calendar:* Sem. plan *Degrees:* A *Prof. Accred.:* Nursing (A), Respiratory Therapy *CEO:* Pres. David A. George
Enroll: 11,029   (619) 346-8041

COLLEGE OF THE REDWOODS
7351 Tompkins Hill Rd., Eureka 95501 *Type:* Public (district) junior *System:* Redwoods Community College District *Accred.:* 1967/1994 (WASC-Jr.) *Calendar:* Sem. plan *Degrees:* A *Prof. Accred.:* Dental Assisting *CEO:* Pres. Cedric A. Sampson
Enroll: 6,803   (707) 445-6700

COLLEGE OF THE SEQUOIAS
915 S. Mooney Blvd., Visalia 93277 *Type:* Public (district) junior *System:* Sequoias Community College District *Accred.:* 1952/

1995 (WASC-Jr.) *Calendar:* Sem. plan
Degrees: A *CEO:* Pres. M. Douglas Kechter
Enroll: 9,086   (209) 730-3700

COLLEGE OF THE SISKIYOUS
800 College Ave., Weed 96094 *Type:* Public
(district) junior *System:* Siskiyou Joint Community College District *Accred.:* 1961/1992
(WASC-Jr.) *Calendar:* Sem. plan *Degrees:*
A *CEO:* Pres. Martha G. Romero
Enroll: 2,774   (916) 938-4462

COLUMBIA COLLEGE
P.O. Box 1849, Columbia 95310 *Type:* Pub-
lic (district) junior *System:* Yosemite Com-
munity College District *Accred.:* 1972/1994
(WASC-Jr.) *Calendar:* Sem. plan *Degrees:*
A *CEO:* Pres. Kenneth B. White
Enroll: 2,338   (209) 533-5100

COLUMBIA COLLEGE HOLLYWOOD
925 N. La Brea Ave., Los Angeles 90038-
2392 *Type:* Private *Accred.:* 1979/1986
(ACCSCT) *Calendar:* Qtr. plan *Degrees:* A,
B *CEO:* Pres. Brianne Murphy
                    (213) 851-0550

COMPTON COMMUNITY COLLEGE
1111 E. Artesia Blvd., Compton 90221 *Type:*
Public (district) junior *System:* Compton
Community College District *Accred.:*
1952/1993 (WASC-Jr.) *Calendar:* Sem. plan
Degrees: A *CEO:* Pres. Byron R. Skinner
Enroll: 5,200   (310) 637-2660

CONCORDE CAREER INSTITUTE
1717 S. Brookhurst St., Anaheim 92804-
6461 *Type:* Private *Accred.:* 1968 (ACC-
SCT) *Degrees:* A *Prof. Accred.:* Medical
Assisting (AMA) *CEO:* Dir. William G.
Carver
                    (714) 635-3450

CONCORDIA UNIVERSITY
1530 Concordia W., Irvine 92715-3299
Type: Private (Lutheran-Missouri Synod)
liberal arts *Accred.:* 1981/1995 (WASC-Sr.)
Calendar: Qtr. plan *Degrees:* A, B, M *CEO:*
Pres. D. Ray Halm
FTE Enroll: 864   (714) 854-8002

CONTRA COSTA COLLEGE
2600 Mission Bell Dr., San Pablo 94806
Type: Public (district) junior *System:* Contra
Costa Community College District *Accred.:*
1952/1989 (WASC-Jr.) *Calendar:* Sem. plan
Degrees: A *Prof. Accred.:* Dental Assisting
CEO: Pres. D. Candy Rose
Enroll: 8,500   (510) 235-7800

COSUMNES RIVER COLLEGE
8401 Center Pkwy., Sacramento 95823 *Type:*
Public (district) junior *System:* Los Rios
Community College District *Accred.:* 1972/
1991 (WASC-Jr.) *Calendar:* Sem. plan
Degrees: A *Prof. Accred.:* Medical Assisting
(AMA), Medical Record Technology, Veteri-
nary Technology *CEO:* Pres. Merrilee Lewis
Enroll: 11,303   (916) 688-7451

CRAFTON HILLS COLLEGE
11711 Sand Canyon Rd., Yucaipa 92399 *Type:*
Public (district) junior *System:* San Bernardino
Community College District *Accred.:* 1975/
1990 (WASC-Jr.) *Calendar:* Sem. plan
Degrees: A *Prof. Accred.:* EMT-Paramedic,
Respiratory Therapy, Respiratory Therapy
Technology *CEO:* Pres. Luis S. Gomez
Enroll: 5,111   (714) 794-2161

CUESTA COLLEGE
P.O. Box 8106, San Luis Obispo 93403 *Type:*
Public (district) junior *System:* San Luis
Obispo Community College District *Accred.:*
1968/1991 (WASC-Jr.) *Calendar:* Sem. plan
Degrees: A *CEO:* Pres. Grace N. Mitchell
Enroll: 7,963   (805) 546-3100

CUYAMACA COLLEGE
2950 Jamacha Rd., El Cajon 92019-4304
Type: Public (district) junior *System:* Grossmont-Cuyamaca Community College District *Accred.:* 1980/1996 (WASC-Jr.) *Calendar:* Sem. plan *Degrees:* A *CEO:* Pres.
Sherrill L. Amador
Enroll: 5,003   (619) 670-5425

CYPRESS COLLEGE
9200 Valley View St., Cypress 90630 *Type:*
Public (district) junior *System:* North Orange
County   Community   College   District
Accred.: 1968/1993 (WASC-Jr.) *Calendar:*

Sem. plan *Degrees:* A *Prof. Accred.:* Dental Assisting, Dental Hygiene, Funeral Service Education (Mortuary Science), Medical Record Technology, Radiography *CEO:* Pres. Christine Johnson
Enroll: 14,780   (714) 527-8238

D-Q UNIVERSITY
P.O. Box 409, Davis 95617 *Type:* Public junior *Accred.:* 1977/1992 (WASC-Jr. probational) *Calendar:* Sem. plan *Degrees:* A *CEO:* Pres. Francis Becenti
Enroll: 535   (916) 758-0470

DE ANZA COLLEGE
21250 Stevens Creek Blvd., Cupertino 95014 *Type:* Public (district) junior *System:* Foothill-DeAnza Community College District *Accred.:* 1969/1994 (WASC-Jr.) *Calendar:* Qtr. plan *Degrees:* A *Prof. Accred.:* Medical Assisting (AMA), Physical Therapy Assisting *CEO:* Pres. Martha J. Kanter
Enroll: 22,915   (408) 864-5678

DEFENSE LANGUAGE INSTITUTE
Presidio of Monterey 93944 *Type:* Public (federal) technical *Accred.:* 1979/1994 (WASC-Jr.) *Degrees:* A *CEO:* Cmdt. Vladimir Sobiochevsky
Enroll: 2,900   (408) 647-5118

DESIGN INSTITUTE OF SAN DIEGO
8555 Commerce Ave., San Diego 92121 *Type:* Private professional *Accred.:* 1995 (ACICS) *Degrees:* B, P *Prof. Accred.:* Interior Design *CEO:* Dir. Gloria Rosenstein
(619) 566-1200

DEVRY INSTITUTE OF TECHNOLOGY—POMONA
901 Corporate Center Dr., Pomona 91768-2642 *Type:* Private *System:* DeVry Institutes *Accred.:* 1981/1992 (NCA) *Calendar:* Sem. plan *Degrees:* A, B *Prof. Accred.:* Engineering Technology (electrical) *CEO:* Pres. RoseMarie Dishman
(909) 622-8866

* Indirect NCA accreditation through DeVry Institutes

LONG BEACH CAMPUS
3880 Kilroy Airport Way, Long Beach 90806 *System:* DeVry Institutes *Degrees:* A, B
(310) 427-0861

DIABLO VALLEY COLLEGE
321 Golf Club Rd., Pleasant Hill 94523 *Type:* Public (district) junior *System:* Contra Costa Community College District *Accred.:* 1952/1991 (WASC-Jr.) *Calendar:* Sem. plan *Degrees:* A *Prof. Accred.:* Dental Assisting, Dental Hygiene *CEO:* Pres. Phyllis L. Peterson
Enroll: 20,000   (510) 685-1230

DOMINICAN COLLEGE OF SAN RAFAEL
50 Acacia St., San Rafael 94901 *Type:* Private (Roman Catholic) liberal arts *Accred.:* 1949/1987 (WASC-Sr.) *Calendar:* Sem. plan *Degrees:* B, M *Prof. Accred.:* Nursing (B) *CEO:* Pres. Joseph R. Fink
FTE Enroll: 1,124   (415) 457-4440

DOMINICAN SCHOOL OF PHILOSOPHY AND THEOLOGY
2401 Ridge Rd., Berkeley 94709 *Type:* Private (Roman Catholic) professional *Accred.:* 1978/1993 (ATS); 1964/1993 (WASC-Sr.) *Calendar:* Sem. plan *Degrees:* B, M, P *CEO:* Pres. Gregory P. Rocca
FTE Enroll: 59   (510) 849-2030

DON BOSCO TECHNICAL INSTITUTE
1151 San Gabriel Blvd., Rosemead 91770 *Type:* Private (Roman Catholic) 2-year *Accred.:* 1972/1996 (WASC-Jr.) *Calendar:* Sem. plan *Degrees:* A *CEO:* Pres. Nicholas Reina
Enroll: 208   (818) 307-6500

EAST LOS ANGELES COLLEGE
1301 Cesar Chavez Ave., Monterey Park 91754 *Type:* Public (district) junior *System:* Los Angeles Community College District *Accred.:* 1952/1992 (WASC-Jr.) *Calendar:* Sem. plan *Degrees:* A *Prof. Accred.:* Medical Record Technology, Respiratory Therapy *CEO:* Pres. Ernest H. Moreno
Enroll: 15,800   (213) 265-8650

EL CAMINO COLLEGE
16007 Crenshaw Blvd., Torrance 90506
Type: Public (district) junior *System:* El
Camino Community College District
Accred.: 1952/1990 (WASC-Jr.) *Calendar:*
Sem. plan *Degrees:* A *Prof. Accred.:* Nursing
(A), Radiography, Respiratory Therapy
CEO: Pres. Thomas Fallo
Enroll: 21,801   (310) 532-3670

EMPEROR'S COLLEGE OF TRADITIONAL
ORIENTAL MEDICINE
1807-B Wilshire Blvd., Santa Monica 90403
Type: Private professional *Calendar:* Qtr.
plan *Degrees:* M *Prof. Accred.:* Acupuncture
(M) *CEO:* Pres. Bong Dal Kim
FTE Enroll: 182   (310) 453-8833

LOS ANGELES CAMPUS
3625 W. 6th St., Ste. 220, Los Angeles
90020
                             (213) 738-8833

EMPIRE COLLEGE
3033 Cleveland Ave., Ste. 102, Santa Rosa
95403 *Type:* Private business *Accred.:*
1969/1987 (ACICS) *Calendar:* Sem. plan
Degrees: A, C *CEO:* Pres. Roy O. Hurd
                             (707) 546-4000

EVERGREEN VALLEY COLLEGE
3095 Yerba Buena Rd., San Jose 95135
Type: Public (district) junior *System:* San
Jose-Evergreen Community College District
Accred.: 1977/1992 (WASC-Jr.) *Calendar:*
Sem. plan *Degrees:* A *Prof. Accred.:* Nursing
(A) *CEO:* Pres. Noelia Vela
Enroll: 10,655   (408) 274-7900

FASHION CAREERS OF CALIFORNIA
1923 Morena Blvd., San Diego 92110 *Type:*
Private business *Accred.:* 1983 (ACICS)
Degrees: A, C *CEO:* Dir. Patricia G. O'Connor
                             (619) 275-4700

THE FASHION INSTITUTE OF DESIGN AND
MERCHANDISING
919 S. Grand Ave., Los Angeles 90015 *Type:*
Private 2-year *Accred.:* 1978/1993 (WASC-
Jr.) *Calendar:* Qtr. plan *Degrees:* A *Prof.*

Accred.: Interior Design *CEO:* Pres. Tonian
Hohberg
Enroll: 2,226   (213) 624-1200

COSTA MESA CAMPUS
3420 S. Bristol St., Costa Mesa 92626
                             (714) 546-0930

SAN DIEGO CAMPUS
1010 Second Ave., Ste. 200, San Diego
92101
                             (619) 235-4515

SAN FRANCISCO CAMPUS
55 Stockton St., San Francisco 94108
                             (415) 433-6691

FEATHER RIVER COLLEGE
P.O. Box 11110, Quincy 95971 *Type:* Public
(district) junior *System:* Feather River Com-
munity College District *Accred.:* 1973/1994
(WASC-Jr.) *Calendar:* Sem. plan *Degrees:*
A *CEO:* Pres. Donald J. Donato
Enroll: 1,435   (916) 283-0202

FIELDING INSTITUTE
2112 Santa Barbara St., Santa Barbara 93105
Type: Private professional *Accred.:* 1982
(WASC-Sr.) *Calendar:* Tri. plan *Degrees:*
M, D *Prof. Accred.:* Clinical Psychology
(provisional) *CEO:* Pres. Donald J. MacIn-
tyre
FTE Enroll: 817   (805) 687-1099

FOOTHILL COLLEGE
12345 El Monte Rd., Los Altos Hills 94022
Type: Public (district) junior *System:*
Foothill-DeAnza Community College Dis-
trict *Accred.:* 1959/1994 (WASC-Jr.) *Calen-
dar:* Qtr. plan *Degrees:* A *Prof. Accred.:*
Dental Assisting, Dental Hygiene, Radiation
Therapy Technology, Radiography, Respira-
tory Therapy, Veterinary Technology *CEO:*
Pres. Bernadine Chuck Fong
Enroll: 19,393   (415) 949-7200

FRANCISCAN SCHOOL OF THEOLOGY
1712 Euclid Ave., Berkeley 94709 *Type:* Private (Roman Catholic) graduate only
Accred.: 1975/1991 (ATS); 1975/1988

(WASC-Sr.) *Calendar:* Qtr. plan *Degrees:* M *CEO:* Pres. William M. Cieslak, O.F.M.
FTE Enroll: 75   (510) 848-5232

FRESNO CITY COLLEGE
1101 E. University Ave., Fresno 93741 *Type:* Public (district) junior *System:* State Center Community College District *Accred.:* 1952/1994 (WASC-Jr.) *Calendar:* Sem. plan *Degrees:* A *Prof. Accred.:* Dental Hygiene, Radiography, Respiratory Therapy *CEO:* Pres. Brice W. Harris
Enroll: 18,243   (209) 442-4600

FRESNO PACIFIC COLLEGE
1717 S. Chestnut Ave., Fresno 93702 *Type:* Private (Mennonite Brethren) liberal arts *Accred.:* 1961/1994 (WASC-Sr.) *Calendar:* Sem. plan *Degrees:* A, B, M *CEO:* Pres. Richard Kriegbaum
FTE Enroll: 1,073   (209) 453-2000

FULLER THEOLOGICAL SEMINARY
135 N. Oakland Ave., Pasadena 91182 *Type:* Private (interdenominational) professional; graduate only *Accred.:* 1957/1990 (ATS); 1969/1990 (WASC-Sr.) *Calendar:* Qtr. plan *Degrees:* M, P, D *Prof. Accred.:* Clinical Psychology, Marriage and Family Therapy (M), Psychology Internship (provisional) *CEO:* Pres. Richard J. Mouw
FTE Enroll: 1,282   (818) 584-5200

FULLERTON COLLEGE
321 E. Chapman Ave., Fullerton 92632 *Type:* Public (district) junior *System:* North Orange County Community College District *Accred.:* 1952/1993 (WASC-Jr.) *Calendar:* Sem. plan *Degrees:* A *CEO:* Pres. Vera Martinez
Enroll: 18,704   (714) 992-7000

GAVILAN COLLEGE
5055 Santa Teresa Blvd., Gilroy 95020 *Type:* Public (district) junior *System:* Gavilan Joint Community College District *Accred.:* 1952/1995 (WASC-Jr.) *Calendar:* Sem. plan *Degrees:* A *CEO:* Pres. Glenn E. Mayle
Enroll: 4,557   (408) 848-4712

GLENDALE COMMUNITY COLLEGE
1500 N. Verdugo Rd., Glendale 91208 *Type:* Public (district) junior *System:* Glendale Community College District *Accred.:* 1952/1992 (WASC-Jr.) *Calendar:* Sem. plan *Degrees:* A *CEO:* Pres. John A. Davitt
Enroll: 14,149   (818) 240-1000

GOLDEN GATE BAPTIST THEOLOGICAL SEMINARY
Strawberry Pt., Mill Valley 94941 *Type:* Private (Southern Baptist) professional; graduate only *Accred.:* 1962/1990 (ATS); 1971/1990 (WASC-Sr.) *Calendar:* Sem. plan *Degrees:* M, P, D *Prof. Accred.:* Music *CEO:* Pres. William O. Crews, Jr.
FTE Enroll: 636   (415) 388-8080

GOLDEN GATE UNIVERSITY
536 Mission St., San Francisco 94105-2968 *Type:* Private business *Accred.:* 1959/1994 (WASC-Sr.) *Calendar:* Tri. plan *Degrees:* A, B, M, P, D *Prof. Accred.:* Law *CEO:* Pres. Thomas M. Stauffer
FTE Enroll: 4,172   (415) 442-7000

GOLDEN WEST COLLEGE
15744 Golden West St., Huntington Beach 92647-0592 *Type:* Public (district) junior *System:* Coast Community College District *Accred.:* 1969/1992 (WASC-Jr.) *Calendar:* Sem. plan *Degrees:* A *Prof. Accred.:* Nursing (A) *CEO:* Interim Pres. Kenneth D. Yglesias
Enroll: 13,094   (714) 892-7711

GOLF ACADEMY OF SAN DIEGO
2022 University Dr., Vista 92083 *Type:* Private business *Accred.:* 1982/1994 (ACICS) *Degrees:* A, C *CEO:* Pres. Dana K. Schwartz
                    (619) 794-2810

GOLF ACADEMY OF THE SOUTH
307 Daneswood Way, Casselberryngs, FL 32707 *Accred.:* 1990 (ACICS)
                    (407) 699-1990

GRADUATE THEOLOGICAL UNION
2400 Ridge Rd., Berkeley 94709 *Type:* Private (interdenominational) graduate only *Accred.:* 1969/1995 (ATS); 1966/1995

(WASC-Sr.) *Calendar:* Sem. plan *Degrees:* M, D *CEO:* Pres. Glenn R. Bucher
FTE Enroll: 421　　　　(510) 649-2400

GROSSMONT COLLEGE
8800 Grossmont College Dr., El Cajon 92020 *Type:* Public (district) junior *System:* Grossmont-Cuyamaca Community College District *Accred.:* 1963/1996 (WASC-Jr.) *Calendar:* Sem. plan *Degrees:* A *Prof. Accred.:* Cardiovascular Technology, Nursing (A), Respiratory Therapy *CEO:* Pres. Richard Sanchez
Enroll: 17,441　　　　(619) 465-1700

HARTNELL COLLEGE
156 Homestead Ave., Salinas 93901 *Type:* Public (district) junior *System:* Hartnell Community College District *Accred.:* 1952/1995 (WASC-Jr.) *Calendar:* Sem. plan *Degrees:* A *Prof. Accred.:* Veterinary Technology *CEO:* Pres. Edward J. Valeau
Enroll: 7,554　　　　(408) 755-6900

HARVEY MUDD COLLEGE
301 E. 12th St., Claremont 91711 *Type:* Private professional *System:* Claremont University Center *Accred.:* 1959/1987 (WASC-Sr.) *Calendar:* Sem. plan *Degrees:* B, M *Prof. Accred.:* Engineering (general) *CEO:* Pres. Henry E. Riggs
FTE Enroll: 645　　　　(909) 621-8000

HEALD BUSINESS COLLEGE—CONCORD
2150 John Glenn Dr., Concord 94520 *Type:* Private business *System:* Heald Colleges *Accred.:* 1983/1994 (WASC-Jr.) *Calendar:* Qtr. plan *Degrees:* A *CEO:* Dir. Steven M. Kinzer
　　　　　　　　　　(510) 827-1300

HEALD BUSINESS COLLEGE—FRESNO
255 W. Bullard Ave., Fresno 93704 *Type:* Private business *System:* Heald Colleges *Accred.:* 1983/1994 (WASC-Jr.) *Calendar:* Qtr. plan *Degrees:* A *CEO:* Dir. Alex Babigan
　　　　　　　　　　(209) 438-4222

HEALD BUSINESS COLLEGE—HAYWARD
777 Southland Dr., Hayward 94545 *Type:* Private business *System:* Heald Colleges

Accred.: 1983/1994 (WASC-Jr.) *Calendar:* Qtr. plan *Degrees:* A *CEO:* Dir. Barbara Gordon
　　　　　　　　　　(510) 784-7000

HEALD BUSINESS COLLEGE—OAKLAND
1000 Broadway, Oakland 94607 *Type:* Private business *System:* Heald Colleges *Accred.:* 1983/1994 (WASC-Jr.) *Calendar:* Qtr. plan *Degrees:* A *CEO:* Dir. Carolyn Greenleaf
　　　　　　　　　　(510) 444-0201

HEALD BUSINESS COLLEGE—SACRAMENTO
2910 Prospect Park Dr., Rancho Cordova 95670 *Type:* Private business *System:* Heald Colleges *Accred.:* 1983/1994 (WASC-Jr.) *Calendar:* Qtr. plan *Degrees:* A *CEO:* Dir. Donald E. Hardenbrook
Enroll: 32　　　　(916) 638-1616

HEALD BUSINESS COLLEGE—SALINAS
1333 Schilling Pl., P.O. Box 3167, Salinas 93901 *Type:* Private business *System:* Heald Colleges *Accred.:* 1983/1994 (WASC-Jr.) *Calendar:* Qtr. plan *Degrees:* A *CEO:* Dir. Chris Tilley
　　　　　　　　　　(408) 757-1700

HEALD BUSINESS COLLEGE—SAN FRANCISCO
1453 Mission St., San Francisco 94103 *Type:* Private business *System:* Heald Colleges *Accred.:* 1983/1994 (WASC-Jr.) *Calendar:* Qtr. plan *Degrees:* A *CEO:* Dir. Linda Sempliner
　　　　　　　　　　(415) 673-5500

HEALD BUSINESS COLLEGE—SAN JOSE
2665 N. First St., Ste. 110, San Jose 95134 *Type:* Private business *System:* Heald Colleges *Accred.:* 1983/1994 (WASC-Jr.) *Calendar:* Qtr. plan *Degrees:* A *CEO:* Dir. Peter Lee
　　　　　　　　　　(408) 955-9555

HEALD BUSINESS COLLEGE—SANTA ROSA
2425 Mendocino Ave., Santa Rosa 95403 *Type:* Private business *System:* Heald Colleges *Accred.:* 1983/1994 (WASC-Jr.) *Calendar:* Qtr. plan *Degrees:* A *CEO:* Dir. Gordon Kent
　　　　　　　　　　(707) 525-1300

HEALD BUSINESS COLLEGE—STOCKTON
1776 W. March La., 3rd Fl., Stockton 95207
Type: Private business *System:* Heald Colleges *Accred.:* 1983/1994 (WASC-Jr.) *Calendar:* Qtr. plan *Degrees:* A *CEO:* Dir. Michael Mallory
　　　　　　　　　　(209) 477-1114

HEALD INSTITUTE OF TECHNOLOGY—HAYWARD
24301 Southland Dr., Ste. 500, Hayward 94545 *Type:* Private technical *System:* Heald Colleges *Accred.:* 1983/1994 (WASC-Jr.) *Calendar:* Qtr. plan *Degrees:* A *CEO:* Dir. Michael Bennett
　　　　　　　　　　(510) 783-2100

HEALD INSTITUTE OF TECHNOLOGY—MARTINEZ
2860 Howe Rd., Martinez 94553 *Type:* Private technical *System:* Heald Colleges *Accred.:* 1983/1994 (WASC-Jr.) *Calendar:* Qtr. plan *Degrees:* A *CEO:* Dir. Douglas Cole
　　　　　　　　　　(510) 228-9000

HEALD INSTITUTE OF TECHNOLOGY—
SACRAMENTO
3737 Marconi Ave., Sacramento 95821 *Type:* Private technical *System:* Heald Colleges *Accred.:* 1983/1994 (WASC-Jr.) *Calendar:* Qtr. plan *Degrees:* A *CEO:* Dir. William Johnson
　　　　　　　　　　(916) 972-0999

HEALD INSTITUTE OF TECHNOLOGY—SAN
FRANCISCO
250 Executive Park Blvd., Ste. 1000, San Francisco 94134 *Type:* Private technical *System:* Heald Colleges *Accred.:* 1983/1994 (WASC-Jr.) *Calendar:* Qtr. plan *Degrees:* A *CEO:* Dir. Timothy Cassady
　　　　　　　　　　(415) 822-2900

HEALD INSTITUTE OF TECHNOLOGY—SAN JOSE
684 El Paseo de Saratoga, Ste. A, San Jose 95130 *Type:* Private technical *System:* Heald Colleges *Accred.:* 1983/1994 (WASC-Jr.) *Calendar:* Qtr. plan *Degrees:* A *CEO:* Dir. Kenneth Heinemann
　　　　　　　　　　(408) 295-8000

HEBREW UNION COLLEGE—JEWISH INSTITUTE OF RELIGION
3077 University Ave., Los Angeles 90007 *Type:* Private (Reform Judaism) *Accred.:* 1960/1995 (WASC-Sr.) *Calendar:* Sem. plan *Degrees:* B, M, D *CEO:* Exec. Vice Pres. Uri D. Herscher
FTE Enroll: 69　　　　(213) 749-3424

HOLY NAMES COLLEGE
3500 Mountain Blvd., Oakland 94619-9989 *Type:* Private (Roman Catholic) liberal arts *Accred.:* 1949/1995 (WASC-Sr.) *Calendar:* Sem. plan *Degrees:* B, M *Prof. Accred.:* Music, Nursing (B) *CEO:* Pres. Mary Alice Muellerleile
FTE Enroll: 805　　　　(510) 436-1000

HUMBOLDT STATE UNIVERSITY
Arcata 95521 *Type:* Public (state) *System:* California State University System *Accred.:* 1949/1990 (WASC-Sr.) *Calendar:* Sem. plan *Degrees:* B, M *Prof. Accred.:* Art, Engineering (environmental/sanitary), Forestry, Journalism (B), Music, Nursing (B), Social Work (B) *CEO:* Pres. Alistair W. McCrone
FTE Enroll: 6,601　　　(707) 826-3011

HUMPHREYS COLLEGE
6650 Inglewood St., Stockton 95207 *Type:* Private *Accred.:* 1992 (WASC-Sr.) *Calendar:* Qtr. plan *Degrees:* A, B, P, C *CEO:* Pres. Robert G. Humphreys
FTE Enroll: 595　　　　(209) 478-0800

IMPERIAL VALLEY COLLEGE
P.O. Box 158, Imperial 92251 *Type:* Public (district) junior *System:* Imperial Community College District *Accred.:* 1952/1995 (WASC-Jr.) *Calendar:* Sem. plan *Degrees:* A *CEO:* Interim Pres. Gilbert Dominguez
Enroll: 6,440　　　　(619) 352-8320

INSTITUTE OF COMPUTER TECHNOLOGY
3200 Wilshire Blvd., No. 400, Los Angeles 90010-1308 *Type:* Private *Accred.:* 1985/1990 (ACCSCT) *Degrees:* A, C *CEO:* Pres. K.C. You
　　　　　　　　　　(213) 381-3333

INTERIOR DESIGNERS INSTITUTE
1061 Camelback Rd., Newport Beach 92660-3228 *Type:* Private *Accred.:* 1987 (ACCSCT) *Degrees:* A, B, C *Prof. Accred.:* Interior Design *CEO:* Exec. Dir. Judy Deaton
Enroll: 248   (714) 675-4451

INTERNATIONAL SCHOOL OF THEOLOGY
24600 Arrowhead Springs, San Bernardino 92414-0001 *Type:* Private (interdenominational) graduate only *Accred.:* 1991/1994 (ATS) *Calendar:* Sem. plan *Degrees:* M *CEO:* Pres. Donald A. Weaver
Enroll: 73   (909) 886-7876

IRVINE VALLEY COLLEGE
5500 Irvine Center Dr., Irvine 92720 *Type:* Public (district) junior *System:* Saddleback Community College District *Accred.:* 1988/1993 (WASC-Jr.) *Calendar:* Sem. plan *Degrees:* A *CEO:* Pres. Daniel Larios
Enroll: 10,284   (714) 559-9300

ITT TECHNICAL INSTITUTE
525 N. Muller Ave., Anaheim 92801 *Type:* Private *Accred.:* 1987 (ACCSCT) *Calendar:* Qtr. plan *Degrees:* A, B *CEO:* Dir. Louis E. Osborn
Enroll: 560   (714) 535-3700

SANTA CLARA CAMPUS
5104 Old Ironsides Dr., Ste. 113, Santa Clara 95054 *Calendar:* Qtr. plan *Degrees:* A
Enroll: 100   (408) 496-0655

ITT TECHNICAL INSTITUTE
2035 E. 223rd St., Carson 90810-1698 *Type:* Private *Accred.:* 1987 (ACCSCT) *Degrees:* A *CEO:* Dir. David Scarbro
       (310) 835-5595

ITT TECHNICAL INSTITUTE
9700 Goethe Rd., Sacramento 95827-5281 *Type:* Private *Accred.:* 1988 (ACCSCT) *Degrees:* A *CEO:* Dir. Jeffrey Ortega
       (916) 366-3900

HAYWARD CAMPUS
26239 Executive Pl., Hayward 94545 *Accred.:* 1994 (ACCSCT) *Calendar:* Qtr. plan *Degrees:* A
Enroll: 200   (510) 785-8522

ITT TECHNICAL INSTITUTE
630 E. Brier Dr., Ste. 150, San Bernardino 92408-2800 *Type:* Private *Accred.:* 1987 (ACCSCT) *Degrees:* A *CEO:* Dir. Michael C. Ackerman
       (909) 889-3800

ITT TECHNICAL INSTITUTE
9680 Granite Ridge Dr., San Diego 92123-2662 *Type:* Private *Accred.:* 1983/1988 (ACCSCT) *Degrees:* A, B *CEO:* Dir. Robert Hammond
       (619) 571-8500

ITT TECHNICAL INSTITUTE
6723 Van Nuys Blvd., Van Nuys 91405-4620 *Type:* Private *Accred.:* 1984/1989 (ACCSCT) *Degrees:* A *CEO:* Dir. Nader Mojtabai
       (818) 989-1177

OXNARD CAMPUS
2051 Solar Dr., Ste. 150, Oxnard 93030 *Accred.:* 1994 (ACCSCT) *Calendar:* Qtr. plan *Degrees:* C
Enroll: 295   (805) 988-0143

ITT TECHNICAL INSTITUTE
1530 W. Cameron Ave., West Covina 91790-2767 *Type:* Private *Accred.:* 1983/1989 (ACCSCT) *Degrees:* A, B *CEO:* Dir. Michele Huggard
       (213) 960-8681

JESUIT SCHOOL OF THEOLOGY AT BERKELEY
1735 LeRoy Ave., Berkeley 94709-1193 *Type:* Private (Roman Catholic) professional; graduate only *Accred.:* 1971/1989 (ATS); 1971/1989 (WASC-Sr.) *Calendar:* Sem. plan *Degrees:* M, P *CEO:* Pres. T. Howland Sanks, S.J.
FTE Enroll: 192   (510) 841-8804

JOHN F. KENNEDY UNIVERSITY
12 Altarinda Rd., Orinda 94563 *Type:* Private liberal arts and professional *Accred.:* 1977/1985 (WASC-Sr.) *Calendar:* Qtr. plan

Degrees: B, M, P *CEO:* Pres. Charles E. Glasser
FTE Enroll: 1,382   (510) 254-0200

KELSEY-JENNEY COLLEGE
7084 Miramar Rd., San Diego 92121 *Type:* Private *Accred.:* 1983/1994 (WASC-Jr.) *Calendar:* Qtr. plan *Degrees:* A *CEO:* Pres. J. Robert Evans
Enroll: 950   (619) 233-7418

KINGS RIVER COMMUNITY COLLEGE
995 N. Reed Ave., Reedley 93654 *Type:* Public (district) junior *System:* State Center Community College District *Accred.:* 1952/1994 (WASC-Jr.) *Calendar:* Sem. plan *Degrees:* A *Prof. Accred.:* Dental Assisting *CEO:* Pres. Richard J. Giese
Enroll: 6,162   (209) 638-3641

LA SIERRA UNIVERSITY
4700 Pierce St., Riverside 92515 *Type:* Private (Seventh-Day Adventist) liberal arts and professional *Accred.:* 1960/1992 (WASC-Sr.) *Calendar:* Qtr. plan *Degrees:* A, B, M, P, D *Prof. Accred.:* Social Work (B) *CEO:* Pres. Lawrence T. Geraty
FTE Enroll: 1,423   (909) 785-2022

LAKE TAHOE COMMUNITY COLLEGE
One College Dr., South Lake Tahoe 96150 *Type:* Public (district) junior *System:* Lake Tahoe Community College District *Accred.:* 1979/1994 (WASC-Jr.) *Calendar:* Qtr. plan *Degrees:* A *CEO:* Pres. Guy F. Lease
Enroll: 2,711   (916) 541-4660

LANEY COLLEGE
900 Fallon St., Oakland 94607 *Type:* Public (district) junior *System:* Peralta Community College District *Accred.:* 1956/1991 (WASC-Jr.) *Calendar:* Sem. plan *Degrees:* A *CEO:* Pres. Odell Johnson
Enroll: 10,484   (510) 834-5740

LAS POSITAS COLLEGE
3033 Collier Canyon Rd., Livermore 94550-9797 *Type:* Public (district) junior *System:* Chabot-Las Positas Community College District *Accred.:* 1991 (WASC-Jr.) *Calen-*dar:* Qtr. plan *Degrees:* A *CEO:* Pres. Susan A. Cota
Enroll: 5,723   (510) 373-5800

LASSEN COLLEGE
P.O. Box 3000, Susanville 96130 *Type:* Public (district) junior *System:* Lassen Community College District *Accred.:* 1952/1990 (WASC-Jr.) *Calendar:* Sem. plan *Degrees:* A *CEO:* Pres. Dennis Adams
Enroll: 3,001   (916) 257-6181

L.I.F.E. BIBLE COLLEGE
1100 Covina Blvd., San Dimas 91773 *Type:* Private (International Church of Foursquare Gospel) *Accred.:* 1980/1990 (AABC) *Calendar:* Sem. plan *Degrees:* A, B, C *CEO:* Pres. Dick Scott
FTE Enroll: 330   (909) 599-5433

LIFE CHIROPRACTIC COLLEGE-WEST
2005 Via Barrett, P.O. Box 367, San Lorenzo 94580 *Type:* Private professional *Calendar:* Sem. plan *Degrees:* P *Prof. Accred.:* Chiropractic Education *CEO:* Pres. Gerard W. Clum, D.C.
                                       (510) 276-9013

LINCOLN UNIVERSITY
281 Masonic Ave., San Francisco 94118 *Type:* Private senior *Accred.:* 1990 (ACICS) *Calendar:* Sem. plan *Degrees:* B, M *CEO:* Acting Pres. Clarence W. Rippel
                                       (415) 221-1212

LOMA LINDA UNIVERSITY
Loma Linda 92350 *Type:* Private (Seventh-Day Adventist) liberal arts and professional *Accred.:* 1960/1992 (WASC-Sr.) *Calendar:* Qtr. plan *Degrees:* A, B, M, P, D *Prof. Accred.:* Clinical Lab Scientist, Cytotechnology, Dental Hygiene, Dentistry, Diagnostic Medical Sonography, Dietetics (coordinated), Endodontics, Marriage and Family Therapy (M), Medical Record Administration, Medicine, Nuclear Medicine Technology, Nursing (B,M), Occupational Therapy, Occupational Therapy Assisting, Oral and Maxillofacial Surgery, Orthodontics, Periodontics, Physical Therapy, Physical Therapy Assisting, Radiation Therapy Technol-

ogy, Radiography, Respiratory Therapy, Social Work (M-candidate), Speech-Language Pathology *CEO:* Pres. B. Lyn Behrens, M.B.B.S.
FTE Enroll: 3,000   (909) 824-4300

LONG BEACH CITY COLLEGE
4901 E. Carson St., Long Beach 90808 *Type:* Public (district) junior *System:* Long Beach Community College District *Accred.:* 1952/1990 (WASC-Jr.) *Calendar:* Sem. plan *Degrees:* A *Prof. Accred.:* Nursing (A-warning), Radiography *CEO:* Pres. Barbara A. Adams
Enroll: 25,137   (310) 420-4111

LOS ANGELES CITY COLLEGE
855 N. Vermont Ave., Los Angeles 90029-3590 *Type:* Public (district) junior *System:* Los Angeles Community College District *Accred.:* 1952/1992 (WASC-Jr.) *Calendar:* Sem. plan *Degrees:* A *Prof. Accred.:* Dental Laboratory Technology (conditional), Radiography *CEO:* Pres. Jose Robledo
Enroll: 16,042   (213) 953-4000

LOS ANGELES COLLEGE OF CHIROPRACTIC
16200 E. Amber Valley Dr., P.O. Box 1166, Whittier 90604 *Type:* Private professional *Accred.:* 1993 (WASC-Sr.) *Calendar:* Sem. plan *Degrees:* B, P *Prof. Accred.:* Chiropractic Education *CEO:* Pres. Reed B. Phillips, DC
FTE Enroll: 791   (310) 947-8755

LOS ANGELES COUNTY MEDICAL CENTER SCHOOL OF NURSING
1200 N. State St., Muir Hall, Rm. 114, Los Angeles 90033 *Type:* Public *Accred.:* 1995 (WASC-Jr.) *Calendar:* Sem. plan *Degrees:* A *CEO:* Dir./Dean Sharon A. Hilton
Enroll: 241   (213) 226-4911

LOS ANGELES HARBOR COLLEGE
1111 Figueroa Pl., Wilmington 90744 *Type:* Public (district) junior *System:* Los Angeles Community College District *Accred.:* 1952/1994 (WASC-Jr.) *Calendar:* Sem. plan *Degrees:* A *CEO:* Pres. James L. Heinselman
Enroll: 8,040   (310) 522-8200

LOS ANGELES MISSION COLLEGE
13356 Eldridge Ave., Sylmar 91342-3244 *Type:* Public (district) junior *System:* Los Angeles Community College District *Accred.:* 1978/1995 (WASC-Jr.) *Calendar:* Sem. plan *Degrees:* A *CEO:* Acting Pres. William E. Norland
Enroll: 7,500   (818) 364-7600

LOS ANGELES PIERCE COLLEGE
6201 Winnetka Ave., Woodland Hills 91371 *Type:* Public (district) junior *System:* Los Angeles Community College District *Accred.:* 1952/1995 (WASC-Jr.) *Calendar:* Sem. plan *Degrees:* A *Prof. Accred.:* Nursing (A), Veterinary Technology (provisional) *CEO:* Pres. Mary E. Lee
Enroll: 14,618   (818) 347-0551

LOS ANGELES SOUTHWEST COLLEGE
1600 W. Imperial Hwy., Los Angeles 90047 *Type:* Public (district) junior *System:* Los Angeles Community College District *Accred.:* 1980/1995 (WASC-Jr.) *Calendar:* Sem. plan *Degrees:* A *CEO:* Pres. Carolyn G. Williams
Enroll: 5,352   (213) 241-5225

LOS ANGELES TRADE-TECHNICAL COLLEGE
400 W. Washington Blvd., Los Angeles 90015 *Type:* Public (district) junior *System:* Los Angeles Community College District *Accred.:* 1952/1992 (WASC-Jr.) *Calendar:* Sem. plan *Degrees:* A *Prof. Accred.:* Nursing (A) *CEO:* Interim Pres. Betty Hartwig
Enroll: 13,925   (213) 744-9000

LOS ANGELES VALLEY COLLEGE
5800 Fulton Ave., Van Nuys 91401 *Type:* Public (district) junior *System:* Los Angeles Community College District *Accred.:* 1952/1995 (WASC-Jr.) *Calendar:* Sem. plan *Degrees:* A *Prof. Accred.:* Nursing (A), Respiratory Therapy *CEO:* Pres. Tyree O. Wieder
Enroll: 16,382   (818) 781-1200

LOS MEDANOS COLLEGE
2700 E. Leland Rd., Pittsburg 94565 *Type:* Public (district) junior *System:* Contra Costa Community College District *Accred.:*

1977/1994 (WASC-Jr.) *Calendar:* Sem. plan *Degrees:* A *CEO:* Interim Pres. Helen Spencer
Enroll: 7,191   (510) 439-2181

LOUISE SALINGER ACADEMY OF FASHION
101 Jessie St., San Francisco 94105-3593 *Type:* Private *Accred.:* 1971/1989 (ACC-SCT) *Calendar:* Qtr. plan *Degrees:* A, B *CEO:* Pres. Esther Herschelle
                    (415) 974-6666

LOYOLA MARYMOUNT UNIVERSITY
Loyola Blvd. at W. 80th St., Los Angeles 90045 *Type:* Private (Roman Catholic) liberal arts and professional *Accred.:* 1949/1993 (WASC-Sr.) *Calendar:* Sem. plan *Degrees:* B, M, P *Prof. Accred.:* Art, Business (B,M), Dance, Engineering (civil, electrical, mechanical), Law, Music (A), Theatre *CEO:* Pres. Thomas P. O'Malley, S.J.
FTE Enroll: 6,247   (310) 338-2700

MARYMOUNT COLLEGE
30800 Palos Verdes Dr. E., Rancho Palos Verdes 90274-6299 *Type:* Private (Roman Catholic) junior *Accred.:* 1971/1995 (WASC-Jr.) *Calendar:* Sem. plan *Degrees:* A *CEO:* Pres. Thomas M. McFadden
Enroll: 1,003   (310) 377-5501

THE MASTER'S COLLEGE AND SEMINARY
21726 W. Placerita Canyon Rd., P.O. Box 221450, Newhall 91322 *Type:* Private (Baptist) liberal arts *Accred.:* 1975/1985 (WASC-Sr.) *Calendar:* Sem. plan *Degrees:* B, M, P *CEO:* Pres. John MacArthur, Jr.
FTE Enroll: 1,118   (805) 259-3540

MASTERS INSTITUTE
50 Airport Pkwy., Ste. 8, San Jose 95110-1011 *Type:* Private *Accred.:* 1984/1989 (ACCSCT) *Degrees:* A, C *CEO:* Pres. David T. Ruggieri
                    (408) 441-1800

MENDOCINO COLLEGE
P.O. Box 3000, Ukiah 95482 *Type:* Public (district) junior *System:* Mendocino-Lake Community College District *Accred.:*

1980/1990 (WASC-Jr.) *Calendar:* Sem. plan *Degrees:* A *CEO:* Pres. Carl J. Ehmann
Enroll: 4,000   (707) 468-3100

MENLO COLLEGE
1000 El Camino Real, Atherton 94027-4185 *Type:* Private *Accred.:* 1952/1987 (WASC-Sr.) *Calendar:* 4-1-4 plan *Degrees:* A, B *CEO:* Pres. James Waddell
FTE Enroll: 440   (415) 323-6141

MENNONITE BRETHREN BIBLICAL SEMINARY
4824 E. Butler Ave., Fresno 93727-5097 *Type:* Private (Mennonite) graduate only *Accred.:* 1977/1991 (ATS); 1972/1992 (WASC-Sr.) *Calendar:* 4-1-4 plan *Degrees:* M *CEO:* Pres. Henry J. Schmidt
FTE Enroll: 99   (209) 251-8628

MERCED COLLEGE
3600 M St., Merced 95348 *Type:* Public (district) junior *System:* Merced Community College District *Accred.:* 1965/1993 (WASC-Jr.) *Calendar:* Sem. plan *Degrees:* A *Prof. Accred.:* Radiography *CEO:* Pres. E. Jan Moser
Enroll: 7,084   (209) 384-6000

MERRITT COLLEGE
12500 Campus Dr., Oakland 94619 *Type:* Public (district) junior *System:* Peralta Community College District *Accred.:* 1956/1991 (WASC-Jr.) *Calendar:* Sem. plan *Degrees:* A *Prof. Accred.:* Radiography *CEO:* Pres. Wise E. Allen
Enroll: 6,023   (510) 531-4911

MILLS COLLEGE
5000 MacArthur Blvd., Oakland 94613 *Type:* Private liberal arts for women *Accred.:* 1949/1992 (WASC-Sr.) *Calendar:* Sem. plan *Degrees:* B, M *CEO:* Pres. Janet L. Holmgren
FTE Enroll: 1,131   (510) 430-2255

MIRA COSTA COLLEGE
One Barnard Dr., Oceanside 92056 *Type:* Public (district) junior *System:* MiraCosta Community College District *Accred.:* 1952/1992 (WASC-Jr.) *Calendar:* Sem. plan *Degrees:* A *CEO:* Pres. Tim Dong
Enroll: 8,433   (619) 757-2121

MISSION COLLEGE
3000 Mission College Blvd., Santa Clara 95054 *Type:* Public (district) junior *System:* West Valley-Mission College District *Accred.:* 1979/1996 (WASC-Jr.) *Calendar:* Sem. plan *Degrees:* A *CEO:* Pres. Michael Rao
Enroll: 9,394   (408) 988-2200

MODESTO JUNIOR COLLEGE
435 College Ave., Modesto 95350 *Type:* Public (district) junior *System:* Yosemite Community College District *Accred.:* 1952/1994 (WASC-Jr.) *Calendar:* Sem. plan *Degrees:* A *Prof. Accred.:* Dental Assisting, EMT-Paramedic, Medical Assisting (AMA), Respiratory Therapy *CEO:* Pres. Maria Sheehan
Enroll: 14,471   (209) 575-6067

MONTEREY INSTITUTE OF INTERNATIONAL STUDIES
425 Van Buren, Monterey 93940 *Type:* Private liberal arts *Accred.:* 1961/1985 (WASC-Sr.) *Calendar:* Sem. plan *Degrees:* B, M *CEO:* Pres. Robert G. Gard, Jr.
FTE Enroll: 668   (408) 647-4100

MONTEREY PENINSULA COLLEGE
980 Fremont St., Monterey 93940 *Type:* Public (district) junior *System:* Monterey Peninsula Community College District *Accred.:* 1952/1992 (WASC-Jr.) *Calendar:* Sem. plan *Degrees:* A *Prof. Accred.:* Dental Assisting, Nursing (A) *CEO:* Pres. Edward O. Gould
Enroll: 8,750   (408) 646-4000

MOORPARK COLLEGE
7075 Campus Rd., Moorpark 93021 *Type:* Public (district) junior *System:* Ventura County Community College District *Accred.:* 1969/1992 (WASC-Jr.) *Calendar:* Sem. plan *Degrees:* A *Prof. Accred.:* Nursing (A), Radiography *CEO:* Pres. James W. Walker
Enroll: 10,228   (805) 378-1400

MOUNT ST. MARY'S COLLEGE
12001 Chalon Rd., Los Angeles 90049 *Type:* Private (Roman Catholic) liberal arts

Accred.: 1949/1992 (WASC-Sr.) *Calendar:* 4-1-4 plan *Degrees:* A, B, M *Prof. Accred.:* Music, Nursing (B), Occupational Therapy Assisting, Physical Therapy, Physical Therapy Assisting *CEO:* Pres. Karen M. Kennelly
FTE Enroll: 1,621   (310) 476-2237

DOHENY CAMPUS
10 Chester Pl., Los Angeles 90007
                                   (310) 746-0450

MOUNT SAN ANTONIO COLLEGE
1100 N. Grand Ave., Walnut 91789 *Type:* Public (district) junior *System:* Mount San Antonio Community College District *Accred.:* 1952/1993 (WASC-Jr.) *Calendar:* Sem. plan *Degrees:* A *Prof. Accred.:* Radiography, Respiratory Therapy, Veterinary Technology (probational) *CEO:* Pres. William H. Feddersen
Enroll: 22,329   (909) 594-5611

MOUNT SAN JACINTO COLLEGE
1499 N. State St., San Jacinto 92583 *Type:* Public (district) junior *System:* Mount San Jacinto Community College District *Accred.:* 1965/1994 (WASC-Jr.) *Calendar:* Sem. plan *Degrees:* A *CEO:* Pres. Roy B. Mason, II
Enroll: 5,688   (909) 672-6752

MTI WESTERN BUSINESS COLLEGE
5221 Madison Ave., Sacramento 95841 *Type:* Private business *Accred.:* 1975/1987 (ACICS) *Degrees:* A, C *CEO:* Pres. John A. Zimmerman
                                   (916) 339-1500

NAPA VALLEY COLLEGE
2277 Napa-Vallejo Hwy., Napa 94558 *Type:* Public (district) junior *System:* Napa Valley Community College District *Accred.:* 1952/1992 (WASC-Jr.) *Calendar:* Sem. plan *Degrees:* A *Prof. Accred.:* Respiratory Therapy *CEO:* Pres. Diane E. Carey
Enroll: 5,932   (707) 253-3000

NATIONAL EDUCATION CENTER—SKADRON CAMPUS
825 E. Hospitality La., San Bernardino 92408 *Type:* Private business *Accred.:* 1962/

1992 (ACICS) *Calendar:* Qtr. plan *Degrees:* A, C *CEO:* Pres. David Corson
(909) 885-3896

THE NATIONAL HISPANIC UNIVERSITY
14271 Story Rd., San Jose 95127-3823 *Type:* Private senior *Accred.:* 1993/1996 (ACICS) *Degrees:* A, B, C *CEO:* Pres. B. Roberto Cruz
(408) 254-6900

NATIONAL UNIVERSITY
4025 Camino del Rio S., San Diego 92108 *Type:* Private business *Accred.:* 1977/1992 (WASC-Sr.) *Calendar:* 12-mos. program *Degrees:* A, B, M, P *CEO:* Pres. Jerry C. Lee *FTE Enroll:* 7,620   (619) 563-7100

NAVAL POSTGRADUATE SCHOOL
One University Cir., Rm. N10, Monterey 93943-5000 *Type:* Public (federal) science and technology *Accred.:* 1955/1990 (WASC-Sr.) *Calendar:* Qtr. plan *Degrees:* B, M, D *Prof. Accred.:* Engineering (aerospace, electrical, mechanical), Public Administration *CEO:* Supt. Marsha J. Evans
FTE Enroll: 1,713   (408) 656-2411

NEW COLLEGE OF CALIFORNIA
50 Fell St., San Francisco 94102 *Type:* Private liberal arts *Accred.:* 1976/1985 (WASC-Sr.) *Calendar:* Sem. plan *Degrees:* B, M, P *CEO:* Pres. Peter Gabel
FTE Enroll: 574   (415) 241-1300

NEW SCHOOL OF ARCHITECTURE
1249 F St., San Diego 92101-6634 *Type:* Private *Accred.:* 1991 (ACCSCT) *Degrees:* A, B *CEO:* Pres. Gordon Bishop
(619) 235-4100

OCCIDENTAL COLLEGE
1600 Campus Rd., Los Angeles 90041-3314 *Type:* Private liberal arts *Accred.:* 1949/1990 (WASC-Sr.) *Calendar:* 3-3 plan *Degrees:* B, M *CEO:* Pres. John B. Slaughter
FTE Enroll: 1,561   (213) 259-2500

OHLONE COLLEGE
43600 Mission Blvd., Fremont 94539 *Type:* Public (district) junior *System:* Fremont-Newark Community College District

Accred.: 1970/1996 (WASC-Jr.) *Calendar:* Sem. plan *Degrees:* A *Prof. Accred.:* Nursing (A), Respiratory Therapy *CEO:* Pres. Floyd Hogue
Enroll: 9,827   (510) 659-6000

ORANGE COAST COLLEGE
2701 Fairview Rd., P.O. Box 5005, Costa Mesa 92628-5005 *Type:* Public (district) junior *System:* Coast Community College District *Accred.:* 1952/1990 (WASC-Jr.) *Calendar:* Sem. plan *Degrees:* A *Prof. Accred.:* Dental Assisting, Diagnostic Medical Sonography, Electroneurodiagnos-tic Technology, Medical Assisting (AMA), Radiography, Respiratory Therapy *CEO:* Interim Pres. James L. McIlwain
Enroll: 25,003   (714) 432-0202

OTIS SCHOOL OF ART AND DESIGN
2401 Wilshire Blvd., Los Angeles 90057 *Type:* Private professional *Accred.:* 1956/1990 (WASC-Sr. probational) *Calendar:* Sem. plan *Degrees:* B, M *Prof. Accred.:* Art *CEO:* Pres. Neil J. Hoffman
FTE Enroll: 719   (213) 251-0500

OXNARD COLLEGE
4000 S. Rose Ave., Oxnard 93033 *Type:* Public (district) junior *System:* Ventura County Community College District *Accred.:* 1978/1993 (WASC-Jr.) *Calendar:* Sem. plan *Degrees:* A *CEO:* Pres. Elise D. Schneider
Enroll: 6,342   (805) 986-5800

PACIFIC CHRISTIAN COLLEGE
2500 E. Nutwood Ave., Fullerton 92631 *Type:* Private (Christian Churches/Churches of Christ) liberal arts *Accred.:* 1969/1994 (WASC-Sr.) *Calendar:* 4-1-4 plan *Degrees:* A, B, M *CEO:* Pres. E. Leroy Lawson
FTE Enroll: 699   (714) 879-3901

PACIFIC COLLEGE OF ORIENTAL MEDICINE
7445 Mission Valley Rd., Ste. 103-106, San Diego 92108-4408 *Type:* Private professional *Calendar:* Tri. plan *Degrees:* M *Prof. Accred.:* Acupuncture (M) *CEO:* Dean Jack Miller
FTE Enroll: 87   (619) 574-6909

NEW YORK CAMPUS
915 Broadway, 3rd Fl., New York, NY 10010 *Prof. Accred.:* Acupuncture (M) (212) 982-3456

PACIFIC GRADUATE SCHOOL OF PSYCHOLOGY
935 E. Meadow Dr., Palo Alto 94303 *Type:* Private professional *Accred.:* 1986/1994 (WASC-Sr.) *Calendar:* Qtr. plan *Degrees:* D *Prof. Accred.:* Clinical Psychology (provisional) *CEO:* Pres. Allen Calvin *FTE Enroll:* 242 (415) 494-7477

PACIFIC LUTHERAN THEOLOGICAL SEMINARY
2770 Marin Ave., Berkeley 94708-5264 *Type:* Private (Evangelical Lutheran Church) graduate only *Accred.:* 1964/1991 (ATS) *Calendar:* Sem. plan *Degrees:* M *CEO:* Pres. Jerry L. Schmalenberger *Enroll:* 134 (510) 524-5264

PACIFIC OAKS COLLEGE
5 Westmoreland Pl., Pasadena 91103 *Type:* Private professional *Accred.:* 1959/1985 (WASC-Sr.) *Calendar:* Sem. plan *Degrees:* B, M *CEO:* Pres. Katherine Gabel *FTE Enroll:* 346 (818) 397-1300

PACIFIC SCHOOL OF RELIGION
1798 Scenic Ave., Berkeley 94709 *Type:* Private (interdenominational) professional; graduate only *Accred.:* 1938/1988 (ATS); 1971/1988 (WASC-Sr.) *Calendar:* Sem. plan *Degrees:* M, P, D *CEO:* Acting Pres. Thomas J. Henderson *FTE Enroll:* 164 (510) 848-0528

PACIFIC UNION COLLEGE
One Angwin Ave., Angwin 94508-9707 *Type:* Private (Seventh-Day Adventist) liberal arts *Accred.:* 1951/1991 (WASC-Sr.) *Calendar:* Qtr. plan *Degrees:* A, B, M *Prof. Accred.:* Music, Nursing (A,B), Social Work (B) *CEO:* Pres. D. Malcolm Maxwell *FTE Enroll:* 1,513 (707) 965-6243

PALMER COLLEGE OF CHIROPRACTIC-WEST
90 E. Tasman Dr., San Jose 95134 *Type:* Private professional *System:* Palmer Chiropractic University System *Calendar:* Qtr. plan *Degrees:* P *Prof. Accred.:* Chiropractic Education *CEO:* Pres. Peter A. Martin, D.C. *Enroll:* 591 (408) 944-6000

PALO VERDE COLLEGE
811 W. Chanslorway, Blythe 92225 *Type:* Public (district) junior *System:* Palo Verde Community College District *Accred.:* 1951/1990 (WASC-Jr.) *Calendar:* Sem. plan *Degrees:* A *CEO:* Pres. Robert L. Wilmoth *Enroll:* 1,386 (619) 922-6168

PALOMAR COLLEGE
1140 W. Mission Rd., San Marcos 92069 *Type:* Public (district) junior *System:* Palomar Community College District *Accred.:* 1951/1991 (WASC-Jr.) *Calendar:* Sem. plan *Degrees:* A *Prof. Accred.:* Dental Assisting, Nursing (A) *CEO:* Pres. George R. Boggs *Enroll:* 21,264 (619) 744-1150

PASADENA CITY COLLEGE
1570 E. Colorado Blvd., Pasadena 91106 *Type:* Public (district) junior *System:* Pasadena Area Community College District *Accred.:* 1952/1991 (WASC-Jr.) *Calendar:* Sem. plan *Degrees:* A *Prof. Accred.:* Dental Assisting, Dental Hygiene, Dental Laboratory Technology, Medical Assisting (AMA), Nursing (A), Radiography *CEO:* Pres. James P. Kossler *Enroll:* 28,000 (818) 585-7123

PATTEN COLLEGE
2433 Coolidge Ave., Oakland 94601 *Type:* Private (Christian Evangelical Church) liberal arts *Accred.:* 1980/1993 (WASC-Sr.) *Calendar:* Sem. plan *Degrees:* A, B *CEO:* Pres. Priscilla C. Benham *FTE Enroll:* 436 (510) 533-8300

PEPPERDINE UNIVERSITY
24255 Pacific Coast Hwy., Malibu 90263 *Type:* Private liberal arts and professional *Accred.:* 1949/1993 (WASC-Sr.) *Calendar:* Tri. plan *Degrees:* B, M, P, D *Prof. Accred.:* Clinical Psychology, Law, Music *CEO:* Pres. David Davenport *FTE Enroll:* 6,404 (310) 456-4000

PHILLIPS COLLEGE INLAND EMPIRE CAMPUS
4300 Central Ave., Riverside 92506 *Type:* Private business *Accred.:* 1982/1994 (ACICS) *Degrees:* A, C *CEO:* Dir. Angela Hughes
(909) 787-9300

PHILLIPS GRADUATE INSTITUTE
5433 Laurel Canyon Blvd., North Hollywood 91607-2193 *Type:* Private *Accred.:* 1983/1988 (WASC-Sr.) *Calendar:* Sem. plan *Degrees:* M *CEO:* Pres. Edwin S. Cox
FTE Enroll: 283   (818) 509-5959

PHILLIPS JUNIOR COLLEGE
8520 Balboa Blvd., Northridge 91325-3561 *Type:* Private *Accred.:* 1984 (ACCSCT) *Degrees:* B *CEO:* Dir. Tom Azim-Zadeh
(818) 895-2220

CARSON CAMPUS
One Civic Plaza, Ste. 200, Carson 90745-2264 *Accred.:* 1991 (ACCSCT)
(310) 518-2600

PHILLIPS JUNIOR COLLEGE—CONDIE CAMPUS
One W. Campbell Ave., Campbell 95008 *Type:* Private junior *Accred.:* 1974/1996 (ACICS); 1991 (WASC-Jr.) *Calendar:* Qtr. plan *Degrees:* A *CEO:* Dir. C. Robert Allen
Enroll: 620   (408) 866-6666

FRESNO CAMPUS
2048 N. Fine Ave., Fresno 93727 *Accred.:* 1989/1991 (ACICS)
(209) 453-1000

PITZER COLLEGE
1050 N. Mills Ave., Claremont 91711-6110 *Type:* Private liberal arts *System:* Claremont University Center *Accred.:* 1965/1990 (WASC-Sr.) *Calendar:* Sem. plan *Degrees:* B *CEO:* Pres. Marilyn Chapin Massey
FTE Enroll: 789   (909) 621-8000

PLATT COLLEGE
10900 E. 183rd St., Ste. 290, Cerritos 90701-5342 *Type:* Private *Accred.:* 1986 (ACC-SCT) *Degrees:* A, C *CEO:* Dir. Margaret Potter Simons
(310) 809-5100

POINT LOMA NAZARENE COLLEGE
3900 Lomaland Dr., San Diego 92106 *Type:* Private (Nazarene) liberal arts *Accred.:* 1949/1990 (WASC-Sr.) *Calendar:* Sem. plan *Degrees:* A, B, M *Prof. Accred.:* Nursing (B) *CEO:* Pres. Jim L. Bond
FTE Enroll: 1,931   (619) 221-2200

POMONA COLLEGE
550 N. College Ave., Claremont 91711 *Type:* Private liberal arts *System:* Claremont University Center *Accred.:* 1949/1992 (WASC-Sr.) *Calendar:* Sem. plan *Degrees:* B *CEO:* Pres. Peter W. Stanley
FTE Enroll: 1,499   (909) 621-8000

PORTERVILLE COLLEGE
100 E. College Ave., Porterville 93257 *Type:* Public (district) junior *System:* Kern Community College District *Accred.:* 1952/1995 (WASC-Jr.) *Calendar:* Sem. plan *Degrees:* A *CEO:* Pres. Bonnie Rogers
Enroll: 2,769   (209) 781-3130

QUEEN OF THE HOLY ROSARY COLLEGE
43326 Mission Blvd., Mission San Jose 94539 *Type:* Private (Roman Catholic) junior *Accred.:* 1979/1994 (WASC-Jr.) *Calendar:* Sem. plan *Degrees:* A *CEO:* Pres. Renilde Cade, O.P.
Enroll: 230   (510) 657-2468

RANCHO SANTIAGO COLLEGE—SANTA ANA
17th and Bristol Sts., Santa Ana 92706 *Type:* Public (district) junior *System:* Rancho Santiago Community College District *Accred.:* 1952/1996 (WASC-Jr.) *Calendar:* Sem. plan *Degrees:* A *CEO:* Chanc. Vivian B. Blevins
Enroll: 23,775   (714) 564-6000

RAND GRADUATE SCHOOL OF POLICY STUDIES
1700 Main St., Santa Monica 90407-2138 *Type:* Private graduate only *Accred.:* 1975/1990 (WASC-Sr.) *Calendar:* Qtr. plan *Degrees:* D *CEO:* Dean Charles Wolf, Jr.
FTE Enroll: 58   (310) 393-0411

RIO HONDO COLLEGE
3600 Workman Mill Rd., Whittier 90608 *Type:* Public (district) junior *System:* Rio Hondo Community College District *Accred.:*

1967/1996 (WASC-Jr.) *Calendar:* Sem. plan *Degrees:* A *CEO:* Pres. Jesus Carreon
Enroll: 15,860   (310) 692-0921

RIVERSIDE COMMUNITY COLLEGE
4800 Magnolia Ave., Riverside 92506-1299 *Type:* Public (district) junior *System:* Riverside Community College District *Accred.:* 1952/1995 (WASC-Jr.) *Calendar:* Sem. plan *Degrees:* A *Prof. Accred.:* Nursing (A) *CEO:* Pres. Salvatore G. Rotella
Enroll: 21,300   (909) 222-8000

ROYAL UNIVERSITY OF AMERICA
1125 W. Sixth St., Los Angeles 90017 *Type:* Private professional *Calendar:* Qtr. plan *Degrees:* M *Prof. Accred.:* Acupuncture (M) *CEO:* Pres. Dae Young Kim
FTE Enroll: 197   (213) 482-6646

SACRAMENTO CITY COLLEGE
3835 Freeport Blvd., Sacramento 95822 *Type:* Public (district) junior *System:* Los Rios Community College District *Accred.:* 1952/1992 (WASC-Jr.) *Calendar:* Sem. plan *Degrees:* A *Prof. Accred.:* Dental Assisting, Dental Hygiene, Occupational Therapy Assisting, Physical Therapy Assisting (candidate) *CEO:* Pres. Robert M. Harris
Enroll: 16,787   (916) 558-2100

SADDLEBACK COLLEGE
28000 Marguerite Pkwy., Mission Viejo 92692 *Type:* Public (district) junior *System:* Saddleback Community College District *Accred.:* 1971/1993 (WASC-Jr.) *Calendar:* Sem. plan *Degrees:* A *Prof. Accred.:* Nursing (A) *CEO:* Pres. Ned Doffoney, Jr.
Enroll: 21,303   (714) 582-4500

ST. JOHN'S SEMINARY
5012 Seminary Rd., Camarillo 93012-2598 *Type:* Private (Roman Catholic) professional; graduate only *Accred.:* 1976/1992 (ATS); 1951/1992 (WASC-Sr.) *Calendar:* Sem. plan *Degrees:* M, P *CEO:* Dean Jeremiah J. McCarthy
Enroll: 102   (805) 482-2755

ST. JOHN'S SEMINARY COLLEGE
5118 E. Seminary Rd., Camarillo 93012 *Type:* Private (Roman Catholic) liberal arts *Accred.:* 1951/1981 (WASC-Sr.) *Calendar:* Sem. plan *Degrees:* B *CEO:* Pres./Rector Edward William Clark
FTE Enroll: 82   (805) 482-2755

ST. MARY'S COLLEGE OF CALIFORNIA
1928 St. Mary's Rd., Moraga 94575 *Type:* Private (Roman Catholic) liberal arts *Accred.:* 1949/1993 (WASC-Sr.) *Calendar:* 4-1-4 plan *Degrees:* A, B, M *Prof. Accred.:* Nursing (B) *CEO:* Pres. Mel T. Anderson, F.S.C.
FTE Enroll: 3,322   (510) 631-4000

ST. PATRICK'S SEMINARY
320 Middlefield Rd., Menlo Park 94025 *Type:* Private (Roman Catholic) professional; graduate only *Accred.:* 1971/1994 (ATS); 1971/1994 (WASC-Sr.) *Calendar:* Sem. plan *Degrees:* M, P *CEO:* Pres./Rector Gerald D. Coleman, S.S.
Enroll: 55   (415) 325-5621

SALVATION ARMY COLLEGE FOR OFFICERS TRAINING
30840 Hawthorne Blvd., Rancho Palos Verdes 90274 *Type:* Private *Accred.:* 1990/1996 (WASC-Jr.) *Calendar:* Qtr. plan *Degrees:* A *CEO:* Trng. Princ. Terry Griffin
Enroll: 83   (310) 377-0481

SAMRA UNIVERSITY OF ORIENTAL MEDICINE
600 St. Paul Ave., Los Angeles 90017 *Type:* Private professional *Calendar:* Qtr. plan *Degrees:* M *Prof. Accred.:* Acupuncture (M) *CEO:* Pres. Norman Bleicher
FTE Enroll: 165   (213) 482-8448

SAMUEL MERRITT COLLEGE
370 Hawthorne Ave., Oakland 94609 *Type:* Private professional *Accred.:* 1984/1990 (WASC-Sr.) *Calendar:* 4-1-4 plan *Degrees:* A, B, M *Prof. Accred.:* Nurse Anesthesia Education, Nursing (B), Occupational Therapy, Physical Therapy *CEO:* Pres. Sharon L. Diaz
FTE Enroll: 517   (510) 420-6011

SAN BERNARDINO VALLEY COLLEGE
701 S. Mt. Vernon Ave., San Bernardino
92410 *Type:* Public (district) junior *System:*
San Bernardino Community College District
Accred.: 1952/1991 (WASC-Jr.) *Calendar:*
Sem. plan *Degrees:* A *Prof. Accred.:* Nursing
(A) *CEO:* Pres. Donald L. Singer
Enroll: 9,415   (909) 888-6511

SAN DIEGO CITY COLLEGE
1313 Twelfth Ave., San Diego 92101 *Type:*
Public (district) junior *System:* San Diego
Community College District *Accred.:* 1952/
1992 (WASC-Jr.) *Calendar:* Sem. plan
Degrees: A *CEO:* Pres. Jerome Hunter
Enroll: 11,500   (619) 230-
2400

SAN DIEGO MESA COLLEGE
7250 Mesa College Dr., San Diego 92111
Type: Public (district) junior *System:* San
Diego Community College District
Accred.: 1966/1992 (WASC-Jr.) *Calendar:*
Sem. plan *Degrees:* A *Prof. Accred.:* Med-
ical Assisting (AMA), Medical Record
Technology, Physical Therapy Assisting,
Radiography, Veterinary Technology (proba-
tional) *CEO:* Pres. Constance M. Carroll
Enroll: 24,101   (619) 627-2600

SAN DIEGO MIRAMAR COLLEGE
10440 Black Mountain Rd., San Diego
92126 *Type:* Public (district) junior *System:*
San Diego Community College District
Accred.: 1982/1992 (WASC-Jr.) *Calendar:*
Sem. plan *Degrees:* A *CEO:* Pres. Louis C.
Murillo
Enroll: 7,342   (619) 536-7800

SAN DIEGO STATE UNIVERSITY
5500 Campanile Dr., San Diego 92182-0763
Type: Public (state) *System:* California State
University System *Accred.:* 1949/1994
(WASC-Sr.) *Calendar:* Sem. plan *Degrees:*
B, M *Prof. Accred.:* Accounting (A,B,C),
Art, Audiology, Business (B,M), Clinical
Psychology, Computer Science, Engineering
(aerospace, civil, electrical, mechanical),
Health Services Administration, Interior
Design, Journalism (B,M), Music, Nursing
(B,M), Public Administration, Recreation

and Leisure Services (B), Rehabilitation
Counseling, Social Work (B,M), Speech-
Language Pathology, Teacher Education,
Theatre, *CEO:* Pres. Thomas B. Day
FTE Enroll: 21,810   (619) 594-5000

SAN FRANCISCO ART INSTITUTE
800 Chestnut St., San Francisco 94133 *Type:*
Private professional *System:* University of
California Office of the President *Accred.:*
1954/1984 (WASC-Sr.) *Calendar:* Sem. plan
Degrees: B, M *Prof. Accred.:* Art *CEO:* Pres.
Ella King Torrey
FTE Enroll: 605   (415) 771-7020

SAN FRANCISCO COLLEGE OF MORTUARY
SCIENCE
1598 Dolores St., San Francisco 94110 *Type:*
Private professional *Accred.:* 1962/1992
(WASC-Jr. probational) *Calendar:* Sem.
plan *Degrees:* A *Prof. Accred.:* Funeral Ser-
vice Education (Mortuary Science) *CEO:*
Pres. Jacquelyn S. Taylor
Enroll: 65   (415) 567-0674

SAN FRANCISCO CONSERVATORY OF MUSIC
1201 Ortega St., San Francisco 94122 *Type:*
Private professional *Accred.:* 1960/1994
(WASC-Sr.) *Calendar:* Sem. plan *Degrees:*
B, M *Prof. Accred.:* Music *CEO:* Pres. Colin
Murdoch
FTE Enroll: 258   (415) 564-8086

SAN FRANCISCO STATE UNIVERSITY
1600 Holloway Ave., San Francisco 94132
Type: Public (state) *System:* California State
University System *Accred.:* 1949/1992
(WASC-Sr.) *Calendar:* Sem. plan *Degrees:*
B, M *Prof. Accred.:* Art, Audiology, Business
(B,M), Clinical Lab Scientist, Computer Sci-
ence, Counseling, Dietetics (internship),
Engineering (civil, electrical, mechanical),
Home Economics, Journalism (B,M), Music,
Nursing (B,M), Physical Therapy, Recreation
and Leisure Services (B), Rehabilitation
Counseling, Social Work (B,M), Speech-
Language Pathology, Teacher Education,
Theatre *CEO:* Pres. Robert A. Corrigan
FTE Enroll: 18,544   (415) 338-1111

SAN FRANCISCO THEOLOGICAL SEMINARY
2 Kensington Rd., San Anselmo 94960 *Type:* Private (Presbyterian) professional; graduate only *Accred.:* 1938/1988 (ATS); 1973/1988 (WASC-Sr.) *Calendar:* Sem. plan *Degrees:* M, P, D *CEO:* Pres. Donald W. McCullough
FTE Enroll: 370   (415) 258-6500

SAN JOAQUIN COLLEGE OF LAW
3385 E. Shields Ave., Fresno 93726 *Type:* Private professional *Accred.:* 1993 (WASC-Sr.) *Calendar:* Sem. plan *Degrees:* M, P, C *CEO:* Dean Janice L. Pearson
FTE Enroll: 237   (209) 225-4953

SAN JOAQUIN DELTA COLLEGE
5151 Pacific Ave., Stockton 95207 *Type:* Public (district) junior *System:* San Joaquin Delta Community College District *Accred.:* 1952/1990 (WASC-Jr.) *Calendar:* Sem. plan *Degrees:* A *Prof. Accred.:* Nursing (A) *CEO:* Pres. L.H. Horton, Jr.
Enroll: 15,333   (209) 474-5151

SAN JOAQUIN VALLEY COLLEGE—BAKERSFIELD
201 New Stine Rd., Bakersfield 93309-2606 *Type:* Private *System:* San Joaquin Valley College System *Accred.:* 1982/1988 (ACCSCT) *Degrees:* A, C *Prof. Accred.:* Medical Assisting *CEO:* Dir. Jane Parker
       (805) 834-0126

SAN JOAQUIN VALLEY COLLEGE—FRESNO
3333 N. Bond St., Fresno 93726-9941 *Type:* Private *System:* San Joaquin Valley College System *Accred.:* 1985 (ACCSCT) *Degrees:* A, C *Prof. Accred.:* Medical Assisting *CEO:* Dir. Richard Muella
       (209) 229-7800

SAN JOAQUIN VALLEY COLLEGE OF AERONAUTICS
4985 E. Andersen Ave., Fresno 93727 *Accred.:* 1993 (ACCSCT)
       (209) 453-0123

SAN JOAQUIN VALLEY COLLEGE—FRESNO
4985 E. Andersen Ave., Fresno 93727-1501 *Type:* Private *System:* San Joaquin Valley College System *Accred.:* 1991/1993 (ACC-SCT); 1995 (WASC-Jr.) *Calendar:* Sem. plan *Degrees:* A *CEO:* Dir. Bob Loogman
Enroll: 50   (209) 453-0380

SAN JOAQUIN VALLEY COLLEGE—VISALIA
8400 W. Mineral King Ave., Visalia 93291-9283 *Type:* Private *System:* San Joaquin Valley College System *Accred.:* 1981/1987 (ACCSCT); 1994/1995 (WASC-Jr.) *Calendar:* Sem. plan *Degrees:* A, C *Prof. Accred.:* Medical Assisting, Respiratory Therapy, Respiratory Therapy Technology *CEO:* Dir. Steve Perry
Enroll: 1,300   (209) 651-2500

SAN JOSE CHRISTIAN COLLEGE
P.O. Box 1090, 790 S. 12th St., San Jose 95112-1281 *Type:* Private (nondenominational) *Accred.:* 1969/1989 (AABC) *Calendar:* Qtr. plan *Degrees:* A, B, C *CEO:* Pres. Bryce L. Jessup
FTE Enroll: 195   (408) 293-9058

SAN JOSE CITY COLLEGE
2100 Moorpark Ave., San Jose 95128 *Type:* Public (district) junior *System:* San Jose-Evergreen Community College District *Accred.:* 1953/1992 (WASC-Jr.) *Calendar:* Sem. plan *Degrees:* A *Prof. Accred.:* Dental Assisting *CEO:* Interim Pres. Raul Rodriguez
Enroll: 12,507   (408) 289-2181

SAN JOSE STATE UNIVERSITY
One Washington Sq., San Jose 95192-0002 *Type:* Public (state) *System:* California State University System *Accred.:* 1949/1995 (WASC-Sr.) *Calendar:* Sem. plan *Degrees:* B, M *Prof. Accred.:* Art, Audiology, Business (B,M), Computer Science, Dance, Engineering (aerospace, chemical, civil, computer, electrical, industrial, materials, mechanical), Journalism (B,M), Librarianship, Music, Nursing (B,M), Occupational Therapy, Planning (M), Public Administration, Recreation and Leisure Services (B), Social Work (B,M), Speech-Language Pathology, Teacher Education, Theatre, *CEO:* Pres. Robert L. Caret
FTE Enroll: 19,188   (408) 924-1000

SANTA BARBARA CITY COLLEGE
721 Cliff Dr., Santa Barbara 93109 *Type:* Public (district) junior *System:* Santa Barbara Community College District *Accred.:* 1952/1991 (WASC-Jr.) *Calendar:* Sem. plan *Degrees:* A *Prof. Accred.:* Dental Assisting, Nursing (A), Radiography *CEO:* Pres. Peter R. MacDougall
Enroll: 11,174   (805) 965-0581

SANTA BARBARA COLLEGE OF ORIENTAL MEDICINE
1919 State St., Ste. 204, Santa Barbara 93101 *Type:* Private professional *Calendar:* Tri. plan *Degrees:* M *Prof. Accred.:* Acupuncture (M) *CEO:* Pres. JoAnn Hickey
FTE Enroll: 40   (805) 898-1180

SANTA CLARA UNIVERSITY
Santa Clara 95053 *Type:* Private (Roman Catholic) liberal arts and professional *Accred.:* 1949/1988 (WASC-Sr.) *Calendar:* Qtr. plan *Degrees:* B, M, P, D *Prof. Accred.:* Business (B,M), Engineering (civil, computer, electrical, mechanical), Law, Music, Theatre *CEO:* Pres. Paul L. Locatelli, S.J.
FTE Enroll: 6,489   (408) 554-4764

SANTA MONICA COLLEGE
1900 Pico Blvd., Santa Monica 90405-1628 *Type:* Public (district) junior *System:* Santa Monica Community College District *Accred.:* 1952/1992 (WASC-Jr.) *Calendar:* Sem. plan *Degrees:* A *Prof. Accred.:* Nursing (A), Respiratory Therapy *CEO:* Pres.Piedad F. Robertson
Enroll: 19,896   (310) 450-5150

SANTA ROSA JUNIOR COLLEGE
1501 Mendocino Ave., Santa Rosa 95401 *Type:* Public (district) junior *System:* Sonoma County Junior College District *Accred.:* 1952/1991 (WASC-Jr.) *Calendar:* Sem. plan *Degrees:* A *Prof. Accred.:* Dental Assisting, Radiography *CEO:* Pres. Robert F. Agrella
Enroll: 28,853   (707) 527-4011

SAYBROOK INSTITUTE
450 Pacific Ave., No. 300, San Francisco 94133 *Type:* Private professional; graduate

only *Accred.:* 1984/1988 (WASC-Sr.) *Calendar:* Sem. plan *Degrees:* M, D *CEO:* Interim Pres. Rudy J. Melone
FTE Enroll: 336   (415) 433-9200

SCHOOL OF THEOLOGY AT CLAREMONT
1325 N. College Ave., Claremont 91711-3199 *Type:* Private (Disciples of Christ/ United Methodist) graduate only *Accred.:* 1944/1993 (ATS); 1971/1994 (WASC-Sr.) *Calendar:* Sem. plan *Degrees:* M, P, D *CEO:* Pres. Robert W. Edgar
FTE Enroll: 257   (909) 626-3521

SCRIPPS COLLEGE
1030 N. Columbia Ave., Claremont 91711 *Type:* Private liberal arts for women *System:* Claremont University Center *Accred.:* 1949/1993 (WASC-Sr.) *Calendar:* Sem. plan *Degrees:* B *CEO:* Pres. Nancy Y. Bekavac
FTE Enroll: 612   (909) 621-8148

THE SCRIPPS RESEARCH INSTITUTE
10666 N. Torrey Pines Rd., La Jolla 92037 *Type:* Private graduate only *Accred.:* 1993 (WASC-Sr.) *Calendar:* 9-mos. program *Degrees:* D *CEO:* Pres. Richard A. Lerner
FTE Enroll: 87   (619) 455-9100

SHASTA COLLEGE
P.O. Box 496006, Redding 96049 *Type:* Public (district) junior *System:* Shasta-Tehama-Trinity Joint Community College District *Accred.:* 1952/1994 (WASC-Jr.) *Calendar:* Sem. plan *Degrees:* A *CEO:* Pres. Douglas M. Treadway
Enroll: 9,619   (916) 225-4600

SIERRA COLLEGE
5000 Rocklin Rd., Rocklin 95677 *Type:* Public (district) junior *System:* Sierra Joint Community College District *Accred.:* 1952/1995 (WASC-Jr.) *Calendar:* Sem. plan *Degrees:* A *CEO:* Pres. Kevin M. Ramirez
Enroll: 13,819   (916) 624-3333

SIMPSON COLLEGE
2211 College View Dr., Redding 96003 *Type:* Private (Christian and Missionary Alliance) liberal arts *Accred.:* 1969/1995

(WASC-Sr.) *Calendar:* 4-1-4 plan *Degrees:* B, M *CEO:* Pres. James M. Grant
FTE Enroll: 712   (916) 222-6360

SKYLINE COLLEGE
3300 College Dr., San Bruno 94066 *Type:* Public (district) junior *System:* San Mateo County Community College District *Accred.:* 1971/1995 (WASC-Jr.) *Calendar:* Sem. plan *Degrees:* A *Prof. Accred.:* Respiratory Therapy *CEO:* Pres. Linda Graef Salter
Enroll: 8,172   (415) 355-7000

SOLANO COMMUNITY COLLEGE
4000 Suisun Valley Rd., Suisun 94585 *Type:* Public (district) junior *System:* Solano County Community College District *Accred.:* 1952/1994 (WASC-Jr.) *Calendar:* Sem. plan *Degrees:* A *CEO:* Pres. Stan Arterbery
Enroll: 10,400   (707) 864-7000

SONOMA STATE UNIVERSITY
1801 E. Cotati Ave., Rohnert Park 94928 *Type:* Public (state) *System:* California State University System *Accred.:* 1963/1989 (WASC-Sr.) *Calendar:* Sem. plan *Degrees:* B, M *Prof. Accred.:* Art, Counseling, Music, Nursing (B,M) *CEO:* Pres. Ruben Arminana
FTE Enroll: 5,175   (707) 664-2880

SOUTH BAYLO UNIVERSITY
1126 N. Brookhurst St., Anaheim 93101 *Type:* Private professional *Calendar:* Qtr. plan *Degrees:* M *Prof. Accred.:* Acupuncture (M) *CEO:* Pres. David Park
FTE Enroll: 235   (714) 533-1495

LOS ANGELES CAMPUS
2727 W. 6th St., Los Angeles 90015 *Prof. Accred.:* Acupuncture (M)
                                   (213) 738-0712

SOUTHERN CALIFORNIA COLLEGE
55 Fair Dr., Costa Mesa 92626 *Type:* Private (Assemblies of God) liberal arts *Accred.:* 1964/1991 (WASC-Sr.) *Calendar:* 4-1-4 plan *Degrees:* B, M *CEO:* Pres. Wayne E. Kraiss
FTE Enroll: 1,023   (714) 556-3610

SOUTHERN CALIFORNIA COLLEGE OF BUSINESS AND LAW
595 W. Lambert Rd., Brea 92621 *Type:* Private junior *Accred.:* 1993/1995 (ACICS) *Degrees:* A, C *CEO:* Pres. Cynthia L. Cramer
                                   (714) 256-8830

SOUTHERN CALIFORNIA COLLEGE OF OPTOMETRY
2575 Yorba Linda Blvd., Fullerton 92631-1699 *Type:* Private professional *Accred.:* 1961/1991 (WASC-Sr.) *Calendar:* Qtr. plan *Degrees:* A, B, P *Prof. Accred.:* Optometric Residency, Optometry *CEO:* Pres. Richard L. Hopping, O.D.
FTE Enroll: 382   (714) 449-7450

SOUTHERN CALIFORNIA INSTITUTE OF ARCHITECTURE
5454 Beethoven St., Los Angeles 90066 *Type:* Private professional *Accred.:* 1991/1995 (WASC-Sr.) *Calendar:* Sem. plan *Degrees:* B, M, P *CEO:* Dir. Michael Rotondi
FTE Enroll: 432   (310) 574-1123

SOUTHWESTERN COLLEGE
900 Otay Lakes Rd., Chula Vista 91910 *Type:* Public (district) junior *System:* Southwestern Community College District *Accred.:* 1964/1991 (WASC-Jr.) *Calendar:* Sem. plan *Degrees:* A *Prof. Accred.:* Surgical Technology *CEO:* Pres. Joseph M. Conte
Enroll: 16,039   (619) 421-6700

SOUTHWESTERN UNIVERSITY SCHOOL OF LAW
675 S. Westmoreland Ave., Los Angeles 90005 *Type:* Private professional *Calendar:* Sem. plan *Degrees:* P *Prof. Accred.:* Law *CEO:* Dean Leigh H. Taylor
Enroll: 1,201   (213) 738-6710

STANFORD UNIVERSITY
Stanford 94305 *Type:* Private liberal arts and professional *Accred.:* 1949/1991 (WASC-Sr.) *Calendar:* Qtr. plan *Degrees:* B, M, P, D *Prof. Accred.:* Business (M), Counseling Psychology, Engineering (aerospace, chemical, civil, electrical, industrial, mechanical, petroleum), Law, Medicine, Physician

Assisting/Surgeon Assisting *CEO:* Pres. Gerhard Casper
FTE Enroll: 13,187   (415) 723-2300

STARR KING SCHOOL FOR THE MINISTRY
2441 LeConte Ave., Berkeley 94709 *Type:* Private (Unitarian Universalist) graduate only *Accred.:* 1978/1988 (ATS) *Calendar:* Sem. plan *Degrees:* M *CEO:* Pres. Rebecca Parker
Enroll: 62   (510) 845-6232

TAFT COLLEGE
29 Emmons Park Dr., Taft 93268 *Type:* Public (district) junior *System:* West Kern Community College District *Accred.:* 1952/1991 (WASC-Jr.) *Calendar:* Sem. plan *Degrees:* A *Prof. Accred.:* Dental Hygiene (provisional) *CEO:* Pres. David Cothrun
Enroll: 1,200   (805) 763-4282

THOMAS AQUINAS COLLEGE
10000 N. Ojai Rd., Santa Paula 93060 *Type:* Private liberal arts *Accred.:* 1980/1993 (WASC-Sr.) *Calendar:* Sem. plan *Degrees:* B *CEO:* Pres. Thomas E. Dillon
FTE Enroll: 221   (805) 525-4417

THOMAS JEFFERSON SCHOOL OF LAW
2121 San Diego Ave., San Diego 92110 *Type:* Private professional *Accred.:* 1976/1994 (WASC-Sr.) *Calendar:* Sem. plan *Degrees:* B, P *CEO:* Pres. John C. Monks
FTE Enroll: 495   (619) 297-9700

UNITED STATES INTERNATIONAL UNIVERSITY
10455 Pomerado Rd., San Diego 92131 *Type:* Private liberal arts and professional *Accred.:* 1956/1984 (WASC-Sr. probational) *Calendar:* Qtr. plan *Degrees:* A, B, M, P, D *Prof. Accred.:* Engineering (civil) *CEO:* Pres. Garry D. Hays
FTE Enroll: 1,996   (619) 271-4300

UNIVERSITY OF CALIFORNIA, BERKELEY
Berkeley 94720 *Type:* Public (state) *System:* University of California Office of the President *Accred.:* 1949/1990 (WASC-Sr.) *Calendar:* Sem. plan *Degrees:* B, M, P, D *Prof. Accred.:* Business (B,M), Clinical Psychology, Computer Science, Dietetics (intern-

ship), Engineering (chemical, civil, computer, electrical, industrial, mechanical, mineral, naval architecture/marine, nuclear), Forestry, Health Services Administration, Interior Design, Journalism (M), Landscape Architecture (M), Law, Librarianship, Optometric Residency, Optometry, Planning (M), Psychology Internship, School Psychology, Social Work (M) *CEO:* Chanc. Chang-Lin Tien
FTE Enroll: 29,086   (510) 642-6000

UNIVERSITY OF CALIFORNIA, DAVIS
Davis 95616 *Type:* Public (state) *System:* University of California Office of the President *Accred.:* 1954/1992 (WASC-Sr.) *Calendar:* Qtr. plan *Degrees:* B, M, P, D *Prof. Accred.:* Business (M), Computer Science, Engineering (aerospace, agricultural, chemical, civil, computer, electrical, materials, mechanical), Landscape Architecture (B), Law, Medicine, Physician Assisting/Surgeon Assisting, Psychology Internship, Veterinary Medicine *CEO:* Chanc. Larry N. Vanderhoef
FTE Enroll: 21,144   (916) 752-1011

UNIVERSITY OF CALIFORNIA, HASTINGS COLLEGE OF THE LAW
200 McAllister St., San Francisco 94102 *Type:* Public (state) professional *System:* University of California Office of the President *Calendar:* Sem. plan *Degrees:* P *Prof. Accred.:* Law *CEO:* Dean Mary Kay Kane
Enroll: 1,253   (415) 565-4600

UNIVERSITY OF CALIFORNIA, IRVINE
Campus Dr., Irvine 92717 *Type:* Public (state) *System:* University of California Office of the President *Accred.:* 1965/1991 (WASC-Sr.) *Calendar:* Qtr. plan *Degrees:* B, M, P, D *Prof. Accred.:* Business (M), Clinical Lab Scientist, Engineering (civil, electrical, mechanical), Medicine, Psychology Internship *CEO:* Chanc. Laurel L. Wilkening
FTE Enroll: 15,070   (714) 824-5011

UNIVERSITY OF CALIFORNIA, LOS ANGELES
405 Hilgard Ave., Los Angeles 90024 *Type:* Public (state) *System:* University of California Office of the President *Accred.:* 1949/1989 (WASC-Sr.) *Calendar:* Qtr. plan

Degrees: B, M, P, D *Prof. Accred.:* Business (M), Clinical Psychology, Combined Prosthodontics, Computer Science, Dentistry, Endodontics, Engineering (aerospace, chemical, civil, computer, electrical, materials, mechanical), General Dentistry, General Practice Residency, Health Services Administration, Interior Design, Law, Librarianship, Maxillofacial Prosthodontics, Medicine, Nurse Anesthesia Education, Nursing (B,M), Oral and Maxillofacial Surgery, Orthodontics, Pediatric Dentistry, Periodontics, Planning (M), Psychology Internship, Social Work (M), *CEO:* Chanc. Charles E. Young
FTE Enroll: 32,797   (310) 825-4321

UNIVERSITY OF CALIFORNIA, RIVERSIDE
Riverside 92521 *Type:* Public (state) *System:* University of California Office of the President *Accred.:* 1956/1988 (WASC-Sr.) *Calendar:* Qtr. plan *Degrees:* B, M, D *Prof. Accred.:* Engineering (electrical) *CEO:* Chanc. Raymond L. Orbach
FTE Enroll: 8,519   (909) 787-1012

UNIVERSITY OF CALIFORNIA, SAN DIEGO
9500 Gilman Dr., Mail Code 0056, La Jolla 92093 *Type:* Public (state) *System:* University of California Office of the President *Accred.:* 1964/1986 (WASC-Sr.) *Calendar:* Qtr. plan *Degrees:* B, M, P, D *Prof. Accred.:* Engineering (bioengineering, chemical, civil, electrical, mechanical, systems), Medicine, Psychology Internship *CEO:* Interim Chanc. Marjorie C. Caserio
FTE Enroll: 15,980   (619) 534-2230

UNIVERSITY OF CALIFORNIA, SAN FRANCISCO
513 Parnassus Ave., San Francisco 94143 *Type:* Public (state) *System:* University of California Office of the President *Accred.:* 1976/1986 (WASC-Sr.) *Calendar:* Qtr. plan *Degrees:* B, M, P, D *Prof. Accred.:* Combined Prosthodontics, Dental Hygiene, Dental Public Health, Dentistry, Dietetics (internship), General Dentistry, Medicine, Nuclear Medicine Technology, Nursing (B,M), Oral and Maxillofacial Surgery, Orthodontics, Pediatric Dentistry, Periodon-

tics, Physical Therapy, Psychology Internship *CEO:* Chanc. Joseph B. Martin
FTE Enroll: 3,729   (415) 476-9000

UNIVERSITY OF CALIFORNIA, SANTA BARBARA
Santa Barbara 93106-2030 *Type:* Public (state) *System:* University of California Office of the President *Accred.:* 1949/1991 (WASC-Sr.) *Calendar:* Qtr. plan *Degrees:* B, M, D *Prof. Accred.:* Combined Professional-Scientific Psychology, Computer Science, Counseling Psychology, Dance, Engineering (chemical, electrical, mechanical, nuclear), Psychology Internship *CEO:* Chanc. Henry T. Yang
FTE Enroll: 17,834   (805) 893-8000

UNIVERSITY OF CALIFORNIA, SANTA CRUZ
1156 High St., Santa Cruz 95064 *Type:* Public (state) *System:* University of California Office of the President *Accred.:* 1965/1994 (WASC-Sr.) *Calendar:* Qtr. plan *Degrees:* B, M, D *Prof. Accred.:* Engineering (computer), Psychology Internship (provisional) *CEO:* Chanc. Karl S. Pister
FTE Enroll: 10,083   (40?) 459-0111

UNIVERSITY OF JUDAISM
15600 Mulholland Dr., Los Angeles 90077 *Type:* Private *Accred.:* 1961/1988 (WASC-Sr.) *Calendar:* Sem. plan *Degrees:* B, M *CEO:* Pres. Robert Wexler
FTE Enroll: 170   (310) 476-9777

UNIVERSITY OF LA VERNE
1950 Third St., La Verne 91750 *Type:* Private liberal arts and professional *Accred.:* 1955/1991 (WASC-Sr.) *Calendar:* 4-1-4 plan *Degrees:* B, M, P, D *CEO:* Pres. Stephen C. Morgan
FTE Enroll: 5,251   (909) 593-3511

UNIVERSITY OF REDLANDS
1200 E. Colton Ave., P.O. Box 3080, Redlands 92373-0999 *Type:* Private liberal arts and professional *Accred.:* 1949/1992 (WASC-Sr.) *Calendar:* 4-1-4 plan *Degrees:* B, M *Prof. Accred.:* Music, Speech-Language Pathology *CEO:* Vice Pres./CEO James R. Appleton
FTE Enroll: 3,835   (909) 793-2121

UNIVERSITY OF SAN DIEGO
    5998 Alcala Park, San Diego 92110-2492
    Type: Private (Roman Catholic) liberal arts
    and professional *Accred.:* 1956/1993
    (WASC-Sr.) *Calendar:* 4-1-4 plan *Degrees:*
    B, M, P, D *Prof. Accred.:* Business (B,M),
    Engineering (electrical), Law, Marriage and
    Family Therapy (M), Nursing (B,M) *CEO:*
    Pres. Alice B. Hayes
    FTE Enroll: 5,324   (619) 260-4600

UNIVERSITY OF SAN FRANCISCO
    2130 Fulton St., San Francisco 94117-1080
    Type: Private (Roman Catholic) liberal arts
    and professional *Accred.:* 1949/1981
    (WASC-Sr.) *Calendar:* Sem. plan *Degrees:*
    B, M, P, D *Prof. Accred.:* Business (B,M),
    Law, Nurse Anesthesia Education, Nursing
    (B) *CEO:* Pres. John P. Schlegel, S.J.
    FTE Enroll: 7,211   (415) 666-6292

UNIVERSITY OF SOUTHERN CALIFORNIA
    University Park, Los Angeles 90089-0012
    Type: Private liberal arts and professional
    Accred.: 1949/1987 (WASC-Sr.) *Calendar:*
    Sem. plan *Degrees:* B, M, P, D *Prof.
    Accred.:* Accounting (A,C), Business (B,M),
    Clinical Psychology, Combined Prosthodon-
    tics, Counseling Psychology, Dental
    Hygiene, Dentistry, Dietetics (internship),
    Endodontics, Engineering (aerospace, chem-
    ical, civil, electrical, industrial, mechanical),
    Health Services Administration, Journalism
    (B,M), Law, Marriage and Family Therapy
    (D), Medicine, Music, Nursing (B), Occupa-
    tional Therapy, Oral and Maxillofacial
    Surgery, Orthodontics, Pediatric Dentistry,
    Periodontics, Physical Therapy, Physician
    Assisting/Surgeon Assisting, Planning (M),
    Psychology Internship, Public Administra-
    tion, Social Work (M-conditional) *CEO:*
    Pres. Steven B. Sample
    FTE Enroll: 24,399   (213) 740-2311

UNIVERSITY OF THE PACIFIC
    3601 Pacific Ave., Stockton 95211 *Type:* Pri-
    vate liberal arts and professional *Accred.:*
    1949/1995 (WASC-Sr.) *Calendar:* Sem. plan
    Degrees: B, M, P, D *Prof. Accred.:* Art, Busi-
    ness (B), Computer Science, Dentistry, Engi-
    neering (civil, computer, electrical, engineer-

ing physics/science, mechanical), General
Dentistry, Law, Music, Orthodontics, Physi-
cal Therapy, Speech-Language Pathology,
Teacher Education *CEO:* Pres. Donald V.
DeRosa
FTE Enroll: 5,501   (209) 946-2011

UNIVERSITY OF WEST LOS ANGELES
    1155 W. Arbor Vitae St., Inglewood 90301-
    2902 *Type:* Private professional *Accred.:* 1983/
    1988 (WASC-Sr.) *Calendar:* Tri. plan *Degrees:*
    B, P *CEO:* Pres. Edward J. Kormondy
    FTE Enroll: 497   (310) 215-3339

VALLEY COMMERCIAL COLLEGE
    1207 I St., Modesto 95354 *Type:* Private busi-
    ness *Accred.:* 1970/1995 (ACICS) *Degrees:*
    A, C *CEO:* Pres./CEO Gregory L. Martin
                                (209) 578-0616

VENTURA COLLEGE
    4667 Telegraph Rd., Ventura 93003 *Type:*
    Public (district) junior *System:* Ventura
    County Community College District
    Accred.: 1952/1990 (WASC-Jr.) *Calendar:*
    Sem. plan *Degrees:* A *CEO:* Interim Pres.
    Larry Calderon
    Enroll: 12,350   (805) 654-6460

VICTOR VALLEY COLLEGE
    18422 Bear Valley Rd., Victorville 92392
    Type: Public (district) junior *System:* Victor
    Valley Community College District *Accred.:*
    1963/1993 (WASC-Jr.) *Calendar:* Sem. plan
    Degrees: A *Prof. Accred.:* Nursing (A), Respi-
    ratory Therapy *CEO:* Interim Pres. Nicholas
    Halisky
    Enroll: 8,071   (619) 245-4271

VISTA COLLEGE
    2020 Milvia St., Berkeley 94704 *Type:* Pub-
    lic (district) junior *System:* Peralta Commu-
    nity College District *Accred.:* 1981/1991
    (WASC-Jr.) *Calendar:* Sem. plan *Degrees:*
    A *CEO:* Pres. Barbara A. Beno
    Enroll: 3,223   (510) 841-8431

WEST COAST UNIVERSITY
    440 S. Shatto Pl., Los Angeles 90020 *Type:*
    Private *Accred.:* 1963/1982 (WASC-Sr. pro-

bational) *Calendar:* Tri. plan *Degrees:* A, B, M *CEO:* Pres. Robert M. L. Baker, Jr.
FTE Enroll: 1,025   (213) 487-4433

WEST HILLS COMMUNITY COLLEGE
300 Cherry La., Coalinga 93210 *Type:* Public (district) junior *System:* West Hills Community College District *Accred.:* 1952/1993 (WASC-Jr.) *Calendar:* Sem. plan *Degrees:* A *CEO:* Pres. Francis P. Gornick
Enroll: 2,378   (209) 935-0801

WEST LOS ANGELES COLLEGE
4800 Freshman Dr., Culver City 90230 *Type:* Public (district) junior *System:* Los Angeles Community College District *Accred.:* 1971/1994 (WASC-Jr.) *Calendar:* Sem. plan *Degrees:* A *Prof. Accred.:* Dental Hygiene *CEO:* Pres. Evelyn C. Wong
Enroll: 7,716   (310) 287-4200

WEST VALLEY COLLEGE
14000 Fruitvale Ave., Saratoga 95070 *Type:* Public (district) junior *System:* West Valley-Mission College District *Accred.:* 1966/1996 (WASC-Jr.) *Calendar:* Sem. plan *Degrees:* A *Prof. Accred.:* Interior Design, Medical Assisting (AMA) *CEO:* Interim Pres. Sam Schauerman
Enroll: 13,084   (408) 867-2200

WESTERN INSTITUTE
120 Avram St., Ste. 102-A, Rohnert Park 94928 *Type:* Private *Accred.:* 1995 (ABHES) *Calendar:* Sem. plan *Degrees:* A *CEO:* Pres. Michael Fanning
Enroll: 52   (707) 664-9267

WESTERN STATE UNIVERSITY COLLEGE OF LAW OF ORANGE COUNTY
1111 N. State College Blvd., Fullerton 92631 *Type:* Private professional *Accred.:* 1976/1995 (WASC-Sr.) *Calendar:* Sem. plan *Degrees:* B, P *CEO:* Pres. John C. Monks
FTE Enroll: 1,486   (714) 738-1000

WESTMINSTER THEOLOGICAL SEMINARY IN CALIFORNIA
1725 Bear Valley Pkwy., Escondido 92027 *Type:* Private (Presbyterian) professional *Accred.:* 1995 (ATS candidate); 1984/1994

(WASC-Sr.) *Calendar:* 4-1-4 plan *Degrees:* M, P *CEO:* Pres. W. Robert Godfrey
FTE Enroll: 126   (619) 480-8474

WESTMONT COLLEGE
955 La Paz Rd., Santa Barbara 93108 *Type:* Private liberal arts *Accred.:* 1957/1995 (WASC-Sr.) *Calendar:* Sem. plan *Degrees:* B *CEO:* Pres. David K. Winter
FTE Enroll: 1,274   (805) 565-6000

WHITTIER COLLEGE
13406 E. Philadelphia St., Whittier 90608 *Type:* Private liberal arts *Accred.:* 1949/1994 (WASC-Sr.) *Calendar:* 4-1-4 plan *Degrees:* B, M, P *Prof. Accred.:* Law, Social Work (B) *CEO:* Pres. James L. Ash, Jr.
FTE Enroll: 1,427   (310) 907-4200

WOODBURY UNIVERSITY
7500 Glen Oaks Blvd., Burbank 91510-7846 *Type:* Private professional *Accred.:* 1961/1991 (WASC-Sr.) *Calendar:* Qtr. plan *Degrees:* B, M *Prof. Accred.:* Interior Design *CEO:* Pres. Paul E. Sago
FTE Enroll: 923   (818) 767-0888

WRIGHT INSTITUTE
2728 Durant Ave., Berkeley 94704 *Type:* Private professional *Accred.:* 1977/1995 (WASC-Sr.) *Calendar:* Qtr. plan *Degrees:* D *Prof. Accred.:* Clinical Psychology *CEO:* Pres. Peter Dybwad
FTE Enroll: 242   (510) 841-9230

YESHIVA OHR ELCHONON-CHABAD/WEST COAST TALMUDIC SEMINARY
7215 Waring Ave., Los Angeles 90046 *Type:* Private professional *Accred.:* 1983/1989 (AARTS) *Calendar:* Sem. plan *Degrees:* B *CEO:* Pres. E. Schocket
Enroll: 35   (213) 937-3763

YO SAN UNIVERSITY OF TRADITIONAL CHINESE MEDICINE
1314 Second St., Santa Monica 90401 *Type:* Private professional *Calendar:* Tri. plan *Degrees:* M *Prof. Accred.:* Acupuncture (M) *CEO:* Pres. Daoshing Ni
FTE Enroll: 26   (310) 917-2202

Y∪BA C∪LLEGE
  2088 N. Beale Rd., Marysville 95901 *Type:*
  Public (district) junior *System:* Yuba Com-
  munity College District *Accred.:* 1952/
  1994 (WASC-Jr.) *Calendar:* Sem. plan
  Degrees: A *Prof. Accred.:* Radiography,
  Veterinary Technology *CEO:* Pres. Stephen
  M. Epler
  Enroll: 9,247   (916) 741-6700

COLORADO

ADAMS STATE COLLEGE
208 Edgemont, Alamosa 81101 *Type:* Public (state) liberal arts and teachers *System:* State Colleges in Colorado *Accred.:* 1950/1987 (NCA) *Calendar:* Sem. plan *Degrees:* A, B, M *Prof. Accred.:* Music, Teacher Education *CEO:* Pres. J. Thomas Gilmore
Enroll: 6,074   (719) 589-7011

AIMS COMMUNITY COLLEGE
5401 W. 20th St., P.O. Box 69, Greeley 80632 *Type:* Public (district) junior *Accred.:* 1977/1989 (NCA) *Calendar:* Qtr. plan *Degrees:* A, C *Prof. Accred.:* Radiography *CEO:* Pres. George R. Conger
Enroll: 6,970   (303) 330-8008

ARAPAHOE COMMUNITY COLLEGE
2500 W. College Dr., P.O. Box 9002, Littleton 80160-9002 *Type:* Public (state) junior *System:* Colorado Community College and Occupational Education System *Accred.:* 1970/1987 (NCA) *Calendar:* Sem. plan *Degrees:* A, C *Prof. Accred.:* Clinical Lab Technology (A), Medical Record Technology, Occupational Therapy Assisting, Physical Therapy Assisting *CEO:* Pres. James F. Weber
Enroll: 7,655   (303) 794-1550

BEL-REA INSTITUTE OF ANIMAL TECHNOLOGY
1681 S. Dayton St., Denver 80231-3048 *Type:* Private *Accred.:* 1975/1993 (ACCSCT) *Calendar:* Qtr. plan *Degrees:* A *Prof. Accred.:* Veterinary Technology *CEO:* Dir. Marc Schapiro
       (800) 950-8001

BETH-EL COLLEGE OF NURSING
2790 N. Academy Blvd., Ste. 200, Colorado Springs 80917-5338 *Type:* Private professional *Accred.:* 1988/1993 (NCA) *Calendar:* Sem. plan *Degrees:* B, M, C *Prof. Accred.:* Nursing (B) *CEO:* Pres./Dean Carole Schoffstall
Enroll: 421   (719) 475-5170

BLAIR JUNIOR COLLEGE
828 Wooten Rd., Colorado Springs 80915 *Type:* Private junior *Accred.:* 1953/1994

(ACICS) *Calendar:* Qtr. plan *Degrees:* A *Prof. Accred.:* Medical Assisting (AMA) *CEO:* Dir. Patricia Draper-Hardy
       (719) 574-1082

COLLEGE FOR FINANCIAL PLANNING
4695 S. Monaco St., Denver 80237-3403 *Type:* Private professional *Accred.:* 1994 (NCA) *Degrees:* M, C *CEO:* Pres. William L. Anthes
Enroll: 839   (303) 220-1200

COLORADO AERO TECH
10851 W. 120th Ave., Broomfield 80021-3465 *Type:* Private *Accred.:* 1972/1987 (ACCSCT) *Degrees:* A *CEO:* Exec. Dir. Erik Brumme
       (800) 888-3995

COLORADO CHRISTIAN UNIVERSITY
180 S. Garrison St., Lakewood 80226 *Type:* Private (interdenominational) *Accred.:* 1981/1995 (NCA) *Calendar:* Sem. plan *Degrees:* A, B, M, C *CEO:* Pres. Ronald Schmidt
Enroll: 1,698   (303) 238-5386

COLORADO COLLEGE
14 E. Cache la Pourde St., Colorado Springs 80903 *Type:* Private liberal arts *Accred.:* 1915/1988 (NCA) *Calendar:* Sem. plan *Degrees:* B, M *CEO:* Pres. Kathryn Mohrman
Enroll: 1,929   (719) 389-6000

COLORADO INSTITUTE OF ART
200 E. Ninth Ave., Denver 80203-9947 *Type:* Private *Accred.:* 1977/1988 (ACCSCT) *Calendar:* Qtr. plan *Degrees:* A, C *CEO:* Pres. Elliot B. Jones, Sr.
       (800) 275-2420

COLORADO MOUNTAIN COLLEGE
Box 10001, 215 Ninth St., Glenwood Springs 81602 *Type:* Public (district) junior *Accred.:* 1974/1992 (NCA) *Calendar:* Qtr. plan *Degrees:* A, C *Prof. Accred.:* Veterinary Technology *CEO:* Pres. Cynthia M. Heelan
Enroll: 7,538   (303) 945-8691

ALPINE CAMPUS
1370 Bob Adams Dr., Steamboat Springs
80477
(303) 879-3288

ROARING FORK CAMPUS
3000 County Rd. 114, Glenwood Springs
81601
(303) 945-7841

TIMBERLINE CAMPUS
901 S. Hwy. 24, Leadville 80461
(719) 486-2015

COLORADO NORTHWESTERN COMMUNITY
COLLEGE
500 Kennedy Dr., Rangely 81648 *Type:* Public (district) junior *Accred.:* 1976/1993 (NCA) *Calendar:* Sem. plan *Degrees:* A, C *Prof. Accred.:* Dental Hygiene (conditional) *CEO:* Pres. Robert A. Anderson, Jr.
Enroll: 1,725   (303) 562-1105

CRAIG CAMPUS
50 College Dr., Craig 81625
(303) 824-7071

COLORADO SCHOOL OF MINES
1500 Illinois St., Golden 80401 *Type:* Public (state) technological *System:* Colorado Commission on Higher Education *Accred.:* 1929/1993 (NCA) *Calendar:* Sem. plan *Degrees:* B, M, D *Prof. Accred.:* Engineering (chemical, engineering physics/science, general, geological/geophysical, metallurgical, mining, petroleum) *CEO:* Pres. George S. Ansell
Enroll: 3,059   (303) 273-3280

COLORADO SCHOOL OF TRADES
1575 Hoyt St., Lakewood 80215-2996 *Type:* Private *Accred.:* 1973/1990 (ACCSCT) *Degrees:* A, C *CEO:* Dir. Robert E. Martin
(303) 233-4697

COLORADO STATE UNIVERSITY
102 Administration Bldg., Fort Collins 80523 *Type:* Public (state) *System:* Colorado Commission on Higher Education *Accred.:* 1925/1994 (NCA) *Calendar:* Sem. plan *Degrees:* B, M, D *Prof. Accred.:* Business (B,M), Construction Education (B), Counseling Psychology, Dietetics (internship),

Engineering (agricultural, chemical, civil, electrical, engineering physics/science, mechanical), Forestry, Interior Design, Journalism (B,M), Landscape Architecture (B), Marriage and Family Therapy (M), Music, Occupational Therapy, Psychology Internship, Recreation and Leisure Services (B), Social Work (B,M), Teacher Education, Veterinary Medicine *CEO:* Pres. Albert C. Yates
Enroll: 18,166   (303) 491-1101

COLORADO TECHNICAL UNIVERSITY
4435 N. Chestnut St., Colorado Springs 80907 *Type:* Private profit *Accred.:* 1980/1991 (NCA) *Calendar:* Qtr. plan *Degrees:* A, B, M, C *Prof. Accred.:* Engineering Technology (bioengineering, electrical) Engineering (electrical) (*CEO:* Pres. David O'Donnell
Enroll: 1,498   (719) 598-0200

COMMUNITY COLLEGE OF AURORA
16000 E. Centretech Pkwy., Aurora 80011 *Type:* Public (state) junior *System:* Colorado Community College and Occupational Education System *Accred.:* 1988/1993 (NCA) *Calendar:* Sem. plan *Degrees:* A, C *CEO:* Pres. Larry D. Carter
Enroll: 4,670   (303) 360-4700

COMMUNITY COLLEGE OF DENVER
Campus Box 250, P.O. Box 173363, Denver 80217-3363 *Type:* Public (state) junior *System:* Colorado Community College and Occupational Education System *Accred.:* 1975/1994 (NCA) *Calendar:* Qtr. plan *Degrees:* A, C *Prof. Accred.:* Nuclear Medicine Technology, Radiation Therapy Technology, Radiography, Surgical Technology *CEO:* Pres. Byron N. McClenney
Enroll: 6,713   (303) 556-2600

DENVER ACADEMY OF COURT REPORTING
7290 Samuel Dr., 2nd Fl., Denver 80221-2792 *Type:* Private business *Accred.:* 1982/1994 (ACICS) *Degrees:* A, C *CEO:* Pres. Charles W. Jarstfer
(303) 427-5292

DENVER BUSINESS COLLEGE
7350 N. Broadway, Denver 80221 *Type:* Private business *Accred.:* 1986/1996 (ACICS) *Calendar:* Qtr. plan *Degrees:* A, C *CEO:* Dir. David Hickey
(303) 426-1000

MESA CAMPUS
1550 S. Alma School Rd., No. 101, Mesa, AZ 85210 *Accred.:* 1988 (ACICS)
(602) 834-1000

HONOLULU CAMPUS
419 South St., Ste. 174, Honolulu, HI 96813 *Accred.:* 1989 (ACICS)
(808) 942-1000

DENVER CONSERVATIVE BAPTIST SEMINARY
P.O. Box 10000, Denver 80250-0100 *Type:* Private (Conservative Baptist) graduate only *Accred.:* 1970/1992 (ATS); 1972/1992 (NCA) *Calendar:* Qtr. plan *Degrees:* M, D *CEO:* Pres. Edward L. Hayes
Enroll: 606
(303) 761-2482

DENVER INSTITUTE OF TECHNOLOGY
7350 N. Broadway, Denver 80221-3653 *Type:* Private *Accred.:* 1968/1990 (ACCSCT) *Calendar:* Qtr. plan *Degrees:* A, C *Prof. Accred.:* Medical Assisting (AMA), Occupational Therapy Assisting *CEO:* Dir. James Z. Turner
(303) 650-5050

HEALTH CAREERS DIVISION CAMPUS
7350 N. Broadway, Annex HCD, Denver 80221-3653 *Accred.:* 1992 (ACCSCT) *Degrees:* A, C
(303) 650-5050

DENVER TECHNICAL COLLEGE
925 S. Niagara St., Denver 80224-1658 *Type:* Private *Accred.:* 1979/1988 (ACCSCT) *Degrees:* A, C *Prof. Accred.:* Medical Assisting, Physical Therapy Assisting *CEO:* Pres. Raul Valdes-Pages
(303) 329-3000

COLORADO SPRINGS CAMPUS
225 S. Union Blvd., Colorado Springs 80910-3138 *Accred.:* 1990 (ACCSCT) *Prof. Accred.:* Medical Assisting
(719) 632-3000

FORT LEWIS COLLEGE
1000 Rim Dr., Durango 81301-3999 *Type:* Public (state) liberal arts *System:* Colorado Commission on Higher Education *Accred.:* 1958/1986 (NCA) *Calendar:* Tri. plan *Degrees:* A, B *Prof. Accred.:* Business (B), Music *CEO:* Pres. Joel M. Jones
Enroll: 4,109
(970) 247-7100

FRONT RANGE COMMUNITY COLLEGE
3645 W. 112th Ave., Westminster 80030 *Type:* Public (state) junior *System:* Colorado Community College and Occupational Education System *Accred.:* 1975/1988 (NCA) *Calendar:* Sem. plan *Degrees:* A, C *Prof. Accred.:* Dental Assisting, Respiratory Therapy *CEO:* Pres. Thomas Gonzales
Enroll: 10,742
(303) 466-8811

ILIFF SCHOOL OF THEOLOGY
2201 S. University Blvd., Denver 80210 *Type:* Private (United Methodist) graduate only *Accred.:* 1938/1987 (ATS); 1973/1988 (NCA) *Calendar:* Qtr. plan *Degrees:* M, D *CEO:* Pres. Donald E. Messer
Enroll: 310
(303) 744-1287

INTERNATIONAL SCHOOL OF INFORMATION MANAGEMENT
PO Box 470640, Aurora 80047 *Type:* Private *Accred.:* 1993 (DETC) *Degrees:* M *CEO:* Pres. Ron Boehm
(800) 441-4746

ITT TECHNICAL INSTITUTE
2121 S. Blackhawk St., Aurora 80014-1416 *Type:* Private *Accred.:* 1985 (ACCSCT) *Degrees:* A, B *CEO:* Dir. Coy D. Ritchie
(303) 695-1913

LITTLE ROCK CAMPUS
4520 South Univ., Little Rock, AR 72204 *Accred.:* 1994 (ACCSCT) *Degrees:* A, C
(501) 565-5550

LAMAR COMMUNITY COLLEGE
2401 S. Main St., Lamar 81052 *Type:* Public (state) junior *System:* Colorado Community College and Occupational Education System *Accred.:* 1976/1992 (NCA) *Calendar:* Qtr. plan *Degrees:* A, C *CEO:* Pres. Marvin E. Lane
Enroll: 863 (719) 336-2248

MESA STATE COLLEGE
P.O. Box 2647, Grand Junction 81502 *Type:* Public (state) *System:* State Colleges in Colorado *Accred.:* 1957/1994 (NCA) *Calendar:* Sem. plan *Degrees:* A, B, C *Prof. Accred.:* Nursing (A,B), Radiography *CEO:* Pres. Raymond N. Kieft
Enroll: 4,638 (970) 248-1020

METROPOLITAN STATE COLLEGE OF DENVER
Campus Box 48, P.O. Box 173362, Denver 80217-3362 *Type:* Public (state) liberal arts *System:* State Colleges in Colorado *Accred.:* 1971/1987 (NCA) *Calendar:* Sem. plan *Degrees:* B, C *Prof. Accred.:* Engineering Technology (civil/construction, electrical, mechanical), Music, Nursing (B), Recreation and Leisure Services (B), Teacher Education *CEO:* Pres. Sheila Kaplan
Enroll: 17,461 (303) 556-3022

MORGAN COMMUNITY COLLEGE
17800 Rd. 20, Fort Morgan 80701 *Type:* Public (state) junior *System:* Colorado Community College and Occupational Education System *Accred.:* 1980/1989 (NCA) *Calendar:* Qtr. plan *Degrees:* A, C *Prof. Accred.:* Occupational Therapy Assisting, Physical Therapy Assisting *CEO:* Pres. Richard Bond
Enroll: 869 (800) 622-0216

THE NAROPA INSTITUTE
2130 Arapahoe Ave., Boulder 80302-6697 *Type:* Private *Accred.:* 1986/1990 (NCA) *Calendar:* Sem. plan *Degrees:* B, M, C *CEO:* Pres. John Whitehouse Cobb
Enroll: 623 (303) 444-0202

NATIONAL TECHNOLOGICAL UNIVERSITY
700 Centre Ave., Fort Collins 80526 *Type:* Private *Accred.:* 1986/1992 (NCA) *Calen-dar:* Sem. plan *Degrees:* M, C *CEO:* Pres. Lionel V. Baldwin
Enroll: 1,943 (970) 495-6400

NATIONAL THEATRE CONSERVATORY
1050 13th St., Denver 80204 *Type:* Private *Accred.:* 1992 (NCA) *Calendar:* Sem. plan *Degrees:* M *CEO:* Exec. Dir. J. Christopher Wineman
Enroll: 28 (303) 893-4000

NAZARENE BIBLE COLLEGE
P.O. Box 15749, 1111 Chapman Dr., Colorado Springs 80916 *Type:* Private (Church of the Nazarene) *Accred.:* 1976/1986 (AABC) *Calendar:* Qtr. plan *Degrees:* A, B, C *CEO:* Pres. Hiram Sanders
FTE Enroll: 329 (719) 596-5110

EMMANUEL BIBLE COLLEGE
1605 E. Elizabeth St., Pasadena, CA 91104 *Degrees:* A, B, C
FTE Enroll: 15 (818) 791-2575

INSTITUTO TEOLOGICO NAZARENO
14254 E. Los Angeles St., Baldwin Park, CA 91706
FTE Enroll: 25 (818) 813-0684

NAZARENE INDIAN BIBLE COLLEGE
2315 Markham Rd., S.W., Albuquerque, NM 87105
FTE Enroll: 44 (505) 877-0240

NORTHEASTERN JUNIOR COLLEGE
Sterling 80751 *Type:* Public (district) junior *Accred.:* 1964/1989 (NCA) *Calendar:* Qtr. plan *Degrees:* A, C *CEO:* Pres. Bruce C. Perryman
Enroll: 2,734 (970) 522-6600

OTERO JUNIOR COLLEGE
1802 Colorado Ave., La Junta 81050 *Type:* Public (state) junior *System:* Colorado Community College and Occupational Education System *Accred.:* 1967/1987 (NCA) *Calendar:* Qtr. plan *Degrees:* A, C *Prof. Accred.:* Nursing (A) *CEO:* Pres. Joe M. Treece
Enroll: 1,091 (719) 384-8721

PARKS JUNIOR COLLEGE
9065 Grant St., Denver 80229 *Type:* Private junior *Accred.:* 1962/1996 (ACICS) *Calendar:* Qtr. plan *Degrees:* A, C *Prof. Accred.:* Medical Assisting (AMA) *CEO:* Dir. Tara B. Pavlakovich
(303) 457-2757

AURORA CAMPUS
6 Abilene St., Aurora 80011 *Accred.:* 1990 (ACICS)
(303) 367-2757

PIKES PEAK COMMUNITY COLLEGE
5675 S. Academy Blvd., Colorado Springs 80906 *Type:* Public (state) junior *System:* Colorado Community College and Occupational Education System *Accred.:* 1975/1994 (NCA) *Calendar:* Sem. plan *Degrees:* A, C *Prof. Accred.:* Dental Assisting (conditional) *CEO:* Pres. Marijane A. Paulsen
Enroll: 6,712　　　　　　(800) 456-6847

PLATT COLLEGE
3100 S. Parker Rd., Aurora 80014-3141 *Type:* Private *Accred.:* 1987 (ACCSCT) *Degrees:* A, C *CEO:* Dir. Jerald Sirbu
(303) 369-5151

PUEBLO COLLEGE OF BUSINESS AND TECHNOLOGY
330 Lake Ave., Pueblo 81004 *Type:* Private business *Accred.:* 1969/1987 (ACICS) *Calendar:* Qtr. plan *Degrees:* A, C *CEO:* Dir. Karen Flockoski
(719) 545-3100

PUEBLO COMMUNITY COLLEGE
900 W. Orman Ave., Pueblo 81004 *Type:* Public (state) junior *System:* Colorado Community College and Occupational Education System *Accred.:* 1979/1991 (NCA) *Calendar:* Sem. plan *Degrees:* A, C *Prof. Accred.:* Dental Assisting (prelim. provisional), Dental Hygiene, Nursing (A), Occupational Therapy Assisting, Physical Therapy Assisting, Radiography, Respiratory Therapy, Surgical Technology *CEO:* Pres. Joe D. May
Enroll: 3,612　　　　　　(719) 549-3200

RED ROCKS COMMUNITY COLLEGE
13300 W. Sixth Ave., Lakewood 80401-5398 *Type:* Public (state) junior *System:* Colorado Community College and Occupational Education System *Accred.:* 1975/1988 (NCA) *Calendar:* Sem. plan *Degrees:* A, C *CEO:* Pres. Dorothy Horrell
Enroll: 6,954　　　　　　(303) 988-6160

REGIS UNIVERSITY
3333 Regis Blvd., Denver 80221-1099 *Type:* Private (Roman Catholic) liberal arts *Accred.:* 1922/1988 (NCA) *Calendar:* Sem. plan *Degrees:* A, B, M, C *Prof. Accred.:* Medical Record Administration, Nursing (B) *CEO:* Pres. Michael J. Sheeran, S.J.
Enroll: 6,616　　　　　　(303) 458-4100

ROCKY MOUNTAIN COLLEGE OF ART AND DESIGN
6875 E. Evans Ave., Denver 80224-2359 *Type:* Private *Accred.:* 1977/1989 (ACCSCT) *Calendar:* Qtr. plan *Degrees:* A, B *CEO:* Pres. Steven M. Steele
(303) 753-6046

TECHNICAL TRADES INSTITUTE
2315 E. Pikes Peak Ave., Colorado Springs 80909 *Type:* Private *Accred.:* 1983/1988 (ACCSCT) *Degrees:* A, C *CEO:* Dir. Frederick W. Harring
(719) 632-7626

EMERY AVIATION COLLEGE
1245A Aviation Way, Colorado Springs 80916 *Accred.:* 1990 (ACCSCT) *Degrees:* A
(719) 591-9488

TECHNICAL TRADES INSTITUTE
772 Horizon Dr., Grand Junction 81501-9977 *Type:* Private *Accred.:* 1987 (ACCSCT) *Degrees:* A, C *CEO:* Dir. Kim E. Rosenquist
(303) 245-8101

TEIKYO LORETTO HEIGHTS UNIVERSITY
3001 South Federal Blvd., Denver 80236 *Type:* Private senior *Accred.:* 1995 (ACICS) *Degrees:* B *CEO:* Pres. Willie T. Nagai
(303) 937-4200

TRINIDAD STATE JUNIOR COLLEGE
600 Prospect St., Trinidad 81082 *Type:* Public (state) junior *System:* Colorado Community College and Occupational Education System *Accred.:* 1962/1988 (NCA) *Calendar:* Qtr. plan *Degrees:* A, C *Prof. Accred.:* Nursing (A) *CEO:* Pres. Harold Deselms
Enroll: 1,614   (719) 846-5011

UNITED STATES AIR FORCE ACADEMY
2354 Fairchild Dr., Ste. 3A15, USAF Academy 80840-6214 *Type:* Public (federal) military and technological *Accred.:* 1959/1989 (NCA) *Calendar:* Sem. plan *Degrees:* B *Prof. Accred.:* Computer Science, Engineering (aerospace, civil, electrical, engineering mechanics, engineering physics/science, mechanical) *CEO:* Supt. Paul E. Stein
Enroll: 4,097   (719) 472-3970

UNIVERSITY OF COLORADO AT BOULDER
Campus Box B-17, Boulder 80309 *Type:* Public (state) *System:* University of Colorado Central Administration *Accred.:* 1913/1990 (NCA) *Calendar:* Sem. plan *Degrees:* B, M, P, D *Prof. Accred.:* Audiology, Business (B,M), Engineering (aerospace, architectural, chemical, civil, computer, electrical), Journalism (B,M), Law, Music, Speech-Language Pathology *CEO:* Chanc. Roderic Park
Enroll: 24,548   (303) 492-1411

UNIVERSITY OF COLORADO AT COLORADO SPRINGS
P.O. Box 7150, Colorado Springs 80933-7150 *Type:* Public (state) *System:* University of Colorado Central Administration *Accred.:* 1970/1987 (NCA) *Calendar:* Sem. plan *Degrees:* B, M, D *Prof. Accred.:* Business (B,M), Computer Science, Engineering (electrical), Public Administration, Teacher Education *CEO:* Chanc. Linda Bunnell Shade
Enroll: 5,862   (719) 593-3000

UNIVERSITY OF COLORADO AT DENVER
P.O. Box 173364, Denver 80217-3364 *Type:* Public (state) *System:* University of Colorado Central Administration *Accred.:* 1970/1991 (NCA) *Calendar:* Sem. plan *Degrees:* B, M, D *Prof. Accred.:* Business (B,M), Counseling, Engineering (civil, electrical, mechanical), Health Services Administration, Landscape Architecture (M), Music, Nursing (B,M), Planning (M), Public Administration, Teacher Education, *CEO:* Chanc. John C. Buechner
Enroll: 12,006   (303) 556-3279

UNIVERSITY OF COLORADO HEALTH SCIENCES CENTER
Campus Box A095, 4200 E. 9th Ave., Denver 80262 *Type:* Public (state) *System:* University of Colorado Central Administration *Accred.:* 1913/1988 (NCA) *Calendar:* Sem. plan *Degrees:* B, M, D *Prof. Accred.:* Clinical Lab Scientist, Clinical Psychology, Dental Hygiene, Dentistry, General Practice Residency, Medicine, Physical Therapy, Physician Assisting/Surgeon Assisting, Psychology Internship *CEO:* Chanc. Vincent A. Fulginiti
Enroll: 2,286   (303) 399-1211

UNIVERSITY OF DENVER
2199 S. University Blvd., Denver 80208 *Type:* Private (United Methodist) *Accred.:* 1914/1991 (NCA) *Calendar:* Qtr. plan *Degrees:* B, M, D, C *Prof. Accred.:* Accounting (A,B,C), Business (B,M), Clinical Psychology, Counseling Psychology, Engineering (electrical, mechanical), Law, Music, Psychology Internship, Social Work (M) *CEO:* Chanc. Daniel L. Ritchie
Enroll: 8,492   (800) 525-9495

UNIVERSITY OF NORTHERN COLORADO
Greeley 80639 *Type:* Public (state) *System:* Colorado Commission on Higher Education *Accred.:* 1916/1995 (NCA) *Calendar:* Sem. plan *Degrees:* B, M, P, D *Prof. Accred.:* Accounting (A), Audiology, Business (B), Counseling, Music, Nursing (B,M), Recreation and Leisure Services (B), Rehabilitation Counseling, School Psychology, Speech-Language Pathology, Teacher Education, *CEO:* Pres. Herman D. Lujan
Enroll: 12,226   (970) 351-1890

UNIVERSITY OF SOUTHERN COLORADO
2200 Bonforte Blvd., Pueblo 81001-4901 *Type:* Public (state) liberal arts and techno-

logical *System:* Colorado Commission on Higher Education *Accred.:* 1951/1987 (NCA) *Calendar:* Sem. plan *Degrees:* B, M *Prof. Accred.:* Engineering Technology (civil/construction, electrical, mechanical), Engineering (industrial), Music, Nursing (B), Social Work (B,M) *CEO:* Pres. Robert C. Shirley
Enroll: 5,182   (719) 549-2100

WESTERN STATE COLLEGE
214 Taylor Hall, Gunnison 81231 *Type:* Public (state) liberal arts *System:* State Colleges in Colorado *Accred.:* 1915/1993 (NCA) *Calendar:* Sem. plan *Degrees:* B *Prof. Accred.:* Music *CEO:* Interim Pres. William M. Fulkerson, Jr.
Enroll: 2,445   (800) 876-5309

YESHIVA TORAS CHAIM TALMUDIC SEMINARY
1400 Quitman St., P.O. Box 4067, Denver 80204 *Type:* Private professional *Accred.:* 1979/1990 (AARTS) *Calendar:* Sem. plan *Degrees:* B, M *CEO:* Pres. S. Beren
Enroll: 22   (303) 629-8200

CONNECTICUT

ALBERTUS MAGNUS COLLEGE
New Haven 06511-1189 *Type:* Private (Roman Catholic) liberal arts *Accred.:* 1932/1995 (NEASC-CIHE) *Calendar:* Sem. plan *Degrees:* A, B, M *CEO:* Pres. Julia M. McNamara
Enroll: 512   (203) 773-8550

ASNUNTUCK COMMUNITY-TECHNICAL COLLEGE
170 Elm St., Enfield 06082 *Type:* Public (state) junior *System:* State of Connecticut Board of Trustees of Community-Technical Colleges *Accred.:* 1976/1986 (NEASC-CIHE) *Calendar:* Sem. plan *Degrees:* A *CEO:* Pres. Harvey S. Irlen
Enroll: 859   (860) 253-3000

BERKELEY DIVINITY SCHOOL
363 St. Ronan St., New Haven 06511 *Type:* Private (Episcopal) graduate only *Accred.:* 1954/1991 (ATS) *Calendar:* Sem. plan *Degrees:* M *CEO:* Dean Philip Turner
(203) 432-6105

BETH BENJAMIN ACADEMY OF CONNECTICUT
132 Prospect St., Stamford 06901 *Type:* Private professional *Accred.:* 1978/1990 (AARTS) *Calendar:* Tri. plan *Degrees:* Talmudic (1st) *CEO:* Pres. S. Schustal
Enroll: 40   (203) 325-4351

BRIARWOOD COLLEGE
2279 Mt. Vernon Rd., Southington 06489 *Type:* Private business *Accred.:* 1982/1995 (NEASC-CTCI) *Calendar:* Sem. plan *Degrees:* A, C *Prof. Accred.:* Dental Assisting, Funeral Service Education (Mortuary Science), Medical Record Technology *CEO:* Pres. Richard G. Rausch
FTE Enroll: 458   (203) 628-4751

CAPITAL COMMUNITY-TECHNICAL COLLEGE
WOODLAND CAMPUS
61 Woodland St., Hartford 06105 *Type:* Public (state) 2-year *System:* State of Connecticut Board of Trustees of Community-Technical Colleges *Accred.:* 1975/1986 (NEASC-CIHE) *Calendar:* Sem. plan *Degrees:* A *Prof. Accred.:* EMT-Paramedic, civil/construction) manufacturing) Nursing (A) *CEO:* Pres. Conrad L. Mallett
Enroll: 1,582   (860) 520-7800

FLATBUSH CAMPUS
401 Flatbush Ave., Hartford 06106 *Prof. Accred.:* Engineering Technology (civil/construction, electrical, manufacturing, mechanical)
(203) 527-4111

CENTRAL CONNECTICUT STATE UNIVERSITY
1615 Stanley St., New Britain 06050 *Type:* Public liberal arts and teachers *System:* Connecticut State University Central Office *Accred.:* 1947/1988 (NEASC-CIHE) *Calendar:* Sem. plan *Degrees:* A, B, M *Prof. Accred.:* Computer Science, Engineering Technology (civil/construction, manufacturing), Nurse Anesthesia Education, Nursing (B), Social Work (B) *CEO:* Interim Pres. Merle W. Harris
Enroll: 7,700   (860) 832-3200

CHARTER OAK STATE COLLEGE
66 Cedar St., Ste. 301, Newington 06111-2646 *Type:* Public (state) liberal arts *System:* State of Connecticut Department of Higher Education *Accred.:* 1981/1987 (NEASC-CIHE) *Calendar:* Sem. plan *Degrees:* A, B *CEO:* Acting Pres. Richard J. Hamilton
Enroll: 1,186   (860) 666-4595

CONNECTICUT COLLEGE
New London 06320 *Type:* Private liberal arts *Accred.:* 1932/1987 (NEASC-CIHE) *Calendar:* Sem. plan *Degrees:* B, M *CEO:* Pres. Claire L. Gaudiani
Enroll: 1,780   (203) 447-1911

EASTERN CONNECTICUT STATE UNIVERSITY
83 Windham St., Willimantic 06226-2295 *Type:* Public liberal arts and teachers *System:* Connecticut State University Central Office *Accred.:* 1958/1990 (NEASC-CIHE) *Calendar:* Sem. plan *Degrees:* A, B, M *CEO:* Pres. David G. Carter
Enroll: 3,188   (860) 465-5000

FAIRFIELD UNIVERSITY
Fairfield 06430-7524 *Type:* Private (Roman Catholic) liberal arts *Accred.:* 1953/1988 (NEASC-CIHE) *Calendar:* Sem. plan *Degrees:* B, M *Prof. Accred.:* Counseling, Engineering (electrical, mechanical), Nursing (B) *CEO:* Pres. Aloysius P. Kelley, S.J. *Enroll:* 3,817 (203) 254-4000

GATEWAY COMMUNITY-TECHNICAL COLLEGE
LONG WHARF CAMPUS
60 Sargent Dr., New Haven 06511 *Type:* Public (state) 2-year *System:* State of Connecticut Board of Trustees of Community-Technical Colleges *Accred.:* 1981/1986 (NEASC-CIHE) *Calendar:* Sem. plan *Degrees:* A *Prof. Accred.:* Nuclear Medicine Technology, Radiation Therapy Technology *CEO:* Interim Pres. Leila Gonzalez-Sullivan *Enroll:* 2,452 (203) 789-7071

NORTH HAVEN CAMPUS
88 Bassett Rd., North Haven 06473 *Prof. Accred.:* Engineering Technology (mechanical)
(203) 234-3300

HARTFORD GRADUATE CENTER
275 Windsor St., Hartford 06120 *Type:* Private graduate only *Accred.:* 1966/1993 (NEASC-CIHE) *Calendar:* Sem. plan *Degrees:* M *CEO:* Pres. Ann Stuart *Enroll:* 884 (203) 548-2400

HARTFORD SEMINARY
77 Sherman St., Hartford 06105 *Type:* Private (interdenominational) graduate only *Accred.:* 1938/1993 (ATS); 1983/1994 (NEASC-CIHE) *Calendar:* Sem. plan *Degrees:* M, D *CEO:* Pres. Barbara Brown Zikmund
Enroll: 64 (203) 232-2451

HOLY APOSTLES COLLEGE AND SEMINARY
Cromwell 06416 *Type:* Private (Roman Catholic) liberal arts for men *Accred.:* 1979/1986 (NEASC-CIHE) *Calendar:* Sem. plan *Degrees:* A, B, M *CEO:* Pres./Rector Ronald D. Lawlor, O.F.M.
Enroll: 33 (203) 635-5311

HOUSATONIC COMMUNITY-TECHNICAL COLLEGE
510 Barnum Ave., Bridgeport 06608 *Type:* Public (state) junior *System:* State of Connecticut Board of Trustees of Community-Technical Colleges *Accred.:* 1972/1992 (NEASC-CIHE) *Calendar:* Sem. plan *Degrees:* A *Prof. Accred.:* Clinical Lab Technology (A), Physical Therapy Assisting *CEO:* Pres. Vincent S. Darnowski *Enroll:* 1,296 (203) 579-6400

KATHARINE GIBBS SCHOOL
142 East Ave., Norwalk 06851 *Type:* Private business *Accred.:* 1975/1991 (ACICS) *Calendar:* Sem. plan *Degrees:* A, C *CEO:* Pres. Frank Bonilla
(203) 838-4173

MANCHESTER COMMUNITY-TECHNICAL COLLEGE
60 Bidwell St., Manchester 06040 *Type:* Public (state) junior *System:* State of Connecticut Board of Trustees of Community-Technical Colleges *Accred.:* 1971/1992 (NEASC-CIHE) *Calendar:* Sem. plan *Degrees:* A *Prof. Accred.:* Clinical Lab Technology (A), Occupational Therapy Assisting, Respiratory Therapy, Surgical Technology *CEO:* Pres. Jonathan M. Daube *Enroll:* 3,235 (860) 647-6000

MIDDLESEX COMMUNITY-TECHNICAL COLLEGE
100 Training Hill Rd., Middletown 06457 *Type:* Public (state) junior *System:* State of Connecticut Board of Trustees of Community-Technical Colleges *Accred.:* 1973/1992 (NEASC-CIHE) *Calendar:* Sem. plan *Degrees:* A *Prof. Accred.:* Nuclear Medicine Technology, Radiography *CEO:* Interim Pres. Robert E. Miller *Enroll:* 1,297 (860) 343-5800

MITCHELL COLLEGE
New London 06320 *Type:* Private junior *Accred.:* 1956/1993 (NEASC-CIHE) *Calendar:* Sem. plan *Degrees:* A *CEO:* Pres. Mary Ellen Jukoski
Enroll: 452 (203) 443-2811

NAUGATUCK VALLEY COMMUNITY-TECHNICAL COLLEGE
750 Chase Pkwy., Waterbury 06708 *Type:* Public (state) 2-year *System:* State of Connecticut

Board of Trustees of Community-Technical Colleges *Accred.:* 1973/1992 (NEASC-CIHE) *Calendar:* Sem. plan *Degrees:* A *Prof. Accred.:* Engineering Technology (chemical, electrical, manufacturing, mechanical, mechanical drafting/design), Nursing (A), Radiography, Respiratory Therapy Technology *CEO:* Pres. Richard L. Sanders
Enroll: 3,014   (203) 575-8040

NORTHWESTERN CONNECTICUT COMMUNITY-
TECHNICAL COLLEGE
Park Pl., Winsted 06098 *Type:* Public (state) junior *System:* State of Connecticut Board of Trustees of Community-Technical Colleges *Accred.:* 1971/1993 (NEASC-CIHE) *Calendar:* Sem. plan *Degrees:* A *Prof. Accred.:* Medical Assisting (AMA) *CEO:* Pres. R. Eileen Baccus
Enroll: 903   (860) 738-6300

NORWALK COMMUNITY-TECHNICAL COLLEGE
188 Richards Ave., Norwalk 06854 *Type:* Public (state) 2-year *System:* State of Connecticut Board of Trustees of Community-Technical Colleges *Accred.:* 1973/1995 (NEASC-CIHE) *Calendar:* Sem. plan *Degrees:* A *Prof. Accred.:* Engineering Technology (architectural, civil/construction, computer, electrical, electromechanical, mechanical), Nursing (A) *CEO:* Pres. William H. Schwab
Enroll: 2,512   (203) 857-7000

PAIER COLLEGE OF ART
20 Gorham Ave., Hamden 06517-4025 *Type:* Private *Accred.:* 1991 (ACCSCT) *Degrees:* B *CEO:* Pres. Jonathan Paier
          (203) 287-3030

QUINEBAUG VALLEY COMMUNITY-TECHNICAL
COLLEGE
742 Upper Maple St., Danielson 06239 *Type:* Public (state) junior *System:* State of Connecticut Board of Trustees of Community-Technical Colleges *Accred.:* 1978/1991 (NEASC-CIHE) *Calendar:* Sem. plan *Degrees:* A *CEO:* Pres. Dianne E. Williams
Enroll: 584   (860) 774-1130

QUINNIPIAC COLLEGE
Hamden 06518-0569 *Type:* Private liberal arts and professional *Accred.:* 1958/1989 (NEASC-CIHE) *Calendar:* Sem. plan *Degrees:* A, B, M, D, Talmudic *Prof. Accred.:* Clinical Lab Scientist, Law (ABA), Nursing (A), Occupational Therapy, Perfusion, Physical Therapy, Radiography, Respiratory Therapy, Veterinary Technology *CEO:* Pres. John L. Lahey
Enroll: 4,987   (203) 288-5251

SACRED HEART UNIVERSITY
5151 Park Ave., Fairfield 06432-1023 *Type:* Private (Roman Catholic) liberal arts *Accred.:* 1969/1993 (NEASC-CIHE) *Calendar:* Sem. plan *Degrees:* A, B, M *Prof. Accred.:* Nursing (B,M), Respiratory Therapy, Social Work (B) *CEO:* Pres. Anthony J. Cernera
Enroll: 3,180   (203) 371-7999

ST. JOSEPH COLLEGE
1678 Asylum Ave., West Hartford 06117 *Type:* Private (Roman Catholic) liberal arts *Accred.:* 1938/1986 (NEASC-CIHE) *Calendar:* Sem. plan *Degrees:* B, M *Prof. Accred.:* Dietetics (coordinated), Dietetics (internship), Marriage and Family Therapy (M), Nursing (B,M), Social Work (B) *CEO:* Pres. Winifred E. Coleman
Enroll: 1,092   (203) 232-4571

ST. VINCENT'S COLLEGE
2800 Main St., Bridgeport 06606 *Type:* Private professional *Accred.:* 1992/1994 (NEASC-CTCI) *Calendar:* Sem. plan *Degrees:* A *CEO:* Pres. Anne T. Avallone
FTE Enroll: 158   (203) 576-5512

SOUTHERN CONNECTICUT STATE UNIVERSITY
501 Crescent St., New Haven 06515-0901 *Type:* Public liberal arts and teachers *System:* Connecticut State University Central Office *Accred.:* 1952/1991 (NEASC-CIHE) *Calendar:* Sem. plan *Degrees:* A, B, M *Prof. Accred.:* Audiology, Computer Science, Counseling, Librarianship, Marriage and Family Therapy (M), Nurse Anesthesia Education (M), Nursing (B,M), Social Work

(B,M), Speech-Language Pathology *CEO:*
Pres. Michael J. Adanti
Enroll: 7,855   (203) 392-5200

SWISS HOSPITALITY INSTITUTE CESAR RITZ
101 Wykeham Rd., Washington 06793 *Type:*
Private business *Accred.:* 1993/1995 (ACICS)
Degrees: A, C *CEO:* Pres. Ann Burton
                                   (860) 868-9555

INSTITUT HOTELIER CESAR RITZ
Le Bouveret Switzerland CH-1897 business *Accred.:* 1989/1995 (ACICS)
                            [41] (25) 813-051

TEIKYO POST UNIVERSITY
Waterbury 06708 *Type:* Private liberal arts
Accred.: 1972/1994 (NEASC-CIHE) *Calen-
dar:* Sem. plan *Degrees:* A, B *CEO:* Pres.
Phyllis C. DeLeo
Enroll: 903   (203) 596-4500

THREE RIVERS COMMUNITY-TECHNICAL
COLLEGE MOHEGAN CAMPUS
P.O. Box 629, Mahan Dr., Norwich 06360
Type: Public (state) 2-year *System:* State of
Connecticut Board of Trustees of Commu-
nity-Technical Colleges *Accred.:* 1973/1992
(NEASC-CIHE) *Calendar:* Sem. plan
Degrees: A *Prof. Accred.:* chemical) manu-
facturing) mechanical drafting/design) *CEO:*
Pres. Booker T. DeVaughn, Jr.
Enroll: 2,000   (860) 886-1931

THAMES VALLEY CAMPUS
574 New London Tpke., Norwich 06360
Prof. Accred.: Engineering Technology
(chemical, electrical, manufacturing,
mechanical, nuclear)
                                   (203) 886-0177

TRINITY COLLEGE
Hartford 06106 *Type:* Private liberal arts
Accred.: 1929/1986 (NEASC-CIHE) *Calen-
dar:* Sem. plan *Degrees:* B, M *Prof. Accred.:*
Engineering (general) *CEO:* Pres. Evan S.
Dobelle
Enroll: 1,939   (203) 297-2000

TUNXIS COMMUNITY-TECHNICAL COLLEGE
271 Scott Swamp Rd., Farmington 06032
Type: Public (state) junior *System:* State of

Connecticut Board of Trustees of Commu-
nity-Technical Colleges *Accred.:* 1975/1991
(NEASC-CIHE) *Calendar:* Sem. plan
Degrees: A *Prof. Accred.:* Dental Assisting,
Dental Hygiene *CEO:* Pres. Cathryn L. Addy
Enroll: 1,832   (860) 677-7701

UNITED STATES COAST GUARD ACADEMY
15 Mohegan Ave., New London 06320-4195
Type: Public (federal) professional *Accred.:*
1952/1990 (NEASC-CIHE) *Calendar:* Sem.
plan *Degrees:* B *Prof. Accred.:* Engineering
(civil, electrical, naval architecture/marine)
CEO: Supt. Paul E. Versaw
FTE Enroll: 906   (203) 444-8444

UNIVERSITY OF BRIDGEPORT
Bridgeport 06602 *Type:* Private *Accred.:*
1951/1989 (NEASC-CIHE) *Calendar:* Sem.
plan *Degrees:* A, B, M, D *Prof. Accred.:* Art,
Chiropractic Education, Dental Hygiene,
Engineering (computer, electrical, mechani-
cal) *CEO:* Pres. Richard L. Rubenstein
Enroll: 1,491   (203) 576-4000

THE UNIVERSITY OF CONNECTICUT
Rt. 195, Storrs 06269 *Type:* Public (state)
System: State of Connecticut Department of
Higher Education *Accred.:* 1931/1987
(NEASC-CIHE) *Calendar:* Sem. plan
Degrees: B, M, D *Prof. Accred.:* Accounting
(A,B), Art, Audiology, Business (B,M), Clin-
ical Psychology (probational), Computer
Science, Dietetics (coordinated), Dietetics
(internship), Engineering (chemical, civil,
computer, electrical, mechanical), Law, Mar-
riage and Family Therapy (M,D), Music,
Nursing (B,M), Physical Therapy, Public
Administration, Recreation and Leisure Ser-
vices (B), Social Work (M), Speech-Language Pathology, Teacher Education, Theatre *CEO:* Pres. Harry J. Hartley
Enroll: 16,269   (860) 486-2000

THE UNIVERSITY OF CONNECTICUT HEALTH
CENTER
263 Farmington Ave., Farmington 06032 *Type:*
Public *System:* State of Connecticut Depart-
ment of Higher Education *Accred.:* 1931/1987
(NEASC-CIHE) *Calendar:* 4-1-4 plan
Degrees: B, P *Prof. Accred.:* Cytotechnology,

Dentistry, Endodontics, General Dentistry, Medicine, Oral and Maxillofacial Surgery, Orthodontics, Pediatric Dentistry, Periodontics *CEO:* Exec. Dir. Leslie S. Cutler
Enroll: 507   (860) 679-2000

UNIVERSITY OF HARTFORD
200 Bloomfield Ave., West Hartford 06117 *Type:* Private *Accred.:* 1961/1991 (NEASC-CIHE) *Calendar:* Sem. plan *Degrees:* A, B, M, D *Prof. Accred.:* Art, Clinical Lab Scientist, Clinical Psychology (provisional), Engineering Technology (electrical), Engineering (civil, electrical, mechanical), Music, Nursing (B), Occupational Therapy, Public Administration, Radiography, Respiratory Therapy, Teacher Education *CEO:* Pres. Humphrey Tonkin
Enroll: 5,673   (860) 768-4100

UNIVERSITY OF NEW HAVEN
West Haven 06516 *Type:* Private *Accred.:* 1966/1990 (NEASC-CIHE) *Calendar:* Sem. plan *Degrees:* A, B, M, D *Prof. Accred.:* Dental Hygiene (conditional), Engineering (civil, electrical, industrial, mechanical) *CEO:* Pres. Lawrence J. DeNardis
Enroll: 3,487   (203) 932-7000

WESLEYAN UNIVERSITY
Middletown 06457 *Type:* Private liberal arts *Accred.:* 1929/1992 (NEASC-CIHE) *Calendar:* Sem. plan *Degrees:* B, M, D *CEO:* Pres. Douglas J. Bennet, Jr.
Enroll: 2,932   (203) 347-9411

WESTERN CONNECTICUT STATE UNIVERSITY
181 White St., Danbury 06810 *Type:* Public liberal arts and teachers *System:* Connecticut State University Central Office *Accred.:* 1954/1994 (NEASC-CIHE) *Calendar:* Sem. plan *Degrees:* A, B, M *Prof. Accred.:* Counseling, Nursing (B,M), Social Work (B) *CEO:* Pres. James R. Roach
Enroll: 3,680   (203) 837-8200

WILCOX COLLEGE OF NURSING
28 Crescent St., Middletown 06547 *Type:* Private *Accred.:* 1993 (NEASC-CTCI) *Calendar:* Sem. plan *Degrees:* A *CEO:* Pres. Kathleen Stolzenberger
FTE Enroll: 197   (203) 344-6407

YALE UNIVERSITY
New Haven 06520 *Type:* Private *Accred.:* 1938/1991 (ATS); 1929/1989 (NEASC-CIHE) *Calendar:* Sem. plan *Degrees:* B, M, D *Prof. Accred.:* Business (M), Clinical Psychology, Engineering (chemical, electrical, mechanical), Forestry, Health Services Administration, Law, Medicine, Music, Nursing (M), Physician Assisting/Surgeon Assisting, Psychology Internship, *CEO:* Pres. Richard C. Levin
Enroll: 10,802   (203) 432-4771

DELAWARE

DELAWARE STATE UNIVERSITY
1200 N. Dupont Hwy., Dover 19901 *Type:*
Public (state) *System:* Delaware Higher Education
Commission *Accred.:* 1945/1992
(MSA) *Calendar:* Sem. plan *Degrees:* B, M
Prof. Accred.: Nursing (B), Social Work
(B,M) *CEO:* Pres. William B. DeLauder
Enroll: 3,389   (302) 739-4901

DELAWARE TECHNICAL AND COMMUNITY
COLLEGE/SOUTHERN CAMPUS
P.O. Box 610, Georgetown 19947 *Type:* Public
(state) 2-year technological *System:*
Delaware Technical and Community College
Office of the President *Accred.:* 1972/1993
(MSA) *Calendar:* Qtr. plan *Degrees:* A, C
Prof. Accred.: Clinical Lab Technology (A),
Occupational Therapy Assisting, Physical
Therapy Assisting, Radiography, Respiratory
Therapy *CEO:* Vice Pres./Campus Dir.
G. Timothy Kavel
Enroll: 3,110   (302) 856-5400

DELAWARE TECHNICAL AND COMMUNITY
COLLEGE STANTON/WILMINGTON CAMPUS
400 Stanton Christiana Rd., Newark 19713
Type: Public (state) 2-year technological
System: Delaware Technical and Community
College Office of the President *Accred.:*
1972/1993 (MSA) *Calendar:* Qtr. plan
Degrees: A, C *Prof. Accred.:* Dental
Hygiene, Engineering Technology (mechanical),
Nuclear Medicine Technology, Nursing
(A), Physical Therapy Assisting, Respiratory
Therapy *CEO:* Vice Pres./Campus
Dir. Lawrence Miller
Enroll: 6,422   (302) 454-3917

DELAWARE TECHNICAL AND COMMUNITY
COLLEGE/TERRY CAMPUS
1832 N. Dupont Pkwy., Dover 19901 *Type:*
Public (state) 2-year technological *System:*
Delaware Technical and Community College
Office of the President *Accred.:* 1972/1993
(MSA) *Calendar:* Qtr. plan *Degrees:* A, C

Prof. Accred.: Diagnostic Medical Sonography,
Histologic Technology, Radiography
CEO: Vice Pres./Campus Dir. Marguerite M.
Johnson
Enroll: 1,824   (302) 739-5321

GOLDEY-BEACOM COLLEGE
4701 Limestone Rd., Wilmington 19808
Type: Private non-profit *Accred.:* 1976/1992
(MSA) *Calendar:* Sem. plan *Degrees:* A, B,
M, C *CEO:* Pres. William R. Baldt
Enroll: 1,708   (302) 998-8814

UNIVERSITY OF DELAWARE
104 Hullihen Hall, Newark 19716 *Type:* Private
(state-related) *System:* Delaware Higher
Education Commission *Accred.:* 1921/1992
(MSA) *Calendar:* 4-1-4 plan *Degrees:* A, B,
M, D *Prof. Accred.:* Accounting (A,C), Business
(B,M), Clinical Lab Scientist, Clinical
Psychology, Dietetics (coordinated), Dietetics
(internship), Engineering Technology
(agricultural, general), Engineering (chemical,
civil, electrical, mechanical), Music,
Nursing (B,M), Physical Therapy, Psychology
Internship, Public Administration *CEO:*
Pres. David P. Roselle
Enroll: 21,585   (302) 831-2000

WESLEY COLLEGE
120 N. State St., Dover 19901 *Type:* Private
(United Methodist) liberal arts *Accred.:*
1950/1993 (MSA) *Calendar:* Sem. plan
Degrees: A, B, C *Prof. Accred.:* Nursing (A)
CEO: Pres. Reed M. Stewart
Enroll: 1,399   (302) 736-2300

WILMINGTON COLLEGE
320 Dupont Hwy., New Castle 19720 *Type:*
Private non-profit *Accred.:* 1975/1991
(MSA) *Calendar:* Tri. plan *Degrees:* A, B,
M, D *Prof. Accred.:* Nursing (B) *CEO:* Pres.
Audrey K. Doberstein
Enroll: 3,229   (302) 328-9401

DISTRICT OF COLUMBIA

THE AMERICAN UNIVERSITY
4400 Massachusetts Ave., N.W., Washington
20016 *Type:* Private (United Methodist)
Accred.: 1928/1994 (MSA) *Calendar:* Sem.
plan *Degrees:* A, B, M, P, D, C *Prof.
Accred.:* Accounting (A,C), Business (B,M),
Clinical Psychology, Journalism (B,M),
Law, Music, Public Administration, Teacher
Education *CEO:* Pres. Benjamin Ladner
Enroll: 10,884   (202) 885-1000

THE CATHOLIC UNIVERSITY OF AMERICA
620 Michigan Ave., N.E., Washington 20064
Type: Private (Roman Catholic) *Accred.:*
1980/1995 (ATS); 1921/1995 (MSA) *Calendar:* Sem. plan *Degrees:* B, M, P, D *Prof.
Accred.:* Clinical Psychology, Engineering
(bioengineering, civil, electrical, mechanical), Law, Librarianship, Music, Nursing
(B,M), Social Work (B,M), Teacher Education *CEO:* Pres. F. Patrick Ellis, F.S.C.
Enroll: 6,128   (202) 319-5000

CORCORAN SCHOOL OF ART
500 17th St., N.W., Washington 20006-4899
Type: Private non-profit *Accred.:* 1985/1991
(MSA) *Calendar:* Sem. plan *Degrees:* B, C
Prof. Accred.: Art *CEO:* Pres./Dir. David C.
Levy
Enroll: 433   (202) 628-9484

DE SALES SCHOOL OF THEOLOGY
721 Lawrence St., N.E., Washington 20017
Type: Private (Roman Catholic) graduate
only *Accred.:* 1976/1992 (ATS); 1976/1992
(MSA) *Calendar:* Sem. plan *Degrees:* M, P
CEO: Pres. John W. Crossin, O.S.F.S.
Enroll: 33   (202) 269-9412

DISTRICT OF COLUMBIA SCHOOL OF LAW
719 13th St., N.W., Washington 20005 *Type:*
Public professional *Calendar:* Sem. plan
Degrees: P *Prof. Accred.:* Law (ABA only)
(provisional) *CEO:* Dean William L. Robinson
Enroll: 243   (202) 727-5225

DOMINICAN HOUSE OF STUDIES
487 Michigan Ave., N.E., Washington 20017
Type: Private (Roman Catholic) graduate for
men *Accred.:* 1976/1992 (ATS); 1976/1992

(MSA) *Calendar:* Sem. plan *Degrees:* M
CEO: Acting Pres. John C. Vidmar
Enroll: 36   (202) 529-5300

GALLAUDET UNIVERSITY
800 Florida Ave., N.E., Washington 20002
Type: Private non-profit *Accred.:* 1957/1991
(MSA) *Calendar:* Sem. plan *Degrees:* A, B,
M, D, C *Prof. Accred.:* Audiology, Counsel-
ing, Recreation and Leisure Services (B),
Rehabilitation Counseling, Social Work
(B,M-candidate), Speech-Language Pathol-
ogy, Teacher Education *CEO:* Pres. Irving
King Jordan
Enroll: 2,068   (202) 651-5000

GEORGE WASHINGTON UNIVERSITY
Washington 20052 *Type:* Private non-profit
Accred.: 1922/1993 (MSA) *Calendar:* Sem.
plan *Degrees:* A, B, M, P, D, C *Prof.
Accred.:* Audiology, Business (B,M), Clini-
cal Lab Scientist, Clinical Psychology, Com-
puter Science, Counseling, Engineering
(civil, computer, electrical, mechanical, sys-
tems), Health Services Administration, Law,
Medical Record Administration, Medicine,
Music, Nuclear Medicine Technology,
Physician Assisting/Surgeon Assisting, Psy-
chology Internship, Public Administration,
Radiation Therapy Technology, Rehabilitation Counseling, Speech-Language Pathology, Teacher Education, *CEO:* Pres. Stephen
Joel Trachtenberg
Enroll: 19,299   (202) 994-4949

GEORGETOWN UNIVERSITY
37th and O Sts., N.W., Washington 20057
Type: Private (Roman Catholic) *Accred.:*
1921/1993 (MSA) *Calendar:* Sem. plan
Degrees: B, M, P, D, C *Prof. Accred.:* Busi-
ness (B,M), Law, Medicine, Nurse Anesthe-
sia Education, Nursing (B,M), Ophthalmic
Medical Technology, Psychology Internship
CEO: Pres. Leo J. O'Donovan, S.J.
Enroll: 12,617   (202) 687-0100

HOWARD UNIVERSITY
2400 Sixth St., N.W., Washington 20059
Type: Private non-profit *Accred.:* 1940/1992

HOWARD UNIVERSITY
2400 Sixth St., N.W., Washington 20059
Type: Private non-profit *Accred.:* 1940/1992
(ATS); 1921/1994 (MSA) *Calendar:* Sem.
plan *Degrees:* B, M, P, D, C *Prof. Accred.:*
Accounting (A), Art, Audiology, Business
(B,M), Clinical Lab Scientist, Clinical Psychology, Computer Science, Dental Hygiene
(conditional), Dentistry, Dietetics (coordinated), Engineering (chemical, civil, electrical, mechanical), General Dentistry, General
Practice Residency, Health Services Administration, Journalism (B), Law, Medicine,
Music, Nursing (B,M), Occupational Therapy, Oral and Maxillofacial Surgery, Orthodontics, Pediatric Dentistry, Physical Therapy, Psychology Internship, School Psychology (probational), Social Work (M), Speech-
Language Pathology *CEO:* Pres. H. Patrick
Swygert
Enroll: 10,952   (202) 806-2500

JOINT MILITARY INTELLIGENCE COLLEGE
Defense Intelligence Analysis, Washington
20340-5100 *Type:* Public (federal) graduate
only *Accred.:* 1983/1994 (MSA) *Calendar:*
Qtr. plan *Degrees:* M, C *CEO:* Pres. A.
Denis Clift
Enroll: 449   (202) 373-3344

MOUNT VERNON COLLEGE
2100 Foxhall Rd., N.W., Washington 20007
Type: Private liberal arts for women *Accred.:*
1958/1993 (MSA) *Degrees:* A, B, M *Prof.
Accred.:* Interior Design *CEO:* Pres.
LucyAnn Geiselman
Enroll: 480   (202) 625-0400

OBLATE COLLEGE
391 Michigan Ave., N.E., Washington
20017-1587 *Type:* Private (Roman Catholic)
Accred.: 1976/1992 (ATS); 1966/1992
(MSA) *Calendar:* Sem. plan *Degrees:* B, M,
P, C *CEO:* Pres. George F. Kirwin, O.M.I.
Enroll: 34   (202) 529-6544

SOUTHEASTERN UNIVERSITY
501 Eye St., S.W., Washington 20024 *Type:*
Private non-profit *Accred.:* 1977 (MSA)

Calendar: Qtr. plan *Degrees:* A, B, M *CEO:*
Interim Pres. Earl M. Mitchell
Enroll: 458   (202) 488-8162

STRAYER COLLEGE
1025 15th St., N.W., Washington 20005
Type: Private business *Accred.:* 1981/1991
(MSA) *Calendar:* Qtr. plan *Degrees:* A, B,
M, C *CEO:* Pres. Ron K. Bailey
Enroll: 6,726   (202) 408-2400

TRINITY COLLEGE
125 Michigan Ave., N.E., Washington 20017
Type: Private (Roman Catholic) liberal arts
for women *Accred.:* 1921/1991 (MSA) *Calendar:* Sem. plan *Degrees:* B, M *CEO:* Pres.
Patricia A. McGuire, J.D.
Enroll: 1,404   (202) 939-5000

UNIVERSITY OF THE DISTRICT OF COLUMBIA
4200 Connecticut Ave., N.W., Washington
20008 *Type:* Public (local) *Accred.:* 1971/
1995 (MSA) *Calendar:* Sem. plan *Degrees:*
A, B, M, C *Prof. Accred.:* Engineering Technology (aerospace, architectural, civil/con-
struction, computer, electrical), Engineering
(civil, electrical, mechanical), Funeral Service Education (Mortuary Science), Nursing
(A,B), Planning (B,M-probational), Radiography Social Work (B) *CEO:* Pres. Tilden J.
LeMelle
Enroll: 10,599   (202) 274-5000

WASHINGTON THEOLOGICAL UNION
6896 Laurel St., NW, Washington 20012
Type: Private (Roman Catholic) graduate
only *Accred.:* 1973/1987 (ATS); 1973/1993
(MSA) *Calendar:* Sem. plan *Degrees:* M, P,
C *CEO:* Pres. Vincent D. Cushing, O.F.M.
Enroll: 230   (202) 726-8800

WESLEY THEOLOGICAL SEMINARY
4500 Massachusetts Ave., N.W., Washington
20016 *Type:* Private (United Methodist)
graduate only *Accred.:* 1940/1990 (ATS);
1975/1991 (MSA) *Calendar:* Sem. plan
Degrees: M, P, D, C *CEO:* Pres. G. Douglass
Lewis
Enroll: 609   (202) 885-8600

FLORIDA

ART INSTITUTE OF FORT LAUDERDALE
1799 S.E. 17th St., Fort Lauderdale 33316-
3000 *Type:* Private *Accred.:* 1971/1988
(ACCSCT) *Calendar:* Qtr. plan *Degrees:* A,
B *CEO:* Pres. David Pauldine
(305) 463-3000

ATI CAREER TRAINING CENTER ELECTRONIC
CAMPUS
2880 N.W. 62nd St., Fort Lauderdale 33309-
9731 *Type:* Private *Accred.:* 1989 (ACC-
SCT) *Calendar:* Qtr. plan *Degrees:* A, C
CEO: Dir. David L. Withers
(305) 973-4760

ATLANTIC COAST INSTITUTE
5225 W. Broward Blvd., Fort Lauderdale
33317 *Type:* Private business *Accred.:* 1985/
1991 (ACICS) *Degrees:* A, C *CEO:* Dir.
Ronald Dooley
(954) 581-2223

BARRY UNIVERSITY
11300 N.E. Second Ave., Miami Shores
33161-6695 *Type:* Private (Roman Catholic)
Accred.: 1947/1993 (SACS-CC) *Calendar:*
Sem. plan *Degrees:* B, M, D *Prof. Accred.:*
Athletic Training, Nurse Anesthesia Educa-
tion (M), Nursing (B,M), Occupational
Therapy, Perfusion, Physical Therapy, Podi-
atry, Social Work (M) *CEO:* Pres. Jeanne
O'Laughlin, O.P.
FTE Enroll: 4,491   (305) 899-3000

BETHUNE-COOKMAN COLLEGE
640 Mary McLeod Bethune Blvd., Daytona
Beach 32114-3099 *Type:* Private liberal arts
(United Methodist) *Accred.:* 1947/1990
(SACS-CC) *Calendar:* Sem. plan *Degrees:*
B *Prof. Accred.:* Clinical Lab Scientist,
Teacher Education *CEO:* Pres. Oswald P.
Bronson, Sr.
FTE Enroll: 2,302   (904) 255-1401

BREVARD COMMUNITY COLLEGE
1519 Clearlake Rd., Cocoa 32922-6597
Type: Public (district) junior *System:* Florida
State Board of Community Colleges
Accred.: 1963/1993 (SACS-CC) *Calendar:*

Sem. plan *Degrees:* A *Prof. Accred.:* Clinical
Lab Technology (A), Dental Assisting, Den-
tal Hygiene, EMT-Paramedic, Radiography,
Respiratory Therapy *CEO:* Pres. Maxwell C.
King
FTE Enroll: 9,974   (407) 632-1111

BROWARD COMMUNITY COLLEGE
225 E. Las Olas Blvd., Fort Lauderdale
33301 *Type:* Public (district) junior *System:*
Florida State Board of Community Colleges
Accred.: 1963/1993 (SACS-CC) *Calendar:*
Sem. plan *Degrees:* A *Prof. Accred.:* Dental
Assisting, Dental Hygiene, Diagnostic Med-
ical Sonography, EMT-Paramedic, Engineer-
ing Technology (electrical), Medical Assist-
ing (AMA), Medical Record Technology,
Nursing (A), Physical Therapy Assisting,
Radiation Therapy Technology, Radiography,
Respiratory Therapy, Respiratory Therapy
Technology *CEO:* Pres. Willis N. Holcombe
FTE Enroll: 25,143   (305) 475-6500

THE CAREER CENTER
1750 45th St., West Palm Beach 33407-2192
Type: Private *Accred.:* 1993 (ACCSCT)
Degrees: A, C *Prof. Accred.:* Medical Assisting *CEO:* Pres. Donald W. Schaefer
(407) 881-0220

CENTRAL FLORIDA COMMUNITY COLLEGE
P.O. Box 1388, 3001 S.W. College Rd.,
Ocala 34478-1388 *Type:* Public (district)
junior *System:* Florida State Board of Com-
munity Colleges *Accred.:* 1964/1995
(SACS-CC) *Calendar:* Sem. plan *Degrees:*
A *Prof. Accred.:* EMT-Paramedic, Nursing
(A), Occupational Therapy Assisting, Physi-
cal Therapy Assisting (candidate), Practical
Nursing, Surgical Technology *CEO:* Pres.
William J. Campion
FTE Enroll: 4,240   (904) 237-2111

CHIPOLA JUNIOR COLLEGE
3094 Indian Cir., Marianna 32446-2053
Type: Public (district) junior *System:* Florida
State Board of Community Colleges
Accred.: 1957/1988 (SACS-CC) *Calendar:*

Sem. plan *Degrees:* A *CEO:* Pres. H. Dale O'Daniel
FTE Enroll: 1,388   (904) 526-2761

CITY COLLEGE
1401 W. Cypress Creek Rd., Fort Lauderdale 33309 *Type:* Private junior *Accred.:* 1986/1996 (ACICS) *Degrees:* A, C *CEO:* Pres. C. M. Fike, II
                                       (305) 492-5353

GAINESVILLE CAMPUS
2400 S.W. 13th St., Gainesville 32608 *Accred.:* 1989 (ACICS)
                                       (904) 335-4000

CLEARWATER CHRISTIAN COLLEGE
3400 Gulf-to-Bay Blvd., Clearwater 34619 *Type:* Private *Accred.:* 1984/1989 (SACS-CC) *Calendar:* Sem. plan *Degrees:* A, B *CEO:* Pres. George D. Youstra
FTE Enroll: 512   (813) 726-1153

COOPER ACADEMY OF COURT REPORTING
2247 Palm Beach Lakes Blvd., Ste. 110, West Palm Beach 33409 *Type:* Private business *Accred.:* 1990 (ACICS) *Degrees:* A *CEO:* Pres. Brenda J. Cooper
                                       (407) 640-6999

DAYTONA BEACH COMMUNITY COLLEGE
P.O. Box 2811, Daytona Beach 32120-2811 *Type:* Public (district) junior *System:* Florida State Board of Community Colleges *Accred.:* 1963/1993 (SACS-CC) *Calendar:* Sem. plan *Degrees:* A *Prof. Accred.:* Dental Assisting, EMT-Paramedic, Medical Record Technology, Nursing (A), Occupational Therapy Assisting, Respiratory Therapy, Respiratory Therapy Technology, Surgical Technology *CEO:* Pres. Philip R. Day, Jr.
FTE Enroll: 7,499   (904) 255-8131

ECKERD COLLEGE
4200 54th Ave. S., St. Petersburg 33711 *Type:* Private (Presbyterian) liberal arts *Accred.:* 1963/1991 (SACS-CC) *Calendar:* 4-1-4 plan *Degrees:* B *CEO:* Pres. Peter H. Armacost
FTE Enroll: 2,261   (813) 867-1166

EDISON COMMUNITY COLLEGE
8099 College Pkwy., S.W., P.O. Box 60210, Fort Myers 33906-6210 *Type:* Public (district) junior *System:* Florida State Board of Community Colleges *Accred.:* 1964/1991 (SACS-CC) *Calendar:* Sem. plan *Degrees:* A *Prof. Accred.:* EMT-Paramedic, Radiography, Respiratory Therapy *CEO:* Pres. Kenneth P. Walker
FTE Enroll: 5,958   (941) 489-9300

EDUCATION AMERICA
2410 E. Busch Blvd., Tampa 33612 *Type:* Private *Accred.:* 1991 (ACCSCT) *Degrees:* A, B *CEO:* Pres. Mark W. Johnson
                                       (813) 935-5700

FORT WORTH CAMPUS
300 E. Loop 820, Fort Worth, TX 76112-1225
                                       (817) 451-0017

EDWARD WATERS COLLEGE
1658 Kings Rd., Jacksonville 32209 *Type:* Private (African Methodist Episcopal) liberal arts and teachers *Accred.:* 1979/1995 (SACS-CC) *Calendar:* Sem. plan *Degrees:* B *CEO:* Interim Pres. Jesse Burns
FTE Enroll: 500   (904) 355-3030

EMBRY-RIDDLE AERONAUTICAL UNIVERSITY
600 S. Clyde Morris Blvd., Daytona Beach 32114-3900 *Type:* Private technological *Accred.:* 1968/1992 (SACS-CC) *Calendar:* Sem. plan *Degrees:* A, B, M *Prof. Accred.:* Engineering Technology (aerospace), Engineering (aerospace, engineering physics/science) *CEO:* Pres. Steven M. Sliwa
FTE Enroll: 13,010   (904) 226-6000

PRESCOTT ARIZONA CAMPUS
3200 N. Willow Creek Rd., Prescott, AZ 86301 *Prof. Accred.:* Engineering (aerospace, electrical)
                                       (904) 226-6000

FLAGLER CAREER INSTITUTE
3225 University Blvd. S., Jacksonville 32216-2736 *Type:* Private *Accred.:* 1980/1993 (ACCSCT) *Calendar:* Qtr. plan *Degrees:* A, C *Prof. Accred.:* Respiratory

Therapy, Respiratory Therapy Technology *CEO:* Exec. Dir. Charles Roth

(704) 721-1622

FLAGLER COLLEGE
P.O. Box 1027, 74 King St., St. Augustine 32085-1027 *Type:* Private liberal arts *Accred.:* 1973/1988 (SACS-CC) *Calendar:* Sem. plan *Degrees:* B *CEO:* Pres. William L. Proctor
FTE Enroll: 1,389　　　　(904) 829-6481

FLORIDA AGRICULTURAL AND MECHANICAL UNIVERSITY
S. Martin Luther King Blvd., 400 Lee Hall, Tallahassee 32307 *Type:* Public (state) *System:* State University System of Florida *Accred.:* 1935/1988 (SACS-CC) *Calendar:* Sem. plan *Degrees:* B, M, D *Prof. Accred.:* Engineering Technology (civil/construction, electrical), Engineering (chemical, civil, electrical, industrial, mechanical), Journalism (B), Medical Record Administration, Nursing (B), Occupational Therapy, Physical Therapy, Respiratory Therapy, Social Work (B), Teacher Education *CEO:* Pres. Frederick S. Humphries
FTE Enroll: 9,503　　　　(904) 599-3000

FLORIDA ATLANTIC UNIVERSITY
777 Glades Rd., Boca Raton 33431-0991 *Type:* Public (state) *System:* State University System of Florida *Accred.:* 1965/1992 (SACS-CC) *Calendar:* Sem. plan *Degrees:* B, M, D *Prof. Accred.:* Business (B,M), Clinical Lab Scientist, Computer Science, Engineering (electrical, mechanical, ocean), Music, Nursing (B,M), Planning (M), Public Administration, Social Work (B), Speech-Language Pathology, Teacher Education *CEO:* Pres. Anthony J. Catanese
FTE Enroll: 11,697　　　　(407) 367-3000

FLORIDA BAPTIST THEOLOGICAL COLLEGE
P.O. Box 1306, Graceville 32440 *Type:* Private (Southern Baptist) *Accred.:* 1981/1987 (SACS-CC) *Calendar:* Sem. plan *Degrees:* B *CEO:* Pres. Thomas A. Kinchen
FTE Enroll: 456　　　　(904) 263-3261

FLORIDA BIBLE COLLEGE
1701 N. Poinciana Blvd., Kissimmee 34758 *Type:* Private (Independent Fundamentalist Churches of America) *Accred.:* 1989/1995 (AABC) *Calendar:* Sem. plan *Degrees:* A, B *CEO:* Pres. James Sheffield
FTE Enroll: 87　　　　(407) 933-4500

FLORIDA CHRISTIAN COLLEGE
1011 Bill Beck Blvd., Kissimmee 34744 *Type:* Private (Christian Churches/Churches of Christ) *Accred.:* 1985/1990 (AABC); 1995 (SACS-CC) *Calendar:* Sem. plan *Degrees:* B *CEO:* Pres. Wayne Lowen
FTE Enroll: 134　　　　(407) 847-8966

FLORIDA COLLEGE
119 Glen Arven Ave., Temple Terrace 33617 *Type:* Private junior *Accred.:* 1954/1988 (SACS-CC) *Calendar:* Sem. plan *Degrees:* A, B (candidate) *CEO:* Pres. Charles G. Caldwell
FTE Enroll: 399　　　　(813) 988-5131

FLORIDA COMMUNITY COLLEGE AT JACKSONVILLE
501 W. State St., Jacksonville 32202-4030 *Type:* Public (district) junior *System:* Florida State Board of Community Colleges *Accred.:* 1969/1994 (SACS-CC) *Calendar:* Sem. plan *Degrees:* A *Prof. Accred.:* Clinical Lab Technology (A), Dental Hygiene, EMT-Paramedic, Histologic Technology, Nursing (A), Respiratory Therapy *CEO:* Pres. Charles C. Spence
FTE Enroll: 12,368　　　　(904) 632-3000

FLORIDA COMPUTER & BUSINESS SCHOOL
8300 Flagler St., Ste. 200, Miami 33144 *Type:* Private business *Accred.:* 1985/1991 (ACICS) *Degrees:* A *CEO:* Dir. David Knobel

(305) 553-6065

FLORIDA INSTITUTE OF TECHNOLOGY
150 W. University Blvd., Melbourne 32901-6988 *Type:* Private technological *Accred.:* 1964/1995 (SACS-CC) *Calendar:* Qtr. plan *Degrees:* A, B, M, D *Prof. Accred.:* Clinical Psychology, Engineering (aerospace, chemical, civil, computer, electrical, mechanical, ocean) *CEO:* Pres. Lynn E. Weaver
FTE Enroll: 3,235　　　　(407) 768-8000

FLORIDA INTERNATIONAL UNIVERSITY
Univ. Park/Tamiami Trail, Miami 33199 *Type:* Public (state) liberal arts *System:* State University System of Florida *Accred.:* 1974/1990 (SACS-CC) *Calendar:* Sem. plan *Degrees:* A, B, M, D *Prof. Accred.:* Accounting (A,C), Business (B,M), Clinical Lab Scientist, Computer Science, Construction Education (B), Dietetics (coordinated), Dietetics (internship), Engineering (civil, electrical, industrial, mechanical), Health Services Administration, Journalism (B,M), Landscape Architecture (M-initial), Medical Record Administration, Nursing (B), Occupational Therapy, Physical Therapy, Public Administration, Social Work (B,M) *CEO:* Pres. Modesto A. Maidique
FTE Enroll: 18,816   (305) 348-2000

FLORIDA KEYS COMMUNITY COLLEGE
5901 W. College Rd., Key West 33040-4397 *Type:* Public (district) junior *System:* Florida State Board of Community Colleges *Accred.:* 1968/1992 (SACS-CC) *Calendar:* Sem. plan *Degrees:* A *CEO:* Pres. William A. Seeker
FTE Enroll: 1,088   (305) 296-9081

FLORIDA MEMORIAL COLLEGE
15800 N.W. 42nd Ave., Miami 33054 *Type:* Private (Baptist) liberal arts *Accred.:* 1951/1992 (SACS-CC) *Calendar:* Sem. plan *Degrees:* B *CEO:* Pres. Albert E. Smith
FTE Enroll: 1,270   (305) 626-3600

FLORIDA METROPOLITAN UNIVERSITY SYSTEM-FORT LAUDERDALE COLLEGE
1040 Bayview Dr., Fort Lauderdale 33304 *Type:* Private senior *System:* Florida Metropolitan University System *Accred.:* 1968/1996 (ACICS) *Calendar:* Qtr. plan *Degrees:* A, B, M *CEO:* Dir. Joel D. Boyd
      (305) 568-1600

FLORIDA METROPOLITAN UNIVERSITY SYSTEM-ORLANDO COLLEGE—NORTH CAMPUS
5421 Diplomat Cir., Orlando 32810 *Type:* Private senior *System:* Florida Metropolitan University System *Accred.:* 1957/1994

(ACICS) *Calendar:* Qtr. plan *Degrees:* A, B, M *CEO:* Pres. Ouida B. Kirby
      (407) 628-5870

MELBOURNE CAMPUS
2410 North Harbor City Blvd, Melbourne 32935 *Accred.:* 1957/1994 (ACICS) *Calendar:* Qtr. plan *Degrees:* A, B, M
FTE Enroll: 283   (407) 254-6459

ORLANDO CAMPUS
2411 Sand Lake Rd., Orlando 32809 *Accred.:* 1987 (ACICS)
      (407) 851-2525

FLORIDA METROPOLITAN UNIVERSITY SYSTEM-TAMPA COLLEGE—PINELLAS CAMPUS
2471 McMullen Booth Rd, Ste. 200, Clearwater 34619 *Type:* Private senior *System:* Florida Metropolitan University System *Accred.:* 1971/1995 (ACICS) *Calendar:* Qtr. plan *Degrees:* A, B, M *CEO:* Pres. Mark Page
      (813) 539-8404

LAKELAND CAMPUS
1200 U.S. Hwy. 98 S., Lakeland 33801 *Accred.:* 1990 (ACICS) *Calendar:* Qtr. plan
      (813) 686-1444

FLORIDA METROPOLITAN UNIVERSITY SYSTEM-TAMPA COLLEGE—W. HILLSBOROUGH COUNTY CAMPUS
3319 W. Hillsborough Ave., Tampa 33614 *Type:* Private *System:* Florida Metropolitan University System *Accred.:* 1966/ 1994 (ACICS) *Calendar:* Qtr. plan *Degrees:* A, B, M *CEO:* Pres. Joyce Meadows
      (813) 879-6000

TAMPA CAMPUS
Sabal Business Ctr., 3924 Coconut Palm Dr., Tampa 33619 *Accred.:* 1990 (ACICS) *Calendar:* Qtr. plan
      (813) 621-0041

FLORIDA SOUTHERN COLLEGE
111 Lake Hollingsworth Dr., Lakeland 33801-5698 *Type:* Private (United Methodist) liberal arts *Accred.:* 1935/1988 (SACS-

CC) *Calendar:* Sem. plan *Degrees:* B, M
CEO: Pres. Thomas L. Reuschling
FTE Enroll: 1,758 (941) 680-4111

FLORIDA STATE UNIVERSITY
Tallahassee 32306 *Type:* Public (state) *System:* State University System of Florida
Accred.: 1915/1994 (SACS-CC) *Calendar:* Sem. plan *Degrees:* A, B, M, D *Prof. Accred.:* Accounting (A,C), Art, Business (B,M), Clinical Psychology, Computer Science, Dance, Engineering (chemical, civil, electrical, industrial, mechanical), Home Economics, Interior Design, Law, Librarianship, Marriage and Family Therapy (D), Music, Nursing (B,M), Planning (M), Public Administration, Recreation and Leisure Services (B), Rehabilitation Counseling, Social Work (B,M), Speech-Language Pathology, Teacher Education, Theatre *CEO:* Pres. Talbot D'Alemberte
FTE Enroll: 25,711 (904) 644-2525

FLORIDA TECHNICAL COLLEGE
8711 Lone Star Rd., Jacksonville 32211 *Type:* Private business *Accred.:* 1984/1988 (ACICS) *Degrees:* A, C *CEO:* Dean Robert M. Myers
(904) 724-2229

FLORIDA TECHNICAL COLLEGE
1819 N. Semoran Blvd., Orlando 32807 *Type:* Private junior *Accred.:* 1982/1988 (ACICS) *Degrees:* A, C *CEO:* Dean Sunil Wadhwa
(407) 678-5600

FLORIDA TECHNICAL COLLEGE
4750 E. Adamo Dr., Tampa 33605 *Type:* Private junior *Accred.:* 1982/1988 (ACICS) *Degrees:* A, C *CEO:* Dean Walter E. Wilfong
(813) 247-1700

FULL SAIL CENTER FOR THE RECORDING ARTS
3300 University Blvd., Winter Park 32792-7429 *Type:* Private *Accred.:* 1986/1993 (ACCSCT) *Degrees:* A *CEO:* Pres. Edward E. Haddock, Jr.
(407) 679-0100

GOODING INSTITUTE OF NURSE ANESTHESIA
Bay Medical Ctr., 615 North Bonita Ave., Panama City 32401 *Type:* Private *Degrees:* M *Prof. Accred.:* Nurse Anesthesia Education *CEO:* Program Dir. Dave Ely
Enroll: 20 (904) 747-6918

GULF COAST COMMUNITY COLLEGE
5230 W. U.S. Hwy. 98, Panama City 32401-1044 *Type:* Public (district) junior *System:* Florida State Board of Community Colleges *Accred.:* 1962/1990 (SACS-CC) *Calendar:* Sem. plan *Degrees:* A *Prof. Accred.:* Dental Assisting, EMT-Paramedic, Nursing (A), Radiography, Respiratory Therapy Technology *CEO:* Pres. Robert L. McSpadden
FTE Enroll: 4,311 (904) 769-1551

HARIN CONSERVATORY OF MUSIC, INC.
2285 Potomac Rd., Boca Raton 33431 *Type:* Private *Calendar:* Sem. plan *Degrees:* B, C *Prof. Accred.:* Dance *CEO:* Dir. Gordon Wright
Enroll: 80 (407) 997-2677

HILLSBOROUGH COMMUNITY COLLEGE
39 Columbia Dr., Tampa 33631-3127 *Type:* Public (district) junior *System:* Florida State Board of Community Colleges *Accred.:* 1971/1986 (SACS-CC) *Degrees:* A *Prof. Accred.:* Diagnostic Medical Sonography, EMT-Paramedic, Nuclear Medicine Technology, Occupational Therapy Assisting, Radiation Therapy Technology, Radiography *CEO:* Pres. Andreas A. Paloumpis
FTE Enroll: 12,172 (813) 253-7000

HOBE SOUND BIBLE COLLEGE
P.O. Box 1065, 11298 S.E. Gomez Ave., Hobe Sound 33455 *Type:* Private (Wesleyan) *Accred.:* 1986/1991 (AABC) *Calendar:* Sem. plan *Degrees:* A, B, C *CEO:* Pres. P. Daniel Stetler
FTE Enroll: 139 (407) 546-5534

INDIAN RIVER COMMUNITY COLLEGE
3209 Virginia Ave., Fort Pierce 34981-5599 *Type:* Public (district) junior *System:* Florida State Board of Community Colleges *Accred.:* 1963/1993 (SACS-CC) *Calendar:* Sem. plan *Degrees:* A *Prof. Accred.:* Clinical Lab Technology (A), Dental Assisting,

Dental Hygiene, Dental Laboratory Technology, EMT-Paramedic, Nursing (A), Radiography, Respiratory Therapy *CEO:* Pres. Edwin R. Massey
FTE Enroll: 4,369   (407) 462-4700

INSTITUTE OF PHYSICAL THERAPY
1690 U.S. 1 S., Ste. 1, St. Augustine 32086
Type: Private *Accred.:* 1993 (DETC)
Degrees: M *Prof. Accred.:* Physical Therapy *CEO:* Pres. Stanley V. Paris
(904) 826-0084

INTERNATIONAL ACADEMY OF MERCHANDISING AND DESIGN
5225 Memorial Hwy., Tampa 33634-7350
Type: Private senior *Accred.:* 1985/1989 (ACICS) *Calendar:* Sem. plan *Degrees:* A, B *Prof. Accred.:* Interior Design *CEO:* Pres. Michael Santoro
(813) 881-0007

INTERNATIONAL COLLEGE
2654 E. Tamiami Tr., Naples 33962-5790
Type: Private senior *Accred.:* 1990 (ACICS) *Calendar:* Sem. plan *Degrees:* A, B *Prof. Accred.:* Medical Record Technology *CEO:* Pres. Terry McMahan
(941) 774-4700

FORT MYERS CAMPUS
8695 College Pkwy., Ste. 120, Fort Myers 33919 *Accred.:* 1993 (ACICS)
(813) 482-0019

INTERNATIONAL FINE ARTS COLLEGE
1737 N. Bayshore Dr., Miami 33132 *Type:* Private *Accred.:* 1979/1995 (SACS-CC) *Calendar:* Sem. plan *Degrees:* A *Prof. Accred.:* Interior Design *CEO:* Pres. Edward Porter
FTE Enroll: 667   (305) 373-4684

ITT TECHNICAL INSTITUTE
2600 Lake Lucien Dr., Maitland 32751-9754
Type: Private *Accred.:* 1990 (ACCSCT)
Degrees: A, B *CEO:* Dir. Gary P. Cosgrove
(407) 660-2900

ITT TECHNICAL INSTITUTE
4809 Memorial Hwy., Tampa 33634-7350
Type: Private *Accred.:* 1983/1988 (ACC-

SCT) *Degrees:* A, B *CEO:* Dir. Dennis Alspaugh
(813) 885-2244

JACKSONVILLE CAMPUS
6600 Youngerman Cir., No. 10, Jacksonville 32244 *Accred.:* 1988 (ACCSCT)
(904) 573-9100

JACKSONVILLE UNIVERSITY
2800 University Blvd. N., Jacksonville 32211 *Type:* Private *Accred.:* 1961/1993 (SACS-CC) *Calendar:* Sem. plan *Degrees:* B, M *Prof. Accred.:* Dance (A), Music, Nursing (B) *CEO:* Pres. Paul S. Tipton, S.J.
FTE Enroll: 2,126   (904) 744-3950

JOHN B. STETSON UNIVERSITY
421 N. Woodland Blvd., DeLand 32720
Type: Private (Southern Baptist) *Accred.:* 1932/1991 (SACS-CC) *Calendar:* 4-1-4 plan *Degrees:* B, M, D *Prof. Accred.:* Law, Music *CEO:* Pres. H. Douglas Lee
FTE Enroll: 2,748   (904) 822-7000

JONES COLLEGE
5353 Arlington Expy., Jacksonville 32211-5588 *Type:* Private senior *Accred.:* 1957/1994 (ACICS) *Calendar:* Sem. plan *Degrees:* A, B, C *CEO:* Exec. Vice Pres. Judy Lima
(904) 743-1122

SOUTH MIAMI CAMPUS
5975 Sunset Dr., Ste. 100, South Miami 33143 *Accred.:* 1988/1994 (ACICS)
(305) 669-9606

KEISER COLLEGE OF TECHNOLOGY
1500 N.W. 49th St., Fort Lauderdale 33309-3779 *Type:* Private *Accred.:* 1991 (SACS-CC) *Calendar:* Sem. plan *Degrees:* A, C *Prof. Accred.:* Clinical Lab Technology (A), Medical Assisting, Medical Laboratory Technology, Radiography *CEO:* Pres. Arthur Keiser
FTE Enroll: 953   (305) 776-4456

MELBOURNE CAMPUS
701 S. Babcock St., Melbourne 32901-1461 *Prof. Accred.:* Medical Assisting
(407) 255-2255

TALLAHASSEE CAMPUS
1605 E. Plaza Dr., Tallahassee 32308 *Prof. Accred.:* Medical Assisting
(904) 942-9494

LAKE CITY COMMUNITY COLLEGE
Rte. 19, Box 1030, Lake City 32305 *Type:* Public (district) junior *System:* Florida State Board of Community Colleges *Accred.:* 1964/1990 (SACS-CC) *Calendar:* Sem. plan *Degrees:* A *Prof. Accred.:* Clinical Lab Technology (A), EMT-Paramedic, Physical Therapy Assisting *CEO:* Pres. Muriel Kay Heimer
FTE Enroll: 2,139 (904) 752-1822

LAKE-SUMTER COMMUNITY COLLEGE
9501 U.S. Hwy. 441 S., Leesburg 34788-8751 *Type:* Public (district) junior *System:* Florida State Board of Community Colleges *Accred.:* 1966/1990 (SACS-CC) *Calendar:* Sem. plan *Degrees:* A *CEO:* Pres. Robert W. Westrick
FTE Enroll: 1,550 (904) 787-3747

LYNN UNIVERSITY
3601 N. Military Tr., Boca Raton 33431 *Type:* Private *Accred.:* 1964/1991 (SACS-CC) *Calendar:* Sem. plan *Degrees:* A, B, M *Prof. Accred.:* Funeral Service Education (Mortuary Science), Physical Therapy Assisting *CEO:* Pres. Donald E. Ross
FTE Enroll: 1,187 (407) 994-0770

MANATEE COMMUNITY COLLEGE
5840 26th St. W., P.O. Box 1849, Bradenton 34207-1849 *Type:* Public (district) junior *System:* Florida State Board of Community Colleges *Accred.:* 1963/1994 (SACS-CC) *Calendar:* Sem. plan *Degrees:* A *Prof. Accred.:* Nursing (A), Radiography, Respiratory Therapy *CEO:* Pres. Stephen J. Korcheck
FTE Enroll: 5,222 (813) 755-1511

MARTIN COLLEGE
1901 N.W. Seventh St., Miami 33125-3462 *Type:* Private *Accred.:* 1978/1986 (ACC-SCT) *Degrees:* A *CEO:* Dir. Fernando A. Alvarez
(305) 541-8140

MIAMI-DADE COMMUNITY COLLEGE
300 N.E. Second Ave., Miami 33132 *Type:* Public (district) junior *System:* Florida State Board of Community Colleges *Accred.:* 1964/1995 (SACS-CC) *Calendar:* Sem. plan *Degrees:* A *Prof. Accred.:* Clinical Lab Technology (A), Dental Hygiene, EMT-Paramedic, Funeral Service Education (Mortuary Science), Medical Record Technology, Nursing (A), Optometric Technician, Physical Therapy Assisting, Radiation Therapy Technology, Radiography, Respiratory Therapy, Respiratory Therapy Technology *CEO:* Pres. Eduardo J. Padron
FTE Enroll: 36,959 (305) 237-3366

NATIONAL EDUCATION CENTER—BAUDER COLLEGE CAMPUS
4801 N. Dixie Hwy., Fort Lauderdale 33334-3971 *Type:* Private *Accred.:* 1970/1988 (ACCSCT) *Calendar:* Qtr. plan *Degrees:* A, B, C *CEO:* Exec. Dir. Peter Crocitto
(305) 491-7171

NORTH FLORIDA COMMUNITY COLLEGE
1000 Turner Davis Dr., Madison 32340-1698 *Type:* Public (district) junior *System:* Florida State Board of Community Colleges *Accred.:* 1963/1994 (SACS-CC) *Calendar:* Sem. plan *Degrees:* A *CEO:* Pres. Beverly M. Grissom
FTE Enroll: 1,073 (904) 973-2288

NOVA SOUTHEASTERN UNIVERSITY
3301 College Ave., Fort Lauderdale 33314 *Type:* Private liberal arts and professional *Accred.:* 1971/1985 (SACS-CC) *Calendar:* Tri. plan *Degrees:* B, M, D *Prof. Accred.:* Clinical Psychology, Law, Marriage and Family Therapy (M-candidate), Occupational Therapy, Physical Therapy, Physician Assisting/Surgeon Assisting, Psychology Internship, Speech-Language Pathology *CEO:* Pres. Ovid C. Lewis
FTE Enroll: 10,424 (305) 475-7300

OKALOOSA-WALTON COMMUNITY COLLEGE
100 College Blvd., Niceville 32578 *Type:* Public (district) junior *System:* Florida State Board of Community Colleges *Accred.:*

1965/1991 (SACS-CC) *Calendar:* Sem. plan *Degrees:* A *CEO:* Pres. James R. Richburg *FTE Enroll:* 3,947   (904) 678-5111

PALM BEACH ATLANTIC COLLEGE
901 S. Flagler Dr., P.O. Box 24708, West Palm Beach 33416-4708 *Type:* Private liberal arts (Baptist) *Accred.:* 1972/1988 (SACS-CC) *Calendar:* Sem. plan *Degrees:* B, M *CEO:* Pres. Paul R. Corts
FTE Enroll: 1,642   (407) 650-7700

PALM BEACH COMMUNITY COLLEGE
4200 Congress Ave., Lake Worth 33461-4796 *Type:* Public (district) junior *System:* Florida State Board of Community Colleges *Accred.:* 1942/1991 (SACS-CC) *Calendar:* Sem. plan *Degrees:* A *Prof. Accred.:* Dental Assisting, Dental Hygiene, Diagnostic Medical Sonography, EMT-Paramedic, Occupational Therapy Assisting, Radiography, Respiratory Therapy, Respiratory Therapy Technology *CEO:* Pres. Edward M. Eissey
FTE Enroll: 10,585   (407) 439-8004

PASCO-HERNANDO COMMUNITY COLLEGE
36727 Blanton Rd., Dade City 33525-7599 *Type:* Public (district) junior *System:* Florida State Board of Community Colleges *Accred.:* 1974/1989 (SACS-CC) *Calendar:* Sem. plan *Degrees:* A *Prof. Accred.:* Dental Hygiene, EMT-Paramedic *CEO:* Pres. Robert W. Judson, Jr.
FTE Enroll: 3,758   (904) 567-6701

PENSACOLA JUNIOR COLLEGE
1000 College Blvd., Pensacola 32504-8998 *Type:* Public (district) junior *System:* Florida State Board of Community Colleges *Accred.:* 1956/1987 (SACS-CC) *Calendar:* Sem. plan *Degrees:* A *Prof. Accred.:* Dental Assisting, Dental Hygiene, EMT-Paramedic, Medical Assisting (AMA), Medical Record Technology, Physical Therapy Assisting, Radiography, Respiratory Therapy, Respiratory Therapy Technology *CEO:* Pres. Horace E. Hartsell
FTE Enroll: 17,341   (904) 484-1000

POLK COMMUNITY COLLEGE
999 Ave. H, N.E., Winter Haven 33881-4299 *Type:* Public (district) junior *System:* Florida State Board of Community Colleges *Accred.:* 1965/1990 (SACS-CC) *Calendar:* Sem. plan *Degrees:* A *Prof. Accred.:* EMT-Paramedic, Nursing (A), Physical Therapy Assisting, Radiography *CEO:* Pres. Maryly VanLeer Peck
FTE Enroll: 4,150   (941) 297-1000

PROSPECT HALL SCHOOL OF BUSINESS
2620 Hollywood Blvd., Hollywood 33020 *Type:* Private business *Accred.:* 1971/1998 (ACICS) *Calendar:* Qtr. plan *Degrees:* A *CEO:* Chair Faisel Morghem
      (305) 923-8100

RINGLING SCHOOL OF ART AND DESIGN
2700 N. Tamiami Tr., Sarasota 34234 *Type:* Private professional *Accred.:* 1979/1995 (SACS-CC) *Calendar:* Sem. plan *Degrees:* B *Prof. Accred.:* Art, Interior Design *CEO:* Pres. Arland F. Christ-Janer
FTE Enroll: 763   (941) 351-5100

ROLLINS COLLEGE
1000 Holt Ave., Winter Park 32789-4499 *Type:* Private liberal arts *Accred.:* 1927/1994 (SACS-CC) *Calendar:* 4-1-4 plan *Degrees:* A, B, M *Prof. Accred.:* Business (M), Counseling, Music *CEO:* Pres. Rita Bornstein
FTE Enroll: 2,624   (407) 646-2000

ST. JOHN VIANNEY COLLEGE SEMINARY
2900 S.W. 87th Ave., Miami 33165 *Type:* Private (Roman Catholic) for men *Accred.:* 1970/1986 (SACS-CC) *Calendar:* Sem. plan *Degrees:* B *CEO:* Pres. George Garcia
FTE Enroll: 50   (305) 223-4561

ST. JOHNS RIVER COMMUNITY COLLEGE
5001 St. Johns Ave., Palatka 32177-3897 *Type:* Public (district) junior *System:* Florida State Board of Community Colleges *Accred.:* 1963/1993 (SACS-CC) *Calendar:* Sem. plan *Degrees:* A *CEO:* Pres. Robert L. McLendon, Jr.
FTE Enroll: 2,379   (904) 328-1571

St. Leo College
P.O. Box 2187, St. Leo 33574 *Type:* Private (Roman Catholic) liberal arts and teachers *Accred.:* 1967/1991 (SACS-CC) *Calendar:* Sem. plan *Degrees:* A, B, M *Prof. Accred.:* Social Work (B) *CEO:* Pres. Frank M. Mouch
FTE Enroll: 5,179 (904) 588-8200

St. Petersburg Junior College
P.O. Box 13489, St. Petersburg 33733-3489 *Type:* Public (district) junior *System:* Florida State Board of Community Colleges *Accred.:* 1931/1990 (SACS-CC) *Calendar:* Sem. plan *Degrees:* A *Prof. Accred.:* Clinical Lab Technology (A), Dental Hygiene, EMT-Paramedic, Engineering Technology (electrical), Funeral Service Education (Mortuary Science), Medical Record Technology, Nursing (A), Physical Therapy Assisting, Radiography, Respiratory Therapy, Veterinary Technology *CEO:* Pres. Carl M. Kuttler, Jr.
FTE Enroll: 12,995 (813) 341-3600

St. Thomas University
16400 N.W. 32nd Ave., Miami 33054 *Type:* Private (Roman Catholic) liberal arts *Accred.:* 1968/1993 (SACS-CC) *Calendar:* Sem. plan *Degrees:* B, M, D *Prof. Accred.:* Law (ABA only) (provisional) *CEO:* Pres. Franklyn M. Casale
FTE Enroll: 2,255 (305) 625-6000

St. Vincent de Paul Regional Seminary
10701 S. Military Tr., Boynton Beach 33436-4899 *Type:* Private (Roman Catholic) graduate only *Accred.:* 1984/1990 (ATS); 1968/1990 (SACS-CC) *Calendar:* Sem. plan *Degrees:* M *CEO:* Rector/Pres. Pablo A. Navarro
Enroll: 84 (407) 732-4424

Santa Fe Community College
3000 N.W. 83rd St., Gainesville 32606-6200 *Type:* Public (district) junior *System:* Florida State Board of Community Colleges *Accred.:* 1968/1992 (SACS-CC) *Calendar:* Sem. plan *Degrees:* A *Prof. Accred.:* Construction Education (A), Dental Assisting, Dental Hygiene, EMT-Paramedic, Engineering Technology (computer), Nuclear Medi-cine Technology, Nursing (A), Radiation Therapy Technology, Radiography, Respiratory Therapy *CEO:* Pres. Lawrence W. Tyree
FTE Enroll: 9,229 (904) 395-5000

Schiller International University
453 Edgewater Dr., Dunedin 34698-4964 *Type:* Private senior *Accred.:* 1982/1991 (ACICS) *Degrees:* A, B, M *CEO:* Acting Provost Cathy Eberhart
(813) 736-5082

Engelberg, Switzerland Campus
Dorfstrasse 40, Engelberg Switzerland 6390 *Accred.:* 1993 (ACICS)
[41] 41-944343

Heidelberg, Germany Campus
Friedrich-Ebert-Anlage 4, Heidelberg Germany 69117 *Accred.:* 1983/1987 (ACICS) *Calendar:* Sem. plan
[49] (62) 211-4010

Kent, England Campus
Wickham Ct., W. Wickham, Kent, England BR4 9HW *Accred.:* 1983/1987 (ACICS)
[44] (181) 777-8069

Leysin, Switzerland Campus
Leysin Switzerland CH-1854 *Accred.:* 1983/1992 (ACICS) *Calendar:* Sem. plan
[41] (25) 342-223

London, England Campus
Royal Waterloo House, 51-55 Waterloo Rd., London, England SE1 8TX *Accred.:* 1983/1987 (ACICS)
[44] (171) 928-1372

Madrid, Spain Campus
Edificio Columina, San Bernardo 97-99, Madrid Spain 28015 *Accred.:* 1983/1987 (ACICS)
[34] (1) 448-2488

Paris, France Campus
32 Blvd. de Vaugirard, Paris France 75015 *Accred.:* 1983/1987 (ACICS)
[33] (14) 538-5601

STRASBOURG, FRANCE CAMPUS
Chateau Pourtales, 161 rue Melanie, Strasbourg France 6700 *Accred.:* 1986 (ACICS)
[33] (88) 45-8464

SCI-NATIONAL INSTITUTE FOR PARALEGAL ARTS AND SCIENCES
164 W. Royal Palm Rd., Boca Raton 33432 *Type:* Private *Accred.:* 1993 (DETC) *Calendar:* 12-mos. program *Degrees:* A *CEO:* Pres. Richard Capezzall
(800) 669-2555

SEMINOLE COMMUNITY COLLEGE
100 Weldon Blvd., Sanford 32773-6199 *Type:* Public (district) junior *System:* Florida State Board of Community Colleges *Accred.:* 1969/1993 (SACS-CC) *Calendar:* Sem. plan *Degrees:* A *Prof. Accred.:* EMT-Paramedic, Interior Design, Nursing (A), Physical Therapy Assisting, Respiratory Therapy, Respiratory Therapy Technology *CEO:* Pres. E. Ann McGee
FTE Enroll: 5,789   (407) 328-4722

SOUTH COLLEGE
1760 N. Congress Ave., West Palm Beach 33409 *Type:* Private junior *Accred.:* 1985/1990 (SACS-CC) 1984/1989 (ACICS) *Calendar:* Qtr. plan *Degrees:* A *Prof. Accred.:* Medical Assisting (AMA) *CEO:* Dir. Thomas Barlow
(407) 697-9200

* Indirect SACS-CC accreditation through South College, Savannah, GA

SOUTH FLORIDA COMMUNITY COLLEGE
600 W. College Dr., Avon Park 33825-9399 *Type:* Public (district) junior *System:* Florida State Board of Community Colleges *Accred.:* 1968/1992 (SACS-CC) *Calendar:* Sem. plan *Degrees:* A *CEO:* Pres. Catherine P. Cornelius
FTE Enroll: 3,002   (813) 453-6661

SOUTHEASTERN COLLEGE OF THE ASSEMBLIES OF GOD
1000 Longfellow Blvd., Lakeland 33801 *Type:* Private (Assemblies of God) *Accred.:* 1954/1992 (AABC); 1986/1991 (SACS-CC

probational) *Calendar:* Sem. plan *Degrees:* B, C *CEO:* Pres. James L. Hennesy
FTE Enroll: 1,105   (813) 665-4404

SOUTHEASTERN UNIVERSITY OF THE HEALTH SCIENCES
1750 N.E. 168th St., North Miami Beach 33162-3097 *Type:* Private professional *Calendar:* Sem. plan *Degrees:* B, M, P, D *Prof. Accred.:* Optometry, Osteopathy *CEO:* Pres. Morton Terry
(305) 949-4000

SOUTHERN COLLEGE
5600 Lake Underhill Rd., Orlando 32807 *Type:* Private junior *Accred.:* 1970/1994 (ACICS) *Calendar:* Qtr. plan *Degrees:* A, C *Prof. Accred.:* Dental Assisting, Dental Laboratory Technology, Interior Design *CEO:* Pres. Daniel F. Moore
(407) 273-1000

SOUTHWEST FLORIDA COLLEGE OF BUSINESS
1685 Medical La., Ste. 200, Fort Myers 33907 *Type:* Private business *Accred.:* 1984/1996 (ACICS) *Calendar:* Qtr. plan *Degrees:* A *CEO:* Dir. Connie Cole
(813) 939-4766

TALLAHASSEE COMMUNITY COLLEGE
444 Appleyard Dr., Tallahassee 32304-2895 *Type:* Public (district) junior *System:* Florida State Board of Community Colleges *Accred.:* 1969/1994 (SACS-CC) *Calendar:* Sem. plan *Degrees:* A *Prof. Accred.:* Dental Hygiene, EMT-Paramedic, Respiratory Therapy *CEO:* Pres. T. K. Wetherell
FTE Enroll: 7,021   (904) 488-9200

TALMUDIC COLLEGE OF FLORIDA
1910 Alton Rd., Miami Beach 33139 *Type:* Private professional *Accred.:* 1977/1994 (AARTS) *Calendar:* Sem. plan *Degrees:* B, M, P, D *CEO:* Pres. Y. Zweig
Enroll: 40   (305) 534-7050

UNIVERSITY OF CENTRAL FLORIDA
4000 Central Florida Blvd., Orlando 32816 *Type:* Public (state) liberal arts and professional *System:* State University System of Florida *Accred.:* 1970/1995 (SACS-CC) *Calendar:* Sem. plan *Degrees:* A, B, M, D

Prof. Accred.: Accounting (A,C), Business (B,M), Clinical Lab Scientist, Computer Science, Engineering Technology (aerospace, civil/construction, computer), Engineering (aerospace, civil, computer, electrical, environmental/sanitary, industrial, mechanical), Medical Record Administration, Music, Nursing (B), Physical Therapy Respiratory Therapy Speech-Language Pathology *CEO:* Pres. John C. Hitt

FTE Enroll: 20,736   (407) 823-2000

UNIVERSITY OF FLORIDA
226 Tigert Hall, Gainesville 32611 *Type:* Public (state) *System:* State University System of Florida *Accred.:* 1913/1993 (SACS-CC) *Calendar:* Sem. plan *Degrees:* A, B, M, D *Prof. Accred.:* Accounting (A,C), Art, Audiology, Business (B,M), Clinical Psychology, Combined Prosthodontics, Construction Education (B), Counseling, Counseling Psychology, Dental Public Health, Dentistry, Endodontics, Engineering (aerospace, agricultural, chemical, civil, computer, electrical, engineering physics/science, environmental/sanitary, industrial, materials, mechanical, nuclear, ocean), Forestry, General Dentistry, Health Services Administration, Interior Design, Journalism (B,M), Landscape Architecture (B,M-initial), Law, Medicine, Music, Nursing (B,M), Occupational Therapy, Ophthalmic Medical Technology, Oral Pathology, Oral and Maxillofacial Surgery, Orthodontics, Pediatric Dentistry, Periodontics, Physical Therapy, Physician Assisting/Surgeon Assisting, Planning (M), Psychology Internship, Recreation and Leisure Services (B), Rehabilitation Counseling, Speech-Language Pathology, Teacher Education, Theatre *CEO:* Pres. John V. Lombardi

FTE Enroll: 32,651   (904) 392-3261

UNIVERSITY OF MIAMI
P.O. Box 248006, Coral Gables 33124-4600 *Type:* Private *Accred.:* 1940/1987 (SACS-CC) *Calendar:* Sem. plan *Degrees:* B, M, D *Prof. Accred.:* Accounting (A,C), Business (B,M), Clinical Psychology, Counseling Psychology (provisional), Cytotechnology, Engineering (architectural, civil, computer,

electrical, industrial, manufacturing, mechanical), General Practice Residency, Health Services Administration, Journalism (B,M), Law, Medicine, Music, Nursing (B,M), Oral and Maxillofacial Surgery, Physical Therapy, Psychology Internship, Teacher Education, Theatre (A), *CEO:* Pres. Edward T. Foote, II

FTE Enroll: 12,496   (305) 284-2211

UNIVERSITY OF NORTH FLORIDA
4567 St. Johns Bluff Rd., S., Jacksonville 32224-2645 *Type:* Public (state) *System:* State University System of Florida *Accred.:* 1974/1989 (SACS-CC) *Calendar:* Sem. plan *Degrees:* B, M, D (candidate) *Prof. Accred.:* Business (B,M), Computer Science, Nursing (B), Physical Therapy, Teacher Education *CEO:* Pres. Adam W. Herbert, Jr.

FTE Enroll: 6,614   (904) 646-2666

THE UNIVERSITY OF SARASOTA
5250 17th St., Sarasota 34235 *Type:* Private professional; graduate only *Accred.:* 1990 (SACS-CC) *Calendar:* Sem. plan *Degrees:* M, D *CEO:* Provost Ned Wilson

FTE Enroll: 154   (941) 379-0404

UNIVERSITY OF SOUTH FLORIDA
4202 E. Flower Ave., Tampa 33620-6100 *Type:* Public (state) *System:* State University System of Florida *Accred.:* 1963/1994 (SACS-CC) *Calendar:* Sem. plan *Degrees:* A, B, M, D *Prof. Accred.:* Accounting (A,C), Audiology, Business (B,M), Clinical Psychology, Computer Science, Engineering (chemical, civil, computer, electrical, industrial, mechanical), Health Services Administration, Journalism (B,M), Librarianship, Medicine, Music, Nursing (B,M), Psychology Internship, Public Administration, Rehabilitation Counseling, Social Work (B,M), Speech-Language Pathology, Teacher Education, Theatre *CEO:* Pres. Betty Castor

FTE Enroll: 31,286   (813) 974-2154

UNIVERSITY OF TAMPA
401 W. Kennedy Blvd., Tampa 33606-1490 *Type:* Private liberal arts *Accred.:* 1951/1995 (SACS-CC) *Calendar:* Sem. plan *Degrees:*

A, B, M *Prof. Accred.:* Music, Nursing (B) *CEO:* Pres. Ronald Vaughn
FTE Enroll: 1,922   (813) 253-3333

UNIVERSITY OF WEST FLORIDA
11000 University Pkwy., Pensacola 32514-5750 *Type:* Public (state) liberal arts and professional *System:* State University System of Florida *Accred.:* 1969/1994 (SACS-CC) *Calendar:* Sem. plan *Degrees:* A, B, M, D *Prof. Accred.:* Business (B,M), Clinical Lab Scientist, Engineering (systems), Journalism (B,M), Music, Nursing (B), Public Administration, Social Work (B) *CEO:* Pres. Morris L. Marx
FTE Enroll: 5,892   (904) 474-2200

VALENCIA COMMUNITY COLLEGE
P.O. Box 3028, Orlando 32802-3028 *Type:* Public (district) junior *System:* Florida State Board of Community Colleges *Accred.:* 1969/1993 (SACS-CC) *Calendar:* Sem. plan *Degrees:* A *Prof. Accred.:* Clinical Lab Technology (A), Dental Hygiene, Diagnostic Medical Sonography, EMT-Paramedic, Nuclear Medicine Technology, Nursing (A), Radiation Therapy Technology, Radiography,

Respiratory Therapy *CEO:* Pres. Paul C. Gianini, Jr.
FTE Enroll: 14,301   (407) 299-5000

VAN DYCK INSTITUTE OF TOURISM
1301 66th St. N., St. Petersburg 33710 *Type:* Private *Accred.:* 1992 (ACCSCT) *Degrees:* A, C *CEO:* Pres. Claus Van Dyck
(813) 347-0074

WARD STONE COLLEGE
9020 S.W. 137th Ave., Miami 33186 *Type:* Private business *Accred.:* 1989/1996 (ACICS) *Degrees:* A *Prof. Accred.:* Medical Assisting *CEO:* Pres. David Higley
(305) 386-9900

WARNER SOUTHERN COLLEGE
5301 U.S. Hwy. 27 S., Lake Wales 33853-8725 *Type:* Private liberal arts (Church of Christ) *Accred.:* 1977/1992 (SACS-CC) *Calendar:* Sem. plan *Degrees:* A, B *CEO:* Pres. Gregory V. Hall
FTE Enroll: 496   (813) 638-1426

WEBBER COLLEGE
P.O. Box 96, Babson Park 33827 *Type:* Private business *Accred.:* 1969/1988 (SACS-CC) *Calendar:* Sem. plan *Degrees:* A, B *CEO:* Pres. Rex R. Yentes
FTE Enroll: 396   (813) 638-1431

GEORGIA

ABRAHAM BALDWIN AGRICULTURAL COLLEGE
ABAC 1,2802 Moore Hwy., Tifton 31794-2601 *Type:* Public (state) junior *System:* Board of Regents of the University System of Georgia *Accred.:* 1953/1986 (SACS-CC) *Calendar:* Qtr. plan *Degrees:* A *Prof. Accred.:* Nursing (A) *CEO:* Pres. Harold J. Loyd
FTE Enroll: 2,410　　　　　(912) 386-3230

AGNES SCOTT COLLEGE
141 E. College Ave., Decatur 30030 *Type:* Private liberal arts for women *Accred.:* 1907/1994 (SACS-CC) *Calendar:* Sem. plan *Degrees:* B, M *CEO:* Pres. Mary Brown Bullock
FTE Enroll: 572　　　　　(404) 638-6000

ALBANY STATE COLLEGE
504 College Dr., Albany 31705-2794 *Type:* Public (state) liberal arts and professional *System:* Board of Regents of the University System of Georgia *Accred.:* 1951/1988 (SACS-CC) *Calendar:* Qtr. plan *Degrees:* B, M *Prof. Accred.:* Nursing (B,M), Teacher Education *CEO:* Pres. Billy C. Black
FTE Enroll: 3,257　　　　　(912) 430-4604

THE AMERICAN COLLEGE
3330 Peachtree Rd., N.E., Atlanta 30326-1016 *Type:* Private professional *Accred.:* 1987/1993 (SACS-CC) *Calendar:* Qtr. plan *Degrees:* A, B, M (candidate) *Prof. Accred.:* Interior Design *CEO:* Pres. Lisa Beers
FTE Enroll: 1,923　　　　　(404) 231-9000

LONDON CAMPUS
110 Marylebone High St., London, England W1M 3DB
　　　　　[44] (071) 486-1772

LOS ANGELES CAMPUS
1651 Westwood Blvd., Los Angeles, CA 90024
　　　　　(310) 477-8640

ANDREW COLLEGE
413 College St., Cuthbert 31740-1395 *Type:* Private (United Methodist) junior *Accred.:*

1927/1995 (SACS-CC) *Calendar:* Qtr. plan *Degrees:* A *CEO:* Pres. Kirk Treible
FTE Enroll: 299　　　　　(912) 732-2171

ARMSTRONG STATE COLLEGE
11935 Abercorn Ext., Savannah 31419-1997 *Type:* Public (state) liberal arts *System:* Board of Regents of the University System of Georgia *Accred.:* 1940/1992 (SACS-CC) *Calendar:* Qtr. plan *Degrees:* A, B, M (candidate) *Prof. Accred.:* Clinical Lab Scientist, Computer Science, Dental Hygiene, Music, Nursing (A,B), Radiation Therapy Technology, Radiography, Respiratory Therapy, Teacher Education *CEO:* Pres. Robert A. Burnett
FTE Enroll: 4,168　　　　　(912) 927-5258

THE ART INSTITUTE OF ATLANTA
3376 Peachtree Rd., N.E., Atlanta 30326 *Type:* Private *Accred.:* 1985/1993 (SACS-CC) *Calendar:* Qtr. plan *Degrees:* A, B *CEO:* Pres. Hal R. Griffith
FTE Enroll: 1,422　　　　　(404) 266-1341

ATHENS AREA TECHNICAL INSTITUTE
800 U.S. Hwy. 29 N., Athens 30610-1500 *Type:* Public (state) 2-year *Accred.:* 1988/1993 (SACS-CC) *Calendar:* Qtr. plan *Degrees:* A *Prof. Accred.:* Engineering Technology (electrical), Radiography, Respiratory Therapy, Respiratory Therapy Technology *CEO:* Pres. Kenneth C. Easom
FTE Enroll: 1,347　　　　　(706) 355-5000

ATLANTA CHRISTIAN COLLEGE
2605 Ben Hill Rd., East Point 30344 *Type:* Private (Christian Churches/Churches of Christ) *Accred.:* 1990/1995 (SACS-CC) *Calendar:* Sem. plan *Degrees:* A, B *CEO:* Pres. Edwin Groover
FTE Enroll: 247　　　　　(404) 761-8861

ATLANTA COLLEGE OF ART
1280 Peachtree St., N.E., Atlanta 30309 *Type:* Private professional *Accred.:* 1969/1992 (SACS-CC) *Calendar:* Sem. plan

Degrees: B *Prof. Accred.:* Art *CEO:* Pres. Ellen L. Meyer
FTE Enroll: 418   (404) 733-5001

ATLANTA METROPOLITAN COLLEGE
1630 Stewart Ave., S.W., Atlanta 30310 *Type:* Public (state) junior *System:* Board of Regents of the University System of Georgia *Accred.:* 1976/1991 (SACS-CC) *Calendar:* Qtr. plan *Degrees:* A *CEO:* Pres. Harold E. Wade
FTE Enroll: 1,475   (404) 756-4000

AUGUSTA COLLEGE
Augusta 30910 *Type:* Public (state) liberal arts *System:* Board of Regents of the University System of Georgia *Accred.:* 1926/1991 (SACS-CC) *Calendar:* Qtr. plan *Degrees:* A, B, M *Prof. Accred.:* Music, Nursing (A), Teacher Education *CEO:* Pres. William A. Bloodworth
FTE Enroll: 4,734   (706) 737-1440

AUGUSTA TECHNICAL INSTITUTE
3116 Deans Bridge Rd., Augusta 30906 *Type:* Public (state) 2-year *Accred.:* 1988/ 1993 (SACS-CC) *Calendar:* Qtr. plan *Degrees:* A *Prof. Accred.:* Cardiovascular Technology, Clinical Lab Technology (A), Dental Assisting, Dental Laboratory Technology, Engineering Technology (mechanical), Medical Assisting (AMA), Practical Nursing, Surgical Technology *CEO:* Pres. Jack B. Patrick
FTE Enroll: 1,857   (706) 771-4000

BAINBRIDGE COLLEGE
Hwy. 84 E., Bainbridge 31717 *Type:* Public (state) junior *System:* Board of Regents of the University System of Georgia *Accred.:* 1975/1990 (SACS-CC) *Calendar:* Qtr. plan *Degrees:* A *CEO:* Pres. Edward D. Mobley
FTE Enroll: 851   (912) 248-2510

BAUDER COLLEGE
Phipps Plaza, 3500 Peachtree Rd., N.E., Atlanta 30326-9975 *Type:* Private *Accred.:* 1973/1985 (ACCSCT); 1985/1990 (SACS-CC) *Calendar:* Qtr. plan *Degrees:* A *CEO:* Dir. Jeanne Moore
FTE Enroll: 410   (404) 237-7573

BERRY COLLEGE
39 Berry Coll., Rome 30149-0039 *Type:* Private liberal arts *Accred.:* 1957/1988 (SACS-CC) *Calendar:* Sem. plan *Degrees:* B, M *Prof. Accred.:* Music, Teacher Education *CEO:* Pres. Gloria M. Shatto
FTE Enroll: 1,693   (770) 232-5374

BRENAU UNIVERSITY
One Centennial Cir., Gainesville 30501 *Type:* Private liberal arts *Accred.:* 1947/1991 (SACS-CC) *Calendar:* Qtr. plan *Degrees:* B, M *Prof. Accred.:* Interior Design, Nursing (B) *CEO:* Pres. John S. Burd
FTE Enroll: 2,120   (770) 534-6299

BREWTON-PARKER COLLEGE
Hwy. 280, Mount Vernon 30445-0197 *Type:* Private (Baptist) liberal arts *Accred.:* 1962/ 1991 (SACS-CC) *Calendar:* Qtr. plan *Degrees:* A, B *Prof. Accred.:* Music (A) *CEO:* Pres. Y. Lynn Holmes
FTE Enroll: 1,934   (912) 583-2241

BRUNSWICK COLLEGE
3700 Altama Ave., Brunswick 31520-3644 *Type:* Public (state) junior *System:* Board of Regents of the University System of Georgia *Accred.:* 1965/1991 (SACS-CC) *Calendar:* Qtr. plan *Degrees:* A *Prof. Accred.:* Clinical Lab Technology (A), Nursing (A), Radiography *CEO:* Pres. Dorothy L. Lord
FTE Enroll: 1,575   (912) 264-7201

CARROLL TECHNICAL INSTITUTE
997 S. Hwy. 16, Carrollton 30117 *Type:* Public (state) *Accred.:* 1973/1992 (COE); 1995 (SACS-CC candidate) *Calendar:* Qtr. plan *Degrees:* A, C *CEO:* Pres. Janet Ayers
FTE Enroll: 882   (404) 834-6800

CHATTAHOCHEE TECHNICAL INSTITUTE
980 S. Cobb Dr., Marietta 30060 *Type:* Public (state) 2-year *Accred.:* 1988/1993 (SACS-CC) *Calendar:* Qtr. plan *Degrees:* A *Prof. Accred.:* Engineering Technology (electrical, electromechanical) *CEO:* Pres. Harlon D. Crimm
FTE Enroll: 1,340   (770) 528-4500

CLARK ATLANTA UNIVERSITY
James P. Brawley Dr. at Fair St, Atlanta 30314 *Type:* Private (United Methodist) *Accred.:* 1990/1995 (SACS-CC) *Calendar:* Sem. plan *Degrees:* B, M, D *Prof. Accred.:* Business (M), Librarianship, Medical Record Administration, Social Work (B,M) *CEO:* Pres. Thomas W. Cole, Jr.
FTE Enroll: 5,128   (404) 880-8000

CLAYTON STATE COLLEGE
5900 N. Lee St., Morrow 30260 *Type:* Public (state) *System:* Board of Regents of the University System of Georgia *Accred.:* 1971/1994 (SACS-CC) *Calendar:* Qtr. plan *Degrees:* A, B *Prof. Accred.:* Dental Hygiene, Nursing (A,B) *CEO:* Pres. Richard Skinner
FTE Enroll: 4,760   (770) 961-3403

COLUMBIA THEOLOGICAL SEMINARY
P.O. Box 520, 701 Columbia Dr., Decatur 30031 *Type:* Private (Presbyterian) graduate only *Accred.:* 1938/1993 (ATS); 1983/1993 (SACS-CC) *Calendar:* 4-1-4 plan *Degrees:* M, D *CEO:* Pres. Douglas W. Oldenburg
Enroll: 640   (404) 378-8821

COLUMBUS COLLEGE
4225 University Ave., Columbus 31907-5645 *Type:* Public (state) liberal arts *System:* Board of Regents of the University System of Georgia *Accred.:* 1963/1995 (SACS-CC) *Calendar:* Qtr. plan *Degrees:* A, B, M *Prof. Accred.:* Clinical Lab Scientist, Counseling, Dental Hygiene, Music, Nursing (A,B), Respiratory Therapy, Teacher Education *CEO:* Pres. Frank D. Brown
FTE Enroll: 5,241   (770) 568-2211

COLUMBUS TECHNICAL INSTITUTE
928 45th St., Columbus 31904-6572 *Type:* Public (state) 2-year *Accred.:* 1990/1995 (SACS-CC) *Calendar:* Qtr. plan *Degrees:* A *Prof. Accred.:* Medical Assisting (AMA) *CEO:* Pres. W.G. Hartline
FTE Enroll: 1,215   (770) 649-1800

COVENANT COLLEGE
Scenic Hwy., Lookout Mountain 30750 *Type:* Private (Reformed Presbyterian) liberal arts *Accred.:* 1971/1987 (SACS-CC)

Calendar: Sem. plan *Degrees:* A, B, M *CEO:* Pres. Frank A. Brock
FTE Enroll: 840   (706) 820-1560

DALTON COLLEGE
213 N. College Dr., Dalton 30720 *Type:* Public (state) junior *System:* Board of Regents of the University System of Georgia *Accred.:* 1969/1994 (SACS-CC) *Calendar:* Qtr. plan *Degrees:* A *Prof. Accred.:* Clinical Lab Technology (A), Nursing (A) *CEO:* Pres. James A. Burran
FTE Enroll: 2,281   (706) 272-4438

DARTON COLLEGE
2400 Gillionville Rd., Albany 31707-3098 *Type:* Public (state) junior *System:* Board of Regents of the University System of Georgia *Accred.:* 1968/1993 (SACS-CC) *Calendar:* Qtr. plan *Degrees:* A *Prof. Accred.:* Clinical Lab Technology (A), Dental Hygiene, Nursing (A) *CEO:* Pres. Peter J. Sireno
FTE Enroll: 2,039   (912) 430-6000

DEKALB COLLEGE
3251 Panthersville Rd., Decatur 30034 *Type:* Public (state) junior *System:* Board of Regents of the University System of Georgia *Accred.:* 1965/1992 (SACS-CC) *Calendar:* Qtr. plan *Degrees:* A *Prof. Accred.:* Dental Hygiene, Nursing (A) *CEO:* Pres. Jacquelyn M. Belcher
FTE Enroll: 12,307   (404) 244-2364

DEKALB TECHNICAL INSTITUTE
495 N. Indian Creek Dr., Clarkston 30021 *Type:* Public (state) 2-year *Accred.:* 1965/1992 (SACS-CC) *Calendar:* Qtr. plan *Degrees:* A *Prof. Accred.:* Clinical Lab Technology (C), Engineering Technology (electrical, electromechanical), Surgical Technology *CEO:* Pres. Paul M. Starnes
FTE Enroll: 1,906   (404) 297-9522

DEVRY INSTITUTE OF TECHNOLOGY—DECATUR
250 N. Arcadia Ave., Decatur 30030 *Type:* Private *System:* DeVry Institutes *Accred.:* 1981/1992 (NCA) *Calendar:* Sem. plan *Degrees:* A, B *Prof. Accred.:* Engineering Technology (electrical) *CEO:* Pres. Ronald W. Bush
          (404) 292-7900

* Indirect NCA accreditation through DeVry Institutes

EAST GEORGIA COLLEGE
131 College Cir., Swainsboro 30401 *Type:* Public (state) junior *System:* Board of Regents of the University System of Georgia *Accred.:* 1975/1990 (SACS-CC) *Calendar:* Qtr. plan *Degrees:* A *CEO:* Pres. Jeremiah J. Ashcroft
FTE Enroll: 779   (912) 237-7831

EMMANUEL COLLEGE
212 Spring St., Franklin Springs 30639 *Type:* Private (Pentacostal Holiness Church) *Accred.:* 1967/1991 (SACS-CC) *Calendar:* Sem. plan *Degrees:* A, B *CEO:* Pres. David R. Hopkins
FTE Enroll: 559   (706) 245-7226

EMORY UNIVERSITY
1380 S. Oxford Rd., Atlanta 30322 *Type:* Private (United Methodist) *Accred.:* 1938/1993 (ATS); 1917/1993 (SACS-CC) *Calendar:* Sem. plan *Degrees:* A, B, M, D *Prof. Accred.:* Anesthesiologist Assisting, Business (B,M), Clinical Psychology, Dietetics (internship), Law, Medicine, Music, Nursing (B,M), Oral Pathology, Oral and Maxillofacial Surgery, Physical Therapy, Physician Assisting/Surgeon Assisting, Psychology Internship, Radiography, *CEO:* Pres. William M. Chace
FTE Enroll: 9,503   (404) 727-6123

FLOYD COLLEGE
P.O. Box 1864, Rome 30162-1864 *Type:* Public (state) junior *System:* Board of Regents of the University System of Georgia *Accred.:* 1972/1987 (SACS-CC) *Calendar:* Qtr. plan *Degrees:* A *Prof. Accred.:* Nursing (A) *CEO:* Pres. H. Lynn Cundiff
FTE Enroll: 2,985   (706) 295-6328

FORT VALLEY STATE COLLEGE
1005 State College Dr., Fort Valley 31030-3298 *Type:* Public (state) liberal arts and teachers *System:* Board of Regents of the University System of Georgia *Accred.:* 1951/1990 (SACS-CC) *Calendar:* Qtr. plan *Degrees:* A, B, M *Prof. Accred.:* Engineering Technology (electrical), Home Economics, Rehabilitation Counseling, Teacher Educa-

tion, Veterinary Technology (probational) *CEO:* Pres. Oscar L. Prater
FTE Enroll: 2,748   (912) 825-6211

GAINESVILLE COLLEGE
Mundy Mill Rd., P.O. Box 1358, Gainesville 30503-1358 *Type:* Public (state) junior *System:* Board of Regents of the University System of Georgia *Accred.:* 1968/1992 (SACS-CC) *Calendar:* Qtr. plan *Degrees:* A *Prof. Accred.:* Dental Assisting, Dental Hygiene *CEO:* Pres. J. Foster Watkins
FTE Enroll: 2,212   (770) 535-6239

GEORGIA BAPTIST COLLEGE OF NURSING
274 Blvd. N.E., P.O. Box 411, Atlanta 30312 *Type:* Private (Southern Baptist) *Accred.:* 1994 (SACS-CC) *Calendar:* Qtr. plan *Degrees:* B *CEO:* Pres. Susan S. Gunby
FTE Enroll: 303   (404) 265-4512

GEORGIA COLLEGE
C.B.X. Box 020, Milledgeville 31061-0490 *Type:* Public (state) liberal arts *System:* Board of Regents of the University System of Georgia *Accred.:* 1925/1994 (SACS-CC) *Calendar:* Qtr. plan *Degrees:* A, B, M *Prof. Accred.:* Music, Nursing (B,M), Public Administration, Teacher Education *CEO:* Pres. Edwin G. Speir, Jr.
FTE Enroll: 4,915   (912) 453-5004

GEORGIA INSTITUTE OF TECHNOLOGY
225 North Ave., N.W., Atlanta 30332-0325 *Type:* Public (state) technological *System:* Board of Regents of the University System of Georgia *Accred.:* 1923/1994 (SACS-CC) *Calendar:* Qtr. plan *Degrees:* B, M, D *Prof. Accred.:* Business (B,M), Computer Science, Engineering (aerospace, ceramic, chemical, civil, computer, electrical, engineering mechanics, environmental/sanitary, industrial, materials, mechanical, nuclear), textile) *CEO:* Pres. Wayne G. Clough
FTE Enroll: 12,946   (404) 894-5051

GEORGIA MILITARY COLLEGE
201 E. Greene St., Milledgeville 31061-3398 *Type:* Public junior *Accred.:* 1940/1987 (SACS-CC) *Calendar:* Qtr. plan *Degrees:* A *CEO:* Pres. Peter J. Boylan
FTE Enroll: 2,419   (912) 454-2700

GEORGIA SOUTHERN UNIVERSITY
Landrum Box 8033, Statesboro 30460-8033
Type: Public (state) liberal arts and teachers
System: Board of Regents of the University
System of Georgia *Accred.:* 1935/1994
(SACS-CC) *Calendar:* Qtr. plan *Degrees:* A,
B, M, D *Prof. Accred.:* Accounting (A),
Business (B,M), Computer Science, Con-
struction Education, Engineering Technol-
ogy (civil/construction, electrical, industrial,
mechanical), Music, Nursing (B,M), Public
Administration, Recreation and Leisure Ser-
vices (B), Teacher Education *CEO:* Pres.
Nicholas L. Henry
FTE Enroll: 13,720   (912) 681-5211

GEORGIA SOUTHWESTERN COLLEGE
800 Wheatley St., Americus 31709-4693
Type: Public (state) liberal arts *System:*
Board of Regents of the University System
of Georgia *Accred.:* 1932/1993 (SACS-CC
warning) *Calendar:* Qtr. plan *Degrees:* A, B,
M *Prof. Accred.:* Nursing (A,B), Teacher
Education *CEO:* Pres. Joan Eliason
FTE Enroll: 2,557   (912) 928-1279

GEORGIA STATE UNIVERSITY
University Plaza, Atlanta 30303-3083 *Type:*
Public (state) *System:* Board of Regents of
the University System of Georgia *Accred.:*
1952/1988 (SACS-CC) *Calendar:* Qtr. plan
Degrees: A, B, M, D *Prof. Accred.:* Account-
ing (A,B,C), Art, Business (B,M), Clinical
Lab Scientist, Clinical Psychology, Counsel-
ing, Counseling Psychology, Dietetics (coor-
dinated), Health Services Administration,
Law, Law (ABA only), Music, Nursing
(B,M), Physical Therapy, Psychology Intern-
ship, Public Administration, Rehabilitation
Counseling, Respiratory Therapy, Respiratory Therapy Technology, School Psychol-
ogy, Social Work (B), Speech-Language
Pathology, Teacher Education *CEO:* Pres.
Carl V. Patton
FTE Enroll: 19,201   (404) 651-2560

GORDON COLLEGE
419 College Dr., Barnesville 30204 *Type:*
Public (state) junior *System:* Board of
Regents of the University System of Georgia
Accred.: 1941/1986 (SACS-CC) *Calendar:*

Qtr. plan *Degrees:* A *Prof. Accred.:* Nursing
(A) *CEO:* Pres. Jerry M. Williamson
FTE Enroll: 1,853   (770) 358-5000

GUPTON-JONES COLLEGE OF FUNERAL SERVICE
5141 Snapfinger Woods Dr., Decatur 30035-
4022 *Type:* Private professional *Degrees:* A,
C *Prof. Accred.:* Funeral Service Education
(Mortuary Science) *CEO:* Pres. Daniel E.
Buchanan
                                        (404) 593-2257

GWINNETT TECHNICAL INSTITUTE
1250 Atkinson Rd., P.O. Box 1505,
Lawrenceville 30246-1505 *Type:* Public
(local) 2-year *Accred.:* 1991 (SACS-CC)
Calendar: Qtr. plan *Degrees:* A, C *Prof.
Accred.:* Dental Assisting, Dental Labora-
tory Technology, Physical Therapy Assist-
ing, Radiography, Respiratory Therapy
Technology *CEO:* Pres. J. Alvin Wilbanks
FTE Enroll: 3,447   (770) 962-7580

INSTITUTE OF PAPER SCIENCE AND TECHNOLOGY
500 10th St., N.W., Atlanta 30318-5794
Type: Private graduate only *Accred.:* 1989/
1992 (SACS-CC) *Calendar:* Qtr. plan
Degrees: M, D *CEO:* Pres. James L. Ferris
FTE Enroll: 78   (404) 894-5700

INTERDENOMINATIONAL THEOLOGICAL CENTER
671 Beckwith St., S.W., Atlanta 30314 *Type:*
Private (interdenominational) graduate only
Accred.: 1960/1991 (ATS); 1984/1991
(SACS-CC) *Calendar:* Sem. plan *Degrees:*
M, D *CEO:* Pres. James H. Costen
Enroll: 398   (404) 527-7700

KENNESAW STATE COLLEGE
1000 Chastain Rd., Kennesaw 30144-5591
Type: Public (state) liberal arts *System:*
Board of Regents of the University System
of Georgia *Accred.:* 1968/1986 (SACS-CC)
Calendar: Qtr. plan *Degrees:* A, B, M *Prof.
Accred.:* Music, Nursing (A,B), Teacher
Education *CEO:* Pres. Betty L. Siegel
FTE Enroll: 9,682   (770) 423-6033

LAGRANGE COLLEGE
601 Broad St., LaGrange 30240-2999 *Type:*
Private (United Methodist) liberal arts
Accred.: 1946/1992 (SACS-CC) *Calendar:*

Qtr. plan *Degrees:* A, B, M *Prof. Accred.:* Nursing (A) *CEO:* Pres. Walter Y. Murphy *FTE Enroll:* 889   (706) 882-2911

LIFE COLLEGE
1269 Barclay Cir., Marietta 30060 *Type:* Private professional *Accred.:* 1986/1991 (SACS-CC) *Calendar:* Qtr. plan *Degrees:* B, M, D *Prof. Accred.:* Chiropractic Education *CEO:* Pres. Sid E. Williams, D.C.
FTE Enroll: 3,384   (770) 424-0554

MACON COLLEGE
100 College Station Dr., Macon 31297 *Type:* Public (state) junior *System:* Board of Regents of the University System of Georgia *Accred.:* 1970/1995 (SACS-CC) *Calendar:* Qtr. plan *Degrees:* A *Prof. Accred.:* Dental Hygiene, Nursing (A) *CEO:* Pres. S. Aaron Hyatt
FTE Enroll: 3,502   (912) 471-2800

MASSEY COLLEGE OF BUSINESS AND TECHNOLOGY
3355 Lenox Rd., Ste. 100, Atlanta 30326 *Type:* Private business *Accred.:* 1977/1987 (ACICS) *Calendar:* Qtr. plan *Degrees:* A *CEO:* Dir. Cathleen Cortese
      (404) 816-4533

HERSING INSTITUTE
1270 Wickham Rd., Ste. 26, Melbourne, FL 32935 *Accred.:* 1994 (ACICS) *Degrees:* C
      (407) 255-9232

HERSING INSTITUTE
120 South Semoran Blvd., Orlando, FL 32807 *Accred.:* 1994 (ACICS)
Enroll: 12   (407) 380-6315

MEADOWS COLLEGE OF BUSINESS
1170 Brown Ave., Columbus 31906 *Type:* Private junior *Accred.:* 1974/1996 (ACICS) *Calendar:* Qtr. plan *Degrees:* A *CEO:* Pres. William F. Meadows, Jr.
      (706) 327-7668

MEDICAL COLLEGE OF GEORGIA
1120 15th St., Augusta 30912 *Type:* Public (state) professional *System:* Board of Regents of the University System of Georgia

Accred.: 1973/1990 (SACS-CC) *Calendar:* Qtr. plan *Degrees:* A, B, M, D *Prof. Accred.:* Clinical Lab Scientist, Combined Prosthodontics, Dental Hygiene, Dentistry, Diagnostic Medical Sonography, Endodontics, General Practice Residency, Medical Illustration, Medical Record Administration, Medical Record Technology, Medicine, Nuclear Medicine Technology, Nurse Anesthesia Education, Nursing (B,M), Occupational Therapy, Occupational Therapy Assisting, Oral and Maxillofacial Surgery, Orthodontics, Pediatric Dentistry, Periodontics, Physical Therapy, Physical Therapy Assisting, Physician Assisting/Surgeon Assisting, Psychology Internship, Radiation Therapy Technology, Radiography, Respiratory Therapy *CEO:* Pres. Francis J. Tedesco
FTE Enroll: 1,998   (706) 721-0211

MERCER UNIVERSITY
1400 Coleman Ave., Macon 31207-0001 *Type:* Private (Baptist) *Accred.:* 1911/1994 (SACS-CC) *Calendar:* Sem. plan *Degrees:* B, M, D *Prof. Accred.:* Engineering (general), Law, Medicine, Music *CEO:* Pres. R. Kirby Godsey
FTE Enroll: 4,704   (912) 752-2700

ATLANTA CAMPUS
3001 Mercer Univ. Dr., Atlanta 30341 Baptist *Accred.:* 1911/1994 (SACS-CC) *Calendar:* Qtr. plan *Degrees:* A, M, D *Enroll:* 6,728   (770) 986-3000

MIDDLE GEORGIA COLLEGE
1100 Second St., S.E., Cochran 31014 *Type:* Public (state) junior *System:* Board of Regents of the University System of Georgia *Accred.:* 1933/1989 (SACS-CC) *Calendar:* Qtr. plan *Degrees:* A *Prof. Accred.:* Nursing (A) *CEO:* Pres. Joe Ben Welch
FTE Enroll: 2,019   (912) 934-3011

MOREHOUSE COLLEGE
830 Westview Dr., S.W., Atlanta 30314 *Type:* Private liberal arts for men *Accred.:* 1932/1988 (SACS-CC) *Calendar:* Sem. plan *Degrees:* B *CEO:* Pres. Walter E. Massey
FTE Enroll: 2,864   (404) 681-2800

MOREHOUSE SCHOOL OF MEDICINE
720 Westview Dr., S.W., Atlanta 30310-1495 *Type:* Private professional *Accred.:* 1986/1991 (SACS-CC) *Calendar:* Sem. plan *Degrees:* D *Prof. Accred.:* Medicine *CEO:* Pres. Louis Sullivan
FTE Enroll: 153   (404) 752-1500

MORRIS BROWN COLLEGE
643 M. L. K., Jr. Dr., NW, Atlanta 30314-4140 *Type:* Private (African Methodist Episcopal) liberal arts *Accred.:* 1941/1989 (SACS-CC) *Calendar:* Sem. plan *Degrees:* B *CEO:* Pres. Samuel D. Jolley, Jr.
FTE Enroll: 1,858   (404) 220-0270

NORTH GEORGIA COLLEGE
College Ave., Dahlonega 30597 *Type:* Public (state) liberal arts and teachers *System:* Board of Regents of the University System of Georgia *Accred.:* 1948/1987 (SACS-CC) *Calendar:* Qtr. plan *Degrees:* A, B, M *Prof. Accred.:* Nursing (A,B), Physical Therapy (candidate), Teacher Education *CEO:* Pres. Delmas J. Allen
FTE Enroll: 2,898   (706) 864-1993

OGLETHORPE UNIVERSITY
4484 Peachtree Rd., N.E., Atlanta 30319-2797 *Type:* Private liberal arts *Accred.:* 1950/1986 (SACS-CC) *Calendar:* Sem. plan *Degrees:* B, M *CEO:* Pres. Donald S. Stanton
FTE Enroll: 988   (404) 261-1441

PAINE COLLEGE
1235 15th St., Augusta 30901-3182 *Type:* Private (United Methodist) liberal arts *Accred.:* 1944/1991 (SACS-CC) *Calendar:* Sem. plan *Degrees:* B *CEO:* Pres. Shirley A.R. Lewis
FTE Enroll: 723   (706) 821-8200

PIEDMONT COLLEGE
P.O. Box 10, Demorest 30535 *Type:* Private liberal arts *Accred.:* 1965/1987 (SACS-CC) *Calendar:* Sem. plan *Degrees:* B *CEO:* Pres. W. Ray Cleere
FTE Enroll: 666   (706) 778-3000

REINHARDT COLLEGE
P.O. Box 128, Waleska 30183 *Type:* Private (United Methodist) *Accred.:* 1953/1988 (SACS-CC) *Calendar:* Qtr. plan *Degrees:* A, B *CEO:* Pres. Floyd A. Falany
FTE Enroll: 765   (770) 720-5600

THE SAVANNAH COLLEGE OF ART AND DESIGN
P.O. Box 3146, Savannah 31402-3146 *Type:* Private professional *Accred.:* 1983/1989 (SACS-CC) *Calendar:* Qtr. plan *Degrees:* B, M *CEO:* Pres. Richard G. Rowan
FTE Enroll: 2,201   (912) 238-2400

SAVANNAH STATE COLLEGE
State College Branch, P.O. Box 20419, Savannah 31404 *Type:* Public (state) liberal arts and professional *System:* Board of Regents of the University System of Georgia *Accred.:* 1951/1991 (SACS-CC) *Calendar:* Qtr. plan *Degrees:* B, M (candidate) *Prof. Accred.:* Engineering Technology (civil/construction, computer, electrical, mechanical), Social Work (B) *CEO:* Pres. John T. Wolfe, Jr.
FTE Enroll: 2,726   (912) 356-2187

SAVANNAH TECHNICAL INSTITUTE
5717 White Bluff Rd., Savannah 31499 *Type:* Public (local) 2-year *Accred.:* 1991 (SACS-CC) *Calendar:* Qtr. plan *Degrees:* A *Prof. Accred.:* Dental Assisting, Engineering Technology (bioengineering, civil/construction, electrical, electromechanical), Medical Assisting (AMA), Practical Nursing, Surgical Technology *CEO:* Interim Pres. Don Stewart
FTE Enroll: 1,350   (912) 351-6362

SHORTER COLLEGE
315 Shorter Ave., Rome 30165-4298 *Type:* Private (Baptist) liberal arts *Accred.:* 1923/1992 (SACS-CC) *Calendar:* Sem. plan *Degrees:* B, M (candidate) *Prof. Accred.:* Music *CEO:* Pres. Larry L. McSwain
FTE Enroll: 1,151   (706) 291-2121

SOUTH COLLEGE
709 Mall Blvd., Savannah 31406 *Type:* Private junior *Accred.:* 1985/1990 (SACS-CC) *Calendar:* Qtr. plan *Degrees:* A, B (candidate)

Prof. Accred.: Medical Assisting (AMA)
CEO: Pres. John T. South, III
FTE Enroll: 730   (912) 651-8100

SOUTH GEORGIA COLLEGE
100 W. College Park Dr., Douglas 31533-5098 *Type:* Public (state) junior *System:* Board of Regents of the University System of Georgia *Accred.:* 1934/1987 (SACS-CC) *Calendar:* Qtr. plan *Degrees:* A *Prof. Accred.:* Nursing (A) *CEO:* Pres. Edward D. Jackson, Jr.
FTE Enroll: 1,145   (912) 383-4380

SOUTHERN COLLEGE OF TECHNOLOGY
1100 S. Marietta Pkwy., Marietta 30060-2896 *Type:* Public (state) *System:* Board of Regents of the University System of Georgia *Accred.:* 1964/1988 (SACS-CC) *Calendar:* Qtr. plan *Degrees:* A, B, M *Prof. Accred.:* Construction Education (B), Engineering Technology (apparel, architectural, civil/construction, computer, electrical, industrial, mechanical) *CEO:* Pres. Stephen R. Cheshier
FTE Enroll: 3,237   (770) 528-7281

SPELMAN COLLEGE
350 Spelman Ln., S.W., Atlanta 30314-4399 *Type:* Private liberal arts for women *Accred.:* 1932/1990 (SACS-CC) *Calendar:* Sem. plan *Degrees:* B *Prof. Accred.:* Music, Teacher Education *CEO:* Pres. Johnnetta B. Cole
FTE Enroll: 2,028   (404) 681-3643

THOMAS COLLEGE
1501 Millpond Rd., Thomasville 31792-7499 *Type:* Private *Accred.:* 1984/1995 (SACS-CC) *Calendar:* Qtr. plan *Degrees:* A, B *CEO:* Pres. Homer R. Pankey
FTE Enroll: 585   (912) 226-1621

TOCCOA FALLS COLLEGE
P.O. Box 800869, Toccoa Falls 30598 *Type:* Private (Christian and Missionary Alliance) *Accred.:* 1957/1987 (AABC); 1983/1989 (SACS-CC) *Calendar:* Sem. plan *Degrees:* A, B, M (candidate) *Prof. Accred.:* Music (A) *CEO:* Pres. Paul L. Alford
FTE Enroll: 858   (706) 886-6831

TRUETT MCCONNELL COLLEGE
100 Alumni Dr., Cleveland 30528 *Type:* Private (Southern Baptist) junior *Accred.:* 1966/1990 (SACS-CC) *Calendar:* Qtr. plan *Degrees:* A *Prof. Accred.:* Music *CEO:* Pres. Thomas Clark Bryan
FTE Enroll: 1,530   (706) 865-2134

THE UNIVERSITY OF GEORGIA
456 E. Broad St., Athens 30602-1661 *Type:* Public (state) *System:* Board of Regents of the University System of Georgia *Accred.:* 1909/1991 (SACS-CC) *Calendar:* Qtr. plan *Degrees:* A, B, M, D *Prof. Accred.:* Accounting (A,B,C), Art, Audiology, Business (B,M), Clinical Psychology, Counseling, Counseling Psychology, Engineering (agricultural), Forestry, Home Economics, Interior Design, Journalism (B,M), Landscape Architecture (B,M), Law, Marriage and Family Therapy (D), Music, Psychology Internship, Public Administration, Recreation and Leisure Services (B), Rehabilitation Counseling, School Psychology, Social Work (B,M), Speech-Language Pathology, Teacher Education, Theatre, Veterinary Medicine *CEO:* Pres. Charles B. Knapp
FTE Enroll: 27,151   (404) 542-3000

VALDOSTA STATE UNIVERSITY
1500 N. Patterson St., Valdosta 31602 *Type:* Public (state) liberal arts and teachers *System:* Board of Regents of the University System of Georgia *Accred.:* 1929/1990 (SACS-CC) *Calendar:* Qtr. plan *Degrees:* A, B, M, D (candidate) *Prof. Accred.:* Art (A), Business (B), Music, Nursing (B,M), Speech-Language Pathology, Teacher Education *CEO:* Pres. Hugh C. Bailey
FTE Enroll: 8,675   (912) 333-5952

WAYCROSS COLLEGE
2001 Francis St., Waycross 31503-9248 *Type:* Public (state) junior *System:* Board of Regents of the University System of Georgia *Accred.:* 1978/1993 (SACS-CC) *Calendar:* Qtr. plan *Degrees:* A *CEO:* Pres. James M. Dye
FTE Enroll: 634   (912) 285-6130

WESLEYAN COLLEGE
4760 Forsyth Rd., Macon 31297-4299 *Type:* Private (United Methodist) liberal arts for women *Accred.:* 1919/1994 (SACS-CC) *Calendar:* Sem. plan *Degrees:* B, M (candidate) *Prof. Accred.:* Music *CEO:* Pres. Robert K. Ackerman
FTE Enroll: 451   (912) 477-1110

WEST GEORGIA COLLEGE
1600 Maple St., Carrollton 30118-0001 *Type:* Public (state) liberal arts and professional *System:* Board of Regents of the University System of Georgia *Accred.:* 1963/1993 (SACS-CC) *Calendar:* Qtr. plan *Degrees:* A, B, M *Prof. Accred.:* Business (B,M), Music, Nursing (A,B), Teacher Education *CEO:* Pres. Beheruz N. Sethna
FTE Enroll: 7,947   (770) 836-6449

YOUNG HARRIS COLLEGE
P.O. Box 98, Young Harris 30582 *Type:* Private (United Methodist) junior *Accred.:* 1938/1991 (SACS-CC) *Calendar:* Qtr. plan *Degrees:* A *CEO:* Pres. Thomas S. Yow, III
FTE Enroll: 524   (706) 379-3111

GUAM

GUAM COMMUNITY COLLEGE

P.O. Box 23069, Guam Main Facility, Main Island 96921 *Type:* Public (territorial) junior *Accred.:* 1979/1994 (WASC-Jr.) *Calendar:* Sem. plan *Degrees:* A *CEO:* Pres. John T. Cruz

Enroll: 4,728   [011] (671) 734-4311

UNIVERSITY OF GUAM

UOG Sta., Mangilao 96923 *Type:* Public (territorial) liberal arts and professional *Accred.:* 1963/1995 (WASC-Sr.) *Calendar:* Sem. plan *Degrees:* A, B, M *CEO:* Pres. John C. Salas

FTE Enroll: 3,740   [011] (671) 734-9230

HAWAII

BRIGHAM YOUNG UNIVERSITY—HAWAII
CAMPUS
   55-220 Kulanui St., Laie, Oahu 96762 *Type:*
   Private (Latter-Day Saints) liberal arts
   Accred.: 1959/1986 (WASC-Sr.) *Degrees:*
   A, B *Prof. Accred.:* Social Work (B) *CEO:*
   Pres. Eric B. Shumway
   FTE Enroll: 2,096   (808) 293-3700

CHAMINADE UNIVERSITY OF HONOLULU
   3140 Waialae Ave., Honolulu 96816-1578
   Type: Private (Roman Catholic) liberal arts
   and professional *Accred.:* 1960/1983
   (WASC-Sr.) *Calendar:* Sem. plan *Degrees:*
   A, B, M *CEO:* Pres. Sue Wesselkamper
   FTE Enroll: 1,279   (808) 735-4711

HAWAII COMMUNITY COLLEGE
   200 W. Kawili St., Hilo 96720-4091 *Type:*
   Public (state) junior *System:* University of
   Hawaii Office of the Chancellor for Com-
   munity Colleges *Accred.:* 1973/1995
   (WASC-Jr.) *Calendar:* Sem. plan *Degrees:*
   A *CEO:* Provost Sandra T. Sakaguchi
   Enroll: 2,354   (808) 933-3311

HAWAII PACIFIC UNIVERSITY
   1166 Fort St., Honolulu 96813 *Type:* Private
   liberal arts and business *Accred.:* 1973/1993
   (WASC-Sr.) *Calendar:* Sem. plan *Degrees:*
   A, B, M *CEO:* Pres. Chatt G. Wright
   FTE Enroll: 6,032   (808) 544-0200

   HAWAII LOA COLLEGE CAMPUS
      45-045 Kamehameha Hwy., Kaneohe
      96744 *Prof. Accred.:* Nursing (B)
                        (808) 235-3641

HEALD BUSINESS COLLEGE—HONOLULU HI
   1500 Kapiolani Rd., Honolulu 96814 *Type:*
   Private *System:* Heald Colleges *Accred.:*
   1983/1994 (WASC-Jr.) *Calendar:* Qtr. plan
   Degrees: A, C *CEO:* Dir. Evelyn Schemmel
                        (808) 955-1500

HONOLULU COMMUNITY COLLEGE
   874 Dillingham Blvd., Honolulu 96817
   Type: Public (state) junior *System:* University of Hawaii Office of the Chancellor for
   Community Colleges *Accred.:* 1970/1995

(WASC-Jr.) *Calendar:* Sem. plan *Degrees:*
A *CEO:* Provost Peter R. Kessinger
Enroll: 4,740   (808) 845-9211

KANSAI GAIDAI HAWAII COLLEGE
   5257 Kalanianaole Hwy., Honolulu 96821
   Type: Private 2-year *Accred.:* 1985/1990
   (WASC-Jr. probational) *Calendar:* Sem.
   plan *Degrees:* A *CEO:* Provost Ben Seale
   Enroll: 215   (808) 377-5402

KAPIOLANI COMMUNITY COLLEGE
   4303 Diamond Head Rd., Honolulu 96816
   Type: Public (state) junior *System:* Univer-
   sity of Hawaii Office of the Chancellor for
   Community Colleges *Accred.:* 1970/1994
   (WASC-Jr.) *Calendar:* Sem. plan *Degrees:*
   A *Prof. Accred.:* Clinical Lab Technology
   (A), Medical Assisting (AMA), Nursing (A),
   Occupational Therapy Assisting, Physical
   Therapy Assisting, Radiography, Respira-
   tory Therapy, Respiratory Therapy Technol-
   ogy *CEO:* Provost John E. Morton
   Enroll: 7,356   (808) 734-9111

KAUAI COMMUNITY COLLEGE
   3-1901 Kaumualii Hwy., Lihue 96766 *Type:*
   Public (state) junior *System:* University of
   Hawaii Office of the Chancellor for Com-
   munity Colleges *Accred.:* 1971/1995
   (WASC-Jr.) *Calendar:* Sem. plan *Degrees:*
   A *Prof. Accred.:* Nursing (A) *CEO:* Campus
   Pres. David Iha
   Enroll: 1,507   (808) 245-8311

LEEWARD COMMUNITY COLLEGE
   96-045 Ala Ike, Pearl City 96782 *Type:* Pub-
   lic (state) junior *System:* University of
   Hawaii Office of the Chancellor for Com-
   munity Colleges *Accred.:* 1971/1995
   (WASC-Jr.) *Calendar:* Sem. plan *Degrees:*
   A *CEO:* Provost Barbara B. Polk
   Enroll: 6,486   (808) 455-0011

MAUI COMMUNITY COLLEGE
   310 Kaahumanu Ave., Kahului 96732 *Type:*
   Public (state) junior *System:* University of
   Hawaii Office of the Chancellor for Community Colleges *Accred.:* 1980/1995

(WASC-Jr.) *Calendar:* Sem. plan *Degrees:* A *Prof. Accred.:* Nursing (A) *CEO:* Provost Clyde M. Sakamoto
Enroll: 1,915   (808) 244-9181

TAI HSUAN FOUNDATION COLLEGE OF ACUPUNCTURE AND HERBAL MEDICINE
2600 S. King St., No. 206, Honolulu 96826 *Type:* Private professional *Calendar:* Sem. plan *Degrees:* M *Prof. Accred.:* Acupuncture (M) *CEO:* Pres. Gayle Todoki
FTE Enroll: 25   (808) 947-4788

TOKAI INTERNATIONAL COLLEGE
2241 Kapiolani Blvd., Honolulu 96826 *Type:* Private Junior *Accred.:* 1994 (WASC-Jr.) *Calendar:* Qtr. plan *Degrees:* A *CEO:* Pres. Richard H. Kosaki
Enroll: 75   (808) 973-4100

UNIVERSITY OF HAWAII AT HILO
Hilo 96720-4091 *Type:* Public (state) liberal arts and professional *System:* University of Hawaii Office of the President *Accred.:* 1976/1994 (WASC-Sr.) *Calendar:* Sem. plan *Degrees:* A, B *CEO:* Chanc. Kenneth L. Perrin
FTE Enroll: 2,290   (808) 933-3445

UNIVERSITY OF HAWAII AT MANOA
2444 Dole St., Honolulu 96822 *Type:* Public (state) liberal arts and professional *System:*

University of Hawaii Office of the President *Accred.:* 1952/1991 (WASC-Sr.) *Calendar:* Sem. plan *Degrees:* A, B, M, P, D *Prof. Accred.:* Audiology, Business (B,M), Clinical Lab Scientist, Clinical Psychology, Dental Hygiene, Dietetics (internship), Engineering (civil, electrical, mechanical, ocean), Journalism (B), Law, Librarianship, Medicine, Music, Nursing (A,B,M), Planning (M), Psychology Internship (provisional), Rehabilitation Counseling, Social Work (B,M), Speech-Language Pathology, *CEO:* Chanc. Kenneth P. Mortimer
FTE Enroll: 16,033   (808) 956-8207

UNIVERSITY OF HAWAII AT WEST OAHU
96-043 Ala Ike, Pearl City 96782 *Type:* Public (state) liberal arts *System:* University of Hawaii Office of the President *Accred.:* 1981 (WASC-Sr.) *Calendar:* Sem. plan *Degrees:* B *CEO:* Chanc. Kenneth L. Perrin
FTE Enroll: 439   (808) 453-6565

WINDWARD COMMUNITY COLLEGE
45-720 Keaahala Rd., Kaneohe 96744 *Type:* Public (state) junior *System:* University of Hawaii Office of the Chancellor for Community Colleges *Accred.:* 1977/1995 (WASC-Jr.) *Calendar:* Sem. plan *Degrees:* A *CEO:* Provost Peter T. Dyer
Enroll: 1,633   (808) 235-0077

IDAHO

ALBERTSON COLLEGE OF IDAHO
2112 Cleveland Blvd., Caldwell 83605 *Type:* Private (United Presbyterian) liberal arts *Accred.:* 1922/1992 (NASC) *Calendar:* 4-1-4 plan *Degrees:* B, M *CEO:* Pres. Robert L. Hendren, Jr.
Enroll: 804　　　　　　　(208) 459-5011

BOISE BIBLE COLLEGE
8695 Marigold St., Boise 83714 *Type:* Private (Christian Churches/Churches of Christ) *Accred.:* 1988/1994 (AABC) *Calendar:* Sem. plan *Degrees:* A, B, C *CEO:* Pres. Charles A. Crane
FTE Enroll: 93　　　　　　(208) 376-7731

BOISE STATE UNIVERSITY
1910 University Dr., Boise 83725 *Type:* Public liberal arts and teachers *System:* State Board of Education and Board of Regents of the University of Idaho *Accred.:* 1941/1994 (NASC) *Calendar:* Sem. plan *Degrees:* A, B, M *Prof. Accred.:* Accounting (A), Business (B,M), Computer Science, Construction Education (B), Dental Assisting, Medical Record Technology, Music, Nursing (A,B), Public Administration, Radiography, Respiratory Therapy, Respiratory Therapy Technology, Social Work (B,M-candidate), Surgical Technology, Teacher Education, Theatre (A) *CEO:* Pres. Charles P. Ruch
Enroll: 15,071　　　　　　(208) 385-1491

COLLEGE OF SOUTHERN IDAHO
315 Falls Ave., P.O. Box 1238, Twin Falls 83301 *Type:* Public (district) junior *System:* State Board of Education and Board of Regents of the University of Idaho *Accred.:* 1968/1994 (NASC) *Calendar:* Sem. plan *Degrees:* A *Prof. Accred.:* Medical Assisting (AMA), Nursing (A) *CEO:* Pres. Gerald R. Meyerhoeffer
Enroll: 4,092　　　　　　(208) 733-9554

EASTERN IDAHO TECHNICAL COLLEGE
1600 S. 2500 E., Idaho Falls 83404 *Type:* Public (district) 2-year *Accred.:* 1982/1992

(NASC) *Calendar:* Qtr. plan *Degrees:* A *CEO:* Dir. Miles LaRowe
Enroll: 411　　　　　　　(208) 524-3000

IDAHO STATE UNIVERSITY
Pocatello 83209-0009 *Type:* Public (state) *System:* State Board of Education and Board of Regents of the University of Idaho *Accred.:* 1923/1994 (NASC) *Calendar:* Sem. plan *Degrees:* A, B, M, D *Prof. Accred.:* Audiology, Business (B,M), Clinical Lab Scientist, Counseling, Dental Hygiene, Dental Laboratory Technology, Dietetics (internship), Engineering (general), Music, Nursing (B,M), Physical Therapy, Radiography, Social Work (B), Speech-Language Pathology, Teacher Education *CEO:* Pres. Richard L. Bowen
Enroll: 11,877　　　　　　(208) 236-3340

ITT TECHNICAL INSTITUTE
950 Lusk St., Boise 83706-2831 *Type:* Private *Accred.:* 1985/1990 (ACCSCT) *Degrees:* A, C *CEO:* Dir. N. Dale Reynolds
　　　　　　　　　　　　(208) 344-8376

LEWIS-CLARK STATE COLLEGE
500 8th Ave., Lewiston 83501 *Type:* Public (state) 4-year liberal arts and teachers *System:* State Board of Education and Board of Regents of the University of Idaho *Accred.:* 1964/1994 (NASC) *Calendar:* Sem. plan *Degrees:* A, B *Prof. Accred.:* Nursing (A,B), Social Work (B-candidate), Teacher Education *CEO:* Pres. James W. Hottois
Enroll: 3,347　　　　　　(208) 799-5272

NORTH IDAHO COLLEGE
Coeur d'Alene 83814 *Type:* Public (district) junior *System:* State Board of Education and Board of Regents of the University of Idaho *Accred.:* 1947/1994 (NASC) *Calendar:* Sem. plan *Degrees:* A *Prof. Accred.:* Nursing (A) *CEO:* Pres. C. Robert Bennett
Enroll: 3,324　　　　　　(208) 769-3300

NORTHWEST NAZARENE COLLEGE
Nampa 83686 *Type:* Private (Nazarene) liberal arts *Accred.:* 1930/1992 (NASC) *Cal-*

endar: Qtr. plan *Degrees:* A, B, M *Prof. Accred.:* Music, Social Work (B), Teacher Education *CEO:* Pres. Richard Hagood
Enroll: 1,280   (208) 467-8011

RICKS COLLEGE

Rexburg 83460 *Type:* Private (Latter-Day Saints) junior *Accred.:* 1936/1994 (NASC) *Calendar:* Sem. plan *Degrees:* A *Prof. Accred.:* Engineering Technology (electrical, manufacturing, mechanical drafting/design), Interior Design, Music *CEO:* Pres. Steven D. Bennion
Enroll: 7,989   (208) 356-2411

UNIVERSITY OF IDAHO

Moscow 83843 *Type:* Public (state) *System:* State Board of Education and Board of Regents of the University of Idaho *Accred.:* 1918/1994 (NASC) *Calendar:* Sem. plan *Degrees:* B, M, D *Prof. Accred.:* Business (B), Computer Science, Counseling, Dietetics (coordinated), Engineering (agricultural, chemical, civil, electrical, geological/geophysical, mechanical, metallurgical, mining), Forestry, Landscape Architecture (B), Law, Music, Recreation and Leisure Services (B), Rehabilitation Counseling, Teacher Education *CEO:* Interim Pres. Thomas O. Bell
Enroll: 11,730   (208) 885-6111

ILLINOIS

ADLER SCHOOL OF PROFESSIONAL PSYCHOLOGY
65 E. Wacker Pl., Chicago 60601 *Type:* Private professional; graduate only *Accred.:* 1978/1995 (NCA) *Calendar:* Tri. plan *Degrees:* M, D, C *CEO:* Pres. Randall L. Thompson
Enroll: 413   (312) 201-5900

AMERICAN ACADEMY OF ART
332 S. Michigan Ave., Ste. 300, Chicago 60604-4301 *Type:* Private *Accred.:* 1974/1989 (ACCSCT) *Calendar:* Sem. plan *Degrees:* A *CEO:* Dir. John Balester
(312) 461-0600

AMERICAN CONSERVATORY OF MUSIC
16 N. Wabash Ave., Ste. 1850, Chicago 60602-4792 *Type:* Private *Degrees:* A, B, M, D, C *Prof. Accred.:* Music *CEO:* Dean Carl L. Waldschmidt
(312) 263-4161

AMERICAN SCHOOLS OF PROFESSIONAL PSYCHOLOGY
220 S. State St., Ste. 609, Chicago 60604 *Type:* Private graduate only *Accred.:* 1981/1991 (NCA) *Calendar:* Sem. plan *Degrees:* M, D *CEO:* Pres. Harold J. O'Donnell
Enroll: 1,625   (312) 922-1025

AMERICAN SCHOOL OF PROFESSIONAL PSYCHOLOGY—HAWAII CAMPUS
Bldg. MDLC, 845 22nd Ave., Honolulu, HI 96816-4521
(808) 735-0109

AMERICAN SCHOOL OF PROFESSIONAL PSYCHOLOGY—VIRGINIA CAMPUS
1400 Wilson Blvd., Ste. 110, Arlington, VA 22209
(703) 243-5300

GEORGIA SCHOOL OF PROFESSIONAL PSYCHOLOGY—ATLANTA
990 Hammond Dr., N.E., Ste. 1100, Atlanta, GA 30328 *Prof. Accred.:* Clinical Psychology (provisional)
(404) 671-1200

ILLINOIS SCHOOL OF PROFESSIONAL PSYCHOLOGY—CHICAGO
Two First National Plaza, 20 S. Clark St., Chicago 60603 *Prof. Accred.:* Clinical Psychology
(312) 341-6500

ILLINOIS SCHOOL OF PROFESSIONAL PSYCHOLOGY—ROLLING MEADOWS
One Continental Towers, 1701 Golf Rd., Ste. 101, Rolling Meadows 60008
(708) 290-7400

MINNESOTA SCHOOL OF PROFESSIONAL PSYCHOLOGY—MINNEAPOLIS
3103 E. 80th St., Ste. 2, Minneapolis, MN 55425 *Prof. Accred.:* Clinical Psychology (provisional)
(612) 858-8800

AUGUSTANA COLLEGE
639 38th St., Rock Island 61201 *Type:* Private (Lutheran) liberal arts *Accred.:* 1913/1986 (NCA) *Calendar:* Qtr. plan *Degrees:* B *Prof. Accred.:* Music, Social Work (B), Teacher Education *CEO:* Pres. Thomas Tredway
Enroll: 2,054   (800) 798-8100

AURORA UNIVERSITY
347 S. Gladstone Ave., Aurora 60506-4892 *Type:* Private (Advent Christian) liberal arts *Accred.:* 1938/1989 (NCA) *Calendar:* Sem. plan *Degrees:* B, M *Prof. Accred.:* Nursing (B), Recreation and Leisure Services (B), Social Work (B,M) *CEO:* Pres. Thomas H. Zarle
Enroll: 1,940   (708) 892-6431

NEW COLLEGE OF AURORA UNIVERSITY—LAKE COUNTY CAMPUS
University Ctr., 14 N. Sheridan Rd., Waukegan 60085
(708) 662-0100

SCHOOL OF NURSING/CHICAGO CAMPUS
300 N. Michigan, Ste. 300, Chicago 60601
(312) 357-1080

WISCONSIN ADMINISTRATIVE OFFICE CAMPUS
P.O. Box 51687, New Berlin, WI 53151
(414) 789-6260

BARAT COLLEGE
700 E. Westleigh Rd., Lake Forest 60045
Type: Private (Roman Catholic) liberal arts
Accred.: 1943/1993 (NCA) *Calendar:* Sem.
plan *Degrees:* B *Prof. Accred.:* Nursing (B)
CEO: Pres. Lucy S. Morros
Enroll: 729   (708) 234-3000

BELLEVILLE AREA COLLEGE
2500 Carlyle Rd., Belleville 62221 *Type:*
Public (district) junior *System:* Illinois Com-
munity College Board *Accred.:* 1961/1993
(NCA) *Calendar:* Sem. plan *Degrees:* A, C
Prof. Accred.: Clinical Lab Technology (A),
Medical Assisting (AMA), Medical Record
Technology, Nursing (A), Physical Therapy
Assisting, Radiography, Respiratory Ther-
apy Technology *CEO:* Pres. Joseph J. Cipfl
Enroll: 15,267   (618) 235-2700

BLACK HAWK COLLEGE
6600 34th Ave., Moline 61265 *Type:* Public
(district) junior *System:* Illinois Community
College Board *Accred.:* 1951/1993 (NCA)
Calendar: Sem. plan *Degrees:* A, C *Prof.
Accred.:* Nursing (A), Physical Therapy
Assisting, Respiratory Therapy, Respiratory
Therapy Technology *CEO:* Pres. Judith A.
Redwine
Enroll: 6,943   (309) 796-1311

BLACKBURN COLLEGE
700 College Ave., Carlinville 62626 *Type:*
Private (United Presbyterian) liberal arts
Accred.: 1918/1986 (NCA) *Calendar:* Sem.
plan *Degrees:* B, M *CEO:* Pres. Miriam R.
Pride
Enroll: 534   (217) 854-3231

BLESSING-RIEMAN COLLEGE OF NURSING
Broadway at 11th St., P.O. Box 7005,
Quincy 62301 *Type:* Private professional
Accred.: 1989/1994 (NCA) *Calendar:* Sem.
plan *Degrees:* B *CEO:* Dean Carole Piles
Enroll: 217   (217) 223-5811

BRADLEY UNIVERSITY
1501 W. Bradley Ave., Peoria 61625 *Type:*
Private *Accred.:* 1913/1990 (NCA) *Calendar:* Sem. plan *Degrees:* B, M *Prof. Accred.:*
Accounting (A), Art, Business (B,M), Construction Education (B), Counseling, Engineering Technology (electrical, manufacturing, mechanical), Engineering (civil, electrical, industrial, manufacturing, mechanical),
Music, Nurse Anesthesia Education (M),
Nursing (B), Physical Therapy, Teacher Education *CEO:* Pres. John R. Brazil
Enroll: 6,024   (309) 676-7611

CARL SANDBURG COLLEGE
2232 S. Lake Storey Rd., Galesburg 61401
Type: Public (district) junior *System:* Illinois
Community College Board *Accred.:* 1974/
1991 (NCA) *Calendar:* Sem. plan *Degrees:*
A, C *Prof. Accred.:* Radiography *CEO:* Pres.
Donald G. Crist
Enroll: 3,540   (309) 344-2518

CATHOLIC THEOLOGICAL UNION
5401 S. Cornell Ave., Chicago 60615-5698
Type: Private (Roman Catholic) graduate
only *Accred.:* 1972/1991 (ATS); 1972/1992
(NCA) *Calendar:* Qtr. plan *Degrees:* M, D
CEO: Pres. Norman E. Bevan, C.S.Sp.
Enroll: 344   (312) 324-8000

CHICAGO COLLEGE OF COMMERCE
11 E. Adams St., Chicago 60603 *Type:* Private business *Accred.:* 1968/1986 (ACICS)
Calendar: Qtr. plan *Degrees:* A, C *CEO:*
Chrmn. of the Bd. Mae S. Glassbrenner
(312) 236-3312

THE CHICAGO SCHOOL OF PROFESSIONAL
PSYCHOLOGY
47 West Polk St., Chicago 60605 *Type:* Private professional; graduate only *Accred.:*
1984/1992 (NCA) *Calendar:* Sem. plan
Degrees: D *Prof. Accred.:* Clinical Psychology *CEO:* Pres. Thomas G. Lynch
Enroll: 265   (312) 786-9443

CHICAGO STATE UNIVERSITY
9501 S. King Dr., Chicago 60628-1598
Type: Public (state) liberal arts and teachers
System: Illinois Board of Governors Universities *Accred.:* 1941/1993 (NCA) *Calendar:*

Tri. plan *Degrees:* B, M *Prof. Accred.:* Medical Record Administration, Nursing (B), Occupational Therapy, Teacher Education *CEO:* Pres. Dolores E. Cross
Enroll: 10,108 (312) 995-2000

CHICAGO THEOLOGICAL SEMINARY
5757 S. University Ave., Chicago 60637 *Type:* Private (United Church of Christ) graduate only *Accred.:* 1938/1986 (ATS); 1982/1987 (NCA) *Calendar:* Qtr. plan *Degrees:* M, D *CEO:* Pres. Kenneth B. Smith
Enroll: 205 (312) 752-5757

COLLEGE OF DUPAGE
22nd St. and Lambert Rd., Glen Ellyn 60137 *Type:* Public (district) junior *System:* Illinois Community College Board *Accred.:* 1932/1994 (NCA) *Calendar:* Qtr. plan *Degrees:* A, C *Prof. Accred.:* Medical Record Technology, Nuclear Medicine Technology, Nursing (A), Occupational Therapy Assisting, Radiography, Respiratory Therapy, Respiratory Therapy Technology *CEO:* Pres. Michael T. Murphy
Enroll: 30,237 (708) 858-2800

COLLEGE OF LAKE COUNTY
19351 W. Washington St., Grayslake 60030 *Type:* Public (district) junior *System:* Illinois Community College Board *Accred.:* 1974/1986 (NCA) *Calendar:* Sem. plan *Degrees:* A, C *Prof. Accred.:* Clinical Lab Technology (A), Medical Record Technology, Nursing (A), Radiography *CEO:* Interim Pres. Gretchen J. Naff
Enroll: 14,994 (708) 223-6601

THE COLLEGE OF OFFICE TECHNOLOGY
2nd Fl., 1514-20 W. Division St., Chicago 60622 *Type:* Private business *Accred.:* 1985/1994 (ACICS) *Degrees:* A, C *CEO:* Dir. Pedro A. Galva
(312) 278-0042

COLLEGE OF ST. FRANCIS
500 N. Wilcox St., Joliet 60435 *Type:* Private (Roman Catholic) liberal arts *Accred.:* 1938/1989 (NCA) *Calendar:* Sem. plan *Degrees:* B, M *Prof. Accred.:* Recreation and Leisure Services (B), Social Work (B) *CEO:* Pres. James A. Doppke
Enroll: 4,295 (815) 740-3360

COLUMBIA COLLEGE
600 S. Michigan Ave., Chicago 60605 *Type:* Private liberal arts *Accred.:* 1974/1989 (NCA) *Calendar:* Sem. plan *Degrees:* B, M *CEO:* Pres. John B. Duff
Enroll: 7,620 (312) 663-1600

CONCORDIA UNIVERSITY
7400 Augusta St., River Forest 60305 *Type:* Private (Lutheran-Missouri Synod) *Accred.:* 1950/1992 (NCA) *Calendar:* Qtr. plan *Degrees:* B, M, C *Prof. Accred.:* Clinical Psychology, Nursing (B), Teacher Education *CEO:* Pres. George C. Heider
Enroll: 2,274 (708) 771-8300

DANVILLE AREA COMMUNITY COLLEGE
2000 E. Main St., Danville 61832 *Type:* Public (district) junior *System:* Illinois Community College Board *Accred.:* 1967/1989 (NCA) *Calendar:* Sem. plan *Degrees:* A, C *CEO:* Pres. Harry J. Braun
Enroll: 2,969 (217) 443-1811

DEPAUL UNIVERSITY
25 E. Jackson Blvd., Chicago 60604 *Type:* Private (Roman Catholic) liberal arts and professional *Accred.:* 1925/1987 (NCA) *Calendar:* Qtr. plan *Degrees:* B, M, D, C *Prof. Accred.:* Accounting (A,B,C), Business (B,M), Clinical Psychology, Law, Music, Nurse Anesthesia Education (M), Nursing (B,M), Teacher Education *CEO:* Pres. John P. Minogue
Enroll: 16,747 (312) 362-8300

DEVRY INSTITUTE OF TECHNOLOGY—ADDISON
1221 N. Swift Rd., Addison 60101-6106 *Type:* Private *System:* DeVry Institutes *Accred.:* 1981/1992 (NCA) *Calendar:* Sem. plan *Degrees:* A, B *Prof. Accred.:* Engineering Technology (electrical) *CEO:* Pres. Jerry R. Dill
(708) 953-1300

* Indirect NCA accreditation through DeVry Institutes

DEVRY INSTITUTE OF TECHNOLOGY—CHICAGO
3300 N. Campbell Ave., Chicago 60618-5994 *Type:* Private *System:* DeVry Institutes *Accred.:* 1981/1992 (NCA) *Calendar:* Sem. plan *Degrees:* A, B *Prof. Accred.:* Engineering Technology (electrical) *CEO:* Pres. E. Arthur Stunard
(312) 929-8500

* Indirect NCA accreditation through DeVry Institutes

DR. WILLIAM M. SCHOLL COLLEGE OF PODIATRIC MEDICINE
1001 N. Dearborn St., Chicago 60610 *Type:* Private professional *Accred.:* 1985/1990 (NCA) *Calendar:* Sem. plan *Degrees:* B, D *Prof. Accred.:* Podiatry *CEO:* Pres. Richard B. Patterson
Enroll: 432   (312) 280-2880

EAST-WEST UNIVERSITY
816 S. Michigan Ave., Chicago 60605 *Type:* Private *Accred.:* 1983/1994 (NCA) *Calendar:* Qtr. plan *Degrees:* A, B *CEO:* Chanc. M. Wasi Khan
Enroll: 285   (312) 939-0111

EASTERN ILLINOIS UNIVERSITY
600 Lincoln Ave., Charleston 61920 *Type:* Public (state) *System:* Illinois Board of Governors Universities *Accred.:* 1915/1995 (NCA) *Calendar:* Sem. plan *Degrees:* B, M, P *Prof. Accred.:* Art, Athletic Training, Business (B,M), Dietetics (internship), Home Economics, Journalism (B), Music, Recreation and Leisure Services (B), Speech-Language Pathology, Teacher Education *CEO:* Pres. David L. Jorns
Enroll: 11,301   (217) 581-5000

ELGIN COMMUNITY COLLEGE
1700 Spartan Dr., Elgin 60123 *Type:* Public (district) junior *System:* Illinois Community College Board *Accred.:* 1968/1986 (NCA) *Calendar:* Sem. plan *Degrees:* A, C *Prof. Accred.:* Dental Assisting, Nursing (A) *CEO:* Pres. Roy Flores
Enroll: 9,085   (708) 697-1000

ELMHURST COLLEGE
190 Prospect St., Elmhurst 60126 *Type:* Private (United Church of Christ) liberal arts *Accred.:* 1924/1989 (NCA) *Calendar:* 4-1-4 plan *Degrees:* B *Prof. Accred.:* Nursing (B), Teacher Education *CEO:* Pres. Bryant L. Cureton
Enroll: 2,775   (708) 617-3500

EUREKA COLLEGE
300 E. College Ave., P.O. Box 280, Eureka 61530-0280 *Type:* Private (Disciples of Christ) liberal arts *Accred.:* 1924/1990 (NCA) *Calendar:* Qtr. plan *Degrees:* B *CEO:* Pres. George A. Hearne
Enroll: 473   (309) 467-3721

FRONTIER COMMUNITY COLLEGE
Lot #2 Frontier Dr., Fairfield 62837 *Type:* Public (district) junior *System:* Illinois Eastern Community Colleges System *Accred.:* 1984/1988 (NCA) *Calendar:* Sem. plan *Degrees:* A, C *Prof. Accred.:* Nursing (A) *CEO:* Pres. Richard L. Mason
(618) 842-3711

* Indirect NCA accreditation through Illinois Eastern Community Colleges System

GARRETT-EVANGELICAL THEOLOGICAL SEMINARY
2121 Sheridan Rd., Evanston 60201 *Type:* Private (United Methodist) graduate only *Accred.:* 1938/1988 (ATS); 1972/1988 (NCA) *Calendar:* Qtr. plan *Degrees:* M, D *CEO:* Pres. Neal F. Fisher
Enroll: 528   (708) 866-3900

GEM CITY COLLEGE
700 State St., Quincy 62301 *Type:* Private business *Accred.:* 1954/1998 (ACICS) *Degrees:* A, C *Prof. Accred.:* Medical Assisting *CEO:* Dir. Russell H. Hagenah
(217) 222-0391

GOVERNORS STATE UNIVERSITY
University Park 60466 *Type:* Public (state) liberal arts *System:* Illinois Board of Governors Universities *Accred.:* 1975/1990 (NCA) *Calendar:* Tri. plan *Degrees:* B, M *Prof. Accred.:* Clinical Lab Scientist, Counseling, Health Services Administration, Nursing

(B,M), Social Work (B), Speech-Language Pathology *CEO:* Pres. Paula Wolff
Enroll: 4,259   (708) 534-5000

GREENVILLE COLLEGE
315 E. College Ave., Greenville 62246 *Type:* Private (Free Methodist) liberal arts *Accred.:* 1948/1986 (NCA) *Calendar:* 4-1-4 plan *Degrees:* B *CEO:* Pres. Robert E. Smith
Enroll: 824   (618) 664-1840

HAROLD WASHINGTON COLLEGE
30 E. Lake St., Chicago 60601 *Type:* Public (city) junior *System:* City Colleges of Chicago *Accred.:* 1967/1994 (NCA) *Calendar:* Sem. plan *Degrees:* A, C *CEO:* Pres. Nancy C. DeSombre
Enroll: 8,119   (312) 553-5600

HARRINGTON INSTITUTE OF INTERIOR DESIGN
410 S. Michigan Ave., Chicago 60605 *Type:* Private professional *Calendar:* Sem. plan *Degrees:* A, P *Prof. Accred.:* Art, Interior Design *CEO:* Pres./Dean Robert C. Marks
          (312) 939-4975

HARRY S TRUMAN COLLEGE
1145 W. Wilson Ave., Chicago 60640 *Type:* Public (city) junior *System:* City Colleges of Chicago *Accred.:* 1967/1990 (NCA) *Calendar:* Sem. plan *Degrees:* A, C *Prof. Accred.:* Medical Record Technology *CEO:* Interim Pres. Donald B. Smith
Enroll: 4,862   (312) 878-1700

HEARTLAND COMMUNITY COLLEGE
1226 Towanda Ave., Bloomington 61701 *Type:* Public (district) junior *System:* Illinois Community College Board *Accred.:* 1994 (NCA) *Calendar:* Sem. plan *Degrees:* A, C *CEO:* Pres. Jonathan M. Astroth
Enroll: 2,779   (309) 827-0500

THE HERMAN M. FINCH UNIVERSITY OF HEALTH SCIENCES/THE CHICAGO MEDICAL SCHOOL
3333 Green Bay Rd., North Chicago 60064 *Type:* Private professional *Accred.:* 1980/1988 (NCA) *Calendar:* Qtr. plan *Degrees:* B, M, D *Prof. Accred.:* Clinical Lab Scientist, Clinical Psychology, Medicine, Nursing (B), Physical Therapy, Physician Assist-

ing/Surgeon Assisting *CEO:* CEO/Pres. Herman Finch
Enroll: 1,285   (708) 578-3000

HIGHLAND COMMUNITY COLLEGE
2998 Pearl City Rd., Freeport 61032-9341 *Type:* Public (district) junior *System:* Illinois Community College Board *Accred.:* 1973/1986 (NCA) *Calendar:* Sem. plan *Degrees:* A, C *CEO:* Pres. Ruth Mercedes Smith
Enroll: 2,682   (815) 235-6121

ILLINOIS BENEDICTINE COLLEGE
5700 College Rd., Lisle 60532 *Type:* Private (Roman Catholic) liberal arts *Accred.:* 1958/1986 (NCA) *Calendar:* Sem. plan *Degrees:* B, M *Prof. Accred.:* Nursing (B) *CEO:* Pres. William Carroll
Enroll: 2,602   (708) 960-1500

ILLINOIS CENTRAL COLLEGE
One College Dr., East Peoria 61635 *Type:* Public (district) junior *System:* Illinois Community College Board *Accred.:* 1972/1992 (NCA) *Calendar:* Sem. plan *Degrees:* A, C *Prof. Accred.:* Clinical Lab Technology (A), Dental Assisting, Dental Hygiene, Music, Nursing (A), Occupational Therapy Assisting, Physical Therapy Assisting, Radiography, Respiratory Therapy, Respiratory Therapy Technology, Surgical Technology *CEO:* Pres. Thomas K. Thomas
Enroll: 11,632   (309) 694-5011

ILLINOIS COLLEGE
1101 W. College St., Jacksonville 62650 *Type:* Private (United Presbyterian/United Church of Christ) liberal arts *Accred.:* 1913/1995 (NCA) *Calendar:* Sem. plan *Degrees:* B *CEO:* Pres. Richard A. Pfau
Enroll: 986   (217) 245-3000

ILLINOIS COLLEGE OF OPTOMETRY
3241 S. Michigan Ave., Chicago 60616 *Type:* Private professional *Accred.:* 1969/1989 (NCA) *Calendar:* Qtr. plan *Degrees:* B, D *Prof. Accred.:* Optometric Residency, Optometry *CEO:* Pres. Boyd B. Banwell
Enroll: 604   (312) 225-1700

ILLINOIS INSTITUTE OF TECHNOLOGY
3300 S. Federal St., Chicago 60616 *Type:* Private *Accred.:* 1941/1987 (NCA) *Calendar:* Sem. plan *Degrees:* B, M, D *Prof. Accred.:* Clinical Psychology, Engineering (aerospace, chemical, civil, electrical, mechanical, metallurgical), Law, Rehabilitation Counseling *CEO:* Pres. Lewis Collens
Enroll: 7,157   (312) 567-3000

DANIEL F. AND ADA L. RICE CAMPUS
201 E. Loop Rd., Wheaton 60187-8489
        (708) 682-6000

DOWNTOWN CENTER CAMPUS
565 W. Adams St., Chicago 60661-3601
        (312) 906-5000

NATIONAL CENTER FOR FOOD SAFETY AND TECHNOLOGY
65th St. & Archer Ave., Summit-Argo 60501-1933
        (708) 563-1576

ILLINOIS STATE UNIVERSITY
Campus Box 1000, Normal 61790-1000 *Type:* Public (state) *System:* Regency Universities System Board of Regents *Accred.:* 1913/1995 (NCA) *Calendar:* Sem. plan *Degrees:* B, M, P, D, C *Prof. Accred.:* Accounting (A,C), Art, Audiology, Business (B,M), Counseling, Home Economics, Medical Record Administration, Music, Psychology Internship, Recreation and Leisure Services (B), Social Work (B), Speech-Language Pathology, Teacher Education, Theatre *CEO:* Pres. David A. Strand
Enroll: 19,604   (309) 438-2111

ILLINOIS VALLEY COMMUNITY COLLEGE
815 N. Orlando Smith Ave., Oglesby 61348 *Type:* Public (district) junior *System:* Illinois Community College Board *Accred.:* 1929/1988 (NCA) *Calendar:* Sem. plan *Degrees:* A, C *Prof. Accred.:* Dental Assisting, Nursing (A) *CEO:* Pres. Alfred E. Wisgoski
Enroll: 4,263   (815) 224-2720

ILLINOIS WESLEYAN UNIVERSITY
P.O. Box 2900, Bloomington 61702 *Type:* Private (United Methodist) *Accred.:* 1916/1993 (NCA) *Calendar:* Sem. plan *Degrees:*

B *Prof. Accred.:* Music, Nursing (B) *CEO:* Pres. Minor Myers, Jr.
Enroll: 1,855   (309) 556-1000

INSTITUTE FOR CLINICAL SOCIAL WORK, INC.
68 E. Wacker Pl., Ste. 1400, Chicago 60601-7202 *Type:* Private professional; graduate only *Accred.:* 1994 (NCA) *Calendar:* Sem. plan *Degrees:* D *CEO:* Pres. Thomas K. Kenemore
Enroll: 72   (312) 726-8480

INTERNATIONAL ACADEMY OF MERCHANDISING AND DESIGN
One N. State St., No. 400, Chicago 60602 *Type:* Private senior *Accred.:* 1981/1998 (ACICS) *Calendar:* Qtr. plan *Degrees:* A, B, C *Prof. Accred.:* Interior Design *CEO:* Pres. Linda Weldon
        (312) 541-3910

JOHN A. LOGAN COLLEGE
Rural Rte. 2, Carterville 62918 *Type:* Public (district) junior *System:* Illinois Community College Board *Accred.:* 1972/1987 (NCA) *Calendar:* Sem. plan *Degrees:* A, C *Prof. Accred.:* Dental Assisting *CEO:* Pres. J. Ray Hancock
Enroll: 4,889   (618) 985-3741

THE JOHN MARSHALL LAW SCHOOL
315 S. Plymouth Ct., Chicago 60604 *Type:* Private professional *Calendar:* Sem. plan *Degrees:* M, P *Prof. Accred.:* Law *CEO:* Dean R. Gilbert Johnston
Enroll: 1,198   (312) 427-2737

JOHN WOOD COMMUNITY COLLEGE
150 S. 48th St., Quincy 62301 *Type:* Public (district) junior *System:* Illinois Community College Board *Accred.:* 1980/1992 (NCA) *Calendar:* Sem. plan *Degrees:* A, C *CEO:* Pres. Robert C. Keys
Enroll: 2,161   (217) 224-6500

JOLIET JUNIOR COLLEGE
1215 Houbolt Rd., Joliet 60431-8938 *Type:* Public (district) junior *System:* Illinois Community College Board *Accred.:* 1917/1992 (NCA) *Calendar:* Sem. plan *Degrees:* A, C

Prof. Accred.: Nursing (A) *CEO:* Pres. Thomas E. Gamble
Enroll: 10,369   (815) 729-9020 x2207

JUDSON COLLEGE
1151 N. State St., Elgin 60123 *Type:* Private *Accred.:* 1973/1988 (NCA) *Calendar:* Tri. plan *Degrees:* B *CEO:* Pres. James W. Didier
Enroll: 706   (708) 695-2500

KANKAKEE COMMUNITY COLLEGE
P.O. Box 888, Kankakee 60901 *Type:* Public (district) junior *System:* Illinois Community College Board *Accred.:* 1974/1994 (NCA) *Calendar:* 4-1-4 plan *Degrees:* A, C *Prof. Accred.:* Clinical Lab Technology (A), Radiography, Respiratory Therapy Technology *CEO:* Pres. Lawrence D. Huffman
Enroll: 3,853   (815) 933-0345

KASKASKIA COLLEGE
27210 College Rd., Centralia 62801 *Type:* Public (district) junior *System:* Illinois Community College Board *Accred.:* 1964/1989 (NCA) *Calendar:* Sem. plan *Degrees:* A, C *Prof. Accred.:* Dental Assisting, Nursing (A), Physical Therapy Assisting, Radiography, Respiratory Therapy Technology *CEO:* Pres. Alice M. Mumaw
Enroll: 3,379   (800) 642-0859

KELLER GRADUATE SCHOOL OF MANAGEMENT
One Tower Ln., Oakbrook Terrace 60181 *Type:* Private professional *Accred.:* 1977/1992 (NCA) *Calendar:* Qtr. plan *Degrees:* M *CEO:* Pres./CEO Ronald L. Taylor
Enroll: 2,578   (708) 571-7700

EAST VALLEY CENTER CAMPUS
1201 S. Alma School Rd., Ste. 5450, Mesa, AZ 85210
          (602) 827-1511

KANSAS CITY DOWNTOWN CAMPUS
City Center Sq., 1100 Main St., Kansas City, MO 64105-2112
          (816) 221-1300

KANSAS CITY SOUTH CAMPUS
11224 Holmes Rd., Kansas City, MO 64131
          (816) 941-2224

MILWAUKEE CENTER CAMPUS
330 E. Kilbourn Ave., Milwaukee, WI 53202-3141
          (414) 278-7677

NORTH SUBURBAN CENTER CAMPUS
Tri-State Intl. Office Ctr., Bldg. 25, Ste. 130, Lincolnshire 60069-4460
          (708) 940-7768

NORTHWEST SUBURBAN CENTER CAMPUS
1051 Perimeter Dr., Schaumburg 60173-5009
          (708) 330-0040

PHOENIX/NORTHWEST CENTER CAMPUS
2149 W. Dunlap Ave., Phoenix, AZ 85021
          (602) 870-0117

SOUTH SUBURBAN CENTER CAMPUS
15255 S. 94th Ave., Orland Park 60462-3823
          (708) 460-9580

WAUKESHA CENTER CAMPUS
20935 Swenson Dr., Waukesha, WI 53186
          (414) 798-9889

WEST SUBURBAN CENTER CAMPUS
1101 31st St., Downers Grove 60515-5515
          (708) 969-6624

KENDALL COLLEGE
2408 Orrington Ave., Evanston 60201 *Type:* Private (United Methodist) liberal arts *Accred.:* 1962/1993 (NCA) *Calendar:* 4-1-4 plan *Degrees:* A, B, C *CEO:* Pres. Thomas J. Kerr, IV
Enroll: 508   (708) 866-1300

KENNEDY-KING COLLEGE
6800 S. Wentworth Ave., Chicago 60621 *Type:* Public (city) junior *System:* City Colleges of Chicago *Accred.:* 1967/1988 (NCA) *Calendar:* Sem. plan *Degrees:* A, C *CEO:* Pres. Wayne D. Watson
Enroll: 2,502   (312) 602-5000

KISHWAUKEE COLLEGE
21193 Malta Rd., Malta 60150 *Type:* Public (district) junior *System:* Illinois Community

College Board *Accred.:* 1974/1989 (NCA) *Calendar:* Sem. plan *Degrees:* A, C *Prof. Accred.:* Radiography *CEO:* Pres. Norman L. Jenkins
Enroll: 3,407   (815) 825-2086

KNOWLEDGE SYSTEMS INSTITUTE
3420 Main St., Skokie 60076 *Type:* Private *Accred.:* 1991 (NCA) *Calendar:* Qtr. plan *Degrees:* M *CEO:* Pres. Shi-Kuo Chang
Enroll: 58   (708) 679-3135

KNOX COLLEGE
Galesburg 61401 *Type:* Private liberal arts *Accred.:* 1913/1989 (NCA) *Calendar:* 3-3 plan *Degrees:* B *CEO:* Pres. Frederick C. Nahm
Enroll: 1,056   (309) 343-0112

LAKE FOREST COLLEGE
555 N. Sheridan Rd., Lake Forest 60045 *Type:* Private (United Presbyterian) liberal arts *Accred.:* 1913/1987 (NCA) *Calendar:* Qtr. plan *Degrees:* B, M *CEO:* Pres. David Spadafora
Enroll: 1,004   (708) 234-3100

LAKE FOREST GRADUATE SCHOOL OF MANAGEMENT
280 N. Sheridan Rd., Lake Forest 60045 *Type:* Private graduate only *Accred.:* 1978/ 1993 (NCA) *Calendar:* Qtr. plan *Degrees:* M *CEO:* Pres. Raymond E. Britt, Jr.
Enroll: 660   (708) 234-5005

LAKE LAND COLLEGE
5001 Lake Land Blvd., Mattoon 61938 *Type:* Public (district) junior *System:* Illinois Community College Board *Accred.:* 1973/1995 (NCA) *Calendar:* Qtr. plan *Degrees:* A, C *Prof. Accred.:* Dental Hygiene, Nursing (A), Physical Therapy Assisting, Practical Nursing *CEO:* Pres. Robert K. Luther
Enroll: 4,831   (217) 234-5253

LAKEVIEW COLLEGE OF NURSING
812 N. Logan Ave., Danville 61832 *Type:* Private professional *Accred.:* 1995 (NCA)

Calendar: Sem. plan *Degrees:* B *CEO:* Pres. Irene A. Steward
Enroll: 122   (217) 443-5238

LEWIS AND CLARK COMMUNITY COLLEGE
5800 Godfrey Rd., Godfrey 62035 *Type:* Public (district) junior *System:* Illinois Community College Board *Accred.:* 1971/1993 (NCA) *Calendar:* Sem. plan *Degrees:* A, C *Prof. Accred.:* Clinical Lab Technology (A), Dental Assisting, Nursing (A) *CEO:* Pres. Dale T. Chapman
Enroll: 5,534   (618) 466-3411

LEWIS UNIVERSITY
Rte. 53, Romeoville 60441 *Type:* Private (Roman Catholic) liberal arts *Accred.:* 1963/ 1987 (NCA) *Calendar:* 4-1-4 plan *Degrees:* A, B, M, C *Prof. Accred.:* Nursing (B,M) *CEO:* Pres. James Gaffney, F.S.C.
Enroll: 4,399   (815) 838-0500

LEXINGTON COLLEGE
10840 S. Western Ave., Chicago 60643 *Type:* Private *Accred.:* 1993 (NCA) *Calendar:* Sem. plan *Degrees:* A *CEO:* Pres. Ana Maria Boza
Enroll: 39   (312) 779-3800

LINCOLN CHRISTIAN COLLEGE
100 Campus View Dr., Lincoln 62656 *Type:* Private (Christian Churches/Churches of Christ) *Accred.:* 1954/1985 (AABC); 1991 (ATS); 1991 (NCA) *Calendar:* Sem. plan *Degrees:* A, B, C *CEO:* Pres. Charles A. McNeely
Enroll: 474   (217) 732-3168

LINCOLN COLLEGE
300 Keokuk St., Lincoln 62656 *Type:* Private junior *Accred.:* 1929/1994 (NCA) *Calendar:* 4-1-4 plan *Degrees:* A, C *CEO:* Pres. Jack D. Nutt
Enroll: 1,105   (217) 732-3155

LINCOLN LAND COMMUNITY COLLEGE
Shepherd Rd., Springfield 62794 *Type:* Public (district) junior *System:* Illinois Community College Board *Accred.:* 1973/1993 (NCA) *Calendar:* Sem. plan *Degrees:* A, C

Prof. Accred.: Nursing (A), Radiography, Respiratory Therapy *CEO:* Pres. Norman L. Stephens
Enroll: 7,473   (217) 786-2200

LINCOLN TRAIL COLLEGE
11220 State Hwy. 1, Robinson 62454 *Type:* Public (district) junior *System:* Illinois Eastern Community Colleges System *Accred.:* 1984/1988 (NCA) *Calendar:* Sem. plan *Degrees:* A, C *Prof. Accred.:* Nursing (A) *CEO:* Interim Pres. John Arabatgis
                                  (618) 544-8657

* Indirect NCA accreditation through Illinois Eastern Community Colleges System

LOYOLA UNIVERSITY OF CHICAGO
820 N. Michigan Ave., Chicago 60611 *Type:* Private (Roman Catholic) *Accred.:* 1921/1995 (NCA) *Calendar:* Sem. plan *Degrees:* B, M, D *Prof. Accred.:* Business (B,M), Clinical Psychology, Counseling Psychology, General Practice Residency, Law, Medicine, Nursing (B,M), Oral and Maxillofacial Surgery, Social Work (B,M), Theatre (A) *CEO:* Pres. John J. Piderit, S.J.
Enroll: 13,806   (312) 915-6000

LUTHERAN SCHOOL OF THEOLOGY AT CHICAGO
1100 E. 55th St., Chicago 60615-5199 *Type:* Private (Evangelical Lutheran) graduate only *Accred.:* 1945/1987 (ATS); 1982/1987 (NCA) *Calendar:* Qtr. plan *Degrees:* M, D, C *CEO:* Pres. William E. Lesher
Enroll: 385   (312) 753-0700

MACCORMAC JUNIOR COLLEGE
506 S. Wabash Ave., Chicago 60605 *Type:* Private *Accred.:* 1979/1989 (NCA) *Calendar:* Qtr. plan *Degrees:* A *CEO:* Pres. John Henry Allen
Enroll: 357   (312) 922-1884

ELMHURST CAMPUS
615 N. West Avenue, Elmhurst 60126 junior *Accred.:* 1979/1989 (NCA) *Calendar:* Qtr. plan *Degrees:* A, C
Enroll: 416   (708) 941-1200

MACMURRAY COLLEGE
447 E. College Ave., Jacksonville 62650 *Type:* Private (United Methodist) liberal arts *Accred.:* 1921/1989 (NCA) *Calendar:* 4-1-4 plan *Degrees:* A, B *Prof. Accred.:* Nursing (B), Social Work (B-candidate) *CEO:* Pres. Edward J. Mitchell
Enroll: 1,382   (217) 479-7025

MALCOLM X COLLEGE
1900 W. Van Buren St., Chicago 60612 *Type:* Public (city) junior *System:* City Colleges of Chicago *Accred.:* 1967/1991 (NCA) *Calendar:* Sem. plan *Degrees:* A, C *Prof. Accred.:* Clinical Lab Technology (A), Funeral Service Education (Mortuary Science), Perfusion, Physician Assisting/Surgeon Assisting, Radiography, Respiratory Therapy *CEO:* Pres. Zerrie D. Campbell
Enroll: 3,185   (312) 850-7000

MCCORMICK THEOLOGICAL SEMINARY
5555 S. Woodlawn Ave., Chicago 60637 *Type:* Private (Presbyterian) graduate only *Accred.:* 1938/1987 (ATS); 1982/1987 (NCA) *Calendar:* Qtr. plan *Degrees:* M, D *CEO:* Pres. Cynthia M. Campbell
Enroll: 561   (312) 947-6300

MCHENRY COUNTY COLLEGE
8900 U.S. Hwy. 14, Crystal Lake 60012-2761 *Type:* Public (district) junior *System:* Illinois Community College Board *Accred.:* 1976/1992 (NCA) *Calendar:* Sem. plan *Degrees:* A, C *CEO:* Pres. Robert C. Bartlett
Enroll: 4,841   (815) 455-3700

MCKENDREE COLLEGE
701 College Rd., Lebanon 62254 *Type:* Private (United Methodist) liberal arts *Accred.:* 1970/1989 (NCA) *Calendar:* 4-1-4 plan *Degrees:* A, B *Prof. Accred.:* Nursing (B) *CEO:* Pres. Jim Dennis
Enroll: 1,632   (618) 537-4481

MEADVILLE/LOMBARD THEOLOGICAL SCHOOL
5701 S. Woodlawn Ave., Chicago 60637 *Type:* Private (Unitarian Universalist) graduate only *Accred.:* 1940/1987 (ATS) *Calendar:* Qtr. plan *Degrees:* M, D *CEO:* Pres./Dean Spencer Lavan
Enroll: 73   (312) 753-3195

MENNONITE COLLEGE OF NURSING
804 N. East St., Bloomington 61701 *Type:*
Private *Accred.:* 1985/1991 (NCA) *Calendar:* Qtr. plan *Degrees:* B *Prof. Accred.:*
Nursing (B) *CEO:* Pres. Kathleen Hogan
Enroll: 166   (309) 829-0715

MIDSTATE COLLEGE
244 S.W. Jefferson St., Peoria 61602 *Type:*
Private junior *Accred.:* 1982/1992 (NCA)
Calendar: Qtr. plan *Degrees:* A, C *Prof.
Accred.:* Medical Assisting (AMA) *CEO:*
Pres. R. Dale Bunch
Enroll: 407   (309) 673-6365

CARTHAGE CAMPUS
30 S. Washington, Carthage 62321
                                (217) 357-6626

MIDWESTERN UNIVERSITY
555 31st St., Downers Grove 60515 *Type:*
Private professional *Accred.:* 1993 (NCA)
Calendar: Sem. plan *Degrees:* B, D *Prof.
Accred.:* Osteopathy, Physician Assisting/
Surgeon Assisting *CEO:* Pres. Jack B.
Kinsinger
Enroll: 1,009   (708) 515-6060

MILLIKIN UNIVERSITY
1184 W. Main St., Decatur 62522 *Type:* Private (United Presbyterian) liberal arts and
professional *Accred.:* 1914/1987 (NCA)
Calendar: 4-1-4 plan *Degrees:* B *Prof.
Accred.:* Music, Nursing (B) *CEO:* Pres.
Curtis L. McCray
Enroll: 1,862   (217) 424-6211

MONMOUTH COLLEGE
700 E. Broadway, Monmouth 61462 *Type:*
Private (United Presbyterian) liberal arts
Accred.: 1913/1988 (NCA) *Calendar:* 3-3
plan *Degrees:* B *CEO:* Pres. Sue A. Huseman
Enroll: 837   (309) 457-2311

MOODY BIBLE INSTITUTE
820 N. La Salle Dr., Chicago 60610 *Type:*
Private (interdenominational) *Accred.:* 1951/
1992 (AABC); 1989/1995 (NCA) *Calendar:*
Sem. plan *Degrees:* A, B, M, C *Prof. Accred.:*
Music *CEO:* Pres. Joseph Stowell, III
Enroll: 5,697   (312) 329-4000

MORAINE VALLEY COMMUNITY COLLEGE
10900 S. 88th Ave., Palos Hills 60465 *Type:*
Public (district) junior *System:* Illinois Community College Board *Accred.:* 1975/1986
(NCA) *Calendar:* Sem. plan *Degrees:* A, C
Prof. Accred.: Clinical Lab Technology (A),
Medical Record Technology, Nursing (A),
Radiography, Respiratory Therapy *CEO:*
Pres. Vernon O. Crawley
Enroll: 13,273   (708) 974-4300

MORRISON INSTITUTE OF TECHNOLOGY
P.O. Box 410, Morrison 61270-0410 *Type:*
Private 2-year *Calendar:* Sem. plan
Degrees: A *Prof. Accred.:* Engineering
Technology (general) *CEO:* CEO Don D.
Vandercreek
Enroll: 250   (815) 772-7218

MORTON COLLEGE
3801 S. Central Ave., Cicero 60650 *Type:*
Public (district) junior *System:* Illinois Community College Board *Accred.:* 1927/1994
(NCA) *Calendar:* Sem. plan *Degrees:* A, C
Prof. Accred.: Dental Assisting, Physical
Therapy Assisting *CEO:* Pres. John Neuhaus
Enroll: 3,977   (708) 656-8000

NAES COLLEGE
2838 W. Peterson Ave., Chicago 60659 *Type:*
Private *Accred.:* 1984/1989 (NCA) *Calendar:* Sem. plan *Degrees:* B *CEO:* Pres. Faith
Smith
Enroll: 118   (312) 761-5000

NATIONAL COLLEGE OF CHIROPRACTIC
200 E. Roosevelt Rd., Lombard 60148 *Type:*
Private professional *Accred.:* 1981/1986
(NCA) *Calendar:* Tri. plan *Degrees:* B, D
Prof. Accred.: Chiropractic Education *CEO:*
Pres. James F. Winterstein
Enroll: 790   (708) 826-6285

NATIONAL-LOUIS UNIVERSITY
2840 Sheridan Rd., Evanston 60201 *Type:*
Private liberal arts and business *Accred.:*
1946/1991 (NCA) *Calendar:* Qtr. plan
Degrees: B, M, P, D, C *Prof. Accred.:* Clinical Lab Scientist, Radiation Therapy Technology, Respiratory Therapy *CEO:* Pres.
Orley R. Herron
Enroll: 2,727   (708) 475-1100

ATLANTA ACADEMIC CENTER CAMPUS
Blackstone Ctr., 1777 N.E. Expressway, Ste. 250, Atlanta, GA 30329
(404) 633-1223

CHICAGO CAMPUS
18 S. Michigan Ave., Chicago 60603
(312) 621-9650

ELGIN FACILITY CAMPUS
400 Federation Pl., Elgin 60123
(708) 695-6070

EVANSTON CAMPUS
2840 Sheridan Rd., Evanston 60201-1796
(708) 475-1100

HEIDELBERG ACADEMIC CENTER CAMPUS
Rohrbacher Strasse 47, Heidelberg Germany 69115
[011] (49) 6221-29025

MILWAUKEE/BELOIT ACADEMIC CENTER CAMPUS
325 N. Corporate Dr., Ste. 200, Brookfield, WI 53045-5861
(414) 792-3699

NORTHERN VIRGINIA/WASHINGTON, DC ACADEMIC CENTER CAMPUS
8000 Westpark Dr., Ste. 125, McLean, VA 22102
(703) 749-3000

ST. LOUIS ACADEMIC CENTER CAMPUS
12412 Powerscourt Dr., Ste. LL20, St. Louis, MO 63131
(314) 822-2110

TAMPA ACADEMIC CENTER CAMPUS
4890 W. Kennedy Blvd., Ste. 145, Tampa, FL 33609
(813) 286-8087

WHEATON CAMPUS
200 S. Naperville Rd., Wheaton 60187
(708) 668-3838

WHEELING CAMPUS
1000 Capitol Dr., Wheeling 60090
(708) 465-0575

NORTH CENTRAL COLLEGE
30 N. Brainard St., P.O. Box 3063, Naperville 60566-7063 *Type:* Private (United Methodist) liberal arts *Accred.:* 1914/1990 (NCA) *Calendar:* 3-3 plan *Degrees:* B, M *CEO:* Pres. Harold R. Wilde *Enroll:* 2,437   (708) 420-3400

NORTH PARK COLLEGE AND THEOLOGICAL SEMINARY
3225 W. Foster Ave., Chicago 60625-4895 *Type:* Private (Evangelical Covenant) liberal arts and theology *Accred.:* 1963/1986 (ATS); 1926/1991 (NCA) *Calendar:* 3-3 plan *Degrees:* B, M *Prof. Accred.:* Music, Nursing (B) *CEO:* Pres. David G. Horner *Enroll:* 1,654   (312) 244-6200

NORTHEASTERN ILLINOIS UNIVERSITY
5500 N. St. Louis Ave., Chicago 60625 *Type:* Public (state) liberal arts and teachers *System:* Illinois Board of Governors Universities *Accred.:* 1961/1987 (NCA) *Calendar:* Tri. plan *Degrees:* B, M *Prof. Accred.:* Counseling, Social Work (B) *CEO:* Acting Pres. Salme H. Steinberg
Enroll: 10,228   (312) 583-4050

NORTHERN BAPTIST THEOLOGICAL SEMINARY
660 E. Butterfield Rd., Lombard 60148 *Type:* Private (Baptist) graduate only *Accred.:* 1968/1992 (ATS); 1947/1993 (NCA) *Calendar:* Qtr. plan *Degrees:* M, D *CEO:* Pres. Ian M. Chapman
Enroll: 233   (708) 620-2100

NORTHERN ILLINOIS UNIVERSITY
Lowden Hall 301, De Kalb 60115 *Type:* Public (state) *System:* Regency Universities System Board of Regents *Accred.:* 1915/1994 (NCA) *Calendar:* Sem. plan *Degrees:* B, M, P, D, C *Prof. Accred.:* Accounting (A,C), Art, Audiology, Business (B,M), Clinical Lab Scientist, Clinical Psychology, Counseling, Dietetics (internship), Engineering (electrical, industrial, mechanical), Journalism (B,M), Law, Marriage and Family Therapy (M), Music, Nursing (B,M), Physical Therapy, Psychology Internship, Public Administration, Rehabilitation Counseling, Speech-Language Pathology, Teacher

Education, Theatre *CEO:* Pres. John E. LaTourette
Enroll: 22,881 (815) 753-9500

NORTHWESTERN BUSINESS COLLEGE
4829 N. Lipps Ave., Chicago 60630 *Type:* Private business *Accred.:* 1974/1998 (ACICS); 1991/1995 (NCA candidate) *Calendar:* Qtr. plan *Degrees:* A, C *Prof. Accred.:* Medical Assisting (AMA) *CEO:* Pres. Lawrence W. Schumacher
Enroll: 1,079 (312) 777-4220

SOUTHWESTERN CAMPUS
8020 W. 87th St., Hickory Hills 60457 *Accred.:* 1989 (ACICS)
(708) 430-0990

NORTHWESTERN UNIVERSITY
633 Clark St., Evanston 60208 *Type:* Private *Accred.:* 1913/1995 (NCA) *Calendar:* Sem. plan *Degrees:* B, M, D *Prof. Accred.:* Audiology, Business (M), Clinical Psychology, Combined Prosthodontics, Counseling Psychology, Dentistry, Endodontics, Engineering (bioengineering, chemical, civil, electrical, environmental/sanitary, industrial, materials, mechanical), General Dentistry, Health Services Administration, Journalism (B,M), Law, Medicine, Music, Oral and Maxillofacial Surgery, Orthodontics, Pediatric Dentistry, Periodontics, Physical Therapy, Psychology Internship, Speech-Language Pathology, Theatre *CEO:* Pres. Henry S. Bienen
Enroll: 17,688 (708) 491-3741

OAKTON COMMUNITY COLLEGE
1600 E. Golf Rd., Des Plaines 60016 *Type:* Public (district) junior *System:* Illinois Community College Board *Accred.:* 1976/ 1988 (NCA) *Calendar:* Sem. plan *Degrees:* A, C *Prof. Accred.:* Clinical Lab Technology (A), Medical Record Technology, Nursing (A), Physical Therapy Assisting *CEO:* Pres. Margaret Lee
Enroll: 11,660 (708) 635-1600

OLIVE-HARVEY COLLEGE
10001 S. Woodlawn Ave., Chicago 60628 *Type:* Public (city) junior *System:* City Colleges of Chicago *Accred.:* 1967/1990 (NCA)

Calendar: Sem. plan *Degrees:* A, C *CEO:* Pres. Lawrence Cox
Enroll: 3,306 (312) 291-6100

OLIVET NAZARENE UNIVERSITY
Kankakee 60901 *Type:* Private (Nazarene) liberal arts *Accred.:* 1956/1995 (NCA) *Calendar:* Sem. plan *Degrees:* A, B, M, C *Prof. Accred.:* Music, Nursing (B), Social Work (B-candidate) *CEO:* Pres. John Carl Bowling
Enroll: 2,259 (815) 939-5011

OLNEY CENTRAL COLLEGE
305 N. West St., Olney 62450 *Type:* Public (district) junior *System:* Illinois Eastern Community Colleges System *Accred.:* 1984/ 1988 (NCA) *Calendar:* Sem. plan *Degrees:* A, C *Prof. Accred.:* Nursing (A), Radiography *CEO:* Pres. Edward J. Covey
Enroll: 1,500 (618) 395-4351

* Indirect NCA accreditation through Illinois Eastern Community Colleges System

PARKLAND COLLEGE
2400 W. Bradley Ave., Champaign 61821 *Type:* Public (district) junior *System:* Illinois Community College Board *Accred.:* 1972/ 1993 (NCA) *Calendar:* Sem. plan *Degrees:* A, C *Prof. Accred.:* Dental Assisting, Dental Hygiene, Engineering Technology (electrical), Nursing (A), Occupational Therapy Assisting, Practical Nursing (warning), Radiation Therapy Technology, Radiography, Respiratory Therapy, Surgical Technology, Veterinary Technology *CEO:* Pres. Zelema M. Harris
Enroll: 8,463 (217) 351-2200

PRAIRIE STATE COLLEGE
202 S. Halsted St., Chicago Heights 60411 *Type:* Public (district) junior *System:* Illinois Community College Board *Accred.:* 1965/ 1989 (NCA) *Calendar:* Sem. plan *Degrees:* A, C *Prof. Accred.:* Dental Hygiene, Nursing (A) *CEO:* Pres. E. Timothy Lightfield
Enroll: 5,301 (708) 756-3110

PRINCIPIA COLLEGE
Elsah 62028 *Type:* Private liberal arts *Accred.:* 1923/1995 (NCA) *Calendar:* Qtr. plan *Degrees:* B *CEO:* Pres. David E. Pfeifer
Enroll: 560   (618) 374-2131

QUINCY UNIVERSITY
1800 College Ave., Quincy 62301 *Type:* Private (Roman Catholic) liberal arts *Accred.:* 1954/1992 (NCA) *Calendar:* Sem. plan *Degrees:* B, M *Prof. Accred.:* Music *CEO:* Pres. James F. Toal, O.F.M.
Enroll: 1,164   (217) 222-8020

RAY COLLEGE OF DESIGN
401 N. Wabash St., Chicago 60611-3532 *Type:* Private *Accred.:* 1975/1988 (ACCSCT) *Calendar:* Sem. plan *Degrees:* A, B *CEO:* Pres. Wade F. Ray
                                           (312) 280-3500

SCHAUMBURG CAMPUS
1051 Perimeter Dr., Schaumburg 60173-5070 *Accred.:* 1988/1993 (ACCSCT)
                                           (708) 619-3450

REND LAKE COLLEGE
Rural Rte. 1, Ina 62846 *Type:* Public (district) junior *System:* Illinois Community College Board *Accred.:* 1969/1989 (NCA) *Calendar:* Sem. plan *Degrees:* A, C *CEO:* Pres. Mark S. Kern
Enroll: 3,195   (618) 437-5321

RICHARD J. DALEY COLLEGE
7500 S. Pulaski Rd., Chicago 60652 *Type:* Public (city) junior *System:* City Colleges of Chicago *Accred.:* 1967/1991 (NCA) *Calendar:* Sem. plan *Degrees:* A, C *CEO:* Pres. Ted Martinez, Jr.
Enroll: 4,749   (312) 838-7500

RICHLAND COMMUNITY COLLEGE
One College Park, Decatur 62521 *Type:* Public (district) junior *System:* Illinois Community College Board *Accred.:* 1978/1993 (NCA) *Calendar:* Qtr. plan *Degrees:* A, C *CEO:* Pres. Charles R. Novak
Enroll: 3,801   (217) 875-7200

ROBERT MORRIS COLLEGE
180 N. La Salle St., Chicago 60601 *Type:* Private *Accred.:* 1986/1991 (NCA) *Calendar:* Qtr. plan *Degrees:* A, B, C *Prof. Accred.:* Medical Assisting (AMA) *CEO:* Pres. Michael P. Viollt
Enroll: 2,974   (312) 836-4888

ROCK VALLEY COLLEGE
3301 N. Mulford Rd., Rockford 61114 *Type:* Public (district) junior *System:* Illinois Community College Board *Accred.:* 1971/1994 (NCA) *Calendar:* Sem. plan *Degrees:* A, C *Prof. Accred.:* Respiratory Therapy, Respiratory Therapy Technology *CEO:* Pres. Karl J. Jacobs
Enroll: 8,906   (815) 654-4250

ROCKFORD BUSINESS COLLEGE
730 N. Church St., Rockford 61103 *Type:* Private business *Accred.:* 1968/1987 (ACICS) *Calendar:* Qtr. plan *Degrees:* A, C *CEO:* Pres./Chrmn. of the Bd. David G. Swank
                                           (815) 965-8616

ROCKFORD COLLEGE
5050 E. State St., Rockford 61108 *Type:* Private liberal arts *Accred.:* 1913/1994 (NCA) *Calendar:* 4-1-4 plan *Degrees:* B, M *Prof. Accred.:* Nursing (B) *CEO:* Pres. William A. Shields
Enroll: 1,591   (815) 226-4000

ROOSEVELT UNIVERSITY
430 S. Michigan Ave., Chicago 60605 *Type:* Private *Accred.:* 1946/1986 (NCA) *Calendar:* Sem. plan *Degrees:* B, M, D, C *Prof. Accred.:* Music, Teacher Education *CEO:* Pres. Theodore L. Gross
Enroll: 6,696   (312) 341-3500

ROSARY COLLEGE
7900 W. Division St., River Forest 60305 *Type:* Private (Roman Catholic) liberal arts *Accred.:* 1919/1995 (NCA) *Calendar:* Sem. plan *Degrees:* B, M, C *Prof. Accred.:* Librarianship *CEO:* Pres. Donna M. Carroll
Enroll: 851   (708) 366-2490

RUSH UNIVERSITY
  1653 W. Congress Pkwy., Chicago 60612
  Type: Private professional *Accred.:* 1974/
  1988 (NCA) *Calendar:* Qtr. plan *Degrees:*
  B, M, D *Prof. Accred.:* Audiology, Clinical
  Lab Scientist, Health Services Administra-
  tion, Medicine, Nurse Anesthesia Education
  (M), Nursing (B,M), Occupational Therapy,
  Perfusion, Speech-Language Pathology
  CEO: Pres. Leo M. Henikoff
  Enroll: 1,321   (312) 942-7120

ST. ANTHONY COLLEGE OF NURSING
  5658 E. State St., Rockford 61108-2468
  Type: Private professional *Accred.:* 1994
  (NCA) *Calendar:* Sem. plan *Degrees:* B
  CEO: Dean Terri Burch
  Enroll: 104   (815) 395-5091

ST. AUGUSTINE COLLEGE
  1333 W. Argyle St., Chicago 60640 *Type:*
  Private (Episcopal) *Accred.:* 1987/1992
  (NCA) *Calendar:* Sem. plan *Degrees:* A, C
  Prof. Accred.: Respiratory Therapy *CEO:*
  Pres. Carlos A. Plazas
  Enroll: 1,346   (312) 878-8756

ST. FRANCIS MEDICAL CENTER COLLEGE OF
NURSING
  511 N.E. Greenleaf St., Peoria 61603 *Type:*
  Private professional *Accred.:* 1991 (NCA)
  Calendar: Qtr. plan *Degrees:* B *Prof.
  Accred.:* Nursing (B) *CEO:* Dean Mary
  Ludgera Pieperbeck
  Enroll: 163   (309) 655-2201

ST. JOSEPH COLLEGE OF NURSING
  290 N. Springfield Ave., Joliet 60435 *Type:*
  Private *Accred.:* 1992 (NCA) *Calendar:* Qtr.
  plan *Degrees:* B *CEO:* Pres. Virginia Keck
  Enroll: 170   (815) 741-7132

ST. XAVIER UNIVERSITY
  3700 W. 103rd St., Chicago 60655 *Type:* Private (Roman Catholic) liberal arts *Accred.:*
  1937/1988 (NCA) *Calendar:* 4-1-4 plan
  Degrees: B, M *Prof. Accred.:* Music (A),
  Nursing (B,M), Speech-Language Pathology (candidate) *CEO:* Pres. Richard A.
  Yanikoski
  Enroll: 4,169   (312) 298-3000

SAUK VALLEY COMMUNITY COLLEGE
  173 Illinois Rte. 2, Dixon 61021 *Type:* Public
  (district) junior *System:* Illinois Community
  College Board *Accred.:* 1972/1992 (NCA)
  Calendar: Sem. plan *Degrees:* A, C *Prof.
  Accred.:* Clinical Lab Technology (A), Radi-
  ography *CEO:* Pres. Richard L. Behrendt
  Enroll: 2,646   (815) 288-5511

SCHOOL OF THE ART INSTITUTE OF CHICAGO
  37 S. Wabash Ave., Chicago 60603 *Type:* Pri-
  vate professional *Accred.:* 1936/1992 (NCA)
  Calendar: Sem. plan *Degrees:* B, M, C *Prof.
  Accred.:* Art *CEO:* Interim Pres. Carol Becker
  Enroll: 1,884   (312) 899-5100

SEABURY-WESTERN THEOLOGICAL SEMINARY
  2122 Sheridan Rd., Evanston 60201 *Type:*
  Private (Episcopal) *Accred.:* 1938/1987
  (ATS); 1981/ 1987 (NCA) *Calendar:* Sem.
  plan *Degrees:* M, D, C *CEO:* Pres./Dean
  Mark S. Sisk
  Enroll: 81   (708) 328-9300

SHAWNEE COMMUNITY COLLEGE
  Shawnee College Rd., Ullin 62992-9725
  Type: Public (district) junior *System:* Illinois
  Community College Board *Accred.:*
  1974/1995 (NCA) *Calendar:* Sem. plan
  Degrees: A, C *CEO:* Pres. Jack D. Hill
  Enroll: 2,233   (618) 634-2242

SHIMER COLLEGE
  P.O. Box A500, 438 N. Sheridan Rd.,
  Waukegan 60079 *Type:* Private liberal arts
  Accred.: 1991/1995 (NCA) *Calendar:* Sem.
  plan *Degrees:* B, C *CEO:* Pres. Don P. Moon
  Enroll: 111   (708) 623-8400

SOUTH SUBURBAN COLLEGE OF COOK COUNTY
  15800 S. State St., South Holland 60473 *Type:*
  Public (district) junior *System:* Illinois Com-
  munity College Board *Accred.:* 1933/ 1989
  (NCA) *Calendar:* Sem. plan *Degrees:* A, C
  Prof. Accred.: Music, Nursing (A), Occupa-
  tional Therapy Assisting, Practical Nursing,
  Radiography *CEO:* Pres. Richard W. Fonte
  Enroll: 8,677   (708) 596-2000

SOUTHEASTERN ILLINOIS COLLEGE
  3575 College Rd., Harrisburg 62946 *Type:*
  Public (district) junior *System:* Illinois

Community College Board *Accred.:* 1976/1988 (NCA) *Calendar:* Sem. plan *Degrees:* A, C *CEO:* Interim Pres. Ben Cullers
Enroll: 3,382 (618) 252-6376

SOUTHERN ILLINOIS COLLEGIATE COMMON MARKET
106 Airway Dr., Marion 62959 *Type:* Private *Degrees:* A *Prof. Accred.:* Medical Record Technology, Occupational Therapy Assisting *CEO:* CEO Ronald K. House
Enroll: 24 (618) 993-5282

SOUTHERN ILLINOIS UNIVERSITY AT CARBONDALE
Carbondale 62901-4333 *Type:* Public (state) *System:* Southern Illinois University System *Accred.:* 1913/1989 (NCA) *Calendar:* Sem. plan *Degrees:* A, B, M, P, D *Prof. Accred.:* Accounting (A,C), Art, Business (B,M), Clinical Psychology, Counseling, Counseling Psychology, Dental Hygiene, Dental Laboratory Technology, Dietetics (internship), Engineering Technology (civil/construction, electrical, mechanical), Engineering (civil, electrical, mechanical, mining), Forestry, Funeral Service Education (Mortuary Science), Interior Design, Journalism (B,M), Law, Medicine, Music, Physical Therapy Assisting, Psychology Internship, Public Administration, Radiography, Recreation and Leisure Services (B), Rehabilitation Counseling, Respiratory Therapy, Social Work (B,M), Speech-Language Pathology, Teacher Education, Theatre *CEO:* Pres. John C. Guyon
Enroll: 23,162 (618) 453-2121

SOUTHERN ILLINOIS UNIVERSITY AT CARBONDALE IN NIIGATA
439-1, Oaza Nagahashikami, Nak, Kitakanbara, Niigata Japan 959-26
[01] (81) 254-43-6205

SOUTHERN ILLINOIS UNIVERSITY AT EDWARDSVILLE
Edwardsville 62026 *Type:* Public (state) *System:* Southern Illinois University System *Accred.:* 1969/1993 (NCA) *Calendar:* Qtr. plan *Degrees:* B, M, P, D *Prof. Accred.:* Accounting (A), Business (B,M), Dentistry,

Engineering (civil, electrical, industrial, mechanical), General Dentistry (prelim. provisional), General Practice Residency, Music, Nurse Anesthesia Education (M), Nursing (B,M), Social Work (B), Speech-Language Pathology, Teacher Education *CEO:* Pres. Nancy Belck
Enroll: 10,938 (618) 692-2000

SPERTUS INSTITUTE OF JEWISH STUDIES
618 S. Michigan Ave., Chicago 60605 *Type:* Private (Jewish) liberal arts and teachers *Accred.:* 1971/1992 (NCA) *Calendar:* Qtr. plan *Degrees:* M, D, C *CEO:* Pres. Howard A. Sulkin
Enroll: 140 (312) 922-9012

SPOON RIVER COLLEGE
Rural Rte. 1, Canton 61520 *Type:* Public (district) junior *System:* Illinois Community College Board *Accred.:* 1977/1992 (NCA) *Calendar:* Sem. plan *Degrees:* A, C *CEO:* Pres. Felix T. Haynes, Jr.
Enroll: 1,860 (309) 647-4645

SPRINGFIELD COLLEGE IN ILLINOIS
1500 N. Fifth St., Springfield 62702 *Type:* Private (Roman Catholic) junior *Accred.:* 1933/1986 (NCA) *Calendar:* 4-1-4 plan *Degrees:* A *CEO:* Pres. H. Brent De Land
Enroll: 457 (217) 525-1420

STATE COMMUNITY COLLEGE OF EAST ST. LOUIS
601 James R. Thompson Blvd. E., St. Louis 62201 *Type:* Public (state) junior *System:* Illinois Community College Board *Accred.:* 1978/1991 (NCA) *Calendar:* Sem. plan *Degrees:* A, C *CEO:* Interim Pres. Janet Finch
Enroll: 1,069 (618) 583-2500

TAYLOR BUSINESS INSTITUTE
36 S. State St., 8th Fl., Chicago 60603 *Type:* Private business *Accred.:* 1973/1990 (ACICS) *Degrees:* A, C *CEO:* Pres. Janice C. Parker
(312) 236-6400

TELSHE YESHIVA-CHICAGO
3535 W. Foster Ave., Chicago 60625 *Type:* Private professional *Accred.:* 1976/1989

(AARTS) *Calendar:* Sem. plan *Degrees:* Rabbinic (1st and 2nd) *CEO:* Pres. A. Levin *Enroll:* 155   (312) 463-7738

TRINITY CHRISTIAN COLLEGE
6601 W. College Dr., Palos Heights 60463 *Type:* Private (Christian Reformed) liberal arts *Accred.:* 1976/1991 (NCA) *Calendar:* Sem. plan *Degrees:* B *Prof. Accred.:* Nursing (B) *CEO:* Pres. Kenneth B. Bootsma *Enroll:* 624   (708) 597-3000

TRINITY COLLEGE
2065 Half Day Rd., Deerfield 60015 *Type:* Private (Evangelical Free Church) liberal arts and professional *System:* Trinity International University *Accred.:* 1969/1994 (NCA) *Calendar:* Sem. plan *Degrees:* B *CEO:* Pres. Gregory L. Waybright *Enroll:* 1,411   (847) 945-8800

SOUTH FLORIDA CAMPUS
500 N.E. First Ave., P.O. Box 019674, Miami, FL 33101-9674 (Evangelical Free Church) *Accred.:* 1993 (NCA) *Calendar:* Sem. plan *Degrees:* A, B *FTE Enroll:* 282   (305) 577-4600

TRINITY EVANGELICAL DIVINITY SCHOOL
2065 Half Day Rd., Deerfield 60015 *Type:* Private (Evangelical Free Church) graduate only *System:* Trinity International University *Accred.:* 1973/1989 (ATS); 1969/1989 (NCA) *Calendar:* Qtr. plan *Degrees:* M, D, C *CEO:* Pres. Greg Waybright *Enroll:* 1,512   (847) 945-8800

TRITON COLLEGE
2000 Fifth Ave., River Grove 60171 *Type:* Public (district) junior *System:* Illinois Community College Board *Accred.:* 1972/1994 (NCA) *Calendar:* Sem. plan *Degrees:* A, C *Prof. Accred.:* Clinical Lab Technology (A), Dental Laboratory Technology, Diagnostic Medical Sonography, Nuclear Medicine Technology, Nursing (A), Ophthalmic Medical Technology, Practical Nursing, Radiography, Respiratory Therapy *CEO:* Pres. George T. Jorndt *Enroll:* 18,026   (708) 456-0300

UNIVERSITY OF CHICAGO
5801 S. Ellis Ave., Chicago 60637 *Type:* Private *Accred.:* 1938/1992 (ATS); 1913/1986 (NCA) *Calendar:* Qtr. plan *Degrees:* B, M, D, C *Prof. Accred.:* Accounting (B), Business (M), General Practice Residency, Health Services Administration, Law, Maxillofacial Prosthodontics, Medicine, Oral and Maxillofacial Surgery, Psychology Internship, Radiation Therapy Technology, Social Work (M) *CEO:* Pres. Hugo Freund Sonnenschein *Enroll:* 11,226   (312) 702-1234

UNIVERSITY OF ILLINOIS AT CHICAGO
P.O. Box 4348, Chicago 60680 *Type:* Public (state) *System:* University of Illinois Central Office *Accred.:* 1970/1987 (NCA) *Calendar:* Qtr. plan *Degrees:* B, M, D *Prof. Accred.:* Art, Blood Bank Technology, Business (B,M), Clinical Lab Scientist, Clinical Psychology, Dentistry, Dietetics (coordinated), Endodontics, Engineering (bioengineering, chemical, civil, computer, electrical, industrial, mechanical, metallurgical), General Practice Residency (prelim. provisional), Medical Illustration, Medical Record Administration, Medicine, Nursing (B,M), Occupational Therapy, Oral and Maxillofacial Surgery, Orthodontics, Pediatric Dentistry, Periodontics, Physical Therapy, Planning (M), Psychology Internship, Public Administration, Social Work (B,M), *CEO:* Pres. James G. Stukel *Enroll:* 24,865   (312) 996-3000

UNIVERSITY OF ILLINOIS AT SPRINGFIELD
Shepherd Rd., Springfield 62794-9243 *Type:* Public (state) liberal arts *System:* Regency Universities System Board of Regents *Accred.:* 1975/1987 (NCA) *Calendar:* Sem. plan *Degrees:* B, M *Prof. Accred.:* Clinical Lab Scientist, Counseling, Nursing (B) *CEO:* Pres. Naomi B. Lynn *Enroll:* 4,384   (217) 786-6600

UNIVERSITY OF ILLINOIS AT URBANA-CHAMPAIGN
601 E. John St., Champaign 61820 *Type:* Public (state) *System:* University of Illinois Central Office *Accred.:* 1913/1989 (NCA)

Calendar: Sem. plan *Degrees:* B, M, D *Prof. Accred.:* Accounting (A,C), Art, Athletic Training, Audiology, Business (B,M), Clinical Psychology, Counseling Psychology, Dance, Engineering (aerospace, agricultural, ceramic, chemical, civil, computer, electrical, engineering mechanics, general, industrial, mechanical, metallurgical, nuclear), Forestry, Journalism (B,M), Landscape Architecture (B,M), Law, Librarianship, Music, Planning (B,M), Psychology Internship, Recreation and Leisure Services (B), Rehabilitation Counseling, Social Work (B,M), Speech-Language Pathology, Theatre, Veterinary Medicine, *CEO:* Chanc. Michael Aiken
Enroll: 36,191   (217) 333-6290

UNIVERSITY OF ST. MARY OF THE LAKE
MUNDELEIN SEMINARY
Rte. 176, Mundelein 60060 *Type:* Private (Roman Catholic) graduate only *Accred.:* 1972/1992 (ATS) *Calendar:* Sem. plan *Degrees:* M, D *CEO:* Pres. Gerald F. Kicanas
Enroll: 194   (708) 566-6401

VANDERCOOK COLLEGE OF MUSIC
3209 S. Michigan Ave., Chicago 60616 *Type:* Private professional *Accred.:* 1971/1995 (NCA) *Calendar:* Sem. plan *Degrees:* B, M *Prof. Accred.:* Music *CEO:* Pres. Roseanne K. Rosenthal
Enroll: 104   (800) 448-2655

WABASH VALLEY COLLEGE
2200 College Dr., Mount Carmel 62863 *Type:* Public (district) junior *System:* Illinois Eastern Community Colleges System *Accred.:* 1984/1988 (NCA) *Calendar:* Sem. plan *Degrees:* A, C *Prof. Accred.:* Nursing (A) *CEO:* Pres. Harry K. Benson
          (618) 262-8641

* Indirect NCA accreditation through Illinois Eastern Community Colleges System

WAUBONSEE COMMUNITY COLLEGE
Illinois Rte. 47 at Harter Rd., Sugar Grove 60554 *Type:* Public (district) junior *System:* Illinois Community College Board *Accred.:*

1972/1986 (NCA) *Calendar:* Sem. plan *Degrees:* A, C *CEO:* Pres. John J. Swalec
Enroll: 6,796   (708) 466-4811

WEST SUBURBAN COLLEGE OF NURSING
Erie St. at Austin Blvd., Oak Park 60302 *Type:* Private professional *Accred.:* 1986/1995 (NCA) *Calendar:* Qtr. plan *Degrees:* B *Prof. Accred.:* Nursing (B) *CEO:* Provost Donna K. Ipema
Enroll: 240   (708) 383-6200

WESTERN ILLINOIS UNIVERSITY
1 University Cir., Macomb 61455-1390 *Type:* Public (state) *System:* Illinois Board of Governors Universities *Accred.:* 1913/1991 (NCA) *Calendar:* Sem. plan *Degrees:* B, M, P *Prof. Accred.:* Audiology, Business (B,M), Counseling, Music, Recreation and Leisure Services (B), Social Work (B-candidate), Speech-Language Pathology, Teacher Education *CEO:* Pres. Donald S. Spencer
Enroll: 12,599   (309) 295-1414

WHEATON COLLEGE
501 E. College Ave., Wheaton 60187 *Type:* Private (interdenominational) *Accred.:* 1913/1994 (NCA) *Calendar:* Sem. plan *Degrees:* B, M, D, C *Prof. Accred.:* Music, Teacher Education *CEO:* Pres. A. Duane Litfin
Enroll: 2,642   (708) 752-5000

WILBUR WRIGHT COLLEGE
4300 N. Narragansett Ave., Chicago 60634 *Type:* Public (city) junior *System:* City Colleges of Chicago *Accred.:* 1967/1992 (NCA) *Calendar:* Sem. plan *Degrees:* A, C *Prof. Accred.:* Diagnostic Medical Sonography, Occupational Therapy Assisting, Radiography *CEO:* Pres. Raymond F. Le Fevour
Enroll: 7,475   (312) 777-7900

WILLIAM RAINEY HARPER COLLEGE
1200 W. Algonquin Rd., Palatine 60067-7398 *Type:* Public (district) junior *System:* Illinois Community College Board *Accred.:* 1971/1988 (NCA) *Calendar:* Sem. plan *Degrees:* A, C *Prof. Accred.:* Dental Hygiene, Medical Assisting (AMA), Music, Nursing (A) *CEO:* Pres. Paul N. Thompson
Enroll: 15,561   (708) 397-3000

INDIANA

ANCILLA COLLEGE
Donaldson 46513 *Type:* Private (Roman Catholic) junior *Accred.:* 1973/1988 (NCA) *Calendar:* Sem. plan *Degrees:* A, C *CEO:* Pres. William J. Shustowski, Jr.
Enroll: 703   (219) 936-8898

ANDERSON UNIVERSITY
1100 E. Fifth St., Anderson 46012-3462 *Type:* Private (Church of God) *Accred.:* 1965/1989 (ATS); 1946/1989 (NCA) *Calendar:* Sem. plan *Degrees:* A, B, M *Prof. Accred.:* Athletic Training, Music, Nursing (B), Social Work (B), Teacher Education *CEO:* Pres. James L. Edwards
Enroll: 2,248   (317) 649-9071

ASSOCIATED MENNONITE BIBLICAL SEMINARY
3003 Benham Ave., Elkhart 46517-1999 *Type:* Private (Mennonite) graduate only *Accred.:* 1958/1989 (ATS); 1974/1989 (NCA) *Calendar:* Sem. plan *Degrees:* M, C *CEO:* Interim Pres. Gerald Gerbrandt
Enroll: 155   (219) 295-3726

BALL STATE UNIVERSITY
2000 University Ave., Muncie 47306 *Type:* Public (state) *System:* Indiana Commission for Higher Education *Accred.:* 1925/1994 (NCA) *Calendar:* Sem. plan *Degrees:* A, B, M, P, D *Prof. Accred.:* Accounting (A), Art, Audiology, Business (B,M), Computer Science, Counseling, Counseling Psychology, Engineering Technology (manufacturing), Journalism (B,M), Landscape Architecture (B,M), Music, Nuclear Medicine Technology, Nursing (B,M), Planning (B,M), Psychology Internship, Radiography, Respiratory Therapy, School Psychology, Social Work (B), Speech-Language Pathology, Teacher Education *CEO:* Pres. John E. Worthen
Enroll: 20,555   (317) 289-1241

BETHANY THEOLOGICAL SEMINARY
615 National Rd. W., Richmond 47374 *Type:* Private (Brethren) graduate only *Accred.:* 1940/1991 (ATS); 1971/1992 (NCA) *Calendar:* Qtr. plan *Degrees:* M, D *CEO:* Pres. Eugene F. Roop
Enroll: 75   (800) 287-8822

BETHEL COLLEGE
1001 W. McKinley Ave., Mishawaka 46545 *Type:* Private (United Missionary) liberal arts *Accred.:* 1971/1991 (NCA) *Calendar:* Sem. plan *Degrees:* A, B, M *Prof. Accred.:* Nursing (A,B) *CEO:* Pres. Norman Bridges
Enroll: 1,200   (219) 257-3313

BUTLER UNIVERSITY
4600 Sunset Ave., Indianapolis 46208 *Type:* Private *Accred.:* 1915/1993 (NCA) *Calendar:* Sem. plan *Degrees:* A, B, M, C *Prof. Accred.:* Dance, Marriage and Family Therapy (M), Music, Psychology Internship (provisional), Teacher Education *CEO:* Pres. Geoffrey Bannister
Enroll: 4,457   (800) 368-6852

CALUMET COLLEGE OF ST. JOSEPH
2400 New York Ave., Whiting 46394 *Type:* Private (Roman Catholic) liberal arts *Accred.:* 1968/1994 (NCA) *Calendar:* Sem. plan *Degrees:* A, B, C *CEO:* Pres. Dennis C. Rittenmeyer
Enroll: 1,125   (219) 473-7770

CHRISTIAN THEOLOGICAL SEMINARY
1000 W. 42nd St., Indianapolis 46208-3301 *Type:* Private (Christian Churches/Disciples of Christ) graduate only *Accred.:* 1944/1988 (ATS); 1973/1988 (NCA) *Calendar:* Sem. plan *Degrees:* M, D *Prof. Accred.:* Marriage and Family Therapy (M) *CEO:* Pres. Richard D.N. Dickinson, Jr.
Enroll: 350   (317) 924-1331

COLLEGE OF COURT REPORTING
111 W. 10th St., Hobart 46342 *Type:* Private business *Accred.:* 1989/1995 (ACICS) *Degrees:* A, C *CEO:* Dir. Kay Moody
       (219) 942-1459

COMMONWEALTH BUSINESS COLLEGE
4200 W. 81st Ave., Merrillville 46410-4388 *Type:* Private business *Accred.:* 1978/1996 (ACICS) *Calendar:* Qtr. plan *Degrees:* A

Prof. Accred.: Medical Assisting *CEO:* Pres. Steven C. Smith

(219) 769-3321

MOLINE CAMPUS
1527 47th Ave., Moline, IL 61265 *Accred.:* 1986/1990 (ACICS)

(309) 762-2100

LAPORTE CAMPUS
8995 N. State Rte. 39, LaPorte 46350 *Accred.:* 1986/1990 (ACICS) *Prof. Accred.:* Medical Assisting

(219) 362-3338

CONCORDIA THEOLOGICAL SEMINARY
6600 N. Clinton St., Fort Wayne 46825-4996 *Type:* Private (Lutheran/Missouri Synod) graduate only *Accred.:* 1968/1991 (ATS); 1981/1991 (NCA) *Calendar:* Qtr. plan *Degrees:* M, D *CEO:* Pres. David G. Schmiel

Enroll: 315   (219) 481-2100

DEPAUW UNIVERSITY
Greencastle 46135 *Type:* Private (United Methodist) *Accred.:* 1915/1988 (NCA) *Calendar:* 4-1-4 plan *Degrees:* B *Prof. Accred.:* Music, Teacher Education *CEO:* Pres. Robert G. Bottoms

Enroll: 2,061   (317) 658-4800

EARLHAM COLLEGE
701 National Rd. W., Richmond 47374-4095 *Type:* Private (Society of Friends) liberal arts *Accred.:* 1973/1986 (ATS); 1915/1994 (NCA) *Calendar:* 3-3 plan *Degrees:* B, M *CEO:* Pres. Richard J. Wood

Enroll: 1,042   (317) 983-1200

FRANKLIN COLLEGE OF INDIANA
501 E. Monroe St., Franklin 46131 *Type:* Private (Baptist) liberal arts *Accred.:* 1915/1992 (NCA) *Calendar:* 4-1-4 plan *Degrees:* A, B *Prof. Accred.:* Teacher Education *CEO:* Pres. William Bryan Martin

Enroll: 889   (317) 738-8000

GOSHEN COLLEGE
1700 S. Main St., Goshen 46526 *Type:* Private (Mennonite) liberal arts *Accred.:* 1941/1995 (NCA) *Calendar:* Tri. plan *Degrees:* B,

C *Prof. Accred.:* Nursing (B), Social Work (B), Teacher Education *CEO:* Pres. Victor E. Stoltzfus

Enroll: 1,123   (219) 535-7000

GRACE COLLEGE AND SEMINARY
200 Seminary Dr., Winona Lake 46590 *Type:* Private (National Fellowship of Brethren Churches) liberal arts *Accred.:* 1976/1994 (NCA) *Calendar:* Sem. plan *Degrees:* A, B, D *CEO:* Acad. Dean Ronald E. Manahan

Enroll: 765   (219) 372-5100

GRACE THEOLOGICAL SEMINARY
200 Seminary Dr., Winona Lake 46590 *Type:* Private (National Fellowship of Brethren Churches) graduate only *Accred.:* 1982/1994 (NCA) *Calendar:* Sem. plan *Degrees:* M, D, C *CEO:* Pres. Ronald E. Manahan

Enroll: 130   (219) 372-5100

HANOVER COLLEGE
P.O. Box 108, Hanover 47243-0108 *Type:* Private (United Presbyterian) liberal arts *Accred.:* 1915/1990 (NCA) *Calendar:* 4-4-x plan *Degrees:* B *Prof. Accred.:* Teacher Education *CEO:* Pres. Russell L. Nichols

Enroll: 1,093   (812) 866-7000

HOLY CROSS COLLEGE
1801 N. Michigan St., Box 308, Notre Dame 46556 *Type:* Private *Accred.:* 1987/1990 (NCA) *Calendar:* Sem. plan *Degrees:* A *CEO:* Pres. Richard B. Gilman, C.S.C.

Enroll: 487   (219) 233-6813

HUNTINGTON COLLEGE
2303 College Ave., Huntington 46750 *Type:* Private (United Brethren in Christ) liberal arts *Accred.:* 1961/1994 (NCA) *Calendar:* 4-1-4 plan *Degrees:* A, B, M, C *Prof. Accred.:* Teacher Education *CEO:* Pres. G. Blair Dowden

Enroll: 638   (219) 356-6000

INDIANA BUSINESS COLLEGE
802 N. Meridian St., Indianapolis 46204 *Type:* Private business *Accred.:* 1980/1986

(ACICS) *Degrees:* A, C *CEO:* Dir. John Mathias

(317) 264-5656

ANDERSON CAMPUS
Applegate Business Park, 1320 E. 53rd St., Ste. 106, Anderson 46103 *Accred.:* 1980/1986 (ACICS)

(317) 644-7414

COLUMBUS CAMPUS
3550 Two Mile House Rd., P.O. Box 1906, Columbus 47201 *Accred.:* 1980/ 1986 (ACICS)

(812) 342-1000

EVANSVILLE CAMPUS
4601 Theater Dr., Evansville 47715 *Accred.:* 1993 (ACICS)

(812) 476-6000

INDIANAPOLIS CAMPUS
5460 Victory Dr., Ste. 100, Indianapolis 46203 *Accred.:* 1993 (ACICS)

(317) 783-5100

LAFAYETTE CAMPUS
1170 S. Creasy Ln., Lafayette 47905 *Accred.:* 1980/1986 (ACICS)

(317) 447-9550

MARION CAMPUS
830 N. Miller Ave., Marion 46952 *Accred.:* 1980/1986 (ACICS)

(317) 662-7497

TERRE HAUTE CAMPUS
3175 S. Third St., Terre Haute 47802 *Accred.:* 1980/1986 (ACICS)

(812) 232-4458

VINCENNES CAMPUS
1431 Willow St., Vincennes 47591 *Accred.:* 1980/1986 (ACICS)

(812) 882-2550

INDIANA BUSINESS COLLEGE
1809 N. Walnut St., Muncie 47303 *Type:* Private business *Accred.:* 1988/1994 (ACICS) *Degrees:* A, C *CEO:* Dir. John E. Burton

(317) 288-8681

INDIANA INSTITUTE OF TECHNOLOGY
1600 E. Washington Blvd., Fort Wayne 46803 *Type:* Private technological *Accred.:* 1962/1986 (NCA) *Calendar:* Sem. plan *Degrees:* A, B, C *CEO:* Pres. Donald J. Andorfer
Enroll: 1,123   (800) 937-2448

INDIANA STATE UNIVERSITY
217 N. Sixth St., Terre Haute 47809 *Type:* Public (state) *System:* Indiana Commission for Higher Education *Accred.:* 1915/1990 (NCA) *Calendar:* Sem. plan *Degrees:* A, B, M, P, D *Prof. Accred.:* Art, Business (B,M), Clinical Lab Technology (A), Clinical Psychology, Construction Education (B), Counseling Psychology, Dietetics (coordinated), Home Economics, Marriage and Family Therapy (M), Music, Nursing (A,B,M), Recreation and Leisure Services (B), School Psychology, Social Work (B-candidate), Speech-Language Pathology, Teacher Education *CEO:* Pres. John W. Moore
Enroll: 11,641   (812) 237-6311

INDIANA UNIVERSITY AT KOKOMO
P.O. Box 9003, 2300 S. Washington St., Kokomo 46904-9003 *Type:* Public (state) *System:* Indiana University System *Accred.:* 1969/1989 (NCA) *Calendar:* Sem. plan *Degrees:* A, B, M, C *Prof. Accred.:* Engineering Technology (electrical), Nursing (A), Teacher Education *CEO:* Chanc. Emita B. Hill
Enroll: 3,257   (317) 455-9200

INDIANA UNIVERSITY AT SOUTH BEND
1700 Mishawaka Ave., P.O. Box 7111, South Bend 46634 *Type:* Public (state) *System:* Indiana University System *Accred.:* 1969/ 1990 (NCA) *Calendar:* Sem. plan *Degrees:* A, B, M, C *Prof. Accred.:* Business (B,M), Dental Assisting, Dental Hygiene, Public Administration, Radiography, Teacher Education *CEO:* Acting Chanc. Lester C. Lamon
Enroll: 7,660   (219) 237-4111

INDIANA UNIVERSITY BLOOMINGTON
Indiana and Kirkwood Ave., Bloomington 47405 *Type:* Public (state) *System:* Indiana University System *Accred.:* 1913/1987

(NCA) *Calendar:* Sem. plan *Degrees:* A, B, M, P, D, C *Prof. Accred.:* Art, Audiology, Business (B,M), Clinical Psychology, Counseling Psychology, Interior Design, Journalism (B,M), Law, Librarianship, Music, Optometric Technician, Optometry, Public Administration, Recreation and Leisure Services (B), School Psychology, Speech-Language Pathology, Teacher Education, Theatre *CEO:* Pres. Myles Brand
Enroll: 35,594   (812) 332-0211

INDIANA UNIVERSITY EAST
2325 N. Chester Blvd., Richmond 47374 *Type:* Public (state) *System:* Indiana University System *Accred.:* 1971/1992 (NCA) *Calendar:* Sem. plan *Degrees:* A, B, C *Prof. Accred.:* Teacher Education *CEO:* Chanc. David J. Fulton
Enroll: 2,387   (317) 973-8200

INDIANA UNIVERSITY NORTHWEST
3400 Broadway, Gary 46408 *Type:* Public (state) *System:* Indiana University System *Accred.:* 1969/1993 (NCA) *Calendar:* Sem. plan *Degrees:* A, B, M, C *Prof. Accred.:* Business (B,M), Clinical Lab Technology (A), Dental Assisting, Dental Hygiene, Medical Record Technology, Nursing (A), Public Administration, Radiation Therapy Technology, Radiography, Respiratory Therapy, Teacher Education *CEO:* Chanc. Hilda Richards
Enroll: 8,279   (219) 980-6500

INDIANA UNIVERSITY-PURDUE UNIVERSITY AT FORT WAYNE
2101 Coliseum Blvd. E., Fort Wayne 46805-1499 *Type:* Public (state) *System:* Indiana University System *Accred.:* 1969/1990 (NCA) *Calendar:* Sem. plan *Degrees:* A, B, M, C *Prof. Accred.:* Business (B,M), Dental Assisting, Dental Hygiene, Dental Laboratory Technology, Engineering Technology (architectural, civil/construction, electrical, industrial, manufacturing, mechanical, mechanical drafting/design), Engineering (electrical, mechanical), Medical Record Technology, Music, Nursing (A,B), Public

Administration, Teacher Education *CEO:* Chanc. Michael A. Wartell
Enroll: 11,513   (219) 481-6100

INDIANA UNIVERSITY-PURDUE UNIVERSITY AT INDIANAPOLIS
355 N. Lansing St., Indianapolis 46202 *Type:* Public (state) *System:* Indiana University System *Accred.:* 1969/1993 (NCA) *Calendar:* Sem. plan *Degrees:* A, B, M, P, D, C *Prof. Accred.:* Art, Clinical Lab Scientist, Combined Maxillofacial Prosthodontics, Combined Prosthodontics, Cytotechnology, Dental Assisting, Dental Hygiene, Dentistry, Dietetics (internship), Endodontics, Engineering Technology (civil/construction, electrical, mechanical, mechanical drafting/design), Engineering (electrical, mechanical), Health Services Administration, Law, Medical Record Administration, Medicine, Nuclear Medicine Technology, Nursing (A,B,M), Occupational Therapy, Occupational Therapy Assisting, Oral Pathology, Oral and Maxillofacial Surgery, Orthodontics, Pediatric Dentistry, Periodontics, Physical Therapy, Psychology Internship, Public Administration, Radiation Therapy Technology, Radiography, Respiratory Therapy *CEO:* Chanc. Gerald L. Bepko
Enroll: 26,766   (317) 274-5555

INDIANA UNIVERSITY SOUTHEAST
4201 Grant Line Rd., New Albany 47150 *Type:* Public (state) *System:* Indiana University System *Accred.:* 1969/1990 (NCA) *Calendar:* Sem. plan *Degrees:* A, B, M, C *Prof. Accred.:* Business (B), mechanical) *CEO:* Chanc. Leon Rand
Enroll: 5,464   (812) 941-2200

INDIANA WESLEYAN UNIVERSITY
4201 S. Washington St., Marion 46953 *Type:* Private (Wesleyan Methodist) liberal arts *Accred.:* 1966/1990 (NCA) *Calendar:* Sem. plan *Degrees:* A, B, M, C *Prof. Accred.:* Clinical Lab Technology (A), Music, Nursing (B,M), Social Work (B), Teacher Education *CEO:* Pres. James Barnes
Enroll: 3,385   (800) 332-6901

INTERNATIONAL BUSINESS COLLEGE
3811 Illinois Rd., Fort Wayne 46804 *Type:*
Private junior *Accred.:* 1953/1986 (ACICS)
Degrees: A, C *Prof. Accred.:* Medical Assisting (AMA) *CEO:* Dir. of Educ. Cheryl Rider
(219) 432-8702

INTERNATIONAL BUSINESS COLLEGE
7205 Shadeland Sta., Indianapolis 46256
Type: Private business *Accred.:* 1986/1994
(ACICS) *Degrees:* A, C *Prof. Accred.:* Medical Assisting (AMA) *CEO:* Dir. of Educ.
Scharme Smith
(317) 841-6400

ITT TECHNICAL INSTITUTE
5115 Oak Grove Rd., Evansville 47715-
2340 *Type:* Private *Accred.:* 1967/1989
(ACCSCT) *Degrees:* A *CEO:* Dir. Thomas
Kielty
(812) 479-1441

FRAMINGHAM CAMPUS
1671 Worcester Rd., Framingham, MA
01701-9456 *Accred.:* 1990 (ACCSCT)
(508) 879-6266

LOUISVILLE CAMPUS
10509 Timberwood Cir., Louisville, KY
40223 *Accred.:* 1993 (ACCSCT)
(502) 327-7424

NORFOLK CAMPUS
863 Glenrock Rd., Norfolk, VA 23502
Accred.: 1991 (ACCSCT)
(804) 466-1260

ITT TECHNICAL INSTITUTE
4919 Coldwater Rd., Fort Wayne 46825-
5532 *Type:* Private *Accred.:* 1968/1990
(ACCSCT) *Degrees:* A, B, C *CEO:* Dir. Jack
Cozad
(219) 484-4107

FORT LAUDERDALE CAMPUS
3401 S. University Dr., Fort Lauderdale,
FL 33328 *Accred.:* 1992 (ACCSCT)
(305) 476-9300

TROY CAMPUS
1225 E. Big Beaver Rd., Troy, MI 48083-
1905 *Accred.:* 1991/1993 (ACCSCT)
(313) 524-1800

ITT TECHNICAL INSTITUTE
9511 Angola Ct., Indianapolis 46268-1119
Type: Private *Accred.:* 1967/1989 (ACC-
SCT) *Degrees:* A, B, C *CEO:* Dir. Steven E.
Brooks
(317) 875-8640

AUSTIN CAMPUS
6330 Hwy. 290 East, Austin, TX 78723
Accred.: 1986 (ACCSCT)
(512) 467-6800

HOFFMAN ESTATES CAMPUS
375 W. Higgins Rd., Hoffman Estates, IL
60195 *Accred.:* 1990 (ACCSCT)
(708) 519-9300

HOUSTON CAMPUS
15621 Blue Ash Dr., Ste. 160, Houston,
TX 77090-5818 *Accred.:* 1988 (ACC-
SCT)
(713) 879-6486

IVY TECH STATE COLLEGE—ANDERSON
104 W. 53rd St., Anderson 46013-1502
Type: Public *System:* Ivy Tech State College—EastCentral Region *Accred.:* 1979/
1984 (NCA) *Calendar:* Sem. plan *Degrees:*
A *CEO:* Exec. Dean Jack Voelz
(317) 643-7133

IVY TECH STATE COLLEGE—BLOOMINGTON
3116 Canterbury Ct., Bloomington 47401-
0393 *Type:* Public *System:* Ivy Tech State
College—Columbus Region *Accred.:* 1978/
1987 (NCA) *Calendar:* Sem. plan *Degrees:*
A *CEO:* Exec. Dean Thomas S. Jordan
(812) 332-1559

IVY TECH STATE COLLEGE—COLUMBUS
4475 Central Ave., Columbus 47203 *Type:*
Public (state) 2-year *System:* Ivy Tech State
College—Columbus Region *Accred.:* 1978/
1987 (NCA) *Calendar:* Sem. plan *Degrees:*
A, C *Prof. Accred.:* Medical Assisting
(AMA) *CEO:* Exec. Dean Gregory K. Flood
Enroll: 2,905   (800) 922-4838

IVY TECH STATE COLLEGE—EAST CHICAGO
410 Columbus Dr., East Chicago 46312-2714 *Type:* Public *System:* Ivy Tech State College Office of the President *Accred.:* 1981/1989 (NCA) *Calendar:* Sem. plan *Degrees:* A *CEO:* Exec. Dean J. Robert Jeffs
(219) 392-3600

IVY TECH STATE COLLEGE—ELKHART
2521 Industrial Pkwy., Elkhart 46516-5430 *Type:* Public *System:* Ivy Tech State College—Northcentral Region *Accred.:* 1970/1990 (NCA) *Calendar:* Sem. plan *Degrees:* A *CEO:* Dir. Jane Perez
(219) 293-4657

IVY TECH STATE COLLEGE—EVANSVILLE
3501 First Ave., Evansville 47710-3398 *Type:* Public (state) 2-year *System:* Ivy Tech State College—Southwest Region *Accred.:* 1977/1986 (NCA) *Calendar:* Sem. plan *Degrees:* A, C *Prof. Accred.:* Medical Assisting (AMA), Nursing (A), Practical Nursing, Surgical Technology *CEO:* Exec. Dean Daniel J. Schenk
Enroll: 2,992   (812) 426-2865

IVY TECH STATE COLLEGE—FT. WAYNE
3800 N. Anthony Blvd., Fort Wayne 46805-1489 *Type:* Public (state) 2-year *System:* Ivy Tech State College—Northeast Region *Accred.:* 1977/1990 (NCA) *Calendar:* Sem. plan *Degrees:* A, C *Prof. Accred.:* Medical Assisting (AMA), Respiratory Therapy, Respiratory Therapy Technology *CEO:* Vice Pres./Chanc. Jon L. Rupright
Enroll: 3,971   (219) 482-9171

IVY TECH STATE COLLEGE—INDIANAPOLIS
One W. 26th St., P.O. Box 1763, Indianapolis 46206-1763 *Type:* Public (state) 2-year *System:* Ivy Tech State College—Central Indiana Region *Accred.:* 1977/1987 (NCA) *Calendar:* Sem. plan *Degrees:* A, C *Prof. Accred.:* Medical Assisting (AMA), Nursing (A), Practical Nursing, Radiography, Respiratory Therapy, Surgical Technology *CEO:* Vice Pres./Chanc. Meredith L. Carter
Enroll: 5,622   (317) 921-4882

IVY TECH STATE COLLEGE—KOKOMO
1815 E. Morgan St., Kokomo 46903-1373 *Type:* Public (state) 2-year *System:* Ivy Tech State College—Kokomo Region *Accred.:* 1978/1987 (NCA) *Calendar:* Sem. plan *Degrees:* A, C *Prof. Accred.:* Medical Assisting (AMA) *CEO:* Exec. Dean Shanon L. Christiansen
Enroll: 1,800   (317) 459-0561

IVY TECH STATE COLLEGE—LAFAYETTE
P.O. Box 6299, Lafayette 46903-6299 *Type:* Public (state) 2-year *System:* Ivy Tech State College—Lafayette Region *Accred.:* 1980/1990 (NCA) *Calendar:* Sem. plan *Degrees:* A, C *Prof. Accred.:* Dental Assisting, Medical Assisting (AMA), Nursing (A), Respiratory Therapy Technology, Surgical Technology *CEO:* Exec. Dean Elizabeth J. Doversberger
Enroll: 1,672   (317) 772-9100

IVY TECH STATE COLLEGE—LAWRENCEBURG
575 Main St., Lawrenceburg 47205-1661 *Type:* Public *System:* Ivy Tech State College—Southeast Region *Accred.:* 1981/1986 (NCA) *Calendar:* Sem. plan *Degrees:* A *CEO:* Site Dir. Gwen Wright
(812) 537-4010

IVY TECH STATE COLLEGE—LOGANSPORT
3001 E Market St., Ste. 7, Logansport 46947-2152 *Type:* Public *System:* Ivy Tech State College—Kokomo Region *Accred.:* 1978/1987 (NCA) *Calendar:* Sem. plan *Degrees:* A *CEO:* Dir. Rebecca Nickoli
(219) 753-5101

IVY TECH STATE COLLEGE—MADISON
590 Ivy Tech Dr., Madison 47250-1881 *Type:* Public (state) 2-year *System:* Ivy Tech State College—Southeast Region *Accred.:* 1981/1986 (NCA) *Calendar:* Sem. plan *Degrees:* A, C *Prof. Accred.:* Medical Assisting (AMA) *CEO:* Exec. Dean Jonathan W. Thomas
Enroll: 931   (812) 265-2580

IVY TECH STATE COLLEGE—MARION
2983 W. 38th St., Marion 46953-9370 *Type:* Public *System:* Ivy Tech State College—EastCentral Region *Accred.:* 1979/1984

(NCA) *Calendar:* Sem. plan *Degrees:* A *CEO:* Dir. James Luttrull

(317) 662-9843

IVY TECH STATE COLLEGE—MUNCIE
4301 S. Cowan Rd., P.O. Box 3100, Muncie 47302-9448 *Type:* Public (state) 2-year *System:* Ivy Tech State College—EastCentral Region *Accred.:* 1979/1984 (NCA) *Calendar:* Sem. plan *Degrees:* A, C *Prof. Accred.:* Medical Assisting (AMA) *CEO:* Interim Exec. Dean James D. Luttrull
Enroll: 2,470   (317) 289-2291

IVY TECH STATE COLLEGE—NORTHWEST TECHNICAL INSTITUTE
1440 E. 35th Ave., Gary 46409-1499 *Type:* Public (state) 2-year *System:* Ivy Tech State College—Northwest Region *Accred.:* 1981/1986 (NCA) *Calendar:* Sem. plan *Degrees:* A, C *CEO:* Vice Pres./Chanc. Darnell E. Cole
Enroll: 2,361   (219) 981-1111

IVY TECH STATE COLLEGE—RICHMOND
2325 Chester Blvd., Richmond 47374 *Type:* Public (state) 2-year *System:* Ivy Tech State College—Whitewater Region *Accred.:* 1981/1986 (NCA) *Calendar:* Sem. plan *Degrees:* A, C *Prof. Accred.:* Nursing (A) *CEO:* Exec. Dean James L. Steck
Enroll: 1,055   (317) 966-2656

IVY TECH STATE COLLEGE—SELLERSBURG
8204 Hwy 311, Sellersburg 47172 *Type:* Public (state) 2-year *System:* Ivy Tech State College—Southcentral Region *Accred.:* 1980/1985 (NCA) *Calendar:* Sem. plan *Degrees:* A, C *Prof. Accred.:* Medical Assisting (AMA) *CEO:* Exec. Dean James R. Wells
Enroll: 2,046   (812) 246-3301

IVY TECH STATE COLLEGE—SOUTH BEND
1534 W. Sample St., South Bend 46619-3892 *Type:* Public (state) 2-year *System:* Ivy Tech State College—Northcentral Region *Accred.:* 1977/1990 (NCA) *Calendar:* Sem. plan *Degrees:* A, C *Prof. Accred.:* Clinical Lab Technology (A), Medical Assisting (AMA), Nursing (A) *CEO:* Exec. Dean Gene Bruce
Enroll: 2,814   (219) 289-7001

IVY TECH STATE COLLEGE—TERRE HAUTE
7999 U.S. Hwy. 41, Terre Haute 47802-4898 *Type:* Public (state) 2-year *System:* Ivy Tech State College—Wabash Valley Region *Accred.:* 1977/1985 (NCA) *Calendar:* Sem. plan *Degrees:* A, C *Prof. Accred.:* Clinical Lab Technology (A), Medical Assisting (AMA), Radiography *CEO:* Exec. Dean Scott Knapp
Enroll: 2,392   (812) 299-1121

IVY TECH STATE COLLEGE—VALPARAISO
2401 Valley Dr., Valparaiso 46383-2520 *Type:* Public *System:* Ivy Tech State College—Northwest Region *Accred.:* 1981/1989 (NCA) *Calendar:* Sem. plan *Degrees:* A *Prof. Accred.:* Medical Assisting (AMA), Practical Nursing, Respiratory Therapy Technology, Surgical Technology *CEO:* Acting Exec. Dir. Jerry Huddleston

(219) 464-8514

IVY TECH STATE COLLEGE—WARSAW
850 E. Smith St., Warsaw 46580-4546 *Type:* Public *System:* Ivy Tech State College—Northcentral Region *Accred.:* 1977/1990 (NCA) *Calendar:* Sem. plan *Degrees:* A *CEO:* Dir. Stephen A. Grill

(219) 267-5428

LINCOLN TECHNICAL INSTITUTE
1201 Stadium Dr., Indianapolis 46202-2194 *Type:* Private *Accred.:* 1968/1988 (ACCSCT) *Degrees:* A, C *CEO:* Exec. Dir. Merlyn Cooper

(317) 632-5553

LUTHERAN COLLEGE OF HEALTH PROFESSIONS
3024 Fairfield Ave., Fort Wayne 46807 *Type:* Private *Accred.:* 1994 (NCA) *Calendar:* Qtr. plan *Degrees:* A, B, C *CEO:* Dean Marilyn R. Wilson
Enroll: 669   (219) 458-2451

MANCHESTER COLLEGE
604 College Ave., North Manchester 46962 *Type:* Private (Church of Brethren) liberal arts *Accred.:* 1932/1993 (NCA) *Calendar:* 4-1-4 plan *Degrees:* A, B, M *Prof. Accred.:* Social Work (B), Teacher Education *CEO:* Pres. Parker G. Marden
Enroll: 1,004   (219) 982-5000

MARIAN COLLEGE
3200 Cold Spring Rd., Indianapolis 46222
Type: Private (Roman Catholic) liberal arts
Accred.: 1956/1986 (NCA) *Calendar:* Sem.
plan *Degrees:* A, B, C *Prof. Accred.:* Nurs-
ing (A,B), Teacher Education *CEO:* Pres.
Daniel A. Felicetti
Enroll: 1,352   (317) 929-0123

MARTIN UNIVERSITY
2171 Avondale Pl., P.O. Box 18567, Indianapolis 46218 *Type:* Private *Accred.:* 1987/
1995 (NCA) *Calendar:* Sem. plan *Degrees:*
B, M *CEO:* Pres. Boniface Hardin
Enroll: 513   (317) 543-3235

MICHIANA COLLEGE
1030 E. Jefferson Blvd., South Bend 46617
Type: Private business *Accred.:* 1961/1997
(ACICS) *Calendar:* Qtr. plan *Degrees:* A, C
Prof. Accred.: Medical Assisting (AMA),
Physical Therapy Assisting *CEO:* Dir. Kelly
Dunnell
                                   (219) 237-0774

FORT WAYNE CAMPUS
4807 Illinois Rd., Fort Wayne 46804
Accred.: 1993 (ACICS)
                                   (219) 436-2738

MID-AMERICA COLLEGE OF FUNERAL SERVICE
3111 Hamburg Pike, Jeffersonville 47130
Type: Private professional *Degrees:* A, C
Prof. Accred.: Funeral Service Education
(Mortuary Science) *CEO:* Pres. Glenn A.
Morton
                                   (812) 288-8878

OAKLAND CITY COLLEGE
143 N. Lucretia St., Oakland City 47660
Type: Private (Baptist) liberal arts *Accred.:*
1977/1993 (NCA) *Calendar:* Sem. plan
Degrees: A, B, M, C *Prof. Accred.:* Teacher
Education *CEO:* Chanc./Pres. James W.
Murray
Enroll: 983   (800) 737-5125

PURDUE UNIVERSITY
Frederick L. Hovde Hall, Rm. 200, West
Lafayette 47907-1031 *Type:* Public (state)
System: Purdue University System *Accred.:*
1913/1990 (NCA) *Calendar:* Sem. plan

Degrees: A, B, M, D, C *Prof. Accred.:* Audiology, Business (B,M), Clinical Psychology,
Construction Education (B), Counseling,
Dietetics (coordinated), Engineering Technology (electrical, mechanical), Engineering
(aerospace, agricultural, chemical, civil,
computer, construction, electrical, food
process, industrial, materials, mechanical,
metallurgical, nuclear), Forestry, Landscape
Architecture (B), Marriage and Family Therapy (D), Nursing (B), Speech-Language
Pathology, Teacher Education, Theatre (A),
Veterinary Medicine *CEO:* Pres. Steven C.
Beering
Enroll: 36,172   (317) 494-4600

PURDUE UNIVERSITY CALUMET
Hammond 46323 *Type:* Public (state) *Sys-
tem:* Purdue University System *Accred.:*
1969/1993 (NCA) *Calendar:* Sem. plan
Degrees: A, B, C *Prof. Accred.:* Engineering
Technology (architectural, civil/construc-
tion, electrical, industrial, manufacturing,
mechanical), Engineering (electrical,
mechanical), Marriage and Family Therapy
(M), Nursing (A,B,M), Teacher Education
CEO: Chanc. James W. Yackel
Enroll: 9,246   (219) 989-2993

PURDUE UNIVERSITY NORTH CENTRAL
1401 S. U.S. Hwy. 421, Westville 46391-
9528 *Type:* Public (state) *System:* Purdue
University System *Accred.:* 1971/1994
(NCA) *Calendar:* Sem. plan *Degrees:* A, B,
M, C *Prof. Accred.:* Engineering Technology
(electrical, industrial, mechanical), Nursing
(A), Radiography *CEO:* Chanc. Dale W.
Alspaugh
Enroll: 3,345   (219) 785-5200

ROSE-HULMAN INSTITUTE OF TECHNOLOGY
5500 Wabash Ave., Terre Haute 47803 *Type:*
Private professional for men *Accred.:* 1916/
1992 (NCA) *Calendar:* Qtr. plan *Degrees:*
B, M *Prof. Accred.:* Engineering (chemical,
civil, electrical, mechanical) *CEO:* Pres.
Samuel F. Hulbert
Enroll: 1,387   (800) 248-7448

ST. FRANCIS COLLEGE
2701 Spring St., Fort Wayne 46808 *Type:* Private (Roman Catholic) liberal arts *Accred.:* 1957/1986 (NCA) *Calendar:* Sem. plan *Degrees:* A, B, M *Prof. Accred.:* Nursing (B), Social Work (B) *CEO:* Pres. M. Elise Kriss
Enroll: 1,005   (219) 434-3100

ST. JOSEPH'S COLLEGE
Rensselaer 47978 *Type:* Private (Roman Catholic) liberal arts *Accred.:* 1932/1992 (NCA) *Calendar:* Sem. plan *Degrees:* A, B, M *Prof. Accred.:* Teacher Education *CEO:* Pres. Albert J. Shannon
Enroll: 1,009   (219) 866-6157

ST. MARY-OF-THE-WOODS COLLEGE
St. Mary-of-the-Woods 47876 *Type:* Private (Roman Catholic) liberal arts for women *Accred.:* 1919/1989 (NCA) *Calendar:* Sem. plan *Degrees:* A, B, M, C *Prof. Accred.:* Music *CEO:* Pres. Barbara Doherty
Enroll: 1,215   (812) 535-5151

ST. MARY'S COLLEGE
Notre Dame 46556 *Type:* Private (Roman Catholic) liberal arts primarily for women *Accred.:* 1922/1986 (NCA) *Calendar:* Sem. plan *Degrees:* B *Prof. Accred.:* Art, Music, Nursing (B), Social Work (B-candidate), Teacher Education *CEO:* Pres. William A. Hickey
Enroll: 1,550   (219) 284-4000

ST. MEINRAD COLLEGE
St. Meinrad 47577 *Type:* Private (Roman Catholic) liberal arts *Accred.:* 1961/1991 (NCA) *Calendar:* Sem. plan *Degrees:* B *CEO:* Pres./Rector Eugene Hensell, O.S.B.
Enroll: 123   (812) 357-6611

ST. MEINRAD SCHOOL OF THEOLOGY
St. Meinrad 47577 *Type:* Private (Roman Catholic) graduate only *Accred.:* 1968/1993 (ATS); 1979/1994 (NCA) *Calendar:* Sem. plan *Degrees:* M *CEO:* Pres./Rector Eugene Hensell, O.S.B.
Enroll: 145   (812) 357-6611

SAWYER COLLEGE, INC.
6040 Hohman Ave., Hammond 46320 *Type:* Private business *Accred.:* 1982/1994 (ACICS) *Calendar:* Qtr. plan *Degrees:* A *Prof. Accred.:* Medical Assisting *CEO:* Dir. Mary Ann Livovich
        (219) 931-0436

MERRIVILLE CAMPUS
3803 E. Lincoln Hwy., Merrillville 46410 *Accred.:* 1985/1988 (ACICS) *Prof. Accred.:* Medical Assisting
        (219) 947-4555

TAYLOR UNIVERSITY
500 W. Reade Ave., Upland 46989 *Type:* Private liberal arts *Accred.:* 1947/1987 (NCA) *Calendar:* Sem. plan *Degrees:* A, B, C *Prof. Accred.:* Music, Social Work (B), Teacher Education *CEO:* Pres. Jay L. Kesler
Enroll: 2,237   (317) 998-2751

FORT WAYNE CAMPUS
1025 W. Rudisill Blvd., Fort Wayne 46807 *Degrees:* A, B, C
        (219) 456-2111

TRI-STATE UNIVERSITY
300 S. Darling, Angola 46703 *Type:* Private business *Accred.:* 1966/1990 (NCA) *Calendar:* Qtr. plan *Degrees:* A, B, C *Prof. Accred.:* Engineering Technology (mechanical drafting/design), Engineering (aerospace, chemical, civil, electrical, mechanical) *CEO:* Pres. R. John Reynolds
Enroll: 1,131   (219) 665-4100

UNIVERSITY OF EVANSVILLE
1800 Lincoln Ave., Evansville 47722 *Type:* Private (United Methodist) *Accred.:* 1931/1986 (NCA) *Calendar:* Qtr. plan *Degrees:* A, B, M, C *Prof. Accred.:* Engineering (electrical, mechanical), Music, Nursing (B,M), Physical Therapy, Physical Therapy Assisting, Teacher Education *CEO:* Pres. James S. Vinson
Enroll: 3,162   (800) 423-8633

THE UNIVERSITY OF INDIANAPOLIS
1400 E. Hanna Ave., Indianapolis 46227-3697 *Type:* Private (United Methodist) liberal arts *Accred.:* 1947/1988 (NCA) *Calendar:*

Qtr. plan *Degrees:* A, B, M *Prof. Accred.:* Music, Nursing (A,B), Occupational Therapy, Physical Therapy, Physical Therapy Assisting, Social Work (B-candidate), Teacher Education *CEO:* Pres. G. Benjamin Lantz, Jr.
Enroll: 3,878   (317) 788-3368

INDIANAPOLIS INTERNATIONAL CAMPUS
29, Voulis St., Syntagma Square, Athens Greece 105 57
                               [30] (132) 39740

INTERCOLLEGE CAMPUS
17 Heroes Ave., P.O. Box 4005, Nicosia Cyprus
                               [35] (723) 57735

UNIVERSITY OF NOTRE DAME
302 Administration Bldg., Notre Dame 46556 *Type:* Private (Roman Catholic) *Accred.:* 1977/1993 (ATS); 1913/1994 (NCA) *Calendar:* Sem. plan *Degrees:* B, M, D *Prof. Accred.:* Accounting (A), Business (B,M), Counseling Psychology, Engineering (aerospace, chemical, civil, electrical, mechanical), Law, Music *CEO:* Pres. Edward A. Malloy, C.S.C.
Enroll: 10,309   (219) 631-5026

UNIVERSITY OF SOUTHERN INDIANA
8600 University Blvd., Evansville 47712 *Type:* Public (state) *System:* Indiana Commission for Higher Education *Accred.:* 1974/1987 (NCA) *Calendar:* Sem. plan *Degrees:* A, B, M, C *Prof. Accred.:* Dental Assisting, Dental Hygiene, Engineering Technology (civil/construction, electrical,

mechanical), Occupational Therapy, Radiography, Respiratory Therapy, Social Work (B), Teacher Education *CEO:* Pres. H. Ray Hoops
Enroll: 7,443   (812) 464-8600

VALPARAISO UNIVERSITY
Valparaiso 46383 *Type:* Private (Lutheran-Missouri Synod) *Accred.:* 1929/1988 (NCA) *Calendar:* Sem. plan *Degrees:* A, B, M, D *Prof. Accred.:* Business (B), Engineering (civil, computer, electrical, mechanical), Law, Music, Nursing (B,M), Social Work (B), Teacher Education *CEO:* Pres. Alan F. Harre
Enroll: 3,480   (219) 464-5000

VINCENNES UNIVERSITY
1002 N. First St., Vincennes 47591-5201 *Type:* Public (state) junior *System:* Indiana Commission for Higher Education *Accred.:* 1958/1986 (NCA) *Calendar:* Sem. plan *Degrees:* A, C *Prof. Accred.:* Art, Clinical Lab Technology (A), Funeral Service Education (Mortuary Science), Medical Record Technology, Nursing (A), Physical Therapy Assisting, Practical Nursing, Respiratory Therapy, Surgical Technology, Theatre *CEO:* Pres. Phillip M. Summers
Enroll: 9,340   (812) 885-4208

WABASH COLLEGE
301 W. Wabash Ave., Crawfordsville 47933 *Type:* Private liberal arts for men *Accred.:* 1913/1993 (NCA) *Calendar:* Sem. plan *Degrees:* B *CEO:* Pres. Andrew T. Ford
Enroll: 783   (317) 362-1400

IOWA

ALLEN COLLEGE OF NURSING
1825 Logan Ave., Waterloo 50703 *Type:* Private *Accred.:* 1995 (NCA) *Calendar:* Sem. plan *Degrees:* B *CEO:* Chanc. Jane Hasek
Enroll: 200   (319) 235-3545

AMERICAN INSTITUTE OF BUSINESS
2500 Fleur Dr., Des Moines 50321 *Type:* Private junior *Accred.:* 1986/1989 (NCA) *Calendar:* Qtr. plan *Degrees:* A, C *CEO:* Pres. Keith Fenton
Enroll: 940   (515) 244-4221

AMERICAN INSTITUTE OF COMMERCE
1801 E. Kimberly Rd., Davenport 52807 *Type:* Private junior *Accred.:* 1957/1995 (ACICS) *Calendar:* Qtr. plan *Degrees:* A, C *Prof. Accred.:* Medical Assisting (AMA) *CEO:* Pres. John Huston
                                 (319) 355-3500

CEDAR FALLS CAMPUS
2302 W. First St., Cedar Falls 50613 *Accred.:* 1987/1989 (ACICS)
                                 (319) 277-0220

BRIAR CLIFF COLLEGE
3303 Rebecca St., Sioux City 51104 *Type:* Private (Roman Catholic) liberal arts *Accred.:* 1945/1995 (NCA) *Calendar:* 3-3 plan *Degrees:* A, B *Prof. Accred.:* Nursing (B), Social Work (B) *CEO:* Pres. Margaret Wick
Enroll: 1,157   (712) 279-5321

BUENA VISTA UNIVERSITY
610 W. Fourth St., Storm Lake 50588 *Type:* Private (United Presbyterian) liberal arts *Accred.:* 1952/1991 (NCA) *Calendar:* Sem. plan *Degrees:* B *Prof. Accred.:* Social Work (B), Teacher Education *CEO:* Pres. Frederick V. Moore
Enroll: 2,367   (712) 749-2103

CENTRAL COLLEGE
812 University, Pella 50219 *Type:* Private (Reformed Church in America) liberal arts *Accred.:* 1942/1994 (NCA) *Calendar:* 3-3

plan *Degrees:* B *Prof. Accred.:* Music *CEO:* Pres. William M. Wiebenga
Enroll: 1,459   (515) 628-9000

CLARKE COLLEGE
1550 Clarke Dr., Dubuque 52001 *Type:* Private (Roman Catholic) liberal arts *Accred.:* 1918/1994 (NCA) *Calendar:* Sem. plan *Degrees:* A, B, M *Prof. Accred.:* Music, Social Work (B), Teacher Education *CEO:* Pres. Catherine Dunn
Enroll: 981   (319) 588-6300

CLINTON COMMUNITY COLLEGE
1000 Lincoln Blvd., Clinton 52732 *Type:* Public (district) junior *System:* Eastern Iowa Community College District *Accred.:* 1983/1993 (NCA) *Calendar:* Qtr. plan *Degrees:* A, C *CEO:* Dean Karen J. Vickers
Enroll: 1,307   (319) 242-6841

* Indirect NCA accreditation through Eastern Iowa Community College District

COE COLLEGE
Cedar Rapids 52402 *Type:* Private (United Presbyterian) liberal arts *Accred.:* 1913/1988 (NCA) *Calendar:* 4-1-4 plan *Degrees:* B, M *Prof. Accred.:* Music, Nursing (B) *CEO:* Acting Pres. James R. Phifer
Enroll: 1,343   (319) 399-8000

CORNELL COLLEGE
600 First St. W., Mount Vernon 52314-1098 *Type:* Private (United Methodist) liberal arts *Accred.:* 1913/1993 (NCA) *Calendar:* Sem. plan *Degrees:* B *Prof. Accred.:* Music *CEO:* Pres. Leslie H. Garner, Jr.
Enroll: 1,134   (800) 747-1112

DES MOINES AREA COMMUNITY COLLEGE
2006 S. Ankeny Blvd., Ankeny 50021 *Type:* Public (district) junior *System:* Iowa Department of Education Division of Community Colleges *Accred.:* 1974/1986 (NCA) *Calendar:* Sem. plan *Degrees:* A, C *Prof. Accred.:* Clinical Lab Technology (A), Dental Assisting, Dental Hygiene, Medical Assisting (AMA), Nursing (A), Practical Nursing,

Respiratory Therapy *CEO:* Pres. Joseph A. Borgen
Enroll: 11,034   (515) 964-6200

DIVINE WORD COLLEGE
102 Jacoby Dr., S.W., Epworth 52045 *Type:* Private liberal arts *Accred.:* 1970/1986 (NCA) *Calendar:* Sem. plan *Degrees:* A, B *CEO:* Pres. Michael Hutchins
Enroll: 74   (319) 876-3353

DORDT COLLEGE
498 4th Ave., N.E., Sioux Center 51250-1697 *Type:* Private (Christian Reformed) liberal arts *Accred.:* 1969/1992 (NCA) *Calendar:* Sem. plan *Degrees:* A, B *Prof. Accred.:* Engineering (general), Social Work (B) *CEO:* Pres. John B. Hulst
Enroll: 1,156   (712) 722-6000

DRAKE UNIVERSITY
26th St. and University Ave., Des Moines 50311 *Type:* Private *Accred.:* 1913/1988 (NCA) *Calendar:* Sem. plan *Degrees:* B, M, P, D *Prof. Accred.:* Art, Business (B,M), Journalism (B,M), Law, Music, Nurse Anesthesia Education (M), Rehabilitation Counseling *CEO:* Pres. Michael R. Ferrari
Enroll: 5,394   (515) 271-2191

ELLSWORTH COMMUNITY COLLEGE
1100 College Ave., Iowa Falls 50126 *Type:* Public (district) junior *System:* Iowa Valley Community College District *Accred.:* 1963/1992 (NCA) *Calendar:* Sem. plan *Degrees:* A, C *CEO:* Dean Duane R. Lloyd
Enroll: 735   (515) 648-4611

EMMAUS BIBLE COLLEGE
2570 Asbury Rd., Dubuque 52001 *Type:* Private (nondenominational) *Accred.:* 1986/1991 (AABC) *Calendar:* Sem. plan *Degrees:* A, B, C *CEO:* Pres. Daniel Smith
FTE Enroll: 222   (319) 588-8000

FAITH BAPTIST BIBLE COLLEGE
1900 N.W. Fourth St., Ankeny 50021 *Type:* Private (General Association of Regular Baptist Churches) *Accred.:* 1969/1989 (AABC) *Calendar:* Sem. plan *Degrees:* A, B, C *CEO:* Pres. Richard Houg
FTE Enroll: 203   (800) 352-0147

GRACELAND COLLEGE
700 College Ave., Lamoni 50140-1698 *Type:* Private (Latter-Day Saints) liberal arts *Accred.:* 1920/1987 (NCA) *Calendar:* 4-1-4 plan *Degrees:* B *Prof. Accred.:* Nursing (B), Teacher Education *CEO:* Pres. William T. Higdon
Enroll: 3,892   (515) 784-5000

GRAND VIEW COLLEGE
1200 Grandview Ave., Des Moines 50316 *Type:* Private (Lutheran) liberal arts *Accred.:* 1959/1995 (NCA) *Calendar:* 4-1-4 plan *Degrees:* A, B *Prof. Accred.:* Nursing (B) *CEO:* Pres. Arthur E. Puotinen
Enroll: 1,418   (800) 444-6083

GRINNELL COLLEGE
P.O. Box 805, Grinnell 50112 *Type:* Private liberal arts *Accred.:* 1913/1989 (NCA) *Calendar:* Sem. plan *Degrees:* B *CEO:* Pres. Pamela A. Ferguson
Enroll: 1,334   (515) 269-4000

HAMILTON BUSINESS COLLEGE
1924 D St., S.W., Cedar Rapids 52404 *Type:* Private business *Accred.:* 1957/1991 (ACICS); 1990/1994 (NCA candidate) *Degrees:* A, C *CEO:* Pres. John Huston
Enroll: 714   (319) 363-0481

DES MOINES CAMPUS
2300 Euclid Ave., Des Moines 50310 *Accred.:* 1989/1991 (ACICS)
                    (515) 279-0253

MASON CITY CAMPUS
100 First St., N.W., Mason City 50401 *Accred.:* 1957/1991 (ACICS)
                    (515) 423-2530

HAMILTON TECHNICAL COLLEGE
1011 E. 53rd St., Davenport 52807-2616 *Type:* Private *Accred.:* 1974/1990 (ACCSCT) *Calendar:* Sem. plan *Degrees:* A, B *CEO:* Pres. MaryAnne Hamilton
                    (319) 386-3570

HAWKEYE COMMUNITY COLLEGE
1501 E. Orange Rd., Box 8015, Waterloo 50704 *Type:* Public (district) junior *System:* Iowa Department of Education Division of

Community Colleges *Accred.:* 1975/1995 (NCA) *Calendar:* Qtr. plan *Degrees:* A, C *Prof. Accred.:* Clinical Lab Technology (A), Dental Assisting, Dental Hygiene, Respiratory Therapy Technology *CEO:* Pres. Phillip O. Barry
Enroll: 3,426   (319) 296-2320

INDIAN HILLS COMMUNITY COLLEGE
525 Grandview Ave., Ottumwa 52501 *Type:* Public (district) junior *System:* Iowa Department of Education Division of Community Colleges *Accred.:* 1977/1990 (NCA) *Calendar:* Qtr. plan *Degrees:* A, C *Prof. Accred.:* Medical Record Technology, Physical Therapy Assisting, Radiography *CEO:* Pres. Lyle Adrian Hellyer
Enroll: 3,336   (515) 683-5111

CENTERVILLE CAMPUS
Centerville 52544
                                   (515) 856-2143

IOWA CENTRAL COMMUNITY COLLEGE
330 Ave. M, Fort Dodge 50501 *Type:* Public (district) junior *System:* Iowa Department of Education Division of Community Colleges *Accred.:* 1974/1991 (NCA) *Calendar:* Sem. plan *Degrees:* A, C *Prof. Accred.:* Medical Assisting (AMA), Radiography *CEO:* Pres. Bob Paxton
Enroll: 2,227   (515) 576-7201

IOWA LAKES COMMUNITY COLLEGE
19 S. 7th St., Estherville 51334 *Type:* Public (district) junior *System:* Iowa Department of Education Division of Community Colleges *Accred.:* 1976/1988 (NCA) *Calendar:* Sem. plan *Degrees:* A, C *CEO:* Pres. James E. Billings
Enroll: 2,057   (800) 242-5106

IOWA STATE UNIVERSITY
117 Beardshear Hall, Ames 50011-2035 *Type:* Public (state) *System:* Iowa State Board of Regents *Accred.:* 1916/1986 (NCA) *Calendar:* Sem. plan *Degrees:* B, M, P, D, C *Prof. Accred.:* Business (B,M), Computer Science, Counseling Psychology, Dietetics (coordinated), Dietetics (internship), Engineering (aerospace, agricultural, ceramic, chemical, civil, computer, construction, electrical, engineering physics/science, industrial, mechanical), Forestry, Home Economics, Interior Design, Journalism (B,M), Landscape Architecture (B), Marriage and Family Therapy (D), Music, Planning (B,M), Psychology Internship Veterinary Medicine *CEO:* Pres. Martin Charles Jischke
Enroll: 24,990   (515) 294-2042

IOWA WESLEYAN COLLEGE
601 N. Main St., Mount Pleasant 52641 *Type:* Private (United Methodist) liberal arts *Accred.:* 1916/1993 (NCA) *Calendar:* 4-1-4 plan *Degrees:* A, B, C *Prof. Accred.:* Nursing (B) *CEO:* Pres. Robert J. Prins
Enroll: 876   (319) 385-8021

IOWA WESTERN COMMUNITY COLLEGE
2700 College Rd., Box 4-C, Council Bluffs 51501 *Type:* Public (district) junior *System:* Iowa Department of Education Division of Community Colleges *Accred.:* 1975/1990 (NCA) *Calendar:* Sem. plan *Degrees:* A, C *Prof. Accred.:* Dental Assisting, Engineering Technology (civil/construction), Medical Assisting (AMA) *CEO:* Pres. Dan D. Kinney
Enroll: 3,581   (712) 325-3200

KIRKWOOD COMMUNITY COLLEGE
6301 Kirkwood Blvd., S.W., P.O. Box 2068, Cedar Rapids 52406-2068 *Type:* Public (district) junior *System:* Iowa Department of Education Division of Community Colleges *Accred.:* 1970/1990 (NCA) *Calendar:* Sem. plan *Degrees:* A, C *Prof. Accred.:* Dental Assisting, Dental Laboratory Technology, Electroneurodiagnostic Technology, Medical Assisting (AMA), Medical Record Technology, Occupational Therapy Assisting, Physical Therapy Assisting, Respiratory Therapy, Veterinary Technology (probational) *CEO:* Pres. Norman R. Nielsen
Enroll: 9,752   (319) 398-5411

LORAS COLLEGE
1450 Alta Vista, Dubuque 52001 *Type:* Private (Roman Catholic) liberal arts *Accred.:* 1917/1990 (NCA) *Calendar:* Sem. plan *Degrees:* A, B, M *Prof. Accred.:* Social Work

(B), Teacher Education *CEO:* Pres. Joachim Froehlich
Enroll: 1,933   (319) 588-7103

LUTHER COLLEGE
Decorah 52101 *Type:* Private (Lutheran) liberal arts *Accred.:* 1915/1989 (NCA) *Calendar:* 4-1-4 plan *Degrees:* B *Prof. Accred.:* Music, Nursing (B), Social Work (B), Teacher Education *CEO:* Interim Pres. David J. Roslien
Enroll: 2,383   (319) 387-1001

MAHARISHI UNIVERSITY OF MANAGEMENT
1000 N. Fourth St., DB 1113, Fairfield 52557-1113 *Type:* Private liberal arts *Accred.:* 1980/1990 (NCA) *Calendar:* Sem. plan *Degrees:* A, B, M, D, C *CEO:* Pres. Bevan Morris
Enroll: 628   (515) 472-5031

MARSHALLTOWN COMMUNITY COLLEGE
3700 S. Center St., Marshalltown 50158 *Type:* Public (district) junior *System:* Iowa Valley Community College District *Accred.:* 1966/1992 (NCA) *Calendar:* Qtr. plan *Degrees:* A, C *Prof. Accred.:* Dental Assisting, Surgical Technology *CEO:* Dean William M. Simpson
Enroll: 1,266   (515) 752-7106

MORNINGSIDE COLLEGE
1501 Morningside Ave., Sioux City 51106 *Type:* Private (United Methodist) liberal arts *Accred.:* 1913/1994 (NCA) *Calendar:* Sem. plan *Degrees:* A, B, M *Prof. Accred.:* Music, Nursing (B), Teacher Education *CEO:* Pres. Jerry M. Israel
Enroll: 1,214   (800) 831-0806

MOUNT MERCY COLLEGE
1330 Elmhurst Dr., N.E., Cedar Rapids 52402 *Type:* Private (Roman Catholic) liberal arts *Accred.:* 1932/1993 (NCA) *Calendar:* 4-1-4 plan *Degrees:* B *Prof. Accred.:* Nursing (B), Social Work (B) *CEO:* Pres. Thomas R. Feld
Enroll: 1,227   (319) 363-8213

MOUNT ST. CLARE COLLEGE
400 N. Bluff Blvd., Clinton 52732 *Type:* Private (Roman Catholic) liberal arts *Accred.:* 1950/1989 (NCA) *Calendar:* Sem. plan *Degrees:* A, B, C *CEO:* Pres. James J. Ross
Enroll: 513   (319) 242-4023

MUSCATINE COMMUNITY COLLEGE
152 Colorado St., Muscatine 52761 *Type:* Public (district) junior *System:* Eastern Iowa Community College District *Accred.:* 1983/1993 (NCA) *Calendar:* Qtr. plan *Degrees:* A, C *CEO:* Pres. Victor G. McAvoy
(319) 263-8250

* Indirect NCA accreditation through Eastern Iowa Community College District

NATIONAL EDUCATION CENTER—NATIONAL INSTITUTE OF TECHNOLOGY CAMPUS
1119 Fifth St., West Des Moines 50265-2698 *Type:* Private *Accred.:* 1968/1986 (ACCSCT) *Calendar:* Qtr. plan *Degrees:* A, C *Prof. Accred.:* Medical Assisting (AMA) *CEO:* Dir. Pat Bishop
(515) 223-1486

NORTH IOWA AREA COMMUNITY COLLEGE
500 College Dr., Mason City 50401 *Type:* Public (district) junior *System:* Iowa Department of Education Division of Community Colleges *Accred.:* 1919/1994 (NCA) *Calendar:* Sem. plan *Degrees:* A, C *Prof. Accred.:* Nursing (A) *CEO:* Pres. David L. Buettner
Enroll: 2,878   (515) 423-1264

NORTHEAST IOWA COMMUNITY COLLEGE
Box 400, Hwy. 150, Calmar 52132 *Type:* Public (district) junior *System:* Iowa Department of Education Division of Community Colleges *Accred.:* 1971/1991 (NCA) *Calendar:* Qtr. plan *Degrees:* A, C *Prof. Accred.:* Dental Assisting, Medical Record Technology, Radiography, Respiratory Therapy Technology *CEO:* Pres. Don Roby
Enroll: 2,586   (800) 728-2256

PEOSTA CAMPUS
10250 Sundown Rd., Peosta 52068
(319) 556-5110

NORTHWEST IOWA COMMUNITY COLLEGE
603 W. Park St., Sheldon 51201 *Type:* Public (district) junior *System:* Iowa Department of Education Division of Community Colleges *Accred.:* 1980/1995 (NCA) *Calendar:* Qtr. plan *Degrees:* A, C *CEO:* Pres. Carl H. Rolf
Enroll: 574   (800) 352-4907

NORTHWESTERN COLLEGE
101 Seventh St., S.W., Orange City 51041 *Type:* Private (Reformed Church in America) liberal arts and teachers *Accred.:* 1953/1986 (NCA) *Calendar:* Sem. plan *Degrees:* A, B, M *Prof. Accred.:* Social Work (B), Teacher Education *CEO:* Pres. James E. Bultman
Enroll: 1,153   (712) 737-7000

PALMER COLLEGE OF CHIROPRACTIC
1000 Brady St., Davenport 52803 *Type:* Private professional *System:* Palmer Chiropractic University System *Accred.:* 1984/1989 (NCA) *Calendar:* Tri. plan *Degrees:* A, B, M, D, C *Prof. Accred.:* Chiropractic Education *CEO:* Interim Pres. Virgil V. Strang
Enroll: 1,974   (800) 722-2586

ST. AMBROSE UNIVERSITY
518 W. Locust St., Davenport 52803 *Type:* Private (Roman Catholic) liberal arts *Accred.:* 1927/1988 (NCA) *Calendar:* Sem. plan *Degrees:* B, M, C *Prof. Accred.:* Engineering (industrial), Occupational Therapy, Physical Therapy *CEO:* Pres. Edward J. Rogalski
Enroll: 2,584   (319) 333-6000

SCOTT COMMUNITY COLLEGE
500 Belmont Rd., Bettendorf 52722 *Type:* Public (district) junior *System:* Eastern Iowa Community College District *Accred.:* 1983/1993 (NCA) *Calendar:* Qtr. plan *Degrees:* A, C *Prof. Accred.:* Clinical Lab Technology (A), Electroneurodiagnostic Technology, Radiography *CEO:* Pres. Lenny E. Stone
(319) 359-7531

* Indirect NCA accreditation through Eastern Iowa Community College District

SIMPSON COLLEGE
701 N. C St., Indianola 50125 *Type:* Private (United Methodist) liberal arts *Accred.:*

1913/1986 (NCA) *Calendar:* 4-1-4 plan *Degrees:* B *Prof. Accred.:* Music *CEO:* Pres. Stephen G. Jennings
Enroll: 1,613   (515) 961-6251

SOUTHEASTERN COMMUNITY COLLEGE
1015 S. Gear Ave., Drawer F, West Burlington 52655 *Type:* Public (district) junior *System:* Iowa Department of Education Division of Community Colleges *Accred.:* 1974/1989 (NCA) *Calendar:* Sem. plan *Degrees:* A, C *Prof. Accred.:* Medical Assisting (AMA) *CEO:* Pres. R. Gene Gardner
Enroll: 2,646   (319) 752-2731

SOUTHWESTERN COMMUNITY COLLEGE
1501 Townline St., P.O. Box 458, Creston 50801 *Type:* Public (district) junior *System:* Iowa Department of Education Division of Community Colleges *Accred.:* 1974/1989 (NCA) *Calendar:* Sem. plan *Degrees:* A, C *CEO:* Pres. Richard L. Byerly
Enroll: 1,191   (515) 782-7081

SPENCER COLLEGE
217 W. Fifth St., P.O. Box 5065, Spencer 51301 *Type:* Private business *Accred.:* 1972/1996 (ACICS) *Calendar:* Qtr. plan *Degrees:* A, C *Prof. Accred.:* Medical Assisting (AMA) *CEO:* Pres. Ferdinand Pane
(712) 262-7290

TEIKYO MARYCREST UNIVERSITY
1607 W. 12th St., Davenport 52804 *Type:* Private liberal arts *Accred.:* 1955/1994 (NCA) *Calendar:* Sem. plan *Degrees:* A, B, M, C *Prof. Accred.:* Nursing (B), Social Work (B) *CEO:* Pres. Lawrence M. Conner
Enroll: 1,266   (319) 326-9512

UNIVERSITY OF DUBUQUE
2000 University Ave., Dubuque 52001 *Type:* Private (Presbyterian) liberal arts *Accred.:* 1944/1989 (ATS); 1921/1989 (NCA) *Calendar:* Sem. plan *Degrees:* A, B, M, D *Prof. Accred.:* Nursing (B), Social Work (B), Teacher Education *CEO:* Pres. John J. Agria
Enroll: 990   (319) 589-3223

UNIVERSITY OF IOWA
101 Jessup Hall, Iowa City 52242-1316 *Type:* Public (state) *System:* Iowa State Board of Regents *Accred.:* 1913/1988 (NCA) *Calendar:* Sem. plan *Degrees:* B, M, P, D *Prof. Accred.:* Accounting (A,C), Athletic Training, Audiology, Business (B,M), Clinical Lab Scientist, Clinical Psychology, Combined Prosthodontics, Counseling, Counseling Psychology, Dental Public Health, Dentistry, Dietetics (internship), Endodontics, Engineering (bioengineering, chemical, civil, electrical, industrial, mechanical), General Dentistry, General Practice Residency, Health Services Administration, Journalism (B,M), Law, Librarianship, Medicine, Music, Nuclear Medicine Technology, Nurse Anesthesia Education (M), Nursing (B,M), Oral Pathology, Oral and Maxillofacial Surgery, Orthodontics, Pediatric Dentistry, Periodontics, Physical Therapy, Physician Assisting/Surgeon Assisting, Planning (M), Psychology Internship, Recreation and Leisure Services (B), Rehabilitation Counseling, School Psychology, Social Work (B,M), Speech-Language Pathology, Theatre *CEO:* Pres. Mary Sue Coleman
Enroll: 26,932   (319) 335-3500

UNIVERSITY OF NORTHERN IOWA
Cedar Falls 50614 *Type:* Public (state) *System:* Iowa State Board of Regents *Accred.:* 1913/1991 (NCA) *Calendar:* Sem. plan *Degrees:* B, M, P, D *Prof. Accred.:* Art, Audiology, Business (B,M), Construction Education (B), Counseling, Home Economics, Music, Recreation and Leisure Services (B), Social Work (B), Speech-Language Pathology *CEO:* Pres. Robert D. Koob
Enroll: 11,560   (319) 273-2311

UNIVERSITY OF OSTEOPATHIC MEDICINE AND HEALTH SCIENCES
3200 Grand Ave., Des Moines 50312 *Type:* Private professional *Accred.:* 1986/1991 (NCA) *Calendar:* Sem. plan *Degrees:* B, M, D, C *Prof. Accred.:* Osteopathy, Physical Therapy, Physician Assisting/Surgeon Assisting, Podiatry *CEO:* Pres. David G. Marker
Enroll: 1,327   (515) 271-1400

UPPER IOWA UNIVERSITY
Box 1857, College and Washington Sts., Fayette 52142 *Type:* Private liberal arts *Accred.:* 1913/1991 (NCA) *Calendar:* 4-1-4 plan *Degrees:* A, B *CEO:* Pres. Ralph L. McKay
Enroll: 3,175   (319) 425-5200

VENNARD COLLEGE
Eighth Ave. E., P.O. Box 29, University Park 52595-9999 *Type:* Private (Wesleyan) *Accred.:* 1948/1995 (AABC) *Calendar:* Sem. plan *Degrees:* A, B, C *CEO:* Pres. Blake J. Neff
FTE Enroll: 107   (515) 673-8391

WALDORF COLLEGE
Forest City 50436 *Type:* Private (Lutheran) junior *Accred.:* 1948/1990 (NCA) *Calendar:* Sem. plan *Degrees:* A, C *CEO:* Pres. William E. Hamm
Enroll: 573   (515) 582-2450

WARTBURG COLLEGE
222 9th St., N.W., Waverly 50677-1003 *Type:* Private (Lutheran) liberal arts *Accred.:* 1948/1987 (NCA) *Calendar:* 4-4-x plan *Degrees:* B, C *Prof. Accred.:* Music, Social Work (B), Teacher Education *CEO:* Pres. Robert L. Vogel
Enroll: 1,405   (319) 352-8450

WARTBURG THEOLOGICAL SEMINARY
333 Wartburg Pl., Dubuque 52003-7797 *Type:* Private (Lutheran) graduate only *Accred.:* 1944/1986 (ATS); 1976/1987 (NCA) *Calendar:* 4-1-4 plan *Degrees:* M, D *CEO:* Pres. Roger W. Fjeld
Enroll: 199   (319) 589-0200

WESTERN IOWA TECH COMMUNITY COLLEGE
4647 Stone Ave., P.O. Box 265, Sioux City 51102-0265 *Type:* Public (district) junior *System:* Iowa Department of Education Division of Community Colleges *Accred.:* 1977/1992 (NCA) *Calendar:* Qtr. plan *Degrees:* A, C *Prof. Accred.:* Dental Assisting, Occupational Therapy Assisting, Physical Therapy Assisting, Practical Nursing, Surgical Technology *CEO:* Pres. Robert E. Dunker
Enroll: 2,664   (712) 274-6400

CHEROKEE CAMPUS
228-1/2 W. Main, Cherokee 51012
(712) 225-0238

DENISON CAMPUS
11 N. 35th St., Denison 51142
(712) 263-3419

WESTMAR UNIVERSITY
1002 Third Ave., S.E., Le Mars 51031 *Type:*
Private (United Methodist) liberal arts
Accred.: 1953/1994 (NCA) *Calendar:* 4-1-4
plan *Degrees:* B, C *CEO:* Pres. Glenn
Balch, Jr.
Enroll: 572
(800) 352-4634

WILLIAM PENN COLLEGE
201 Trueblood Ave., Oskaloosa 52577 *Type:*
Private (Society of Friends) liberal arts
Accred.: 1913/1994 (NCA) *Calendar:* Sem.
plan *Degrees:* B *CEO:* Pres. John A. Fallon, III
Enroll: 576
(515) 673-1001

KANSAS

ALLEN COUNTY COMMUNITY COLLEGE
1801 North Central, Iola 66749 *Type:* Public (district) junior *System:* Kansas State Board of Education *Accred.:* 1974/1989 (NCA) *Calendar:* Sem. plan *Degrees:* A, C *CEO:* Pres. John Masterson
Enroll: 1,558   (316) 365-5116

BAKER UNIVERSITY
606 W. 8th St., P.O. Box 65, Baldwin City 66006-0065 *Type:* Private (United Methodist) liberal arts *Accred.:* 1913/1992 (NCA) *Calendar:* 4-1-4 plan *Degrees:* A, B, M *Prof. Accred.:* Music (A), Nursing (A,B) *CEO:* Pres. Daniel M. Lambert
Enroll: 1,997   (913) 594-6451

SCHOOL OF NURSING CAMPUS
Stormont-Vail Medical Ctr., 1500 S.W. 10th St., Topeka 66604-1353
(913) 354-5850

SCHOOL OF PROFESSIONAL AND GRADUATE STUDIES CAMPUS
6600 Coll. Blvd., Ste. 340, Overland Park 66211
(913) 491-4432

BARCLAY COLLEGE
607 N. Kingman, Haviland 67059 *Type:* Private (Evangelical Friends International) *Accred.:* 1975/1985 (AABC) *Calendar:* 4-1-4 plan *Degrees:* B, C *CEO:* Pres. Walter Moody
FTE Enroll: 93   (316) 862-5252

BARTON COUNTY COMMUNITY COLLEGE
Rural Rte. 3, Box 136Z, Great Bend 67530 *Type:* Public (district) junior *System:* Kansas State Board of Education *Accred.:* 1974/1993 (NCA) *Calendar:* Sem. plan *Degrees:* A, C *Prof. Accred.:* Clinical Lab Technology (A), Occupational Therapy Assisting *CEO:* Pres. Jimmie L. Downing
Enroll: 4,567   (800) 748-7594

BENEDICTINE COLLEGE
1020 N. Second St., Atchison 66002 *Type:* Private (Roman Catholic) liberal arts *Accred.:* 1971/1993 (NCA) *Calendar:* 4-1-4 plan *Degrees:* A, B, M *Prof. Accred.:* Music, Teacher Education *CEO:* Pres. Daniel Carey
Enroll: 867   (913) 367-5340

BETHANY COLLEGE
421 N. First St., Lindsborg 67456 *Type:* Private (Lutheran) liberal arts *Accred.:* 1932/1990 (NCA) *Calendar:* 4-1-4 plan *Degrees:* B *Prof. Accred.:* Music, Social Work (B), Teacher Education *CEO:* Pres. Joel M. McKean
Enroll: 743   (913) 227-3311

BETHEL COLLEGE
300 E. 27th St., North Newton 67117 *Type:* Private (Mennonite) liberal arts *Accred.:* 1938/1989 (NCA) *Calendar:* 4-1-4 plan *Degrees:* B *Prof. Accred.:* Nursing (B), Social Work (B) *CEO:* Pres. Douglas A. Penner
Enroll: 644   (316) 283-2500

THE BROWN MACKIE COLLEGE
126 S. Santa Fe Ave., Salina 67401 *Type:* Private business *Accred.:* 1980/1995 (NCA) *Calendar:* Qtr. plan *Degrees:* A, C *CEO:* Pres. M. Gary Talley
Enroll: 547   (913) 825-5422

OVERLAND CAMPUS
8000 W. 110th St., Ste. 200, Overland Park 66210
(913) 451-3856

BUTLER COUNTY COMMUNITY COLLEGE
901 S. Haverhill Rd., El Dorado 67042 *Type:* Public (district) junior *System:* Kansas State Board of Education *Accred.:* 1970/1990 (NCA) *Calendar:* Sem. plan *Degrees:* A, C *Prof. Accred.:* Nursing (A) *CEO:* Pres. Jacqueline A. Vietti
Enroll: 7,447   (316) 312-2222

CENTRAL BAPTIST THEOLOGICAL SEMINARY
741 N. 31st St., Kansas City 66102-3964 *Type:* Private (Baptist) graduate only *Accred.:* 1962/1984 (ATS); 1979/1990 (NCA) *Calendar:* Sem. plan *Degrees:* M *CEO:* Pres. Thomas E. Clifton
Enroll: 84   (800) 677-2287

CENTRAL COLLEGE
1200 S. Main St., McPherson 67460 *Type:* Private (Free Methodist) *Accred.:* 1975/1994 (NCA) *Calendar:* 4-1-4 plan *Degrees:* A, B, C *CEO:* Pres. John A. Martin
Enroll: 304   (316) 241-0723

CLOUD COUNTY COMMUNITY COLLEGE
2221 Campus Dr., P.O. Box 1002, Concordia 66901-1002 *Type:* Public (district) junior *System:* Kansas State Board of Education *Accred.:* 1977/1991 (NCA) *Calendar:* Sem. plan *Degrees:* A, C *Prof. Accred.:* Nursing (A), Practical Nursing *CEO:* Pres. James P. Ihrig
Enroll: 2,513   (800) 729-5101

COFFEYVILLE COMMUNITY COLLEGE
400 W. 11th St., Coffeyville 67337 *Type:* Public (district) junior *System:* Kansas State Board of Education *Accred.:* 1972/1995 (NCA) *Calendar:* Sem. plan *Degrees:* A, C *CEO:* Pres. Ronald Thomas
Enroll: 2,008   (316) 251-7700

COLBY COMMUNITY COLLEGE
1255 S. Range, Colby 67701 *Type:* Public (district) junior *System:* Kansas State Board of Education *Accred.:* 1972/1995 (NCA) *Calendar:* Sem. plan *Degrees:* A, C *Prof. Accred.:* Nursing (A), Physical Therapy Assisting, Practical Nursing, Veterinary Technology *CEO:* Pres. Mikel V. Ary
Enroll: 2,132   (913) 462-3984

COWLEY COUNTY COMMUNITY COLLEGE
125 S. Second St., P.O. Box 1147, Arkansas City 67005 *Type:* Public (district) junior *System:* Kansas State Board of Education *Accred.:* 1975/1990 (NCA) *Calendar:* Sem. plan *Degrees:* A, C *CEO:* Pres. Patrick J. McAtee
Enroll: 3,059   (800) 593-2222

DODGE CITY COMMUNITY COLLEGE
2501 N. 14th St., Dodge City 67801 *Type:* Public (district) junior *System:* Kansas State Board of Education *Accred.:* 1966/1986 (NCA) *Calendar:* Sem. plan *Degrees:* A, C *Prof. Accred.:* Medical Record Technology,

Nursing (A), Practical Nursing *CEO:* Interim Pres. Carl L. Heinrich
Enroll: 2,277   (800) 262-4565

DONNELLY COLLEGE
608 N. 18th St., Kansas City 66102 *Type:* Private (Roman Catholic) junior *Accred.:* 1958/1989 (NCA) *Calendar:* Sem. plan *Degrees:* A, C *CEO:* Pres. John P. Murry
Enroll: 455   (913) 621-6070

EMPORIA STATE UNIVERSITY
1200 Commercial St., Emporia 66801-5087 *Type:* Public (state) liberal arts and teachers *System:* Kansas Board of Regents *Accred.:* 1915/1995 (NCA) *Calendar:* Sem. plan *Degrees:* B, M, P, D *Prof. Accred.:* Librarianship, Music, Rehabilitation Counseling, Teacher Education *CEO:* Pres. Robert E. Glennen, Jr.
Enroll: 6,075   (316) 343-1200

FORT HAYS STATE UNIVERSITY
600 Park St., Hays 67601 *Type:* Public (state) liberal arts and teachers *System:* Kansas Board of Regents *Accred.:* 1915/1992 (NCA) *Calendar:* Sem. plan *Degrees:* A, B, M, P *Prof. Accred.:* Music, Nursing (B), Radiography, Speech-Language Pathology, Teacher Education *CEO:* Pres. Edward H. Hammond
Enroll: 5,496   (913) 628-4000

FORT SCOTT COMMUNITY COLLEGE
2108 S. Horton St., Fort Scott 66701 *Type:* Public (district) junior *System:* Kansas State Board of Education *Accred.:* 1976/1993 (NCA) *Calendar:* Sem. plan *Degrees:* A, C *Prof. Accred.:* Nursing (A) *CEO:* Pres. Laura Meeks
Enroll: 1,694   (316) 223-2700

FRIENDS UNIVERSITY
2100 University Ave., Wichita 67213 *Type:* Private (Friends) liberal arts *Accred.:* 1915/1991 (NCA) *Calendar:* Sem. plan *Degrees:* A, B, M *Prof. Accred.:* Marriage and Family Therapy (M), Music, Teacher Education *CEO:* Pres. Biff Green
Enroll: 2,330   (316) 261-5800

GARDEN CITY COMMUNITY COLLEGE
801 Campus Dr., Garden City 67846 *Type:* Public (district) junior *System:* Kansas State Board of Education *Accred.:* 1975/1995 (NCA) *Calendar:* Sem. plan *Degrees:* A, C *Prof. Accred.:* Nursing (A) *CEO:* Pres. James H. Tangeman
Enroll: 2,219   (800) 658-1696

HASKELL INDIAN NATIONS UNIVERSITY
155 Indian Ave., Ste.1305, Lawrence 66046-4800 *Type:* Public (federal) junior *Accred.:* 1979/1993 (NCA) *Calendar:* Sem. plan *Degrees:* A, B *CEO:* Pres. Bob Martin
Enroll: 793   (913) 749-8404

HESSTON COLLEGE
P.O. Box 3000, Hesston 67062 *Type:* Private (Mennonite) junior *Accred.:* 1964/1991 (NCA) *Calendar:* 4-1-4 plan *Degrees:* A *Prof. Accred.:* Nursing (A) *CEO:* Pres. Loren E. Swartzendruber
Enroll: 462   (316) 327-4221

HIGHLAND COMMUNITY COLLEGE
Box 68, Highland 66035 *Type:* Public (district) junior *System:* Kansas State Board of Education *Accred.:* 1977/1989 (NCA) *Calendar:* Sem. plan *Degrees:* A, C *CEO:* Pres. Betty Stevens
Enroll: 2,294   (913) 442-3236

HUTCHINSON COMMUNITY COLLEGE
1300 N. Plum St., Hutchinson 67501 *Type:* Public (district) junior *System:* Kansas State Board of Education *Accred.:* 1960/1994 (NCA) *Calendar:* Sem. plan *Degrees:* A, C *Prof. Accred.:* Medical Record Technology, Nursing (A), Radiography *CEO:* Pres. Edward E. Berger
Enroll: 3,830   (800) 289-3501

INDEPENDENCE COMMUNITY COLLEGE
College Ave. and Brookside Dr., P.O. Box 708, Independence 67301 *Type:* Public (district) junior *System:* Kansas State Board of Education *Accred.:* 1957/1988 (NCA) *Calendar:* Sem. plan *Degrees:* A, C *CEO:* Pres. Don Schoening
Enroll: 890   (316) 331-4100

JOHNSON COUNTY COMMUNITY COLLEGE
12345 College Blvd., Overland Park 66210 *Type:* Public (district) junior *System:* Kansas State Board of Education *Accred.:* 1975/1987 (NCA) *Calendar:* Sem. plan *Degrees:* A, C *Prof. Accred.:* Dental Hygiene, EMT-Paramedic, Nursing (A), Respiratory Therapy *CEO:* Pres. Charles J. Carlsen
Enroll: 15,302   (913) 469-8500

KANSAS CITY KANSAS COMMUNITY COLLEGE
7250 State Ave., Kansas City 66112 *Type:* Public (district) junior *System:* Kansas State Board of Education *Accred.:* 1951/1986 (NCA) *Calendar:* Sem. plan *Degrees:* A, C *Prof. Accred.:* Funeral Service Education (Mortuary Science), Nursing (A) *CEO:* Pres. Thomas R. Burke
Enroll: 5,918   (913) 334-1100

KANSAS NEWMAN COLLEGE
3100 McCormick Ave., Wichita 67213-2097 *Type:* Private (Roman Catholic) liberal arts *Accred.:* 1967/1987 (NCA) *Calendar:* Sem. plan *Degrees:* A, B, M *Prof. Accred.:* Nursing (A,B), Occupational Therapy *CEO:* Pres. Tarcisia Roths, Sr.
Enroll: 1,954   (800) 736-7585

KANSAS STATE UNIVERSITY
Anderson Hall 110, Manhattan 66506-0113 *Type:* Public (state) *System:* Kansas Board of Regents *Accred.:* 1916/1992 (NCA) *Calendar:* Sem. plan *Degrees:* A, B, M, D, C *Prof. Accred.:* Accounting (A,C), Business (B,M), Computer Science, Construction Education (B), Dietetics (coordinated), Engineering Technology (civil/construction, electrical, mechanical), Engineering (agricultural, architectural, chemical, civil, computer, electrical, industrial, manufacturing, mechanical, nuclear), Home Economics, Interior Design, Journalism (B,M), Landscape Architecture (B,M), Marriage and Family Therapy (M,D), Music, Planning (M), Psychology Internship, Public Administration, Recreation and Leisure Services (B), Social Work (B), Speech-Language Pathology, Teacher Education, Theatre, Veterinary Medicine *CEO:* Pres. Jon Wefald
Enroll: 20,664   (913) 532-6011

SALINA COLLEGE OF TECHNOLOGY
2409 Scanlan Ave., Salina 67401-8196
Prof. Accred.: Engineering Technology
(chemical, civil/construction, computer)
mechanical)
(913) 825-0275

KANSAS WESLEYAN UNIVERSITY
100 E. Clafin, Salina 67401-6196 *Type:* Private (United Methodist) liberal arts *Accred.:*
1916/1990 (NCA) *Calendar:* 4-1-4 plan
Degrees: A, B *Prof. Accred.:* Nursing (A,B)
CEO: Pres. Marshall P. Stanton
Enroll: 720 (800) 874-1154

LABETTE COMMUNITY COLLEGE
200 S. 14th St., Parsons 67357 *Type:* Public
(district) junior *System:* Kansas State Board
of Education *Accred.:* 1976/1988 (NCA)
Calendar: Sem. plan *Degrees:* A, C *Prof.
Accred.:* Nursing (A), Radiography, Respiratory Therapy, Respiratory Therapy Technology *CEO:* Pres. Joe Birmingham
Enroll: 2,023 (316) 421-6700

MANHATTAN CHRISTIAN COLLEGE
1415 Anderson Ave., Manhattan 66502
Type: Private (Christian Churches/Churches
of Christ) *Accred.:* 1948/1986 (AABC) *Calendar:* Sem. plan *Degrees:* A, B, C *CEO:*
Pres. Kenneth D. Cable
FTE Enroll: 236 (913) 539-3571

MCPHERSON COLLEGE
1600 E. Euclid, P.O. Box 1402, McPherson
67460 *Type:* Private (Church of Brethren)
liberal arts *Accred.:* 1921/1995 (NCA) *Calendar:* 4-1-4 plan *Degrees:* A, B, C *CEO:*
Pres. Paul W. Hoffman
Enroll: 459 (316) 241-0731

MIDAMERICA NAZARENE COLLEGE
2030 E. College Way, Olathe 66062-1899
Type: Private (Nazarene) liberal arts
Accred.: 1974/1989 (NCA) *Calendar:* Sem.
plan *Degrees:* A, B, M *Prof. Accred.:* Music
(A), Nursing (B) *CEO:* Pres. Richard L.
Spindle
Enroll: 1,445 (913) 782-3750

NEOSHO COUNTY COMMUNITY COLLEGE
1000 S. Allen, Chanute 66720 *Type:* Public
(district) junior *System:* Kansas State Board
of Education *Accred.:* 1976/1986 (NCA)
Calendar: Sem. plan *Degrees:* A, C *Prof.
Accred.:* Nursing (A) *CEO:* Pres. Theodore
W. Wischropp
Enroll: 1,606 (316) 431-2820

OTTAWA UNIVERSITY
1001 S. Cedar, Ottawa 66067-3399 *Type:*
Private (Baptist) liberal arts *Accred.:* 1914/
1994 (NCA) *Calendar:* Sem. plan *Degrees:*
B, M *CEO:* Pres. Harold D. Germer
Enroll: 4,337 (913) 242-5200

KANSAS CITY CAMPUS
10865 Grandview, Bldg. 20, Overland
Park 66210
(913) 451-1431

MILWAUKEE CAMPUS
300 N. Corporate Dr., Ste. 110, Brookfield, WI 53045
(414) 879-0200

PHOENIX CAMPUS
2340 W. Mission Ln., Phoenix, AZ 85021
(602) 371-1188

PITTSBURG STATE UNIVERSITY
1701 S. Broadway, Pittsburg 66762 *Type:*
Public (state) liberal arts and professional
System: Kansas Board of Regents *Accred.:*
1915/1993 (NCA) *Calendar:* Sem. plan
Degrees: A, B, M, P, C *Prof. Accred.:* Counseling, Engineering Technology (civil/construction, electrical, manufacturing, mechanical, plastics), Music, Nursing (B), Social
Work (B), Teacher Education *CEO:* Pres.
John R. Darling
Enroll: 6,489 (316) 231-7000

PRATT COMMUNITY COLLEGE
348 N.E. SR 61, Pratt 67124 *Type:* Public
(district) junior *System:* Kansas State Board
of Education *Accred.:* 1976/1995 (NCA)
Calendar: Sem. plan *Degrees:* A, C *Prof.
Accred.:* Nursing (A) *CEO:* Pres. William A.
Wojciechowski
Enroll: 1,291 (316) 672-5641

ST. MARY COLLEGE
4100 S. 4th St. Trafficway, Leavenworth 66048-5082 *Type:* Private (Roman Catholic) liberal arts primarily for women *Accred.:* 1928/1987 (NCA) *Calendar:* Sem. plan *Degrees:* A, B, M *Prof. Accred.:* Nursing (B), Teacher Education *CEO:* Pres. James F. Reid
Enroll: 899   (913) 758-6102

SEWARD COUNTY COMMUNITY COLLEGE
1801 N. Kansas St., Box 1137, Liberal 67901 *Type:* Public (district) junior *System:* Kansas State Board of Education *Accred.:* 1975/1990 (NCA) *Calendar:* Sem. plan *Degrees:* A, C *Prof. Accred.:* Clinical Lab Technology (A), Nursing (A), Practical Nursing, Respiratory Therapy, Respiratory Therapy Technology *CEO:* Pres. James R. Grote
Enroll: 1,631   (316) 624-1951

SOUTHWESTERN COLLEGE
100 College St., Winfield 67156 *Type:* Private (United Methodist) liberal arts *Accred.:* 1918/1995 (NCA) *Calendar:* 4-1-4 plan *Degrees:* B, M, C *Prof. Accred.:* Music, Nursing (B), Social Work (B) *CEO:* Pres. Carl E. Martin
Enroll: 752   (316) 221-4150

STERLING COLLEGE
Cooper at Broadway, Sterling 67579 *Type:* Private (United Presbyterian) liberal arts *Accred.:* 1928/1994 (NCA) *Calendar:* 4-1-4 plan *Degrees:* A, B *CEO:* Interim Pres. J. Robert Campbell
Enroll: 841   (316) 278-2173

TABOR COLLEGE
400 S. Jefferson St., Hillsboro 67063 *Type:* Private liberal arts *Accred.:* 1965/1995 (NCA) *Calendar:* Sem. plan *Degrees:* A, B *Prof. Accred.:* Music *CEO:* Pres. David Brandt
Enroll: 503   (316) 947-3121

UNITED STATES ARMY COMMAND AND GENERAL STAFF COLLEGE
Fort Leavenworth 66027 *Type:* Public (federal) *Accred.:* 1976/1995 (NCA) *Calendar:* Sem. plan *Degrees:* M, C *CEO:* Cmdt. Leonard D. Holder, Jr.
Enroll: 1,200   (913) 684-2741

UNIVERSITY OF KANSAS
203 Strong Hall, Lawrence 66045 *Type:* Public (state) *System:* Kansas Board of Regents *Accred.:* 1913/1995 (NCA) *Calendar:* Sem. plan *Degrees:* B, M, P, D, C *Prof. Accred.:* Art, Audiology, Business (B,M), Clinical Psychology, Counseling Psychology, Engineering (aerospace, architectural, chemical, civil, computer, electrical, engineering physics/science, mechanical, petroleum), Health Services Administration, Journalism (B,M), Law, Music, Planning (M), Public Administration, School Psychology, Social Work (B,M), Speech-Language Pathology, Teacher Education *CEO:* Chanc. Robert E. Hemenway
Enroll: 28,046   (913) 864-2700

UNIVERSITY OF KANSAS MEDICAL CENTER
3901 Rainbow Blvd., Kansas City 66160 *Type:* Public *Degrees:* B, M, C *Prof. Accred.:* Clinical Lab Scientist, Cytotechnology, Dietetics (internship), Medical Record Administration, Medicine, Nuclear Medicine Technology, Nurse Anesthesia Education (M), Nursing (B,M), Occupational Therapy, Physical Therapy, Radiation Therapy Technology, Respiratory Therapy *CEO:* Exec. Vice Chanc. Donald S. Hagen
                    (913) 588-1401

WASHBURN UNIVERSITY OF TOPEKA
17th and College Sts., Topeka 66621 *Type:* Public (local) *Accred.:* 1913/1988 (NCA) *Calendar:* Sem. plan *Degrees:* A, B, M, D, C *Prof. Accred.:* Art (A), Law, Medical Record Technology, Music, Nursing (B), Physical Therapy Assisting, Radiation Therapy Technology, Radiography, Respiratory Therapy, Respiratory Therapy Technology, Social Work (B,M-candidate), Teacher Education *CEO:* Pres. Hugh L. Thompson
Enroll: 6,439   (913) 231-1010

WICHITA STATE UNIVERSITY

1845 Fairmont St., Wichita 67260 *Type:* Public (state) *System:* Kansas Board of Regents *Accred.:* 1927/1987 (NCA) *Calendar:* Sem. plan *Degrees:* A, B, M, P, D *Prof. Accred.:* Audiology, Business (B,M), Clinical Lab Scientist, Dance (A), Dental Hygiene, Engineering (aerospace, electrical, industrial, mechanical), Music, Nursing (B,M), Physical Therapy, Physician Assisting/Surgeon Assisting, Respiratory Therapy, Social Work (B), Speech-Language Pathology, Teacher Education *CEO:* Pres. Eugene M. Hughes

Enroll: 14,556   (800) 362-2594

KENTUCKY

ALICE LLOYD COLLEGE
100 Purpose Rd., Pippa Passes 41844 *Type:*
Private liberal arts *Accred.:* 1952/1987
(SACS-CC) *Calendar:* Sem. plan *Degrees:*
B *CEO:* Pres. Timothy T. Siebert
FTE Enroll: 604   (606) 368-2101

ASBURY COLLEGE
One Macklem Dr., Wilmore 40390-1198
Type: Private liberal arts and teachers
Accred.: 1940/1989 (SACS-CC) *Calendar:*
Sem. plan *Degrees:* B *Prof. Accred.:* Music
CEO: Pres. David Gyertson
FTE Enroll: 1,141   (606) 858-3511

ASBURY THEOLOGICAL SEMINARY
204 N. Lexington Ave., Wilmore 40390-
1199 *Type:* Private (interdenominational)
graduate only *Accred.:* 1946/1994 (ATS);
1984/1994 (SACS-CC) *Calendar:* 4-1-4
plan *Degrees:* M, D *CEO:* Pres. Maxie D.
Dunnam
Enroll: 969   (606) 858-3581

ASHLAND COMMUNITY COLLEGE
1400 College Dr., Ashland 41101-3683
Type: Public (state) junior *System:* University of Kentucky Community College System *Accred.:* 1957/1991 (SACS-CC) *Calendar:* Sem. plan *Degrees:* A *CEO:* Pres.
Charles R. Dassance
FTE Enroll: 2,451   (606) 329-2999

BELLARMINE COLLEGE
2001 Newburg Rd., Louisville 40205 *Type:*
Private (Roman Catholic) liberal arts
Accred.: 1949/1988 (SACS-CC) *Calendar:*
Sem. plan *Degrees:* A, B, M *Prof. Accred.:*
Nursing (B), Teacher Education *CEO:* Pres.
Joseph J. McGowan, Jr.
FTE Enroll: 1,805   (502) 452-8211

BEREA COLLEGE
Berea 40404 *Type:* Private liberal arts
Accred.: 1926/1995 (SACS-CC) *Calendar:*
4-1-4 plan *Degrees:* B *Prof. Accred.:* Nurs-
ing (B), Teacher Education *CEO:* Pres. Larry
D. Shinn
FTE Enroll: 1,570   (606) 986-9341

BRESCIA COLLEGE
717 Frederica St., Owensboro 42301-3023
Type: Private (Roman Catholic) liberal arts
Accred.: 1957/1989 (SACS-CC) *Calendar:*
Sem. plan *Degrees:* A, B, M (candidate)
CEO: Pres. Vivian M. Bowles
FTE Enroll: 569   (502) 685-3131

CAMPBELLSVILLE COLLEGE
200 W. College St., Campbellsville 42718-
2799 *Type:* Private (Southern Baptist) liberal
arts *Accred.:* 1963/1994 (SACS-CC) *Calendar:* Sem. plan *Degrees:* A, B, M *Prof.
Accred.:* Music (A) *CEO:* Pres. Kenneth W.
Winters
FTE Enroll: 1,029   (502) 465-8158

CENTRE COLLEGE
600 W. Walnut St., Danville 40422-1394
Type: Private liberal arts *Accred.:* 1904/1985
(SACS-CC) *Calendar:* 4-1-4 plan *Degrees:*
B *CEO:* Pres. Michael F. Adams
FTE Enroll: 947   (606) 238-5200

CLEAR CREEK BAPTIST BIBLE COLLEGE
300 Clear Creek Rd., Pineville 40977 *Type:*
Private (Southern Baptist Convention)
Accred.: 1986/1991 (AABC) *Calendar:*
Sem. plan *Degrees:* A, B, C *CEO:* Pres. Bill
Whittaker
FTE Enroll: 121   (606) 337-3196

CUMBERLAND COLLEGE
6190 College Station Dr., Williamsburg
40769 *Type:* Private (Baptist) liberal arts and
teachers *Accred.:* 1964/1995 (SACS-CC)
Calendar: Sem. plan *Degrees:* A, B, M *Prof.
Accred.:* Music *CEO:* Pres. James H. Taylor
FTE Enroll: 1,384   (606) 549-2200

EASTERN KENTUCKY UNIVERSITY
Lancaster Ave., Richmond 40475-3101 *Type:*
Public (state) *System:* Kentucky Council on
Higher Education *Accred.:* 1928/1986
(SACS-CC) *Calendar:* Sem. plan *Degrees:*
A, B, M *Prof. Accred.:* Clinical Lab Scientist,
Clinical Lab Technology (A), Computer Sci-
ence, Construction Education (B), EMT-Para-
medic, Medical Assisting (AMA), Medical

Record Administration, Medical Record Technology, Music, Nursing (A,B), Occupational Therapy, Public Administration, Recreation and Leisure Services (B), Social Work (B), Speech-Language Pathology, Teacher Education *CEO:* Pres. H. Hanly Funderburk, Jr.
FTE Enroll: 14,611　　　　(606) 622-1000

ELIZABETHTOWN COMMUNITY COLLEGE
600 College Street Rd., Elizabethtown 42701-3053 *Type:* Public (state) junior *System:* University of Kentucky Community College System *Accred.:* 1964/1991 (SACS-CC) *Calendar:* Sem. plan *Degrees:* A *Prof. Accred.:* Dental Hygiene, Nursing (A) *CEO:* Pres. Charles E. Stebbins
FTE Enroll: 2,737　　　　(502) 769-2371

FUGAZZI COLLEGE
406 Lafayette Ave., Lexington 40502 *Type:* Private junior *Accred.:* 1957/1998 (ACICS) *Calendar:* Qtr. plan *Degrees:* A, C *Prof. Accred.:* Medical Assisting (AMA) *CEO:* Dir. Sarah Wilkins
　　　　　　　　　　　　(606) 266-0401

BRANCH CAMPUS
5042 Lindbar Dr., Ste 200, Nashville, TN 37211 *Accred.:* 1991 (ACICS)
　　　　　　　　　　　　(615) 333-3344

GEORGETOWN COLLEGE
400 E. College St., Georgetown 40324 *Type:* Private (Southern Baptist) liberal arts *Accred.:* 1919/1992 (SACS-CC) *Calendar:* Sem. plan *Degrees:* B, M *CEO:* Pres. William H. Crouch, Jr.
FTE Enroll: 1,328　　　　(502) 863-8011

HAZARD COMMUNITY COLLEGE
One Community College Dr., Hazard 41701 *Type:* Public (state) junior *System:* University of Kentucky Community College System *Accred.:* 1968/1991 (SACS-CC) *Calendar:* Sem. plan *Degrees:* A *Prof. Accred.:* Radiography *CEO:* Pres. G. Edward Hughes
FTE Enroll: 1,530　　　　(606) 436-5721

HENDERSON COMMUNITY COLLEGE
2660 S. Green St., Henderson 42420 *Type:* Public (state) junior *System:* University of

Kentucky Community College System *Accred.:* 1960/1991 (SACS-CC) *Calendar:* Sem. plan *Degrees:* A *Prof. Accred.:* Clinical Lab Technology (A), Nursing (A) *CEO:* Pres. Patrick R. Lake
FTE Enroll: 961　　　　(502) 827-1867

HOPKINSVILLE COMMUNITY COLLEGE
P.O. Box 2100, Hopkinsville 42241-2100 *Type:* Public (state) junior *System:* University of Kentucky Community College System *Accred.:* 1965/1991 (SACS-CC) *Calendar:* Sem. plan *Degrees:* A *CEO:* Pres. A. James Kerley
FTE Enroll: 1,726　　　　(502) 886-3921

INSTITUTE OF ELECTRONIC TECHNOLOGY
509 S. 30th St., Paducah 42001-0161 *Type:* Private *Accred.:* 1968/1989 (ACCSCT) *Calendar:* Sem. plan *Degrees:* A *CEO:* Dir. of Educ. Don Johnson
　　　　　　　　　　　　(502) 444-9676

LEXINGTON ELECTRONICS INSTITUTE
Clays Mill Shopping Ctr., 3340 Holwyn Rd., Lexington 40503-9938 *Accred.:* 1991 (ACCSCT)
　　　　　　　　　　　　(606) 223-9608

JEFFERSON COMMUNITY COLLEGE
109 E. Broadway, Louisville 40202 *Type:* Public (state) junior *System:* University of Kentucky Community College System *Accred.:* 1968/1991 (SACS-CC) *Calendar:* Sem. plan *Degrees:* A *Prof. Accred.:* Nursing (A), Physical Therapy Assisting, Respiratory Therapy *CEO:* Pres. Richard Green
FTE Enroll: 6,962　　　　(502) 584-0181

KENTUCKY CAREER INSTITUTE
P.O. Box 143, 8095 Connector Dr., Florence 41022 *Type:* Private business *Accred.:* 1993 (ACICS) *Degrees:* A, C *CEO:* Pres. Harry Beck
FTE Enroll: 92　　　　(606) 371-9393

KENTUCKY CHRISTIAN COLLEGE
100 Academic Pkwy., Grayson 41143-2205 *Type:* Private (Christian Churches) *Accred.:* 1962/1991 (AABC); 1984/1989 (SACS-CC)

Calendar: Sem. plan *Degrees:* A, B *CEO:* Pres. Keith P. Keeran
FTE Enroll: 465   (606) 474-3000

KENTUCKY COLLEGE OF BUSINESS
628 E. Main St., Lexington 40508 *Type:* Private junior *Accred.:* 1970/1995 (ACICS) *Calendar:* Qtr. plan *Degrees:* A, C *Prof. Accred.:* Medical Assisting (AMA) *CEO:* Dir. Kim Thomasson
          (606) 253-0621

DANVILLE CAMPUS
115 E. Lexington Ave., Danville 40422 *Accred.:* 1977/1995 (ACICS)
          (606) 236-6991

FLORENCE CAMPUS
7627 Ewing Blvd., Florence 41042 *Accred.:* 1977/1995 (ACICS)
          (606) 525-6510

LOUISVILLE CAMPUS
3950 Dixie Hwy., Louisville 40216 *Accred.:* 1970/1995 (ACICS)
          (502) 447-7665

PIKEVILLE CAMPUS
198 S. Mayo Tr., Pikeville 41501 *Accred.:* 1977/1995 (ACICS)
          (606) 432-5477

RICHMOND CAMPUS
139 Killarney La., Richmond 40475 *Accred.:* 1970/1995 (ACICS)
          (606) 623-8956

KENTUCKY MOUNTAIN BIBLE COLLEGE
855 Hwy. 541, P.O. Box 10, Vancleve 41385 *Type:* Private (Kentucky Mountain Holiness Asscociation) *Accred.:* 1994 (AABC) *Calendar:* Sem. plan *Degrees:* A, B *CEO:* Pres. Philip Speas
FTE Enroll: 53   (606) 666-5000

KENTUCKY STATE UNIVERSITY
400 E. Main St., Frankfort 40601 *Type:* Public (state) liberal arts and teachers *System:* Kentucky Council on Higher Education *Accred.:* 1939/1989 (SACS-CC) *Calendar:* Sem. plan *Degrees:* A, B, M *Prof. Accred.:*

Music, Nursing (A), Social Work (B), Teacher Education *CEO:* Pres. Mary L. Smith
FTE Enroll: 1,953   (502) 227-6000

KENTUCKY WESLEYAN COLLEGE
3000 Frederica St., P.O. Box 1039, Owensboro 42302-1039 *Type:* Private (United Methodist) liberal arts *Accred.:* 1948/1988 (SACS-CC) *Calendar:* Sem. plan *Degrees:* A, B *CEO:* Pres. Wesley H. Poling
FTE Enroll: 723   (502) 926-3111

LEES COLLEGE
601 Jefferson Ave., Jackson 41339 *Type:* Private (Presbyterian) *Accred.:* 1951/1989 (SACS-CC probational) *Calendar:* Sem. plan *Degrees:* A *CEO:* Pres. Charles M. Derrickson
FTE Enroll: 624   (606) 666-7521

LEXINGTON COMMUNITY COLLEGE
Oswald Bldg., Cooper Dr., Lexington 40506-0235 *Type:* Public (state) junior *System:* University of Kentucky Community College System *Accred.:* 1965/1991 (SACS-CC) *Calendar:* Sem. plan *Degrees:* A *Prof. Accred.:* Dental Hygiene, Dental Laboratory Technology, Nuclear Medicine Technology, Nursing (A), Radiography, Respiratory Therapy *CEO:* Pres. Janice Friedd
FTE Enroll: 3,828   (606) 257-4831

LEXINGTON THEOLOGICAL SEMINARY
631 S. Limestone St., Lexington 40508 *Type:* Private (Disciples of Christ) graduate only *Accred.:* 1938/1995 (ATS); 1984/1995 (SACS-CC) *Calendar:* Sem. plan *Degrees:* M, D *CEO:* Pres. Richard L. Harrison, Jr.
Enroll: 190   (606) 252-0361

LINDSEY WILSON COLLEGE
210 Lindsey Wilson St., Columbia 42728 *Type:* Private (United Methodist) *Accred.:* 1951/1993 (SACS-CC) *Calendar:* Sem. plan *Degrees:* A, B, M *CEO:* Pres. John B. Begley
FTE Enroll: 1,277   (502) 384-2126

LOUISVILLE PRESBYTERIAN THEOLOGICAL SEMINARY
1044 Alta Vista Rd., Louisville 40205 *Type:* Private (Presbyterian) graduate only

Accred.: 1938/1989 (ATS); 1973/1989 (SACS-CC) *Calendar:* 4-1-4 plan *Degrees:* M, D *Prof. Accred.:* Marriage and Family Therapy (M) *CEO:* Pres. John M. Mulder
Enroll: 265   (502) 895-3411

LOUISVILLE TECHNICAL INSTITUTE
3901 Atkinson Dr., Louisville 40218-4528 *Type:* Private *Accred.:* 1968/1992 (ACC-SCT) *Calendar:* Qtr. plan *Degrees:* A, C *CEO:* Exec. Dir. David B. Keene
                    (502) 456-6509

MADISONVILLE COMMUNITY COLLEGE
2000 College Dr., Madisonville 42431 *Type:* Public (state) junior *System:* University of Kentucky Community College System *Accred.:* 1968/1991 (SACS-CC) *Calendar:* Sem. plan *Degrees:* A *Prof. Accred.:* Engineering Technology (electrical), Respiratory Therapy *CEO:* Pres. Arthur D. Stumpf
FTE Enroll: 1,680   (502) 821-2250

MAYSVILLE COMMUNITY COLLEGE
1755 U.S. 68, Maysville 41056 *Type:* Public (state) junior *System:* University of Kentucky Community College System *Accred.:* 1968/1991 (SACS-CC) *Calendar:* Sem. plan *Degrees:* A *CEO:* Pres. James C. Shires
FTE Enroll: 1,037   (606) 759-7141

MID-CONTINENT BAPTIST BIBLE COLLEGE
P.O. Box 7010, Mayfield 42066 *Type:* Private (Baptist) professional *Accred.:* 1987/1992 (SACS-CC) *Calendar:* Sem. plan *Degrees:* B *CEO:* Pres. LaVerne Butler
FTE Enroll: 88   (502) 247-8521

MIDWAY COLLEGE
512 E. Stephens St., Midway 40347-1120 *Type:* Private *Accred.:* 1949/1994 (SACS-CC) *Calendar:* Sem. plan *Degrees:* A, B *Prof. Accred.:* Nursing (A,B) *CEO:* Pres. Robert R. Botkin
FTE Enroll: 658   (606) 846-4421

MOREHEAD STATE UNIVERSITY
University Blvd., Morehead 40351 *Type:* Public (state) *System:* Kentucky Council on Higher Education *Accred.:* 1930/1990 (SACS-CC) *Calendar:* Sem. plan *Degrees:* A, B, M *Prof. Accred.:* Music, Nursing (A,B), Radiography, Social Work (B), Teacher Education, Veterinary Technology *CEO:* Pres. Ronald G. Eaglin
FTE Enroll: 7,620   (606) 783-2221

MURRAY STATE UNIVERSITY
One Murray St., Murray 42071-3305 *Type:* Public (state) *System:* Kentucky Council on Higher Education *Accred.:* 1928/1994 (SACS-CC) *Calendar:* Sem. plan *Degrees:* A, B, M *Prof. Accred.:* Art, Business (B,M), Counseling, Engineering Technology (civil/construction, electrical, manufacturing), Journalism (B,M), Music, Nurse Anesthesia Education (M), Nursing (B), Social Work (B), Speech-Language Pathology, Teacher Education, Veterinary Technology *CEO:* Pres. Kern Alexander
FTE Enroll: 7,134   (502) 762-3011

NATIONAL EDUCATION CENTER—KENTUCKY COLLEGE OF TECHNOLOGY
300 High Rise Dr., Louisville 40213-3200 *Type:* Private *Accred.:* 1968/1986 (ACC-SCT) *Degrees:* A, C *CEO:* Exec. Dir. Greg Cawthon
                    (502) 966-5555

NORTHERN KENTUCKY UNIVERSITY
Nunn Dr., Highland Heights 41099 *Type:* Public (state) *System:* Kentucky Council on Higher Education *Accred.:* 1973/1988 (SACS-CC) *Calendar:* Sem. plan *Degrees:* A, B, M, D *Prof. Accred.:* Law, Music (A), Nursing (A,B), Radiography, Respiratory Therapy Technology, Social Work (B), Teacher Education *CEO:* Pres. Leon E. Boothe
FTE Enroll: 9,416   (606) 572-5100

OWENSBORO COMMUNITY COLLEGE
4800 New Hartford Rd., Owensboro 42303 *Type:* Public (state) junior *System:* University of Kentucky Community College System *Accred.:* 1990/1995 (SACS-CC) *Calendar:* Sem. plan *Degrees:* A *Prof. Accred.:* Radiography *CEO:* Pres. John M. McGuire
FTE Enroll: 1,813   (502) 686-4400

OWENSBORO JUNIOR COLLEGE OF BUSINESS
1515 E. 18th St., Owensboro 42303 *Type:* Private junior *Accred.:* 1969/1996 (ACICS)

Calendar: Tri. plan *Degrees:* A *CEO:* Pres. Mark Gabis
(502) 926-4040

PADUCAH COMMUNITY COLLEGE
P.O. Box 7380, Paducah 42002-7380 *Type:* Public (state) junior *System:* University of Kentucky Community College System *Accred.:* 1932/1991 (SACS-CC) *Calendar:* Sem. plan *Degrees:* A *Prof. Accred.:* Nursing (A), Physical Therapy Assisting *CEO:* Pres. Leonard F. O'Hara
FTE Enroll: 1,983   (502) 554-9200

PIKEVILLE COLLEGE
214 Sycamore St., Pikeville 41501 *Type:* Private (United Presbyterian) liberal arts *Accred.:* 1961/1992 (SACS-CC) *Calendar:* Sem. plan *Degrees:* A, B *CEO:* Pres. William H. Owens
FTE Enroll: 846   (606) 432-9200

PRESTONSBURG COMMUNITY COLLEGE
One Bert T. Combs Dr., Prestonsburg 41653 *Type:* Public (state) junior *System:* University of Kentucky Community College System *Accred.:* 1964/1991 (SACS-CC) *Calendar:* Sem. plan *Degrees:* A *CEO:* Pres. Deborah Lee Floyd
FTE Enroll: 2,388   (606) 886-3863

RETS ELECTRONIC INSTITUTE
4146 Outer Loop, Louisville 40219-9977 *Type:* Private *Accred.:* 1978/1988 (ACC-SCT) *Calendar:* Sem. plan *Degrees:* A *CEO:* Dir. Barry McConaghy
(502) 968-7191

ST. CATHARINE COLLEGE
2735 Bardstown Rd., St. Catharine 40061 *Type:* Private (Roman Catholic) junior *Accred.:* 1957/1988 (SACS-CC) *Calendar:* Sem. plan *Degrees:* A *CEO:* Pres. Martha L. Collins
FTE Enroll: 386   (606) 336-5082

SOMERSET COMMUNITY COLLEGE
808 Monticello Rd., Somerset 42501 *Type:* Public (state) junior *System:* University of Kentucky Community College System *Accred.:* 1965/1991 (SACS-CC) *Calendar:* Sem. plan *Degrees:* A *Prof. Accred.:* Clinical Lab Technology (A) *CEO:* Pres. Rollin J. Watson
FTE Enroll: 2,145   (606) 679-8501

SOUTHEAST COMMUNITY COLLEGE
300 College Rd., Cumberland 40823-1099 *Type:* Public (state) junior *System:* University of Kentucky Community College System *Accred.:* 1960/1991 (SACS-CC) *Calendar:* Sem. plan *Degrees:* A *CEO:* Pres. W. Bruce Ayers
FTE Enroll: 2,208   (606) 589-2145

THE SOUTHERN BAPTIST THEOLOGICAL SEMINARY
2825 Lexington Rd., Louisville 40280 *Type:* Private (Southern Baptist) graduate only *Accred.:* 1938/1992 (ATS); 1968/1993 (SACS-CC) *Calendar:* Sem. plan *Degrees:* M, D *Prof. Accred.:* Music, Social Work (M) *CEO:* Pres. R. Albert Mohler, Jr.
Enroll: 1,770   (502) 897-4011

SOUTHWESTERN COLLEGE OF BUSINESS
2929 S. Dixie Hwy., Crestview Hills 41017 *Type:* Private business *Accred.:* 1980/1997 (ACICS) *Calendar:* Qtr. plan *Degrees:* A, C *Prof. Accred.:* Medical Assisting *CEO:* Dir. Bruce Budesheim
(606) 341-6633

SPALDING UNIVERSITY
851 S. Fourth St., Louisville 40203-2115 *Type:* Private (Roman Catholic) liberal arts *Accred.:* 1938/1986 (SACS-CC) *Calendar:* Sem. plan *Degrees:* A, B, M, D *Prof. Accred.:* Clinical Psychology, Dietetics (internship), Nursing (B,M), Social Work (B), Teacher Education *CEO:* Pres. Thomas Oates
FTE Enroll: 925   (502) 585-9911

SPENCERIAN COLLEGE
4627 Dixie Hwy., P.O. Box 16418, Louisville 40216 *Type:* Private business *Accred.:* 1954/1994 (ACICS); 1977/1999 (COE) *Calendar:* Qtr. plan *Degrees:* A, C *Prof. Accred.:* Medical Assisting (AMA) *CEO:* Exec. Dir. David E. Gray
FTE Enroll: 350   (502) 447-1000

SUE BENNETT COLLEGE
151 College St., London 40741 *Type:* Private (United Methodist) *Accred.:* 1932/1992

(SACS-CC) *Calendar:* Sem. plan *Degrees:* A, B *CEO:* Pres. Paul G. Bunnell
FTE Enroll: 497　　　　　　(606) 864-2238

SULLIVAN COLLEGE
3101 Bardstown Rd., Louisville 40205 *Type:* Private senior *Accred.:* 1965/1995 (ACICS); 1979/1994 (SACS-CC) *Calendar:* Qtr. plan *Degrees:* A, B *CEO:* Chanc. A. R. Sullivan
FTE Enroll: 1,850　　　　　(502) 456-6504

LEXINGTON CAMPUS
2659 Regency Rd., Lexington 40503 *Accred.:* 1985/1991 (ACICS)
　　　　　　　　　　　　　(606) 276-4357

THOMAS MORE COLLEGE
333 Thomas More Pkwy., Crestview Hills 41017 *Type:* Private (Roman Catholic) liberal arts *Accred.:* 1959/1990 (SACS-CC) *Calendar:* Sem. plan *Degrees:* A, B, M (candidate) *Prof. Accred.:* Nursing (B) *CEO:* Interim Pres. William F. Cleves
FTE Enroll: 929　　　　　　(606) 341-5800

TRANSYLVANIA UNIVERSITY
300 N. Broadway, Lexington 40508-1797 *Type:* Private liberal arts *Accred.:* 1915/1993 (SACS-CC) *Calendar:* 4-4-x plan *Degrees:* B *CEO:* Pres. Charles L. Shearer
FTE Enroll: 886　　　　　　(606) 233-8300

UNION COLLEGE
310 College St., Barbourville 40906 *Type:* Private (United Methodist) liberal arts *Accred.:* 1932/1994 (SACS-CC) *Calendar:* Sem. plan *Degrees:* A, B, M *CEO:* Pres. Jack C. Phillips
FTE Enroll: 825　　　　　　(606) 546-4151

UNIVERSITY OF KENTUCKY
206 Administration Bldg., Lexington 40506-0032 *Type:* Public (state) *System:* Kentucky Council on Higher Education *Accred.:* 1915/1992 (SACS-CC) *Calendar:* Sem. plan *Degrees:* A, B, M, D *Prof. Accred.:* Accounting (A,C), Business (B,M), Clinical Lab Scientist, Clinical Psychology, Counseling Psychology, Dentistry, Dietetics (coordinated), Dietetics (internship), Engineering (agricultural, chemical, civil, electrical, materials, mechanical, metallurgical), Forestry, General

Practice Residency, Health Services Administration, Home Economics, Interior Design, Journalism (B), Landscape Architecture (B), Law, Librarianship, Marriage and Family Therapy (M), Medicine, Music, Nursing (B,M), Oral and Maxillofacial Surgery, Orthodontics, Pediatric Dentistry, Periodontics, Physical Therapy, Physician Assisting/Surgeon Assisting, Public Administration, Radiation Therapy Technology, Rehabilitation Counseling, School Psychology, Social Work (B,M), Speech-Language Pathology *CEO:* Pres. Charles T. Wethington, Jr.
FTE Enroll: 19,429　　　　(606) 257-9000

UNIVERSITY OF LOUISVILLE
2301 S. Third St., Louisville 40292-0001 *Type:* Public (state) *System:* Kentucky Council on Higher Education *Accred.:* 1915/1987 (SACS-CC) *Calendar:* Sem. plan *Degrees:* A, B, M, D *Prof. Accred.:* Accounting (A), Audiology, Business (B,M), Clinical Lab Scientist, Clinical Psychology, Combined Prosthodontics, Cytotechnology, Dental Hygiene, Dentistry, Endodontics, Engineering (chemical, civil, computer, electrical, industrial, mechanical), General Dentistry, General Practice Residency, Law, Marriage and Family Therapy (post-D), Medicine, Music, Nuclear Medicine Technology, Nursing (B,M), Oral and Maxillofacial Surgery, Orthodontics, Physical Therapy, Psychology Internship, Radiography, Respiratory Therapy, Social Work (M), Speech-Language Pathology, Teacher Education *CEO:* Pres. John W. Shumaker
FTE Enroll: 16,354　　　　(502) 852-5555

WESTERN KENTUCKY UNIVERSITY
1526 Bid Red Way, Bowling Green 42101 *Type:* Public (state) *System:* Kentucky Council on Higher Education *Accred.:* 1926/1994 (SACS-CC) *Calendar:* Sem. plan *Degrees:* A, B, M *Prof. Accred.:* Art, Business (B), Computer Science, Dental Hygiene, Engineering Technology (civil/construction, electrical, mechanical), Journalism (B), Medical Record Technology, Music, Nursing (A,B), Recreation and Leisure Services (B), Social Work (B), Speech-Language Pathology, Teacher Education *CEO:* Pres. Thomas C. Meredith
FTE Enroll: 12,841　　　　(502) 745-0111

LOUISIANA

BATON ROUGE SCHOOL OF COMPUTERS
9255 Interline Ave., Baton Rouge 70809-1971 *Type:* Private *Accred.:* 1982/1988 (ACCSCT) *Degrees:* A, C *CEO:* Pres. Betty Truxillo
(504) 923-2525

BOSSIER PARISH COMMUNITY COLLEGE
2719 Airline Dr. at I-220, Bossier City 71111 *Type:* Public (local) junior *Accred.:* 1983/ 1989 (SACS-CC) *Calendar:* Sem. plan *Degrees:* A *Prof. Accred.:* Respiratory Therapy Technology *CEO:* Chanc. Tom Carleton
FTE Enroll: 3,012   (318) 746-9851

CENTENARY COLLEGE OF LOUISIANA
P.O. Box 41188, Shreveport 71134-1188 *Type:* Private (United Methodist) liberal arts *Accred.:* 1925/1987 (SACS-CC) *Calendar:* Sem. plan *Degrees:* B, M *Prof. Accred.:* Music *CEO:* Pres. Kenneth L. Schwab
FTE Enroll: 874   (318) 869-5011

DELGADO COMMUNITY COLLEGE
501 City Park Ave., New Orleans 70119-4399 *Type:* Public (state/local) junior *System:* University of Louisiana System *Accred.:* 1971/1986 (SACS-CC) *Calendar:* Sem. plan *Degrees:* A *Prof. Accred.:* Engineering Technology (electrical), Funeral Service Education (Mortuary Science), Nuclear Medicine Technology, Physical Therapy Assisting, Radiography, Respiratory Therapy, Respiratory Therapy Technology, Surgical Technology *CEO:* Pres. Ione H. Elioff
FTE Enroll: 10,952   (504) 483-4114

DELTA SCHOOL OF BUSINESS AND TECHNOLOGY
517 Broad St., Lake Charles 70601 *Type:* Private business *Accred.:* 1976/1995 (ACICS) *Degrees:* A, C *CEO:* Pres. Gary J. Holt
(318) 439-5765

DILLARD UNIVERSITY
2601 Gentilly Blvd., New Orleans 70122 *Type:* Private (United Methodist) liberal arts *Accred.:* 1937/1989 (SACS-CC) *Calendar:* Sem. plan *Degrees:* B *Prof. Accred.:* Nursing (B-warning) *CEO:* Pres. Samuel D. Cook
FTE Enroll: 1,561   (504) 283-8822

GRAMBLING STATE UNIVERSITY
P.O. Drawer 607, Grambling 71245 *Type:* Public (state) liberal arts and professional *System:* University of Louisiana System *Accred.:* 1949/1990 (SACS-CC warning) *Calendar:* Sem. plan *Degrees:* A, B, M, D *Prof. Accred.:* Journalism (B), Music, Nursing (B), Recreation and Leisure Services (B), Social Work (B-conditional,M), Teacher Education, Theatre (A) *CEO:* Pres. Raymond A. Hicks
FTE Enroll: 7,833   (318) 274-2000

GRANTHAM COLLEGE OF ENGINEERING
34641 Grantham College Rd., P.O. Box 5700, Slidell 70469-5700 *Type:* Private home study *Accred.:* 1961/1991 (DETC) *Degrees:* A, B *CEO:* Pres. Donald J. Grantham
(504) 649-4191

ITI TECHNICAL COLLEGE
13944 Airline Hwy., Baton Rouge 70817-5998 *Type:* Private *Accred.:* 1981/1988 (ACCSCT) *Degrees:* A, C *CEO:* Pres. Earl J. Martin, Jr.
(504) 752-4233

LOUISIANA COLLEGE
1140 College Dr., Pineville 71359 *Type:* Private (Southern Baptist) liberal arts *Accred.:* 1923/1991 (SACS-CC) *Calendar:* Sem. plan *Degrees:* A, B *Prof. Accred.:* Music, Nursing (B), Social Work (B) *CEO:* Pres. Robert L. Lynn
FTE Enroll: 989   (318) 487-7011

LOUISIANA STATE UNIVERSITY AND AGRICULTURAL AND MECHANICAL COLLEGE
Baton Rouge 70803 *Type:* Public (state) *System:* Louisiana State University System *Accred.:* 1913/1995 (SACS-CC) *Calendar:* Sem. plan *Degrees:* B, M, D *Prof. Accred.:*

Art, Audiology, Business (B,M), Clinical Psychology, Construction Education (B), Engineering (agricultural, chemical, civil, computer, electrical, industrial, mechanical, petroleum), Forestry, Home Economics, Interior Design, Journalism (B,M), Landscape Architecture (B,M), Law, Librarianship, Music, Social Work (M), Speech-Language Pathology, Teacher Education, Veterinary Medicine *CEO:* Chanc. William E. Davis
FTE Enroll: 22,951   (504) 388-3202

LOUISIANA STATE UNIVERSITY AT ALEXANDRIA
8100 Hwy. 71 S., Alexandria 71302-9121 *Type:* Public (state) junior *System:* Louisiana State University System *Accred.:* 1960/1994 (SACS-CC) *Calendar:* Sem. plan *Degrees:* A *Prof. Accred.:* Nursing (A) *CEO:* Chanc. Robert Cavanaugh
FTE Enroll: 1,961   (318) 445-3672

LOUISIANA STATE UNIVERSITY AT EUNICE
P.O. Box 1129, Eunice 70535 *Type:* Public (state) junior *System:* Louisiana State University System *Accred.:* 1967/1994 (SACS-CC) *Calendar:* Sem. plan *Degrees:* A *Prof. Accred.:* Radiography, Respiratory Therapy Technology *CEO:* Chanc. Michael Smith
FTE Enroll: 2,105   (318) 457-7311

LOUISIANA STATE UNIVERSITY IN SHREVEPORT
One University Plaza, Shreveport 71115-2399 *Type:* Public (state) *System:* Louisiana State University System *Accred.:* 1975/1994 (SACS-CC) *Calendar:* Sem. plan *Degrees:* B, M *Prof. Accred.:* Business (B,M), Computer Science, Medicine, Teacher Education *CEO:* Chanc. Vince Marsala
FTE Enroll: 3,451   (318) 797-5000

LOUISIANA STATE UNIVERSITY MEDICAL CENTER
433 Bolivar St., New Orleans 70112-2223 *Type:* Public (state) *System:* Louisiana State University System *Accred.:* 1931/1994 (SACS-CC) *Calendar:* Sem. plan *Degrees:* A, B, M, D *Prof. Accred.:* Audiology, Clinical Lab Scientist, Combined Prosthodontics, Dental Hygiene, Dental Laboratory Technology, Dentistry, Endodontics, Medicine,

Nursing (A,B,M), Occupational Therapy, Ophthalmic Medical Technology, Oral and Maxillofacial Surgery, Orthodontics, Pediatric Dentistry, Periodontics, Physical Therapy, Rehabilitation Counseling, Respiratory Therapy, Speech-Language Pathology *CEO:* Chanc. Mervin L. Trail
FTE Enroll: 3,074   (504) 568-4808

LOUISIANA TECH UNIVERSITY
P.O. Box 3168, Tech Sta., Ruston 71272 *Type:* Public (state) *System:* University of Louisiana System *Accred.:* 1927/1995 (SACS-CC) *Calendar:* Qtr. plan *Degrees:* A, B, M, D *Prof. Accred.:* Accounting (A,B,C), Art, Audiology, Business (B,M), Computer Science, Dietetics (internship), Engineering Technology (civil/construction, electrical), Engineering (bioengineering, chemical, civil, electrical, industrial, mechanical, petroleum), Forestry, Home Economics, Interior Design, Medical Record Administration, Medical Record Technology, Music, Nursing (A), Speech-Language Pathology, Teacher Education *CEO:* Pres. Daniel D. Reneau
FTE Enroll: 8,636   (318) 257-0211

LOYOLA UNIVERSITY
6363 St. Charles Ave., New Orleans 70118 *Type:* Private (Roman Catholic) *Accred.:* 1929/1985 (SACS-CC) *Calendar:* Sem. plan *Degrees:* B, M, D *Prof. Accred.:* Business (B,M), Law, Music, Nursing (B) *CEO:* Pres. Bernard P. Knoth
FTE Enroll: 4,485   (504) 865-2011

MCNEESE STATE UNIVERSITY
P.O. Box 93300, Lake Charles 70609-3300 *Type:* Public (state) liberal arts *System:* University of Louisiana System *Accred.:* 1954/1986 (SACS-CC) *Calendar:* Sem. plan *Degrees:* A, B, M *Prof. Accred.:* Business (B,M), Dietetics (internship), Engineering (general), Home Economics (provisional), Journalism, Music, Nursing (B), Radiography, Teacher Education *CEO:* Pres. Robert D. Hebert
FTE Enroll: 7,382   (318) 446-8111

NEW ORLEANS BAPTIST THEOLOGICAL
SEMINARY
  3939 Gentilly Blvd., New Orleans 70126-
  4858 *Type:* Private (Southern Baptist) graduate
  only *Accred.:* 1954/1986 (ATS); 1965/ 1986
  (SACS-CC) *Calendar:* Sem. plan *Degrees:*
  A, M, D *Prof. Accred.:* Music *CEO:* Interim
  Pres. Billy K. Smith
  Enroll: 2,483   (504) 282-4455

NICHOLLS STATE UNIVERSITY
  P.O. Box 2001, Thibodaux 70310 *Type:* Pub-
  lic (state) liberal arts and teachers *System:*
  University of Louisiana System *Accred.:*
  1964/1995 (SACS-CC) *Calendar:* Sem. plan
  Degrees: A, B, M *Prof. Accred.:* Business
  (B,M), Home Economics, Journalism (B,M),
  Music, Nursing (A,B), Respiratory Therapy
  Technology, Teacher Education *CEO:* Pres.
  Donald J. Ayo
  FTE Enroll: 6,008   (504) 448-8111

NORTHEAST LOUISIANA UNIVERSITY
  700 University Ave., Monroe 71209 *Type:*
  Public (state) *System:* University of
  Louisiana System *Accred.:* 1955/1989
  (SACS-CC) *Calendar:* Sem. plan *Degrees:*
  A, B, M, D *Prof. Accred.:* Business (B,M),
  Computer Science, Construction Education
  (B), Counseling, Dental Hygiene, Home
  Economics, Journalism, Marriage and Fam-
  ily Therapy (M), Music, Nursing (B), Occu-
  pational Therapy, Occupational Therapy
  Assisting, Radiography, Social Work (B),
  Speech-Language Pathology, Teacher Edu-
  cation *CEO:* Pres. Lawson L. Swearingen, Jr.
  FTE Enroll: 10,975   (318) 342-1000

NORTHWESTERN STATE UNIVERSITY
  College Ave., Natchitoches 71497 *Type:*
  Public (state) liberal arts and professional
  System: University of Louisiana System
  Accred.: 1941/1986 (SACS-CC) *Calendar:*
  Sem. plan *Degrees:* A, B, M, D *Prof.
  Accred.:* Counseling, Music, Nursing
  (A,B,M), Radiography, Social Work (B),
  Teacher Education, Veterinary Technology
  CEO: Pres. Robert A. Alost
  FTE Enroll: 7,375   (318) 357-6361

NOTRE DAME SEMINARY
  2901 S. Carrollton Ave., New Orleans
  70118-4391 *Type:* Private (Roman Catholic)
  graduate only *Accred.:* 1979/1986 (ATS);
  1951/1986 (SACS-CC) *Calendar:* Sem. plan
  Degrees: M *CEO:* Rector/Pres. Gregory M.
  Aymond
  FTE Enroll: 116   (504) 866-7426

NUNEZ COMMUNITY COLLEGE
  3700 LaFontaine St., Chalmette 70043 *Type:*
  Public (state) *System:* University of Louis-
  iana System *Accred.:* 1992/1993 (SACS-CC)
  Calendar: Sem. plan *Degrees:* A *CEO:* Pres.
  Carol F. Hopson
  FTE Enroll: 852   (504) 278-7440

NEW ORLEANS CAMPUS
  901 Delery St., New Orleans 70117
                                 (504) 278-7440

PORT SULPHUR CAMPUS
  P.O. Drawer 944, Port Sulphur 70083
                                 (504) 564-2701

OUR LADY OF HOLY CROSS COLLEGE
  4123 Woodland Dr., New Orleans 70131-
  7399 *Type:* Private (Roman Catholic) liberal
  arts and teachers *Accred.:* 1972/1986
  (SACS-CC) *Calendar:* Sem. plan *Degrees:*
  A, B, M *Prof. Accred.:* Nursing (B) *CEO:*
  Pres. Thomas E. Chambers
  FTE Enroll: 1,053   (504) 394-7744

OUR LADY OF THE LAKE COLLEGE
  5345 Brittany Dr., Baton Rouge 70808 *Type:*
  Private *Accred.:* 1994 (SACS-CC) *Calen-
  dar:* Sem. plan *Degrees:* A *Prof. Accred.:*
  Radiography, Surgical Technology *CEO:*
  Pres. James W. Firnberg
  FTE Enroll: 364   (504) 768-1700

REMINGTON COLLEGE
  303 Rue Louis XIV, Lafayette 70508 *Type:*
  Private business *Accred.:* 1988/1994
  (ACICS) *Calendar:* Qtr. plan *Degrees:* A, C
  CEO: Provost Rosalie Lampone
                                 (318) 981-4010

RETS TRAINING CENTER
  3321 Hessmer Ave., Metairie 70002-4726
  Type: Private *Accred.:* 1976/1993 (ACC-

SCT) *Degrees:* A *CEO:* Pres. Harold M. Zlatnicky

(504) 888-6848

ST. JOSEPH SEMINARY COLLEGE
75376 River Rd., St. Benedict 70457-9990 *Type:* Private (Roman Catholic) liberal arts *Accred.:* 1956/1993 (SACS-CC) *Calendar:* Sem. plan *Degrees:* B *CEO:* Pres./Rector Scott J. Underwood
FTE Enroll: 80   (504) 892-1800

SOUTHEASTERN LOUISIANA UNIVERSITY
SLU 784, Hammond 70402 *Type:* Public (state) liberal arts and professional *System:* University of Louisiana System *Accred.:* 1946/1994 (SACS-CC) *Calendar:* Sem. plan *Degrees:* A, B, M *Prof. Accred.:* Accounting (A), Business (B.M), Music, Nursing (B), Respiratory Therapy Technology, Social Work (B), Speech-Language Pathology, Teacher Education *CEO:* Pres. Sally Clausen
FTE Enroll: 11,851   (504) 549-2000

SOUTHERN UNIVERSITY AND AGRICULTURAL AND MECHANICAL COLLEGE AT BATON ROUGE
P.O. Box 9374, Baton Rouge 70813 *Type:* Public (state) *System:* Southern University and Agricultural and Mechanical College System *Accred.:* 1938/1991 (SACS-CC) *Calendar:* Sem. plan *Degrees:* A, B, M, D *Prof. Accred.:* Computer Science, Engineering (civil, electrical, mechanical), Home Economics (provisional), Journalism, Law (ABA only), Music, Nursing (B), Rehabilitation Counseling, Social Work (B), Speech-Language Pathology, Teacher Education *CEO:* Chanc. Marvin L. Yates
FTE Enroll: 9,596   (504) 771-4500

SOUTHERN UNIVERSITY AT NEW ORLEANS
6400 Press Dr., New Orleans 70126 *Type:* Public (state) *System:* Southern University and Agricultural and Mechanical College System *Accred.:* 1958/1990 (SACS-CC) *Calendar:* Sem. plan *Degrees:* A, B, M *Prof. Accred.:* Social Work (B,M) *CEO:* Chanc. Robert B. Gex
FTE Enroll: 3,809   (504) 286-5000

SOUTHERN UNIVERSITY IN SHREVEPORT
3050 Martin Luther King, Jr. D, Shreveport 71107 *Type:* Public (state) junior *System:* Southern University and Agricultural and Mechanical College System *Accred.:* 1964/ 1991 (SACS-CC) *Calendar:* Sem. plan *Degrees:* A *Prof. Accred.:* Clinical Lab Technology (A), Radiography, Respiratory Therapy *CEO:* Chanc. Jerome Greene, Jr.
FTE Enroll: 916   (318) 674-3300

TULANE UNIVERSITY
6823 St. Charles Ave., New Orleans 70118 *Type:* Private *Accred.:* 1903/1990 (SACS-CC) *Calendar:* Sem. plan *Degrees:* B, M, D *Prof. Accred.:* Business (B,M), Computer Science, Engineering (bioengineering, chemical, civil, electrical, mechanical), Health Services Administration, Law, Medicine, Psychology Internship, School Psychology (provisional), Social Work (M) *CEO:* Pres. Eamon M. Kelly
FTE Enroll: 10,064   (504) 865-5000

UNIVERSITY OF NEW ORLEANS
Lakefront, New Orleans 70148 *Type:* Public (state) *System:* Louisiana State University System *Accred.:* 1958/1994 (SACS-CC) *Calendar:* Sem. plan *Degrees:* A, B, M, D *Prof. Accred.:* Accounting (A,C), Art, Business (B,M), Computer Science, Counseling, Engineering (civil, electrical, mechanical, naval architecture/marine), Music, Planning (M), Teacher Education *CEO:* Chanc. Gregory M. St. L. O'Brien
FTE Enroll: 12,446   (504) 286-6000

UNIVERSITY OF SOUTHWESTERN LOUISIANA
E. University Ave., Lafayette 70504 *Type:* Public (state) *System:* University of Louisiana System *Accred.:* 1925/1990 (SACS-CC) *Calendar:* Sem. plan *Degrees:* A, B, M, D *Prof. Accred.:* Audiology, Computer Science, EMT-Paramedic, Engineering (chemical, civil, electrical, mechanical, petroleum), Home Economics, Interior Design, Journalism (B,M), Medical Record Administration, Music, Nursing (B), Speech-Language Pathology, Teacher Education *CEO:* Pres. Ray P. Authement
FTE Enroll: 14,314   (318) 482-1000

XAVIER UNIVERSITY OF LOUISIANA

7325 Palmetto St., New Orleans 70125 *Type:* Private (Roman Catholic) *Accred.:* 1937/ 1990 (SACS-CC) *Calendar:* Sem. plan *Degrees:* B, M, D *Prof. Accred.:* Music, Nurse Anesthesia Education (M) *CEO:* Pres. Norman C. Francis

FTE Enroll: 3,166   (504) 486-7411

MAINE

ANDOVER COLLEGE
901 Washington Ave., Portland 04103 *Type:*
Private junior *Accred.:* 1970/1986 (ACICS);
1995 (NEASC-CTCI candidate) *Calendar:*
Qtr. plan *Degrees:* A, C *CEO:* CEO Lee C.
Jenkins
(207) 774-6126

BANGOR THEOLOGICAL SEMINARY
300 Union St., Bangor 04401 *Type:* Private
(United Church of Christ) graduate only
Accred.: 1974/1986 (ATS); 1968/1986
(NEASC-CIHE) *Calendar:* Sem. plan
Degrees: M, D *CEO:* Pres. Ansley Coe
Throckmorton
Enroll: 116   (207) 942-6781

BATES COLLEGE
Lewiston 04240 *Type:* Private liberal arts
Accred.: 1929/1990 (NEASC-CIHE) *Calendar:* Sem. plan *Degrees:* B *CEO:* Pres.
Donald W. Harward
Enroll: 1,612   (207) 786-6255

BEAL COLLEGE
629 Main St., Bangor 04401 *Type:* Private
junior *Accred.:* 1966/1995 (ACICS)
Degrees: A *Prof. Accred.:* Medical Assisting
(AMA) *CEO:* Pres. Allen T. Stehle
(207) 947-4591

BOWDOIN COLLEGE
Brunswick 04011 *Type:* Private liberal arts
Accred.: 1929/1987 (NEASC-CIHE) *Calendar:* Sem. plan *Degrees:* B, M *CEO:* Pres.
Robert H. Edwards
Enroll: 1,476   (207) 725-3000

CASCO BAY COLLEGE
477 Congress St., Portland 04101 *Type:* Private junior *Accred.:* 1968/1986 (ACICS)
Calendar: Sem. plan *Degrees:* A, C *CEO:*
Pres. Gene F. Stearns
(207) 772-0196

CENTRAL MAINE MEDICAL CENTER SCHOOL OF
NURSING
Lewiston 04240 *Type:* Private 2-year technical *Accred.:* 1978/1994 (NEASC-CTCI)

Calendar: Sem. plan *Degrees:* A *Prof.
Accred.:* Nursing (A) *CEO:* Dir. Fay E.
Ingersoll
FTE Enroll: 78   (207) 795-2840

CENTRAL MAINE TECHNICAL COLLEGE
1250 Turner St., Auburn 04210 *Type:* Public
(state) 2-year *Accred.:* 1976/1991 (NEASC-
CTCI) *Calendar:* Sem. plan *Degrees:* A, C
Prof. Accred.: Engineering Technology
(civil/construction), Nursing (A) *CEO:* Pres.
William J. Hierstein
FTE Enroll: 735   (207) 784-2385

COLBY COLLEGE
Waterville 04901 *Type:* Private liberal arts
Accred.: 1929/1988 (NEASC-CIHE) *Calendar:* 4-1-4 plan *Degrees:* B *CEO:* Pres.
William R. Cotter
Enroll: 1,650   (207) 872-3000

COLLEGE OF THE ATLANTIC
103 Eden St., Bar Harbor 04609 *Type:* Private liberal arts *Accred.:* 1976/1988
(NEASC-CIHE) *Calendar:* Tri. plan
Degrees: B, M *CEO:* Pres. Steven Katona
Enroll: 225   (207) 288-5015

EASTERN MAINE TECHNICAL COLLEGE
354 Hogan Rd., Bangor 04401 *Type:* Public
(state) 2-year *Accred.:* 1973/1994 (NEASC-
CTCI) *Calendar:* Sem. plan *Degrees:* A
Prof. Accred.: Clinical Lab Technology (A),
Nursing (A), Radiography *CEO:* Pres. Joyce
B. Hedlund
FTE Enroll: 785   (207) 941-4691

HUSSON COLLEGE
Bangor 04401 *Type:* Private 4-year business
and professional *Accred.:* 1974/1993
(NEASC-CIHE) *Calendar:* Sem. plan
Degrees: A, B, M *Prof. Accred.:* Nursing (B)
CEO: Pres. William H. Beardsley
Enroll: 1,419   (207) 947-1121

KENNEBEC VALLEY TECHNICAL COLLEGE
Fairfield 04937 *Type:* Public (state) 2-year
Accred.: 1979/1994 (NEASC-CTCI) *Calendar:* Sem. plan *Degrees:* A *Prof. Accred.:*

Nursing (A), Occupational Therapy Assisting, Physical Therapy Assisting *CEO:* Pres. Barbara W. Woodlee
FTE Enroll: 792   (207) 453-9762

MAINE COLLEGE OF ART
Portland 04101 *Type:* Private 4-year professional *Accred.:* 1978/1995 (NEASC-CIHE) *Calendar:* Sem. plan *Degrees:* B *Prof. Accred.:* Art *CEO:* Pres. Roger Gilmore
Enroll: 252   (207) 775-3052

MAINE MARITIME ACADEMY
Castine 04420 *Type:* Public (state) professional *Accred.:* 1971/1986 (NEASC-CIHE) *Calendar:* Sem. plan *Degrees:* B, M *Prof. Accred.:* Engineering Technology (naval architecture/marine), Engineering (naval architecture/marine) *CEO:* Pres. Leonard H. Tyler, Jr.
Enroll: 666   (207) 326-4311

MID-STATE COLLEGE
88 E. Hardscrabble Rd., Auburn 04210 *Type:* Private business *Accred.:* 1970/1987 (ACICS) *Calendar:* Sem. plan *Degrees:* A, C *CEO:* Dir. Marylin Newell
                                  (207) 783-1478

AUGUSTA CAMPUS
218 Water St., Augusta 04330 *Accred.:* 1977/1987 (ACICS)
                                  (207) 623-3962

NORTHERN MAINE TECHNICAL COLLEGE
33 Edgemont Dr., Presque Isle 04769 *Type:* Public (state) 2-year *Accred.:* 1975/1989 (NEASC-CTCI) *Calendar:* Sem. plan *Degrees:* A *Prof. Accred.:* Nursing (A) *CEO:* Pres. Durward R. Huffman
FTE Enroll: 694   (207) 769-2461

ST. JOSEPH'S COLLEGE
Windham 04084-5263 *Type:* Private (Roman Catholic) liberal arts *Accred.:* 1961/1991 (NEASC-CIHE) *Calendar:* Sem. plan *Degrees:* B, M *Prof. Accred.:* Nursing (B) *CEO:* Pres. David B. House
Enroll: 1,868   (207) 892-6766

SOUTHERN MAINE TECHNICAL COLLEGE
Fort Rd., South Portland 04106 *Type:* Public (state) 2-year *Accred.:* 1974/1994 (NEASC-CTCI) *Calendar:* Sem. plan *Degrees:* A *Prof. Accred.:* Nursing (A), Radiation Therapy Technology, Radiography, Respiratory Therapy *CEO:* Pres. Wayne H. Ross
FTE Enroll: 1,991   (207) 767-9500

THOMAS COLLEGE
Waterville 04901 *Type:* Private liberal arts and business *Accred.:* 1969/1994 (NEASC-CIHE) *Calendar:* Sem. plan *Degrees:* A, B, M *CEO:* Pres. George R. Spann
Enroll: 565   (207) 873-0771

UNITY COLLEGE
Unity 04988-9502 *Type:* Private liberal arts *Accred.:* 1974/1992 (NEASC-CIHE) *Degrees:* A, B *CEO:* Pres. Wilson G. Hess
Enroll: 484   (207) 948-3131

UNIVERSITY OF MAINE
Orono 04469-0102 *Type:* Public (state) *System:* University of Maine System *Accred.:* 1929/1988 (NEASC-CIHE) *Calendar:* Sem. plan *Degrees:* A, B, M, D *Prof. Accred.:* Business (B,M), Clinical Psychology, Dental Assisting, Dental Hygiene, Dietetics (internship), Engineering Technology (civil/construction, electrical, mechanical), Engineering (agricultural, chemical, civil, electrical, engineering physics/science, forest, mechanical, surveying), Forestry, Medical Record Technology, Music, Nursing (B), Psychology Internship, Public Administration, Social Work (B,M), Speech-Language Pathology, Teacher Education, Veterinary Technology *CEO:* Pres. Frederick E. Hutchinson
Enroll: 8,567   (207) 581-1512

UNIVERSITY OF MAINE AT AUGUSTA
Augusta 04330 *Type:* Public (state) *System:* University of Maine System *Accred.:* 1973/1985 (NEASC-CIHE) *Calendar:* Sem. plan *Degrees:* A, B *Prof. Accred.:* Clinical Lab Technology (A), Nursing (A) *CEO:* Acting Pres. Charles MacRoy
Enroll: 2,216   (207) 621-3403

UNIVERSITY OF MAINE AT FARMINGTON
86 Main St., Farmington 04938 *Type:* Public (state) liberal arts and teachers *System:* University of Maine System *Accred.:* 1958/1992 (NEASC-CIHE) *Calendar:* Sem. plan *Degrees:* A, B *Prof. Accred.:* Teacher Education *CEO:* Pres. Theodora J. Kalikow
Enroll: 2,035   (207) 778-7000

UNIVERSITY OF MAINE AT FORT KENT
Pleasant St., Fort Kent 04743 *Type:* Public (state) liberal arts and teachers *System:* University of Maine System *Accred.:* 1970/1986 (NEASC-CIHE) *Calendar:* Sem. plan *Degrees:* A, B *Prof. Accred.:* Nursing (B) *CEO:* Pres. Richard G. Dumont
Enroll: 515   (207) 834-3162

UNIVERSITY OF MAINE AT MACHIAS
Machias 04654 *Type:* Public (state) liberal arts and teachers *System:* University of Maine System *Accred.:* 1970/1994 (NEASC-CIHE) *Calendar:* Sem. plan *Degrees:* A, B *Prof. Accred.:* Recreation and Leisure Services (B) *CEO:* Pres. Paul E. Nordstrom
Enroll: 703   (207) 255-3313

UNIVERSITY OF MAINE AT PRESQUE ISLE
181 Main St., Presque Isle 04769 *Type:* Public (state) liberal arts and teachers *System:* University of Maine System *Accred.:* 1968/1994 (NEASC-CIHE) *Calendar:* Sem. plan *Degrees:* A, B *Prof. Accred.:* Clinical Lab Technology (A), Recreation and Leisure Services (B), Social Work (B-candidate) *CEO:* Pres. W. Michael Easton
Enroll: 1,053   (207) 764-0311

UNIVERSITY OF NEW ENGLAND
11 Hills Beach Rd., Biddeford 04005 *Type:* Private liberal arts and professional *Accred.:* 1966/1986 (NEASC-CIHE) *Calendar:* 4-1-4 plan *Degrees:* A, B, M, D *Prof. Accred.:* Nurse Anesthesia Education (M), Nursing (A), Occupational Therapy, Osteopathy, Physical Therapy, Social Work (M) *CEO:* Pres. Sandra G. Featherman
Enroll: 1,571   (207) 283-0171

UNIVERSITY OF SOUTHERN MAINE
96 Falmouth St., Portland 04103 *Type:* Public (state) liberal arts and professional *System:* University of Maine System *Accred.:* 1960/1991 (NEASC-CIHE) *Calendar:* Sem. plan *Degrees:* A, B, M, D *Prof. Accred.:* Art, Computer Science, Counseling, Engineering (electrical), Law, Music, Nursing (B,M), Public Administration, Rehabilitation Counseling, Social Work (B), Teacher Education *CEO:* Pres. Richard L. Pattenaude
Enroll: 5,834   (207) 780-4141

WASHINGTON COUNTY TECHNICAL COLLEGE
Calais 04619 *Type:* Public (state) 2-year *Accred.:* 1976/1989 (NEASC-CTCI) *Calendar:* Sem. plan *Degrees:* A *CEO:* Pres. Ronald P. Renaud
FTE Enroll: 267   (207) 454-2144

WESTBROOK COLLEGE
Stevens Ave., Portland 04103 *Type:* Private liberal arts *Accred.:* 1934/1984 (NEASC-CIHE) *Calendar:* Sem. plan *Degrees:* A, B *Prof. Accred.:* Dental Hygiene, Nursing (B) *CEO:* Pres. William D. Andrews
Enroll: 259   (207) 797-7261

MARYLAND

ALLEGANY COMMUNITY COLLEGE
Willowbrook Rd., Cumberland 21502 *Type:*
Public county/state *System:* Maryland Higher
Education Commission *Accred.:* 1965/ 1990
(MSA) *Calendar:* Sem. plan *Degrees:* A, C
Prof. Accred.: Clinical Lab Technology (A),
Dental Hygiene, Occupational Therapy
Assisting, Radiography, Respiratory Therapy *CEO:* Pres. Donald L. Alexander
Enroll: 2,877   (301) 724-7700

ANNE ARUNDEL COMMUNITY COLLEGE
101 College Pkwy., Arnold 21012 *Type:*
Public (local/state) two-year *System:* Maryland Higher Education Commission *Accred.:*
1968/1994 (MSA) *Calendar:* Sem. plan
Degrees: A, C *Prof. Accred.:* Nursing (A),
Radiography *CEO:* Pres. Martha A. Smith
Enroll: 12,387   (410) 647-7100

BALTIMORE CITY COMMUNITY COLLEGE
2901 Liberty Heights Ave., Baltimore 21215
Type: Public (state) two-year *System:* Maryland Higher Education Commission *Accred.:*
1963/1993 (MSA) *Calendar:* Sem. plan
Degrees: A, C *Prof. Accred.:* Dental
Hygiene, Medical Record Technology, Nursing (A), Physical Therapy Assisting, Respiratory Therapy *CEO:* Pres. James D.
Tschechtelin
Enroll: 6,500   (410) 333-5555

HARBOR CAMPUS
600 E. Lombard St., Baltimore 21202
                                   (410) 333-8348

BALTIMORE HEBREW UNIVERSITY
5800 Park Heights Ave., Baltimore 21215
Type: Private non-profit *Accred.:* 1974/1995
(MSA) *Calendar:* Sem. plan *Degrees:* B, M,
D *CEO:* Acting Pres. Robert O. Freedman
Enroll: 339   (410) 578-6900

BALTIMORE INTERNATIONAL CULINARY
COLLEGE
19-21 S. Gay St., Baltimore 21202-1503
Type: Private non-profit *Accred.:* 1985/1991
(ACCSCT); 1989 (MSA candidate) *Calen-*

dar: Sem. plan *Degrees:* A, C *CEO:* Pres.
Roger Chylinski
Enroll: 557   (410) 752-1446

BOWIE STATE UNIVERSITY
14000 Jericho Park Rd., Bowie 20715-9465
Type: Public (state) *System:* University of
Maryland System *Accred.:* 1961/1992
(MSA) *Calendar:* Sem. plan *Degrees:* B, M
Prof. Accred.: Nursing (B), Social Work (B),
Teacher Education *CEO:* Pres. Nathanael
Pollard, Jr.
Enroll: 4,896   (301) 464-3000

CAPITOL COLLEGE
11301 Springfield Rd., Laurel 20708 *Type:*
Private non-profit *Accred.:* 1976/1991
(MSA) *Calendar:* Sem. plan *Degrees:* A, B,
M, C *Prof. Accred.:* Engineering Technology
(computer, electrical) *CEO:* Pres. G. William
Troxler
Enroll: 794   (301) 953-0060

CATONSVILLE COMMUNITY COLLEGE
800 S. Rolling Rd., Catonsville 21228 *Type:*
Public (local) two-year *System:* Community
Colleges of Baltimore County *Accred.:*
1966/1991 (MSA) *Calendar:* Sem. plan
Degrees: A, C *Prof. Accred.:* Funeral Service
Education (Mortuary Science), Occupational
Therapy Assisting *CEO:* Pres. Frederick J.
Walsh
Enroll: 10,295   (410) 455-6050

CECIL COMMUNITY COLLEGE
1000 North East Rd., North East 21901-1999
Type: Public (local) two-year *System:* Maryland Higher Education Commission *Accred.:*
1974/1990 (MSA) *Calendar:* Sem. plan
Degrees: A, C *Prof. Accred.:* Nursing (A)
CEO: Pres. Robert L. Gell
Enroll: 1,348   (410) 287-6060

CHARLES COUNTY COMMUNITY COLLEGE
Mitchell Rd., P.O. Box 910, La Plata 20646-
0910 *Type:* Public (state) two-year *System:*
Maryland Higher Education Commission
Accred.: 1969/1994 (MSA) *Calendar:* Sem.
plan *Degrees:* A, C *Prof. Accred.:* Nursing

(A), Practical Nursing *CEO:* Pres. John M. Sine
Enroll: 5,925   (301) 934-2251

CHESAPEAKE COLLEGE
P.O. Box 8, Wye Mills 21679-0008 *Type:* Public (local/state) two-year *System:* Maryland Higher Education Commission *Accred.:* 1970/1995 (MSA) *Calendar:* Sem. plan *Degrees:* A, C *Prof. Accred.:* Radiography *CEO:* Pres. John R. Kotula
Enroll: 2,086   (410) 822-5400

COLLEGE OF NOTRE DAME OF MARYLAND
4701 N. Charles St., Baltimore 21210 *Type:* Private (Roman Catholic) liberal arts primarily for women *Accred.:* 1925/1992 (MSA) *Calendar:* Sem. plan *Degrees:* B, M *Prof. Accred.:* Nursing (B) *CEO:* Pres. Rosemarie T. Nassif
Enroll: 3,208   (410) 435-0100

COLUMBIA UNION COLLEGE
7600 Flower Ave., Takoma Park 20912 *Type:* Private (Seventh-Day Adventist) liberal arts *Accred.:* 1942/1992 (MSA) *Calendar:* Sem. plan *Degrees:* A, B *Prof. Accred.:* Clinical Lab Scientist, Clinical Lab Technology (A), Nursing (B), Respiratory Therapy *CEO:* Pres. Charles Scriven
Enroll: 933   (301) 891-4000

COPPIN STATE COLLEGE
2500 W. North Ave., Baltimore 21216-3698 *Type:* Public (state) *System:* University of Maryland System *Accred.:* 1962/1993 (MSA) *Calendar:* Sem. plan *Degrees:* B, M *Prof. Accred.:* Nursing (B), Rehabilitation Counseling, Social Work (B), Teacher Education *CEO:* Pres. Calvin W. Burnett
Enroll: 3,380   (410) 383-5585

DUNDALK COMMUNITY COLLEGE
7200 Sollers Point Rd., Dundalk 21222-4692 *Type:* Public (local) two-year *System:* Community Colleges of Baltimore County *Accred.:* 1975/1994 (MSA) *Calendar:* Sem. plan *Degrees:* A, C *CEO:* Pres. Harold D. McAninch
Enroll: 3,444   (410) 282-6700

ESSEX COMMUNITY COLLEGE
7201 Rossville Blvd., Baltimore 21237-3899 *Type:* Public (local) two-year *System:* Community Colleges of Baltimore County *Accred.:* 1966/1992 (MSA) *Calendar:* Sem. plan *Degrees:* A, C *Prof. Accred.:* Clinical Lab Technology (A), Diagnostic Medical Sonography, Medical Record Technology, Music, Nuclear Medicine Technology, Nursing (A), Physician Assisting/Surgeon Assisting, Radiation Therapy Technology, Radiography, Respiratory Therapy Technology, Theatre, Veterinary Technology *CEO:* Pres. Donald J. Slowinski
Enroll: 9,653   (410) 682-6000

FREDERICK COMMUNITY COLLEGE
7932 Oppossumtown Pike, Frederick 21702-2097 *Type:* Public (local) two-year *System:* Maryland Higher Education Commission *Accred.:* 1971/1991 (MSA) *Calendar:* Sem. plan *Degrees:* A, C *CEO:* Pres. Lee John Betts
Enroll: 4,356   (301) 846-2400

FROSTBURG STATE UNIVERSITY
Frostburg 21532-1099 *Type:* Public (state) *System:* University of Maryland System *Accred.:* 1953/1991 (MSA) *Calendar:* Sem. plan *Degrees:* B, M, C *Prof. Accred.:* Social Work (B-candidate) *CEO:* Pres. Catherine R. Gira
Enroll: 5,443   (301) 687-4000

GARRETT COMMUNITY COLLEGE
P.O. Box 151, Mosser Rd., McHenry 21541 *Type:* Public (local) two-year *System:* Maryland Higher Education Commission *Accred.:* 1975/1993 (MSA) *Calendar:* Sem. plan *Degrees:* A, C *CEO:* Pres. Stephen J. Herman
Enroll: 710   (301) 387-3000

GOUCHER COLLEGE
1021 Dulaney Valley Rd., Baltimore 21204-2794 *Type:* Private liberal arts primarily for women *Accred.:* 1921/1993 (MSA) *Calendar:* Sem. plan *Degrees:* B, M *CEO:* Pres. Judy Jolly Mohraz
Enroll: 1,130   (410) 337-6000

HAGERSTOWN BUSINESS COLLEGE
18618 Crestwood Dr., Hagerstown 21742
Type: Private junior *Accred.:* 1968/1996
(ACICS) *Calendar:* Qtr. plan *Degrees:* A
Prof. Accred.: Medical Record Technology
CEO: Pres. James Gifford
(301) 739-2670

HAGERSTOWN JUNIOR COLLEGE
11400 Robinwood Dr., Hagerstown 21740-6590 *Type:* Public (local/state) two-year *System:* Maryland Higher Education Commission *Accred.:* 1968/1994 (MSA) *Calendar:* Sem. plan *Degrees:* A, C *Prof. Accred.:* Radiography *CEO:* Pres. Norman P. Shea
Enroll: 3,035   (301) 790-2800

HARFORD COMMUNITY COLLEGE
401 Thomas Run Rd., Bel Air 21015-1698
Type: Public (local/state) two-year *System:* Maryland Higher Education Commission *Accred.:* 1967/1992 (MSA) *Calendar:* Sem. plan *Degrees:* A, C *Prof. Accred.:* Histologic Technology, Nursing (A) *CEO:* Pres. Claudia E. Chiesi
Enroll: 5,304   (410) 836-4000

HOME STUDY INTERNATIONAL
12501 Old Columbia Pike, P.O. Box 4437, Silver Spring 20914-4437 *Type:* Private home study *Accred.:* 1967/1993 (DETC) *Degrees:* A, B, C *CEO:* Pres. Joseph E. Gurubatham
(301) 680-6570

GRIGGS UNIVERSITY
12501 Old Columbia Pike, P.O. Box 4437, Silver Spring 20914-4437 *Accred.:* 1994 (DETC) *Degrees:* A, B
(301) 680-6570

HOOD COLLEGE
401 Rosemont Ave., Frederick 21701-8575
Type: Private liberal arts primarily for women *Accred.:* 1922/1992 (MSA) *Calendar:* Sem. plan *Degrees:* B, M *Prof. Accred.:* Home Economics, Social Work (B) *CEO:* Pres. Shirley Peterson
Enroll: 2,022   (301) 663-3131

HOWARD COMMUNITY COLLEGE
10901 Little Patuxent Pkwy., Columbia 21044 *Type:* Public (local/state) two-year *System:* Maryland Higher Education Commission *Accred.:* 1975/1990 (MSA) *Calendar:* Sem. plan *Degrees:* A, C *Prof. Accred.:* Nursing (A) *CEO:* Pres. Dwight A. Burrill
Enroll: 4,991   (410) 992-4800

JOHNS HOPKINS UNIVERSITY
34th and N. Charles Sts., Baltimore 21218
Type: Private non-profit *Accred.:* 1921/1994 (MSA) *Calendar:* Sem. plan *Degrees:* A, B, M, P, D *Prof. Accred.:* Engineering Technology (industrial hygiene), Engineering (bioengineering, chemical, civil, electrical, engineering mechanics, materials, mechanical), General Practice Residency, Health Services Administration, Medical Illustration, Medicine, Nursing (B,M) *CEO:* Interim Pres. Daniel Nathans
Enroll: 16,120   (410) 516-8068

COLUMBIA CENTER CAMPUS
6740 Alexander Bell Dr., Columbia 21046
(410) 290-1777

PEABODY INSTITUTE OF THE JOHNS HOPKINS UNIVERSITY
One E. Mount Vernon Pl., Baltimore 21202-2397 *Prof. Accred.:* Music
(410) 659-8150

SCHOOL OF ADVANCED INTERNATIONAL STUDIES
1740 Massachusetts Ave., N.W., Washington, DC 20036
(202) 663-5600

LOYOLA COLLEGE IN MARYLAND
4501 N. Charles St., Baltimore 21210 *Type:* Private (Roman Catholic) *Accred.:* 1931/1990 (MSA) *Calendar:* Sem. plan *Degrees:* B, M, D, C *Prof. Accred.:* Accounting (A), Business (B,M), Computer Science, Counseling, Engineering (engineering physics/science), Speech-Language Pathology *CEO:* Pres. Harold E. Ridley, S.J.
Enroll: 6,261   (410) 617-2000

THE MARYLAND COLLEGE OF ART AND DESIGN
10500 Georgia Ave., Silver Spring 20902
Type: Private professional *Calendar:* Qtr.
plan *Degrees:* A *Prof. Accred.:* Art *CEO:*
Pres. Edward Glynn
Enroll: 85　　　　　　　　　　(301) 649-4454

THE MARYLAND INSTITUTE COLLEGE OF ART
1300 W. Mt. Royal Ave., Baltimore 21217
Type: Private professional *Accred.:* 1967/
1993 (MSA) *Calendar:* Sem. plan *Degrees:*
B, M, C *Prof. Accred.:* Art, Interior Design
CEO: Pres. Fred Lazarus, IV
Enroll: 913　　　　　　　　　(410) 669-9200

MONTGOMERY COLLEGE—GERMANTOWN
CAMPUS
20200 Observation Dr., Germantown 20876
Type: Public (local) two-year *System:* Mont-
gomery College Central Administration
Accred.: 1980/1992 (MSA) *Calendar:* Sem.
plan *Degrees:* A, C *CEO:* Provost Noreen A.
Lyne
Enroll: 3,731　　　　　　　　(301) 353-7700

MONTGOMERY COLLEGE—ROCKVILLE CAMPUS
51 Mannakee St., Rockville 20850 *Type:*
Public (local) two-year *System:* Mont-
gomery College Central Administration
Accred.: 1968/1992 (MSA) *Calendar:* Sem.
plan *Degrees:* A, C *Prof. Accred.:* Clinical
Lab Technology (A), Diagnostic Medical
Sonography, Engineering Technology (elec-
trical), Medical Record Technology, Music,
Radiography *CEO:* Acting Provost Floyd
Cumberbatch
Enroll: 13,624　　　　　　　(301) 279-5000

MONTGOMERY COLLEGE—TAKOMA PARK
CAMPUS
Takoma Ave. and Fenton St., Takoma Park
20912 *Type:* Public (local) two-year *System:*
Montgomery College Central Administra-
tion *Accred.:* 1950/1992 (MSA) *Calendar:*
Sem. plan *Degrees:* A, C *Prof. Accred.:*
Nursing (A), Physical Therapy Assisting
CEO: Provost Heijia L. Wheeler
Enroll: 4,050　　　　　　　　(301) 650-1300

MORGAN STATE UNIVERSITY
Hillen Rd. and Cold Spring Ln., Baltimore
21239 *Type:* Public (state) liberal arts *Sys-*

tem: Maryland Higher Education Commis-
sion *Accred.:* 1925/1994 (MSA) *Calendar:*
Sem. plan *Degrees:* B, M, D *Prof. Accred.:*
Clinical Lab Scientist, Engineering (civil,
electrical, industrial), Landscape Architec-
ture (M-initial), Music, Planning (M), Social
Work (B) *CEO:* Pres. Earl S. Richardson
Enroll: 5,766　　　　　　　　(410) 319-3333

MOUNT ST. MARY'S COLLEGE AND SEMINARY
Emmitsburg 21727 *Type:* Private (Roman
Catholic) *Accred.:* 1987/1992 (ATS); 1922/
1990 (MSA) *Calendar:* Sem. plan *Degrees:*
B, M *CEO:* Pres. George R. Houston, Jr.
Enroll: 1,807　　　　　　　　(301) 447-6122

NER ISRAEL RABBINICAL COLLEGE
400 Mount Wilson La., Baltimore 21208
Type: Private professional *Accred.:* 1974/
1992 (AARTS) *Calendar:* Sem. plan
Degrees: B, M, D *CEO:* Pres. Herman N.
Neuberger
Enroll: 425　　　　　　　　　(410) 484-7200

POTOMAC COLLEGE
11710 Hunters Ln., Ste. 9, Rockville 20852
Type: Private senior *Accred.:* 1994 (ACICS)
Calendar: Sem. plan *Degrees:* A *CEO:* Pres.
Edward Shapiro
　　　　　　　　　　　　　　(301) 231-7358

PRINCE GEORGE'S COMMUNITY COLLEGE
301 Largo Rd., Largo 20772-2199 *Type:*
Public (local) two-year *System:* Maryland
Higher Education Commission *Accred.:*
1969/1995 (MSA) *Calendar:* Sem. plan
Degrees: A *Prof. Accred.:* Engineering Tech-
nology (electrical), Medical Record Tech-
nology, Nuclear Medicine Technology,
Nursing (A), Radiography, Respiratory
Therapy *CEO:* Pres. Robert I. Bickford
Enroll: 12,201　　　　　　　(301) 336-6000

RETS TECHNICAL TRAINING CENTER
1520 S. Caton Ave., Baltimore 21227-1063
Type: Private *Accred.:* 1973/1988 (ACC-
SCT) *Degrees:* A *CEO:* Pres. H.V. Leslie
　　　　　　　　　　　　　　(410) 644-6400

ST. JOHN'S COLLEGE
60 College Ave., P.O. Box 2800, Annapolis
21404 *Type:* Private liberal arts *Accred.:*

1923/1994 (MSA) *Calendar:* Sem. plan *Degrees:* B, M *CEO:* Pres. Christopher B. Nelson
Enroll: 457   (410) 263-2371

ST. MARY'S COLLEGE OF MARYLAND
St. Mary's City 20686 *Type:* Public (state) liberal arts *System:* Maryland Higher Education Commission *Accred.:* 1959/1990 (MSA) *Calendar:* Sem. plan *Degrees:* B *Prof. Accred.:* Music *CEO:* Pres. Edward T. Lewis
Enroll: 1,565   (301) 862-0200

ST. MARY'S SEMINARY AND UNIVERSITY
5400 Roland Ave., Baltimore 21210 *Type:* Private (Roman Catholic) *Accred.:* 1971/ 1991 (ATS); 1951/1991 (MSA) *Calendar:* Sem. plan *Degrees:* B, M, P *CEO:* Pres./ Rector Robert F. Leavitt
Enroll: 241   (410) 323-3200

SALISBURY STATE UNIVERSITY
1101 Camden Ave., Salisbury 21801-6837 *Type:* Public (state) *System:* University of Maryland System *Accred.:* 1956/1991 (MSA) *Calendar:* Sem. plan *Degrees:* B, M *Prof. Accred.:* Business (B,M), Clinical Lab Scientist, Nursing (B,M), Respiratory Therapy, Social Work (B) *CEO:* Interim Pres. K. Nelson Butler
Enroll: 6,048   (410) 543-6000

SOJOURNER-DOUGLASS COLLEGE
500 N. Caroline St., Baltimore 21205 *Type:* Private *Accred.:* 1980/1995 (MSA) *Calendar:* Tri. plan *Degrees:* B *CEO:* Pres. Charles W. Simmons
Enroll: 350   (410) 276-0306

TOWSON STATE UNIVERSITY
Towson 21204-7097 *Type:* Public (state) *System:* University of Maryland System *Accred.:* 1949/1994 (MSA) *Calendar:* Sem. plan *Degrees:* B, M, C *Prof. Accred.:* Accounting (A), Audiology, Business (B), Computer Science, Dance, Music, Nursing (B), Occupational Therapy, Psychology Internship, Speech-Language Pathology *CEO:* Pres. Hoke L. Smith
Enroll: 14,551   (410) 830-2000

TRADITIONAL ACUPUNCTURE INSTITUTE
American City Bldg., Ste. 100, 10227 Wincopin Cir., Columbia 21044-3422 *Type:* Private professional *Calendar:* Sem. plan *Degrees:* M *Prof. Accred.:* Acupuncture (M) *CEO:* Pres. Robert M. Duggan
FTE Enroll: 48   (410) 596-6006

UNIFORMED SERVICES UNIVERSITY OF THE HEALTH SCIENCES
4301 Jones Bridge Rd., Bethesda 20814 *Type:* Public (federal) graduate only *Accred.:* 1984/1993 (MSA) *Degrees:* M, P, D *Prof. Accred.:* Medicine, Nurse Anesthesia Education, *CEO:* Pres. James A. Zimble
Enroll: 725   (301) 295-3030

UNITED STATES NAVAL ACADEMY
121 Blake Rd., Annapolis 21402-5000 *Type:* Public (federal) military *Accred.:* 1947/1991 (MSA) *Calendar:* Sem. plan *Degrees:* B *Prof. Accred.:* Computer Science, Engineering (aerospace, electrical, mechanical, naval architecture/marine, ocean, systems) *CEO:* Supt. Charles R. Larson, U.S.N.
Enroll: 4,107   (410) 293-1000

UNIVERSITY OF BALTIMORE
1420 N. Charles St., Baltimore 21201-5779 *Type:* Public (state) *System:* University of Maryland System *Accred.:* 1971/1992 (MSA) *Calendar:* Sem. plan *Degrees:* B, M, P, C *Prof. Accred.:* Business (B,M), Law, Public Administration *CEO:* Pres. H. Mebane Turner
Enroll: 5,204   (410) 837-4200

UNIVERSITY OF MARYLAND AT BALTIMORE
520 W. Lombard St., Baltimore 21201-1627 *Type:* Public (state) *System:* University of Maryland System *Accred.:* 1921/1991 (MSA) *Calendar:* 4-1-4 plan *Degrees:* B, M, P, D, C *Prof. Accred.:* Clinical Lab Scientist, Combined Prosthodontics, Dental Hygiene, Dentistry, Dietetics (internship), Endodontics, Engineering (chemical, mechanical), General Dentistry (prelim. provisional), General Practice Residency, Law, Medicine, Nursing (B,M), Oral Pathology, Oral and Maxillofacial Surgery, Orthodontics, Pediatric Dentistry, Periodontics,

Physical Therapy, Social Work (M) *CEO:* Pres. David J. Ramsay
Enroll: 5,609   (410) 706-3100

UNIVERSITY OF MARYLAND BALTIMORE COUNTY
5401 Wilkens Ave., Baltimore 21228-5398 *Type:* Public (state) *System:* University of Maryland System *Accred.:* 1966/1991 (MSA) *Calendar:* 4-1-4 plan *Degrees:* B, M, D *Prof. Accred.:* Clinical Psychology, Diagnostic Medical Sonography, EMT-Paramedic, Psychology Internship (provisional), Public Administration, Social Work (B) *CEO:* Pres. Freeman A. Hrabowski, III
Enroll: 10,315   (410) 455-1000

UNIVERSITY OF MARYLAND COLLEGE PARK
Rte. 1, Baltimore Blvd., College Park 20742 *Type:* Public (state) *System:* University of Maryland System *Accred.:* 1921/1992 (MSA) *Calendar:* Sem. plan *Degrees:* B, M, D, C *Prof. Accred.:* Audiology, Business (B,M), Clinical Psychology, Counseling, Counseling Psychology, Engineering (aerospace, agricultural, chemical, civil, electrical, fire protection, general, mechanical, nuclear), Journalism (B,M), Librarianship, Marriage and Family Therapy (M), Music, Planning (M), Psychology Internship, Rehabilitation Counseling, School Psychology, Speech-Language Pathology, Teacher Education, Veterinary Medicine *CEO:* Pres. William E. Kirwan
Enroll: 32,493   (301) 405-1000

UNIVERSITY OF MARYLAND EASTERN SHORE
Princess Anne 21853-1299 *Type:* Public (state) *System:* University of Maryland System *Accred.:* 1937/1991 (MSA) *Calendar:* Sem. plan *Degrees:* B, M, D *Prof. Accred.:* Construction Education (B), Physical Therapy *CEO:* Pres. William P. Hytche
Enroll: 2,925   (410) 651-2200

UNIVERSITY OF MARYLAND UNIVERSITY COLLEGE
University Blvd. at Adelphi Rd, College Park 20742-1600 *Type:* Public (state) *System:* University of Maryland System *Accred.:* 1946/1991 (MSA) *Calendar:* Sem. plan *Degrees:* A, B, M, C *CEO:* Pres. T. Benjamin Massey
Enroll: 36,302   (301) 985-7000

VILLA JULIE COLLEGE
1525 Green Spring Valley Rd., Stevenson 21153 *Type:* Private liberal arts *Accred.:* 1962/1993 (MSA) *Calendar:* Sem. plan *Degrees:* A, B *Prof. Accred.:* Clinical Lab Technology (A) *CEO:* Pres. Carolyn Manuszak
Enroll: 1,830   (410) 486-7000

WASHINGTON BIBLE COLLEGE
6511 Princess Garden Pkwy., Lanham 20706 *Type:* Private (nondenominational) *Accred.:* 1962/1991 (AABC) *Calendar:* Sem. plan *Degrees:* A, B, C *CEO:* Pres. Homer Heater, Jr.
FTE Enroll: 221   (301) 552-1400

WASHINGTON COLLEGE
300 Washington Ave., Chestertown 21620 *Type:* Private liberal arts *Accred.:* 1925/1994 (MSA) *Calendar:* Sem. plan *Degrees:* B, M, C *CEO:* Pres. John S. Toll
Enroll: 914   (410) 778-2800

WESTERN MARYLAND COLLEGE
2 College Hill, Westminster 21157 *Type:* Private liberal arts *Accred.:* 1922/1993 (MSA) *Calendar:* Sem. plan *Degrees:* B, M *Prof. Accred.:* Social Work (B) *CEO:* Pres. Robert Hunter Chambers, III
Enroll: 2,357   (410) 848-7000

WOR-WIC COMMUNITY COLLEGE
32000 Campus Dr., Salisbury 21801 *Type:* Public (local) two-year *System:* Maryland Higher Education Commission *Accred.:* 1980/1995 (MSA) *Calendar:* Sem. plan *Degrees:* A, C *Prof. Accred.:* Radiography *CEO:* Pres. Arnold H. Maner
Enroll: 1,968   (410) 334-2800

MASSACHUSETTS

ALLSTATE INSTITUTE OF TECHNOLOGY
165 Front St., Door D, 5th Fl., Chicopee 01013 *Type:* Private *Accred.:* 1993 (ACC-SCT) *Degrees:* A, B, C *CEO:* Dir./Owner Bart O'Connor, Jr.
(413) 594-8248

AMERICAN INTERNATIONAL COLLEGE
1000 State St., Springfield 01109-3189 *Type:* Private liberal arts and professional *Accred.:* 1933/1989 (NEASC-CIHE) *Calendar:* Sem. plan *Degrees:* B, M, D *Prof. Accred.:* Nursing (B) *CEO:* Pres. Harry J. Courniotes
Enroll: 1,490   (413) 737-7000

AMHERST COLLEGE
Amherst 01002 *Type:* Private liberal arts *Accred.:* 1929/1988 (NEASC-CIHE) *Calendar:* Sem. plan *Degrees:* B *CEO:* Pres. Tom Gerety
Enroll: 1,606   (413) 542-2000

ANDOVER NEWTON THEOLOGICAL SCHOOL
210 Herrick Rd., Newton Centre 02159 *Type:* Private Private (Baptist) graduate only *Accred.:* 1938/1988 (ATS); 1978/1988 (NEASC-CIHE) *Calendar:* Sem. plan *Degrees:* M, D *CEO:* Pres. Benjamin Griffin
Enroll: 286   (617) 964-1100

ANNA MARIA COLLEGE
Paxton 01612-1198 *Type:* Private (Roman Catholic) liberal arts *Accred.:* 1955/1988 (NEASC-CIHE) *Calendar:* Sem. plan *Degrees:* A, B, M *Prof. Accred.:* Clinical Lab Technology (A), Music, Nursing (B), Social Work (B) *CEO:* Interim Pres. William R. Dill
Enroll: 1,073   (508) 849-3300

AQUINAS COLLEGE AT MILTON
303 Adams St., Milton 02186 *Type:* Private *Accred.:* 1975/1991 (NEASC-CTCI) *Degrees:* A *Prof. Accred.:* Medical Assisting (AMA) *CEO:* Acting Pres. Sarah Barrett
FTE Enroll: 180   (617) 696-3100

AQUINAS COLLEGE AT NEWTON
15 Walnut Park, Newton 02158 *Type:* Private *Accred.:* 1975/1991 (NEASC-CTCI) *Calendar:* Sem. plan *Degrees:* A *CEO:* Pres. Marian Batho, C.S.J.
FTE Enroll: 210   (617) 969-4400

ART INSTITUTE OF BOSTON
700 Beacon St., Boston 02215 *Type:* Private professional *Calendar:* Sem. plan *Degrees:* B, C *Prof. Accred.:* Art *CEO:* Pres. Stan Trecker
Enroll: 350   (617) 262-1223

ARTHUR D. LITTLE MANAGEMENT EDUCATION INSTITUTE, INC.
Cambridge 02140-2390 *Type:* Private specialized graduate *Accred.:* 1976/1986 (NEASC-CIHE) *Calendar:* 10-mos. program *Degrees:* M *CEO:* Pres. Ranganeth P. Nayak
Enroll: 60   (617) 498-6200

ASSUMPTION COLLEGE
500 Salisbury St., Worcester 01615-0005 *Type:* Private (Roman Catholic) liberal arts *Accred.:* 1949/1991 (NEASC-CIHE) *Calendar:* Sem. plan *Degrees:* A, B, M *Prof. Accred.:* Nursing (B), Rehabilitation Counseling *CEO:* Pres. Joseph H. Hagan
Enroll: 2,151   (508) 752-5615

ATLANTIC UNION COLLEGE
P.O. Box 1000, South Lancaster 01561 *Type:* Private (Seventh-Day Adventist) liberal arts *Accred.:* 1945/1988 (NEASC-CIHE) *Calendar:* Sem. plan *Degrees:* A, B, M *Prof. Accred.:* Music, Nursing (A,B), Social Work (B) *CEO:* Pres. James J. Londis
Enroll: 886   (508) 368-2000

BABSON COLLEGE
Babson Park, Wellesley 02157 *Type:* Private professional *Accred.:* 1950/1991 (NEASC-CIHE) *Calendar:* Sem. plan *Degrees:* B, M *Prof. Accred.:* Business (B,M) *CEO:* Pres. William F. Glavin
Enroll: 2,476   (617) 235-1200

BAY PATH COLLEGE
Longmeadow 01106 *Type:* Private for women *Accred.:* 1965/1985 (NEASC-CIHE) *Calendar:* Sem. plan *Degrees:* A, B *Prof. Accred.:* Occupational Therapy Assisting *CEO:* Pres. Carol A. Leary
Enroll: 501   (413) 567-0621

BAY STATE COLLEGE
122 Commonwealth Ave., Boston 02116 *Type:* Private *Accred.:* 1989 (NEASC-CTCI) *Calendar:* Sem. plan *Degrees:* A, C *Prof. Accred.:* Medical Assisting, Physical Therapy Assisting *CEO:* Pres. Robert Keegan
FTE Enroll: 654   (617) 236-8000

BECKER COLLEGE
61 Sever St., Worcester 01615 *Type:* Private *Accred.:* 1976/1992 (NEASC-CIHE) *Calendar:* Sem. plan *Degrees:* A, B *Prof. Accred.:* Nursing (A), Occupational Therapy Assisting, Physical Therapy Assisting *CEO:* Pres. Arnold C. Weller, Jr.
Enroll: 1,143   (508) 791-9241

LEICESTER CAMPUS
3 Paxton St., Leicester 01524 *Prof. Accred.:* Veterinary Technology
(508) 791-9241

BENTLEY COLLEGE
175 Forest St., Waltham 02154-4705 *Type:* Private professional *Accred.:* 1966/1992 (NEASC-CIHE) *Calendar:* Sem. plan *Degrees:* A, B, M *Prof. Accred.:* Business (B,M) *CEO:* Pres. Joseph M. Cronin
Enroll: 4,820   (617) 891-2000

BERKLEE COLLEGE OF MUSIC
1140 Boylston St., Boston 02215 *Type:* Private professional *Accred.:* 1973/1993 (NEASC-CIHE) *Calendar:* Sem. plan *Degrees:* B *CEO:* Pres. Lee Eliot Berk
Enroll: 2,495   (617) 266-1400

BERKSHIRE COMMUNITY COLLEGE
West St., Pittsfield 01201 *Type:* Public (state) junior *System:* Commonwealth of Massachusetts Higher Education Coordinating Council *Accred.:* 1964/1989 (NEASC-CIHE) *Calendar:* Sem. plan *Degrees:* A *Prof. Accred.:* Nursing (A), Physical Therapy

Assisting, Respiratory Therapy *CEO:* Pres. Barbara A. Viniar
Enroll: 1,375   (413) 499-4660

BOSTON ARCHITECTURAL CENTER
320 Newbury St., Boston 02115 *Type:* Private professional *Accred.:* 1991 (NEASC-CIHE) *Degrees:* B *CEO:* Pres. George B. Terrien
Enroll: 567   (617) 536-3170

BOSTON COLLEGE
Chestnut Hill 02167-3934 *Type:* Private (Roman Catholic) *Accred.:* 1935/1986 (NEASC-CIHE) *Calendar:* Sem. plan *Degrees:* B, M, D *Prof. Accred.:* Business (B,M), Counseling Psychology, Law, Nursing (B,M), Social Work (M), Teacher Education *CEO:* Pres. J. Donald Monan, S.J.
Enroll: 12,855   (617) 552-8000

BOSTON CONSERVATORY
8 The Fenway, Boston 02215 *Type:* Private *Accred.:* 1968/1988 (NEASC-CIHE) *Calendar:* Sem. plan *Degrees:* B, M *Prof. Accred.:* Music *CEO:* Pres. William A. Seymour
Enroll: 393   (617) 536-6340

BOSTON UNIVERSITY
147 Bay State Rd., Boston 02215 *Type:* Private *Accred.:* 1938/1991 (ATS); 1929/1989 (NEASC-CIHE) *Calendar:* Sem. plan *Degrees:* B, M, D *Prof. Accred.:* Business (B,M), Clinical Psychology, Combined Prosthodontics, Counseling Psychology, Dental Public Health, Dentistry, Endodontics, Engineering (aerospace, bioengineering, computer, electrical, manufacturing, mechanical, systems), General Dentistry, Health Services Administration, Law, Medicine, Music, Occupational Therapy, Ophthalmic Medical Technology, Oral and Maxillofacial Surgery, Orthodontics, Pediatric Dentistry, Periodontics, Physical Therapy, Psychology Internship, Rehabilitation Counseling, Social Work (B,M), Speech-Language Pathology *CEO:* Pres. John R. Silber
Enroll: 22,876   (617) 353-2000

BRADFORD COLLEGE
Bradford 01830 *Type:* Private *Accred.:* 1931/1986 (NEASC-CIHE) *Calendar:* 4-1-4 plan *Degrees:* A, B *CEO:* Pres. Joseph Short
Enroll: 505   (508) 372-7161

BRANDEIS UNIVERSITY
Waltham 02254-9110 *Type:* Private *Accred.:* 1953/1987 (NEASC-CIHE) *Calendar:* Sem. plan *Degrees:* B, M, D *CEO:* Pres. Jehuda Reinharz
Enroll: 3,897   (617) 736-2000

BRIDGEWATER STATE COLLEGE
Bridgewater 02324 *Type:* Public (state) liberal arts and teachers *System:* Commonwealth of Massachusetts Higher Education Coordinating Council *Accred.:* 1953/1992 (NEASC-CIHE) *Calendar:* Sem. plan *Degrees:* B, M *Prof. Accred.:* Social Work (B), Teacher Education *CEO:* Pres. Adrian Tinsley
Enroll: 6,120   (508) 697-1200

BRISTOL COMMUNITY COLLEGE
777 Elsbree St., Fall River 02720-7395 *Type:* Public (state) junior *System:* Commonwealth of Massachusetts Higher Education Coordinating Council *Accred.:* 1970/1994 (NEASC-CIHE) *Calendar:* Sem. plan *Degrees:* A *Prof. Accred.:* Clinical Lab Technology (A), Dental Hygiene, Nursing (A) *CEO:* Pres. Eileen T. Farley
Enroll: 3,071   (508) 678-2811

BUNKER HILL COMMUNITY COLLEGE
Rutherford Ave., Boston 02129 *Type:* Public (state) junior *System:* Commonwealth of Massachusetts Higher Education Coordinating Council *Accred.:* 1976/1990 (NEASC-CIHE) *Calendar:* Sem. plan *Degrees:* A *Prof. Accred.:* Nuclear Medicine Technology, Nursing (A), Radiography *CEO:* Interim Pres. Maurice O'Shea
Enroll: 3,553   (617) 228-2000

BURDETT SCHOOL
745 Boylston St., Boston 02116 *Type:* Private business *Accred.:* 1954/1996 (ACICS) *Degrees:* A, C *CEO:* Pres. James L. Godkins
                                              (617) 859-1900

WORCESTER CAMPUS
100 Front St., Worcester 01608 *Accred.:* 1993 (ACICS)
                                              (508) 849-1900

CAMBRIDGE COLLEGE
1000 Massachusetts Ave., Ste.128, Cambridge 02138-5304 *Type:* Private *Accred.:* 1981/1987 (NEASC-CIHE) *Calendar:* Sem. plan *Degrees:* M *CEO:* Pres. Eileen M. Brown
Enroll: 17,971   (617) 492-5108

AURORA COLORADO CAMPUS
11059 E. Bethany Dr., Ste. 110, Aurora, CO 80014 *Accred.:* 1994 (ACCSCT) *Prof. Accred.:* Medical Assisting
Enroll: 211   (303) 338-9700

CAPE COD COMMUNITY COLLEGE
Rte. 132, West Barnstable 02668 *Type:* Public (state) junior *System:* Commonwealth of Massachusetts Higher Education Coordinating Council *Accred.:* 1967/1988 (NEASC-CIHE) *Calendar:* Sem. plan *Degrees:* A *Prof. Accred.:* Dental Hygiene, Nursing (A), Physical Therapy Assisting (candidate) *CEO:* Pres. Richard A. Kraus
Enroll: 2,035   (508) 362-2131

CLARK UNIVERSITY
Worcester 01610-1477 *Type:* Private *Accred.:* 1929/1986 (NEASC-CIHE) *Degrees:* B, M, D *Prof. Accred.:* Business (B,M), Clinical Psychology, Health Services Administration *CEO:* Pres. Richard P. Traina
Enroll: 2,581   (508) 793-7711

COLLEGE OF OUR LADY OF THE ELMS
291 Springfield St., Chicopee 01013-2839 *Type:* Private (Roman Catholic) liberal arts for women *Accred.:* 1942/1992 (NEASC-CIHE) *Calendar:* Sem. plan *Degrees:* B, M *Prof. Accred.:* Nursing (B), Social Work (B) *CEO:* Pres. Kathleen Keating, S.S.J.
Enroll: 829   (413) 594-2761

COLLEGE OF THE HOLY CROSS
Worcester 01610-2395 *Type:* Private (Roman Catholic) liberal arts *Accred.:* 1930/1990 (NEASC-CIHE) *Calendar:* Sem.

plan *Degrees:* B, M *CEO:* Pres. Gerard Reedy, S.J.
Enroll: 2,720   (508) 793-2011

CONWAY SCHOOL OF LANDSCAPE DESIGN
Delabarre Ave., Conway 01341 *Type:* Private *Accred.:* 1989/1994 (NEASC-CIHE) *Calendar:* Tri. plan *Degrees:* M *CEO:* Dir. Mollie Babize
Enroll: 11   (413) 369-4044

CURRY COLLEGE
Milton 02186 *Type:* Private liberal arts and teachers *Accred.:* 1970/1992 (NEASC-CIHE) *Calendar:* Sem. plan *Degrees:* B, M *Prof. Accred.:* Nursing (B) *CEO:* Pres. Catherine W. Ingold
Enroll: 1,158   (617) 333-0500

DEAN COLLEGE
Franklin 02038 *Type:* Private *Accred.:* 1957/1986 (NEASC-CIHE) *Calendar:* Sem. plan *Degrees:* A *CEO:* Pres. Paula M. Rooney
Enroll: 1,334   (508) 528-9100

EASTERN NAZARENE COLLEGE
23 E. Elm Ave., Quincy 02170-2999 *Type:* Private (Nazarene) liberal arts *Accred.:* 1943/1990 (NEASC-CIHE) *Calendar:* 4-1-4 plan *Degrees:* A, B, M *Prof. Accred.:* Social Work (B) *CEO:* Pres. Kent R. Hill
Enroll: 1,287   (617) 773-6350

EMERSON COLLEGE
100 Beacon St., Boston 02116-1596 *Type:* Private liberal arts *Accred.:* 1950/1992 (NEASC-CIHE) *Calendar:* Sem. plan *Degrees:* B, M, D *Prof. Accred.:* Speech-Language Pathology *CEO:* Pres. Jacqueline Liebergott
Enroll: 2,763   (617) 578-8500

EUROPEAN INSTITUTE FOR INTERNATIONAL COMMUNICATION
Brusselsestraat 84, Maastricht Netherlands 6211 PH
                    [31] (043) 25 82 82

EMMANUEL COLLEGE
400 The Fenway, Boston 02115 *Type:* Private (Roman Catholic) liberal arts primarily

for women *Accred.:* 1933/1992 (NEASC-CIHE) *Calendar:* Sem. plan *Degrees:* B, M *Prof. Accred.:* Nursing (B) *CEO:* Pres. Janet Eisner, S.N.D.
Enroll: 1,131   (617) 277-9430

ENDICOTT COLLEGE
Beverly 01915 *Type:* Private liberal arts *Accred.:* 1952/1987 (NEASC-CIHE) *Calendar:* Sem. plan *Degrees:* A, B *Prof. Accred.:* Interior Design, Nursing (A), Physical Therapy Assisting *CEO:* Pres. Richard E. Wylie
Enroll: 1,014   (508) 927-0585

EPISCOPAL DIVINITY SCHOOL
99 Brattle St., Cambridge 02138 *Type:* Private (Episcopal) graduate only *Accred.:* 1938/1988 (ATS) *Calendar:* Sem. plan *Degrees:* M, D *CEO:* Pres./Dean William W. Rankin
Enroll: 121   (617) 868-3450

ESSEX AGRICULTURAL AND TECHNICAL INSTITUTE
562 Maple St., Hathorne 01937 *Type:* Public (state) *Accred.:* 1979/1994 (NEASC-CTCI) *Calendar:* Sem. plan *Degrees:* A, C *CEO:* Dir. Gustave D. Olson, Jr.
FTE Enroll: 501   (508) 774-0050

FISHER COLLEGE
118 Beacon St., Boston 02116 *Type:* Private *Accred.:* 1970/1990 (NEASC-CIHE) *Calendar:* Sem. plan *Degrees:* A *Prof. Accred.:* Physical Therapy Assisting *CEO:* Pres. Christian Fisher
Enroll: 2,417   (617) 262-3240

FITCHBURG STATE COLLEGE
160 Pearl St., Fitchburg 01420 *Type:* Public *System:* Commonwealth of Massachusetts Higher Education Coordinating Council *Accred.:* 1953/1992 (NEASC-CIHE) *Calendar:* Sem. plan *Degrees:* B, M *Prof. Accred.:* Clinical Lab Scientist, Nursing (B) *CEO:* Pres. Michael P. Riccards
Enroll: 3,604   (508) 345-2151

FRAMINGHAM STATE COLLEGE
100 State St., Framingham 01701-9101 *Type:* Public liberal arts and teachers *System:* Commonwealth of Massachusetts Higher

Education Coordinating Council *Accred.:* 1950/1994 (NEASC-CIHE) *Calendar:* Sem. plan *Degrees:* B, M *Prof. Accred.:* Dietetics (coordinated), Dietetics (internship), Home Economics, Nursing (B) *CEO:* Interim Pres. Helen Heineman
Enroll: 3,624   (508) 626-1220

FRANKLIN INSTITUTE OF BOSTON
Boston 02116 *Type:* Private 2-year technical *Accred.:* 1970/1990 (NEASC-CTCI) *Calendar:* Sem. plan *Degrees:* A *Prof. Accred.:* Engineering Technology (architectural, civil/construction, computer, electrical, mechanical) *CEO:* Pres. Richard P. D'Onofrio
FTE Enroll: 376   (617) 423-4630

GORDON COLLEGE
Wenham 01984 *Type:* Private liberal arts *Accred.:* 1961/1992 (NEASC-CIHE) *Calendar:* Tri. plan *Degrees:* B *Prof. Accred.:* Music, Social Work (B) *CEO:* Pres. R. Judson Carleberg
Enroll: 1,159   (508) 927-2300

GORDON-CONWELL THEOLOGICAL SEMINARY
130 Essex St., South Hamilton 01982 *Type:* Private (interdenominational) graduate only *Accred.:* 1964/1995 (ATS); 1985 (NEASC-CIHE) *Calendar:* Sem. plan *Degrees:* M, D *CEO:* Pres. Robert E. Cooley
Enroll: 544   (508) 468-7111

GREENFIELD COMMUNITY COLLEGE
One College Dr., Greenfield 01301 *Type:* Public (state) junior *System:* Commonwealth of Massachusetts Higher Education Coordinating Council *Accred.:* 1966/1990 (NEASC-CIHE) *Calendar:* Sem. plan *Degrees:* A *Prof. Accred.:* Nursing (A) *CEO:* Pres. Charles Wall
Enroll: 1,810   (413) 774-3131

HAMPSHIRE COLLEGE
Amherst 01002 *Type:* Private liberal arts *Accred.:* 1974/1988 (NEASC-CIHE) *Calendar:* 4-1-4 plan *Degrees:* B *CEO:* Pres. Gregory S. Prince, Jr.
Enroll: 1,087   (413) 549-4600

HARVARD UNIVERSITY
Cambridge 02138 *Type:* Private (interdenominational) *Accred.:* 1940/1991 (ATS); 1929/1987 (NEASC-CIHE) *Calendar:* Sem. plan *Degrees:* A, B, M, P, D *Prof. Accred.:* Business (M), Combined Prosthodontics, Dental Public Health, Dentistry, Engineering Technology (industrial hygiene), Engineering (engineering physics/science), Landscape Architecture (M), Law, Medicine, Oral Pathology (conditional), Orthodontics, Periodontics, Planning, Psychology Internship *CEO:* Pres. Neil Rudenstine
Enroll: 17,971   (617) 495-1000

HEBREW COLLEGE
43 Hawes St., Brookline 02146 *Type:* Private (Jewish) teachers *Accred.:* 1955/1988 (NEASC-CIHE) *Calendar:* Sem. plan *Degrees:* B, M *CEO:* Pres. David M. Gordis
Enroll: 38   (617) 232-8710

HELLENIC COLLEGE/HOLY CROSS GREEK ORTHODOX SCHOOL OF THEOLOGY
50 Goddard Ave., Brookline 02146 *Type:* Private (Greek Orthodox) liberal arts and professional *Accred.:* 1974/1991 (ATS); 1974/1991 (NEASC-CIHE) *Calendar:* Sem. plan *Degrees:* B, M *CEO:* Pres. Alkiviadis C. Calivas
Enroll: 154   (617) 731-3500

HOLYOKE COMMUNITY COLLEGE
303 Homestead Ave., Holyoke 01040 *Type:* Public (state) junior *System:* Commonwealth of Massachusetts Higher Education Coordinating Council *Accred.:* 1970/1990 (NEASC-CIHE) *Calendar:* Sem. plan *Degrees:* A *Prof. Accred.:* Medical Record Technology, Nursing (A), Radiography, Veterinary Technology (probational) *CEO:* Pres. David M. Bartley
Enroll: 3,199   (413) 538-7000

KATHARINE GIBBS SCHOOL
126 Newbury St., Boston 02116 *Type:* Private junior *Accred.:* 1967/1998 (ACICS) *Calendar:* Sem. plan *Degrees:* A, C *CEO:* Pres. Robert Moon
                    (617) 578-7100

LABOURE COLLEGE
2120 Dorchester Ave., Boston 02124 *Type:*
Private (Roman Catholic) 2-year *Accred.:*
1975/1991 (NEASC-CTCI) *Calendar:* Sem.
plan *Degrees:* A *Prof. Accred.:* Electroneuro-
diagnostic Technology, Medical Record
Technology, Nursing (A), Radiation Therapy
Technology *CEO:* Pres. Clarisse Correia,
D.C.
FTE Enroll: 474   (617) 296-8300

LASELL COLLEGE
Newton 02166 *Type:* Private liberal arts for
women *Accred.:* 1932/1992 (NEASC-CIHE)
Calendar: Sem. plan *Degrees:* A, B *Prof.
Accred.:* Physical Therapy Assisting *CEO:*
Pres. Thomas E.J. de Witt
Enroll: 502   (617) 243-2000

LESLEY COLLEGE
29 Everett St., Cambridge 02138-2790 *Type:*
Private teachers for women *Accred.:* 1952/
1994 (NEASC-CIHE) *Calendar:* Sem. plan
Degrees: A, B, M, D *CEO:* Pres. Margaret
A. McKenna
Enroll: 2,858   (617) 868-9600

MARIAN COURT JUNIOR COLLEGE
35 Little's Point Rd., Swampscott 01907
Type: Private (Roman Catholic) *Accred.:*
1982/1992 (NEASC-CTCI) *Calendar:* Sem.
plan *Degrees:* A *CEO:* Pres. Joanne Bibeau,
R.S.M.
FTE Enroll: 203   (617) 595-6768

MASSACHUSETTS BAY COMMUNITY COLLEGE
50 Oakland St., Wellesley Hills 02181-5399
Type: Public (state) junior *System:* Common-
wealth of Massachusetts Higher Education
Coordinating Council *Accred.:* 1967/1995
(NEASC-CIHE) *Calendar:* Sem. plan
Degrees: A *Prof. Accred.:* Occupational
Therapy Assisting, Physical Therapy Assist-
ing, Radiography *CEO:* Pres. Roger A. Van
Winkle
Enroll: 3,336   (617) 237-1100

MASSACHUSETTS COLLEGE OF ART
621 Huntington Ave., Boston 02115 *Type:*
Public (state) teachers and professional *System:* Commonwealth of Massachusetts
Higher Education Coordinating Council

Accred.: 1954/1994 (NEASC-CIHE) *Calen-
dar:* Sem. plan *Degrees:* B, M *Prof. Accred.:*
Art *CEO:* Pres. William F. O'Neil
Enroll: 1,430   (617) 232-1555

MASSACHUSETTS COLLEGE OF PHARMACY AND
ALLIED HEALTH SCIENCES
179 Longwood Ave., Boston 02115 *Type:*
Private professional *Accred.:* 1974/1987
(NEASC-CIHE) *Calendar:* Sem. plan
Degrees: A, B, M, D *Prof. Accred.:* Nuclear
Medicine Technology, Nursing (B), Radia-
tion Therapy Technology *CEO:* Pres. Sum-
ner M. Robinson
Enroll: 1,424   (617) 732-2800

MASSACHUSETTS INSTITUTE OF TECHNOLOGY
Cambridge 02139 *Type:* Private *Accred.:*
1929/1989 (NEASC-CIHE) *Calendar:* Sem.
plan *Degrees:* B, M, D *Prof. Accred.:* Business (B,M), Engineering (aerospace, chemical, civil, computer, electrical, environmen-
tal/sanitary, materials, mechanical, nuclear,
ocean), Planning (M) *CEO:* Pres. Charles M.
Vest
Enroll: 9,568   (617) 253-1000

MASSACHUSETTS MARITIME ACADEMY
101 Academy Dr., Buzzards Bay 02532
Type: Public (state) professional *System:*
Commonwealth of Massachusetts Higher
Education Coordinating Council *Accred.:*
1974/1990 (NEASC-CIHE) *Calendar:* Qtr.
plan *Degrees:* B *CEO:* Pres. Peter M.
Mitchell
Enroll: 880   (508) 830-5000

MASSACHUSETTS SCHOOL OF PROFESSIONAL
PSYCHOLOGY
221 Rivermoor St., Boston 02132 *Type:* Private professional; graduate only *Accred.:*
1984/1992 (NEASC-CIHE) *Calendar:* Sem.
plan *Degrees:* D *Prof. Accred.:* Clinical Psychology *CEO:* Pres. Bruce J. Weiss
Enroll: 131   (617) 327-6777

MASSASOIT COMMUNITY COLLEGE
One Massasoit Blvd., Brockton 02402 *Type:*
Public (state) junior *System:* Commonwealth
of Massachusetts Higher Education Coordi-
nating Council *Accred.:* 1971/1987
(NEASC-CIHE) *Calendar:* Sem. plan

Degrees: A *Prof. Accred.:* Clinical Lab Technology (A), Dental Assisting, Nursing (A), Physical Therapy Assisting, Radiography, Respiratory Therapy *CEO:* Pres. Gerard F. Burke
Enroll: 3,377   (508) 588-9100

MERRIMACK COLLEGE
North Andover 01845 *Type:* Private (Roman Catholic) liberal arts *Accred.:* 1953/1991 (NEASC-CIHE) *Calendar:* Sem. plan *Degrees:* A, B *Prof. Accred.:* Engineering (civil, computer) *CEO:* Pres. Richard J. Santagati
Enroll: 2,204   (508) 837-5000

MGH INSTITUTE OF HEALTH PROFESSIONS
101 Merrimac St., Boston 02114-4719 *Type:* Private professional *Accred.:* 1985/1990 (NEASC-CIHE) *Calendar:* Sem. plan *Degrees:* M *Prof. Accred.:* Nursing (M), Speech-Language Pathology *CEO:* Pres. Maureen W. Groer
Enroll: 322   (617) 726-8002

MIDDLESEX COMMUNITY COLLEGE
Springs Rd., Bedford 01730 *Type:* Public (state) junior *System:* Commonwealth of Massachusetts Higher Education Coordinating Council *Accred.:* 1973/1995 (NEASC-CIHE) *Calendar:* Sem. plan *Degrees:* A *Prof. Accred.:* Clinical Lab Technology (A), Dental Assisting, Dental Hygiene, Dental Laboratory Technology, Diagnostic Medical Sonography, Nursing (A), Radiography *CEO:* Pres. Carole A. Cowan
Enroll: 4,213   (617) 280-3200

LOWELL CAMPUS
Kearney Sq., Lowell 01852
                                     (508) 656-3200

MONTSERRAT COLLEGE OF ART
Dunham Rd., Box 26, Beverly 01915 *Type:* Private 4-year professional *Accred.:* 1982 (NEASC-CTCI) *Calendar:* Sem. plan *Degrees:* B, C *Prof. Accred.:* Art *CEO:* Pres. Paul G. Marks
FTE Enroll: 249   (508) 922-8222

MOUNT HOLYOKE COLLEGE
South Hadley 01075 *Type:* Private liberal arts for women *Accred.:* 1929/1988

(NEASC-CIHE) *Calendar:* Sem. plan *Degrees:* B, M *CEO:* Pres. Joanne V. Creighton
Enroll: 1,920   (413) 538-2000

MOUNT IDA COLLEGE
777 Dedham St., Newton Centre 02159 *Type:* Private *Accred.:* 1970/1988 (NEASC-CIHE) *Degrees:* A, B *Prof. Accred.:* Dental Assisting (conditional), Funeral Service Education (Mortuary Science) (1993), Interior Design, Occupational Therapy Assisting, Veterinary Technology *CEO:* Pres. Bryan E. Carlson
Enroll: 1,639   (617) 969-7000

MOUNT WACHUSETT COMMUNITY COLLEGE
444 Green St., Gardner 01440 *Type:* Public (state) junior *System:* Commonwealth of Massachusetts Higher Education Coordinating Council *Accred.:* 1968/1992 (NEASC-CIHE) *Calendar:* Sem. plan *Degrees:* A *Prof. Accred.:* Clinical Lab Technology (A), Nursing (A) *CEO:* Pres. Daniel M. Asquino
Enroll: 1,317   (508) 632-6600

THE NEW ENGLAND BANKING INSTITUTE
One Lincoln Plaza, 89 South St., Boston 02111 *Type:* Private *Accred.:* 1985 (NEASC-CTCI) *Calendar:* Sem. plan *Degrees:* A *CEO:* Pres. Robert A. Regan
FTE Enroll: 439   (617) 951-2350

NEW ENGLAND COLLEGE OF OPTOMETRY
424 Beacon St., Boston 02115 *Type:* Private professional *Accred.:* 1976/1986 (NEASC-CIHE) *Calendar:* Sem. plan *Degrees:* B, P, D *Prof. Accred.:* Optometry *CEO:* Pres. Larry R. Clausen
Enroll: 404   (617) 266-2030

NEW ENGLAND CONSERVATORY OF MUSIC
290 Huntington Ave., Boston 02115 *Type:* Private professional *Accred.:* 1951/1988 (NEASC-CIHE) *Calendar:* Sem. plan *Degrees:* B, M, D *Prof. Accred.:* Music *CEO:* Pres. Laurence Lesser
Enroll: 691   (617) 262-1120

NEW ENGLAND SCHOOL OF ART AND DESIGN
28 Newbury St., Boston 02116-3276 *Type:* Private *Calendar:* Sem. plan *Degrees:* B, C

Prof. Accred.: Interior Design *CEO:* Chair of Int. Des. Curtis M. Estes
(617) 536-0383

NEW ENGLAND SCHOOL OF LAW
154 Stuart St., Boston 02116 *Type:* Private professional *Calendar:* Sem. plan *Degrees:* P *Prof. Accred.:* Law (ABA only) *CEO:* Dean John F. O'Brien
Enroll: 1,121   (617) 451-0010

NEWBURY COLLEGE
129 Fisher Ave., Brookline 02146 *Type:* Private *Accred.:* 1995/1995 (NEASC-CIHE candidate); 1977/1992 (NEASC-CTCI) *Calendar:* Sem. plan *Degrees:* A *Prof. Accred.:* Physical Therapy Assisting, Respiratory Therapy, Respiratory Therapy Technology *CEO:* Pres. Edward J. Tassinari
FTE Enroll: 2,425   (617) 730-7000

NICHOLS COLLEGE
Dudley 01571 *Type:* Private business *Accred.:* 1965/1995 (NEASC-CIHE) *Calendar:* Sem. plan *Degrees:* A, B, M *CEO:* Pres. Lowell C. Smith
Enroll: 1,037   (508) 943-1560

NORTH ADAMS STATE COLLEGE
North Adams 01247 *Type:* Public teachers *System:* Commonwealth of Massachusetts Higher Education Coordinating Council *Accred.:* 1953/1993 (NEASC-CIHE) *Calendar:* 4-1-4 plan *Degrees:* B, M *CEO:* Pres. Thomas D. Aceto
Enroll: 1,457   (413) 664-4511

NORTH SHORE COMMUNITY COLLEGE
1 Ferncroft Rd., Danvers 01923-4093 *Type:* Public (state) junior *System:* Commonwealth of Massachusetts Higher Education Coordinating Council *Accred.:* 1969/1989 (NEASC-CIHE) *Calendar:* Sem. plan *Degrees:* A *Prof. Accred.:* Nursing (A), Occupational Therapy Assisting, Physical Therapy Assisting, Radiography, Respiratory Therapy *CEO:* Pres. George Traicoff
Enroll: 3,097   (508) 762-4000

NORTHEASTERN UNIVERSITY
244 Hampton Plaza, Boston 02115-5095 *Type:* Private *Accred.:* 1940/1988 (NEASC-CIHE) *Calendar:* Qtr. plan *Degrees:* A, B, M, P, D *Prof. Accred.:* Audiology, Business (B,M), Clinical Lab Scientist, Clinical Lab Technology (A), Computer Science, Engineering Technology (electrical, mechanical), Engineering (chemical, civil, electrical, industrial, mechanical), Law, Medical Record Administration, Nurse Anesthesia Education (M), Nursing (B,M), Perfusion, Physical Therapy, Physician Assisting/Surgeon Assisting, Public Administration, Radiography, Rehabilitation Counseling, Respiratory Therapy, Speech-Language Pathology *CEO:* Pres. John A. Curry
Enroll: 18,459   (617) 373-2000

NORTHERN ESSEX COMMUNITY COLLEGE
100 Elliott Way, Haverhill 01830-2399 *Type:* Public (state) junior *System:* Commonwealth of Massachusetts Higher Education Coordinating Council *Accred.:* 1969/1990 (NEASC-CIHE) *Calendar:* Sem. plan *Degrees:* A *Prof. Accred.:* Dental Assisting, Medical Assisting (AMA), Medical Record Technology, Nursing (A), Practical Nursing, Radiography, Respiratory Therapy, Respiratory Therapy Technology *CEO:* Pres. David Hartled
Enroll: 3,588   (508) 374-3900

PINE MANOR COLLEGE
400 Heath St., Chestnut Hill 02167 *Type:* Private liberal arts for women *Accred.:* 1939/1993 (NEASC-CIHE) *Calendar:* Sem. plan *Degrees:* A, B *CEO:* Pres. Rosemary Ashby
Enroll: 389   (617) 731-7000

POPE JOHN XXIII NATIONAL SEMINARY
558 South Ave., Weston 02193-2699 *Type:* Private (Roman Catholic) graduate only *Accred.:* 1983/1988 (ATS) *Calendar:* Sem. plan *Degrees:* M *CEO:* Rector Francis D. Kelly
Enroll: 62   (617) 899-5500

QUINCY COLLEGE
34 Coddington St., Quincy 02169 *Type:* Public (city) junior *Accred.:* 1980/1987 (NEASC-CIHE) *Calendar:* Sem. plan *Degrees:* A *Prof. Accred.:* Nursing (A), Practical Nursing, Surgical Technology *CEO:* Interim Pres. Stephen Kenney
Enroll: 2,842   (617) 984-1600

QUINSIGAMOND COMMUNITY COLLEGE
670 W. Boylston St., Worcester 01606 *Type:* Public (state) junior *System:* Commonwealth of Massachusetts Higher Education Coordinating Council *Accred.:* 1967/1994 (NEASC-CIHE) *Calendar:* Sem. plan *Degrees:* A *Prof. Accred.:* Dental Hygiene, Nursing (A), Occupational Therapy Assisting, Radiography, Respiratory Therapy *CEO:* Pres. Sandra L. Kurtinitus
Enroll: 2,583   (508) 853-2300

RADCLIFFE COLLEGE
10 Garden St., Cambridge 02138 *Type:* Private primarily for women *Accred.:* 1929/1987 (NEASC-CIHE) *Calendar:* Sem. plan *Degrees:* A, B *CEO:* Pres. Linda S. Wilson
Enroll: 2,692   (617) 495-8601

* Indirect NEASC-CIHE accreditation through Harvard University

REGIS COLLEGE
Weston 02193 *Type:* Private (Roman Catholic) liberal arts for women *Accred.:* 1933/1986 (NEASC-CIHE) *Calendar:* Sem. plan *Degrees:* B, M *Prof. Accred.:* Nursing (B), Social Work (B) *CEO:* Pres. Sheila E. Megley, R.S.M.
Enroll: 802   (617) 893-1820

ROXBURY COMMUNITY COLLEGE
1234 Columbus Ave., Roxbury Crossing 02120-3400 *Type:* Public (state) junior *System:* Commonwealth of Massachusetts Higher Education Coordinating Council *Accred.:* 1981/1995 (NEASC-CIHE) *Calendar:* Sem. plan *Degrees:* A *CEO:* Pres. Grace Carolyn Brown
Enroll: 1,898   (617) 427-0060

ST. HYACINTH COLLEGE AND SEMINARY
Granby 01033 *Type:* Private (Roman Catholic Order of Friars Minor Conventual) for men *Accred.:* 1967/1988 (NEASC-CIHE) *Calendar:* Sem. plan *Degrees:* B *CEO:* Pres. Jude Surowiec, OFM
Enroll: 23   (413) 467-7191

ST. JOHN'S SEMINARY
127 Lake St., Brighton 02135 *Type:* Private (Roman Catholic) *Accred.:* 1970/1989 (ATS); 1969/1989 (NEASC-CIHE) *Calendar:* Sem. plan *Degrees:* B, M, P *CEO:* Rector Timothy J. Moran
Enroll: 114   (617) 254-2610

SALEM STATE COLLEGE
352 Lafayette St., Salem 01970-4589 *Type:* Public liberal arts and professional *System:* Commonwealth of Massachusetts Higher Education Coordinating Council *Accred.:* 1953/1991 (NEASC-CIHE) *Calendar:* Sem. plan *Degrees:* B, M *Prof. Accred.:* Art, Nuclear Medicine Technology, Nursing (B,M), Social Work (B,M), Teacher Education *CEO:* Pres. Nancy D. Harrington
Enroll: 6,824   (508) 741-6000

SCHOOL OF THE MUSEUM OF FINE ARTS, BOSTON
230 The Fenway, Boston 02115-9975 *Type:* Private professional *Calendar:* Sem. plan *Degrees:* B, M, C *Prof. Accred.:* Art *CEO:* Pres. Bruce K. MacDonald
                                   (617) 267-6100

SIMMONS COLLEGE
Boston 02115 *Type:* Private liberal arts and professional for women *Accred.:* 1929/1990 (NEASC-CIHE) *Calendar:* Sem. plan *Degrees:* B, M, D *Prof. Accred.:* Health Services Administration, Librarianship, Nursing (B,M), Physical Therapy, Social Work (M) *CEO:* Acting Pres. Barbara Graham
Enroll: 2,595   (617) 738-2000

SIMON'S ROCK COLLEGE OF BARD
Great Barrington 01230-9702 *Type:* Private liberal arts *Accred.:* 1974/1986 (NEASC-CIHE) *Calendar:* Sem. plan *Degrees:* A, B *CEO:* Pres. Leon Botstein
Enroll: 321   (413) 528-0771

SMITH COLLEGE
Northampton 01063 *Type:* Private liberal arts for women *Accred.:* 1929/1988 (NEASC-CIHE) *Calendar:* Sem. plan *Degrees:* B, M, D *Prof. Accred.:* Social Work (M) *CEO:* Pres. Ruth J. Simmons
Enroll: 2,548   (413) 584-2700

SOUTHERN NEW ENGLAND SCHOOL OF LAW
333 Faunce Corner Rd., N. Dartmouth 02747-1252 *Type:* Private *Accred.:* 1995 (NEASC-CIHE) *Degrees:* P *CEO:* Dean Francis J. Larkin
Enroll: 179   (5080 998-9600

SPRINGFIELD COLLEGE
Springfield 01109 *Type:* Private liberal arts and professional *Accred.:* 1930/1989 (NEASC-CIHE) *Calendar:* Qtr. plan *Degrees:* B, M, D *Prof. Accred.:* Occupational Therapy, Physical Therapy, Recreation and Leisure Services (B), Rehabilitation Counseling, Social Work (M) *CEO:* Pres. Randolph W. Bromery
Enroll: 3,159   (413) 748-3000

SPRINGFIELD TECHNICAL COMMUNITY COLLEGE
One Armory Sq., Springfield 01105 *Type:* Public (state) 2-year *System:* Commonwealth of Massachusetts Higher Education Coordinating Council *Accred.:* 1971/1991 (NEASC-CIHE) *Calendar:* Sem. plan *Degrees:* A *Prof. Accred.:* Clinical Lab Technology (A), Dental Assisting, Dental Hygiene, Medical Assisting (AMA), Nuclear Medicine Technology, Nursing (A), Occupational Therapy Assisting, Physical Therapy Assisting, Radiation Therapy Technology, Radiography, Respiratory Therapy, Surgical Technology *CEO:* Pres. Andrew M. Scibelli
Enroll: 3,686   (413) 781-7822

STONEHILL COLLEGE
North Easton 02357 *Type:* Private (Roman Catholic) liberal arts *Accred.:* 1959/1989 (NEASC-CIHE) *Calendar:* Sem. plan *Degrees:* B *Prof. Accred.:* Teacher Education *CEO:* Pres. Bartley MacPhaidin, C.S.C.
Enroll: 2,210   (508) 238-1081

SUFFOLK UNIVERSITY
8 Ashburton Pl., Beacon Hill, Boston 02108 *Type:* Private *Accred.:* 1952/1992 (NEASC-CIHE) *Calendar:* Sem. plan *Degrees:* A, B, M, P, D *Prof. Accred.:* Business (B,M), Law, Public Administration *CEO:* Pres. David J. Sargent
Enroll: 9,703   (617) 723-4700

TUFTS UNIVERSITY
Medford 02155 *Type:* Private liberal arts *Accred.:* 1929/1992 (NEASC-CIHE) *Calendar:* Sem. plan *Degrees:* B, M, P, D *Prof. Accred.:* Combined Prosthodontics, Dentistry, Dietetics (internship), Endodontics (conditional), Engineering (chemical, civil, computer, electrical, environmental/sanitary, mechanical), General Practice Residency, Medicine, Occupational Therapy, Oral and Maxillofacial Surgery, Orthodontics, Pediatric Dentistry, Periodontics, Psychology Internship, Veterinary Medicine *CEO:* Pres. John A. DiBiaggio
Enroll: 7,905   (617) 628-5000

UNIVERSITY OF MASSACHUSETTS AT AMHERST
Amherst 01003 *Type:* Public (state) *System:* University of Massachusetts President's Office *Accred.:* 1932/1988 (NEASC-CIHE) *Calendar:* Sem. plan *Degrees:* A, B, M, P, D *Prof. Accred.:* Audiology, Business (B,M), Clinical Psychology, Combined Professional-Scientific Psychology, Counseling Psychology, Engineering (chemical, civil, computer, electrical, environmental/sanitary, industrial, manufacturing, mechanical), Forestry, Interior Design, Landscape Architecture (B-initial,M), Music, Nursing (B,M), Planning (M), Psychology Internship, Public Administration, Speech-Language Pathology, Teacher Education, Theatre *CEO:* Chanc. David K. Scott
Enroll: 21,061   (413) 545-0111

UNIVERSITY OF MASSACHUSETTS BOSTON
Harbor Campus, 100 Morrisey Blvd., Boston 02125-3393 *Type:* Public (state) *System:* University of Massachusetts President's Office *Accred.:* 1972/1995 (NEASC-CIHE) *Calendar:* Sem. plan *Degrees:* B, M, D *Prof. Accred.:* Clinical Psychology, Nursing

(B,M), Rehabilitation Counseling *CEO:* Pres. Sherry H. Penney
Enroll: 8,907   (617) 287-6800

UNIVERSITY OF MASSACHUSETTS DARTMOUTH
North Dartmouth 02747 *Type:* Public (state) *System:* University of Massachusetts President's Office *Accred.:* 1964/1990 (NEASC-CIHE) *Calendar:* Sem. plan *Degrees:* B, M *Prof. Accred.:* Art, Clinical Lab Scientist, Computer Science, Engineering Technology (electrical, mechanical), Engineering (civil, computer, electrical, mechanical), Nursing (B,M) *CEO:* Chanc. Peter Cressy
Enroll: 5,422   (508) 999-8004

UNIVERSITY OF MASSACHUSETTS LOWELL
One University Ave., Lowell 01854 *Type:* Public (state) *System:* University of Massachusetts President's Office *Accred.:* 1975/ 1994 (NEASC-CIHE) *Calendar:* Sem. plan *Degrees:* A, B, M, D *Prof. Accred.:* Art (A), Business (B,M), Clinical Lab Scientist, Computer Science, Engineering Technology (civil/construction, electrical, mechanical), Engineering (chemical, civil, electrical, mechanical, nuclear, plastics), Music, Nursing (B,M), Physical Therapy, Teacher Education *CEO:* Chanc. William T. Hogan
Enroll: 8,525   (508) 934-4000

UNIVERSITY OF MASSACHUSETTS MEDICAL CENTER AT WORCESTER
55 Lake Ave., N., Worcester 01605 *Type:* Public (state) *System:* University of Massachusetts President's Office *Calendar:* Sem. plan *Degrees:* B, M, P *Prof. Accred.:* Medicine, Nuclear Medicine Technology, Nursing (M), Radiation Therapy Technology *CEO:* Chanc. Aaron Lazare
Enroll: 407   (508) 856-8100

WELLESLEY COLLEGE
Wellesley 02181 *Type:* Private liberal arts for women *Accred.:* 1929/1989 (NEASC-CIHE) *Calendar:* 4-1-4 plan *Degrees:* B *CEO:* Pres. Diana Chapman Walsh
Enroll: 2,225   (617) 235-0320

WENTWORTH INSTITUTE OF TECHNOLOGY
Boston 02115 *Type:* Private technological *Accred.:* 1967/1991 (NEASC-CIHE) *Calen-

dar:* Sem. plan *Degrees:* A, B *Prof. Accred.:* Engineering Technology (aerospace, architectural, civil/construction, computer, electrical, manufacturing, mechanical), mechanical drafting/design) *CEO:* Pres. John F. Van Domelen
Enroll: 2,105   (617) 442-9010

WESTERN NEW ENGLAND COLLEGE
Springfield 01119 *Type:* Private liberal arts and professional *Accred.:* 1965/1992 (NEASC-CIHE) *Calendar:* Sem. plan *Degrees:* B, M, P, D *Prof. Accred.:* Engineering (electrical, industrial, mechanical), Law, Social Work (B) *CEO:* Pres. Beverly W. Miller
Enroll: 2,339   (413) 782-3111

WESTFIELD STATE COLLEGE
Western Ave., Westfield 01086 *Type:* Public (state) liberal arts and teachers *System:* Commonwealth of Massachusetts Higher Education Coordinating Council *Accred.:* 1957/1991 (NEASC-CIHE) *Calendar:* Sem. plan *Degrees:* B, M *Prof. Accred.:* Teacher Education *CEO:* Pres. Ronald L. Applbaum
Enroll: 3,709   (413) 568-3311

WESTON JESUIT SCHOOL OF THEOLOGY
3 Phillips Pl., Cambridge 02138-3495 *Type:* Private (Roman Catholic) graduate only *Accred.:* 1968/1988 (ATS) *Calendar:* Sem. plan *Degrees:* M *CEO:* Pres. Robert A. Wild, S.J.
Enroll: 209   (617) 492-1960

WHEATON COLLEGE
Norton 02766 *Type:* Private liberal arts *Accred.:* 1929/1989 (NEASC-CIHE) *Calendar:* Sem. plan *Degrees:* B *CEO:* Pres. Dale Rogers Marshall
Enroll: 1,313   (508) 285-7722

WHEELOCK COLLEGE
200 The Riverway, Boston 02215-4176 *Type:* Private teachers for women *Accred.:* 1950/1995 (NEASC-CIHE) *Calendar:* Tri. plan *Degrees:* A, B, M *Prof. Accred.:* Social Work (B), Teacher Education *CEO:* Acting Pres. Marjorie Bakken
Enroll: 1,076   (617) 734-5200

WILLIAMS COLLEGE
Williamstown 01267 *Type:* Private liberal arts *Accred.:* 1929/1988 (NEASC-CIHE) *Calendar:* 4-1-4 plan *Degrees:* B, M *CEO:* Pres. Harry C. Payne
Enroll: 2,072   (413) 597-3131

WORCESTER POLYTECHNIC INSTITUTE
100 Institute Rd., Worcester 01609-2280 *Type:* Private technological *Accred.:* 1937/1991 (NEASC-CIHE) *Calendar:* Sem. plan *Degrees:* B, M, D *Prof. Accred.:* Computer Science, Engineering (chemical, civil, electrical, manufacturing, mechanical) *CEO:* Pres. Edward A. Parrish, Jr.
Enroll: 3,345   (508) 831-5000

WORCESTER STATE COLLEGE
486 Chandler St., Worcester 01602-2597 *Type:* Public (state) liberal arts and teachers *System:* Commonwealth of Massachusetts Higher Education Coordinating Council *Accred.:* 1957/1992 (NEASC-CIHE) *Calendar:* Sem. plan *Degrees:* B, M *Prof. Accred.:* Nuclear Medicine Technology, Nursing (B), Occupational Therapy, Radiation Therapy Technology, Speech-Language Pathology *CEO:* Pres. Kalyan K. Ghosh
Enroll: 3,750   (508) 793-8000

MICHIGAN

ADRIAN COLLEGE
110 S. Madison St., Adrian 49221 *Type:* Private (United Methodist) liberal arts *Accred.:* 1916/1989 (NCA) *Calendar:* Sem. plan *Degrees:* A, B *CEO:* Pres. Stanley P. Caine
Enroll: 1,059   (800) 877-2246

ALBION COLLEGE
611 E. Porter St., Albion 49224 *Type:* Private (United Methodist) liberal arts *Accred.:* 1915/1991 (NCA) *Calendar:* Sem. plan *Degrees:* B *Prof. Accred.:* Music *CEO:* Pres. Melvin L. Vulgamore
Enroll: 1,668   (517) 629-1000

ALMA COLLEGE
Alma 48801 *Type:* Private (United Presbyterian) liberal arts *Accred.:* 1916/1990 (NCA) *Calendar:* 4-4-x plan *Degrees:* B *Prof. Accred.:* Music *CEO:* Pres. Alan J. Stone
Enroll: 1,404   (517) 463-7111

ALPENA COMMUNITY COLLEGE
666 Johnson St., Alpena 49707 *Type:* Public (district) junior *System:* Michigan Department of Education *Accred.:* 1963/1988 (NCA) *Calendar:* Sem. plan *Degrees:* A, C *CEO:* Pres. Donald L. Newport
Enroll: 1,942   (517) 356-9021

ANDREWS UNIVERSITY
Berrien Springs 49104 *Type:* Private (Seventh-Day Adventist) liberal arts and professional *Accred.:* 1970/1989 (ATS); 1922/1994 (NCA) *Calendar:* Qtr. plan *Degrees:* A, B, M, P, D *Prof. Accred.:* Clinical Lab Scientist, Counseling, Music, Nursing (B,M), Physical Therapy, Social Work (B), Teacher Education *CEO:* Pres. Niels-Erik A. Andreasen
Enroll: 5,548   (616) 471-7771

AQUINAS COLLEGE
1607 Robinson Rd., S.E., Grand Rapids 49506 *Type:* Private (Roman Catholic) liberal arts *Accred.:* 1946/1987 (NCA) *Calendar:* Sem. plan *Degrees:* A, B, M *CEO:* Pres. R. Paul Nelson
Enroll: 2,443   (800) 678-9593

BAKER COLLEGE CENTER FOR GRADUATE STUDIES
1050 W. Bristol Rd., Flint 48507-5508 *Type:* Private *System:* Baker College System *Accred.:* 1985/1990 (NCA) *Calendar:* Qtr. plan *Degrees:* M *CEO:* Dir. Steven L. Williams
Enroll: 10,185   (810) 766-4390

BAKER COLLEGE CORPORATE SERVICES
1050 W. Bristol Rd., Flint 48507-5508 *Type:* Private *System:* Baker College System *Accred.:* 1985/1990 (NCA) *Calendar:* Qtr. plan *Degrees:* A, B *CEO:* Co-Dir. Pamela L. Baker *CEO:* Co-Dir. James Kullman
      (810) 766-4242

BAKER COLLEGE OF AUBURN HILLS
1500 University Dr., Auburn Hills 48326-2642 *Type:* Private *System:* Baker College System *Accred.:* 1985/1990 (NCA) *Calendar:* Qtr. plan *Degrees:* A, B *CEO:* Campus Dir./Dean Sandra Kay Krug
      (810) 340-0600

BAKER COLLEGE OF CADILLAC
9600 E. 13th St., Cadillac 49601-9600 *Type:* Private *System:* Baker College System *Accred.:* 1985/1990 (NCA) *Calendar:* Qtr. plan *Degrees:* A, B *CEO:* Campus Dir./Dean Maynard W. Thompson
      (616) 775-8458

BAKER COLLEGE OF FLINT
1050 W. Bristol Rd., Flint 48507-5508 *Type:* Private *System:* Baker College System *Accred.:* 1985/1990 (NCA) *Calendar:* Qtr. plan *Degrees:* A, B *Prof. Accred.:* Medical Assisting (AMA), Medical Record Technology, Physical Therapy Assisting *CEO:* Pres. Julianne T. Princinsky
Enroll: 10,185   (810) 767-7600

BAKER COLLEGE OF JACKSON
2800 Springport Rd., Jackson 49202-1299 *Type:* Private *System:* Baker College System

Accred.: 1985/1990 (NCA) *Calendar:* Qtr. plan *Degrees:* A, B *CEO:* Pres. Jack D. Bunce

(517) 789-6123

BAKER COLLEGE OF MOUNT CLEMENS
34950 Little Mack Ave., Clinton Township 48035-6611 *Type:* Private *System:* Baker College System *Accred.:* 1985/1990 (NCA) *Calendar:* Qtr. plan *Degrees:* A, B *CEO:* Campus Dir./Dean Rodolfo Morales, Jr.

(810) 791-6610

BAKER COLLEGE OF MUSKEGON
123 E. Apple Ave., Muskegon 49442-3497 *Type:* Private *System:* Baker College System *Accred.:* 1985/1990 (NCA) *Calendar:* Qtr. plan *Degrees:* A, B *Prof. Accred.:* Medical Assisting (AMA), Medical Record Technology, Occupational Therapy Assisting, Physical Therapy Assisting, Surgical Technology *CEO:* Pres. Rick E. Amidon

(616) 726-4904

BAKER COLLEGE OF OWOSSO
1020 S. Washington St., Owosso 48867-4400 *Type:* Private *System:* Baker College System *Accred.:* 1985/1990 (NCA) *Calendar:* Qtr. plan *Degrees:* A, B *Prof. Accred.:* Medical Assisting (AMA) *CEO:* Pres. Denise A. Bannan

(517) 723-5251

BAKER COLLEGE OF PORT HURON
3403 Lapeer Rd., Port Huron 48060-2597 *Type:* Private *System:* Baker College System *Accred.:* 1985/1990 (NCA) *Calendar:* Qtr. plan *Degrees:* A, B *CEO:* Campus Dir./Dean Donald R. Torline

(810) 985-7000

BAY DE NOC COMMUNITY COLLEGE
2001 N. Lincoln Rd., Escanaba 49829 *Type:* Public (district) junior *System:* Michigan Department of Education *Accred.:* 1976/1991 (NCA) *Calendar:* Sem. plan *Degrees:* A, C *CEO:* Pres. Dwight E. Link
Enroll: 2,248   (800) 221-2001

BAY MILLS COMMUNITY COLLEGE
Rte. 1, Box 315A, Brimley 49715 *Type:* Public (district) junior *Accred.:* 1995 (NCA)

Calendar: Sem. plan *Degrees:* A, C *CEO:* Pres. Martha McLeod
Enroll: 495   (906) 248-3354

CALVIN COLLEGE
3201 Burton St., S.E., Grand Rapids 49546 *Type:* Private (Christian Reformed) liberal arts *Accred.:* 1930/1995 (NCA) *Calendar:* 4-1-4 plan *Degrees:* B, M *Prof. Accred.:* Engineering (general), Music (associate), Social Work (B), Teacher Education *CEO:* Pres. Gaylen J. Byker
Enroll: 3,783   (800) 688-0122

CALVIN THEOLOGICAL SEMINARY
3233 Burton St., S.E., Grand Rapids 49546 *Type:* Private (Christian Reformed) graduate only *Accred.:* 1944/1988 (ATS) *Calendar:* Qtr. plan *Degrees:* M, D *CEO:* Pres. James A. De Jong
Enroll: 242   (616) 957-6036

THE CENTER FOR CREATIVE STUDIES—COLLEGE OF ART AND DESIGN
245 E. Kirby St., Detroit 48202-4013 *Type:* Private professional *Accred.:* 1982/1993 (NCA) *Calendar:* Sem. plan *Degrees:* B *Prof. Accred.:* Art *CEO:* Pres. Richard Rogers
Enroll: 851   (313) 872-3118

CENTER FOR HUMANISTIC STUDIES
40 E. Ferry Ave., Detroit 48202-3802 *Type:* Private professional; graduate only *Accred.:* 1984/1989 (NCA) *Calendar:* Qtr. plan *Degrees:* M, P *CEO:* Pres. Clark Moustakas
Enroll: 68   (313) 875-7440

CENTRAL MICHIGAN UNIVERSITY
Warriner 165, Mount Pleasant 48859 *Type:* Public (state) *System:* Michigan Department of Education *Accred.:* 1915/1986 (NCA) *Calendar:* Sem. plan *Degrees:* B, M, P, D, C *Prof. Accred.:* Accounting (A), Athletic Training, Audiology, Business (B,M), Clinical Psychology (provisional), Dietetics (internship), Music, Physical Therapy, Recreation and Leisure Services (B), Speech-Language Pathology, Teacher Education *CEO:* Pres. Leonard E. Plachta
Enroll: 24,500   (517) 774-4000

CHARLES STEWART MOTT COMMUNITY
COLLEGE
1401 E. Court St., Flint 48502-2394 *Type:*
Public (district) junior *System:* Michigan
Department of Education *Accred.:* 1926/
1990 (NCA) *Calendar:* Sem. plan *Degrees:*
A, C *Prof. Accred.:* Dental Assisting, Dental
Hygiene, Nursing (A), Occupational
Therapy Assisting, Respiratory Therapy
CEO: Pres. Allen D. Arnold
Enroll: 10,434 (810) 762-0200

CLEARY COLLEGE
2170 Washtenaw Ave., Ypsilanti 48197
Type: Private *Accred.:* 1988/1991 (NCA)
Calendar: Qtr. plan *Degrees:* A, B, C *CEO:*
Pres. Thomas P. Sullivan
Enroll: 807 (800) 686-1883

LIVINGSTONE CAMPUS
3750 Cleary Dr., Howell
(517) 548-1979

CONCORDIA COLLEGE
4090 Geddes Rd., Ann Arbor 48105 *Type:*
Private (Lutheran-Missouri Synod) liberal
arts *Accred.:* 1968/1991 (NCA) *Calendar:*
Sem. plan *Degrees:* A, B *CEO:* Pres. James
M. Koerschen
Enroll: 588 (313) 995-7300

CORNERSTONE COLLEGE AND GRAND RAPIDS
BAPTIST SEMINARY
1001 E. Beltline Ave., N.E., Grand Rapids
49505 *Type:* Private (Baptist) liberal arts and
professional *Accred.:* 1977/1992 (NCA)
Calendar: Sem. plan *Degrees:* A, B, M, D, C
CEO: Pres. Rex M. Rogers
Enroll: 933 (616) 949-5300

CRANBROOK ACADEMY OF ART
1221 Woodward Ave., Box 801, Bloomfield
Hills 48303-0801 *Type:* Private professional;
graduate only *Accred.:* 1960/1989 (NCA)
Calendar: Sem. plan *Degrees:* M *Prof.
Accred.:* Art *CEO:* Acting Dir. Gerhart
Knodel
Enroll: 142 (810) 645-3300

DAVENPORT COLLEGE OF BUSINESS
415 E. Fulton St., Grand Rapids 49503 *Type:*
Private *Accred.:* 1976/1988 (NCA) *Calendar:*

Qtr. plan *Degrees:* A, B, C *Prof. Accred.:*
Medical Assisting (AMA) *CEO:* Pres.
Donald W. Maine
Enroll: 9,306 (800) 632-9569

GRANGER CAMPUS
7121 Grape Rd., Granger, IN 46530 *Prof.
Accred.:* Medical Assisting
(219) 277-8447

MERRIVILLE CAMPUS
8200 Georgia St., Merrillville, IN 46410
Prof. Accred.: Medical Assisting
(219) 769-5556

HOMMAND CAMPUS
643 Waverly Rd., Holland 49423
(616) 395-4600

KALAMAZOO CAMPUS
4123 N. Main St., Kalamazoo 49006 *Prof.
Accred.:* Medical Assisting, Medical
Record Technology
(616) 382-2835

LANSING CAMPUS
220 E. Kalamazoo St., Lansing 48933
(517) 484-2600

DELTA COLLEGE
Delta and Mackinow Rds., University
Center 48710 *Type:* Public (district) junior
System: Michigan Department of Education
Accred.: 1968/1984 (NCA) *Calendar:* Sem.
plan *Degrees:* A, C *Prof. Accred.:* Dental
Assisting, Dental Hygiene, Engineering
Technology (electrical, mechanical),
Nursing (A), Physical Therapy Assisting,
Radiography, Respiratory Therapy, Surgical
Technology *CEO:* Pres. Peter D. Boyse
Enroll: 13,024 (517) 686-9000

DETROIT COLLEGE OF BUSINESS
4801 Oakman Blvd., Dearborn 48126 *Type:*
Private business *Accred.:* 1986/1990 (NCA)
Calendar: Qtr. plan *Degrees:* A, B, C *CEO:*
Sr. Vice Pres. James Mendola
Enroll: 5,598 (313) 581-4400

FLINT CAMPUS
3115 Lawndale Ave., Flint 48504-2699
(810) 239-1443

WARREN CAMPUS
27500 Dequindre Rd., Warren 48092-5209
(810) 558-8700

DETROIT COLLEGE OF LAW
130 E. Elizabeth St., Detroit 48201 *Type:* Private professional *Calendar:* Sem. plan *Degrees:* P *Prof. Accred.:* Law *CEO:* Dean Arthur J. Lombard
Enroll: 791   (313) 226-0100

EASTERN MICHIGAN UNIVERSITY
202 Welch Hall, Ypsilanti 48197 *Type:* Public (state) *System:* Michigan Department of Education *Accred.:* 1915/1991 (NCA) *Calendar:* Sem. plan *Degrees:* B, M, P, D, C *Prof. Accred.:* Business (B,M), Clinical Lab Scientist, Construction Education (B), Counseling, Dietetics (coordinated), Interior Design, Music, Nursing (B), Occupational Therapy, Public Administration, Recreation and Leisure Services (B), Social Work (B,M-candidate), Speech-Language Pathology, Teacher Education *CEO:* Pres. William E. Shelton
Enroll: 23,321   (313) 487-1849

FERRIS STATE UNIVERSITY
Big Rapids 49307 *Type:* Public (state) professional and technical *System:* Michigan Department of Education *Accred.:* 1959/1995 (NCA) *Calendar:* Qtr. plan *Degrees:* A, B, M, D, C *Prof. Accred.:* Clinical Lab Scientist, Clinical Lab Technology (A), Construction Education (B), Dental Hygiene, Dental Laboratory Technology, Engineering (surveying), Medical Record Administration, Medical Record Technology, Nuclear Medicine Technology, Nursing (B), Optometric Technician, Optometry, Radiography, Respiratory Therapy, Social Work (B) *CEO:* Pres. William A. Sederburg
Enroll: 10,258   (616) 592-2100

NORTHERN MICHIGAN REGIONAL CENTER CAMPUS
1701 Front St., Traverse City 49684-3061
(616) 922-1734

SOUTHEAST MICHIGAN REGIONAL CENTER CAMPUS
1401 E. Court St., Flint 48503-2018
(810) 762-0461

SOUTHWEST MICHIGAN REGIONAL CENTER CAMPUS
Applied Technology Ctr., 151 Fountain N.E., Grand Rapids 49503-3263
(616) 771-3770

GLEN OAKS COMMUNITY COLLEGE
62249 Shimmel Rd., Centreville 49032 *Type:* Public (district) junior *System:* Michigan Department of Education *Accred.:* 1975/1993 (NCA) *Calendar:* Sem. plan *Degrees:* A, C *CEO:* Pres. Philip G. Ward
Enroll: 1,212   (616) 467-9945

GMI ENGINEERING AND MANAGEMENT INSTITUTE
1700 W. Third Ave., Flint 48504-4898 *Type:* Private technological *Accred.:* 1962/1987 (NCA) *Calendar:* Sem. plan *Degrees:* B, M *Prof. Accred.:* Engineering (electrical, industrial, manufacturing, mechanical) *CEO:* Pres. James E. A. John
Enroll: 3,271   (810) 762-9864

GOGEBIC COMMUNITY COLLEGE
E-4946 Jackson Rd., Ironwood 49938 *Type:* Public (district) junior *System:* Michigan Department of Education *Accred.:* 1949/1992 (NCA) *Calendar:* Sem. plan *Degrees:* A, C *Prof. Accred.:* Medical Record Technology *CEO:* Pres. Donald J. Foster
Enroll: 1,276   (906) 932-4231

GRACE BIBLE COLLEGE
1011 Aldon St., S.W., P.O. Box 910, Wyoming 49509-9990 *Type:* Private (Grace Gospel Fellowship) *Accred.:* 1964/1995 (AABC); 1990 (NCA) *Calendar:* Sem. plan *Degrees:* A, B, C *CEO:* Pres. E. Bruce Kemper
Enroll: 153   (616) 538-2330

GRAND RAPIDS COMMUNITY COLLEGE
143 Bostwick St., N.E., Grand Rapids 49503 *Type:* Public (district) junior *System:* Michigan Department of Education *Accred.:* 1917/1991 (NCA) *Calendar:* Sem. plan

Accredited Degree Granting Institutions

Degrees: A, C *Prof. Accred.:* Dental Assisting, Dental Hygiene, Music, Nursing (A), Occupational Therapy Assisting, Practical Nursing, Radiography *CEO:* Pres. Richard W. Calkins
Enroll: 13,726   (616) 771-4000

GRAND VALLEY STATE UNIVERSITY
One Campus Dr., Allendale 49401 *Type:* Public (state) liberal arts *System:* Michigan Department of Education *Accred.:* 1968/ 1989 (NCA) *Calendar:* Sem. plan *Degrees:* B, M *Prof. Accred.:* Art, Athletic Training, Engineering (general), Music, Nursing (B,M), Physical Therapy, Psychology Internship (provisional), Public Administration, Social Work (B,M), Teacher Education *CEO:* Pres. Arend D. Lubbers
Enroll: 13,553   (616) 895-6611

GREAT LAKES CHRISTIAN COLLEGE
6211 W. Willow Hwy., Lansing 48917 *Type:* Private (Christian Churches/Churches of Christ) *Accred.:* 1977/1987 (AABC) *Calendar:* Sem. plan *Degrees:* A, B, C *CEO:* Pres. Jerry Paul
FTE Enroll: 204   (517) 321-0242

GREAT LAKES JUNIOR COLLEGE
310 S. Washington Ave., Saginaw 48607 *Type:* Private junior *Accred.:* 1993 (NCA) *Calendar:* Qtr. plan *Degrees:* A, C *CEO:* Pres. William Guerriero
Enroll: 1,769   (517) 755-3455

HENRY FORD COMMUNITY COLLEGE
5101 Evergreen Rd., Dearborn 48128 *Type:* Public (district) junior *System:* Michigan Department of Education *Accred.:* 1949/ 1995 (NCA) *Calendar:* Sem. plan *Degrees:* A, C *Prof. Accred.:* Medical Assisting (AMA), Medical Record Technology, Nursing (A), Physical Therapy Assisting, Respiratory Therapy *CEO:* Pres. Andrew A. Mazzara
Enroll: 14,174   (313) 271-2750

HIGHLAND PARK COMMUNITY COLLEGE
Glendale Ave. at Third St., Highland Park 48203 *Type:* Public (district) junior *System:* Michigan Department of Education *Accred.:* 1921/1987 (NCA) *Calendar:* Sem. plan

Degrees: A, C *Prof. Accred.:* ◌ Technology (A), Surgical Technol◌ Pres. Thomas Lloyd
Enroll: 1,822   (313) 25◌

HILLSDALE COLLEGE
33 E. College Ave., Hillsdale 49242 *Type* Private liberal arts *Accred.:* 1915/1988 (NCA) *Calendar:* Sem. plan *Degrees:* B, C *CEO:* Pres. George Charles Roche, III
Enroll: 1,144   (517) 437-7341

HOPE COLLEGE
141 E. 12th St., P.O. Box 9000, Holland 49422-9000 *Type:* Private (Reformed Church in America) liberal arts *Accred.:* 1915/1994 (NCA) *Calendar:* Sem. plan *Degrees:* B *Prof. Accred.:* Art, Dance, Music, Nursing (B), Social Work (B-candidate), Teacher Education, Theatre (A) *CEO:* Pres. John H. Jacobson
Enroll: 2,825   (616) 395-7000

JACKSON COMMUNITY COLLEGE
2111 Emmons Rd., Jackson 49201 *Type:* Public (district) junior *System:* Michigan Department of Education *Accred.:* 1933/ 1986 (NCA) *Calendar:* Sem. plan *Degrees:* A, C *Prof. Accred.:* Diagnostic Medical Sonography, Medical Assisting (AMA), Radiography *CEO:* Pres. E. Lee Howser
Enroll: 7,521   (517) 787-0800

KALAMAZOO COLLEGE
1200 Academy St., Kalamazoo 49006-3295 *Type:* Private (Baptist) liberal arts *Accred.:* 1915/1993 (NCA) *Calendar:* Qtr. plan *Degrees:* B *CEO:* Pres. Lawrence D. Bryan
Enroll: 1,241   (616) 337-7000

KALAMAZOO VALLEY COMMUNITY COLLEGE
P.O. Box 4070, Kalamazoo 49003-4070 *Type:* Public (district) junior *System:* Michigan Department of Education *Accred.:* 1972/1986 (NCA) *Calendar:* Sem. plan *Degrees:* A, C *Prof. Accred.:* Dental Hygiene, Medical Assisting (AMA), Respiratory Therapy *CEO:* Pres. Marilyn J. Schlack
Enroll: 9,202   (616) 372-5000

Michigan

...E 49017-3397
...ior *System:*
...ion *Accred.:*
...ar:* Sem. plan
...ccred.:* Clinical Lab
Dental Hygiene, Physical
...isting, Radiography *CEO:* Pres.
... Ohm
Enroll: 5,175   (616) 965-3931

KENDALL COLLEGE OF ART AND DESIGN
111 Division Ave. N., Grand Rapids 49503
Type: Private *Accred.:* 1981/1993 (NCA)
Calendar: Sem. plan *Degrees:* B *Prof.*
Accred.: Art, Interior Design *CEO:* Acting
Pres. Oliver H. Evans
Enroll: 574   (800) 676-2787

KIRTLAND COMMUNITY COLLEGE
10775 N. St. Helen Rd., Roscommon 48653
Type: Public (district) junior *System:*
Michigan Department of Education *Accred.:*
1976/1989 (NCA) *Calendar:* Sem. plan
Degrees: A, C *CEO:* Pres. Dorothy N.
Franke
Enroll: 1,350   (517) 275-5121

LAKE MICHIGAN COLLEGE
2755 E. Napier St., Benton Harbor 49022
Type: Public (district) junior *System:*
Michigan Department of Education *Accred.:*
1962/1989 (NCA) *Calendar:* Sem. plan
Degrees: A, C *Prof. Accred.:* Dental
Assisting, Nursing (A), Occupational
Therapy Assisting, Radiography *CEO:* Pres.
Richard J. Pappas
Enroll: 3,402   (616) 927-3571

LAKE SUPERIOR STATE UNIVERSITY
1000 College Dr., Sault Ste. Marie 49783
Type: Public (state) liberal arts *System:*
Michigan Department of Education *Accred.:*
1968/1991 (NCA) *Calendar:* Qtr. plan
Degrees: A, B, M, C *Prof. Accred.:*
Engineering Technology (automated sys-
tems, computer, electrical, industrial,
mechanical, mechanical drafting/design),
Nursing (B) *CEO:* Pres. Robert D. Arbuckle
Enroll: 3,314   (906) 632-6841

LANSING COMMUNITY COLLEGE
521 N. Washington Sq., Box 40010, Lansing
48901-7210 *Type:* Public (district) junior
System: Michigan Department of Education
Accred.: 1964/1994 (NCA) *Calendar:* Qtr.
plan *Degrees:* A, C *Prof. Accred.:* Dental
Assisting, Dental Hygiene, EMT-Paramedic,
Nursing (A), Radiation Therapy Technology,
Radiography, Respiratory Therapy, Respi-
ratory Therapy Technology *CEO:* Pres. Abel
B. Sykes, Jr.
Enroll: 16,816   (517) 483-1851

LAWRENCE TECHNOLOGICAL UNIVERSITY
21000 W. Ten Mile Rd., Ste. M351,
Southfield 48075 *Type:* Private professional
and technological *Accred.:* 1967/1991
(NCA) *Calendar:* Qtr. plan *Degrees:* A, B,
M *Prof. Accred.:* Engineering Technology
(civil/construction, electrical, industrial,
mechanical), Engineering (civil, construction, electrical), mechanical) *CEO:* Pres.
Charles M. Chambers
Enroll: 4,159   (810) 204-4000

LEWIS COLLEGE OF BUSINESS
17370 Meyers Rd., Detroit 48235 *Type:*
Private business *Accred.:* 1978/1995 (NCA)
Calendar: Tri. plan *Degrees:* A, C *CEO:*
Pres. Marjorie L. Harris
Enroll: 272   (313) 862-6300

MACOMB COMMUNITY COLLEGE
14500 E. Twelve Mile Rd., Warren 48093-
3896 *Type:* Public (district) junior *System:*
Michigan Department of Education *Accred.:*
1970/1987 (NCA) *Calendar:* Sem. plan
Degrees: A, C *Prof. Accred.:* Medical
Assisting (AMA), Nursing (A), Physical
Therapy Assisting, Respiratory Therapy,
Veterinary Technology *CEO:* Pres. Albert L.
Lorenzo
Enroll: 25,185   (810) 445-7999

MADONNA UNIVERSITY
36600 Schoolcraft Rd., Livonia 48150 *Type:*
Private (Roman Catholic) liberal arts
Accred.: 1959/1988 (NCA) *Calendar:* Sem.
plan *Degrees:* A, B, M, C *Prof. Accred.:*
Nursing (B,M), Social Work (B), Teacher

Education *CEO:* Pres. Mary Francilene, C.S.S.F.
Enroll: 4,155   (800) 852-4951

MARYGROVE COLLEGE
8425 W. McNichols Rd., Detroit 48221
Type: Private (Roman Catholic) liberal arts
Accred.: 1926/1987 (NCA) *Calendar:* Sem.
plan *Degrees:* A, B, M, C *Prof. Accred.:*
Radiography, Respiratory Therapy, Social
Work (B), Teacher Education *CEO:* Pres.
John E. Shay, Jr.
Enroll: 1,090   (313) 864-8000

MICHIGAN CHRISTIAN COLLEGE
800 W. Avon Rd., Rochester Hills 48307
Type: Private (Church of Christ) *Accred.:*
1974/1989 (NCA) *Calendar:* Sem. plan
Degrees: A, B, C *CEO:* Pres. Kenneth L.
Johnson
Enroll: 411   (800) 521-6010

MICHIGAN STATE UNIVERSITY
450 Administration Bldg., East Lansing
48824 *Type:* Public (state) *System:* Michigan
Department of Education *Accred.:* 1915/
1986 (NCA) *Calendar:* Qtr. plan *Degrees:*
B, M, P, D *Prof. Accred.:* Accounting (Type
A,B), Audiology, Business (B,M), Clinical
Lab Scientist, Clinical Psychology,
Counseling Psychology, Engineering (agri-
cultural, chemical, civil, electrical, materials,
mechanical), Forestry, Interior Design,
Journalism (B,M), Landscape Architecture
(B), Medicine, Music, Nursing (B,M),
Osteopathy, Planning (B,M), Psychology
Internship, Public Administration,
Recreation and Leisure Services (B,Oct.88
to Oct.98), Rehabilitation Counseling,
School Psychology, Social Work (B,M),
Speech-Language Pathology, Theatre,
Veterinary Medicine, Veterinary Technology
CEO: Pres. M. Peter McPherson
Enroll: 40,254   (517) 355-1855

MICHIGAN TECHNOLOGICAL UNIVERSITY
1400 Townsend Dr., Houghton 49931 *Type:*
Public (state) *System:* Michigan Department
of Education *Accred.:* 1928/1988 (NCA)
Calendar: Qtr. plan *Degrees:* A, B, M, D, C
Prof. Accred.: Engineering Technology

(civil/construction, electrical, electromechanical), Engineering (chemical, civil,
electrical, environmental/sanitary, general,
geological/geophysical, materials, mechanical) mining) *CEO:* Pres. Curtis J. Tompkins
Enroll: 6,460   (906) 487-1885

MID MICHIGAN COMMUNITY COLLEGE
1375 S. Clare Ave., Harrison 48625 *Type:*
Public (district) junior *System:* Michigan
Department of Education *Accred.:* 1974/
1992 (NCA) *Calendar:* Sem. plan *Degrees:*
A, C *Prof. Accred.:* Radiography *CEO:* Pres.
Charles J. Corrigan, Ph.D.
Enroll: 2,240   (517) 386-6622

MONROE COUNTY COMMUNITY COLLEGE
1555 S. Raisinville Rd., Monroe 48161
Type: Public (district) junior *System:*
Michigan Department of Education *Accred.:*
1972/1990 (NCA) *Calendar:* Sem. plan
Degrees: A, C *Prof. Accred.:* Nursing (A),
Respiratory Therapy, Respiratory Therapy
Technology *CEO:* Pres. Gerald D. Welch
Enroll: 3,923   (313) 242-7300

MONTCALM COMMUNITY COLLEGE
2800 College Dr., S.W., P.O. Box 300,
Sidney 48885-0300 *Type:* Public (district)
junior *System:* Michigan Department of
Education *Accred.:* 1974/1986 (NCA)
Calendar: Sem. plan *Degrees:* A, C *CEO:*
Pres. Donald C. Burns
Enroll: 2,211   (517) 328-2111

MUSKEGON COMMUNITY COLLEGE
221 S. Quarterline Rd., Muskegon 49442
Type: Public (district) junior *System:*
Michigan Department of Education *Accred.:*
1929/1991 (NCA) *Calendar:* Sem. plan
Degrees: A, C *Prof. Accred.:* Respiratory
Therapy, Respiratory Therapy Technology
CEO: Pres. Frank Marczak
Enroll: 4,649   (616) 777-0311

NORTH CENTRAL MICHIGAN COLLEGE
1515 Howard St., Petoskey 49770 *Type:*
Public (district) junior *System:* Michigan
Department of Education *Accred.:*
1972/1995 (NCA) *Calendar:* Sem. plan
Degrees: A, C *CEO:* Pres. Robert B. Graham
Enroll: 2,086   (616) 348-6600

NORTHERN MICHIGAN UNIVERSITY
1401 Presque Isle Ave., Marquette 49855
Type: Public (state) *System:* Michigan
Department of Education *Accred.:* 1916/
1995 (NCA) *Calendar:* Sem. plan *Degrees:*
A, B, M, P, C *Prof. Accred.:* Clinical Lab
Scientist, Clinical Lab Technology (A),
Music, Nursing (B,M), Social Work (B),
Speech-Language Pathology, Teacher
Education *CEO:* Pres. William E.
Vandament
Enroll: 7,898   (906) 227-1000

NORTHWESTERN MICHIGAN COLLEGE
1701 E. Front St., Traverse City 49686-3061
Type: Public (district) junior *System:*
Michigan Department of Education *Accred.:*
1961/1990 (NCA) *Calendar:* Qtr. plan
Degrees: A, C *Prof. Accred.:* Dental
Assisting *CEO:* Pres. Timothy G. Quinn
Enroll: 3,928   (616) 922-1010

NORTHWOOD UNIVERSITY
3225 Cook Rd., Midland 48640 *Type:*
Private business *Accred.:* 1974/1986 (NCA)
Calendar: Qtr. plan *Degrees:* A, B, M, C
CEO: Pres. David E. Fry
Enroll: 8,544   (517) 837-4200

OAKLAND COMMUNITY COLLEGE
2480 Opdyke Rd., Bloomfield Hills 48304-
2266 *Type:* Public (district) junior *System:*
Michigan Department of Education *Accred.:*
1971/1988 (NCA) *Calendar:* Tri. plan
Degrees: A, C *Prof. Accred.:* Diagnostic
Medical Sonography, Radiography, Respi-
ratory Therapy *CEO:* Interim Chanc.
Anthony D. Jarson
Enroll: 27,129   (810) 540-1500

AUBURN HILLS CAMPUS
2900 Featherstone Rd., Auburn Hills
48326
                                   (313) 360-3032

HIGHLAND LAKES CAMPUS
7350 Cooley Lake Rd., Waterford 48327-
4187 *Prof. Accred.:* Dental Hygiene,
Medical Assisting (AMA), Nursing (A)
                                   (313) 540-1500

ORCHARD RIDGE CAMPUS
27055 Orchard Lake Rd., Farmington
Hills 48334
                                   (313) 471-7500

ROYAL OAK CAMPUS
739 S. Washington, Royal Oak 48067-
3898
                                   (810) 54-5542

SOUTHFIELD CAMPUS
22322 Rutland Dr., Southfield 48075
                                   (313) 552-2600

OAKLAND UNIVERSITY
Rochester 48309 *Type:* Public (state) liberal
arts and professional *System:* Michigan
Department of Education *Accred.:* 1959/
1989 (NCA) *Calendar:* Tri. plan *Degrees:* B,
M, P, D *Prof. Accred.:* Accounting (A),
Business (B,M), Computer Science,
Counseling, Engineering (computer, electri-
cal, mechanical, systems), Nurse Anesthesia
Education, Nursing (B,M), Physical
Therapy, Public Administration, Teacher
Education *CEO:* Interim Pres. Gary D. Russi
Enroll: 13,165   (810) 370-2100

OLIVET COLLEGE
Dole Hall, Olivet 49076 *Type:* Private
(United Church of Christ) liberal arts
Accred.: 1913/1995 (NCA) *Calendar:* Sem.
plan *Degrees:* B *CEO:* Pres. Michael S.
Bassis
Enroll: 791   (616) 749-7000

REFORMED BIBLE COLLEGE
3333 E. Beltline Ave., N.E., Grand Rapids
49505 *Type:* Private (Reformed) *Accred.:*
1964/1995 (AABC); 1995 (NCA) *Calendar:*
Sem. plan *Degrees:* A, B, C *CEO:* Pres.
Nicholas V. Kroeze
Enroll: 181   (616) 363-2050

SACRED HEART MAJOR SEMINARY
2701 Chicago Blvd., Detroit 48206 *Type:*
Private (Roman Catholic) *Accred.:* 1991
(ATS); 1960/1994 (NCA) *Calendar:* Tri.

plan *Degrees:* A, B, M *CEO:* Pres. Allen H. Vigneron
Enroll: 213   (313) 883-8500

SAGINAW VALLEY STATE UNIVERSITY
7400 Bay Rd., University Center 48710 *Type:* Public (state) liberal arts *System:* Michigan Department of Education *Accred.:* 1970/1994 (NCA) *Calendar:* Tri. plan *Degrees:* B, M *Prof. Accred.:* Engineering (electrical, mechanical), Nursing (B,M), Occupational Therapy, Social Work (B), Teacher Education *CEO:* Pres. Eric R. Gilbertson
Enroll: 7,066   (517) 790-4000

ST. CLAIR COUNTY COMMUNITY COLLEGE
323 Erie St., P.O. Box 5015, Port Huron 48061-5015 *Type:* Public (district) junior *System:* Michigan Department of Education *Accred.:* 1930/1987 (NCA) *Calendar:* Sem. plan *Degrees:* A, C *CEO:* Pres. R. Ernest Dear
Enroll: 4,593   (810) 984-3881

ST. MARY'S COLLEGE
3535 Indian Tr., Orchard Lake 48324 *Type:* Private (Roman Catholic) liberal arts *Accred.:* 1976/1993 (NCA) *Calendar:* Sem. plan *Degrees:* B, C *CEO:* Pres. Edward D. Meyer
Enroll: 288   (810) 683-0504

SCHOOLCRAFT COLLEGE
18600 Haggerty Rd., Livonia 48152-2696 *Type:* Public (district) junior *System:* Michigan Department of Education *Accred.:* 1968/1991 (NCA) *Calendar:* Sem. plan *Degrees:* A, C *Prof. Accred.:* Medical Record Technology, Occupational Therapy Assisting *CEO:* Pres. Richard W. McDowell
Enroll: 9,498   (313) 462-4400

SIENA HEIGHTS COLLEGE
1247 E. Siena Heights Dr., Adrian 49221 *Type:* Private (Roman Catholic) liberal arts *Accred.:* 1940/1992 (NCA) *Calendar:* Sem. plan *Degrees:* A, B, M, C *Prof. Accred.:* Art *CEO:* Pres. Richard B. Artman
Enroll: 1,846   (517) 263-0731

SOUTHWESTERN MICHIGAN COLLEGE
58900 Cherry Grove Rd., Dowagiac 49047-9793 *Type:* Public (state) junior *System:* Michigan Department of Education *Accred.:* 1971/1991 (NCA) *Calendar:* 4-1-4 plan *Degrees:* A, C *CEO:* Pres. David C. Briegel
Enroll: 2,665   (616) 782-5113

SPRING ARBOR COLLEGE
Spring Arbor 49283 *Type:* Private (Free Methodist) liberal arts *Accred.:* 1960/1987 (NCA) *Calendar:* Sem. plan *Degrees:* A, B, M *Prof. Accred.:* Social Work (B-candidate), Teacher Education *CEO:* Pres. Allen Carden
Enroll: 1,972   (517) 750-1200

SUOMI COLLEGE
601 Quincy St., Hancock 49930-1882 *Type:* Private (Lutheran) junior *Accred.:* 1969/1989 (NCA) *Calendar:* Sem. plan *Degrees:* A, C *CEO:* Pres. Robert A. Ubbelohde
Enroll: 405   (800) 682-7604

THOMAS M. COOLEY LAW SCHOOL
217 S. Capitol Ave., P.O. Box 13038, Lansing 48901-3038 *Type:* Private professional *Calendar:* Sem. plan *Degrees:* P *Prof. Accred.:* Law (ABA only) *CEO:* Pres. Thomas E. Brennan
Enroll: 1,536   (517) 371-5140

UNIVERSITY OF DETROIT MERCY
4001 W. McNichols Rd., P.O. Box 19900, Detroit 48219-0900 *Type:* Private (Roman Catholic) liberal arts *Accred.:* 1931/1993 (NCA) *Calendar:* Sem. plan *Degrees:* A, B, M, P, D, C *Prof. Accred.:* Business (B,M), Clinical Psychology, Dental Hygiene, Dentistry, Endodontics, Engineering (chemical, civil, electrical, mechanical), General Practice Residency, Law, Medical Record Administration, Medical Record Technology, Nurse Anesthesia Education (M), Orthodontics, Physician Assisting/Surgeon Assisting, Social Work (B) *CEO:* Pres. Maureen A. Fay, O.P.
Enroll: 7,461   (313) 993-1000

UNIVERSITY OF MICHIGAN
2068 Administration Bldg., Ann Arbor 48109 *Type:* Public (state) *System:* University of

Michigan System *Accred.:* 1913/1990 (NCA) *Calendar:* Tri. plan *Degrees:* B, M, P, D, C *Prof. Accred.:* Art, Business (B,M), Clinical Psychology, Combined Prosthodontics, Dental Hygiene, Dentistry, Dietetics (internship), Endodontics, Engineering Technology (industrial hygiene), Engineering (aerospace, chemical, civil, computer, electrical, environmental/sanitary, industrial, materials, mechanical, naval architecture/marine, nuclear), Forestry, General Dentistry, General Practice Residency, Health Services Administration, Landscape Architecture (M), Law, Librarianship, Medical Illustration, Medicine, Music, Nursing (B,M), Oral and Maxillofacial Surgery, Orthodontics, Pediatric Dentistry, Periodontics, Planning (M), Psychology Internship, Radiation Therapy Technology, Social Work (M) *CEO:* Pres. James J. Duderstadt
Enroll: 36,543   (313) 764-1817

UNIVERSITY OF MICHIGAN—DEARBORN
4901 Evergreen Rd., Dearborn 48128-1491 *Type:* Public (state) *System:* University of Michigan System *Accred.:* 1970/1994 (NCA) *Calendar:* Tri. plan *Degrees:* B, M *Prof. Accred.:* Engineering (electrical, industrial, mechanical) *CEO:* Chanc. James C. Renick
Enroll: 8,185   (313) 593-5000

UNIVERSITY OF MICHIGAN—FLINT
Flint 48502-2186 *Type:* Public (state) *System:* University of Michigan System *Accred.:* 1970/1990 (NCA) *Calendar:* Sem. plan *Degrees:* B, M, C *Prof. Accred.:* Business (B,M), Music, Nurse Anesthesia Education (M), Nursing (B), Physical Therapy *CEO:* Chanc. Charlie Nelms
Enroll: 6,236   (810) 762-3000

WALSH COLLEGE OF ACCOUNTANCY AND BUSINESS ADMINISTRATION
3838 Livernois Rd., P.O. Box 7006, Troy 48007-7006 *Type:* Private professional *Accred.:* 1975/1992 (NCA) *Calendar:* Sem. plan *Degrees:* B, M *CEO:* Pres. David A. Spencer
Enroll: 3,915   (313) 689-8282

NOVI CAMPUS
41700 Gardenbrook, Novi 48375-1320
     (810) 349-5454

PORT HURON CAMPUS
Bayview Office Bldg., 805-B 10th Ave., Port Huron 48060
     (810) 984-4444

UNIVERSITY CENTER CAMPUS
Macomb CC, 44575 Garfield Rd., Clinton Township 48038-1139
     (810) 263-6630

WASHTENAW COMMUNITY COLLEGE
4800 E. Huron River Dr., P.O. Box D-1, Ann Arbor 48106-0978 *Type:* Public (district) junior *System:* Michigan Department of Education *Accred.:* 1973/1990 (NCA) *Calendar:* Sem. plan *Degrees:* A, C *Prof. Accred.:* Dental Assisting, Radiography, Respiratory Therapy *CEO:* Pres. Gunder A. Myran
Enroll: 10,455   (313) 973-3300

WAYNE COUNTY COMMUNITY COLLEGE
801 W. Fort St., Detroit 48226-3010 *Type:* Public (district) junior *System:* Michigan Department of Education *Accred.:* 1976/1993 (NCA) *Calendar:* Sem. plan *Degrees:* A, C *Prof. Accred.:* Dental Assisting, Dental Hygiene, Occupational Therapy Assisting, Veterinary Technology *CEO:* Pres. Curtis L. Ivery
Enroll: 9,284   (313) 496-2510

WAYNE STATE UNIVERSITY
4200 Administration Bldg., Detroit 48202 *Type:* Public (state) *System:* Michigan Department of Education *Accred.:* 1915/1987 (NCA) *Calendar:* Sem. plan *Degrees:* B, M, P, D, C *Prof. Accred.:* Audiology, Business (B,M), Clinical Lab Scientist, Clinical Psychology, Counseling, Cytotechnology, Dietetics (coordinated), Engineering (chemical, civil, electrical, industrial, materials, mechanical), Funeral Service Education (Mortuary Science), Law, Librarianship, Medicine, Music, Nurse Anesthesia Education (M), Nursing (B,M), Occupational Therapy, Physical Therapy, Planning, Psychology Internship, Public

Administration, Radiation Therapy Technology, Rehabilitation Counseling, Social Work (B,M), Speech-Language Pathology, Teacher Education, Theatre *CEO:* Pres. David W. Adamany
Enroll: 34,280 (313) 577-2424

WEST SHORE COMMUNITY COLLEGE
3000 N. Stiles Rd., P.O. Box 277, Scottville 49454 *Type:* Public (district) junior *System:* Michigan Department of Education *Accred.:* 1974/1986 (NCA) *Calendar:* Sem. plan *Degrees:* A, C *CEO:* Pres. William M. Anderson
Enroll: 1,487 (616) 845-6211

WESTERN MICHIGAN UNIVERSITY
Kalamazoo 49008 *Type:* Public (state) *System:* Michigan Department of Education *Accred.:* 1915/1991 (NCA) *Calendar:* Tri. plan *Degrees:* B, M, P, D *Prof. Accred.:* Art, Audiology, Business (B,M), Clinical Psychology, Computer Science, Counseling, Counseling Psychology, Dance, Engineering Technology (manufacturing), Engineering (computer, electrical, industrial, mechanical), Music, Occupational Therapy, Physician Assisting/Surgeon Assisting, Social Work (B,M), Speech-Language Pathology, Teacher Education, Theatre *CEO:* Pres. Diether H. Haenicke
Enroll: 25,673 (616) 387-1000

BATTLE CREEK REGIONAL CENTER/KENDALL CENTER CAMPUS
50 W. Jackson Street, Battle Creek 49017
(616) 965-5380

GRAND RAPIDS REGIONAL CENTER CAMPUS
2333 E. Beltline, S.E., Grand Rapids 49546
(616) 771-9470

LANSING REGIONAL CENTER CAMPUS
300 N. Washington Sq., Ste. 200, Lansing 48933
(517) 372-8114

MUSKEGON REGIONAL CENTER CAMPUS
221 S. Quarterline Rd., Muskegon 49442
(616) 777-0500

SOUTHWEST REGIONAL CENTER CAMPUS
2510 Lakeview Ave., St. Joseph 49085
(616) 983-1968

WESTERN THEOLOGICAL SEMINARY
101 E. 13th St., Holland 49423 *Type:* Private (Reformed Church) graduate only *Accred.:* 1940/1993 (ATS) *Calendar:* Sem. plan *Degrees:* M, D *CEO:* Pres. Dennis N. Voskuil
Enroll: 139 (616) 392-8555

WILLIAM TYNDALE COLLEGE
35700 W. Twelve Mile Rd., Farmington Hills 48331 *Type:* Private *Accred.:* 1988/1993 (NCA) *Calendar:* Sem. plan *Degrees:* A, B, C *CEO:* Pres. James Clark McHann, Jr.
Enroll: 565 (810) 553-7200

YESHIVA BETH YEHUDA-YESHIVA GEDOLAH OF GREATER DETROIT
24600 Greenfield St., Oak Park 48237 *Type:* Private professional *Accred.:* 1986/1991 (AARTS) *Calendar:* Sem. plan *Degrees:* B, M, P, D *CEO:* Pres. Saul Weingarden
Enroll: 43 (810) 968-3360

MINNESOTA

ACADEMY EDUCATION CENTER
3050 Metro Dr., Ste. 200, Minneapolis 55425 *Type:* Private business *Accred.:* 1976/1995 (ACICS) *Degrees:* A, C *CEO:* Pres. Nancy Grazzini-Olson
(612) 851-0066

ALEXANDRIA TECHNICAL COLLEGE
1601 Jefferson St., Alexandria 56308 *Type:* Public (state) 2-year *Accred.:* 1980/1994 (NCA) *Calendar:* Qtr. plan *Degrees:* A, C *Prof. Accred.:* Clinical Lab Technology (A), Interior Design *CEO:* Pres. Larry Shellito
Enroll: 1,689   (800) 253-9884

ALFRED ADLER INSTITUTE OF MINNESOTA
1001 Hwy. 7, Ste. 344, Hopkins 55305 *Type:* Private professional; graduate only *Accred.:* 1991/1994 (NCA) *Calendar:* Qtr. plan *Degrees:* M, C *CEO:* Pres. Larry Hedberg
Enroll: 467   (612) 988-4170

ANOKA-HENNEPIN TECHNICAL COLLEGE
1355 W. Hwy. 10, Anoka 55303 *Type:* Private *Degrees:* A, C *Prof. Accred.:* Electroneurodiagnostic Technology, Medical Assisting (AMA), Medical Record Technology, Occupational Therapy Assisting, Physical Therapy Assisting, Practical Nursing, Surgical Technology *CEO:* Interim Pres. Cliff Korkowski
(612) 427-1880

ANOKA-RAMSEY COMMUNITY COLLEGE
11200 Mississippi Blvd. NW, Coon Rapids 55433-3499 *Type:* Public (state) junior *System:* Minnesota State Colleges and Universities *Accred.:* 1975/1987 (NCA) *Calendar:* Qtr. plan *Degrees:* A, C *Prof. Accred.:* Nursing (A) *CEO:* Pres. Patrick M. Johns
Enroll: 5,860   (612) 427-2600

CAMBRIDGE COMMUNITY COLLEGE CENTER
33270 Polk St. N.E., Cambridge 55008 *System:* Minnesota State Colleges and

Universities *Accred.:* 1975/1987 (NCA) *Calendar:* Qtr. plan *Degrees:* A, C *FTE Enroll:* 1,272   (612) 689-7000

AUGSBURG COLLEGE
2211 Riverside Ave., Minneapolis 55454 *Type:* Private (Lutheran) liberal arts *Accred.:* 1954/1987 (NCA) *Calendar:* 4-1-4 plan *Degrees:* B, M *Prof. Accred.:* Music, Nursing (B), Social Work (B,M-candidate), Teacher Education *CEO:* Pres. Charles S. Anderson
Enroll: 2,964   (612) 330-1000

AUSTIN COMMUNITY COLLEGE
1600 8th Ave., N.W., Austin 55912-1407 *Type:* Public (state) junior *System:* Minnesota State Colleges and Universities *Accred.:* 1971/1995 (NCA) *Calendar:* Qtr. plan *Degrees:* A *Prof. Accred.:* Nursing (A), Occupational Therapy Assisting *CEO:* Pres. Vicky R. Smith
Enroll: 1,357   (800) 747-6941

BEMIDJI STATE UNIVERSITY
1500 Birchmont Dr., N.E., Bemidji 56601-2699 *Type:* Public (state) liberal arts and teachers *System:* Minnesota State Colleges and Universities *Accred.:* 1943/1990 (NCA) *Calendar:* Qtr. plan *Degrees:* A, B, M *Prof. Accred.:* Music (A), Nursing (B), Social Work (B), Teacher Education *CEO:* Pres. M. James Bensen
Enroll: 4,813   (218) 755-2000

BETHANY LUTHERAN COLLEGE
734 Marsh St., Mankato 56001 *Type:* Private (Lutheran) junior *Accred.:* 1974/1989 (NCA) *Calendar:* Sem. plan *Degrees:* A *CEO:* Pres. Marvin G. Meyer
Enroll: 358   (507) 625-2977

BETHEL COLLEGE
3900 Bethel Dr., St. Paul 55112 *Type:* Private (Baptist) liberal arts *Accred.:* 1959/1990 (NCA) *Calendar:* Sem. plan *Degrees:* A, B, M *Prof. Accred.:* Nursing (B), Social Work

(B), Teacher Education *CEO:* Pres. George K. Brushaber
Enroll: 2,201   (612) 638-6400

BETHEL THEOLOGICAL SEMINARY
3949 Bethel Dr., St. Paul 55112 *Type:* Private (Baptist) graduate only *Accred.:* 1966/1991 (ATS); 1976/1991 (NCA) *Calendar:* Qtr. plan *Degrees:* M, D *CEO:* Exec. Vice Pres./Dean Leland V. Eliason
Enroll: 488   (612) 638-6180

WEST CAMPUS
6116 Arosa St., San Diego, CA 92115
(619) 582-8188

CARLETON COLLEGE
One N. College St., Northfield 55057 *Type:* Private liberal arts *Accred.:* 1913/1989 (NCA) *Calendar:* 3-3 plan *Degrees:* B *CEO:* Pres. Stephen R. Lewis, Jr.
Enroll: 1,932   (507) 663-4000

CENTRAL LAKES COLLEGE
501 W. College Dr., Brainerd 56401-3900 *Type:* Public (state) junior *System:* Minnesota State Colleges and Universities *Accred.:* 1977/1993 (NCA) *Calendar:* Qtr. plan *Degrees:* A *CEO:* Pres. Sally Jane Ihne
Enroll: 2,027   (218) 828-2525

STAPLES CAMPUS
Airport Rd., Staples 56479 *Calendar:* Qtr. plan *Degrees:* A, C
FTE Enroll: 600   (218) 894-1052

TECHNICAL COLLEGE CAMPUS
300 Quince St., Brainerd 56401 *Degrees:* A, C *Prof. Accred.:* Dental Assisting
(218) 828-5344

COLLEGE OF ST. BENEDICT
37 S. College Ave., St. Joseph 56374 *Type:* Private (Roman Catholic) liberal arts for women *Accred.:* 1933/1989 (NCA) *Calendar:* 4-1-4 plan *Degrees:* B *Prof. Accred.:* Dietetics (coordinated), Music (A), Nursing (B), Social Work (B), Teacher Education *CEO:* Pres. Colman O'Connell
Enroll: 2,026   (612) 363-5011

COLLEGE OF ST. CATHERINE
2004 Randolph Ave., St. Paul 55105 *Type:* Private (Roman Catholic) liberal arts for women *Accred.:* 1916/1993 (NCA) *Calendar:* 4-1-4 plan *Degrees:* A, B, M, C *Prof. Accred.:* Diagnostic Medical Sonography, Medical Record Technology, Music, Nursing (B), Occupational Therapy, Radiography, Respiratory Therapy, Social Work (B,M), Teacher Education *CEO:* Pres. Anita M. Pampusch
Enroll: 4,035   (612) 690-6000

ST. MARY'S CAMPUS
2500 S. Sixth St., Minneapolis 55454-1494 *Prof. Accred.:* Nursing (A), Occupational Therapy Assisting, Physical Therapy, Physical Therapy Assisting
(612) 690-7702

COLLEGE OF ST. SCHOLASTICA
1200 Kenwood Ave., Duluth 55811 *Type:* Private (Roman Catholic) liberal arts *Accred.:* 1931/1993 (NCA) *Calendar:* Qtr. plan *Degrees:* B, M, C *Prof. Accred.:* Clinical Lab Scientist, Medical Record Administration, Nursing (B,M), Occupational Therapy, Physical Therapy, Social Work (B) *CEO:* Pres. Daniel H. Pilon
Enroll: 1,849   (800) 447-5444

COLLEGE OF VISUAL ARTS
344 Summit Ave., St. Paul 55102-2199 *Type:* Private *Accred.:* 1978/1988 (ACCSCT); 1994 (NCA candidate) *Calendar:* Sem. plan *Degrees:* B, C *CEO:* Pres. Chris R. Kabella
Enroll: 206   (612) 224-3416

CONCORDIA COLLEGE
901 S. 8th St., Moorhead 56562 *Type:* Private (Lutheran) liberal arts *Accred.:* 1927/1994 (NCA) *Calendar:* Tri. plan *Degrees:* B *Prof. Accred.:* Music, Social Work (B), Teacher Education *CEO:* Pres. Paul J. Dovre
Enroll: 2,971   (218) 299-4000

CONCORDIA COLLEGE
275 N. Syndicate St., St. Paul 55104 *Type:* Private (Lutheran-Missouri Synod) liberal arts and teachers *Accred.:* 1959/1988 (NCA) *Calendar:* Qtr. plan *Degrees:* A, B, M *Prof.*

Accred.: Teacher Education *CEO:* Pres. Robert A. Holst
Enroll: 1,275   (612) 641-8278

CROWN COLLEGE
6425 County Rd. 30, St. Bonifacius 55375 *Type:* Private (Christian and Missionary Alliance) *Accred.:* 1950/1992 (AABC); 1980/1992 (NCA) *Calendar:* Sem. plan *Degrees:* A, B, C *CEO:* Pres. Bill W. Lanpher
Enroll: 620   (612) 446-4100

DAKOTA COUNTY TECHNICAL COLLEGE
1300 145th St. E., Rosemount 55068 *Type:* Public professional *Accred.:* 1994 (NCA candidate) *Degrees:* A, P *Prof. Accred.:* Dental Assisting (Provisional), Interior Design, Practical Nursing *CEO:* Pres. David Schroeder
Enroll: 2,590   (612) 423-8200

DULUTH BUSINESS UNIVERSITY
412 W. Superior St., Duluth 55802 *Type:* Private business *Accred.:* 1970/1987 (ACICS) *Calendar:* Qtr. plan *Degrees:* A, C *Prof. Accred.:* Medical Assisting (AMA) *CEO:* Pres. James R. Gessner
                                   (218) 722-3361

DUNWOODY INDUSTRIAL INSTITUTE
818 Dunwoody Blvd., Minneapolis 55403-1192 *Type:* Private *Accred.:* 1972/1988 (ACCSCT); 1994 (NCA candidate) *Degrees:* A, C *CEO:* Pres. Frank Starke
Enroll: 915   (612) 374-5800

FERGUS FALLS COMMUNITY COLLEGE
1414 College Way, Fergus Falls 56537-1009 *Type:* Public (state) junior *System:* Minnesota State Colleges and Universities *Accred.:* 1972/1993 (NCA) *Calendar:* Qtr. plan *Degrees:* A, C *Prof. Accred.:* Clinical Lab Technology (A), Histologic Technology *CEO:* Pres. Daniel F. True
Enroll: 1,440   (218) 739-7500

FOND DU LAC TRIBAL AND COMMUNITY COLLEGE
2101 14th Street, Cloquet 55720 *Type:* Public junior *System:* Minnesota State Colleges

and Universities *Accred.:* 1982/1989 (NCA) *Degrees:* A, C *CEO:* Pres. Lester J. Briggs
                                   (218) 879-0800

GLOBE COLLEGE OF BUSINESS
Box 60, 175 Fifth St. E., Ste. 201, St. Paul 55101-2901 *Type:* Private business *Accred.:* 1953/1996 (ACICS) *Calendar:* Qtr. plan *Degrees:* A *Prof. Accred.:* Medical Assisting (AMA) *CEO:* Pres. Terry L. Myhre
                                   (612) 224-4378

GUSTAVUS ADOLPHUS COLLEGE
800 W. College Ave., St. Peter 56082 *Type:* Private (Lutheran) liberal arts *Accred.:* 1915/1993 (NCA) *Calendar:* 4-1-4 plan *Degrees:* B *Prof. Accred.:* Athletic Training, Music, Nursing (B), Teacher Education *CEO:* Pres. Axel D. Steuer
Enroll: 2,362   (507) 933-8000

HAMLINE UNIVERSITY
1536 Hewitt Ave., St. Paul 55104 *Type:* Private (United Methodist) liberal arts *Accred.:* 1914/1988 (NCA) *Calendar:* 4-1-4 plan *Degrees:* B, M, D *Prof. Accred.:* Law, Music, Teacher Education *CEO:* Pres. Larry G. Osnes
Enroll: 2,562   (612) 641-2800

HENNEPIN TECHNICAL COLLEGE
9000 Brooklyn Blvd., Brooklyn Park 55455 *Type:* Public *System:* Minnesota State Colleges and Universities *Calendar:* Qtr. plan *Degrees:* A *Prof. Accred.:* Dental Assisting, Practical Nursing *CEO:* Pres. Sharon Grossbach
                                   (612) 425-3800

EDEN PRAIRIE CAMPUS
9200 Flying Cloud Dr., Eden Prairie 55344 *Calendar:* Qtr. plan *Degrees:* A, C *FTE Enroll:* 12,945   (612) 944-2222

HIBBING COMMUNITY COLLEGE
1515 E. 25th St., Hibbing 55746-3354 *Type:* Public (state) junior *System:* Minnesota State Colleges and Universities *Accred.:* 1982/1989 (NCA) *Calendar:* Qtr. plan *Degrees:* A, C *Prof. Accred.:* Occupational

Therapy Assisting *CEO:* Pres. Anthony J. Kuznik

(218) 262-6700

HUTCHINSON-WILLMAR TECHNICAL COLLEGE
P.O. Box 1097, Willmar 56201 *Type:* Public (state) 2-year *Accred.:* 1976/1992 (NCA) *Calendar:* Tri. plan *Degrees:* A, C *Prof. Accred.:* Medical Assisting (AMA), Practical Nursing, Veterinary Technology (provisional) *CEO:* Pres. Ronald A. Erpelding
Enroll: 2,208   (612) 235-5114

HUTCHINSON CAMPUS
2 Century Ave., Hutchinson 55350
(612) 587-9019

INVER HILLS COMMUNITY COLLEGE
2500 80th St. E., Inver Grove Heights 55076-3224 *Type:* Public (state) junior *System:* Minnesota State Colleges and Universities *Accred.:* 1976/1988 (NCA) *Calendar:* Qtr. plan *Degrees:* A, C *Prof. Accred.:* Nursing (A) *CEO:* Pres. Steven R. Wallace
Enroll: 5,453   (612) 450-8500

ITASCA COMMUNITY COLLEGE
1851 E. Hwy. 169, Grand Rapids 55744-3361 *Type:* Public (state) junior *System:* Minnesota State Colleges and Universities *Accred.:* 1982/1989 (NCA) *Calendar:* Qtr. plan *Degrees:* A, C *CEO:* Exec. Dean James Clarke

(218) 327-4461

LAKE SUPERIOR COLLEGE
2101 Trinity Rd., Duluth 55811-3399 *Type:* Public *System:* Minnesota State Colleges and Universities *Accred.:* 1988 (NCA) *Calendar:* Qtr. plan *Degrees:* A *Prof. Accred.:* Clinical Lab Technology (A), Dental Hygiene, Occupational Therapy Assisting, Physical Therapy Assisting *CEO:* Pres. Harold P. Erickson
FTE Enroll: 1,290   (218) 722-2801

EAST CAMPUS
1309 Rice Lake Rd., Duluth 55811 *Accred.:* 1988 (NCA) *Calendar:* Qtr. plan *Degrees:* A, C *Prof. Accred.:* Radiography
FTE Enroll: 1,290   (218) 723-4796

CENTURY COMMUNITY AND TECHNICAL COLLEGE
3401 Century Ave., White Bear Lake 55110-5655 *Type:* Public (state) junior *System:* Minnesota State Colleges and Universities *Accred.:* 1974/1986 (NCA) *Calendar:* Qtr. plan *Degrees:* A *Prof. Accred.:* Nursing (A), Radiography *CEO:* Pres. James Meznek
Enroll: 5,747   (612) 779-3200

EAST CAMPUS
3300 Century Ave. N., White Bear Lake 55110 *Prof. Accred.:* Dental Assisting, Dental Hygiene (provisional), Dental Laboratory Technology, EMT-Paramedic, Medical Assisting (AMA)
Enroll: 2,653   (612) 779-5740

LOWTHIAN COLLEGE
825 2nd Ave., S., Minneapolis 55402 *Type:* Private business *Accred.:* 1971/1999 (ACICS) *Degrees:* A *CEO:* Pres. Petrena Lowthian

(612) 332-3361

LUTHER SEMINARY
2481 Como Ave., St. Paul 55108 *Type:* Private (Evangelical Lutheran) graduate only *Accred.:* 1944/1994 (ATS); 1979/1995 (NCA) *Calendar:* Sem. plan *Degrees:* M, D *CEO:* Pres. David L. Tiede
Enroll: 814   (612) 641-3456

MACALESTER COLLEGE
1600 Grand Ave., St. Paul 55105 *Type:* Private (United Presbyterian) liberal arts *Accred.:* 1913/1986 (NCA) *Calendar:* 4-1-4 plan *Degrees:* B *Prof. Accred.:* Teacher Education *CEO:* Pres. Robert M. Gavin, Jr.
Enroll: 1,796   (612) 696-6000

MANKATO STATE UNIVERSITY
PO Box 8400, Mankato 56002-8400 *Type:* Public (state) liberal arts and professional *System:* Minnesota State Colleges and Universities *Accred.:* 1916/1986 (NCA) *Calendar:* Qtr. plan *Degrees:* A, B, M, P, C *Prof. Accred.:* Art, Counseling, Dental Hygiene, Engineering Technology (electrical, manufacturing), Engineering (electrical), Music, Nursing (B), Recreation and Leisure Services (B), Rehabilitation Counseling, Social

Work (B), Speech-Language Pathology, Teacher Education *CEO:* Pres. Richard R. Rush
Enroll: 13,473   (800) 722-0544

MARTIN LUTHER COLLEGE
1995 Luther Ct., New Ulm 56073 *Type:* Private (Evangelical Lutheran Synod) *Accred.:* 1980/1992 (NCA) *Calendar:* Sem. plan *Degrees:* B *CEO:* Pres. Theodore B. Olsen
Enroll: 571   (507) 354-8221

MAYO GRADUATE SCHOOL
200 First St., S.W., Rochester 55905 *Type:* Private professional *Accred.:* 1984/1989 (NCA) *Calendar:* Sem. plan *Degrees:* M, D, C *Prof. Accred.:* Clinical Lab Technology (C), Combined Maxillofacial Prosthodontics, Cytotechnology, Diagnostic Medical Sonography, Medicine, Nuclear Medicine Technology, Nurse Anesthesia Education (C,M), Oral and Maxillofacial Surgery, Orthodontics, Periodontics, Physical Therapy, Radiation Therapy Technology, Radiography *CEO:* CEO Robert R. Waller
Enroll: 588   (507) 284-2511

MESABI COMMUNITY COLLEGE
1001 West Chestnut St., Virginia 55792 *Type:* Public (state) junior *System:* Minnesota State Colleges and Universities *Accred.:* 1982/1989 (NCA) *Calendar:* Qtr. plan *Degrees:* A, C *CEO:* Pres. Jon Harris
                                    (218) 749-7700

METROPOLITAN STATE UNIVERSITY
700 E. 7th St., 2nd Fl. New Main, St. Paul 55106-5000 *Type:* Public (state) liberal arts *System:* Minnesota State Colleges and Universities *Accred.:* 1975/1995 (NCA) *Calendar:* Qtr. plan *Degrees:* B, M *Prof. Accred.:* Nursing (B) *CEO:* Pres. Susan A. Cole
Enroll: 5,510   (612) 772-7777

MINNEAPOLIS BUSINESS COLLEGE
1711 W. County Rd. B, Roseville 55113 *Type:* Private business *Accred.:* 1962/1995 (ACICS) *Degrees:* A, C *Prof. Accred.:* Medical Assisting (AMA) *CEO:* Pres. David Whitman
                                    (612) 636-7406

MINNEAPOLIS COLLEGE OF ART AND DESIGN
2501 Stevens Ave. S., Minneapolis 55404 *Type:* Private professional *Accred.:* 1960/1995 (NCA) *Calendar:* Sem. plan *Degrees:* B, M *Prof. Accred.:* Art *CEO:* Pres. John S. Slorp
Enroll: 543   (612) 874-3700

MINNEAPOLIS COMMUNITY AND TECHNICAL COLLEGE
1501 Hennepin Ave., Minneapolis 55403-1779 *Type:* Public (state) junior *System:* Minnesota State Colleges and Universities *Accred.:* 1977/1993 (NCA) *Calendar:* Qtr. plan *Degrees:* A, C *Prof. Accred.:* Nursing (A) *CEO:* Pres. Diann Schindler
Enroll: 4,498   (612) 341-7000

MINNESOTA BIBLE COLLEGE
920 Mayowood Rd, S.W., Rochester 55902 *Type:* Private (Christian Churches/Churches of Christ) *Accred.:* 1948/1994 (AABC) *Calendar:* Qtr. plan *Degrees:* A, B *CEO:* Interim Pres. Robert Cash
FTE Enroll: 92   (507) 288-4563

MINNESOTA SCHOOL OF BUSINESS
1401 W. 76th St., Ste. 500, Richfield 55423 *Type:* Private business *Accred.:* 1953/1994 (ACICS) *Calendar:* Qtr. plan *Degrees:* A, C *Prof. Accred.:* Medical Assisting (AMA) *CEO:* Dir. Kathy Metcalf
                                    (612) 861-2000

BROOKLYN CENTER CAMPUS
6120 Earle Brown Dr., Brooklyn Center 55430
                                    (612) 566-7777

MINNESOTA RIVERLAND TECHNICAL COLLEGE
1255 S.W. 3rd St., Faribault 55021 *Type:* Public (state) junior *Accred.:* 1995(NCA) *Calendar:* Qtr. plan *Degrees:* A, C *CEO:* Vice Pres./Campus CEO Gary Swanson
                                    (507) 334-3965

AUSTIN CAMPUS
1900 Eighth Ave., N.W., Austin 55912
                                    (507) 433-0600

ROCHESTER CAMPUS
1926 College View Rd., S.E., Ave., Rochester 55904
(507) 285-8631

MOORHEAD STATE UNIVERSITY
1104 7th Ave. S., Moorhead 56563 *Type:* Public (state) liberal arts and teachers *System:* Minnesota State Colleges and Universities *Accred.:* 1916/1987 (NCA) *Calendar:* Sem. plan *Degrees:* A, B, M, P *Prof. Accred.:* Art, Music, Nursing (B), Social Work (B), Speech-Language Pathology, Teacher Education *CEO:* Pres. Roland E. Barden
Enroll: 7,025   (218) 236-2011

NATIONAL EDUCATION CENTER—BROWN INSTITUTE CAMPUS
2225 E. Lake St., Minneapolis 55407-1900 *Type:* Private *Accred.:* 1967/1988 (ACCSCT) *Degrees:* A *CEO:* Pres. Bonnie Hugeback
(612) 721-2481

NORMANDALE COMMUNITY COLLEGE
9700 France Ave. S., Bloomington 55431-4309 *Type:* Public (state) junior *System:* Minnesota State Colleges and Universities *Accred.:* 1973/1991 (NCA) *Calendar:* Qtr. plan *Degrees:* A, C *Prof. Accred.:* Dental Assisting, Dental Hygiene, Nursing (A) *CEO:* Pres. Thomas A. Horak
Enroll: 8,171   (612) 832-6000

NORTH CENTRAL BIBLE COLLEGE
910 Elliot Ave. S., Minneapolis 55404 *Type:* Private (Assemblies of God) *Accred.:* 1986/1991 (NCA) *Calendar:* Sem. plan *Degrees:* A, B, C *CEO:* Pres. Gordon L. Anderson
Enroll: 1,340   (612) 332-3491

NORTH HENNEPIN COMMUNITY COLLEGE
7411 85th Ave. N., Brooklyn Park 55445-2231 *Type:* Public (state) junior *System:* Minnesota State Colleges and Universities *Accred.:* 1972/1994 (NCA) *Calendar:* Qtr. plan *Degrees:* A, C *Prof. Accred.:* Clinical Lab Technology (A), Nursing (A) *CEO:* Pres. Katherine H. Sloan
Enroll: 5,744   (612) 424-0811

NORTHLAND COMMUNITY AND TECHNICAL COLLEGE
1301 Hwy. 1 E., Thief River Falls 56701-2598 *Type:* Public (state) junior *System:* Minnesota State Colleges and Universities *Accred.:* 1976/1993 (NCA) *Calendar:* Qtr. plan *Degrees:* A *CEO:* Pres. Orley Gunderson
Enroll: 812   (218) 681-0701

NORTHWEST TECHNICAL COLLEGE
905 Grant Ave., S.E., Bemidji 56601 *Type:* Public (state) *Accred.:* 1995 (NCA) *Calendar:* Qtr. plan *Degrees:* A, C *CEO:* Pres. Ray Cross
Enroll: 4,502   (218) 755-4270

DETROIT LAKES CAMPUS
900 Hwy. 34 E., Detroit Lakes 56501
(218) 847-1341

EAST GRAND FORKS CAMPUS
Hwy. 220 N., East Grand Forks 56721
(218) 773-3441

MOORHEAD CAMPUS
1900 28th Ave., S., Moorhead 56560
(218) 236-6277

WADENA CAMPUS
405 S.W. Colfax, P.O. Box 56, Wadena 56482
(218) 631-3530

NORTHWESTERN COLLEGE
3003 N. Snelling Ave., St. Paul 55113-1598 *Type:* Private liberal arts *Accred.:* 1978/1989 (NCA) *Calendar:* Qtr. plan *Degrees:* A, B, C *Prof. Accred.:* Music *CEO:* Pres. Donald O. Ericksen
Enroll: 1,269   (612) 631-5100

NORTHWESTERN COLLEGE OF CHIROPRACTIC
2501 W. 84th St., Bloomington 55431-1599 *Type:* Private professional *Accred.:* 1988/1993 (NCA) *Calendar:* Tri. plan *Degrees:* B, D *Prof. Accred.:* Chiropractic Education *CEO:* Pres. John F. Allenburg
Enroll: 625   (612) 888-4777

OAK HILLS BIBLE COLLEGE
1600 Oak Hills Rd., S.W., Bemidji 56601 *Type:* Private (interdenominational) *Accred.:* 1990 (AABC) *Calendar:* Qtr. plan *Degrees:* A, B, C *CEO:* Pres. Mark Hovestol
FTE Enroll: 134   (218) 751-8670

PINE TECHNICAL COLLEGE
1100 Fourth St., Pine City 55063 *Type:* Public *System:* Minnesota State Colleges and Universities *Accred.:* 1994 (NCA) *Calendar:* Qtr. plan *Degrees:* A, C *CEO:* Pres. Eugene Biever
Enroll: 732   (612) 629-6764

RAINY RIVER COMMUNITY COLLEGE
1501 Hwy. 71, International Falls 56649-2160 *Type:* Public (state) junior *System:* Minnesota State Colleges and Universities *Accred.:* 1982/1989 (NCA) *Calendar:* Qtr. plan *Degrees:* A, C *CEO:* Pres. Allen Rasmussen
         (218) 285-7722

RANGE TECHNICAL COLLEGE—HIBBING
2900 E. Beltline, Hibbing 55746 *Type:* Public *System:* Minnesota State Colleges and Universities *Accred.:* 1995 (NCA) *Calendar:* Qtr. plan *Degrees:* A, C *Prof. Accred.:* Clinical Lab Technology (A), Dental Assisting *CEO:* Pres. Joe Sertich
         (218) 262-7200

EVELETH CAMPUS
1100 Industrial Park Dr., P.O. Box 0648, Eveleth 55734-0648
Enroll: 900   (507) 454-4600

RASMUSSEN COLLEGE EAGAN
3500 Federal Dr., Eagan 55122 *Type:* Private business *Accred.:* 1953/1996 (ACICS) *Degrees:* A, C *CEO:* Dir. Laurie Hinze
         (612) 687-9000

RASMUSSEN COLLEGE MANKATO
501 Holly Lane, Mankato 56001 *Type:* Private business *Accred.:* 1973/1986 (ACICS) *Degrees:* A, C *CEO:* Dir. Douglas Gardner
         (507) 625-6556

RASMUSSEN COLLEGE MINNETONKA
12450 Wayzata Blvd., Ste. 315, Minnetonka 55305-9845 *Type:* Private business *Accred.:* 1973/1990 (ACICS); 1995 (NCA candidate) *Degrees:* A, C *Prof. Accred.:* Medical Record Technology *CEO:* Dir. Mary Ellen Schmidt
         (612) 545-2000

RASMUSSEN COLLEGE ST. CLOUD
245 N. 37th Ave., St. Cloud 56303 *Type:* Private business *Accred.:* 1969/1987 (ACICS) *Calendar:* Qtr. plan *Degrees:* A, C *CEO:* Dir. Cathy Wogen
         (612) 251-5600

RED WING/WINONA TECHNICAL COLLEGE
308 Pioneer Rd. & Hwy. 58, Red Wing 55066 *Type:* Public *System:* Minnesota State Colleges and Universities *Accred.:* 1995 (NCA) *Calendar:* Qtr. plan *Degrees:* A, C *CEO:* Vice Pres./CEO Ron Matuska
Enroll: 1,918   (612) 388-8271

WINONA CAMPUS
1250 Homer Rd., P.O. Box 409, Winona 55987-0409 *Accred.:* 1995 (NCA) *Calendar:* Qtr. plan *Degrees:* A, C *CEO:* Interim Pres. Jim Johnson
Enroll: 900   (507) 454-4600

ROCHESTER COMMUNITY COLLEGE
851 30th Ave., S.E., Rochester 55904-4915 *Type:* Public (state) junior *System:* Minnesota State Colleges and Universities *Accred.:* 1923/1991 (NCA) *Calendar:* Qtr. plan *Degrees:* A, C *Prof. Accred.:* Dental Assisting, Dental Hygiene, Engineering Technology (civil/construction, electrical), Medical Assisting (AMA), Nursing (A), Respiratory Therapy *CEO:* Pres. Karen E. Nagle
Enroll: 3,940   (507) 285-7210

ST. CLOUD STATE UNIVERSITY
720 Fourth Ave. S., St. Cloud 56301-4498 *Type:* Public (state) liberal arts and professional *System:* Minnesota State Colleges and Universities *Accred.:* 1915/1987 (NCA) *Calendar:* Qtr. plan *Degrees:* A, B, M, P *Prof. Accred.:* Art, Business (B,M), Com-

puter Science, Engineering Technology (manufacturing), Engineering (electrical), Journalism (B,M), Music, Rehabilitation Counseling, Social Work (B), Speech-Language Pathology, Teacher Education *CEO:* Pres. Bruce F. Grube
Enroll: 14,673   (612) 255-0121

ST. CLOUD TECHNICAL COLLEGE
1540 Northway Dr., St. Cloud 56303 *Type:* Public (state) 2-year *Accred.:* 1985/1990 (NCA) *Calendar:* Qtr. plan *Degrees:* A, C *Prof. Accred.:* Dental Assisting, Practical Nursing, Surgical Technology *CEO:* Pres. Larry Barnhardt
Enroll: 2,369   (612)654-5000

ST. JOHN'S UNIVERSITY
Collegeville 56321 *Type:* Private (Roman Catholic) liberal arts and seminary for men *Accred.:* 1969/1988 (ATS); 1950/1989 (NCA) *Calendar:* 4-1-4 plan *Degrees:* B, M *Prof. Accred.:* Nursing (B), Social Work (B), Teacher Education *CEO:* Pres. Dietrich Reinhart, O.S.B.
Enroll: 1,820   (612) 363-2011

ST. MARY'S UNIVERSITY OF MINNESOTA
700 Terrace Hgts., Ste. 30, Winona 55987-1399 *Type:* Private (Roman Catholic) liberal arts *Accred.:* 1934/1987 (NCA) *Calendar:* Sem. plan *Degrees:* B, M *Prof. Accred.:* Nuclear Medicine Technology, Nurse Anesthesia Education *CEO:* Pres. Louis De Thomasis
Enroll: 7,623   (800) 635-5987

ST. OLAF COLLEGE
1520 St. Olaf Ave., Northfield 55057 *Type:* Private (Lutheran) liberal arts *Accred.:* 1915/1993 (NCA) *Calendar:* 4-1-4 plan *Degrees:* B *Prof. Accred.:* Dance, Music, Nursing (B), Social Work (B), Teacher Education, Theatre *CEO:* Pres. Mark V. Edwards
Enroll: 2,958   (507) 646-2222

ST. PAUL TECHNICAL COLLEGE
235 Marshall Ave., St. Paul 55102 *Type:* Public (local) 2-year *Accred.:* 1983/1993 (NCA) *Calendar:* Qtr. plan *Degrees:* A, C *Prof. Accred.:* Clinical Lab Technology (A),

Practical Nursing, Respiratory Therapy *CEO:* Pres. Donovan Schwichtenberg
Enroll: 3,692   (612) 221-1300

SOUTH CENTRAL TECHNICAL
1920 Lee Blvd., North Mankato 56003 *Type:* Public *System:* Minnesota State Colleges and Universities *Accred.:* 1995 (NCA) *Calendar:* Qtr. plan *Degrees:* A, C *CEO:* Pres. Ken Mills
Enroll: 3,239   (507) 389-7200

ALBERT LEA CAMPUS
2200 Tech Dr., Albert Lea 56007-3499 *Prof. Accred.:* Dental Assisting, Physical Therapy Assisting
     (507) 373-0656

SOUTHWEST STATE UNIVERSITY
1501 State St., Marshall 56258 *Type:* Public (state) liberal arts *System:* Minnesota State Colleges and Universities *Accred.:* 1972/1993 (NCA) *Calendar:* Qtr. plan *Degrees:* A, B *Prof. Accred.:* Music, Social Work (B-candidate) *CEO:* Pres. Douglas Sweetland
Enroll: 2,575   (800) 642-0684

SOUTHWESTERN TECHNICAL COLLEGE
1593 11th Ave., Granite Falls 56241 *Type:* Public (state) *System:* Minnesota State Colleges and Universities *Accred.:* 1991/1994 (NCA) *Calendar:* Qtr. plan *Degrees:* A, C *CEO:* Pres./ CEO Ralph Knapp
Enroll: 2,575   (800) 642-0684

CANBY CAMPUS
1011 First St., W., Canby 56220*P*
     (507) 223-7252

JACKSON CAMPUS
401 West St., W., Jackson 56143*P*
     (507) 847-3320

PIPESTONE CAMPUS
1314 N. Hiawatha Ave., P.O. Box 250 Pipestone 56164-0250
     (507) 825-5470

UNITED THEOLOGICAL SEMINARY OF THE TWIN CITIES
3000 Fifth St., N.W., New Brighton 55112 *Type:* Private (United Church of Christ)

Accred.: 1966/1992 (ATS); 1977/1992 (NCA) *Calendar:* Qtr. plan *Degrees:* M, D, C *CEO:* Pres. Benjamin Griffin
Enroll: 256   (612) 633-4311

UNIVERSITY OF MINNESOTA—CROOKSTON
Hwys. 2 and 75 N., Crookston 56716 *Type:* Public (state) *System:* University of Minnesota System *Accred.:* 1971/1995 (NCA) *Calendar:* Qtr. plan *Degrees:* A, B *CEO:* Chanc. Donald G. Sargeant
Enroll: 1,557   (218) 281-6510

UNIVERSITY OF MINNESOTA—DULUTH
515 Darland Admin. Bldg., 10 University Dr., Duluth 55812 *Type:* Public (state) *System:* University of Minnesota System *Accred.:* 1968/1988 (NCA) *Calendar:* Qtr. plan *Degrees:* B, M, C *Prof. Accred.:* Computer Science, Counseling, Engineering (chemical, computer, industrial), Medicine, Music, Social Work (M), Speech-Language Pathology, Teacher Education *CEO:* Chanc. Kathryn A. Martin
Enroll: 7,497   (218) 726-8000

UNIVERSITY OF MINNESOTA—MORRIS
600 E. Fourth St., Morris 56267 *Type:* Public (state) *System:* University of Minnesota System *Accred.:* 1970/1990 (NCA) *Calendar:* Qtr. plan *Degrees:* B *Prof. Accred.:* Teacher Education *CEO:* Chanc. David C. Johnson
Enroll: 1,924   (612) 589-2211

UNIVERSITY OF MINNESOTA—TWIN CITIES
202 Morrill Hall, 100 Church St., S.E., Minneapolis 55455 *Type:* Public (state) *System:* University of Minnesota System *Accred.:* 1913/1986 (NCA) *Calendar:* Qtr. plan *Degrees:* B, M, P, D, C *Prof. Accred.:* Accounting (A), Audiology, Business (B,M), Clinical Lab Scientist, Clinical Psychology, Combined Prosthodontics, Counseling Psychology, Dance (A), Dental Hygiene, Dentistry, Dietetics (coordinated), Dietetics (internship), Endodontics, Engineering (aerospace, agricultural, chemical, civil, electrical, geological/geophysical, materials, mechanical), Forestry, Funeral Service Education (Mortuary Science), General Dentistry, General Practice Residency, Health Services Administration, Interior Design, Journalism (B,M), Landscape Architecture (B,M-initial), Law, Marriage and Family Therapy (D), Medicine, Music, Nurse Anesthesia Education, Nursing (B,M), Occupational Therapy, Oral Pathology, Oral and Maxillofacial Surgery, Orthodontics, Pediatric Dentistry, Perfusion, Periodontics, Physical Therapy, Planning (M), Psychology Internship, Radiation Therapy Technology, Radiography, Recreation and Leisure Services, School Psychology, Social Work (M), Speech-Language Pathology, Teacher Education, Theatre, Veterinary Medicine *CEO:* Pres. Nils Hasselmo
Enroll: 39,078   (612) 625-5000

UNIVERSITY OF ST. THOMAS
2115 Summit Ave., St. Paul 55105 *Type:* Private (Roman Catholic) liberal arts *Accred.:* 1974/1994 (ATS); 1916/1994 (NCA) *Calendar:* 4-1-4 plan *Degrees:* B, M, P, D *Prof. Accred.:* Music, Social Work (B,M), Teacher Education *CEO:* Pres. Dennis J. Dease
Enroll: 10,161   (612) 962-5000

GAINEY CONFERENCE CENTER CAMPUS
RR2 Box 1, Owatonna 55060
                                       (612) 962-4444

MINNEAPOLIS CAMPUS
1000 LaSalle Ave., Ste. 201, Minneapolis 55403
                                       (612) 962-4000

THE MEETING POINT CAMPUS
1107 Hazeltine Blvd., Chaska 55318
                                       (612) 448-8800

VERMILION COMMUNITY COLLEGE
1900 E. Camp St., Ely 55731-1918 *Type:* Public (state) junior *System:* Minnesota State Colleges and Universities *Accred.:* 1982/1989 (NCA) *Calendar:* Qtr. plan *Degrees:* A, C *CEO:* Pres. Jon Harris
                                       (218) 365-7200

WALDEN UNIVERSITY
155 S. Fifth Ave., Minneapolis 55401 *Type:* Private graduate only *Accred.:* 1990/1994

(NCA) *Calendar:* Tri. plan *Degrees:* D *CEO:* Pres. Dave Palmer
Enroll: 879   (800) 444-6795

WILLIAM MITCHELL COLLEGE OF LAW
875 Summit Ave., St. Paul 55105 *Type:* Private professional *Calendar:* Sem. plan *Degrees:* P *Prof. Accred.:* Law *CEO:* Pres./Dean Harry J. Haynsworth, IV
Enroll: 1,156   (612) 227-9171

WILLMAR COMMUNITY COLLEGE
County Rd., P.O. Box 797, Willmar 56201-0797 *Type:* Public (state) junior *System:* Minnesota State Colleges and Universities *Accred.:* 1972/1995 (NCA) *Calendar:* Qtr. plan *Degrees:* A *CEO:* Pres. Mary E. Retterer
Enroll: 1,341   (612) 231-5102

WINONA STATE UNIVERSITY
Winona 55987 *Type:* Public (state) liberal arts and teachers *System:* Minnesota State Colleges and Universities *Accred.:* 1913/1991 (NCA) *Calendar:* Qtr. plan *Degrees:* A, B, M, P, C *Prof. Accred.:* Engineering (materials), Music, Nursing (B,M), Social Work (B), Teacher Education *CEO:* Pres. Darrell W. Krueger
Enroll: 7,192   (800) 342-5978

ROCHESTER CENTER CAMPUS
Hwy. 14 E., 859 30th Ave., S.E., Rochester 55904
                                        (507) 285-7100

WORTHINGTON COMMUNITY COLLEGE
1450 College Way, Worthington 56187-3024 *Type:* Public (state) junior *System:* Minnesota State Colleges and Universities *Accred.:* 1973/1990 (NCA) *Calendar:* Qtr. plan *Degrees:* A, C *CEO:* Pres. C. W. Burchill
Enroll: 904   (507) 372-2107

MISSISSIPPI

ALCORN STATE UNIVERSITY
1000 Oakland Cir., Lorman 39096-9402 *Type:* Public (state) teachers *System:* Mississippi Board of Trustees of State Institutions of Higher Learning *Accred.:* 1948/1991 (SACS-CC) *Calendar:* Sem. plan *Degrees:* A, B, M *Prof. Accred.:* Home Economics, Music, Nursing (A,B), Teacher Education *CEO:* Pres. Clinton Bristow, Jr.
FTE Enroll: 2,712   (601) 877-6100

BELHAVEN COLLEGE
1500 Peachtree St., Jackson 39202 *Type:* Private (Presbyterian) liberal arts *Accred.:* 1946/1987 (SACS-CC) *Calendar:* Sem. plan *Degrees:* B, M (candidate) *Prof. Accred.:* Art, Music *CEO:* Pres. Roger Parrott
FTE Enroll: 905   (601) 968-5928

BLUE MOUNTAIN COLLEGE
P.O. Box 338, Blue Mountain 38610 *Type:* Private (Southern Baptist) liberal arts *Accred.:* 1927/1994 (SACS-CC) *Calendar:* Sem. plan *Degrees:* B *CEO:* Pres. E. Harold Fisher
FTE Enroll: 320   (601) 685-4771

COAHOMA COMMUNITY COLLEGE
3240 Friars Pt. Rd., Clarksdale 38614 *Type:* Public (district) junior *System:* Mississippi State Board for Community and Junior Colleges *Accred.:* 1975/1990 (SACS-CC) *Calendar:* Sem. plan *Degrees:* A *CEO:* Pres. Vivian M. Presley
FTE Enroll: 915   (601) 627-2571

COPIAH-LINCOLN COMMUNITY COLLEGE
P.O. Box 457, Wesson 39191 *Type:* Public (district) junior *System:* Mississippi State Board for Community and Junior Colleges *Accred.:* 1936/1995 (SACS-CC) *Calendar:* Sem. plan *Degrees:* A *Prof. Accred.:* Clinical Lab Technology (A), Radiography *CEO:* Pres. Billy B. Thames
FTE Enroll: 2,231   (601) 643-5101

DELTA STATE UNIVERSITY
Hwy. 8 W., Cleveland 38733 *Type:* Public (state) liberal arts and teachers *System:* Mississippi Board of Trustees of State Institutions of Higher Learning *Accred.:* 1930/1994 (SACS-CC) *Calendar:* Sem. plan *Degrees:* A, B, M, D *Prof. Accred.:* Art (A), Counseling, Home Economics, Music, Nursing (B), Social Work (B), Teacher Education *CEO:* Pres. F. Kent Wyatt
FTE Enroll: 3,357   (601) 846-3000

EAST CENTRAL COMMUNITY COLLEGE
P.O. Box 129, Decatur 39327-0129 *Type:* Public (district) junior *System:* Mississippi State Board for Community and Junior Colleges *Accred.:* 1939/1991 (SACS-CC) *Calendar:* Sem. plan *Degrees:* A *CEO:* Pres. Eddie M. Smith
FTE Enroll: 1,144   (601) 635-2111

EAST MISSISSIPPI COMMUNITY COLLEGE
P.O. Box 158, Scooba 39358 *Type:* Public (district) junior *System:* Mississippi State Board for Community and Junior Colleges *Accred.:* 1949/1987 (SACS-CC) *Calendar:* Sem. plan *Degrees:* A *Prof. Accred.:* Funeral Service Education (Mortuary Science) *CEO:* Pres. Thomas L. Davis, Jr.
FTE Enroll: 1,056   (601) 476-8442

HINDS COMMUNITY COLLEGE
505 E. Main St., Raymond 39154-9799 *Type:* Public (district) junior *System:* Mississippi State Board for Community and Junior Colleges *Accred.:* 1928/1986 (SACS-CC) *Calendar:* Sem. plan *Degrees:* A *Prof. Accred.:* Clinical Lab Technology (A), Dental Assisting, Medical Record Technology, Nursing (A), Physical Therapy Assisting, Respiratory Therapy, Respiratory Therapy Technology, Surgical Technology, Veterinary Technology (probational) *CEO:* Pres. V. Clyde Muse
FTE Enroll: 7,663   (601) 857-5261

HOLMES COMMUNITY COLLEGE
P.O. Box 369, Goodman 39079 *Type:* Public (district) junior *System:* Mississippi State Board for Community and Junior Colleges *Accred.:* 1934/1995 (SACS-CC) *Calendar:*

Sem. plan *Degrees:* A *Prof. Accred.:* Nursing (A) *CEO:* Pres. Starkey A. Morgan, Sr.
FTE Enroll: 1,914   (601) 472-2312

ITAWAMBA COMMUNITY COLLEGE
602 W. Hill St., Fulton 38843-1099 *Type:* Public (district) junior *System:* Mississippi State Board for Community and Junior Colleges *Accred.:* 1955/1988 (SACS-CC) *Calendar:* Sem. plan *Degrees:* A *Prof. Accred.:* Nursing (A), Physical Therapy Assisting, Radiography, Respiratory Therapy, Respiratory Therapy Technology *CEO:* Pres. David Cole
FTE Enroll: 2,702   (601) 862-3101

JACKSON STATE UNIVERSITY
1400 J. R. Lynch St., Jackson 39217 *Type:* Public (state) liberal arts and teachers *System:* Mississippi Board of Trustees of State Institutions of Higher Learning *Accred.:* 1948/1991 (SACS-CC) *Calendar:* Sem. plan *Degrees:* B, M, D *Prof. Accred.:* Art, Journalism (B), Music, Public Administration, Rehabilitation Counseling, Social Work (B), Teacher Education *CEO:* Pres. James E. Lyons, Sr.
FTE Enroll: 5,772   (601) 968-2121

JONES COUNTY JUNIOR COLLEGE
900 Court St., Ellisville 39437 *Type:* Public (district) junior *System:* Mississippi State Board for Community and Junior Colleges *Accred.:* 1940/1987 (SACS-CC) *Calendar:* Sem. plan *Degrees:* A *Prof. Accred.:* EMT-Paramedic, Nursing (A), Radiography *CEO:* Pres. T. Terrell Tisdale
FTE Enroll: 3,968   (601) 477-4000

MAGNOLIA BIBLE COLLEGE
P.O. Box 1109, 822 S. Huntington, Kosciusko 39090 *Type:* Private (Churches of Christ) *Accred.:* 1989/1995 (AABC); 1990/1995 (SACS-CC) *Calendar:* Sem. plan *Degrees:* B *CEO:* Pres. Cecil May, Jr.
FTE Enroll: 26   (601) 289-2896

MARY HOLMES COLLEGE
P.O. Box 1257, Hwy. 50 W., West Point 39773 *Type:* Private (United Presbyterian) 2-year *Accred.:* 1973/1989 (SACS-CC) *Cal-*

endar: Sem. plan *Degrees:* A *CEO:* Pres. Sammie Potts
FTE Enroll: 314   (601) 494-6820

MERIDIAN COMMUNITY COLLEGE
910 Hwy. 19 N., Meridian 39307 *Type:* Public (district) junior *System:* Mississippi State Board for Community and Junior Colleges *Accred.:* 1942/1991 (SACS-CC) *Calendar:* Sem. plan *Degrees:* A *Prof. Accred.:* Clinical Lab Technology (A), Dental Hygiene, Medical Record Technology, Nursing (A), Practical Nursing, Radiography, Respiratory Therapy Technology *CEO:* Pres. William F. Scaggs
FTE Enroll: 1,950   (601) 483-8241

MILLSAPS COLLEGE
1701 N. State St., Jackson 39210 *Type:* Private (United Methodist) liberal arts *Accred.:* 1912/1992 (SACS-CC) *Calendar:* Sem. plan *Degrees:* B, M *Prof. Accred.:* Business (B,M), Teacher Education *CEO:* Pres. George M. Harmon
FTE Enroll: 1,240   (601) 974-1000

MISSISSIPPI COLLEGE
P.O. Box 4186, Clinton 39058 *Type:* Private (Southern Baptist) liberal arts *Accred.:* 1922/1992 (SACS-CC) *Degrees:* B, M, D *Prof. Accred.:* Law, Music, Nursing (B), Social Work (B-candidate), Teacher Education *CEO:* Pres. Howell W. Todd
FTE Enroll: 2,857   (601) 925-3000

MISSISSIPPI DELTA COMMUNITY COLLEGE
P.O. Box 668, Moorhead 38761 *Type:* Public (district) junior *System:* Mississippi State Board for Community and Junior Colleges *Accred.:* 1930/1987 (SACS-CC) *Calendar:* Sem. plan *Degrees:* A *Prof. Accred.:* Clinical Lab Technology (A), Nursing (A), Radiography *CEO:* Pres. Bobby S. Garvin
FTE Enroll: 3,491   (601) 246-6322

MISSISSIPPI GULF COAST COMMUNITY COLLEGE
P.O. Box 67, Perkinston 39573 *Type:* Public (district) junior *System:* Mississippi State Board for Community and Junior Colleges *Accred.:* 1929/1989 (SACS-CC) *Calendar:* Sem. plan *Degrees:* A *Prof. Accred.:* Clinical

Lab Technology (A), EMT-Paramedic, Nursing (A), Radiography, Respiratory Therapy Technology *CEO:* Pres. Barry L. Mellinger
FTE Enroll: 7,234   (601) 928-5211

MISSISSIPPI STATE UNIVERSITY
Mississippi State 39762 *Type:* Public (state) *System:* Mississippi Board of Trustees of State Institutions of Higher Learning *Accred.:* 1926/1993 (SACS-CC) *Calendar:* Sem. plan *Degrees:* B, M, D *Prof. Accred.:* Accounting (A,C), Art, Business (B,M), Computer Science, Counseling, Engineering (aerospace, agricultural, bioengineering, chemical, civil, computer, electrical, industrial, mechanical, nuclear), Forestry, Home Economics, Interior Design, Landscape Architecture (B), Music (A), Public Administration, Rehabilitation Counseling, Social Work (B-candidate), Teacher Education *CEO:* Pres. Donald W. Zacharias
FTE Enroll: 13,651   (601) 325-3920

MISSISSIPPI UNIVERSITY FOR WOMEN
P.O. Box W-1602, Columbus 39701 *Type:* Public (state) liberal arts and teachers for women *System:* Mississippi Board of Trustees of State Institutions of Higher Learning *Accred.:* 1921/1993 (SACS-CC) *Calendar:* Sem. plan *Degrees:* A, B, M *Prof. Accred.:* Art (A), Home Economics, Music, Nursing (A,B,M), Teacher Education *CEO:* Pres. Clyda S. Rent
FTE Enroll: 2,033   (601) 329-4750

MISSISSIPPI VALLEY STATE UNIVERSITY
14000 Hwy. 82 W., Itta Bena 38941-1400 *Type:* Public (state) teachers *System:* Mississippi Board of Trustees of State Institutions of Higher Learning *Accred.:* 1968/1992 (SACS-CC) *Calendar:* Sem. plan *Degrees:* B, M *Prof. Accred.:* Art, Music (A), Social Work (B), Teacher Education *CEO:* Pres. William W. Sutton
FTE Enroll: 2,329   (601) 254-3997

NORTHEAST MISSISSIPPI COMMUNITY COLLEGE
101 Cunningham Blvd., Booneville 38829 *Type:* Public (district) junior *System:* Mississippi State Board for Community and Junior Colleges *Accred.:* 1956/1991 (SACS-CC)

Calendar: Sem. plan *Degrees:* A *Prof. Accred.:* Clinical Lab Technology (A), Dental Hygiene, Medical Assisting (AMA), Nursing (A), Respiratory Therapy Technology *CEO:* Pres. Joe M. Childers
FTE Enroll: 2,734   (601) 728-7751

NORTHWEST MISSISSIPPI COMMUNITY COLLEGE
510 N. Panola, Senatobia 38668 *Type:* Public (district) junior *System:* Mississippi State Board for Community and Junior Colleges *Accred.:* 1953/1988 (SACS-CC) *Calendar:* Sem. plan *Degrees:* A *Prof. Accred.:* Funeral Service Education (Mortuary Science), Nursing (A), Respiratory Therapy, Respiratory Therapy Technology *CEO:* Pres. David M. Haraway
FTE Enroll: 3,425   (601) 562-3200

PEARL RIVER COMMUNITY COLLEGE
101 Hwy. 11 N., Station A, Poplarville 39470-2298 *Type:* Public (district) junior *System:* Mississippi State Board for Community and Junior Colleges *Accred.:* 1929/1995 (SACS-CC) *Calendar:* Sem. plan *Degrees:* A *Prof. Accred.:* Dental Assisting, Dental Hygiene, Nursing (A), Respiratory Therapy Technology *CEO:* Pres. Ted J. Alexander
FTE Enroll: 2,383   (601) 795-6801

HATTIESBURG CAMPUS
5448 U.S. Hwy. 495, Hattiesburg 39401 *Calendar:* Sem. plan *Prof. Accred.:* Physical Therapy Assisting
                 (601) 795-6801

REFORMED THEOLOGICAL SEMINARY
5422 Clinton Blvd., Jackson 39209 *Type:* Private (interdenominational) graduate only *Accred.:* 1977/1991 (ATS); 1977/1992 (SACS-CC) *Calendar:* Sem. plan *Degrees:* M, D *Prof. Accred.:* Marriage and Family Therapy (M) *CEO:* Pres. Luder G. Whitlock, Jr.
FTE Enroll: 507   (601) 922-4988

RUST COLLEGE
150 E. Rust Ave., Holly Springs 38635 *Type:* Private (United Methodist) liberal arts *Accred.:* 1970/1994 (SACS-CC) *Calendar:*

Sem. plan *Degrees:* A, B *CEO:* Pres. David L. Beckley
FTE Enroll: 1,180   (601) 252-4661

SOUTHEASTERN BAPTIST COLLEGE
4229 Hwy. 15 N., Laurel 39440 *Type:* Private (Baptist Missionary Association) *Accred.:* 1988/1994 (AABC) *Calendar:* Sem. plan *Degrees:* A, B, C *CEO:* Pres. Gerald Kellar
FTE Enroll: 56   (601) 426-6346

SOUTHWEST MISSISSIPPI COMMUNITY COLLEGE
Summit 39666-9704 *Type:* Public (district) junior *System:* Mississippi State Board for Community and Junior Colleges *Accred.:* 1958/1990 (SACS-CC) *Calendar:* Sem. plan *Degrees:* A *CEO:* Pres. Horace C. Holmes
FTE Enroll: 1,492   (601) 276-2000

TOUGALOO COLLEGE
500 W. County Line Rd., Tougaloo 39174 *Type:* Private liberal arts *Accred.:* 1953/1990 (SACS-CC) *Calendar:* Sem. plan *Degrees:* A, B *CEO:* Pres. Joe A. Lee
FTE Enroll: 1,153   (601) 977-7700

UNIVERSITY OF MISSISSIPPI
109 Lyceum Bldg., University 38677 *Type:* Public (state) *System:* Mississippi Board of Trustees of State Institutions of Higher Learning *Accred.:* 1895/1989 (SACS-CC) *Calendar:* Sem. plan *Degrees:* B, M, D *Prof. Accred.:* Accounting (A,C), Art, Audiology, Business (B,M), Clinical Psychology, Computer Science, Engineering (chemical, civil, electrical, geological/geophysical, mechanical), Home Economics, Journalism (B,M), Law, Music, Nursing (B,M), Psychology Internship, Social Work (B), Speech-Language Pathology, Teacher Education *CEO:* Chanc. Robert C. Khayat
FTE Enroll: 9,883   (601) 232-7211

UNIVERSITY OF MISSISSIPPI MEDICAL CENTER
2500 N. State St., Jackson 39216-4505 *Type:* Public (state) *System:* Mississippi Board of Trustees of State Institutions of Higher Learning *Accred.:* 1991 (SACS-CC) *Calendar:* Qtr. plan *Degrees:* B, M, D *Prof. Accred.:* Clinical Lab Scientist, Cytotechnology, Dental Hygiene, Dentistry, EMT-Para-

medic, General Dentistry (prelim. provisional), General Practice Residency, Medical Record Administration, Medicine, Nuclear Medicine Technology, Occupational Therapy, Physical Therapy, Radiation Therapy Technology, Radiography, Respiratory Therapy *CEO:* Vice Chanc. A. Wallace Conerly
FTE Enroll: 1,758   (601) 984-1000

THE UNIVERSITY OF SOUTHERN MISSISSIPPI
Southern Sta., Box 5001, Hattiesburg 39406-5001 *Type:* Public (state) *System:* Mississippi Board of Trustees of State Institutions of Higher Learning *Accred.:* 1929/1995 (SACS-CC) *Calendar:* Sem. plan *Degrees:* B, M, D *Prof. Accred.:* Art, Audiology, Business (B,M), Clinical Lab Scientist, Clinical Psychology, Computer Science, Counseling, Counseling Psychology, Dance, Dietetics (coordinated), Engineering Technology (architectural, civil/construction, computer, electrical, industrial, mechanical), Home Economics, Interior Design, Journalism (B), Librarianship, Marriage and Family Therapy (M), Music, Nursing (B,M), Recreation and Leisure Services (B), School Psychology, Social Work (B-candidate,M), Speech-Language Pathology, Teacher Education, Theatre *CEO:* Pres. Aubrey K. Lucas
FTE Enroll: 10,465   (601) 266-4111

GULF PARK CAMPUS
E. Beach Blvd., Long Beach 39560 *Prof. Accred.:* Engineering Technology (electrical)
          (601) 865-4500

WESLEY BIBLICAL SEMINARY
5980 Floral Dr., Jackson 39206 *Type:* Private (interdenominational) graduate only *Accred.:* 1991/1994 (ATS) *Calendar:* Sem. plan *Degrees:* M *CEO:* Pres. Robert R. Lawrence
Enroll: 94   (601) 957-1314

WESLEY COLLEGE
111 Wesley Cir., P.O. Box 1070, Florence 39073 *Type:* Private (Congregational Methodist Church) *Accred.:* 1979/1989 (AABC)

Calendar: Sem. plan *Degrees:* B, C *CEO:* Pres. Samuel Bruce
FTE Enroll: 86   (601) 845-2265

WILLIAM CAREY COLLEGE
498 Tuscan Ave., Hattiesburg 39401-5499 *Type:* Private (Southern Baptist) liberal arts *Accred.:* 1958/1990 (SACS-CC) *Calendar:* Tri. plan *Degrees:* B, M *Prof. Accred.:* Music, Nursing (B) *CEO:* Pres. James W. Edwards
FTE Enroll: 2,194   (601) 582-5051

WOOD COLLEGE
Wood College Rd., Mathiston 39752 *Type:* Private (United Methodist) junior *Accred.:* 1956/1990 (SACS-CC) *Calendar:* Sem. plan *Degrees:* A *CEO:* Pres. Doyce Gunter
FTE Enroll: 476   (601) 263-5352

MISSOURI

AQUINAS INSTITUTE OF THEOLOGY
3642 Lindell Blvd., St. Louis 63108-3396
Type: Private (Roman Catholic) graduate only *Accred.:* 1968/1986 (ATS); 1964/1986 (NCA) *Calendar:* 4-1-4 plan *Degrees:* M, D
CEO: Pres. Charles E. Bouchard, O.P.
Enroll: 122   (314) 658-3882

ASSEMBLIES OF GOD THEOLOGICAL SEMINARY
1445 Boonville Ave., Springfield 65802
Type: Private (Assemblies of God) graduate only *Accred.:* 1992 (ATS); 1978/1995 (NCA) *Calendar:* 4-4-x plan *Degrees:* M
CEO: Pres. Delbert H. Tarr, Jr.
Enroll: 400   (417) 862-3344

AVILA COLLEGE
11901 Wornall Rd., Kansas City 64145
Type: Private (Roman Catholic) liberal arts *Accred.:* 1946/1988 (NCA) *Calendar:* Sem. plan *Degrees:* A, B, M, C *Prof. Accred.:* Clinical Lab Scientist, Nursing (B), Radiography, Social Work (B) *CEO:* Pres. Larry Kramer
Enroll: 1,429   (816) 942-8400

BAPTIST BIBLE COLLEGE
628 E. Kearney St., Springfield 65803 *Type:* Private (Baptist Bible Fellowship) *Accred.:* 1978/1988 (AABC) *Calendar:* Sem. plan *Degrees:* A, B, C *CEO:* Pres. Leland R. Kennedy
FTE Enroll: 797   (417) 869-9811

BARNES COLLEGE
416 S. Kingshighway Blvd., St. Louis 63110
Type: Private *Accred.:* 1994 (NCA) *Calendar:* Sem. plan *Degrees:* B *CEO:* Acting Chf. Admin. Ofcr. William Behrendt
Enroll: 443   (314) 362-5225

BEREAN UNIVERSITY
1445 Boonville Ave., Springfield 65802
Type: Private home study *Accred.:* 1985/1990 (DETC) *Degrees:* A, B, M *CEO:* Pres. Zenas J. Bicket
                                 (417) 862-2781

CALVARY BIBLE COLLEGE
15800 Calvary Rd., Kansas City 64147-1341
Type: Private (nondenominational) *Accred.:* 1961/1989 (AABC) *Calendar:* Sem. plan *Degrees:* A, B, C *CEO:* Interim Pres. Warren Bathke
FTE Enroll: 202   (816) 322-0110

CENTRAL BIBLE COLLEGE
3000 N. Grant Ave., Springfield 65803 *Type:* Private (Assemblies of God) *Accred.:* 1948/1985 (AABC) *Calendar:* Sem. plan *Degrees:* A, B, C *CEO:* Pres. H. Maurice Lednicky
FTE Enroll: 985   (417) 833-2551

CENTRAL CHRISTIAN COLLEGE OF THE BIBLE
911 Urbandale Dr. E., Moberly 65270 *Type:* Private (Christian Churches/Churches of Christ) *Accred.:* 1982/1992 (AABC) *Calendar:* Sem. plan *Degrees:* A, B, C *CEO:* Pres. Lloyd M. Pelfrey
FTE Enroll: 91   (816) 263-3900

CENTRAL METHODIST COLLEGE
Fayette 65248 *Type:* Private (United Methodist) liberal arts *Accred.:* 1913/1991 (NCA) *Calendar:* 4-1-4 plan *Degrees:* A, B *Prof. Accred.:* Music *CEO:* Pres. Marianne Inman
Enroll: 1,131   (816) 248-3391

CENTRAL MISSOURI STATE UNIVERSITY
Warrensburg 64093 *Type:* Public (state) liberal arts and teachers *System:* Missouri Coordinating Board for Higher Education *Accred.:* 1915/1994 (NCA) *Calendar:* Qtr. plan *Degrees:* A, B, M, P, C *Prof. Accred.:* Art, Audiology, Construction Education (B), Home Economics, Music, Nursing (B), Social Work (B), Speech-Language Pathology, Teacher Education *CEO:* Pres. Ed M. Elliott
Enroll: 10,805   (816) 543-4111

CLEVELAND CHIROPRACTIC COLLEGE
6401 Rockhill Rd., Kansas City 64131 *Type:* Private professional *Accred.:* 1984/1989 (NCA) *Calendar:* Tri. plan *Degrees:* D *Prof.*

Accred.: Chiropractic Education *CEO:* Pres. Carl S. Cleveland, III
Enroll: 502   (800) 274-0617

COLLEGE OF THE OZARKS
Point Lookout 65726 *Type:* Private (Presbyterian) liberal arts *Accred.:* 1961/ 1991 (NCA) *Calendar:* Tri. plan *Degrees:* B *Prof. Accred.:* Teacher Education *CEO:* Pres. Jerry C. Davis
Enroll: 1,541   (800) 222-0525

COLUMBIA COLLEGE
1001 Rogers St., Columbia 65216 *Type:* Private (Disciples of Christ) *Accred.:* 1918/ 1993 (NCA) *Calendar:* Sem. plan *Degrees:* A, B *Prof. Accred.:* Social Work (B) *CEO:* Pres. Gerald Brouder
Enroll: 6,337   (800) 231-2391

CONCEPTION SEMINARY COLLEGE
P.O. Box 502, Conception 64433 *Type:* Private (Roman Catholic) *Accred.:* 1960/1994 (NCA) *Calendar:* Sem. plan *Degrees:* B, C *CEO:* Pres./Rector Gregory J. Polan
Enroll: 80   (816) 944-2218

CONCORDIA SEMINARY
801 De Mun Ave., St. Louis 63105 *Type:* Private (Lutheran/Missouri Synod) graduate only *Accred.:* 1963/1993 (ATS); 1978/1994 (NCA) *Calendar:* Qtr. plan *Degrees:* M, D, C *CEO:* Pres. John Franklin Johnson
Enroll: 573   (314) 721-5934

COTTEY COLLEGE
1000 W. Austin St., Nevada 64772 *Type:* Private junior for women *Accred.:* 1918/ 1993 (NCA) *Calendar:* Sem. plan *Degrees:* A *Prof. Accred.:* Music *CEO:* Pres. Helen R. Washburn
Enroll: 356   (417) 667-8181

COVENANT THEOLOGICAL SEMINARY
12330 Conway Rd., St. Louis 63141 *Type:* Private (Presbyterian) graduate only *Accred.:* 1983/1987 (ATS); 1973/1988 (NCA) *Calendar:* Sem. plan *Degrees:* M, D, C *CEO:* Pres. Bryan Chapell
Enroll: 587   (314) 434-4044

CROWDER COLLEGE
601 Laclede, Neosho 64850 *Type:* Public (district) junior *System:* Missouri Coordinating Board for Higher Education *Accred.:* 1977/1992 (NCA) *Calendar:* Sem. plan *Degrees:* A, C *CEO:* Pres. Kent Farnsworth
Enroll: 1,702   (417) 451-3223

CULVER-STOCKTON COLLEGE
Canton 63435 *Type:* Private (Disciples of Christ) liberal arts *Accred.:* 1924/1992 (NCA) *Calendar:* Sem. plan *Degrees:* B *CEO:* Pres. Edwin B. Strong, Jr.
Enroll: 1,057   (217) 231-6000

DEACONESS COLLEGE OF NURSING
6150 Oakland Ave., St. Louis 63139 *Type:* Private professional *Accred.:* 1985/1990 (NCA) *Calendar:* Sem. plan *Degrees:* A, B *Prof. Accred.:* Nursing (B) *CEO:* Pres. Elizabeth Anne Krekorian
Enroll: 405   (314) 768-3044

DEVRY INSTITUTE OF TECHNOLOGY—KANSAS CITY
11224 Holmes Rd., Kansas City 64131 *Type:* Private *System:* DeVry Institutes *Accred.:* 1981/1992 (NCA) *Calendar:* Sem. plan *Degrees:* A, B *Prof. Accred.:* Engineering Technology (electrical) *CEO:* Pres. Charles Robert Levalley
                    (816) 941-0430

* Indirect NCA accreditation through DeVry Institutes

DRURY COLLEGE
900 N. Benton Ave., Springfield 65802 *Type:* Private (United Church of Christ) liberal arts *Accred.:* 1915/1991 (NCA) *Calendar:* Sem. plan *Degrees:* A, B, M *Prof. Accred.:* Teacher Education *CEO:* Pres. John E. Moore, Jr.
Enroll: 3,429   (417) 873-7879

FORT LEONARD WOOD CAMPUS
Truman Ed. Ctr., Bldg. 499, Fort Leonard Wood 65473
                    (314) 873-7399

EAST CENTRAL COLLEGE
P.O. Box 529, Union 63084 *Type:* Public
(district) junior *System:* Missouri Coordinating Board for Higher Education *Accred.:*
1976/1990 (NCA) *Calendar:* Sem. plan
Degrees: A, C *Prof. Accred.:* Dental Assisting *CEO:* Pres. Dale L. Gibson
Enroll: 3,051   (314) 583-5193

EDEN THEOLOGICAL SEMINARY
475 E. Lockwood Ave., St. Louis 63119-
3192 *Type:* Private (United Church of
Christ) graduate only *Accred.:* 1938/1988
(ATS); 1973/1989 (NCA) *Calendar:* 4-1-4
plan *Degrees:* M, D, C *CEO:* Pres. Charles
R. Kniker
Enroll: 235   (314) 961-3627

ELECTRONIC INSTITUTE
15329 Kensington Ave., Kansas City 64147-
1212 *Type:* Private *Accred.:* 1971/1987
(ACCSCT) *Calendar:* Qtr. plan *Degrees:* A
CEO: Pres./Owner Jeff Freeman
(816) 331-5700

EVANGEL COLLEGE
1111 N. Glenstone Ave., Springfield 65802
Type: Private (Assemblies of God) liberal
arts *Accred.:* 1965/1988 (NCA) *Calendar:*
Sem. plan *Degrees:* A, B *Prof. Accred.:*
Music, Teacher Education *CEO:* Pres.
Robert H. Spence
Enroll: 1,541   (417) 865-2811

FONTBONNE COLLEGE
6800 Wydown Blvd., St. Louis 63105 *Type:*
Private (Roman Catholic) liberal arts
Accred.: 1926/1993 (NCA) *Calendar:* Sem.
plan *Degrees:* B, M *Prof. Accred.:* Home
Economics, Speech-Language Pathology
CEO: Pres. Dennis C. Golden
Enroll: 1,681   (314) 862-3456

FOREST INSTITUTE OF PROFESSIONAL
PSYCHOLOGY
1322 S. Campbell Ave., Springfield 65807
Type: Private *Accred.:* 1983/1994 (NCA)
Calendar: Tri. plan *Degrees:* M, D *CEO:*
Pres. Richard H. Cox
Enroll: 157   (800) 424-7793

HANNIBAL-LAGRANGE COLLEGE
2800 Palmyra Rd., Hannibal 63401 *Type:*
Private (Southern Baptist) liberal arts
Accred.: 1958/1993 (NCA) *Calendar:* Sem.
plan *Degrees:* A, B, C *Prof. Accred.:* Nurs-
ing (A) *CEO:* Interim Pres. Woodrow W.
Burt
Enroll: 931   (314) 221-3675

HARRIS-STOWE STATE COLLEGE
3026 Laclede Ave., St. Louis 63103 *Type:*
Public (state) teachers *System:* Missouri
Coordinating Board for Higher Education
Accred.: 1924/1991 (NCA) *Calendar:* Sem.
plan *Degrees:* B *Prof. Accred.:* Teacher Edu-
cation *CEO:* Pres. Henry Givens, Jr.
Enroll: 1,909   (314) 340-3366

HICKEY SCHOOL
940 W. Port Plaza, St. Louis 63146 *Type:*
Private business *Accred.:* 1971/1995
(ACICS) *Degrees:* A, C *CEO:* Pres. Joyce
Johnson
(314) 434-2212

ITT TECHNICAL INSTITUTE
13505 Lakefront Dr., Earth City 63045-1416
Type: Private *Accred.:* 1965/1988 (ACC-
SCT) *Degrees:* A, B *CEO:* Dir. Karen
Finkenkeller
(314) 298-7800

MEMPHIS CAMPUS
1255 Lynnfield Rd., Ste. 192, Memphis,
TN 38119 *Accred.:* 1994 (ACCSCT) *Calendar:* Qtr. plan
Enroll: 180   (901) 762-0556

OMAHA CAMPUS
9814 M St., Omaha, NE 68127-2056
Accred.: 1991 (ACCSCT)
(402) 331-2900

JEFFERSON COLLEGE
1000 Viking Dr., Hillsboro 63050-1000
Type: Public (district) junior *System:* Mis-
souri Coordinating Board for Higher Educa-
tion *Accred.:* 1969/1989 (NCA) *Calendar:*
Sem. plan *Degrees:* A, C *Prof. Accred.:*
Music (A), Veterinary Technology *CEO:*
Pres. Gregory D. Adkins
Enroll: 3,962   (314) 789-3951

JEWISH HOSPITAL COLLEGE OF NURSING AND
ALLIED HEALTH
  306 S. Kingshighway Blvd., St. Louis 63110-
  1091 *Type:* Private professional *Accred.:*
  1995 (NCA) *Calendar:* Sem. plan *Degrees:*
  A, B, C *CEO:* Pres. Sharon L. Pontius
  Enroll: 371   (314) 454-7055

KANSAS CITY ART INSTITUTE
  4415 Warwick Blvd., Kansas City 64111
  Type: Private professional *Accred.:* 1964/
  1990 (NCA) *Calendar:* Sem. plan *Degrees:*
  B *Prof. Accred.:* Art *CEO:* Interim Pres.
  Ronald E. Cattelino
  Enroll: 559   (816) 561-4852

KEMPER MILITARY SCHOOL AND COLLEGE
  701 Third St., Boonville 65233 *Type:* Private
  junior for men *Accred.:* 1927/1990 (NCA)
  Calendar: Sem. plan *Degrees:* A *CEO:* Pres.
  Charles W. Stewart
  Enroll: 255   (816) 882-5623

KENRICK-GLENNON SEMINARY
  5200 Glennon Dr., St. Louis 63119-4399
  Type: Private (Roman Catholic) graduate
  only *Accred.:* 1973/1989 (ATS); 1964/1989
  (NCA) *Calendar:* Sem. plan *Degrees:* M
  CEO: Pres./Rector George J. Lucas
  Enroll: 53   (314) 644-0266

KIRKSVILLE COLLEGE OF OSTEOPATHIC
MEDICINE
  800 W. Jefferson Ave., Kirksville 63501
  Type: Private professional *Accred.:* 1994
  (NCA) *Calendar:* Qtr. plan *Degrees:* D *Prof.
  Accred.:* Osteopathy *CEO:* Pres. Fred C.
  Tinning
  Enroll: 584   (816) 626-2121

LINCOLN UNIVERSITY
  820 Chestnut St., Jefferson City 65102-0029
  Type: Public (state) liberal arts and profes-
  sional *System:* Missouri Coordinating Board
  for Higher Education *Accred.:* 1926/1993
  (NCA) *Calendar:* Sem. plan *Degrees:* A, B,
  M *Prof. Accred.:* Music, Nursing (A),
  Teacher Education *CEO:* Pres. Wendell G.
  Rayburn, Sr.
  Enroll: 3,512   (314) 681-5000

LINDENWOOD COLLEGE
  209 S. Kingshighway Blvd., St. Charles
  63301 *Type:* Private (United Presbyterian)
  liberal arts *Accred.:* 1918/1994 (NCA) *Calendar:* 4-1-4 plan *Degrees:* B, M *Prof.
  Accred.:* Teacher Education *CEO:* Pres.
  Dennis C. Spellmann
  Enroll: 2,362   (314) 949-2000

LOGAN COLLEGE OF CHIROPRACTIC
  1851 Schoettler Rd., P.O. Box 1065,
  Chesterfield 63006-1065 *Type:* Private pro-
  fessional *Accred.:* 1987/1992 (NCA) *Calen-
  dar:* Sem. plan *Degrees:* B, D *Prof. Accred.:*
  Chiropractic Education *CEO:* Pres. George
  A. Goodman
  Enroll: 777   (800) 782-3344

LONGVIEW COMMUNITY COLLEGE
  500 Longview Rd., Lee's Summit 64081
  Type: Public (district) junior *System:* Metro-
  politan Community College District
  Accred.: 1986 (NCA) *Calendar:* Sem. plan
  Degrees: A, C *CEO:* Pres. Aldo W. Leker
                                   (816) 672-2000

* Indirect NCA accreditation through Metropolitan Community College District

MAPLE WOODS COMMUNITY COLLEGE
  2601 N.E. Barry Rd., Kansas City 64156
  Type: Public (district) junior *System:* Metro-
  politan Community College District
  Accred.: 1986 (NCA) *Calendar:* Sem. plan
  Degrees: A, C *Prof. Accred.:* Veterinary
  Technology *CEO:* Pres. Stephen R. Brainard
                                   (816) 437-3000

* Indirect NCA accreditation through Metropolitan Community College District

MARYVILLE UNIVERSITY OF ST. LOUIS
  13550 Conway Rd., St. Louis 63141-7299
  Type: Private liberal arts *Accred.:* 1941/1995
  (NCA) *Calendar:* 4-4-x plan *Degrees:* B, M,
  C *Prof. Accred.:* Art (A), Interior Design,
  Nursing (B), Physical Therapy, Teacher Edu-
  cation *CEO:* Pres. Keith H. Lovin
  Enroll: 3,425   (314) 529-9300

METRO BUSINESS COLLEGE
1732 N. Kingshighway Blvd., Cape Girardeau 63701 *Type:* Private business *Accred.:* 1979/1997 (ACICS) *Degrees:* A, C *Prof. Accred.:* Medical Assisting *CEO:* Dir. Mary Emmerderfer
(314) 334-9181

JEFFERSON CITY CAMPUS
1407 Southwest Blvd., Jefferson City 65109 *Accred.:* 1986 (ACICS) *Prof. Accred.:* Medical Assisting
(314) 635-6600

ROLLA CAMPUS
1202 E. Hwy. 72, Rolla 65401 business *Accred.:* 1985/1990 (ACICS) *Prof. Accred.:* Medical Assisting
(314) 364-8464

MIDWESTERN BAPTIST THEOLOGICAL SEMINARY
5001 N. Oak St. Trafficway, Kansas City 64118 *Type:* Private (Southern Baptist) *Accred.:* 1964/1992 (ATS); 1971/1992 (NCA) *Calendar:* Sem. plan *Degrees:* A, M, D *CEO:* Pres. Mark Coppenger
Enroll: 441   (816) 453-4600

MINERAL AREA COLLEGE
P.O. Box 1000, Hwy. 67 and 32, Park Hills 63601 *Type:* Public (district) junior *System:* Missouri Coordinating Board for Higher Education *Accred.:* 1971/1988 (NCA) *Calendar:* Sem. plan *Degrees:* A, C *Prof. Accred.:* Dental Assisting *CEO:* Pres. Dixie A. Kohn
Enroll: 2,588   (314) 431-4593

MISSOURI BAPTIST COLLEGE
One College Park Dr., St. Louis 63141-8698 *Type:* Private (Southern Baptist) liberal arts *Accred.:* 1978/1990 (NCA) *Calendar:* Sem. plan *Degrees:* A, B, C *CEO:* Pres. R. Alton Lacey
Enroll: 1,913   (314) 434-1115

MISSOURI COLLEGE
10121 Manchester Rd., St. Louis 63122-1583 *Type:* Private *Accred.:* 1970/1988 (ACCSCT) *Degrees:* A *Prof. Accred.:* Med-

ical Assisting *CEO:* Assoc. Dir. Michael Vander Velde
(314) 821-7700

MISSOURI SOUTHERN STATE COLLEGE
3950 E. Newman Rd., Joplin 64801-1595 *Type:* Public (state) liberal arts and teachers *System:* Missouri Coordinating Board for Higher Education *Accred.:* 1949/1988 (NCA) *Calendar:* Sem. plan *Degrees:* A, B *Prof. Accred.:* Dental Hygiene, Nursing (A,B), Radiography, Teacher Education *CEO:* Pres. Julio S. Leon
Enroll: 5,334   (417) 624-9300

MISSOURI TECHNICAL SCHOOL
1167 Corporate Lake Dr., St. Louis 63132-2907 *Type:* Private *Accred.:* 1985/1990 (ACCSCT) *Degrees:* A, B *CEO:* Dir. Paul C. Dodge
(314) 569-3600

MISSOURI VALLEY COLLEGE
500 E. College Dr., Marshall 65340 *Type:* Private (Presbyterian) liberal arts *Accred.:* 1916/1992 (NCA) *Calendar:* Sem. plan *Degrees:* A, B *CEO:* Pres. J. Kenneth Bryant
Enroll: 1,297   (816) 886-6924

MISSOURI WESTERN STATE COLLEGE
4525 Downs Dr., St. Joseph 64507 *Type:* Public (state) *System:* Missouri Coordinating Board for Higher Education *Accred.:* 1919/1990 (NCA) *Calendar:* Sem. plan *Degrees:* A, B, C *Prof. Accred.:* Engineering Technology (civil/construction, electrical), Music, Nursing (B), Social Work (B), Teacher Education *CEO:* Pres. Janet G. Murphy
Enroll: 5,124   (816) 271-4200

MOBERLY AREA COMMUNITY COLLEGE
College and Rollins Sts., Moberly 65270 *Type:* Public (district) junior *System:* Missouri Coordinating Board for Higher Education *Accred.:* 1980/1992 (NCA) *Calendar:* Sem. plan *Degrees:* A, C *CEO:* Pres. Andrew Komar, Jr.
Enroll: 1,613   (816) 263-4110

NAZARENE THEOLOGICAL SEMINARY
1700 E. Meyer Blvd., Kansas City 64131 *Type:* Private (Nazarene) graduate only

Accred.: 1970/1989 (ATS) *Calendar:* Sem. plan *Degrees:* M, D *CEO:* Pres. A. Gordon Wetmore
Enroll: 277   (816) 333-6254

NORTH CENTRAL MISSOURI COLLEGE
1301 Main St., Trenton 64683 *Type:* Public (district) junior *System:* Missouri Coordinating Board for Higher Education *Accred.:* 1983/1992 (NCA) *Calendar:* Sem. plan *Degrees:* A, C *CEO:* Pres. James E. Selby
Enroll: 1,142   (816) 359-3948

NORTHEAST MISSOURI STATE UNIVERSITY
200 McClain Hall, Kirksville 63501-9980 *Type:* Public (state) liberal arts and teachers *System:* Missouri Coordinating Board for Higher Education *Accred.:* 1914/1995 (NCA) *Calendar:* Sem. plan *Degrees:* B, M *Prof. Accred.:* Counseling, Music, Nursing (B), Speech-Language Pathology, Teacher Education *CEO:* Interim Pres. W. Jack Magruder
Enroll: 6,317   (816) 785-4000

NORTHWEST MISSOURI STATE UNIVERSITY
800 University Dr., Maryville 64468-6001 *Type:* Public (state) liberal arts and teachers *System:* Missouri Coordinating Board for Higher Education *Accred.:* 1921/1988 (NCA) *Calendar:* Sem. plan *Degrees:* B, M, P, C *Prof. Accred.:* Home Economics, Music, Teacher Education *CEO:* Pres. L. Hubbard
Enroll: 5,901   (816) 562-1212

OZARK CHRISTIAN COLLEGE
1111 N. Main St., Joplin 64801 *Type:* Private (Christian Churches/Churches of Christ) *Accred.:* 1988/1994 (AABC) *Calendar:* Sem. plan *Degrees:* A, B, C *CEO:* Pres. Kenneth Idleman
FTE Enroll: 527   (417) 624-2518

OZARKS TECHNICAL COMMUNITY COLLEGE
1417 N. Jefferson Ave., Springfield 65802 *Type:* Public (district) 2-year *System:* Missouri Coordinating Board for Higher Education *Accred.:* 1992/1994 (NCA candidate) *Calendar:* Sem. plan *Degrees:* A, C *Prof. Accred.:* Dental Assisting, Medical Record Technology, Respiratory Therapy, Respira-

tory Therapy Technology *CEO:* Pres. Norman K. Myers
Enroll: 2,934   (417) 895-7000

PARK COLLEGE
8700 River Park Dr., Parkville 64152 *Type:* Private (Latter-Day Saints) liberal arts *Accred.:* 1913/1995 (NCA) *Calendar:* 4-1-4 plan *Degrees:* A, B, M *CEO:* Pres. Donald J. Breckon
Enroll: 8,494   (816) 741-2000

FORD MOTOR COMPANY ON-SITE PROGRAM
KC City Assembly Plant, P.O. Box 11009, Kansas City 64119
                                (816) 459-1138

GRADUATE SCHOOL OF RELIGION CAMPUS
P.O. Box 1059, Independence 64051-1059
                                (816) 833-1000

INDEPENDENCE CAMPUS
2200 S. 291 Hwy., Independence 64057
                                (816) 252-9065

METROPARK CAMPUS
934 Wyandotte St., Kansas City 64105-1630
                                (816) 842-6182

PATRICIA STEVENS COLLEGE
1415 Olive St., St. Louis 63103 *Type:* Private business *Accred.:* 1968/1988 (ACICS) *Calendar:* Qtr. plan *Degrees:* A, C *CEO:* Exec. Dir. Richard R. Harvey
                                (314) 421-0949

PENN VALLEY COMMUNITY COLLEGE
3201 S.W. Trafficway, Kansas City 64111 *Type:* Public (district) junior *System:* Metropolitan Community College District *Accred.:* 1986 (NCA) *Calendar:* Sem. plan *Degrees:* A, C *Prof. Accred.:* Medical Record Technology, Nursing (A), Occupational Therapy Assisting, Physical Therapy Assisting, Radiography *CEO:* Pres. E. Paul Williams
                                (816) 759-4000

* Indirect NCA accreditation through Metropolitan Community College District

PHILLIPS JUNIOR COLLEGE
1010 W. Sunshine St., Springfield 65807
Type: Private junior *Accred.:* 1981/1994
(ACICS) *Calendar:* Qtr. plan *Degrees:* A
Prof. Accred.: Medical Assisting (AMA)
CEO: Pres. Barbara Loven
(417) 864-7220

RANKEN TECHNICAL COLLEGE
4431 Finney Ave., St. Louis 63113 *Type:* Private *Accred.:* 1989/1994 (NCA) *Calendar:*
Tri. plan *Degrees:* A, C *CEO:* Pres. Ben H.
Ernst
Enroll: 1,511   (314) 371-0236

RESEARCH COLLEGE OF NURSING
2316 E. Meyer Blvd., Kansas City 64132
Type: Private professional *Accred.:* 1987/
1992 (NCA) *Calendar:* Sem. plan *Degrees:*
B *Prof. Accred.:* Nursing (B) *CEO:* Dean
Nancy O. Debasio
Enroll: 247   (816) 276-4700

ROCKHURST COLLEGE
1100 Rockhurst Rd., Kansas City 64110
Type: Private (Roman Catholic) liberal arts
Accred.: 1934/1993 (NCA) *Calendar:* Sem.
plan *Degrees:* B, M *Prof. Accred.:* Nursing
(B), Occupational Therapy, Physical Therapy *CEO:* Pres. Thomas J. Savage, S.J.
Enroll: 2,658   (816) 926-4000

ST. CHARLES COUNTY COMMUNITY COLLEGE
4601 Mid Rivers Mall Dr., P.O. Box 76975,
St. Peters 63376 *Type:* Public (district)
junior *System:* Missouri Coordinating Board
for Higher Education *Accred.:* 1991 (NCA)
Calendar: Sem. plan *Degrees:* A, C *Prof.*
Accred.: Medical Record Technology, Nursing (A) *CEO:* Pres. Donald D. Shook
Enroll: 4,567   (314) 922-8000

ST. LOUIS CHRISTIAN COLLEGE
1360 Grandview Dr., Florissant 63033 *Type:*
Private (Christian Churches/Churches of
Christ) *Accred.:* 1977/1987 (AABC) *Calendar:* Sem. plan *Degrees:* A, B, C *CEO:* Pres.
Kenneth Beck
FTE Enroll: 143   (314) 837-6777

ST. LOUIS COLLEGE OF PHARMACY
4588 Parkview Pl., St. Louis 63110 *Type:*
Private professional *Accred.:* 1967/1987
(NCA) *Calendar:* Sem. plan *Degrees:* B, M,
D *CEO:* Pres. Thomas F. Patton
Enroll: 799   (314) 367-8700

ST. LOUIS COMMUNITY COLLEGE AT FLORISSANT VALLEY
3400 Pershall Rd., Ferguson 63135 *Type:*
Public (district) junior *System:* St. Louis
Community College District *Accred.:* 1988
(NCA) *Calendar:* Sem. plan *Degrees:* A, C
Prof. Accred.: Art, civil/construction)
mechanical) *CEO:* Pres. Irving P. McPhail
(314) 595-4200

* Indirect NCA accreditation through St. Louis
Community College District

ST. LOUIS COMMUNITY COLLEGE AT FOREST PARK
5600 Oakland Ave., St. Louis 63110 *Type:*
Public (district) junior *System:* St. Louis
Community College District *Accred.:* 1988
(NCA) *Calendar:* Sem. plan *Degrees:* A, C
Prof. Accred.: Clinical Lab Technology (A),
Dental Hygiene, Diagnostic Medical Sonography, Funeral Service Education (Mortuary
Science), Nursing (A), Radiography, Respiratory Therapy, Surgical Technology *CEO:*
Pres. Henry D. Shannon
(314) 644-9100

* Indirect NCA accreditation through St. Louis
Community College District

ST. LOUIS COMMUNITY COLLEGE AT MERAMEC
11333 Big Bend Blvd., Kirkwood 63122
Type: Public (district) junior *System:* St.
Louis Community College District *Accred.:*
1988 (NCA) *Calendar:* Sem. plan *Degrees:*
A, C *Prof. Accred.:* Dental Laboratory Technology, Nursing (A), Occupational Therapy
Assisting, Physical Therapy Assisting *CEO:*
Pres. Richard A. Black
(314) 984-7500

* Indirect NCA accreditation through St. Louis
Community College District

ST. LOUIS UNIVERSITY
221 N. Grand Blvd., St. Louis 63103 *Type:* Private (Roman Catholic) *Accred.:* 1916/1992 (NCA) *Calendar:* Sem. plan *Degrees:* A, B, M, P, D, C *Prof. Accred.:* Business (B,M), Clinical Lab Scientist, Clinical Psychology, Dietetics (internship), Health Services Administration, Law, Medical Record Administration, Medicine, Nuclear Medicine Technology, Nursing (B,M), Occupational Therapy, Orthodontics, Perfusion, Physical Therapy, Physician Assisting/Surgeon Assisting, Public Administration, Social Work (B,M), Speech-Language Pathology, Teacher Education *CEO:* Pres. Lawrence Biondi, S.J.
Enroll: 11,317   (314) 658-2222

PARKS COLLEGE
Falling Springs Rd., Cahokia, IL 62206 *Prof. Accred.:* Engineering (aerospace, electrical)
                    (618) 337-7500

ST. LUKE'S COLLEGE
4426 Wornall Rd., Kansas City 64111 *Type:* Private liberal arts *Accred.:* 1994 (NCA) *Calendar:* Sem. plan *Degrees:* B *CEO:* Pres. Helen A. Jepson
Enroll: 108   (816) 932-2233

ST. PAUL SCHOOL OF THEOLOGY
5123 Truman Rd., Kansas City 64127 *Type:* Private (United Methodist) graduate only *Accred.:* 1964/1991 (ATS); 1976/1992 (NCA) *Calendar:* Sem. plan *Degrees:* M, D *CEO:* Pres. Lovett H. Weems, Jr.
Enroll: 288   (816) 483-9600

SANFORD-BROWN COLLEGE
12006 Manchester Rd., Des Peres 63131 *Type:* Private business *Accred.:* 1982/1994 (ACICS); 1992 (NCA candidate) *Calendar:* Sem. plan *Degrees:* A, C *Prof. Accred.:* Medical Assisting *CEO:* Dir. Christa Jones
                    (314) 822-7100

GRANITE CITY CAMPUS
3237 W. Chain of Rocks Rd., Granite City, IL 62040 business *Accred.:* 1988/1994

(ACICS) *Degrees:* A, C *Prof. Accred.:* Medical Assisting
                    (618) 931-0300

HAZELWOOD, MISSOURI CAMPUS
355 Brooks Dr., Hazelwood 63042 *Accred.:* 1990 (ACICS) *Degrees:* A, C *Prof. Accred.:* Medical Assisting, Occupational Therapy Assisting, Physical Therapy Assisting
                    (314) 731-1101

KANSAS CITY, MISSOURI CAMPUS
2702 Rockcreek Pkwy., Ste. 300, North Kansas City 64117 *Accred.:* 1992 (ACICS)
                    (816) 221-6463

ST. CHARLES, MISSOURI CAMPUS
3555 Franks Dr., St. Charles 63301 *Accred.:* 1988 (ACICS) *Degrees:* A, C *Prof. Accred.:* Medical Assisting
                    (314) 724-7100

SOUTHEAST MISSOURI STATE UNIVERSITY
One University Plaza, Cape Girardeau 63701 *Type:* Public (state) liberal arts and teachers *System:* Missouri Coordinating Board for Higher Education *Accred.:* 1915/1991 (NCA) *Calendar:* Sem. plan *Degrees:* A, B, M, P, C *Prof. Accred.:* Music, Nursing (A,B), Recreation and Leisure Services (B), Social Work (B), Speech-Language Pathology, Teacher Education *CEO:* Pres. William L. Atchley
Enroll: 7,921   (314) 651-2000

SOUTHWEST BAPTIST UNIVERSITY
1600 University Ave., Bolivar 65613-2496 *Type:* Private (Southern Baptist) liberal arts *Accred.:* 1957/1990 (NCA) *Calendar:* Sem. plan *Degrees:* A, B, M, C *Prof. Accred.:* Music *CEO:* Pres. Roy Blunt
Enroll: 3,202   (417) 326-5281

SOUTHWEST MISSOURI STATE UNIVERSITY
901 S. National Ave., Springfield 65804 *Type:* Public (state) liberal arts and teachers *System:* Missouri Coordinating Board for Higher Education *Accred.:* 1915/1986 (NCA) *Calendar:* Sem. plan *Degrees:* A, B, M, P, C *Prof. Accred.:* Accounting (A,C),

Athletic Training, Audiology (candidate), Business (B,M), Computer Science, Home Economics, Music, Nursing (A,B), Public Administration, Recreation and Leisure Services (B), Social Work (B), Speech-Language Pathology, Teacher Education *CEO:* Pres. John H. Keiser
Enroll: 17,210   (800) 492-7900

WEST PLAINS CAMPUS
128 Garfield, West Plains 65775 *Accred.:* 1994 (NCA) *Calendar:* Sem. plan *Degrees:* A
Enroll: 990   (417) 256-5761

STATE FAIR COMMUNITY COLLEGE
3201 W. 16th St., Sedalia 65301 *Type:* Public (district) junior *System:* Missouri Coordinating Board for Higher Education *Accred.:* 1977/1989 (NCA) *Calendar:* Sem. plan *Degrees:* A, C *Prof. Accred.:* Respiratory Therapy Technology *CEO:* Pres. Marvin R. Fielding
Enroll: 2,384   (816) 530-5800

STEPHENS COLLEGE
Columbia 65215 *Type:* Private liberal arts *Accred.:* 1918/1988 (NCA) *Calendar:* Sem. plan *Degrees:* A, B, C *Prof. Accred.:* Medical Record Administration *CEO:* Pres. Marcia Kierscht
Enroll: 962   (314) 876-7100

THREE RIVERS COMMUNITY COLLEGE
2080 Three Rivers Blvd., Poplar Bluff 63901 *Type:* Public (district) junior *System:* Missouri Coordinating Board for Higher Education *Accred.:* 1974/1987 (NCA) *Calendar:* Sem. plan *Degrees:* A, C *Prof. Accred.:* Clinical Lab Technology (A), Nursing (A) *CEO:* Pres. Stephen M. Poort
Enroll: 2,405   (314) 840-9600

THE UNIVERSITY OF HEALTH SCIENCES
2105 Independence Blvd., Kansas City 64124 *Type:* Private professional *Calendar:* Tri. plan *Degrees:* P *Prof. Accred.:* Osteopathy *CEO:* Pres. John P. Perrin
Enroll: 500   (816) 283-2000

UNIVERSITY OF MISSOURI—COLUMBIA
105 Jesse Hall, Columbia 65211 *Type:* Public (state) *System:* University of Missouri System *Accred.:* 1913/1995 (NCA) *Calendar:* Sem. plan *Degrees:* B, M, P, D *Prof. Accred.:* Accounting (A,C), Business (B,M), Clinical Psychology, Counseling Psychology, Dietetics (coordinated), Engineering (agricultural, chemical, civil, computer, electrical, industrial, mechanical), Forestry, Health Services Administration, Interior Design, Journalism (B,M), Law, Librarianship, Medicine, Music, Nuclear Medicine Technology, Nursing (B,M), Occupational Therapy, Physical Therapy, Psychology Internship, Public Administration, Radiography, Recreation and Leisure Services, Rehabilitation Counseling, Respiratory Therapy, Social Work (B,M), Speech-Language Pathology, Veterinary Medicine *CEO:* Chanc. Charles A. Kiesler
Enroll: 22,175   (314) 882-2121

UNIVERSITY OF MISSOURI—KANSAS CITY
5100 Rockhill Rd., Kansas City 64110 *Type:* Public (state) *System:* University of Missouri System *Accred.:* 1938/1989 (NCA) *Calendar:* Sem. plan *Degrees:* B, M, P, D, C *Prof. Accred.:* Business (B,M), Combined Prosthodontics, Counseling Psychology, Dental Hygiene, Dentistry, Engineering (civil, electrical, mechanical), General Dentistry, General Practice Residency (prelim. provisional), Law, Maxillofacial Prosthodontics, Medicine, Music, Nurse Anesthesia Education, Nursing (B,M), Oral and Maxillofacial Surgery, Orthodontics, Pediatric Dentistry, Periodontics, Psychology Internship, Public Administration, Teacher Education, Theatre *CEO:* Chanc. Eleanor B. Schwartz
Enroll: 9,962   (816) 235-1000

UNIVERSITY OF MISSOURI—ROLLA
206 Parker Hall, Rolla 65401 *Type:* Public (state) *System:* University of Missouri System *Accred.:* 1913/1989 (NCA) *Calendar:* Sem. plan *Degrees:* B, M, D *Prof. Accred.:* Computer Science, Engineering (aerospace, ceramic, chemical, civil, electrical, engineering management, geological/geophysical,

mechanical, metallurgical, mining, nuclear) *CEO:* Chanc. John T. Park
Enroll: 5,472   (314) 341-4114

UNIVERSITY OF MISSOURI—ST. LOUIS
8001 Natural Bridge Rd., St. Louis 63121 *Type:* Public (state) *System:* University of Missouri System *Accred.:* 1960/1989 (NCA) *Calendar:* Sem. plan *Degrees:* B, M, D *Prof. Accred.:* Business (B,M), Clinical Psychology, Music (A), Nursing (B), Optometry, Public Administration, Social Work (B), Teacher Education *CEO:* Chanc. Blanche M. Touhill
Enroll: 15,588   (314) 516-5000

VATTEROTT COLLEGE
3925 Industrial Dr., St. Ann 63074-1807 *Type:* Private *Accred.:* 1982/1987 (ACC-SCT) *Degrees:* A *CEO:* Dir. Turner Brooks
                         (314) 428-5900

INDEPENDENCE CAMPUS
210 S. Main St., Independence 64050 *Accred.:* 1987 (ACCSCT)
                         (816) 252-3997

JOPLIN CAMPUS
Rte. 3, Box 834, Joplin 64801 *Accred.:* 1987 (ACCSCT)
                         (417) 781-5633

SPRINGFIELD CAMPUS
1258 E. Trafficway, Springfield 65801 *Accred.:* 1987 (ACCSCT)
                         (417) 831-8116

WASHINGTON UNIVERSITY
One Brookings Dr., Box 1192, St. Louis 63130 *Type:* Private *Accred.:* 1913/1994 (NCA) *Calendar:* Sem. plan *Degrees:* B, M, D, C *Prof. Accred.:* Art, Audiology, Business (B,M), Clinical Psychology, Engineering (chemical, civil, computer, electrical, general, mechanical, systems), Health Services Administration, Law, Medicine, Occupa-

tional Therapy, Physical Therapy, Social Work (M), Speech-Language Pathology *CEO:* Chanc. Mark S. Wrighton
Enroll: 11,655   (314) 935-5000

WEBSTER UNIVERSITY
470 E. Lockwood Ave., St. Louis 63119 *Type:* Private liberal arts *Accred.:* 1925/1988 (NCA) *Calendar:* Sem. plan *Degrees:* B, M, D, C *Prof. Accred.:* Music, Nursing (B) *CEO:* Pres. Richard S. Meyers
Enroll: 10,834   (314) 968-6900

WENTWORTH MILITARY ACADEMY AND JUNIOR COLLEGE
Washington Ave., Lexington 64067 *Type:* Private junior *Accred.:* 1930/1991 (NCA) *Calendar:* Sem. plan *Degrees:* A, C *CEO:* Supt. Jerry E. Brown
Enroll: 827   (816) 259-2221

WESTMINSTER COLLEGE
501 Westminster Ave., Fulton 65251-1299 *Type:* Private (Presbyterian) liberal arts *Accred.:* 1913/1995 (NCA) *Calendar:* Sem. plan *Degrees:* B *CEO:* Pres. James F. Traer
Enroll: 667   (314) 642-3361

WILLIAM JEWELL COLLEGE
500 College Hill, Liberty 64068 *Type:* Private (Southern Baptist) liberal arts *Accred.:* 1915/1991 (NCA) *Calendar:* 4-1-4 plan *Degrees:* B *Prof. Accred.:* Music, Nursing (B) *CEO:* Pres. W. Christian Sizemore
Enroll: 1,735   (816) 781-7700

WILLIAM WOODS UNIVERSITY
200 W. 12th St., Fulton 65251 *Type:* Private (Disciples of Christ) liberal arts for women *Accred.:* 1919/1987 (NCA) *Calendar:* Sem. plan *Degrees:* A, B, M *Prof. Accred.:* Social Work (B) *CEO:* Pres. Jahnae H. Barnett
Enroll: 900   (314) 642-2251

MONTANA

BILLINGS BUSINESS COLLEGE
2520 Fifth Ave., S., Billings 59101 *Type:* Private business *Accred.:* 1990/1996 (ACICS) *Degrees:* A, C *CEO:* Pres. James Anderson
(406) 256-1000

BLACKFEET COMMUNITY COLLEGE
P.O. Box 819, Browning 59417 *Type:* Private (tribal) junior *Accred.:* 1985/1995 (NASC probational) *Calendar:* Qtr. plan *Degrees:* A *CEO:* Pres. Carol Murray
Enroll: 565   (406) 338-2587

CARROLL COLLEGE
1601 N. Benton Avenue, Helena 59625 *Type:* Private (Roman Catholic) liberal arts *Accred.:* 1949/1994 (NASC) *Calendar:* Sem. plan *Degrees:* B *Prof. Accred.:* Medical Record Administration, Nursing (B), Social Work (B) *CEO:* Pres. Matthew J. Quinn
Enroll: 1,438   (406) 447-4300

DAWSON COMMUNITY COLLEGE
Box 421, Glendive 59330 *Type:* Public junior *System:* Montana University System *Accred.:* 1969/1994 (NASC) *Calendar:* Sem. plan *Degrees:* A *CEO:* Pres. Donald H. Kettner
Enroll: 467   (406) 365-3396

FLATHEAD VALLEY COMMUNITY COLLEGE
777 Grandview Dr., Kalispell 59901 *Type:* Public junior *System:* Montana University System *Accred.:* 1970/1994 (NASC) *Calendar:* Qtr. plan *Degrees:* A *CEO:* Pres. David Beyer
Enroll: 1,614   (406) 756-3822

FORT BELKNAP COLLEGE
P.O. Box 159, Harlem 59526-0159 *Type:* Private (tribal) junior *Accred.:* 1993/1995 (NASC) *Calendar:* Sem. plan *Degrees:* A *CEO:* Pres. Margaret C. Perez
Enroll: 559   (406) 353-2205

FORT PECK COMMUNITY COLLEGE
P.O. Box 1027, Poplar 59255 *Type:* Private (tribal) junior *Accred.:* 1991/1993 (NASC) *Calendar:* Sem. plan *Degrees:* A *CEO:* Pres. James E. Shanley
Enroll: 355   (406) 768-5551

HELENA COLLEGE OF TECHNOLOGY OF THE UNIVERSITY OF MONTANA
1115 N. Roberts St., Helena 59601 *Type:* Public (state) 2-year *System:* Montana University System *Accred.:* 1977/1994 (NASC) *Calendar:* Sem. plan *Degrees:* A *CEO:* Dean Alex Capdeville
Enroll: 498   (406) 444-6800

LITTLE BIG HORN COLLEGE
P.O. Box 370, Crow Agency 59022 *Type:* Private (tribal) junior *Accred.:* 1990/1995 (NASC) *Calendar:* Sem. plan *Degrees:* A *CEO:* Pres. Janine Pease-Pretty On Top
Enroll: 299   (406) 638-7211

MILES COMMUNITY COLLEGE
2715 Dickinson, Miles City 59301 *Type:* Public (district) junior *System:* Montana University System *Accred.:* 1971/1993 (NASC) *Calendar:* Sem. plan *Degrees:* A *CEO:* Pres. Frank Williams
Enroll: 642   (406) 232-3031

MONTANA STATE UNIVERSITY—BILLINGS
1500 N. 30th St., Billings 59101 *Type:* Public (state) liberal arts and teachers *System:* Montana University System *Accred.:* 1932/1995 (NASC) *Calendar:* Sem. plan *Degrees:* B, M *Prof. Accred.:* Art, Music, Rehabilitation Counseling, Teacher Education *CEO:* Chanc. Ronald Sexton
Enroll: 4,092   (406) 657-2011

COLLEGE OF TECHNOLOGY CAMPUS
3803 Central Ave., Billings 59102 (state) 2-year *Accred.:* 1979/1994 (NASC) *Calendar:* Sem. plan *Degrees:* A
Enroll: 422   (406) 656-4445

MONTANA STATE UNIVERSITY—BOZEMAN
Bozeman 59717 *Type:* Public (state) *System:* Montana University System *Accred.:* 1932/1995 (NASC) *Calendar:* Sem. plan *Degrees:* B, M, D *Prof. Accred.:* Art, Business (B), Computer Science, Counseling, Engineering Technology (civil/construction, electrical, mechanical), Engineering (agricultural, chemical, civil, electrical, industrial,

mechanical), Music, Nursing (B,M), Psychology Internship, Teacher Education *CEO:* Pres. Michael P. Malone
Enroll: 10,962   (406) 994-0211

MONTANA STATE UNIVERSITY COLLEGE OF
TECHNOLOGY—GREAT FALLS
2100 16th Ave., S., Great Falls 59405 *Type:* Public (state) 2-year *System:* Montana University System *Accred.:* 1979/1995 (NASC) *Calendar:* Sem. plan *Degrees:* A *Prof. Accred.:* Dental Assisting, Occupational Therapy Assisting, Respiratory Therapy, Respiratory Therapy Technology *CEO:* Dean Willard R. Weaver
Enroll: 924   (406) 771-1240

MONTANA STATE UNIVERSITY—NORTHERN
P.O. Box 7751, Havre 59501 *Type:* Public (state) teachers *System:* Montana University System *Accred.:* 1932/1992 (NASC) *Calendar:* Qtr. plan *Degrees:* A, B, M *Prof. Accred.:* Nursing (A,B) *CEO:* Chanc. William Daehling
Enroll: 1,830   (406) 265-3700

MONTANA TECH OF THE UNIVERSITY OF
MONTANA
1300 W. Park St., Butte 59701-8997 *Type:* Public (state) technological *System:* Montana University System *Accred.:* 1932/1995 (NASC) *Calendar:* Sem. plan *Degrees:* B, M *Prof. Accred.:* Engineering (engineering physics/science, environmental/sanitary, geological/geophysical, metallurgical, mining, petroleum) *CEO:* Chanc. Lindsay D. Norman
Enroll: 1,806   (406) 496-4101

DIVISION OF TECHNOLOGY CAMPUS
25 Basin Creek Rd., Butte 59701 (state) 2-year *Accred.:* 1984/1993 (NASC) *Calendar:* Sem. plan *Degrees:* A
Enroll: 322   (406) 494-2894

ROCKY MOUNTAIN COLLEGE
1511 Poly Dr., Billings 59102 *Type:* Private liberal arts *Accred.:* 1949/1995 (NASC) *Calendar:* Sem. plan *Degrees:* A, B *CEO:* Pres. Arthur H. DeRosier, Jr.
Enroll: 804   (406) 657-1020

SALISH KOOTENAI COLLEGE
P.O. Box 117, Pablo 59855 *Type:* Private (tribal) junior *Accred.:* 1984/1995 (NASC) *Calendar:* Qtr. plan *Degrees:* A, B *Prof. Accred.:* Dental Assisting, Medical Record Technology, Nursing (A) *CEO:* Pres. Joseph F. McDonald
Enroll: 994   (406) 675-4800

STONE CHILD COMMUNITY COLLEGE
RR 1, Box 1082, Box Elder 59521-9796 *Type:* Private (tribal) junior *Accred.:* 1993/1995 (NASC) *Calendar:* Sem. plan *Degrees:* A *CEO:* Pres. Luanne Belcourt
Enroll: 276   (406) 395-4313

UNIVERSITY OF GREAT FALLS
1301 20th St., S., Great Falls 59405 *Type:* Private (Roman Catholic) liberal arts *Accred.:* 1935/1994 (NASC) *Calendar:* Sem. plan *Degrees:* B, M *CEO:* Pres. Frederick W. Gilliard
Enroll: 1,342   (406) 791-5301

THE UNIVERSITY OF MONTANA—MISSOULA
Missoula 59812 *Type:* Public (state) *System:* Montana University System *Accred.:* 1932/1994 (NASC) *Calendar:* Qtr. plan *Degrees:* A, B, M, D *Prof. Accred.:* Art, Business (B,M), Clinical Psychology, Forestry, Journalism (B,M), Law, Music, Physical Therapy, Recreation and Leisure Services (B), Social Work (B), Teacher Education, Theatre *CEO:* Pres. George M. Dennison
Enroll: 11,062   (406) 243-0211

COLLEGE OF TECHNOLOGY CAMPUS
909 South Ave., W., Missoula 59801 (state) 2-year *Accred.:* 1974/1994 (NASC) *Calendar:* Sem. plan *Degrees:* A, C *Prof. Accred.:* Respiratory Therapy Technology, Surgical Technology
Enroll: 612   (406) 243-7811

WESTERN MONTANA COLLEGE OF THE
UNIVERSITY OF MONTANA
710 S. Atlantic St., Dillon 59725-3511 *Type:* Public (state) teachers *System:* Montana University System *Accred.:* 1932/1989 (NASC) *Calendar:* Sem. plan *Degrees:* A, B *CEO:* Chanc. Sheila M. Stearns
Enroll: 1,150   (406) 683-7151

NEBRASKA

BELLEVUE UNIVERSITY
Galvin Rd. at Harvell Dr., Bellevue 68005
Type: Private liberal arts *Accred.:* 1977/1992
(NCA) *Calendar:* Sem. plan *Degrees:* B, M
CEO: Pres. John B. Muller
Enroll: 2,159   (402) 291-8100

CENTRAL COMMUNITY COLLEGE
P.O. Box 4903, Grand Island 68802-4903
Type: Public (state) 2-year technical *System:*
Nebraska Coordinating Commission for
Postsecondary Education *Accred.:* 1980/
1995 (NCA) *Calendar:* Qtr. plan *Degrees:* A,
C *Prof. Accred.:* Medical Assisting (AMA),
Nursing (A) *CEO:* Pres. Joseph W. Preusser
Enroll: 11,128   (308) 384-5220

GRAND ISLAND CAMPUS
P.O. Box 4903, Grand Island 68802-4903
System: Nebraska Coordinating Commis-
sion for Postsecondary Education *Accred.:*
1980/1988 (NCA) *Calendar:* Sem. plan
Enroll: 3,710   (308) 384-5220

HASTINGS CAMPUS
P.O. Box 1024, Hastings 68902-1024 *Sys-
tem:* Nebraska Coordinating Commission
for Postsecondary Education *Accred.:*
1980/1988 (NCA) *Calendar:* Sem. plan
Prof. Accred.: Dental Assisting, Dental
Hygiene, Dental Laboratory Technology
Enroll: 2,430   (402) 463-9811

PLATTE CAMPUS
4500 63rd St., P.O. Box 1027, Columbus
68601 *System:* Nebraska Coordinating
Commission for Postsecondary Education
Accred.: 1980/1988 (NCA) *Calendar:*
Sem. plan
Enroll: 3,179   (402) 564-7132

CHADRON STATE COLLEGE
1000 Main St., Chadron 69337 *Type:* Public
(state) liberal arts and teachers *System:*
Nebraska Coordinating Commission for
Postsecondary Education *Accred.:* 1915/
1987 (NCA) *Calendar:* Sem. plan *Degrees:*
A, B, M, P *Prof. Accred.:* Social Work (B),

Teacher Education *CEO:* Pres. Samuel H.
Rankin, Jr.
Enroll: 2,625   (308) 432-6000

CLARKSON COLLEGE
101 S. 42nd St., Omaha 68131 *Type:* Private
professional *Accred.:* 1984/1989 (NCA)
Calendar: Sem. plan *Degrees:* A, B, M, C
Prof. Accred.: Nursing (B), Physical Ther-
apy Assisting, Radiography *CEO:* Pres. Fay
Bower
Enroll: 554   (800) 647-5500

COLLEGE OF ST. MARY
1901 S. 72nd St., Omaha 68124 *Type:* Pri-
vate (Roman Catholic) liberal arts *Accred.:*
1958/1995 (NCA) *Calendar:* Sem. plan
Degrees: A, B, C *Prof. Accred.:* Medical
Record Administration, Medical Record
Technology, Nursing (A,B) *CEO:* Pres.
Gretchen Von Loewe Kreuter
Enroll: 1,172   (800) 926-5534

CONCORDIA COLLEGE
800 N. Columbia Ave., Seward 68434 *Type:*
Private (Lutheran) *Accred.:* 1953/1988 (NCA)
Calendar: Sem. plan *Degrees:* B, M, C *Prof.
Accred.:* Teacher Education *CEO:* Pres.
Orville C. Walz
Enroll: 954   (800) 535-5494

CREIGHTON UNIVERSITY
2500 California Plaza, Omaha 68178 *Type:*
Private (Roman Catholic) *Accred.:* 1916/
1987 (NCA) *Calendar:* Sem. plan *Degrees:*
A, B, M, D, C *Prof. Accred.:* Accounting
(A), Business (B,M), Dentistry, EMT-Paramedic, Law, Medicine, Nursing (B,M),
Occupational Therapy, Physical Therapy
(candidate), Social Work (B), Teacher Education *CEO:* Pres. Michael G. Morrison, S.J.
Enroll: 4,097   (402) 280-2700

DANA COLLEGE
2848 College Dr., Blair 68008 *Type:* Private
(Lutheran) liberal arts and professional
Accred.: 1958/1992 (NCA) *Calendar:* 4-1-4
plan *Degrees:* B *Prof. Accred.:* Social Work

(B), Teacher Education *CEO:* Pres. Myrvin Christopherson
Enroll: 650   (402) 426-9000

DOANE COLLEGE
1014 Boswell Ave., Crete 68333 *Type:* Private (United Church of Christ) liberal arts *Accred.:* 1913/1992 (NCA) *Calendar:* Sem. plan *Degrees:* B, M *Prof. Accred.:* Teacher Education *CEO:* Pres. Frederic D. Brown
Enroll: 1,476   (800) 333-6263

GATEWAY COLLEGE
808 S. 74th Plaza, Ste. 200, Omaha 68114-4666 *Type:* Private *Accred.:* 1973/1995 (ACCSCT) *Calendar:* Qtr. plan *Degrees:* A, C *CEO:* Dir. John E. Queen
                                            (402) 398-0900

LINCOLN CAMPUS
1033 O St., Ste. 130, Lincoln 68508-3126 *Accred.:* 1985/1990 (ACCSCT)
                                            (402) 434-6060

GRACE UNIVERSITY
Ninth & William, Omaha 68108 *Type:* Private *Accred.:* 1948/1995 (AABC); 1994 (NCA) *Calendar:* Sem. plan *Degrees:* A, B, C *CEO:* Pres. Neal F. McBride
Enroll: 414   (402) 449-2800

HASTINGS COLLEGE
720 N. Turner Ave., P.O. Box 269, Hastings 68902-0269 *Type:* Private (United Presbyterian) liberal arts *Accred.:* 1916/1995 (NCA) *Calendar:* 4-1-4 plan *Degrees:* B, M *Prof. Accred.:* Music, Teacher Education *CEO:* Pres. Richard E. Hoorer
Enroll: 992   (402) 463-2402

LINCOLN SCHOOL OF COMMERCE
P.O. Box 82826, 1821 K St., Lincoln 68501-2826 *Type:* Private junior *Accred.:* 1966/1987 (ACICS) *Calendar:* Sem. plan *Degrees:* A *CEO:* Pres. Scott Rhude
                                            (402) 474-5315

MCCOOK COMMUNITY COLLEGE
1205 E. Third St., McCook 69001 *Type:* Public (state) 2-year *System:* Mid-Plains Community College Area *Accred.:* 1980/1992

(NCA) *Calendar:* Sem. plan *Degrees:* A, C *CEO:* Pres. Robert G. Smallfoot
                                            (308) 345-6303

* Indirect NCA accreditation through Mid-Plains Community College Area

METROPOLITAN COMMUNITY COLLEGE
P.O. Box 3777, Omaha 68103 *Type:* Public (local) junior *System:* Nebraska Coordinating Commission for Postsecondary Education *Accred.:* 1979/1993 (NCA) *Calendar:* Qtr. plan *Degrees:* A, C *Prof. Accred.:* Dental Assisting, Nursing (A), Respiratory Therapy, Respiratory Therapy Technology, Surgical Technology *CEO:* Pres. J. Richard Gilliland
Enroll: 10,686   (800) 228-9553

MID-PLAINS COMMUNITY COLLEGE
601 W. State Farm Rd., North Platte 69101 *Type:* Public (local) 2-year technical *System:* Mid-Plains Community College Area *Accred.:* 1986/1992 (NCA) *Calendar:* Sem. plan *Degrees:* A, C *Prof. Accred.:* Clinical Lab Technology (A), Dental Assisting *CEO:* Chanc. Gregory G. Fitch
Enroll: 3,260   (308) 532-8980

* Indirect NCA accreditation through Mid-Plains Community College Area

MIDLAND LUTHERAN COLLEGE
900 Clarkson St., Fremont 68025 *Type:* Private (Lutheran) liberal arts *Accred.:* 1947/1989 (NCA) *Calendar:* 4-1-4 plan *Degrees:* A, B *Prof. Accred.:* Nursing (B) *CEO:* Pres. Carl L. Hansen
Enroll: 1,019   (800) 642-8382

NEBRASKA CHRISTIAN COLLEGE
1800 Syracuse St., Norfolk 68701 *Type:* Private (Christian Churches/Churches of Christ) *Accred.:* 1985/1990 (AABC) *Calendar:* Sem. plan *Degrees:* A, B *CEO:* Pres. Ray Stites
FTE Enroll: 119   (402) 371-5960

NEBRASKA COLLEGE OF BUSINESS
3636 California St., Omaha 68131 *Type:* Private junior *Accred.:* 1968/1987 (ACICS)

Calendar: Qtr. plan *Degrees:* A, C *CEO:* Dir. Thomas Loggins

(402) 553-8500

NEBRASKA COLLEGE OF TECHNICAL AGRICULTURE
Curtis 69025 *Type:* Private *Calendar:* Sem. plan *Degrees:* A *Prof. Accred.:* Veterinary Technology *CEO:* Dir. Ricky Sue Barnes-Wach

(308) 367-4124

NEBRASKA INDIAN COMMUNITY COLLEGE
P.O. Box 752, Winnebago 68071 *Type:* Public (federal) 2-year *Accred.:* 1986/1992 (NCA) *Calendar:* Sem. plan *Degrees:* A, C *CEO:* Pres. Yvonne Bushyhead
Enroll: 320   (402) 878-2414

NEBRASKA METHODIST COLLEGE OF NURSING AND ALLIED HEALTH
8501 W. Dodge Rd., Omaha 68114 *Type:* Private professional *Accred.:* 1989/1993 (NCA) *Calendar:* Sem. plan *Degrees:* A, B, C *Prof. Accred.:* Nursing (B), Respiratory Therapy *CEO:* Pres. Roger Koehler
Enroll: 378   (402) 390-4879

NEBRASKA WESLEYAN UNIVERSITY
5000 St. Paul Ave., Lincoln 68504 *Type:* Private (United Methodist) liberal arts *Accred.:* 1914/1990 (NCA) *Calendar:* Sem. plan *Degrees:* B *Prof. Accred.:* Music, Nursing (B), Social Work (B), Teacher Education *CEO:* Pres. John W. White, Jr.
Enroll: 1,610   (402) 466-2371

NORTHEAST COMMUNITY COLLEGE
801 E. Benjamin Ave., P.O. Box 469, Norfolk 68702-0469 *Type:* Public (local) junior *System:* Nebraska Coordinating Commission for Postsecondary Education *Accred.:* 1979/1994 (NCA) *Calendar:* Sem. plan *Degrees:* A, C *Prof. Accred.:* Physical Therapy Assisting *CEO:* Pres. James C. Underwood
Enroll: 3,612   (402) 371-2020

PERU STATE COLLEGE
Peru 68421 *Type:* Public (state) liberal arts and teachers *System:* Nebraska Coordinating Commission for Postsecondary Education *Accred.:* 1915/1991 (NCA) *Calendar:* Sem.

plan *Degrees:* A, B, M *Prof. Accred.:* Teacher Education *CEO:* Pres. Robert Burns
Enroll: 1,351   (402) 872-3815

SOUTHEAST COMMUNITY COLLEGE
8800 O St., Lincoln 68520 *Type:* Public (state/local) 2-year *System:* Nebraska Coordinating Commission for Postsecondary Education *Accred.:* 1983/1993 (NCA) *Calendar:* Qtr. plan *Degrees:* A, C *Prof. Accred.:* Clinical Lab Technology (A), Dental Assisting, Medical Assisting (AMA), Practical Nursing, Radiography, Respiratory Therapy, Respiratory Therapy Technology, Surgical Technology *CEO:* Chanc. Jack Huck
Enroll: 6,647   (402) 437-2500

SPENCER SCHOOL OF BUSINESS
P.O. Box 399, 410 W. Second St., Grand Island 68802 *Type:* Private business *Accred.:* 1972/1994 (ACICS) *Calendar:* Qtr. plan *Degrees:* A, C *Prof. Accred.:* Medical Assisting (AMA) *CEO:* Dir. Connie J. Collin

(308) 382-8044

UNION COLLEGE
3800 S. 48th St., Lincoln 68506 *Type:* Private (Seventh-Day Adventist) liberal arts *Accred.:* 1923/1990 (NCA) *Calendar:* Sem. plan *Degrees:* A, B *Prof. Accred.:* Nursing (B), Social Work (B), Teacher Education *CEO:* Pres. John G. Kerbs
Enroll: 598   (402) 488-2331

UNIVERSITY OF NEBRASKA AT KEARNEY
905 W. 25th St., Kearney 68849 *Type:* Public (state) *System:* University of Nebraska *Accred.:* 1916/1994 (NCA) *Calendar:* Sem. plan *Degrees:* B, M, P *Prof. Accred.:* Music, Nursing (B), Social Work (B), Speech-Language Pathology, Teacher Education *CEO:* Chanc. Gladys Styles Johnston
Enroll: 6,452   (308) 236-8441

UNIVERSITY OF NEBRASKA AT OMAHA
60th and Dodge, Omaha 68182-0108 *Type:* Public (state) *System:* University of Nebraska *Accred.:* 1939/1987 (NCA) *Calendar:* Sem. plan *Degrees:* B, M, P, D, C *Prof. Accred.:* Business (B,M), Counseling, Engineering Technology (civil/construction, electrical, general drafting/design), Engineering

(civil), Music (A), Public Administration, Social Work (B,M) Teacher Education *CEO:* Chanc. Delbert D. Weber
Enroll: 12,344   (402) 554-2200

UNIVERSITY OF NEBRASKA—LINCOLN
14th and R Sts, Lincoln 68588-0419 *Type:* Public (state) *System:* University of Nebraska *Accred.:* 1913/1987 (NCA) *Calendar:* Sem. plan *Degrees:* A, B, M, P, D, C *Prof. Accred.:* Accounting (A,C), Art, Audiology, Business (B,M), Clinical Psychology, Combined Prosthodontics, Construction Education (B), Counseling Psychology, Dental Hygiene, Dentistry, Endodontics, Engineering (agricultural, bioengineering, chemical, civil, electrical, industrial, mechanical), General Dentistry, General Practice Residency, Home Economics, Interior Design, Journalism (B,M), Law, Marriage and Family Therapy (M), Music, Oral and Maxillofacial Surgery, Orthodontics, Pediatric Dentistry, Periodontics, Planning (M), School Psychology, Speech-Language Pathology, Teacher Education, Theatre *CEO:* Chanc. James C. Moeser
Enroll: 18,700   (402) 472-7211

UNIVERSITY OF NEBRASKA MEDICAL CENTER
600 S. 42nd St., Omaha 68198-6605 *Type:* Public (state) *System:* University of Nebraska *Accred.:* 1913/1987 (NCA) *Calendar:* Sem. plan *Degrees:* B, M, D, C *Prof. Accred.:* Clinical Lab Scientist, Diagnostic

Medical Sonography, Dietetics (internship), Medicine, Nuclear Medicine Technology, Nursing (B,M), Perfusion, Physical Therapy, Physician Assisting/Surgeon Assisting, Radiation Therapy Technology, Radiography *CEO:* Chanc. Carol A. Aschenbrener
Enroll: 976   (402) 559-4200

WAYNE STATE COLLEGE
1111 Main St., Wayne 68787 *Type:* Public (state) liberal arts and teachers *System:* Nebraska Coordinating Commission for Postsecondary Education *Accred.:* 1917/1992 (NCA) *Calendar:* Sem. plan *Degrees:* B, M, P *Prof. Accred.:* Teacher Education *CEO:* Pres. Donald J. Mash
Enroll: 3,318   (402) 375-7000

WESTERN NEBRASKA COMMUNITY COLLEGE
1601 E. 27th St., Scottsbluff 69361 *Type:* Public (local) junior *System:* Nebraska Coordinating Commission for Postsecondary Education *Accred.:* 1988/1990 (NCA) *Calendar:* Sem. plan *Degrees:* A, C *Prof. Accred.:* Practical Nursing *CEO:* Pres. John N. Harms
Enroll: 1,910   (308) 635-3606

YORK COLLEGE
9th and Kiplinger, York 68467 *Type:* Private (Church of Christ) *Accred.:* 1970/1994 (NCA) *Calendar:* Sem. plan *Degrees:* A, B, C *CEO:* Pres. Garrett E. Baker
Enroll: 509   (402) 362-4441

NEVADA

CAREER COLLEGE OF NORTHERN NEVADA
1195-A Corporate Blvd., Reno 89502-2331
Type: Private *Accred.:* 1989 (ACCSCT)
Degrees: A, C *CEO:* Pres. Larry F. Clark
(702) 856-2266

COMMUNITY COLLEGE OF SOUTHERN NEVADA
3200 E. Cheyenne Ave., North Las Vegas
89106 *Type:* Public (district) junior *System:*
University and Community College System
of Nevada *Accred.:* 1975/1995 (NASC) *Calendar:* Sem. plan *Degrees:* A *Prof. Accred.:*
Clinical Lab Technology (A), Dental
Hygiene, Medical Record Technology, Nursing (A), Physical Therapy Assisting, Practical Nursing *CEO:* Pres. Richard Moore
Enroll: 17,113   (702) 651-4491

DEEP SPRINGS COLLEGE
HC 72, Box 45001, Dyer 89010-9803 *Type:*
Private junior for men *Accred.:* 1952/1993
(WASC-Jr.) *Calendar:* Sem. plan *Degrees:*
A *CEO:* Pres. L. Jackson Newell
Enroll: 27   (619) 872-2000

EDUCATION DYNAMICS INSTITUTE
2635 N. Decatur Blvd., Las Vegas 89108-
2913 *Type:* Private *Accred.:* 1973/1988
(ACCSCT) *Degrees:* A, C *CEO:* Exec. Dir.
Robert McCart
(702) 648-1522

EDUCATION DYNAMICS INSTITUTE
953 E. Sahara Ave., Bldg. 35-B, Ste. 102, Las
Vegas 89108-2906 *Type:* Private *Accred.:*
1990 (ACCSCT) *Degrees:* A, C *CEO:* Dir.
Erick Mendoza
(702) 731-6421

GREAT BASIN COLLEGE
1500 College Parkway, Elko 89801 *Type:*
Public (district) junior *System:* University
and Community College System of Nevada
Accred.: 1974/1994 (NASC) *Calendar:*
Sem. plan *Degrees:* A *Prof. Accred.:* Nursing
(A) *CEO:* Pres. Ronald K. Remington
Enroll: 2,414   (702) 738-8493

MORRISON COLLEGE—RENO
140 Washington St., Reno 89503 *Type:* Private senior *Accred.:* 1990/1994 (ACICS)
Calendar: Qtr. plan *Degrees:* A, B *CEO:*
Pres. Mary Morrison
(702) 323-4145

PHILLIPS COLLEGE
3320 E. Flamingo Rd., Ste. 30, Las Vegas
89121-4306 *Type:* Private business *Accred.:*
1983/1996 (ACICS) *Calendar:* Qtr. plan
Degrees: A *CEO:* Dir. Warren Strand
(702) 434-0486

SIERRA NEVADA COLLEGE
P.O. Box 4269, Incline Village 89450-4269
Type: Private liberal arts *Accred.:* 1977/1995
(NASC) *Calendar:* Sem. plan *Degrees:* B
CEO: Pres. Mark Hurtubise
Enroll: 483   (702) 831-1314

TRUCKEE MEADOWS COMMUNITY COLLEGE
7000 Dandini Blvd., Reno 89512 *Type:* Public (district) junior *System:* University and
Community College System of Nevada
Accred.: 1980/1995 (NASC) *Calendar:*
Sem. plan *Degrees:* A *Prof. Accred.:* Dental
Assisting (conditional), Radiography *CEO:*
Pres. Kenneth E. Wright
Enroll: 9,223   (702) 673-7000

UNIVERSITY OF NEVADA, LAS VEGAS
4505 Maryland Pkwy., Las Vegas 89154
Type: Public (state) *System:* University and
Community College System of Nevada
Accred.: 1964/1995 (NASC) *Calendar:*
Sem. plan *Degrees:* A, B, M, D *Prof.
Accred.:* Accounting (A,C), Art, Business
(B,M), Clinical Lab Scientist, Computer Science, Counseling, Engineering (civil, electrical, mechanical), Music, Nuclear Medicine
Technology, Nursing (B,M), Public Administration, Radiography, Social Work (B,M),
Teacher Education, Theatre *CEO:* Pres.
Carol C. Harter
Enroll: 20,239   (702) 895-3011

UNIVERSITY OF NEVADA, RENO
Reno 89557 *Type:* Public (state) *System:* University and Community College System of Nevada *Accred.:* 1938/1993 (NASC) *Calendar:* Sem. plan *Degrees:* A, B, M, D *Prof. Accred.:* Business (B,M), Clinical Lab Scientist, Clinical Lab Technology (C), Clinical Psychology, Counseling, Dietetics (internship), Engineering (chemical, civil, electrical, geological/geophysical, mechanical, metallurgical, mining), Journalism (B,M), Medicine, Music, Nursing (B,M), Social Work (B,M), Speech-Language Pathology, Teacher Education *CEO:* Pres. Joseph N. Crowley
Enroll: 11,746   (702) 784-1105

WESTERN NEVADA COMMUNITY COLLEGE
2201 W. College Pkwy., Carson City 89703 *Type:* Public (district) junior *System:* University and Community College System of Nevada *Accred.:* 1975/1995 (NASC) *Calendar:* Sem. plan *Degrees:* A *Prof. Accred.:* Nursing (A) *CEO:* Pres. James R. Randolph
Enroll: 4,689   (702) 887-3000

NEW HAMPSHIRE

CASTLE COLLEGE
Searles Rd., Windham 03087 *Type:* Private *Accred.:* 1985/1989 (NEASC-CTCI) *Calendar:* Qtr. plan *Degrees:* A *CEO:* Pres. Sheila L. Garvey
FTE Enroll: 362　　　　(603) 893-6111

COLBY-SAWYER COLLEGE
100 Main St., New London 03257 *Type:* Private *Accred.:* 1933/1995 (NEASC-CIHE) *Calendar:* Sem. plan *Degrees:* A, B *Prof. Accred.:* Nursing (B) *CEO:* Pres. Anne Ponder
Enroll: 659　　　　(603) 526-2010

COLLEGE FOR LIFELONG LEARNING
125 N. State St., Concord 03301-6430 *Type:* Public (state) *System:* University System of New Hampshire *Accred.:* 1980/1986 (NEASC-CIHE) *Calendar:* Sem. plan *Degrees:* A, B *CEO:* Dean Victor B. Montana
Enroll: 1,337　　　　(603) 228-3000

DANIEL WEBSTER COLLEGE
Nashua 03063 *Type:* Private *Accred.:* 1972/1986 (NEASC-CIHE) *Calendar:* Tri. plan *Degrees:* A, B *CEO:* Pres. Hannah M. McCarthy
Enroll: 743　　　　(603) 883-3556

DARTMOUTH COLLEGE
Hanover 03755 *Type:* Private liberal arts *Accred.:* 1929/1988 (NEASC-CIHE) *Calendar:* Qtr. plan *Degrees:* B, M, P, D *Prof. Accred.:* Business (M), Engineering (general), Medicine, Psychology Internship, Theatre *CEO:* Pres. James O. Freedman
Enroll: 5,171　　　　(603) 646-1110

FRANKLIN PIERCE COLLEGE
College Rd., Rindge 03461 *Type:* Private liberal arts *Accred.:* 1968/1988 (NEASC-CIHE) *Calendar:* Sem. plan *Degrees:* B *CEO:* Pres. George J. Hagerty
Enroll: 2,324　　　　(603) 899-5111

FRANKLIN PIERCE LAW CENTER
2 White St., Concord 03301 *Type:* Private professional *Calendar:* Sem. plan *Degrees:*
P *Prof. Accred.:* Law (ABA only) *CEO:* Pres. Robert M. Viles
Enroll: 418　　　　(603) 228-1541

HESSER COLLEGE
3 Sundial Ave., Manchester 03103 *Type:* Private junior business *Accred.:* 1985/1989 (NEASC-CTCI) *Calendar:* Sem. plan *Degrees:* A *CEO:* Pres. Linwood W. Galeucia
FTE Enroll: 1,987　　　　(603) 668-6660

KEENE STATE COLLEGE
229 Main St., Keene 03435-1502 *Type:* Public (state) liberal arts and teachers *System:* University System of New Hampshire *Accred.:* 1949/1990 (NEASC-CIHE) *Calendar:* Sem. plan *Degrees:* A, B, M *Prof. Accred.:* Music (A), Teacher Education *CEO:* Pres. Stanley J. Yarosewick
Enroll: 3,951　　　　(603) 352-1909

MCINTOSH COLLEGE
23 Cataract Ave., Dover 03820 *Type:* Private junior business *Accred.:* 1988 (NEASC-CTCI) *Calendar:* Sem. plan *Degrees:* A, C *CEO:* Pres. Robert J. DeColfmacker
FTE Enroll: 751　　　　(603) 742-1234

NEW ENGLAND COLLEGE
Henniker 03242-0788 *Type:* Private liberal arts *Accred.:* 1967/1995 (NEASC-CIHE) *Calendar:* 4-1-4 plan *Degrees:* B, M *Prof. Accred.:* Engineering (civil) *CEO:* Pres. William G. Ellis
Enroll: 795　　　　(603) 428-2211

NEW HAMPSHIRE COLLEGE
2500 N. River Rd., Manchester 03104-1394 *Type:* Private *Accred.:* 1973/1991 (NEASC-CIHE) *Calendar:* Sem. plan *Degrees:* A, B, M *CEO:* Pres. Richard A. Gustafson
Enroll: 3,738　　　　(603) 668-2211

NEW HAMPSHIRE TECHNICAL COLLEGE—BERLIN
2020 Riverside Dr., Berlin 03570 *Type:* Public (state) 2-year technical *System:* New Hampshire Department of Regional Community-Technical Colleges *Accred.:* 1974/

1994 (NEASC-CTCI) *Calendar:* Sem. plan *Degrees:* A *CEO:* Pres. Alex Easton
FTE Enroll: 593   (603) 752-1113

NEW HAMPSHIRE TECHNICAL COLLEGE—
CLAREMONT
One College Dr., Claremont 03743-9707 *Type:* Public (state) 2-year technical *System:* New Hampshire Department of Regional Community-Technical Colleges *Accred.:* 1973/1994 (NEASC-CTCI) *Calendar:* Sem. plan *Degrees:* A *Prof. Accred.:* Clinical Lab Technology (A), Medical Assisting (AMA), Medical Record Technology, Nursing (A), Occupational Therapy Assisting, Physical Therapy Assisting, Respiratory Therapy *CEO:* Pres. Keith Bird
FTE Enroll: 510   (603) 542-7744

NEW HAMPSHIRE TECHNICAL COLLEGE—
LACONIA
Prescott Hill, Rte. 106, Laconia 03246 *Type:* Public (state) 2-year technical *System:* New Hampshire Department of Regional Community-Technical Colleges *Accred.:* 1974/1994 (NEASC-CTCI) *Calendar:* Sem. plan *Degrees:* A *CEO:* Pres. Alex Easton
FTE Enroll: 861   (603) 524-3207

NEW HAMPSHIRE TECHNICAL COLLEGE—
MANCHESTER
1066 Front St., Manchester 03102 *Type:* Public (state) 2-year technical *System:* New Hampshire Department of Regional Community-Technical Colleges *Accred.:* 1974/1994 (NEASC-CTCI) *Calendar:* Sem. plan *Degrees:* A *CEO:* Pres. Jane Power Kilcoyne
FTE Enroll: 1,045   (603) 668-6706

NEW HAMPSHIRE TECHNICAL COLLEGE—
NASHUA
505 Amherst St., P.O. Box 2052, Nashua 03061-2052 *Type:* Public (state) 2-year technical *System:* New Hampshire Department of Regional Community-Technical Colleges *Accred.:* 1974/1989 (NEASC-CTCI) *Calendar:* Sem. plan *Degrees:* A *CEO:* Pres. Keith Bird
FTE Enroll: 774   (603) 882-6923

NEW HAMPSHIRE TECHNICAL COLLEGE—
STRATHAM
P.O. Box 365, Stratham 03885 *Type:* Public (state) 2-year technical *System:* New Hampshire Department of Regional Community-Technical Colleges *Accred.:* 1975/1990 (NEASC-CTCI) *Calendar:* Sem. plan *Degrees:* A *CEO:* Pres. Jane P. Kilcoyne
FTE Enroll: 600   (603) 772-1194

NEW HAMPSHIRE TECHNICAL INSTITUTE
11 Institute Dr., Concord 03301-7412 *Type:* Public (state) 2-year technical *System:* New Hampshire Department of Regional Community-Technical Colleges *Accred.:* 1969/1991 (NEASC-CTCI) *Calendar:* Sem. plan *Degrees:* A *Prof. Accred.:* Dental Assisting, Dental Hygiene, EMT-Paramedic, Engineering Technology (architectural, computer, electrical, manufacturing, mechanical), Nursing (A), Radiography *CEO:* Interim Pres. William Simonton
FTE Enroll: 2,208   (603) 225-1800

NOTRE DAME COLLEGE
Manchester 03104-2299 *Type:* Private (Roman Catholic) liberal arts *Accred.:* 1970/1992 (NEASC-CIHE) *Calendar:* Sem. plan *Degrees:* A, B, M *CEO:* Pres. Carol J. Descoteaux, C.S.C.
Enroll: 980   (603) 669-4298

PLYMOUTH STATE COLLEGE
Plymouth 03264-1567 *Type:* Public (state) liberal arts and professional *System:* University System of New Hampshire *Accred.:* 1955/1994 (NEASC-CIHE) *Calendar:* Sem. plan *Degrees:* A, B, M *Prof. Accred.:* Social Work (B-candidate), Teacher Education *CEO:* Pres. Donald P. Wharton
Enroll: 3,837   (603) 535-5000

RIVIER COLLEGE
420 S. Main St., Nashua 03060-5086 *Type:* Private (Roman Catholic) liberal arts *Accred.:* 1948/1992 (NEASC-CIHE) *Calendar:* Sem. plan *Degrees:* A, B, M *Prof. Accred.:* Nursing (A,B) *CEO:* Pres. Jeanne Perreault
Enroll: 1,579   (603) 888-1311

ST. ANSELM COLLEGE
100 St. Anselm Dr., Manchester 03102-1310 *Type:* Private (Roman Catholic) liberal arts *Accred.:* 1941/1989 (NEASC-CIHE) *Calendar:* Sem. plan *Degrees:* A, B *Prof. Accred.:* Nursing (B) *CEO:* Pres. Jonathan P. DeFelice, O.S.B.
Enroll: 1,875　　　　　　　　(603) 641-7000

UNIVERSITY OF NEW HAMPSHIRE
Durham 03824-3547 *Type:* Public (state) *System:* University System of New Hampshire *Accred.:* 1929/1994 (NEASC-CIHE) *Calendar:* Sem. plan *Degrees:* A, B, M, D *Prof. Accred.:* Business (B,M), Clinical Lab Scientist, Computer Science, Dietetics (internship), Engineering Technology (electrical, mechanical), Engineering (chemical, civil, electrical, mechanical), Forestry, Health Services Administration, Marriage and Family Therapy (M), Music, Nursing (B,M), Occupational Therapy, Psychology Internship, Recreation and Leisure Services (B), Social Work (B), Speech-Language Pathology *CEO:* Interim Pres. Walter R. Peterson
Enroll: 12,668　　　　　　　(603) 862-1234

MANCHESTER CAMPUS
R.F.D. 4, Hackett Hill Rd., Manchester 03102
　　　　　　　　　　　　　　(603) 668-0700

WHITE PINES COLLEGE
Chester 03036 *Type:* Private junior *Accred.:* 1975/1994 (NEASC-CIHE) *Calendar:* Sem. plan *Degrees:* A *CEO:* Pres. Mary Scerra
Enroll: 51　　　　　　　　　(603) 887-4401

NEW JERSEY

ASSUMPTION COLLEGE FOR SISTERS
350 Bernardsville Rd., Mallinckrodt Convent, Mendham 07945-0800 *Type:* Private (Roman Catholic) *Accred.:* 1965/1995 (MSA) *Calendar:* Sem. plan *Degrees:* A, C *CEO:* Pres. Julitta Heinen
Enroll: 28   (201) 543-6528

ATLANTIC COMMUNITY COLLEGE
5100 Black Horse Pike, Mays Landing 08330-2699 *Type:* Public (local/state) junior *System:* New Jersey Commission on Higher Education *Accred.:* 1971/1991 (MSA) *Calendar:* Sem. plan *Degrees:* A, C *Prof. Accred.:* Clinical Lab Technology (A), Dental Assisting (conditional), Engineering Technology (electrical), Nursing (A), Occupational Therapy Assisting, Physical Therapy Assisting *CEO:* Pres. John T. May
Enroll: 6,342   (609) 343-4900

BERGEN COMMUNITY COLLEGE
400 Paramus Rd., Paramus 07652 *Type:* Public (local) junior *System:* New Jersey Commission on Higher Education *Accred.:* 1972/1991 (MSA) *Calendar:* Sem. plan *Degrees:* A, C *Prof. Accred.:* Clinical Lab Technology (A), Dental Hygiene, Diagnostic Medical Sonography, Medical Assisting (AMA), Nursing (A), Radiography, Respiratory Therapy, Surgical Technology *CEO:* Pres. Judith K. Winn
Enroll: 12,886   (201) 447-7100

BERKELEY COLLEGE OF BUSINESS
44 Rifle Camp Rd., West Paterson 07424 *Type:* Private junior *Accred.:* 1983/1990 (MSA) *Calendar:* Qtr. plan *Degrees:* A, C *CEO:* Pres. Kevin L. Luing
Enroll: 1,458   (201) 278-5400

BERGEN CAMPUS
100 W. Prospect St., Waldwick 07463
                          (201) 652-0388

MIDDLESEX CAMPUS
430 Rahway Ave., Woodbridge 07095
                          (908) 750-1800

BETH MEDRASH GOVOHA
617 Sixth St., Lakewood 08701 *Type:* Private professional *Accred.:* 1974/1991 (AARTS) *Calendar:* Sem. plan *Degrees:* B, M *CEO:* Pres. M. Kotler
Enroll: 1,800   (908) 367-1060

BLOOMFIELD COLLEGE
467 Franklin St., Bloomfield 07003 *Type:* Private (Presbyterian) liberal arts *Accred.:* 1960/1992 (MSA) *Calendar:* 4-1-4 plan *Degrees:* B, C *Prof. Accred.:* Nursing (B) *CEO:* Pres. John F. Noonan
Enroll: 2,148   (201) 748-9000

BROOKDALE COMMUNITY COLLEGE
765 Newman Springs Rd., Lincroft 07738 *Type:* Public (local) junior *System:* New Jersey Commission on Higher Education *Accred.:* 1972/1993 (MSA) *Calendar:* Sem. plan *Degrees:* A, C *Prof. Accred.:* Clinical Lab Technology (A), Nursing (A), Respiratory Therapy *CEO:* Pres. Peter F. Burnham
Enroll: 12,264   (908) 842-1900

BURLINGTON COUNTY COLLEGE
County Rte. 530, Pemberton 08068-1599 *Type:* Public (local/state) junior *System:* New Jersey Commission on Higher Education *Accred.:* 1972/1994 (MSA) *Calendar:* Sem. plan *Degrees:* A, C *Prof. Accred.:* Clinical Lab Technology (A), Engineering Technology (electrical), Medical Record Technology *CEO:* Pres. Robert C. Messina, Jr.
Enroll: 6,798   (609) 894-9311

CALDWELL COLLEGE
9 Ryerson Ave., Caldwell 07006-6195 *Type:* Private (Roman Catholic) liberal arts *Accred.:* 1952/1993 (MSA) *Calendar:* Sem. plan *Degrees:* B, C *CEO:* Pres. Patrice Werner, O.P.
Enroll: 1,609   (201) 228-4424

CAMDEN COUNTY COLLEGE
P.O. Box 200, Blackwood 08012 *Type:* Public (local/state) junior *System:* New Jersey Commission on Higher Education *Accred.:* 1972/1992 (MSA) *Calendar:* Sem. plan *Degrees:* A, C *Prof. Accred.:* Clinical Lab

Technology (A), Dental Assisting, Dental Hygiene, Veterinary Technology *CEO:* Pres. Phyllis Della Vecchia
Enroll: 14,543   (609) 227-7200

CAMDEN CAMPUS
Seventh and Cooper Sts., Camden 08102
(609) 338-1817

CENTENARY COLLEGE
400 Jefferson St., Hackettstown 07840 *Type:* Private liberal arts *Accred.:* 1932/1995 (MSA) *Calendar:* Sem. plan *Degrees:* A, B *CEO:* Pres. Stephanie M. Bennett-Smith
Enroll: 922   (908) 852-1400

COLLEGE OF ST. ELIZABETH
2 Convent Rd., Morristown 07960-6989 *Type:* Private (Roman Catholic) liberal arts for women *Accred.:* 1921/1995 (MSA) *Calendar:* Sem. plan *Degrees:* B, C *Prof. Accred.:* Dietetics (internship), Nursing (B) *CEO:* Pres. Jacqueline Burns, S.C.
Enroll: 1,599   (201) 292-6300

COUNTY COLLEGE OF MORRIS
Rte. 10 and Center Grove Rd., Randolph 07869 *Type:* Public (local/state) junior *System:* New Jersey Commission on Higher Education *Accred.:* 1972/1993 (MSA) *Calendar:* Sem. plan *Degrees:* A, C *Prof. Accred.:* Clinical Lab Technology (A), Engineering Technology (electrical, mechanical), Nursing (A) *CEO:* Pres. Edward J. Yaw
Enroll: 9,627   (201) 328-5000

CUMBERLAND COUNTY COLLEGE
College Dr., P.O. Box 517, Vineland 08360 *Type:* Public (local/state) junior *System:* New Jersey Commission on Higher Education *Accred.:* 1970/1991 (MSA) *Calendar:* Sem. plan *Degrees:* A, C *Prof. Accred.:* Nursing (A), Radiography *CEO:* Pres. Roland J. Chapdelaine
Enroll: 2,680   (609) 691-8600

DEVRY TECHNICAL INSTITUTE—WOODBRIDGE
479 Green St., Woodbridge 07095 *Type:* Private *System:* DeVry Institutes *Accred.:* 1981/ 1992 (NCA) *Calendar:* Sem. plan *Degrees:*

A, C *Prof. Accred.:* Engineering Technology (electrical) *CEO:* Pres. Robert M. Bocchino
(908) 634-3460

* Indirect NCA accreditation through DeVry Institutes

DREW UNIVERSITY
Madison Ave., Rte. 24, Madison 07940 *Type:* Private liberal arts *Accred.:* 1938/1991 (ATS); 1932/1991 (MSA) *Calendar:* Sem. plan *Degrees:* B, M, P, D *CEO:* Pres. Thomas H. Kean
Enroll: 2,036   (201) 408-3000

ESSEX COUNTY COLLEGE
303 University Ave., Newark 07102 *Type:* Public (local/state) junior *System:* New Jersey Commission on Higher Education *Accred.:* 1974/1992 (MSA) *Calendar:* Sem. plan *Degrees:* A, C *Prof. Accred.:* Nursing (A), Physical Therapy Assisting, Radiography *CEO:* Pres. A. Zachary Yamba
Enroll: 8,686   (201) 877-3000

WEST ESSEX BRANCH CAMPUS
730 Bloomfield Ave., West Caldwell 07006
(201) 228-3970

FAIRLEIGH DICKINSON UNIVERSITY
Dickinson Hall, 1000 River Road, Teaneck 07666 *Type:* Private non-profit *Accred.:* 1948/1992 (MSA) *Calendar:* Sem. plan *Degrees:* A, B, M, P, D *Prof. Accred.:* Clinical Psychology, Computer Science, Engineering Technology (civil/construction, electrical, mechanical), Engineering (electrical), Respiratory Therapy *CEO:* Pres. Francis J. Mertz
Enroll: 9,976   (201) 692-7100

FLORHAM-MADISON CAMPUS
285 Madison Ave., Madison 07940 *Prof. Accred.:* Physical Therapy Assisting
(201) 593-8500

MONMOUTH COUNTY GRADUATE CENTER
One Main St., Ste. 103, Eatontown 07724
(908) 542-4118

FELICIAN COLLEGE
262 S. Main St., Lodi 07644 *Type:* Private (Roman Catholic) liberal arts *Accred.:* 1974/1990 (MSA) *Calendar:* Sem. plan *Degrees:* A, B, C *Prof. Accred.:* Clinical Lab Technology (A), Nursing (A,B) *CEO:* Pres. Theresa Mary Martin
Enroll: 1,066   (201) 778-1190

GEORGIAN COURT COLLEGE
900 Lakewood Ave., Lakewood 08701 *Type:* Private (Roman Catholic) *Accred.:* 1922/1994 (MSA) *Calendar:* Sem. plan *Degrees:* B, M *Prof. Accred.:* Social Work (B-candidate) *CEO:* Pres. Barbara Williams, R.S.M.
Enroll: 2,539   (908) 364-2200

GLOUCESTER COUNTY COLLEGE
Tanyard and Salisnas Rds., Sewell 08080 *Type:* Public (local/state) junior *System:* New Jersey Commission on Higher Education *Accred.:* 1973/1993 (MSA) *Calendar:* Sem. plan *Degrees:* A, C *Prof. Accred.:* Diagnostic Medical Sonography, Nuclear Medicine Technology, Nursing (A), Respiratory Therapy Technology *CEO:* Pres. Richard H. Jones
Enroll: 5,292   (609) 468-5000

HUDSON COUNTY COMMUNITY COLLEGE
168 Sip Avenue, Jersey City 07306 *Type:* Public (local/state) junior *System:* New Jersey Commission on Higher Education *Accred.:* 1981/1986 (MSA) *Calendar:* Sem. plan *Degrees:* A, C *Prof. Accred.:* Engineering Technology (electrical), Medical Assisting (AMA), Medical Record Technology *CEO:* Pres. Glen Gabert
Enroll: 3,959   (201) 656-2020

IMMACULATE CONCEPTION SEMINARY
400 S. Orange Ave., South Orange 07079 *Type:* Private (Roman Catholic) graduate only *Accred.:* 1977/1994 (ATS) *Calendar:* Sem. plan *Degrees:* M *CEO:* Rector/Dean John W. Flesey
Enroll: 173   (201) 761-9575

JERSEY CITY STATE COLLEGE
2039 Kennedy Blvd., Jersey City 07305-1597 *Type:* Public (state) *System:* New Jersey Commission on Higher Education *Accred.:* 1959/1990 (MSA) *Calendar:* Sem. plan *Degrees:* B, M, C *Prof. Accred.:* Art, Music, Nursing (B), Teacher Education *CEO:* Pres. Carlos Hernandez
Enroll: 8,670   (201) 200-2000

KATHARINE GIBBS SCHOOL
33 Plymouth St., Montclair 07042 *Type:* Private junior *Accred.:* 1967/1988 (ACICS) *Calendar:* Sem. plan *Degrees:* A, C *CEO:* Pres. Mary Jo Greco
          (201) 744-6967

PISCATAWAY CAMPUS
80 Kingsbridge Rd., Piscataway 08854 *Accred.:* 1985 (ACICS)
          (908) 885-1580

KEAN COLLEGE OF NEW JERSEY
1000 Morris Ave., Union 07083 *Type:* Public (state) *System:* New Jersey Commission on Higher Education *Accred.:* 1960/1991 (MSA) *Calendar:* Sem. plan *Degrees:* B, M *Prof. Accred.:* Construction Education (B), Medical Record Administration, Music, Nursing (B), Occupational Therapy, Physical Therapy, Public Administration, Social Work (B), Speech-Language Pathology, Teacher Education *CEO:* Interim Pres. Henry J. Ross
Enroll: 11,386   (908) 527-2000

MERCER COUNTY COMMUNITY COLLEGE
1200 Old Trenton Rd., Trenton 08690-0182 *Type:* Public (local/state) junior *System:* New Jersey Commission on Higher Education *Accred.:* 1967/1995 (MSA) *Calendar:* Sem. plan *Degrees:* A, C *Prof. Accred.:* Clinical Lab Technology (A), Engineering Technology (civil/construction, electrical, mechanical), Funeral Service Education (Mortuary Science), Nursing (A), Radiography *CEO:* Pres. Thomas D. Sepe
Enroll: 8,441   (609) 586-4800

JAMES KERNEY CAMPUS
N. Broad and Academy Sts., Trenton 08690
          (609) 586-4800

MIDDLESEX COUNTY COLLEGE
155 Mill Rd., P.O. Box 3050, Edison 08818-3050 *Type:* Public (local/state) junior *System:* New Jersey Commission on Higher Education *Accred.:* 1970/1991 (MSA) *Calendar:* Sem. plan *Degrees:* A, C *Prof. Accred.:* Clinical Lab Technology (A), Dental Hygiene, Engineering Technology (civil/construction, electrical, mechanical), Nursing (A), Radiography *CEO:* Interim Pres. John Bakum
Enroll: 11,941   (908) 548-6000

MONMOUTH UNIVERSITY
Norwood and Cedar Aves., West Long Branch 07764-1898 *Type:* Private non-profit *Accred.:* 1952/1991 (MSA) *Calendar:* Sem. plan *Degrees:* A, B, M *Prof. Accred.:* Engineering (electrical), Nursing (B), Social Work (B) *CEO:* Pres. Rebecca Stafford
Enroll: 4,422   (908) 571-3400

MONTCLAIR STATE UNIVERSITY
Valley Rd. and Normal Ave., Upper Montclair 07043-1624 *Type:* Public (state) *System:* New Jersey Commission on Higher Education *Accred.:* 1937/1992 (MSA) *Calendar:* Sem. plan *Degrees:* B, M *Prof. Accred.:* Art (A), Computer Science, Dance, Home Economics, Music, Recreation and Leisure Services (B), Speech-Language Pathology, Teacher Education, Theatre *CEO:* Pres. Irvin D. Reid
Enroll: 12,674   (201) 655-4000

NEW BRUNSWICK THEOLOGICAL SEMINARY
17 Seminary Pl., New Brunswick 08901-1196 *Type:* Private (Reformed Church) graduate only *Accred.:* 1938/1986 (ATS) *Calendar:* Sem. plan *Degrees:* M *CEO:* Pres. Norman J. Kansfield
Enroll: 211   (908) 247-5241

NEW JERSEY INSTITUTE OF TECHNOLOGY
27 Eberhardt Hall, University Heights, Newark 07102-1982 *Type:* Public (state) technological *System:* New Jersey Commission on Higher Education *Accred.:* 1934/1992 (MSA) *Calendar:* Sem. plan *Degrees:* B, M, D *Prof. Accred.:* Computer Science, Engineering Technology (civil/construction, electrical, manufacturing, mechanical, surveying), Engineering (chemical, civil, electrical, industrial, mechanical) *CEO:* Pres. Saul K. Fenster
Enroll: 7,504   (201) 596-3000

OCEAN COUNTY COLLEGE
College Dr., P.O. Box 2001, Toms River 08754-2001 *Type:* Public (local/state) junior *System:* New Jersey Commission on Higher Education *Accred.:* 1969/1994 (MSA) *Calendar:* Sem. plan *Degrees:* A, C *Prof. Accred.:* Clinical Lab Technology (C), Engineering Technology (electrical), Nursing (A) *CEO:* Pres. Milton Shaw
Enroll: 8,162   (908) 255-4000

PASSAIC COUNTY COMMUNITY COLLEGE
College Blvd., Paterson 07509 *Type:* Public (local/state) junior *System:* New Jersey Commission on Higher Education *Accred.:* 1978/1994 (MSA) *Calendar:* Sem. plan *Degrees:* A, C *Prof. Accred.:* Nursing (A), Radiography, Respiratory Therapy Technology *CEO:* Pres. Elliott Collins
Enroll: 3,707   (201) 684-6800

PRINCETON THEOLOGICAL SEMINARY
64 Mercer St., P.O. Box 821, Princeton 08542-0803 *Type:* Private (Presbyterian) graduate only *Accred.:* 1938/1987 (ATS); 1968/1993 (MSA) *Calendar:* Sem. plan *Degrees:* M, P, D *CEO:* Pres. Thomas W. Gillespie
Enroll: 827   (609) 921-8300

PRINCETON UNIVERSITY
Nassau Hall, Princeton 08544-0015 *Type:* Private non-profit *Accred.:* 1921/1994 (MSA) *Calendar:* Sem. plan *Degrees:* B, M, D *Prof. Accred.:* Engineering (aerospace, chemical, civil, electrical, engineering physics/science, geological/geophysical, mechanical) *CEO:* Pres. Harold T. Shapiro
Enroll: 6,342   (609) 258-3000

RABBINICAL COLLEGE OF AMERICA
226 Sussex Ave., Morristown 07960 *Type:* Private professional *Accred.:* 1979/1990

(AARTS) *Calendar:* Sem. plan *Degrees:* B *CEO:* Pres. M. Herson
Enroll: 188   (201) 267-9404

RAMAPO COLLEGE OF NEW JERSEY
505 Ramapo Valley Rd., Mahwah 07430-1680 *Type:* Public (state) liberal arts *System:* New Jersey Commission on Higher Education *Accred.:* 1975/1990 (MSA) *Calendar:* Sem. plan *Degrees:* B *Prof. Accred.:* Social Work (B) *CEO:* Pres. Robert A. Scott
Enroll: 4,674   (201) 529-7500

RARITAN VALLEY COMMUNITY COLLEGE
P.O. Box 3300, Somerville 08876 *Type:* Public (local/state) junior *System:* New Jersey Commission on Higher Education *Accred.:* 1972/1992 (MSA) *Calendar:* Sem. plan *Degrees:* A, C *Prof. Accred.:* Nursing (A) *CEO:* Pres. Cary A. Israel
Enroll: 5,664   (908) 526-1200

RICHARD STOCKTON COLLEGE OF NEW JERSEY
Jim Leeds Rd., Pomona 08240 *Type:* Public (state) *System:* New Jersey Commission on Higher Education *Accred.:* 1975/1991 (MSA) *Calendar:* Sem. plan *Degrees:* B *Prof. Accred.:* Nursing (B), Physical Therapy, Social Work (B) *CEO:* Pres. Vera King Farris
Enroll: 5,701   (609) 652-1776

RIDER UNIVERSITY
2083 Lawrenceville Rd., Lawrenceville 08648-3099 *Type:* Private non-profit *Accred.:* 1955/1991 (MSA) *Calendar:* 4-1-4 plan *Degrees:* A, B, M, C *Prof. Accred.:* Business (B,M), Teacher Education *CEO:* Pres. J. Barton Luedeke
Enroll: 5,580   (609) 896-5000

WESTMINSTER CHOIR COLLEGE
101 Walnut Ln., Princeton 08540 *Prof. Accred.:* Music
         (609) 921-7100

ROWAN COLLEGE OF NEW JERSEY
201 Mullica Hill Rd., Glassboro 08028-1701 *Type:* Public (state) *System:* New Jersey Commission on Higher Education *Accred.:* 1958/1994 (MSA) *Calendar:* Sem. plan

Degrees: B, M, C *Prof. Accred.:* Art, Music, Teacher Education *CEO:* Pres. Herman D. James
Enroll: 8,936   (609) 256-4100

CAMDEN CAMPUS
One Broadway, Camden 08102
         (609) 757-2857

RUTGERS, THE STATE UNIVERSITY OF NEW JERSEY CAMDEN CAMPUS
Armitage Hall, Camden 08102 *Type:* Public (state) *System:* Rutgers, The State University of New Jersey Central Office *Accred.:* 1950/1993 (MSA) *Calendar:* Sem. plan *Degrees:* B, M, P *Prof. Accred.:* Law, Nursing (B), Physical Therapy, Public Administration, Social Work (B,M) *CEO:* Provost Walter K. Gordon
Enroll: 9,456   (609) 225-6095

RUTGERS, THE STATE UNIVERSITY OF NEW JERSEY NEW BRUNSWICK CAMPUS
18 Bishop Pl., New Brunswick 08903 *Type:* Public (state) *System:* Rutgers, The State University of New Jersey Central Office *Accred.:* 1921/1993 (MSA) *Calendar:* Sem. plan *Degrees:* B, M, P, D *Prof. Accred.:* Accounting (A), Art, Business (B), Clinical Psychology, Dance (A), Engineering (agricultural, ceramic, chemical, civil, electrical, industrial, mechanical), Landscape Architecture (B), Librarianship, Music, Planning (M), School Psychology, Social Work (B,M), Theatre *CEO:* Provost Joseph A. Potenza
Enroll: 33,415   (908) 932-7461

RUTGERS, THE STATE UNIVERSITY OF NEW JERSEY NEWARK CAMPUS
15 Washington St., Newark 07102 *Type:* Public (state) *System:* Rutgers, The State University of New Jersey Central Office *Accred.:* 1946/1993 (MSA) *Calendar:* Sem. plan *Degrees:* B, M, P *Prof. Accred.:* Business (B,M), Law, Nursing (B,M), Public Administration, Social Work (B,M) *CEO:* Provost Norman Samuels
Enroll: 9,459   (201) 648-1766

ST. PETER'S COLLEGE
2641 Kennedy Blvd., Jersey City 07306 *Type:* Private (Roman Catholic) *Accred.:* 1935/1993 (MSA) *Calendar:* Sem. plan *Degrees:* A, B, M, C *Prof. Accred.:* Nursing (B) *CEO:* Pres. James N. Loughran, S.J.
Enroll: 3,561　　　　　　(201) 915-9000

ENGLEWOOD CLIFFS CAMPUS
Hudson Terrace, Englewood Cliffs 07632
　　　　　　　　　　(201) 568-7730

SALEM COMMUNITY COLLEGE
460 Hollywood Ave., Carneys Point 08069-2799 *Type:* Public (local/state) junior *System:* New Jersey Commission on Higher Education *Accred.:* 1979/1995 (MSA) *Calendar:* Sem. plan *Degrees:* A, C *CEO:* Pres. Linda C. Jolly
Enroll: 1,428　　　　　　(609) 299-2100

SETON HALL UNIVERSITY
400 S. Orange Ave., South Orange 07079 *Type:* Private (Roman Catholic) *Accred.:* 1932/1994 (MSA) *Calendar:* Sem. plan *Degrees:* B, M, P, D, C *Prof. Accred.:* Business (B,M), Nursing (B,M), Physical Therapy, Public Administration, Social Work (B), Teacher Education *CEO:* Pres. Robert T. Sheeran
Enroll: 10,312　　　　　　(201) 761-9000

SCHOOL OF LAW CAMPUS
One Newark Ctr., Newark 07102-5210 *Prof. Accred.:* Law
Enroll: 1,326　　　　　　(201) 642-8500

STEVENS INSTITUTE OF TECHNOLOGY
Castle Point on the Hudson, Hoboken 07030 *Type:* Private research *Accred.:* 1927/1993 (MSA) *Calendar:* Sem. plan *Degrees:* B, M, D *Prof. Accred.:* Computer Science, Engineering (chemical, civil, computer, electrical, engineering management, engineering physics/science, general, mechanical, metallurgical) *CEO:* Pres. Harold J. Raveche
Enroll: 2,914　　　　　　(201) 216-5100

SUSSEX COUNTY COMMUNITY COLLEGE
College Hill, Newton 07860 *Type:* Public (local/state) junior *System:* New Jersey Commission on Higher Education *Accred.:* 1993/1993 (MSA) *Calendar:* Sem. plan *Degrees:* A, C *CEO:* Pres. William A. Connor
Enroll: 2,213　　　　　　(201) 300-2100

TALMUDICAL ACADEMY OF NEW JERSEY
Rte. 524, Adelphia 07710 *Type:* Private professional *Accred.:* 1980/1993 (AARTS) *Calendar:* Sem. plan *Degrees:* B *CEO:* Pres. Charles Semah
Enroll: 16　　　　　　(201) 431-1600

THOMAS A. EDISON STATE COLLEGE
101 W. State St., Trenton 08608-1176 *Type:* Public (state) *System:* New Jersey Commission on Higher Education *Accred.:* 1977/1992 (MSA) *Calendar:* Sem. plan *Degrees:* A, B, P, C *Prof. Accred.:* Nursing (B) *CEO:* Pres. George A. Pruitt
Enroll: 8,619　　　　　　(609) 984-1100

TRENTON STATE COLLEGE
Hillwood Lakes, P.O. Box 4700, Trenton 08650-4700 *Type:* Public (state) *System:* New Jersey Commission on Higher Education *Accred.:* 1939/1995 (MSA) *Calendar:* Sem. plan *Degrees:* B, M, C *Prof. Accred.:* Audiology, Counseling, Engineering Technology (industrial, mechanical), Interior Design, Music, Nursing (B), Speech-Language Pathology, Teacher Education *CEO:* Pres. Harold W. Eickhoff
Enroll: 6,981　　　　　　(609) 771-1855

UNION COUNTY COLLEGE
1033 Springfield Ave., Cranford 07016 *Type:* Public (local/state) two-year *System:* New Jersey Commission on Higher Education *Accred.:* 1957/1992 (MSA) *Calendar:* Sem. plan *Degrees:* A, C *Prof. Accred.:* Clinical Lab Technology (A), Occupational Therapy Assisting, Physical Therapy Assisting, Respiratory Therapy *CEO:* Pres. Thomas H. Brown
Enroll: 10,457　　　　　　(908) 709-7000

ELIZABETH CAMPUS
12 W. Jersey St., Elizabeth 07206
　　　　　　　　　　(908) 965-6090

PLAINFIELD CAMPUS
232 E. Second St., Plainfield 07060 *Prof. Accred.:* Practical Nursing
(908) 889-8500

UNIVERSITY OF MEDICINE AND DENTISTRY OF NEW JERSEY
30 Bergen St., Newark 07107-3007 *Type:* Public (state) professional *System:* New Jersey Commission on Higher Education *Accred.:* 1979/1995 (MSA) *Calendar:* Sem. plan *Degrees:* A, B, M, P, D, C *Prof. Accred.:* Clinical Lab Scientist, Cytotechnology, Diagnostic Medical Sonography, Nuclear Medicine Technology, Nursing (A), Physician Assisting/Surgeon Assisting, Psychology Internship, Radiography, Respiratory Therapy, Respiratory Therapy Technology, Surgical Technology *CEO:* Pres. Stanley S. Bergen, Jr.
Enroll: 4,032   (201) 982-4300

GRADUATE SCHOOL OF BIOMEDICAL SCIENCES
185 S. Orange Ave., Newark 07103
Enroll: 734   (201) 456-4511

NEW JERSEY DENTAL SCHOOL
110 Bergen St., Newark 07103 *Prof. Accred.:* Combined Prosthodontics, Dental Assisting, Dental Hygiene, Dentistry, Endodontics, General Dentistry, General Practice Residency, Oral and Maxillofacial Surgery, Orthodontics, Pediatric Dentistry, Periodontics
Enroll: 353   (201) 456-4633

NEW JERSEY MEDICAL SCHOOL
185 S. Orange Ave., Newark 07103 *Prof. Accred.:* Medicine, Psychology Internship
Enroll: 703   (201) 465-4539

NEW JERSEY SCHOOL OF OSTEOPATHIC MEDICINE
Academic Ctr., One Medical Center Dr., Stratford 08084 *Prof. Accred.:* Osteopathy
Enroll: 231   (609) 566-6995

ROBERT WOOD JOHNSON MEDICAL SCHOOL
671 Hoes Ln., Piscataway 08854 *Prof. Accred.:* Medicine, Psychology (internship)
Enroll: 599   (908) 463-4557

SCHOOL OF HEALTH-RELATED PROFESSIONS
65 Bergen St., Newark 07107 *Prof. Accred.:* Dietetics (internship)
Enroll: 637   (201) 456-5453

WARREN COUNTY COMMUNITY COLLEGE
Box 55A, Rte. 57 W., R.D. 1, Washington 07882 *Type:* Public (local/state) junior *System:* New Jersey Commission on Higher Education *Accred.:* 1993 (MSA) *Calendar:* Sem. plan *Degrees:* A, C *CEO:* Pres. Vincent De Sanctis
Enroll: 831   (908) 689-1090

WILLIAM PATERSON COLLEGE OF NEW JERSEY
300 Pompton Rd., Wayne 07470 *Type:* Public (state) *System:* New Jersey Commission on Higher Education *Accred.:* 1958/1991 (MSA) *Calendar:* Sem. plan *Degrees:* B, M *Prof. Accred.:* Music, Nursing (B), Speech-Language Pathology, Teacher Education *CEO:* Pres. Arnold Speert
Enroll: 9,671   (201) 595-2000

NEW MEXICO

ALBUQUERQUE TECHNICAL VOCATIONAL
INSTITUTE
525 Buena Vista Dr., S.E., Albuquerque
87106 *Type:* Public 2-year *System:* New
Mexico Commission on Higher Education
Accred.: 1978/1993 (NCA) *Calendar:* Tri.
plan *Degrees:* A, C *Prof. Accred.:* Clinical
Lab Technology (A), Engineering Technol-
ogy (electrical, general drafting/design),
Nursing (A), Practical Nursing, Respiratory
Therapy *CEO:* Pres. Alex A. Sanchez
Enroll: 14,905   (505) 224-3000

CLOVIS COMMUNITY COLLEGE
417 Schepps Blvd., Clovis 88101 *Type:* Public (state) junior *System:* New Mexico Commission on Higher Education *Accred.:* 1987/
1992 (NCA) *Calendar:* Sem. plan *Degrees:*
A, C *Prof. Accred.:* Nursing (A), Radiography *CEO:* Pres. Jay Gurley
Enroll: 3,743   (505) 769-2811

THE COLLEGE OF SANTA FE
1600 St. Michael's Dr., Santa Fe 87501
Type: Private (Roman Catholic) liberal arts
Accred.: 1965/1991 (NCA) *Calendar:* Sem.
plan *Degrees:* A, B, M *CEO:* Pres. James A.
Fries
Enroll: 1,394   (800) 456-2673

COLLEGE OF THE SOUTHWEST
6610 Lovington Hwy., Hobbs 88240 *Type:*
Private liberal arts *Accred.:* 1980/1993
(NCA) *Calendar:* Sem. plan *Degrees:* B
CEO: Pres. Joan M. Tucker
Enroll: 431   (800) 530-4400

EASTERN NEW MEXICO UNIVERSITY
Campus Station No. 1, Portales 88130 *Type:*
Public (state) *System:* New Mexico Com-
mission on Higher Education *Accred.:* 1947/
1987 (NCA) *Calendar:* Sem. plan *Degrees:*
A, B, M *Prof. Accred.:* Music, Speech-Lan-
guage Pathology *CEO:* Pres. Everett L. Frost
Enroll: 3,296   (505) 562-2121

ROSWELL CAMPUS
P.O. Box 6000, Roswell 88202 (state)
Accred.: 1971/1992 (NCA) *Calendar:*

Sem. plan *Degrees:* A, C *Prof. Accred.:*
EMT-Paramedic, Nursing (A), Occupa-
tional Therapy Assisting
Enroll: 2,448   (505) 624-7000

INSTITUTE OF AMERICAN INDIAN AND ALASKAN
NATIVE CULTURE AND ARTS DEVELOPMENT
St. Michael's Dr., Box 20007, Santa Fe
87504 *Type:* Public (federal) *Accred.:* 1984/
1995 (NCA) *Calendar:* Sem. plan *Degrees:*
A *Prof. Accred.:* Art *CEO:* Pres. Perry G.
Horse
Enroll: 240   (505) 988-6463

INTERNATIONAL INSTITUTE OF CHINESE
MEDICINE
P.O. Box 4991, Santa Fe 87502 *Type:* Private
professional *Calendar:* Sem. plan *Degrees:*
M *Prof. Accred.:* Acupuncture *CEO:* Pres.
Michael Zeng
FTE Enroll: 85   (505) 473-5233

INTERNATIONAL SCHOOL
301 Victory Ln., Sunland 88063 *Type:* Private *Accred.:* 1990 (ACCSCT) *Degrees:* A
CEO: Owner Bob C. Lewis
                                         (505) 589-1414

LUNA VOCATIONAL TECHNICAL INSTITUTE
P.O. Drawer K, Las Vegas 87701 *Type:* Pub-
lic 2-year *System:* New Mexico Commission
on Higher Education *Accred.:* 1982/1995
(NCA) *Calendar:* Tri. plan *Degrees:* A, C
CEO: Pres. Samuel F. Vigil
Enroll: 1,373   (505) 454-2500

NEW MEXICO HIGHLANDS UNIVERSITY
National Ave., Las Vegas 87701 *Type:* Public
(state) liberal arts and professional *System:*
New Mexico Commission on Higher Educa-
tion *Accred.:* 1926/1991 (NCA) *Calendar:*
Sem. plan *Degrees:* A, B, M *Prof. Accred.:*
electrical) *CEO:* Pres. Selimo Rael
Enroll: 2,015   (505) 454-3229

NEW MEXICO INSTITUTE OF MINING AND
TECHNOLOGY
Brown Hall, Socorro 87801 *Type:* Public
(state) technological *System:* New Mexico
Commission on Higher Education *Accred.:*

1914/1995 (NCA) *Calendar:* Sem. plan *Degrees:* A, B, M, D *Prof. Accred.:* Engineering (electrical, environmental/sanitary, materials, petroleum) *CEO:* Pres. Daniel H. Lopez
Enroll: 1,405   (505) 835-5500

NEW MEXICO JUNIOR COLLEGE
5317 Lovington Hwy., Hobbs 88240 *Type:* Public (district) junior *System:* New Mexico Commission on Higher Education *Accred.:* 1970/1986 (NCA) *Calendar:* Sem. plan *Degrees:* A, C *Prof. Accred.:* Clinical Lab Technology (A), Nursing (A) *CEO:* Pres. Charles D. Hays, Jr.
Enroll: 2,829   (505) 392-4510

NEW MEXICO MILITARY INSTITUTE
100 W. College Blvd., Roswell 88201 *Type:* Public (state) junior *System:* New Mexico Commission on Higher Education *Accred.:* 1938/1991 (NCA) *Calendar:* Sem. plan *Degrees:* A *CEO:* Supt. Winfield W. Scott, Jr.
Enroll: 440   (800) 421-5376

NEW MEXICO STATE UNIVERSITY
Box 30001, Dept. 3Z, Las Cruces 88003 *Type:* Public (state) *System:* New Mexico Commission on Higher Education *Accred.:* 1926/1988 (NCA) *Calendar:* Sem. plan *Degrees:* A, B, M, P, D, C *Prof. Accred.:* Accounting (A,C), Business (B,M), Engineering Technology (civil/construction, electrical, mechanical), Engineering (agricultural, chemical, civil, electrical, geological/geophysical, industrial, mechanical), Music, Nursing (A,B), Public Administration, Social Work (B,M), Speech-Language Pathology, Teacher Education *CEO:* Pres. J. Michael Orenduff
Enroll: 17,461   (505) 646-0111

ALAMOGORDO BRANCH COMMUNITY COLLEGE
P.O. Box 477, Alamogordo 88311-0477 (state) *Accred.:* 1973/1993 (NCA) *Calendar:* Sem. plan *Degrees:* A, C *Prof. Accred.:* Clinical Lab Technology (A), Nursing (A)
Enroll: 2,330   (505) 439-3600

CARLSBAD BRANCH COMMUNITY COLLEGE
1500 University Dr., Carlsbad 88220 (state) *Accred.:* 1980/1992 (NCA) *Calendar:* Sem. plan *Degrees:* A, C *Prof. Accred.:* Nursing (A)
Enroll: 1,240   (505) 885-8831

DONA ANA BRANCH COMMUNITY COLLEGE
Box 30001, Las Cruces 88003 2-year *Degrees:* A, C *Prof. Accred.:* Radiography
                    (505) 527-7510

GRANTS BRANCH COMMUNITY COLLEGE
1500 3rd St., Grants 87020
                    (505) 287-7981

NORTHERN NEW MEXICO COMMUNITY COLLEGE
1002 N. Onate St., Espanola 87532 *Type:* Public (state) junior *System:* New Mexico Commission on Higher Education *Accred.:* 1982/1994 (NCA) *Calendar:* Sem. plan *Degrees:* A, C *Prof. Accred.:* Radiography *CEO:* Pres. Connie A. Valdez
Enroll: 1,641   (505) 747-2100

PARKS COLLEGE
1023 Tijeras Ave., N.W., Albuquerque 87102 *Type:* Private junior *Accred.:* 1981/1995 (ACICS) *Calendar:* Qtr. plan *Degrees:* A, C *CEO:* Pres. Cynthia S. Welch
                    (505) 843-7500

TUCSON CAMPUS
6922 E. Broadway, Tucson, AZ 85710 *Accred.:* 1987 (ACICS)
                    (520) 886-7979

ST. JOHN'S COLLEGE
Santa Fe 87501-4599 *Type:* Private liberal arts *Accred.:* 1969/1989 (NCA) *Calendar:* Sem. plan *Degrees:* B, M *CEO:* Pres. John Agresto
Enroll: 391   (505) 984-6000

SAN JUAN COLLEGE
4601 College Blvd., Farmington 87402 *Type:* Public (state) junior *System:* New Mexico Commission on Higher Education *Accred.:* 1973/1994 (NCA) *Calendar:* Sem. plan *Degrees:* A, C *Prof. Accred.:* Engineering Technology (mechanical drafting/

design), Nursing (A), Physical Therapy Assisting *CEO:* Pres. James C. Henderson
Enroll: 4,254   (800) 241-6327

SANTA FE COMMUNITY COLLEGE
P.O. Box 4187, Santa Fe 87502-4187 *Type:* Public (state) junior *System:* New Mexico Commission on Higher Education *Accred.:* 1988/1993 (NCA) *Calendar:* Sem. plan *Degrees:* A, C *Prof. Accred.:* Nursing (A) *CEO:* Pres. Leonardo de la Garza
Enroll: 5,114   (505) 471-8200

SOUTHWEST ACUPUNCTURE COLLEGE
325 Paseo De Peralta, Ste. 500, Santa Fe 87501 *Type:* Private professional *Calendar:* Tri. plan *Degrees:* M *Prof. Accred.:* Acupuncture *CEO:* Pres. Anthony Abbate
FTE Enroll: 65   (505) 988-3538

ALBUQUERQUE CAMPUS
4308 Carlisle Blvd., N.E., Ste. 205, Albuquerque 87107
                                   (505) 888-8898

SOUTHWESTERN INDIAN POLYTECHNIC INSTITUTE
9169 Coors Rd., N.W., Box 10146, Albuquerque 87184 *Type:* Public (federal) 2-year *Accred.:* 1975/1993 (NCA) *Calendar:* Qtr. plan *Degrees:* A, C *CEO:* Pres. Carolyn Elgin
Enroll: 586   (505) 897-5340

THE UNIVERSITY OF NEW MEXICO
Scholes Hall 160, Albuquerque 87131 *Type:* Public (state) *System:* New Mexico Commission on Higher Education *Accred.:* 1922/1989 (NCA) *Calendar:* Sem. plan *Degrees:* A, B, M, P, D, C *Prof. Accred.:* Audiology, Business (B,M), Clinical Lab Scientist, Clinical Psychology, Computer Science, Construction Education, Counseling, Dance, Dental Hygiene, Diagnostic Medical Sonography, EMT-Paramedic, Engineering (chemical, civil, computer, construction, electrical, mechanical, nuclear), Journalism (B,M), Law, Medicine, Music, Nuclear Medicine Technology, Nursing (B,M), Occupational Therapy, Physical Therapy, Planning (M), Psychology Internship, Public Administration, Radiation Therapy Technology, Radiography, Speech-Language Pathology, Teacher Education, Theatre *CEO:* Pres. Richard E. Peck
Enroll: 24,832   (505) 277-0111

GALLUP CAMPUS
200 College Rd., Gallup 87301 *Prof. Accred.:* Clinical Lab Technology (A), Dental Assisting (prelim. provisional), Nursing (A)
                                   (505) 843-7783

LOS ALAMOS CAMPUS
4000 University Dr., Los Alamos 87544
                                   (505) 867-2379

TAOS EDUCATION CENTER CAMPUS
115 Civic Plaza Dr., Taos 87571
                                   (505) 758-7667

VALENCIA CAMPUS
280 La Entrada, Los Lunas 87031
                                   (505) 865-1639

WESTERN NEW MEXICO UNIVERSITY
P.O. Box 680, 1000 W. College Ave., Silver City 88062 *Type:* Public (state) liberal arts and professional *System:* New Mexico Commission on Higher Education *Accred.:* 1926/1992 (NCA) *Calendar:* Sem. plan *Degrees:* A, B, M, C *Prof. Accred.:* Nursing (A), Occupational Therapy Assisting, Social Work (B-candidate) *CEO:* Pres. John E. Counts
Enroll: 1,979   (800) 222-9668

NEW YORK

ADELPHI UNIVERSITY
South Ave., Garden City 11530 *Type:* Private
non-profit *Accred.:* 1921/1993 (MSA) *Cal-
endar:* Sem. plan *Degrees:* A, B, M, D, C
Prof. Accred.: Audiology, Clinical Psychol-
ogy, Nursing (B,M), Social Work (B,M),
Speech-Language Pathology *CEO:* Pres.
Peter Diamandopoulos
Enroll: 7,979   (516) 877-3000

ADIRONDACK COMMUNITY COLLEGE
Bay Rd., Queensbury 12804 *Type:* Public
(local/state) junior *System:* State University
of New York Office of Community Colleges
Accred.: 1971/1993 (MSA) *Calendar:* Sem.
plan *Degrees:* A *Prof. Accred.:* Medical
Record Technology *CEO:* Pres. Roger C.
Andersen
Enroll: 3,475   (518) 743-2200

ALBANY COLLEGE OF PHARMACY OF UNION
UNIVERSITY
106 New Scotland Ave., Albany 12208 *Type:*
Private professional *Accred.:* 1921/1992
(MSA) *Calendar:* Sem. plan *Degrees:* B, P,
D *CEO:* Pres. Claire Lathers
Enroll: 666   (518) 445-7200

ALBANY MEDICAL COLLEGE OF UNION
UNIVERSITY
47 New Scotland Ave., Albany 12208 *Type:*
Private professional *Accred.:* 1921/1989
(MSA) *Calendar:* Sem. plan *Degrees:* M, P,
D *Prof. Accred.:* Cytotechnology, Medicine,
Nurse Anesthesia Education (M), Physician
Assisting/Surgeon Assisting, Psychology
Internship *CEO:* Interim Dean Richard
Edmonds
Enroll: 674   (518) 262-4970

ALFRED UNIVERSITY
26 North Main St., Alfred 14802-1232 *Type:*
Private non-profit *Accred.:* 1921/1994
(MSA) *Calendar:* Sem. plan *Degrees:* B, M,
D *Prof. Accred.:* Business (B) *CEO:* Pres.
Edward G. Coll, Jr.
Enroll: 2,363   (607) 871-2111

NEW YORK STATE COLLEGE OF CERAMICS AT
ALFRED UNIVERSITY
Alfred 14802 *System:* State University of
New York System Office *Prof. Accred.:*
Art, Engineering (ceramic, electrical,
industrial)
       (607) 871-2411

AMERICAN ACADEMY MCALLISTER INSTITUTE
OF FUNERAL SERVICE, INC.
450 W. 56th St., New York 10019 *Type:* Private professional *Degrees:* A, C *Prof.
Accred.:* Funeral Service Education (Mortuary Science) *CEO:* Pres. Meg Dunn
       (212) 757-1190

AMERICAN ACADEMY OF DRAMATIC ARTS
120 Madison Ave., New York 10016 *Type:*
Private 2-year professional *Accred.:* 1983/
1993 (MSA) *Calendar:* Sem. plan *Degrees:*
A *Prof. Accred.:* Theatre *CEO:* Pres. George
Cuttingham
Enroll: 412   (212) 686-9244

AUDREY COHEN COLLEGE
345 Hudson St., New York 10014-4598
Type: Private professional *Accred.:* 1984/
1994 (MSA) *Calendar:* Sem. plan *Degrees:*
B, M *CEO:* Pres. Audrey C. Cohen
Enroll: 1,048   (212) 989-2002

BANK STREET COLLEGE OF EDUCATION
610 W. 112th St., New York 10025 *Type:* Pri-
vate graduate only *Accred.:* 1960/1992
(MSA) *Calendar:* Sem. plan *Degrees:* M, P,
C *CEO:* Pres. Augusta Souza Kappner
Enroll: 903   (212) 875-4400

BARD COLLEGE
Annandale-on-Hudson 12504 *Type:* Private
liberal arts *Accred.:* 1922/1992 (MSA) *Cal-
endar:* Sem. plan *Degrees:* B, M *CEO:* Pres.
Leon Botstein
Enroll: 1,233   (914) 758-6822

BARNARD COLLEGE
3009 Broadway, New York 10027-6598
Type: Private liberal arts for women *Accred.:*

1921/1991 (MSA) *Calendar:* Sem. plan *Degrees:* B *CEO:* Pres. Judith Shapiro *Enroll:* 2,274 (212) 854-5262

BERKELEY COLLEGE
W. Red Oak Ln., White Plains 10604 *Type:* Private 2-year *Accred.:* 1988/1994 (MSA) *Calendar:* Qtr. plan *Degrees:* A, C *CEO:* Pres. Rose Mary Healy
Enroll: 563 (914) 694-1122

BERKELEY COLLEGE OF NEW YORK CITY
3 E. 43rd St., New York 10017 *Type:* Private 2-year *Accred.:* 1993 (MSA) *Calendar:* Qtr. plan *Degrees:* A, C *CEO:* Pres. Robert J. Hurd
Enroll: 795 (212) 986-4343

BERNARD M. BARUCH COLLEGE
17 Lexington Ave., New York 10010 *Type:* Public (local/state) *System:* City University of New York Office of the Chancellor *Accred.:* 1968/1990 (MSA) *Calendar:* Sem. plan *Degrees:* B, M *Prof. Accred.:* Accounting (A,B), Business (B,M), Public Administration *CEO:* Pres. Matthew Goldstein
Enroll: 15,091 (212) 802-2000

BETH HAMEDRASH SHAAREI YOSHER
4102 16th Ave., Brooklyn 11204 *Type:* Private professional *Accred.:* 1982/1990 (AARTS) *Calendar:* Sem. plan *Degrees:* Talmudic (1st and 2nd) *CEO:* Pres. Y. Mayer
Enroll: 121 (718) 854-2290

BETH HATALMUD RABBINICAL COLLEGE
2127 82nd St., Brooklyn 11214 *Type:* Private professional *Accred.:* 1978/1990 (AARTS) *Calendar:* Sem. plan *Degrees:* Talmudic (1st and 2nd) *CEO:* Pres. E. Meyer
Enroll: 230 (718) 259-2525

BORICUA COLLEGE
3755 Broadway, New York 10032 *Type:* Private liberal arts *Accred.:* 1980/1993 (MSA) *Calendar:* Tri. plan *Degrees:* A, B *CEO:* Pres. Victor G. Alicea
Enroll: 1,039 (212) 694-1000

BOROUGH OF MANHATTAN COMMUNITY COLLEGE
199 Chambers St., New York 10007 *Type:* Public (local/state) two-year *System:* City University of New York Office of the Chancellor *Accred.:* 1964/1993 (MSA) *Calendar:* Sem. plan *Degrees:* A *Prof. Accred.:* Medical Record Technology, Nursing (A), Respiratory Therapy *CEO:* Pres. Antonio Perez
Enroll: 16,728 (212) 346-8000

BRIARCLIFFE SCHOOL, INC.
250 Crossways Park Dr., Woodbury 11797-2015 *Type:* Private junior *Accred.:* 1977/1991 (ACICS); 1989 (MSA candidate) *Calendar:* Sem. plan *Degrees:* A, C *CEO:* Pres. Richard Turan
Enroll: 1,252 (516) 364-2055

LYNBROOK CAMPUS
10 Peninsula Blvd., Lynbrook 11563 *Accred.:* 1989 (ACICS)
(516) 596-1313

PATCHOGUE CAMPUS
10 Lake St., Patchogue 11772 *Accred.:* 1989 (ACICS)
(516) 654-5300

BRONX COMMUNITY COLLEGE
W. 181st St. and University Av, Bronx 10453 *Type:* Public (local/state) two-year *System:* City University of New York Office of the Chancellor *Accred.:* 1961/1994 (MSA) *Calendar:* Sem. plan *Degrees:* A, C *Prof. Accred.:* Engineering Technology (electrical), Nuclear Medicine Technology, Nursing (A), Radiography *CEO:* Acting Pres. Leo A. Corbie
Enroll: 8,357 (718) 220-6920

BROOKLYN COLLEGE
2900 Bedford Ave., Brooklyn 11210-2889 *Type:* Public (local/state) *System:* City University of New York Office of the Chancellor *Accred.:* 1933/1994 (MSA) *Calendar:* Sem. plan *Degrees:* B, M, C *Prof. Accred.:* Audiology, Nurse Anesthesia Education, Speech-Language Pathology *CEO:* Pres. Vernon E. Lattin
Enroll: 15,984 (718) 951-5000

BROOKLYN LAW SCHOOL
250 Joralemon St., Brooklyn 11201 *Type:* Private professional *Calendar:* Sem. plan *Degrees:* P *Prof. Accred.:* Law *CEO:* Dean David G. Trager
Enroll: 1,457   (718) 625-2200

BROOME COMMUNITY COLLEGE
Upper Front St., P.O. Box 1017, Binghamton 13902 *Type:* Public (local/state) two year *System:* State University of New York Office of Community Colleges *Accred.:* 1960/1990 (MSA) *Calendar:* Sem. plan *Degrees:* A, C *Prof. Accred.:* Clinical Lab Technology (A), Dental Hygiene, Engineering Technology (chemical, civil/construction, electrical, mechanical), Medical Assisting (AMA), Medical Record Technology, Nursing (A), Physical Therapy Assisting, Radiography *CEO:* Pres. Donald A. Dellow
Enroll: 6,011   (607) 778-5000

BRYANT AND STRATTON BUSINESS INSTITUTE
1259 Central Ave., Albany 12205 *Type:* Private business *Accred.:* 1953/1994 (ACICS) *Calendar:* Qtr. plan *Degrees:* A *CEO:* Dir. Beth A. Tarquino
     (518) 437-1802

BRYANT AND STRATTON BUSINESS INSTITUTE
1028 Main St., Buffalo 14202 *Type:* Private business *Accred.:* 1953/1996 (ACICS) *Calendar:* Qtr. plan *Degrees:* A, C *Prof. Accred.:* Medical Assisting (AMA) *CEO:* Dir. William B. Schatt
     (716) 884-9120

LACKAWANNA CAMPUS
1214 Abbott Rd., Lackawanna 14218 *Accred.:* 1990 (ACICS)
     (716) 821-9331

WILLIAMSVILLE CAMPUS
200 Bryant and Stratton Way, Williamsville 14221 *Accred.:* 1981 (ACICS)
     (716) 631-0260

BRYANT AND STRATTON BUSINESS INSTITUTE
82 St. Paul St., Rochester 14604-1381 *Type:* Private business *Accred.:* 1975/1988 (ACICS) *Calendar:* Qtr. plan *Degrees:* A, C

Prof. Accred.: Medical Assisting (AMA) *CEO:* Dir. Eric B. Donaldson
     (716) 325-6010

ROCHESTER CAMPUS
1225 Jefferson Rd., Rochester 14623 *Accred.:* 1993 (ACICS) *Prof. Accred.:* Medical Assisting (AMA)
     (716) 292-5627

BRYANT AND STRATTON BUSINESS INSTITUTE
953 James St., Syracuse 13203-2502 *Type:* Private business *Accred.:* 1968/1987 (ACICS) *Calendar:* Qtr. plan *Degrees:* A, C *Prof. Accred.:* Medical Assisting (AMA) *CEO:* Dir. Edward J. Heinrich
     (315) 472-6603

CICERO CAMPUS
5775 S. Bay Rd., Cicero 13039 *Accred.:* 1984 (ACICS)
     (315) 452-1105

CANISIUS COLLEGE
2001 Main St., Buffalo 14208 *Type:* Private non-profit *Accred.:* 1921/1995 (MSA) *Calendar:* Sem. plan *Degrees:* A, B, M *Prof. Accred.:* Business (B,M), Teacher Education *CEO:* Pres. Vincent M. Cooke, S.J.
Enroll: 4,787   (716) 883-7000

CAYUGA COUNTY COMMUNITY COLLEGE
Franklin St., Auburn 13021 *Type:* Public (local/state) two year *System:* State University of New York Office of Community Colleges *Accred.:* 1965/1991 (MSA) *Calendar:* Sem. plan *Degrees:* A, C *Prof. Accred.:* Nursing (A) *CEO:* Pres. Lawrence H. Poole
Enroll: 2,823   (315) 255-1743

CAZENOVIA COLLEGE
Seminary St., Cazenovia 13035 *Type:* Private liberal arts *Accred.:* 1961/1992 (MSA) *Calendar:* Sem. plan *Degrees:* A, B *CEO:* Pres. Adelaide Van Titus, Ed.D.
Enroll: 913   (315) 655-8283

CENTRAL YESHIVA TOMCHEI TMIMIM-LUBAVITCH
841-853 Ocean Pkwy., Brooklyn 11230 *Type:* Private professional *Accred.:* 1976/1994 (AARTS) *Calendar:* Sem. plan

Degrees: Rabbinic (1st and 2nd), Talmudic (1st and 2nd) *CEO:* Pres. J. Korf
Enroll: 450   (718) 434-0784

CHRIST THE KING SEMINARY
711 Knox Rd., P.O. Box 607, East Aurora 14052-0607 *Type:* Private (Roman Catholic) *Accred.:* 1977/1992 (ATS); 1974/1993 (MSA) *Calendar:* Sem. plan *Degrees:* M, P *CEO:* Pres./Rector Frederick D. Leising
Enroll: 95   (716) 652-8900

THE CITY COLLEGE
Convent Ave. at 138th St., New York 10031 *Type:* Public (local/state) *System:* City University of New York Office of the Chancellor *Accred.:* 1921/1992 (MSA) *Calendar:* Sem. plan *Degrees:* B, M, C *Prof. Accred.:* Clinical Psychology, Computer Science, Engineering (chemical, civil, electrical, mechanical), Landscape Architecture (B), Nursing (B) *CEO:* Pres. Yolanda T. Moses
Enroll: 14,885   (212) 650-7000

CITY UNIVERSITY SCHOOL OF LAW AT QUEENS COLLEGE
65-21 Main St., Flushing 11367 *Type:* Public *System:* City University of New York Office of the Chancellor *Calendar:* Sem. plan *Degrees:* P *Prof. Accred.:* Law (ABA only) *CEO:* Dean Kristin Booth Glen
Enroll: 447   (718) 575-4200

CLARKSON UNIVERSITY
Box 5500, Potsdam 13699-5500 *Type:* Private technological *Accred.:* 1927/1993 (MSA) *Calendar:* Sem. plan *Degrees:* B, M, D *Prof. Accred.:* Business (B,M), Engineering (chemical, civil, computer, electrical, mechanical) *CEO:* Pres. Dennis G. Brown
Enroll: 2,601   (315) 268-6400

CLINTON COMMUNITY COLLEGE
136 Clinton Point Dr., Box 8A, Plattsburgh 12901-9573 *Type:* Public (local/state) two year *System:* State University of New York Office of Community Colleges *Accred.:* 1975/1992 (MSA) *Calendar:* Sem. plan *Degrees:* A, C *Prof. Accred.:* Clinical Lab Technology (A), Nursing (A) *CEO:* Pres. Jay L. Fennell
Enroll: 2,119   (518) 562-4200

COLGATE ROCHESTER DIVINITY SCHOOL/BEXLEY HALL/CROZER THEOLOGICAL SEMINARY
1100 S. Goodman St., Rochester 14620 *Type:* Private (interdenominational) graduate only *Accred.:* 1938/1993 (ATS) *Calendar:* Sem. plan *Degrees:* M, D *CEO:* Pres. James H. Evans, Jr.
Enroll: 167   (716) 271-1320

COLGATE UNIVERSITY
13 Oak Dr., Hamilton 13346 *Type:* Private liberal arts *Accred.:* 1921/1993 (MSA) *Calendar:* Sem. plan *Degrees:* B, M *CEO:* Pres. Neil R. Grabois
Enroll: 2,795   (315) 824-1000

COLLEGE OF AERONAUTICS
La Guardia Airport Sta., Flushing 11371 *Type:* Private technical *Accred.:* 1969/1992 (MSA) *Calendar:* Tri. plan *Degrees:* A, B *Prof. Accred.:* Engineering Technology (aerospace) *CEO:* Pres. Richard B. Goetze, Jr.
Enroll: 978   (718) 429-6600

COLLEGE OF INSURANCE
101 Murray St., New York 10007 *Type:* Private professional *Accred.:* 1967/1994 (MSA) *Calendar:* Sem. plan *Degrees:* A, B, M, C *CEO:* Pres. Ellen Thrower
Enroll: 546   (212) 962-4111

COLLEGE OF MOUNT ST. VINCENT
6301 Riverdale Ave., Riverdale 10471 *Type:* Private liberal arts *Accred.:* 1921/1992 (MSA) *Calendar:* Sem. plan *Degrees:* A, B, M, C *Prof. Accred.:* Nursing (B) *CEO:* Pres. Mary C. Stuart
Enroll: 1,337   (212) 405-3200

COLLEGE OF NEW ROCHELLE
29 Castle Pl., New Rochelle 10805 *Type:* Private non-profit *Accred.:* 1921/1992 (MSA) *Calendar:* Sem. plan *Degrees:* B, M, C *Prof. Accred.:* Nursing (B,M), Social Work (B) *CEO:* Pres. Dorothy Ann Kelly, O.S.U.
Enroll: 6,243   (914) 632-5300

BROOKLYN CAMPUS
1368 Fulton St., Brooklyn 11216
(718) 638-2500

CO-OP CITY CAMPUS
950 Baychester Ave., Bronx 10475
(212) 320-0300

DC 37 CAMPUS
125 Barclay St., New York 10007
(212) 815-1710

NEW YORK THEOLOGICAL SEMINARY CAMPUS
5 W. 29th St., New York 10001
(212) 689-6208

ROSA PARKS CAMPUS
144 W. 125th St., New York 10024
(212) 662-7500

SOUTH BRONX CAMPUS
332 E. 149th St., Bronx 10451
(212) 665-1310

THE COLLEGE OF ST. ROSE
432 Western Ave., Albany 12203 *Type:* Private *Accred.:* 1928/1994 (MSA) *Calendar:* Sem. plan *Degrees:* B, M *Prof. Accred.:* Art, Speech-Language Pathology *CEO:* Pres. Louis C. Vaccaro
Enroll: 3,879   (518) 454-5111

COLLEGE OF STATEN ISLAND
2800 Victory Blvd., Staten Island 10314 *Type:* Public (local/state) *System:* City University of New York Office of the Chancellor *Accred.:* 1963/1990 (MSA) *Calendar:* Sem. plan *Degrees:* A, B, M, C *Prof. Accred.:* Clinical Lab Technology (A), Computer Science, Engineering Technology (civil/construction, electrical, electromechanical, industrial), Engineering (engineering physics/science), Nursing (A,B) *CEO:* Pres. Marlene Springer
Enroll: 12,512   (718) 982-2000

SUNNYSIDE CAMPUS
715 Ocean Terr., Staten Island 10301
(718) 390-7664

COLUMBIA-GREENE COMMUNITY COLLEGE
P.O. Box 1000, Hudson 12534 *Type:* Public (local/state) two year *System:* State University of New York Office of Community Colleges *Accred.:* 1975/1991 (MSA) *Calendar:* Sem. plan *Degrees:* A *Prof. Accred.:* Nursing (A) *CEO:* Pres. Terry A. Cline
Enroll: 1,711   (518) 828-4181

COLUMBIA UNIVERSITY
116th St. and Broadway, New York 10027 *Type:* Private non-profit *Accred.:* 1921/1991 (MSA) *Calendar:* Sem. plan *Degrees:* B, M, P, D, C *Prof. Accred.:* Business (M), Combined Maxillofacial Prosthodontics (prelim. provisional), Combined Prosthodontics, Dance, Dentistry, Endodontics, Engineering (chemical, civil, electrical, industrial, materials, mechanical, metallurgical), Journalism (M), Law, Medicine, Nurse Anesthesia Education (M), Nursing (B,M), Occupational Therapy, Orthodontics, Pediatric Dentistry, Periodontics, Physical Therapy, Planning (M), Social Work (M) *CEO:* Pres. George Rupp
Enroll: 19,064   (212) 854-1754

CONCORDIA COLLEGE
171 White Plains Rd., Bronxville 10708-1923 *Type:* Private (Lutheran) liberal arts *Accred.:* 1941/1991 (MSA) *Calendar:* Sem. plan *Degrees:* A, B *Prof. Accred.:* Social Work (B) *CEO:* Pres. Ralph C. Schultz
Enroll: 522   (914) 337-9300

THE COOPER UNION FOR THE ADVANCEMENT OF SCIENCE AND ART
30 Cooper Sq., New York 10003 *Type:* Private non-profit *Accred.:* 1946/1993 (MSA) *Calendar:* Sem. plan *Degrees:* B, M, C *Prof. Accred.:* Art, Engineering (chemical, civil, electrical, mechanical) *CEO:* Pres. John J. Iselin
Enroll: 1,064   (212) 254-6300

CORNELL UNIVERSITY
300 Day Hall, Ithaca 14853 *Type:* Private non-profit *Accred.:* 1921/1992 (MSA) *Calendar:* Sem. plan *Degrees:* B, M, P, D *Prof. Accred.:* Business (M), Engineering (agricultural, chemical, civil, electrical, engineering

physics/science, industrial, materials, mechanical), Health Services Administration, Interior Design, Landscape Architecture (B,M), Law, Medicine, Physician Assisting/Surgeon Assisting, Planning (M), Social Work (B), Surgeon Assisting *CEO:* Pres. Hunter R. Rawlings, III
Enroll: 8,615   (607) 255-2000

SUNY College of Agriculture and Life Sciences
Ithica 14853 *System:* State University of New York System Office *Accred.:* 1921/1991 (MSA) *Calendar:* Sem. plan *Degrees:* B, M, D
Enroll: 4,294   (607) 255-2241

SUNY College of Veterinary Medicine
Ithica 14853 *System:* State University of New York System Office *Accred.:* 1921/1991 (MSA) *Calendar:* Sem. plan *Degrees:* M, D
Enroll: 418   (607) 253-3771

SUNY College of Human Ecology
Ithica 14853 *System:* State University of New York System Office *Accred.:* 1921/1991 (MSA) *Calendar:* Sem. plan *Degrees:* B, M, D
Enroll: 1,534   (607) 255-2138

SUNY School of Industrial and Labor Relations
Ithica 14853 *System:* State University of New York System Office *Accred.:* 1921/1991 (MSA) *Calendar:* Sem. plan *Degrees:* B, M, D
Enroll: 1,947   (607) 255-2185

Corning Community College
Spencer Hill, Corning 14830 *Type:* Public (local/state) junior *System:* State University of New York Office of Community Colleges *Accred.:* 1964/1995 (MSA) *Calendar:* Sem. plan *Degrees:* A, C *Prof. Accred.:* Nursing (A) *CEO:* Pres. Eduardo J. Marti
Enroll: 5,522   (607) 962-9011

Culinary Institute of America
433 S. Albany Post Rd., Hyde Park 12538-1499 *Type:* Private *Accred.:* 1983/1988

(ACCSCT) *Degrees:* A, B, C *CEO:* Pres. Ferdinand E. Metz
                    (914) 452-9600

Daemen College
4380 Main St., Amherst 14226-3592 *Type:* Private liberal arts *Accred.:* 1956/1991 (MSA) *Calendar:* Sem. plan *Degrees:* B, M *Prof. Accred.:* Clinical Lab Scientist, Medical Record Administration, Nursing (B), Physical Therapy, Social Work (B) *CEO:* Pres. Martin J. Anisman
Enroll: 2,122   (716) 839-3600

Darkei No'am Rabbinical College
2822 Ave. J, Brooklyn 11210 *Type:* Private professional *Accred.:* 1983/1988 (AARTS) *Calendar:* Sem. plan *Degrees:* Rabbinic (1st and 2nd) *CEO:* Pres. Chaim Scharf
Enroll: 55   (718) 338-6464

Dominican College of Blauvelt
470 Western Hwy., Orangeburg 10962 *Type:* Private liberal arts *Accred.:* 1972/1992 (MSA) *Calendar:* Sem. plan *Degrees:* A, B, C *Prof. Accred.:* Nursing (B), Occupational Therapy, Social Work (B) *CEO:* Pres. Kathleen Sullivan, O.P.
Enroll: 1,735   (914) 359-7800

Dowling College
Idle Hour Blvd., Oakdale 11769-1999 *Type:* Private non-profit *Accred.:* 1971/1993 (MSA) *Calendar:* Sem. plan *Degrees:* B, M *CEO:* Pres. Victor P. Meskill
Enroll: 5,683   (516) 244-3000

Dutchess Community College
53 Pendell Rd., Poughkeepsie 12601-1595 *Type:* Public (local/state) two year *System:* State University of New York Office of Community Colleges *Accred.:* 1964/1995 (MSA) *Calendar:* Sem. plan *Degrees:* A, C *Prof. Accred.:* Clinical Lab Technology (A), Nursing (A) *CEO:* Pres. D. David Conklin
Enroll: 6,693   (914) 431-8000

Fishkill Campus
Southern Dutchess Ext. Site, Blodgett House, Fishkill 12524
                    (914) 896-5775

POUGHKEEPSIE CAMPUS
Martha Lawrence Ext. Site, Spackenhill Rd., Poughkeepsie 12603
(914) 462-0063

SOUTHERN DUTCHESS EXTENTION SITE
Hollowbrook Park, Bldg. No. 4, Myers Corners Rd., Wappingers Falls 12590
(914) 298-0755

D'YOUVILLE COLLEGE
320 Porter Ave., Buffalo 14201 *Type:* Private liberal arts *Accred.:* 1928/1995 (MSA) *Calendar:* Sem. plan *Degrees:* B, M *Prof. Accred.:* Dietetics (coordinated), Nursing (B,M), Occupational Therapy, Physical Therapy, Physician Assisting/Surgeon Assisting, Social Work (B) *CEO:* Pres. Denise A. Roche
Enroll: 1,825   (716) 881-3200

ELMIRA COLLEGE
Park Pl., Elmira 14901 *Type:* Private liberal arts *Accred.:* 1921/1994 (MSA) *Calendar:* Sem. plan *Degrees:* A, B, M *Prof. Accred.:* Nursing (B) *CEO:* Pres. Thomas K. Meier
Enroll: 1,923   (607) 735-1800

ERIE COMMUNITY COLLEGE CITY CAMPUS
121 Ellicott St., Buffalo 14203 *Type:* Public (local/state) two year *System:* State University of New York Office of Community Colleges *Accred.:* 1981/1990 (MSA) *Calendar:* Sem. plan *Degrees:* A, C *Prof. Accred.:* Clinical Lab Technology (A), Medical Assisting (AMA), Nursing (A), Occupational Therapy Assisting, Radiation Therapy Technology, Respiratory Therapy *CEO:* Pres. Louis M. Ricci
Enroll: 3,515   (716) 851-1001

SOUTH CAMPUS
S-4041 Southwestern Blvd., Orchard Park 14127-2199 (local/state) two year *Accred.:* 1981/1990 (MSA) *Calendar:* Sem. plan *Degrees:* A, C *Prof. Accred.:* Dental Laboratory Technology
Enroll: 3,427   (716) 851-1003

NORTH (AMHERST) CAMPUS
6205 Main St., Williamsville 14221-7095 (local/state) two year *Accred.:* 1972/1990 (MSA) *Calendar:* Sem. plan *Degrees:* A, C *Prof. Accred.:* Dental Hygiene, Engineering Technology (civil/construction, electrical, mechanical), Nursing (A)
Enroll: 6,868   (716) 851-1002

FASHION INSTITUTE OF TECHNOLOGY
Seventh Ave. at 27th St., New York 10001-5992 *Type:* Public (local/state) professional *System:* State University of New York Office of Community Colleges *Accred.:* 1957/1992 (MSA) *Calendar:* 4-1-4 plan *Degrees:* A, B, M, C *Prof. Accred.:* Art, Interior Design *CEO:* Pres. Allan F. Hershfield
Enroll: 12,708   (212) 760-7700

FINGER LAKES COMMUNITY COLLEGE
4355 Lake Shore Dr., Canandaigua 14424 *Type:* Public (local/state) junior *System:* State University of New York Office of Community Colleges *Accred.:* 1977/1992 (MSA) *Calendar:* Sem. plan *Degrees:* A, C *Prof. Accred.:* Nursing (A) *CEO:* Pres. Daniel T. Hayes
Enroll: 4,075   (716) 394-3500

FIVE TOWNS COLLEGE
305 N. Service Rd., Dix Hills 11746-6055 *Type:* Private for-profit *Accred.:* 1988/1993 (MSA) *Calendar:* Sem. plan *Degrees:* A, B *CEO:* Pres. Stanley G. Cohen
Enroll: 721   (516) 424-7000

FORDHAM UNIVERSITY
E. Fordham Rd., Bronx 10458 *Type:* Private non-profit *Accred.:* 1921/1995 (MSA) *Calendar:* Sem. plan *Degrees:* B, M, P, D, C *Prof. Accred.:* Business (B,M), Clinical Psychology, Counseling Psychology, Law, School Psychology, Social Work (M), Teacher Education *CEO:* Pres. Joseph A. O'Hare, S.J.
Enroll: 14,423   (718) 817-1000

FULTON-MONTGOMERY COMMUNITY COLLEGE
2805 State Hwy., 67, Johnstown 12095 *Type:* Public (local/state) junior *System:* State University of New York Office of Community

Colleges *Accred.:* 1969/1991 (MSA) *Calendar:* Sem. plan *Degrees:* A *CEO:* Pres. Priscilla J. Bell
Enroll: 1,694   (518) 762-4651

THE GENERAL THEOLOGICAL SEMINARY
175 Ninth Ave., New York 10011-4977 *Type:* Private (Episcopal) graduate only *Accred.:* 1938/1994 (ATS) *Calendar:* Sem. plan *Degrees:* M, D *CEO:* Pres. Craig Anderson
Enroll: 97   (212) 243-5150

GENESEE COMMUNITY COLLEGE
One College Rd., Batavia 14020 *Type:* Public (local/state) junior *System:* State University of New York Office of Community Colleges *Accred.:* 1971/1992 (MSA) *Calendar:* Sem. plan *Degrees:* A, C *Prof. Accred.:* Nursing (A), Occupational Therapy Assisting, Physical Therapy Assisting *CEO:* Pres. Stuart Steiner
Enroll: 4,521   (716) 343-0055

GRADUATE SCHOOL AND UNIVERSITY CENTER
33 W. 42nd St., New York 10036 *Type:* Public (local/state) graduate only *System:* City University of New York Office of the Chancellor *Accred.:* 1961/1994 (MSA) *Calendar:* Sem. plan *Degrees:* M, D *CEO:* Pres. Frances Degen Horowitz
Enroll: 4,180   (212) 642-2000

HAMILTON COLLEGE
198 College Hill Rd., Clinton 13323 *Type:* Private liberal arts *Accred.:* 1921/1991 (MSA) *Calendar:* Sem. plan *Degrees:* B *CEO:* Pres. Eugene M. Tobin
Enroll: 1,664   (315) 859-4011

HARTWICK COLLEGE
Oneonta 13820 *Type:* Private liberal arts *Accred.:* 1949/1994 (MSA) *Calendar:* 4-1-4 plan *Degrees:* B *Prof. Accred.:* Art (A), Music, Nursing (B) *CEO:* Pres. Rick Detweiler
Enroll: 1,502   (607) 431-4200

HEBREW UNION COLLEGE—JEWISH INSTITUTE OF RELIGION
One W. Fourth St., New York 10012 *Type:* Private (Jewish) graduate only *Accred.:* 1960/1993 (MSA) *Calendar:* Sem. plan *Degrees:* M, P, D, C *CEO:* Pres. Alfred Gottschalk
Enroll: 158   (212) 674-5300

HELENE FULD SCHOOL OF NURSING
1879 Madison Ave., New York 10035 *Type:* Private professional *Accred.:* 1988/1993 (MSA) *Calendar:* Qtr. plan *Degrees:* A *Prof. Accred.:* Nursing (A) *CEO:* Dir. Margaret Wines
Enroll: 193   (212) 423-1000

HERBERT H. LEHMAN COLLEGE
Bedford Park Blvd. W., Bronx 10468 *Type:* Public (local/state) *System:* City University of New York Office of the Chancellor *Accred.:* 1968/1994 (MSA) *Calendar:* Sem. plan *Degrees:* B, M *Prof. Accred.:* Audiology, Nursing (B,M), Social Work (B), Speech-Language Pathology *CEO:* Pres. Ricardo R. Fernandez
Enroll: 10,577   (718) 960-8000

HERKIMER COUNTY COMMUNITY COLLEGE
Reservoir Rd., Herkimer 13350 *Type:* Public (local/state) junior *System:* State University of New York Office of Community Colleges *Accred.:* 1972/1993 (MSA) *Calendar:* Sem. plan *Degrees:* A, C *Prof. Accred.:* Occupational Therapy Assisting, Physical Therapy Assisting *CEO:* Pres. Ronald F. Williams
Enroll: 2,542   (315) 866-0300

HILBERT COLLEGE
5200 S. Park Ave., Hamburg 14075-1597 *Type:* Private liberal arts *Accred.:* 1976/1991 (MSA) *Calendar:* Sem. plan *Degrees:* A, B, C *CEO:* Pres. Edmunette Paczesny, F.S.S.J.
Enroll: 847   (716) 649-7900

HOBART AND WILLIAM SMITH COLLEGES
Geneva 14456 *Type:* Private liberal arts *Accred.:* 1921/1994 (MSA) *Calendar:* Tri. plan *Degrees:* B *CEO:* Pres. Richard H. Hersh
Enroll: 1,797   (315) 789-5500

HOFSTRA UNIVERSITY
Hempstead 11550 *Type:* Private non-profit
Accred.: 1940/1994 (MSA) *Calendar:* Sem.
plan *Degrees:* A, B, M, P, D, C *Prof. Accred.:*
Audiology, Business (B,M), Combined Professional-Scientific Psychology, Engineering
(electrical, engineering physics/ science,
mechanical), Law, Rehabilitation Counseling, Speech-Language Pathology, Teacher
Education *CEO:* Pres. James M. Shuart
Enroll: 11,545   (516) 463-6600

HOSTOS COMMUNITY COLLEGE
475 Grand Concourse, Bronx 10451 *Type:*
Public (local/state) *System:* City University
of New York Office of the Chancellor
Accred.: 1974/1990 (MSA) *Calendar:* Sem.
plan *Degrees:* A *Prof. Accred.:* Radiography
CEO: Pres. Isaura Santiago
Enroll: 5,273   (718) 518-4246

HOUGHTON COLLEGE
Houghton 14744 *Type:* Private (Wesleyan)
liberal arts *Accred.:* 1935/1995 (MSA) *Cal-
endar:* Sem. plan *Degrees:* A, B *Prof.
Accred.:* Music *CEO:* Pres. Daniel R.
Chamberlain
Enroll: 1,389   (716) 567-9200

BUFFALO SUBURBAN CAMPUS
910 Union Rd., West Seneca 14224
(716) 674-6363

HUDSON VALLEY COMMUNITY COLLEGE
80 Vandenburgh Ave., Troy 12180 *Type:*
Public (local/state) junior *System:* State University of New York Office of Community
Colleges *Accred.:* 1969/1994 (MSA) *Calendar:* Sem. plan *Degrees:* A, C *Prof. Accred.:*
Clinical Lab Technology (A), Construction
Education (A), Dental Hygiene, Diagnostic
Medical Sonography, Engineering Technology (civil/construction, electrical, mechanical), Funeral Service Education (Mortuary
Science), Nursing (A), Physician Assist-
ing/Surgeon Assisting, Radiography, Respi-
ratory Therapy *CEO:* Pres. Joseph J. Bulmer
Enroll: 10,086   (518) 283-1100

HUNTER COLLEGE
695 Park Ave., New York 10021 *Type:* Pub-
lic (local/state) *System:* City University of
New York Office of the Chancellor *Accred.:*
1921/1992 (MSA) *Calendar:* Sem. plan
Degrees: B, M, C *Prof. Accred.:* Audiology,
Nursing (B,M), Physical Therapy, Planning
(M), Rehabilitation Counseling, Social Work
(M), Speech-Language Pathology *CEO:*
Pres. David A. Caputo
Enroll: 19,663   (212) 772-4000

IONA COLLEGE
715 North Ave., New Rochelle 10801-1890
Type: Private non-profit *Accred.:* 1952/1992
(MSA) *Calendar:* Sem. plan *Degrees:* A, B,
M, C *Prof. Accred.:* Nursing (A), Practical
Nursing, Social Work (B) *CEO:* Pres. James
A. Liguori
Enroll: 6,194   (914) 633-2000

MANHATTAN CAMPUS
425 W. 33rd St., New York 10001
(212) 714-9444

ROCKLAND CAMPUS
One Dutch Hill Rd., Orangeburg 10962
(914) 359-2252

YONKERS CAMPUS
1061 N. Broadway, Yonkers 10701
(914) 378-8000

ITHACA COLLEGE
Danby Rd., Ithaca 14850 *Type:* Private non-
profit *Accred.:* 1955/1992 (MSA) *Calendar:*
Sem. plan *Degrees:* B, M *Prof. Accred.:*
Audiology, Medical Record Administration,
Music, Physical Therapy, Recreation and
Leisure Services (B), Speech-Language
Pathology, Theatre *CEO:* Pres. James J.
Whalen
Enroll: 5,688   (607) 274-3013

JAMESTOWN COMMUNITY COLLEGE
525 Falconer St., Jamestown 14701 *Type:*
Public (local/state) junior *System:* State University of New York Office of Community
Colleges *Accred.:* 1956/1991 (MSA) *Calendar:* Sem. plan *Degrees:* A, C *Prof. Accred.:*

Nursing (A) *CEO:* Pres. Gregory T. DeCinque
Enroll: 4,110 (716) 665-5220

CATTARAUGUS COUNTY CAMPUS
244 N. Union St., Olean 14760
(716) 372-1661

JEFFERSON COMMUNITY COLLEGE
Outer Coffeen St., Watertown 13601 *Type:* Public (local/state) junior *System:* State University of New York Office of Community Colleges *Accred.:* 1969/1995 (MSA) *Calendar:* Sem. plan *Degrees:* A, C *Prof. Accred.:* Nursing (A) *CEO:* Pres. John W. Deans
Enroll: 3,038 (315) 786-2230

JEWISH THEOLOGICAL SEMINARY OF AMERICA
3080 Broadway, New York 10027 *Type:* Private (Jewish) *Accred.:* 1954/1991 (MSA) *Calendar:* Sem. plan *Degrees:* B, M, P, D *CEO:* Chanc. Ismar Schorsch
Enroll: 476 (212) 678-8000

JOHN JAY COLLEGE OF CRIMINAL JUSTICE
899 10th Ave., New York 10019 *Type:* Public (local/state) *System:* City University of New York Office of the Chancellor *Accred.:* 1965/1993 (MSA) *Calendar:* Sem. plan *Degrees:* A, B, M, C *Prof. Accred.:* Public Administration *CEO:* Pres. Gerald W. Lynch
Enroll: 10,313 (212) 237-8000

THE JUILLIARD SCHOOL
60 Lincoln Center Plaza, New York 10023-6588 *Type:* Private professional *Accred.:* 1956/1993 (MSA) *Calendar:* Sem. plan *Degrees:* B, M, D, C *CEO:* Pres. Joseph W. Polisi
Enroll: 783 (212) 799-5000

KATHARINE GIBBS SCHOOL
535 Broad Hollow Rd., Melville 11747 *Type:* Private business *Accred.:* 1973/1997 (ACICS) *Calendar:* Sem. plan *Degrees:* A, C *CEO:* Pres. David Schuchman
(516) 293-2460

KATHARINE GIBBS SCHOOL
200 Park Ave., New York 10166 *Type:* Private business *Accred.:* 1967/1992 (ACICS) *Degrees:* A, C *CEO:* Pres. Julia Slick
(212) 867-9300

KEHILATH YAKOV RABBINICAL SEMINARY
206 Wilson St., Brooklyn 11211 *Type:* Private professional *Accred.:* 1980/1991 (AARTS) *Calendar:* Sem. plan *Degrees:* Rabbinic (1st and 2nd) *CEO:* Pres. Sandor Schwartz
Enroll: 120 (718) 963-3940

KEUKA COLLEGE
Keuka Park 14478 *Type:* Private liberal arts primarily for women *Accred.:* 1927/1992 (MSA) *Calendar:* 4-1-4 plan *Degrees:* B *Prof. Accred.:* Nursing (B), Occupational Therapy, Social Work (B) *CEO:* Pres. Arthur F. Kirk, Jr.
Enroll: 905 (315) 536-4411

KINGSBOROUGH COMMUNITY COLLEGE
2001 Oriental Blvd., Manhattan Beach, Brooklyn 11235 *Type:* Public (local/state) *System:* City University of New York Office of the Chancellor *Accred.:* 1964/1991 (MSA) *Calendar:* Sem. plan *Degrees:* A *Prof. Accred.:* Nursing (A) *CEO:* Pres. Leon M. Goldstein
Enroll: 15,464 (718) 368-5000

LA GUARDIA COMMUNITY COLLEGE
31-10 Thomson Ave., Long Island City 11101 *Type:* Public (local/state) *System:* City University of New York Office of the Chancellor *Accred.:* 1974/1992 (MSA) *Calendar:* Qtr. plan *Degrees:* A, C *Prof. Accred.:* Nursing (A), Occupational Therapy Assisting, Physical Therapy Assisting, Veterinary Technology *CEO:* Pres. Raymond C. Bowen
Enroll: 10,437 (718) 482-7200

LABORATORY INSTITUTE OF MERCHANDISING
12 E. 53rd St., New York 10022 *Type:* Private for-profit *Accred.:* 1977/1992 (MSA) *Calendar:* 4-1-4 plan *Degrees:* A, B *CEO:* Pres. Adrian G. Marcuse
Enroll: 173 (212) 752-1530

LE MOYNE COLLEGE
Le Moyne Heights, Syracuse 13214 *Type:* Private liberal arts *Accred.:* 1953/1992 (MSA) *Calendar:* Sem. plan *Degrees:* B, M *CEO:* Pres. Robert A. Mitchell, S.J.
Enroll: 2,757 (315) 445-4100

LONG ISLAND UNIVERSITY
Northern Blvd., Brookville 11548 *Type:* Private *Accred.:* 1955/1994 (MSA) *Calendar:* Sem. plan *Degrees:* A, B, M, D, C *Prof. Accred.:* Clinical Lab Scientist, Clinical Psychology, Dietetics (internship), Librarianship, Medical Record Administration, Radiography, Respiratory Therapy *CEO:* Pres. David J. Steinberg
Enroll: 19,222   (516) 299-2501

BRENTWOOD CAMPUS
Second Ave., Brentwood 11717
     (516) 273-5112

BROOKLYN CAMPUS
University Plaza, Brooklyn 11201 *Prof. Accred.:* Nursing (A,B), Physical Therapy
     (718) 488-1000

C.W. POST CAMPUS
Greenvale 11548 *Prof. Accred.:* Counseling, Nursing (B), Public Administration, Speech-Language Pathology
     (516) 299-0200

ROCKLAND CAMPUS
Rte. 340, Orangeburg 10962
     (914) 359-7200

SOUTHAMPTON CAMPUS
Southampton 11968
     (516) 283-4000

WESTCHESTER CAMPUS
555 Broadway, Dobbs Ferry 10522
     (914) 674-4000

MACHZIKEI HADATH RABBINICAL COLLEGE
5407 16th Ave., Brooklyn 11204 *Type:* Private professional *Accred.:* 1980/1995 (AARTS) *Calendar:* Sem. plan *Degrees:* Talmudic (1st and 2nd) *CEO:* Pres. Avi Klein
Enroll: 118   (718) 854-8777

MANHATTAN COLLEGE
Manhattan College Pkwy., Riverdale 10471 *Type:* Private *Accred.:* 1921/1992 (MSA) *Calendar:* Sem. plan *Degrees:* A, B, M *Prof. Accred.:* Engineering (chemical, civil, electrical, environmental/sanitary, mechanical),

Nuclear Medicine Technology *CEO:* Pres. Thomas J. Scanlan
Enroll: 3,250   (718) 920-0100

MANHATTAN SCHOOL OF MUSIC
120 Claremont Ave., New York 10027 *Type:* Private professional *Accred.:* 1956/1993 (MSA) *Calendar:* Sem. plan *Degrees:* B, M, D, C *CEO:* Pres. Marta Istomin
Enroll: 895   (212) 749-2802

MANHATTANVILLE COLLEGE
2900 Purchase St., Purchase 10577 *Type:* Private liberal arts *Accred.:* 1926/1990 (MSA) *Calendar:* Sem. plan *Degrees:* B, M *CEO:* Pres. Richard A. Berman
Enroll: 1,626   (914) 694-2200

MARIA COLLEGE OF ALBANY
700 New Scotland Ave., Albany 12208-1798 *Type:* Private junior for women *Accred.:* 1973/1993 (MSA) *Calendar:* Sem. plan *Degrees:* A *Prof. Accred.:* Nursing (A), Occupational Therapy Assisting, Physical Therapy Assisting *CEO:* Pres. Laureen Fitzgerald, R.S.M.
Enroll: 860   (518) 438-7170

MARIST COLLEGE
290 North Rd., Poughkeepsie 12601 *Type:* Private non-profit *Accred.:* 1964/1993 (MSA) *Calendar:* Sem. plan *Degrees:* B, M, C *Prof. Accred.:* Clinical Lab Scientist, Social Work (B) *CEO:* Pres. Dennis J. Murray
Enroll: 4,694   (914) 575-3000

MARYMOUNT COLLEGE
100 Marymount Ave., Tarrytown 10591-3796 *Type:* Private liberal arts *Accred.:* 1927/1990 (MSA) *Calendar:* Sem. plan *Degrees:* B *Prof. Accred.:* Social Work (B) *CEO:* Pres. Brigid Driscoll, R.S.H.M.
Enroll: 1,031   (914) 631-3200

MARYMOUNT MANHATTAN COLLEGE
221 E. 71st St., New York 10021 *Type:* Private liberal arts *Accred.:* 1961/1994 (MSA) *Calendar:* 4-1-4 plan *Degrees:* B *CEO:* Pres. Regina S. Peruggi
Enroll: 1,943   (212) 517-0400

MATER DEI COLLEGE
Rural Rte. 2, Box 45, Ogdensburg 13669-1034
Type: Private junior *Accred.:* 1974/1990
(MSA) *Calendar:* Sem. plan *Degrees:* A, C
CEO: Pres. Ronald M. Mrozinski, O.F.M.
Enroll: 490   (315) 393-5930

MEDAILLE COLLEGE
18 Agassiz Cir., Buffalo 14214 *Type:* Private
liberal arts *Accred.:* 1951/1993 (MSA) *Calendar:* Sem. plan *Degrees:* A, B, C *CEO:*
Pres. Kevin I. Sullivan
Enroll: 1,129   (716) 884-3281

MEDGAR EVERS COLLEGE
1650 Bedford Ave., Brooklyn 11225 *Type:*
Public (local/state) *System:* City University
of New York Office of the Chancellor
Accred.: 1976/1992 (MSA) *Calendar:* Sem.
plan *Degrees:* A, B, C *Prof. Accred.:* Nursing (B) *CEO:* Pres. Edison O. Jackson
Enroll: 5,217   (718) 270-4900

MERCY COLLEGE
555 Broadway, Dobbs Ferry 10522 *Type:*
Private non-profit *Accred.:* 1968/1994
(MSA) *Calendar:* Sem. plan *Degrees:* A, B,
M, C *Prof. Accred.:* Nursing (B,M), Occupa-
tional Therapy, Veterinary Technology *CEO:*
Pres. Jay Sexter
Enroll: 4,932   (914) 693-4500

BRONX CAMPUS
50 Antin Pl., Bronx 10462
                    (212) 798-8952

WHITE PLAINS CAMPUS
Martine Ave. and S. Broadway, White
Plains 10601
                    (914) 948-3666

YORKTOWN CAMPUS
2651 Stang Blvd., Yorktown Heights
10598
                    (914) 245-6100

MESIVTA OF EASTERN PARKWAY RABBINICAL
SEMINARY
510 Dahill Rd., Brooklyn 11218 *Type:* Private professional *Accred.:* 1980/1991
(AARTS) *Calendar:* Sem. plan *Degrees:*

Talmudic (1st and 2nd) *CEO:* Pres. Joseph
D. Epstein
Enroll: 65   (718) 438-1002

MESIVTA TIFERETH JERUSALEM OF AMERICA
141 E. Broadway, New York 10002 *Type:*
Private professional *Accred.:* 1979/1994
(AARTS) *Calendar:* Sem. plan *Degrees:* Tal-
mudic (1st and 2nd) *CEO:* Pres. D. Feinstein
Enroll: 80   (212) 964-2830

MESIVTA TORAH VODAATH SEMINARY
425 E. 9th St., Brooklyn 11218 *Type:* Private
professional *Accred.:* 1976/1995 (AARTS)
Calendar: Sem. plan *Degrees:* Talmudic (1st
and 2nd) *CEO:* Dean Chaim Leshkowitz
Enroll: 400   (718) 941-8000

MIRRER YESHIVA CENTRAL INSTITUTE
1795 Ocean Pkwy., Brooklyn 11223 *Type:*
Private professional *Accred.:* 1975/1988
(AARTS) *Calendar:* Sem. plan *Degrees:*
Talmudic (1st and 2nd) *CEO:* Pres. S.M.
Kalmanowitz
Enroll: 183   (718) 645-0536

MOHAWK VALLEY COMMUNITY COLLEGE
1101 Sherman Dr., Utica 13501 *Type:* Public
(local/state) junior *System:* State University
of New York Office of Community Colleges
Accred.: 1960/1993 (MSA) *Calendar:* Sem.
plan *Degrees:* A, C *Prof. Accred.:* Engineering Technology (civil/construction, electrical, mechanical), Medical Record Technology, Nursing (A) *CEO:* Pres. Michael I.
Schafer
Enroll: 6,033   (315) 792-5400

ROME CAMPUS
Floyd Ave., Rome 13440
                    (315) 339-3470

MOLLOY COLLEGE
1000 Hempstead Ave., Rockville Centre
11571-5002 *Type:* Private non-profit *Accred.:* 1967/1993 (MSA) *Calendar:* 4-1-4
plan *Degrees:* A, B, M *Prof. Accred.:*
Nuclear Medicine Technology, Nursing
(B,M), Respiratory Therapy, Respiratory

Therapy Technology, Social Work (B) *CEO:* Pres. Janet A. Fitzgerald, O.P.
Enroll: 2,116   (516) 678-5000

MONROE COLLEGE
29 E. Fordham Rd., Bronx 10468 *Type:* Private junior *Accred.:* 1990/1995 (MSA) *Calendar:* Sem. plan *Degrees:* A *CEO:* Pres. Stephen J. Jerome
Enroll: 1,926   (718) 933-6700

NEW ROCHELLE CAMPUS
434 Main St., New Rochelle 10801
                                   (914) 632-5400

MONROE COMMUNITY COLLEGE
1000 E. Henrietta Rd., Rochester 14623 *Type:* Public (local/state) junior *System:* State University of New York Office of Community Colleges *Accred.:* 1965/1991 (MSA) *Calendar:* Sem. plan *Degrees:* A, C *Prof. Accred.:* Dental Hygiene, Engineering Technology (electrical), Medical Record Technology, Nursing (A), Radiography *CEO:* Pres. Peter A. Spina
Enroll: 13,731   (716) 292-2100

DAEMON CITY CENTER CAMPUS
228 E. Main St., Rochester 14604
                                   (716) 262-1610

MOUNT ST. MARY COLLEGE
330 Powell Ave., Newburgh 12550 *Type:* Private liberal arts *Accred.:* 1968/1992 (MSA) *Calendar:* Sem. plan *Degrees:* B, M *Prof. Accred.:* Nursing (B) *CEO:* Pres. Ann Sakac, O.P.
Enroll: 1,909   (914) 561-0800

MOUNT SINAI SCHOOL OF MEDICINE
One Gustave L. Levy Pl., New York 10029 *Type:* Private *System:* City University of New York Office of the Chancellor *Calendar:* Sem. plan *Degrees:* B, M, P, D *Prof. Accred.:* Health Services Administration, Medicine *CEO:* Pres. John W. Rowe
Enroll: 483   (212) 241-8888

NASSAU COMMUNITY COLLEGE
One Education Dr., Garden City 11530 *Type:* Public (local/state) junior *System:* State University of New York Office of Community

Colleges *Accred.:* 1967/1994 (MSA) *Calendar:* Sem. plan *Degrees:* A *Prof. Accred.:* Engineering Technology (civil/construction), Funeral Service Education (Mortuary Science), Music, Nursing (A), Physical Therapy Assisting, Radiation Therapy Technology, Radiography, Respiratory Therapy, Surgical Technology *CEO:* Pres. Sean A. Fanelli
Enroll: 27,260   (516) 572-7205

NAZARETH COLLEGE OF ROCHESTER
4245 East Ave., Rochester 14618-3790 *Type:* Private non-profit *Accred.:* 1930/1991 (MSA) *Calendar:* Sem. plan *Degrees:* B, M *Prof. Accred.:* Music, Nursing (B), Social Work (B), Speech-Language Pathology *CEO:* Pres. Rose Marie Beston
Enroll: 2,723   (716) 586-2525

NEW SCHOOL FOR SOCIAL RESEARCH
66 W. 12th St., New York 10011 *Type:* Private non-profit *Accred.:* 1960/1991 (MSA) *Calendar:* Sem. plan *Degrees:* A, B, M, D, C *Prof. Accred.:* Clinical Psychology (probational), Public Administration *CEO:* Pres. Jonathan F. Fanton
Enroll: 6,498   (212) 229-5600

PARSONS SCHOOL OF DESIGN—NEW YORK
66 Fifth Ave., New York 10011 *Prof. Accred.:* Art
                                   (212) 229-8950

PARSONS SCHOOL OF DESIGN—PARIS, FRANCE
14 Rue Letellier, Paris France 75015 *Prof. Accred.:* Art
                                   [33] (14) 577-3966

NEW YORK CHIROPRACTIC COLLEGE
2360 State Rte. 89, Seneca Falls 13148-0800 *Type:* Private professional *Accred.:* 1985/1995 (MSA) *Calendar:* Tri. plan *Degrees:* P *Prof. Accred.:* Chiropractic Education *CEO:* Pres. Kenneth W. Padgett, D.C.
Enroll: 920   (315) 568-3000

NEW YORK CITY TECHNICAL COLLEGE
300 Jay St., Brooklyn 11201 *Type:* Public (local/state) *System:* City University of New

York Office of the Chancellor *Accred.:* 1957/ 1992 (MSA) *Calendar:* Sem. plan *Degrees:* A, B, C *Prof. Accred.:* Clinical Lab Technology (A), Dental Hygiene, Dental Laboratory Technology, Engineering Technology (civil/ construction, electrical, electromechanical, mechanical), Nursing (A), Radiography *CEO:* Pres. Charles W. Merideth
Enroll: 10,765   (718) 260-5000

NEW YORK COLLEGE OF PODIATRIC MEDICINE
53 E. 124th St., New York 10035 *Type:* Private professional *Calendar:* Sem. plan *Degrees:* P *Prof. Accred.:* Podiatry *CEO:* Acting Pres. Monroe Seifer
Enroll: 554   (212) 410-8000

NEW YORK INSTITUTE OF TECHNOLOGY
268 Wheatley Rd., Old Westbury 11568-1036 *Type:* Private professional *Accred.:* 1969/1993 (MSA) *Calendar:* Sem. plan *Degrees:* A, B, M, P, C *Prof. Accred.:* Clinical Lab Scientist, Engineering Technology (electrical), Engineering (electrical, mechanical), Interior Design, Osteopathy *CEO:* Pres. Matthew Schure
Enroll: 5,754   (516) 686-7516

CENTRAL ISLIP CAMPUS
211 Carleton Ave., Central Islip 11722
                (516) 348-3000

MANHATTAN CAMPUS
1855 Broadway, New York 10023 *Prof. Accred.:* Engineering Technology (electrical), Engineering (electrical)
                (212) 399-8300

NEW YORK LAW SCHOOL
57 Worth St., New York 10013 *Type:* Private *Calendar:* Sem. plan *Degrees:* P *Prof. Accred.:* Law *CEO:* Dean Harry H. Wellington
Enroll: 1,383   (212) 431-2840

NEW YORK MEDICAL COLLEGE
Sunshine Cottage, Administration Bldg., Valhalla 10595 *Type:* Private (Roman Catholic) professional *Accred.:* 1991/1995 (MSA candidate) *Calendar:* Sem. plan *Degrees:* M, P, D *Prof. Accred.:* Dietetics (internship), General Practice Residency,

Medicine, Oral and Maxillofacial Surgery *CEO:* Pres./CEO Harry C. Barrett
Enroll: 1,595   (914) 993-4000

NEW YORK SCHOOL OF INTERIOR DESIGN
170 70th St., New York 10021 *Type:* Private professional *Degrees:* B, P, C *Prof. Accred.:* Interior Design *CEO:* Dean Frank Koe
                (212) 753-5365

NEW YORK THEOLOGICAL SEMINARY
5 W. 29th St., New York 10001-4599 *Type:* Private (interdenominational) graduate only *Accred.:* 1958/1994 (ATS) *Calendar:* 4-1-4 plan *Degrees:* M, D *CEO:* Pres. M. William Howard, Jr.
Enroll: 331   (212) 532-4012

NEW YORK UNIVERSITY
70 Washington Square. S., New York 10012 *Type:* Private non-profit *Accred.:* 1921/1994 (MSA) *Calendar:* Sem. plan *Degrees:* A, B, M, P, D, C *Prof. Accred.:* Accounting (A,B,C), Business (B,M), Clinical Psychology, Combined Prosthodontics, Counseling Psychology, Cytotechnology, Dance, Dental Assisting, Dental Hygiene, Dentistry, Diagnostic Medical Sonography, Endodontics, General Dentistry, Health Services Administration, Journalism (B,M), Law, Medicine, Music, Nuclear Medicine Technology, Nursing (B,M), Occupational Therapy, Oral and Maxillofacial Surgery, Orthodontics, Pediatric Dentistry, Periodontics, Physical Therapy, Physical Therapy Assisting, Planning (M), Psychology Internship, Public Administration, Rehabilitation Counseling, Respiratory Therapy, School Psychology, Social Work (B,M), Speech-Language Pathology*CEO:* Pres. L. Jay Oliva
Enroll: 35,439   (212) 998-1212

NIAGARA COUNTY COMMUNITY COLLEGE
3111 Saunders Settlement Rd., Sanborn 14132 *Type:* Public (local/state) junior *System:* State University of New York Office of Community Colleges *Accred.:* 1970/1991 (MSA) *Calendar:* Sem. plan *Degrees:* A, C *Prof. Accred.:* Electroneurodiagnostic Technology, Engineering Technology (electrical, mechanical), Nursing (A), Physical Therapy

Assisting, Radiography, Surgical Technology *CEO:* Pres. Gerald L. Miller
Enroll: 5,702   (716) 731-3271

NIAGARA UNIVERSITY
Niagara University 14109 *Type:* Private non-profit *Accred.:* 1922/1992 (MSA) *Calendar:* Sem. plan *Degrees:* A, B, M, C *Prof. Accred.:* Nursing (B), Social Work (B), Teacher Education *CEO:* Pres. Paul L. Golden, CM
Enroll: 2,862   (716) 285-1212

NORTH COUNTRY COMMUNITY COLLEGE
20 Winona Ave., P.O. Box 89, Saranac Lake 12983 *Type:* Public (local/state) junior *System:* State University of New York Office of Community Colleges *Accred.:* 1975/1990 (MSA) *Calendar:* Sem. plan *Degrees:* A, C *Prof. Accred.:* Radiography *CEO:* Pres. Gail Rogers Rice
Enroll: 1,397   (518) 891-2915

MALONECAMPUS
College Ave., Malone 12953
         (518) 483-4550

TICONDEROGA CAMPUS
Montcalm St., Ticonderoga 12883
         (518) 585-4454

NYACK COLLEGE
One South Blvd., Nyack 10960-3698 *Type:* Private (Christian and Missionary Alliance) liberal arts *Accred.:* 1990 (ATS); 1962/1994 (MSA) *Calendar:* Sem. plan *Degrees:* A, B, M *Prof. Accred.:* Music *CEO:* Pres. David E. Schroeder
Enroll: 1,027   (914) 358-1710

OHR HAMEIR THEOLOGICAL SEMINARY
Furnace Woods Rd., P.O. Box 2130, Peekskill 10566 *Type:* Private professional *Accred.:* 1979/1989 (AARTS) *Calendar:* Sem. plan *Degrees:* Talmudic (1st and 2nd) *CEO:* Pres. E. Kanarek
Enroll: 71   (914) 736-1500

OHR SOMAYACH-TANENBAUM EDUCATIONAL CENTER
P.O. Box 334, Monsey 10952 *Type:* Private professional *Accred.:* 1984/1989 (AARTS)

Calendar: Tri. plan *Degrees:* Talmudic (1st and 2nd) *CEO:* Pres. Emil Tauber
Enroll: 70   (914) 425-1370

OLEAN BUSINESS INSTITUTE
301 N. Union St., Olean 14760 *Type:* Private business *Accred.:* 1969/1988 (ACICS) *Calendar:* Sem. plan *Degrees:* A *CEO:* Dir. Patrick J. McCarthy
         (716) 372-7978

ONONDAGA COMMUNITY COLLEGE
Rte. 173, Syracuse 13215 *Type:* Public (local/state) junior *System:* State University of New York Office of Community Colleges *Accred.:* 1972/1994 (MSA) *Calendar:* Sem. plan *Degrees:* A *Prof. Accred.:* Dental Hygiene, Engineering Technology (computer, electrical), Medical Record Technology, Nursing (A), Physical Therapy Assisting, Respiratory Therapy, Respiratory Therapy Technology, Surgical Technology *CEO:* Pres. Bruce H. Leslie
Enroll: 7,697   (315) 469-7741

ORANGE COUNTY COMMUNITY COLLEGE
115 South St., Middletown 10940 *Type:* Public (local/state) junior *System:* State University of New York Office of Community Colleges *Accred.:* 1962/1993 (MSA) *Calendar:* Sem. plan *Degrees:* A, C *Prof. Accred.:* Clinical Lab Technology (A), Dental Hygiene, Engineering Technology (electrical), Nursing (A), Occupational Therapy Assisting, Physical Therapy Assisting, Radiography *CEO:* Pres. William F. Messner
Enroll: 5,632   (914) 341-4701

PACE UNIVERSITY
One Pace Plaza, New York 10038 *Type:* Private non-profit *Accred.:* 1957/1988 (MSA) *Calendar:* Sem. plan *Degrees:* A, B, M, P, D, C *Prof. Accred.:* Computer Science, Psychology Internship, School Psychology *CEO:* Pres. Patricia O'Donnell Ewers
Enroll: 7,764   (212) 346-1200

PLEASANTVILLE/BRIARCLIFF CAMPUS
861 Bedford Rd., Pleasantville 10570 *Prof. Accred.:* Nursing (A,B,M)
         (914) 773-3200

WHITE PLAINS CAMPUS
78 N. Broadway, White Plains 10603
Prof. Accred.: Law
(914) 422-4213

PAUL SMITH'S COLLEGE
Paul Smiths 12970 *Type:* Private junior
Accred.: 1977/1993 (MSA) *Calendar:* Sem.
plan *Degrees:* A *Prof. Accred.:* Engineering
Technology (surveying) *CEO:* Pres. Arthur
E. Linkins, III
Enroll: 823   (518) 327-6211

PHILLIPS BETH ISRAEL SCHOOL OF NURSING
310 E. 22nd St., New York 10010 *Type:* Private *Calendar:* Sem. plan *Degrees:* A *Prof.
Accred.:* Nursing (A) *CEO:* Dean Julianne
M. Hart
(212) 614-6104

POLYTECHNIC UNIVERSITY
6 MetroTech Ctr., Brooklyn 11201 *Type:* Private non-profit *Accred.:* 1927/1994 (MSA)
Calendar: Sem. plan *Degrees:* B, M, D *Prof.
Accred.:* Computer Science, Engineering
(aerospace, chemical, civil, computer, electrical, industrial, mechanical, metallurgical)
CEO: Pres. David C. Chang
Enroll: 3,399   (718) 260-3600

LONG ISLAND CENTER CAMPUS
Rte. 110, Farmingdale 11735
(516) 755-4400

WESTCHESTER GRADUATE CENTER CAMPUS
36 Saw Mill River Rd., Hawthorne 10532
(914) 347-6940

PRACTICAL BIBLE COLLEGE
400 Riverside Dr., P.O. Box 601, Johnson
City 13737-0601 *Type:* Private (Baptist)
Accred.: 1985/1990 (AABC) *Calendar:*
Sem. plan *Degrees:* A, B, C *CEO:* Pres. Dale
Linebaugh
FTE Enroll: 187   (607) 729-1581

PRATT INSTITUTE
200 Willoughby Ave., Brooklyn 11205 *Type:*
Private non-profit *Accred.:* 1950/1992
(MSA) *Calendar:* 4-1-4 plan *Degrees:* A, B,
M, C *Prof. Accred.:* Art, electrical) Interior

Design Planning (M) *CEO:* Pres. Thomas F.
Schutte
Enroll: 3,041   (718) 636-3600

QUEENS COLLEGE
65-40 Kissena Blvd., Flushing 11367 *Type:*
Public (local/state) *System:* City University
of New York Office of the Chancellor
Accred.: 1941/1991 (MSA) *Calendar:* Sem.
plan *Degrees:* B, M, P *Prof. Accred.:* Audiology, Home Economics, Law (ABA only),
Librarianship *CEO:* Pres. Allen L. Sessoms
Enroll: 17,958   (718) 997-5000

QUEENSBOROUGH COMMUNITY COLLEGE
222-05 56th Ave., Bayside 11364-1497
Type: Public (local/state) *System:* City University of New York Office of the Chancellor
Accred.: 1963/1994 (MSA) *Calendar:* Sem.
plan *Degrees:* A, C *Prof. Accred.:* Engineering Technology (computer, electrical,
mechanical), Nursing (A) *CEO:* Pres. Kurt
R. Schmeller
Enroll: 11,888   (718) 631-6262

RABBINICAL ACADEMY MESIVTA RABBI CHAIM
BERLIN
1593 Coney Island Ave., Brooklyn 11230
Type: Private professional *Accred.:* 1975/
1993 (AARTS) *Calendar:* Sem. plan
Degrees: Talmudic (1st and 2nd) *CEO:* Pres.
A.M. Schechter
Enroll: 400   (718) 377-0777

RABBINICAL COLLEGE BETH SHRAGA
28 Saddle River Rd., Monsey 10952 *Type:*
Private professional *Accred.:* 1978/1995
(AARTS) *Calendar:* Sem. plan *Degrees:*
Talmudic (1st and 2nd) *CEO:* Pres. S. Schiff
Enroll: 25   (914) 356-1980

RABBINICAL COLLEGE BOBOVER YESHIVA B'NEI
ZION
1577 48th St., Brooklyn 11219 *Type:* Private
professional *Accred.:* 1979/1991 (AARTS)
Calendar: Sem. plan *Degrees:* Rabbinic
(1st), Talmudic (1st and 2nd) *CEO:* Pres. N.
Halberstam
Enroll: 387   (718) 438-2018

RABBINICAL COLLEGE CH'SAN SOFER
1876 50th St., Brooklyn 11204 *Type:* Private professional *Accred.:* 1979/1990 (AARTS) *Calendar:* Sem. plan *Degrees:* Talmudic (1st and 2nd) *CEO:* Pres. Jacob Hershkowitz
Enroll: 81   (718) 236-1171

RABBINICAL COLLEGE OF LONG ISLAND
201 Magnolia Blvd., Long Beach 11561 *Type:* Private professional *Accred.:* 1979/1990 (AARTS) *Calendar:* Sem. plan *Degrees:* Talmudic (1st) *CEO:* Pres. Y. Feigelstock
Enroll: 97   (516) 431-7304

RABBINICAL SEMINARY ADAS YEREIM
185 Wilson St., Brooklyn 11211 *Type:* Private professional *Accred.:* 1979/1990 (AARTS) *Calendar:* Sem. plan *Degrees:* Talmudic (1st) *CEO:* Pres. A. Schonberger
Enroll: 80   (718) 388-1751

RABBINICAL SEMINARY M'KOR CHAIM
1571 55th St., Brooklyn 11219 *Type:* Private professional *Accred.:* 1979/1990 (AARTS) *Calendar:* Sem. plan *Degrees:* Talmudic (1st and 2nd) *CEO:* Pres. Benjamin Lederer
Enroll: 78   (718) 851-0183

RABBINICAL SEMINARY OF AMERICA
92-15 69th Ave., Forest Hills 11375 *Type:* Private professional *Accred.:* 1975/1992 (AARTS) *Calendar:* Sem. plan *Degrees:* Talmudic (1st and 2nd) *CEO:* Pres. A.H. Leibowitz
Enroll: 229   (718) 268-4700

REGENTS COLLEGE OF THE UNIVERSITY OF THE STATE OF NEW YORK
7 Columbia Cir., Albany 12203-5159 *Type:* Private non-profit *Accred.:* 1977/1992 (MSA) *Calendar:* Sem. plan *Degrees:* A, B *Prof. Accred.:* Nursing (A,B) *CEO:* Pres. Richard P. Mills
Enroll: 17,269   (518) 464-8500

RENSSELAER POLYTECHNIC INSTITUTE
110 Eighth St., Troy 12180-3590 *Type:* Private non-profit *Accred.:* 1927/1991 (MSA) *Calendar:* Sem. plan *Degrees:* B, M, D *Prof. Accred.:* Business (B,M), Engineering (aerospace, bioengineering, chemical, civil, computer, electrical, engineering physics/science, environmental/sanitary, industrial, materials, mechanical, nuclear) *CEO:* Pres. R. Byron Pipes
Enroll: 6,339   (518) 276-6000

ROBERTS WESLEYAN COLLEGE
2301 Westside Dr., Rochester 14624-1997 *Type:* Private liberal arts *Accred.:* 1963/1990 (MSA) *Calendar:* Sem. plan *Degrees:* A, B, M *Prof. Accred.:* Art, Music, Nursing (B), Social Work (B) *CEO:* Pres. William C. Crothers
Enroll: 1,181   (716) 594-6000

ROCHESTER BUSINESS INSTITUTE
1850 Ridge Rd. E., Rochester 14622 *Type:* Private business *Accred.:* 1966/1996 (ACICS) *Calendar:* Qtr. plan *Degrees:* A *CEO:* Pres. Tom Conte
      (716) 266-0430

ROCHESTER INSTITUTE OF TECHNOLOGY
P.O. Box 9887, One Lomb Memorial Dr., Rochester 14623 *Type:* Private non-profit *Accred.:* 1958/1992 (MSA) *Calendar:* Qtr. plan *Degrees:* A, B, M, D, C *Prof. Accred.:* Art, Business (B,M), Computer Science, Diagnostic Medical Sonography, Dietetics (coordinated), Engineering Technology (architectural, civil/construction, computer, electrical, electromechanical, energy, manufacturing, mechanical, mechanical drafting/design), Engineering (computer, electrical, industrial, mechanical), Medical Record Technology, Nuclear Medicine Technology, Physician Assisting/Surgeon Assisting, Social Work (B) *CEO:* Pres. Albert J. Simone
Enroll: 12,250   (716) 475-2400

ROCKLAND COMMUNITY COLLEGE
145 College Rd., Suffern 10901 *Type:* Public (local/state) junior *System:* State University of New York Office of Community Colleges *Accred.:* 1968/1991 (MSA) *Calendar:* Sem. plan *Degrees:* A, C *Prof. Accred.:* Medical Record Technology, Nursing (A), Occupational Therapy Assisting, Respiratory Therapy *CEO:* Pres. Neal A. Raisman
Enroll: 7,321   (914) 574-4000

HAVERSTRAW LEARNING CENTER CAMPUS
36-39 Main St., Haberstraw 10927
(914) 942-0624

NYACK LEARNING CENTER CAMPUS
92-94 Main St., Nyack 10960
(914) 358-9392

SPRING VALLEY LEARNING CENTER CAMPUS
185 N. Main St., Spring Valley 10977
(914) 352-5535

THE SAGE COLLEGES
45 Ferry St., Troy 12180 *Type:* Private non-profit *Accred.:* 1928/1990 (MSA) *Calendar:* Sem. plan *Degrees:* A, B, M *Prof. Accred.:* Nursing (B,M), Occupational Therapy, Physical Therapy *CEO:* Pres. Jeanne Neff
Enroll: 4,203   (518) 270-2000

SAGE JUNIOR COLLEGE OF ALBANY
140 New Scotland Ave., Albany 12208
Prof. Accred.: Art, Nursing (A)
(518) 445-1711

ST. BERNARD'S INSTITUTE
1100 S. Goodman St., Rochester 14620 *Type:* Private (Roman Catholic) graduate only *Accred.:* 1970/1993 (ATS) *Calendar:* Sem. plan *Degrees:* M *CEO:* Pres. Patricia A. Schoelles
Enroll: 113   (716) 271-1320

ST. BONAVENTURE UNIVERSITY
Rte. 417, St. Bonaventure 14778 *Type:* Private non-profit *Accred.:* 1924/1989 (MSA) *Calendar:* Sem. plan *Degrees:* B, M *CEO:* Pres. Robert J. Wickenheiser
Enroll: 2,489   (716) 375-2000

ST. FRANCIS COLLEGE
180 Remsen St., Brooklyn 11201 *Type:* Private liberal arts *Accred.:* 1959/1994 (MSA) *Calendar:* Sem. plan *Degrees:* A, B, C *CEO:* Interim Pres. John Hawes
Enroll: 2,166   (718) 522-2300

ST. JOHN FISHER COLLEGE
3690 East Ave., Rochester 14618 *Type:* Private non-profit *Accred.:* 1957/1991 (MSA)

Calendar: Sem. plan *Degrees:* B, M *CEO:* Pres. William L. Pickett
Enroll: 2,110   (716) 385-8000

ST. JOHN'S UNIVERSITY
Grand Central and Utopia Pkwys., Jamaica 11439 *Type:* Private (Roman Catholic) *Accred.:* 1921/1991 (MSA) *Calendar:* Sem. plan *Degrees:* A, B, M, P, D, C *Prof. Accred.:* Audiology, Business (B,M), Clinical Psychology, Law, Librarianship, Speech-Language Pathology *CEO:* Pres. Donald J. Harrington, C.M.
Enroll: 17,476   (718) 990-6161

STATEN ISLAND CAMPUS
300 Howard Ave., Staten Island 10301
(718) 390-4545

ST. JOSEPH'S COLLEGE
245 Clinton Ave., Brooklyn 11205-3688 *Type:* Private liberal arts *Accred.:* 1928/1992 (MSA) *Calendar:* Sem. plan *Degrees:* B, C *Prof. Accred.:* Nursing (B) *CEO:* Pres. George Aquin O'Connor, C.S.J.
Enroll: 1,343   (718) 636-6800

SUFFOLK CAMPUS
155 Roe Blvd., Patchogue 11772
(516) 447-3200

ST. JOSEPH'S SEMINARY
201 Seminary Ave., Yonkers 10704 *Type:* Private (Roman Catholic) graduate only *Accred.:* 1973/1993 (ATS); 1961/1993 (MSA) *Calendar:* Sem. plan *Degrees:* M, P *CEO:* Rector/Pres. Edwin O'Brien
Enroll: 68   (914) 968-6200

ST. LAWRENCE UNIVERSITY
Canton 13617 *Type:* Private liberal arts *Accred.:* 1921/1993 (MSA) *Calendar:* Sem. plan *Degrees:* B, M *CEO:* Pres. Patti McGill Peterson
Enroll: 1,920   (315) 379-5011

ST. THOMAS AQUINAS COLLEGE
125 Rte. 340, Sparkill 10976-1050 *Type:* Private *Accred.:* 1972/1992 (MSA) *Calendar:* Sem. plan *Degrees:* A, B, M *CEO:* Pres. Margaret M. Fitzpatrick
Enroll: 2,075   (914) 398-4000

St. Vladimir's Orthodox Theological
Seminary
575 Scarsdale Rd., Crestwood 10707 *Type:*
Private (Orthodox Church in America) grad-
uate only *Accred.:* 1973/1993 (ATS) *Calen-
dar:* Sem. plan *Degrees:* M, D *CEO:* Pres.
Metropolitan Theodosius
Enroll: 77   (914) 961-8313

Sarah Lawrence College
One Meadway, Bronxville 10708 *Type:* Pri-
vate liberal arts *Accred.:* 1937/1992 (MSA)
Calendar: Sem. plan *Degrees:* B, M *CEO:*
Pres. Alice Stone Ilchman
Enroll: 1,306   (914) 337-0700

Schenectady County Community College
78 Washington Ave., Schenectady 12305
Type: Public (local/state) junior *System:*
State University of New York Office of
Community Colleges *Accred.:* 1974/1994
(MSA) *Calendar:* Sem. plan *Degrees:* A, C
Prof. Accred.: Music *CEO:* Pres. Gabriel J.
Basil
Enroll: 3,642   (518) 346-6211

School of Visual Arts
209 E. 23rd St., New York 10010 *Type:* Pri-
vate professional *Accred.:* 1978/1992 (MSA)
Calendar: Sem. plan *Degrees:* B, M *Prof.
Accred.:* Art *CEO:* Pres. David J. Rhodes
Enroll: 5,211   (212) 592-2000

Seminary of the Immaculate Conception
440 W. Neck Rd., Huntington 11743 *Type:*
Private (Roman Catholic) graduate only
Accred.: 1976/1991 (ATS); 1976/1992
(MSA) *Calendar:* Sem. plan *Degrees:* M, P,
D, C *CEO:* Rector Vincent F. Fullam
Enroll: 192   (516) 423-0483

Sh'or Yoshuv Rabbinical College
1526 Central Ave., Far Rockaway 11691
Type: Private professional *Accred.:* 1979/
1992 (AARTS) *Calendar:* Sem. plan *Degrees:*
Talmudic (1st and 2nd) *CEO:* Pres. Maurice
Friedman
Enroll: 110   (718) 327-2048

Siena College
515 Loudon Rd., Loudonville 12211-1462
Type: Private non-profit *Accred.:* 1943/1994
(MSA) *Calendar:* Sem. plan *Degrees:* B
Prof. Accred.: Social Work (B) *CEO:* Pres.
William E. McConville, O.F.M.
Enroll: 3,232   (518) 783-2300

Simmons Institute of Funeral Service
1828 South Ave., Syracuse 13207 *Type:* Private professional *Calendar:* 16-mos. program *Degrees:* A *Prof. Accred.:* Funeral Service Education (Mortuary Science) *CEO:*
Pres. Thomas R. Taggart
                                 (315) 475-5142

Skidmore College
814 N. Broadway, Saratoga Springs 12866-
1632 *Type:* Private liberal arts *Accred.:*
1925/1989 (MSA) *Calendar:* Sem. plan
Degrees: B, M *Prof. Accred.:* Art, Social
Work (B) *CEO:* Pres. David H. Porter
Enroll: 2,600   (518) 584-5000

State University of New York at Albany
1400 Washington Ave., Albany 12222 *Type:*
Public (state) *System:* State University of
New York System Office *Accred.:* 1938/
1990 (MSA) *Calendar:* Sem. plan *Degrees:*
B, M, D, C *Prof. Accred.:* Business (B,M),
Clinical Psychology, Computer Science,
Counseling Psychology, Librarianship, Pub-
lic Administration, Rehabilitation Counsel-
ing, School Psychology, Social Work (B,M)
CEO: Interim Pres. Karen R. Hitchcock
Enroll: 16,616   (518) 442-3300

State University of New York at
Binghamton
P.O. Box 6000, Binghamton 13902-6000
Type: Public (state) *System:* State University
of New York System Office *Accred.:* 1952/
1991 (MSA) *Calendar:* Sem. plan *Degrees:*
B, M, D, C *Prof. Accred.:* Business (B,M),
Clinical Psychology, Computer Science,
mechanical) Engineering (Engineering
(mechanical) *CEO:* Pres. Lois B. DeFleur
Enroll: 12,089   (607) 777-2000

STATE UNIVERSITY OF NEW YORK AT BUFFALO
Capen Hall, Buffalo 14260 *Type:* Public
(state) *System:* State University of New York
System Office *Accred.:* 1921/1994 (MSA)
Calendar: Sem. plan *Degrees:* B, M, P, D, C
Prof. Accred.: Accounting (A,B), Art, Audi-
ology, Business (B,M), Clinical Psychology,
Combined Prosthodontics, Counseling Psy-
chology, Dental Assisting, Dentistry,
Endodontics, Engineering (aerospace, chem-
ical, civil, electrical, industrial, mechanical),
General Dentistry, General Practice Resi-
dency, Law, Librarianship, Medicine, Music,
Nurse Anesthesia Education (M), Nursing
(B,M), Oral and Maxillofacial Surgery,
Orthodontics, Periodontics, Physical Ther-
apy, Planning (M), Psychology Internship,
Rehabilitation Counseling, Social Work (M),
Speech-Language Pathology *CEO:* Pres.
William R. Greiner
Enroll: 24,943   (716) 645-2000

STATE UNIVERSITY OF NEW YORK AT STONY
BROOK
Nicolls Rd., Stony Brook 11794-0701 *Type:*
Public (state) *System:* State University of
New York System Office *Accred.:* 1957/
1994 (MSA) *Calendar:* Sem. plan *Degrees:*
B, M, P, D, C *Prof. Accred.:* Clinical Lab
Scientist, Clinical Psychology, Dentistry,
Engineering (computer, electrical, engineer-
ing physics/science, mechanical), General
Dentistry, General Practice Residency, Med-
icine, Nursing (B,M), Orthodontics, Peri-
odontics, Physical Therapy, Physician
Assisting/Surgeon Assisting, Psychology
Internship, Radiation Therapy Technology,
Respiratory Therapy, Social Work (B,M),
Theatre (A) *CEO:* Pres. Shirley Strum
Kenny
Enroll: 17,621   (516) 689-6000

STATE UNIVERSITY OF NEW YORK COLLEGE AT
BROCKPORT
350 New Campus Dr., Brockport 14420
Type: Public (state) *System:* State University
of New York System Office *Accred.:*
1952/1992 (MSA) *Calendar:* Sem. plan
Degrees: B, M, C *Prof. Accred.:* Computer
Science, Counseling, Dance, Nursing (B),
Public Administration, Recreation and

Leisure Services, Social Work (B) *CEO:*
Pres. John E. Van de Wetering
Enroll: 9,148   (716) 395-2211

STATE UNIVERSITY OF NEW YORK COLLEGE AT
BUFFALO
1300 Elmwood Ave., Buffalo 14222 *Type:*
Public (state) *System:* State University of
New York System Office *Accred.:* 1948/
1992 (MSA) *Calendar:* Sem. plan *Degrees:*
B, M, C *Prof. Accred.:* Clinical Lab Scien-
tist, Dietetics (coordinated), Engineering
Technology (electrical, mechanical),
Nuclear Medicine Technology, Occupational
Therapy, Social Work (B), Speech-Language
Pathology, Teacher Education *CEO:* Interim
Pres. Muriel A. Moore
Enroll: 11,528   (716) 878-4000

STATE UNIVERSITY OF NEW YORK COLLEGE AT
CORTLAND
P.O. Box 2000, Cortland 13045 *Type:* Public
(state) *System:* State University of New York
System Office *Accred.:* 1948/1992 (MSA)
Calendar: Sem. plan *Degrees:* B, M, C *Prof.
Accred.:* Recreation and Leisure Services
CEO: Pres. Judson H. Taylor
Enroll: 6,827   (607) 753-2201

STATE UNIVERSITY OF NEW YORK COLLEGE AT
FREDONIA
Fredonia 14063 *Type:* Public (state) *System:*
State University of New York System Office
Accred.: 1952/1990 (MSA) *Calendar:* Sem.
plan *Degrees:* B, M, C *Prof. Accred.:* Audi-
ology, Music, Speech-Language Pathology,
Theatre (A) *CEO:* Pres. Donald A. MacPhee
Enroll: 4,892   (716) 673-3111

STATE UNIVERSITY OF NEW YORK COLLEGE AT
GENESEO
Geneseo 14454 *Type:* Public (state) *System:*
State University of New York System Office
Accred.: 1952/1992 (MSA) *Calendar:* Sem.
plan *Degrees:* B, M *Prof. Accred.:* Speech-
Language Pathology *CEO:* Pres. Christopher
C. Dahl
Enroll: 5,754   (716) 245-5501

STATE UNIVERSITY OF NEW YORK COLLEGE AT NEW PALTZ

New Paltz 12561 *Type:* Public (state) *System:* State University of New York System Office *Accred.:* 1950/1991 (MSA) *Calendar:* Sem. plan *Degrees:* B, M, C *Prof. Accred.:* Audiology, Computer Science, Engineering (electrical), Music, Nursing (B), Speech-Language Pathology *CEO:* Pres. Alice Chandler
Enroll: 7,852   (914) 257-2121

STATE UNIVERSITY OF NEW YORK COLLEGE AT OLD WESTBURY

P.O. Box 210, Old Westbury 11568 *Type:* Public (state) *System:* State University of New York System Office *Accred.:* 1976/1991 (MSA) *Calendar:* Sem. plan *Degrees:* B, C *CEO:* Pres. L. Eudora Pettigrew
Enroll: 4,226   (516) 876-3000

STATE UNIVERSITY OF NEW YORK COLLEGE AT ONEONTA

Oneonta 13820-4015 *Type:* Public (state) *System:* State University of New York System Office *Accred.:* 1949/1993 (MSA) *Calendar:* Sem. plan *Degrees:* B, M, C *Prof. Accred.:* Home Economics *CEO:* Pres. Alan B. Donovan
Enroll: 5,829   (607) 436-2500

STATE UNIVERSITY OF NEW YORK COLLEGE AT OSWEGO

Oswego 13126 *Type:* Public (state) *System:* State University of New York System Office *Accred.:* 1950/1992 (MSA) *Calendar:* Sem. plan *Degrees:* B, M, C *Prof. Accred.:* Music *CEO:* Acting Pres. Deborah F. Stanley
Enroll: 8,817   (315) 341-2500

STATE UNIVERSITY OF NEW YORK COLLEGE AT PLATTSBURG

Plattsburgh 12901 *Type:* Public (state) *System:* State University of New York System Office *Accred.:* 1952/1992 (MSA) *Calendar:* Sem. plan *Degrees:* B, M, C *Prof. Accred.:* Audiology, Counseling, Nursing (B), Speech-Language Pathology *CEO:* Pres. Horace A. Judson
Enroll: 6,182   (518) 564-2000

STATE UNIVERSITY OF NEW YORK COLLEGE AT PURCHASE

735 Anderson Hill Rd., Purchase 10577-1400 *Type:* Public (state) *System:* State University of New York System Office *Accred.:* 1976/1993 (MSA) *Calendar:* Sem. plan *Degrees:* B, M, C *CEO:* Pres. Bill Lacy
Enroll: 3,751   (914) 251-6000

STATE UNIVERSITY OF NEW YORK COLLEGE OF AGRICULTURE AND TECHNOLOGY AT COBLESKILL

Cobleskill 12043 *Type:* Public (state) *System:* State University of New York System Office *Accred.:* 1952/1991 (MSA) *Calendar:* Sem. plan *Degrees:* A, B *Prof. Accred.:* Histologic Technology *CEO:* Pres. Kenneth E. Wing
Enroll: 2,597   (518) 234-5111

STATE UNIVERSITY OF NEW YORK COLLEGE OF AGRICULTURE AND TECHNOLOGY AT MORRISVILLE

Morrisville 13408 *Type:* Public (state) *System:* State University of New York System Office *Accred.:* 1952/1992 (MSA) *Calendar:* Sem. plan *Degrees:* A, C *Prof. Accred.:* Engineering Technology (electrical, mechanical), Nursing (A) *CEO:* Pres. Frederick W. Woodward
Enroll: 3,151   (315) 684-6000

STATE UNIVERSITY OF NEW YORK COLLEGE OF ENVIRONMENTAL SCIENCE AND FORESTRY

Syracuse 13210 *Type:* Public (state) *System:* State University of New York System Office *Accred.:* 1952/1992 (MSA) *Calendar:* Sem. plan *Degrees:* A, B, M, D *Prof. Accred.:* Engineering (forest), Forestry, Landscape Architecture (B,M) *CEO:* Pres. Ross S. Whaley
Enroll: 1,566   (315) 470-5000

STATE UNIVERSITY OF NEW YORK COLLEGE OF OPTOMETRY

100 E. 24th St., New York 10010 *Type:* Public (state) *System:* State University of New York System Office *Accred.:* 1976/1992 (MSA) *Calendar:* Qtr. plan *Degrees:* M, P, D *Prof. Accred.:* Optometric Residency, Optometry *CEO:* Pres. Alden N. Haffner
Enroll: 264   (212) 780-4900

STATE UNIVERSITY OF NEW YORK COLLEGE OF TECHNOLOGY AT ALFRED
  Huntington Bldg., Alfred 14802 *Type:* Public (state) *System:* State University of New York System Office *Accred.:* 1952/1991 (MSA) *Calendar:* Sem. plan *Degrees:* A, B, C *Prof. Accred.:* Clinical Lab Technology (A), Engineering Technology (air conditioning, architectural, civil/construction, electrical, electromechanical, general drafting/design, mechanical), Medical Record Technology *CEO:* Pres. William D. Rezak
  Enroll: 3,493   (607) 587-4111

  WELLSVILLE CAMPUS
    Wellsville 14895
                                      (607) 587-3105

STATE UNIVERSITY OF NEW YORK COLLEGE OF TECHNOLOGY AT CANTON
  Cornell Dr., Canton 13617 *Type:* Public (state) *System:* State University of New York System Office *Accred.:* 1952/1992 (MSA) *Calendar:* Sem. plan *Degrees:* A, C *Prof. Accred.:* Clinical Lab Technology (A), Engineering Technology (air conditioning, civil/construction, electrical, mechanical), Funeral Service Education (Mortuary Science), Nursing (A), Veterinary Technology *CEO:* Pres. Joseph L. Kennedy
  Enroll: 2,081   (315) 386-7204

STATE UNIVERSITY OF NEW YORK COLLEGE OF TECHNOLOGY AT DELHI
  Delhi 13753 *Type:* Public (state) *System:* State University of New York System Office *Accred.:* 1952/1992 (MSA) *Calendar:* Sem. plan *Degrees:* A, C *Prof. Accred.:* Veterinary Technology *CEO:* Pres. Mary Ellen Duncan
  Enroll: 2,184   (607) 746-4111

STATE UNIVERSITY OF NEW YORK COLLEGE OF TECHNOLOGY AT FARMINGDALE
  Melville Rd., Farmingdale 11735 *Type:* Public (state) *System:* State University of New York System Office *Accred.:* 1952/1991 (MSA) *Calendar:* Sem. plan *Degrees:* A, B *Prof. Accred.:* Clinical Lab Technology (A), Dental Hygiene, Engineering Technology (air conditioning, automotive, bioengineering, civil/construction, electrical), manufac-

turing) Nursing (A) *CEO:* Pres. Frank A. Cipriani
  Enroll: 6,717   (516) 420-2000

STATE UNIVERSITY OF NEW YORK EMPIRE STATE COLLEGE
  One Union Ave., Saratoga Springs 12866 *Type:* Public (state) *System:* State University of New York System Office *Accred.:* 1974/1990 (MSA) *Calendar:* Sem. plan *Degrees:* A, B, M *CEO:* Pres. James W. Hall
  Enroll: 7,199   (518) 587-2100

  COLLEGEWIDE PROGRAMS CAMPUS
    28 Union Ave., Saratoga Springs 12866-4309
                                      (518) 587-2100

  GENESSEE VALLEY REGIONAL CENTER CAMPUS
    8 Prince St., Rochester 14607
                                      (716) 244-3641

  HUDSON VALLEY REGIONAL CENTER CAMPUS
    200 N. Central Ave., Hartsdale 10530
                                      (914) 948-6206

  LONG ISLAND REGIONAL CENTER CAMPUS
    Trainor House, P.O. Box 130, Old Westbury 11568
                                      (516) 997-4700

  METROPOLITAN REGIONAL CENTER CAMPUS
    666 Broadway, New York 10012
                                      (212) 598-0640

  NIAGARA FRONTIER REGIONAL CENTER CAMPUS
    564 Franklin St., Buffalo 14202
                                      (716) 886-8020

  NORTHEAST CENTER CAMPUS
    845 Central Ave., Albany 12206
                                      (518) 485-5964

STATE UNIVERSITY OF NEW YORK HEALTH SCIENCE CENTER AT BROOKLYN
  450 Clarkson Ave., Brooklyn 11203 *Type:* Public (state) *System:* State University of New York System Office *Accred.:* 1952/1991 (MSA) *Calendar:* Sem. plan *Degrees:* B, M, P, D, C *Prof. Accred.:* Diagnostic Medical Sonography, Medical Record Adminis-

tration, Medicine, Nuclear Medicine Technology, Nursing (B,M), Occupational Therapy, Perfusion, Physical Therapy, Physician Assisting/Surgeon Assisting, Radiography *CEO:* Pres. Russell L. Miller
Enroll: 1,672   (718) 270-1000

STATE UNIVERSITY OF NEW YORK HEALTH SCIENCE CENTER AT SYRACUSE
750 E. Adams St., Syracuse 13210 *Type:* Public (state) *System:* State University of New York System Office *Accred.:* 1952/1994 (MSA) *Calendar:* Sem. plan *Degrees:* A, B, M, P, D *Prof. Accred.:* Blood Bank Technology, Clinical Lab Scientist, Cytotechnology, General Practice Residency, Medicine, Nuclear Medicine Technology, Nursing (B,M), Perfusion, Physical Therapy, Psychology Internship, Radiation Therapy Technology, Radiography, Respiratory Therapy *CEO:* Pres. Gregory L. Eastwood
Enroll: 1,123   (315) 464-5540

STATE UNIVERSITY OF NEW YORK INSTITUTE OF TECHNOLOGY AT UTICA/ROME
P.O. Box 3050, Utica 13504-3050 *Type:* Public (state) *System:* State University of New York System Office *Accred.:* 1979/1994 (MSA) *Calendar:* Sem. plan *Degrees:* B, M *Prof. Accred.:* Engineering Technology (computer, electrical, industrial, mechanical), Medical Record Administration, Nursing (B,M) *CEO:* Pres. Peter J. Cayan
Enroll: 2,544   (315) 792-7400

STATE UNIVERSITY OF NEW YORK MARITIME COLLEGE
Fort Schuyler, Throggs Neck 10465 *Type:* Public (state) *System:* State University of New York System Office *Accred.:* 1952/1991 (MSA) *Calendar:* Sem. plan *Degrees:* B, M *Prof. Accred.:* Engineering (electrical, naval architecture/marine) *CEO:* Pres. David C. Brown
Enroll: 822   (212) 409-7200

STATE UNIVERSITYN OF NEW YORK COLLEGE AT POSTDAM
Pierrepont Ave., Potsdam 13676 *Type:* Public (state) *System:* State University of New

York System Office *Accred.:* 1952/1992 (MSA) *Calendar:* Sem. plan *Degrees:* B, M *Prof. Accred.:* Music *CEO:* Pres. William C. Merwin
Enroll: 4,294   (315) 267-2000

SUFFOLK COUNTY COMMUNITY COLLEGE AMMERMAN CAMPUS
533 College Rd., Selden 11784 *Type:* Public (local/state) junior *System:* Suffolk County Community College Central Administration *Accred.:* 1966/1992 (MSA) *Calendar:* Sem. plan *Degrees:* A *Prof. Accred.:* Nursing (A), Physical Therapy Assisting *CEO:* Provost N. Patricia Yarborough
Enroll: 12,468   (516) 451-4110

SUFFOLK COUNTY COMMUNITY COLLEGE EASTERN CAMPUS
Speonk-Riverhead Rd., Riverhead 11901 *Type:* Public (local/state) junior *System:* Suffolk County Community College Central Administration *Accred.:* 1982/1992 (MSA) *Calendar:* Sem. plan *Degrees:* A *CEO:* Provost Elizabeth Blake
Enroll: 2,614   (516) 548-2500

SUFFOLK COUNTY COMMUNITY COLLEGE WESTERN CAMPUS
Crooked Hill Rd., Brentwood 11717 *Type:* Public (local/state) junior *System:* Suffolk County Community College Central Administration *Accred.:* 1981/1992 (MSA) *Calendar:* Sem. plan *Degrees:* A *Prof. Accred.:* Nursing (A) *CEO:* Provost Salvatore La Lima
Enroll: 6,133   (516) 434-6789

SULLIVAN COUNTY COMMUNITY COLLEGE
P.O. Box 4002, Loch Sheldrake 12759-4002 *Type:* Public (local/state) junior *System:* State University of New York Office of Community Colleges *Accred.:* 1968/1992 (MSA) *Calendar:* 4-1-4 plan *Degrees:* A, C *Prof. Accred.:* Nursing (A) *CEO:* Pres. Jeffrey B. Willens
Enroll: 2,085   (914) 434-5750

SYRACUSE UNIVERSITY
300 Tolley Administration Bldg, Syracuse 13244 *Type:* Private non-profit *Accred.:*

1921/1993 (MSA) *Calendar:* Sem. plan *Degrees:* A, B, M, P, D, C *Prof. Accred.:* Art, Audiology, Business (B,M), Clinical Psychology, Counseling, Dietetics (coordinated), Engineering (aerospace, bioengineering, chemical, civil, computer, electrical, mechanical), Interior Design, Journalism (B,M), Law, Librarianship, Marriage and Family Therapy (M,D-candidate), Music, Nursing (B,M), Public Administration, Rehabilitation Counseling, School Psychology, Social Work (B,M), Speech-Language Pathology *CEO:* Pres./Chanc. Kenneth A. Shaw
Enroll: 18,972   (315) 443-1870

TALMUDICAL SEMINARY OHOLEI TORAH
667 Eastern Pkwy., Brooklyn 11213 *Type:* Private professional *Accred.:* 1979/1990 (AARTS) *Calendar:* Sem. plan *Degrees:* Talmudic (1st) *CEO:* Pres. Yaakov Pinson
Enroll: 232   (718) 778-3340

TAYLOR BUSINESS INSTITUTE
120 West 30th St, New York 10001 *Type:* Private business *Accred.:* 1962/1994 (ACICS) *Calendar:* Sem. plan *Degrees:* A *CEO:* Pres. Patricia Martin
                             (212) 279-0510

TEACHERS COLLEGE OF COLUMBIA UNIVERSITY
525 W. 120th St., New York 10027 *Type:* Private professional; graduate only *Accred.:* 1921/1991 (MSA) *Calendar:* Sem. plan *Degrees:* M, D *Prof. Accred.:* Clinical Psychology, Counseling Psychology, Nursing (M), School Psychology, Speech-Language Pathology *CEO:* Pres. Arthur E. Levine
Enroll: 4,559   (212) 678-3000

TECHNICAL CAREER INSTITUTE
320 W. 31st St., New York 10001 *Type:* Private *Calendar:* Sem. plan *Degrees:* A *Prof. Accred.:* Engineering Technology (electrical) *CEO:* Pres. David M. Goodman
                             (212) 594-4000

TOMPKINS CORTLAND COMMUNITY COLLEGE
P.O. Box 139, 170 North St., Dryden 13053 *Type:* Public (local/state) junior *System:* State University of New York Office of

Community Colleges *Accred.:* 1973/1993 (MSA) *Calendar:* Sem. plan *Degrees:* A, C *Prof. Accred.:* Nursing (A) *CEO:* Pres. Carl E. Haynes
Enroll: 2,925   (607) 844-8211

TORAH TEMIMAH TALMUDICAL SEMINARY
507 Ocean Pkwy., Brooklyn 11218 *Type:* Private professional *Accred.:* 1981/1991 (AARTS) *Calendar:* Sem. plan *Degrees:* Talmudic (1st and 2nd) *CEO:* Pres./Dean L. Margulies
Enroll: 248   (718) 853-8500

TOURO COLLEGE
Empire State Bldg., Ste. 5122, 350 Fifth Ave., New York 10118 *Type:* Private nonprofit *Accred.:* 1976/1992 (MSA) *Calendar:* Sem. plan *Degrees:* A, B, M, P, C *Prof. Accred.:* Law, Medical Record Administration, Occupational Therapy, Physical Therapy *CEO:* Pres. Bernard Lander
Enroll: 6,717   (212) 643-0700

HUNTINGTON BRANCH CAMPUS
300 Nassau Rd., Huntington 11743 *Prof. Accred.:* Law (ABA only)
Enroll: 896   (516) 421-2244

TAINO TOWERS CAMPUS
844 Ave. of the Americas, New York 10001
                             (212) 447-0700

TROCAIRE COLLEGE
110 Red Jacket Pkwy., Buffalo 14220 *Type:* Private junior *Accred.:* 1974/1989 (MSA) *Calendar:* Sem. plan *Degrees:* A, C *Prof. Accred.:* Clinical Lab Technology (A), Medical Record Technology, Nursing (A), Radiography, Surgical Technology *CEO:* Pres. Barbara Ciarico, R.S.M.
Enroll: 1,169   (716) 826-1200

ULSTER COUNTY COMMUNITY COLLEGE
Stone Ridge 12484 *Type:* Public (local/state) junior *System:* State University of New York Office of Community Colleges *Accred.:* 1971/1991 (MSA) *Calendar:* Sem. plan *Degrees:* A, C *CEO:* Pres. Robert T. Brown
Enroll: 2,741   (914) 687-5000

UNION COLLEGE
Schenectady 12308 *Type:* Private liberal arts
Accred.: 1921/1991 (MSA) *Calendar:* Sem.
plan *Degrees:* B, M, D *Prof. Accred.:* Engi-
neering (civil, electrical, mechanical),
Health Services Administration *CEO:* Pres.
Roger H. Hull
Enroll: 2,570   (518) 388-6000

UNION THEOLOGICAL SEMINARY
3041 Broadway, New York 10027-0003
Type: Private (interdenominational) graduate
only *Accred.:* 1938/1988 (ATS); 1967/1994
(MSA) *Calendar:* Sem. plan *Degrees:* M, P,
D *CEO:* Pres. Holland L. Hendrix
Enroll: 283   (212) 662-7100

UNION UNIVERSITY—ALBANY LAW SCHOOL
80 New Scotland Ave., Albany 12208 *Type:*
Private professional *Calendar:* Sem. plan
Degrees: P, D *Prof. Accred.:* Law *CEO:*
Pres./Dean Thomas H. Sponsler
Enroll: 785   (518) 445-2321

UNITED STATES MERCHANT MARINE ACADEMY
Steamboat Rd., Kings Point 11024 *Type:* Public (federal) technological *Accred.:* 1949/
1990 (MSA) *Calendar:* Qtr. plan *Degrees:* B
Prof. Accred.: Engineering (naval architec-
ture/marine) *CEO:* Supt. Thomas T. Matteson
Enroll: 950   (516) 773-5000

UNITED STATES MILITARY ACADEMY
West Point 10996-5000 *Type:* Public (fed-
eral) professional *Accred.:* 1949/1989
(MSA) *Calendar:* Sem. plan *Degrees:* B
Prof. Accred.: Engineering (civil, electrical,
engineering management, mechanical)
CEO: Supt. Howard D. Graves
Enroll: 4,061   (914) 938-4011

UNITED TALMUDICAL ACADEMY
82 Lee Ave., Brooklyn 11211 *Type:* Private
professional *Accred.:* 1979/1993 (AARTS)
Calendar: Sem. plan *Degrees:* Rabbinic (1st
and 2nd) *CEO:* Pres. L. Lefkowitz
Enroll: 1,508   (718) 963-9260

UNIVERSITY OF ROCHESTER
River Sta., Rochester 14627 *Type:* Private
non-profit *Accred.:* 1921/1992 (MSA) *Cal-*

endar: Sem. plan *Degrees:* B, M, P, D, C
Prof. Accred.: Business (M), Clinical Psy-
chology, Engineering (chemical, electrical,
mechanical), General Practice Residency,
Marriage and Family Therapy (post-D),
Medicine, Music, Nursing (B,M), Oral and
Maxillofacial Surgery, Psychology Intern-
ship, Radiation Therapy Technology *CEO:*
Pres. Thomas Jackson
Enroll: 9,632   (716) 275-2121

UTICA COLLEGE OF SYRACUSE UNIVERSITY
1600 Burrstone Rd., Utica 13502-4892 *Type:*
Private liberal arts *Accred.:* 1946/1993
(MSA) *Calendar:* Sem. plan *Degrees:* B
Prof. Accred.: Nursing (B), Occupational
Therapy *CEO:* Pres. Michael K. Simpson
Enroll: 1,841   (315) 792-3111

UTICA SCHOOL OF COMMERCE
201 Bleecker St., Utica 13501 *Type:* Private
business *Accred.:* 1969/1988 (ACICS) *Cal-*
endar: Sem. plan *Degrees:* A *CEO:* Pres.
Philip M. Williams
                                  (315) 733-2307

CANASTOTA CAMPUS
P.O. Box 462, Rte. 5, Canastota 13032
Accred.: 1993 (ACICS)
                                  (315) 697-8200

ONEONTA CAMPUS
17-19 Elm St., Oneonta 13820 *Accred.:*
1993 (ACICS)
                                  (607) 432-7003

VASSAR COLLEGE
Raymond Ave., Box 1, Poughkeepsie 12601
Type: Private liberal arts *Accred.:* 1921/1994
(MSA) *Calendar:* Sem. plan *Degrees:* B, M
CEO: Pres. Frances D. Fergusson
Enroll: 2,312   (914) 437-7000

VILLA MARIA COLLEGE OF BUFFALO
240 Pine Ridge Rd., Buffalo 14225-3999
Type: Private junior *Accred.:* 1972/1994
(MSA) *Calendar:* Sem. plan *Degrees:* A, C
Prof. Accred.: Interior Design *CEO:* Pres.
Marcella Marie Garus, C.S.S.F.
Enroll: 372   (716) 896-0700

WADHAMS HALL SEMINARY/COLLEGE
R.D. 4, Box 80, Ogdensburg 13669 *Type:* Private (Roman Catholic) *Accred.:* 1972/ 1992 (MSA) *Calendar:* Sem. plan *Degrees:* B *CEO:* Pres. Richard W. Siepka
Enroll: 31   (315) 393-4231

WAGNER COLLEGE
Howard Ave. and Campus Rd., Staten Island 10301 *Type:* Private liberal arts *Accred.:* 1931/1991 (MSA) *Calendar:* Sem. plan *Degrees:* B, M *Prof. Accred.:* Nursing (B-warning,M) *CEO:* Pres. Norman R. Smith
Enroll: 1,856   (718) 390-3100

WEBB INSTITUTE OF NAVAL ARCHITECTURE
Crescent Beach Rd., Glen Cove 11542 *Type:* Private technological *Accred.:* 1930/1990 (MSA) *Calendar:* Sem. plan *Degrees:* B *Prof. Accred.:* Engineering (naval architecture/marine) *CEO:* Pres. James J. Conti
Enroll: 75   (516) 671-2213

WELLS COLLEGE
Aurora 13026-0500 *Type:* Private liberal arts for women *Accred.:* 1921/1992 (MSA) *Calendar:* 4-1-4 plan *Degrees:* B *CEO:* Pres. Robert A. Plane
Enroll: 398   (315) 364-3265

WESTCHESTER BUSINESS INSTITUTE
325 Central Ave., White Plains 10606 *Type:* Private business *Accred.:* 1966/1996 (ACICS) *Calendar:* Qtr. plan *Degrees:* A, C *CEO:* Exec. Vice Pres. Karen Smith
                                        (914) 948-4442

WESTCHESTER COMMUNITY COLLEGE
75 Grasslands Rd., Valhalla 10595 *Type:* Public (local/state) junior *System:* State University of New York Office of Community Colleges *Accred.:* 1970/1990 (MSA) *Calendar:* Sem. plan *Degrees:* A *Prof. Accred.:* Radiography, Respiratory Therapy *CEO:* Pres. Joseph N. Hankin
Enroll: 11,347   (914) 785-6600

YESHIVA DERECH CHAIM
1573 39th St., Brooklyn 11218 *Type:* Private professional *Accred.:* 1984/1993 (AARTS) *Calendar:* Sem. plan *Degrees:* Talmudic (1st and 2nd) *CEO:* Pres. Mordechai Rennert
Enroll: 165   (718) 438-5476

YESHIVA KARLIN STOLIN BETH AARON V'ISRAEL RABBINICAL INSTITUTE
1818 54th St., Brooklyn 11204 *Type:* Private professional *Accred.:* 1975/1990 (AARTS) *Calendar:* Sem. plan *Degrees:* Talmudic (1st and 2nd) *CEO:* Pres. Meyer Pilchick
Enroll: 40   (718) 232-7800

YESHIVA MIKDASH MELECH
1326 Ocean Pkwy., Brooklyn 11230-5655 *Type:* Private professional *Accred.:* 1979/ 1993 (AARTS) *Calendar:* Sem. plan *Degrees:* Rabbinic (1st and 2nd) *CEO:* Pres. Haim Benoliel
Enroll: 80   (718) 339-1090

YESHIVA OF NITRA—RABBINICAL COLLEGE YESHIVA FARM SETTLEMENT
Pines Bridge Rd., Mount Kisco 10549 *Type:* Private professional *Accred.:* 1980/1991 (AARTS) *Calendar:* Sem. plan *Degrees:* Rabbinic (1st and 2nd), Talmudic (1st and 2nd) *CEO:* Pres. Alexander Fischer
Enroll: 190   (718) 387-0422

YESHIVA SHAAR HATORAH TALMUDIC RESEARCH INSTITUTE
83-96 117th St., Kew Gardens 11415 *Type:* Private professional *Accred.:* 1984/1991 (AARTS) *Calendar:* Sem. plan *Degrees:* Rabbinic (1st), Talmudic (1st and 2nd) *CEO:* Pres. Z. Epstein
Enroll: 142   (718) 846-1940

YESHIVA UNIVERSITY
500 W. 185th St., New York 10033-3299 *Type:* Private non-profit *Accred.:* 1948/1991 (MSA) *Calendar:* Sem. plan *Degrees:* A, B, M, P, D, C *Prof. Accred.:* Clinical Psychology, Combined Prosthodontics, General Practice Residency, Law, Medicine, Oral and Maxillofacial Surgery, Orthodontics, Pediatric Dentistry, Psychology Internship, School Psychology, Social Work (M) *CEO:* Pres. Norman Lamm
Enroll: 5,279   (212) 960-5400

YESHIVAS NOVOMINSK
1569 47th St., Brooklyn 11219 *Type:* Private professional *Accred.:* 1992 (AARTS) *Calendar:* Sem. plan *Degrees:* Talmudic (1st) *CEO:* Pres. Abraham Frankel
Enroll: 113   (718) 438-2727

YESHIVATH VIZNITZ
15 Elyon Rd., Monsey 10952 *Type:* Private professional *Accred.:* 1980/1991 (AARTS) *Calendar:* Sem. plan *Degrees:* A, Rabbinic (1st and advanced) *CEO:* Pres. Gershon Neiman
Enroll: 343   (914) 356-1010

YESIVATH ZICHRON MOSHE
Laurel Park Rd., South Fallsburg 12779 *Type:* Private professional *Accred.:* 1979/ 1992 (AARTS) *Calendar:* Sem. plan *Degrees:* Talmudic (1st and 2nd) *CEO:* Pres. A. Gorelick
Enroll: 120   (914) 434-5240

YORK COLLEGE
94-20 Guy R. Brewer Blvd., Jamaica 11451 *Type:* Public (local/state) *System:* City University of New York Office of the Chancellor *Accred.:* 1967/1993 (MSA) *Calendar:* Sem. plan *Degrees:* B *Prof. Accred.:* Nursing (B), Occupational Therapy, Social Work (B) *CEO:* Acting Pres. Thomas K. Minter
Enroll: 6,889   (718) 262-2000

NORTH CAROLINA

ALAMANCE COMMUNITY COLLEGE
P.O. Box 8000, Graham 27253-8000 *Type:*
Public (district) junior *System:* North Carolina Community College System *Accred.:*
1969/1993 (SACS-CC) *Calendar:* Qtr. plan
Degrees: A *Prof. Accred.:* Clinical Lab Technology (A), Dental Assisting *CEO:* Pres. W.
Ronald McCarter
FTE Enroll: 2,293   (910) 578-2002

ANSON COMMUNITY COLLEGE
P.O. Box 126, Polkton 28135 *Type:* Public
(district) junior *System:* North Carolina
Community College System *Accred.:* 1977/
1993 (SACS-CC) *Calendar:* Qtr. plan
Degrees: A *CEO:* Pres. Donald P. Altieri
FTE Enroll: 590   (704) 272-7635

APPALACHIAN STATE UNIVERSITY
Boone 28608 *Type:* Public (state) *System:*
University of North Carolina General
Administration *Accred.:* 1942/1992 (SACS-CC) *Calendar:* Sem. plan *Degrees:* B, M, D
(candidate) *Prof. Accred.:* Athletic Training,
Business (B,M), Computer Science, Counseling, Dietetics (internship), Home Economics, Marriage and Family Therapy (M-candidate), Music, Social Work (B), Speech-Language Pathology, Teacher Education
CEO: Chanc. Francis T. Borkowski
FTE Enroll: 11,373   (704) 262-2000

ASHEVILLE-BUNCOMBE TECHNICAL COMMUNITY
COLLEGE
340 Victoria Rd., Asheville 28801 *Type:*
Public (district) junior *System:* North Carolina Community College System *Accred.:*
1969/1994 (SACS-CC) *Calendar:* Qtr. plan
Degrees: A *Prof. Accred.:* Clinical Lab Technology (A), Dental Assisting, Dental
Hygiene, Radiography *CEO:* Pres. K. Ray
Bailey
FTE Enroll: 2,764   (704) 254-1921

BARBER-SCOTIA COLLEGE
145 Cabarrus Ave., W., Concord 28025
Type: Private (Presbyterian) liberal arts and
teachers *Accred.:* 1949/1993 (SACS-CC

probational) *Calendar:* Sem. plan *Degrees:*
B *CEO:* Pres. Mabel P. McLean
FTE Enroll: 445   (704) 786-5171

BARTON COLLEGE
College Sta., Wilson 27893 *Type:* Private
(Disciples of Christ) liberal arts *Accred.:*
1955/1988 (SACS-CC) *Calendar:* Sem. plan
Degrees: B *Prof. Accred.:* Nursing (B),
Social Work (B-candidate), Teacher Education *CEO:* Pres. James B. Hemby, Jr.
FTE Enroll: 1,338   (919) 399-6300

BEAUFORT COUNTY COMMUNITY COLLEGE
P.O. Box 1069, Washington 27889 *Type:*
Public (district) junior *System:* North Carolina Community College System *Accred.:*
1973/1988 (SACS-CC) *Calendar:* Qtr. plan
Degrees: A *Prof. Accred.:* Clinical Lab Technology (A) *CEO:* Pres. U. Ronald Champion
FTE Enroll: 851   (919) 946-6194

BELMONT ABBEY COLLEGE
100 Belmont-Mount Holly Rd., Belmont
28012-2795 *Type:* Private (Roman Catholic)
liberal arts *Accred.:* 1957/1989 (SACS-CC)
Calendar: Sem. plan *Degrees:* B, M *Prof.
Accred.:* Teacher Education *CEO:* Pres.
Robert A. Preston
FTE Enroll: 815   (704) 825-6700

BENNETT COLLEGE
900 E. Washington St., Greensboro 27401-3239 *Type:* Private (United Methodist) liberal arts for women *Accred.:* 1935/1990
(SACS-CC) *Calendar:* Sem. plan *Degrees:*
B *Prof. Accred.:* Social Work (B), Teacher
Education *CEO:* Pres. Gloria Randall Scott
FTE Enroll: 655   (910) 273-4431

BLADEN COMMUNITY COLLEGE
P.O. Box 266, Dublin 28332-0266 *Type:*
Public (district) junior *System:* North Carolina Community College System *Accred.:*
1976/1992 (SACS-CC) *Calendar:* Qtr. plan
Degrees: A *CEO:* Pres. Lynn G. King
FTE Enroll: 555   (910) 862-2164

BLUE RIDGE COMMUNITY COLLEGE
College Dr., Box 133A, Flat Rock 28731-9624 *Type:* Public (district) junior *System:* North Carolina Community College System *Accred.:* 1973/1988 (SACS-CC) *Calendar:* Qtr. plan *Degrees:* A *CEO:* Pres. David W. Sink, Jr.
FTE Enroll: 1,126　　　(704) 692-3572

BREVARD COLLEGE
400 N. Broad St., Brevard 28712-3306 *Type:* Private (United Methodist) junior *Accred.:* 1949/1986 (SACS-CC) *Calendar:* Sem. plan *Degrees:* A, B (candidate) *Prof. Accred.:* Music *CEO:* Pres. J. Thomas Bertrand
FTE Enroll: 715　　　(704) 883-8292

BRUNSWICK COMMUNITY COLLEGE
P.O. Box 30, Supply 28462-0030 *Type:* Public (district) junior *System:* North Carolina Community College System *Accred.:* 1983/1988 (SACS-CC) *Calendar:* Qtr. plan *Degrees:* A *CEO:* Pres. W. Michael Reaves
FTE Enroll: 639　　　(910) 754-6900

CALDWELL COMMUNITY COLLEGE AND TECHNICAL INSTITUTE
100 Hickory Blvd., Lenoir 28645 *Type:* Public (district) junior *System:* North Carolina Community College System *Accred.:* 1969/1986 (SACS-CC) *Calendar:* Qtr. plan *Degrees:* A *Prof. Accred.:* Diagnostic Medical Sonography, Occupational Therapy Assisting, Physical Therapy Assisting, Radiography *CEO:* Pres. Kenneth A. Boham
FTE Enroll: 1,864　　　(704) 726-2200

CAMPBELL UNIVERSITY
P.O. Box 97, Buies Creek 27506 *Type:* Private (Southern Baptist) liberal arts *Accred.:* 1941/1990 (SACS-CC) *Calendar:* Sem. plan *Degrees:* B, M, D *Prof. Accred.:* Law (ABA only), Social Work (B-candidate), Teacher Education *CEO:* Pres. Norman A. Wiggins
FTE Enroll: 4,194　　　(910) 893-1200

CAPE FEAR COMMUNITY COLLEGE
411 N. Front St., Wilmington 28401-3993 *Type:* Public (district) junior *System:* North Carolina Community College System *Accred.:* 1971/1986 (SACS-CC) *Calendar:*
Qtr. plan *Degrees:* A *Prof. Accred.:* Dental Assisting *CEO:* Pres. Eric B. McKeithan
FTE Enroll: 2,730　　　(910) 251-5100

CARTERET COMMUNITY COLLEGE
3505 Arendell St., Morehead City 28557 *Type:* Public (district) junior *System:* North Carolina Community College System *Accred.:* 1974/1989 (SACS-CC) *Calendar:* Qtr. plan *Degrees:* A *Prof. Accred.:* Medical Assisting (AMA), Radiography, Respiratory Therapy, Respiratory Therapy Technology *CEO:* Pres. Donald W. Bryant
FTE Enroll: 1,439　　　(919) 247-6000

CATAWBA COLLEGE
1300 W. Innes St., Salisbury 28144 *Type:* Private (United Church of Christ) liberal arts *Accred.:* 1928/1995 (SACS-CC) *Calendar:* Sem. plan *Degrees:* B, M *Prof. Accred.:* Teacher Education *CEO:* Pres. J. Fred Corriher, Jr.
FTE Enroll: 966　　　(704) 637-4111

CATAWBA VALLEY COMMUNITY COLLEGE
2550 Hwy. 70 S.E., Hickory 28602-9699 *Type:* Public (district) junior *System:* North Carolina Community College System *Accred.:* 1969/1994 (SACS-CC) *Calendar:* Qtr. plan *Degrees:* A *Prof. Accred.:* EMT-Paramedic, Engineering Technology (architectural, electrical, industrial, mechanical), Medical Record Technology, Nursing (A), Respiratory Therapy Technology, Surgical Technology *CEO:* Pres. Cuyler A. Dunbar
FTE Enroll: 2,408　　　(704) 327-7000

CECILS COLLEGE
1567 Patton Ave., Asheville 28806 *Type:* Private junior *Accred.:* 1971/1997 (ACICS) *Calendar:* Sem. plan *Degrees:* A *CEO:* Pres. John T. South, Jr.
　　　　　　　　　　(704) 252-2486

CENTRAL CAROLINA COMMUNITY COLLEGE
1105 Kelly Dr., Sanford 27330 *Type:* Public (district) junior *System:* North Carolina Community College System *Accred.:* 1972/1987 (SACS-CC) *Calendar:* Qtr. plan *Degrees:* A *Prof. Accred.:* Veterinary Technology *CEO:* Pres. Marvin R. Joyner
FTE Enroll: 2,204　　　(919) 775-5401

CENTRAL PIEDMONT COMMUNITY COLLEGE
P.O. Box 35009, Charlotte 28235 *Type:* Public (district) junior *System:* North Carolina Community College System *Accred.:* 1969/ 1993 (SACS-CC) *Calendar:* Qtr. plan *Degrees:* A *Prof. Accred.:* Cytotechnology, Dental Assisting, Dental Hygiene, Engineering Technology (architectural, civil/construction, computer, electrical, manufacturing, mechanical), Medical Assisting (AMA), Medical Record Technology, Physical Therapy Assisting, Respiratory Therapy *CEO:* Pres. Paul Anthony Zeiss
FTE Enroll: 10,916   (704) 342-6633

CHOWAN COLLEGE
P.O. Box 1848, Murfreesboro 27855 *Type:* Private (Southern Baptist) *Accred.:* 1956/ 1988 (SACS-CC) *Calendar:* Sem. plan *Degrees:* A, B *CEO:* Interim Pres. Herman E. Collier, Jr.
FTE Enroll: 802   (919) 398-4101

CLEVELAND COMMUNITY COLLEGE
137 S. Post Rd., Shelby 28150 *Type:* Public (district) junior *System:* North Carolina Community College System *Accred.:* 1975/ 1991 (SACS-CC) *Calendar:* Qtr. plan *Degrees:* A *Prof. Accred.:* Radiography *CEO:* Pres. L. Steve Thornburg
FTE Enroll: 1,608   (704) 484-4000

CMHA SCHOOL OF NURSING
P.O. Box 32861, 1416 East Morehead St., Charlotte 28232-2861 *Type:* Public *Accred.:* 1995 (SACS-CC) *Calendar:* Sem. plan *Degrees:* A *CEO:* Admin./Dir. Clara B. Smith
FTE Enroll: 129   (704) 355-5043

COASTAL CAROLINA COMMUNITY COLLEGE
444 Western Blvd., Jacksonville 28546-6877 *Type:* Public (district) junior *System:* North Carolina Community College System *Accred.:* 1972/1987 (SACS-CC) *Calendar:* Qtr. plan *Degrees:* A *Prof. Accred.:* Clinical Lab Technology (A), Dental Assisting, Dental Hygiene, Surgical Technology *CEO:* Pres. Ronald K. Lingle
FTE Enroll: 2,725   (910) 455-1221

COLLEGE OF THE ALBEMARLE
P.O. Box 2327, Elizabeth City 27906-2327 *Type:* Public (district) junior *System:* North Carolina Community College System *Accred.:* 1968/1993 (SACS-CC) *Calendar:* Qtr. plan *Degrees:* A *CEO:* Pres. Larry R. Donnithorne
FTE Enroll: 1,421   (919) 335-0821

CRAVEN COMMUNITY COLLEGE
800 College Ct., New Bern 28562 *Type:* Public (district) junior *System:* North Carolina Community College System *Accred.:* 1971/1986 (SACS-CC) *Calendar:* Qtr. plan *Degrees:* A *CEO:* Pres. Lewis S. Redd
FTE Enroll: 1,545   (919) 638-4131

DAVIDSON COLLEGE
P.O. Box 1719, Davidson 28036 *Type:* Private (Presbyterian) liberal arts *Accred.:* 1917/1986 (SACS-CC) *Calendar:* Sem. plan *Degrees:* B *Prof. Accred.:* Teacher Education *CEO:* Pres. John W. Kuykendall
FTE Enroll: 1,607   (704) 892-2000

DAVIDSON COUNTY COMMUNITY COLLEGE
P.O. Box 1287, Lexington 27293-1287 *Type:* Public (district) junior *System:* North Carolina Community College System *Accred.:* 1968/1992 (SACS-CC) *Calendar:* Qtr. plan *Degrees:* A *Prof. Accred.:* Engineering Technology (electrical), Medical Record Technology, Nursing (A) *CEO:* Pres. J. Bryan Brooks
FTE Enroll: 1,803   (704) 249-8186

DUKE UNIVERSITY
P.O. Box 90001, Durham 27708-0001 *Type:* Private liberal arts and professional (United Methodist) *Accred.:* 1938/1994 (ATS); 1895/1988 (SACS-CC) *Calendar:* Sem. plan *Degrees:* A, B, M, D *Prof. Accred.:* Blood Bank Technology, Business (M), Clinical Lab Scientist, Clinical Psychology, Engineering (bioengineering, civil, electrical, mechanical), Forestry, Health Services Administration, Law, Medicine, Nursing (M), Ophthalmic Medical Technology, Physical Therapy, Physician Assisting/Surgeon

Assisting, Psychology Internship, Teacher Education *CEO:* Pres. Nannerl O. Keohane
FTE Enroll: 10,982　　　　(919) 684-8111

DURHAM TECHNICAL COMMUNITY COLLEGE
1637 Lawson St., Durham 27703 *Type:* Public (district) junior *System:* North Carolina Community College System *Accred.:* 1971/1986 (SACS-CC) *Calendar:* Qtr. plan *Degrees:* A *Prof. Accred.:* Dental Laboratory Technology, Occupational Therapy Assisting, Respiratory Therapy, Respiratory Therapy Technology *CEO:* Pres. Phail Wynn, Jr.
FTE Enroll: 3,183　　　　(919) 598-9222

EAST CAROLINA UNIVERSITY
E. Fifth St., Greenville 27858-4353 *Type:* Public (state) *System:* University of North Carolina General Administration *Accred.:* 1927/1992 (SACS-CC) *Calendar:* Sem. plan *Degrees:* B, M, D *Prof. Accred.:* Art, Audiology, Business (B,M), Clinical Lab Scientist, Construction Education, Cytotechnology, Dietetics (internship), General Practice Residency, Marriage and Family Therapy (M), Medical Record Administration, Medicine, Music, Nursing (B,M), Occupational Therapy, Physical Therapy, Public Administration, Recreation and Leisure Services (B), Rehabilitation Counseling, Social Work (B,M), Speech-Language Pathology, Teacher Education *CEO:* Chanc. Richard R. Eakin
FTE Enroll: 16,176　　　　(919) 328-6131

EAST COAST BIBLE COLLEGE
6900 Wilkinson Blvd., Charlotte 28214 *Type:* Private (Church of God) *Accred.:* 1985/1995 (AABC); 1989 (SACS-CC warning) *Calendar:* Sem. plan *Degrees:* A, B *CEO:* Pres. A. Lawrence Leonhardt
FTE Enroll: 206　　　　(704) 394-2307

EDGECOMBE COMMUNITY COLLEGE
2009 W. Wilson St., Tarboro 27886 *Type:* Public (district) junior *System:* North Carolina Community College System *Accred.:* 1973/1988 (SACS-CC) *Calendar:* Qtr. plan *Degrees:* A *Prof. Accred.:* Radiography, Respiratory Therapy, Respiratory Therapy Technology *CEO:* Pres. Hartwell Fuller, Jr.
FTE Enroll: 1,328　　　　(919) 823-5166

ELIZABETH CITY STATE UNIVERSITY
1704 Weeksville Rd., Elizabeth City 27909 *Type:* Public (state) liberal arts and teachers *System:* University of North Carolina General Administration *Accred.:* 1947/1991 (SACS-CC) *Calendar:* Sem. plan *Degrees:* B *Prof. Accred.:* Teacher Education *CEO:* Interim Chanc. Mickey L. Burnim
FTE Enroll: 2,057　　　　(919) 335-3400

ELON COLLEGE
Campus Box 2185, Elon College 27244-2010 *Type:* Private (United Church of Christ) liberal arts *Accred.:* 1947/1992 (SACS-CC) *Calendar:* Sem. plan *Degrees:* B, M *Prof. Accred.:* Teacher Education *CEO:* Pres. J. Fred Young
FTE Enroll: 3,279　　　　(910) 584-2200

FAYETTEVILLE STATE UNIVERSITY
1200 Murchison Rd., Newbold Sta., Fayetteville 28301-4298 *Type:* Public (state) liberal arts and teachers *System:* University of North Carolina General Administration *Accred.:* 1947/1991 (SACS-CC) *Calendar:* Sem. plan *Degrees:* A, B, M, D (candidate) *Prof. Accred.:* Teacher Education *CEO:* Chanc. Willis B. McLeod
FTE Enroll: 3,476　　　　(910) 486-1111

FAYETTEVILLE TECHNICAL COMMUNITY COLLEGE
P.O. Box 35236, 2201 Hull Rd., Fayetteville 28303-0236 *Type:* Public (district) junior *System:* North Carolina Community College System *Accred.:* 1967/1991 (SACS-CC) *Calendar:* Qtr. plan *Degrees:* A *Prof. Accred.:* Dental Assisting, Dental Hygiene, Engineering Technology (civil/construction, electrical), Funeral Service Education (Mortuary Science), Nursing (A), Physical Therapy Assisting, Radiography, Respiratory Therapy, Surgical Technology *CEO:* Pres. Robert Craig Allen
FTE Enroll: 5,515　　　　(910) 678-8400

FORSYTH TECHNICAL COMMUNITY COLLEGE
2100 Silas Creek Pkwy., Winston-Salem 27103-5150 *Type:* Public (district) junior *System:* North Carolina Community College System *Accred.:* 1968/1992 (SACS-CC)

Calendar: Qtr. plan *Degrees:* A *Prof. Accred.:* Diagnostic Medical Sonography, Engineering Technology (electrical, manufacturing, mechanical drafting/design), Nuclear Medicine Technology, Radiation Therapy Technology, Radiography, Respiratory Therapy *CEO:* Pres. Desna L. Wallin
FTE Enroll: 4,963   (910) 723-0371

GARDNER-WEBB UNIVERSITY
P.O. Box 997, Boiling Springs 28017 *Type:* Private (Southern Baptist) liberal arts *Accred.:* 1948/1986 (SACS-CC) *Calendar:* Sem. plan *Degrees:* A, B, M *Prof. Accred.:* Music, Nursing (A,B), Teacher Education *CEO:* Pres. M. Christopher White
FTE Enroll: 1,971   (704) 434-2361

GASTON COLLEGE
201 Hwy. 321 S., Dallas 28034-1499 *Type:* Public (district) junior *System:* North Carolina Community College System *Accred.:* 1967/1991 (SACS-CC) *Calendar:* Qtr. plan *Degrees:* A *Prof. Accred.:* Engineering Technology (civil/construction, electrical, industrial, mechanical), Medical Assisting (AMA) *CEO:* Pres. Patricia Skinner
FTE Enroll: 3,047   (704) 922-6200

GREENSBORO COLLEGE
815 W. Market St., P.O. Box 26050, Greensboro 27401-6050 *Type:* Private (United Methodist) liberal arts *Accred.:* 1926/1995 (SACS-CC) *Calendar:* Sem. plan *Degrees:* B *Prof. Accred.:* Teacher Education *CEO:* Pres. Craven E. Williams
FTE Enroll: 875   (910) 272-7102

GUILFORD COLLEGE
5800 W. Friendly Ave., Greensboro 27410-4171 *Type:* Private liberal arts (Quaker) *Accred.:* 1926/1986 (SACS-CC) *Calendar:* Sem. plan *Degrees:* A, B *Prof. Accred.:* Teacher Education *CEO:* Pres. William R. Rogers
FTE Enroll: 1,558   (910) 316-2000

GUILFORD TECHNICAL COMMUNITY COLLEGE
P.O. Box 309, Jamestown 27282 *Type:* Public (district) junior *System:* North Carolina Community College System *Accred.:* 1969/1994 (SACS-CC) *Calendar:* Qtr. plan

Degrees: A *Prof. Accred.:* Dental Assisting, Dental Hygiene, Engineering Technology (civil/construction, electrical), mechanical drafting/design) *CEO:* Pres. Donald W. Cameron
FTE Enroll: 6,481   (910) 334-4822

HALIFAX COMMUNITY COLLEGE
P.O. Drawer 809, Weldon 27890 *Type:* Public (district) junior *System:* North Carolina Community College System *Accred.:* 1975/1990 (SACS-CC) *Calendar:* Qtr. plan *Degrees:* A *Prof. Accred.:* Clinical Lab Technology (A) *CEO:* Pres. Elton L. Newbern, Jr.
FTE Enroll: 993   (919) 536-2551

HAYWOOD COMMUNITY COLLEGE
1 Freedlander Dr., Clyde 28721 *Type:* Public (district) junior *System:* North Carolina Community College System *Accred.:* 1973/1988 (SACS-CC) *Calendar:* Qtr. plan *Degrees:* A *Prof. Accred.:* Medical Assisting (AMA) *CEO:* Pres. Dan W. Moore
FTE Enroll: 1,281   (704) 627-2821

HIGH POINT UNIVERSITY
University Sta., Montlieu Ave., High Point 27262-3598 *Type:* Private (United Methodist) liberal arts *Accred.:* 1951/1995 (SACS-CC) *Calendar:* Sem. plan *Degrees:* B, M *Prof. Accred.:* Athletic Training, Teacher Education *CEO:* Pres. Jacob C. Martinson, Jr.
FTE Enroll: 2,245   (910) 841-9000

ISOTHERMAL COMMUNITY COLLEGE
P.O. Box 804, Spindale 28160 *Type:* Public (district) junior *System:* North Carolina Community College System *Accred.:* 1970/1995 (SACS-CC) *Calendar:* Qtr. plan *Degrees:* A *CEO:* Pres. Willard L. Lewis, III
FTE Enroll: 1,166   (704) 286-3636

JAMES SPRUNT COMMUNITY COLLEGE
P.O. Box 398, Kenansville 28349-0398 *Type:* Public (district) junior *System:* North Carolina Community College System *Accred.:* 1973/1988 (SACS-CC) *Calendar:* Qtr. plan *Degrees:* A *CEO:* Pres. Donald L. Reichard
FTE Enroll: 788   (910) 296-2400

JOHN WESLEY COLLEGE
2314 N. Centennial St., High Point 27265
Type: Private (Wesleyan) *Accred.:* 1982/
1992 (AABC) *Calendar:* Sem. plan *Degrees:*
A, B, C *CEO:* Pres. Brian C. Donley
FTE Enroll: 114   (910) 889-2262

JOHNSON C. SMITH UNIVERSITY
100 Beatties Ford Rd., Charlotte 28216
Type: Private (Presbyterian) liberal arts
Accred.: 1933/1986 (SACS-CC) *Calendar:*
Sem. plan *Degrees:* B *Prof. Accred.:* Teacher
Education *CEO:* Pres. Dorothy Cowser
Yancy
FTE Enroll: 1,391   (704) 378-1000

JOHNSTON COMMUNITY COLLEGE
P.O. Box 2350, Smithfield 27577 *Type:* Pub-
lic (district) junior *System:* North Carolina
Community College System *Accred.:* 1977/
1992 (SACS-CC) *Calendar:* Qtr. plan
Degrees: A *Prof. Accred.:* Radiography
CEO: Pres. John L. Tart
FTE Enroll: 1,953   (919) 934-3051

LEES-MCRAE COLLEGE
P.O. Box 128, Banner Elk 28604 *Type:* Private (Presbyterian) liberal arts *Accred.:*
1953/1995 (SACS-CC) *Calendar:* Sem. plan
Degrees: A, B *Prof. Accred.:* Teacher Education *CEO:* Pres. James A. Schobel
FTE Enroll: 657   (704) 898-5241

LENOIR COMMUNITY COLLEGE
P.O. Box 188, Kinston 28501 *Type:* Public
(district) junior *System:* North Carolina
Community College System *Accred.:* 1968/
1993 (SACS-CC) *Calendar:* Qtr. plan
Degrees: A *Prof. Accred.:* Surgical Technol-
ogy *CEO:* Pres. Lonnie H. Blizzard
FTE Enroll: 1,545   (919) 527-6223

LENOIR-RHYNE COLLEGE
7th Ave. and 8th St., NE, Box 7163, Hickory
28603 *Type:* Private (Lutheran) liberal arts
Accred.: 1928/1992 (SACS-CC) *Calendar:*
Sem. plan *Degrees:* B, M *Prof. Accred.:*
Nursing (B), Teacher Education *CEO:* Pres.
Ryan A. LaHurd
FTE Enroll: 1,309   (704) 328-1741

LIVINGSTONE COLLEGE
701 W. Monroe St., Salisbury 28144 *Type:*
Private (African Methodist Episcopal) liberal
arts *Accred.:* 1944/1991 (SACS-CC warning)
Calendar: Sem. plan *Degrees:* B, M *Prof.
Accred.:* Social Work (B), Teacher Education
CEO: Interim Pres. Roy D. Hudson
FTE Enroll: 826   (704) 638-5500

LOUISBURG COLLEGE
501 N. Main St., Louisburg 27549 *Type:* Private (United Methodist) junior *Accred.:*
1952/1986 (SACS-CC) *Calendar:* Sem. plan
Degrees: A *CEO:* Pres. Ronald L. May
FTE Enroll: 568   (919) 496-2521

MARS HILL COLLEGE
50 Marshall St., Mars Hill 28754 *Type:* Pri-
vate (Southern Baptist) liberal arts *Accred.:*
1926/1991 (SACS-CC) *Calendar:* Sem. plan
Degrees: B *Prof. Accred.:* Music, Social
Work (B), Teacher Education, Theatre (A)
CEO: Pres. A. Max Lennon
FTE Enroll: 1,184   (704) 689-1111

MARTIN COMMUNITY COLLEGE
1161 Kehukee Park Rd., Williamston 27892
Type: Public (district) junior *System:* North
Carolina Community College System
Accred.: 1972/1988 (SACS-CC) *Calendar:*
Qtr. plan *Degrees:* A *Prof. Accred.:* Physical
Therapy Assisting *CEO:* Pres. Martin H.
Nadelman
FTE Enroll: 638   (919) 792-1521

MAYLAND COMMUNITY COLLEGE
P.O. Box 547, Spruce Pine 28777 *Type:* Pub-
lic (district) junior *System:* North Carolina
Community College System *Accred.:* 1978/
1994 (SACS-CC) *Calendar:* Qtr. plan
Degrees: A *CEO:* Pres. Nathan L. Hodges
FTE Enroll: 672   (704) 765-7351

MCDOWELL TECHNICAL COMMUNITY COLLEGE
Rte. 1, Box 170, Marion 28752 *Type:* Public
(district) junior *System:* North Carolina
Community College System *Accred.:* 1975/
1990 (SACS-CC) *Calendar:* Qtr. plan
Degrees: A *CEO:* Pres. Robert M. Boggs
FTE Enroll: 619   (704) 652-6021

MEREDITH COLLEGE
3800 Hillsborough St., Raleigh 27607-5298
Type: Private (Southern Baptist) liberal arts
for women *Accred.:* 1921/1990 (SACS-CC)
Calendar: Sem. plan *Degrees:* B, M *Prof.
Accred.:* Dietetics (internship), Interior
Design, Music, Social Work (B), Teacher
Education *CEO:* Pres. John Edgar Weems
FTE Enroll: 2,011   (919) 829-6000

METHODIST COLLEGE
5400 Ramsey St., Fayetteville 28311-1420
Type: Private (United Methodist) liberal arts
Accred.: 1964/1989 (SACS-CC) *Calendar:*
Sem. plan *Degrees:* A, B *Prof. Accred.:*
Social Work (B-candidate), Teacher Educa-
tion *CEO:* Pres. M. Elton Hendricks
FTE Enroll: 1,701   (910) 630-7000

MITCHELL COMMUNITY COLLEGE
500 W. Broad St., Statesville 28677 *Type:*
Public (district) junior *System:* North Carolina Community College System *Accred.:*
1955/1989 (SACS-CC) *Calendar:* Qtr. plan
Degrees: A *CEO:* Pres. Douglas O. Eason
FTE Enroll: 1,167   (704) 878-3200

MONTGOMERY COMMUNITY COLLEGE
P.O. Box 787, Troy 27371 *Type:* Public (dis-
trict) junior *System:* North Carolina Commu-
nity College System *Accred.:* 1978/1993
(SACS-CC) *Calendar:* Qtr. plan *Degrees:* A
CEO: Pres. Theodore H. Gasper, Jr.
FTE Enroll: 420   (910) 576-6222

MONTREAT COLLEGE
P.O. Box 1267, Montreat 28757 *Type:* Pri-
vate (Presbyterian) liberal arts *Accred.:*
1960/1990 (SACS-CC) *Calendar:* Sem. plan
Degrees: A, B, M (candidate) *CEO:* Pres.
William W. Hurt
FTE Enroll: 324   (704) 669-8011

MOUNT OLIVE COLLEGE
634 Henderson St., Mount Olive 28365
Type: Private (Free Will Baptist) liberal arts
Accred.: 1960/1991 (SACS-CC warning)
Calendar: Sem. plan *Degrees:* A, B *CEO:*
Pres. J. William Byrd
FTE Enroll: 738   (919) 658-2502

NASH COMMUNITY COLLEGE
P.O. Box 7488, Rocky Mount 27804-7488
Type: Public (district) junior *System:* North
Carolina Community College System
Accred.: 1976/1991 (SACS-CC) *Calendar:*
Qtr. plan *Degrees:* A *Prof. Accred.:* Physi-
cal Therapy Assisting *CEO:* Pres. J. Reid
Parrott, Jr.
FTE Enroll: 1,248   (919) 443-4011

NORTH CAROLINA AGRICULTURAL AND
TECHNICAL STATE UNIVERSITY
1601 E. Market St., Greensboro 27411 *Type:*
Public (state) *System:* University of North
Carolina General Administration *Accred.:*
1936/1990 (SACS-CC) *Calendar:* Sem. plan
Degrees: B, M, D (candidate) *Prof. Accred.:*
Accounting (A), Business (B), Computer
Science, Engineering (aerospace, agricul-
tural, architectural, chemical, civil, electrical,
industrial), Home Economics (provisional),
Landscape Architecture (B-initial), Music
(A), Nursing (B), Social Work (B), Teacher
Education *CEO:* Chanc. Edward B. Fort
FTE Enroll: 7,299   (910) 334-7500

NORTH CAROLINA CENTRAL UNIVERSITY
1801 Fayetteville St., Durham 27707 *Type:*
Public (state) liberal arts and professional
System: University of North Carolina Gen-
eral Administration *Accred.:* 1937/1989
(SACS-CC) *Calendar:* Sem. plan *Degrees:*
B, M *Prof. Accred.:* Law (ABA only),
Librarianship, Nursing (B), Speech-Lan-
guage Pathology, Teacher Education *CEO:*
Chanc. Julius L. Chambers
FTE Enroll: 4,893   (919) 560-6100

NORTH CAROLINA SCHOOL OF THE ARTS
200 Waughtown St., P.O. Box 12189, Winston-Salem 27117-2189 *Type:* Public (state)
professional *System:* University of North
Carolina General Administration *Accred.:*
1970/1995 (SACS-CC) *Calendar:* Tri. plan
Degrees: B, M *CEO:* Chanc. Alexander C.
Ewing
FTE Enroll: 589   (910) 770-3399

NORTH CAROLINA STATE UNIVERSITY
P.O. Box 7001, Raleigh 27695-7001 *Type:*
Public (state) *System:* University of North

Carolina General Administration *Accred.:* 1928/1994 (SACS-CC) *Calendar:* Sem. plan *Degrees:* A, B, M, D *Prof. Accred.:* Computer Science, Counseling, Engineering (aerospace, agricultural, chemical, civil, computer, construction, electrical, industrial, materials, mechanical, nuclear, textile), Forestry, Landscape Architecture (M), Public Administration, Recreation and Leisure Services (B), School Psychology, Social Work (B), Teacher Education, Veterinary Medicine *CEO:* Chanc. Larry K. Monteith
FTE Enroll: 22,176   (919) 515-2011

NORTH CAROLINA WESLEYAN COLLEGE
3400 N. Wesleyan Blvd., Rocky Mount 27804 *Type:* Private (United Methodist) liberal arts *Accred.:* 1963/1990 (SACS-CC) *Calendar:* Sem. plan *Degrees:* B *Prof. Accred.:* Teacher Education *CEO:* Pres. John B. White
FTE Enroll: 1,170   (919) 985-5100

PAMLICO COMMUNITY COLLEGE
P.O. Box 185, Hwy. 306 S., Grantsboro 28529 *Type:* Public (district) junior *System:* North Carolina Community College System *Accred.:* 1977/1992 (SACS-CC) *Calendar:* Qtr. plan *Degrees:* A *CEO:* Pres. E. Douglas Kearney, Jr.
FTE Enroll: 163   (919) 249-1851

PEACE COLLEGE
15 E. Peace St., Raleigh 27604 *Type:* Private (Presbyterian) junior for women *Accred.:* 1947/1995 (SACS-CC) *Calendar:* Sem. plan *Degrees:* A, B (candidate) *CEO:* Pres. Garrett Briggs
FTE Enroll: 437   (919) 508-2000

PEMBROKE STATE UNIVERSITY
P.O. Box 1510, One University Dr., Pembroke 28372-1510 *Type:* Public (state) liberal arts and teachers *System:* University of North Carolina General Administration *Accred.:* 1951/1990 (SACS-CC) *Calendar:* Sem. plan *Degrees:* B, M *Prof. Accred.:* Music, Social Work (B), Teacher Education *CEO:* Chanc. Joseph B. Oxendine
FTE Enroll: 2,582   (910) 521-6000

PFEIFFER COLLEGE
P.O. Box 960, Misenheimer 28109-0960 *Type:* Private (United Methodist) liberal arts *Accred.:* 1959/1992 (SACS-CC) *Calendar:* Sem. plan *Degrees:* B, M *Prof. Accred.:* Music, Teacher Education *CEO:* Pres. Zane E. Eargle
FTE Enroll: 829   (704) 463-1360

PIEDMONT BIBLE COLLEGE
716 Franklin St., Winston-Salem 27101 *Type:* Private (Baptist) *Accred.:* 1956/1995 (AABC) *Calendar:* Sem. plan *Degrees:* A, B, C *CEO:* Pres. Howard L. Wilburn
FTE Enroll: 242   (910) 725-8344

PIEDMONT COMMUNITY COLLEGE
P.O. Box 1197, Roxboro 27573 *Type:* Public (district) junior *System:* North Carolina Community College System *Accred.:* 1977/1992 (SACS-CC) *Calendar:* Qtr. plan *Degrees:* A *CEO:* Pres. H. James Owen
FTE Enroll: 919   (910) 599-1181

PITT COMMUNITY COLLEGE
P.O. Drawer 7007, Greenville 27835 *Type:* Public (district) junior *System:* North Carolina Community College System *Accred.:* 1969/1993 (SACS-CC) *Calendar:* Qtr. plan *Degrees:* A *Prof. Accred.:* Diagnostic Medical Sonography, Medical Assisting (AMA), Medical Record Technology, Nuclear Medicine Technology, Occupational Therapy Assisting, Radiation Therapy Technology, Radiography, Respiratory Therapy *CEO:* Pres. Charles E. Russell
FTE Enroll: 3,358   (919) 321-4200

QUEENS COLLEGE
1900 Selwyn Ave., Charlotte 28274 *Type:* Private (Presbyterian) liberal arts for women *Accred.:* 1932/1991 (SACS-CC) *Calendar:* Sem. plan *Degrees:* B, M *Prof. Accred.:* Music, Nursing (B), Teacher Education *CEO:* Pres. Billy O. Wireman
FTE Enroll: 1,058   (704) 337-2200

RANDOLPH COMMUNITY COLLEGE
P.O. Box 1009, Asheboro 27204-1009 *Type:* Public (district) junior *System:* North Car-

olina Community College System *Accred.:* 1974/1989 (SACS-CC) *Calendar:* Qtr. plan *Degrees:* A *Prof. Accred.:* Nursing (A) *CEO:* Pres. Larry K. Linker
FTE Enroll: 1,098   (910) 629-1471

RICHMOND COMMUNITY COLLEGE
P.O. Box 1189, Hamlet 28345 *Type:* Public (district) junior *System:* North Carolina Community College System *Accred.:* 1969/1993 (SACS-CC) *Calendar:* Qtr. plan *Degrees:* A *CEO:* Pres. Joseph W. Grimsley
FTE Enroll: 864   (910) 582-7000

ROANOKE BIBLE COLLEGE
714 First St., Elizabeth City 27909 *Type:* Private (Christian Churches/Churches of Christ) *Accred.:* 1979/1989 (AABC); 1995 (SACS-CC candidate) *Calendar:* Sem. plan *Degrees:* A, B, C *CEO:* Pres. William A. Griffin
FTE Enroll: 119   (919) 338-5191

ROANOKE-CHOWAN COMMUNITY COLLEGE
Rte. 2, Box 46-A, Ahoskie 27910 *Type:* Public (district) junior *System:* North Carolina Community College System *Accred.:* 1976/1992 (SACS-CC) *Calendar:* Qtr. plan *Degrees:* A *CEO:* Pres. Harold E. Mitchell
FTE Enroll: 799   (919) 332-5921

ROBESON COMMUNITY COLLEGE
P.O. Box 1420, Lumberton 28359 *Type:* Public (district) junior *System:* North Carolina Community College System *Accred.:* 1975/1990 (SACS-CC) *Calendar:* Qtr. plan *Degrees:* A *CEO:* Pres. Frederick G. Williams, Jr.
FTE Enroll: 1,271   (919) 738-7101

ROCKINGHAM COMMUNITY COLLEGE
P.O. Box 38, Wentworth 27375-0038 *Type:* Public (district) junior *System:* North Carolina Community College System *Accred.:* 1968/1993 (SACS-CC) *Calendar:* Qtr. plan *Degrees:* A *CEO:* Pres. N. Jerry Owens, Jr.
FTE Enroll: 2,030   (910) 342-4261

ROWAN-CABARRUS COMMUNITY COLLEGE
P.O. Box 1595, Salisbury 28145-1595 *Type:* Public (district) junior *System:* North Carolina Community College System *Accred.:*

1970/1995 (SACS-CC) *Calendar:* Qtr. plan *Degrees:* A *Prof. Accred.:* Dental Assisting, Nursing (A), Radiography *CEO:* Pres. Richard L. Brownell
FTE Enroll: 2,299   (704) 637-0760

ST. ANDREWS PRESBYTERIAN COLLEGE
1700 Dogwood Mile, Laurinburg 28352 *Type:* Private (Presbyterian) liberal arts *Accred.:* 1961/1990 (SACS-CC probational) *Calendar:* 4-1-4 plan *Degrees:* B *Prof. Accred.:* Teacher Education *CEO:* Pres. Warren L. Board
FTE Enroll: 762   (910) 277-5000

ST. AUGUSTINE'S COLLEGE
1315 Oakwood Ave., Raleigh 27610-2298 *Type:* Private (Episcopal) liberal arts *Accred.:* 1942/1991 (SACS-CC) *Calendar:* Sem. plan *Degrees:* B *Prof. Accred.:* Teacher Education *CEO:* Pres. Bernard W. Franklin
FTE Enroll: 2,681   (919) 516-4000

ST. MARY'S COLLEGE
900 Hillsborough St., Raleigh 27603-1689 *Type:* Private (Episcopal) junior for women *Accred.:* 1927/1989 (SACS-CC) *Calendar:* Sem. plan *Degrees:* A *CEO:* Pres. Clauston L. Jenkins
FTE Enroll: 215   (919) 839-4100

SALEM COLLEGE
Salem Sta., P.O. Box 10548, Winston-Salem 27108 *Type:* Private liberal arts for women *Accred.:* 1922/1990 (SACS-CC) *Calendar:* 4-1-4 plan *Degrees:* B, M *Prof. Accred.:* Music, Teacher Education *CEO:* Pres. Julianne Still Thrift
FTE Enroll: 737   (910) 721-2600

SAMPSON COMMUNITY COLLEGE
P.O. Drawer 318, Clinton 28328 *Type:* Public (district) junior *System:* North Carolina Community College System *Accred.:* 1977/1993 (SACS-CC) *Calendar:* Qtr. plan *Degrees:* A *CEO:* Pres. Clifton W. Paderick
FTE Enroll: 903   (910) 592-8081

SANDHILLS COMMUNITY COLLEGE
2200 Airport Rd., Pinehurst 28374 *Type:* Public (district) junior *System:* North Carolina Community College System *Accred.:* 1968/1993 (SACS-CC) *Calendar:* Qtr. plan

Degrees: A *Prof. Accred.:* Clinical Lab Technology (A), Nursing (A), Radiography, Respiratory Therapy, Surgical Technology *CEO:* Pres. John R. Dempsey
FTE Enroll: 2,401   (910) 692-6185

SHAW UNIVERSITY
118 E. South St., Raleigh 27601 *Type:* Private liberal arts (Baptist) *Accred.:* 1994 (ATS candidate); 1943/1993 (SACS-CC) *Calendar:* Sem. plan *Degrees:* A, B *Prof. Accred.:* Teacher Education *CEO:* Pres. Talbert O. Shaw
FTE Enroll: 2,437   (919) 546-8200

SOUTHEASTERN BAPTIST THEOLOGICAL
SEMINARY
P.O. Box 1889, 222 N. Wingate St., Wake Forest 27588-1889 *Type:* Private (Southern Baptist) *Accred.:* 1958/1994 (ATS); 1978/1993 (SACS-CC) *Calendar:* Sem. plan *Degrees:* A, M, D *CEO:* Pres. L. Paige Patterson
Enroll: 906   (919) 556-3101

SOUTHEASTERN COMMUNITY COLLEGE
P.O. Box 151, Whiteville 28472 *Type:* Public (district) junior *System:* North Carolina Community College System *Accred.:* 1967/1991 (SACS-CC) *Calendar:* Qtr. plan *Degrees:* A *CEO:* Pres. Stephen C. Scott
FTE Enroll: 1,318   (910) 642-7141

SOUTHWESTERN COMMUNITY COLLEGE
275 Webster Rd., Sylva 28779 *Type:* Public (district) junior *System:* North Carolina Community College System *Accred.:* 1971/1986 (SACS-CC) *Calendar:* Qtr. plan *Degrees:* A *Prof. Accred.:* Clinical Lab Technology (A), Occupational Therapy Assisting, Physical Therapy Assisting, Radiography, Respiratory Therapy, Respiratory Therapy Technology *CEO:* Pres. Barry W. Russell
FTE Enroll: 1,140   (704) 586-4091

STANLY COMMUNITY COLLEGE
141 College Dr., Albemarle 28001 *Type:* Public (district) junior *System:* North Carolina Community College System *Accred.:* 1979/1994 (SACS-CC) *Calendar:* Qtr. plan *Degrees:* A *Prof. Accred.:* Occupational Therapy Assisting, Physical Therapy Assist-

ing, Respiratory Therapy, Respiratory Therapy Technology *CEO:* Pres. Jan J. Crawford
FTE Enroll: 1,651   (704) 982-0121

SURRY COMMUNITY COLLEGE
S. Maine St., Dobson 27017 *Type:* Public (district) junior *System:* North Carolina Community College System *Accred.:* 1969/1994 (SACS-CC) *Calendar:* Qtr. plan *Degrees:* A *CEO:* Pres. James M. Reeves
FTE Enroll: 1,822   (910) 386-8121

TRI-COUNTY COMMUNITY COLLEGE
2300 Hwy. 64 E., Murphy 28906 *Type:* Public (district) junior *System:* North Carolina Community College System *Accred.:* 1975/1990 (SACS-CC) *Calendar:* Qtr. plan *Degrees:* A *CEO:* Interim Pres. Frank D. Slagle
FTE Enroll: 547   (704) 847-6810

THE UNIVERSITY OF NORTH CAROLINA AT
ASHEVILLE
One University Heights, Asheville 28804-3299 *Type:* Public liberal arts *System:* University of North Carolina General Administration *Accred.:* 1958/1992 (SACS-CC) *Calendar:* Sem. plan *Degrees:* B, M *Prof. Accred.:* Teacher Education *CEO:* Chanc. Patsy B. Reed
FTE Enroll: 2,585   (704) 251-6600

THE UNIVERSITY OF NORTH CAROLINA AT
CHAPEL HILL
CB 9100, 103 S. Bldg., Chapel Hill 27599-9100 *Type:* Public (state) *System:* University of North Carolina General Administration *Accred.:* 1895/1995 (SACS-CC) *Calendar:* Sem. plan *Degrees:* B, M, D *Prof. Accred.:* Audiology, Business (B,M), Clinical Lab Scientist, Clinical Psychology, Combined Prosthodontics, Counseling, Counseling Psychology, Cytotechnology, Dental Assisting, Dental Hygiene, Dentistry, Dietetics (coordinated), Endodontics, Engineering Technology (industrial hygiene), Engineering (environmental/sanitary), General Dentistry, General Practice Residency, Health Services Administration, Journalism (B,M), Law, Librarianship, Medicine, Nursing (B,M), Occupational Therapy, Oral and Maxillofacial Surgery, Orthodontics, Pedi-

atric Dentistry, Periodontics, Physical Therapy, Planning (M), Psychology Internship, Public Administration, Radiography, Recreation and Leisure Services (B), Rehabilitation Counseling, School Psychology, Social Work (M), Speech-Language Pathology, Teacher Education *CEO:* Chanc. Michael K. Hooker
FTE Enroll: 21,540   (919) 962-2211

THE UNIVERSITY OF NORTH CAROLINA AT CHARLOTTE
University City Blvd., Charlotte 28223 *Type:* Public (state) *System:* University of North Carolina General Administration *Accred.:* 1957/1992 (SACS-CC) *Calendar:* Sem. plan *Degrees:* B, M, D *Prof. Accred.:* Accounting (A), Business (B,M), Counseling, Engineering Technology (civil/construction, electrical, manufacturing, mechanical), Engineering (civil, electrical, mechanical), Nurse Anesthesia Education (M), Nursing (B,M), Public Administration, Social Work (B-candidate), Teacher Education *CEO:* Chanc. James H. Woodward, Jr.
FTE Enroll: 13,151   (704) 547-2000

THE UNIVERSITY OF NORTH CAROLINA AT GREENSBORO
1000 Spring Garden St., Greensboro 27412 *Type:* Public (state) *System:* University of North Carolina General Administration *Accred.:* 1921/1993 (SACS-CC) *Calendar:* Sem. plan *Degrees:* B, M, D *Prof. Accred.:* Audiology, Business (B,M), Clinical Psychology, Computer Science, Counseling, Dietetics (internship), Interior Design, Librarianship, Music, Nurse Anesthesia Education, Nursing (B,M), Public Administration, Recreation and Leisure Services (B), Social Work (B), Speech-Language Pathology, Teacher Education, Theatre (A) *CEO:* Chanc. Patricia A. Sullivan
FTE Enroll: 10,236   (910) 334-5000

THE UNIVERSITY OF NORTH CAROLINA AT WILMINGTON
601 S. College Rd., Wilmington 28403-3297 *Type:* Public (state) *System:* University of North Carolina General Administration *Accred.:* 1952/1992 (SACS-CC) *Calendar:*

Sem. plan *Degrees:* B, M *Prof. Accred.:* Business (B,M), Music, Nursing (B), Recreation and Leisure Services (B), Teacher Education *CEO:* Chanc. James R. Leutze
FTE Enroll: 7,463   (910) 395-3000

VANCE-GRANVILLE COMMUNITY COLLEGE
P.O. Box 917, Henderson 27536 *Type:* Public (district) junior *System:* North Carolina Community College System *Accred.:* 1977/1993 (SACS-CC) *Calendar:* Qtr. plan *Degrees:* A *Prof. Accred.:* Radiography *CEO:* Pres. Benjamin F. Currin
FTE Enroll: 2,226   (919) 492-2061

WAKE FOREST UNIVERSITY
P.O. Box 7373 Reynolda Sta., Winston-Salem 27109 *Type:* Private *Accred.:* 1921/1987 (SACS-CC) *Calendar:* Sem. plan *Degrees:* B, M, D *Prof. Accred.:* Accounting (A), Business (B,M), Clinical Lab Scientist, Counseling, General Practice Residency, Law, Medicine, Physician Assisting/Surgeon Assisting, Teacher Education *CEO:* Pres. Thomas K. Hearn, Jr.
FTE Enroll: 5,496   (910) 759-5000

WAKE TECHNICAL COMMUNITY COLLEGE
9101 Fayetteville Rd., Raleigh 27603-5696 *Type:* Public (district) junior *System:* North Carolina Community College System *Accred.:* 1970/1995 (SACS-CC) *Calendar:* Qtr. plan *Degrees:* A *Prof. Accred.:* Clinical Lab Technology (A), Dental Assisting, Engineering Technology (civil/construction, computer, electrical, mechanical), Medical Assisting (AMA), Radiography *CEO:* Pres. Bruce I. Howell
FTE Enroll: 4,030   (919) 662-3400

WARREN WILSON COLLEGE
P.O. Box 9000, Asheville 28815-9000 *Type:* Private (United Presbyterian) liberal arts *Accred.:* 1952/1994 (SACS-CC) *Calendar:* Sem. plan *Degrees:* B, M *Prof. Accred.:* Social Work (B), Teacher Education *CEO:* Pres. Douglas M. Orr, Jr.
FTE Enroll: 540   (704) 298-3325

WAYNE COMMUNITY COLLEGE
Caller Box 8002, Goldsboro 27533-8002 *Type:* Public (district) junior *System:* North

Carolina Community College System *Accred.:* 1970/1995 (SACS-CC) *Calendar:* Qtr. plan *Degrees:* A *Prof. Accred.:* Dental Assisting, Dental Hygiene *CEO:* Pres. Edward H. Wilson, Jr.
FTE Enroll: 2,237   (919) 735-5151

WESTERN CAROLINA UNIVERSITY
Cullowhee 28723 *Type:* Public (state) *System:* University of North Carolina General Administration *Accred.:* 1946/1986 (SACS-CC) *Calendar:* Sem. plan *Degrees:* B, M *Prof. Accred.:* Business (B,M), Clinical Lab Scientist, Counseling, EMT-Paramedic, Engineering Technology (electrical, manufacturing), Home Economics, Medical Record Administration, Music, Nursing (B), Social Work (B), Speech-Language Pathology, Teacher Education *CEO:* Chanc. John W. Bardo
FTE Enroll: 5,881   (704) 227-7211

WESTERN PIEDMONT COMMUNITY COLLEGE
1001 Burkemont Ave., Morganton 28655-9978 *Type:* Public (district) junior *System:* North Carolina Community College System *Accred.:* 1968/1993 (SACS-CC) *Calendar:* Qtr. plan *Degrees:* A *Prof. Accred.:* Clinical Lab Technology (A), Dental Assisting, Medical Assisting (AMA), Nursing (A) *CEO:* Pres. James A. Richardson
FTE Enroll: 1,676   (704) 438-6000

WILKES COMMUNITY COLLEGE
P.O. Box 120, Collegiate Dr., Wilkesboro 28697-0120 *Type:* Public (district) junior *System:* North Carolina Community College

System *Accred.:* 1970/1995 (SACS-CC) *Calendar:* Qtr. plan *Degrees:* A *Prof. Accred.:* Dental Assisting *CEO:* Interim Pres. Swanson Richards
FTE Enroll: 1,322   (910) 651-8600

WILSON TECHNICAL COMMUNITY COLLEGE
P.O. Box 4305, 902 Herring Ave. Woodard Sta., Wilson 27893 *Type:* Public (district) junior *System:* North Carolina Community College System *Accred.:* 1969/1994 (SACS-CC) *Calendar:* Qtr. plan *Degrees:* A *CEO:* Pres. Frank L. Eagles
FTE Enroll: 818   (919) 291-1195

WINGATE UNIVERSITY
Wingate 28174-0157 *Type:* Private (Southern Baptist) liberal arts *Accred.:* 1951/1995 (SACS-CC) *Calendar:* Sem. plan *Degrees:* A, B, M *Prof. Accred.:* Medical Assisting (AMA), Music, Nursing (B), Teacher Education *CEO:* Pres. Jerry E. McGee
FTE Enroll: 1,414   (704) 233-8000

WINSTON-SALEM STATE UNIVERSITY
601 Martin Luther King, Jr. Dr, Winston-Salem 27110 *Type:* Public (state) liberal arts and teachers *System:* University of North Carolina General Administration *Accred.:* 1947/1990 (SACS-CC) *Calendar:* Sem. plan *Degrees:* B *Prof. Accred.:* Clinical Lab Scientist, Computer Science, Music, Nursing (B), Physical Therapy, Teacher Education *CEO:* Chanc. Alvin J. Schexnider
FTE Enroll: 2,465   (910) 750-2000

NORTH DAKOTA

BISMARCK STATE COLLEGE
1500 Edwards Ave., Bismarck 58501-1299
Type: Public (state) *System:* North Dakota
University System *Accred.:* 1966/1988
(NCA) *Calendar:* Sem. plan *Degrees:* A, C
Prof. Accred.: Clinical Lab Technology (A)
CEO: Pres. Donna S. Thigpen
Enroll: 2,349   (701) 224-5400

DICKINSON STATE UNIVERSITY
291 Campus Dr., Dickinson 58601-4896
Type: Public (state) liberal arts and teachers
System: North Dakota University System
Accred.: 1928/1995 (NCA) *Calendar:* Sem.
plan *Degrees:* A, B, C *Prof. Accred.:*
Nursing (B), Teacher Education *CEO:* Pres.
Philip W. Conn
Enroll: 1,591   (800) 227-2507

FORT BERTHOLD COMMUNITY COLLEGE
P.O. Box 490, New Town 58763 *Type:*
Public (tribal) junior *Accred.:* 1988/1991
(NCA) *Calendar:* Sem. plan *Degrees:* A, C
CEO: Pres. Karen J. Gillis
Enroll: 260   (701) 627-4738

JAMESTOWN COLLEGE
600 College Ln., Jamestown 58405 *Type:*
Private (United Presbyterian) liberal arts
Accred.: 1920/1991 (NCA) *Calendar:* 4-1-4
plan *Degrees:* B *Prof. Accred.:* Nursing (B)
CEO: Pres. James S. Walker
Enroll: 1,083   (800) 336-2554

LITTLE HOOP COMMUNITY COLLEGE
P.O. Box 269, Fort Totten 58335 *Type:*
Public (tribal) junior *Accred.:* 1990/1993
(NCA) *Calendar:* Sem. plan *Degrees:* A, C
CEO: Pres. Merrill Berg
Enroll: 318   (701) 766-4415

MAYVILLE STATE UNIVERSITY
330 3rd St., N.E., Mayville 58257-1299
Type: Public (state) liberal arts and teachers
System: North Dakota University System
Accred.: 1917/1986 (NCA) *Calendar:* Sem.
plan *Degrees:* A, B, C *Prof. Accred.:* Teacher
Education *CEO:* Pres. Ellen E. Chaffee
Enroll: 778   (701) 786-2301

MEDCENTER ONE COLLEGE OF NURSING
512 N. Seventh St., Bismarck 58501 *Type:*
Private professional *Accred.:* 1990 (NCA)
Calendar: Sem. plan *Degrees:* B *Prof.
Accred.:* Nursing (B) *CEO:* Provost/Dean
Karen Kristensen
Enroll: 91   (701) 224-6731

MINOT STATE UNIVERSITY
500 University Ave., W., Minot 58707-0001
Type: Public (state) liberal arts and teachers
System: North Dakota University System
Accred.: 1917/1988 (NCA) *Calendar:* Sem.
plan *Degrees:* A, B, M *Prof. Accred.:*
Audiology, Music, Nursing (B), Social Work
(B), Speech-Language Pathology, Teacher
Education *CEO:* Pres. H. Erik Shaar
Enroll: 3,673   (701) 858-3000

NORTH DAKOTA STATE COLLEGE OF SCIENCE
800 N. 6th St., Wahpeton 58076-0001 *Type:*
Public (state) junior *System:* North Dakota
University System *Accred.:* 1971/1991
(NCA) *Calendar:* Sem. plan *Degrees:* A, C
Prof. Accred.: Dental Assisting, Dental
Hygiene, Medical Record Technology,
Occupational Therapy Assisting, Practical
Nursing *CEO:* Pres. Jerry C. Olson
Enroll: 2,429   (701) 671-2221

NORTH DAKOTA STATE UNIVERSITY
State University. Sta., Fargo 58105 *Type:*
Public (state) *System:* North Dakota
University System *Accred.:* 1915/1986
(NCA) *Calendar:* Sem. plan *Degrees:* B, M,
P, D *Prof. Accred.:* Computer Science,
Construction Education (B), Dietetics (coor-
dinated), Engineering (agricultural, civil,
construction, electrical, industrial, mechani-
cal), Home Economics, Interior Design,
Landscape Architecture (B-initial), Music,
Nursing (B), Respiratory Therapy, Teacher
Education *CEO:* Pres. Thomas R. Plough
Enroll: 8,688   (701) 231-8011

NORTH DAKOTA STATE UNIVERSITY—
BOTTINEAU
First and Simrall Blvd., Bottineau 58318-
1198 *Type:* Public (state) junior *System:*

North Dakota University System *Accred.:* 1971/1989 (NCA) *Calendar:* Sem. plan *Degrees:* A, C *CEO:* Exec. Dean J.W. Smith
Enroll: 339 (701) 228-2277

STANDING ROCK COLLEGE
HC1, Box 4, Fort Yates 58538 *Type:* Public (tribal) *Accred.:* 1984/1991 (NCA) *Calendar:* Sem. plan *Degrees:* A, C *CEO:* Pres. Dave Archambault
Enroll: 221 (701) 854-3861

TRI-COLLEGE UNIVERSITY
306 Ceres Hall, North Dakota State Univ., Fargo 58105-5630 *Type:* Private graduate only *Accred.:* 1979/1984 (NCA) *Calendar:* Sem. plan *Degrees:* M, P *Prof. Accred.:* Nursing (B), Teacher Education *CEO:* Provost Jean Strandness
Enroll: 243 (701) 237-8170

TRINITY BIBLE COLLEGE
50 S. Sixth St., Ellendale 58436-7105 *Type:* Private (Assemblies of God) *Accred.:* 1980/1990 (AABC); 1991/1995 (NCA) *Calendar:* Sem. plan *Degrees:* A, B, C *CEO:* Pres. Howard Young
Enroll: 482 (701) 349-3621

TURTLE MOUNTAIN COMMUNITY COLLEGE
P.O. Box 340, Belcourt 58316-0340 *Type:* Private (tribal) junior *Accred.:* 1984/1994 (NCA) *Calendar:* Sem. plan *Degrees:* A, C *CEO:* Pres. Gerald E. Monette
Enroll: 585 (701) 477-5605

UNITED TRIBES TECHNICAL COLLEGE
3315 University Dr., Bismarck 58504 *Type:* Private (tribal) *Accred.:* 1982/1990 (NCA) *Calendar:* Qtr. plan *Degrees:* A, C *CEO:* Pres. David M. Gipp
Enroll: 246 (701) 255-3285

UNIVERSITY OF MARY
7500 University Dr., Bismarck 58504 *Type:* Private (Roman Catholic) liberal arts *Accred.:* 1969/1993 (NCA) *Calendar:* 4-1-4 plan *Degrees:* A, B, M *Prof. Accred.:* Athletic Training, Nursing (B,M), Social Work (B) *CEO:* Pres. Thomas Welder, O.S.B.
Enroll: 1,651 (701) 255-7500

UNIVERSITY OF NORTH DAKOTA
Box 8193, University Sta., Grand Forks 58202-8193 *Type:* Public (state) *System:* North Dakota University System *Accred.:* 1913/1994 (NCA) *Calendar:* Sem. plan *Degrees:* B, M, P, D *Prof. Accred.:* Art, Business (B,M), Clinical Lab Scientist, Clinical Psychology, Computer Science, Counseling Psychology (provisional), Cytotechnology, Dietetics (coordinated), Engineering (chemical, civil, electrical, geological/geophysical, mechanical), Home Economics, Law, Medicine, Music, Nurse Anesthesia Education, Nursing (B,M), Occupational Therapy, Physical Therapy, Physician Assisting/Surgeon Assisting, Social Work (B,M), Speech-Language Pathology, Teacher Education *CEO:* Pres. Kendall L. Baker
Enroll: 9,550 (701) 777-2011

UNIVERSITY OF NORTH DAKOTA—LAKE REGION
1801 N. College Dr., Devils Lake 58301-1598 *Type:* Public (state) *System:* North Dakota University System *Accred.:* 1974/1991 (NCA) *Calendar:* Sem. plan *Degrees:* A, C *CEO:* Exec. Dean Sharon L. Etemad
Enroll: 1,195 (701) 662-1600

UNIVERSITY OF NORTH DAKOTA—WILLISTON
P.O. Box 1326, Williston 58802-1326 *Type:* Public (state) *System:* North Dakota University System *Accred.:* 1972/1990 (NCA) *Calendar:* Sem. plan *Degrees:* A, C *Prof. Accred.:* Physical Therapy Assisting (candidate) *CEO:* Exec. Dean Garvin L. Stevens
Enroll: 814 (701) 774-4200

VALLEY CITY STATE UNIVERSITY
101 College St. S.E., Valley City 58072-4195 *Type:* Public (state) liberal arts and teachers *System:* North Dakota University System *Accred.:* 1915/1992 (NCA) *Calendar:* Sem. plan *Degrees:* A, B *Prof. Accred.:* Teacher Education *CEO:* Pres. Ellen E. Chaffee
Enroll: 986 (701) 845-7122

OHIO

ACA COLLEGE OF DESIGN
2528 Kemper Ln., Cincinnati 45206-2014
Type: Private *Accred.:* 1979/1989 (ACC-
SCT) *Calendar:* Qtr. plan *Degrees:* A, C
CEO: Pres. Marion Allman
(513) 751-1206

ACADEMY OF COURT REPORTING
614 Superior Ave., N.W., Cleveland 44113
Type: Private business *Accred.:* 1980/1996
(ACICS) *Degrees:* A, C *CEO:* Pres. Ken
Endies
(216) 861-3222

SOUTHFIELD CAMPUS
26111 Evergreen Rd., Ste. 101, Southfield, MI 48076 *Accred.:* 1989 (ACICS)
(810) 353-4880

AKRON CAMPUS
2930 W. Market St., Akron 44313
Accred.: 1986 (ACICS)
(216) 867-4030

COLUMBUS CAMPUS
630 E. Broad St., Columbus 43215
Accred.: 1988 (ACICS)
(614) 221-7770

AIR FORCE INSTITUTE OF TECHNOLOGY
AFIT/CC Bldg. 125, 2950 P St., Wright-Pat-
terson AFB 45433-7765 *Type:* Public (federal) technological; graduate only *Accred.:*
1960/1991 (NCA) *Calendar:* Qtr. plan
Degrees: M, D *Prof. Accred.:* Engineering
(aerospace, computer, electrical, engineering
physics/science, nuclear, systems) *CEO:*
Cmdt. Ronald D. Townsend
Enroll: 625   (513) 255-2321

ANTIOCH UNIVERSITY
150 E. South College St., Yellow Springs
45387 *Type:* Private liberal arts and professional *Accred.:* 1927/1993 (NCA) *Calendar:*
Sem. plan *Degrees:* B, M, D *CEO:* Chanc.
Alan E. Guskin
Enroll: 1,610   (513) 767-6494

ANTIOCH COLLEGE
795 Livermore St., Yellow Springs 45387
Calendar: Qtr. plan
(513) 767-7331

ANTIOCH NEW ENGLAND GRADUATE SCHOOL
Roxbury St., Keene, NH 03431 *Prof.
Accred.:* Clinical Psychology, Marriage
and Family Therapy (M)
(603) 357-3122

ANTIOCH SEATTLE
2607 Second Ave., Seattle, WA 98121
(206) 441-5352

ANTIOCH SOUTHERN CALIFORNIA—LOS
ANGELES
13274 Fiji Way, Marina del Rey, CA
90292
(310) 578-1080

ANTIOCH SOUTHERN CALIFORNIA—SANTA
BARBARA
801 Garden St., Santa Barbara, CA 93101
(805) 962-8179

GEORGE MEANY CENTER FOR LABOR
STUDIES
10000 New Hampshire Ave., Silver
Spring, MD 20903
(301) 431-6400

THE MCGREGOR SCHOOL OF ANTIOCH
UNIVERSITY
800 Livermore St., Yellow Springs 45387
(513) 767-6321

ANTONELLI COLLEGE
124 E. Seventh St., Cincinnati 45202-2592
Type: Private *Accred.:* 1975/1990 (ACC-
SCT) *Calendar:* Qtr. plan *Degrees:* A *CEO:*
Dir. Christy Connolly
(513) 241-4338

ART ACADEMY OF CINCINNATI
1125 St. Gregory St., Cincinnati 45202
Type: Private professional *Accred.:*
1990/1995 (NCA) *Calendar:* Sem. plan

Degrees: A, B, C *Prof. Accred.:* Art *CEO:* Dir. Gregory Allgire Smith
Enroll: 187   (513) 721-5205

ART ADVERTISING ACADEMY
4343 Bridgetown Rd., Cincinnati 45211-4427 *Type:* Private *Accred.:* 1984/1989 (ACCSCT) *Degrees:* A, C *CEO:* Owner/Dir. Jerry E. Neff
         (513) 574-1010

ASHLAND UNIVERSITY
401 College Ave., Ashland 44805 *Type:* Private (Brethren) liberal arts *Accred.:* 1969/1988 (ATS); 1930/1988 (NCA) *Calendar:* Sem. plan *Degrees:* A, B, M, D *Prof. Accred.:* Music, Nursing (B), Social Work (B), Teacher Education *CEO:* Pres. G. William Benz
Enroll: 3,155   (419) 289-5161

ATHENAEUM OF OHIO
6616 Beechmont Ave., Cincinnati 45230-2091 *Type:* Private (Roman Catholic) graduate only *Accred.:* 1972/1992 (ATS); 1959/1993 (NCA) *Calendar:* Qtr. plan *Degrees:* M, C *CEO:* Pres. Robert J. Mooney
Enroll: 257   (513) 231-2223

BALDWIN-WALLACE COLLEGE
275 Eastland Rd., Berea 44017 *Type:* Private (United Methodist) liberal arts *Accred.:* 1913/1988 (NCA) *Calendar:* Qtr. plan *Degrees:* B, M, C *Prof. Accred.:* Music, Teacher Education *CEO:* Pres. Neal Malicky
Enroll: 4,105   (216) 826-2900

BELMONT TECHNICAL COLLEGE
120 Fox-Shannon Pl., St. Clairsville 43950 *Type:* Public (state) 2-year *System:* Ohio Board of Regents *Accred.:* 1978/1988 (NCA) *Calendar:* Qtr. plan *Degrees:* A, C *Prof. Accred.:* Medical Assisting (AMA) *CEO:* Pres. Wesley R. Channell
Enroll: 1,689   (614) 695-9500

BLUFFTON COLLEGE
280 W. College Ave., Bluffton 45817-1196 *Type:* Private (Mennonite) liberal arts *Accred.:* 1953/1989 (NCA) *Calendar:* 4-1-4

plan *Degrees:* B *Prof. Accred.:* Music, Social Work (B) *CEO:* Pres. Elmer Neufeld
Enroll: 899   (800) 488-3257

BOHECKER'S BUSINESS COLLEGE
326 E. Main St., Ravenna 44266 *Type:* Private business *Accred.:* 1985/1994 (ACICS) *Degrees:* A *CEO:* Owner John Fitzpatrick
         (216) 297-7319

BOWLING GREEN STATE UNIVERSITY
Bowling Green 43403 *Type:* Public (state) *System:* Ohio Board of Regents *Accred.:* 1916/1993 (NCA) *Calendar:* Sem. plan *Degrees:* A, B, M, P, D *Prof. Accred.:* Art, Audiology, Business (B,M), Clinical Lab Scientist, Clinical Psychology, Construction Education, Journalism (B,M), Medical Record Technology, Music, Nursing (B,M), Physical Therapy, Recreation and Leisure Services (candidate), Rehabilitation Counseling, Respiratory Therapy, Social Work (B), Speech-Language Pathology, Teacher Education, Theatre *CEO:* Pres. Sidney A. Ribeau
Enroll: 15,709   (419) 372-2531

FIRELANDS COLLEGE
901 Rye Beach Rd., Huron 44839
         (419) 433-5560

BRADFORD SCHOOL
6170 Busch Blvd., Columbus 43229 *Type:* Private business *Accred.:* 1960/1988 (ACICS) *Calendar:* Qtr. plan *Degrees:* A, C *Prof. Accred.:* Medical Assisting (AMA) *CEO:* Dir. of Educ. Janet DeHorre
         (614) 846-9410

BRYANT & STRATTON BUSINESS INSTITUTE
12955 Snow Rd., Parma 44130-1013 *Type:* Private business *Accred.:* 1984/1996 (ACICS) *Calendar:* Qtr. plan *Degrees:* A, C *CEO:* Dir. Alan J. Hyers
         (216) 265-3151

RICHMOND HEIGHTS CAMPUS
691 Richmond Rd., Sears Bldg., 3rd Fl., Richmond Heights 44143 *Accred.:* 1988/1990 (ACICS)
         (216) 461-3151

CAPITAL UNIVERSITY
2199 E. Main St., Columbus 43209 *Type:* Private (Lutheran) liberal arts and professional *Accred.:* 1921/1993 (NCA) *Calendar:* 4-1-4 plan *Degrees:* B, M, D, C *Prof. Accred.:* Law, Music, Nursing (B), Social Work (B), Teacher Education *CEO:* Pres. Josiah H. Blackmore
Enroll: 2,708   (800) 289-6289

CASE WESTERN RESERVE UNIVERSITY
10900 Euclid Ave., Cleveland 44106-7001 *Type:* Private *Accred.:* 1913/1995 (NCA) *Calendar:* Sem. plan *Degrees:* B, M, D *Prof. Accred.:* Accounting (A,C), Anesthesiologist Assisting, Business (B,M), Clinical Psychology, Dentistry, Endodontics, Engineering (bioengineering, chemical, civil, computer, electrical, engineering physics/science, materials, mechanical, polymer, systems), General Dentistry, Law, Medicine, Music, Nurse Anesthesia Education, Nursing (B,M), Oral and Maxillofacial Surgery, Orthodontics, Pediatric Dentistry, Periodontics, Social Work (M), Speech-Language Pathology *CEO:* Pres. Agnar Pytte
Enroll: 3,658   (800) 444-6984

CEDARVILLE COLLEGE
N. Main St., Box 601, Cedarville 45314-0601 *Type:* Private (Baptist) liberal arts *Accred.:* 1975/1987 (NCA) *Calendar:* Qtr. plan *Degrees:* A, B, C *Prof. Accred.:* Nursing (B) *CEO:* Pres. Paul Dixon
Enroll: 2,378   (800) 777-2211

CENTRAL OHIO TECHNICAL COLLEGE
1179 University Dr., Newark 43055-1767 *Type:* Public (district) 2-year *System:* Ohio Board of Regents *Accred.:* 1975/1988 (NCA) *Calendar:* Qtr. plan *Degrees:* A, C *Prof. Accred.:* Diagnostic Medical Sonography, Nursing (A), Physical Therapy Assisting, Radiography *CEO:* Pres. Rafael L. Cortada
Enroll: 1,712   (614) 366-1351

CENTRAL STATE UNIVERSITY
1400 Brush Row Rd., Wilberforce 45384 *Type:* Public (state) *System:* Ohio Board of Regents *Accred.:* 1949/1989 (NCA) *Calendar:* Qtr. plan *Degrees:* A, B, M *Prof.

Accred.: Engineering (manufacturing), Music *CEO:* Pres. Herman B. Smith, Jr.
Enroll: 2,735   (513) 376-6011

CHATFIELD COLLEGE
20918 State Rte. 251, St. Martin 45118 *Type:* Private liberal arts *Accred.:* 1971/1994 (NCA) *Calendar:* Sem. plan *Degrees:* A *CEO:* Pres. Ellen Doyle
Enroll: 148   (513) 875-3344

CINCINNATI BIBLE COLLEGE AND SEMINARY
2700 Glenway Ave., Cincinnati 45204-3200 *Type:* Private (Christian Churches/Churches of Christ) *Accred.:* 1966/1995 (AABC); 1989/1994 (NCA) *Calendar:* Sem. plan *Degrees:* A, B *CEO:* Pres. J. David Grubbs
Enroll: 632   (513) 244-8100

CINCINNATI COLLEGE OF MORTUARY SCIENCE
Cohen Ctr., 3860 Pacific Ave., Cincinnati 45207-1033 *Type:* Private professional *Accred.:* 1982/1991 (NCA) *Calendar:* Qtr. plan *Degrees:* A, B *Prof. Accred.:* Funeral Service Education (Mortuary Science) *CEO:* Pres. Dan L. Flory
Enroll: 207   (513) 745-3631

CINCINNATI STATE TECHNICAL AND COMMUNITY COLLEGE
3520 Central Pkwy., Cincinnati 45223 *Type:* Public (state) 2-year *System:* Ohio Board of Regents *Accred.:* 1976/1991 (NCA) *Calendar:* Qtr. plan *Degrees:* A, C *Prof. Accred.:* Clinical Lab Technology (A), Engineering Technology (bioengineering, civil/construction, computer, electrical, electromechanical, mechanical), Medical Assisting (AMA), Medical Record Technology, Occupational Therapy Assisting, Respiratory Therapy, Surgical Technology *CEO:* Pres. James P. Long
Enroll: 5,486   (513) 569-1500

CIRCLEVILLE BIBLE COLLEGE
1476 Lancaster Pike, Circleville 43113 *Type:* Private (Churches of Christ in Christian Union) *Accred.:* 1976/1986 (AABC) *Calendar:* Sem. plan *Degrees:* A, B *CEO:* Pres. John Conley
FTE Enroll: 164   (614) 474-8896

CLARK STATE COMMUNITY COLLEGE
570 E. Leffels Ln., P.O. Box 570, Springfield 45505 *Type:* Public (state) 2-year *System:* Ohio Board of Regents *Accred.:* 1974/1989 (NCA) *Calendar:* Qtr. plan *Degrees:* A, C *Prof. Accred.:* Clinical Lab Technology (A), Engineering Technology (general drafting/ design), mechanical drafting/ design) *CEO:* Pres. Albert A. Salerno
Enroll: 2,826   (513) 325-0691

CLEVELAND COLLEGE OF JEWISH STUDIES
26500 Shaker Blvd., Beachwood 44122 *Type:* Private (Jewish) *Accred.:* 1988/1993 (NCA) *Calendar:* Sem. plan *Degrees:* B, M *CEO:* Pres. David S. Ariel
Enroll: 16   (216) 464-4050

CLEVELAND INSTITUTE OF ART
11141 East Blvd., Cleveland 44106 *Type:* Private professional *Accred.:* 1970/1991 (NCA) *Calendar:* Sem. plan *Degrees:* B *Prof. Accred.:* Art *CEO:* Pres. Robert A. Mayer
Enroll: 520   (216) 421-7400

CLEVELAND INSTITUTE OF ELECTRONICS, INC.
1776 E. 17th St., Cleveland 44114 *Type:* Private home study *Accred.:* 1956/1992 (DETC) *Degrees:* A, C *CEO:* Pres. John R. Drinko
                             (216) 781-9400

WORLD COLLEGE
Lake Shores Plaza, 5193 Shore Dr. Ste. 113, Virginia Beach, VA 23455-2500 *Accred.:* 1993 (DETC) *Degrees:* B
                             (804) 464-4600

CLEVELAND INSTITUTE OF MUSIC
11021 East Blvd., Cleveland 44106 *Type:* Private professional *Accred.:* 1980/1986 (NCA) *Calendar:* Sem. plan *Degrees:* B, M, D, C *Prof. Accred.:* Music *CEO:* Pres. David Cerone
Enroll: 275   (216) 791-5000

CLEVELAND STATE UNIVERSITY
Euclid Ave. at E. 24th St., Cleveland 44115 *Type:* Public (state) *System:* Ohio Board of Regents *Accred.:* 1940/1990 (NCA) *Calen-*

dar: Qtr. plan *Degrees:* B, M, P, D *Prof. Accred.:* Accounting (A,C), Audiology, Business (B,M), Counseling, Engineering (chemical, civil, electrical, industrial, mechanical), Health Services Administration, Law, Music, Nursing (B), Occupational Therapy, Physical Therapy, Public Administration, Social Work (B), Speech-Language Pathology, Teacher Education *CEO:* Pres. Claire A. Van Ummersen
Enroll: 11,341   (216) 687-2000

COLLEGE OF MOUNT ST. JOSEPH
5701 Delhi Rd., Cincinnati 45233 *Type:* Private (Roman Catholic) liberal arts primarily for women *Accred.:* 1932/1989 (NCA) *Calendar:* Sem. plan *Degrees:* A, B, M, C *Prof. Accred.:* Music, Nursing (B), Social Work (B-candidate) *CEO:* Pres. Francis Marie Thrailkill, O.S.U.
Enroll: 2,295   (800) 654-9314

COLLEGE OF WOOSTER
Wooster 44691 *Type:* Private independent *Accred.:* 1915/1993 (NCA) *Calendar:* Sem. plan *Degrees:* B *Prof. Accred.:* Music *CEO:* Acting Pres. R. Stanton Hales
Enroll: 1,667   (216) 263-2000

COLUMBUS COLLEGE OF ART AND DESIGN
107 N. Ninth St., Columbus 43215 *Type:* Private professional *Accred.:* 1986/1991 (NCA) *Calendar:* Sem. plan *Degrees:* B *Prof. Accred.:* Art *CEO:* Pres. Charles L. Deihl
Enroll: 1,726   (614) 224-9101

COLUMBUS STATE COMMUNITY COLLEGE
550 E. Spring St., P.O. Box 1609, Columbus 43215-1722 *Type:* Public (state) 2-year *System:* Ohio Board of Regents *Accred.:* 1973/ 1990 (NCA) *Calendar:* Qtr. plan *Degrees:* A, C *Prof. Accred.:* Clinical Lab Technology (A), Dental Laboratory Technology, EMT-Paramedic, Engineering Technology (electrical), Histologic Technology, Medical Record Technology, Nursing (A), Respiratory Therapy, Respiratory Therapy Technology, Veterinary Technology *CEO:* Pres. Marvin G. Gutter
Enroll: 17,042   (800) 621-6407

CUYAHOGA COMMUNITY COLLEGE
700 Carnegie Ave., Cleveland 44115 *Type:* Public (county) 2-year *System:* Ohio Board of Regents *Accred.:* 1979/1989 (NCA) *Calendar:* Qtr. plan *Degrees:* A, C *Prof. Accred.:* Clinical Lab Technology (A), Medical Assisting (AMA), Medical Record Technology, Occupational Therapy Assisting, Physician Assisting/Surgeon Assisting, Radiography, Respiratory Therapy *CEO:* Pres. Jerry Sue Thornton
Enroll: 24,758   (216) 987-6000

EASTERN CAMPUS
4250 Richmond Rd., Highland Hills 44122 *Prof. Accred.:* Nursing (A)
(216) 987-2000

METROPOLITAN CAMPUS
2900 Community College Ave., Cleveland 44115 *Prof. Accred.:* Dental Assisting, Dental Hygiene, Dental Laboratory Technology, Nursing (A), Physical Therapy Assisting
(216) 987-4000

WESTERN CAMPUS
11000 W. Pleasant Valley Rd., Parma 44130 *Prof. Accred.:* Nursing (A)
(216) 987-5000

DAVID N. MYERS COLLEGE
112 Prospect Ave., S.E., Cleveland 44115 *Type:* Private *Accred.:* 1978/1995 (NCA) *Calendar:* Tri. plan *Degrees:* A, B, C *CEO:* Pres./Chief Oper. Exec. Arnold G. Tew
Enroll: 1,362   (216) 696-9000

DAVIS COLLEGE
4747 Monroe St., Toledo 43623 *Type:* Private junior *Accred.:* 1991/1994 (NCA) *Calendar:* Qtr. plan *Degrees:* A, C *Prof. Accred.:* Medical Assisting (AMA) *CEO:* Pres. Diane Brunner
Enroll: 462   (419) 473-2700

THE DEFIANCE COLLEGE
701 N. Clinton St., Defiance 43512 *Type:* Private (United Church of Christ) liberal arts *Accred.:* 1916/1993 (NCA) *Calendar:* 4-1-4

plan *Degrees:* A, B, M *Prof. Accred.:* Social Work (B) *CEO:* Pres. Jim Harris
Enroll: 884   (419) 784-4010

DENISON UNIVERSITY
P.O. Box B, Granville 43023 *Type:* Private (Baptist) liberal arts *Accred.:* 1913/1990 (NCA) *Calendar:* Sem. plan *Degrees:* B *CEO:* Pres. Michele Tolela Myers
Enroll: 1,736   (614) 587-0810

DEVRY INSTITUTE OF TECHNOLOGY—COLUMBUS
1350 Alum Creek Dr., Columbus 43209-2705 *Type:* Private *System:* DeVry Institutes *Accred.:* 1981/1992 (NCA) *Calendar:* Sem. plan *Degrees:* A, B *Prof. Accred.:* Engineering Technology (electrical) *CEO:* Pres. Richard A. Czerniak
(614) 253-7291

* Indirect NCA accreditation through DeVry Institutes

EDISON STATE COMMUNITY COLLEGE
1973 Edison Dr., Piqua 45356 *Type:* Public (state) 2-year *System:* Ohio Board of Regents *Accred.:* 1981/1994 (NCA) *Calendar:* Qtr. plan *Degrees:* A, C *Prof. Accred.:* Nursing (A) *CEO:* Pres. Kenneth A. Yowell
Enroll: 2,755   (800) 922-3722

ETI TECHNICAL COLLEGE
4300 Euclid Ave., Cleveland 44103-9932 *Type:* Private *Accred.:* 1969/1989 (ACCSCT) *Calendar:* Qtr. plan *Degrees:* A, B, C *CEO:* Pres. Jack Baron
(216) 431-4300

NILES CAMPUS
2076-86 Youngstown-Warren Rd., Niles 44446-4398 *Accred.:* 1989 (ACCSCT)
(216) 652-9919

ETI TECHNICAL COLLEGE
1320 W. Maple St., N.W., North Canton 44720-2854 *Type:* Private *Accred.:* 1987 (ACCSCT) *Calendar:* Qtr. plan *Degrees:* A, C *CEO:* Dir. Al Jablonski
(216) 494-1214

FRANCISCAN UNIVERSITY OF STEUBENVILLE
100 Franciscan Way, Steubenville 43952 *Type:* Private (Roman Catholic) liberal arts *Accred.:* 1960/1995 (NCA) *Calendar:* Sem. plan *Degrees:* A, B, M *Prof. Accred.:* Nursing (B) *CEO:* Pres. Michael Scanlan
Enroll: 1,538   (614) 283-3771

FRANKLIN UNIVERSITY
201 S. Grant Ave., Columbus 43215 *Type:* Private liberal arts and technical *Accred.:* 1976/1988 (NCA) *Calendar:* Tri. plan *Degrees:* A, B, M *Prof. Accred.:* Engineering Technology (electrical, mechanical), Nursing (B) *CEO:* Pres. Paul J. Otte
Enroll: 3,886   (614) 341-6237

GOD'S BIBLE SCHOOL AND COLLEGE
1810 Young St., Cincinnati 45210 *Type:* Private (Wesleyan) *Accred.:* 1986/1991 (AABC) *Calendar:* Sem. plan *Degrees:* B *CEO:* Pres. Michael Avery
FTE Enroll: 170   (513) 721-7944

HEBREW UNION COLLEGE—JEWISH INSTITUTE OF RELIGION
3101 Clifton Ave., Cincinnati 45220 *Type:* Private (Union of Hebrew Congregations) primarily for men *Accred.:* 1960/1991 (NCA) *Calendar:* Qtr. plan *Degrees:* M, P, D *CEO:* Pres. Sheldon Zimmerman
Enroll: 130   (513) 221-1875

HEIDELBERG COLLEGE
310 E. Market St., Tiffin 44883 *Type:* Private (United Church of Christ) liberal arts *Accred.:* 1913/1995 (NCA) *Calendar:* Sem. plan *Degrees:* B, M *Prof. Accred.:* Music *CEO:* Pres. William C. Cassell
Enroll: 1,139   (419) 448-2000

HIRAM COLLEGE
Hiram 44234 *Type:* Private (Disciples of Christ) liberal arts *Accred.:* 1914/1990 (NCA) *Calendar:* Qtr. plan *Degrees:* B *Prof. Accred.:* Music *CEO:* Pres. G. Benjamin Oliver
Enroll: 1,257   (216) 569-3211

HOCKING TECHNICAL COLLEGE
3301 Hocking Pkwy., Nelsonville 45764 *Type:* Public (state) 2-year *System:* Ohio Board of Regents *Accred.:* 1976/1991 (NCA) *Calendar:* Qtr. plan *Degrees:* A, C *Prof. Accred.:* Engineering Technology (ceramic), Medical Assisting (AMA), Medical Record Technology, Nursing (A), Practical Nursing *CEO:* Pres. John J. Light
Enroll: 5,995   (614) 753-3591

HONDROS CAREER CENTERS
4807 Evanswood Dr., Columbus 43229 *Type:* Private business *Accred.:* 1993/1996 (ACICS) *Degrees:* A, C *CEO:* Dir. Carol Hartsfield
(614) 888-7277

AKRON CAMPUS
2383 S. Main St., Akron 44319 *Accred.:* 1993 (ACICS)
(216) 773-9299

CINCINNATI CAMPUS
4675 Cornell Rd., Ste. 175, Cincinnati 45241 *Accred.:* 1993 (ACICS)
(513) 247-9711

INDEPENDENCE CAMPUS
6533 Brecksville Rd., Independence 44131-2131 *Accred.:* 1993 (ACICS)
(216) 524-1143

MAYFIELD VILLAGE CAMPUS
Cleveland E., 777 Beta Dr., Mayfield Village 44143-2326 *Accred.:* 1993 (ACICS)
(216) 461-7900

ITT TECHNICAL INSTITUTE
3325 Stop Eight Rd., Dayton 45414-9915 *Type:* Private *Accred.:* 1969/1991 (ACCSCT) *Degrees:* A *CEO:* Dir. William R. Miles
(513) 454-2267

ITT TECHNICAL INSTITUTE
1030 North Meridian Rd., Youngstown 44509 *Type:* Private business *Accred.:* 1971/1995 (ACICS) *Degrees:* A, C *CEO:* Dir. Michael L. Seifert
(216) 270-1600

PITTSBURGH CAMPUS
8 Parkway Ctr., Pittsburgh, PA 15220
Accred.: 1992/1995 (ACICS)
(412) 937-9150

JEFFERSON COMMUNITY COLLEGE
4000 Sunset Blvd., Steubenville 43952 *Type:*
Public (state) 2-year *System:* Ohio Board of
Regents *Accred.:* 1973/1989 (NCA) *Calendar:* Qtr. plan *Degrees:* A, C *Prof. Accred.:*
Clinical Lab Technology (A), Dental Assisting, Medical Assisting (AMA), Radiography, Respiratory Therapy *CEO:* Pres.
Edward L. Florak
Enroll: 1,528   (614) 264-5591

JOHN CARROLL UNIVERSITY
20700 N. Park Blvd., University Heights
44118 *Type:* Private (Roman Catholic) liberal arts and business *Accred.:* 1922/1994
(NCA) *Calendar:* Sem. plan *Degrees:* B, M,
C *Prof. Accred.:* Accounting (A), Business
(B,M), Teacher Education *CEO:* Pres. John
J. Shea
Enroll: 3,482   (216) 397-1886

KENT STATE UNIVERSITY
P.O. Box 5190, Kent 44242 *Type:* Public
(state) *System:* Ohio Board of Regents
Accred.: 1915/1994 (NCA) *Calendar:* Sem.
plan *Degrees:* A, B, M, P, D *Prof. Accred.:*
Art, Audiology, Business (B,M), Clinical
Psychology, Counseling, Counseling Psychology, Interior Design, Journalism (B,M),
Librarianship, Music, Nursing (A,B,M),
Occupational Therapy Assisting, Psychology
Internship (probational), Public Administration, Radiography, Recreation and Leisure
Services (B), Rehabilitation Counseling,
School Psychology, Speech-Language
Pathology, Teacher Education *CEO:* Pres.
Carol A. Cartwright
Enroll: 26,796   (216) 672-3000

ASHTABULA CAMPUS
3325 W. 13th St., Ashtabula 44004 *Prof.
Accred.:* Nursing (A)
(216) 964-3322

EAST LIVERPOOL CAMPUS
400 E. Fourth St., East Liverpool 43920
Prof. Accred.: Nursing (A), Physical Therapy Assisting
(216) 385-3805

GEUAGA CAMPUS
14111 Claridon-Troy Rd., Burton Township 44021
(216) 834-4187

SALEM CAMPUS
2491 State Rte. 45 S., Salem 44460
(216) 332-0361

STARK CAMPUS
6000 Frank Ave., N.W., Canton 44720
(216) 499-9600

TRUMBULL CAMPUS
4314 Mahoning Ave., N.W., Warren
44483
(216) 678-4281

TUSCARAWAS CAMPUS
University Dr., N.E., New Philadelphia
44663 *Prof. Accred.:* Engineering Technology (electrical, electromechanical),
mechanical)
(216) 339-3391

KENYON COLLEGE
Gambier 43022-9623 *Type:* Private (Episcopal) liberal arts *Accred.:* 1913/1991 (NCA)
Calendar: Sem. plan *Degrees:* B *CEO:* Pres.
Robert A. Oden, Jr.
Enroll: 1,518   (614) 427-5000

KETTERING COLLEGE OF MEDICAL ARTS
3737 Southern Blvd., Kettering 45429 *Type:*
Private (Seventh-Day Adventist) junior
Accred.: 1974/1990 (NCA) *Calendar:* Sem.
plan *Degrees:* A, C *Prof. Accred.:* Diagnostic Medical Sonography, Nursing (A), Physician Assisting/Surgeon Assisting, Radiography, Respiratory Therapy *CEO:* Pres. Peter
D.H. Bath
Enroll: 619   (513) 296-7218

LAKE ERIE COLLEGE
391 W. Washington St., Painesville 44077
Type: Private liberal arts *Accred.:* 1913/1994

(NCA) *Calendar:* Sem. plan *Degrees:* B, M *CEO:* Pres. Harold F. Laydon
Enroll: 578   (216) 352-3361

LAKELAND COMMUNITY COLLEGE
7700 Clocktower Dr., Kirkland 44094-5198 *Type:* Public (district) 2-year *System:* Ohio Board of Regents *Accred.:* 1973/1990 (NCA) *Calendar:* 4-1-4 plan *Degrees:* A, C *Prof. Accred.:* Clinical Lab Technology (A), Dental Hygiene, Nursing (A), Radiography, Respiratory Therapy *CEO:* Pres. Ralph R. Doty
Enroll: 8,698   (800) 589-8520

LIMA TECHNICAL COLLEGE
4240 Campus Dr., Lima 45804 *Type:* Public (state) 2-year *System:* Ohio Board of Regents *Accred.:* 1979/1992 (NCA) *Calendar:* Qtr. plan *Degrees:* A, C *Prof. Accred.:* Dental Hygiene, Engineering Technology (electrical), Nursing (A), Physical Therapy Assisting, Radiography, Respiratory Therapy, Respiratory Therapy Technology *CEO:* Pres. James J. Countryman
Enroll: 2,583   (419) 221-1112

LORAIN COUNTY COMMUNITY COLLEGE
1005 N. Abbe Rd., Elyria 44035 *Type:* Public (district) 2-year *System:* Ohio Board of Regents *Accred.:* 1971/1994 (NCA) *Calendar:* Qtr. plan *Degrees:* A, C *Prof. Accred.:* Clinical Lab Technology (A), Nursing (A), Practical Nursing (warning), Radiography *CEO:* Pres. Roy A. Church
Enroll: 7,297   (800) 955-5222

LOURDES COLLEGE
6832 Convent Blvd., Sylvania 43560 *Type:* Private (Roman Catholic) liberal arts *Accred.:* 1964/1992 (NCA) *Calendar:* Sem. plan *Degrees:* A, B, C *Prof. Accred.:* Nursing (B), Occupational Therapy Assisting, Social Work (B) *CEO:* Pres. Ann Francis Klimkowski, O.S.F.
Enroll: 1,662   (419) 885-3211

MALONE COLLEGE
515 25th St., N.W., Canton 44709 *Type:* Private (Friends) liberal arts *Accred.:* 1964/1994 (NCA) *Calendar:* Sem. plan *Degrees:*

A, B, M *Prof. Accred.:* Nursing (B), Social Work (B) *CEO:* Pres. Ronald G. Johnson
Enroll: 1,894   (216) 471-8100

MARIETTA COLLEGE
215 5th St., Marietta 45750 *Type:* Private liberal arts *Accred.:* 1913/1986 (NCA) *Calendar:* Sem. plan *Degrees:* A, B, M, C *Prof. Accred.:* Engineering (petroleum) *CEO:* Pres. Lauren Wilson
Enroll: 1,267   (614) 376-4643

MARION TECHNICAL COLLEGE
1467 Mt. Vernon Ave., Marion 43302-5694 *Type:* Public (state) 2-year *System:* Ohio Board of Regents *Accred.:* 1977/1987 (NCA) *Calendar:* Qtr. plan *Degrees:* A, C *Prof. Accred.:* Clinical Lab Technology (A), Nursing (A) *CEO:* Pres. John Richard Bryson
Enroll: 1,801   (614) 389-4636

MEDICAL COLLEGE OF OHIO
3000 Arlington, P.O. Box 10008, Toledo 43699-0008 *Type:* Public (state) professional *System:* Ohio Board of Regents *Accred.:* 1980/1991 (NCA) *Calendar:* Sem. plan *Degrees:* M, D *Prof. Accred.:* General Practice Residency, Medicine, Nursing (B,M), Occupational Therapy, Physical Therapy, Psychology Internship *CEO:* Pres. Roger C. Bone
Enroll: 1,029   (419) 381-4267

MERCY COLLEGE OF NORTHWEST OHIO
2238 Jefferson Ave., Toledo 43624-1197 *Type:* Private professional *Accred.:* 1995 (NCA) *Calendar:* Sem. plan *Degrees:* A *CEO:* Pres. Patricia Ann Dahlke
Enroll: 167   (419) 259-1279

METHODIST THEOLOGICAL SCHOOL IN OHIO
P.O. Box 1204, 3081 Columbus Pike, Delaware 43015-0391 *Type:* Private (United Methodist) graduate only *Accred.:* 1965/1987 (ATS); 1976/1988 (NCA) *Calendar:* Qtr. plan *Degrees:* M *CEO:* Pres. Norman E. Dewire
Enroll: 244   (614) 363-1146

MIAMI-JACOBS COLLEGE
P.O. Box 1433, 400 E. Second St., Dayton 45401 *Type:* Private junior *Accred.:* 1957/ 1986 (ACICS) *Calendar:* Qtr. plan *Degrees:* A, C *CEO:* Pres. Charles G. Campbell
(513) 461-5174

MIAMI UNIVERSITY
201 Roudebush Hall, Oxford 45056 *Type:* Public (state) *System:* Ohio Board of Regents *Accred.:* 1913/1995 (NCA) *Calendar:* Sem. plan *Degrees:* A, B, M, P, D *Prof. Accred.:* Accounting (A,C), Art, Audiology, Business (B,M), Clinical Psychology, Engineering (manufacturing), Music, Nursing (B), Speech-Language Pathology, Teacher Education, Theatre (A) *CEO:* Acting Pres. Anne H. Hopkins
Enroll: 17,461   (513) 529-1809

HAMILTON CAMPUS
1601 Peck Blvd., Hamilton 45011 *Prof. Accred.:* Nursing (A)
(513) 863-8833

MIDDLETOWN CAMPUS
4200 E. University Blvd., Middletown 45042 *Prof. Accred.:* Nursing (A)
(513) 424-4444

MOUNT CARMEL COLLEGE OF NURSING
127 S. Davis Ave., Columbus 43222 *Type:* Private professional *Accred.:* 1994 (NCA) *Calendar:* Sem. plan *Degrees:* B *Prof. Accred.:* Dietetics (internship) *CEO:* Pres./Dean Ann E. Schiele
Enroll: 320   (614) 225-5800

MOUNT UNION COLLEGE
1972 Clark Ave., Alliance 44601 *Type:* Private (United Methodist) liberal arts *Accred.:* 1913/1992 (NCA) *Calendar:* Sem. plan *Degrees:* B, C *Prof. Accred.:* Music *CEO:* Pres. Harold M. Kolenbrander
Enroll: 1,532   (216) 821-5320

MOUNT VERNON NAZARENE COLLEGE
800 Martinsburg Rd., Mount Vernon 43050 *Type:* Private (Nazarene) liberal arts *Accred.:* 1972/1989 (NCA) *Calendar:* 4-1-4

plan *Degrees:* A, B, M *CEO:* Pres. E. LeBron Fairbanks
Enroll: 1,329   (614) 397-1244

MTI BUSINESS COLLEGE
1140 Euclid Ave., Cleveland 44115-1603 *Type:* Private business *Accred.:* 1980/1995 (ACICS) *Degrees:* A, C *Prof. Accred.:* Medical Assisting (AMA) *CEO:* Pres. Charles M. Kramer
(216) 621-8228

MUSKINGUM AREA TECHNICAL COLLEGE
1555 Newark Rd., Zanesville 43701 *Type:* Public (state) 2-year *System:* Ohio Board of Regents *Accred.:* 1975/1988 (NCA) *Calendar:* Qtr. plan *Degrees:* A, C *Prof. Accred.:* Engineering Technology (electrical), Medical Assisting (AMA), Occupational Therapy Assisting, Radiography *CEO:* Pres. Lynn H. Willett
Enroll: 2,135   (800) 686-8324

MUSKINGUM COLLEGE
Montgomery Hall, New Concord 43762 *Type:* Private (United Presbyterian) liberal arts *Accred.:* 1919/1993 (NCA) *Calendar:* Sem. plan *Degrees:* B, M *Prof. Accred.:* Music *CEO:* Pres. Samuel W. Speck, Jr.
Enroll: 1,189   (614) 826-8211

NORTH CENTRAL TECHNICAL COLLEGE
P.O. Box 698, Mansfield 44901-0698 *Type:* Public (state) 2-year *System:* Ohio Board of Regents *Accred.:* 1976/1988 (NCA) *Calendar:* Qtr. plan *Degrees:* A, C *Prof. Accred.:* Nursing (A), Physical Therapy Assisting, Radiography, Respiratory Therapy *CEO:* Pres. Byron E. Kee
Enroll: 2,857   (419) 755-4800

NORTHEASTERN OHIO UNIVERSITIES COLLEGE OF MEDICINE
4209 State Rte. 44, P.O. Box 95, Rootstown 44272-0095 *Type:* Public (state) professional *System:* Ohio Board of Regents *Calendar:* Sem. plan *Degrees:* P *Prof. Accred.:* Medicine, Psychology Internship *CEO:* Pres./ Dean Robert S. Blacklow
Enroll: 420   (216) 325-2511

NORTHWEST STATE COMMUNITY COLLEGE
22-600 State Rte. 34, Archbold 43502 *Type:*
Public (state) 2-year *System:* Ohio Board of
Regents *Accred.:* 1977/1989 (NCA) *Calendar:* Qtr. plan *Degrees:* A, C *Prof. Accred.:*
Engineering Technology (electrical) *CEO:*
Pres. Larry G. McDougle
Enroll: 1,832   (419) 267-5511

NORTHWESTERN COLLEGE
1441 N. Cable Rd., Lima 45805 *Type:* Private *Accred.:* 1987/1991 (NCA) *Calendar:*
Qtr. plan *Degrees:* A, C *CEO:* Pres. Loren R.
Jarvis
Enroll: 1,523   (419) 227-3141

NOTRE DAME COLLEGE
4545 College Rd., South Euclid 44121 *Type:*
Private (Roman Catholic) liberal arts for
women *Accred.:* 1931/1991 (NCA) *Calendar:* Sem. plan *Degrees:* A, B, M, C *CEO:*
Pres. Gay Culverhouse
Enroll: 642   (216) 381-1680

OBERLIN COLLEGE
Oberlin 44074 *Type:* Private liberal arts
Accred.: 1913/1988 (NCA) *Calendar:* 4-1-4
plan *Degrees:* B, M, C *Prof. Accred.:* Music
CEO: Pres. Nancy Schrom Dye
Enroll: 2,745   (216) 775-8400

OHIO COLLEGE OF PODIATRIC MEDICINE
10515 Carnegie Ave., Cleveland 44106
Type: Private professional *Accred.:* 1987/
1992 (NCA) *Calendar:* Sem. plan *Degrees:*
D *Prof. Accred.:* Podiatry *CEO:* Pres.
Thomas V. Melillo
Enroll: 469   (216) 231-3300

OHIO DOMINICAN COLLEGE
1216 Sunbury Rd., Columbus 43219 *Type:*
Private (Roman Catholic) liberal arts
Accred.: 1934/1988 (NCA) *Calendar:* Sem.
plan *Degrees:* A, B, C *CEO:* Pres. Mary
Andrew Matesich, O.P.
Enroll: 1,713   (614) 251-4690

OHIO INSTITUTE OF PHOTOGRAPHY AND
TECHNOLOGY
2029 Edgefield Rd., Dayton 45439-1984
Type: Private *Accred.:* 1976/1993 (ACC-

SCT) *Calendar:* Sem. plan *Degrees:* A *CEO:*
Pres. Terry Guthrie
										(513) 294-6155

OHIO NORTHERN UNIVERSITY
525 N. Main St., Ada 45810 *Type:* Private
(United Methodist) *Accred.:* 1958/1995
(NCA) *Calendar:* Qtr. plan *Degrees:* B, D
Prof. Accred.: Engineering (civil, electrical,
mechanical), Law, Music, Teacher Education
CEO: Pres. DeBow Freed
Enroll: 2,506   (419) 772-2030

THE OHIO STATE UNIVERSITY
205 Bricker Hall, 190 N. Oval Dr., Columbus 43210 *Type:* Public (state) *System:* Ohio
Board of Regents *Accred.:* 1913/1987
(NCA) *Calendar:* Qtr. plan *Degrees:* A, B,
M, D *Prof. Accred.:* Accounting (A,B), Art,
Audiology, Blood Bank Technology, Business (B,M), Clinical Lab Scientist, Clinical
Psychology, Combined Prosthodontics,
Counseling Psychology, Dance, Dental
Hygiene, Dentistry, Dietetics (coordinated),
Dietetics (internship), Endodontics, Engineering (aerospace, agricultural, ceramic,
chemical, civil, electrical, environmental/
sanitary, industrial, materials, mechanical,
metallurgical, welding), Forestry, General
Dentistry, General Practice Residency,
Health Services Administration, Interior
Design, Journalism (B,M), Landscape Architecture (B,M), Law, Medical Record Administration, Medicine, Music, Nuclear Medicine Technology, Nursing (B,M), Occupational Therapy, Optometry, Oral Pathology,
Oral and Maxillofacial Surgery, Orthodontics, Pediatric Dentistry, Perfusion, Periodontics, Physical Therapy, Planning (M),
Psychology Internship, Public Administration, Radiation Therapy Technology, Radiography, Rehabilitation Counseling, Respiratory Therapy, Social Work (B,M), Speech-
Language Pathology, Teacher Education,
Theatre *CEO:* Pres. E. Gordon Gee
Enroll: 41,817   (614) 292-6446

LIMA CAMPUS
4240 Campus Dr., Lima 45804
										(419) 221-1641

MANSFIELD CAMPUS
1680 University Dr., Mansfield 44906
(419) 755-4011

MARION CAMPUS
1465 Mount Vernon Ave., Marion 43302-5695
(614) 389-2361

NEWARK CAMPUS
1179 University Dr., Newark 43055-1797
(614) 366-3321

OHIO STATE UNIVERSITY—AGRICULTURAL TECHNICAL INSTITUTE
1328 Dover Rd., Wooster 44691 *Accred.:* 1978/1993 (NCA) *Degrees:* A
Enroll: 740   (216) 264-3911

OHIO UNIVERSITY
Athens 45701 *Type:* Public (state) *System:* Ohio Board of Regents *Accred.:* 1913/1994 (NCA) *Calendar:* Qtr. plan *Degrees:* A, B, M, D, C *Prof. Accred.:* Audiology, Business (B,M), Clinical Psychology, Counseling, Dance, Engineering (chemical, civil, electrical, industrial, mechanical), Home Economics, Interior Design, Journalism (B,M), Music, Nursing (B), Osteopathy, Physical Therapy, Rehabilitation Counseling, Social Work (B), Speech-Language Pathology, Teacher Education *CEO:* Pres. Robert Glidden
Enroll: 24,309   (614) 593-1000

CHILLICOTHE CAMPUS
571 W. 5th St., Chillicothe 45601
(614) 774-7200

EASTERN CAMPUS
National Rd., W. St., St. Clairsville 43950
(614) 695-1720

LANCASTER CAMPUS
1570 Granville Pike, Lancaster 43130
(614) 654-6711

SOUTHERN CAMPUS
1804 Liberty Ave., Ironton 43701
(614) 533-4600

ZANESVILLE CAMPUS
1425 Neward Rd., Zanesville 43701 *Prof. Accred.:* Nursing (A)
(614) 453-0762

OHIO VALLEY BUSINESS COLLEGE
P.O. Box 7000, 500 Maryland Ave., East Liverpool 43920 *Type:* Private business *Accred.:* 1985/1995 (ACICS) *Degrees:* A *Prof. Accred.:* Medical Assisting (AMA) *CEO:* Pres. Debra Sanford
(216) 385-1070

OHIO WESLEYAN UNIVERSITY
61 S. Sanusky St., Delaware 43015 *Type:* Private (United Methodist) liberal arts *Accred.:* 1913/1989 (NCA) *Calendar:* 4-1-4 plan *Degrees:* B *Prof. Accred.:* Music, Nursing (B) *CEO:* Pres. Thomas B. Courtice
Enroll: 1,731   (614) 368-2000

OTTERBEIN COLLEGE
Westerville 43081 *Type:* Private (United Methodist) liberal arts *Accred.:* 1913/1995 (NCA) *Calendar:* 3-3 plan *Degrees:* B, M *Prof. Accred.:* Music, Nursing (A,B), Teacher Education *CEO:* Pres. C. Brent DeVore
Enroll: 2,488   (800) 488-8144

OWENS COMMUNITY COLLEGE
P.O. Box 10000, Toledo 43699 *Type:* Public (state) 2-year *System:* Ohio Board of Regents *Accred.:* 1976/1991 (NCA) *Calendar:* Sem. plan *Degrees:* A, C *Prof. Accred.:* Dental Hygiene, Diagnostic Medical Sonography, Engineering Technology (architectural, bioengineering, civil/construction, computer, electrical, electromechanical, industrial), Nursing (A), Optometric Technician, Physical Therapy Assisting, Radiation Therapy Technology Surgical Technology *CEO:* Pres. Daniel H. Brown
Enroll: 10,255   (419) 661-7000

FINDLAY CAMPUS
300 Davis St., Findlay 45840-3600 *Prof. Accred.:* Engineering Technology (mechanical drafting/design)
(419) 423-6827

PAYNE THEOLOGICAL SEMINARY
1230 Wilberforce Clifton Rd., Wilberforce 45384 *Type:* Private African Methodist Episcopal *Accred.:* 1995 (ATS) *Degrees:* M *CEO:* Pres. Louis Charles Harvey
Enroll: 46   (513) 376-2946

PONTIFICAL COLLEGE JOSEPHINUM
7625 N. High St., Columbus 43235 *Type:* Private (Roman Catholic) liberal arts and professional *Accred.:* 1970/1991 (ATS); 1977/1991 (NCA) *Calendar:* Sem. plan *Degrees:* B, M *CEO:* Pres./Rector Blase J. Cupich
Enroll: 53   (614) 885-5585

RABBINICAL COLLEGE OF TELSHE
28400 Euclid Ave., Wickliffe 44092-2523 *Type:* Private professional *Accred.:* 1974/1993 (AARTS) *Calendar:* Sem. plan *Degrees:* M, D *CEO:* Pres. M. Gifter
Enroll: 150   (216) 943-5300

RETS TECH CENTER
P.O. Box 130, Centerville 45459-6120 *Type:* Private *Accred.:* 1974/1989 (ACCSCT) *Calendar:* Qtr. plan *Degrees:* A, C *CEO:* Pres. Michael A. LeMaster
                               (513) 433-3410

ST. MARY SEMINARY
28700 Euclid Ave., Wickliffe 44092-2585 *Type:* Private (Roman Catholic) graduate only *Accred.:* 1970/1995 (ATS); 1981/1986 (NCA) *Calendar:* Qtr. plan *Degrees:* M *CEO:* Pres./Rector Allan R. Laubenthal
Enroll: 73   (800) 949-7874

SAWYER COLLEGE OF BUSINESS
13027 Lorain Ave., Cleveland 44111 *Type:* Private business *Accred.:* 1979/1994 (ACICS) *Calendar:* Qtr. plan *Degrees:* A, C *CEO:* Dir. Betty Gray
                               (216) 941-7666

SAWYER COLLEGE OF BUSINESS
3150 Mayfield Rd., Cleveland Heights 44118 *Type:* Private business *Accred.:* 1973/1997 (ACICS) *Calendar:* Qtr. plan *Degrees:* A, C *CEO:* Dir. Bruce T. Shields
                               (216) 932-0911

SHAWNEE STATE UNIVERSITY
940 Second St., Portsmouth 45662 *Type:* Public (state) 2-year *System:* Ohio Board of Regents *Accred.:* 1975/1993 (NCA) *Calendar:* Qtr. plan *Degrees:* A, B, C *Prof. Accred.:* Clinical Lab Technology (A), Dental Hygiene, Occupational Therapy, Occupational Therapy Assisting, Physical Therapy Assisting, Radiography, Respiratory Therapy *CEO:* Pres. Clive C. Veri
Enroll: 3,185   (614) 354-3205

SINCLAIR COMMUNITY COLLEGE
444 W. Third St., Dayton 45402 *Type:* Public (district) 2-year *System:* Ohio Board of Regents *Accred.:* 1970/1988 (NCA) *Calendar:* Qtr. plan *Degrees:* A, C *Prof. Accred.:* Dental Hygiene, Engineering Technology (electrical, industrial, mechanical, packaging), Medical Assisting (AMA), Medical Record Technology, Nursing (A), Occupational Therapy Assisting, Physical Therapy Assisting, Radiography, Respiratory Therapy, Surgical Technology *CEO:* Pres. David H. Ponitz
Enroll: 20,075   (513) 226-2500

SOUTHEASTERN BUSINESS COLLEGE
1855 Western Ave., Chillicothe 45601 *Type:* Private business *Accred.:* 1976/1986 (ACICS) *Degrees:* A *CEO:* Exec. Dir. John T. Danicki
                               (614) 774-6300

JACKSON CAMPUS
420 E. Main St., Jackson 45640 *Accred.:* 1976 (ACICS)
                               (614) 286-1554

LANCASTER CAMPUS
1522 Sheridan Dr., Lancaster 43130 *Accred.:* 1985 (ACICS)
                               (614) 687-6126

NEW BOSTON CAMPUS
3879 Rhodes Ave., New Boston 45662 *Accred.:* 1981 (ACICS)
                               (614) 456-4124

SOUTHEASTERN BUSINESS COLLEGE
1176 Jackson Pike, Ste. 312, Gallipolis 45631 *Type:* Private business *Accred.:* 1983/1989 (ACICS) *Degrees:* A *CEO:* Pres./Owner Robert Shirey
(614) 446-4367

SOUTHEASTERN BUSINESS COLLEGE
1907 N. Ridge Rd., Lorain 44055 *Type:* Private business *Accred.:* 1991 (ACICS) *Degrees:* A *CEO:* Dir. Ellen Robbin
(216) 277-0021

SANDUSKY CAMPUS
4020 Milan Rd., Sandusky 44870 *Accred.:* 1992 (ACICS)
(419) 627-8345

SOUTHERN OHIO COLLEGE
1011 Glendale-Milford Rd, Cincinnati 45215-1107 *Type:* Private junior *Accred.:* 1964/1996 (ACICS); 1983/1995 (NCA) *Calendar:* Qtr. plan *Degrees:* A, C *Prof. Accred.:* Medical Assisting (AMA) *CEO:* Pres. Stephen Coppock
Enroll: 1,035   (513) 242-3791

AKRON CAMPUS
2791 Mogadore Rd., Akron 44312 *Accred.:* 1980/1990 (ACICS) *Prof. Accred.:* Medical Assisting (AMA)
(216) 733-8766

FAIRFIELD CAMPUS
4641 Bach La., Fairfield 45014 *Accred.:* 1983/1990 (ACICS) *Prof. Accred.:* Medical Assisting (AMA)
(513) 829-7100

NORTHERN KENTUCKY CAMPUS
309 Buttermilk Pike, Fort Mitchell, KY 41017 *Accred.:* 1988/1990 (ACICS)
(606) 341-5627

SOUTHERN STATE COMMUNITY COLLEGE
200 Hobart Dr., Hillsboro 45133 *Type:* Public (state) 2-year *System:* Ohio Board of Regents *Accred.:* 1981/1990 (NCA) *Calendar:* Qtr. plan *Degrees:* A, C *Prof. Accred.:* Medical Assisting (AMA), Nursing (A) *CEO:* Pres. Lawrence N. Dukes
Enroll: 1,560   (513) 393-3431

SOUTHWESTERN COLLEGE OF BUSINESS
225 W. First St., Dayton 45402 *Type:* Private business *Accred.:* 1973/1995 (ACICS) *Calendar:* Qtr. plan *Degrees:* A, C *Prof. Accred.:* Medical Assisting *CEO:* Dir. Cherie Dixon
(513) 224-0061

MIDDLETOWN CAMPUS
631 S. Briel Blvd., Middletown 45044 *Accred.:* 1982/1995 (ACICS) *Prof. Accred.:* Medical Assisting
(513) 423-3346

VINE STREET CAMPUS
632 Vine St., Ste 200, Cincinnati 45202 *Accred.:* 1982/1995 (ACICS) *Prof. Accred.:* Medical Assisting
(513) 421-3212

SOUTHWESTERN COLLEGE OF BUSINESS
9910 Princeton-Glendale Rd., Cincinnati 45246 business *Accred.:* 1982/1991 (ACICS) *Calendar:* Qtr. plan *Degrees:* A *Prof. Accred.:* Medical Assisting *CEO:* Dir. Susan Hatfield
(513) 874-0432

STARK TECHNICAL COLLEGE
6200 Frank Ave., N.W., Canton 44720 *Type:* Public (state) 2-year *System:* Ohio Board of Regents *Accred.:* 1976/1991 (NCA) *Calendar:* Qtr. plan *Degrees:* A, C *Prof. Accred.:* Clinical Lab Technology (A), Engineering Technology (civil/construction, electrical, mechanical, mechanical drafting/design), Medical Assisting (AMA), Medical Record Technology, Occupational Therapy Assisting, Physical Therapy Assisting, Respiratory Therapy *CEO:* Pres. John J. McGrath, Jr.
Enroll: 4,207   (216) 494-6170

STAUTZENBERGER COLLEGE—FINDLAY
1637 Tiffin Ave., Ste. 150, Findlay 54840 *Type:* Private business *Accred.:* 1986/1995 (ACICS) *Degrees:* A, C *CEO:* Dir. Dan Harper
(419) 423-2211

STAUTZENBERGER COLLEGE—SOUTH
5355 Southwyck Blvd., Toledo 43614 *Type:*
Private business *Accred.:* 1987 (ACICS)
Degrees: A, C *CEO:* Pres. Charles Hawes
(419) 866-0261

TERRA STATE COMMUNITY COLLEGE
2830 Napoleon Rd., Fremont 43420 *Type:*
Public (state) 2-year *System:* Ohio Board of
Regents *Accred.:* 1975/1987 (NCA) *Calendar:* Qtr. plan *Degrees:* A, C *CEO:* Pres.
Charlotte J. Lee
Enroll: 2,397   (419) 334-8400

TIFFIN UNIVERSITY
155 Miami St., Tiffin 44883 *Type:* Private
Accred.: 1985/1990 (NCA) *Calendar:* Sem.
plan *Degrees:* A, B, M, C *CEO:* Pres.
George Kidd, Jr.
Enroll: 1,023   (419) 447-6442

TRINITY LUTHERAN SEMINARY
2199 E. Main St., Columbus 43209-2334
Type: Private (Evangelical Lutheran) graduate only *Accred.:* 1940/1992 (ATS); 1974/
1992 (NCA) *Calendar:* Sem. plan *Degrees:*
M *CEO:* Pres. Dennis A. Anderson
Enroll: 259   (614) 235-4136

TRUMBULL BUSINESS COLLEGE
3200 Ridge Rd., Warren 44484 *Type:* Private
business *Accred.:* 1976/1994 (ACICS)
Degrees: A, C *CEO:* Pres. Dennis R. Griffith
(216) 369-3200

THE UNION INSTITUTE
440 E. McMillan St., Cincinnati 45206-1947
Type: Private *Accred.:* 1985/1990 (NCA)
Calendar: Qtr. plan *Degrees:* B, D *CEO:*
Pres. Robert T. Conley
Enroll: 482   (513) 861-6400

UNITED THEOLOGICAL SEMINARY
1810 Harvard Blvd., Dayton 45406 *Type:*
Private (United Methodist) graduate only
Accred.: 1938/1990 (ATS); 1975/1991
(NCA) *Calendar:* 4-1-4 plan *Degrees:* M, D
CEO: Interim Chanc. Emerson Colaw
Enroll: 559   (513) 278-5817

THE UNIVERSITY OF AKRON
302 Buchtel Common, Akron 44325 *Type:*
Public (state) *System:* Ohio Board of
Regents *Accred.:* 1914/1987 (NCA) *Calendar:* Sem. plan *Degrees:* A, B, M, D, C *Prof.*
Accred.: Accounting (A,B), Art, Audiology,
Business (B,M), Counseling, Counseling
Psychology, Dance, Dietetics (coordinated),
Engineering Technology (civil/construction,
electrical, mechanical, surveying), Engineering (chemical, civil, electrical, mechanical),
Home Economics, Law, Medical Assisting
(AMA), Music, Nurse Anesthesia Education,
Nursing (B,M), Psychology Internship, Public Administration, Respiratory Therapy,
Social Work (B), Speech-Language Pathology, Surgical Technology, Teacher Education *CEO:* Pres. Peggy Gordon Elliott
Enroll: 20,275   (216) 972-7111

UNIVERSITY OF AKRON—WAYNE COLLEGE
1901 Smucker Rd., Orrville 44667 *Type:*
Public (state) *System:* Ohio Board of
Regents *Accred.:* 1972/1991 (NCA) *Calendar:* Qtr. plan *Degrees:* A, C *CEO:* Dean
Tyrone M. Turning
Enroll: 1,521   (800) 221-8308

UNIVERSITY OF CINCINNATI
P.O. Box 210063, Cincinnati 45221-0063
Type: Public (state) *System:* Ohio Board of
Regents *Accred.:* 1913/1989 (NCA) *Calendar:* Qtr. plan *Degrees:* A, B, M, D, C *Prof.*
Accred.: Art, Audiology, Blood Bank Technology, Business (B,M), Clinical Lab Scientist, Clinical Psychology, Construction Education (B), Counseling, Dental Hygiene,
Dietetics (internship), EMT-Paramedic,
Engineering Technology (architectural,
chemical, civil/construction, electrical,
industrial hygiene, manufacturing, mechanical), Engineering (aerospace, chemical,
civil, computer, electrical, engineering
mechanics, environmental/sanitary, industrial, materials, mechanical, nuclear), Interior Design, Law, Medicine, Music, Nuclear
Medicine Technology, Nurse Anesthesia
Education, Nursing (B,M), Oral and Maxillofacial Surgery, Physical Therapy Assisting, Planning (B,M), Psychology Internship,
Radiation Therapy Technology, Radiogra-

phy, School Psychology, Social Work (B,M), Speech-Language Pathology, Teacher Education, Theatre *CEO:* Pres. Joseph A. Steger
Enroll: 26,982　　　　(513) 556-2201

UNIVERSITY OF CINCINNATI - RAYMOND WALTERS COLLEGE
9555 Plainfield Rd., Cincinnati 45236 *Type:* Public (state) *System:* Ohio Board of Regents *Accred.:* 1969/1989 (NCA) *Calendar:* Qtr. plan *Degrees:* A, C *Prof. Accred.:* Dental Hygiene, Nursing (A), Veterinary Technology *CEO:* Dean Barbara A. Bardes
Enroll: 3,850　　　　(513) 745-5600

UNIVERSITY OF CINCINNATI— CLERMONT COLLEGE
725 College Dr., Batavia 45103 *Type:* Public (state) *System:* Ohio Board of Regents *Accred.:* 1978/1989 (NCA) *Calendar:* Qtr. plan *Degrees:* A, C *CEO:* Dean Roger J. Barry
Enroll: 1,918　　　　(513) 732-5200

UNIVERSITY OF DAYTON
300 College Park Ave., Dayton 45469 *Type:* Private (Roman Catholic) *Accred.:* 1928/ 1988 (NCA) *Calendar:* Tri. plan *Degrees:* B, M, P, D, C *Prof. Accred.:* Accounting (A), Business (B,M), Clinical Lab Scientist, Computer Science, Engineering Technology (electrical, industrial, manufacturing, mechanical), Engineering (chemical, civil, electrical, mechanical), Law, Music, Teacher Education *CEO:* Pres. Raymond L. Fitz, S.M.
Enroll: 6,435　　　　(513) 229-1000

UNIVERSITY OF FINDLAY
1000 N. Main St., Findlay 45840 *Type:* Private (Churches of God) liberal arts *Accred.:* 1933/1994 (NCA) *Calendar:* Sem. plan *Degrees:* A, B, M *Prof. Accred.:* Nuclear Medicine Technology, Social Work (B-candidate), Teacher Education *CEO:* Pres. Kenneth E. Zirkle
Enroll: 3,318　　　　(419) 424-8313

UNIVERSITY OF RIO GRANDE
E. College Ave., Rio Grande 45674 *Type:* Private liberal arts *Accred.:* 1969/1995 (NCA) *Calendar:* Qtr. plan *Degrees:* A, B,

M, C *Prof. Accred.:* Clinical Lab Technology (A), Nursing (A), Social Work (B) *CEO:* Pres. Barry M. Dorsey
Enroll: 1,951　　　　(614) 245-5353

UNIVERSITY OF TOLEDO
2801 W. Bancroft St., Toledo 43606 *Type:* Public (state) *System:* Ohio Board of Regents *Accred.:* 1922/1992 (NCA) *Calendar:* Qtr. plan *Degrees:* A, B, M, P, D, C *Prof. Accred.:* Business (B,M), Cardiovascular Technology, Clinical Psychology, Computer Science, Counseling, Engineering Technology (civil/construction, electrical, industrial, mechanical, mechanical drafting/design), Engineering (chemical, civil, computer, electrical, engineering physics/ science, industrial, mechanical), Law, Medical Assisting (AMA), Music, Nursing (A,B,M), Physical Therapy, Public Administration, Recreation and Leisure Services (B), Respiratory Therapy, Respiratory Therapy Technology, Social Work (B), Speech-Language Pathology, Teacher Education *CEO:* Pres. Frank E. Horton
Enroll: 19,854　　　　(419) 537-2072

URBANA UNIVERSITY
One College Way, Urbana 43078 *Type:* Private (Swedenborgian) liberal arts *Accred.:* 1975/1991 (NCA) *Calendar:* Sem. plan *Degrees:* A, B *CEO:* Pres. Francis E. Hazard
Enroll: 1,000　　　　(513) 652-1301

URSULINE COLLEGE
2550 Lander Rd., Pepper Pike 44124 *Type:* Private (Roman Catholic) liberal arts primarily for women *Accred.:* 1931/1992 (NCA) *Calendar:* Sem. plan *Degrees:* B, M, C *Prof. Accred.:* Nursing (B), Social Work (B-candidate) *CEO:* Pres. Anne Marie Diederich, O.S.U.
Enroll: 1,300　　　　(216) 449-4200

VIRGINIA MARTI COLLEGE OF FASHION AND ART
P.O. Box 580, Lakewood 44107-3002 *Type:* Private *Accred.:* 1975/1990 (ACCSCT) *Degrees:* A, C *CEO:* Dir. Virginia Marti
　　　　(216) 221-8584

WALSH UNIVERSITY
2020 Easton St., N.W., Canton 44720 *Type:* Private (Roman Catholic) liberal arts *Accred.:* 1970/1990 (NCA) *Calendar:* Sem. plan *Degrees:* A, B, M *Prof. Accred.:* Nursing (A,B) *CEO:* Pres. Richard J. Mucowski, O.F.M.
Enroll: 1,241   (216) 499-7090

WASHINGTON STATE COMMUNITY COLLEGE
710 Colegate Dr., Marietta 45750 *Type:* Public (state) 2-year *System:* Ohio Board of Regents *Accred.:* 1979/1995 (NCA) *Calendar:* Qtr. plan *Degrees:* A, C *Prof. Accred.:* Clinical Lab Technology (A) *CEO:* Pres. Carson K. Miller
Enroll: 2,152   (614) 374-8716

WEST SIDE INSTITUTE OF TECHNOLOGY
9801 Walford Ave., Cleveland 44102-4758 *Type:* Private *Accred.:* 1969/1988 (ACC-SCT) *Degrees:* A *CEO:* Dir. Richard R. Pountney
                                   (216) 651-1656

WILBERFORCE UNIVERSITY
1055 N. Bickett Rd., Wilberforce 45384 *Type:* Private (African Methodist Episcopal) liberal arts *Accred.:* 1939/1992 (NCA) *Calendar:* Tri. plan *Degrees:* B *CEO:* Pres. John L. Henderson
Enroll: 958   (513) 376-2911

WILMINGTON COLLEGE
P.O. Box 1185, Wilmington 45177 *Type:* Private (Quaker) liberal arts *Accred.:* 1944/1994 (NCA) *Calendar:* Sem. plan *Degrees:* A, B *CEO:* Pres. Daniel A. DiBiasio
Enroll: 2,033   (513) 382-6661

WINEBRENNER THEOLOGICAL SEMINARY
701 E. Melrose Ave., P.O. Box 478, Findlay 45839 *Type:* Private (Churches of God) graduate only *Accred.:* 1991/1994 (ATS); 1986/1994 (NCA) *Calendar:* Sem. plan *Degrees:* M, C *CEO:* Pres. David E. Draper
Enroll: 29   (419) 422-4824

WITTENBERG UNIVERSITY
P.O. Box 720, Springfield 45501 *Type:* Private (Lutheran) *Accred.:* 1916/1987 (NCA)

Calendar: 3-3 plan *Degrees:* B *Prof. Accred.:* Music *CEO:* Pres. L. Baird Tipson
Enroll: 2,180   (513) 327-6231

WRIGHT STATE UNIVERSITY
3640 Colonel Glenn Hwy., Dayton 45435 *Type:* Public (state) *System:* Ohio Board of Regents *Accred.:* 1968/1986 (NCA) *Calendar:* Qtr. plan *Degrees:* A, B, M, P, D, C *Prof. Accred.:* Accounting (A), Business (B,M), Clinical Lab Scientist, Clinical Psychology, Computer Science, Counseling, Engineering (bioengineering, computer, electrical, engineering physics/science, materials, mechanical), Medicine, Music, Nursing (B,M), Psychology Internship, Rehabilitation Counseling, Social Work (B), Teacher Education *CEO:* Pres. Harley E. Flack
Enroll: 12,828   (513) 873-3333

LAKE CAMPUS
7600 State Rte. 703, Celina 45822
                                   (419) 586-2365

XAVIER UNIVERSITY
3800 Victory Pkwy., Cincinnati 45207 *Type:* Private (Roman Catholic) *Accred.:* 1925/1989 (NCA) *Calendar:* Sem. plan *Degrees:* A, B, M *Prof. Accred.:* Business (B,M), Health Services Administration, Nursing (A,B), Occupational Therapy, Radiography, Social Work (B) *CEO:* Pres. James E. Hoff, S.J.
Enroll: 3,927   (513) 745-3000

YOUNGSTOWN STATE UNIVERSITY
410 Wick Ave., Youngstown 44555 *Type:* Public (state) *System:* Ohio Board of Regents *Accred.:* 1945/1988 (NCA) *Calendar:* Qtr. plan *Degrees:* A, B, M, D, C *Prof. Accred.:* Art (A), Clinical Lab Technology (A), Counseling, Dental Hygiene, Dietetics (coordinated), EMT-Paramedic, Engineering Technology (civil/construction, electrical, mechanical), Engineering (chemical, civil, electrical, environmental/sanitary, industrial, mechanical), Music, Nursing (B), Respiratory Therapy, Social Work (B), Teacher Education *CEO:* Pres. Leslie H. Cochran
Enroll: 12,833   (216) 742-3000

OKLAHOMA

BACONE COLLEGE
2299 Old Bacone Rd., Muskogee 74403-1597 *Type:* Private (Baptist) junior *Accred.:* 1965/1989 (NCA) *Calendar:* Sem. plan *Degrees:* A, C *Prof. Accred.:* Nursing (A), Radiography *CEO:* Pres. Dennis Tanner
Enroll: 576   (918) 683-4581

BARTLESVILLE WESLEYAN COLLEGE
2201 Silver Lake Rd., Bartlesville 74006 *Type:* Private (Wesleyan) liberal arts *Accred.:* 1978/1991 (NCA) *Calendar:* Sem. plan *Degrees:* A, B, C *CEO:* Pres. Paul R. Mills
Enroll: 504   (918) 333-6212

CAMERON UNIVERSITY
2800 Gore Blvd., Lawton 73505-6377 *Type:* Public (state) liberal arts and professional *System:* Oklahoma State Regents for Higher Education *Accred.:* 1973/1991 (NCA) *Calendar:* Sem. plan *Degrees:* A, B, M *Prof. Accred.:* Music, Nursing (A), Teacher Education *CEO:* Pres. Don Davis
Enroll: 5,452   (405) 581-2200

CARL ALBERT STATE COLLEGE
1507 S. McKenna, Poteau 74953-5208 *Type:* Public (state) junior *System:* Oklahoma State Regents for Higher Education *Accred.:* 1978/1993 (NCA) *Calendar:* Sem. plan *Degrees:* A, C *Prof. Accred.:* Nursing (A) *CEO:* Pres. Joe E. White
Enroll: 1,943   (918) 647-1200

CONNORS STATE COLLEGE
Rte. 1, Box 1000, Warner 74469-9700 *Type:* Public (state) junior *System:* Oklahoma State Regents for Higher Education *Accred.:* 1963/1990 (NCA) *Calendar:* Sem. plan *Degrees:* A, C *Prof. Accred.:* Nursing (A) *CEO:* Pres. Ron Garner
Enroll: 2,411   (918) 463-2931

EAST CENTRAL UNIVERSITY
Ada 74820-6899 *Type:* Public (state) liberal arts and teachers *System:* Oklahoma State Regents for Higher Education *Accred.:* 1922/1992 (NCA) *Calendar:* Sem. plan *Degrees:* B, M *Prof. Accred.:* Medical Record Administration, Nursing (B), Rehabilitation Counseling, Social Work (B), Teacher Education *CEO:* Pres. Bill S. Cole
Enroll: 3,884   (405) 332-8000

EASTERN OKLAHOMA STATE COLLEGE
1301 W. Main St., Wilburton 74578-4999 *Type:* Public (state) junior *System:* Oklahoma State Regents for Higher Education *Accred.:* 1954/1986 (NCA) *Calendar:* Sem. plan *Degrees:* A, C *Prof. Accred.:* Nursing (A) *CEO:* Pres. Bill H. Hill
Enroll: 2,209   (918) 465-2361

LANGSTON UNIVERSITY
P.O. Box 907, Langston 73050-0907 *Type:* Public (state) liberal arts and professional *System:* Oklahoma State Regents for Higher Education *Accred.:* 1948/1987 (NCA) *Calendar:* Sem. plan *Degrees:* A, B, M *Prof. Accred.:* Nursing (B), Physical Therapy, Teacher Education *CEO:* Pres. Ernest L. Holloway
Enroll: 3,958   (405) 466-2231

MID-AMERICA BIBLE COLLEGE
3500 S.W. 119th St., Oklahoma City 73170 *Type:* Private (Church of God) *Accred.:* 1968/1988 (AABC); 1985/1992 (NCA) *Calendar:* Sem. plan *Degrees:* A, B *CEO:* Pres. Forrest Robinson
Enroll: 452   (405) 691-3800

MURRAY STATE COLLEGE
1100 S. Murray, Tishomingo 73460-3130 *Type:* Public (state) junior *System:* Oklahoma State Regents for Higher Education *Accred.:* 1964/1994 (NCA) *Calendar:* Sem. plan *Degrees:* A, C *Prof. Accred.:* Nursing (A), Veterinary Technology *CEO:* Pres. Glen Pedersen
Enroll: 1,571   (405) 371-2371

NATIONAL EDUCATION CENTER—SPARTAN
SCHOOL OF AERONAUTICS
P.O. Box 582833, Tulsa 74158-2833 *Type:*
Private *Accred.:* 1969/1986 (ACCSCT)
Degrees: A *CEO:* Pres. Ross L. Alloway
(918) 836-6886

NORTHEASTERN OKLAHOMA A&M COLLEGE
200 I St. N.E., Miami 74354-6497 *Type:*
Public (state) junior *System:* Oklahoma State
Regents for Higher Education *Accred.:*
1925/1987 (NCA) *Calendar:* Sem. plan
Degrees: A, C *Prof. Accred.:* Clinical Lab
Technology (A), Nursing (A), Surgical Tech-
nology *CEO:* Pres. Jerry D. Carroll
Enroll: 2,381   (918) 542-8441

NORTHEASTERN STATE UNIVERSITY
Tahlequah 74464-7099 *Type:* Public (state)
liberal arts and teachers *System:* Oklahoma
State Regents for Higher Education *Accred.:*
1922/1992 (NCA) *Calendar:* Sem. plan
Degrees: B, M, D, C *Prof. Accred.:* Nursing
(B), Optometric Residency, Optometry,
Social Work (B), Speech-Language Pathol-
ogy (initial), Teacher Education *CEO:* Pres.
W. Roger Webb
Enroll: 7,676   (918) 456-5511

MUSKOGEE CAMPUS
P.O. Box 549, Muskogee 74402-0549
(918) 683-0641

NORTHERN OKLAHOMA COLLEGE
P.O. Box 310, Tonkawa 74653-0310 *Type:*
Public (state) junior *System:* Oklahoma State
Regents for Higher Education *Accred.:*
1948/1988 (NCA) *Calendar:* Sem. plan
Degrees: A, C *Prof. Accred.:* Nursing (A)
CEO: Pres. Joe M. Kinzer, Jr.
Enroll: 2,260   (405) 628-6200

NORTHWESTERN OKLAHOMA STATE UNIVERSITY
709 Oklahoma Blvd., Alva 73717-9848
Type: Public (state) liberal arts and teachers
System: Oklahoma State Regents for Higher
Education *Accred.:* 1922/1994 (NCA) *Cal-
endar:* Sem. plan *Degrees:* B, M, C *Prof.
Accred.:* Nursing (B), Teacher Education
CEO: Pres. Joe J. Struckle
Enroll: 1,606   (405) 327-1700

OKLAHOMA BAPTIST UNIVERSITY
500 W. University, Shawnee 74801 *Type:*
Private (Southern Baptist) liberal arts and
professional *Accred.:* 1952/1988 (NCA)
Calendar: 4-1-4 plan *Degrees:* A, B, M, C
Prof. Accred.: Music, Nursing (B), Teacher
Education *CEO:* Pres. Bob R. Agee
Enroll: 2,412   (405) 275-2850

OKLAHOMA CHRISTIAN UNIVERSITY OF SCIENCE
AND ARTS
Box 11000, Oklahoma City 73136 *Type:* Pri-
vate (Church of Christ) liberal arts *Accred.:*
1966/1986 (NCA) *Calendar:* Tri. plan
Degrees: B, M *Prof. Accred.:* Engineering
(electrical, mechanical), Music (A), Teacher
Education *CEO:* Pres. Kevin E. Jacobs
Enroll: 1,445   (405) 425-5000

CASCADE COLLEGE
9101 E. Burnside St., Portland, OR
97216-1515 *Degrees:* B
(503) 257-1365

OKLAHOMA CITY COMMUNITY COLLEGE
7777 S. May Ave., Oklahoma City 73159-
4444 *Type:* Public (district) junior *System:*
Oklahoma State Regents for Higher Educa-
tion *Accred.:* 1977/1992 (NCA) *Calendar:*
Sem. plan *Degrees:* A, C *Prof. Accred.:*
Nursing (A), Occupational Therapy Assist-
ing, Physical Therapy Assisting *CEO:* Pres.
Robert P. Todd
Enroll: 9,694   (405) 682-1611

OKLAHOMA CITY UNIVERSITY
2501 N. Blackwelder Ave., Oklahoma City
73106 *Type:* Private (United Methodist)
Accred.: 1951/1992 (NCA) *Calendar:* Sem.
plan *Degrees:* A, B, M, D *Prof. Accred.:* Law
(ABA only), Music, Nursing (B) *CEO:* Pres.
Jerald C. Walker
Enroll: 2,237   (405) 521-5000

OKLAHOMA PANHANDLE STATE UNIVERSITY
Box 430, Goodwell 73939-9728 *Type:* Pub-
lic (state) liberal arts *System:* Oklahoma
State Regents for Higher Education
Accred.: 1926/1985 (NCA) *Calendar:* Sem.
plan *Degrees:* A, B, C *CEO:* Pres. John W.
Goodwin
Enroll: 1,262   (405) 349-2611

OKLAHOMA STATE UNIVERSITY
101 Whitehurst Hall, Stillwater 74078 *Type:* Public (state) *System:* Oklahoma State University Office of the President *Accred.:* 1916/1986 (NCA) *Calendar:* Sem. plan *Degrees:* B, M, P, D, C *Prof. Accred.:* Accounting (A,C), Business (B,M), Clinical Psychology, Counseling Psychology (provisional), Dietetics (internship), Engineering Technology (civil/construction, electrical, fire protection/safety, manufacturing, mechanical), Engineering (aerospace, agricultural, architectural, chemical, civil, electrical, general, industrial, mechanical), Forestry, Home Economics, Interior Design, Journalism (B,M), Landscape Architecture (B), Marriage and Family Therapy (M), Music, Recreation and Leisure Services (B), Speech-Language Pathology, Veterinary Medicine *CEO:* Pres. James E. Halligan
Enroll: 14,281   (405) 744-5000

COLLEGE OF OSTEOPATHIC MEDICINE
1111 W. 17th St., Tulsa 74107 (state) professional *Calendar:* Sem. plan *Degrees:* P *Prof. Accred.:* Osteopathy
Enroll: 271   (918) 582-1972

OKLAHOMA CITY CAMPUS
900 N. Portland Ave., Oklahoma City 73107 (state) junior *Accred.:* 1975/1990 (NCA) *Calendar:* Sem. plan *Degrees:* A, C *Prof. Accred.:* Nursing (A)
Enroll: 4,159   (405) 947-4421

OKMULGEE CAMPUS
1801 E. Fourth St., Okmulgee 74447 (state) junior *Accred.:* 1975/1990 (NCA) *Calendar:* Tri. plan *Degrees:* A, C
Enroll: 2,188   (918) 756-6211

ORAL ROBERTS UNIVERSITY
7777 S. Lewis Ave., Tulsa 74171 *Type:* Private (interdenominational) liberal arts and professional *Accred.:* 1980/1987 (ATS); 1971/1992 (NCA) *Calendar:* Sem. plan *Degrees:* B, M, D, C *Prof. Accred.:* Engineering (general), Music, Nursing (B,M), Social Work (B) *CEO:* Pres. Richard L. Roberts
Enroll: 2,880   (918) 495-6161

PHILLIPS THEOLOGICAL SEMINARY
102 University Dr., P.O. Box 2335, University Sta., Enid 73702 *Type:* Private (Disciples of Christ) *Accred.:* 1952/1991 (ATS); 1992 (NCA) *Calendar:* Sem. plan *Degrees:* M, D *CEO:* Pres. William Tabbernee
Enroll: 215   (405) 548-2238

PHILLIPS UNIVERSITY
100 S. University Ave., Enid 73701 *Type:* Private *Accred.:* 1919/1994 (NCA) *Calendar:* Sem. plan *Degrees:* A, B, M *Prof. Accred.:* Music *CEO:* Pres. Donald Heath
Enroll: 1,606   (405) 237-4433

REDLANDS COMMUNITY COLLEGE
1300 S. Country Club Rd., El Reno 73036-5304 *Type:* Public (state) junior *System:* Oklahoma State Regents for Higher Education *Accred.:* 1978/1991 (NCA) *Calendar:* Sem. plan *Degrees:* A, C *Prof. Accred.:* Nursing (A) *CEO:* Pres. Larry F. Devane
Enroll: 2,139   (405) 262-2552

ROGERS STATE COLLEGE
Will Rogers and College Hill, Claremore 74017-2099 *Type:* Public (state) junior *System:* Oklahoma State Regents for Higher Education *Accred.:* 1950/1995 (NCA) *Calendar:* Sem. plan *Degrees:* A, C *Prof. Accred.:* Nursing (A) *CEO:* Acting Pres. Danette McNamara-Boyle
Enroll: 3,538   (918) 343-7500

ROSE STATE COLLEGE
6420 S.E. 15th St., Midwest City 73110-2799 *Type:* Public (state) junior *System:* Oklahoma State Regents for Higher Education *Accred.:* 1975/1988 (NCA) *Calendar:* Sem. plan *Degrees:* A, C *Prof. Accred.:* Clinical Lab Technology (A), Dental Assisting, Dental Hygiene, Medical Record Technology, Nursing (A), Radiography, Respiratory Therapy *CEO:* Pres. Larry Nutter
Enroll: 9,083   (405) 733-7311

ST. GREGORY'S COLLEGE
1900 W. MacArthur, Shawnee 74801 *Type:* Private (Roman Catholic) junior *Accred.:* 1969/1989 (NCA) *Calendar:* Sem. plan *Degrees:* A *CEO:* Pres. Frank Pfaff
Enroll: 268   (405) 878-5100

SEMINOLE JUNIOR COLLEGE
P.O. Box 351, Seminole 74868-0351 *Type:*
Public (state) junior *System:* Oklahoma State
Regents for Higher Education *Accred.:*
1975/1990 (NCA) *Calendar:* Tri. plan
Degrees: A, C *Prof. Accred.:* Clinical Lab
Technology (A), Nursing (A) *CEO:* Pres.
James J. Cook
Enroll: 1,598   (405) 382-9950

SOUTHEASTERN OKLAHOMA STATE UNIVERSITY
Sta. A, Durant 74701-0609 *Type:* Public
(state) liberal arts and teachers *System:* Okla-
homa State Regents for Higher Education
Accred.: 1922/1994 (NCA) *Calendar:* Sem.
plan *Degrees:* B, M, C *Prof. Accred.:* Music,
Teacher Education *CEO:* Pres. Larry
Williams
Enroll: 3,650   (405) 924-0121

SOUTHERN NAZARENE UNIVERSITY
6729 N.W. 39th Expy., Bethany 73008 *Type:*
Private (Nazarene) liberal arts *Accred.:*
1956/1990 (NCA) *Calendar:* Sem. plan
Degrees: A, B, M *Prof. Accred.:* Nursing
(B), Teacher Education *CEO:* Pres. Loren P.
Gresham, Ph.D.
Enroll: 1,535   (405) 789-6400

SOUTHWESTERN COLLEGE OF CHRISTIAN
MINISTRIES
7210 N.W. 39th Expy., P.O. Box 340,
Bethany 73008-0340 *Type:* Private (Pente-
costal Holiness) liberal arts *Accred.:*
1973/1991 (NCA) *Calendar:* Sem. plan
Degrees: A, B, M *CEO:* Pres. Ronald Q.
Moore
Enroll: 183   (405) 789-7661

SOUTHWESTERN OKLAHOMA STATE UNIVERSITY
100 Campus Dr., Weatherford 73096-3098
Type: Public (state) liberal arts and profes-
sional *System:* Oklahoma State Regents for
Higher Education *Accred.:* 1922/1991
(NCA) *Calendar:* Sem. plan *Degrees:* A, B,
M, C *Prof. Accred.:* Medical Record Admin-
istration, Music, Nursing (B), Radiography,
Teacher Education *CEO:* Pres. Joe Anna
Hibler
Enroll: 4,724   (405) 772-6611

SAYRE CAMPUS
409 E. Mississippi, Sayre 73662 *Prof.
Accred.:* Medical Laboratory Technology,
Physical Therapy Assisting
                                   (405) 928-5533

TULSA JUNIOR COLLEGE
6111 E. Skelly Dr., Rm. 200, Tulsa 74135-
6198 *Type:* Public (state) junior *System:*
Oklahoma State Regents for Higher Education *Accred.:* 1974/1989 (NCA) *Calendar:*
Sem. plan *Degrees:* A, C *Prof. Accred.:* Clinical Lab Technology (A), Dental Hygiene,
Medical Assisting (AMA), Nursing (A),
Occupational Therapy Assisting, Physical
Therapy Assisting, Radiography, Respiratory Therapy, Respiratory Therapy Technology *CEO:* Pres. Dean P. Van Trease
Enroll: 21,005   (918) 595-7000

UNIVERSITY OF CENTRAL OKLAHOMA
100 N. University Dr., Edmond 73060-0170
Type: Public (state) liberal arts and teachers
System: Oklahoma State Regents for Higher
Education *Accred.:* 1921/1993 (NCA) *Cal-
endar:* Sem. plan *Degrees:* B, M, C *Prof.
Accred.:* Dietetics (internship), Funeral Ser-
vice Education (Mortuary Science), Nursing
(B), Speech-Language Pathology, Teacher
Education *CEO:* Pres. George Nigh
Enroll: 12,376   (405) 341-2980

UNIVERSITY OF OKLAHOMA
660 Parrington Oval, Ste. 110, Norman
73019-0390 *Type:* Public (state) *System:*
University of Oklahoma President's Office
Accred.: 1913/1992 (NCA) *Calendar:* Sem.
plan *Degrees:* B, M, D, C *Prof. Accred.:*
Accounting (A,C), Business (B,M), Construction Education (B), Counseling Psychology, Engineering (aerospace, chemical,
civil, electrical, engineering physics/science,
environmental/sanitary, general, industrial,
mechanical, petroleum), Health Services
Administration, Interior Design, Journalism
(B,M), Landscape Architecture, Law, Librar-
ianship, Music, Planning (M), Social Work
(B,M), Teacher Education *CEO:* Pres. David
L. Boren
Enroll: 16,456   (405) 325-0311

UNIVERSITY OF OKLAHOMA HEALTH SCIENCES
CENTER
P.O. Box 26901, Oklahoma City 73126-0901
Type: Public (state) *System:* University of
Oklahoma President's Office *Calendar:*
Sem. plan *Degrees:* A, B, M, P, D *Prof.
Accred.:* Audiology, Clinical Lab Scientist,
Combined Prosthodontics, Cytotechnology,
Dental Hygiene, Dentistry, Diagnostic Med-
ical Sonography, Dietetics (coordinated),
Dietetics (internship), General Dentistry,
Medicine, Nuclear Medicine Technology,
Nursing (B,M), Occupational Therapy, Oral
and Maxillofacial Surgery, Orthodontics,
Periodontics, Physical Therapy, Physician
Assisting/Surgeon Assisting, Psychology
Internship, Radiation Therapy Technology,
Radiography, Speech-Language Pathology
CEO: Interim Provost Joseph Ferretti
Enroll: 2,313   (405) 271-4000

UNIVERSITY OF SCIENCE AND ARTS OF
OKLAHOMA
P.O. Box 82345, Chickasha 73018-0001
Type: Public (state) liberal arts and teachers
System: Oklahoma State Regents for Higher
Education *Accred.:* 1920/1989 (NCA) *Cal-
endar:* Tri. plan *Degrees:* B *Prof. Accred.:*
Music, Teacher Education *CEO:* Pres. Roy
Troutt
Enroll: 1,687   (405) 224-3140

UNIVERSITY OF TULSA
600 S. College Ave., Tulsa 74104 *Type:* Private (United Presbyterian) *Accred.:* 1929/
1988 (NCA) *Calendar:* 4-1-4 plan *Degrees:*
B, M, D *Prof. Accred.:* Business (B,M),
Clinical Psychology (provisional), Computer
Science, Engineering (chemical, electrical,
engineering physics/science, mechanical,
petroleum), Law, Music, Nursing (B),
Speech-Language Pathology, Teacher Education *CEO:* Pres. Robert H. Donaldson
Enroll: 3,168   (918) 631-2000

WESTERN OKLAHOMA STATE COLLEGE
2801 N. Main St., Altus 73521-1397 *Type:*
Public (state) junior *System:* Oklahoma State
Regents for Higher Education *Accred.:*
1976/1988 (NCA) *Calendar:* Sem. plan
Degrees: A, C *CEO:* Pres. M. Ray Brown
Enroll: 1,703   (405) 477-2000

OREGON

BASSIST COLLEGE
2000 S.W. Fifth Ave., Portland 97201 *Type:* Private technical *Accred.:* 1977/1991 (NASC) *Calendar:* Qtr. plan *Degrees:* A, B *CEO:* Pres. Donald H. Bassist
Enroll: 134   (503) 228-6528

BLUE MOUNTAIN COMMUNITY COLLEGE
P.O. Box 100, Pendleton 97801 *Type:* Public (district) junior *System:* Oregon Office of Community College Services *Accred.:* 1968/1994 (NASC) *Calendar:* Qtr. plan *Degrees:* A *Prof. Accred.:* Dental Assisting, Engineering Technology (electrical) *CEO:* Pres. Ronald L. Daniels
Enroll: 5,117   (541) 276-1260

CENTRAL OREGON COMMUNITY COLLEGE
Bend 97701-5998 *Type:* Public (district) junior *System:* Oregon Office of Community College Services *Accred.:* 1966/1992 (NASC) *Calendar:* Qtr. plan *Degrees:* A *Prof. Accred.:* Medical Record Technology *CEO:* Pres. Robert L. Barber
Enroll: 3,137   (541) 383-7700

CHEMEKETA COMMUNITY COLLEGE
P.O. Box 14007, Salem 97309 *Type:* Public (district) junior *System:* Oregon Office of Community College Services *Accred.:* 1972/1992 (NASC) *Calendar:* Qtr. plan *Degrees:* A *Prof. Accred.:* Dental Assisting, Medical Assisting (AMA), Nursing (A) *CEO:* Pres. Gerard J. Berger
Enroll: 18,054   (503) 399-5000

CLACKAMAS COMMUNITY COLLEGE
19600 S. Molalla Ave., Oregon City 97045 *Type:* Public (district) junior *System:* Oregon Office of Community College Services *Accred.:* 1971/1991 (NASC) *Calendar:* Qtr. plan *Degrees:* A *Prof. Accred.:* Nursing (A) *CEO:* Pres. John S. Keyser
Enroll: 12,339   (503) 657-6958

CLATSOP COMMUNITY COLLEGE
1653 Jerome Ave., Astoria 97103 *Type:* Public (district) junior *System:* Oregon Office of Community College Services *Accred.:* 1965/

1993 (NASC) *Calendar:* Qtr. plan *Degrees:* A *CEO:* Pres. John W. Wubben
Enroll: 5,790   (503) 325-0910

CONCORDIA UNIVERSITY
2811 N.E. Holman St., Portland 97211 *Type:* Private (Lutheran) liberal arts *Accred.:* 1962/1993 (NASC) *Calendar:* Qtr. plan *Degrees:* A, B *CEO:* Pres. Charles E. Schlimpert
Enroll: 1,095   (503) 288-9371

EASTERN OREGON STATE COLLEGE
La Grande 97850 *Type:* Public (state) liberal arts and teachers *System:* Oregon State System of Higher Education *Accred.:* 1931/1993 (NASC) *Calendar:* Qtr. plan *Degrees:* A, B, M *Prof. Accred.:* Teacher Education *CEO:* Pres. David E. Gilbert
Enroll: 1,917   (541) 962-3512

EUGENE BIBLE COLLEGE
2155 Bailey Hill Rd., Eugene 97405 *Type:* Private (Open Bible Standard Churches) *Accred.:* 1983/1994 (AABC) *Calendar:* Qtr. plan *Degrees:* B, C *CEO:* Pres. Jeffrey Farmer
FTE Enroll: 192   (503) 485-1780

GEORGE FOX COLLEGE
Newberg 97132 *Type:* Private liberal arts *Accred.:* 1959/1994 (NASC) *Calendar:* Sem. plan *Degrees:* B, M, D *Prof. Accred.:* Music *CEO:* Pres. Edward F. Stevens
Enroll: 1,658   (503) 538-8383

ITT TECHNICAL INSTITUTE
6035 N.E. 78th Ct., Portland 97218-2854 *Type:* Private *Accred.:* 1973/1988 (ACCSCT) *Degrees:* A, B *CEO:* Dir. James Horner
                    (503) 255-6500

LANE COMMUNITY COLLEGE
4000 E. 30th Ave., Eugene 97405 *Type:* Public (district) junior *System:* Oregon Office of Community College Services *Accred.:* 1968/1994 (NASC) *Calendar:* Qtr. plan *Degrees:* A *Prof. Accred.:* Dental Assisting,

Dental Hygiene, Nursing (A), Respiratory Therapy *CEO:* Pres. Jerry Moskus
Enroll: 9,917   (541) 747-4501

LEWIS AND CLARK COLLEGE
0615 S.W. Palatine Hill Rd., Portland 97219 *Type:* Private (United Presbyterian) liberal arts *Accred.:* 1943/1993 (NASC) *Calendar:* Qtr. plan *Degrees:* B, M *Prof. Accred.:* Law, Music *CEO:* Pres. Michael J. Mooney
Enroll: 3,234   (503) 768-7680

LINFIELD COLLEGE
McMinnville 97128 *Type:* Private (Baptist) liberal arts *Accred.:* 1928/1993 (NASC) *Calendar:* 4-1-4 plan *Degrees:* B, M *Prof. Accred.:* Music, Nursing (B) *CEO:* Pres. Vivian A. Bull
Enroll: 2,876   (503) 434-2408

LINN-BENTON COMMUNITY COLLEGE
Albany 97321 *Type:* Public (district) junior *System:* Oregon Office of Community College Services *Accred.:* 1972/1992 (NASC) *Calendar:* Qtr. plan *Degrees:* A *Prof. Accred.:* Dental Assisting, Nursing (A) *CEO:* Pres. Jon Carnahan
Enroll: 5,738   (541) 917-4999

MARYLHURST COLLEGE
P.O. Box 261, Marylhurst 97036 *Type:* Private (Roman Catholic) liberal arts *Accred.:* 1977/1991 (NASC) *Calendar:* Qtr. plan *Degrees:* B, M *Prof. Accred.:* Music *CEO:* Pres. Nancy A. Wilgenbusch
Enroll: 1,305   (503) 636-8141

MOUNT ANGEL SEMINARY
St. Benedict 97373 *Type:* Private (Roman Catholic) *Accred.:* 1978/1985 (ATS); 1929/1992 (NASC) *Calendar:* Sem. plan *Degrees:* B, M *CEO:* Pres. Patrick S. Brennan
Enroll: 150   (503) 845-3951

MOUNT HOOD COMMUNITY COLLEGE
26000 S.E. Stark St., Gresham 97030 *Type:* Public (district) junior *System:* Oregon Office of Community College Services *Accred.:* 1972/1992 (NASC) *Calendar:* Qtr. plan *Degrees:* A *Prof. Accred.:* Dental Hygiene, Funeral Service Education (Mortuary Science), Medical Assisting (AMA), Nursing (A), Occupational Therapy Assisting, Physical Therapy Assisting, Respiratory Therapy, Surgical Technology *CEO:* Pres. Paul E. Kreider
Enroll: 12,844   (503) 667-6422

MULTNOMAH BIBLE COLLEGE
8435 N.E. Glisan St., Portland 97220 *Type:* Private (interdenominational) *Accred.:* 1953/1994 (AABC); 1993 (ATS candidate) *Calendar:* Sem. plan *Degrees:* A, B, C *CEO:* Pres. Joseph C. Aldrich
Enroll: 189   (503) 255-0332

NORTHWEST CHRISTIAN COLLEGE
Eugene 97401 *Type:* Private (Disciples of Christ) liberal arts *Accred.:* 1962/1994 (NASC) *Calendar:* Qtr. plan *Degrees:* A, B, M *CEO:* Pres. James E. Womack
Enroll: 379   (541) 343-1641

OREGON COLLEGE OF ORIENTAL MEDICINE
10525 Cherry Blossom Dr., Portland 97216 *Type:* Private professional *Calendar:* Qtr. plan *Degrees:* M *Prof. Accred.:* Acupuncture *CEO:* Pres. Elizabeth Goldblatt
FTE Enroll: 110   (503) 253-3443

OREGON GRADUATE INSTITUTE OF SCIENCE AND TECHNOLOGY
P.O. Box 91000, 20000 N.W. Walker Rd., Beaverton 97006 *Type:* Private graduate only *Accred.:* 1973/1994 (NASC) *Calendar:* Qtr. plan *Degrees:* M, D *CEO:* Pres. Paul Bragdon
Enroll: 651   (503) 690-1020

OREGON HEALTH SCIENCES UNIVERSITY
3181 S.W. Sam Jackson Park Rd., Portland 97201 *Type:* Public (state) professional *System:* Oregon State System of Higher Education *Accred.:* 1980/1995 (NASC) *Calendar:* Qtr. plan *Degrees:* A, B, M, D *Prof. Accred.:* Clinical Lab Scientist, Dental Hygiene, Dentistry, Dietetics (internship), EMT-Paramedic, Endodontics, Medicine, Nursing (B,M), Oral and Maxillofacial Surgery, Orthodontics, Pediatric Dentistry, Periodontics, Psychology

Internship, Radiation Therapy Technology
CEO: Pres. Peter O. Kohler, M.D.
Enroll: 1,757 (503) 494-8252

OREGON INSTITUTE OF TECHNOLOGY
Klamath Falls 97601-8801 *Type:* Public
(state) technological *System:* Oregon State
System of Higher Education *Accred.:*
1962/1992 (NASC) *Calendar:* Qtr. plan
Degrees: A, B *Prof. Accred.:* Dental
Hygiene, Engineering Technology (civil/
construction, computer, electrical, manufac-
turing, mechanical), Nursing (B) *CEO:* Pres.
Lawrence J. Wolf
Enroll: 2,478 (541) 885-1103

OREGON POLYTECHNIC INSTITUTE
900 S.E. Sandy Blvd., Portland 97214 *Type:*
Private *Accred.:* 1977/1986 (ACCSCT) *Calendar:* Qtr. plan *Degrees:* A *CEO:* Dir.
Mardell Lanfranco
(503) 234-9333

OREGON STATE UNIVERSITY
Corvallis 97331 *Type:* Public (state) *System:*
Oregon State System of Higher Education
Accred.: 1924/1995 (NASC) *Calendar:* Qtr.
plan *Degrees:* B, M, D *Prof. Accred.:*
Accounting (A), Athletic Training, Business
(B,M), Construction Education (B), Coun-
seling, Engineering (chemical, civil, com-
puter, electrical, industrial, manufacturing,
mechanical, nuclear), Forestry, Health Ser-
vices Administration, Home Economics,
Teacher Education *CEO:* Pres. Paul G.
Risser
Enroll: 14,323 (541) 737-2565

PACIFIC NORTHWEST COLLEGE OF ART
1219 S.W. Park Ave., Portland 97205 *Type:*
Private professional *Accred.:* 1961/1993
(NASC) *Calendar:* Sem. plan *Degrees:* B
Prof. Accred.: Art *CEO:* Dir./CEO Sally C.
Lawrence
Enroll: 269 (503) 226-4391

PACIFIC UNIVERSITY
2043 College Way, Forest Grove 97116
Type: Private (United Church of Christ)
Accred.: 1929/1993 (NASC) *Calendar:*
Sem. plan *Degrees:* B, M, D *Prof. Accred.:*

Clinical Psychology, Music, Occupational
Therapy, Optometry, Physical Therapy
CEO: Pres. Faith Gabelnick
Enroll: 1,840 (503) 357-6151

PORTLAND COMMUNITY COLLEGE
P.O. Box 19000, Portland 97219-0990 *Type:*
Public (district) junior *System:* Oregon Office
of Community College Services *Accred.:*
1970/1995 (NASC) *Calendar:* Qtr. plan
Degrees: A *Prof. Accred.:* Clinical Lab Tech-
nology (A), Dental Assisting, Dental
Hygiene, Dental Laboratory Technology,
Engineering Technology (electrical), Medical
Assisting (AMA), Medical Record Technol-
ogy, Nursing (A), Radiography, Veterinary
Technology *CEO:* Pres. Daniel F. Moriarty
Enroll: 38,004 (503) 244-6111

PORTLAND STATE UNIVERSITY
P.O. Box 751, Portland 97207 *Type:* Public
(state) *System:* Oregon State System of
Higher Education *Accred.:* 1955/1995
(NASC) *Calendar:* Qtr. plan *Degrees:* B, M,
D *Prof. Accred.:* Accounting (A), Audiology,
Business (B,M), Computer Science, Coun-
seling, Engineering (civil, electrical,
mechanical), Music, Planning (M), Public
Administration, Rehabilitation Counseling,
Social Work (M), Speech-Language Pathol-
ogy, Teacher Education *CEO:* Pres. Judith A.
Ramaley
Enroll: 15,818 (503) 725-4419

REED COLLEGE
3203 S.E. Woodstock Blvd., Portland 97202-
8199 *Type:* Private liberal arts *Accred.:*
1920/1994 (NASC) *Calendar:* Sem. plan
Degrees: B, M *CEO:* Pres. Steven S. Koblik
Enroll: 1,279 (503) 771-1112

ROGUE COMMUNITY COLLEGE
3345 Redwood Hwy., Grants Pass 97527
Type: Public (district) junior *System:* Oregon
Office of Community College Services
Accred.: 1976/1991 (NASC) *Calendar:* Qtr.
plan *Degrees:* A *Prof. Accred.:* Respiratory
Therapy, Respiratory Therapy Technology
CEO: Pres. Harvey Bennett
Enroll: 5,370 (541) 479-5541

SOUTHERN OREGON STATE COLLEGE
Ashland 97520 *Type:* Public (state) liberal arts and teachers *System:* Oregon State System of Higher Education *Accred.:* 1928/1995 (NASC) *Calendar:* Qtr. plan *Degrees:* B, M *Prof. Accred.:* Music, Nursing (B), Teacher Education *CEO:* Pres. Stephen J. Reno
Enroll: 4,554   (541) 552-6111

SOUTHWESTERN OREGON COMMUNITY COLLEGE
1988 Newmark, Coos Bay 97420 *Type:* Public (district) junior *System:* Oregon Office of Community College Services *Accred.:* 1966/1994 (NASC) *Calendar:* Qtr. plan *Degrees:* A *CEO:* Pres. Stephen Kridelbaugh
Enroll: 4,570   (541) 888-2525

TREASURE VALLEY COMMUNITY COLLEGE
Ontario 97914 *Type:* Public (district) junior *System:* Oregon Office of Community College Services *Accred.:* 1966/1995 (NASC) *Calendar:* Qtr. plan *Degrees:* A *CEO:* Pres. Berton Glandon
Enroll: 3,084   (541) 889-6493

UMPQUA COMMUNITY COLLEGE
Roseburg 97470 *Type:* Public (district) junior *System:* Oregon Office of Community College Services *Accred.:* 1970/1995 (NASC) *Calendar:* Qtr. plan *Degrees:* A *Prof. Accred.:* Nursing (A) *CEO:* Pres. James M. Kraby
Enroll: 6,885   (541) 440-4600

UNIVERSITY OF OREGON
Eugene 97403-1226 *Type:* Public (state) *System:* Oregon State System of Higher Education *Accred.:* 1918/1992 (NASC) *Calendar:* Qtr. plan *Degrees:* B, M, D *Prof. Accred.:* Accounting (Type A), Business (B,M), Clinical Psychology, Counseling, Counseling Psychology, Interior Design, Journalism (B,M), Landscape Architecture (B), Law, Music, Planning (M), Psychology Internship, Public Administration, Speech-Language Pathology *CEO:* Pres. David B. Frohnmayer
Enroll: 16,681   (541) 346-3036

UNIVERSITY OF PORTLAND
5000 N. Willamette Blvd., Portland 97203 *Type:* Private (Roman Catholic) *Accred.:*
1931/1995 (NASC) *Calendar:* Sem. plan *Degrees:* B, M *Prof. Accred.:* Business (B,M), Engineering (civil, electrical, mechanical), Nursing (B,M) *CEO:* Pres. David T. Tyson, CSC
Enroll: 2,600   (503) 283-7205

WARNER PACIFIC COLLEGE
2219 S.E. 68th Ave., Portland 97215 *Type:* Private (Church of God) liberal arts *Accred.:* 1961/1990 (NASC probational) *Calendar:* Sem. plan *Degrees:* A, B, M *CEO:* Pres. Marshall K. Christensen
Enroll: 692   (503) 775-4366

WESTERN BAPTIST COLLEGE
5000 Deer Park Dr., S.E., Salem 97301-9330 *Type:* Private (General Association of Regular Baptist Churches) *Accred.:* 1959/1991 (AABC); 1971/1995 (NASC) *Calendar:* Sem. plan *Degrees:* A, B, C *CEO:* Pres. David F. Miller
Enroll: 579   (503) 375-7500

WESTERN BUSINESS COLLEGE
425 S.W. Washington St., Portland 97204 *Type:* Private business *Accred.:* 1969/1997 (ACICS) *Calendar:* Qtr. plan *Degrees:* A, C *CEO:* Dir. Randy Rogers
                                   (503) 222-3225

VANCOUVER CAMPUS
6625 E. Mill Plain Blvd., Vancouver, WA 98661 *Accred.:* 1987 (ACICS)
                                   (360) 694-3225

WESTERN (CONSERVATIVE BAPTIST) SEMINARY
5511 S.E. Hawthorne Blvd., Portland 97215 *Type:* Private (Conservative Baptist) graduate only *Accred.:* 1969/1993 (NASC) *Calendar:* Sem. plan *Degrees:* M, D *CEO:* Pres. Ronald E. Hawkins
Enroll: 448   (503) 233-8561

WESTERN EVANGELICAL SEMINARY
P.O. Box 23939, Portland 97281-3939 *Type:* Private (interdenominational) graduate only *Accred.:* 1974/1994 (ATS); 1976/1994 (NASC) *Calendar:* Qtr. plan *Degrees:* M *CEO:* Pres. David C. Le Shana
Enroll: 213   (503) 639-0559

WESTERN OREGON STATE COLLEGE
345 N. Monmouth Ave., Monmouth 97361 *Type:* Public (state) *System:* Oregon State System of Higher Education *Accred.:* 1924/1993 (NASC) *Calendar:* Qtr. plan *Degrees:* A, B, M *Prof. Accred.:* Music, Rehabilitation Counseling, Teacher Education *CEO:* Pres. Betty J. Youngblood
Enroll: 4,008   (503) 838-8215

WESTERN STATES CHIROPRACTIC COLLEGE
2900 N.E. 132nd Ave., Portland 97230 *Type:* Private professional *Accred.:* 1986/1990

(NASC) *Calendar:* Qtr. plan *Degrees:* B, D *Prof. Accred.:* Chiropractic Education *CEO:* Pres. William H. Dallas
Enroll: 427   (503) 256-3180

WILLAMETTE UNIVERSITY
Salem 97301 *Type:* Private (United Methodist) *Accred.:* 1924/1991 (NASC) *Calendar:* Sem. plan *Degrees:* B, M *Prof. Accred.:* Law, Music, Public Administration *CEO:* Pres. Jerry E. Hudson
Enroll: 2,464   (503) 370-6300

PENNSYLVANIA

ACADEMY OF THE NEW CHURCH
P.O. Box 711, Bryn Athyn 19009 *Type:* Private (Church of New Jersualem) *Accred.:* 1952/1993 (MSA) *Calendar:* Tri. plan *Degrees:* A, B, P *CEO:* Pres. Daniel W. Goodenough
Enroll: 130   (215) 947-4200

ALBRIGHT COLLEGE
P.O. Box 15234, Reading 19612-5234 *Type:* Private (United Methodist) liberal arts *Accred.:* 1926/1995 (MSA) *Calendar:* 4-1-4 plan *Degrees:* B *Prof. Accred.:* Social Work (B) *CEO:* Pres. Ellen S. Hurwitz
Enroll: 1,218   (610) 921-2381

ALLEGHENY COLLEGE
520 N. Main St., Meadville 16335 *Type:* Private liberal arts *Accred.:* 1921/1994 (MSA) *Calendar:* Tri. plan *Degrees:* B, C *CEO:* Pres. Daniel F. Sullivan
Enroll: 1,854   (814) 332-3100

ALLENTOWN COLLEGE OF ST. FRANCIS DE SALES
Station Ave., Center Valley 18034 *Type:* Private (Roman Catholic) liberal arts *Accred.:* 1970/1993 (MSA) *Calendar:* Sem. plan *Degrees:* B, M *Prof. Accred.:* Nursing (B,M) *CEO:* Pres. Daniel G. Gambet, O.S.F.S.
Enroll: 2,424   (610) 282-1100

ALTOONA SCHOOL OF COMMERCE
508 58th St., Altoona 16602 *Type:* Private business *Accred.:* 1971/1995 (ACICS) *Calendar:* Qtr. plan *Degrees:* A *CEO:* Dir. J. William Laughlin
                                 (814) 944-6134

ALVERNIA COLLEGE
400 St. Bernadine St., Reading 19607 *Type:* Private (Roman Catholic) liberal arts *Accred.:* 1967/1995 (MSA) *Calendar:* Sem. plan *Degrees:* A, B *Prof. Accred.:* Nursing (A), Physical Therapy Assisting *CEO:* Pres. Daniel N. DeLucca
Enroll: 1,296   (610) 796-8200

THE AMERICAN COLLEGE
270 Bryn Mawr Ave., Bryn Mawr 19010 *Type:* Private professional *Accred.:* 1978/1993 (MSA) *Calendar:* Sem. plan *Degrees:* M, C *CEO:* Pres. Samuel H. Weese
Enroll: 17,423   (215) 526-1000

AMERICAN INSTITUTE OF DESIGN
1616 Orthodox St., Philadelphia 19124-3706 *Type:* Private *Accred.:* 1972/1987 (ACCSCT) *Calendar:* Qtr. plan *Degrees:* A, C *CEO:* Pres. Peter Klein
                                 (215) 288-8200

ANTONELLI INSTITUTE
2910 Jolly Rd., Plymouth Meeting 19462-0570 *Type:* Private *Accred.:* 1975/1990 (ACCSCT) *Calendar:* Sem. plan *Degrees:* A *CEO:* Dir. Thomas Treacy
                                 (215) 275-3040

ART INSTITUTE OF PHILADELPHIA
1622 Chestnut St., Philadelphia 19103-5198 *Type:* Private *Accred.:* 1973/1988 (ACCSCT) *Calendar:* Qtr. plan *Degrees:* A *CEO:* Pres. Robert P. Gioella
                                 (215) 567-7080

ART INSTITUTE OF PITTSBURGH
526 Penn Ave., Pittsburgh 15222-3269 *Type:* Private *Accred.:* 1970/1990 (ACCSCT) *Calendar:* Qtr. plan *Degrees:* A *CEO:* Pres. Saundra Van Dyke
                                 (412) 263-6600

BAPTIST BIBLE COLLEGE OF PENNSYLVANIA
538 Venard Rd., Clarks Summit 18411 *Type:* Private (Baptist) *Accred.:* 1968/1984 (AABC); 1984/1995 (MSA) *Calendar:* Sem. plan *Degrees:* A, B, C *CEO:* Pres. Milo Thompson
FTE Enroll: 529   (717) 586-2400

BEAVER COLLEGE
450 South Easton Rd., Glenside 19038-3295 *Type:* Private (United Presbyterian) *Accred.:* 1946/1994 (MSA) *Calendar:* 4-1-4 plan *Degrees:* A, B, M, P, C *Prof. Accred.:*

Art, Physical Therapy *CEO:* Pres. Bette E. Landman
Enroll: 2,641   (215) 572-2900

BEREAN INSTITUTE
1901 W. Girard Ave., Philadelphia 19130-1599 *Type:* Private business *Accred.:* 1974/1990 (ACCSCT); 1974/1995 (ACICS) *Calendar:* Sem. plan *Degrees:* A *CEO:* Pres. Norman K. Spencer
                                   (215) 763-4833

BIBLICAL THEOLOGICAL SEMINARY
200 N. Main St., Hatfield 19440 *Type:* Private (interdenominational) professional *Accred.:* 1994 (ATS candidate); 1990 (MSA) *Calendar:* Sem. plan *Degrees:* M, P, C *CEO:* Pres. David G. Dunbar
Enroll: 252   (215) 368-5000

BLOOMSBURG UNIVERSITY OF PENNSYLVANIA
400 East 2nd St., Bloomsburg 17815 *Type:* Public (state) *System:* Pennsylvania State System of Higher Education *Accred.:* 1950/1994 (MSA) *Calendar:* Sem. plan *Degrees:* A, B, M, C *Prof. Accred.:* Audiology, Nursing (B,M), Social Work (B), Speech-Language Pathology, Teacher Education *CEO:* Pres. Jessica S. Kozloff
Enroll: 7,277   (717) 389-4000

BRADFORD SCHOOL
707 Grant St., Gulf Tower, Pittsburgh 15219 *Type:* Private business *Accred.:* 1970/1988 (ACICS) *Degrees:* A, C *Prof. Accred.:* Medical Assisting (AMA) *CEO:* Dir. Vincent S. Graziano
                                   (412) 391-6710

BRADLEY ACADEMY FOR THE VISUAL ARTS
625 E. Philadelphia St., York 17403-1625 *Type:* Private *Accred.:* 1983/1988 (ACCSCT) *Calendar:* Sem. plan *Degrees:* A *CEO:* Dir. Loren H. Kroh
                                   (717) 848-1447

BRYN MAWR COLLEGE
101 N. Merion Ave., Bryn Mawr 19010-2899 *Type:* Private liberal arts for women *Accred.:* 1921/1993 (MSA) *Calendar:* Sem. plan *Degrees:* B, M, D, C *Prof. Accred.:*

Social Work (M) *CEO:* Pres. Mary Patterson McPherson
Enroll: 1,778   (610) 526-5000

BUCKNELL UNIVERSITY
Lewisburg 17837-2086 *Type:* Private liberal arts *Accred.:* 1921/1994 (MSA) *Calendar:* 4-1-4 plan *Degrees:* B, M *Prof. Accred.:* Computer Science, Engineering (chemical, civil, electrical, mechanical), Music *CEO:* Pres. William D. Adams
Enroll: 3,678   (717) 523-1271

BUCKS COUNTY COMMUNITY COLLEGE
Swamp Rd., Newtown 18940 *Type:* Public (local/state) junior *Accred.:* 1968/1992 (MSA) *Calendar:* Sem. plan *Degrees:* A, C *Prof. Accred.:* Art, Music (A), Nursing (A) *CEO:* Pres. James J. Linksz
Enroll: 10,354   (215) 968-8000

BUSINESS INSTITUTE OF PENNSYLVANIA
335 Boyd Dr., Sharon 16146 *Type:* Private business *Accred.:* 1977/1986 (ACICS) *Degrees:* A *CEO:* Dir. Patricia McMahon
                                   (412) 983-0700

MEADVILLE CAMPUS
628 Arch St., Ste B105, Meadville 16335 *Accred.:* 1993 (ACICS)
                                   (814) 724-0700

PULASKI CAMPUS
Rd. 1 School House Rd., Pulaski 16143 *Accred.:* 1985 (ACICS)
                                   (412) 964-0700

BUTLER COUNTY COMMUNITY COLLEGE
College Dr., Oak Hills, P.O. Box 1203, Butler 16003-1203 *Type:* Public (local/state) junior *Accred.:* 1971/1992 (MSA) *Calendar:* Sem. plan *Degrees:* A, C *Prof. Accred.:* Physical Therapy Assisting *CEO:* Pres. Fred F. Bartok
Enroll: 3,045   (412) 287-8711

CABRINI COLLEGE
610 King of Prussia Rd., Radnor 19087-3699 *Type:* Private (Roman Catholic) liberal arts for women *Accred.:* 1965/1995 (MSA)

Calendar: Sem. plan *Degrees:* B, M *CEO:* Pres./CEO Antoinette Iadarola
Enroll: 2,021　　　　　(610) 902-8100

CALIFORNIA UNIVERSITY OF PENNSYLVANIA
250 University Ave., California 15419-1934 *Type:* Public (state) *System:* Pennsylvania State System of Higher Education *Accred.:* 1951/1990 (MSA) *Calendar:* Sem. plan *Degrees:* A, B, M *Prof. Accred.:* Nurse Anesthesia Education, Nursing (B), Social Work (B), Speech-Language Pathology, Teacher Education *CEO:* Pres. Angelo Armenti, Jr.
Enroll: 6,215　　　　　(412) 938-4000

CAMBRIA-ROWE BUSINESS COLLEGE
221 Central Ave., Johnstown 15902 *Type:* Private business *Accred.:* 1959/1994 (ACICS) *Calendar:* Qtr. plan *Degrees:* A *CEO:* Pres. Bill Coward
　　　　　(814) 536-5168

INDIANA CAMPUS
422 S. 13th St., Indiana 15701 *Accred.:* 1993 (ACICS)
　　　　　(412) 463-0222

CARLOW COLLEGE
3333 Fifth Ave., Pittsburgh 15213-3165 *Type:* Private (Roman Catholic) liberal arts for women *Accred.:* 1935/1991 (MSA) *Calendar:* Sem. plan *Degrees:* B, M, C *Prof. Accred.:* Nursing (B) *CEO:* Pres. Grace Ann Geibel, R.S.M.
Enroll: 2,084　　　　　(412) 578-6000

CARNEGIE MELLON UNIVERSITY
5000 Forbes Ave., Pittsburgh 15213 *Type:* Private non-profit *Accred.:* 1921/1993 (MSA) *Calendar:* Sem. plan *Degrees:* B, M, D *Prof. Accred.:* Art, Business (B,M), Engineering (chemical, civil, computer, electrical, general, mechanical), Music *CEO:* Pres. Robert Mehrabian
Enroll: 7,141　　　　　(412) 268-2000

CEDAR CREST COLLEGE
100 College Dr., Allentown 18104 *Type:* Private (United Church of Christ) liberal arts for women *Accred.:* 1944/1993 (MSA) *Calendar:* Sem. plan *Degrees:* B *Prof. Accred.:*

Nuclear Medicine Technology, Nursing (B), Social Work (B) *CEO:* Pres. Dorothy Gulbenkian Blaney
Enroll: 1,625　　　　　(610) 437-4471

CENTRAL PENNSYLVANIA BUSINESS SCHOOL
College Hill Rd., Summerdale 17093-0309 *Type:* Private *Accred.:* 1977/1993 (MSA) *Calendar:* Tri. plan *Degrees:* A *Prof. Accred.:* Medical Assisting (AMA), Physical Therapy Assisting *CEO:* Pres. Todd A. Milano
Enroll: 577　　　　　(717) 732-0702

CHATHAM COLLEGE
Woodland Rd., Pittsburgh 15232 *Type:* Private liberal arts for women *Accred.:* 1924/1993 (MSA) *Calendar:* 4-1-4 plan *Degrees:* B, M *Prof. Accred.:* Occupational Therapy, Physical Therapy *CEO:* Pres. Esther L. Barazzone
Enroll: 704　　　　　(412) 365-1100

CHESTNUT HILL COLLEGE
Germantown and Northwestern Aves., Philadelphia 19118-2695 *Type:* Private (Roman Catholic) liberal arts for women *Accred.:* 1930/1992 (MSA) *Calendar:* Sem. plan *Degrees:* A, B, M, C *CEO:* Pres. Carol Jean Vale, Ph.D.
Enroll: 1,196　　　　　(215) 248-7000

CHEYNEY UNIVERSITY OF PENNSYLVANIA
Cheyney and Creek Rds., Cheyney 19319 *Type:* Public (state) *System:* Pennsylvania State System of Higher Education *Accred.:* 1951/1991 (MSA) *Calendar:* Sem. plan *Degrees:* A, B, M *Prof. Accred.:* Teacher Education *CEO:* Interim Pres. Donald L. Mullett
Enroll: 1,357　　　　　(610) 399-2000

CHI INSTITUTE
520 Street Rd., Southampton 18966-3787 *Type:* Private *Accred.:* 1985/1990 (ACCSCT) *Degrees:* A, C *CEO:* Dir. Glenn B. Murray
　　　　　(215) 357-5100

THE CHUBB INSTITUTE—KEYSTONE SCHOOL
965 Baltimore Pike, Springfield 19064 *Type:* Private business *Accred.:* 1968/1996

(ACICS) *Calendar:* Sem. plan *Degrees:* A *CEO:* Dir. Jane Chadwick

(215) 543-1747

CHURCHMAN BUSINESS SCHOOL
355 Spring Garden St., Easton 18042 *Type:* Private business *Accred.:* 1954/1987 (ACICS) *Calendar:* Tri. plan *Degrees:* A *CEO:* Pres. Charles W. Churchman, Jr.

(610) 258-5345

CLARION UNIVERSITY OF PENNSYLVANIA
Clarion 16214 *Type:* Public (state) *System:* Pennsylvania State System of Higher Education *Accred.:* 1948/1993 (MSA) *Calendar:* Sem. plan *Degrees:* A, B, M *Prof. Accred.:* Audiology, Librarianship, Speech-Language Pathology, Teacher Education *CEO:* Pres. Diane L. Reinhard
Enroll: 5,637   (814) 226-2000

VENANGO CAMPUS
W. First St., Oil City 16301 *Prof. Accred.:* Nursing (A,B)

(814) 676-6591

THE CLARISSA SCHOOL OF FASHION DESIGN
Warner Ctr., 332 Fifth Ave., Pittsburgh 15222-2411 *Type:* Private *Accred.:* 1976/1987 (ACCSCT) *Calendar:* Sem. plan *Degrees:* A, C *CEO:* Dir. Penelope N. Smith

(412) 471-4414

COLLEGE MISERICORDIA
301 Lake St., Dallas 18612-1098 *Type:* Private (Roman Catholic) liberal arts primarily for women *Accred.:* 1935/1994 (MSA) *Calendar:* Sem. plan *Degrees:* A, B, M, C *Prof. Accred.:* Nursing (B,M), Occupational Therapy, Physical Therapy, Radiography, Social Work (B) *CEO:* Pres. Albert B. Anderson
Enroll: 1,831   (717) 674-6400

COMMUNITY COLLEGE OF ALLEGHENY COUNTY
ALLEGHENY CAMPUS
808 Ridge Ave., Pittsburgh 15212 *Type:* Public (local/state) junior *System:* Community College of Allegheny County College Office *Accred.:* 1970/1994 (MSA) *Calendar:* Sem. plan *Degrees:* A, C *Prof. Accred.:* Medical Assisting (AMA), Medical Record Technology, Nuclear Medicine Technology, Nursing

(A), Radiation Therapy Technology, Respiratory Therapy, Respiratory Therapy Technology *CEO:* Exec. Dean/Vice Pres. J. David Griffin
Enroll: 6,146   (412) 237-2525

COMMUNITY COLLEGE OF ALLEGHENY COUNTY
BOYCE CAMPUS
595 Beatty Rd., Monroeville 15146 *Type:* Public (local/state) junior *System:* Community College of Allegheny County College Office *Accred.:* 1970/1994 (MSA) *Calendar:* Sem. plan *Degrees:* A, C *Prof. Accred.:* Diagnostic Medical Sonography, Occupational Therapy Assisting, Physical Therapy Assisting, Radiography, Surgical Technology *CEO:* Vice Pres./Exec. Dean Jacqueline D. Taylor
Enroll: 3,971   (412) 371-8651

COMMUNITY COLLEGE OF ALLEGHENY COUNTY
NORTH CAMPUS
8701 Perry Hwy., Pittsburgh 15237 *Type:* Public (local/state) junior *System:* Community College of Allegheny County College Office *Accred.:* 1979/1994 (MSA) *Calendar:* Sem. plan *Degrees:* A, C *CEO:* Vice Pres./Exec. Dean Patricia A. McDonald
Enroll: 4,494   (412) 366-7000

COMMUNITY COLLEGE OF ALLEGHENY COUNTY
SOUTH CAMPUS
1750 Clairton Rd., Rte. 885, West Mifflin 15122 *Type:* Public (local/state) junior *System:* Community College of Allegheny County College Office *Accred.:* 1973/1994 (MSA) *Calendar:* Sem. plan *Degrees:* A, C *Prof. Accred.:* Clinical Lab Technology (A) *CEO:* Exec. Dean/Vice Pres. Thomas A. Juravich
Enroll: 4,889   (412) 469-1100

COMMUNITY COLLEGE OF BEAVER COUNTY
One Campus Dr., Monaca 15061-2588 *Type:* Public (local/state) junior *Accred.:* 1972/1995 (MSA) *Calendar:* Sem. plan *Degrees:* A, C *Prof. Accred.:* Clinical Lab Technology (A), Nursing (A) *CEO:* Pres. Margaret J. Williams-Betlyn
Enroll: 2,635   (412) 775-8561

COMMUNITY COLLEGE OF PHILADELPHIA
1700 Spring Garden St., Philadelphia 19130-3991 *Type:* Public (local/state) junior *Accred.:* 1968/1994 (MSA) *Calendar:* Sem. plan *Degrees:* A, C *Prof. Accred.:* Clinical Lab Technology (A), Dental Assisting, Dental Hygiene, Medical Assisting (AMA), Medical Record Technology, Nursing (A), Radiography, Respiratory Therapy *CEO:* Pres. Frederick W. Capshaw
Enroll: 18,305   (215) 751-8000

COMPUTER TECH
107 Sixth St., Fulton Bldg., Pittsburgh 15222 *Type:* Private business *Accred.:* 1971/1995 (ACICS) *Degrees:* A, C *CEO:* Pres. Edward J. Boyd
                        (412) 391-4197

FAIRMONT CAMPUS
Country Club Rd. Ext., 217 Marion Sq., Fairmont, WV 26554 *Accred.:* 1989/1995 (ACICS)
                        (304) 363-5100

CONSOLIDATED SCHOOL OF BUSINESS
2124 Ambassador Cir., Lancaster 17603 *Type:* Private business *Accred.:* 1987/1996 (ACICS) *Degrees:* A, C *CEO:* Exec. Dir. Robert L. Safran, Jr.
                        (717) 394-6211

CONSOLIDATED SCHOOL OF BUSINESS
1605 Clugston Rd., York 17404 *Type:* Private business *Accred.:* 1984/1996 (ACICS) *Degrees:* A, C *CEO:* Exec. Dir. Betty J. Johnson
                        (717) 764-9950

THE CRAFT INSTITUTE
9 S. 12th St., Philadelphia 19107-3644 *Type:* Private *Accred.:* 1980/1993 (ACCSCT) *Degrees:* A, C *Prof. Accred.:* Medical Assisting *CEO:* Dir. Colleen Russo
                        (215) 665-8546

THE CURTIS INSTITUTE OF MUSIC
1726 Locust St., Philadelphia 19103 *Type:* Private professional *Accred.:* 1993 (MSA) *Calendar:* Sem. plan *Degrees:* B, M *Prof. Accred.:* Music *CEO:* Dir. Gary Graffman
Enroll: 154   (215) 893-5252

DEAN INSTITUTE OF TECHNOLOGY
1501 W. Liberty Ave., Pittsburgh 15226-1197 *Type:* Private *Accred.:* 1969/1990 (ACCSCT) *Calendar:* Qtr. plan *Degrees:* A, C *CEO:* Dir. James S. Dean
                        (412) 531-4433

DELAWARE COUNTY COMMUNITY COLLEGE
901 S. Media Line Rd., Media 19063 *Type:* Public (local/state) junior *Accred.:* 1970/1991 (MSA) *Calendar:* Sem. plan *Degrees:* A, C *Prof. Accred.:* Medical Assisting (AMA), Nursing (A), Surgical Technology *CEO:* Pres. Richard D. DeCosmo
Enroll: 10,127   (610) 359-5000

DELAWARE VALLEY COLLEGE OF SCIENCE AND AGRICULTURE
700 E. Butler Ave., Doylestown 18901-2697 *Type:* Private non-profit *Accred.:* 1962/1993 (MSA) *Calendar:* Sem. plan *Degrees:* A, B *CEO:* Interim Pres. Joshua Feldstein
Enroll: 2,225   (215) 345-1500

DICKINSON COLLEGE
P.O. Box 1773, Carlisle 17013-2896 *Type:* Private liberal arts *Accred.:* 1921/1992 (MSA) *Calendar:* Sem. plan *Degrees:* B *CEO:* Pres. A. Lee Fritschler
Enroll: 1,875   (717) 243-5121

DICKINSON SCHOOL OF LAW
150 S. College St., Carlisle 17013 *Type:* Private *Calendar:* Sem. plan *Degrees:* P *Prof. Accred.:* Law *CEO:* Dean John Maher
Enroll: 521   (717) 243-4611

DOUGLAS SCHOOL OF BUSINESS
130 Seventh St., Monessen 15062 *Type:* Private business *Accred.:* 1977/1998 (ACICS) *Calendar:* Tri. plan *Degrees:* A, C *CEO:* Pres. Jeffrey D. Imbrescia
                        (412) 684-3684

DREXEL UNIVERSITY
32nd and Chestnut Sts., Philadelphia 19104 *Type:* Private non-profit *Accred.:* 1927/1991 (MSA) *Calendar:* Qtr. plan *Degrees:* B, M, D *Prof. Accred.:* Business (B,M), Computer Science, Engineering (architectural, chemical, civil, electrical, materials, mechanical),

Librarianship *CEO:* Pres. Constantine N. Papadakis
Enroll: 9,782   (215) 895-2000

DUBOIS BUSINESS COLLEGE
One Beaver Dr., DuBois 15801 *Type:* Private business *Accred.:* 1954/1994 (ACICS) *Calendar:* Tri. plan *Degrees:* A *CEO:* Dir. Jackie D. Syktich
                                   (814) 371-6920

DUFF'S BUSINESS INSTITUTE
110 Ninth St., Pittsburgh 15222 *Type:* Private business *Accred.:* 1961/1996 (ACICS) *Calendar:* Qtr. plan *Degrees:* A, C *Prof. Accred.:* Medical Assisting (AMA) *CEO:* Dir. Mark A. Scott
                                   (412) 261-4520

DUQUESNE UNIVERSITY
600 Forbes Ave., Pittsburgh 15282 *Type:* Private (Roman Catholic) *Accred.:* 1935/1993 (MSA) *Calendar:* Sem. plan *Degrees:* A, B, M, P, D *Prof. Accred.:* Business (B,M), Counseling, Law, Music, Nursing (B,M), Occupational Therapy, Perfusion, Physical Therapy, Physician Assisting/Surgeon Assisting *CEO:* Pres. John E. Murray, Jr.
Enroll: 8,969   (412) 434-6000

EAST STROUDSBURG UNIVERSITY OF PENNSYLVANIA
200 Prospect St., East Stroudsburg 18301 *Type:* Public (state) *System:* Pennsylvania State System of Higher Education *Accred.:* 1950/1992 (MSA) *Calendar:* Sem. plan *Degrees:* A, B, M *Prof. Accred.:* Nursing (B), Recreation and Leisure Services (B) *CEO:* Pres. James E. Gilbert
Enroll: 5,652   (717) 422-3211

THE EASTERN BAPTIST THEOLOGICAL SEMINARY
6 Lancaster Ave., Wynnewood 19096-3494 *Type:* Private (Baptist) graduate only *Accred.:* 1954/1992 (ATS); 1954/1993 (MSA) *Calendar:* 4-1-4 plan *Degrees:* M, P, D *CEO:* Pres. Manfred T. Brauch
Enroll: 355   (610) 896-5000

EASTERN COLLEGE
10 Fairview Dr., St. Davids 19087-3696 *Type:* Private (Baptist) liberal arts *Accred.:*

1954/1992 (MSA) *Calendar:* Sem. plan *Degrees:* A, B, M, C *Prof. Accred.:* Cardiovascular Technology, Nursing (B), Social Work (B) *CEO:* Pres. Roberta Hestenes
Enroll: 2,065   (610) 341-5800

EDINBORO UNIVERSITY OF PENNSYLVANIA
Edinboro 16444 *Type:* Public (state) *System:* Pennsylvania State System of Higher Education *Accred.:* 1949/1993 (MSA) *Calendar:* Sem. plan *Degrees:* A, B, M, C *Prof. Accred.:* Dietetics (coordinated), Music (A), Nursing (B), Rehabilitation Counseling, Social Work (B), Speech-Language Pathology *CEO:* Pres. Foster F. Diebold
Enroll: 7,484   (814) 732-2000

ELECTRONIC INSTITUTES
19 Jamesway Plaza, Middletown 17057-4851 *Type:* Private *Accred.:* 1967/1987 (ACCSCT) *Degrees:* A, C *CEO:* Dir. William F. Margut
                                   (717) 944-2731

ELECTRONIC INSTITUTES
4634 Browns Hill Rd., Pittsburgh 15217-2919 *Type:* Private *Accred.:* 1971/1986 (ACCSCT) *Degrees:* A, C *CEO:* Pres. Philip Chosky
                                   (412) 521-8686

ELIZABETHTOWN COLLEGE
One Alpha Dr., Elizabethtown 17022-2298 *Type:* Private (Church of Brethren) liberal arts *Accred.:* 1948/1994 (MSA) *Calendar:* Sem. plan *Degrees:* B, C *Prof. Accred.:* Music, Occupational Therapy, Social Work (B) *CEO:* Pres. Gerhard E. Spiegler
Enroll: 1,795   (717) 367-1000

ERIE BUSINESS CENTER
246 W. Ninth St., Erie 16501 *Type:* Private business *Accred.:* 1954/1994 (ACICS) *Degrees:* A *CEO:* Pres. Charles P. McGeary
                                   (814) 456-7504

NEW CASTLE CAMPUS
700 Moravia St., New Castle 16101 *Accred.:* 1985/1990 (ACICS)
                                   (412) 658-9066

ERIE INSTITUTE OF TECHNOLOGY
2221 Peninsula Dr., Erie 16506-2954 *Type:* Private *Accred.:* 1979/1989 (ACCSCT) *Degrees:* A, C *CEO:* Pres./Dir. Clinton L. Oviatt, Jr.
(814) 838-2711

EVANGELICAL SCHOOL OF THEOLOGY
121 S. College St., Myerstown 17067 *Type:* Private (Evangelical Congregational Church) graduate only *Accred.:* 1987/1990 (ATS); 1984/1991 (MSA) *Calendar:* Sem. plan *Degrees:* M, P *CEO:* Interim Pres. Kirby N. Keller
Enroll: 97   (717) 866-5775

FRANKLIN & MARSHALL COLLEGE
P.O. Box 3003, Lancaster 17604-3003 *Type:* Private liberal arts *Accred.:* 1921/1994 (MSA) *Calendar:* Sem. plan *Degrees:* B *CEO:* Pres. A. Richard Kneedler
Enroll: 1,774   (717) 291-3911

GANNON UNIVERSITY
University Sq., Erie 16541 *Type:* Private (Roman Catholic) *Accred.:* 1951/1993 (MSA) *Calendar:* Sem. plan *Degrees:* A, B, M, C *Prof. Accred.:* Dietetics (coordinated), Engineering (electrical, mechanical), Nurse Anesthesia Education, Nursing (A,B,M), Physical Therapy, Physician Assisting/Surgeon Assisting, Radiography, Respiratory Therapy, Social Work (B) *CEO:* Pres. David A. Rubino
Enroll: 3,669   (814) 871-7000

GENEVA COLLEGE
College Ave., Beaver Falls 15010 *Type:* Private (Reformed Presbyterian) liberal arts *Accred.:* 1922/1993 (MSA) *Calendar:* Sem. plan *Degrees:* A, B, M *CEO:* Pres. John H. White
Enroll: 1,679   (412) 846-5100

GETTYSBURG COLLEGE
N. Washington St., Gettysburg 17325-1486 *Type:* Private liberal arts *Accred.:* 1921/1994 (MSA) *Calendar:* Sem. plan *Degrees:* B *CEO:* Pres. Gordon A. Haaland
Enroll: 2,108   (717) 337-6000

GRATZ COLLEGE
Old York Rd. and Melrose Ave., Melrose Park 19126 *Type:* Private liberal arts *Accred.:* 1967/1992 (MSA) *Calendar:* Sem. plan *Degrees:* B, M, C *CEO:* Pres. Gary S. Schiff
Enroll: 147   (215) 635-7300

GROVE CITY COLLEGE
100 Campus Dr., Grove City 16127-2104 *Type:* Private liberal arts *Accred.:* 1922/1990 (MSA) *Calendar:* Sem. plan *Degrees:* B *Prof. Accred.:* Engineering (electrical, mechanical) *CEO:* Interim Pres. Garth E. Runion
Enroll: 2,280   (412) 458-2000

GWYNEDD-MERCY COLLEGE
Gwynedd Valley 19437 *Type:* Private liberal arts primarily for women *Accred.:* 1958/1991 (MSA) *Calendar:* Sem. plan *Degrees:* A, B, M, C *Prof. Accred.:* Cardiovascular Technology, Medical Record Administration, Medical Record Technology, Nursing (A,B), Radiation Therapy Technology, Respiratory Therapy, Respiratory Therapy Technology *CEO:* Pres. Linda M. Bevilacqua, O.P.
Enroll: 1,856   (215) 646-7300

HARCUM COLLEGE
Morris and Montgomery Aves., Bryn Mawr 19010 *Type:* Private junior for women *Accred.:* 1970/1990 (MSA) *Calendar:* Sem. plan *Degrees:* A *Prof. Accred.:* Clinical Lab Technology (A), Dental Assisting, Dental Hygiene, Medical Assisting (AMA), Occupational Therapy Assisting, Physical Therapy Assisting, Veterinary Technology *CEO:* Pres. Patricia M. Ryan
Enroll: 688   (610) 526-4100

HARRISBURG AREA COMMUNITY COLLEGE
One HACC Dr., Harrisburg 17110-2999 *Type:* Public (local/state) junior *Accred.:* 1967/1992 (MSA) *Calendar:* Sem. plan *Degrees:* A *Prof. Accred.:* Clinical Lab Technology (A), Dental Assisting, Dental Hygiene, EMT-Paramedic, Engineering Technology (electrical, mechanical), Nursing (A), Practical Nursing, Respiratory Therapy,

Respiratory Therapy Technology *CEO:* Pres.
Mary L. Fifield
Enroll: 8,512   (717) 780-2300

LANCASTER CAMPUS
1008 New Holland Ave., Lancaster 17604
(717) 293-5000

LEBANON CAMPUS
731 Cumberland St., Lebanon 17042
(717) 270-4222

HAVERFORD COLLEGE
370 Lancaster Ave., Haverford 19041-1392
Type: Private liberal arts *Accred.:* 1921/1993
(MSA) *Calendar:* Sem. plan *Degrees:* B
CEO: Pres. Tom G. Kessinger
Enroll: 1,109   (610) 896-1000

HIRAM G. ANDREWS CENTER
727 Goucher St., Johnstown 15905-3092
Type: Private *Accred.:* 1987 (ACCSCT)
Degrees: A, C *CEO:* Dir. Joseph Rizzo, Sr.
(814) 255-8200

HOLY FAMILY COLLEGE
Grant and Frankford Aves., Philadelphia
19114-2094 *Type:* Private (Roman Catholic)
liberal arts *Accred.:* 1961/1991 (MSA) *Cal-
endar:* Sem. plan *Degrees:* A, B, M *Prof.
Accred.:* Nursing (B), Radiography *CEO:*
Pres. M. Francesca Onley
Enroll: 2,569   (215) 637-7700

HUSSIAN SCHOOL OF ART
1118 Market St., Philadelphia 19107-3679
Type: Private *Accred.:* 1972/1989 (ACC-
SCT) *Calendar:* Sem. plan *Degrees:* A *CEO:*
Dir. Ronald Dove
(215) 238-9000

ICM SCHOOL OF BUSINESS
10 Wood St., Pittsburgh 15222 *Type:* Private
business *Accred.:* 1967/1992 (ACICS)
Degrees: A, C *Prof. Accred.:* Medical Assisting (AMA) *CEO:* Dir. Gerry Kosentos
(412) 261-2647

ICS LEARNING SYSTEMS
925 Oak St., Scranton 18515 *Type:* Private
home study *Accred.:* 1956/1995 (DETC)
Degrees: A, C *CEO:* Pres. Gary M. Keisling
(717) 342-7701

THE ENGLISH LANGUAGE INSTITUTE OF
AMERICA, INC.
925 Oak St., Scranton 18515 *Accred.:*
1981/1990 (DETC)
(717) 941-3406

ICS CENTER FOR DEGREE STUDIES
925 Oak St., Scranton 18515 *Accred.:*
1994 (DETC) *Degrees:* A
(717) 342-7701

NORTH AMERICAN CORRESPONDENCE
SCHOOLS
925 Oak St., Scranton 18515
(717) 342-7701

IMMACULATA COLLEGE
Immaculata 19345 *Type:* Private (Roman
Catholic) liberal arts for women *Accred.:*
1928/1994 (MSA) *Calendar:* Sem. plan
Degrees: A, B, M, D *Prof. Accred.:* Dietetics
(internship), Music, Nursing (B) *CEO:* Pres.
Marie Roseanne Bonfini, I.H.M.
Enroll: 2,088   (610) 647-4400

INDIANA UNIVERSITY OF PENNSYLVANIA
Indiana 15705 *Type:* Public (state) *System:*
Pennsylvania State System of Higher Educa-
tion *Accred.:* 1941/1990 (MSA) *Calendar:*
Sem. plan *Degrees:* A, B, M, D, C *Prof.
Accred.:* Clinical Psychology, Music, Nurs-
ing (B,M), Respiratory Therapy, Speech-
Language Pathology, Teacher Education
CEO: Pres. Lawrence K. Pettit
Enroll: 13,814   (412) 357-2100

ARMSTRONG COUNTY CAMPUS
Kittanning 16201
(814) 543-1078

PUNXSUTAWNEY CAMPUS
Punxsutawney 15767
(814) 938-6711

INFORMATION COMPUTER SYSTEMS INSTITUTE
2201 Hangar Pl., Allentown 18103-9504
Type: Private *Accred.:* 1984/1989 (ACC-
SCT) *Degrees:* A, C *CEO:* Owner/Pres.
William Barber
                                    (215) 264-8029

JOHNSON TECHNICAL INSTITUTE
3427 N. Main Ave., Scranton 18508-1495
Type: Private *Accred.:* 1979/1989 (ACC-
SCT) *Calendar:* Sem. plan *Degrees:* A *CEO:*
Pres. Thomas W. Krause
                                    (717) 342-6404

BRANCH CAMPUS
200 Shady La., Philipsburg 16866 *Accred.:*
1991 (ACCSCT)
                                    (814) 342-5680

JUNIATA COLLEGE
1700 Moore St., Huntingdon 16652 *Type:*
Private liberal arts *Accred.:* 1922/1993
(MSA) *Calendar:* Sem. plan *Degrees:* B
Prof. Accred.: Social Work (B) *CEO:* Pres.
Robert W. Neff
Enroll: 1,038   (814) 643-4310

KEYSTONE COLLEGE
P.O. Box 50, La Plume 18440-0200 *Type:*
Private junior *Accred.:* 1936/1993 (MSA)
Calendar: Sem. plan *Degrees:* A, C *Prof.
Accred.:* Physical Therapy Assisting *CEO:*
Pres. Edward G. Boehm, Jr.
Enroll: 849   (717) 945-5141

KING'S COLLEGE
133 N. River St., Wilkes-Barre 18711 *Type:*
Private (Roman Catholic) liberal arts
Accred.: 1955/1994 (MSA) *Calendar:* Sem.
plan *Degrees:* A, B, M, C *Prof. Accred.:*
Physician Assisting/Surgeon Assisting *CEO:*
Pres. James R. Lackenmier, C.S.C.
Enroll: 2,271   (717) 826-5900

KUTZTOWN UNIVERSITY OF PENNSYLVANIA
Kutztown 19530 *Type:* Public (state) *System:*
Pennsylvania State System of Higher Educa-
tion *Accred.:* 1944/1993 (MSA) *Calendar:*
Sem. plan *Degrees:* B, M *Prof. Accred.:*
Nursing (B), Teacher Education *CEO:* Pres.
David E. McFarland
Enroll: 7,916   (610) 683-4000

LA ROCHE COLLEGE
9000 Babcock Blvd., Pittsburgh 15237 *Type:*
Private (Roman Catholic) *Accred.:* 1973/
1994 (MSA) *Calendar:* Sem. plan *Degrees:*
B, M, C *Prof. Accred.:* Art (A), Interior
Design, Nurse Anesthesia Education, Nurs-
ing (B,M) *CEO:* Pres. William A. Kerr
Enroll: 1,685   (412) 367-9300

LA SALLE UNIVERSITY
1900 W. Olney Ave., Philadelphia 19141
Type: Private (Roman Catholic) *Accred.:*
1930/1991 (MSA) *Calendar:* Sem. plan
Degrees: A, B, M *Prof. Accred.:* Nursing
(B,M), Social Work (B) *CEO:* Pres. Joseph
F. Burke, F.S.C.
Enroll: 5,522   (215) 951-1000

LACKAWANNA JUNIOR COLLEGE
901 Prospect Ave., Scranton 18505 *Type:*
Private junior *Accred.:* 1973/1978 (MSA)
Calendar: Sem. plan *Degrees:* A, C *CEO:*
Pres. Raymond S. Angeli
Enroll: 842   (717) 961-7810

LAFAYETTE COLLEGE
High St., Easton 18042 *Type:* Private liberal
arts *Accred.:* 1921/1994 (MSA) *Calendar:*
Sem. plan *Degrees:* B *Prof. Accred.:* Engineering (chemical, civil, electrical, mechanical) *CEO:* Pres. Arthur J. Rothkopf
Enroll: 2,219   (610) 250-5000

LAKE ERIE COLLEGE OF OSTEOPATHIC
MEDICINE
1858 W. Grandview Blvd., Erie 16509 *Type:*
Private *Calendar:* Sem. plan *Degrees:* P
Prof. Accred.: Osteopathy (provisional)
CEO: Pres. Joseph John Namey
                                    (814) 866-6641

LANCASTER BIBLE COLLEGE
901 Eden Rd., Lancaster 17601 *Type:* Private *Accred.:* 1964/1989 (AABC); 1982/
1992 (MSA) *Calendar:* Sem. plan *Degrees:*
A, B, C *CEO:* Pres. Gilbert A. Peterson
Enroll: 460   (717) 569-7071

LANCASTER THEOLOGICAL SEMINARY
555 W. James St., Lancaster 17603-2897
Type: Private (United Church of Christ)
graduate only *Accred.:* 1938/1994 (ATS);

1978/1994 (MSA) *Calendar:* 3-3 plan *Degrees:* M, P, D *CEO:* Pres. Peter M. Schmiechen
Enroll: 141   (717) 393-0654

LANSDALE SCHOOL OF BUSINESS
201 Church Rd., North Wales 19454 *Type:* Private junior *Accred.:* 1967/1986 (ACICS) *Degrees:* A *CEO:* Pres. Marlon D. Keller
                    (215) 699-5700

LAUREL BUSINESS INSTITUTE
11-15 Penn St., Uniontown 15401 *Type:* Private business *Accred.:* 1987/1992 (ACICS) *Degrees:* A, C *CEO:* Pres. Christopher D. Decker
                    (412) 439-4900

LEBANON VALLEY COLLEGE
101 N. College Ave., Annville 17003-0501 *Type:* Private (United Methodist) liberal arts *Accred.:* 1922/1993 (MSA) *Calendar:* Sem. plan *Degrees:* A, B, M *Prof. Accred.:* Music *CEO:* Pres. John A. Synodinos
Enroll: 1,744   (717) 867-6100

LEHIGH CARBON COMMUNITY COLLEGE
4525 Education Park Dr., Schnecksville 18078-2598 *Type:* Public (local/state) junior *Accred.:* 1972/1993 (MSA) *Calendar:* Sem. plan *Degrees:* A, C *Prof. Accred.:* Medical Assisting (AMA), Medical Record Technology, Nursing (A), Occupational Therapy Assisting, Physical Therapy Assisting, Respiratory Therapy, Respiratory Therapy Technology *CEO:* Pres. James R. Davis
Enroll: 4,860   (610) 799-2121

LEHIGH UNIVERSITY
27 Memorial Dr. W., Bethlehem 18015 *Type:* Private non-profit *Accred.:* 1921/1993 (MSA) *Calendar:* Sem. plan *Degrees:* B, M, D *Prof. Accred.:* Accounting (A), Business (B,M), Computer Science, Counseling Psychology, Engineering (chemical, civil, computer, electrical, industrial, materials, mechanical), School Psychology, Theatre *CEO:* Pres. Peter Likins, Jr.
Enroll: 6,447   (610) 758-3000

LINCOLN TECHNICAL INSTITUTE
5151 Tilghman St., Allentown 18104-3298 *Type:* Private *Accred.:* 1967/1988 (ACCSCT) *Degrees:* A *CEO:* Exec. Dir. Michael Zuccheri
                    (610) 398-5301

LINCOLN UNIVERSITY
Lincoln University 19352-0999 *Type:* Private (state) liberal arts *Accred.:* 1922/1993 (MSA) *Calendar:* Sem. plan *Degrees:* A, B, M *Prof. Accred.:* Recreation and Leisure Services (B) *CEO:* Pres. Niara Sudarkasa
Enroll: 1,372   (610) 932-8300

LOCK HAVEN UNIVERSITY OF PENNSYLVANIA
Lock Haven 17745 *Type:* Public (state) *System:* Pennsylvania State System of Higher Education *Accred.:* 1949/1990 (MSA) *Calendar:* Sem. plan *Degrees:* A, B, M, C *Prof. Accred.:* Nursing (A), Social Work (B), Teacher Education *CEO:* Pres. Craig D. Willis
Enroll: 3,690   (717) 893-2011

LUTHERAN THEOLOGICAL SEMINARY AT GETTYSBURG
61 N.W. Confederate Ave., Gettysburg 17325-1795 *Type:* Private (Evangelical Lutheran Church) graduate only *Accred.:* 1938/1990 (ATS); 1971/1991 (MSA) *Calendar:* Qtr. plan *Degrees:* M, P *CEO:* Pres. Darold H. Beekmann
Enroll: 224   (717) 334-6286

LUTHERAN THEOLOGICAL SEMINARY AT PHILADELPHIA
7301 Germantown Ave., Philadelphia 19119 *Type:* Private (Evangelical Lutheran Church) graduate only *Accred.:* 1938/1992 (ATS); 1971/1992 (MSA) *Calendar:* Sem. plan *Degrees:* M, P, D *CEO:* Pres. Robert G. Hughes
Enroll: 248   (215) 248-4616

LUZERNE COUNTY COMMUNITY COLLEGE
133 S. Prospect St., Nanticoke 18634 *Type:* Public (local/state) junior *Accred.:* 1975 /1991 (MSA) *Calendar:* Tri. plan *Degrees:* A *Prof. Accred.:* Dental Hygiene, Nursing

(A), Respiratory Therapy Technology *CEO:* Interim Pres. Thomas J. Moran
Enroll: 7,001   (717) 829-7300

LYCOMING COLLEGE
700 College Pl., Williamsport 17701 *Type:* Private (United Methodist) liberal arts *Accred.:* 1934/1991 (MSA) *Calendar:* Sem. plan *Degrees:* B *Prof. Accred.:* Nursing (B) *CEO:* Pres. James E. Douthat
Enroll: 1,507   (717) 321-4000

MANOR JUNIOR COLLEGE
700 Fox Chase Rd., Jenkintown 19046 *Type:* Private (Ukrainian Catholic) for women *Accred.:* 1967/1993 (MSA) *Calendar:* Sem. plan *Degrees:* A, C *Prof. Accred.:* Clinical Lab Technology (A), Dental Assisting, Veterinary Technology (probational) *CEO:* Pres. Mary Cecilia Jurasinski, O.S.B.M.
Enroll: 654   (215) 885-2360

MANSFIELD UNIVERSITY OF PENNSYLVANIA
Academy St., Mansfield 16933 *Type:* Public (state) *System:* Pennsylvania State System of Higher Education *Accred.:* 1942/1992 (MSA) *Calendar:* Sem. plan *Degrees:* A, B, M *Prof. Accred.:* Music, Radiography, Respiratory Therapy, Social Work (B), Teacher Education *CEO:* Pres. Rodney C. Kelchner
Enroll: 2,992   (717) 662-4000

MARYWOOD COLLEGE
2300 Adams Ave., Scranton 18509 *Type:* Private (Roman Catholic) liberal arts primarily for women *Accred.:* 1921/1991 (MSA) *Calendar:* Sem. plan *Degrees:* B, M *Prof. Accred.:* Art, Dietetics (coordinated), Music, Nursing (B), Social Work (B,M), Teacher Education *CEO:* Pres. Mary Reap, I.H.M.
Enroll: 3,068   (717) 348-6231

MCCANN SCHOOL OF BUSINESS
Main and Pine Sts., Mahanoy City 17948 *Type:* Private business *Accred.:* 1962/1995 (ACICS) *Calendar:* Tri. plan *Degrees:* A *CEO:* Dir. Thomas Fletcher
                                   (717) 773-1820

POTTSVILLE CAMPUS
101 North Centre St., Pottsville 17910 *Accred.:* 1987/1995 (ACICS)
                                   (717) 622-7622

MCCARRIE SCHOOL OF HEALTH SCIENCES AND TECHNOLOGY INC.
512-20 South Broad St., Philadelphia 19146-1613 *Type:* Private technical *Accred.:* 1983/1995 (ABHES); 1973/1989 (ACC-SCT) *Degrees:* A, C *Prof. Accred.:* Medical Assisting, Medical Laboratory Technology *CEO:* Exec. Vice Pres. Robert J. Walder
                                   (215) 545-7772

MEDIAN SCHOOL OF ALLIED HEALTH CAREERS
125 Seventh St., Pittsburgh 15222-3400 *Type:* Private *Accred.:* 1970/1986 (ACC-SCT) *Calendar:* Qtr. plan *Degrees:* A, C *Prof. Accred.:* Dental Assisting, Medical Assisting (AMA) *CEO:* Pres. William B. Mosle, Jr.
                                   (412) 391-7021

MEDICAL COLLEGE OF PENNSYLVANIA AND HAHNEMANN UNIVERSITY
3300 Henry Ave., Philadelphia 19129 *Type:* Private professional *Accred.:* 1984/1992 (MSA) *Calendar:* Sem. plan *Degrees:* A, B, M, P, D *Prof. Accred.:* Clinical Lab Scientist, Clinical Lab Technology (A), Clinical Psychology, General Practice Residency, Marriage and Family Therapy (M), Medicine, Nurse Anesthesia Education, Nursing (A,B), Oral and Maxillofacial Surgery, Perfusion, Physical Therapy, Physical Therapy Assisting, Physician Assisting/Surgeon Assisting, Psychology Internship, Radiography *CEO:* Provost Leonard L. Ross
Enroll: 3,133   (215) 842-6000

MERCYHURST COLLEGE
501 E. 38th St., Erie 16546 *Type:* Private (Roman Catholic) liberal arts *Accred.:* 1931/1992 (MSA) *Calendar:* Sem. plan *Degrees:* A, B, M *Prof. Accred.:* Dietetics (coordinated), Social Work (B) *CEO:* Pres. William P. Garvey
Enroll: 2,444   (814) 824-2000

MESSIAH COLLEGE
Grantham 17027 *Type:* Private (Brethren in Christ) *Accred.:* 1963/1993 (MSA) *Calendar:* Sem. plan *Degrees:* B *Prof. Accred.:* Engineering (electrical), Music, Nursing (B), Social Work (B) *CEO:* Pres. Rodney J. Sawatsky
Enroll: 2,320   (717) 766-2511

CITY CAMPUS
2026 N. Broad St., Philadelphia 19121
(215) 769-2526

MILLERSVILLE UNIVERSITY OF PENNSYLVANIA
P.O. Box 1002, Millersville 17551-1002 *Type:* Public (state) *System:* Pennsylvania State System of Higher Education *Accred.:* 1950/1990 (MSA) *Calendar:* Sem. plan *Degrees:* A, B, M *Prof. Accred.:* Music, Nursing (B), Respiratory Therapy, Social Work (B), Teacher Education *CEO:* Pres. Joseph A. Caputo
Enroll: 7,417   (717) 872-3024

MONTGOMERY COUNTY COMMUNITY COLLEGE
340 DeKalb Pike, Blue Bell 19422 *Type:* Public (local/state) junior *Accred.:* 1970/1991 (MSA) *Calendar:* Sem. plan *Degrees:* A, C *Prof. Accred.:* Clinical Lab Technology (A), Dental Hygiene, Nursing (A) *CEO:* Pres. Edward M. Sweitzer
Enroll: 9,206   (215) 641-6300

MOORE COLLEGE OF ART AND DESIGN
The Parkway at 20th St., Philadelphia 19103 *Type:* Private professional for women *Accred.:* 1958/1992 (MSA) *Calendar:* Sem. plan *Degrees:* B, C *Prof. Accred.:* Art, Interior Design *CEO:* Pres. Barbara G. Price
Enroll: 337   (215) 568-4515

MORAVIAN COLLEGE
1200 Main St., Bethlehem 18018 *Type:* Private (Moravian Church) *Accred.:* 1954/1988 (ATS); 1922/1993 (MSA) *Calendar:* 4-1-4 plan *Degrees:* B, M *Prof. Accred.:* Music *CEO:* Pres. Roger H. Martin
Enroll: 1,840   (610) 861-1300

MOUNT ALOYSIUS COLLEGE
One College Dr., Cresson 16630 *Type:* Private (Roman Catholic) liberal arts *Accred.:*
1943/1995 (MSA) *Calendar:* Sem. plan *Degrees:* A, B, C *Prof. Accred.:* Clinical Lab Technology (A), Medical Assisting (AMA), Nursing (A), Occupational Therapy Assisting, Physical Therapy Assisting, Surgical Technology *CEO:* Pres. Edward F. Pierce
Enroll: 1,958   (814) 886-4131

MUHLENBERG COLLEGE
24th and Chew Sts., Allentown 18104 *Type:* Private (Lutheran) liberal arts *Accred.:* 1921/1991 (MSA) *Calendar:* Sem. plan *Degrees:* A, B *CEO:* Pres. Arthur R. Taylor
Enroll: 2,117   (215) 821-3100

NATIONAL EDUCATION CENTER ALLENTOWN CAMPUS
1501 Lehigh St., Allentown 18103 *Type:* Private business *Accred.:* 1968/1988 (ACICS) *Calendar:* Sem. plan *Degrees:* A, C *CEO:* Dir. Virginia Carpenter
(215) 791-5100

NATIONAL EDUCATION CENTER THOMPSON CAMPUS
5650 Derry St., Harrisburg 17111-4112 *Type:* Private business *Accred.:* 1962/1990 (ACICS) *Calendar:* Qtr. plan *Degrees:* A, C *CEO:* Pres. Rita A. Girondi
(717) 564-8710

PHILADELPHIA CAMPUS
University City Science Ctr., 3440 Market St., Philadelphia 19104 *Accred.:* 1983 (ACICS)
(215) 387-1530

NATIONAL EDUCATION CENTER—VALE TECHNICAL INSTITUTE CAMPUS
135 W. Market St., Blairsville 15717-1389 *Type:* Private *Accred.:* 1967/1993 (ACCSCT) *Degrees:* A, C *CEO:* Dir. Gary A. McGee
(412) 459-9500

NATIONAL EDUCATION CENTER—CLEVELAND CAMPUS
14445 Broadway Ave., Cleveland, OH 44125 *Accred.:* 1990 (ACCSCT)
(216) 475-7520

NEUMANN COLLEGE
Concord Rd., Aston 19014 *Type:* Private (Roman Catholic) liberal arts *Accred.:* 1972/ 1991 (MSA) *Calendar:* Sem. plan *Degrees:* A, B, M *Prof. Accred.:* Clinical Lab Scientist, Nursing (B) *CEO:* Pres. Nan B. Hechenberger
Enroll: 1,336   (610) 459-0905

NEW CASTLE SCHOOL OF TRADES
New Castle Youngstown Rd., Rte. 422, R.D. 1, Pulaski 16143-9721 *Type:* Private *Accred.:* 1973/1988 (ACCSCT) *Degrees:* A, C *CEO:* Dir. Jason Whitehead
(412) 964-8811

NEWPORT BUSINESS INSTITUTE
945 Greensburg Rd., New Kensington 15068 *Type:* Private business *Accred.:* 1959/1992 (ACICS) *Calendar:* Qtr. plan *Degrees:* A *CEO:* Dir. Kenneth Huselton
(412) 339-7542

NORTHAMPTON COUNTY AREA COMMUNITY COLLEGE
3835 Green Pond Rd., Bethlehem 18017 *Type:* Public (local/state) junior *Accred.:* 1970/1995 (MSA) *Calendar:* Sem. plan *Degrees:* A, C *Prof. Accred.:* Clinical Lab Technology (A), Dental Hygiene, Funeral Service Education (Mortuary Science), Nursing (A), Practical Nursing, Radiography *CEO:* Pres. Robert J. Kopecek
Enroll: 6,130   (610) 861-5300

MONROE COUNTY BRANCH CAMPUS
P.O. Box 639, Tannersville 18372
(717) 620-9221

PACE INSTITUTE
606 Court St., Reading 19601 *Type:* Private business *Accred.:* 1984/1996 (ACICS) *Degrees:* A, C *CEO:* Pres. Rhoda E. Dersh
(215) 375-1212

PEIRCE COLLEGE
1420 Pine St., Philadelphia 19102 *Type:* Private junior *Accred.:* 1971/1987 (MSA) *Calendar:* Sem. plan *Degrees:* A, C *CEO:* Pres. Arthur J. Lendo, Jr.
Enroll: 1,217   (215) 545-6400

PENN COMMERCIAL COLLEGE
82 S. Main St., Washington 15301 *Type:* Private business *Accred.:* 1960/1998 (ACICS) *Calendar:* Qtr. plan *Degrees:* A, C *CEO:* Dir. Robert Bazant
(412) 222-5330

PENN TECHNICAL INSTITUTE
110 Ninth St., Pittsburgh 15222-3618 *Type:* Private *Accred.:* 1967/1988 (ACCSCT) *Calendar:* Qtr. plan *Degrees:* A *CEO:* Dir. Louis A. Dimasi
(412) 355-0455

PENNCO TECH
3815 Otter St., Bristol 19007-3696 *Type:* Private *Accred.:* 1969/1993 (ACCSCT) *Degrees:* A, C *CEO:* Pres. John A. Hobyak
(215) 824-3200

PENNSYLVANIA ACADEMY OF THE FINE ARTS
118 N. Broad St., Philadelphia 19102 *Type:* Private professional *Degrees:* M, C *Prof. Accred.:* Art *CEO:* Dir. Frederick S. Osborne, Jr.
(215) 972-7623

PENNSYLVANIA COLLEGE OF OPTOMETRY
1200 W. Godfrey Ave., Philadelphia 19141 *Type:* Private professional *Accred.:* 1954/ 1993 (MSA) *Calendar:* Sem. plan *Degrees:* B, M, P, C *Prof. Accred.:* Optometric Residency, Optometry *CEO:* Pres. Thomas L. Lewis, O.D.
Enroll: 652   (215) 276-6200

PENNSYLVANIA COLLEGE OF PODIATRIC MEDICINE
8th and Race Sts., Philadelphia 19107 *Type:* Private professional *Accred.:* 1990/1995 (MSA) *Calendar:* Sem. plan *Degrees:* P, D *Prof. Accred.:* Podiatry *CEO:* Pres. John F. D'Aprix
Enroll: 422   (215) 629-0300

PENNSYLVANIA COLLEGE OF TECHNOLOGY
One College Ave., Williamsport 17701 *Type:* Public (state) junior *Accred.:* 1970/1992 (MSA) *Calendar:* Sem. plan *Degrees:* A, B, C *Prof. Accred.:* Dental Hygiene, Engineering Technology (civil/construction), Nursing

(A), Occupational Therapy Assisting, Radiography *CEO:* Pres. Robert L. Breuder
Enroll: 4,638   (717) 326-3761

NORTH CAMPUS
Mansfield Rd., Wellsboro 16901
                         (717) 724-7703

PENNSYLVANIA INSTITUTE OF TECHNOLOGY
800 Manchester Ave., Media 19063 *Type:*
Private 2-year *Accred.:* 1983/1991 (MSA)
Calendar: Qtr. plan *Degrees:* A, C *CEO:*
Pres. Edward R. D'Alessio
Enroll: 487   (215) 565-7900

THE PENNSYLVANIA STATE UNIVERSITY
314 Old Main, University Park 16802 *Type:*
Public (state) *Accred.:* 1921/1987 (MSA)
Calendar: Sem. plan *Degrees:* A, B, M, D, C
Prof. Accred.: Accounting (A,B,C), Art,
Audiology, Business (B,M), Clinical Psychology, Counseling Psychology, Engineering (aerospace, agricultural, architectural,
ceramic, chemical, civil, computer, electrical, engineering physics/science, industrial,
mechanical, metallurgical, mining, nuclear,
petroleum), Forestry, Health Services
Administration, Journalism (B,M), Landscape Architecture (B), Music, Nursing
(B,M), Occupational Therapy Assisting,
Psychology Internship, Recreation and
Leisure Services (B), Rehabilitation Counseling, School Psychology, Social Work (B),
Speech-Language Pathology, Teacher Education *CEO:* Pres. Graham B. Spanier
Enroll: 38,294   (814) 865-4700

ALLENTOWN CAMPUS
8380 Mohr Ln., Fogelsville 18051-9999
                         (610) 285-5000

ALTOONA CAMPUS
Ivyside Park, Altoona 16601-3760 *Prof.
Accred.:* Engineering Technology (electrical, mechanical)
                         (814) 949-5000

BEAVER CAMPUS
Brodhead Rd., Monaca 15061 *Prof.
Accred.:* Engineering Technology (electrical, mechanical)
                         (412) 773-3500

BEHREND COLLEGE
Station Rd., Erie 16563-0101 *Prof.
Accred.:* Engineering Technology (electrical, mechanical, plastics)
                         (814) 898-6000

BERKS CAMPUS
Tulpehocken Rd., P.O. Box 7009, Reading
19610 *Prof. Accred.:* Engineering Technology (electrical, mechanical)
                         (610) 320-4800

CAPITAL COLLEGE
777 W. Harrisburg Pk., Middletown
17057-4898 *Prof. Accred.:* Engineering
Technology (civil/construction, electrical,
environmental/sanitary, mechanical), Public Administration
                         (717) 948-6000

DELAWARE COUNTY CAMPUS
25 Yearsley Mill Rd., Media 19063-5596
                         (610) 892-1350

DUBOIS CAMPUS
College Pl., DuBois 15801 *Prof. Accred.:*
Engineering Technology (electrical,
mechanical)
                         (814) 375-4700

FAYETTE CAMPUS
P.O. Box 519, Rte. 119 N., Uniontown
15401 *Prof. Accred.:* Engineering Technology (air conditioning, architectural,
electrical)
                         (412) 430-4100

GREAT VALLEY GRADUATE CENTER
30 E. Swedesford Rd., Malvern 19355
                         (610) 648-3200

HAZLETON CAMPUS
Highacres, Hazleton 18201 *Prof. Accred.:*
Clinical Lab Technology (A), Engineering
Technology (electrical, mechanical),
Physical Therapy Assisting
                         (717) 450-3000

HERSHEY MEDICAL CENTER
500 University Dr., P.O. Box 850, Hershey 17033 *Prof. Accred.:* Medicine
                         (717) 531-8521

MCKEESPORT CAMPUS
University Dr., McKeesport 15132 *Prof.
Accred.:* Engineering Technology (electrical, mechanical)
(412) 675-9000

MONT ALTO CAMPUS
Campus Dr., Mont Alto 17237-9703 *Prof.
Accred.:* Physical Therapy Assisting
(717) 749-6000

NEW KENSINGTON CAMPUS
3550 Seventh Street Rd., New Kensington
15068 *Prof. Accred.:* Clinical Lab Technology (A), Engineering Technology (bioengineering, electrical, mechanical), Radiography
(412) 339-5466

OGONTZ CAMPUS
1600 Woodland Rd., Abington 19001
Prof. Accred.: Engineering Technology
(electrical, mechanical)
(215) 881-7300

SCHUYLKILL CAMPUS
200 University Dr., Schuylkill Haven
17972-2208 *Prof. Accred.:* Engineering
Technology (computer, electrical), Radiography
(717) 385-6000

SHENANGO CAMPUS
147 Shenango Ave., Sharon 16146 *Prof.
Accred.:* Engineering Technology (electrical, mechanical)
(412) 983-5800

WILKES-BARRE CAMPUS
P.O. Box PSU, Lehman 18627 *Prof.
Accred.:* Engineering Technology (bioengineering, electrical, mechanical, surveying)
(717) 675-2171

WORTHINGTON-SCRANTON CAMPUS
120 Ridge View Dr., Dunmore 18512
Prof. Accred.: Engineering Technology
(architectural, electrical)
(717) 963-4757

YORK CAMPUS
1031 Edgecomb Ave., York 17403 *Prof.
Accred.:* Engineering Technology (electrical, mechanical)
(717) 771-4000

PHILADELPHIA COLLEGE OF BIBLE
200 Manor Ave., Langhorne 19047-2990
Type: Private (interdenominational) *Accred.:*
1950/1986 (AABC); 1967/1995 (MSA) *Calendar:* Sem. plan *Degrees:* A, B, C *Prof.
Accred.:* Music, Social Work (B) *CEO:* Pres.
W. Sherrill Babb
FTE Enroll: 780   (215) 752-5800

NEW JERSEY CAMPUS
P.O. Box 204, Liberty Corner, NJ 07938
(908) 604-2707

WISCONSIN WILDERNESS CAMPUS
HC 60, Box 60, Cable, WI 54821
(715) 798-3525

PHILADELPHIA COLLEGE OF OSTEOPATHIC
MEDICINE
4150 City Ave., Philadelphia 19131 *Type:*
Private professional *Calendar:* Sem. plan
Degrees: M, P, D *Prof. Accred.:* Osteopathy
CEO: Pres. Leonard H. Finkelstein, D.O.
Enroll: 808   (215) 871-2800

PHILADELPHIA COLLEGE OF PHARMACY AND
SCIENCE
600 S. 43rd St., Philadelphia 19104-4495
Type: Private professional *Accred.:* 1962/
1993 (MSA) *Calendar:* Sem. plan *Degrees:*
B, M, P, D *Prof. Accred.:* Physical Therapy
CEO: Pres. Phillip P. Gerbino
Enroll: 1,939   (215) 596-8800

PHILADELPHIA COLLEGE OF TEXTILES AND
SCIENCE
Schoolhouse Ln. and Henry Ave., Philadelphia 19144 *Type:* Private professional
Accred.: 1955/1991 (MSA) *Calendar:* Sem.
plan *Degrees:* A, B, M *Prof. Accred.:* Interior Design *CEO:* Pres. James P. Gallagher
Enroll: 3,308   (215) 951-2700

PITTSBURGH INSTITUTE OF AERONAUTICS
P.O. Box 10897, Pittsburgh 15236-0897
Type: Private *Accred.:* 1970/1993 (ACC-

SCT) *Calendar:* Qtr. plan *Degrees:* A, C *CEO:* CEO John Graham

(412) 466-1022

PITTSBURGH INSTITUTE OF MORTUARY SCIENCE
5808 Baum Blvd., Pittsburgh 15206 *Type:* Private professional *Degrees:* A, C *Prof. Accred.:* Funeral Service Education (Mortuary Science) *CEO:* Pres. Eugene C. Ogrodnik

(412) 362-8500

PITTSBURGH TECHNICAL INSTITUTE
635 Smithfield St., Pittsburgh 15222-2560 *Type:* Private *Accred.:* 1970/1991 (ACC-SCT) *Calendar:* Sem. plan *Degrees:* A *CEO:* Pres. J.R. McCartan

(412) 471-1011

PITTSBURGH THEOLOGICAL SEMINARY
616 N. Highland Ave., Pittsburgh 15206 *Type:* Private (Presbyterian) graduate only *Accred.:* 1938/1992 (ATS); 1970/1993 (MSA) *Calendar:* Qtr. plan *Degrees:* M, P, D *CEO:* Pres. Carnegie Samuel Calian
Enroll: 313   (412) 362-5610

POINT PARK COLLEGE
201 Wood St., Pittsburgh 15222 *Type:* Private *Accred.:* 1968/1994 (MSA) *Calendar:* Sem. plan *Degrees:* A, B, M, C *Prof. Accred.:* Engineering Technology (civil/construction, electrical, mechanical) *CEO:* Pres. James O. Hunter
Enroll: 2,397   (412) 391-4100

READING AREA COMMUNITY COLLEGE
P.O. Box 1706, 10 S. 2nd St., Reading 19603-1706 *Type:* Public (state) junior *Accred.:* 1979/1993 (MSA) *Calendar:* Tri. plan *Degrees:* A, C *Prof. Accred.:* Clinical Lab Technology (A), Respiratory Therapy, Respiratory Therapy Technology *CEO:* Pres. Gust Zogas
Enroll: 3,231   (610) 372-4721

RECONSTRUCTIONIST RABBINICAL COLLEGE
Greenwood Ave. and Church Rd., Wyncote 19095 *Type:* Private (Jewish) professional *Accred.:* 1990/1995 (MSA) *Calendar:* Sem.

plan *Degrees:* M, P *CEO:* Pres. David A. Teutsch
Enroll: 73   (215) 576-0800

REFORMED PRESBYTERIAN THEOLOGICAL SEMINARY
7418 Penn Ave., Pittsburgh 15208 *Type:* Private (Presbyterian) graduate only *Accred.:* 1994 (ATS) *Calendar:* Sem. plan *Degrees:* M *CEO:* Pres. Jerry F. O'Neill
Enroll: 89   (412) 731-8690

THE RESTAURANT SCHOOL
4207 Walnut St., Philadelphia 19104-3518 *Type:* Private *Accred.:* 1982/1987 (ACCSCT) *Degrees:* A *CEO:* Pres. Daniel Liberatoscioli

(215) 222-4200

RETS EDUCATION CENTER
2641 W. Chester Pike, Broomall 19008-1999 *Type:* Private *Accred.:* 1973/1988 (ACCSCT) *Degrees:* A, C *CEO:* Dir. Jane Chadwick

(215) 353-7630

ROBERT MORRIS COLLEGE
Narrows Run Rd., Coraopolis 15108 *Type:* Private *Accred.:* 1968/1992 (MSA) *Calendar:* Tri. plan *Degrees:* A, B, M *CEO:* Pres. Edward A. Nicholson
Enroll: 5,346   (412) 262-8200

PITTSBURGH CAMPUS
600 Fifth Ave., Pittsburgh 15219
(412) 227-6800

ROSEMONT COLLEGE
1400 Montgomery Ave., Rosemont 19010-1699 *Type:* Private (Roman Catholic) liberal arts for women *Accred.:* 1930/1990 (MSA) *Calendar:* Sem. plan *Degrees:* B, M, C *CEO:* Pres. Margaret M. Healy
Enroll: 589   (215) 527-0200

ST. CHARLES BORROMEO SEMINARY
1000 E. Wynnewood Rd., Overbrook 19096-3099 *Type:* Private (Roman Catholic) *Accred.:* 1970/1991 (ATS); 1971/1991 (MSA) *Calendar:* Sem. plan *Degrees:* B, M, P, C *CEO:* Pres./Rector James E. Molloy
Enroll: 508   (610) 667-3394

ST. FRANCIS COLLEGE
Loretto 15940 *Type:* Private (Roman Catholic) *Accred.:* 1939/1991 (MSA) *Calendar:* Sem. plan *Degrees:* A, B, M *Prof. Accred.:* Nursing (B), Physician Assisting/Surgeon Assisting, Social Work (B) *CEO:* Pres. Christian Oravec
Enroll: 1,983   (814) 472-3000

ST. JOSEPH'S UNIVERSITY
5600 City Line Ave., Philadelphia 19131 *Type:* Private (Roman Catholic) *Accred.:* 1922/1994 (MSA) *Calendar:* Sem. plan *Degrees:* A, B, M, C *Prof. Accred.:* Nurse Anesthesia Education *CEO:* Pres. Nicholas S. Rashford, S.J.
Enroll: 10,667   (610) 660-1000

ST. VINCENT COLLEGE AND SEMINARY
300 Frazier Purchase Rd., Latrobe 15650 *Type:* Private (Roman Catholic) liberal arts *Accred.:* 1984/1988 (ATS); 1921/1993 (MSA) *Calendar:* Sem. plan *Degrees:* B, M, P, C *CEO:* Pres. Martin R. Bartel, O.S.B.
Enroll: 1,316   (412) 539-9761

THE SAWYER SCHOOL
717 Liberty Ave., Ste. 800, Pittsburgh 15222 *Type:* Private business *Accred.:* 1973/1997 (ACICS) *Degrees:* A *Prof. Accred.:* Medical Assisting, Medical Assisting (AMA) *CEO:* Pres. Thomas B. Sapienza
       (412) 261-5700

SCHUYLKILL BUSINESS INSTITUTE
2400 W. End Ave., Pottsville 17901 *Type:* Private business *Accred.:* 1980/1998 (ACICS) *Degrees:* A *CEO:* Pres. James Tarity, Jr.
       (717) 622-4835

SETON HILL COLLEGE
Greensburg 15601 *Type:* Private (Roman Catholic) liberal arts for women *Accred.:* 1921/1992 (MSA) *Calendar:* Sem. plan *Degrees:* B, C *Prof. Accred.:* Dietetics (coordinated), Music *CEO:* Pres. JoAnne W. Boyle
Enroll: 925   (412) 834-2200

SHIPPENSBURG UNIVERSITY OF PENNSYLVANIA
Shippensburg 17257 *Type:* Public (state) *System:* Pennsylvania State System of Higher Education *Accred.:* 1939/1994 (MSA) *Calendar:* Sem. plan *Degrees:* B, M *Prof. Accred.:* Business (B), Counseling, Social Work (B), Teacher Education *CEO:* Pres. Anthony F. Ceddia
Enroll: 6,603   (717) 532-9121

SLIPPERY ROCK UNIVERSITY OF PENNSYLVANIA
Slippery Rock 16057 *Type:* Public (state) *System:* Pennsylvania State System of Higher Education *Accred.:* 1943/1991 (MSA) *Calendar:* Sem. plan *Degrees:* B, M *Prof. Accred.:* Athletic Training, Music, Nurse Anesthesia Education, Nursing (B), Physical Therapy, Recreation and Leisure Services, Social Work (B), Teacher Education *CEO:* Pres. Robert N. Aebersold
Enroll: 7,563   (412) 738-0512

SOUTH HILLS BUSINESS SCHOOL
480 Waupelani Dr., State College 16801-4516 *Type:* Private business *Accred.:* 1976/1991 (ACICS) *Calendar:* Tri. plan *Degrees:* A *Prof. Accred.:* Medical Record Technology *CEO:* Dir. Maralyn J. Mazza
       (814) 234-7755

SUSQUEHANNA UNIVERSITY
Selinsgrove 17870 *Type:* Private (Lutheran) *Accred.:* 1930/1994 (MSA) *Calendar:* Sem. plan *Degrees:* A, B *Prof. Accred.:* Business (B), Music *CEO:* Pres. Joel L. Cunningham
Enroll: 1,608   (717) 374-0101

SWARTHMORE COLLEGE
500 College Ave., Swarthmore 19081 *Type:* Private liberal arts *Accred.:* 1921/1989 (MSA) *Calendar:* Sem. plan *Degrees:* B, M *Prof. Accred.:* Engineering (general) *CEO:* Pres. Alfred H. Bloom
Enroll: 1,390   (215) 328-8000

TALMUDICAL YESHIVA OF PHILADELPHIA
6063 Drexel Rd., Philadelphia 19131 *Type:* Private professional *Accred.:* 1975/1995 (AARTS) *Calendar:* Sem. plan *Degrees:* Rabbinic (1st), Talmudic (1st and 2nd) *CEO:* Pres. Erwin Weinberg
Enroll: 105   (215) 473-1212

TEMPLE UNIVERSITY
Broad and Montgomery Sts., Philadelphia
19122 *Type:* Private (state-related) *Accred.:*
1921/1994 (MSA) *Calendar:* Sem. plan
Degrees: A, B, M, P, D, C *Prof. Accred.:* Art,
Audiology, Business (B,M), Clinical Psychology, Combined Prosthodontics, Counseling Psychology, Dance, Dentistry,
Endodontics, Engineering Technology (civil/
construction, electrical, mechanical), Engineering (civil, electrical, mechanical), General Dentistry, Health Services Administration, Journalism (B,M), Landscape Architecture (B), Law, Medical Record Administration, Medicine, Music, Nursing (B), Occupational Therapy, Oral and Maxillofacial
Surgery, Orthodontics, Periodontics, Physical
Therapy, Psychology Internship, Recreation
and Leisure Services (B), School Psychology,
Social Work (B,M), Speech-Language
Pathology, Teacher Education, Theatre *CEO:*
Pres. Peter J. Liacouras
Enroll: 29,616   (215) 204-7000

THADDEUS STEVENS STATE SCHOOL OF
TECHNOLOGY
750 E. King St., Lancaster 17602 *Type:* Public (state) junior *Accred.:* 1991 (MSA) *Calendar:* Sem. plan *Degrees:* A, C *CEO:* Pres.
Alan K. Cohen
Enroll: 456   (717) 299-7730

THIEL COLLEGE
75 College Ave., Greenville 16125 *Type:* Pri-
vate (Lutheran) liberal arts *Accred.:* 1922/
1992 (MSA) *Calendar:* Sem. plan *Degrees:* A,
B, C *Prof. Accred.:* Nursing (B), Respiratory
Therapy Technology *CEO:* Pres. C. Carlyle
Haaland
Enroll: 968   (412) 589-2000

THOMAS JEFFERSON UNIVERSITY
11th and Walnut Sts., Philadelphia 19107
Type: Private professional *Accred.:* 1976/
1993 (MSA) *Calendar:* Qtr. plan *Degrees:*
A, B, M, P, D, C *Prof. Accred.:* Clinical Lab
Scientist, Cytotechnology, Diagnostic Medical Sonography, General Practice Residency, Medicine, Nursing (B,M), Occupational Therapy, Oral and Maxillofacial

Surgery, Physical Therapy, Radiography
CEO: Pres. Paul C. Brucker
Enroll: 2,624   (215) 955-6000

TRI-STATE BUSINESS INSTITUTE
5757 W. 26th St., Erie 16506 *Type:* Private
business *Accred.:* 1990/1997 (ACICS)
Degrees: A, C *CEO:* Vice Pres. Guy M.
Euliano
          (814) 838-7673

TRIANGLE TECH
P.O. Box 551, DuBois 15801-9990 *Type:* Pri-
vate *Accred.:* 1981/1986 (ACCSCT) *Degrees:*
A, C *CEO:* Dir. Branda McCullough
          (814) 371-2090

TRIANGLE TECH
2000 Liberty St., Erie 16502-9987 *Type:* Private *Accred.:* 1978/1988 (ACCSCT) *Degrees:* A, C *CEO:* Dir. Mary M. Gill
          (814) 453-6016

TRIANGLE TECH
222 Pittsburgh St., Ste. A, Greensburg 15601
Type: Private *Accred.:* 1979/1990 (ACC-
SCT) *Degrees:* A, C *CEO:* Dir. Jayne Kalp
          (412) 832-1050

BUSINESS CAREERS INSTITUTE
222 East Pittsburg St., Greensburg 15601-
2394 *Accred.:* 1991 (ACCSCT)
          (412) 834-1258

TRIANGLE TECH
1940 Perrysville Ave., Pittsburgh 15214-
3897 *Type:* Private *Accred.:* 1970/1990
(ACCSCT) *Degrees:* A, C *CEO:* Dir. Brian
James
          (412) 359-1000

MONROEVILLE SCHOOL OF BUSINESS
105 Mall Blvd., Expo Mart, 3rd Fl., Monroeville 15146-2229 *Accred.:* 1990 (ACC-
SCT) *Degrees:* A, C
          (412) 856-8040

TRINITY EPISCOPAL SCHOOL FOR MINISTRY
311 Eleventh St., Ambridge 15003 *Type:* Private (Episcopal) graduate only *Accred.:*

1985/1990 (ATS) *Calendar:* Sem. plan *Degrees:* M *CEO:* Pres. William C. Frey *Enroll:* 119   (412) 266-3838

UNIVERSITY OF PENNSYLVANIA
34th and Spruce Sts., Philadelphia 19104 *Type:* Private non-profit *Accred.:* 1921/1989 (MSA) *Calendar:* Sem. plan *Degrees:* A, B, M, P, D, C *Prof. Accred.:* Business (B,M), Clinical Psychology, Combined Professional-Scientific Psychology, Dentistry, Endodontics, Engineering (bioengineering, chemical, civil, electrical, materials, mechanical, systems), General Dentistry, General Practice Residency, Health Services Administration, Landscape Architecture (M), Law, Medicine, Nursing (B,M), Oral and Maxillofacial Surgery, Orthodontics, Periodontics, Planning (M), Practical Nursing, Psychology Internship, Social Work (M), Veterinary Medicine *CEO:* Pres. Judith Rodin
Enroll: 22,720   (215) 898-5000

UNIVERSITY OF PITTSBURGH
4200 Fifth Ave., Pittsburgh 15260 *Type:* Public (state-related) *Accred.:* 1921/1991 (MSA) *Calendar:* Tri. plan *Degrees:* B, M, P, D, C *Prof. Accred.:* Audiology, Business (B,M), Clinical Lab Scientist, Clinical Psychology, Combined Prosthodontics, Counseling, Counseling Psychology (provisional), Dental Hygiene, Dentistry, Dietetics (coordinated), Endodontics, Engineering (chemical, civil, electrical, engineering physics/science, industrial, materials, mechanical, metallurgical), General Dentistry, Health Services Administration, Law, Librarianship, Maxillofacial Prosthodontics, Medical Record Administration, Medicine, Nurse Anesthesia Education, Nursing (B,M), Occupational Therapy, Oral and Maxillofacial Surgery, Orthodontics, Pediatric Dentistry, Periodontics, Physical Therapy, Planning (M), Psychology Internship, Public Administration, Rehabilitation Counseling, Social Work (B,M), Speech-Language Pathology, Theatre, *CEO:* Interim Chanc. Mark A. Nordenberg
Enroll: 26,328   (412) 624-4141

BRADFORD CAMPUS
Bradford 16701 *Prof. Accred.:* Nursing (A)
                    (814) 362-7500

GREENSBURG CAMPUS
1150 Mount Pleasant Rd., Greensburg 15601
                    (412) 837-7040

JOHNSTOWN CAMPUS
Johnstown 15904 *Prof. Accred.:* Engineering Technology (civil/construction, electrical, mechanical), Respiratory Therapy
                    (814) 269-7000

TITUSVILLE CAMPUS
504 E. Main St., Titusville 16354
                    (814) 827-4400

UNIVERSITY OF SCRANTON
800 Linden St., Scranton 18510-4501 *Type:* Private (Roman Catholic) *Accred.:* 1927/1993 (MSA) *Calendar:* 4-1-4 plan *Degrees:* A, B, M, C *Prof. Accred.:* Computer Science, Counseling, Health Services Administration, Nursing (B), Physical Therapy, Rehabilitation Counseling *CEO:* Pres. Joseph A. Panuska, S.J.
Enroll: 4,946   (717) 941-7500

UNIVERSITY OF THE ARTS
Broad and Pine Sts., Philadelphia 19102 *Type:* Private professional *Accred.:* 1969/1993 (MSA) *Calendar:* Sem. plan *Degrees:* A, B, M, C *Prof. Accred.:* Art, Music *CEO:* Pres. Peter Solmssen
Enroll: 1,298   (215) 875-4800

URSINUS COLLEGE
Box 1000, Collegeville 19426-1000 *Type:* Private liberal arts *Accred.:* 1921/1994 (MSA) *Calendar:* Sem. plan *Degrees:* A, B *CEO:* Pres. John R. Strassburger
Enroll: 2,370   (610) 489-4111

VALLEY FORGE CHRISTIAN COLLEGE
1401 Charlestown Rd., VFCC Box 51, Phoenixville 19460 *Type:* Private (Assemblies of God) *Accred.:* 1967/1987 (AABC) *Calendar:* Sem. plan *Degrees:* B, C *CEO:* Pres. Wesley W. Smith
FTE Enroll: 506   (215) 935-0450

VALLEY FORGE MILITARY COLLEGE
1001 Eagle Rd., Wayne 19087-3695 *Type:* Private junior for men *Accred.:* 1954/1992 (MSA) *Calendar:* 4-1-4 plan *Degrees:* A *CEO:* Pres. Virgil L. Hill, Jr.
Enroll: 205　　　　　　　(610) 688-1800

VILLANOVA UNIVERSITY
800 Lancaster Ave., Villanova 19085 *Type:* Private (Roman Catholic) *Accred.:* 1921/1991 (MSA) *Calendar:* Sem. plan *Degrees:* A, B, M, P, D *Prof. Accred.:* Accounting (A), Business (B,M), Computer Science, Engineering (chemical, civil, electrical, mechanical), Law, Nursing (B,M) *CEO:* Pres. Edmund J. Dobbin, O.S.A.
Enroll: 10,735　　　　　　(610) 519-4500

WASHINGTON AND JEFFERSON COLLEGE
60 South Lincoln St., Washington 15301 *Type:* Private liberal arts *Accred.:* 1921/1994 (MSA) *Calendar:* 4-1-4 plan *Degrees:* A, B, M *CEO:* Pres. Howard J. Burnett
Enroll: 1,224　　　　　　　(412) 222-4400

WAYNESBURG COLLEGE
51 W. College St., Waynesburg 15370 *Type:* Private (United Presbyterian) liberal arts *Accred.:* 1950/1995 (MSA) *Calendar:* Sem. plan *Degrees:* A, B, M *Prof. Accred.:* Nursing (B) *CEO:* Pres. Timothy R. Thyreen
Enroll: 1,319　　　　　　　(412) 627-8191

WELDER TRAINING AND TESTING INSTITUTE
729 E. Highland St., Allentown 18103-1263 *Type:* Private *Accred.:* 1973/1988 (ACCSCT) *Degrees:* A, C *CEO:* Dir. Patrick F. Dorris
　　　　　　　　　　　　　　(215) 437-9720

WEST CHESTER UNIVERSITY OF PENNSYLVANIA
S. High St., West Chester 19383 *Type:* Public (state) *System:* Pennsylvania State System of Higher Education *Accred.:* 1946/1990 (MSA) *Calendar:* Sem. plan *Degrees:* A, B, M *Prof. Accred.:* Music, Nursing (B), Respiratory Therapy, Social Work (B), Speech-Language Pathology, Teacher Education *CEO:* Pres. Madeleine Wing Adler
Enroll: 11,168　　　　　　(610) 436-1000

WESTMINSTER COLLEGE
S. Market St., New Wilmington 16172 *Type:* Private (Presbyterian) liberal arts *Accred.:* 1921/1991 (MSA) *Calendar:* 4-1-4 plan *Degrees:* B, M *Prof. Accred.:* Music *CEO:* Chanc. Oscar E. Remick
Enroll: 1,540　　　　　　　(412) 946-8761

WESTMINSTER THEOLOGICAL SEMINARY
Church Rd. and Willow Grove Av, Glenside 19118 *Type:* Private (interdenominational) graduate only *Accred.:* 1986/1991 (ATS); 1954/1992 (MSA) *Calendar:* 4-1-4 plan *Degrees:* M, P, D *CEO:* Pres. Samuel T. Logan, Jr.
Enroll: 533　　　　　　　(215) 887-5511

WESTMORELAND COUNTY COMMUNITY COLLEGE
Armbrust Rd., Youngwood 15697-1895 *Type:* Public (local/state) junior *Accred.:* 1978/1993 (MSA) *Calendar:* Sem. plan *Degrees:* A, C *Prof. Accred.:* Dental Hygiene *CEO:* Pres. Daniel C. Krezenski
Enroll: 6,277　　　　　　　(412) 925-4000

WIDENER UNIVERSITY
One University Pl., Chester 19013-5792 *Type:* Private *Accred.:* 1954/1991 (MSA) *Calendar:* Sem. plan *Degrees:* A, B, M, P, D, C *Prof. Accred.:* Clinical Psychology, Engineering (chemical, civil, electrical, general), Health Services Administration, Nursing (B,M), Physical Therapy (candidate), Psychology Internship *CEO:* Pres. Robert J. Bruce
Enroll: 8,543　　　　　　　(610) 499-4000

HARRISBURG CAMPUS
3800 Vartan Way, Harrisburg 17110-9450 *Prof. Accred.:* Law (ABA only)
Enroll: 797　　　　　　　(717) 541-3900

SCHOOL OF LAW CAMPUS
4601 Concord Pike, P.O. Box 7474, Wilmington, DE 19803-0474 *Prof. Accred.:* Law
Enroll: 1,404　　　　　　　(302) 477-2100

WILKES UNIVERSITY
170 S. Franklin St., Wilkes-Barre 18766 *Type:* Private non-profit *Accred.:* 1937/1990 (MSA) *Calendar:* Sem. plan *Degrees:* B, M

Prof. Accred.: Engineering (electrical, materials), Nursing (B) *CEO:* Pres. Christopher N. Breiseth
Enroll: 3,065   (717) 824-4651

THE WILLIAMSON FREE SCHOOL OF
MECHANICAL TRADES
106 S. New Middletown Rd., Media 19063-5299 *Type:* Private *Accred.:* 1970/1993 (ACCSCT) *Degrees:* A, C *CEO:* Pres. Barry G. Schuler
                              (610) 566-1776

WILLIAMSPORT SCHOOL OF COMMERCE
941 W. Third St., Williamsport 17701 *Type:* Private business *Accred.:* 1963/1986 (ACICS) *Calendar:* Qtr. plan *Degrees:* A *CEO:* Dir. Benjamin H. Comfort, III
                              (717) 326-2869

WILMA BOYD CAREER SCHOOLS
One Chatham Ctr., Pittsburgh 15219 *Type:* Private business *Accred.:* 1975/1996 (ACICS); 1979/1994 (DETC) *Degrees:* A, C *CEO:* Pres./Dir. Ruth A. Delach
                              (412) 456-1800

WILSON COLLEGE
1015 Philadelphia Ave., Chambersburg 17201-1285 *Type:* Private (Presbyterian) liberal arts for women *Accred.:* 1922/

1994 (MSA) *Calendar:* 4-1-4 plan *Degrees:* A, B, C *Prof. Accred.:* Veterinary Technology *CEO:* Pres. Gwendolyn Evans Jensen
Enroll: 861   (717) 264-4141

YESHIVA BETH MOSHE
930 Hickory St., Scranton 18505 *Type:* Private professional *Accred.:* 1976/1994 (AARTS) *Calendar:* Sem. plan *Degrees:* Talmudic (1st and 2nd) *CEO:* Pres. David Fink
Enroll: 55   (717) 346-1747

YORK COLLEGE OF PENNSYLVANIA
Country Club Rd., York 17405-7199 *Type:* Private *Accred.:* 1959/1991 (MSA) *Calendar:* Sem. plan *Degrees:* A, B, M *Prof. Accred.:* Medical Record Administration, Nursing (B), Recreation and Leisure Services, Respiratory Therapy, Respiratory Therapy Technology *CEO:* Pres. George W. Waldner
Enroll: 4,870   (717) 846-7788

YORKTOWNE BUSINESS INSTITUTE
W. Seventh Ave., York 17404 *Type:* Private business *Accred.:* 1979/1991 (ACICS) *Degrees:* A, C *CEO:* Pres. James P. Murphy
                              (717) 846-5000

PUERTO RICO

AMERICAN UNIVERSITY OF PUERTO RICO
P.O. Box 2037, Bayamon 00619 *Type:* Private liberal arts *Accred.:* 1982/1993 (MSA) *Calendar:* Sem. plan *Degrees:* A, B *CEO:* Pres. Juan B. Nazario-Negron
Enroll: 1,794   (809) 798-2022

MANATI CAMPUS
P.O. Box 1082, Manati 00701
                                   (809) 854-2835

ATLANTIC COLLEGE
Box 1774, Guaynabo 00651-1774 *Type:* Private senior *Accred.:* 1987/1995 (ACICS) *Calendar:* Sem. plan *Degrees:* A, B, C *CEO:* Pres. Teresa de Dios
                                   (809) 720-1022

BAYAMON CENTRAL UNIVERSITY
P.O. Box 1725, Bayamon 00960-1725 *Type:* Private (Roman Catholic) *Accred.:* 1971/1993 (MSA) *Calendar:* Sem. plan *Degrees:* A, B, M *CEO:* Pres. Vincent A.M. Van Rooij, O.P.
Enroll: 3,269   (809) 786-3030

CARIBBEAN CENTER FOR ADVANCED STUDIES
Apartado 3711, Old San Juan Sta., San Juan 00904-3711 *Type:* Private professional *Accred.:* 1974/1989 (MSA) *Calendar:* Sem. plan *Degrees:* M, P, D *CEO:* Pres. Salvador Santiago-Negron
Enroll: 426   (809) 725-6500

MIAMI INSTITUTE OF PSYCHOLOGY
8180 N.W. 36th St., 2nd Fl., Miami, FL 33166-6653 professional *Accred.:* 1981/1989 (MSA) *Calendar:* Sem. plan *Degrees:* B, M, D, C *Prof. Accred.:* Clinical Psychology (provisional)
Enroll: 295   (305) 593-1223

CARIBBEAN UNIVERSITY
Box 493, Rd. 167 km. 21.2, Forest Hills, Bayamon 00960-0493 *Type:* Private liberal arts *Accred.:* 1977/1991 (MSA) *Calendar:* Qtr. plan *Degrees:* A, B, M *CEO:* Pres. Angel E. Juan-Ortega
Enroll: 1,840   (809) 780-0070

CENTRO DE ESTUDIOS AVANZADOS DE PUERTO RICO Y EL CARIBE
Del Cristo St., No. 52, Box S 4467, San Juan 00904 *Type:* Private graduate only *Accred.:* 1982/1992 (MSA) *Calendar:* Sem. plan *Degrees:* M *CEO:* Exec. Dir. Ricardo Alegria
Enroll: 155   (809) 723-4481

COLEGIO BIBLICO PENTECOSTAL
Carretera 848, Km 0.5, P.O. Box 901, St. Just 00978 *Type:* Private (Church of God) *Accred.:* 1990 (AABC) *Calendar:* Sem. plan *Degrees:* B, C *CEO:* Pres. Ismael Lopez Borrero
FTE Enroll: 144   (809) 761-0640

COLEGIO UNIVERSITARIO DEL ESTE
P.O. Box 2010, Carolina 00983-2010 *Type:* Private liberal arts *System:* Sistema Universitario Ana G. Mendez Central Office *Accred.:* 1959/1995 (MSA) *Calendar:* Sem. plan *Degrees:* A, B *Prof. Accred.:* Medical Record Technology *CEO:* Chanc. Alberto Maldonado Ruiz
Enroll: 3,759   (809) 257-7373

COLUMBIA COLLEGE
P.O. Box 8517, Carretera 183, KM 1.7, Caguas 00726 *Type:* Private senior *Accred.:* 1976/1995 (ACICS) *Calendar:* Tri. plan *Degrees:* A, B, C *CEO:* Pres. Rafael Ramirez
                                   (809) 743-4041

RIO GRANDE CAMPUS
Public Sq., San Jose St., Rio Grande 00745 *Accred.:* 1976/1995 (ACICS)
                                   (809) 743-4041

YAUCO CAMPUS
Box 3062, Yauco 00698 *Accred.:* 1976/1995 (ACICS)
                                   (809) 856-0845

CONSERVATORY OF MUSIC OF PUERTO RICO
P.O. Box 41227, Minillas Sta., Santurce 00940 *Type:* Public (state) *Accred.:* 1975/

1989 (MSA) *Calendar:* Sem. plan *Degrees:* B *CEO:* Rector Raymond Torres Santos
Enroll: 302   (809) 751-0160

ELECTRONIC DATA PROCESSING COLLEGE
P.O. Box 2303, Hato Rey 00919 *Type:* Private senior *Accred.:* 1976/1995 (ACICS) *Degrees:* A, B *CEO:* Pres. Anibal N. Nieves
         (809) 765-3560

SAN SEBASTIAN CAMPUS
48 Betances St., P.O. Box 1674, San Sebastian 00685 *Accred.:* 1979/1995 (ACICS)
         (809) 896-2137

EVANGELICAL SEMINARY OF PUERTO RICO
776 Ponce de Leon Ave., San Juan 00925-9907 *Type:* Private (interdenominational) graduate only *Accred.:* 1982/1987 (ATS); 1989/1995 (MSA candidate) *Calendar:* Sem. plan *Degrees:* M, P *CEO:* Pres. Samuel Pagan
Enroll: 169   (809) 751-6483

HUERTAS JUNIOR COLLEGE
Box 8429, Caguas 00726 *Type:* Private junior *Accred.:* 1977/1995 (ACICS) *Calendar:* Qtr. plan *Degrees:* A, C *CEO:* Dir. Felix Rodriguez Matos
         (809) 743-2156

HUMACAO COMMUNITY COLLEGE
101-103 Cruz Ortiz Stella, Box 8948, Humacao 00792 *Type:* Private business *Accred.:* 1979/1988 (ACICS) *Degrees:* A, C *CEO:* Pres. Gilberto Rivera-Ortiz
         (809) 852-1430

FAJARDO CAMPUS
P.O. Box 1185, Gerrido Morales No. 52, Fajardo 00738 *Accred.:* 1987 (ACICS)
         (809) 863-5210

INSTITUTO COMERCIAL DE PUERTO RICO JUNIOR COLLEGE
558 Munoz Rivera Ave., Box 304, Hato Rey 00919 *Type:* Private junior *Accred.:* 1985/1992 (MSA) *Calendar:* Tri. plan *Degrees:* A, C *CEO:* Chanc. Genoveva Christian
Enroll: 1,728   (809) 763-1010

ARECIBO CAMPUS
Rd. 2, KM 80.4, San Daniel Box 1606, Arecibo 00612-1606
         (809) 878-0524

MAYAGUEZ CAMPUS
Mendez Vigo No. 55, P.O. Box 1108, Mayaguez 00708-1108
         (809) 832-2250

INTER AMERICAN UNIVERSITY OF PUERTO RICO AGUADILLA CAMPUS
P.O. Box 20000, Aguadilla 00605-2000 *Type:* Private liberal arts *System:* Inter American University of Puerto Rico Central Administration *Accred.:* 1957/1993 (MSA) *Calendar:* Sem. plan *Degrees:* A, B, C *CEO:* Chanc. Hilda M. Baco
Enroll: 3,889   (809) 891-0925

INTER AMERICAN UNIVERSITY OF PUERTO RICO ARECIBO CAMPUS
P.O. Box 4050, Arecibo 00614-4050 *Type:* Private liberal arts *System:* Inter American University of Puerto Rico Central Administration *Accred.:* 1957/1993 (MSA) *Calendar:* Sem. plan *Degrees:* A, B, C *CEO:* Chanc. Zaida Vega-Lugo
Enroll: 4,633   (809) 878-5475

INTER AMERICAN UNIVERSITY OF PUERTO RICO BARRANQUITAS CAMPUS
P.O. Box 517, Barranquitas 00794-0517 *Type:* Private liberal arts *System:* Inter American University of Puerto Rico Central Administration *Accred.:* 1957/1993 (MSA) *Calendar:* Sem. plan *Degrees:* A, B, C *CEO:* Chanc. Irene Fernandez
Enroll: 1,657   (809) 857-2585

INTER AMERICAN UNIVERSITY OF PUERTO RICO BAYAMON CAMPUS
Urb. Industrial Minillas, Carr. 174 #172, Bayamon 00959-1911 *Type:* Private liberal arts *System:* Inter American University of Puerto Rico Central Administration *Accred.:* 1960/1993 (MSA) *Calendar:* Sem. plan *Degrees:* A, B, C *CEO:* Chanc. Felix Torres-Leon
Enroll: 4,862   (809) 780-4040

INTER AMERICAN UNIVERSITY OF PUERTO RICO
FAJARDO CAMPUS
P.O. Box 1029, Fajardo 00738-1029 *Type:*
Private liberal arts *System:* Inter American
University of Puerto Rico Central Adminis-
tration *Accred.:* 1961/1993 (MSA) *Calen-
dar:* Sem. plan *Degrees:* A, B, C *CEO:*
Chanc. Yolanda Robles-Garcia
Enroll: 1,983   (809) 863-2390

INTER AMERICAN UNIVERSITY OF PUERTO RICO
GUAYAMA CAMPUS
P.O. Box 10004, Guayama 00785 *Type:* Pri-
vate liberal arts *System:* Inter American Uni-
versity of Puerto Rico Central Administra-
tion *Accred.:* 1957/1993 (MSA) *Calendar:*
Sem. plan *Degrees:* A, B, C *CEO:* Chanc.
Samuel F. Febres
Enroll: 1,898   (809) 864-2222

INTER AMERICAN UNIVERSITY OF PUERTO RICO
METROPOLITAN CAMPUS
P.O. Box 191293, San Juan 00919-1293
Type: Private liberal arts *System:* Inter Amer-
ican University of Puerto Rico Central
Administration *Accred.:* 1960/1993 (MSA)
Calendar: Sem. plan *Degrees:* A, B, M, P, D
Prof. Accred.: Clinical Lab Scientist, Nurs-
ing (B), Optometry, Social Work (B) *CEO:*
Chanc. Manuel J. Fernos
Enroll: 14,323   (809) 250-1912

INTER AMERICAN UNIVERSITY OF PUERTO RICO
PONCE CAMPUS
Bo. Sabanetas, Carr. 1, Mercedita 00715
Type: Private liberal arts *System:* Inter Amer-
ican University of Puerto Rico Central
Administration *Accred.:* 1962/1993 (MSA)
Calendar: Sem. plan *Degrees:* A, B *CEO:*
Chanc. Marilina L. Wayland
Enroll: 3,663   (809) 284-1912

INTER AMERICAN UNIVERSITY OF PUERTO RICO
SAN GERMAN CAMPUS
P.O. Box 5100, San German 00683-9801
Type: Private liberal arts *System:* Inter Amer-
ican University of Puerto Rico Central
Administration *Accred.:* 1944/1993 (MSA)
Calendar: Sem. plan *Degrees:* A, B, M *Prof.
Accred.:* Clinical Lab Scientist, Medical

Record Technology *CEO:* Chanc. Agnes
Mojica
Enroll: 6,392   (809) 264-1912

INTER AMERICAN UNIVERSITY OF PUERTO RICO
SCHOOL OF LAW
P.O. Box 70351, San Juan 00936-8351 *Type:*
Private professional *System:* Inter American
University of Puerto Rico Central Adminis-
tration *Accred.:* 1961/1995 (MSA) *Calen-
dar:* Sem. plan *Degrees:* P *Prof. Accred.:*
Law (ABA only) *CEO:* Dean Carlos E.
Ramos-Gonzalez
Enroll: 647   (809) 751-1912

INTER AMERICAN UNIVERSITY OF PUERTO RICO
SCHOOL OF OPTOMETRY
P.O. Box 191049, San Juan 00919-1049
Type: Private professional *System:* Inter
American University of Puerto Rico Central
Administration *Accred.:* 1985/1994 (MSA)
Calendar: Sem. plan *Degrees:* P *CEO:* Dean
Arthur J. Afanador
Enroll: 265   (809) 765-1915

INTERNATIONAL JUNIOR COLLEGE
1254 Ponce de Leon Ave., San Juan 00910
Type: Private junior *Accred.:* 1984/1988
(ACICS) *Degrees:* A *CEO:* Chanc. Providencia
Vales Mendez
                                   (809) 725-8718

CAGUAS CAMPUS
Plaza San Alfonso, 2nd Fl., Caguas 00627
Accred.: 1984 (ACICS)
                                   (809) 746-3777

HUMACAO CAMPUS
Humacao Shopping Ctr., Font Martelo St.,
Humacao 00971 *Accred.:* 1993 (ACICS)
                                   (809) 850-0055

NATIONAL COLLEGE OF BUSINESS AND
TECHNOLOGY
Ramos Bldg., Hwy. No. 2, P.O. Box 2036,
Bayamon 00960 *Type:* Private business
Accred.: 1983/ 2001 (ACICS) *Calendar:*
Qtr. plan *Degrees:* A, C *CEO:* Dir. Jesus
Siverio Orta
                                   (809) 780-5134

ARECIBO CAMPUS
Ave. Gonzalo Marin, Ste. 109, Arecibo 00612 *Accred.:* 1983/1989 (ACICS)
(809) 879-5044

PONCE SCHOOL OF MEDICINE
Ponce 00732 *Type:* Private professional *Calendar:* Sem. plan *Degrees:* P *Prof. Accred.:* Medicine *CEO:* Pres./Dean Jaime Rivera-Dueno
Enroll: 177   (809) 843-8288

THE PONTIFICAL CATHOLIC UNIVERSITY OF PUERTO RICO
Las Americas Ave., Sta. 6, Ponce 00732 *Type:* Private (Roman Catholic) *Accred.:* 1953/1993 (MSA) *Calendar:* Sem. plan *Degrees:* A, B, M, P, C *Prof. Accred.:* Clinical Lab Scientist, Law (ABA only), Nursing (B,M), Social Work (B) *CEO:* Pres. Tosello O. Giangiacomo, C.S.Sp.
Enroll: 8,399   (809) 841-2000

ARECIBO CAMPUS
P.O. Box 495, Arecibo 00613
(809) 881-1212

GUAYAMA CAMPUS
P.O. Box 809, Guayama 00654
(809) 864-0550

MAYAGUEZ CAMPUS
P.O. Box 1326, Mayaguez 00709
(809) 834-5151

PUERTO RICO TECHNICAL JUNIOR COLLEGE
Ave. Ponce de Leon No. 703, Hato Rey 00917 *Type:* Private *Accred.:* 1992 (ACC-SCT) *Degrees:* A, C *CEO:* Pres. Jose M. Muriente-Grana
(809) 751-0133

RAMIREZ COLLEGE OF BUSINESS AND TECHNOLOGY
P.O. Box 8340, 103 Munoz Rivera Ave., San Juan 00910 *Type:* Private junior *Accred.:* 1975/1994 (ACICS) *Calendar:* Tri. plan *Degrees:* A *CEO:* CEO Rogena Kyles
(809) 763-3120

TECHNOLOGICAL COLLEGE OF THE MUNICIPALITY OF SAN JUAN
Jose Oliver St., Industrial Park, Hato Rey 00918 *Type:* Public (local) junior *Accred.:* 1978/1992 (MSA) *Calendar:* Sem. plan *Degrees:* A *Prof. Accred.:* Nursing (A) *CEO:* Acting Chanc. Juan Camacho
Enroll: 967   (809) 250-7111

UNIVERSIDAD ADVENTISTA DE LAS ANTILLAS
P.O. Box 118, Mayaguez 00681 *Type:* Private (Seventh-Day Adventist) liberal arts *Accred.:* 1978/1987 (MSA) *Calendar:* Sem. plan *Degrees:* A, B *CEO:* Pres. Miguel Munoz
Enroll: 780   (809) 834-9595

UNIVERSIDAD CENTRAL DEL CARIBE
Call Box 60-327, Cayey 00621-6032 *Type:* Private professional *Degrees:* A, P *Prof. Accred.:* Medicine, Radiography *CEO:* Pres. Raul A. Marcial-Rojas
(809) 798-3001

UNIVERSIDAD DEL TURABO
Box 3030, Gurabo 00778 *Type:* Private non-profit *System:* Sistema Universitario Ana G. Mendez Central Office *Accred.:* 1974/1994 (MSA) *Calendar:* Sem. plan *Degrees:* A, B, M *CEO:* Rector Dennis Aliceo Rodriguez
Enroll: 7,744   (809) 743-7979

UNIVERSIDAD METROPOLITANA
Box 21150, Rio Piedras 00928 *Type:* Private *System:* Sistema Universitario Ana G. Mendez Central Office *Accred.:* 1983/1992 (MSA) *Calendar:* Sem. plan *Degrees:* A, B, M *Prof. Accred.:* Nursing (A,B), Respiratory Therapy *CEO:* Chanc. Rene L. Labarca Bonnet
Enroll: 5,066   (809) 766-1717

UNIVERSIDAD POLITECNICA DE PUERTO RICO
Ponce De Leon Ave., No. 405, Hato Rey 00918 *Type:* Private non-profit *Accred.:* 1985/1995 (MSA) *Calendar:* Qtr. plan *Degrees:* B, M *CEO:* Pres. Ernesto Vasquez-Barquet
Enroll: 4,678   (809) 754-8000

UNIVERSITY OF PUERTO RICO—AGUADILLA REGIONAL COLLEGE
P.O. Box 250160, Aguadilla 00604-0160 *Type:* Public (state) junior *System:* Univer-

sity of Puerto Rico Regional Colleges Administration *Accred.:* 1976/1992 (MSA) *Calendar:* Sem. plan *Degrees:* A *CEO:* Dean/Dir. Juana Segarra-Jaramillo
Enroll: 1,874 (809) 890-2681

UNIVERSITY OF PUERTO RICO—ARECIBO
TECHNOLOGICAL UNIVERSITY COLLEGE
P.O. Box 1806, Arecibo 00613 *Type:* Public (state) *System:* University of Puerto Rico Regional Colleges Administration *Accred.:* 1967/1994 (MSA) *Calendar:* Sem. plan *Degrees:* A, B *Prof. Accred.:* Nursing (A) *CEO:* Dir. Juan Ramirez
Enroll: 3,837 (809) 828-2830

UNIVERSITY OF PUERTO RICO—BAYAMON
TECHNOLOGICAL UNIVERSITY COLLEGE
Bayamon Gardens Sta., Bayamon 00959-1919 *Type:* Public (state) *System:* University of Puerto Rico Regional Colleges Administration *Accred.:* 1960/1992 (MSA) *Calendar:* Sem. plan *Degrees:* A, B *CEO:* Dean/Dir. Carmen Ana Rivera
Enroll: 4,261 (809) 786-6840

UNIVERSITY OF PUERTO RICO—CAROLINA
REGIONAL COLLEGE
P.O. Box 4800, Carolina 00984-4800 *Type:* Public (state) junior *System:* University of Puerto Rico Regional Colleges Administration *Accred.:* 1978/1992 (MSA) *Calendar:* Sem. plan *Degrees:* A *CEO:* Acting Dean/Dir. Myrna Mayol
Enroll: 2,318 (809) 257-0000

UNIVERSITY OF PUERTO RICO—CAYEY CAMPUS
Antonio R. Barcelo Ave., Cayey 00633 *Type:* Public (state) liberal arts *System:* University of Puerto Rico Central Administration *Accred.:* 1967/1995 (MSA) *Calendar:* Sem. plan *Degrees:* A, B *CEO:* Chanc. Jose Luis Monserrate
Enroll: 3,149 (809) 738-2161

UNIVERSITY OF PUERTO RICO—HUMACAO
CAMPUS
CUH Sta., Humacao 00661 *Type:* Public (state) liberal arts *System:* University of Puerto Rico Central Administration *Accred.:* 1962/1994 (MSA) *Calendar:* Sem. plan

Degrees: A, B *Prof. Accred.:* Nursing (A,B), Occupational Therapy Assisting, Physical Therapy Assisting, Social Work (B) *CEO:* Chanc. Roberto Marrero-Corletto
Enroll: 3,925 (809) 850-0000

UNIVERSITY OF PUERTO RICO—LA MONTANA
REGIONAL COLLEGE
P.O. Box 2500, Utuado 00641 *Type:* Public (state) junior *System:* University of Puerto Rico Regional Colleges Administration *Accred.:* 1986/1990 (MSA) *Calendar:* Sem. plan *Degrees:* A *CEO:* Acting Dean/Dir. Ramon Colon Murphy
Enroll: 1,082 (809) 894-2828

UNIVERSITY OF PUERTO RICO—MAYAGUEZ
CAMPUS
P.O. Box 5000, College Sta., Mayaguez 00681 *Type:* Public (state) *System:* University of Puerto Rico Central Administration *Accred.:* 1946/1995 (MSA) *Calendar:* Sem. plan *Degrees:* A, B, M, D *Prof. Accred.:* Engineering (chemical, civil, electrical, industrial, mechanical), Nursing (A,B) *CEO:* Chanc. Stuart Ramos
Enroll: 11,123 (809) 834-4040

UNIVERSITY OF PUERTO RICO—MEDICAL
SCIENCES CAMPUS
P.O. Box 365067, San Juan 00936-5067 *Type:* Public (state) *System:* University of Puerto Rico Central Administration *Accred.:* 1949/1992 (MSA) *Calendar:* Sem. plan *Degrees:* A, B, M, P, D, C *Prof. Accred.:* Clinical Lab Scientist, Combined Prosthodontics, Cytotechnology, Dental Assisting, Dental Hygiene (provisional), Dentistry, Dietetics (internship), General Practice Residency, Health Services Administration, Medical Record Administration, Medicine, Nuclear Medicine Technology, Nurse Anesthesia Education, Nursing (B,M), Occupational Therapy, Oral and Maxillofacial Surgery, Pediatric Dentistry, Physical Therapy, Radiography, Respiratory Therapy *CEO:* Chanc. Jorge L. Sanchez-Colon
Enroll: 2,722 (809) 758-2525

UNIVERSITY OF PUERTO RICO—PONCE
TECHNOLOGICAL UNIVERSITY COLLEGE
P.O. Box 7186, Ponce 00732 *Type:* Public
(state) *System:* University of Puerto Rico
Regional Colleges Administration *Accred.:*
1970/1995 (MSA) *Calendar:* Sem. plan
Degrees: A, B *Prof. Accred.:* Physical Ther-
apy Assisting *CEO:* Dir. Antonia Lopez
Enroll: 2,918   (809) 844-8181

UNIVERSITY OF PUERTO RICO—RIO PIEDRAS
CAMPUS
Ponce de Leon Ave., Stop 38, San Juan 00931
Type: Public (state) *System:* University of
PuertoRico Central Administration *Accred.:*
1946/1995 (MSA) *Calendar:* Sem. plan *De-
grees:* B, M, P, D, C *Prof. Accred.:* Law,
Librarianship, Planning (M), Rehabilitation
Counseling, Social Work (B,M), Teacher Edu-
cation *CEO:* Chanc. Efrain Gonzalez Tejera
Enroll: 18,690   (809) 764-0000

UNIVERSITY OF THE SACRED HEART
Box 12383, Loiza Sta., Santurce 00914 *Type:*
Private   (Roman   Catholic)   *Accred.:*
1950/1992 (MSA) *Calendar:* Sem. plan
Degrees: A, B, M, C *Prof. Accred.:* Clinical
Lab Scientist, Nursing (A,B), Social Work
(B) *CEO:* Pres. Jose Jaime Rivera
Enroll: 5,199   (809) 728-1515

RHODE ISLAND

BROWN UNIVERSITY
Providence 02912 *Type:* Private *Accred.:* 1929/1988 (NEASC-CIHE) *Calendar:* Sem. plan *Degrees:* B, M, P, D *Prof. Accred.:* Engineering (bioengineering, chemical, civil, electrical, materials, mechanical), Medicine, Psychology Internship *CEO:* Pres. Vartan Gregorian
Enroll: 7,418   (401) 863-1000

BRYANT COLLEGE
1150 Douglas Pike, Smithfield 02917-1284 *Type:* Private *Accred.:* 1964/1990 (NEASC-CIHE) *Calendar:* Sem. plan *Degrees:* A, B, M *Prof. Accred.:* Business (B,M) *CEO:* Interim Pres. James A. Norton
Enroll: 2,970   (401) 232-6000

COMMUNITY COLLEGE OF RHODE ISLAND
400 East Ave., Warwick 02886-1805 *Type:* Public (state) *System:* State of Rhode Island Office of Higher Education *Accred.:* 1969/1994 (NEASC-CIHE) *Calendar:* Sem. plan *Degrees:* A, C *Prof. Accred.:* Clinical Lab Technology (A), Dental Assisting, Dental Hygiene, Nursing (A), Physical Therapy Assisting, Practical Nursing, Radiography, Respiratory Therapy *CEO:* Pres. Edward J. Liston
Enroll: 8,627   (401) 825-2188

JOHNSON & WALES UNIVERSITY
8 Abbott Park Pl., Providence 02903 *Type:* Private senior *Accred.:* 1954/1999 (ACICS); 1994 (NEASC-CIHE) *Calendar:* Tri. plan *Degrees:* A, B, M, P *CEO:* Pres. John A. Yena
Enroll: 9,195   (401) 598-1000

CHARLESTON CAMPUS
701 E. Bay St., PCC Box 1409, Charleston, SC 29403 *Accred.:* 1984/1987 (ACICS)
                                     (401) 598-1000

NORFOLK CAMPUS
2428 Almeda Ave., Stes. 316-318, Norfolk, VA 23513 *Accred.:* 1987 (ACICS)
                                     (804) 853-3508

NORTH MIAMI CAMPUS
1701 N.E. 127th St., North Miami, FL 33181 *Accred.:* 1993 (ACICS)
                                     (305) 892-7000

VAIL CAMPUS
616 W. Lionshead Cir., Ste. 101, Vail, CO 81657 *Accred.:* 1993 (ACICS)
                                     (970) 476-2993

KATHARINE GIBBS SCHOOL
178 Butler Ave., Providence 02906 *Type:* Private business *Accred.:* 1967/1997 (ACICS) *Calendar:* Sem. plan *Degrees:* A, C *CEO:* Dir. Elaine K. Carroll
                                     (401) 861-1420

NAVAL WAR COLLEGE
Newport 02841-5010 *Type:* Public (federal) *Accred.:* 1989/1995 (NEASC-CIHE) *Calendar:* Sem. plan *Degrees:* M *CEO:* Pres. James R. Stark
Enroll: 472   (401) 841-2266

NEW ENGLAND TECHNICAL COLLEGE
2500 Post Rd., Warwick 02886-2251 *Type:* Private *Accred.:* 1982/1993 (NEASC-CTCI) *Calendar:* Qtr. plan *Degrees:* A, B *CEO:* Pres. Richard I. Gouse
FTE Enroll: 2,041   (401) 739-5000

PROVIDENCE COLLEGE
Providence 02918 *Type:* Private (Roman Catholic) liberal arts *Accred.:* 1933/1987 (NEASC-CIHE) *Calendar:* Sem. plan *Degrees:* B, M, D *Prof. Accred.:* Social Work (B) *CEO:* Pres. Philip A. Smith, O.P.
Enroll: 3,699   (401) 865-1000

RHODE ISLAND COLLEGE
Providence 02908 *Type:* Public (state) liberal arts and teachers *System:* State of Rhode Island Office of Higher Education *Accred.:* 1958/1990 (NEASC-CIHE) *Calendar:* Sem. plan *Degrees:* B, M *Prof. Accred.:* Art, Music, Nursing (B), Social Work (B,M), Teacher Education *CEO:* Pres. John Nazarian
Enroll: 6,496   (401) 456-8100

RHODE ISLAND SCHOOL OF DESIGN
2 College St., Providence 02903 *Type:* Private professional *Accred.:* 1949/1986 (NEASC-CIHE) *Calendar:* Sem. plan *Degrees:* B, M *Prof. Accred.:* Art, Landscape Architecture (B) *CEO:* Pres. Roger Mandle
Enroll: 2,148   (401) 454-6402

ROGER WILLIAMS UNIVERSITY
One Old Ferry Rd., Bristol 02809-2921 *Type:* Private liberal arts *Accred.:* 1972/1986 (NEASC-CIHE) *Calendar:* Sem. plan *Degrees:* A, B, P *CEO:* Pres. Anthony J. Santoro
Enroll: 2,720   (401) 253-1040

SALVE REGINA UNIVERSITY
100 Ochre Point Ave., Newport 02840-4192 *Type:* Private (Roman Catholic) liberal arts *Accred.:* 1956/1991 (NEASC-CIHE) *Calendar:* Sem. plan *Degrees:* A, B, M, D *Prof.*
Accred.: Art, Nursing (B), Social Work (B) *CEO:* Pres. M. Therese Antone, RSM
Enroll: 1,838   (401) 847-6650

UNIVERSITY OF RHODE ISLAND
Kingston 02881-0806 *Type:* Public (state) *System:* State of Rhode Island Office of Higher Education *Accred.:* 1930/1987 (NEASC-CIHE) *Calendar:* Sem. plan *Degrees:* A, B, M, D *Prof. Accred.:* Accounting (A,C), Audiology, Business (B,M), Clinical Psychology, Dental Hygiene, Engineering (chemical, civil, computer, electrical, industrial, manufacturing, mechanical), Landscape Architecture (B), Librarianship, Marriage and Family Therapy (M), Music, Nursing (B,M), Physical Therapy, Planning (M), School Psychology, Speech-Language Pathology, Teacher Education *CEO:* Pres. Robert L. Carothers
Enroll: 11,302   (401) 792-2444

SOUTH CAROLINA

AIKEN TECHNICAL COLLEGE
P.O. Box 696, Aiken 29802-0696 *Type:* Public (state) 2-year *System:* South Carolina State Board for Technical and Comprehensive Education *Accred.:* 1975/1990 (SACS-CC) *Calendar:* Qtr. plan *Degrees:* A *Prof. Accred.:* Dental Assisting *CEO:* Pres. Kathleen A. Noble
FTE Enroll: 1,715   (803) 593-9231

ALLEN UNIVERSITY
1530 Harden St., Columbia 29204 *Type:* Private (African Methodist Episcopal) liberal arts and teachers *Accred.:* 1992 (SACS-CC) *Calendar:* Sem. plan *Degrees:* B *CEO:* Pres. David T. Shannon
FTE Enroll: 306   (803) 254-4165

ANDERSON COLLEGE
316 Blvd., Anderson 29621 *Type:* Private (Southern Baptist) *Accred.:* 1959/1990 (SACS-CC) *Calendar:* Sem. plan *Degrees:* A, B *Prof. Accred.:* Music (A) *CEO:* Pres. Lee G. Royce
FTE Enroll: 983   (803) 231-2000

BENEDICT COLLEGE
Harden and Blanding Sts., Columbia 29204 *Type:* Private liberal arts (Baptist) *Accred.:* 1946/1991 (SACS-CC) *Calendar:* Sem. plan *Degrees:* B *Prof. Accred.:* Social Work (B) *CEO:* Pres. David H. Swinton
FTE Enroll: 1,230   (803) 253-4220

CENTRAL CAROLINA TECHNICAL COLLEGE
506 N. Guignard Dr., Sumter 29150-2499 *Type:* Public (state) 2-year *System:* South Carolina State Board for Technical and Comprehensive Education *Accred.:* 1970/ 1995 (SACS-CC) *Calendar:* Sem. plan *Degrees:* A *Prof. Accred.:* Engineering Technology (civil/construction) *CEO:* Pres. Herbert C. Robbins
FTE Enroll: 1,701   (803) 778-1961

CHARLESTON SOUTHERN UNIVERSITY
P.O. Box 1108087, 9200 University Blvd., Charleston 29422-8087 *Type:* Private (Southern Baptist) liberal arts and teachers *Accred.:* 1970/1995 (SACS-CC) *Calendar:* 4-1-4 plan *Degrees:* A, B, M *Prof. Accred.:* Music *CEO:* Pres. Jairy C. Hunter, Jr.
FTE Enroll: 1,962   (803) 863-7000

CHESTERFIELD-MARLBORO TECHNICAL COLLEGE
1201 Chesterfield Hwy., Cheraw 29520-1007 *Type:* Public (state) 2-year *System:* South Carolina State Board for Technical and Comprehensive Education *Accred.:* 1973/1988 (SACS-CC) *Calendar:* Qtr. plan *Degrees:* A *CEO:* Pres. Ronald W. Hampton
FTE Enroll: 689   (803) 921-6900

THE CITADEL
Citadel Sta., 171 Moultrie St., Charleston 29409-0205 *Type:* Public (state) primarily for men *System:* South Carolina Commission on Higher Education *Accred.:* 1924/ 1994 (SACS-CC) *Calendar:* Sem. plan *Degrees:* B, M *Prof. Accred.:* Engineering (civil, electrical), Teacher Education *CEO:* Pres. Claudius E. Watts, III
FTE Enroll: 3,007   (803) 353-5000

CLAFLIN COLLEGE
400 Magnolia St., Orangeburg 29115 *Type:* Private (United Methodist) liberal arts *Accred.:* 1947/1991 (SACS-CC) *Calendar:* Sem. plan *Degrees:* B *CEO:* Pres. Henry N. Tisdale
FTE Enroll: 991   (803) 534-2710

CLEMSON UNIVERSITY
201 Sikes Hall, Clemson 29634 *Type:* Public (state) liberal arts *System:* South Carolina Commission on Higher Education *Accred.:* 1927/1991 (SACS-CC) *Calendar:* Sem. plan *Degrees:* B, M, D *Prof. Accred.:* Accounting (A,C), Business (B,M), Computer Science, Construction Education (B), Engineering (agricultural, ceramic, chemical, civil, computer, electrical, environmental/sanitary, industrial, mechanical), Forestry, Landscape Architecture (B-initial), Nursing (B,M), Planning (M), Recreation and Leisure Services

(B), Teacher Education *CEO:* Pres. Constantine W. Curris
FTE Enroll: 15,669   (803) 656-3311

COASTAL CAROLINA UNIVERSITY
P.O. Box 1954, Myrtle Beach 29526 *Type:* Public (state) *System:* South Carolina Commission on Higher Education *Accred.:* 1976/ 1991 (SACS-CC) *Calendar:* Sem. plan *Degrees:* A, B, M (candidate) *CEO:* Chanc. Ronald R. Ingle
FTE Enroll: 3,665   (803) 347-3161

COKER COLLEGE
300 E. College Ave., Hartsville 29550 *Type:* Private liberal arts *Accred.:* 1923/1995 (SACS-CC) *Calendar:* Sem. plan *Degrees:* B *Prof. Accred.:* Music *CEO:* Pres. James D. Daniels
FTE Enroll: 800   (803) 383-8000

COLLEGE OF CHARLESTON
66 George St., Charleston 29424 *Type:* Public (state) liberal arts *System:* South Carolina Commission on Higher Education *Accred.:* 1916/1986 (SACS-CC) *Calendar:* Sem. plan *Degrees:* B, M *Prof. Accred.:* Accounting (A), Business (B), Computer Science, Public Administration *CEO:* Pres. Alexander M. Sanders, Jr.
FTE Enroll: 8,464   (803) 953-5507

COLUMBIA COLLEGE
1301 Columbia College Dr., Columbia 29203 *Type:* Private (United Methodist) liberal arts for women *Accred.:* 1938/1991 (SACS-CC) *Calendar:* Sem. plan *Degrees:* B, M *Prof. Accred.:* Music, Social Work (B) *CEO:* Pres. Peter T. Mitchell
FTE Enroll: 1,095   (803) 786-3012

COLUMBIA INTERNATIONAL UNIVERSITY
7435 Monticello Rd., P.O. Box 3122, Columbia 29230 *Type:* Private (interdenominational) *Accred.:* 1948/1994 (AABC); 1985/1990 (ATS); 1982/1988 (SACS-CC) *Calendar:* Sem. plan *Degrees:* A, B, M, D, C *CEO:* Pres. Johnny V. Miller
FTE Enroll: 883   (803) 754-4100

COLUMBIA JUNIOR COLLEGE OF BUSINESS
P.O. Box 1196, 3810 Main St., Columbia 29202 *Type:* Private junior *Accred.:* 1964/ 1987 (ACICS) *Calendar:* Qtr. plan *Degrees:* A, C *CEO:* Pres. Michael Gorman
                    (803) 799-9082

CONVERSE COLLEGE
580 E. Main St., Spartanburg 29302-0006 *Type:* Private liberal arts primarily for women *Accred.:* 1912/1986 (SACS-CC) *Calendar:* Sem. plan *Degrees:* B, M *Prof. Accred.:* Music *CEO:* Pres. Sandra C. Thomas
FTE Enroll: 899   (803) 596-9000

DENMARK TECHNICAL COLLEGE
P.O. Box 327, Denmark 29042-0327 *Type:* Public (state) 2-year *System:* South Carolina State Board for Technical and Comprehensive Education *Accred.:* 1979/1984 (SACS-CC warning) *Calendar:* Sem. plan *Degrees:* A *CEO:* Pres. Joann R. G. Boyd-Scotland
FTE Enroll: 780   (803) 793-3301

ERSKINE COLLEGE
2 Washington St., Due West 29639 *Type:* Private (Presbyterian) liberal arts *Accred.:* 1981/1992 (ATS); 1925/1992 (SACS-CC) *Calendar:* 4-1-4 plan *Degrees:* A, B, M, D *CEO:* Pres. James W. Strobel
FTE Enroll: 750   (803) 379-2131

FLORENCE-DARLINGTON TECHNICAL COLLEGE
P.O. Box 100548, Florence 29501-0548 *Type:* Public (state) 2-year *System:* South Carolina State Board for Technical and Comprehensive Education *Accred.:* 1970/ 1995 (SACS-CC) *Calendar:* Sem. plan *Degrees:* A *Prof. Accred.:* Clinical Lab Technology (A), Dental Assisting, Dental Hygiene, Engineering Technology (civil/ construction, electrical, mechanical drafting/design), Medical Record Technology, Nursing (A), Radiography, Respiratory Therapy, Respiratory Therapy Technology, Surgical Technology *CEO:* Pres. Charles W. Gould
FTE Enroll: 2,187   (803) 661-8324

FORREST JUNIOR COLLEGE
601 E. River St., Anderson 29624 *Type:* Private junior *Accred.:* 1965/1995 (ACICS)

Calendar: Qtr. plan *Degrees:* A *Prof. Accred.:* Medical Assisting (AMA) *CEO:* Dir. John Re

(803) 225-7653

FRANCIS MARION UNIVERSITY
P.O. Box 100547, Florence 29501-0547 *Type:* Public (state) liberal arts *System:* South Carolina Commission on Higher Education *Accred.:* 1972/1987 (SACS-CC) *Calendar:* Sem. plan *Degrees:* A, B, M *CEO:* Pres. Lee A. Vickers
FTE Enroll: 3,630   (803) 661-1362

FURMAN UNIVERSITY
3300 Poinsett Hwy., Greenville 29613 *Type:* Private (Southern Baptist) liberal arts *Accred.:* 1924/1987 (SACS-CC) *Calendar:* 3-3 plan *Degrees:* B, M *Prof. Accred.:* Music *CEO:* Pres. David E. Shi
FTE Enroll: 2,782   (803) 294-2000

GREENVILLE TECHNICAL COLLEGE
P.O. Box 5616, Sta. B, Greenville 29606-5616 *Type:* Public (state) 2-year *System:* South Carolina State Board for Technical and Comprehensive Education *Accred.:* 1968/1992 (SACS-CC) *Calendar:* Sem. plan *Degrees:* A *Prof. Accred.:* Clinical Lab Technology (A), Dental Assisting, Dental Hygiene, EMT-Paramedic, Engineering Technology (architectural, electrical, mechanical), Nursing (A), Physical Therapy Assisting, Practical Nursing, Radiography, Respiratory Therapy, Respiratory Therapy Technology, Surgical Technology *CEO:* Pres. Thomas E. Barton, Jr.
FTE Enroll: 6,387   (803) 250-8000

HORRY-GEORGETOWN TECHNICAL COLLEGE
P.O. Box 1966, Conway 29526-1966 *Type:* Public (state) 2-year *System:* South Carolina State Board for Technical and Comprehensive Education *Accred.:* 1972/1988 (SACS-CC) *Calendar:* Sem. plan *Degrees:* A *Prof. Accred.:* Engineering Technology (electrical), Radiography *CEO:* Pres. D. Kent Sharples
FTE Enroll: 2,122   (803) 347-3186

LANDER UNIVERSITY
320 Stanley Ave., Greenwood 29649-2099 *Type:* Public (state) liberal arts *System:* South Carolina Commission on Higher Education *Accred.:* 1952/1986 (SACS-CC) *Calendar:* Sem. plan *Degrees:* B, M *Prof. Accred.:* Nursing (B) *CEO:* Pres. William C. Moran
FTE Enroll: 2,579   (803) 229-8200

LIMESTONE COLLEGE
1115 College Dr., Gaffney 29340 *Type:* Private liberal arts *Accred.:* 1928/1990 (SACS-CC) *Calendar:* Sem. plan *Degrees:* B *Prof. Accred.:* Music *CEO:* Pres. Walt Griffin
FTE Enroll: 1,155   (803) 489-7151

LUTHERAN THEOLOGICAL SOUTHERN SEMINARY
4201 N. Main St., Columbia 29203 *Type:* Private (Evangelical Lutheran Church) professional; graduate only *Accred.:* 1944/1993 (ATS); 1983/1993 (SACS-CC) *Calendar:* Sem. plan *Degrees:* M, D *CEO:* Pres. H. Frederick Reisz, Jr.
Enroll: 198   (803) 786-5150

MEDICAL UNIVERSITY OF SOUTH CAROLINA
171 Ashley Ave., Charleston 29425 *Type:* Public (state) professional *System:* South Carolina Commission on Higher Education *Accred.:* 1971/1986 (SACS-CC) *Calendar:* Sem. plan *Degrees:* B, M, D *Prof. Accred.:* Clinical Lab Scientist, Cytotechnology, Dentistry, General Dentistry (prelim. provisional), General Practice Residency, Health Services Administration, Medical Record Administration, Medicine, Nurse Anesthesia Education, Nursing (B,M), Occupational Therapy, Oral and Maxillofacial Surgery, Pediatric Dentistry, Perfusion, Periodontics, Physical Therapy, Psychology Internship, Radiation Therapy Technology *CEO:* Pres. James B. Edwards
FTE Enroll: 2,032   (803) 792-2211

MIDLANDS TECHNICAL COLLEGE
P.O. Box 2408, Columbia 29202-2408 *Type:* Public (state) 2-year *System:* South Carolina State Board for Technical and Comprehensive Education *Accred.:* 1974/1989 (SACS-CC) *Calendar:* Sem. plan *Degrees:* A *Prof.*

Accred.: Clinical Lab Technology (A), Dental Assisting, Dental Hygiene, Engineering Technology (architectural, civil/construction, electrical, mechanical), Medical Record Technology, Nuclear Medicine Technology, Nursing (A), Practical Nursing, Radiography, Respiratory Therapy, Respiratory Therapy Technology, Surgical Technology *CEO:* Pres. James L. Hudgins
FTE Enroll: 6,808   (803) 738-1400

MORRIS COLLEGE
100 W. College St., Sumter 29150-3599
Type: Private (Baptist) liberal arts *Accred.:* 1978/1993 (SACS-CC) *Calendar:* Sem. plan
Degrees: B *CEO:* Pres. Luns C. Richardson
FTE Enroll: 932   (803) 775-9371

NEWBERRY COLLEGE
2100 College St., Newberry 29108-2197
Type: Private (Lutheran) liberal arts *Accred.:* 1936/1992 (SACS-CC) *Calendar:* Sem. plan
Degrees: B *Prof. Accred.:* Music, Teacher Education *CEO:* Pres. Peter L. French
FTE Enroll: 637   (803) 276-5010

NIELSEN ELECTRONICS INSTITUTE
1600 Meeting St., Charleston 29405-9987
Type: Private *Accred.:* 1974/1989 (ACC-SCT) *Calendar:* Qtr. plan *Degrees:* A, C
CEO: Pres. Robert R. Nielsen
          (803) 722-2344

NORTH GREENVILLE COLLEGE
P.O. Box 1892, Tigerville 29688 *Type:* Private (Southern Baptist) *Accred.:* 1957/1989 (SACS-CC) *Calendar:* Sem. plan *Degrees:* A, B *CEO:* Pres. James B. Epting
FTE Enroll: 599   (803) 895-1410

ORANGEBURG-CALHOUN TECHNICAL COLLEGE
3250 St. Matthews Rd., N.E., Orangeburg 29118 *Type:* Public (state) 2-year *System:* South Carolina State Board for Technical and Comprehensive Education *Accred.:* 1970/1995 (SACS-CC) *Calendar:* Sem. plan *Degrees:* A *Prof. Accred.:* Clinical Lab Technology (A), Nursing (A), Practical Nursing, Radiography, Respiratory Therapy Technology *CEO:* Pres. Jeffery R. Olson
FTE Enroll: 1,482   (803) 536-0311

PIEDMONT TECHNICAL COLLEGE
P.O. Drawer 1467, Greenwood 29648-1467
Type: Public (state) 2-year *System:* South Carolina State Board for Technical and Comprehensive Education *Accred.:* 1972/1987 (SACS-CC) *Calendar:* Sem. plan
Degrees: A *Prof. Accred.:* Engineering Technology (electrical, general drafting/design), Radiography, Respiratory Therapy, Respiratory Therapy Technology *CEO:* Pres. Lex D. Walters
FTE Enroll: 2,990   (803) 941-8324

PRESBYTERIAN COLLEGE
S. Broad St., P.O. Box 975, Clinton 29325
Type: Private (Presbyterian) liberal arts *Accred.:* 1949/1986 (SACS-CC) *Calendar:* Sem. plan *Degrees:* B *CEO:* Pres. Kenneth B. Orr
FTE Enroll: 1,159   (803) 833-2820

SHERMAN COLLEGE OF STRAIGHT CHIROPRACTIC
2020 Springfield Rd., P.O. Box 1452, Spartanburg 29304 *Type:* Private professional *Calendar:* Tri. plan *Degrees:* D *Prof. Accred.:* Chiropractic Education *CEO:* Pres. Thomas A. Gelardi
FTE Enroll: 151   (803) 578-8770

SOUTH CAROLINA STATE UNIVERSITY
300 College Ave. N.E., Orangeburg 29117
Type: Public (state) liberal arts *System:* South Carolina Commission on Higher Education *Accred.:* 1941/1990 (SACS-CC) *Calendar:* Sem. plan *Degrees:* B, M, D *Prof. Accred.:* Engineering Technology (civil/construction, electrical, industrial, mechanical), Home Economics, Music, Rehabilitation Counseling, Social Work (B), Speech-Language Pathology, Teacher Education *CEO:* Interim Pres. Leroy Davis
FTE Enroll: 4,255   (803) 536-7000

SOUTHERN WESLEYAN UNIVERSITY
P.O. Box 1020, One Wesleyan Dr., Central 29630-1020 *Type:* Private (Wesleyan Methodist) liberal arts and teachers *Accred.:* 1973/1989 (SACS-CC) *Calendar:* Sem. plan *Degrees:* A, B, M *CEO:* Pres. David J. Spittal
FTE Enroll: 1,365   (803) 639-2453

SPARTANBURG METHODIST COLLEGE
1200 Textile Rd., Spartanburg 29301-0009
Type: Private (United Methodist) junior
Accred.: 1957/1988 (SACS-CC) *Calendar:*
Sem. plan *Degrees:* A *CEO:* Pres. George D.
Fields, Jr.
FTE Enroll: 808   (803) 587-4000

SPARTANBURG TECHNICAL COLLEGE
P.O. Drawer 4386, Spartanburg 29305-4386
Type: Public (state) 2-year *System:* South
Carolina State Board for Technical and
Comprehensive Education *Accred.:* 1970/
1995 (SACS-CC) *Calendar:* Sem. plan
Degrees: A *Prof. Accred.:* Clinical Lab Tech-
nology (A), Dental Assisting, Engineering
Technology (civil/construction, electrical,
mechanical), Radiography, Respiratory
Therapy, Respiratory Therapy Technology,
Surgical Technology *CEO:* Pres. Jack A.
Powers
FTE Enroll: 2,199   (803) 591-3600

TECHNICAL COLLEGE OF THE LOWCOUNTRY
921 S. Ribaut Rd., P.O. Box 1288, Beaufort
29901-1288 *Type:* Public (state) 2-year *System:* South Carolina State Board for Technical and Comprehensive Education *Accred.:*
1978/1994 (SACS-CC) *Calendar:* Sem. plan
Degrees: A *Prof. Accred.:* Nursing (A) *CEO:*
Pres. Anne S. McNutt
FTE Enroll: 959   (803) 525-8324

TRI-COUNTY TECHNICAL COLLEGE
P.O. Box 587, Highway 76, Pendleton
29670-0587 *Type:* Public (state) 2-year *System:* South Carolina State Board for Technical and Comprehensive Education *Accred.:*
1971/1986 (SACS-CC) *Calendar:* Sem. plan
Degrees: A *Prof. Accred.:* Clinical Lab Technology (A), Dental Assisting, Engineering
Technology (electrical), Surgical Technology, Veterinary Technology *CEO:* Pres. Don
C. Garrison
FTE Enroll: 2,487   (803) 646-8361

TRIDENT TECHNICAL COLLEGE
P.O. Box 118067, Charleston 29423-8067
Type: Public (state) 2-year *System:* South
Carolina State Board for Technical and
Comprehensive Education *Accred.:* 1974/

1990 (SACS-CC) *Calendar:* Sem. plan
Degrees: A *Prof. Accred.:* Clinical Lab Technology (A), Dental Assisting, Dental
Hygiene, Engineering Technology (chemical, civil/construction, electrical, mechanical), Medical Assisting (AMA), Nursing (A-
warning), Occupational Therapy Assisting,
Physical Therapy Assisting, Radiography,
Respiratory Therapy *CEO:* Pres. Mary Dellamura Thornley
FTE Enroll: 6,578   (803) 572-6111

UNIVERSITY OF SOUTH CAROLINA—AIKEN
171 University Pkwy., Aiken 29801 *Type:*
Public (state) *System:* University of South
Carolina Central Office *Accred.:* 1961/1991
(SACS-CC) *Calendar:* Sem. plan *Degrees:*
A, B, M *Prof. Accred.:* Nursing (A,B) *CEO:*
Chanc. Robert E. Alexander
FTE Enroll: 2,500   (803) 648-6851

UNIVERSITY OF SOUTH CAROLINA—COLUMBIA
Columbia 29208 *Type:* Public (state) *System:*
University of South Carolina Central Office
Accred.: 1917/1991 (SACS-CC) *Calendar:*
Sem. plan *Degrees:* A, B, M, D *Prof.
Accred.:* Accounting (A,C), Audiology,
Business (B,M), Clinical Psychology, Com-
puter Science, Counseling, Engineering
(chemical, civil, electrical, mechanical),
Health Services Administration, Journalism
(B,M), Law, Librarianship, Medicine,
Music, Nurse Anesthesia Education, Nursing
(B,M), Psychology Internship, Public
Administration, Rehabilitation Counseling,
School Psychology, Social Work (M),
Speech-Language Pathology, Teacher Edu-
cation, Theatre *CEO:* Pres. John M. Palms
FTE Enroll: 23,557   (803) 777-7000

UNIVERSITY OF SOUTH CAROLINA—
BEAUFORT
801 Carteret St., Beaufort 29902 (state) 2-
year *System:* University of South Carolina
Central Office *Accred.:* 1917/1991 (SACS-
CC) *Calendar:* Sem. plan *Degrees:* A
Enroll: 1,070   (803) 521-4100

UNIVERSITY OF SOUTH CAROLINA—
LANCASTER
   P.O. Box 889, Lancaster 29721 (state) 2-
   year *System:* University of South Carolina
   Central Office *Accred.:* 1917/1991 (SACS-
   CC) *Calendar:* Sem. plan *Degrees:* A
   Enroll: 1,031   (803) 285-7471

UNIVERSITY OF SOUTH CAROLINA—
SALKEHATCHIE
   P.O. Box 617, Allendale 29810 (state) 2-
   year *System:* University of South Carolina
   Central Office *Accred.:* 1917/1991 (SACS-
   CC) *Calendar:* Sem. plan *Degrees:* A
   Enroll: 1,006   (803) 584-3446

UNIVERSITY OF SOUTH CAROLINA—SUMTER
   200 Miller Rd., Sumter 29150 (state) 2-
   year *System:* University of South Carolina
   Central Office *Accred.:* 1917/1991 (SACS-
   CC) *Calendar:* Sem. plan *Degrees:* A
   Enroll: 1,620   (803) 775-6341

UNIVERSITY OF SOUTH CAROLINA—UNION
   P.O. Drawer 729, Union 29379 (state) 2-
   year *System:* University of South Carolina
   Central Office *Accred.:* 1917/1991 (SACS-
   CC) *Calendar:* Sem. plan *Degrees:* A
   Enroll: 432   (803) 429-8728

UNIVERSITY OF SOUTH CAROLINA—
SPARTANBURG
   800 University Way, Spartanburg 29303 *Type:*
   Public (state) *System:* University of South
   Carolina Central Office *Accred.:* 1976/1991
   (SACS-CC) *Calendar:* Sem. plan *Degrees:* A,
   B, M (candidate) *Prof. Accred.:* Nursing (A,B)
   CEO: Chanc. John C. Stockwell
   FTE Enroll: 2,732   (803) 599-2000

VOORHEES COLLEGE
   1141 Voorhees Rd., Denmark 29042 *Type:*
   Private (Episcopal) liberal arts *Accred.:*
   1946/1992 (SACS-CC) *Calendar:* Sem.

plan *Degrees:* A, B *CEO:* Pres. Leonard E.
Dawson
FTE Enroll: 712   (803) 793-3351

WILLIAMSBURG TECHNICAL COLLEGE
   601 Martin Luther King Jr. Ave., Kingstree
   29556-4197 *Type:* Public (state) 2-year *System:* South Carolina State Board for Technical
   and Comprehensive Education *Accred.:*
   1977/1992 (SACS-CC) *Calendar:* Sem. plan
   Degrees: A *CEO:* Pres. Norman Scott
   FTE Enroll: 273   (803) 354-2021

WINTHROP UNIVERSITY
   701 Oakland Ave., Rock Hill 29733 *Type:*
   Public (state) liberal arts *System:* South Car-
   olina Commission on Higher Education
   Accred.: 1923/1991 (SACS-CC) *Calendar:*
   Sem. plan *Degrees:* B, M *Prof. Accred.:* Art,
   Business (B,M), Computer Science, Dietet-
   ics (internship), Interior Design, Music,
   Social Work (B), Teacher Education *CEO:*
   Pres. Anthony J. DiGiorgio
   FTE Enroll: 4,316   (803) 323-2211

WOFFORD COLLEGE
   429 N. Church St., Spartanburg 29303-3663
   Type: Private (United Methodist) liberal arts
   for men *Accred.:* 1917/1986 (SACS-CC)
   Calendar: 4-1-4 plan *Degrees:* B *CEO:* Pres.
   Joab M. Lesesne, Jr.
   FTE Enroll: 1,093   (803) 597-4000

YORK TECHNICAL COLLEGE
   452 S. Anderson Rd., Rock Hill 29730-3395
   Type: Public (state) 2-year *System:* South
   Carolina State Board for Technical and Com-
   prehensive Education *Accred.:* 1970/ 1995
   (SACS-CC) *Calendar:* Sem. plan *Degrees:* A
   Prof. Accred.: Clinical Lab Technology (A),
   Dental Assisting, Dental Hygiene (condi-
   tional), Engineering Technology (electrical,
   mechanical drafting/ design), Radiography
   CEO: Pres. Dennis F. Merrell
   FTE Enroll: 2,297   (803) 327-8000

SOUTH DAKOTA

AUGUSTANA COLLEGE
29th St. and Summit Ave., Sioux Falls 57197
Type: Private (Lutheran) liberal arts *Accred.:*
1931/1992 (NCA) *Calendar:* 4-1-4 plan
Degrees: A, B, M *Prof. Accred.:* Music,
Nursing (B), Social Work (B), Teacher Education *CEO:* Pres. Ralph H. Wagoner
Enroll: 1,624   (800) 727-2844

BLACK HILLS STATE UNIVERSITY
1200 University Ave., Spearfish 57799-9500
Type: Public (state) liberal arts and teachers
System: South Dakota Board of Regents
Accred.: 1928/1993 (NCA) *Calendar:* Sem.
plan *Degrees:* A, B, M, C *Prof. Accred.:*
Music, Teacher Education *CEO:* Pres.
Thomas O. Flickema
Enroll: 3,925   (605) 642-6011

DAKOTA STATE UNIVERSITY
820 N. Washington St., Madison 57042
Type: Public (state) liberal arts and teachers
System: South Dakota Board of Regents
Accred.: 1920/1991 (NCA) *Calendar:* Sem.
plan *Degrees:* A, B *Prof. Accred.:* Medical
Record Administration, Medical Record
Technology, Respiratory Therapy *CEO:*
Pres. Jerald A. Tunheim
Enroll: 1,438   (605) 256-5111

DAKOTA WESLEYAN UNIVERSITY
1200 W. University, Mitchell 57301 *Type:*
Private (United Methodist) liberal arts
Accred.: 1916/1987 (NCA) *Calendar:* Sem.
plan *Degrees:* A, B, M *Prof. Accred.:* Nursing (A) *CEO:* Pres. John L. Ewing, Jr.
Enroll: 702   (605) 995-2600

HURON UNIVERSITY
333 Ninth St., S.W., Huron 57350 *Type:* Private liberal arts *Accred.:* 1915/1990 (NCA)
Calendar: Sem. plan *Degrees:* A, B, M, C
Prof. Accred.: Nursing (A) *CEO:* Pres. Rich
Buckles
Enroll: 1,213   (800) 942-5826

LONDON CAMPUS
58 Prince's Gate, South Kensington, London, England SW7-2PG
[011] (44) 71-584-9696

SIOUX FALLS CAMPUS
2900 E. 26th St., Sioux Falls 57103
(605) 331-5159

TOKYO CAMPUS
1-1-7 Kamiochiai, Shinjuju-ku, Tokyo
Japan 161
[011] (81) 3-3367-4141

KILIAN COMMUNITY COLLEGE
224 N. Phillips Ave., Sioux Falls 57102
Type: Private *Accred.:* 1986/1990 (NCA)
Calendar: Qtr. plan *Degrees:* A, C *CEO:*
Pres. Jane Doyle Bromert
Enroll: 167   (605) 336-1711

LAKE AREA TECHNICAL INSTITUTE
230 11th St., N.E., Watertown 57201 *Type:*
Public (district) junior *Accred.:* 1980/1990
(NCA) *Calendar:* Qtr. plan *Degrees:* A, C
Prof. Accred.: Clinical Lab Technology (A),
Dental Assisting, Medical Assisting (AMA),
Physical Therapy Assisting, Practical Nursing *CEO:* Dir. Gary D. Williams
Enroll: 1,174   (800) 657-4344

MITCHELL TECHNICAL INSTITUTE
821 N. Capital St., Mitchell 57301 *Type:*
Public (district) junior *Accred.:* 1980/1995
(NCA) *Calendar:* Sem. plan *Degrees:* A, C
Prof. Accred.: Clinical Lab Technology (A)
CEO: Dir. Chris A. Paustian
Enroll: 650   (605) 995-3024

MOUNT MARTY COLLEGE
1105 W. Eighth St., Yankton 57078 *Type:*
Private (Roman Catholic) liberal arts
Accred.: 1961/1993 (NCA) *Calendar:* Sem.
plan *Degrees:* A, B, M, C *Prof. Accred.:*
Nurse Anesthesia Education, Nursing (B)
CEO: Pres. Jacquelyn Ernster
Enroll: 985   (800) 685-4552

NATIONAL COLLEGE
321 Kansas City St., P.O. Box 1780, Rapid
City 57701 *Type:* Private *Accred.:* 1985/ 1994
(NCA) *Calendar:* Qtr. plan *Degrees:* A, B, C
Prof. Accred.: Medical Assisting (AMA),

Medical Record Technology, Veterinary Technology *CEO:* Pres. Jerry L. Gallentine
Enroll: 1,904   (605) 394-4800

ALBUQUERQUE CAMPUS
1202 Penn. Ave., N.W., Albuquerque, NM 87110
(505) 265-7517

COLORADO SPRINGS CAMPUS
2577 N. Chelton, Colorado Springs, CO 80909
(719) 471-4205

DENVER CAMPUS
1325 S. Colorado Blvd., #100, Denver, CO 80222
(303) 758-6700

ELLSWORTH AFB EXTENSION CAMPUS
P.O. Box 1780, Rapid City 57709
(605) 923-5856

KANSAS CITY CAMPUS
Blue Ridge Mall, 4200 Blue Ridge Blvd., Kansas City, MO 64133
(816) 353-4554

SIOUX FALLS CAMPUS
3109 S. Kiwanis Ave., Sioux Falls 57105
(605) 334-5430

ST. PAUL CAMPUS
1380 Energy Ln., Ste. 13, St. Paul, MN 55108-5271
(612) 644-1265

NETTLETON JUNIOR COLLEGE
100 S. Spring Ave., Sioux Falls 57104 *Type:* Private business *Accred.:* 1953/1994 (ACICS) *Degrees:* A, C *CEO:* Dir. Warren Strand
(605) 336-1837

NORTH AMERICAN BAPTIST SEMINARY
1525 S. Grange Ave., Sioux Falls 57105 *Type:* Private (Baptist) graduate only *Accred.:* 1968/1994 (ATS); 1979/1994 (NCA) *Calendar:* Sem. plan *Degrees:* M, D, C *CEO:* Pres. Charles M. Hiatt
Enroll: 170   (605) 336-6588

NORTHERN STATE UNIVERSITY
1200 S. Jay St., Aberdeen 57401 *Type:* Public (state) liberal arts and teachers *System:* South Dakota Board of Regents *Accred.:* 1918/1987 (NCA) *Calendar:* Sem. plan *Degrees:* A, B, M, C *Prof. Accred.:* Music *CEO:* Pres. John Hutchinson
Enroll: 2,705   (605) 626-2521

OGLALA LAKOTA COLLEGE
P.O. Box 490, Kyle 57752 *Type:* Public (tribal) *Accred.:* 1983/1993 (NCA) *Calendar:* Sem. plan *Degrees:* A, B, M, C *CEO:* Pres. Tom Shortbull
Enroll: 882   (605) 455-2321

PRESENTATION COLLEGE
1500 N. Main St., Aberdeen 57401 *Type:* Private (Roman Catholic) *Accred.:* 1971/1994 (NCA) *Calendar:* Sem. plan *Degrees:* A, B, C *Prof. Accred.:* Clinical Lab Technology (A), Nursing (A), Social Work (B-candidate), Surgical Technology *CEO:* Pres. Alexander J. Popovics
Enroll: 441   (605) 225-8404

LAKOTA CAMPUS
P.O. Box 1070, Eagle Butte 57625
(605) 964-4071

SINTE GLESKA UNIVERSITY
P.O. Box 490, Rosebud 57570 *Type:* Public (tribal) *Accred.:* 1983/1993 (NCA) *Calendar:* Sem. plan *Degrees:* A, B, M *CEO:* Pres. Lionel R. Bordeaux
Enroll: 694   (605) 747-2263

SISSETON-WAHPETON COMMUNITY COLLEGE
P.O. Box 689, Old Agency, Sisseton 57262 *Type:* Public (tribal) junior *Accred.:* 1990/1994 (NCA) *Calendar:* Qtr. plan *Degrees:* A *CEO:* Pres. Chris Cavender
Enroll: 222   (605) 698-3966

SOUTH DAKOTA SCHOOL OF MINES AND TECHNOLOGY
501 E. St. Joseph St., Rapid City 57701 *Type:* Public (state) technological *System:* South Dakota Board of Regents *Accred.:* 1925/1986 (NCA) *Calendar:* Sem. plan *Degrees:* B, M, D *Prof. Accred.:* Computer

Science, Engineering (chemical, civil, electrical, geological/geophysical, industrial, mechanical, metallurgical, mining) *CEO:* Pres. Richard J. Gowen
Enroll: 2,225   (605) 394-2511

SOUTH DAKOTA STATE UNIVERSITY
Box 2201, University Sta., Brookings 57007 *Type:* Public (state) *System:* South Dakota Board of Regents *Accred.:* 1916/1990 (NCA) *Calendar:* Sem. plan *Degrees:* A, B, M, D *Prof. Accred.:* Counseling, Engineering (agricultural, civil, electrical, mechanical), Home Economics, Journalism (B), Music, Nursing (B,M), Teacher Education *CEO:* Pres. Robert T. Wagner
Enroll: 8,296   (605) 688-4151

SOUTHEAST TECHNICAL INSTITUTE
2301 Career Pl., Sioux Falls 57107 *Type:* Public (district) 2-year *Accred.:* 1981/1993 (NCA) *Calendar:* Qtr. plan *Degrees:* A, C *Prof. Accred.:* Nuclear Medicine Technology *CEO:* Dir. Terrence Sullivan
Enroll: 1,581   (605) 331-7624

STENOTYPE INSTITUTE OF SOUTH DAKOTA
705 West Ave. N., Sioux Falls 57104 *Type:* Private business *Accred.:* 1975/1995 (ACICS) *Degrees:* A, C *CEO:* Pres. Linda Clauson
                                  (605) 336-1442

UNIVERSITY OF SIOUX FALLS
1101 West 22nd St, Sioux Falls 57105-1699 *Type:* Private (Baptist) liberal arts *Accred.:* 1931/1992 (NCA) *Calendar:* 4-1-4 plan *Degrees:* A, B, M *Prof. Accred.:* Social Work (B), Teacher Education *CEO:* Pres. Thomas F. Johnson
Enroll: 842   (605) 331-5000

THE UNIVERSITY OF SOUTH DAKOTA
414 E. Clark St., Vermillion 57069-2390 *Type:* Public (state) *System:* South Dakota Board of Regents *Accred.:* 1913/1991 (NCA) *Calendar:* Sem. plan *Degrees:* A, B, M, P, D *Prof. Accred.:* Art, Audiology (initial), Business (B,M), Clinical Psychology, Counseling, Dental Hygiene, Law, Medicine, Music, Nurse Anesthesia Education, Nursing (A), Occupational Therapy, Physical Therapy, Public Administration, Social Work (B), Speech-Language Pathology, Teacher Education, Theatre (A) *CEO:* Pres. Betty Turner Asher
Enroll: 6,028   (605) 677-5276

WESTERN DAKOTA TECHNICAL INSTITUTE
1600 Sedivy Ln., Rapid City 57701-4178 *Type:* Public (district) junior *Accred.:* 1983/1993 (NCA) *Calendar:* Qtr. plan *Degrees:* A, C *CEO:* Dir. Ken Gifford
Enroll: 891   (605) 394-4034

TENNESSEE

AMERICAN ACADEMY OF NUTRITION
1429 Cherokee Blvd., Knoxville 37919
Type: Private home study *Accred.:* 1989
(DETC) *Degrees:* A, C *CEO:* Admin. Peter
Berwick
(423) 524-8079

AMERICAN BAPTIST COLLEGE
1800 Baptist World Ctr., Nashville 37207
Type: Private (National Baptist/Southern
Baptist Conventions) *Accred.:* 1971/1992
(AABC) *Calendar:* Sem. plan *Degrees:* A,
B, C *CEO:* Pres. Bernard Lafayette, Jr.
FTE Enroll: 171   (615) 228-7877

AMERICAN TECHNICAL INSTITUTE
P.O. Box 8, Brunswick 38014 *Type:* Private
Calendar: Sem. plan *Degrees:* B *Prof.
Accred.:* Engineering Technology (nuclear)
CEO: Pres. D. Wayne Jones
FTE Enroll: 150   (901) 382-4847

AQUINAS COLLEGE
4210 Harding Rd., Nashville 37205 *Type:*
Private (Roman Catholic) 2-year *Accred.:*
1971/1986 (SACS-CC) *Calendar:* Sem. plan
Degrees: A, B (candidate) *Prof. Accred.:*
Nursing (A) *CEO:* Pres. Mary Evelyn Potts
FTE Enroll: 334   (615) 297-7545

AUSTIN PEAY STATE UNIVERSITY
601 College St., Clarksville 37044 *Type:*
Public (state) *System:* Tennessee Board of
Regents *Accred.:* 1947/1994 (SACS-CC)
Calendar: Sem. plan *Degrees:* A, B, M *Prof.
Accred.:* Art (A), Clinical Lab Scientist,
Music, Nursing (B), Social Work (B),
Teacher Education *CEO:* Pres. Sal D.
Rinella
FTE Enroll: 6,330   (615) 648-7011

BELMONT UNIVERSITY
1900 Belmont Blvd., Nashville 37212-3757
Type: Private (Baptist) liberal arts *Accred.:*
1959/1990 (SACS-CC) *Calendar:* Sem. plan
Degrees: A, B, M *Prof. Accred.:* Music,
Nursing (A), Teacher Education *CEO:* Pres.
William E. Troutt
FTE Enroll: 2,400   (615) 383-7001

BETHEL COLLEGE
325 Cherry St., McKenzie 38201 *Type:* Private (Presbyterian) liberal arts *Accred.:*
1952/1988 (SACS-CC) *Calendar:* Sem. plan
Degrees: B, M *CEO:* Pres. Bill J. Elkins
FTE Enroll: 439   (901) 352-1000

BRYAN COLLEGE
Box 7000, Dayton 37321 *Type:* Private lib-
eral arts *Accred.:* 1969/1994 (SACS-CC)
Calendar: Sem. plan *Degrees:* A, B *CEO:*
Pres. William E. Brown
FTE Enroll: 417   (615) 775-2041

CARSON-NEWMAN COLLEGE
1646 Russell Ave., P.O. Box 557, Jefferson
City 37760 *Type:* Private (Southern Baptist)
liberal arts *Accred.:* 1927/1993 (SACS-CC)
Calendar: Sem. plan *Degrees:* B, M *Prof.
Accred.:* Art (A), Home Economics, Music,
Nursing (B), Teacher Education *CEO:* Pres.
J. Cordell Maddox
FTE Enroll: 2,126   (615) 475-4000

CHATTANOOGA STATE TECHNICAL COMMUNITY
COLLEGE
4501 Amnicola Hwy., Chattanooga 37406
Type: Public (state) 2-year *System:* Ten-
nessee Board of Regents *Accred.:* 1967/1991
(SACS-CC) *Calendar:* Sem. plan *Degrees:*
A *Prof. Accred.:* Dental Assisting, Dental
Hygiene, Engineering Technology (com-
puter, electrical, mechanical), Medical
Record Technology, Nuclear Medicine Tech-
nology, Nursing (A), Physical Therapy
Assisting, Radiation Therapy Technology,
Radiography, Respiratory Therapy *CEO:*
Pres. James L. Catanzaro
FTE Enroll: 6,297   (423) 697-4400

CHRISTIAN BROTHERS UNIVERSITY
650 East Pkwy. S., Memphis 38104 *Type:*
Private (Roman Catholic) liberal arts
Accred.: 1958/1990 (SACS-CC) *Calendar:*
Sem. plan *Degrees:* A, B, M *Prof. Accred.:*
Engineering (chemical, civil, electrical,
mechanical) *CEO:* Chief Academic Offi-
cer.Michael J. McGinniss, F.S.C.
FTE Enroll: 1,362   (901) 722-0200

THE CHURCH OF GOD SCHOOL OF THEOLOGY
900 Walker St., N.E., P.O. Box 3330, Cleveland 37320-3330 *Type:* Private (Church of God) graduate only *Accred.:* 1989/1991 (ATS); 1984/1989 (SACS-CC) *Calendar:* 4-1-4 plan *Degrees:* M *CEO:* Pres. Cecil B. Knight
Enroll: 250   (423) 478-1131

CLEVELAND STATE COMMUNITY COLLEGE
P.O. Box 3570, Cleveland 37320-3570 *Type:* Public (state) junior *System:* Tennessee Board of Regents *Accred.:* 1969/1994 (SACS-CC) *Calendar:* Sem. plan *Degrees:* A *Prof. Accred.:* Clinical Lab Technology (A), Nursing (A) *CEO:* Pres. Owen F. Cargol
FTE Enroll: 1,472   (423) 472-7141

COLUMBIA STATE COMMUNITY COLLEGE
P.O. Box 1315, 1665 Hampshire Pike, Columbia 38402-1315 *Type:* Public (state) junior *System:* Tennessee Board of Regents *Accred.:* 1968/1993 (SACS-CC) *Calendar:* Sem. plan *Degrees:* A *Prof. Accred.:* Clinical Lab Technology (A), Nursing (A), Radiography, Respiratory Therapy, Veterinary Technology *CEO:* Pres. L. Paul Sands
FTE Enroll: 2,517   (615) 540-2722

CRICHTON COLLEGE
P.O. Box 757830, Memphis 38175-7830 *Type:* Private *Accred.:* 1986/1992 (SACS-CC warning) *Calendar:* Sem. plan *Degrees:* B *CEO:* Pres. Larry R. Brooks
FTE Enroll: 457   (901) 367-9800

CUMBERLAND UNIVERSITY
S. Greenwood St., Lebanon 37087-3554 *Type:* Private *Accred.:* 1962/1990 (SACS-CC) *Calendar:* Sem. plan *Degrees:* A, B, M *CEO:* Pres. Clair E. Martin
FTE Enroll: 832   (615) 444-2562

DAVID LIPSCOMB UNIVERSITY
3901 Granny White Pike, Nashville 37204-3951 *Type:* Private (Churches of Christ) liberal arts *Accred.:* 1954/1986 (SACS-CC) *Calendar:* Sem. plan *Degrees:* B, M *Prof. Accred.:* Music, Social Work (B) *CEO:* Pres. Harold Hazelip
FTE Enroll: 2,372   (615) 269-1000

DRAUGHONS JUNIOR COLLEGE
Plus Park at Pavilion Blvd., PO Box 17386, Nashville 37217 *Type:* Private junior *Accred.:* 1954/1996 (ACICS) *Calendar:* Qtr. plan *Degrees:* A *CEO:* Chrmn. Charles W. Davidson
                        (615) 361-7555

BOWLING GREEN CAMPUS
2424 Airway Dr. and Lovers Ln., Bowling Green, KY 42103 *Accred.:* 1954/1990 (ACICS)
                        (502) 843-6750

CLARKSVILLE CAMPUS
1860 Wilma Rudolph Blvd., Clarksville 37040 *Accred.:* 1988/1990 (ACICS)
                        (615) 552-7600

DYERSBURG STATE COMMUNITY COLLEGE
1510 Lake Rd., Dyersburg 38024 *Type:* Public (state) junior *System:* Tennessee Board of Regents *Accred.:* 1971/1986 (SACS-CC) *Calendar:* Sem. plan *Degrees:* A *Prof. Accred.:* Nursing (A) *CEO:* Pres. Karen A. Bowyer
FTE Enroll: 1,496   (901) 286-3200

EAST TENNESSEE STATE UNIVERSITY
P.O. Box 70734, Johnson City 37614-0734 *Type:* Public (state) *System:* Tennessee Board of Regents *Accred.:* 1927/1993 (SACS-CC) *Calendar:* Sem. plan *Degrees:* A, B, M, D *Prof. Accred.:* Accounting (A,C), Art, Audiology, Business (B,M), Clinical Lab Technology (A), Computer Science, Dental Assisting, Dental Hygiene, Dental Laboratory Technology, Dietetics (internship), Engineering Technology (civil/construction, electrical, general drafting/design), Journalism (B), Medical Assisting (AMA), Medicine, Music, Nursing (A,B,M), Radio-graphy, Respiratory Therapy Technology, Social Work (B) Surgical Technology *CEO:* Pres. Roy S. Nicks
FTE Enroll: 8,916   (423) 929-4112

ELECTRONIC COMPUTER PROGRAMMING COLLEGE
3805 Brainerd Rd., Chattanooga 37411-3798 *Type:* Private *Accred.:* 1982/1987 (ACCSCT) *Degrees:* A, C *CEO:* Dir. Jo Ann Pearson
                        (615) 624-0077

EMMANUEL SCHOOL OF RELIGION
One Walker Dr., Johnson City 37601 *Type:* Private (Christian Churches/Churches of Christ) graduate only *Accred.:* 1981/1986 (ATS); 1986 (SACS-CC) *Calendar:* Sem. plan *Degrees:* M *CEO:* Pres. C. Robert Wetzel
Enroll: 121   (615) 926-1186

FISK UNIVERSITY
1000 17th Ave. N., Nashville 37208-3051 *Type:* Private liberal arts *Accred.:* 1930/1989 (SACS-CC) *Calendar:* Sem. plan *Degrees:* B, M *Prof. Accred.:* Music *CEO:* Pres. Henry P. Ponder
FTE Enroll: 850   (615) 329-8500

FREE WILL BAPTIST BIBLE COLLEGE
P.O. Box 50117, 3606 W. End Ave., Nashville 37205 *Type:* Private (National Association of Free Will Baptist Churches) *Accred.:* 1958/1988 (AABC); 1994 (SACS-CC candidate) *Calendar:* Sem. plan *Degrees:* A, B *CEO:* Pres. Thomas Malone
FTE Enroll: 339   (615) 383-1340

FREED-HARDEMAN UNIVERSITY
158 E. Main St., Henderson 38340-2399 *Type:* Private (Church of Christ) liberal arts *Accred.:* 1956/1991 (SACS-CC) *Calendar:* Sem. plan *Degrees:* B, M *Prof. Accred.:* Social Work (B), Teacher Education *CEO:* Pres. Milton R. Sewell
FTE Enroll: 1,301   (901) 989-6000

HIWASSEE COLLEGE
225 Hiwassee College Dr., Madisonville 37354 *Type:* Private (United Methodist) junior *Accred.:* 1958/1990 (SACS-CC) *Calendar:* Sem. plan *Degrees:* A *CEO:* Pres. Stephen E. Fritz
FTE Enroll: 538   (615) 442-2091

ITT TECHNICAL INSTITUTE
10208 Technology Dr., Knoxville 37919-9875 *Type:* Private *Accred.:* 1990 (ACC-SCT) *Degrees:* A *CEO:* Dir. David Reynolds
(423) 691-8111

BIRMINGHAM CAMPUS
500 Riverhills Business Pk., Birmingham, AL 35242 *Accred.:* 1994 (ACCSCT) *Calendar:* Qtr. plan *Degrees:* C
Enroll: 160   (205) 991-5410

ITT TECHNICAL INSTITUTE
441 Donelson Pike, Nashville 37214-8029 *Type:* Private *Accred.:* 1985/1990 (ACC-SCT) *Degrees:* A, B *CEO:* Dir. Nathan Blaede
(615) 889-8700

GREENVILLE CAMPUS
Patewood Business Ctr., One Marcus Dr., Greenville, SC 29615 *Accred.:* 1993 (ACCSCT)
(803) 288-0777

JACKSON STATE COMMUNITY COLLEGE
2046 North Pkwy., Jackson 38301-3797 *Type:* Public (state) junior *System:* Tennessee Board of Regents *Accred.:* 1969/1994 (SACS-CC warning) *Calendar:* Sem. plan *Degrees:* A *Prof. Accred.:* Clinical Lab Technology (A), EMT-Paramedic, Physical Therapy Assisting, Radiography, Respiratory Therapy *CEO:* Pres. Walter L. Nelms
FTE Enroll: 2,406   (901) 424-3520

JOHN A. GUPTON COLLEGE
1616 Church Street, Nashville 37203 *Type:* Private 2-year *Accred.:* 1971/1986 (SACS-CC) *Calendar:* Sem. plan *Degrees:* A *Prof. Accred.:* Funeral Service Education (Mortuary Science) *CEO:* Pres. B. Steven Spann
FTE Enroll: 73   (615) 327-3927

JOHNSON BIBLE COLLEGE
7900 Johnson Dr., Knoxville 37998 *Type:* Private (Christian Churches/Churches of Christ) *Accred.:* 1970/1990 (AABC); 1979/1995 (SACS-CC) *Calendar:* Sem. plan *Degrees:* A, B, M *CEO:* Pres. David L. Eubanks
FTE Enroll: 388   (615) 573-4517

KING COLLEGE
1350 King College Rd., Bristol 37620-2699 *Type:* Private (Presbyterian) liberal arts *Accred.:* 1947/1988 (SACS-CC) *Calendar:*

4-1-4 plan *Degrees:* B *CEO:* Pres. Richard Stanislaw
FTE Enroll: 548　　　　　　　(615) 968-1187

KNOXVILLE BUSINESS COLLEGE
720 N. Fifth Ave., Knoxville 37917 *Type:* Private junior *Accred.:* 1955/1995 (ACICS) *Calendar:* Qtr. plan *Degrees:* A *CEO:* Pres. Stephen A. South
　　　　　　　　　　　　　(423) 524-3043

KNOXVILLE COLLEGE
901 College St., Knoxville 37921 *Type:* Private (Presbyterian) liberal arts *Accred.:* 1948/1992 (SACS-CC probational) *Calendar:* Sem. plan *Degrees:* A, B *Prof. Accred.:* Medical Assisting (AMA) *CEO:* Pres. Roland A. Harris, Jr.
FTE Enroll: 704　　　　　　　(423) 524-6500

LAMBUTH UNIVERSITY
705 Lambuth Blvd., Jackson 38301 *Type:* Private (United Methodist) liberal arts *Accred.:* 1954/1989 (SACS-CC) *Calendar:* Sem. plan *Degrees:* B *CEO:* Pres. Thomas F. Boyd
FTE Enroll: 931　　　　　　　(901) 425-2500

LANE COLLEGE
545 Lane Ave., Jackson 38301-4598 *Type:* Private (Christian Methodist Episcopal) liberal arts *Accred.:* 1949/1992 (SACS-CC) *Calendar:* Sem. plan *Degrees:* B *CEO:* Pres. Wesley Cornelious McClure
FTE Enroll: 744　　　　　　　(901) 426-7500

LEE COLLEGE
P.O. Box 3450, Cleveland 37320-3450 *Type:* Private (Churches of God) liberal arts *Accred.:* 1960/1994 (SACS-CC) *Calendar:* Sem. plan *Degrees:* B, M (candidate) *Prof. Accred.:* Music (A) *CEO:* Pres. Charles Paul Conn
FTE Enroll: 2,011　　　　　　(615) 472-2111

LEMOYNE-OWEN COLLEGE
807 Walker Ave., Memphis 38126 *Type:* Private (United Church of Christ/Baptist) liberal arts *Accred.:* 1960/1993 (SACS-CC) *Calendar:* Sem. plan *Degrees:* B, M *CEO:* Sr. Vice Pres. Earl Vinson
FTE Enroll: 1,321　　　　　　(901) 774-9090

LINCOLN MEMORIAL UNIVERSITY
Cumberland Gap Pkwy., Harrogate 37752-0901 *Type:* Private liberal arts *Accred.:* 1936/1989 (SACS-CC) *Calendar:* Sem. plan *Degrees:* A, B, M *Prof. Accred.:* Clinical Lab Scientist, Nursing (A), Veterinary Technology *CEO:* Pres. Scott D. Miller
FTE Enroll: 1,445　　　　　　(615) 869-3611

MARTIN METHODIST COLLEGE
433 W. Madison St., Pulaski 38478 *Type:* Private (United Methodist) *Accred.:* 1952/1989 (SACS-CC) *Calendar:* Sem. plan *Degrees:* A, B *CEO:* Pres. George P. Miller, III
FTE Enroll: 496　　　　　　　(615) 369-7456

MARYVILLE COLLEGE
502 E. Lamar Alexander Pkwy., Maryville 37804-5907 *Type:* Private (United Presbyterian) liberal arts *Accred.:* 1922/1993 (SACS-CC) *Calendar:* Sem. plan *Degrees:* B *Prof. Accred.:* Music *CEO:* Pres. Gerald W. Gibson
FTE Enroll: 752　　　　　　　(615) 981-8000

MEHARRY MEDICAL COLLEGE
1005 D. B. Todd Blvd., Nashville 37208 *Type:* Private professional (United Methodist) *Accred.:* 1972/1988 (SACS-CC) *Calendar:* Sem. plan *Degrees:* M, D *Prof. Accred.:* Dental Hygiene, Dentistry (conditional), General Practice Residency, Health Services Administration, Medicine *CEO:* Pres. John E. Maupin
FTE Enroll: 697　　　　　　　(615) 327-6200

MEMPHIS COLLEGE OF ART
Overton Park, 1930 Poplar Avenue, Memphis 38104-2764 *Type:* Private professional *Accred.:* 1963/1994 (SACS-CC) *Calendar:* Sem. plan *Degrees:* B, M *Prof. Accred.:* Art *CEO:* Pres. Jeffrey D. Nesin
FTE Enroll: 230　　　　　　　(901) 726-4085

MEMPHIS THEOLOGICAL SEMINARY
168 East Pkwy. S., Memphis 38104-4395 *Type:* Private (Cumberland Presbyterian) graduate only *Accred.:* 1973/1988 (ATS); 1988 (SACS-CC) *Calendar:* Sem. plan *Degrees:* M, D *CEO:* Pres. J. David Hester
Enroll: 232　　　　　　　　(901) 458-8232

MID-AMERICA BAPTIST THEOLOGICAL SEMINARY
2216 Germantown Rd., S., Germantown 38138 *Type:* Private (Baptist) professional *Accred.:* 1981/1986 (SACS-CC) *Calendar:* Sem. plan *Degrees:* A, M, D *CEO:* Pres. B. Gray Allison
FTE Enroll: 361   (901) 751-8453

MIDDLE TENNESSEE SCHOOL OF ANESTHESIA
P.O. Box 6414, Madison 37116 *Type:* Private *Accred.:* 1994 (SACS-CC) *Calendar:* Qtr. plan *Degrees:* M *Prof. Accred.:* Nurse Anesthesia Education *CEO:* Vice Pres./Dean Mary E. DeVasher
Enroll: 66   (615) 868-6503

MIDDLE TENNESSEE STATE UNIVERSITY
1301 E. Main St., Murfreesboro 37132 *Type:* Public (state) *System:* Tennessee Board of Regents *Accred.:* 1928/1995 (SACS-CC) *Calendar:* Sem. plan *Degrees:* A, B, M, D *Prof. Accred.:* Business (B,M), Computer Science, Home Economics, Journalism (B), Music, Nursing (B), Recreation and Leisure Services (B), Social Work (B), Teacher Education *CEO:* Pres. James E. Walker
FTE Enroll: 14,984   (615) 898-2300

MILLER-MOTTE BUSINESS COLLEGE
1820 Business Park Dr., Clarksville 37040-0415 *Type:* Private *Accred.:* 1987/1995 (ACICS); 1990 (COE) *Degrees:* A, C *Prof. Accred.:* Medical Assisting (AMA) *CEO:* Dir. Raymond M. Green
FTE Enroll: 462   (615) 553-0071

WILMINGTON CAMPUS
606 S. College Rd., Wilmington, NC 28403 *Prof. Accred.:* Medical Assisting (AMA)
                                   (910) 392-4660

MILLIGAN COLLEGE
P.O. Box 9, Milligan College 37682 *Type:* Private liberal arts (Christian Church) *Accred.:* 1960/1992 (SACS-CC) *Calendar:* Sem. plan *Degrees:* A, B, M *Prof. Accred.:* Teacher Education *CEO:* Pres. Marshall J. Leggett
FTE Enroll: 737   (615) 461-8700

MOTLOW STATE COMMUNITY COLLEGE
P.O. Box 88100, Ledford Mill Rd., Tullahoma 37388-8100 *Type:* Public (state) junior *System:* Tennessee Board of Regents *Accred.:* 1971/1986 (SACS-CC) *Calendar:* Sem. plan *Degrees:* A *Prof. Accred.:* Nursing (A) *CEO:* Pres. A. Frank Glass
FTE Enroll: 2,376   (615) 393-1500

NASHVILLE AUTO DIESEL COLLEGE
1524 Gallatin Rd., Nashville 37206-3298 *Type:* Private *Accred.:* 1967/1990 (ACCSCT) *Degrees:* A, C *CEO:* Pres. Thomas Hooper
                                   (615) 226-3990

NASHVILLE STATE TECHNICAL INSTITUTE
120 White Bridge Rd., Nashville 37209-4515 *Type:* Public (state) 2-year *System:* Tennessee Board of Regents *Accred.:* 1972/1987 (SACS-CC) *Calendar:* Sem. plan *Degrees:* A *Prof. Accred.:* Engineering Technology (architectural, civil/construction, computer, electrical, industrial, mech-anical), Occupational Therapy Assisting *CEO:* Pres. George H. Van Allen
FTE Enroll: 3,248   (615) 353-3333

NORTHEAST STATE TECHNICAL COMMUNITY COLLEGE
P.O. Box 246, 2425 Hwy. 75, Blountville 37617-0246 *Type:* Public (state) 2-year *System:* Tennessee Board of Regents *Accred.:* 1984/1989 (SACS-CC) *Calendar:* Sem. plan *Degrees:* A *Prof. Accred.:* EMT-Paramedic, Engineering Technology (computer, electrical, instrumentation) *CEO:* Pres. R. Wade Powers
FTE Enroll: 2,594   (423) 323-3191

NOSSI COLLEGE OF ART
907 Two Mile Pkwy., Goodlettsville 37072 *Type:* Private *Accred.:* 1988 (ACCSCT) *Degrees:* A, C *CEO:* Exec. Dir. Nossi Vatandoost
                                   (615) 851-1088

PELLISSIPPI STATE TECHNICAL COMMUNITY COLLEGE
10915 Hardin Valley Rd., P.O. Box 22990, Knoxville 37933-0990 *Type:* Public (state) 2-year *System:* Tennessee Board of Regents

Accred.: 1977/1992 (SACS-CC) *Calendar:* Sem. plan *Degrees:* A *Prof. Accred.:* Engineering Technology (chemical, civil/ construction, electrical, industrial, manufacturing, mechanical, mechanical drafting/ design) *CEO:* Pres. Allen G. Edwards
FTE Enroll: 5,669   (423) 694-6400

RHODES COLLEGE
2000 North Pkwy., Memphis 38112 *Type:* Private (Presbyterian) liberal arts *Accred.:* 1911/1990 (SACS-CC) *Calendar:* Sem. plan *Degrees:* B, M *CEO:* Pres. James H. Daughdrill, Jr.
FTE Enroll: 1,382   (901) 726-3000

ROANE STATE COMMUNITY COLLEGE
276 Patton Ln., Harriman 37748 *Type:* Public (state) 2-year *System:* Tennessee Board of Regents *Accred.:* 1974/1989 (SACS-CC) *Calendar:* Sem. plan *Degrees:* A *Prof. Accred.:* Clinical Lab Technology (A), Dental Hygiene, EMT-Paramedic, Medical Record Technology, Nursing (A), Occupational Therapy Assisting, Physical Therapy Assisting, Radiography, Respiratory Therapy *CEO:* Pres. Sherry L. Hoppe
FTE Enroll: 4,133   (423) 354-3000

SHELBY STATE COMMUNITY COLLEGE
P.O. Box 40568, Memphis 38174-0568 *Type:* Public (state) junior *System:* Tennessee Board of Regents *Accred.:* 1974/1989 (SACS-CC) *Calendar:* Sem. plan *Degrees:* A *Prof. Accred.:* Clinical Lab Technology (A), EMT-Paramedic, Medical Assisting (AMA), Nursing (A), Physical Therapy Assisting, Radiography *CEO:* Interim Pres. Mark L. Stansbury
FTE Enroll: 5,269   (901) 544-5000

SOUTHEAST COLLEGE OF TECHNOLOGY
2731 Nonconnah Blvd., Memphis 38132-2199 *Type:* Private *Accred.:* 1987 (ACCSCT) *Degrees:* A, C *CEO:* Pres. David A. Podesta
                              (901) 345-1000

SOUTHERN COLLEGE OF OPTOMETRY
1245 Madison Ave., Memphis 38104 *Type:* Private professional *Accred.:* 1967/1992 (SACS-CC) *Calendar:* Qtr. plan *Degrees:* D

Prof. Accred.: Optometric Residency, Optometry *CEO:* Pres. William E. Cochran
FTE Enroll: 407   (901) 722-3200

SOUTHERN COLLEGE OF SEVENTH-DAY ADVENTISTS
P.O. Box 370, Collegedale 37315-0370 *Type:* Private (Seventh-Day Adventist) liberal arts *Accred.:* 1950/1992 (SACS-CC) *Calendar:* Sem. plan *Degrees:* A, B *Prof. Accred.:* Music, Nursing (A,B) *CEO:* Pres. Donald R. Sahly
FTE Enroll: 1,388   (615) 238-2111

STATE TECHNICAL INSTITUTE AT MEMPHIS
5983 Macon Cove, Memphis 38134-7693 *Type:* Public (state) 2-year *System:* Tennessee Board of Regents *Accred.:* 1969/1994 (SACS-CC) *Calendar:* Sem. plan *Degrees:* A *Prof. Accred.:* Engineering Technology (architectural, bioengineering, chemical, civil/construction, computer, electrical, industrial, mechanical) *CEO:* Pres. Doug Call
FTE Enroll: 6,149   (901) 383-4111

TENNESSEE INSTITUTE OF ELECTRONICS
3202 Tazewell Pike, Knoxville 37918-2530 *Type:* Private *Accred.:* 1967/1987 (ACCSCT) *Calendar:* Qtr. plan *Degrees:* A *CEO:* Pres. Ronald R. Rackley
                              (615) 688-9422

TENNESSEE STATE UNIVERSITY
3500 John Merritt Blvd., Nashville 37209-1561 *Type:* Public (state) *System:* Tennessee Board of Regents *Accred.:* 1946/1990 (SACS-CC) *Calendar:* Sem. plan *Degrees:* A, B, M, D *Prof. Accred.:* Business (B,M), Clinical Lab Scientist, Dental Hygiene, Engineering (architectural, civil, electrical, mechanical), Home Economics (provisional), Medical Record Administration, Music, Nursing (A,B), Occupational Therapy, Physical Therapy, Public Administration, Respiratory Therapy, Social Work (B), Speech-Language Pathology *CEO:* Pres. James A. Hefner
FTE Enroll: 6,111   (615) 963-5000

TENNESSEE TECHNOLOGICAL UNIVERSITY
N. Dixie Ave., Campus Box 5007, Cookeville 38505 *Type:* Public (state) *Sys-*

tem: Tennessee Board of Regents *Accred.:* 1939/1995 (SACS-CC) *Calendar:* Sem. plan *Degrees:* A, B, M, D *Prof. Accred.:* Accounting (A), Business (B,M), Engineering (chemical, civil, electrical, industrial, mechanical), Music, Nursing (B), Teacher Education *CEO:* Pres. Angelo A. Volpe
FTE Enroll: 6,835　　　(615) 372-3101

TENNESSEE TEMPLE UNIVERSITY
1815 Union Ave., Chattanooga 37404 *Type:* Private (Baptist) *Accred.:* 1984/1995 (AABC) *Calendar:* Sem. plan *Degrees:* A, B, C *CEO:* Interim Pres. Roger Stiles
FTE Enroll: 475　　　(615) 493-4100

TENNESSEE WESLEYAN COLLEGE
P.O. Box 40, Athens 37371 *Type:* Private (United Methodist) liberal arts *Accred.:* 1958/1990 (SACS-CC) *Calendar:* Sem. plan *Degrees:* B *CEO:* Pres. B. James Dawson
FTE Enroll: 522　　　(423) 745-7504

TREVECCA NAZARENE UNIVERSITY
333 Murfreesboro Rd., Nashville 37210-2877 *Type:* Private (Nazarene) liberal arts and teachers *Accred.:* 1969/1993 (SACS-CC) *Calendar:* Sem. plan *Degrees:* A, B, M *Prof. Accred.:* Music, Physician Assisting/Surgeon Assisting, Social Work (B-candidate) *CEO:* Pres. Millard Reed
FTE Enroll: 1,357　　　(615) 248-1200

TUSCULUM COLLEGE
P.O. Box 5093, Greeneville 37743 *Type:* Private (Presbyterian) liberal arts *Accred.:* 1926/1991 (SACS-CC) *Calendar:* Sem. plan *Degrees:* B, M *CEO:* Pres. Robert E. Knott
FTE Enroll: 1,117　　　(615) 636-7300

UNION UNIVERSITY
2447 Hwy. 45 By-Pass, Jackson 38305 *Type:* Private (Southern Baptist) liberal arts *Accred.:* 1948/1987 (SACS-CC) *Calendar:* Sem. plan *Degrees:* A, B, M *Prof. Accred.:* Music, Nursing (A,B) *CEO:* Pres. Hyran E. Barefoot
FTE Enroll: 2,477　　　(901) 668-1818

THE UNIVERSITY OF MEMPHIS
Memphis 38152 *Type:* Public (state) *System:* Tennessee Board of Regents *Accred.:* 1927/

1994 (SACS-CC) *Calendar:* Sem. plan *Degrees:* B, M, D *Prof. Accred.:* Accounting (A,B,C), Art, Audiology, Business (B,M), Clinical Psychology, Counseling, Counseling Psychology, Dietetics (internship), Engineering Technology (architectural, computer, electrical, manufacturing), Engineering (civil, electrical, mechanical), Health Services Administration, Home Economics, Journalism (B,M), Law (ABA only), Music, Nursing (B), Planning (M), Psychology Internship, Public Administration, Rehabilitation Counseling, Social Work (B), Speech-Language Pathology, Teacher Education *CEO:* Pres. V. Lane Rawlins
FTE Enroll: 16,474　　　(901) 678-2000

THE UNIVERSITY OF TENNESSEE AT CHATTANOOGA
615 McCallie Ave., Chattanooga 37403-2598 *Type:* Public (state) *System:* University of Tennessee System *Accred.:* 1910/1991 (SACS-CC) *Calendar:* Sem. plan *Degrees:* B, M *Prof. Accred.:* Art, Business (B,M), Engineering (general), Music, Nurse Anesthesia Education, Nursing (B), Physical Therapy, Social Work (B), Teacher Education *CEO:* Chanc. Frederick W. Obear
FTE Enroll: 6,972　　　(423) 744-4111

THE UNIVERSITY OF TENNESSEE AT MARTIN
University St., Martin 38238 *Type:* Public (state) *System:* University of Tennessee System *Accred.:* 1951/1992 (SACS-CC) *Calendar:* Sem. plan *Degrees:* A, B, M *Prof. Accred.:* Engineering Technology (civil/construction, electrical, mechanical), Home Economics, Music, Nursing (B), Social Work (B), Teacher Education *CEO:* Chanc. Margaret N. Perry
FTE Enroll: 6,715　　　(901) 587-7000

THE UNIVERSITY OF TENNESSEE, KNOXVILLE
527 Andy Holt Tower, Knoxville 37996-0150 *Type:* Public (state) *System:* University of Tennessee System *Accred.:* 1897/1992 (SACS-CC) *Calendar:* Sem. plan *Degrees:* B, M, D *Prof. Accred.:* Accounting (A,C), Art, Audiology, Business (B,M), Clinical Psychology, Counseling, Counseling Psychology, Dietetics (internship), Engineering

(aerospace, agricultural, chemical, civil, electrical, engineering physics/science, industrial, materials, mechanical, nuclear), Forestry, General Practice Residency, Home Economics, Interior Design, Journalism (B,M), Law, Librarianship, Music, Nurse Anesthesia Education, Nursing (B,M), Oral and Maxillofacial Surgery, Planning (M), Psychology Internship, Recreation and Leisure Services, Rehabilitation Counseling, School Psychology, Social Work (B,M-conditional), Speech-Language Pathology, Teacher Education, Veterinary Medicine, *CEO:* Chanc. William T. Snyder
FTE Enroll: 22,998   (615) 974-1000

THE UNIVERSITY OF TENNESSEE, MEMPHIS
800 Madison Ave., Memphis 38163 *Type:* Public (state) *System:* University of Tennessee System *Accred.:* 1897/1993 (SACS-CC) *Calendar:* Sem. plan *Degrees:* B, M, D *Prof. Accred.:* Clinical Lab Scientist, Cytotechnology, Dental Hygiene, Dentistry, General Dentistry, Medical Record Administration, Medicine, Nursing (B,M), Occupational Therapy, Oral and Maxillofacial Surgery, Orthodontics, Pediatric Dentistry, Periodontics, Physical Therapy, Psychology Internship, Social Work (M) *CEO:* Chanc. William R. Rice
FTE Enroll: 1,985   (901) 448-5500

THE UNIVERSITY OF THE SOUTH
735 University Ave., Sewanee 37383-1000 *Type:* Private (Episcopal) liberal arts *Accred.:* 1958/1995 (ATS); 1895/1995 (SACS-CC) *Calendar:* Sem. plan *Degrees:* B, M, D *CEO:* Pres. Samuel R. Williamson, Jr.
FTE Enroll: 1,218   (615) 598-1000

VANDERBILT UNIVERSITY
2201 W. End Ave., Nashville 37240 *Type:* Private (interdenominational) *Accred.:* 1938/1994 (ATS); 1895/1986 (SACS-CC) *Calendar:* Sem. plan *Degrees:* B, M, D *Prof. Accred.:* Audiology, Business (M), Clinical Lab Scientist, Clinical Psychology, Counseling, Dietetics (internship), Engineering (bioengineering, chemical, civil, electrical, mechanical), General Practice Residency, Law, Medicine, Music, Nuclear Medicine Technology, Nursing (M), Oral and Maxillofacial Surgery, Perfusion, Psychology Internship, Radiation Therapy Technology, Speech-Language Pathology, Teacher Education *CEO:* Chanc. Joe B. Wyatt
FTE Enroll: 9,536   (615) 322-7311

VOLUNTEER STATE COMMUNITY COLLEGE
1360 Nashville Pike, Gallatin 37066 *Type:* Public (state) 2-year *System:* Tennessee Board of Regents *Accred.:* 1973/1989 (SACS-CC) *Calendar:* Sem. plan *Degrees:* A *Prof. Accred.:* Dental Assisting, EMT-Paramedic, Medical Record Technology, Physical Therapy Assisting, Radiography, Respiratory Therapy Technology *CEO:* Pres. Hal R. Ramer
FTE Enroll: 4,070   (615) 452-8600

WALTERS STATE COMMUNITY COLLEGE
500 S. Davy Crockett Pkwy., Morristown 37813-6899 *Type:* Public (state) junior *System:* Tennessee Board of Regents *Accred.:* 1972/1987 (SACS-CC) *Calendar:* Sem. plan *Degrees:* A *Prof. Accred.:* Nursing (A), Physical Therapy Assisting, Respiratory Therapy Technology *CEO:* Pres. Jack E. Campbell
FTE Enroll: 3,849   (615) 585-2600

WATKINS INSTITUTE SCHOOL OF INTERIOR DESIGN
601 Church St., Nashville 37219-2390 *Type:* Private *Calendar:* Sem. plan *Degrees:* A *Prof. Accred.:* Interior Design *CEO:* Pres. Brien McQuiston
Enroll: 400   (615) 242-1851

TEXAS

ABILENE CHRISTIAN UNIVERSITY
ACU Sta., Box 7000, Abilene 79699 *Type:* Private (Church of Christ) liberal arts *Accred.:* 1951/1991 (SACS-CC) *Calendar:* Sem. plan *Degrees:* A, B, M, D *Prof. Accred.:* Marriage and Family Therapy (M), Music, Social Work (B) *CEO:* Pres. Royce Money
FTE Enroll: 3,405   (915) 674-2000

ABILENE INTERCOLLEGIATE SCHOOL OF NURSING
2149 Hickory, Abilene 79601 *Type:* Private professional *Calendar:* Sem. plan *Degrees:* B *Prof. Accred.:* Nursing (B) *CEO:* Dean Corine Bonnet
                              (915) 672-2441

ALVIN COMMUNITY COLLEGE
3110 Mustang Rd., Alvin 77511-4898 *Type:* Public (district) junior *System:* Texas Higher Education Coordinating Board *Accred.:* 1959/1990 (SACS-CC) *Calendar:* Sem. plan *Degrees:* A *Prof. Accred.:* Clinical Lab Technology (A), Nursing (A), Respiratory Therapy, Respiratory Therapy Technology *CEO:* Pres. A. Rodney Allbright
FTE Enroll: 3,949   (713) 331-6111

AMARILLO COLLEGE
P.O. Box 447, Amarillo 79178 *Type:* Public (district) junior *System:* Texas Higher Education Coordinating Board *Accred.:* 1933/1992 (SACS-CC) *Calendar:* Sem. plan *Degrees:* A *Prof. Accred.:* Clinical Lab Technology (A), Dental Hygiene, Engineering Technology (electrical), Music, Nursing (A), Occupational Therapy Assisting, Physical Therapy Assisting, Radiation Therapy Technology, Radiography, Respiratory Therapy, Surgical Technology *CEO:* Pres. Luther Bud Joyner
FTE Enroll: 4,700   (806) 371-5000

AMARILLO TECHNICAL CENTER
P.O. Box 11197, Amarillo 79111 (state) 2-year *Accred.:* 1970/1985 (SACS-CC) *Calendar:* Qtr. plan *Degrees:* A
FTE Enroll: 439   (806) 335-2316

AMBASSADOR UNIVERSITY
P.O. Box 111, Big Sandy 75755 *Type:* Private (Church of God) liberal arts *Accred.:* 1994 (SACS-CC) *Calendar:* Sem. plan *Degrees:* A, B *CEO:* Pres. Russell Duke
FTE Enroll: 1,112   (903) 636-2000

AMBER UNIVERSITY
1700 Eastgate Dr., Garland 75041 *Type:* Private (Church of Christ) *Accred.:* 1981/1987 (SACS-CC) *Calendar:* Tri. plan *Degrees:* B, M *CEO:* Pres. Douglas W. Warner
FTE Enroll: 1,520   (214) 279-6511

ANGELINA COLLEGE
P.O. Box 1768, Lufkin 75902 *Type:* Public (district) junior *System:* Texas Higher Education Coordinating Board *Accred.:* 1970/1995 (SACS-CC) *Calendar:* Sem. plan *Degrees:* A *Prof. Accred.:* Radiography, Respiratory Therapy Technology *CEO:* Pres. Larry M. Phillips
FTE Enroll: 2,577   (409) 639-1301

ANGELO STATE UNIVERSITY
2601 West Ave. N., San Angelo 76909 *Type:* Public (state) liberal arts *System:* Texas State University System *Accred.:* 1936/1992 (SACS-CC) *Calendar:* Sem. plan *Degrees:* A, B, M *Prof. Accred.:* Music, Nursing (A,B) *CEO:* Pres. James Hindman
FTE Enroll: 5,227   (915) 942-2073

ARLINGTON BAPTIST COLLEGE
3001 W. Division St., Arlington 76012-3425 *Type:* Private (World Baptist Fellowship) *Accred.:* 1981/1991 (AABC) *Calendar:* Sem. plan *Degrees:* B *CEO:* Pres. David Bryant
FTE Enroll: 158   (817) 461-8741

ART INSTITUTE OF DALLAS
Two NorthPark E., 8080 Park La., Dallas 75231-9959 *Type:* Private *Accred.:* 1986/1990 (ACCSCT) *Calendar:* Qtr. plan *Degrees:* A *CEO:* Pres. Thomas M. Hauser
                              (214) 692-8080

ART INSTITUTE OF HOUSTON
1900 Yorktown St., Houston 77056 *Type:* Private *Accred.:* 1979/1993 (ACCSCT) *Calendar:* Qtr. plan *Degrees:* A, C *CEO:* Pres. Steve R. Gregg

(713) 623-2040

AUSTIN COLLEGE
900 N. Grand Ave., P.O. Box 1177, Sherman 75090-4440 *Type:* Private (Presbyterian) liberal arts *Accred.:* 1947/1989 (SACS-CC) *Calendar:* 4-1-4 plan *Degrees:* B, M *CEO:* Pres. Oscar C. Page
FTE Enroll: 1,184   (903) 813-2000

AUSTIN COMMUNITY COLLEGE
5930 Middle Fiskville Rd., Austin 78752-4390 *Type:* Public (district) junior *System:* Texas Higher Education Coordinating Board *Accred.:* 1978/1993 (SACS-CC) *Calendar:* Sem. plan *Degrees:* A *Prof. Accred.:* Clinical Lab Technology (A), Diagnostic Medical Sonography, EMT-Paramedic, Nursing (A), Occupational Therapy Assisting, Physical Therapy Assisting, Radiography, Surgical Technology *CEO:* Pres. William E. Segura
FTE Enroll: 14,949   (512) 483-7598

AUSTIN PRESBYTERIAN THEOLOGICAL SEMINARY
100 E. 27th St., Austin 78705-5797 *Type:* Private (Presbyterian) graduate only *Accred.:* 1940/1989 (ATS); 1973/1989 (SACS-CC) *Calendar:* 4-1-4 plan *Degrees:* M, D *CEO:* Pres. Jack L. Stotts
Enroll: 210   (512) 472-6736

BAPTIST MISSIONARY ASSOCIATION
THEOLOGICAL SEMINARY
1530 E. Pine St., Jacksonville 75766 *Type:* Private (Baptist) professional *Accred.:* 1986/1991 (SACS-CC) *Calendar:* Sem. plan *Degrees:* A, B, M *CEO:* Pres. Philip R. Bryan
FTE Enroll: 56   (903) 586-2501

BAYLOR COLLEGE OF DENTISTRY
3302 Gaston Ave., Dallas 75246 *Type:* Public *Accred.:* 1976/1989 (SACS-CC) *Calendar:* Qtr. plan *Degrees:* M, D *Prof. Accred.:* Combined Prosthodontics, Dental Hygiene, Dentistry, Dietetics (internship), Endodontics, General Dentistry, General Practice Residency (prelim. provisional), Oral and Maxillofacial Surgery, Orthodontics, Pediatric Dentistry, Periodontics *CEO:* Pres. Dominick P. DePaola
FTE Enroll: 466   (214) 828-8100

BAYLOR COLLEGE OF MEDICINE
One Baylor Plaza, Houston 77030-3498 *Type:* Private professional; graduate only *Accred.:* 1970/1995 (SACS-CC) *Calendar:* Qtr. plan *Degrees:* M, D *Prof. Accred.:* Audiology (candidate), Medicine, Nuclear Medicine Technology, Nurse Anesthesia Education, Perfusion, Physician Assisting/Surgeon Assisting, Psychology Internship, Speech-Language Pathology *CEO:* Pres. Ralph D. Feigin
FTE Enroll: 1,116   (713) 798-4951

BAYLOR UNIVERSITY
Waco 76798 *Type:* Private (Southern Baptist) *Accred.:* 1914/1986 (SACS-CC) *Calendar:* Sem. plan *Degrees:* B, M, D *Prof. Accred.:* Accounting (A), Audiology (candidate), Business (B,M), Clinical Psychology, Computer Science, Engineering (general), Health Services Administration, Home Economics, Law, Music, Nursing (B), Physical Therapy, Recreation and Leisure Services (candidate), Social Work (B), Speech-Language Pathology, Teacher Education *CEO:* Pres. Robert B. Sloan, Jr.
FTE Enroll: 11,681   (817) 755-1011

BEE COUNTY COLLEGE
3800 Charco Rd., Beeville 78102 *Type:* Public (district) junior *System:* Texas Higher Education Coordinating Board *Accred.:* 1969/1994 (SACS-CC) *Calendar:* Sem. plan *Degrees:* A *Prof. Accred.:* Dental Hygiene *CEO:* Pres. Norman E. Wallace
FTE Enroll: 2,126   (512) 358-3130

BLINN COLLEGE
902 College Ave., Brenham 77833 *Type:* Public (district) junior *System:* Texas Higher Education Coordinating Board *Accred.:* 1950/1994 (SACS-CC) *Calendar:* Sem. plan *Degrees:* A *Prof. Accred.:* Nursing (A), Radiography *CEO:* Pres. Donald Voelter
FTE Enroll: 6,816   (409) 830-4000

BRAZOSPORT COLLEGE
500 College Dr., Lake Jackson 77566 *Type:* Public (district) junior *System:* Texas Higher Education Coordinating Board *Accred.:* 1970/1995 (SACS-CC) *Calendar:* Sem. plan *Degrees:* A *CEO:* Pres. John R. Grable
FTE Enroll: 1,860   (409) 266-3000

BROOKHAVEN COLLEGE
3939 Valley View Ln., Farmers Branch 75244-4997 *Type:* Public (district) junior *System:* Dallas County Community College District *Accred.:* 1979/1993 (SACS-CC) *Calendar:* Sem. plan *Degrees:* A *CEO:* Pres. Walter G. Bumphus
FTE Enroll: 5,379   (214) 620-4700

CEDAR VALLEY COLLEGE
3030 N. Dallas Ave., Lancaster 75134 *Type:* Public (district) junior *System:* Dallas County Community College District *Accred.:* 1979/1993 (SACS-CC) *Calendar:* Sem. plan *Degrees:* A *Prof. Accred.:* Veterinary Technology *CEO:* Pres. Carol J. Spencer
FTE Enroll: 1,956   (214) 372-8200

CENTER FOR ADVANCED LEGAL STUDIES
3015 Richmond Ave., Houston 77098 *Type:* Private *Accred.:* 1989/1990 (COE) *Degrees:* A, C *CEO:* Dir. Doyle Happe
FTE Enroll: 103   (713) 529-2778

CENTRAL TEXAS COLLEGE
P.O. Box 1800, Killeen 76540-9990 *Type:* Public (district) junior *System:* Texas Higher Education Coordinating Board *Accred.:* 1969/1994 (SACS-CC) *Calendar:* Sem. plan *Degrees:* A *Prof. Accred.:* Clinical Lab Technology (A), Nursing (A) *CEO:* Chanc. James R. Anderson
FTE Enroll: 10,768   (817) 526-7161

CISCO JUNIOR COLLEGE
Rte. 3, Box 3, Cisco 76437 *Type:* Public (district) junior *System:* Texas Higher Education Coordinating Board *Accred.:* 1958/1989 (SACS-CC) *Calendar:* Sem. plan *Degrees:* A *Prof. Accred.:* Medical Assisting (AMA), Practical Nursing *CEO:* Pres. Roger C. Schustereit
FTE Enroll: 2,190   (817) 442-2567

CLARENDON COLLEGE
P.O. Box 968, Clarendon 79226 *Type:* Public (district) junior *System:* Texas Higher Education Coordinating Board *Accred.:* 1970/1995 (SACS-CC) *Calendar:* Sem. plan *Degrees:* A *CEO:* Pres. Scott Elliott
FTE Enroll: 613   (806) 874-3571

THE COLLEGE OF ST. THOMAS MOORE
3001 Lubbock Ave., Fort Worth 76109 *Type:* Private (Roman Catholic) *Accred.:* 1994 (SACS-CC) *Calendar:* Sem. plan *Degrees:* A *CEO:* Provost James A. Patrick
FTE Enroll: 16   (817) 923-8459

COLLEGE OF THE MAINLAND
1200 Amburn Rd., Texas City 77591 *Type:* Public (district) junior *System:* Texas Higher Education Coordinating Board *Accred.:* 1969/1993 (SACS-CC) *Calendar:* Sem. plan *Degrees:* A *Prof. Accred.:* Nursing (A) *CEO:* Pres. Larry L. Stanley
FTE Enroll: 2,600   (409) 938-1211

COLLIN COUNTY COMMUNITY COLLEGE
2200 W. University Dr., McKinney 75070-8001 *Type:* Public (district) junior *System:* Texas Higher Education Coordinating Board *Accred.:* 1989/1994 (SACS-CC) *Calendar:* Sem. plan *Degrees:* A *Prof. Accred.:* Respiratory Therapy, Respiratory Therapy Technology *CEO:* Pres. John H. Anthony
FTE Enroll: 6,098   (214) 548-6790

COMMONWEALTH INSTITUTE OF FUNERAL SERVICE
415 Barren Springs Dr., Houston 77090 *Type:* Private professional *Calendar:* Qtr. plan *Degrees:* A, C *Prof. Accred.:* Funeral Service Education (Mortuary Science) *CEO:* Pres. Terry McEnany
                    (713) 873-0262

CONCORDIA UNIVERSITY AT AUSTIN
3400 I.H. 35 N., Austin 78705 *Type:* Private (Lutheran) liberal arts *Accred.:* 1968/1988 (SACS-CC) *Calendar:* Sem. plan *Degrees:* A, B *CEO:* Pres. David Zeisen
FTE Enroll: 622   (512) 452-7661

COURT REPORTING INSTITUTE OF DALLAS
N., 8585 N. Stemmons Fwy., Ste. 200, Dallas 75247 *Type:* Private business *Accred.:* 1986/1998 (ACICS) *Degrees:* A, C *CEO:* Dir. Carolyn S. Willard
(214) 350-9722

THE CRISWELL COLLEGE
4010 Gaston Ave., Dallas 75246 *Type:* Private (Baptist) *Accred.:* 1985/1990 (SACS-CC) *Calendar:* Sem. plan *Degrees:* A, B, M *CEO:* Pres. Richard R. Melick, Jr.
FTE Enroll: 233   (214) 821-5433

DALLAS BAPTIST UNIVERSITY
3000 Mountain Creek Pkwy., Dallas 75211-9299 *Type:* Private (Southern Baptist) liberal arts *Accred.:* 1959/1988 (SACS-CC) *Calendar:* Sem. plan *Degrees:* B, M *Prof. Accred.:* Nursing (B) *CEO:* Pres. Gary R. Cook
FTE Enroll: 1,902   (214) 331-8311

DALLAS CHRISTIAN COLLEGE
2700 Christian Pkwy., Dallas 75234 *Type:* Private (Christian Churches/Churches of Christ) *Accred.:* 1978/1988 (AABC) *Calendar:* Sem. plan *Degrees:* A, B, C *CEO:* Interim Pres. Keith Ray
FTE Enroll: 82   (214) 241-3371

DALLAS THEOLOGICAL SEMINARY
3909 Swiss Ave., Dallas 75204 *Type:* Private (interdenominational) graduate only *Accred.:* 1993 (ATS); 1969/1993 (SACS-CC) *Calendar:* Sem. plan *Degrees:* M, D *CEO:* Pres. Charles R. Swindoll
Enroll: 1,358   (214) 824-3094

DEL MAR COLLEGE
Baldwin and Ayers, Corpus Christi 78404-3897 *Type:* Public (district) junior *System:* Texas Higher Education Coordinating Board *Accred.:* 1946/1990 (SACS-CC) *Calendar:* Sem. plan *Degrees:* A *Prof. Accred.:* Art, Clinical Lab Technology (A), Dental Assisting, Dental Hygiene (provisional), Diagnostic Medical Sonography, Engineering Technology (electrical), Music, Nursing (A), Radiography, Respiratory Therapy, Respiratory Therapy Technology, Surgical Technology *CEO:* Pres. Terry L. Dicianna
FTE Enroll: 7,388   (512) 886-1200

DEVRY INSTITUTE OF TECHNOLOGY—IRVING
4801 Regent Blvd., Irving 75063-2440 *Type:* Private *System:* DeVry Institutes *Accred.:* 1981/1992 (NCA) *Calendar:* Sem. plan *Degrees:* A, B *Prof. Accred.:* Engineering Technology (electrical) *CEO:* Pres. Francis V. Cannon
(214) 929-6777

* Indirect NCA accreditation through DeVry Institutes

EAST TEXAS BAPTIST UNIVERSITY
1209 N. Grove Ave., Marshall 75670-1498 *Type:* Private (Southern Baptist) liberal arts *Accred.:* 1957/1989 (SACS-CC) *Calendar:* 4-1-4 plan *Degrees:* A, B, M *Prof. Accred.:* Music *CEO:* Pres. Bob E. Riley
FTE Enroll: 1,253   (214) 935-7963

EAST TEXAS STATE UNIVERSITY
ETSU Sta., Commerce 75429-3011 *Type:* Public (state) *System:* Texas Higher Education Coordinating Board *Accred.:* 1925/1993 (SACS-CC) *Calendar:* Sem. plan *Degrees:* B, M, D *Prof. Accred.:* Business (B,M), Counseling, Music, Social Work (B) *CEO:* Pres. Jerry D. Morris
FTE Enroll: 6,502   (903) 886-5102

EAST TEXAS STATE UNIVERSITY AT TEXARKANA
P.O. Box 5518, Texarkana 75505-0518 *Type:* Public (state) *System:* Texas Higher Education Coordinating Board *Accred.:* 1979/1995 (SACS-CC) *Calendar:* Sem. plan *Degrees:* B, M *CEO:* Pres. Stephen R. Hensley
FTE Enroll: 759   (903) 838-6514

EASTFIELD COLLEGE
3737 Motley Dr., Mesquite 75150-2099 *Type:* Public (district) junior *System:* Dallas County Community College District *Accred.:* 1972/1993 (SACS-CC) *Calendar:* Sem. plan *Degrees:* A *CEO:* Pres. Robert Aguero
FTE Enroll: 5,510   (214) 324-7100

EL CENTRO COLLEGE
Main and Lamar Sts., Dallas 75202-3604 *Type:* Public (district) junior *System:* Dallas County Community College District *Accred.:* 1968/1993 (SACS-CC) *Calendar:* Sem. plan *Degrees:* A *Prof. Accred.:* Clinical Lab Tech-

nology (A), Diagnostic Medical Sonography, Interior Design, Nursing (A), Radiography, Respiratory Therapy, Respiratory Therapy Technology, Surgical Technology *CEO:* Pres. Wright L. Lassiter, Jr.
FTE Enroll: 3,034   (214) 746-2010

EL PASO COMMUNITY COLLEGE
P.O. Box 20500, El Paso 79998 *Type:* Public (district) junior *System:* Texas Higher Education Coordinating Board *Accred.:* 1978/ 1994 (SACS-CC) *Calendar:* Sem. plan *Degrees:* A *Prof. Accred.:* Clinical Lab Technology (A), Dental Assisting, Dental Hygiene, Diagnostic Medical Sonography, Medical Assisting (AMA), Medical Record Technology, Nuclear Medicine Technology, Nursing (A), Physical Therapy Assisting, Radiation Therapy Technology, Radiography, Respiratory Therapy, Surgical Technology *CEO:* Pres. Adriana D. Barrera
FTE Enroll: 14,047   (915) 594-2000

THE EPISCOPAL THEOLOGICAL SEMINARY OF THE SOUTHWEST
P.O. Box 2247, 606 Rathervue Pl., Austin 78768-2247 *Type:* Private (Episcopal) graduate only *Accred.:* 1958/1993 (ATS); 1983/ 1993 (SACS-CC) *Calendar:* 4-1-4 plan *Degrees:* M *CEO:* Dean Durstan R. McDonald
Enroll: 66   (512) 472-4133

EXECUTIVE SECRETARIAL SCHOOL
4849 Greenville Ave., Ste. 200, Dallas 75206-4125 *Type:* Private business *Accred.:* 1969/1999 (ACICS); 1977/1992 (COE) *Calendar:* Tri. plan *Degrees:* A, C *CEO:* Chrmn. of the Bd. Jan V. Friedheim
(214) 369-9009

FRANK PHILLIPS COLLEGE
P.O. Box 5118, Borger 79008-5118 *Type:* Public (district) junior *System:* Texas Higher Education Coordinating Board *Accred.:* 1958/1989 (SACS-CC) *Calendar:* Sem. plan *Degrees:* A *CEO:* Pres. William A. Griffin, Jr.
FTE Enroll: 1,160   (806) 274-5311

GALVESTON COLLEGE
4015 Ave. Q, Galveston 77550 *Type:* Public (district) junior *System:* Texas Higher Education Coordinating Board *Accred.:* 1969/1994

(SACS-CC) *Calendar:* Sem. plan *Degrees:* A *Prof. Accred.:* Nuclear Medicine Technology, Nursing (A), Radiation Therapy Technology, Radiography *CEO:* Pres. Carlisle B. Rathburn, III
FTE Enroll: 1,468   (409) 763-6551

GRAYSON COUNTY COLLEGE
6101 Grayson Dr., Denison 75020 *Type:* Public (district) junior *System:* Texas Higher Education Coordinating Board *Accred.:* 1967/1991 (SACS-CC) *Calendar:* Sem. plan *Degrees:* A *Prof. Accred.:* Clinical Lab Technology (A), Dental Assisting, Nursing (A) *CEO:* Pres. James M. Williams, Jr.
FTE Enroll: 2,586   (903) 465-6030

HALLMARK INSTITUTE OF TECHNOLOGY
10401 IH 10 W., San Antonio 78230 *Type:* Private *Accred.:* 1973/1987 (ACCSCT) *Degrees:* A *CEO:* Pres. Richard H. Fessler
(210) 924-8551

HALLMARK INSTITUTE OF TECHNOLOGY
1130 99th St., San Antonio 78214-9985 *Type:* Private *Accred.:* 1971/1988 (ACCSCT) *Degrees:* A *CEO:* Dir. Jeanne C. Martin
(210) 690-9000

HARDIN-SIMMONS UNIVERSITY
2200 Hickory St., Abilene 79698 *Type:* Private (Southern Baptist) *Accred.:* 1927/1987 (SACS-CC) *Calendar:* Sem. plan *Degrees:* A, B, M *Prof. Accred.:* Music, Social Work (B) *CEO:* Pres. Edwin L. Hall
FTE Enroll: 1,702   (915) 670-1000

HILL COLLEGE
112 Lamar Dr., Hillsboro 76645 *Type:* Public (district) junior *System:* Texas Higher Education Coordinating Board *Accred.:* 1963/1990 (SACS-CC) *Calendar:* Sem. plan *Degrees:* A *CEO:* Pres. William R. Auvenshine
FTE Enroll: 1,541   (817) 582-2555

HOUSTON BAPTIST UNIVERSITY
7502 Fondren Rd., Houston 77074-3298 *Type:* Private (Southern Baptist) liberal arts *Accred.:* 1968/1991 (SACS-CC) *Calendar:* Qtr. plan *Degrees:* A, B, M *Prof. Accred.:* Nursing (A,B) *CEO:* Pres. E. Douglas Hodo
FTE Enroll: 2,174   (713) 774-7661

HOUSTON COMMUNITY COLLEGE SYSTEM
P.O. Box 7849, Houston 77270-7849 *Type:*
Public (district) junior *System:* Texas Higher
Education Coordinating Board *Accred.:*
1977/1992 (SACS-CC) *Calendar:* Sem. plan
Degrees: A *Prof. Accred.:* Clinical Lab Tech-
nology (A), Dental Assisting, Engineering
Technology (electrical), Medical Record
Technology, Nuclear Medicine Technology,
Occupational Therapy Assisting, Physical
Therapy Assisting, Radiography, Respira-
tory Therapy, Respiratory Therapy Technol-
ogy, Surgical Technology *CEO:* Interim
Chanc. James Harding
FTE Enroll: 23,331   (713) 869-5021

CENTRAL COLLEGE
1300 Holman Ave., Houston 77004
                            (713) 630-7205

COLLEGE WITHOUT WALLS
4310 Dunlavy St., Houston 77270
                            (713) 868-0795

NORTHEAST COLLEGE
4638 Airline Dr., P.O. Box 7849, Houston
77270-7849
                            (713) 694-5384

NORTHWEST COLLEGE
16360 Park Ten Pl., Houston 77084
                            (713) 578-3487

SOUTHEAST COLLEGE
6815 Rustic St., Houston 77012
                            (713) 641-2725

SOUTHWEST COLLEGE
5407 Gulfton St., Houston 77081
                            (713) 661-4589

HOUSTON GRADUATE SCHOOL OF THEOLOGY
6910 Fannin St., Ste. 207, Houston 77030-
3802 *Type:* Private Religious Society of
Friends *Accred.:* 1994 (ATS candidate); 1986/
1991 (SACS-CC) *Calendar:* Sem. plan
Degrees: M, D (candidate) *CEO:* Pres. Delbert
P. Vaughn
Enroll: 168   (713) 791-9505

HOWARD COLLEGE
1001 Birdwell Ln., Big Spring 79720 *Type:*
Public (district) junior *System:* Howard
County Junior College District *Accred.:*
1955/1986 (SACS-CC) *Calendar:* Sem. plan
Degrees: A *Prof. Accred.:* Dental Hygiene,
Medical Record Technology, Nursing (A),
Respiratory Therapy Technology *CEO:* Pres.
Cheryl T. Sparks
FTE Enroll: 1,765   (915) 264-5000

HOWARD PAYNE UNIVERSITY
1000 Fisk Ave., Brownwood 76801 *Type:*
Private (Southern Baptist) liberal arts
Accred.: 1948/1994 (SACS-CC) *Calendar:*
Sem. plan *Degrees:* B *Prof. Accred.:* Music
(A), Social Work (B-candidate) *CEO:* Pres.
Don Newbury, Jr.
FTE Enroll: 1,415   (915) 646-2502

HUSTON-TILLOTSON COLLEGE
900 Chicon St., Austin 78702 *Type:* Private
(United Methodist/United Church of Christ)
liberal arts *Accred.:* 1943/1990 (SACS-CC)
Calendar: Sem. plan *Degrees:* B *CEO:* Pres.
Joseph T. McMillan, Jr.
FTE Enroll: 539   (512) 505-3000

ICI UNIVERSITY
6300 N. Belt Line Rd., Irving 75063 *Type:*
Private home study *Accred.:* 1977/1993
(DETC) *Degrees:* A, B, M, C *CEO:* Pres.
George M. Flattery
                            (800) 444-0424

INCARNATE WORD COLLEGE
4301 Broadway, San Antonio 78209 *Type:*
Private (Roman Catholic) liberal arts
Accred.: 1925/1995 (SACS-CC) *Calendar:*
Sem. plan *Degrees:* B, M *Prof. Accred.:*
Nuclear Medicine Technology, Nursing
(B,M) *CEO:* Pres. Louis J. Agnese, Jr.
FTE Enroll: 2,764   (210) 829-6000

INSTITUTE FOR CHRISTIAN STUDIES
1909 University Ave., Austin 78705 *Type:*
Private (Church of Christ) *Accred.:* 1987/
1992 (SACS-CC) *Calendar:* Sem. plan
Degrees: B *CEO:* Pres. David Worley
FTE Enroll: 36   (512) 476-2772

ITT TECHNICAL INSTITUTE
2201 Arlington Downs Rd., Arlington 76011-6319 *Type:* Private *Accred.:* 1983/ 1988 (ACCSCT) *Degrees:* A *CEO:* Dir. Tom D. Marley
(817) 640-7100

ITT TECHNICAL INSTITUTE
1640 Eastgate Dr., #100, Garland 75041- 5585 *Type:* Private *Accred.:* 1989 (ACC-SCT) *Degrees:* A *CEO:* Dir. Maureen K. Clements
(214) 279-0500

ITT TECHNICAL INSTITUTE
9421 W. Sam Houston Pkwy., Houston 77099-1849 *Type:* Private *Accred.:* 1984/ 1988 (ACCSCT) *Degrees:* A *CEO:* Dir. Louis Christensen
(713) 270-1634

ITT TECHNICAL INSTITUTE
4242 Piedras Dr. E., Ste. 100, San Antonio 78228-1414 *Type:* Private *Accred.:* 1988 (ACCSCT) *Degrees:* A *CEO:* Dir. Barry S. Simich
(210) 737-1881

JACKSONVILLE COLLEGE
105 B.J. Albritton Dr., Jacksonville 75766- 4798 *Type:* Private (Baptist) junior *Accred.:* 1974/1989 (SACS-CC) *Calendar:* Sem. plan *Degrees:* A *CEO:* Pres. Edwin Crank
FTE Enroll: 252   (903) 586-2518

JARVIS CHRISTIAN COLLEGE
P.O. Drawer G, Hwy. 80E, Hawkins 75765- 9989 *Type:* Private (Disciples of Christ) lib-eral arts *Accred.:* 1967/1993 (SACS-CC) *Calendar:* Sem. plan *Degrees:* A, B *CEO:* Pres. Sebetha Jenkins
FTE Enroll: 378   (903) 769-5700

KD STUDIO
2600 Stemmons Fwy., No. 117, Dallas 75207 *Type:* Private *Calendar:* Sem. plan *Degrees:* A *Prof. Accred.:* Theatre *CEO:* Pres. Kathy Tyner
(214) 638-0484

KILGORE COLLEGE
1100 Broadway, Kilgore 75662-3299 *Type:* Public (district) junior *System:* Texas Higher Education Coordinating Board *Accred.:* 1939/1989 (SACS-CC) *Calendar:* Sem. plan *Degrees:* A *Prof. Accred.:* Clinical Lab Tech-nology (A), Nursing (A), Physical Therapy Assisting, Radiography, Surgical Technol-ogy *CEO:* Pres. J. Frank Thornton
FTE Enroll: 3,423   (903) 984-8531

LAMAR UNIVERSITY
P.O. Box 10001, Beaumont 77710 *Type:* Public (state) *System:* Texas State University System *Accred.:* 1955/1988 (SACS-CC) *Calendar:* Sem. plan *Degrees:* A, B, M, D *Prof. Accred.:* Audiology, Business (B,M), Dental Hygiene, Engineering (chemical, civil, electrical, industrial, mechanical), Music, Nursing (A,B), Radiography, Respi-ratory Therapy, Respiratory Therapy Tech-nology, Social Work (B), Speech-Language Pathology, Teacher Education *CEO:* Pres. Rex L. Cottle
FTE Enroll: 6,672   (409) 880-7011

LAMAR UNIVERSITY—INSTITUTE OF TECHNOLOGY
P.O. Box 10001, Beaumont 77710 *Type:* Public *System:* Texas State University Sys-tem *Accred.:* 1955/1988 (SACS-CC) *Calen-dar:* Sem. plan *Degrees:* A, C *CEO:* Pres. Robert Krienke
Enroll: 1,500   (409) 880-8185

LAMAR UNIVERSITY—ORANGE
410 W. Front St., Orange 77630 *Type:* Public (state) junior *System:* Texas State University System *Accred.:* 1989/1994 (SACS-CC) *Calendar:* Sem. plan *Degrees:* A *CEO:* Pres. J. Michael Shahan
FTE Enroll: 1,035   (409) 883-7750

LAMAR UNIVERSITY—PORT ARTHUR
P.O. Box 310, Port Arthur 77641-0310 *Type:* Public (state) junior *System:* Texas State University System *Accred.:* 1988/1993 (SACS-CC warning) *Calendar:* Sem. plan *Degrees:* A *CEO:* Pres. W. Sam Monroe
FTE Enroll: 1,726   (409) 983-4921

LAREDO COMMUNITY COLLEGE
W. End Washington St., Laredo 78040-4395
Type: Public (district) junior *System:* Texas
Higher Education Coordinating Board
Accred.: 1957/1989 (SACS-CC) *Calendar:*
Sem. plan *Degrees:* A *Prof. Accred.:* Clinical
Lab Technology (A), Nursing (A), Physical
Therapy Assisting, Radiography *CEO:* Pres.
Ramon H. Dovalina
FTE Enroll: 5,333   (210) 722-0521

LEE COLLEGE
P.O. Box 818, Baytown 77522-0818 *Type:*
Public (district) junior *System:* Texas Higher
Education Coordinating Board *Accred.:*
1948/1995 (SACS-CC) *Calendar:* Sem. plan
Degrees: A *Prof. Accred.:* Medical Record
Technology, Nursing (A) *CEO:* Pres. Jackson
N. Sasser
FTE Enroll: 2,691   (713) 427-5611

LETOURNEAU UNIVERSITY
2100 Mobberly Ave., P.O. Box 7001,
Longview 75607-7001 *Type:* Private liberal
arts and professional *Accred.:* 1970/1995
(SACS-CC) *Calendar:* Sem. plan *Degrees:*
A, B, M *Prof. Accred.:* Engineering (gen-
eral) *CEO:* Pres. Alvin O. Austin
FTE Enroll: 1,955   (903) 753-0231

LON MORRIS COLLEGE
800 College Ave., Jacksonville 75766 *Type:*
Private (United Methodist) junior *Accred.:*
1927/1994 (SACS-CC) *Calendar:* Sem. plan
Degrees: A *CEO:* Pres. Clifford M. Lee
FTE Enroll: 247   (903) 589-4000

LUBBOCK CHRISTIAN UNIVERSITY
5601 19th St., Lubbock 79407-2099 *Type:*
Private (Church of Christ) liberal arts
Accred.: 1963/1988 (SACS-CC) *Calendar:*
Sem. plan *Degrees:* A, B, M *Prof. Accred.:*
Social Work (B) *CEO:* Pres. Ken Jones
FTE Enroll: 992   (806) 796-8800

MCLENNAN COMMUNITY COLLEGE
1400 College Dr., Waco 76708 *Type:* Public
(district) junior *System:* Texas Higher Education Coordinating Board *Accred.:* 1968/ 1992
(SACS-CC) *Calendar:* Sem. plan *Degrees:* A

Prof. Accred.: Clinical Lab Technology (A),
Nursing (A), Physical Therapy Assisting,
Radiography, Respiratory Therapy Technol-
ogy *CEO:* Pres. Dennis F. Michaelis
FTE Enroll: 4,036   (817) 756-0934

MCMURRY UNIVERSITY
S. 14th St. and Sayles Blvd., Abilene 79697
Type: Private (United Methodist) liberal arts
Accred.: 1949/1989 (SACS-CC) *Calendar:*
Sem. plan *Degrees:* A, B *CEO:* Pres. Robert
E. Shimp
FTE Enroll: 1,095   (915) 691-6200

MICROCOMPUTER TECHNOLOGY INSTITUTE
7277 Regency Square Blvd., Houston
77036-3163 *Type:* Private *Accred.:* 1983/
1988 (ACCSCT) *Degrees:* A, C *CEO:* Dir.
Barbara Andrews
                                      (713) 974-7181

FRIENDSWOOD CAMPUS
17164 Blackhawk Blvd., Friendswood
77546-3446 *Accred.:* 1988 (ACCSCT)
Degrees: A, C
                                      (713) 996-8180

MIDLAND COLLEGE
3600 N. Garfield St., Midland 79705 *Type:*
Public (district) junior *System:* Texas Higher
Education Coordinating Board *Accred.:*
1975/1990 (SACS-CC) *Calendar:* Sem. plan
Degrees: A *Prof. Accred.:* Nursing (A),
Radiography, Respiratory Therapy, Respira-
tory Therapy Technology, Veterinary Tech-
nology (probational) *CEO:* Pres. David E.
Daniel
FTE Enroll: 2,430   (915) 685-4500

MIDWESTERN STATE UNIVERSITY
3410 Taft Blvd., Wichita Falls 76308-2099
Type: Public (state) *System:* Texas Higher
Education Coordinating Board *Accred.:*
1950/1992 (SACS-CC) *Calendar:* Sem. plan
Degrees: A, B, M *Prof. Accred.:* Dental
Hygiene, Engineering Technology (manu-
facturing), Music, Nursing (B), Radiogra-
phy, Social Work (B-candidate), Teacher
Education *CEO:* Pres. Louis J. Rodriguez
FTE Enroll: 5,794   (817) 689-4000

MISS WADE'S FASHION MERCHANDISING
COLLEGE
P.O. Box 586343, Ste. M5120, Int'l. Apparel
Mart, Dallas 75258 *Type:* Private *Accred.:*
1985/1990 (SACS-CC) *Calendar:* Tri. plan
Degrees: A *CEO:* Pres. Frank J. Tortoriello, Jr.
FTE Enroll: 279   (214) 637-3530

MOUNTAIN VIEW COLLEGE
4849 W. Illinois Ave., Dallas 75211-6599
Type: Public (district) junior *System:* Dallas
County Community College District
Accred.: 1972/1993 (SACS-CC) *Calendar:*
Sem. plan *Degrees:* A *CEO:* Pres. Monique
Amerman
FTE Enroll: 3,897   (214) 333-8700

NATIONAL EDUCATION CENTER—BRYMAN
CAMPUS
16416 Northchase Dr., Ste. 300, Houston
77060-2020 *Type:* Private *Accred.:* 1973/
1988 (ACCSCT) *Degrees:* A, C *CEO:* Dir.
Ray White
                              (713) 447-6656

NATIONAL EDUCATION CENTER—NATIONAL
INSTITUTE OF TECHNOLOGY CAMPUS
10945 Estates Ln., Dallas 75238-2378 *Type:*
Private *Accred.:* 1969/1988 (ACCSCT) *Cal-
endar:* Qtr. plan *Degrees:* A, C *Prof.
Accred.:* Medical Assisting (AMA) *CEO:*
Dir. Paulette Gallerson
                              (214) 503-9373

NAVARRO COLLEGE
3200 W. Seventh Ave., Corsicana 75110
Type: Public (district) junior *System:* Texas
Higher Education Coordinating Board
Accred.: 1954/1995 (SACS-CC) *Calendar:*
Sem. plan *Degrees:* A *Prof. Accred.:* Med-
ical Assisting, Medical Laboratory Technol-
ogy *CEO:* Pres. Gerald E. Burson
FTE Enroll: 2,525   (903) 874-6501

NORTH CENTRAL TEXAS COMMUNITY COLLEGE
1525 W. California St., Gainesville 76240-
4699 *Type:* Public (district) junior *System:*
Texas Higher Education Coordinating Board
Accred.: 1961/1991 (SACS-CC) *Calendar:*
Sem. plan *Degrees:* A *Prof. Accred.:* Nursing

(A), Occupational Therapy Assisting *CEO:*
Pres. Ronnie Glasscock
FTE Enroll: 2,710   (817) 668-7731

NORTH HARRIS MONTGOMERY COMMUNITY
COLLEGE DISTRICT
250 N. Sam Houston Pkwy., E., Houston
77060 *Type:* Public (district) junior *System:*
Texas Higher Education Coordinating Board
Accred.: 1976/1991 (SACS-CC) *Calendar:*
Sem. plan *Degrees:* A *Prof. Accred.:* Nursing
(A) *CEO:* Chanc. John E. Pickelman
FTE Enroll: 15,653   (713) 591-3500

HOUSTON BRANCH
2700 W. W. Thorne Dr., Houston 77073
System: North Harris Montgomery Community College District *Accred.:* 1976/
1991 (SACS-CC) *Calendar:* Sem. plan
                              (713) 443-5400

KINGWOOD COLLEGE
20000 Kingwood Dr., Kingwood 77339
Accred.: 1976/1991 (SACS-CC) *Calendar:* Sem. plan *Prof. Accred.:* Respiratory
Therapy, Respiratory Therapy Technology
                              (713) 359-1600

MONTGOMERY COLLEGE
3200 Hwy. 242, College Park Dr., Conroe
77384 *System:* North Harris Montgomery
Community College District *Accred.:*
1976/1991 (SACS-CC) *Calendar:* Sem.
plan *Degrees:* A
                              (409) 273-2900

TOMBALL COLLEGE
30555 Tomball Pkwy., Tomball 77375-
4036 *Accred.:* 1976/1991 (SACS-CC)
Calendar: Sem. plan *Prof. Accred.:* Veterinary Technology
                              (713) 351-3300

NORTH LAKE COLLEGE
5001 N. MacArthur Blvd., Irving 75038-
3899 *Type:* Public (district) junior *System:*
Dallas County Community College District
Accred.: 1979/1993 (SACS-CC) *Calendar:*
Sem. plan *Degrees:* A *Prof. Accred.:* Con-
struction Education (A) *CEO:* Pres. James F.
Horton, Jr.
FTE Enroll: 4,590   (214) 659-5229

NORTHEAST TEXAS COMMUNITY COLLEGE
P.O. Drawer 1307, Mount Pleasant 75456-1307 *Type:* Public (district) junior *System:* Texas Higher Education Coordinating Board *Accred.:* 1987/1992 (SACS-CC) *Calendar:* Sem. plan *Degrees:* A *CEO:* Pres. Charles Florio
FTE Enroll: 1,513   (903) 572-1911

OBLATE SCHOOL OF THEOLOGY
285 Oblate Dr., San Antonio 78216-6693 *Type:* Private (Roman Catholic) graduate only *Accred.:* 1982/1989 (ATS); 1968/1989 (SACS-CC) *Calendar:* Sem. plan *Degrees:* M, D (candidate) *CEO:* Pres. J. William Morell
Enroll: 125   (210) 341-1366

ODESSA COLLEGE
201 W. University Blvd., Odessa 79764 *Type:* Public (district) junior *System:* Texas Higher Education Coordinating Board *Accred.:* 1952/1992 (SACS-CC) *Calendar:* Sem. plan *Degrees:* A *Prof. Accred.:* Clinical Lab Technology (A), Music, Nursing (A), Physical Therapy Assisting, Radiography, Respiratory Therapy, Respiratory Therapy Technology, Surgical Technology *CEO:* Pres. Vance Gipson
FTE Enroll: 3,024   (915) 335-6400

OUR LADY OF THE LAKE UNIVERSITY
411 S.W. 24th St., San Antonio 78207-4689 *Type:* Private (Roman Catholic) liberal arts *Accred.:* 1923/1992 (SACS-CC) *Calendar:* Sem. plan *Degrees:* B, M, D *Prof. Accred.:* Marriage and Family Therapy (M), Social Work (B,M), Speech-Language Pathology *CEO:* Pres. Elizabeth Anne Sueltenfuss
FTE Enroll: 2,275   (210) 434-6711

PALO ALTO COLLEGE
1400 W. Villaret Blvd., San Antonio 78224-2499 *Type:* Public (district) junior *System:* Alamo Community College District *Accred.:* 1987/1993 (SACS-CC) *Calendar:* Sem. plan *Degrees:* A *CEO:* Pres. Joel E. Vela
FTE Enroll: 4,576   (210) 921-5260

PANOLA COLLEGE
1109 W. Panola St., Carthage 75633 *Type:* Public (district) junior *System:* Texas Higher Education Coordinating Board *Accred.:* 1960/1990 (SACS-CC) *Calendar:* Sem. plan *Degrees:* A *CEO:* Pres. William Edmonson
FTE Enroll: 1,247   (903) 693-2022

PARIS JUNIOR COLLEGE
2400 Clarksville St., Paris 75460 *Type:* Public (district) junior *System:* Texas Higher Education Coordinating Board *Accred.:* 1934/1992 (SACS-CC) *Calendar:* Sem. plan *Degrees:* A *Prof. Accred.:* Nursing (A) *CEO:* Pres. Bobby R. Walters
FTE Enroll: 1,736   (903) 784-9370

PARKER COLLEGE OF CHIROPRACTIC
2500 Walnut Hill Ln., Dallas 75229-5668 *Type:* Private professional *Accred.:* 1987/1992 (SACS-CC warning) *Calendar:* Tri. plan *Degrees:* B, D *Prof. Accred.:* Chiropractic Education *CEO:* Pres. James W. Parker
FTE Enroll: 1,007   (214) 438-6932

PAUL QUINN COLLEGE
3837 Simpson Stuart Rd., Dallas 75241 *Type:* Private (African Methodist Episcopal) liberal arts *Accred.:* 1972/1987 (SACS-CC) *Calendar:* Sem. plan *Degrees:* B *CEO:* Pres. Lee E. Monroe
FTE Enroll: 665   (214) 302-3547

PRAIRIE VIEW A&M UNIVERSITY
P.O. Box 188, Prairie View 77429 *Type:* Public (state) *System:* Texas A&M University System *Accred.:* 1934/1990 (SACS-CC) *Calendar:* Sem. plan *Degrees:* B, M *Prof. Accred.:* Computer Science, Engineering Technology (computer, electrical), Engineering (chemical, civil, electrical, mechanical), Home Economics, Nursing (B), Social Work (B), Teacher Education *CEO:* Pres. Charles A. Hines
FTE Enroll: 5,432   (409) 857-3311

RANGER COLLEGE
College Cir., Ranger 76470-3298 *Type:* Public (district) junior *System:* Texas Higher Education Coordinating Board *Accred.:* 1968/1992 (SACS-CC) *Calendar:* Sem. plan *Degrees:* A *CEO:* Pres. Joe Mills
FTE Enroll: 645   (817) 647-3234

RICHLAND COLLEGE
12800 Abrams Rd., Dallas 75243-2199 *Type:* Public (district) junior *System:* Dallas County Community College District *Accred.:* 1974/1993 (SACS-CC) *Calendar:* Sem. plan *Degrees:* A *CEO:* Pres. Stephen K. Mittelstet
FTE Enroll: 8,009   (214) 238-6194

ST. EDWARD'S UNIVERSITY
3001 S. Congress Ave., Austin 78704 *Type:* Private liberal arts and teachers (Roman Catholic) *Accred.:* 1958/1987 (SACS-CC) *Calendar:* Sem. plan *Degrees:* B, M *Prof. Accred.:* Social Work (B) *CEO:* Pres. Patricia A. Hayes
FTE Enroll: 2,414   (512) 448-8400

ST. MARY'S UNIVERSITY
One Camino Santa Maria, San Antonio 78228-8572 *Type:* Private (Roman Catholic) *Accred.:* 1949/1994 (SACS-CC) *Calendar:* Sem. plan *Degrees:* B, M, D *Prof. Accred.:* Engineering (electrical, industrial), Law, Marriage and Family Therapy (M), Music (A) *CEO:* Pres. John H. Moder, S.M.
FTE Enroll: 3,591   (210) 436-3011

ST. PHILIP'S COLLEGE
211 Nevada St., San Antonio 78203 *Type:* Public (district) junior *System:* Alamo Community College District *Accred.:* 1951/1995 (SACS-CC) *Calendar:* Sem. plan *Degrees:* A *Prof. Accred.:* Clinical Lab Technology (A), Medical Record Technology, Occupational Therapy Assisting, Physical Therapy Assisting, Practical Nursing, Radiography, Respiratory Therapy Technology, Surgical Technology *CEO:* Pres. Charles A. Taylor
FTE Enroll: 5,101   (210) 531-3500

SAM HOUSTON STATE UNIVERSITY
Huntsville 77341 *Type:* Public (state) liberal arts and teachers *System:* Texas State University System *Accred.:* 1925/1989 (SACS-CC) *Calendar:* Sem. plan *Degrees:* B, M, D *Prof. Accred.:* Music, Teacher Education *CEO:* Interim Pres. B.K. Marks
FTE Enroll: 11,316   (409) 294-1111

SAN ANTONIO COLLEGE
1300 San Pedro Ave., San Antonio 78284 *Type:* Public (district) junior *System:* Alamo Community College District *Accred.:* 1952/1995 (SACS-CC) *Calendar:* Sem. plan *Degrees:* A *Prof. Accred.:* Dental Assisting, Funeral Service Education (Mortuary Science), Medical Assisting (AMA), Nursing (A) *CEO:* Pres. Ruth Burgos-Sasscer
FTE Enroll: 14,194   (210) 733-2000

SAN JACINTO COLLEGE DISTRICT
4624 Fairmont Pwy., Ste. 200, Pasadena 77504 *Type:* Public (district) junior *System:* Texas Higher Education Coordinating Board *Accred.:* 1963/1989 (SACS-CC) *Calendar:* Sem. plan *Degrees:* A *Prof. Accred.:* Clinical Lab Technology (A), Nursing (A), Radiography, Respiratory Therapy, Respiratory Therapy Technology, Surgical Technology *CEO:* Chanc. J.B. Whiteley
FTE Enroll: 12,428   (713) 998-6100

SCHREINER COLLEGE
2100 Memorial Blvd., Kerrville 78028 *Type:* Private (Presbyterian) *Accred.:* 1934/1989 (SACS-CC) *Calendar:* Sem. plan *Degrees:* A, B *CEO:* Pres. Sam M. Junkin
FTE Enroll: 571   (210) 896-5411

SOUTH PLAINS COLLEGE
1401 College Ave., Levelland 79336 *Type:* Public (district) junior *System:* Texas Higher Education Coordinating Board *Accred.:* 1963/1993 (SACS-CC) *Calendar:* Sem. plan *Degrees:* A *Prof. Accred.:* Medical Record Technology, Nursing (A), Radiography, Respiratory Therapy, Respiratory Therapy Technology, Surgical Technology *CEO:* Pres. Gary D. McDaniel
FTE Enroll: 4,528   (806) 894-9611

SOUTH TEXAS COLLEGE OF LAW
1303 San Jacinto St., Houston 77002-7000 *Type:* Private professional *Calendar:* Sem. plan *Degrees:* P *Prof. Accred.:* Law (ABA only) *CEO:* Pres./Dean Frank T. Read
Enroll: 1,352   (713) 659-8040

SOUTH TEXAS COMMUNITY COLLEGE
3201 W. Pecan, McAllen 78501 *Type:* Public state *Accred.:* 1995 (SACS-CC) *Calendar:* Qtr. plan *Degrees:* A *CEO:* Pres. Shirley Reed
Enroll: 4,000   (210) 618-8365

SOUTHERN METHODIST UNIVERSITY
6425 Boaz St., P.O. Box 296, Dallas 75275
Type: Private (United Methodist) *Accred.:*
1938/1991 (ATS); 1921/1991 (SACS-CC)
Calendar: Sem. plan *Degrees:* B, M, D *Prof.
Accred.:* Business (B,M), Dance, Engineering (civil, computer, electrical), Law, Music
CEO: Pres. R. Gerald Turner
FTE Enroll: 7,623   (214) 768-2000

SOUTHWEST INSTITUTE OF MERCHANDISING AND
DESIGN
9611 Acer Ave., El Paso 79925-6744 *Type:*
Private *Accred.:* 1975/1990 (ACCSCT) *Degrees:* A *CEO:* Pres. Mary F. Simon
                           (915) 593-7328

SOUTHWEST SCHOOL OF ELECTRONICS
5424 Hwy. 290 W., Ste. 200, Austin 78735-8800 *Type:* Private *Accred.:* 1978/1988
(ACCSCT) *Degrees:* A *CEO:* Dir. Joan Uribe
                           (512) 892-2640

SOUTHWEST TEXAS JUNIOR COLLEGE
2401 Garner Field Rd., Uvalde 78801-6297
Type: Public (district) junior *System:* Texas
Higher Education Coordinating Board *Accred.:* 1964/1995 (SACS-CC) *Calendar:*
Sem. plan *Degrees:* A *CEO:* Pres. Billy Word
FTE Enroll: 2,258   (210) 278-4401

SOUTHWEST TEXAS STATE UNIVERSITY
P.O. Box 1002, SWTSU Station, San Marcos
78666-4616 *Type:* Public (state) liberal arts
and teachers *System:* Texas State University
System *Accred.:* 1925/1989 (SACS-CC)
Calendar: Sem. plan *Degrees:* A, B, M *Prof.
Accred.:* Clinical Lab Scientist, Health Services Administration, Home Economics,
Interior Design, Medical Record Administration, Music, Physical Therapy, Public
Administration, Respiratory Therapy, Respiratory Therapy Technology, Social Work
(B), Speech-Language Pathology *CEO:*
Pres. Jerome H. Supple
FTE Enroll: 18,174   (512) 245-2121

SOUTHWESTERN ADVENTIST COLLEGE
P.O. Box 567, Keene 76059 *Type:* Private
(Seventh-Day Adventist) liberal arts and
teachers *Accred.:* 1958/1995 (SACS-CC)
Calendar: Sem. plan *Degrees:* A, B, M

Prof. Accred.: Nursing (A,B), Social Work
(B-candidate) *CEO:* Pres. Marvin E.
Anderson
FTE Enroll: 764   (817) 645-3921

SOUTHWESTERN ASSEMBLIES OF GOD
UNIVERSITY
1200 Sycamore St., Waxahachie 75165
Type: Private (Assemblies of God) *Accred.:*
1948/1995 (AABC); 1968/1992 (SACS-CC)
Calendar: Sem. plan *Degrees:* A, B, M (candidate) *CEO:* Pres. Delmer R. Guynes
FTE Enroll: 923   (214) 937-4010

SOUTHWESTERN BAPTIST THEOLOGICAL
SEMINARY
2001 W. Seminary Dr., P.O. Box 22000, Fort
Worth 76122 *Type:* Private (Southern Baptist) *Accred.:* 1944/1991 (ATS); 1969/1991
(SACS-CC) *Calendar:* Sem. plan *Degrees:*
A, B, M, D *Prof. Accred.:* Music *CEO:* Pres.
Kenneth S. Hemphill
Enroll: 3,254   (817) 923-1921

SOUTHWESTERN CHRISTIAN COLLEGE
P.O. Box 10, Terrell 75160 *Type:* Private
(Church of Christ) liberal arts *Accred.:*
1973/1989 (SACS-CC) *Calendar:* Sem. plan
Degrees: A, B *CEO:* Pres. Jack Evans, Sr.
FTE Enroll: 182   (214) 524-3341

SOUTHWESTERN UNIVERSITY
University Ave. at Maple St., P.O. Box 770,
Georgetown 78627 *Type:* Private liberal arts
(United Methodist) *Accred.:* 1915/1992
(SACS-CC) *Calendar:* Sem. plan *Degrees:*
B *Prof. Accred.:* Music *CEO:* Pres. Roy B.
Shilling, Jr.
FTE Enroll: 1,218   (512) 863-6511

STEPHEN F. AUSTIN STATE UNIVERSITY
P.O. Box 6078, SFA Sta., Nacogdoches
75962 *Type:* Public (state) liberal arts and
teachers *System:* Texas Higher Education
Coordinating Board *Accred.:* 1927/1990
(SACS-CC) *Calendar:* Sem. plan *Degrees:*
B, M, D *Prof. Accred.:* Business (B,M),
Counseling, Forestry, Home Economics,
Interior Design, Music, Nursing (B), Rehabilitation Counseling, Social Work (B),

Speech-Language Pathology, Teacher Education, Theatre *CEO:* Pres. Daniel D. Angel
FTE Enroll: 11,486   (409) 468-2201

SUL ROSS STATE UNIVERSITY
Hwy. 90, Alpine 79832 *Type:* Public (state) liberal arts and teachers *System:* Texas State University System *Accred.:* 1929/1989 (SACS-CC) *Calendar:* Sem. plan *Degrees:* A, B, M *Prof. Accred.:* Veterinary Technology *CEO:* Pres. R. Victor Morgan
FTE Enroll: 2,884   (915) 837-8011

UVALDE CAMPUS
Uvalde Ctr., Uvalde 78801
                             (512) 278-3339

TARLETON STATE UNIVERSITY
1333 W. Washington St., Tarleton Sta., Stephenville 76402 *Type:* Public (state) liberal arts and professional *System:* Texas A&M University System *Accred.:* 1926/1990 (SACS-CC) *Calendar:* Sem. plan *Degrees:* A, B, M *Prof. Accred.:* Clinical Lab Scientist, Music (A), Social Work (B) *CEO:* Pres. Dennis P. McCabe
FTE Enroll: 5,785   (817) 968-9100

TARRANT COUNTY JUNIOR COLLEGE
1500 Houston St., Fort Worth 76102-6599 *Type:* Public (district) junior *System:* Texas Higher Education Coordinating Board *Accred.:* 1969/1993 (SACS-CC) *Calendar:* Sem. plan *Degrees:* A *Prof. Accred.:* Clinical Lab Technology (A), Dental Hygiene, Medical Record Technology, Nursing (A), Physical Therapy Assisting, Radiography, Respiratory Therapy, Surgical Technology *CEO:* Chanc. C.A. Roberson
FTE Enroll: 18,021   (817) 336-7851

NORTHEAST CAMPUS
828 Harwood Rd., Hurst 76054
                             (817) 281-7860

NORTHWEST CAMPUS
4801 Marine Creek Pkwy., Fort Worth 76179
                             (817) 232-2900

SOUTH CAMPUS
5301 Campus Dr., Fort Worth 76119
                             (817) 531-4501

SOUTHEAST CAMPUS
2100 TCJC Pkwy., Arlington 76018
                             (817) 336-7851

TEMPLE JUNIOR COLLEGE
2600 S. First St., Temple 76504-7435 *Type:* Public (district) junior *System:* Texas Higher Education Coordinating Board *Accred.:* 1959/1990 (SACS-CC) *Calendar:* Sem. plan *Degrees:* A *Prof. Accred.:* Clinical Lab Technology (A), Respiratory Therapy, Surgical Technology *CEO:* Pres. Marc A. Nigliazzo
FTE Enroll: 2,544   (817) 773-9961

TEXARKANA COLLEGE
2500 N. Robinson Rd., Texarkana 75501 *Type:* Public (district) junior *System:* Texas Higher Education Coordinating Board *Accred.:* 1931/1995 (SACS-CC) *Calendar:* Sem. plan *Degrees:* A *Prof. Accred.:* Nursing (A) *CEO:* Pres. Carl M. Nelson
FTE Enroll: 3,313   (903) 838-4541

TEXAS A&M INTERNATIONAL UNIVERSITY
5201 University Blvd., Laredo 78041 *Type:* Public (state) *System:* Texas A&M University System *Accred.:* 1970/1995 (SACS-CC) *Calendar:* Sem. plan *Degrees:* B, M *CEO:* Interim Pres. Hose Garcia
FTE Enroll: 1,712   (210) 326-2001

TEXAS A&M UNIVERSITY
College Sta., 77843 *Type:* Public (state) *System:* Texas A&M University System *Accred.:* 1924/1993 (SACS-CC) *Calendar:* Sem. plan *Degrees:* B, M, D *Prof. Accred.:* Accounting (A,C), Business (B,M), Clinical Psychology, Computer Science, Construction Education (B), Counseling Psychology, Dietetics (internship), Engineering Technology (electrical, manufacturing, mechanical), Engineering (aerospace, agricultural, bioengineering, chemical, civil, electrical, industrial, mechanical, nuclear, ocean, petroleum, radiological health), Forestry, Journalism (B), Landscape Architecture (B,M), Medicine, Planning (M), Psychology Internship, Public Administration, School Psychol-

ogy, Teacher Education, Veterinary Medicine *CEO:* Pres. Ray M. Bowen
FTE Enroll: 39,405   (409) 845-3211

TEXAS A&M UNIVERSITY AT GALVESTON
P.O. Box 1675, Galveston 77553 *Type:* Public (state) *System:* Texas A&M University System *Accred.:* 1978/1983 (SACS-CC) *Calendar:* Sem. plan *Degrees:* B *Prof. Accred.:* Engineering (naval architecture/marine) *CEO:* Pres. Robert A. Duce
FTE Enroll: 1,337   (409) 740-4400

* Indirect SACS-CC accreditation through Texas A&M University

TEXAS A&M UNIVERSITY—CORPUS CHRISTI
6300 Ocean Dr., Corpus Christi 78412 *Type:* Public (state) liberal arts *System:* Texas A&M University System *Accred.:* 1975/1990 (SACS-CC) *Calendar:* Sem. plan *Degrees:* A, B, M, D *Prof. Accred.:* Clinical Lab Scientist, Music, Nursing (B,M) *CEO:* Pres. Robert R. Furgason
FTE Enroll: 3,769   (512) 991-5700

TEXAS A&M UNIVERSITY—KINGSVILLE
Campus Box 101, Kingsville 78363 *Type:* Public (state) *System:* Texas A&M University System *Accred.:* 1933/1995 (SACS-CC) *Calendar:* Sem. plan *Degrees:* B, M, D *Prof. Accred.:* Dietetics (internship), Engineering (chemical, civil, electrical, mechanical, petroleum), Music *CEO:* Pres. Manuel L. Ibanez
FTE Enroll: 5,775   (512) 595-2111

TEXAS CHIROPRACTIC COLLEGE
5912 Spencer Hwy., Pasadena 77505 *Type:* Private professional *Accred.:* 1984/1990 (SACS-CC) *Calendar:* Tri. plan *Degrees:* B, D *Prof. Accred.:* Chiropractic Education *CEO:* Pres. Shelby M. Elliott
FTE Enroll: 442   (713) 487-1170

TEXAS CHRISTIAN UNIVERSITY
2800 S. University Dr., Fort Worth 76129 *Type:* Private (Christian Church/Disciples of Christ) *Accred.:* 1942/1989 (ATS); 1922/1993 (SACS-CC) *Calendar:* Sem. plan *Degrees:* B, M, D *Prof. Accred.:* Accounting (A), Athletic Training, Business (B,M),

Computer Science, Dietetics (coordinated), Interior Design, Journalism (B,M), Music, Nursing (B), Social Work (B), Speech-Language Pathology *CEO:* Chanc. William E. Tucker
FTE Enroll: 6,654   (817) 921-7000

TEXAS COLLEGE
2404 N. Grand Ave., Tyler 75712 *Type:* Private liberal arts and teachers (Christian Methodist Episcopal) *Accred.:* 1970/1984 (SACS-CC probational) *Calendar:* Sem. plan *Degrees:* B *CEO:* Pres. Haywood L. Strickland
FTE Enroll: 258   (903) 593-8311

TEXAS LUTHERAN COLLEGE
1000 W. Court St., Seguin 78155 *Type:* Private (Lutheran) liberal arts *Accred.:* 1953/1988 (SACS-CC) *Calendar:* Sem. plan *Degrees:* A, B *Prof. Accred.:* Social Work (B-candidate) *CEO:* Pres. Jon N. Moline
FTE Enroll: 1,065   (210) 372-8001

TEXAS SOUTHERN UNIVERSITY
3100 Cleburne St., Houston 77004 *Type:* Public *System:* Texas Higher Education Coordinating Board *Accred.:* 1948/1990 (SACS-CC) *Calendar:* Sem. plan *Degrees:* B, M, D *Prof. Accred.:* Clinical Lab Scientist, Law (ABA only), Medical Record Administration, Respiratory Therapy, Social Work (B) *CEO:* Pres. James M. Douglas
FTE Enroll: 6,915   (713) 527-7011

TEXAS SOUTHMOST COLLEGE
80 Fort Brown St., Brownsville 78520 *Type:* Public (district) junior *System:* Texas Higher Education Coordinating Board *Accred.:* 1930/1994 (SACS-CC) *Calendar:* Sem. plan *Degrees:* A *Prof. Accred.:* Clinical Lab Technology (A), Nursing (A), Radiography, Respiratory Therapy, Respiratory Therapy Technology *CEO:* District Exec. Dir. Michael Putegnat
FTE Enroll: 4,815   (210) 544-8200

* Indirect SACS-CC accreditation through University of Texas at Brownsville/Texas Southmost College Partnership

TEXAS STATE TECHNICAL COLLEGE—
HARLINGEN
2424 Boxwood St., Harlingen 78550 *Type:* Public (state) 2-year *System:* Texas State Technical College System *Accred.:* 1968/ 1995 (SACS-CC) *Calendar:* Qtr. plan *Degrees:* A *Prof. Accred.:* Medical Record Technology *CEO:* Pres. J. Gilbert Leal
FTE Enroll: 2,363   (210) 425-4922

TEXAS STATE TECHNICAL COLLEGE—
SWEETWATER
Rte. 3, Box 18, Sweetwater 79556 *Type:* Public (state) 2-year *System:* Texas State Technical College System *Accred.:* 1979/1994 (SACS-CC) *Calendar:* Qtr. plan *Degrees:* A *CEO:* Pres. Clay G. Johnson
FTE Enroll: 972   (915) 235-7300

TEXAS STATE TECHNICAL COLLEGE—WACO
3801 Campus Dr., Waco 76705 *Type:* Public (state) 2-year *System:* Texas State Technical College System *Accred.:* 1968/1993 (SACS-CC) *Calendar:* Qtr. plan *Degrees:* A *Prof. Accred.:* Dental Assisting *CEO:* Pres. Fred L. Williams
FTE Enroll: 2,928   (817) 799-3611

TEXAS TECH UNIVERSITY
P.O. Box 4349, Lubbock 79409 *Type:* Public (state) *System:* Texas Higher Education Coordinating Board *Accred.:* 1928/1994 (SACS-CC) *Calendar:* Sem. plan *Degrees:* B, M, D *Prof. Accred.:* Accounting (A,B,C), Art, Audiology, Business (B,M), Clinical Psychology, Counseling Psychology, Dietetics (internship), Engineering Technology (civil/construction), Engineering (agricultural, chemical, civil, electrical, engineering physics/science, industrial, mechanical, petroleum), Health Services Administration, Home Economics, Interior Design, Journalism (B), Landscape Architecture (B), Law, Marriage and Family Therapy (D), Music, Psychology Internship (probational), Public Administration, Social Work (B) Teacher Education *CEO:* Pres. Robert W. Lawless
FTE Enroll: 21,948   (806) 742-2011

TEXAS TECH UNIVERSITY HEALTH SCIENCES
CENTER
3601 Fourth St., Lubbock 79430 *Type:* Public (state) *System:* Texas Higher Education Coordinating Board *Calendar:* Sem. plan *Degrees:* B, M, D *Prof. Accred.:* Clinical Lab Scientist, EMT-Paramedic, Medicine, Nursing (B,M), Occupational Therapy, Physical Therapy *CEO:* Pres. Robert W. Lawless
Enroll: 876   (806) 743-3111

TEXAS WESLEYAN UNIVERSITY
1201 Wesleyan St., Fort Worth 76105-1536 *Type:* Private (United Methodist) liberal arts *Accred.:* 1949/1993 (SACS-CC) *Calendar:* Sem. plan *Degrees:* B, M, D *Prof. Accred.:* Music, Nurse Anesthesia Education *CEO:* Pres. Jake B. Schrum
FTE Enroll: 2,147   (817) 531-4444

TEXAS WOMAN'S UNIVERSITY
P.O. Box 425587, Denton 76204-3587 *Type:* Public (state) for women *System:* Texas Higher Education Coordinating Board *Accred.:* 1923/1993 (SACS-CC) *Calendar:* Sem. plan *Degrees:* B, M, D *Prof. Accred.:* Dental Hygiene, Dietetics (internship), Health Services Administration, Journalism, Librarianship, Music, Nursing (B,M), Occupational Therapy, Physical Therapy, Psychology Internship, Social Work (B), Speech-Language Pathology *CEO:* Pres. Carol D. Surles
FTE Enroll: 7,423   (817) 898-3201

TRINITY UNIVERSITY
715 Stadium Dr., San Antonio 78212-7200 *Type:* Private (Presbyterian) *Accred.:* 1946/ 1987 (SACS-CC) *Calendar:* Sem. plan *Degrees:* B, M *Prof. Accred.:* Engineering (engineering physics/science), Health Services Administration, Music *CEO:* Pres. Ronald K. Calgaard
FTE Enroll: 2,465   (210) 736-7011

TRINITY VALLEY COMMUNITY COLLEGE
500 S. Prairieville, Athens 75751 *Type:* Public (district) junior *System:* Texas Higher Education Coordinating Board *Accred.:* 1952/1986 (SACS-CC) *Calendar:* Sem. plan

Degrees: A *Prof. Accred.:* Nursing (A), Surgical Technology *CEO:* Pres. Ronald C. Baugh
FTE Enroll: 3,143   (903) 677-8822

TYLER JUNIOR COLLEGE
P.O. Box 9020, Tyler 75711 *Type:* Public (district) junior *System:* Texas Higher Education Coordinating Board *Accred.:* 1931/1990 (SACS-CC) *Calendar:* Sem. plan *Degrees:* A *Prof. Accred.:* Clinical Lab Technology (A), Dental Hygiene, Medical Record Technology, Radiography, Respiratory Therapy, Respiratory Therapy Technology *CEO:* Interim Pres. William R. Crowe
FTE Enroll: 6,027   (903) 510-2200

UNIVERSAL TECHNICAL INSTITUTE
721 Lockhaven Dr., Houston 77073-5598 *Type:* Private *Accred.:* 1983 (ACCSCT) *Degrees:* A, C *CEO:* Dir. Wendell Crabb
                             (713) 443-6262

UNIVERSITY OF CENTRAL TEXAS
P.O. Box 1416, 1901 Clear Creek Rd., Killeen 76540-1416 *Type:* Private *Accred.:* 1976/1995 (SACS-CC) *Calendar:* Sem. plan *Degrees:* B, M *Prof. Accred.:* Social Work (B-candidate) *CEO:* Pres. Jack W. Fuller
FTE Enroll: 583   (817) 526-8262

THE UNIVERSITY OF DALLAS
1845 E. Northgate Dr., Irving 75062-4799 *Type:* Private (Roman Catholic) *Accred.:* 1963/1994 (SACS-CC) *Calendar:* Sem. plan *Degrees:* B, M, D *CEO:* Interim Pres. Milam Joseph
FTE Enroll: 2,217   (214) 721-5000

UNIVERSITY OF HOUSTON
4800 Calhoun Blvd., Houston 77004 *Type:* Public (state) *System:* University of Houston System *Accred.:* 1954/1987 (SACS-CC) *Calendar:* Sem. plan *Degrees:* B, M, D *Prof. Accred.:* Accounting (A,B,C), Business (B,M), Clinical Psychology, Computer Science, Counseling Psychology, Dietetics (internship), Engineering Technology (civil/construction, computer, electrical, mechanical), Engineering (chemical, civil, electrical, industrial, mechanical), Law, Music, Optometry, Psychology Internship, Social Work

(M), Speech-Language Pathology, Teacher Education *CEO:* Pres. Glenn A. Goerke
FTE Enroll: 25,986   (713) 749-1000

UNIVERSITY OF HOUSTON—CLEAR LAKE
2700 Bay Area Blvd., Houston 77058 *Type:* Public (state) *System:* University of Houston System *Accred.:* 1976/1992 (SACS-CC) *Calendar:* Sem. plan *Degrees:* B, M *Prof. Accred.:* Accounting (A,C), Business (B,M), Health Services Administration, Marriage and Family Therapy (M), Public Administration, Teacher Education *CEO:* Pres. William A. Staples
FTE Enroll: 7,194   (713) 488-7170

UNIVERSITY OF HOUSTON—DOWNTOWN
One Main St., Houston 77002 *Type:* Public (state) *System:* University of Houston System *Accred.:* 1976/1995 (SACS-CC) *Calendar:* Sem. plan *Degrees:* B *Prof. Accred.:* Business (B), Engineering Technology (process/piping design) *CEO:* Pres. Max Castillo
FTE Enroll: 5,829   (713) 221-8000

UNIVERSITY OF HOUSTON—VICTORIA
2506 E. Red River, Victoria 77901-4450 *Type:* Public (state) *System:* University of Houston System *Accred.:* 1978/1993 (SACS-CC) *Calendar:* Sem. plan *Degrees:* B, M *CEO:* Interim Pres. Karen Haynes
FTE Enroll: 689   (512) 576-3151

UNIVERSITY OF MARY HARDIN-BAYLOR
Box 800 11th and College St., Belton 76513 *Type:* Private (Southern Baptist) liberal arts primarily for women *Accred.:* 1926/1993 (SACS-CC) *Calendar:* Sem. plan *Degrees:* B, M *Prof. Accred.:* Nursing (B), Social Work (B-candidate) *CEO:* Pres. Jerry G. Bawcom
FTE Enroll: 1,824   (817) 939-8642

UNIVERSITY OF NORTH TEXAS
P.O. Box 13737, Denton 76203 *Type:* Public (state) *System:* Texas Higher Education Coordinating Board *Accred.:* 1925/1995 (SACS-CC) *Calendar:* Sem. plan *Degrees:* B, M, D *Prof. Accred.:* Accounting (A,C), Audiology, Business (B,M), Clinical Psychology, Computer Science, Counseling,

Counseling Psychology, Interior Design, Journalism (B,M), Librarianship, Music, Public Administration, Recreation and Leisure Services (B), Rehabilitation Counseling, Social Work (B), Speech-Language Pathology *CEO:* Chanc. Alfred F. Hurley
FTE Enroll: 25,759   (817) 565-2000

UNIVERSITY OF NORTH TEXAS HEALTH SCIENCE CENTER AT FORT WORTH
3500 Camp Bowie Blvd., Fort Worth 76107-2970 *Type:* Public (state) professional *System:* Texas Higher Education Coordinating Board *Accred.:* 1995 (SACS-CC) *Calendar:* Sem. plan *Degrees:* P, D *Prof. Accred.:* Osteopathy *CEO:* Pres. David M. Richards
Enroll: 379   (817) 735-2000

UNIVERSITY OF ST. THOMAS
3800 Montrose Blvd., Houston 77006 *Type:* Private (Roman Catholic) liberal arts *Accred.:* 1990/1993 (ATS); 1954/1994 (SACS-CC) *Calendar:* Sem. plan *Degrees:* B, M, D *Prof. Accred.:* Engineering (manufacturing) *CEO:* Pres. Joseph M. McFadden
FTE Enroll: 1,751   (713) 522-7911

THE UNIVERSITY OF TEXAS AT ARLINGTON
701 S. Nedderman, Arlington 76019 *Type:* Public (state) *System:* University of Texas System *Accred.:* 1964/1986 (SACS-CC) *Calendar:* Sem. plan *Degrees:* B, M, D *Prof. Accred.:* Accounting (A,B,C), Business (B,M), Computer Science, Engineering (aerospace, civil, computer, electrical, industrial, mechanical), Interior Design, Music, Nursing (B,M), Planning (M), Social Work (B,M) *CEO:* Pres. Robert E. Witt
FTE Enroll: 18,482   (817) 273-3365

THE UNIVERSITY OF TEXAS AT AUSTIN
University Sta., Austin 78712 *Type:* Public (state) *System:* University of Texas System *Accred.:* 1901/1988 (SACS-CC) *Calendar:* Sem. plan *Degrees:* B, M, D *Prof. Accred.:* Accounting (A,C), Audiology, Business (B,M), Clinical Psychology, Counseling Psychology, Dance (A), Dietetics (coordinated), Engineering (aerospace, architectural, chemical, civil, computer, electrical, environmental/sanitary, mechanical, petro-

leum), Home Economics, Interior Design, Journalism (B,M), Law, Librarianship, Music, Nursing (B,M), Planning (M), Psychology Internship, Public Administration, Rehabilitation Counseling, School Psychology, Social Work (B,M), Speech-Language Pathology *CEO:* Pres. Robert M. Berdahl
FTE Enroll: 44,850   (512) 471-3434

THE UNIVERSITY OF TEXAS AT BROWNSVILLE/ TEXAS SOUTHMOST COLLEGE PARTNERSHIP
80 Fort Brown, Brownsville 78520 *Type:* Public (state) *System:* University of Texas System *Accred.:* 1988 (SACS-CC) *Calendar:* Sem. plan *Degrees:* A, B, M *CEO:* Pres. Juliet V. Garcia
FTE Enroll: 6,700   (210) 544-8200

THE UNIVERSITY OF TEXAS AT DALLAS
P.O. Box 830688, Richardson 75083-0688 *Type:* Public (state) *System:* University of Texas System *Accred.:* 1972/1988 (SACS-CC) *Calendar:* Sem. plan *Degrees:* B, M, D *Prof. Accred.:* Audiology, Engineering (electrical), Speech-Language Pathology *CEO:* Pres. Franklyn G. Jenifer
FTE Enroll: 5,918   (214) 883-2111

THE UNIVERSITY OF TEXAS AT EL PASO
500 W. University Ave., El Paso 79968-0500 *Type:* Public (state) *System:* University of Texas System *Accred.:* 1936/1986 (SACS-CC) *Calendar:* Sem. plan *Degrees:* B, M, D *Prof. Accred.:* Accounting (A,C), Business (B,M), Clinical Lab Scientist, Computer Science, Engineering (civil, electrical, industrial, mechanical, metallurgical), Music, Nursing (B,M), Public Administration, Social Work (B-candidate), Speech-Language Pathology *CEO:* Pres. Diana S. Natalicio
FTE Enroll: 14,098   (915) 747-5000

THE UNIVERSITY OF TEXAS AT SAN ANTONIO
6900 N. Loop 1604 W., San Antonio 78249-0617 *Type:* Public (state) *System:* University of Texas System *Accred.:* 1974/1990 (SACS-CC) *Calendar:* Sem. plan *Degrees:* B, M, D *Prof. Accred.:* Art, Business (B,M), Engineering (civil, electrical, mechanical),

Music, Nursing (B,M) *CEO:* Pres. Samuel A. Kirkpatrick
FTE Enroll: 14,189   (210) 691-4100

THE UNIVERSITY OF TEXAS AT TYLER
3900 University Blvd., Tyler 75799 *Type:* Public (state) *System:* University of Texas System *Accred.:* 1974/1990 (SACS-CC) *Calendar:* Sem. plan *Degrees:* B, M *Prof. Accred.:* Clinical Lab Scientist, Nursing (B,M) *CEO:* Pres. George F. Hamm
FTE Enroll: 1,833   (903) 566-7000

THE UNIVERSITY OF TEXAS HEALTH SCIENCE CENTER AT HOUSTON
P.O. Box 20036, Houston 77225 *Type:* Public (state) *System:* University of Texas System *Accred.:* 1973/1990 (SACS-CC) *Calendar:* Sem. plan *Degrees:* B, M, D *Prof. Accred.:* Clinical Lab Scientist, Combined Prosthodontics, Cytotechnology, Dental Hygiene, Dietetics (coordinated), Endodontics, General Dentistry (prelim. provisional), General Practice Residency, Maxillofacial Prosthodontics, Medicine, Nurse Anesthesia Education, Nursing (B,M), Oral and Maxillofacial Surgery, Orthodontics, Pediatric Dentistry, Periodontics, Psychology Internship *CEO:* Pres. M. David Low
FTE Enroll: 2,817   (713) 792-2121

THE UNIVERSITY OF TEXAS HEALTH SCIENCE CENTER AT SAN ANTONIO
7703 Floyd Curl Dr., San Antonio 78284-7834 *Type:* Public (state) *System:* University of Texas System *Accred.:* 1973/1989 (SACS-CC) *Calendar:* Sem. plan *Degrees:* B, M, D *Prof. Accred.:* Clinical Lab Scientist, Combined Prosthodontics, Dental Hygiene, Dental Laboratory Technology, Dental Public Health, Dentistry, EMT-Paramedic, Endodontics, General Dentistry, General Practice Residency, Medicine, Nurse Anesthesia Education, Occupational Therapy, Oral Pathology, Oral and Maxillofacial Surgery, Pediatric Dentistry, Periodontics, Physical Therapy, Psychology Internship *CEO:* Pres. John P. Howe, III
FTE Enroll: 2,465   (210) 567-7000

THE UNIVERSITY OF TEXAS MEDICAL BRANCH AT GALVESTON
301 University Blvd., Ste. 604, Galveston 77550 *Type:* Public (state) *System:* University of Texas System *Accred.:* 1973/1988 (SACS-CC) *Calendar:* Sem. plan *Degrees:* B, M, D *Prof. Accred.:* Blood Bank Technology, Clinical Lab Scientist, Medical Record Administration, Medicine, Nursing (B,M), Occupational Therapy, Oral and Maxillofacial Surgery (conditional), Physical Therapy, Physician Assisting/Surgeon Assisting, Psychology Internship *CEO:* Pres. Thomas N. James
FTE Enroll: 1,940   (409) 761-1011

THE UNIVERSITY OF TEXAS OF THE PERMIAN BASIN
4901 E. University Blvd., Odessa 79762 *Type:* Public (state) *System:* University of Texas System *Accred.:* 1975/1990 (SACS-CC) *Calendar:* Sem. plan *Degrees:* B, M *CEO:* Pres. Charles A. Sorber
FTE Enroll: 1,602   (915) 552-2020

THE UNIVERSITY OF TEXAS—PAN AMERICAN
1201 W. University Dr., Edinburg 78539-2999 *Type:* Public (state) liberal arts *System:* University of Texas System *Accred.:* 1956/1986 (SACS-CC) *Calendar:* Sem. plan *Degrees:* A, B, M, D (candidate) *Prof. Accred.:* Business (B,M), Clinical Lab Scientist, Dietetics (coordinated), Nursing (A,B), Social Work (B), Speech-Language Pathology *CEO:* Pres. Miguel A. Nevarez
FTE Enroll: 11,093   (210) 381-2011

THE UNIVERSITY OF TEXAS SOUTHWESTERN MEDICAL CENTER AT DALLAS
5323 Harry Hines Blvd., Dallas 75235-9002 *Type:* Public (state) *System:* University of Texas System *Accred.:* 1973/1989 (SACS-CC) *Calendar:* Sem. plan *Degrees:* B, M, D *Prof. Accred.:* Blood Bank Technology, Clinical Lab Scientist, Clinical Psychology, Dietetics (coordinated), EMT-Paramedic, Medical Illustration, Medicine, Oral and Maxillofacial Surgery, Physical Therapy, Physician Assisting/Surgeon Assisting, Psy-

chology Internship, Rehabilitation Counseling *CEO:* Pres. C. Kern Wildenthal
FTE Enroll: 1,658   (214) 648-3111

VERNON REGIONAL JUNIOR COLLEGE
4400 College Dr., Vernon 76384-4092 *Type:* Public (district) junior *System:* Texas Higher Education Coordinating Board *Accred.:* 1974/1989 (SACS-CC) *Calendar:* Sem. plan *Degrees:* A *CEO:* Pres. R. Wade Kirk
FTE Enroll: 1,176   (817) 552-6291

THE VICTORIA COLLEGE
2200 E. Red River St., Victoria 77901-4494 *Type:* Public (district) junior *System:* Texas Higher Education Coordinating Board *Accred.:* 1951/1993 (SACS-CC) *Calendar:* Sem. plan *Degrees:* A *Prof. Accred.:* Clinical Lab Technology (A), Nursing (A), Respiratory Therapy, Respiratory Therapy Technology *CEO:* Pres. Jimmy L. Goodson
FTE Enroll: 2,419   (512) 573-3291

WAYLAND BAPTIST UNIVERSITY
1900 W. Seventh St., Plainview 79072 *Type:* Private (Southern Baptist) liberal arts *Accred.:* 1956/1989 (SACS-CC) *Calendar:* Sem. plan *Degrees:* A, B, M *CEO:* Pres. Wallace E. Davis, Jr.
FTE Enroll: 2,510   (806) 296-5521

WEATHERFORD COLLEGE
308 E. Park Ave., Weatherford 76086 *Type:* Public (district) junior *System:* Texas Higher Education Coordinating Board *Accred.:* 1956/1991 (SACS-CC) *Calendar:* Sem. plan *Degrees:* A *CEO:* Pres. James Boyd
FTE Enroll: 1,894   (817) 594-5471

WEST TEXAS A&M UNIVERSITY
2501 Fourth Ave., P.O. Box 997, W.T. Station, Canyon 79016 *Type:* Public (state) liberal arts and professional *System:* Texas A&M University System *Accred.:* 1925/1995 (SACS-CC) *Calendar:* Sem. plan *Degrees:* B, M *Prof. Accred.:* Music, Nursing (B,M), Social Work (B) *CEO:* Pres. Russell C. Long
FTE Enroll: 5,565   (806) 656-2100

WESTERN TECHNICAL INSTITUTE
1000 Texas Ave., El Paso 79901-1536 *Type:* Private *Accred.:* 1978/1986 (ACCSCT) *Degrees:* A, C *Prof. Accred.:* Medical Assisting (AMA) *CEO:* Dir. Allan Sharpe
                                       (915) 532-3737

BRANCH CAMPUS
4710 Alabama St., El Paso 79930-2610 *Accred.:* 1990 (ACCSCT)
                                       (915) 566-9621

WESTERN TEXAS COLLEGE
6200 S. College Ave., Snyder 79549 *Type:* Public (district) junior *System:* Texas Higher Education Coordinating Board *Accred.:* 1973/1988 (SACS-CC) *Calendar:* Sem. plan *Degrees:* A *CEO:* Pres. Harry L. Krenek
FTE Enroll: 804   (915) 573-8511

WHARTON COUNTY JUNIOR COLLEGE
911 Boling Hwy., Wharton 77488 *Type:* Public (district) junior *System:* Texas Higher Education Coordinating Board *Accred.:* 1951/1988 (SACS-CC) *Calendar:* Sem. plan *Degrees:* A *Prof. Accred.:* Clinical Lab Technology (A), Dental Hygiene, Medical Record Technology, Physical Therapy Assisting, Radiography *CEO:* Pres. Frank R. Vivelo
FTE Enroll: 2,706   (409) 532-4560

WILEY COLLEGE
711 Wiley Ave., Marshall 75670 *Type:* Private (United Methodist) liberal arts and teachers *Accred.:* 1933/1993 (SACS-CC) *Calendar:* Sem. plan *Degrees:* A, B *CEO:* Pres. Lamore J. Carter
FTE Enroll: 564   (903) 927-3300

WILLIAM MARSH RICE UNIVERSITY
6100 S. Main St., P.O. Box 1892, Houston 77251 *Type:* Private *Accred.:* 1914/1995 (SACS-CC) *Calendar:* Sem. plan *Degrees:* B, M, D *Prof. Accred.:* Engineering (chemical, civil, electrical, materials, mechanical) *CEO:* Pres. S. Malcolm Gillis
FTE Enroll: 4,120   (713) 527-8101

UTAH

BRIGHAM YOUNG UNIVERSITY
Provo 84602 *Type:* Private (Latter-Day Saints) *Accred.:* 1923/1991 (NASC) *Calendar:* Sem. plan *Degrees:* A, B, M, D *Prof. Accred.:* Accounting (A,C), Art (A), Audiology, Business (B,M), Clinical Lab Scientist, Clinical Psychology, Computer Science, Construction Education (B), Dance (A), Dietetics (coordinated), Engineering Technology (electrical, manufacturing, mechanical drafting/design), Engineering (chemical, civil, electrical, manufacturing, mechanical), Journalism (B,M), Law, Marriage and Family Therapy (M,D), Music, Nursing (B,M), Psychology Internship, Public Administration, Recreation and Leisure Services (B), Social Work (B,M), Speech-Language Pathology, Teacher Education, Theatre, Veterinary Technology *CEO:* Pres. Merrill J. Bateman
Enroll: 30,413   (801) 378-4668

CERTIFIED CAREERS INSTITUTE
1455 W. 2200 S., No. 200, Salt Lake City 84119 *Type:* Private *Accred.:* 1988 (ACCSCT) *Degrees:* A, C *CEO:* CEO Gene Curtis
                            (801) 973-7008

OGDEN CAMPUS
2661 Washington Blvd., Ste. 104, Ogden 84401-3697 *Accred.:* 1988 (ACCSCT)
                            (801) 621-4925

COLLEGE OF EASTERN UTAH
Price 84501 *Type:* Public (state) junior *System:* Utah System of Higher Education *Accred.:* 1945/1992 (NASC) *Calendar:* Qtr. plan *Degrees:* A *CEO:* Pres. Michael A. Petersen
Enroll: 3,123   (801) 637-2120

DIXIE COLLEGE
St. George 84770 *Type:* Public (state) junior *System:* Utah System of Higher Education *Accred.:* 1945/1992 (NASC) *Calendar:* Qtr. plan *Degrees:* A *Prof. Accred.:* Nursing (A) *CEO:* Pres. Robert C. Huddleston
Enroll: 4,374   (801) 652-7501

ITT TECHNICAL INSTITUTE
920 W. LeVoy Dr., Murray 84123-2500 *Type:* Private *Accred.:* 1986/1990 (ACCSCT) *Degrees:* A, B *CEO:* Dir. Dean L. Dalby
                            (801) 263-3313

LDS BUSINESS COLLEGE
411 E. S. Temple St., Salt Lake City 84111 *Type:* Private (Latter-Day Saints) *Accred.:* 1977/1995 (NASC) *Calendar:* Qtr. plan *Degrees:* A *Prof. Accred.:* Medical Assisting (AMA) *CEO:* Pres. Stephen K. Woodhouse
Enroll: 831   (801) 524-8100

PHILLIPS JUNIOR COLLEGE
3098 Highland Dr., Salt Lake City 84106 *Type:* Private junior *Accred.:* 1985/1996 (ACICS) *Degrees:* A *CEO:* Pres. Wayne Wilson
                            (801) 485-0221

SALT LAKE COMMUNITY COLLEGE
P.O. Box 30808, Salt Lake City 84130 *Type:* Public (state) junior *System:* Utah System of Higher Education *Accred.:* 1969/1994 (NASC) *Calendar:* Qtr. plan *Degrees:* A *Prof. Accred.:* Clinical Lab Technology (A), Medical Assisting (AMA), Nursing (A), Occupational Therapy Assisting, Physical Therapy Assisting, Practical Nursing, Radiography, Surgical Technology *CEO:* Pres. Frank W. Budd
Enroll: 17,212   (801) 957-4227

SNOW COLLEGE
Ephraim 84627 *Type:* Public (state) junior *System:* Utah System of Higher Education *Accred.:* 1953/1992 (NASC) *Calendar:* Qtr. plan *Degrees:* A *CEO:* Pres. Gerald J. Day
Enroll: 2,996   (801) 283-4021

SOUTHERN UTAH UNIVERSITY
Cedar City 84720 *Type:* Public (state) liberal arts and teachers *System:* Utah System of Higher Education *Accred.:* 1933/1993 (NASC) *Calendar:* Qtr. plan *Degrees:* A, B, M *Prof. Accred.:* Music, Nursing (A) *CEO:* Pres. Gerald R. Sherratt
Enroll: 5,026   (801) 586-7701

STEVENS-HENAGER COLLEGE OF BUSINESS
2168 Washington Blvd., Ogden 84401-1467
Type: Private junior *Accred.:* 1962/1995
(ACICS) *Calendar:* Qtr. plan *Degrees:* A, C
CEO: Dir. Vicky Dewsnup
(801) 394-7791

PROVO CAMPUS
25 E. 1700 S., Provo 84606-6157 *Accred.:*
1993 (ACICS)
(801) 375-5455

UNIVERSITY OF UTAH
Salt Lake City 84112 *Type:* Public (state)
System: Utah System of Higher Education
Accred.: 1933/1991 (NASC) *Calendar:* Qtr.
plan *Degrees:* A, B, M, D *Prof. Accred.:*
Accounting (A,C), Audiology, Business
(B,M), Clinical Lab Scientist, Clinical Psy-
chology, Counseling Psychology, Cytotech-
nology, Dietetics (coordinated), Engineering
Technology (industrial hygiene), Engineer-
ing (chemical, civil, electrical, geological/
geophysical, materials, mechanical, metal-
lurgical, mining), General Dentistry, General
Practice Residency, Journalism (B,M), Law,
Medicine, Music, Nuclear Medicine Technology, Nursing (B,M), Physical Therapy,
Physician Assisting/Surgeon Assisting, Psychology Internship, Public Administration,
Radiation Therapy Technology, Recreation
and Leisure Services (B), School Psychology, Social Work (M), Speech-Language
Pathology *CEO:* Pres. Arthur K. Smith
Enroll: 26,914   (801) 581-5701

UTAH STATE UNIVERSITY
Logan 84322-1400 *Type:* Public (state) *System:* Utah System of Higher Education
Accred.: 1924/1993 (NASC) *Calendar:* Qtr.
plan *Degrees:* A, B, M, D *Prof. Accred.:*
Accounting (A,C), Audiology, Business
(B,M), Combined Professional-Scientific Psychology, Dietetics (coordinated), Engineering
(agricultural, civil, electrical, manufacturing,

mechanical), Forestry, Home Economics, Inte-
rior Design, Landscape Architecture (B,M),
Marriage and Family Therapy (M-candidate),
Music, Nursing (A), Recreation and Leisure
Services, Rehabilitation Counseling, Social
Work (B), Speech-Language Pathology,
Teacher Education *CEO:* Pres. George H.
Emert
Enroll: 20,371   (801) 797-1157

UTAH VALLEY STATE COLLEGE
800 W. 1200 S., Orem 84058 *Type:* Public
(state) junior *System:* Utah System of Higher
Education *Accred.:* 1969/1995 (NASC) *Calendar:* Sem. plan *Degrees:* A, B *Prof.
Accred.:* Engineering Technology (electrical) *CEO:* Pres. Kerry D. Romesburg
Enroll: 15,190   (801) 222-8133

WEBER STATE UNIVERSITY
3750 Harrison Blvd., Ogden 84408-1004
Type: Public (state) liberal arts and teachers
System: Utah System of Higher Education
Accred.: 1932/1994 (NASC) *Calendar:* Qtr.
plan *Degrees:* A, B, M *Prof. Accred.:* Busi-
ness (B,M), Clinical Lab Scientist, Clinical
Lab Technology (A), Dental Hygiene, Diag-
nostic Medical Sonography, EMT-Para-
medic, Engineering Technology (automo-
tive, electrical, manufacturing), Medical
Record Technology, Music, Nuclear Medi-
cine Technology, Nursing (A,B), Practical
Nursing, Radiation Therapy Technology,
Radiography, Respiratory Therapy, Respiratory Therapy Technology *CEO:* Pres. Paul
H. Thompson
Enroll: 14,230   (801) 626-6001

WESTMINSTER COLLEGE OF SALT LAKE CITY
1840 S. 1300 E., Salt Lake City 84105 *Type:*
Private liberal arts and professional *Accred.:*
1936/1993 (NASC) *Calendar:* 4-1-4 plan
Degrees: B, M *Prof. Accred.:* Nursing (B)
CEO: Pres. Peggy A. Stock
Enroll: 2,113   (801) 488-4298

VERMONT

BENNINGTON COLLEGE
Bennington 05201 *Type:* Private liberal arts *Accred.:* 1935/1994 (NEASC-CIHE) *Degrees:* B, M *CEO:* Pres. Elizabeth Coleman
Enroll: 433   (802) 442-5401

BURLINGTON COLLEGE
95 N. Ave., Burlington 05401-8477 *Type:* Private *Accred.:* 1982/1987 (NEASC-CIHE) *Calendar:* Tri. plan *Degrees:* A, B *CEO:* Pres. Daniel Casey
Enroll: 127   (802) 862-9616

CASTLETON STATE COLLEGE
Castleton 05735 *Type:* Public (state) liberal arts and teachers *System:* Vermont State Colleges *Accred.:* 1960/1991 (NEASC-CIHE) *Calendar:* Sem. plan *Degrees:* A, B, M *Prof. Accred.:* Nursing (A), Social Work (B) *CEO:* Pres. Martha K. Farmer
Enroll: 2,199   (802) 468-5611

CHAMPLAIN COLLEGE
P.O. Box 670, Burlington 05402-0670 *Type:* Private *Accred.:* 1972/1990 (NEASC-CIHE) *Calendar:* Sem. plan *Degrees:* A, B *Prof. Accred.:* Radiography *CEO:* Pres. Roger H. Perry
Enroll: 1,411   (802) 658-0800

COLLEGE OF ST. JOSEPH
Rutland 05701 *Type:* Private (Roman Catholic) teachers *Accred.:* 1972/1986 (NEASC-CIHE) *Calendar:* Sem. plan *Degrees:* A, B, M *CEO:* Pres. Frank G. Miglorie, Jr.
Enroll: 296   (802) 773-5900

COMMUNITY COLLEGE OF VERMONT
Waterbury 05676 *Type:* Public (state) junior *System:* Vermont State Colleges *Accred.:* 1975/1992 (NEASC-CIHE) *Calendar:* Tri. plan *Degrees:* A *CEO:* Pres. Barbara E. Murphy
Enroll: 2,136   (802) 241-3535

GODDARD COLLEGE
Plainfield 05667 *Type:* Private liberal arts *Accred.:* 1959/1992 (NEASC-CIHE) *Calendar:* Sem. plan *Degrees:* B, M *CEO:* Pres. Richard E. Greene
FTE Enroll: 497   (802) 454-8311

GREEN MOUNTAIN COLLEGE
Poultney 05764 *Type:* Private (United Methodist) liberal arts *Accred.:* 1934/1987 (NEASC-CIHE) *Calendar:* 4-1-4 plan *De-grees:* A, B *Prof. Accred.:* Recreation and Leisure Services (B) *CEO:* Pres. Thomas Benson
Enroll: 629   (802) 287-9313

JOHNSON STATE COLLEGE
Johnson 05656 *Type:* Public (state) liberal arts and teachers *System:* Vermont State Colleges *Accred.:* 1961/1986 (NEASC-CIHE) *Calendar:* Sem. plan *Degrees:* A, B, M *CEO:* Pres. Robert T. Hahn
Enroll: 1,453   (802) 635-2356

LANDMARK COLLEGE
Putney 05346 *Type:* Private junior *Accred.:* 1991 (NEASC-CIHE) *Calendar:* Sem. plan *Degrees:* A *CEO:* Pres. Lynda J. Katz
Enroll: 100   (802) 387-4767

LYNDON STATE COLLEGE
Vail Hill, Lyndonville 05851 *Type:* Public (state) liberal arts and teachers *System:* Vermont State Colleges *Accred.:* 1965/1989 (NEASC-CIHE) *Calendar:* Sem. plan *Degrees:* A, B, M *Prof. Accred.:* Recreation and Leisure Services (B) *CEO:* Pres. Margaret R. (Peggy) Williams
Enroll: 1,082   (802) 626-9371

MARLBORO COLLEGE
Marlboro 05344-0300 *Type:* Private liberal arts *Accred.:* 1965/1994 (NEASC-CIHE) *Calendar:* Sem. plan *Degrees:* B, M *CEO:* Pres. Roderick M. Gander
Enroll: 259   (802) 257-4333

MIDDLEBURY COLLEGE
Middlebury 05753 *Type:* Private liberal arts *Accred.:* 1929/1990 (NEASC-CIHE) *Calendar:* Sem. plan *Degrees:* B, M, D *CEO:* Pres. John McCardell
Enroll: 2,028   (802) 388-3711

NEW ENGLAND CULINARY INSTITUTE
250 Main St., Montpelier 05602-9720 *Type:* Private *Accred.:* 1984/1989 (ACCSCT) *Degrees:* A, B *CEO:* Pres. Francis Voigt
(802) 223-6324

ESSEX CAMPUS
1700 Troy Ave., No. 1, Colchester 05446-3105
(802) 655-0808

NORWICH UNIVERSITY
Northfield 05663 *Type:* Private liberal arts *Accred.:* 1933/1990 (NEASC-CIHE) *Calendar:* Sem. plan *Degrees:* A, B, M, D *Prof. Accred.:* Engineering Technology (environmental/sanitary), Engineering (civil, electrical, mechanical) *CEO:* Pres. Richard W. Schneider *Enroll:* 2,387 (802) 485-2000

VERMONT COLLEGE
College St., Montpelier 05602 *Prof. Accred.:* Nursing (A,B)
(802) 485-2000

ST. MICHAEL'S COLLEGE
Winooski Park, Colchester 05439 *Type:* Private (Roman Catholic) *Accred.:* 1939/1990 (NEASC-CIHE) *Calendar:* Sem. plan *Degrees:* B, M *CEO:* Pres. Paul J. Reiss *Enroll:* 2,084 (802) 655-2000

SCHOOL FOR INTERNATIONAL TRAINING
P.O. Box 676, Brattleboro 05301-0676 *Type:* Private liberal arts *Accred.:* 1974/ 1992 (NEASC-CIHE) *Calendar:* Sem. plan *Degrees:* B, M *CEO:* Pres. A. Neal Mangham *Enroll:* 903 (802) 257-7751

SOUTHERN VERMONT COLLEGE
Bennington 05201 *Type:* Private *Accred.:* 1979/1989 (NEASC-CIHE) *Calendar:* Sem. plan *Degrees:* A, B *Prof. Accred.:* Nursing (A) *CEO:* Pres. William A. Glasser *Enroll:* 497 (802) 442-5427

STERLING COLLEGE
Craftsbury Common 05827 *Type:* Private 2-year *Accred.:* 1987/1994 (NEASC-CTCI) *Calendar:* Qtr. plan *Degrees:* A *CEO:* Pres. John S. Devens
FTE Enroll: 75 (802) 586-7711

TRINITY COLLEGE OF VERMONT
208 Colchester Ave., Burlington 05401 *Type:* Private (Roman Catholic) liberal arts for women *Accred.:* 1952/1991 (NEASC-CIHE) *Calendar:* Sem. plan *Degrees:* B, M *Prof. Accred.:* Social Work (B) *CEO:* Pres. Janice E. Ryan, R.S.M.
Enroll: 676 (802) 658-0337

UNIVERSITY OF VERMONT
Burlington 05405-0160 *Type:* Public (state) *Accred.:* 1929/1988 (NEASC-CIHE) *Calendar:* Sem. plan *Degrees:* A, B, M, P, D *Prof. Accred.:* Athletic Training, Business (B,M), Clinical Lab Scientist, Clinical Psychology, Counseling, Dental Hygiene, Engineering (civil, electrical, mechanical), Forestry, Medicine, Nuclear Medicine Technology, Nursing (A,B,M), Physical Therapy, Radiation Therapy Technology, Social Work (B,M), Speech-Language Pathology, Teacher Education *CEO:* Pres. Thomas P. Salmon
Enroll: 8,761 (802) 656-3131

VERMONT LAW SCHOOL
Chelsea St., P.O. Box 96, South Royalton 05068 *Type:* Private professional *Accred.:* 1980/1995 (NEASC-CIHE) *Calendar:* Sem. plan *Degrees:* P, D *Prof. Accred.:* Law *CEO:* Pres. R. Allan Paul
Enroll: 513 (802) 763-8303

VERMONT TECHNICAL COLLEGE
Randolph Ctr., 05061 *Type:* Public (state) 2-year *System:* Vermont State Colleges *Accred.:* 1970/1994 (NEASC-CTCI) *Calendar:* Sem. plan *Degrees:* A *Prof. Accred.:* Engineering Technology (architectural, civil/construction, computer, electrical), mechanical) *CEO:* Pres. Robert G. Clarke
FTE Enroll: 627 (802) 728-3391

WOODBURY COLLEGE
660 Elm St., Montpelier 05602 *Type:* Private *Accred.:* 1984 (NEASC-CTCI) *Calendar:* Sem. plan *Degrees:* A *CEO:* Pres. Lawrence H. Mandell
FTE Enroll: 88 (802) 229-0516

VIRGIN ISLANDS

UNIVERSITY OF THE VIRGIN ISLANDS
St. Thomas 00802 *Type:* Public (state)
Accred.: 1971/1991 (MSA) *Calendar:* Sem.
plan *Degrees:* A, B, M *Prof. Accred.:*
Nursing (A,B) *CEO:* Pres. Orville E. Kean
Enroll: 1,915   (809) 776-9200

ST. CROIX CAMPUS
   St. Croix 00850
                    (809) 778-1620

VIRGINIA

AMERICAN MILITARY UNIVERSITY
9104 P Manassas Dr., Manassas 22110 *Type:* Private *Accred.:* 1995 (DETC) *Calendar:* Sem. plan *Degrees:* M *CEO:* Pres. James Etter
Enroll: 480 (703) 330-5398

ATLANTIC UNIVERSITY
Atlantic Ave. and 67th St., P.O. Box 595, Virginia Beach 23451 *Type:* Public *Accred.:* 1994 (DETC) *Calendar:* Qtr. plan *Degrees:* M *CEO:* Pres. Jerry Cardwell
(800) 428-1512

AVERETT COLLEGE
420 W. Main St., Danville 24541 *Type:* Private (Southern Baptist) liberal arts *Accred.:* 1928/1987 (SACS-CC) *Calendar:* Sem. plan *Degrees:* B, M *CEO:* Pres. Frank R. Campbell
FTE Enroll: 1,640 (804) 791-5600

BLUE RIDGE COMMUNITY COLLEGE
P.O. Box 80, Weyers Cave 24486 *Type:* Public (state) junior *System:* Virginia Community College System *Accred.:* 1969/1994 (SACS-CC) *Calendar:* Sem. plan *Degrees:* A *Prof. Accred.:* Veterinary Technology *CEO:* Pres. James R. Perkins
FTE Enroll: 2,500 (703) 234-9261

BLUEFIELD COLLEGE
3000 College Dr., Bluefield 24605 *Type:* Private (Southern Baptist) liberal arts *Accred.:* 1949/1993 (SACS-CC) *Calendar:* Sem. plan *Degrees:* A, B *CEO:* Pres. Roy A. Dobyns
FTE Enroll: 680 (703) 326-3682

BRIDGEWATER COLLEGE
Bridgewater 22812 *Type:* Private (Church of Brethren) liberal arts *Accred.:* 1925/1991 (SACS-CC) *Calendar:* 3-3 plan *Degrees:* B *CEO:* Pres. Phillip C. Stone
FTE Enroll: 901 (540) 828-2501

CENTRAL VIRGINIA COMMUNITY COLLEGE
3506 Wards Rd., Lynchburg 24502-2498 *Type:* Public (state) junior *System:* Virginia Community College System *Accred.:* 1969/1994 (SACS-CC) *Calendar:* Sem. plan

Degrees: A *Prof. Accred.:* Medical Record Technology, Radiography, Respiratory Therapy Technology *CEO:* Pres. Belle S. Whelan
FTE Enroll: 2,309 (804) 386-4500

CHRISTENDOM COLLEGE
2101 Shenandoah Shores Rd., Front Royal 22630 *Type:* Private (Roman Catholic) liberal arts *Accred.:* 1987/1992 (SACS-CC) *Calendar:* Sem. plan *Degrees:* A, B *CEO:* Pres. Timothy O'Donnell
FTE Enroll: 171 (703) 636-2900

CHRISTOPHER NEWPORT UNIVERSITY
50 Shoe Ln., Newport News 23606-2998 *Type:* Public (state) liberal arts *System:* Commonwealth of Virginia Council of Higher Education *Accred.:* 1971/1986 (SACS-CC) *Calendar:* Sem. plan *Degrees:* B, M *Prof. Accred.:* Nursing (B), Social Work (B) *CEO:* Pres. Paul S. Trible, Jr.
FTE Enroll: 3,737 (804) 594-7000

CLINCH VALLEY COLLEGE OF THE UNIVERSITY OF VIRGINIA
College Ave., Wise 24293 *Type:* Public (state) liberal arts and teachers *System:* University of Virginia Central Office *Accred.:* 1970/1995 (SACS-CC) *Calendar:* Sem. plan *Degrees:* B *CEO:* Chanc. L. Jay Lemons
FTE Enroll: 1,324 (703) 328-0100

THE COLLEGE OF WILLIAM AND MARY
P.O. Box 8795, Williamsburg 23187-8795 *Type:* Public (state) liberal arts *System:* College of William and Mary Central Office *Accred.:* 1921/1995 (SACS-CC) *Calendar:* Sem. plan *Degrees:* A, B, M, D *Prof. Accred.:* Accounting (A), Business (B,M), Law, Teacher Education *CEO:* Pres. Timothy J. Sullivan
FTE Enroll: 6,876 (804) 221-4000

COMMONWEALTH COLLEGE
301 Centre Pointe Dr., Virginia Beach 23462 *Type:* Private junior *Accred.:* 1970/1996 (ACICS); 1984/1995 (COE warning) *Calendar:* Sem. plan *Degrees:* A, C *CEO:* Pres. Maritza Samoorian
(804) 499-9000

HAMPTON CAMPUS
1120 W. Mercury Blvd., Hampton 23666-3309 *Accred.:* 1984/1988 (ACICS)
(804) 499-7900

NORFOLK CAMPUS
300 Boush St., Norfolk 23510-1216 *Accred.:* 1964/1991 (ACICS)
(804) 625-5891

RICHMOND CAMPUS
8141 Hull Street Rd., Richmond 23235-6411 *Accred.:* 1983/1991 (ACICS)
(804) 745-2444

COMMUNITY HOSPITAL OF ROANOKE VALLEY COLLEGE OF HEALTH SCIENCES
P.O. Box 13186, Roanoke 24031-3186 *Type:* Private *Accred.:* 1986/1991 (SACS-CC) *Calendar:* Sem. plan *Degrees:* A, B *Prof. Accred.:* EMT-Paramedic, Medical Record Technology, Nursing (A), Occupational Therapy Assisting, Physical Therapy Assisting, Respiratory Therapy *CEO:* Pres. Harry C. Nickens
FTE Enroll: 375   (703) 985-8483

DABNEY S. LANCASTER COMMUNITY COLLEGE
P.O. Box 1000, Clifton Forge 24422-1000 *Type:* Public (state) junior *System:* Virginia Community College System *Accred.:* 1969/1994 (SACS-CC) *Calendar:* Sem. plan *Degrees:* A *Prof. Accred.:* Nursing (A) *CEO:* Pres. Richard R. Teaff
FTE Enroll: 917   (540) 862-4246

DANVILLE COMMUNITY COLLEGE
1008 S. Main St., Danville 24541 *Type:* Public (state) junior *System:* Virginia Community College System *Accred.:* 1970/1995 (SACS-CC) *Calendar:* Sem. plan *Degrees:* A *CEO:* Pres. B. Carlyle Ramsey
FTE Enroll: 1,895   (804) 797-2222

EASTERN MENNONITE UNIVERSITY
1200 Park Rd., Harrisonburg 22801-2462 *Type:* Private (Mennonite) liberal arts *Accred.:* 1986/1990 (ATS); 1959/1990 (SACS-CC) *Calendar:* Sem. plan *Degrees:* A, B, M *Prof. Accred.:* Nursing (B), Social

Work (B), Teacher Education *CEO:* Pres. Joseph L. Lapp
FTE Enroll: 1,028   (703) 432-4000

EASTERN SHORE COMMUNITY COLLEGE
29300 Lankford Hwy., Melfa 23410 *Type:* Public (state) junior *System:* Virginia Community College System *Accred.:* 1973/1988 (SACS-CC) *Calendar:* Sem. plan *Degrees:* A *CEO:* Pres. John C. Fiege
FTE Enroll: 430   (804) 787-5900

ECPI COMPUTER INSTITUTE
5555 Greenwich Rd., Ste. 300, Virginia Beach 23462-6542 *Type:* Private *Accred.:* 1971/1991 (ACCSCT); 1984/1989 (COE) *Degrees:* A, C *CEO:* Dir. Mark B. Dreyfus
FTE Enroll: 1,062   (804) 671-7171

CHARLOTTE CAMPUS
1121 Wood Ridge Center Dr., Ste. 150, Charlotte, NC 28217-1986 *Accred.:* 1986 (ACCSCT) *Degrees:* C
(704) 357-0077

GREENSBORO CAMPUS
7015-G Albert Pick Rd., Greensboro, NC 27409-9654 *Accred.:* 1986 (ACCSCT) *Degrees:* C
(910) 665-1400

HAMPTON CAMPUS
1919 Commerce Ave., No. 200, Hampton 23666-4246 *Accred.:* 1986 (ACCSCT) *Degrees:* A, C
(804) 838-9191

RALEIGH CAMPUS
4509 Creedmoor Rd., Raleigh, NC 27612 *Accred.:* 1986/1991 (ACCSCT) *Degrees:* C
(919) 571-0057

ECPI COMPUTER INSTITUTE—RICHMOND
4303 W. Broad St., Richmond 23230-3305 *Type:* Private *Accred.:* 1986/1991 (ACCSCT); 1990/1991 (COE) *Degrees:* A, C *CEO:* Dir. Bruce Misiaszek
FTE Enroll: 368   (804) 359-3535

ECPI COMPUTER INSTITUTE—ROAKOKE
1030 Jefferson St., S.E., Roanoke 24016 *Type:* Private *Accred.:* 1986 (ACCSCT);

1992 (COE) *Degrees:* A, C *CEO:* Dir. Elmer F. Haas
FTE Enroll: 121   (703) 343-5566

EMORY AND HENRY COLLEGE
P.O. Box 947, Emory 24327 *Type:* Private (United Methodist) liberal arts *Accred.:* 1925/1987 (SACS-CC) *Calendar:* Sem. plan *Degrees:* B *CEO:* Pres. Thomas R. Morris, Jr.
FTE Enroll: 831   (504) 944-4121

FERRUM COLLEGE
Ferrum 24088 *Type:* Private (United Methodist) liberal arts *Accred.:* 1960/1991 (SACS-CC) *Calendar:* Sem. plan *Degrees:* A, B *Prof. Accred.:* Recreation and Leisure Services (B), Social Work (B) *CEO:* Pres. Jerry M. Boone
FTE Enroll: 1,072   (703) 365-2121

GEORGE MASON UNIVERSITY
4400 University Dr., Fairfax 22030-4444 *Type:* Public (state) *System:* Commonwealth of Virginia Council of Higher Education *Accred.:* 1957/1991 (SACS-CC) *Calendar:* Sem. plan *Degrees:* B, M, D *Prof. Accred.:* Accounting (A,C), Business (B,M), Clinical Psychology, Computer Science, Engineering (electrical), Law, Music (A), Nursing (B,M), Public Administration, Social Work (B), Teacher Education *CEO:* Pres. George W. Johnson
FTE Enroll: 15,052   (703) 993-1000

GERMANNA COMMUNITY COLLEGE
P.O. Box 339, Locust Grove 22508 *Type:* Public (state) junior *System:* Virginia Community College System *Accred.:* 1972/1987 (SACS-CC) *Calendar:* Sem. plan *Degrees:* A *Prof. Accred.:* Nursing (A) *CEO:* Pres. Francis S. Turnage
FTE Enroll: 1,490   (540) 423-1333

HAMPDEN-SYDNEY COLLEGE
P.O. Box 128, Hampden-Sydney 23943 *Type:* Private (Presbyterian) liberal arts for men *Accred.:* 1919/1986 (SACS-CC) *Calendar:* Sem. plan *Degrees:* B *CEO:* Pres. Samuel V. Wilson
FTE Enroll: 946   (804) 223-6000

HAMPTON UNIVERSITY
E. Queen St., Hampton 23668 *Type:* Private liberal arts *Accred.:* 1932/1988 (SACS-CC) *Calendar:* Sem. plan *Degrees:* B, M, D *Prof. Accred.:* Computer Science, Engineering (chemical, electrical), Journalism, Music, Nursing (B,M), Social Work (B), Speech-Language Pathology, Teacher Education *CEO:* Pres. William R. Harvey
FTE Enroll: 5,388   (804) 727-5000

HOLLINS COLLEGE
P.O. Box 9688, Roanoke 24020 *Type:* Private liberal arts primarily for women *Accred.:* 1932/1986 (SACS-CC) *Calendar:* 4-1-4 plan *Degrees:* B, M *CEO:* Pres. Jane M. O'Brien
FTE Enroll: 948   (703) 362-6000

INSTITUTE OF TEXTILE TECHNOLOGY
2551 Ivy Rd., Charlottesville 22903-4614 *Type:* Private professional; graduate only *Accred.:* 1987/1992 (SACS-CC) *Calendar:* Qtr. plan *Degrees:* M *CEO:* Pres. Michael Ted Waroblak
FTE Enroll: 34   (804) 296-5511

J. SARGEANT REYNOLDS COMMUNITY COLLEGE
P.O. Box 85622, Richmond 23285-5622 *Type:* Public (state) junior *System:* Virginia Community College System *Accred.:* 1974/1989 (SACS-CC) *Calendar:* Sem. plan *Degrees:* A *Prof. Accred.:* Clinical Lab Technology (A), Dental Assisting, Dental Laboratory Technology, Nursing (A), Occupational Therapy Assisting, Respiratory Therapy, Respiratory Therapy Technology *CEO:* Pres. S.A. Burnette
FTE Enroll: 5,843   (804) 371-3200

JAMES MADISON UNIVERSITY
Harrisonburg 22807 *Type:* Public (state) liberal arts and teachers *System:* Commonwealth of Virginia Council of Higher Education *Accred.:* 1927/1992 (SACS-CC) *Calendar:* Sem. plan *Degrees:* B, M, D *Prof. Accred.:* Accounting (A,C), Art, Audiology, Business (B,M), Counseling, Music, Nursing (B), Social Work (B), Speech-Language

Pathology, Teacher Education, Theatre
CEO: Pres. Ronald E. Carrier
FTE Enroll: 10,709   (703) 568-6211

JOHN TYLER COMMUNITY COLLEGE
13101 Jefferson Davis Hwy., Chester 23831-
5399 *Type:* Public (state) junior *System:* Virginia Community College System *Accred.:*
1969/1993 (SACS-CC) *Calendar:* Sem. plan
Degrees: A *Prof. Accred.:* Engineering Technology (architectural), Funeral Service Education (Mortuary Science), Nursing (A)
CEO: Pres. Marshall W. Smith
FTE Enroll: 2,878   (804) 796-4000

THE JUDGE ADVOCATE GENERAL'S SCHOOL
600 Massie Rd., Charlottesville 22903-1781
Type: Public (federal) professional *Calen-
dar:* Sem. plan *Degrees:* P *Prof. Accred.:*
Law (ABA only) *CEO:* Cmdt. John T.
Edwards
Enroll: 76   (804) 972-6310

LIBERTY UNIVERSITY
P.O. Box 20000, Lynchburg 24506-8001
Type: Private (Baptist) liberal arts *Accred.:*
1980/1986 (SACS-CC warning) *Calendar:*
Sem. plan *Degrees:* A, B, M, D *Prof.
Accred.:* Nursing (A) *CEO:* Pres. A. Pierre
Guillermin
FTE Enroll: 6,820   (804) 582-2000

LONGWOOD COLLEGE
201 High St., Farmville 23909 *Type:* Public
(state) liberal arts and teachers for women
System: Commonwealth of Virginia Council
of Higher Education *Accred.:* 1927/1993
(SACS-CC) *Calendar:* Sem. plan *Degrees:*
B, M *Prof. Accred.:* Music, Recreation and
Leisure Services (B), Social Work (B),
Teacher Education *CEO:* Pres. William F.
Dorrill
FTE Enroll: 3,237   (804) 395-2000

LORD FAIRFAX COMMUNITY COLLEGE
P.O. Box 47, Middletown 22645 *Type:* Pub-
lic (state) junior *System:* Virginia Commu-
nity College System *Accred.:* 1972/1987
(SACS-CC) *Calendar:* Sem. plan *Degrees:*
A *CEO:* Pres. Marilyn C. Beck
FTE Enroll: 1,691   (703) 869-1120

LYNCHBURG COLLEGE
1501 Lakeside Dr., Lynchburg 24501-3199
Type: Private (Disciples of Christ) liberal
arts *Accred.:* 1927/1993 (SACS-CC) *Calen-
dar:* Sem. plan *Degrees:* B, M *Prof. Accred.:*
Counseling, Nursing (B) *CEO:* Pres. Charles
O. Warren
FTE Enroll: 1,895   (804) 522-8100

MARY BALDWIN COLLEGE
Frederick and New St., Staunton 24401
Type: Private (Presbyterian) liberal arts for
women *Accred.:* 1931/1988 (SACS-CC)
Calendar: Sem. plan *Degrees:* B, M *CEO:*
Pres. Cynthia H. Tyson
FTE Enroll: 1,118   (703) 887-7000

MARY WASHINGTON COLLEGE
1301 College Ave., Fredericksburg 22401
Type: Public (state) liberal arts *System:*
Commonwealth of Virginia Council of
Higher Education *Accred.:* 1930/1993
(SACS-CC) *Calendar:* Sem. plan *Degrees:*
B, M *Prof. Accred.:* Music *CEO:* Pres.
William M. Anderson, Jr.
FTE Enroll: 3,355   (703) 898-4100

MARYMOUNT UNIVERSITY
2807 N. Glebe Rd., Arlington 22207-4299
Type: Private (Roman Catholic) *Accred.:*
1958/1988 (SACS-CC) *Calendar:* Sem. plan
Degrees: A, B, M *Prof. Accred.:* Interior
Design, Nursing (A,B,M), Teacher Educa-
tion *CEO:* Pres. Eymard Gallagher,
R.S.H.M.
FTE Enroll: 2,854   (703) 522-5600

MEDICAL COLLEGE OF HAMPTON ROADS
825 Fairfax Ave., Norfolk 23507 *Type:* Pri-
vate professional *Accred.:* 1984/1990
(SACS-CC) *Calendar:* Sem. plan *Degrees:*
M, D *Prof. Accred.:* Medicine, Psychology
Internship *CEO:* Pres. Edward E. Brickell
FTE Enroll: 527   (804) 446-5600

MOUNTAIN EMPIRE COMMUNITY COLLEGE
P.O. Drawer 700, Big Stone Gap 24219 *Type:*
Public (state) junior *System:* Virginia Com-
munity College System *Accred.:* 1974/ 1989
(SACS-CC) *Calendar:* Sem. plan *Degrees:* A
Prof. Accred.: Nursing (A), Respiratory

Therapy Technology *CEO:* Pres. Robert H. Sandel
FTE Enroll: 1,843   (703) 523-2400

NATIONAL BUSINESS COLLEGE
1813 E. Main St., Salem 24153 *Type:* Private senior *Accred.:* 1954/1998 (ACICS) *Calendar:* Qtr. plan *Degrees:* A *Prof. Accred.:* Medical Assisting (AMA) *CEO:* Pres. Anna Marie Counts
                                       (703) 986-1800

BLUEFIELD CAMPUS
100 Logan St., Bluefield 24605 *Accred.:* 1984 (ACICS)
                                       (703) 326-3621

BRISTOL CAMPUS
300A Piedmont Ave., Bristol 24201 *Accred.:* 1993 (ACICS)
                                       (540) 669-5333

CHARLOTTESVILLE CAMPUS
1819 Emmet St., Charlottesville 22903 *Accred.:* 1979 (ACICS)
                                       (804) 295-0136

DANVILLE CAMPUS
734 Main St., Danville 24541 *Accred.:* 1984 (ACICS)
                                       (804) 793-6822

HARRISONBURG CAMPUS
51-B Burgess Rd., Harrisonburg 22801 *Accred.:* 1988 (ACICS)
                                       (703) 432-0943

LYNCHBURG CAMPUS
104 Candlewood Ct., Lynchburg 24502 *Accred.:* 1987 (ACICS)
                                       (804) 239-3500

MARTINSVILLE CAMPUS
10 Church St., Martinsville 24114 *Accred.:* 1987 (ACICS)
                                       (703) 632-5621

NEW RIVER COMMUNITY COLLEGE
P.O. Drawer 1127, Dublin 24084 *Type:* Public (state) junior *System:* Virginia Community College System *Accred.:* 1972/1987 (SACS-CC) *Calendar:* Sem. plan *Degrees:*

A *Prof. Accred.:* Nursing (A) *CEO:* Pres. Edwin L. Barnes
FTE Enroll: 2,340   (703) 674-3600

NORFOLK STATE UNIVERSITY
2401 Corprew Ave., Norfolk 23504 *Type:* Public (state) liberal arts and teachers *System:* Commonwealth of Virginia Council of Higher Education *Accred.:* 1967/1988 (SACS-CC) *Calendar:* Sem. plan *Degrees:* A, B, M, D (candidate) *Prof. Accred.:* Business (B), Clinical Lab Scientist, Computer Science, Medical Record Administration, Music, Nursing (A,B), Social Work (B,M), Teacher Education *CEO:* Pres. Harrison B. Wilson
FTE Enroll: 8,652   (804) 683-8600

NORTHERN VIRGINIA COMMUNITY COLLEGE
4001 Wakefield Chapel Rd., Annandale 22003-3723 *Type:* Public (state) junior *System:* Virginia Community College System *Accred.:* 1968/1992 (SACS-CC) *Calendar:* Sem. plan *Degrees:* A *Prof. Accred.:* Clinical Lab Technology (A), Dental Hygiene, EMT-Paramedic, Medical Record Technology, Nursing (A), Physical Therapy Assisting, Radiography, Respiratory Therapy, Respiratory Therapy Technology *CEO:* Pres. Richard J. Ernst
FTE Enroll: 21,503   (703) 323-3000

ALEXANDRIA CAMPUS
3001 N. Beauregard St., Alexandria 22311
                                       (703) 845-6200

ANNANDALE CAMPUS
8333 Little River Tpke., Annandale 22003
                                       (703) 323-3010

LOUDOUN CAMPUS
1000 Harry Flood Byrd Hwy., Sterling 22170 *Prof. Accred.:* Veterinary Technology
                                       (703) 450-2500

MANASSAS CAMPUS
6901 Sudley Rd., Manassas 22110
                                       (703) 257-6600

WOODBRIDGE CAMPUS
15200 Neabsco Mills Rd., Woodbridge 22191
(703) 878-5700

NOTRE DAME INSTITUTE
4407 Sano St., Alexandria 22312 *Type:* Private graduate only *Accred.:* 1994 (SACS-CC) *Calendar:* Sem. plan *Degrees:* M *CEO:* Pres. William P. Saunders
FTE Enroll: 121   (703) 658-4304

OLD DOMINION UNIVERSITY
5215 Hampton Blvd., Norfolk 23529 *Type:* Public (state) liberal arts and professional *System:* Commonwealth of Virginia Council of Higher Education *Accred.:* 1961/1992 (SACS-CC) *Calendar:* Sem. plan *Degrees:* B, M, D *Prof. Accred.:* Accounting (A), Business (B,M), Clinical Lab Scientist, Computer Science, Cytotechnology, Dental Assisting, Dental Hygiene, Engineering Technology (civil/construction, electrical, mechanical), Engineering (civil, computer, electrical, mechanical), Music, Nuclear Medicine Technology, Nurse Anesthesia Education, Nursing (B,M), Ophthalmic Medical Technology, Physical Therapy, Public Administration, Recreation and Leisure Services (B), Speech-Language Pathology, Teacher Education, Theatre *CEO:* Pres. James V. Koch
FTE Enroll: 12,602   (804) 683-3000

PATRICK HENRY COMMUNITY COLLEGE
P.O. Drawer 5311, Martinsville 24114 *Type:* Public (state) junior *System:* Virginia Community College System *Accred.:* 1972/1987 (SACS-CC) *Calendar:* Sem. plan *Degrees:* A *Prof. Accred.:* Nursing (A) *CEO:* Pres. Max F. Wingett
FTE Enroll: 1,536   (703) 638-8777

PAUL D. CAMP COMMUNITY COLLEGE
100 N. College Rd., P.O. Box 737, Franklin 23851 *Type:* Public (state) junior *System:* Virginia Community College System *Accred.:* 1973/1988 (SACS-CC) *Calendar:* Sem. plan *Degrees:* A *CEO:* Pres. Jerome J. Friga
FTE Enroll: 842   (804) 569-6700

PIEDMONT VIRGINIA COMMUNITY COLLEGE
Rte. 6, Box 1, Charlottesville 22902-8714 *Type:* Public (state) junior *System:* Virginia Community College System *Accred.:* 1974/1989 (SACS-CC) *Calendar:* Sem. plan *Degrees:* A *Prof. Accred.:* Nursing (A) *CEO:* Pres. Deborah M. DiCroce
FTE Enroll: 2,084   (804) 977-3900

PRESBYTERIAN SCHOOL OF CHRISTIAN EDUCATION
1205 Palmyra Ave., Richmond 23227 *Type:* Private (Presbyterian) graduate only *Accred.:* 1964/1988 (ATS); 1951/1988 (SACS-CC) *Calendar:* 4-1-4 plan *Degrees:* M, D *CEO:* Pres. Wayne G. Boulton
Enroll: 150   (804) 359-5031

PROTESTANT EPISCOPAL THEOLOGICAL SEMINARY IN VIRGINIA
3737 Seminary Rd., Alexandria 22304 *Type:* Private (Episcopal) graduate only *Accred.:* 1938/1993 (ATS) *Calendar:* Sem. plan *Degrees:* M, D *CEO:* Pres. Martha J. Horne
Enroll: 215   (703) 370-6600

RADFORD UNIVERSITY
Box 6890, Radford 24142 *Type:* Public (state) liberal arts and teachers *System:* Commonwealth of Virginia Council of Higher Education *Accred.:* 1928/1993 (SACS-CC) *Calendar:* Sem. plan *Degrees:* B, M *Prof. Accred.:* Audiology, Business (B,M), Computer Science, Music, Nursing (B,M), Recreation and Leisure Services (B), Social Work (B,M-candidate), Speech-Language Pathology, Teacher Education *CEO:* Pres. H. Douglas Covington
FTE Enroll: 8,934   (703) 831-5000

RANDOLPH-MACON COLLEGE
P.O. Box 5005, Ashland 23005-5505 *Type:* Private (United Methodist) liberal arts *Accred.:* 1904/1987 (SACS-CC) *Calendar:* 4-1-4 plan *Degrees:* B *CEO:* Pres. Ladell Payne
FTE Enroll: 1,120   (804) 798-8372

RANDOLPH-MACON WOMAN'S COLLEGE
2500 Rivermont Ave., Lynchburg 24503 *Type:* Private (United Methodist) liberal arts

for women *Accred.:* 1902/1990 (SACS-CC) *Calendar:* Sem. plan *Degrees:* B *CEO:* Pres. Kathleen Gill Bowman
FTE Enroll: 715   (804) 947-8000

RAPPAHANNOCK COMMUNITY COLLEGE
P.O. Box 287, Glenns 23149 *Type:* Public (state) junior *System:* Virginia Community College System *Accred.:* 1973/1988 (SACS-CC) *Calendar:* Sem. plan *Degrees:* A *CEO:* Pres. John H. Upton
FTE Enroll: 1,032   (804) 758-6700

REGENT UNIVERSITY
1000 Regent University Dr., Virginia Beach 23464 *Type:* Private (interdenominational) graduate only *Accred.:* 1992 (ATS); 1984/1989 (SACS-CC) *Calendar:* Sem. plan *Degrees:* M, D *Prof. Accred.:* Law (ABA only) (provisional) *CEO:* Pres. Terrence Lindvall
FTE Enroll: 1,155   (804) 579-4000

RICHARD BLAND COLLEGE
11301 Johnson Rd., Petersburg 23805 *Type:* Public (state) junior *System:* College of William and Mary Central Office *Accred.:* 1961/1988 (SACS-CC) *Calendar:* Sem. plan *Degrees:* A *CEO:* Pres. Clarence Maze, Jr.
FTE Enroll: 875   (804) 862-6213

ROANOKE COLLEGE
221 College Ln., Salem 24153-3794 *Type:* Private (Lutheran) liberal arts *Accred.:* 1927/1991 (SACS-CC) *Calendar:* Sem. plan *Degrees:* B *CEO:* Pres. David M. Gring
FTE Enroll: 1,586   (703) 375-2500

ST. PAUL'S COLLEGE
406 Winsor Ave., Lawrenceville 23868 *Type:* Private (Episcopal) liberal arts and teachers *Accred.:* 1950/1990 (SACS-CC warning) *Calendar:* Sem. plan *Degrees:* B *CEO:* Pres. Thomas M. Law
FTE Enroll: 639   (804) 848-3111

SHENANDOAH UNIVERSITY
1460 College Dr., Winchester 22602 *Type:* Private (United Methodist) *Accred.:* 1973/1989 (SACS-CC) *Calendar:* Sem. plan *Degrees:* A, B, M, D (candidate) *Prof.*

Accred.: Music, Nursing (A), Occupational Therapy, Physical Therapy, Respiratory Therapy *CEO:* Pres. James A. Davis
FTE Enroll: 1,434   (703) 665-4500

SOUTHERN VIRGINIA COLLEGE
One College Hill Dr., Buena Vista 24416 *Type:* Private for women *Accred.:* 1962/1983 (SACS-CC probational) *Calendar:* Sem. plan *Degrees:* A *CEO:* Pres. John W. Ripley
FTE Enroll: 129   (703) 261-8400

SOUTHSIDE VIRGINIA COMMUNITY COLLEGE
109 Campus Dr., Alberta 23821 *Type:* Public (state) junior *System:* Virginia Community College System *Accred.:* 1972/1987 (SACS-CC) *Calendar:* Sem. plan *Degrees:* A *CEO:* Pres. John J. Cavan
FTE Enroll: 2,176   (804) 949-1000

SOUTHWEST VIRGINIA COMMUNITY COLLEGE
P.O. Box SVCC, Richlands 24641 *Type:* Public (state) junior *System:* Virginia Community College System *Accred.:* 1970/1995 (SACS-CC) *Calendar:* Sem. plan *Degrees:* A *Prof. Accred.:* Nursing (A), Radiography, Respiratory Therapy, Respiratory Therapy Technology *CEO:* Pres. Charles R. King
FTE Enroll: 2,752   (703) 964-2555

SWEET BRIAR COLLEGE
P.O. Box C, Sweet Briar 24595 *Type:* Private liberal arts for women *Accred.:* 1920/1990 (SACS-CC) *Calendar:* Sem. plan *Degrees:* B *CEO:* Pres. Barbara A. Hill
FTE Enroll: 685   (804) 381-6100

THOMAS NELSON COMMUNITY COLLEGE
P.O. Box 9407, Hampton 23670 *Type:* Public (state) junior *System:* Virginia Community College System *Accred.:* 1970/1995 (SACS-CC) *Calendar:* Sem. plan *Degrees:* A *Prof. Accred.:* Clinical Lab Technology (A) *CEO:* Pres. Shirley Robinson Pippins
FTE Enroll: 4,795   (804) 825-2700

TIDEWATER COMMUNITY COLLEGE
7000 College Dr., Portsmouth 23703 *Type:* Public (state) junior *System:* Virginia Community College System *Accred.:* 1971/1986 (SACS-CC) *Calendar:* Sem. plan *Degrees:*

A *Prof. Accred.:* Diagnostic Medical Sonography, Medical Record Technology, Nursing (A), Physical Therapy Assisting, Radiography, Respiratory Therapy, Respiratory Therapy Technology *CEO:* Pres. Larry L. Whitworth
FTE Enroll: 10,653   (804) 484-2121

UNION THEOLOGICAL SEMINARY IN VIRGINIA
3401 Brook Rd., Richmond 23227 *Type:* Private (Presbyterian) graduate only *Accred.:* 1938/1986 (ATS); 1971/1986 (SACS-CC) *Calendar:* Sem. plan *Degrees:* M, D *CEO:* Pres. Louis B. Weeks
Enroll: 244   (804) 355-0671

UNIVERSITY OF RICHMOND
Richmond 23173 *Type:* Private (Southern Baptist) liberal arts *Accred.:* 1910/1988 (SACS-CC) *Calendar:* Sem. plan *Degrees:* A, B, M, D *Prof. Accred.:* Accounting (A), Business (B,M), Law, Music *CEO:* Pres. Richard L. Morrill
FTE Enroll: 3,679   (804) 289-8000

UNIVERSITY OF VIRGINIA
P.O. Box 9011, Charlottesville 22906 *Type:* Public (state) *System:* University of Virginia Central Office *Accred.:* 1904/1986 (SACS-CC) *Calendar:* Sem. plan *Degrees:* B, M, D *Prof. Accred.:* Accounting (A,C), Audiology, Business (B,M), Clinical Psychology, Counseling, Dietetics (internship), Engineering (aerospace, chemical, civil, electrical, mechanical, nuclear, systems), General Practice Residency, Landscape Architecture (M), Law, Medicine, Nursing (B,M), Planning (B,M), Psychology Internship, Speech-Language Pathology, Teacher Education *CEO:* Pres. John T. Casteen, III
FTE Enroll: 18,797   (804) 924-3337

VIRGINIA COMMONWEALTH UNIVERSITY
910 W. Franklin St., VCU Box 842520, Richmond 23284-2525 *Type:* Public (state) *System:* Commonwealth of Virginia Council of Higher Education *Accred.:* 1953/1994 (SACS-CC) *Calendar:* Sem. plan *Degrees:* A, B, M, D *Prof. Accred.:* Accounting (A,C), Art, Business (B,M), Clinical Lab Scientist, Clinical Psychology, Combined Prosthodon-

tics, Computer Science, Counseling Psychology, Dental Hygiene, Dentistry, Dietetics (internship), Endodontics, General Dentistry (prelim. provisional), Health Services Administration, Interior Design, Journalism (B,M), Medicine, Music, Nuclear Medicine Technology, Nurse Anesthesia Education, Nursing (B,M), Occupational Therapy, Oral and Maxillofacial Surgery, Orthodontics, Pediatric Dentistry, Periodontics, Physical Therapy, Planning (M), Psychology Internship, Public Administration, Radiation Therapy Technology, Radiography, Recreation and Leisure Services (B), Rehabilitation Counseling, Social Work (B,M), Teacher Education *CEO:* Pres. Eugene P. Trani
FTE Enroll: 15,049   (804) 828-0100

VIRGINIA HIGHLANDS COMMUNITY COLLEGE
P.O. Box 828, State Rte. 372 off Rte. 140, Abingdon 24212-0828 *Type:* Public (state) junior *System:* Virginia Community College System *Accred.:* 1972/1987 (SACS-CC) *Calendar:* Sem. plan *Degrees:* A *Prof. Accred.:* Nursing (A) *CEO:* Pres. F. David Wilkin
FTE Enroll: 1,469   (703) 628-6094

VIRGINIA INTERMONT COLLEGE
1013 Moore St., Bristol 24201 *Type:* Private (Southern Baptist) liberal arts *Accred.:* 1925/1987 (SACS-CC) *Calendar:* Sem. plan *Degrees:* A, B *Prof. Accred.:* Social Work (B) *CEO:* Pres. Gary M. Poulton
FTE Enroll: 669   (703) 669-6101

VIRGINIA MILITARY INSTITUTE
Smith Hall, Lexington 24450 *Type:* Public (state) primarily for men *System:* Commonwealth of Virginia Council of Higher Education *Accred.:* 1926/1986 (SACS-CC) *Calendar:* Sem. plan *Degrees:* B *Prof. Accred.:* Engineering (civil, electrical, mechanical) *CEO:* Superint. Josiah Bunting, III
FTE Enroll: 1,191   (703) 464-7000

VIRGINIA POLYTECHNIC INSTITUTE AND STATE UNIVERSITY
210 Burruss Hall, Blacksburg 24061-0131 *Type:* Public (state) *System:* Commonwealth of Virginia Council of Higher Education

Accred.: 1923/1988 (SACS-CC) *Calendar:* Sem. plan *Degrees:* A, B, M, D *Prof. Accred.:* Accounting (A,C), Business (B,M), Clinical Psychology, Construction Education (B), Engineering (aerospace, agricultural, chemical, civil, computer, electrical, engineering mechanics, environmental/sanitary, industrial, materials, mechanical, mining, ocean), Forestry, Home Economics, Interior Design, Landscape Architecture (B,M), Marriage and Family Therapy (D), Planning (M), Public Administration, Teacher Education, Theatre *CEO:* Pres. Paul E. Torgersen
FTE Enroll: 26,030   (703) 231-6000

VIRGINIA STATE UNIVERSITY
1 Hayden Pl., Box 9001, Petersburg 23806 *Type:* Public (state) liberal arts and professional *System:* Commonwealth of Virginia Council of Higher Education *Accred.:* 1933/1988 (SACS-CC) *Calendar:* Sem. plan *Degrees:* B, M *Prof. Accred.:* Dietetics (internship), Engineering Technology (electrical, mechanical), Music, Social Work (B), Teacher Education *CEO:* Pres. Eddie N. Moore, Jr.
FTE Enroll: 3,531   (804) 524-5000

VIRGINIA UNION UNIVERSITY
1500 N. Lombardy St., Richmond 23220-1711 *Type:* Private (Baptist) liberal arts *Accred.:* 1971/1987 (ATS); 1935/1990 (SACS-CC) *Calendar:* Sem. plan *Degrees:* B, M, D *Prof. Accred.:* Social Work (B) *CEO:* Pres. S. Dallas Simmons
FTE Enroll: 1,549   (804) 257-5600

VIRGINIA WESLEYAN COLLEGE
1584 Wesleyan Dr., Norfolk 23502-5599 *Type:* Private (United Methodist) liberal arts and teachers *Accred.:* 1970/1995 (SACS-CC) *Calendar:* Sem. plan *Degrees:* B *Prof. Accred.:* Recreation and Leisure Services (B) *CEO:* Pres. William T. Greer, Jr.
FTE Enroll: 1,297   (804) 455-3200

VIRGINIA WESTERN COMMUNITY COLLEGE
3095 Colonial Ave., S.W., P.O. Box 14045, Roanoke 24038 *Type:* Public (state) junior *System:* Virginia Community College System *Accred.:* 1969/1993 (SACS-CC) *Calendar:* Sem. plan *Degrees:* A *Prof. Accred.:* Dental Hygiene, Engineering Technology (electrical), Nursing (A), Radiography *CEO:* Pres. Charles L. Downs
FTE Enroll: 3,526   (703) 857-7311

WASHINGTON AND LEE UNIVERSITY
Washington St., Lexington 24450 *Type:* Private liberal arts *Accred.:* 1895/1990 (SACS-CC) *Calendar:* 4-4-x plan *Degrees:* B, D *Prof. Accred.:* Business (B), Journalism (B), Law *CEO:* Pres. John W. Elrod
FTE Enroll: 1,945   (703) 463-8400

WYTHEVILLE COMMUNITY COLLEGE
1000 E. Main St., Wytheville 24382 *Type:* Public (state) junior *System:* Virginia Community College System *Accred.:* 1970/1995 (SACS-CC) *Calendar:* Sem. plan *Degrees:* A *Prof. Accred.:* Clinical Lab Technology (A), Dental Assisting, Dental Hygiene, Nursing (A), Physical Therapy Assisting *CEO:* Pres. William F. Snyder
FTE Enroll: 1,548   (703) 228-5541

WASHINGTON

THE ART INSTITUTE OF SEATTLE
2323 Elliott Ave., Seattle 98121-1633 *Type:* Private *Accred.:* 1983 (ACCSCT); 1993/1995 (NASC candidate) *Calendar:* Qtr. plan *Degrees:* A, C *CEO:* Pres. Leslie E. Pritchard
Enroll: 1,781   (206) 448-0900

BASTYR UNIVERSITY
144 N.E. 54th St., Seattle 98105 *Type:* Private professional *Accred.:* 1989/1995 (NASC) *Calendar:* Qtr. plan *Degrees:* B, M, D *Prof. Accred.:* Acupuncture (M) *CEO:* Pres. Joseph E. Pizzorno, Jr.
Enroll: 741   (206) 517-3535

BELLEVUE COMMUNITY COLLEGE
3000 Landerholm Cir., S.E., Bellevue 98007-6484 *Type:* Public (district) junior *System:* Washington State Board for Community and Technical Colleges *Accred.:* 1970/1995 (NASC) *Calendar:* Qtr. plan *Degrees:* A *Prof. Accred.:* Diagnostic Medical Sonography, Nuclear Medicine Technology, Nursing (A), Radiation Therapy Technology, Radiography *CEO:* Pres. B. Jean Floten
Enroll: 10,249   (206) 641-0111

BIG BEND COMMUNITY COLLEGE
7662 Chanute St., Moses Lake 98837-3299 *Type:* Public (district) junior *System:* Washington State Board for Community and Technical Colleges *Accred.:* 1965/1994 (NASC) *Calendar:* Qtr. plan *Degrees:* A *CEO:* Pres. William C. Bonaudi
Enroll: 3,072   (509) 762-5351

CENTRAL WASHINGTON UNIVERSITY
208 Bouillon, Ellensburg 98926 *Type:* Public (state) liberal arts and teachers *System:* Washington Higher Education Coordinating Board *Accred.:* 1918/1994 (NASC) *Calendar:* Qtr. plan *Degrees:* B, M *Prof. Accred.:* Clinical Lab Scientist, Construction Education (B), Dietetics (internship), EMT-Paramedic, Engineering Technology (electrical), Music, Recreation and Leisure Services (B), Teacher Education *CEO:* Pres. Ivory V. Nelson
Enroll: 8,468   (509) 963-1111

CENTRALIA COLLEGE
600 W. Locust, Centralia 98531 *Type:* Public (district) junior *System:* Washington State Board for Community and Technical Colleges *Accred.:* 1948/1995 (NASC) *Calendar:* Qtr. plan *Degrees:* A *CEO:* Pres. Henry P. Kirk
Enroll: 3,086   (360) 736-9391

CITY UNIVERSITY
335 116th Ave S.E., Bellevue 98004 *Type:* Private *Accred.:* 1978/1995 (NASC) *Calendar:* Qtr. plan *Degrees:* A, B, M *CEO:* Pres. Michael A. Pastore
Enroll: 6,166   (206) 643-2000

CLARK COLLEGE
1800 E. McLoughlin Blvd., Vancouver 98663 *Type:* Public (district) junior *System:* Washington State Board for Community and Technical Colleges *Accred.:* 1948/1994 (NASC) *Calendar:* Qtr. plan *Degrees:* A *Prof. Accred.:* Dental Hygiene, Nursing (A) *CEO:* Pres. Earl P. Johnson
Enroll: 10,804   (360) 992-2000

COLUMBIA BASIN COLLEGE
2600 N. 20th Ave., Pasco 99301-3397 *Type:* Public (district) junior *System:* Washington State Board for Community and Technical Colleges *Accred.:* 1960/1994 (NASC) *Calendar:* Qtr. plan *Degrees:* A *CEO:* Pres. Lee R. Thornton
Enroll: 7,392   (509) 547-0511

CORNISH COLLEGE OF THE ARTS
710 E. Roy St., Seattle 98102 *Type:* Private professional *Accred.:* 1977/1994 (NASC) *Calendar:* Sem. plan *Degrees:* B *CEO:* Pres. Sergei P. Tschernisch
Enroll: 623   (206) 323-1400

EASTERN WASHINGTON UNIVERSITY
Cheney 99004 *Type:* Public (state) liberal arts and teachers *System:* Washington Higher Education Coordinating Board *Accred.:*

1919/1993 (NASC) *Calendar:* Qtr. plan *Degrees:* B, M *Prof. Accred.:* Business (B,M), Computer Science, Counseling, Dental Hygiene, Engineering Technology (computer, mechanical), Music, Nursing (B,M), Physical Therapy, Planning (B,M), Recreation and Leisure Services (B), Social Work (B,M), Speech-Language Pathology, Teacher Education *CEO:* Pres. Marshall E. Drummond
Enroll: 8,360　　　　　(509) 359-6200

EDMONDS COMMUNITY COLLEGE
20000 68th Ave. W., Lynnwood 98036 *Type:* Public (district) junior *System:* Washington State Board for Community and Technical Colleges *Accred.:* 1973/1993 (NASC) *Calendar:* Qtr. plan *Degrees:* A *Prof. Accred.:* Medical Assisting (AMA) *CEO:* Pres. Carleton M. Opgaard
Enroll: 8,696　　　　　(206) 640-1500

EVERETT COMMUNITY COLLEGE
801 Wetmore Ave., Everett 98201-1327 *Type:* Public (district) junior *System:* Washington State Board for Community and Technical Colleges *Accred.:* 1948/1995 (NASC) *Calendar:* Qtr. plan *Degrees:* A *Prof. Accred.:* Nursing (A), Practical Nursing *CEO:* Pres. Susan C. Carroll
Enroll: 8,174　　　　　(206) 388-9100

EVERGREEN STATE COLLEGE
Olympia 98505 *Type:* Public (state) liberal arts *System:* Washington Higher Education Coordinating Board *Accred.:* 1974/1994 (NASC) *Calendar:* Qtr. plan *Degrees:* B, M *CEO:* Pres. Jane L. Jervis
Enroll: 3,614　　　　　(206) 866-6000

GONZAGA UNIVERSITY
Spokane 99258 *Type:* Private (Roman Catholic) *Accred.:* 1927/1994 (NASC) *Calendar:* Sem. plan *Degrees:* B, M, D *Prof. Accred.:* Business (B,M), Engineering (civil, electrical, mechanical), Law, Nurse Anesthesia Education, Nursing (B), Teacher Education *CEO:* Pres. Bernard J. Coughlin, S.J.
Enroll: 4,697　　　　　(509) 328-4220

GRAYS HARBOR COLLEGE
1620 Edward P. Smith Dr., Aberdeen 98520 *Type:* Public (district) junior *System:* Washing-

ton State Board for Community and Technical Colleges *Accred.:* 1948/1991 (NASC) *Calendar:* Qtr. plan *Degrees:* A *CEO:* Pres. Jewell C. Manspeaker
Enroll: 3,201　　　　　(360) 538-4000

GREEN RIVER COMMUNITY COLLEGE
12401 S.E. 320th St., Auburn 98002 *Type:* Public (district) junior *System:* Washington State Board for Community and Technical Colleges *Accred.:* 1967/1995 (NASC) *Calendar:* Qtr. plan *Degrees:* A *Prof. Accred.:* Occupational Therapy Assisting *CEO:* Pres. Richard A. Rutkowski
Enroll: 6,808　　　　　(206) 833-9111

HENRY COGSWELL COLLEGE
10626 N.E. 37th Cir., Kirkland 98033 *Type:* Private technical *Accred.:* 1992/1995 (NASC candidate) *Calendar:* Tri. plan *Degrees:* A, B *Prof. Accred.:* Engineering Technology (electrical, mechanical), Engineering (electrical) *CEO:* Pres. Ron Hundley
Enroll: 191　　　　　(206) 822-3137

HERITAGE COLLEGE
3240 Fort Rd., Toppenish 98948 *Type:* Private (Roman Catholic) liberal arts *Accred.:* 1986/1994 (NASC) *Calendar:* Sem. plan *Degrees:* A, B, M *CEO:* Pres. Kathleen Ross, S.N.J.M.
Enroll: 1,114　　　　　(509) 865-2244

HIGHLINE COMMUNITY COLLEGE
P.O. Box 98000, Des Moines 98198-9800 *Type:* Public (district) junior *System:* Washington State Board for Community and Technical Colleges *Accred.:* 1965/1995 (NASC) *Calendar:* Qtr. plan *Degrees:* A *Prof. Accred.:* Dental Assisting, Medical Assisting (AMA), Nursing (A), Respiratory Therapy *CEO:* Pres. Edward M. Command
Enroll: 8,711　　　　　(206) 878-3710

ITT TECHNICAL INSTITUTE
12720 Gateway Dr., Ste. 100, Seattle 98168-3333 *Type:* Private *Accred.:* 1977/1988 (ACC-SCT) *Degrees:* A, B *CEO:* Dir. Carol A. Menck
　　　　　(206) 244-3300

ITT TECHNICAL INSTITUTE
N. 1050 Argonne Rd., Spokane 99212-2610
Type: Private *Accred.:* 1984/1988 (ACC-SCT) *Degrees:* A *CEO:* Dir. Ralph Oscarson
(509) 926-2900

BOTHELL CAMPUS
2525-223rd St., S.E., Bothell 98021 *Accred.:*
1994 (ACCSCT) *Calendar:* Qtr. plan
Degrees: A
Enroll: 222   (206) 485-0303

LAKE WASHINGTON TECHNICAL COLLEGE
11605 132nd Ave., N.E., Kirkland 98034
Type: Public (district) *System:* Washington
State Board for Community and Technical
Colleges *Accred.:* 1981/1991 (NASC) *Calendar:* Sem. plan *Degrees:* A *Prof. Accred.:* Dental Assisting *CEO:* Pres. Donald W. Fowler
Enroll: 4,087   (206) 828-5600

LOWER COLUMBIA COLLEGE
1600 Maple, Longview 98632-0310 *Type:*
Public (district) junior *System:* Washington
State Board for Community and Technical
Colleges *Accred.:* 1948/1995 (NASC) *Calendar:* Qtr. plan *Degrees:* A *Prof. Accred.:*
Nursing (A), Practical Nursing *CEO:* Pres.
Vernon R. Pickett
Enroll: 4,091   (360) 577-2300

LUTHERAN BIBLE INSTITUTE OF SEATTLE
Providence Heights, Issaquah 98027 *Type:*
Private (Lutheran) professional *Accred.:*
1982/1993 (NASC) *Calendar:* Qtr. plan
Degrees: A, B *CEO:* Pres. James A. Bergquist
Enroll: 169   (206) 392-0400

NORTH SEATTLE COMMUNITY COLLEGE
9600 College Way N., Seattle 98103 *Type:*
Public (district) junior *System:* Seattle Community College District *Accred.:* 1973/1993
(NASC) *Calendar:* Qtr. plan *Degrees:* A
Prof. Accred.: Medical Assisting (AMA)
CEO: Pres. Constance W. Rice
Enroll: 8,802   (206) 527-3600

NORTHWEST COLLEGE OF ART
16464 State Hwy. 305, Poulsbo 98370-0932
Type: Private *Accred.:* 1989 (ACCSCT)
Degrees: A, B *CEO:* Pres. Craig Freeman
(206) 779-9993

NORTHWEST COLLEGE OF THE ASSEMBLIES OF
GOD
P.O. Box 579, 5520 108th Ave., N.E., Kirkland 98083 *Type:* Private (Assemblies of
God) *Accred.:* 1973/1995 (NASC) *Calendar:* Sem. plan *Degrees:* A, B *CEO:* Pres.
Dennis A. Davis
FTE Enroll: 839   (206) 822-8266

NORTHWEST INDIAN COLLEGE
Bellingham 98226 *Type:* Private (tribal)
junior *Accred.:* 1993/1995 (NASC) *Calendar:* Sem. plan *Degrees:* A *CEO:* Pres.
Robert J. Lorence
Enroll: 1,416   (360) 676-2772

NORTHWEST INSTITUTE OF ACUPUNCTURE AND
ORIENTAL MEDICINE
1307 N. 45th St., Seattle 98103 *Type:* Private
professional *Calendar:* Qtr. plan *Degrees:* M
Prof. Accred.: Acupuncture *CEO:* Pres.
Frederick O. Lanphear
FTE Enroll: 60   (206) 633-2419

OLYMPIC COLLEGE
1600 Chester Ave., Bremerton 98310 *Type:*
Public (district) junior *System:* Washington
State Board for Community and Technical
Colleges *Accred.:* 1948/1994 (NASC) *Calendar:* Qtr. plan *Degrees:* A *CEO:* Interim
Pres. Donna Allen
Enroll: 5,943   (360) 478-4544

PACIFIC LUTHERAN UNIVERSITY
Tacoma 98447-0003 *Type:* Private (Lutheran)
Accred.: 1936/1994 (NASC) *Calendar:* 4-1-4 plan *Degrees:* B, M *Prof. Accred.:*
Accounting (A), Business (B,M), Computer
Science, Marriage and Family Therapy (M),
Music, Nursing (B), Social Work (B),
Teacher Education *CEO:* Pres. Loren J.
Anderson
Enroll: 3,434   (206) 531-6900

PENINSULA COLLEGE
1502 E. Lauridsen Blvd., Port Angeles
98362 *Type:* Public (district) junior *System:*
Washington State Board for Community and
Technical Colleges *Accred.:* 1965/1992
(NASC) *Calendar:* Qtr. plan *Degrees:* A
CEO: Pres. Wallace H. Sigmar
Enroll: 3,823   (360) 417-6500

PIERCE COLLEGE
9401 Farwest Dr., S.W., Tacoma 98498 *Type:* Public (district) junior *System:* Washington State Board for Community and Technical Colleges *Accred.:* 1972/1992 (NASC) *Calendar:* Qtr. plan *Degrees:* A *Prof. Accred.:* Dental Hygiene, Veterinary Technology *CEO:* Pres. George A. Delaney
Enroll: 10,533   (206) 964-6500

PUGET SOUND CHRISTIAN COLLEGE
410 Fourth Ave. N., Edmonds 98020 *Type:* Private (Christian Churches/Churches of Christ) *Accred.:* 1979/1989 (AABC) *Calendar:* Qtr. plan *Degrees:* A, B, C *CEO:* Pres. R. Allan Dunbar
FTE Enroll: 82   (206) 775-8686

RENTON TECHNICAL COLLEGE
3000 Fourth St., N.E., Renton 98056 *Type:* Public (district) *System:* Washington State Board for Community and Technical Colleges *Accred.:* 1978/1993 (NASC) *Calendar:* Sem. plan *Degrees:* A *Prof. Accred.:* Dental Assisting, Surgical Technology *CEO:* Pres. Robert C. Roberts
Enroll: 6,514   (206) 235-2352

RESOURCE CENTER FOR THE HANDICAPPED
20150 45th Ave., N.E., Seattle 98155-1700 *Type:* Private *Accred.:* 1987/1993 (ACC-SCT) *Degrees:* A *CEO:* Dir. Cindi Strong
(206) 368-3327

ST. MARTIN'S COLLEGE
Lacey 98503 *Type:* Private (Roman Catholic) liberal arts *Accred.:* 1933/1992 (NASC) *Calendar:* Sem. plan *Degrees:* A, B, M *Prof. Accred.:* Engineering (civil), Nursing (B) *CEO:* Pres. David R. Spangler
Enroll: 1,345   (206) 491-4700

SEATTLE CENTRAL COMMUNITY COLLEGE
1701 Broadway, Seattle 98122 *Type:* Public (district) junior *System:* Seattle Community College District *Accred.:* 1970/1995 (NASC) *Calendar:* Qtr. plan *Degrees:* A *Prof. Accred.:* Nursing (A), Respiratory Therapy, Surgical Technology *CEO:* Pres. Charles H. Mitchell
Enroll: 8,902   (206) 587-3800

SEATTLE PACIFIC UNIVERSITY
3307 Third Ave. W., Seattle 98119 *Type:* Private (Methodist) liberal arts *Accred.:* 1933/1995 (NASC) *Calendar:* Qtr. plan *Degrees:* B, M, D *Prof. Accred.:* Engineering (electrical), Music, Nursing (B), Teacher Education *CEO:* Provost Philip Eaton
Enroll: 7,282   (206) 281-2000

SEATTLE UNIVERSITY
12th Ave. and E. Columbia St., Seattle 98122 *Type:* Private (Roman Catholic) Accredited: 1993 (ATS); 1935/1994 (NASC) *Calendar:* Qrt. plan Degrees: B, M, D *Prof. Accred.:* Business (B, M), Diagnostic Medical Sonography, Engineering (civil, electrical, mechanical), Nursing (B), Teacher Education *CEO:* Pres. William J. Sullivan, S.J.
Enroll: 6,091   (206) 296-6000

SHORELINE COMMUNITY COLLEGE
16101 Greenwood Ave. N., Seattle 98133 *Type:* Public (district) junior *System:* Washington State Board for Community and Technical Colleges *Accred.:* 1966/1992 (NASC) *Calendar:* Qtr. plan *Degrees:* A *Prof. Accred.:* Clinical Lab Technology (A), Dental Hygiene, Histologic Technology, Medical Record Technology, Nursing (A) *CEO:* Pres. Gary L. Oertli
Enroll: 8,440   (206) 546-4101

SKAGIT VALLEY COLLEGE
2405 College Way, Mount Vernon 98273 *Type:* Public (district) junior *System:* Washington State Board for Community and Technical Colleges *Accred.:* 1948/1994 (NASC) *Calendar:* Qtr. plan *Degrees:* A *Prof. Accred.:* Nursing (A), Practical Nursing *CEO:* Pres. Lydia Ledesma
Enroll: 6,893   (360) 428-1261

SOUTH PUGET SOUND COMMUNITY COLLEGE
2011 Mottman Rd., S.W., Olympia 98512 *Type:* Public (district) junior *System:* Washington State Board for Community and Technical Colleges *Accred.:* 1975/1995 (NASC) *Calendar:* Qtr. plan *Degrees:* A *Prof. Accred.:* Dental Assisting, Nursing (A) *CEO:* Pres. Kenneth J. Minnaert
Enroll: 5,313   (360) 754-7711

SOUTH SEATTLE COMMUNITY COLLEGE
6000 16th Ave., S.W., Seattle 98106 *Type:*
Public (district) junior *System:* Seattle Community College District *Accred.:* 1975/1995
(NASC) *Calendar:* Qtr. plan *Degrees:* A
CEO: Pres. Peter C. Ku
Enroll: 6,554   (206) 764-5300

SPOKANE COMMUNITY COLLEGE
N. 1810 Greene St., Spokane 99207 *Type:*
Public (district) junior *System:* Community
Colleges of Spokane *Accred.:* 1967/1995
(NASC) *Calendar:* Qtr. plan *Degrees:* A
Prof. Accred.: Cardiovascular Technology,
Dental Assisting, EMT-Paramedic, Medical
Record Technology, Nursing (A), Optometric Technician, Respiratory Therapy, Surgical Technology *CEO:* Pres. James Williams
Enroll: 6,914   (509) 533-7000

SPOKANE FALLS COMMUNITY COLLEGE
W. 3410 Fort George Wright Dr., Spokane
99204 *Type:* Public (district) junior *System:*
Community Colleges of Spokane *Accred.:*
1967/1993 (NASC) *Calendar:* Qtr. plan
Degrees: A *CEO:* Pres. Vern Jerome Loland
Enroll: 6,721   (509) 533-3500

TACOMA COMMUNITY COLLEGE
5900 S. 12th St., Tacoma 98465 *Type:* Public (district) junior *System:* Washington State
Board for Community and Technical Colleges *Accred.:* 1967/1994 (NASC) *Calendar:* Qtr. plan *Degrees:* A *Prof. Accred.:*
EMT-Paramedic, Medical Record Technology, Nursing (A), Radiography, Respiratory
Therapy, Respiratory Therapy Technology
CEO: Pres. Raymond J. Needham
Enroll: 8,037   (206) 566-5000

UNIVERSITY OF PUGET SOUND
Tacoma 98416 *Type:* Private (United Methodist) *Accred.:* 1923/1994 (NASC) *Calendar:* 4-1-4 plan *Degrees:* B, M *Prof. Accred.:* Law,
Music, Occupational Therapy, Physical Therapy *CEO:* Pres. Susan Resneck Pierce
Enroll: 3,163   (206) 756-3100

UNIVERSITY OF WASHINGTON
Seattle 98195 *Type:* Public (state) *System:*
Washington Higher Education Coordinating
Board *Accred.:* 1918/1993 (NASC) *Calendar:* Qtr. plan *Degrees:* B, M, P, D *Prof.
Accred.:* Accounting (A,C), Audiology,
Business (B,M), Clinical Lab Scientist, Clinical Psychology, Combined Prosthodontics,
Construction Education (B), Dentistry,
Endodontics, Engineering (aerospace,
ceramic, chemical, civil, computer, electrical, industrial, mechanical, metallurgical),
Forestry, General Practice Residency, Health
Services Administration, Journalism (B,M),
Landscape Architecture (B,M), Law, Librarianship, Medical Record Administration,
Medicine, Music, Nursing (B,M), Occupational Therapy, Oral and Maxillofacial
Surgery, Orthodontics, Pediatric Dentistry
(prelim. provisional), Periodontics, Physical
Therapy, Physician Assisting/Surgeon
Assisting, Planning (M), Psychology Internship, School Psychology, Social Work
(B,M), Speech-Language Pathology, Teacher Education, Theatre *CEO:* Pres. Richard L.
McCormick
Enroll: 33,719   (206) 543-2100

WALLA WALLA COLLEGE
204 S. College Ave., College Place 99324-1198 *Type:* Private (Seventh-Day Adventist)
liberal arts *Accred.:* 1932/1992 (NASC) *Calendar:* Qtr. plan *Degrees:* A, B, M *Prof.
Accred.:* Engineering (general), Music,
Nursing (B), Social Work (B,M) *CEO:* Pres.
W.G. Nelson
Enroll: 1,725   (509) 527-2615

WALLA WALLA COMMUNITY COLLEGE
500 Tausick Way, Walla Walla 99362 *Type:*
Public (district) junior *System:* Washington
State Board for Community and Technical
Colleges *Accred.:* 1969/1995 (NASC) *Calendar:* Qtr. plan *Degrees:* A *Prof. Accred.:*
Nursing (A), Respiratory Therapy *CEO:*
Pres. Steven L. Van Ausdle
Enroll: 5,641   (509) 522-2500

WASHINGTON STATE UNIVERSITY
Pullman 99164-1046 *Type:* Public (state)
System: Washington Higher Education Coordinating Board *Accred.:* 1918/1995 (NASC)
Calendar: Sem. plan *Degrees:* B, M, P, D
Prof. Accred.: Accounting (A,C), Athletic
Training, Audiology, Business (B,M), Clini-

cal Psychology, Construction Education (B), Counseling Psychology, Dietetics (coordinated), Engineering (agricultural, chemical, civil, electrical, geological/geophysical, materials), Forestry, Interior Design, Landscape Architecture (B), Music, Nursing (B,M), Psychology Internship, Recreation and Leisure Services (B), Speech-Language Pathology, Teacher Education *CEO:* Pres. Samuel H. Smith
Enroll: 19,035   (509) 335-3564

SPOKANE CAMPUS
601 W. First Ave., Spokane 99204-0399 *System:* Washington Higher Education Coordinating Board *Accred.:* 1989 (NASC) *Calendar:* Sem. plan *Degrees:* B, M
FTE Enroll: 314   (509) 358-7500

TRI CITIES CAMPUS
100 Sprout Rd., Richland 99352-1643 *System:* Washington Higher Education Coordinating Board *Accred.:* 1989 (NASC) *Calendar:* Sem. plan *Degrees:* B, M
Enroll: 1,300   (509) 372-7000

VANCOUVER CAMPUS
1812 E. McLoughlin Blvd., Vancouver 98663-3597 *System:* Washington Higher Education Coordinating Board *Accred.:* 1989 (NASC) *Calendar:* Sem. plan *Degrees:* B, M
Enroll: 900   (360) 737-2010

WENATCHEE VALLEY COLLEGE
1300 Fifth St., Wenatchee 98801 *Type:* Public (district) junior *System:* Washington State Board for Community and Technical Colleges *Accred.:* 1948/1995 (NASC) *Calendar:* Qtr. plan *Degrees:* A *Prof. Accred.:* Clinical Lab Technology (A), Radiography *CEO:* Interim Pres. Woody Ahn
Enroll: 3,737   (509) 662-1651

WESTERN WASHINGTON UNIVERSITY
Bellingham 98225 *Type:* Public (state) liberal arts and teachers *System:* Washington

Higher Education Coordinating Board *Accred.:* 1921/1993 (NASC) *Calendar:* Qtr. plan *Degrees:* B, M *Prof. Accred.:* Audiology, Business (B,M), Computer Science, Counseling, Engineering Technology (electrical, manufacturing), Music, Recreation and Leisure Services (B), Speech-Language Pathology, Teacher Education *CEO:* Pres. Karen W. Morse
Enroll: 10,598   (360) 650-3000

WHATCOM COMMUNITY COLLEGE
237 W. Kellogg Rd., Bellingham 98226 *Type:* Public (district) junior *System:* Washington State Board for Community and Technical Colleges *Accred.:* 1976/1991 (NASC) *Calendar:* Qtr. plan *Degrees:* A *Prof. Accred.:* Physical Therapy Assisting *CEO:* Pres. Harold G. Heiner
Enroll: 4,706   (360) 676-2170

WHITMAN COLLEGE
345 Boyer, Walla Walla 99362 *Type:* Private liberal arts *Accred.:* 1918/1994 (NASC) *Calendar:* Sem. plan *Degrees:* B *CEO:* Pres. Thomas Cronin
Enroll: 1,350   (509) 527-5111

WHITWORTH COLLEGE
Spokane 99251-0002 *Type:* Private (United Presbyterian) liberal arts *Accred.:* 1933/1994 (NASC) *Calendar:* 4-1-4 plan *Degrees:* B, M *Prof. Accred.:* Music, Nursing (B,M), Teacher Education *CEO:* Pres. William P. Robinson
Enroll: 2,003   (509) 466-1000

YAKIMA VALLEY COMMUNITY COLLEGE
P.O. Box 1647, Yakima 98907 *Type:* Public (district) junior *System:* Washington State Board for Community and Technical Colleges *Accred.:* 1948/1993 (NASC) *Calendar:* Qtr. plan *Degrees:* A, Talmudic, C *Prof. Accred.:* Dental Hygiene, Nursing (A), Occupational Therapy Assisting, Radiography *CEO:* Pres. Linda Kaminski
Enroll: 6,051   (509) 575-2350

WEST VIRGINIA

ALDERSON-BROADDUS COLLEGE
Philippi 26416 *Type:* Private (Baptist) liberal arts *Accred.:* 1959/1993 (NCA) *Calendar:* Sem. plan *Degrees:* A, B, M *Prof. Accred.:* Nursing (B), Physician Assisting/Surgeon Assisting, Teacher Education *CEO:* Pres. Stephen E. Markwood
Enroll: 899   (304) 457-1700

APPALACHIAN BIBLE COLLEGE
100 N. Sand Branch Rd., P.O. Box ABC, Bradley 25818 *Type:* Private (Baptist) *Accred.:* 1967/1987 (AABC) *Calendar:* Sem. plan *Degrees:* A, B, C *CEO:* Pres. Daniel L. Anderson
FTE Enroll: 204   (304) 877-6428

BETHANY COLLEGE
Bethany 26032 *Type:* Private (Disciples of Christ) liberal arts *Accred.:* 1926/1989 (NCA) *Calendar:* Sem. plan *Degrees:* B *Prof. Accred.:* Social Work (B), Teacher Education *CEO:* Pres. D. Duane Cummins
Enroll: 743   (304) 829-7000

BLUEFIELD STATE COLLEGE
219 Rock St., Bluefield 24701 *Type:* Public (state) liberal arts and teachers *System:* State College System of West Virginia *Accred.:* 1951/1992 (NCA) *Calendar:* Sem. plan *Degrees:* A, B, C *Prof. Accred.:* Engineering Technology (architectural, civil/construction, electrical, mechanical, mining), Nursing (A), Radiography, Teacher Education *CEO:* Pres. Robert E. Moore
Enroll: 2,609   (800) 344-8892

GREENBRIER COMMUNITY COLLEGE CENTER
Drawer 151, Lewisburg 24901
                                 (304) 645-3303

THE COLLEGE OF WEST VIRGINIA
609 S. Kanawha St., Beckley 25801 *Type:* Private *Accred.:* 1981/1994 (NCA) *Calendar:* Sem. plan *Degrees:* A, B, C *Prof. Accred.:* Respiratory Therapy *CEO:* Pres. Charles H. Polk
Enroll: 1,919   (800) 766-6067

CONCORD COLLEGE
P.O. Box 1000, Athens 24712 *Type:* Public (state) liberal arts and teachers *System:* State College System of West Virginia *Accred.:* 1931/1988 (NCA) *Calendar:* Sem. plan *Degrees:* A, B *Prof. Accred.:* Social Work (B), Teacher Education *CEO:* Pres. Jerry L. Beasley
Enroll: 2,623   (304) 384-3115

DAVIS & ELKINS COLLEGE
100 Campus Dr., Elkins 26241 *Type:* Private (Presbyterian) liberal arts *Accred.:* 1946/1990 (NCA) *Calendar:* 4-1-4 plan *Degrees:* A, B, M, C *Prof. Accred.:* Nursing (A) *CEO:* Pres. Dorothy I. MacConkey
Enroll: 877   (800) 624-3157

FAIRMONT STATE COLLEGE
Locust Ave., Fairmont 26554 *Type:* Public (state) liberal arts and professional *System:* State College System of West Virginia *Accred.:* 1928/1992 (NCA) *Calendar:* Sem. plan *Degrees:* A, B, C *Prof. Accred.:* Clinical Lab Technology (A), Engineering Technology (civil/construction, electrical, mechanical, mechanical drafting/design), Medical Record Technology, Nursing (A), Teacher Education *CEO:* Pres. Robert J. Dillman
Enroll: 6,355   (800) 641-5678

GLENVILLE STATE COLLEGE
200 High St., Glenville 26351 *Type:* Public (state) liberal arts and teachers *System:* State College System of West Virginia *Accred.:* 1949/1992 (NCA) *Calendar:* Sem. plan *Degrees:* A, B *Prof. Accred.:* Teacher Education *CEO:* Pres. William K. Simmons
Enroll: 2,269   (800) 344-4407

HUNTINGTON JUNIOR COLLEGE OF BUSINESS
900 Fifth Ave., Huntington 25701 *Type:* Private junior *Accred.:* 1969/1994 (ACICS); 1993/1995 (NCA candidate) *Calendar:* Qtr. plan *Degrees:* A, C *CEO:* Dir. Carolyn Smith
Enroll: 534   (800) 344-4522

MARSHALL UNIVERSITY
400 Hal Greer Blvd., Huntington 25755 *Type:* Public (state) *System:* University System of West Virginia *Accred.:* 1928/1986 (NCA) *Calendar:* Sem. plan *Degrees:* A, B, M, P, D, C *Prof. Accred.:* Clinical Lab Scientist, Clinical Lab Technology (A), Journalism, Medical Record Technology, Medicine, Music, Nursing (A,B), Recreation and Leisure Services (B), Social Work (B), Speech-Language Pathology, Teacher Education *CEO:* Pres. J. Wade Gilley
Enroll: 10,303   (800) 642-3463

MOUNTAIN STATE COLLEGE
Spring at 16th St., Parkersburg 26101 *Type:* Private business *Accred.:* 1977/2000 (ACICS) *Calendar:* Qtr. plan *Degrees:* A, C *CEO:* Dir. Judith Sutton
                                   (304) 485-5487

NATIONAL EDUCATION CENTER—CROSS LANES NATIONAL INSTITUTE OF TECHNOLOGY CAMPUS
5514 Big Tyler Rd., Cross Lanes 25311-9998 *Type:* Private *Accred.:* 1971/1986 (ACCSCT) *Degrees:* A, C *CEO:* Dir. Dennis Hirsch
                                   (304) 776-6290

OHIO VALLEY COLLEGE
College Pkwy., Parkersburg 26101 *Type:* Private (Churches of Christ) *Accred.:* 1978/1993 (NCA) *Calendar:* Sem. plan *Degrees:* A, B, C *CEO:* Pres. E. Keith Stotts
Enroll: 282   (304) 485-7384

POTOMAC STATE COLLEGE OF WEST VIRGINIA UNIVERSITY
Fort Ave., Keyser 26726 *Type:* Public (state) junior *System:* University System of West Virginia *Accred.:* 1926/1994 (NCA) *Calendar:* Sem. plan *Degrees:* A, C *CEO:* Pres. Kathrine Brailer
Enroll: 1,056   (800) 262-7332

SALEM-TEIKYO UNIVERSITY
223 W. Main St., Salem 26426 *Type:* Private liberal arts *Accred.:* 1963/1995 (NCA) *Calendar:* Sem. plan *Degrees:* A, B, M *CEO:* Pres. Ronald E. Ohl
Enroll: 738   (304) 782-5011

SHEPHERD COLLEGE
Shepherdstown 25443 *Type:* Public (state) liberal arts and teachers *System:* State College System of West Virginia *Accred.:* 1950/1992 (NCA) *Calendar:* Sem. plan *Degrees:* A, B *Prof. Accred.:* Music, Nursing (A,B), Social Work (B), Teacher Education *CEO:* Interim Pres. John P. Watkins
Enroll: 3,648   (304) 876-2511

SOUTHERN WEST VIRGINIA COMMUNITY AND TECHNICAL COLLEGE
P.O. Box 2900, Mount Gay 25637 *Type:* Public (state) junior *System:* State College System of West Virginia *Accred.:* 1971/1990 (NCA) *Calendar:* Sem. plan *Degrees:* A, C *Prof. Accred.:* Nursing (A), Radiography *CEO:* Pres. Travis P. Kirkland
Enroll: 3,231   (304) 792-7098

THE UNIVERSITY OF CHARLESTON
2300 MacCorkle Ave., Charleston 25304 *Type:* Private liberal arts *Accred.:* 1958/1995 (NCA) *Calendar:* Sem. plan *Degrees:* A, B, M *Prof. Accred.:* Nursing (A,B), Radiography, Respiratory Therapy, Teacher Education *CEO:* Pres. Edwin H. Welch
Enroll: 1,363   (304) 357-4800

WEBSTER COLLEGE
412 Fairmont Ave., Fairmont 26554 *Type:* Private junior *Accred.:* 1968/1999 (ACICS) *Calendar:* Qtr. plan *Degrees:* A, C *CEO:* Dir. Todd A. Matthews, Sr.
                                   (304) 363-8824

PIERCE CAMPUS
N. Bridge Plaza, 2192 N. U.S. Rte. 1, Fort Pierce, FL 34946 *Accred.:* 1988 (ACICS)
                                   (407) 464-7474

GAINESVILLE CAMPUS
2002 N.W. 13th St., Gainesville, FL 32609 *Accred.:* 1987 (ACICS)
                                   (904) 375-8014

BEW PORT RICHEY CAMPUS
5623 U.S. Hwy. 19, Ste. 300, New Port Richey, FL 34652 *Accred.:* 1993 (ACICS)
                                   (813) 849-4993

OCALA CAMPUS
1530 S.W. Third Ave., Ocala, FL 34474 *Accred.:* 1985/1987 (ACICS)
(904) 629-1941

WEST LIBERTY STATE COLLEGE
West Liberty 26074 *Type:* Public (state) liberal arts and professional *System:* State College System of West Virginia *Accred.:* 1942/1988 (NCA) *Calendar:* Sem. plan *Degrees:* A, B *Prof. Accred.:* Clinical Lab Scientist, Dental Hygiene, Music, Teacher Education *CEO:* Interim Pres. Donald C. Danton
Enroll: 2,381   (304) 336-5000

WEST VIRGINIA BUSINESS COLLEGE
1052 Main St., Wheeling 26003 *Type:* Private business *Accred.:* 1990/1996 (ACICS) *Degrees:* A, C *CEO:* Pres. Teddy Tarr
(304) 232-0631

CLARKSBURG CAMPUS
215 W. Main St., Clarksburg 26301 business *Accred.:* 1966/1990 (ACICS) *Calendar:* Qtr. plan
(304) 624-7695

WEST VIRGINIA CAREER COLLEGE
1000 Virginia St., E., Charleston 25301 *Type:* Private business *Accred.:* 1971/1995 (ACICS) *Calendar:* Qtr. plan *Degrees:* A, C *CEO:* Exec. Vice Pres. Thomas A. Crouse
(304) 345-2820

DAYTONA BEACH CAMPUS
Nova Village Market Plaza, 1104 Beville Rd., Ste. J, Daytona Beach, FL 32114 *Accred.:* 1989 (ACICS)
(904) 255-0175

WEST VIRGINIA CAREER COLLEGE
148 Willey St., Morgantown 26505 *Type:* Private business *Accred.:* 1953/1995 (ACICS) *Calendar:* Qtr. plan *Degrees:* A, C *CEO:* Exec. Dir. Patricia A. Callen
(304) 296-8282

FURNACE CAMPUS
200 College Dr., Lemont Furnace, PA 15456 *Accred.:* 1987 (ACICS)
(412) 437-4600

WEST VIRGINIA GRADUATE COLLEGE
100 Angus E. Peyton Dr., S., Charleston 25303-1600 *Type:* Public (state) graduate only *System:* University System of West Virginia *Accred.:* 1972/1991 (NCA) *Calendar:* Sem. plan *Degrees:* M, P, C *Prof. Accred.:* Nurse Anesthesia Education, Teacher Education *CEO:* Pres. Dennis P. Prisk
Enroll: 2,736   (800) 642-9842

WEST VIRGINIA INSTITUTE OF TECHNOLOGY
405 Fayette Pike, Montgomery 25136 *Type:* Public (state) *System:* State College System of West Virginia *Accred.:* 1956/1994 (NCA) *Calendar:* Sem. plan *Degrees:* A, B, M, C *Prof. Accred.:* Dental Hygiene, Engineering Technology (civil/construction, electrical, mechanical, mechanical drafting/design), Engineering (chemical, civil, electrical, mechanical) *CEO:* Pres. John P. Carrier
Enroll: 2,678   (304) 442-3071

WEST VIRGINIA NORTHERN COMMUNITY COLLEGE
1704 Market St., Wheeling 26003 *Type:* Public (state) junior *System:* State College System of West Virginia *Accred.:* 1972/1993 (NCA) *Calendar:* Sem. plan *Degrees:* A, C *Prof. Accred.:* Clinical Lab Technology (A), Nursing (A), Respiratory Therapy, Surgical Technology *CEO:* Pres. Linda S. Dunn
Enroll: 2,921   (304) 233-5900

WEST VIRGINIA SCHOOL OF OSTEOPATHIC MEDICINE
400 N. Lee St., Lewisburg 24901 *Type:* Public (state) professional *System:* University System of West Virginia *Calendar:* Sem. plan *Degrees:* P *Prof. Accred.:* Osteopathy *CEO:* Pres. Olen E. Jones, Jr.
Enroll: 233   (304) 645-6270

WEST VIRGINIA STATE COLLEGE
P.O. Box 399, Institute 25112 *Type:* Public (state) liberal arts and professional *System:* State College System of West Virginia *Accred.:* 1927/1995 (NCA) *Calendar:* Sem. plan *Degrees:* A, B *Prof. Accred.:* Engineering Technology (electrical), Nuclear Medicine Technology, Recreation and Leisure

Services (B), Social Work (B), Teacher Education *CEO:* Pres. Hazo W. Carter, Jr.
Enroll: 4,519   (304) 766-3000

WEST VIRGINIA UNIVERSITY
Box 6201, Morgantown 26506-6201 *Type:* Public (state) *System:* University System of West Virginia *Accred.:* 1926/1994 (NCA) *Calendar:* Sem. plan *Degrees:* B, M, D *Prof. Accred.:* Art, Audiology, Business (B,M), Clinical Lab Scientist, Clinical Psychology, Counseling, Counseling Psychology, Dental Hygiene, Dentistry, Dietetics (internship), Endodontics, Engineering (aerospace, chemical, civil, computer, electrical, industrial, mechanical, mining, petroleum), Forestry, General Dentistry, General Practice Residency, Interior Design, Journalism (B,M), Landscape Architecture (B), Law, Medicine, Music, Nursing (B,M), Oral and Maxillofacial Surgery, Orthodontics, Physical Therapy, Psychology Internship, Public Administration, Recreation and Leisure Services (B), Rehabilitation Counseling, Social Work (B,M), Speech-Language Pathology, Teacher Education, Theatre *CEO:* Pres. David C. Hardesty, Jr.
Enroll: 15,383   (304) 293-0111

WEST VIRGINIA UNIVERSITY AT PARKERSBURG
Rte. 5, Box 167-A, Parkersburg 26101 *Type:* Public (state) *System:* University System of West Virginia *Accred.:* 1971/1994 (NCA) *Calendar:* Sem. plan *Degrees:* A, B, C *Prof. Accred.:* Nursing (A) *CEO:* Pres. Eldon L. Miller
Enroll: 3,651   (304) 424-8000

WEST VIRGINIA WESLEYAN COLLEGE
College Ave., Buckhannon 26201 *Type:* Private (United Methodist) liberal arts *Accred.:* 1927/1990 (NCA) *Calendar:* 4-1-4 plan *Degrees:* B, M *Prof. Accred.:* Music, Nursing (B), Teacher Education *CEO:* Pres. Willliam R. Haden
Enroll: 1,620   (304) 473-8000

WHEELING JESUIT COLLEGE
316 Washington Ave., Wheeling 26003 *Type:* Private (Roman Catholic) liberal arts *Accred.:* 1962/1989 (NCA) *Calendar:* Sem. plan *Degrees:* B, M *Prof. Accred.:* Nuclear Medicine Technology, Nursing (B), Physical Therapy, Respiratory Therapy *CEO:* Pres. Thomas S. Acker, S.J.
Enroll: 1,296   (304) 243-2000

WISCONSIN

ALVERNO COLLEGE
3401 S. 39th St., P.O. Box 343922, Milwaukee 53234-3922 *Type:* Private (Roman Catholic) liberal arts primarily for women *Accred.:* 1951/1987 (NCA) *Calendar:* 4-1-4 plan *Degrees:* A, B, C *Prof. Accred.:* Music, Nursing (B), Teacher Education *CEO:* Pres. Joel Read, O.S.F.
Enroll: 2,457　　　　　　(414) 382-6000

BELLIN COLLEGE OF NURSING
725 S. Webster Ave., P.O. Box 23400, Green Bay 54305-3400 *Type:* Private professional *Accred.:* 1989/1994 (NCA) *Calendar:* 4-1-4 plan *Degrees:* B, C *Prof. Accred.:* Nursing (B) *CEO:* Pres. Joyce A. McCollum
Enroll: 217　　　　　　　(414) 433-3560

BELOIT COLLEGE
700 College St., Beloit 53511 *Type:* Private liberal arts *Accred.:* 1913/1987 (NCA) *Calendar:* Sem. plan *Degrees:* B, M, C *CEO:* Pres. Victor E. Ferrall, Jr.
Enroll: 1,246　　　　　　(608) 363-2000

BLACKHAWK TECHNICAL COLLEGE
P.O. Box 5009, Janesville 53547-5009 *Type:* Public (district) 2-year *Accred.:* 1978/1990 (NCA) *Calendar:* Sem. plan *Degrees:* A, C *Prof. Accred.:* Dental Assisting, Medical Assisting (AMA), Nursing (A), Physical Therapy Assisting *CEO:* Pres. James C. Catania
Enroll: 2,338　　　　　　(608) 756-4121

CARDINAL STRITCH COLLEGE
6801 N. Yates Rd., Milwaukee 53217 *Type:* Private (Roman Catholic) liberal arts *Accred.:* 1953/1994 (NCA) *Calendar:* Sem. plan *Degrees:* A, B, M, C *Prof. Accred.:* Nursing (A,B), Teacher Education *CEO:* Pres. Mary Lea Schneider, O.S.F.
Enroll: 3,017　　　　　(800) 347-8822

EDINA CAMPUS
3300 Edinborough Way, Ste. 505, Edina, MN 55435
　　　　　　　　　　　(612) 835-6418

MADISON CAMPUS
8071 Excelsior Dr., Madison 53717
　　　　　　　　　　　(608) 831-2722

CARROLL COLLEGE
100 N. East Ave., Waukesha 53186 *Type:* Private (Presbyterian) liberal arts *Accred.:* 1913/1988 (NCA) *Calendar:* 4-1-4 plan *Degrees:* B, M *Prof. Accred.:* Nursing (B), Social Work (B) *CEO:* Pres. Frank S. Falcone
Enroll: 2,243　　　　　　(414) 547-1211

CARTHAGE COLLEGE
2001 Alford Dr., Kenosha 53140 *Type:* Private (Lutheran) liberal arts *Accred.:* 1916/1995 (NCA) *Calendar:* 4-1-4 plan *Degrees:* B, M *Prof. Accred.:* Music, Social Work (B) *CEO:* Pres. F. Gregory Campbell
Enroll: 2,071　　　　　　(414) 551-8500

CHIPPEWA VALLEY TECHNICAL COLLEGE
620 W. Clairemont Ave., Eau Claire 54701 *Type:* Public (district) 2-year *Accred.:* 1973/1993 (NCA) *Calendar:* Sem. plan *Degrees:* A, C *Prof. Accred.:* Clinical Lab Technology (A), Diagnostic Medical Sonography, Histologic Technology, Medical Record Technology, Nursing (A), Radiography *CEO:* Pres. William A. Ihlenfeldt
Enroll: 3,465　　　　　　(715) 833-6200

COLUMBIA COLLEGE OF NURSING
2121 E. Newport Ave., Milwaukee 53211 *Type:* Private professional *Accred.:* 1988/1993 (NCA) *Calendar:* Sem. plan *Degrees:* B *CEO:* Dean/CEO Marion H. Snyder
Enroll: 397　　　　　　　(414) 961-3530

CONCORDIA UNIVERSITY WISCONSIN
12800 N. Lake Shore Dr., 9 W., Mequon 53092-2402 *Type:* Private (Lutheran) *Accred.:* 1964/1991 (NCA) *Calendar:* 4-1-4 plan *Degrees:* A, B, M *Prof. Accred.:* Nursing (B), Physical Therapy, Social Work (B-candidate) *CEO:* Pres. R. John Buuck
Enroll: 2,957　　　　　　(414) 243-5700

EDGEWOOD COLLEGE
855 Woodrow St., Madison 53711 *Type:* Private (Roman Catholic) liberal arts *Accred.:*

1958/1988 (NCA) *Calendar:* Sem. plan *Degrees:* A, B, M *Prof. Accred.:* Nursing (B), Teacher Education *CEO:* Pres. James A. Ebben
Enroll: 1,468   (800) 444-4861

Fox Valley Technical College
1825 N. Bluemound Dr., P.O. Box 2277, Appleton 54913-2277 *Type:* Public (district) 2-year *Accred.:* 1974/1986 (NCA) *Calendar:* Sem. plan *Degrees:* A, C *Prof. Accred.:* Dental Assisting, Nursing (A), Occupational Therapy Assisting *CEO:* Pres./District Dir. H. Victor Baldi
Enroll: 8,108   (414) 735-5600

Gateway Technical College
3520 30th Ave., Kenosha 53144 *Type:* Public (district) 2-year *Accred.:* 1970/1990 (NCA) *Calendar:* Sem. plan *Degrees:* A, C *Prof. Accred.:* Dental Assisting, Medical Assisting (AMA), Medical Record Technology, Nursing (A), Surgical Technology *CEO:* Pres. Carole Johnson
Enroll: 8,513   (414) 656-6900

ITT Technical Institute
6300 W. Layton Ave., Greenfield 53220-4612 *Type:* Private *Accred.:* 1989/1991 (ACCSCT) *Degrees:* A *CEO:* Dir. Elizabeth A. Franck
                                  (414) 282-9494

Lac Courte Oreilles Ojibwa Community College
Rte. 2, Box 2357, Hayward 54843 *Type:* Public (tribal) junior *Accred.:* 1993 (NCA) *Calendar:* Sem. plan *Degrees:* A, C *CEO:* Pres. Jasjit S. Minhas
Enroll: 468   (715) 634-4790

Lakeland College
P.O. Box 359, Sheboygan 53082-0359 *Type:* Private (United Church of Christ) liberal arts *Accred.:* 1961/1992 (NCA) *Calendar:* 4-1-4 plan *Degrees:* A, B, M *CEO:* Pres. David R. Black
Enroll: 3,299   (414) 565-2111

Lakeshore Technical College
1290 North Ave., Cleveland 53015 *Type:* Public (district) 2-year *Accred.:* 1977/1992

(NCA) *Calendar:* Sem. plan *Degrees:* A, C *Prof. Accred.:* Dental Assisting, Medical Assisting (AMA), Nursing (A), Radiography *CEO:* Pres./District Dir. Dennis Ladwig
Enroll: 2,516   (800) 443-2129

Lawrence University
P.O. Box 599, Appleton 54912 *Type:* Private liberal arts *Accred.:* 1913/1989 (NCA) *Calendar:* Qtr. plan *Degrees:* B *Prof. Accred.:* Music *CEO:* Pres. Richard Warch
Enroll: 1,146   (414) 832-7000

Madison Area Technical College
3550 Anderson St., Madison 53703 *Type:* Public (district) 2-year *Accred.:* 1969/1993 (NCA) *Calendar:* Sem. plan *Degrees:* A, C *Prof. Accred.:* Clinical Lab Technology (A), Dental Assisting, Dental Hygiene, Medical Assisting (AMA), Nursing (A), Occupational Therapy Assisting, Radiography, Respiratory Therapy, Surgical Technology, Veterinary Technology *CEO:* Pres. Beverly S. Simone
Enroll: 15,178   (608) 246-6676

Madison Junior College of Business
31 South Henry St., Madison 53703-3110 *Type:* Private junior *Accred.:* 1953/1995 (ACICS); 1992/1994 (NCA candidate) *Calendar:* Tri. plan *Degrees:* A, C *CEO:* Pres. Jeffry S. Sears
Enroll: 176   (608) 251-6522

Marantha Baptist Bible College
745 W. Main St., P.O. Box 438, Watertown 53094 *Type:* Private *Accred.:* 1993 (NCA) *Calendar:* Sem. plan *Degrees:* A, B, M, C *CEO:* Pres. Arno Q. Weniger
Enroll: 600   (414) 261-9300

Marian College of Fond du Lac
45 S. National Ave., Fond du Lac 54935 *Type:* Private (Roman Catholic) liberal arts *Accred.:* 1960/1989 (NCA) *Calendar:* Sem. plan *Degrees:* B, M *Prof. Accred.:* Nursing (B), Social Work (B), Teacher Education *CEO:* Pres. Matthew G. Flanigan
Enroll: 1,852   (414) 923-7600

MARQUETTE UNIVERSITY
P.O. Box 1881, 615 N. 11th St., Milwaukee
53233 *Type:* Private (Roman Catholic)
Accred.: 1922/1993 (NCA) *Calendar:* Sem.
plan *Degrees:* A, B, M, P, D *Prof. Accred.:*
Accounting (A), Business (B,M), Combined
Prosthodontics, Dental Hygiene, Dentistry,
Endodontics, Engineering (bioengineering,
civil, electrical, industrial, mechanical),
General Dentistry (prelim. provisional),
Journalism (B,M), Law, Nursing (B,M),
Orthodontics, Physical Therapy, Social Work
(B), Speech-Language Pathology, Teacher
Education *CEO:* Pres. Albert J. DiUlio, S.J.
Enroll: 7,722   (414) 288-7223

MEDICAL COLLEGE OF WISCONSIN
8701 Watertown Plank Rd., Milwaukee
53226 *Type:* Private *Accred.:* 1922/1987
(NCA) *Calendar:* Sem. plan *Degrees:* M, D,
C *Prof. Accred.:* Medicine, Oral and Maxillofacial Surgery, Radiation Therapy Technology, *CEO:* Pres. T. Michael Bolger
Enroll: 1,243   (414) 456-8296

MID-STATE TECHNICAL COLLEGE
500 32nd St. N., Wisconsin Rapids 54494
Type: Public (district) 2-year *Accred.:* 1979/
1994 (NCA) *Calendar:* Sem. plan *Degrees:*
A, C *Prof. Accred.:* Medical Assisting
(AMA), Respiratory Therapy, Surgical Tech-
nology *CEO:* Pres. Brian Oehler
Enroll: 4,287   (715) 423-5650

MILWAUKEE AREA TECHNICAL COLLEGE
700 W. State St., Milwaukee 53233 *Type:*
Public (district) 2-year *Accred.:* 1959/1989
(NCA) *Calendar:* Sem. plan *Degrees:* A, C
Prof. Accred.: Clinical Lab Technology (A),
Dental Hygiene, Dental Laboratory Technol-
ogy, Funeral Service Education (Mortuary
Science), Medical Assisting (AMA), Nurs-
ing (A), Occupational Therapy Assisting,
Physical Therapy Assisting, Practical Nurs-
ing, Radiography, Respiratory Therapy, Res-
piratory Therapy Technology, Surgical Tech-
nology *CEO:* Pres. John R. Birkholz
Enroll: 23,995   (414) 278-6600

MILWAUKEE INSTITUTE OF ART AND DESIGN
273 E. Erie St., Milwaukee 53202 *Type:* Pri-
vate professional *Accred.:* 1987/1993 (NCA)
Calendar: Sem. plan *Degrees:* B, C *Prof.
Accred.:* Art *CEO:* Pres. Terrence J. Coffman
Enroll: 511   (414) 276-7889

MILWAUKEE SCHOOL OF ENGINEERING
1025 N. Broadway, Milwaukee 53202-3109
Type: Private professional *Accred.:* 1971/
1994 (NCA) *Calendar:* Qtr. plan *Degrees:*
A, B, M, C *Prof. Accred.:* Engineering Technology (electrical, manufacturing, mechanical), Engineering (architectural, bioengineering, computer, electrical, industrial,
mechanical) *CEO:* Pres. Hermann Viets
Enroll: 2,195   (414) 277-7100

MORAINE PARK TECHNICAL COLLEGE
235 N. National Ave., P.O. Box 1940, Fond du
Lac 54936-1940 *Type:* Public (district) 2-year
Accred.: 1975/1995 (NCA) *Calendar:* Sem.
plan *Degrees:* A, C *Prof. Accred.:* Medical
Record Technology, Nursing (A), Practical
Nursing *CEO:* Pres. John J. Shanahan
Enroll: 6,100   (414) 922-8611

MOUNT MARY COLLEGE
2900 N. Menomonee River Pkwy., Milwaukee 53222 *Type:* Private (Roman Catholic)
liberal arts primarily for women *Accred.:*
1926/1993 (NCA) *Calendar:* Sem. plan
Degrees: B, M *Prof. Accred.:* Dietetics
(coordinated), Interior Design, Occupational
Therapy, Social Work (B), Teacher Education *CEO:* Interim Pres. Sally Mahoney
Enroll: 1,383   (414) 258-4810

MOUNT SENARIO COLLEGE
1500 W. College Ave., Ladysmith 54848
Type: Private liberal arts *Accred.:* 1975/1992
(NCA) *Calendar:* Sem. plan *Degrees:* A, B
Prof. Accred.: Social Work (B-candidate)
CEO: Pres. Norman L. Stewart
Enroll: 1,066   (715) 532-5511

NASHOTAH HOUSE
2777 Mission Rd., Nashotah 53058-9793
Type: Private (Episcopal) graduate only
Accred.: 1954/1988 (ATS) *Calendar:* Sem.
plan *Degrees:* M *CEO:* Pres. Gary W. Kriss
Enroll: 31   (414) 646-3371

NICOLET AREA TECHNICAL COLLEGE
Box 518, Rhinelander 54501 *Type:* Public (district) junior *Accred.:* 1975/1995 (NCA) *Calendar:* Sem. plan *Degrees:* A, C *Prof. Accred.:* Nursing (A) *CEO:* Pres. Adrian Lorbetske
Enroll: 1,826   (800) 544-3039

NORTHCENTRAL TECHNICAL COLLEGE
1000 Campus Dr., Wausau 54401 *Type:* Public (district) 2-year *Accred.:* 1970/1988 (NCA) *Calendar:* Sem. plan *Degrees:* A, C *Prof. Accred.:* Dental Hygiene, Nursing (A), Radiography, Surgical Technology *CEO:* Pres. Robert Ernst
Enroll: 3,459   (715) 675-3331

NORTHEAST WISCONSIN TECHNICAL COLLEGE
P.O. Box 19042, 2740 W. Mason St., Green Bay 54307-9042 *Type:* Public (district) 2-year *Accred.:* 1976/1991 (NCA) *Calendar:* Sem. plan *Degrees:* A, C *Prof. Accred.:* Dental Assisting, Dental Hygiene, Medical Assisting (AMA), Medical Record Technology, Nursing (A), Physical Therapy Assisting, Respiratory Therapy, Surgical Technology *CEO:* Pres. Gerald Prindiville
Enroll: 5,004   (414) 498-5400

MARINETTE CAMPUS
1601 University Ave., Marinette 54143
(715) 735-9361

STURGEON BAY CAMPUS
229 N. 14th Ave., Sturgeon Bay 54235-1317
(414) 743-2207

NORTHLAND COLLEGE
1411 Ellis Ave., Ashland 54806 *Type:* Private (United Church of Christ) liberal arts *Accred.:* 1957/1991 (NCA) *Calendar:* 4-1-4 plan *Degrees:* B *CEO:* Pres. Robert R. Parsonage
Enroll: 813   (715) 682-1699

RIPON COLLEGE
300 Seward St., P.O. Box 248, Ripon 54971 *Type:* Private liberal arts *Accred.:* 1913/1990 (NCA) *Calendar:* Sem. plan *Degrees:* B *CEO:* Pres. Paul B. Ranslow
Enroll: 732   (414) 748-8115

SACRED HEART SCHOOL OF THEOLOGY
P.O. Box 429, 7335 S. Hwy. 100, Hales Corners 53130-0429 *Type:* Private (Roman Catholic) graduate only *Accred.:* 1981/1988 (ATS); 1995 (NCA) *Calendar:* Sem. plan *Degrees:* M *CEO:* Pres. John A. Kasparek
Enroll: 116   (414) 425-8300

ST. FRANCIS SEMINARY
3257 S. Lake Dr., St. Francis 53235 *Type:* Private (Roman Catholic) *Accred.:* 1975/1990 (ATS); 1963/1991 (NCA) *Calendar:* Sem. plan *Degrees:* M *CEO:* Rector Andrew L. Nelson
Enroll: 90   (414) 747-6400

ST. NORBERT COLLEGE
100 Grant St., De Pere 54115-2099 *Type:* Private (Roman Catholic) liberal arts *Accred.:* 1934/1992 (NCA) *Calendar:* Sem. plan *Degrees:* B, M *CEO:* Pres. Thomas A. Manion
Enroll: 2,059   (800) 236-4878

SILVER LAKE COLLEGE
2406 S. Alverno Rd., Manitowoc 54220 *Type:* Private (Roman Catholic) liberal arts *Accred.:* 1959/1988 (NCA) *Calendar:* Sem. plan *Degrees:* A, B, M *Prof. Accred.:* Music, Nursing (B), Teacher Education *CEO:* Pres. Barbara Belinske, O.S.F.
Enroll: 829   (800) 236-4752

SOUTHWEST WISCONSIN TECHNICAL COLLEGE
1800 Bronson Blvd., Fennimore 53809 *Type:* Public (district) 2-year *Accred.:* 1976/1988 (NCA) *Calendar:* Sem. plan *Degrees:* A, C *Prof. Accred.:* Nursing (A), Practical Nursing *CEO:* Pres./District Dir. Richard A. Rogers
Enroll: 1,988   (608) 822-3262

STRATTON COLLEGE
1300 N. Jackson St., Milwaukee 53202-2608 *Type:* Private junior *Accred.:* 1966/1999 (ACICS) *Calendar:* Qtr. plan *Degrees:* A, C *Prof. Accred.:* Medical Assisting (AMA) *CEO:* Dir. Robert H. Ley
(414) 276-5200

UNIVERSITY OF WISCONSIN CENTERS
780 Regent St., P.O. Box 8680, Madison
53708-8680 *Type:* Public (state) *System:*
University of Wisconsin System *Accred.:*
1977/1993 (NCA) *Calendar:* Sem. plan
Degrees: A *CEO:* Chanc. Lee E. Grugel
Enroll: 9,919   (608) 262-1783

BARABOO-SAUK COUNTY CAMPUS
1006 Connie Rd., Baraboo 53913-1098
                        (608) 356-8351

BARRON COUNTY CAMPUS
1800 College Dr., Rice Lake 54868-2497
                        (715) 234-8176

FOND DU LAC CAMPUS
400 Campus Dr., Fond du Lac 54935-
2998
                        (414) 929-3600

FOX VALLEY CAMPUS
1478 Midway Rd., P.O. Box 8002,
Menasha 54952-8002
                        (414) 832-2600

MANITOWOC COUNTY CAMPUS
705 Viebahn St., Manitowoc 54220-6699
                        (414) 683-4700

MARATHON COUNTY CAMPUS
518 S. Seventh Ave., Wausau 54401-9602
                        (715) 845-9602

MARINETTE COUNTY CAMPUS
750 W. Bay Shore St., Marinette 54143-
4300
                        (715) 735-4300

MARSHFIELD-WOOD COUNTY CAMPUS
P.O. Box 150, 2000 W. 5th St., Marshfield
54449-0150
                        (715) 387-1147

RICHLAND CAMPUS
Hwy. 14 W., Richland Center 53581-1399
                        (608) 647-6186

ROCK COUNTY CAMPUS
2909 Kellogg Ave., Janesville 53545-5699
                        (608) 758-6565

SHEBOYGAN COUNTY CAMPUS
One University Dr., Sheboygan 53081-
4789
                        (414) 459-6600

WASHINGTON COUNTY CAMPUS
400 University Dr., West Bend 53095-
3699
                        (414) 335-5200

WAUKESHA COUNTY CAMPUS
1500 University Dr., Waukesha 53188-
2799
                        (414) 521-5200

UNIVERSITY OF WISCONSIN—EAU CLAIRE
P.O. Box 4004, Eau Claire 54701 *Type:* Pub-
lic (state) liberal arts and teachers *System:*
University of Wisconsin System *Accred.:*
1950/1990 (NCA) *Calendar:* Sem. plan
Degrees: A, B, M *Prof. Accred.:* Business
(B), Journalism (B), Music, Nursing (B,M),
Social Work (B), Speech-Language Pathol-
ogy *CEO:* Chanc. Larry G. Schnack
Enroll: 9,801   (715) 836-2637

UNIVERSITY OF WISCONSIN—GREEN BAY
2420 Nicolet Dr., Green Bay 54311-7001
Type: Public (state) liberal arts and teachers
System: University of Wisconsin System
Accred.: 1972/1988 (NCA) *Calendar:* Sem.
plan *Degrees:* A, B, M *Prof. Accred.:* Music,
Nursing (B), Social Work (B) *CEO:* Chanc.
Mark Perkins
Enroll: 5,268   (414) 465-2000

UNIVERSITY OF WISCONSIN—LA CROSSE
1725 State St., La Crosse 54601 *Type:* Pub-
lic (state) liberal arts and teachers *System:*
University of Wisconsin System *Accred.:*
1928/1986 (NCA) *Calendar:* Sem. plan
Degrees: A, B, M *Prof. Accred.:* Business
(B,M), Music, Nurse Anesthesia Education,
Physical Therapy, Recreation and Leisure
Services (B), Social Work (B), Teacher Edu-
cation *CEO:* Chanc. Judith L. Kuipers
Enroll: 8,005   (608) 785-8000

UNIVERSITY OF WISCONSIN—MADISON
500 Lincoln Dr., Madison 53706 *Type:* Public (state) liberal arts and teachers *System:*
University of Wisconsin System *Accred.:*

1913/1989 (NCA) *Calendar:* Sem. plan *Degrees:* B, M, P, D, C *Prof. Accred.:* Accounting (A,B,C), Art, Audiology, Business (B,M), Clinical Lab Scientist, Clinical Psychology, Construction Education (B), Counseling Psychology, Dietetics (coordinated), Dietetics (internship), Engineering (agricultural, chemical, civil, electrical, engineering mechanics, industrial, mechanical, metallurgical, nuclear, surveying), Forestry, Health Services Administration, Interior Design, Journalism (B,M), Landscape Architecture (B), Law, Librarianship, Medicine, Music, Nursing (B,M), Occupational Therapy, Physical Therapy, Physician Assisting/Surgeon Assisting, Planning (M), Psychology Internship, Public Administration, Rehabilitation Counseling, School Psychology, Social Work (B,M), Speech-Language Pathology, Theatre, Veterinary Medicine *CEO:* Chanc. David Ward
Enroll: 26,207   (608) 262-1234

UNIVERSITY OF WISCONSIN—MILWAUKEE
P.O. Box 413, Milwaukee 53201 *Type:* Public (state) liberal arts and teachers *System:* University of Wisconsin System *Accred.:* 1969/1995 (NCA) *Calendar:* Sem. plan *Degrees:* B, M, P, D *Prof. Accred.:* Business (B,M), Clinical Lab Scientist, Clinical Psychology, Engineering (civil, electrical, industrial, materials, mechanical), Librarianship, Medical Record Administration, Music, Nursing (B,M), Occupational Therapy, Planning (M), Public Administration, Rehabilitation Counseling, Social Work (B,M), Speech-Language Pathology *CEO:* Chanc. John H. Schroeder
Enroll: 18,244   (414) 229-4331

UNIVERSITY OF WISCONSIN—OSHKOSH
800 Algoma Blvd., Oshkosh 54901 *Type:* Public (state) liberal arts and teachers *System:* University of Wisconsin System *Accred.:* 1915/1987 (NCA) *Calendar:* Sem. plan *Degrees:* A, B, M *Prof. Accred.:* Audiology, Business (B,M), Counseling, Journalism (B), Music, Nursing (B,M), Social Work (B), Speech-Language Pathology *CEO:* Chanc. John E. Kerrigan
Enroll: 9,098   (414) 424-1234

UNIVERSITY OF WISCONSIN—PARKSIDE
Box 2000, Kenosha 53141-2000 *Type:* Public (state) liberal arts and teachers *System:* University of Wisconsin System *Accred.:* 1972/1993 (NCA) *Calendar:* Sem. plan *Degrees:* B, M *CEO:* Chanc. Eleanor J. Smith
Enroll: 4,827   (414) 595-2345

UNIVERSITY OF WISCONSIN—PLATTEVILLE
One University Plaza, Platteville 53818-3099 *Type:* Public (state) liberal arts and teachers *System:* University of Wisconsin System *Accred.:* 1918/1987 (NCA) *Calendar:* Sem. plan *Degrees:* A, B, M *Prof. Accred.:* Engineering (civil, electrical, industrial, mechanical), Music (A), Teacher Education *CEO:* Chanc. Robert G. Culbertson
Enroll: 4,916   (608) 342-1234

UNIVERSITY OF WISCONSIN—RIVER FALLS
410 S. 3rd St., River Falls 54022 *Type:* Public (state) liberal arts and teachers *System:* University of Wisconsin System *Accred.:* 1935/1988 (NCA) *Calendar:* Qtr. plan *Degrees:* A, B, M *Prof. Accred.:* Journalism (B), Music, Social Work (B), Speech-Language Pathology, Teacher Education *CEO:* Chanc. Gary A. Thibodeau
Enroll: 4,944   (715) 425-3201

UNIVERSITY OF WISCONSIN—STEVENS POINT
2100 Main St., Stevens Point 54481 *Type:* Public (state) liberal arts and teachers *System:* University of Wisconsin System *Accred.:* 1916/1988 (NCA) *Calendar:* Sem. plan *Degrees:* A, B, M *Prof. Accred.:* Art (A), Audiology, Dance, Forestry, Music, Speech-Language Pathology, Theatre (A) *CEO:* Interim Chanc. Howard Thoyre
Enroll: 7,983   (715) 346-0123

UNIVERSITY OF WISCONSIN—STOUT
328 Administration Bldg., P.O. Box 790, Menomonie 54751-0790 *Type:* Public (state) liberal arts and teachers *System:* University of Wisconsin System *Accred.:* 1928/1986 (NCA) *Calendar:* Sem. plan *Degrees:* B, M, P *Prof. Accred.:* Art, Construction Education, Marriage and Family Therapy (M),

Rehabilitation Counseling, Teacher Education *CEO:* Chanc. Charles W. Sorensen
Enroll: 6,756   (800) 447-8688

UNIVERSITY OF WISCONSIN—SUPERIOR
1800 Grand Ave., Superior 54880 *Type:* Public (state) liberal arts and teachers *System:* University of Wisconsin System *Accred.:* 1916/1993 (NCA) *Calendar:* Sem. plan *Degrees:* A, B, M, P *Prof. Accred.:* Music, Social Work (B) *CEO:* Acting Chanc. Jan G. Womack
Enroll: 2,123   (715) 394-8101

UNIVERSITY OF WISCONSIN—WHITEWATER
800 W. Main St., Whitewater 53190 *Type:* Public (state) liberal arts and teachers *System:* University of Wisconsin System *Accred.:* 1915/1986 (NCA) *Calendar:* Sem. plan *Degrees:* A, B, M *Prof. Accred.:* Business (B,M), Music, Social Work (B), Speech-Language Pathology, Teacher Education *CEO:* Chanc. H. Gaylon Greenhill
Enroll: 9,228   (414) 472-1918

VITERBO COLLEGE
815 S. Ninth St., La Crosse 54601 *Type:* Private (Roman Catholic) liberal arts *Accred.:* 1954/1989 (NCA) *Calendar:* Sem. plan *Degrees:* B, M *Prof. Accred.:* Dietetics (coordinated), Music, Nursing (B), Teacher Education *CEO:* Pres. William J. Medland
Enroll: 1,548   (608) 791-0040

WAUKESHA COUNTY TECHNICAL COLLEGE
800 Main St., Pewaukee 53072 *Type:* Public (district) 2-year *Accred.:* 1975/1990 (NCA) *Calendar:* Sem. plan *Degrees:* A, C *Prof. Accred.:* Medical Assisting (AMA), Nursing (A), Surgical Technology *CEO:* Pres. Richard Todd Anderson
Enroll: 5,876   (414) 691-5566

WESTERN WISCONSIN TECHNICAL COLLEGE
304 N. Sixth St., Box 908, La Crosse 54602 *Type:* Public (district) 2-year *Accred.:* 1972/1992 (NCA) *Calendar:* Qtr. plan *Degrees:* A, C *Prof. Accred.:* Clinical Lab Technology (A), Dental Assisting, Electroneurodiagnostic Technology, Medical Assisting (AMA), Medical Record Technology, Nursing (A), Physical Therapy Assisting, Radiography, Respiratory Therapy, Surgical Technology *CEO:* Pres. James Lee Rasch
Enroll: 4,230   (608) 785-9200

WISCONSIN INDIANHEAD TECHNICAL COLLEGE
HCR 69, Box 10B, 505 Pine Ridge Rd., Shell Lake 54871 *Type:* Public (district) 2-year *Accred.:* 1979/1994 (NCA) *Calendar:* Sem. plan *Degrees:* A, C *Prof. Accred.:* Medical Assisting (AMA), Nursing (A) *CEO:* Pres./District Dir. David R. Hildebrand
Enroll: 3,127   (715) 468-2815

WISCONSIN LUTHERAN COLLEGE
8830 W. Bluemond Rd., Milwaukee 53226 *Type:* Private (Lutheran) *Accred.:* 1987/1990 (NCA) *Calendar:* Sem. plan *Degrees:* B *CEO:* Pres. Gary J. Greenfield
Enroll: 373   (414) 774-8620

WISCONSIN SCHOOL OF ELECTRONICS
1227 N. Sherman Ave., Madison 53704 *Type:* Private *Accred.:* 1970/1993 (ACCSCT) *Calendar:* Qtr. plan *Degrees:* A *CEO:* Dir. Donald G. Madelung
          (608) 249-6611

WISCONSIN SCHOOL OF PROFESSIONAL PSYCHOLOGY
9120 W. Hampton Ave., Ste. 212, Milwaukee 53225 *Type:* Private professional *Accred.:* 1987/1995 (NCA) *Calendar:* Sem. plan *Degrees:* D *CEO:* Pres. Samuel H. Friedman
Enroll: 91   (414) 464-9777

WYOMING

CASPER COLLEGE
125 College Dr., Casper 82601 *Type:* Public (district) junior *System:* Wyoming Community College Commission *Accred.:* 1960/1989 (NCA) *Calendar:* Sem. plan *Degrees:* A, C *Prof. Accred.:* Music, Nursing (A), Radiography *CEO:* Pres. Leroy Strausner
Enroll: 3,917   (307) 268-2547

CENTRAL WYOMING COLLEGE
2660 Peck Ave., Riverton 82501 *Type:* Public (district) junior *System:* Wyoming Community College Commission *Accred.:* 1976/1988 (NCA) *Calendar:* Sem. plan *Degrees:* A, C *Prof. Accred.:* Nursing (A) *CEO:* Pres. Jo Anne McFarland
Enroll: 1,550   (307) 856-9291

EASTERN WYOMING COLLEGE
3200 W. C St., Torrington 82240 *Type:* Public (district) junior *System:* Wyoming Community College Commission *Accred.:* 1976/1991 (NCA) *Calendar:* Sem. plan *Degrees:* A, C *Prof. Accred.:* Veterinary Technology *CEO:* Pres. Jack Bottenfield
Enroll: 1,650   (307) 532-8200

LARAMIE COUNTY COMMUNITY COLLEGE
1400 E. College Dr., Cheyenne 82007 *Type:* Public (district) junior *System:* Wyoming Community College Commission *Accred.:* 1975/1990 (NCA) *Calendar:* Sem. plan *Degrees:* A, C *Prof. Accred.:* Dental Hygiene, Nursing (A), Practical Nursing, Radiography *CEO:* Pres. Charles H. Bohlen
Enroll: 4,256   (307) 778-5222

NORTHWEST COLLEGE
231 W. Sixth St., Powell 82435 *Type:* Public (district) junior *System:* Wyoming Community College Commission *Accred.:* 1964/1991 (NCA) *Calendar:* Sem. plan *Degrees:* A, C *Prof. Accred.:* Nursing (A), Practical Nursing *CEO:* Pres. John P. Hanna
Enroll: 1,991   (307) 754-6111

SHERIDAN COLLEGE
P.O. Box 1500, Sheridan 82801 *Type:* Public (district) junior *System:* Wyoming Community College Commission *Accred.:* 1968/1988 (NCA) *Calendar:* Sem. plan *Degrees:* A, C *Prof. Accred.:* Dental Assisting, Dental Hygiene, Nursing (A), Practical Nursing *CEO:* Pres. Stephen J. Maier
Enroll: 2,508   (307) 674-6446

GILLETTE CAMPUS
720 W. 8th St., Gillette 82716 *Prof. Accred.:* Nursing (A)
(307) 686-0254

UNIVERSITY OF WYOMING
P.O. Box 3434, University Sta., Laramie 82071 *Type:* Public (state) *Accred.:* 1976/1990 (NCA) *Calendar:* Sem. plan *Degrees:* B, M, P, D *Prof. Accred.:* Audiology, Business (B,M), Clinical Lab Scientist, Clinical Psychology, Counseling, Engineering (agricultural, architectural, chemical, civil, electrical, mechanical), Law, Music, Nursing (B,M), Psychology Internship, Social Work (B), Speech-Language Pathology *CEO:* Pres. Terry P. Roark
Enroll: 9,111   (307) 766-4121

WESTERN WYOMING COMMUNITY COLLEGE
P.O. Box 428, Rock Springs 82902-0428 *Type:* Public (district) junior *System:* Wyoming Community College Commission *Accred.:* 1976/1994 (NCA) *Calendar:* Sem. plan *Degrees:* A, C *Prof. Accred.:* Radiography, Respiratory Therapy, Respiratory Therapy Technology *CEO:* Pres. Tex Boggs
Enroll: 2,797   (307) 382-1600

OUTSIDE THE UNITED STATES

CANADA

ACADIA DIVINITY COLLEGE
Wolfville B0P 1X0 *Type:* Private (Baptist)
graduate only *Accred.:* 1984/1990 (ATS)
Calendar: Sem. plan *Degrees:* M, D *CEO:*
Princ. Andrew D. MacRae
FTE Enroll: 157   (902) 542-2285

ATLANTIC SCHOOL OF THEOLOGY
640 Francklyn St., Halifax B3H 3B5 *Type:*
Private (interdenominational) graduate only
Accred.: 1976/1993 (ATS) *Calendar:* Sem.
plan *Degrees:* M *CEO:* Interim Pres. Gordon
E. MacDermid
FTE Enroll: 107   (902) 423-6939

BETHANY BIBLE COLLEGE
26 Western St., Sussex E0E 1P0 *Type:* Pri-
vate (Wesleyan) *Accred.:* 1987/1992
(AABC) *Calendar:* Sem. plan Degrees: B, C
CEO: Pres. David Medders
FTE Enroll: 127   (506) 432-4400

BRIERCREST BIBLE COLLEGE
510 College Dr., Caronport S0H 0S0 *Type:*
Private *Accred.:* 1976/1986 (AABC) *Calen-
dar:* Sem. plan *Degrees:* A, B, C *CEO:* Pres.
John Barkman
FTE Enroll: 673   (306) 756-3200

CANADIAN BIBLE COLLEGE
4400 Fourth Ave., Regina S4T 0H8 *Type:*
Private (Christian and Missionary Alliance)
Accred.: 1961/1994 (AABC); 1989/1994
(ATS) *Calendar:* Sem. plan *Degrees:* A, B
CEO: Pres. Robert A. Rose
FTE Enroll: 123   (306) 545-1515

CATHERINE BOOTH BIBLE COLLEGE
447 Webb Pl., Winnipeg R3B 2P2 *Type:* Pri-
vate (Salvation Army) *Accred.:* 1991
(AABC) *Calendar:* Sem. plan *Degrees:* A,
B, C *CEO:* Pres. Lloyd Hetherington
FTE Enroll: 82   (204) 947-6701

COLUMBIA BIBLE COLLEGE
2940 Clearbrook Rd., Clearbrook V2T 2Z8
Type: Private (Mennonite Brethren/ Conference of Mennonites) *Accred.:* 1991 (AABC)

Calendar: Sem. plan *Degrees:* B, C *CEO:*
Pres. Walter Unger
FTE Enroll: 249   (604) 853-3358

DALHOUSIE UNIVERSITY
Halifax B3H 3J5 *Type:* Private *Calendar:*
Sem. plan *Degrees:* B, M, P, D Prof. Accred.:
Dentistry, Health Services Administration,
Librarianship, Medicine, Oral and Maxillo-
facial Surgery, Periodontics *CEO:* Pres./Vice
Chanc. Howard C. Clark
Enroll: 11,046   (902) 424-2211

EASTERN PENTECOSTAL BIBLE COLLEGE
780 Argyle St., Peterborough K9H 5T2
Type: Private (Pentacostal Assemblies of
Canada) *Accred.:* 1989/1995 (AABC) *Cal-
endar:* Sem. plan *Degrees:* B, C *CEO:* Pres.
Carl Verge
FTE Enroll: 506   (705) 748-9111

EMMANUEL BIBLE COLLEGE
100 Fergus Ave., Kitchener N2A 2H2 *Type:*
Private (Missionary Church) *Accred.:* 1982/
1992 (AABC) *Calendar:* Sem. plan
Degrees: B, C *CEO:* Pres. Thomas Dow
FTE Enroll: 211   (519) 894-8900

EMMANUEL COLLEGE OF VICTORIA UNIVERSITY
75 Queen's Park Crescent, E., Toronto M5S
1K7 *Type:* Private (United Church of
Canada) graduate only *Accred.:* 1938/1991
(ATS) *Calendar:* Sem. plan *Degrees:* M, D
CEO: Princ. John C. Hoffman
FTE Enroll: 237   (416) 585-4539

HURON COLLEGE FACULTY OF THEOLOGY
1349 Western Rd., London N6G 1H3 *Type:*
Private (Anglican) graduate only *Accred.:*
1981/1995 (ATS) *Calendar:* Sem. plan
Degrees: M *CEO:* Princ. Charles J. Jago
Enroll: 67   (519) 438-7224

JOINT BOARD OF THEOLOGICAL COLLEGES
3473 University St., Montreal H3A 2A8 *Type:*
Private (interdenominational) graduate only
Accred.: 1989/1993 (ATS) Calendar: Sem.
plan *Degrees:* M *CEO:* Pres. William Klempa
FTE Enroll: 13   (514) 849-8511

KNOX COLLEGE
59 St. George St., Toronto M5S 2E6 *Type:* Private (Presbyterian Church in Canada) graduate only *Accred.:* 1948/1991 (ATS) *Calendar:* Sem. plan *Degrees:* M, D *CEO:* Princ. Arthur Van Seters
Enroll: 123   (416) 978-4500

LUTHERAN THEOLOGICAL SEMINARY
114 Seminary Crescent, Saskatoon S7N 0X3 *Type:* Private (Evangelical Lutheran Church) graduate only *Accred.:* 1976/1988 (ATS) *Calendar:* Sem. plan *Degrees:* M *CEO:* Pres. Roger W. Nostbakken
Enroll: 94   (306) 975-7004

MCGILL UNIVERSITY
845 Sherbrooke St. W., Montreal H3A 2T5 *Type:* Private (interdenominational) *Accred.:* 1952/1990 (ATS) *Calendar:* Sem. plan *Degrees:* B, M, D *Prof. Accred.:* Clinical Psychology, Dentistry, Librarianship, Medicine, Oral and Maxillofacial Surgery, Physical Therapy, Psychology Internship *CEO:* Princ./Vice Chanc. D.L. Johnston
Enroll: 30,314   (514) 398-4455

MCMASTER UNIVERSITY
Hamilton L8S 4L8 *Type:* Private Union Baptist Accred.: 1954/1987 (ATS) *Calendar:* Sem. plan *Degrees:* M, P, D *Prof. Accred.:* Medicine *CEO:* Pres./Vice Chanc. Peter George
Enroll: 16,628   (416) 525-9140

MEMORIAL UNIVERSITY OF NEWFOUNDLAND
St. John's A1B 3V6 *Type:* Public *Calendar:* Sem. plan *Degrees:* B, M, P, D *Prof. Accred.:* Medicine *CEO:* Pres. Arthur May
Enroll: 15,606   (709) 737-8000

NER ISRAEL YESHIVA COLLEGE OF TORONTO
8950 Bathurst St., P.O. Box 5002, Thornhill L3T 6K1 *Type:* Private professional *Accred.:* 1980/1993 (AARTS) *Calendar:* Sem. plan *Degrees:* B *CEO:* Pres. A. Bleeman
Enroll: 150   (905) 731-1224

NEWMAN THEOLOGICAL COLLEGE
15611 St. Albert Tr., Edmonton T5L 4H8 *Type:* Private (Roman Catholic) graduate only *Accred.:* 1991 (ATS) *Calendar:* Sem. plan *Degrees:* M *CEO:* Pres. Kevin Carr
Enroll: 231   (403) 447-2993

NORTH AMERICAN BAPTIST COLLEGE
11525 23rd Ave., Edmonton T6J 4T3 *Type:* Private (North American Baptist Conference) *Accred.:* 1969/1989 (AABC) *Calendar:* Sem. plan *Degrees:* A, B, C *CEO:* Pres. Paul Siewert
FTE Enroll: 240   (403) 437-1960

NORTHWEST BAPTIST THEOLOGICAL COLLEGE
22606 76A Ave., P.O. Box 790, Langley V3A 8B8 *Type:* Private (Fellowship of Evangelical Baptist Churches) *Accred.:* 1989/1995 (AABC) *Calendar:* Sem. plan *Degrees:* A, B, C *CEO:* Pres. Doug Harris
FTE Enroll: 214   (604) 888-3310

ONTARIO BIBLE COLLEGE AND THEOLOGICAL SEMINARY
25 Ballyconnor Ct., North York M2M 4B3 *Type:* Private (interdenominational) *Accred.:* 1966/1994 (AABC); 1989 (ATS) *Calendar:* Sem. plan *Degrees:* B, C *CEO:* Pres. Bruce Gordon
Enroll: 533   (416) 226-6380

PROVIDENCE COLLEGE AND SEMINARY
Otterburne R0A 1G0 *Type:* Private (interdenominational) *Accred.:* 1973/1994 (AABC); 1992 (ATS) *Calendar:* Sem. plan *Degrees:* B, C *CEO:* Pres. Larry McKinney
Enroll: 219   (204) 433-7488

QUEEN'S THEOLOGICAL COLLEGE
Kingston K7L 3N6 *Type:* Private (United Church of Canada) graduate only *Accred.:* 1986/1991 (ATS) *Calendar:* Sem. plan *Degrees:* M *CEO:* Princ. Hallett E. Llewellyn
Enroll: 93   (613) 545-2110

QUEEN'S UNIVERSITY AT KINGSTON
Kingston K7L 3N6 *Type:* Private *Calendar:* Sem. plan *Degrees:* M, D *Prof. Accred.:* Clinical Psychology, Medicine *CEO:* Chanc. Agnes M. Benidickson
                    (613) 545-2000

REGENT COLLEGE
5800 University Blvd., Vancouver V6T 2E4
Type: Private (interdenominational) graduate
only *Accred.:* 1985/1990 (ATS) *Calendar:*
Sem. plan *Degrees:* M *CEO:* Pres. Walter C.
Wright, Jr.
FTE Enroll: 652   (604) 224-3245

REGIS COLLEGE
15 St. Mary St., Toronto M4Y 2R5 *Type:* Private (Roman Catholic) graduate only *Accred.:*
1970/1991 (ATS) *Calendar:* Sem. plan
Degrees: M, D *CEO:* Pres. John E. Costello
FTE Enroll: 174   (416) 922-5474

ROCKY MOUNTAIN COLLEGE
4039 Brentwood Rd., N.W., Calgary T2L 1L1
Type: Private (Evangelical Church in Canada)
Accred.: 1989 (AABC) *Calendar:* Sem. plan
Degrees: B, C *CEO:* Pres. Randy Steinwand
FTE Enroll: 184   (403) 284-5100

RYERSON POLYTECHNIC UNIVERSITY
350 Victoria St., Toronto M5B 2K3 *Type:*
Public *Degrees:* B *Prof. Accred.:* Interior
Design *CEO:* Pres./Vice Chanc. Claude
Lajeunesse
                          (416) 979-5000

ST. AUGUSTINE'S SEMINARY OF TORONTO
2661 Kingston Rd., Scarborough, M1M
1M3 *Type:* Private (Roman Catholic) graduate only *Accred.:* 1980/1991 (ATS) *Calendar:* Sem. plan *Degrees:* M *CEO:* Pres./Rec-
tor John A. Boissoneau
Enroll: 134   (416) 261-7207

ST. PETER'S SEMINARY
1040 Waterloo St. N., London N6A 3Y1
Type: Private (Roman Catholic) graduate
only *Accred.:* 1986/1991 (ATS) *Calendar:*
Sem. plan *Degrees:* M *CEO:* Rector/Dean
Thomas C. Collins
Enroll: 61   (519) 432-1824

SIMON FRASER UNIVERSITY
Burnaby V5A 1S6 *Type:* Private *Calendar:*
Sem. plan *Degrees:* A, B, C *Prof. Accred.:*
Clinical Psychology *CEO:* Chanc. Barbara
Rae
                          (604) 291-3111

STEINBACH BIBLE COLLEGE
Hwy. 12 N., Box 1420, Steinbach R0A 2A0
Type: Private (Mennonite Churches)
Accred.: 1991 (AABC) *Calendar:* Sem. plan
Degrees: B, C *CEO:* Chrmn. Stan Plett
FTE Enroll: 71   (204) 326-6451

TORONTO SCHOOL OF THEOLOGY
47 Queen's Park Crescent, E., Toronto M5S
2C3 *Type:* Private (interdenominational)
graduate only *Accred.:* 1980/1992 (ATS)
Calendar: Sem. plan *Degrees:* M, D *CEO:*
Dir. Jean-Marc Laporte
                          (416) 978-4039

TRINITY COLLEGE
6 Hoskin Ave., Toronto M5S 1H8 *Type:* Private (Anglican Church of Canada) graduate
only *Accred.:* 1938/1991 (ATS) *Calendar:*
Sem. plan *Degrees:* M, D *CEO:* Acting Dean
Donald Wiebe
Enroll: 109   (416) 978-2133

UNIVERSITE DE MONTREAL
Case Postal 6128, Succursale A, Montreal
H3C 3J7 *Type:* Private *Calendar:* Sem. plan
Degrees: B, M, P, D *Prof. Accred.:* Dentistry,
Health Services Administration, Librarian-
ship, Medicine, Optometry, Orthodontics,
Pediatric Dentistry, Planning (B,M), Veteri-
nary Medicine *CEO:* Rector G.G. Cloutier
Enroll: 49,837   (514) 343-6111

UNIVERSITE DE SHERBROOKE
2500 Blvd. de l'Universite, Sherbrooke J1K
2R1 *Type:* Private *Calendar:* Sem. plan
Degrees: B, M, P, D *Prof. Accred.:* Medicine
CEO: Rector A. Cabana
Enroll: 17,411   (819) 821-7000

UNIVERSITE LAVAL
Cite Universitaire, Quebec City G1K 7P4
Type: Private *Calendar:* Sem. plan *Degrees:*
B, M, P, D *Prof. Accred.:* Dentistry, Medi-
cine, Oral and Maxillofacial Surgery *CEO:*
Rector Michel Gervais
Enroll: 35,373   (418) 656-2131

UNIVERSITY OF ALBERTA
Edmonton T6G 2E1 *Type:* Public *Calendar:*
Sem. plan *Degrees:* B, M, P, D *Prof.
Accred.:* Business (B,M), Dentistry, Health

Services Administration, Librarianship, Medicine, Orthodontics *CEO:* Pres./Vice Chanc. P. Davenport
Enroll: 29,536   (403) 492-3111

UNIVERSITY OF BRITISH COLUMBIA
2075 Westbrook Mall, Vancouver V6T 1W5 *Type:* Public *Calendar:* Sem. plan *Degrees:* B, M, P, D *Prof. Accred.:* Clinical Psychology, Counseling, Dentistry, Librarianship, Medicine, Periodontics, Planning (M), Psychology Internship *CEO:* Pres./Vice Chanc. D.W. Strangway
Enroll: 28,461   (604) 228-2375

UNIVERSITY OF CALGARY
2500 University Dr., N.W., Calgary T2N 1N4 *Type:* Public *Calendar:* Sem. plan *Degrees:* B, M, P, D *Prof. Accred.:* Business (B,M), Medicine *CEO:* Pres. Murry Frazier
Enroll: 20,541   (403) 220-5110

UNIVERSITY OF GUELPH
Guelph N1G 2W1 *Type:* Public *Calendar:* Sem. plan *Degrees:* B, M *Prof. Accred.:* Landscape Architecture (B,M), Marriage and Family Therapy (M), Veterinary Medicine *CEO:* Pres./Vice Chanc. B. Segal
Enroll: 12,723   (519) 824-4120

UNIVERSITY OF MANITOBA
Winnipeg R3T 2N2 *Type:* Public *Calendar:* Sem. plan *Degrees:* B, M, P, D *Prof. Accred.:* Clinical Psychology, Dentistry, Interior Design, Medicine, Oral and Maxillofacial Surgery, Orthodontics, Periodontics, Psychology Internship *CEO:* Pres./Vice Chanc. Arnold Naimark
Enroll: 23,462   (204) 474-8880

UNIVERSITY OF OTTAWA
Ottawa K1N 6N5 *Type:* Public *Calendar:* Sem. plan *Degrees:* B, M, P, D *Prof. Accred.:* Clinical Psychology, Health Services Administration, Medicine, Psychology Internship, Recreation and Leisure Services (candidate) *CEO:* Rector/Vice Chanc. M. Hamelin
Enroll: 23,694   (613) 564-3311

UNIVERSITY OF PRINCE EDWARD ISLAND
550 University Ave., Charlottetown C1A 4P3 *Type:* Private *Calendar:* Sem. plan

Degrees: A, B, C *Prof. Accred.:* Veterinary Medicine *CEO:* Chanc. G. L. Bennett
                (902) 566-0439

UNIVERSITY OF ST. MICHAEL'S COLLEGE
81 St. Mary St., Toronto M5S 1J4 *Type:* Private (Roman Catholic) graduate only *Accred.:* 1972/1991 (ATS) *Calendar:* Sem. plan *Degrees:* M, D *CEO:* Dean Michael A. Fahey
Enroll: 245   (416) 926-7140

UNIVERSITY OF SASKATCHEWAN
Saskatoon S7N 0W0 *Type:* Public *Calendar:* Sem. plan *Degrees:* B, M, P, D *Prof. Accred.:* Clinical Psychology, Dentistry, Medicine, Veterinary Medicine *CEO:* Pres./Vice Chanc. J. W. G. Ivany
Enroll: 15,546   (306) 244-4343

UNIVERSITY OF TORONTO
Toronto M5S 1A1 *Type:* Public *Calendar:* Sem. plan *Degrees:* B, M, P, D *Prof. Accred.:* Combined Maxillofacial Prosthodontics, Dental Public Health, Dentistry, Health Services Administration, Landscape Architecture (B), Librarianship, Medicine, Oral Pathology, Oral and Maxillofacial Surgery, Orthodontics, Pediatric Dentistry, Periodontics *CEO:* Pres. J.R.S Prichard
Enroll: 53,313   (416) 978-2011

UNIVERSITY OF VICTORIA
Victoria V8W 3P5 *Type:* Public *Calendar:* Qtr. plan *Degrees:* B, M, D *Prof. Accred.:* Clinical Psychology *CEO:* Pres. David F. Strong
Enroll: 15,000   (604) 721-7211

UNIVERSITY OF WATERLOO
University Ave., Waterloo N2L 3G1 *Type:* Private *Calendar:* Sem. plan *Degrees:* B, M, P *Prof. Accred.:* Clinical Psychology, Optometry *CEO:* Pres./Vice Chanc. D. T. Wright
Enroll: 25,337   (519) 885-1211

UNIVERSITY OF WESTERN ONTARIO
London N6A 3K7 *Type:* Private *Calendar:* Sem. plan *Degrees:* B, M, P, D *Prof. Accred.:* Clinical Psychology, Dentistry, Librarianship,

Medicine, Oral Pathology, Orthodontics
CEO: Pres./Vice Chanc. K.G. Pedersen
Enroll: 22,450　　　　(519) 679-2111

UNIVERSITY OF WINDSOR
Windsor N9B 3P4 *Type:* Public *Calendar:*
Sem. plan *Degrees:* B, M, P, D *Prof.*
Accred.: Clinical Psychology *CEO:*
Pres./Vice Chanc. R.W. Ianni
Enroll: 14,079　　　　(519) 253-4232

VANCOUVER SCHOOL OF THEOLOGY
6000 Iona Dr., Vancouver V6T 1L4 *Type:* Private (interdenominational) graduate only
Accred.: 1976/1992 (ATS) *Calendar:* Sem.
plan *Degrees:* M *CEO:* Princ. William J.
Phillips
Enroll: 128　　　　(604) 228-9031

WATERLOO LUTHERAN SEMINARY
75 University Ave., W., Waterloo N2L 3C5
Type: Private (Evangelical Luthern Church)
graduate only *Accred.:* 1982/1987 (ATS)
Calendar: Sem. plan *Degrees:* M *CEO:*
Princ. Richard C. Crossman
Enroll: 155　　　　(519) 884-1970

WESTERN PENTECOSTAL BIBLE COLLEGE
35235 Straiton Rd., P.O. Box 1700, Abbotsford V2S 7E7 *Type:* Private (Pentecostal
Assemblies of Canada) *Accred.:* 1980/1990
(AABC) *Calendar:* Sem. plan *Degrees:* B, C
CEO: Pres. James Richards
FTE Enroll: 177　　　　(604) 853-7491

WYCLIFFE COLLEGE
5 Hoskin Ave., Toronto M5S 1H7 *Type:* Private (Anglican) graduate only *Accred.:* 1978/
1991 (ATS) *Calendar:* Sem. plan *Degrees:*
M, D *CEO:* Princ. Michael Pountney
Enroll: 162　　　　(416) 979-2870

CAYMAN ISLANDS

INTERNATIONAL COLLEGE
P.O. Box Savannah, Newlands, Grand Cayman *Type:* Private senior *Accred.:* 1979/
1996 (ACICS) *Calendar:* Qtr. plan *Degrees:*
A, B, M, C *CEO:* Pres. Elsa M. Cummings
　　　　(809) 947-1100

COSTA RICA

INSTITUTO CENTROAMERICANO DE
ADMINISTRACION DE EMPRESAS
4050 Alajuela, La Garita, Alajuela 960 *Type:*
Private graduate only *Accred.:* 1994 (SACS-
CC) *Calendar:* Tri. plan *Degrees:* M *CEO:*
Rector Brizio Biondi-Morra
FTE Enroll: 478　　　　[011] (506) 443-0506

EGYPT

AMERICAN UNIVERSITY IN CAIRO
113 Sharia Dasr El Aini, Cairo *Type:* Private
Accred.: 1982/1994 (MSA) *Calendar:* Sem.
plan *Degrees:* B, M *CEO:* Pres. Donald
McDonald
Enroll: 4,109　　　　[20] 354-1830

FRANCE

THE AMERICAN UNIVERSITY OF PARIS
31 Ave. Bosquet, Paris 75007 *Type:* Private
liberal arts *Accred.:* 1973/1995 (MSA) *Calendar:* Sem. plan *Degrees:* B, C *CEO:* Pres.
Lee W. Heubner
Enroll: 262　　　　[33] (1) 40 62 06 00

GREECE

COLLEGE OF SOUTHEASTERN EUROPE
22 Academia St., Athens 10671 *Type:* Private *Accred.:* 1995 (ACICS) *Degrees:* B, M
CEO: Pres. Achilles C. Kanellopoulos
　　　　[30] (1) 361-7861

DEREE COLLEGE
P.O. Box 60018, 10 Agnia, Paraskevi Attikis
GR-153 *Type:* Private liberal arts *Accred.:*
1981/1986 (NEASC-CIHE) *Calendar:* 4-1-
4 plan *Degrees:* A, B *CEO:* Pres. John S.
Bailey
Enroll: 4,164　　　　[30] (1) 639-3250

ITALY

AMERICAN UNIVERSITY OF ROME
Via Pietro Roselli 4, Rome 00153 *Type:* Private senior *Accred.:* 1993/1995 *(ACICS)*

Degrees: A, B, C CEO: Pres. Alessandro C. De Bosis

[39] (6) 5833-0919

JAPAN

AKITA CAMPUS OF MINNESOTA STATE COLLEGES AND UNIVERSITIES
193-2 Oku-Tsubakidai, Yuwa-Machi, Akita 010-12 *Type:* Public *System:* Minnesota State Colleges and Universities *Accred.:* 1990 (NCA) *Calendar:* Qtr. plan *Degrees:* A, C *CEO:* Provost John Norris
Enroll: 400   (612) 296-5284

* Indirect NCA accreditation through Minnesota State Colleges and Universities

MARSHALL ISLANDS

COLLEGE OF THE MARSHALL ISLANDS
P.O. Box 1258, Majuro 96960 *Type:* Public junior *Accred.:* 1991 (WASC-Jr.) *Calendar:* Sem. plan *Degrees:* A *CEO:* Pres. Dorothy Rae Nadeau
Enroll: 405   (692) 625-3394

MEXICO

FUNDACION UNIVERSIDAD DE LAS AMERICAS - PUEBLA
Apartado Postal 100, Sta. Catarina Martir, Cholula, Puebla 72820 *Type:* Private *Accred.:* 1959/1994 (SACS-CC) *Calendar:* Sem. plan *Degrees:* B, M *CEO:* Rector Enrique Cardenas
FTE Enroll: 6,138   [011] (522) 229-2000

INSTITUTO TECNOLOGICO Y DE ESTUDIOS SUPERIORES DE MONTERREY
Ave. Eugenio Garza Sada, 2501 Sur, Monterrey, N.L. 64849 *Type:* Private *Accred.:* 1950/1989 (SACS-CC) *Calendar:* Sem. plan *Degrees:* B, M, D *CEO:* Pres. Rafael Rangel-Sostmann
FTE Enroll: 45,135   [011] (528) 358-2133

UNIVERSIDAD DE LAS AMERICAS, A.C.
Calle de Puebla No. 223, Col. Roma, Mexico D.F. 06700 *Type:* Private *Accred.:* 1991

(SACS-CC) *Calendar:* Sem. plan *Degrees:* B, M *CEO:* Pres. Alejandro Gertz Manero
FTE Enroll: 1,593   [011] (525) 208-0247

MICRONESIA

COLLEGE OF MICRONESIA
P.O. Box 159, Kolonia, Pohnpei 96941 *Type:* Public junior *Accred.:* 1978/1992 (WASC-Jr.) *Calendar:* Sem. plan *Degrees:* A *CEO:* Pres. Susan J. Moses
Enroll: 1,367   (691) 320-2480

NIGERIA

THE NIGERIAN BAPTIST THEOLOGICAL SEMINARY
P.O. Box 30, Ogbomoso Oyo State *Type:* Private (Southern Baptist) professional *Accred.:* 1983/1988 (SACS-CC) *Calendar:* Sem. plan *Degrees:* B *CEO:* Pres. Yusufu Ameh Obaje
FTE Enroll: 225   (038) 710-0110

NORTHERN MARIANAS

NORTHERN MARIANAS COLLEGE
Box 1250, Saipan 96950 *Type:* Public junior *Accred.:* 1985/1990 (WASC-Jr.) *Calendar:* Sem. plan *Degrees:* A *CEO:* Pres. Agnes M. McPhetres
Enroll: 1,072   (670) 234-6932

PALAU

PALAU COMMUNITY COLLEGE
P.O. Box 9, Koror 96940 *Type:* Public vocational *Accred.:* 1977/1992 (WASC-Jr.) *Calendar:* Sem. plan *Degrees:* A *CEO:* Pres. Francis M. Matsutaro
Enroll: 403   (680) 488-2471

PANAMA

PANAMA CANAL COLLEGE
DoDDS, Panama Region, Unit No. 9025, APO Miami, FL 34002 *Type:* Public (federal) junior *Accred.:* 1941/1990 (MSA) *Calendar:* Sem. plan *Degrees:* A *CEO:* Dean Ronald G. Woodbury
Enroll: 1,590   (507) 52-3304

SWITZERLAND

FRANKLIN COLLEGE SWITZERLAND
Via Ponte Tresa 29, Sorengo (Lugano) 6924
Type: Private liberal arts *Accred.:* 1975/1990
(MSA) *Calendar:* Sem. plan *Degrees:* A, B
CEO: Pres. Erik Nielsen
Enroll: 219   [41] (9) 155-0101

UNITED KINGDOM

IMC-INTERNATIONAL MANAGEMENT CENTRES
Castle St., Buckingham, England MK18
1BP *Type:* Private distance education
Accred.: 1989/1995 (DETC) *Degrees:* M, C
CEO: Princ. Gordon Wills
                                [44] (280) 81-7222

RICHMOND COLLEGE, THE AMERICAN
INTERNATIONAL UNIVERSITY IN LONDON
Queens Rd., Richmond, Surrey, England
TW10 6JP *Type:* Private liberal arts *Accred.:*
1981/1991 (MSA) *Calendar:* Sem. plan
Degrees: A, B, M *CEO:* Pres. Walter J.
McCann
Enroll: 998   [0] (81) 332-8200

Accredited Non-Degree Granting Institutions

ALABAMA

ALABAMA STATE COLLEGE OF BARBER STYLING
9480 Parkway E., Birmingham 35215-8308
Type: Private *Accred.:* 1990 (ACCSCT)
Degrees: C *CEO:* Owner/Dir. Donald S.
Mathews
(205) 836-2404

ARMY ORDNANCE MISSILE AND MUNITIONS
CENTER AND SCHOOL
Redstone Arsenal, Huntsville 35897-6200
Type: Public (federal) technical *Accred.:*
1976/1990 (COE) *Degrees:* C *CEO:* Cmdt.
Thomas A. Hooper
FTE Enroll: 2,849   (205) 876-3349

CAPPS COLLEGE
3100 Cottage Hill Rd., Bldg. 5, Mobile
36606 *Type:* Private *Accred.:* 1986/1992
(ABHES) *Degrees:* C *Prof. Accred.:*
Medical Assisting *CEO:* Pres. Morgan
Landry
(205) 473-1393

CAREER DEVELOPMENT INSTITUTE
2233 Fourth Ave., N., Birmingham 35203
Type: Private *Accred.:* 1988/1993 (COE)
Calendar: Qtr. plan *Degrees:* C *CEO:* Dir.
Darlene Mosley
FTE Enroll: 146   (205) 252-6396

BESSEMER CAMPUS
2314 Ninth Ave., N., Bessemer 35020
(205) 425-6757

CAREER DEVELOPMENT INSTITUTE
1060 Springhill Ave., Mobile 36604 *Type:*
Private *Accred.:* 1988/1993 (COE probation-
al) *Calendar:* Qtr. plan *Degrees:* C *CEO:*
Dir. Bertha George
FTE Enroll: 119   (205) 433-5042

CAREER DEVELOPMENT INSTITUTE
505 and 507 Montgomery St., Montgomery
36101-0766 *Type:* Private *Accred.:* 1988/
1993 (COE) *Calendar:* Qtr. plan *Degrees:* C
CEO: Dir. Amie Garrett
FTE Enroll: 140   (205) 262-3131

EXTENSION COURSE INSTITUTE OF THE UNITED
STATES AIR FORCE
50 S. Turner Blvd., Gunter Annex, Maxwell
Air Force Base 36118-5643 *Type:* Public
(federal) distance education *Accred.:* 1975/
1995 (DETC) *Degrees:* C *CEO:* Cmdt. Mark
D. Schultz
(205) 416-4252

GADSDEN BUSINESS COLLEGE
750 Forrest Ave., P.O. Box 1544, Gadsden
35901 *Type:* Private business *Accred.:* 1962/
1991 (ACICS) *Calendar:* Qtr. plan *Degrees:*
C *CEO:* Vice Pres. Michael Beecham
(205) 546-2863

ANNISTON CAMPUS
P.O. Box 1575, 630 S. Wilmer Ave.,
Anniston 36202-1575 *Accred.:* 1962/1991
(ACICS)
(205) 237-7517

HUNTSVILLE BUSINESS INSTITUTE SCHOOL OF
COURT REPORTING
3315 S. Memorial Pkwy., No. 5, Huntsville
35801 *Type:* Private *Accred.:* 1990 (COE)
Degrees: C *CEO:* Dir. Bonnie Gray
FTE Enroll: 20   (205) 880-7530

JOHN POPE EDEN AREA VOCATIONAL
EDUCATION CENTER
Rte. 2, Box 1855, Ashville 35953 *Type:*
Public (state) *Accred.:* 1984/1989 (COE)
Degrees: C *CEO:* Dir. John Hazelwood
FTE Enroll: 169   (205) 594-7055

J.R. PITTARD AREA VOCATIONAL SCHOOL
22401 Alabama Hwy. 21, Alpine 35014
Type: Public (state) *Accred.:* 1990 (SACS-
CC) *Degrees:* C *CEO:* Dir. L. C. McMurphy
FTE Enroll: 124   (205) 539-8161

MITCHELL COSMETOLOGY COLLEGE
116 First St., S., Alabaster 35007 *Type:*
Private *Accred.:* 1993 (COE) *Degrees:* C
CEO: Pres. Timothy Mitchell
FTE Enroll: 33   (205) 663-7126

PRINCE INSTITUTE OF PROFESSIONAL STUDIES
7735 Atlanta Hwy., Montgomery 36117
Type: Private business *Accred.:* 1984/1996
(ACICS) *Degrees:* C *CEO:* Pres. Sara Prince
(205) 271-1670

RICE COLLEGE
2116 Bessemer Rd., Birmingham 35208
Type: Private *Accred.:* 1983/1988 (COE)
Degrees: C *CEO:* Dir. Darrell Glaze
FTE Enroll: 152   (205) 781-8600

SOUTHERN COMMUNITY COLLEGE
205 S. Main St., Tuskegee 36083 *Type:*
Private *Accred.:* 1983/1993 (COE) *Degrees:*
C *Prof. Accred.:* Practical Nursing *CEO:*
Pres. Lawrence F. Haygood, Jr.
FTE Enroll: 11   (334) 727-5220

TALLAPOOSA-ALEXANDER CITY AREA
VOCATIONAL CENTER
100 E. Junior College Dr., Alexander City
35010 *Type:* Public (state) *Accred.:* 1984/
1989 (SACS-CC) *Degrees:* C *CEO:* Dir. Joe
Martin
FTE Enroll: 144   (205) 329-8448

WINSTON COUNTY TECHNICAL CENTER
Holly Grove Rd., Double Springs 35553
Type: Public (state) *Accred.:* 1985/1990
(SACS-CC) *Degrees:* C *CEO:* Dir. Betty
Porter
FTE Enroll: 95   (205) 489-2121

ALASKA

THE CAREER ACADEMY
1415 E. Tudor Rd., Anchorage 99507-1033
Type: Private *Accred.:* 1987 (ACCSCT) *Degrees:* C *CEO:* Pres. Jennifer A. Deitz
(907) 563-7575

ARIZONA

AMERICAN INSTITUTE OF TECHNOLOGY
440 S. 54th Ave., Phoenix 85043 *Type:* Private *Accred.:* 1985/1990 (ACCSCT) *Degrees:* C *CEO:* Dir. R. Wade Murphree
(602) 233-2222

APOLLO COLLEGE—WESTSIDE
2701 West Bethany Home Rd., Phoenix 85017 *Type:* Private *Accred.:* 1991 (AB-HES) *Prof. Accred.:* Medical Assisting *CEO:* Dir. Bernie Fortunoff
(602) 433-1333

ARIZONA COLLEGE OF ALLIED HEALTH
7900 E. Greenway Rd., Ste. 210, Scottsdale 85260 *Type:* Private *Accred.:* 1994 (AB-HES) *Degrees:* C *CEO:* Pres. C. Larkin Hicks
FTE Enroll: 19   (602) 951-0629

ARIZONA PARALEGAL TRAINING PROGRAM
First American Title Bldg., 111 West Monroe Ave, Ste 800, Phoenix 85003 *Type:* Private business *Accred.:* 1981/1996 (ACICS) *Degrees:* C *CEO:* Dir. Raylene Dillon
(602) 252-2171

AZTECH COLLEGE
941 S. Dobson Rd., Ste. 120, Mesa 85202 *Type:* Private *Accred.:* 1973 (ACCSCT) *Degrees:* C *CEO:* Dir. David Brown
(602) 897-9898

ALBUQUERQUE CAMPUS
2201 San Pedro Dr., N.E., Bldg. 3, Albuquerque, NM 87110-9877
(505) 884-8371

THE BRYMAN SCHOOL
4343 N. 16th St., Phoenix 85016-5338 *Type:* Private *Accred.:* 1989 (ACCSCT) *Degrees:* C *Prof. Accred.:* Medical Assisting, Medical Assisting (AMA) *CEO:* Dir. Carole Miller
(602) 274-4300

CLINTON TECHNICAL INSTITUTE
2844 W. Deer Valley Rd., Phoenix 85027-9951 *Type:* Private *Accred.:* 1979/1986

(ACCSCT) *Degrees:* C *CEO:* Dir. Gary Green
(602) 869-9644

MOTORCYCLE/MARINE MECHANICS INSTITUTE
9751 Delegates Dr., Orlando, FL 32837-9835 *Accred.:* 1991 (ACCSCT)
(407) 240-2422

CONSERVATORY OF RECORDING ARTS AND SCIENCES
2300 E. Broadway Rd., Tempe 85282 *Type:* Private *Accred.:* 1990 (ACCSCT) *Degrees:* C *CEO:* Admin. Dir. Kirt R. Hamm
(602) 265-5566

DESERT INSTITUTE OF THE HEALING ARTS
639 N. Sixth Ave., Tucson 85705-8330 *Type:* Private *Accred.:* 1987 (ACCSCT) *Degrees:* C *CEO:* Admin. Dir. Janice Hollender
(602) 882-0899

DISTANCE LEARNING INTERNATIONAL
500 N. Kimball Ave., Southdale 79029 *Type:* Private distance education *Accred.:* 1981/1995 (DETC) *Degrees:* C *CEO:* Admin. Laura Orman Fabricant
(817) 488-6797

LONG MEDICAL INSTITUTE
4126 N. Black Canyon Hwy., Phoenix 85017-4394 *Type:* Private *Accred.:* 1981/1987 (ACCSCT) *Degrees:* C *Prof. Accred.:* Respiratory Therapy Technology *CEO:* Dir. Carol Martin
(602) 279-9333

MODERN SCHOOLS OF AMERICA, INC.
500 N. Kimball Ave., Southdale 79029 *Type:* Private distance education *Accred.:* 1980/1990 (DETC) *Degrees:* C *CEO:* Admin. Laura Fabricant
(817) 488-6797

MUNDUS INSTITUTE
4745 N. Seventh St., Ste. 100, Phoenix 85032-3669 *Type:* Private *Accred.:* 1989 (ACCSCT) *Degrees:* C *CEO:* Dir. Ann Marie Crawford
(602) 248-8548

NORTH AMERICAN TECHNICAL COLLEGE
1131 W. Broadway, Tempe 85282 *Type:* Private *Accred.:* 1994 (ACCSCT) *Degrees:* C *CEO:* Pres. Daniel Martinez
(602) 829-1903

NORTHERN ARIZONA COLLEGE OF HEALTH CAREERS
2575 E. Seventh Ave., Flagstaff 86004 *Type:* Private *Accred.:* 1982/1995 (ABHES) *Degrees:* C *CEO:* Pres./Dir. Betty McCarty
(520) 526-0763

ROBERTO-VENN SCHOOL OF LUTHIERY
4011 S. 16th St., Phoenix 85040-1314 *Type:* Private *Accred.:* 1979/1989 (ACCSCT) *Degrees:* C *CEO:* Dir. John H. Roberts
(602) 243-1179

TUCSON COLLEGE
7302-10 E. 22nd St., Tucson 85710 *Type:* Private business *Accred.:* 1966/1996 (ACICS) *Degrees:* C *Prof. Accred.:* Medical Assisting *CEO:* Dir. Elaine Bellcourt
(602) 296-3261

ARKANSAS

ARKANSAS COLLEGE OF BARBERING AND HAIR DESIGN
200 Washington Ave., North Little Rock 72114-5615 *Type:* Private *Accred.:* 1990 (AC-CSCT) *Degrees:* C *CEO:* Pres. Larry M. Little
(501) 376-9696

ARKANSAS VALLEY TECHNICAL INSTITUTE
1311 S. I St., Fort Smith 72901 *Type:* Private *Degrees:* C *Prof. Accred.:* Respiratory Therapy Technology *CEO:* Pres. Carl Jones
Enroll: 45   (501) 441-5256

CARTI SCHOOL OF RADIATION THERAPY TECHNOLOGY
P.O. Box 5210, Little Rock 72215 *Type:* Private *Degrees:* C *Prof. Accred.:* Radiation Therapy Technology *CEO:* Pres. Edward Rensch, Jr.
Enroll: 15   (501) 664-8573

COTTON BOLL TECHNICAL INSTITUTE
Box 36, Burdette 72321 *Type:* Private *Prof. Accred.:* Dental Assisting *CEO:* Pres. William Nelson
(501) 763-1486

EASTERN COLLEGE OF HEALTH VOCATIONS
6423 Forbing Rd., Little Rock 72209 *Type:* Private *Accred.:* 1984/1990 (ABHES) *Degrees:* C *CEO:* Pres. Susan M. Dalto
(501) 568-0211

NEW TYLER BARBER COLLEGE INC.
1221 E. Seventh St., North Little Rock 72114-4973 *Type:* Private *Accred.:* 1984/1989 (ACCSCT) *Degrees:* C *CEO:* Pres. Daniel Bryant
(501) 375-0377

REMINGTON COLLEGE
7601 Scott Hamilton Dr., Little Rock 72209 *Type:* Private business *Accred.:* 1988/1994 (ACICS) *Calendar:* Qtr. plan *Degrees:* C *CEO:* Dir. Byron Thompson
(501) 565-7000

FAYETTEVILLE CAMPUS
3348 N. College St., Fayetteville 72703 *Accred.:* 1988 (ACICS)
(501) 442-2364

CALIFORNIA

ACADEMY PACIFIC BUSINESS AND TRAVEL
COLLEGE
1777 N. Vine St., Hollywood 90028-5218
Type: Private *Accred.:* 1973/1990 (ACC-
SCT) *Degrees:* C *CEO:* Pres. Marsha Toy
(213) 462-3211

AMERICAN CAREER COLLEGE
4021 Rosewood Ave., Los Angeles 90004-
2932 *Type:* Private *Accred.:* 1983/1995
(ABHES); 1989 (ACCSCT) *Degrees:* C
CEO: Pres./Dir. David A. Pyle
(213) 383-2862

AMERICAN COLLEGE OF HOTEL AND
RESTAURANT MANAGER
11336 Camarillo St., North Hollywood
91602 *Type:* Private business *Accred.:* 1995
(ACICS) *Degrees:* C *CEO:* Pres. Robert
Toren
Enroll: 75   (818) 505-9800

AMERITECH COLLEGES
6843 Lennox Ave., Van Nuys 91405-4059
Type: Private *Accred.:* 1983 (ACCSCT)
Degrees: C *CEO:* Dir. Jari Simpson
(818) 901-7311

ANDON COLLEGE AT MODESTO
1314 H St., Modesto 95354 *Type:* Private
Accred.: 1985/1994 (ABHES) *Degrees:* C
CEO: Pres. Gary D. Kerber
(209) 571-8777

ANDON COLLEGE AT STOCKTON
1201 N. El Dorado St., Stockton 95202
Type: Private *Accred.:* 1988/1994 (ABHES)
Degrees: C *CEO:* Pres. Gary D. Kerber
(209) 462-8777

ASSOCIATED TECHNICAL COLLEGE
1177 N. Magnolia Ave., Anaheim 92801-
2606 *Type:* Private *Accred.:* 1984 (ACC-
SCT) *Degrees:* C *CEO:* Dir. Ali Khalaj
(714) 229-8785

ASSOCIATED TECHNICAL COLLEGE
1670 Wilshire Blvd., Los Angeles 90017-
1690 *Type:* Private *Accred.:* 1969/1987

(ACCSCT) *Degrees:* C *CEO:* Dir. Antonio
Sanges
(213) 484-2444

ASSOCIATED TECHNICAL COLLEGE
395 N. E St., San Bernardino 92401-1488
Type: Private *Accred.:* 1988 (ACCSCT)
Degrees: C *CEO:* Dir. Antonio Sanchez
(909) 885-1888

ASSOCIATED TECHNICAL COLLEGE
1475 Sixth Ave., San Diego 92101-3245
Type: Private *Accred.:* 1984/1989 (ACC-
SCT) *Degrees:* C *CEO:* Dir. Ali Pourhosseini
(619) 234-2181

BRYAN COLLEGE OF COURT REPORTING
2511 Beverly Blvd., Los Angeles 90057
Type: Private business *Accred.:* 1971/1995
(ACICS) *Degrees:* C *CEO:* Admin. Ned
Branch
(213) 484-8850

BRYAN COLLEGE-SAN FRANCISCO
731 Market St., San Francisco 94103 *Type:*
Private business *Accred.:* 1995 (ACICS)
Degrees: C *CEO:* Dir. Ned Branch
(415) 957-0663

CABOT COLLEGE
41 E. 12th St., National City 91950 *Type:*
Private business *Accred.:* 1988/1995
(ACICS) *Degrees:* C *CEO:* Pres. Wayne Cox
(619) 474-8017

CALIFORNIA ACADEMY OF MERCHANDISING,
ART AND DESIGN
2035 Hurley Way No. 300, Sacramento
95825 *Type:* Private business *Accred.:* 1986/
1995 (ACICS) *Degrees:* C *CEO:* Dir. Jeannie
Folsom
(916) 649-8168

CALIFORNIA CAREER SCHOOLS
392 W. Cerritos Ave., Anaheim 92805-6550
Type: Private *Accred.:* 1987 (ACCSCT)
Degrees: C *CEO:* Owner Sidney Smith
(714) 635-6585

CALIFORNIA INSTITUTE OF LOCKSMITHING
14721 Oxnard St., Van Nuys 91411 *Type:* Private *Accred.:* 1990 (ACCSCT) *Degrees:* C *CEO:* Dir. Charles H. Merchant, Sr.
(818) 994-7426

CALIFORNIA NANNIE COLLEGE
910 Howe Ave., Sacramento 95825-3979 *Type:* Private *Accred.:* 1987 (ACCSCT) *Degrees:* C *CEO:* Owner Larry Lionetli
(916) 921-2400

CALIFORNIA PARAMEDICAL & TECHNICAL COLLEGE
3745 Long Beach Blvd., Long Beach 90807-3377 *Type:* Private *Accred.:* 1980/1987 (ACCSCT) *Degrees:* C *Prof. Accred.:* Respiratory Therapy Technology, Surgical Technology *CEO:* Dir. Julia Morally
(310) 426-9359

CALIFORNIA PARAMEDICAL AND TECHNICAL COLLEGE
4550 LaSierra Ave., Riverside 92505-2907 *Type:* Private *Accred.:* 1982/1987 (ACCSCT) *Degrees:* C *Prof. Accred.:* Medical Assisting, Respiratory Therapy Technology *CEO:* Dir. Julia Morally
(909) 687-9006

CALIFORNIA SCHOOL OF COURT REPORTING
3510 Adams St., Riverside 92504 *Type:* Private business *Accred.:* 1986/1994 (ACICS) *Degrees:* C *CEO:* Pres. Virginia Wilcke
(714) 359-0293

CAREER MANAGEMENT INSTITUTE
1855 W. Katella Ave., Ste. 150, Orange 92667 *Type:* Private *Accred.:* 1993 (ACCSCT) *Degrees:* C *CEO:* Owner Nino Duccini
(714) 771-5077

CAREER WEST ACADEMY
2505B Zanella Way, Chico 95928 *Type:* Private *Accred.:* 1991 (ACCSCT) *Degrees:* C *CEO:* Admin. Christine Howell Payton
(916) 893-1481

CENTRAL CALIFORNIA SCHOOL OF CONTINUING EDUCATION
3195 McMillan St., Ste. F, San Luis Obispo 93401 *Type:* Private *Accred.:* 1992 (ACC-

SCT) *Degrees:* C *CEO:* Admin. Gene R. Appleby
(805) 543-9123

CHAMPION INSTITUTE OF COSMETOLOGY
72261 Hwy. 111, Palm Desert 92260 *Type:* Private *Accred.:* 1993 (ACCSCT) *Degrees:* C *CEO:* Pres. Virginia Slough
(619) 322-2227

CHAMPION INSTITUTE OF COSMETOLOGY
559 S. Palm Canyon Dr., Palm Desert 92260 *Type:* Private *Accred.:* 1993 (ACCSCT) *Degrees:* C *CEO:* Pres. Virginia Slough
(619) 322-2227

COLLEGE FOR RECORDING ARTS
665 Harrison St., San Francisco 94107-1312 *Type:* Private *Accred.:* 1977/1990 (ACCSCT) *Calendar:* Sem. plan *Degrees:* C *CEO:* Pres. Leo de Gar Kulka
(415) 781-6306

COLLEGEAMERICA—SAN FRANCISCO
814 Mission St., Ste. 300, San Francisco 94103-9748 *Type:* Private *Accred.:* 1969 (ACCSCT) *Degrees:* C *CEO:* Dir. Tami Freedman
(415) 882-4545

COMBAT SYSTEMS TECHNICAL SCHOOLS COMMAND
Mare Island, Vallejo 94592-5050 *Type:* Public (federal) technical *Accred.:* 1986/1990 (COE) *Degrees:* C *CEO:* Cmd. Ofcr. Shannon R. Butler
FTE Enroll: 397   (707) 554-8550

COMPUTER LEARNING CENTER
222 S. Harbor Blvd., Anaheim 92805 *Type:* Private business *Accred.:* 1990 (ACICS) *Degrees:* C *CEO:* Dir. Mary Langdon
(714) 956-8060

COMPUTER LEARNING CENTER
3130 Wilshire Blvd., Los Angeles 90010 *Type:* Private business *Accred.:* 1990 (ACICS) *Degrees:* C *CEO:* Dir. Michael Nielsen
(213) 386-6311

COMPUTER LEARNING CENTER
661 Howard St., San Francisco 94105 *Type:* Private business *Accred.:* 1980/1992 (ACICS) *Degrees:* C *CEO:* Dir. Jo-Ann Meron
(415) 498-0800

COMPUTER LEARNING CENTER
111 N. Market St., Ste. 105, San Jose 95113 *Type:* Private business *Accred.:* 1990 (ACICS) *Degrees:* C *CEO:* Dir. Harry Mauz, Jr.
(408) 983-5950

CONCORDE CAREER INSTITUTE
4150 Lankershim Blvd., North Hollywood 91602-2896 *Type:* Private *Accred.:* 1973 (ACCSCT) *Degrees:* C *Prof. Accred.:* Respiratory Therapy Technology, Surgical Technology *CEO:* Dir. Jeri Weinstein
(818) 766-8151

CONCORDE CAREER INSTITUTE
570 W. Fourth St., Ste. 107, San Bernardino 92416 *Type:* Private *Accred.:* 1968 (ACCSCT) *Degrees:* C *Prof. Accred.:* Medical Assisting (AMA) *CEO:* Dir. Mary Ellen Kontra
(909) 884-8891

CONCORDE CAREER INSTITUTE
123 Camino de la Reina, San Diego 92108 *Type:* Private *Accred.:* 1969 (ACCSCT) *Degrees:* C *CEO:* Dir. Nelson Melchior
(619) 688-0800

CONCORDE CAREER INSTITUTE
1290 N. First St., San Jose 95112-4709 *Type:* Private *Accred.:* 1989 (ACCSCT) *Degrees:* C *Prof. Accred.:* Respiratory Therapy Technology *CEO:* Dir. Rosalie Lampone
(408) 441-6411

CONSOLIDATED WELDING SCHOOLS
4343 E. Imperial Hwy., Lynwood 90262-2396 *Type:* Private *Accred.:* 1985/1990 (ACCSCT) *Degrees:* C *CEO:* Pres. Robert Swanson
(310) 638-0418

DELL'ARTE SCHOOL OF PHYSICAL THEATRE
P.O. Box 816, Blue Lake 95525 *Type:* Private *Degrees:* C *Prof. Accred.:* Theatre (A) *CEO:* Dir. Peter Buckley
(707) 668-5663

DICKINSON-WARREN BUSINESS COLLEGE
2702 Clayton Rd., Ste 201, Concord 94519 *Type:* Private business *Accred.:* 1979/1995 (ACICS) *Degrees:* C *CEO:* Pres. Ramon Flores
(510) 609-1770

EAST LOS ANGELES OCCUPATIONAL CENTER
2100 Marengo St., Los Angeles 90033 *Type:* Private professional *Degrees:* C *Prof. Accred.:* Dental Assisting *CEO:* Princ. Joe Tijerina
(213) 223-1283

EDUCORP CAREER COLLEGE
230 E. Third St., Long Beach 90802-3140 *Type:* Private *Accred.:* 1975/1987 (ACCSCT) *Degrees:* C *CEO:* Dir. Kenneth Boyle
(310) 437-0501

EDUTEK PROFESSIONAL COLLEGES
1541 Broadway, San Diego 92101-5788 *Type:* Private *Accred.:* 1981/1991 (ACCSCT) *Degrees:* C *CEO:* Exec. Dir. Carol Ruiz
(619) 239-4138

EDUTEK PROFESSIONAL COLLEGES
5952 El Cajon Blvd., San Diego 92120-4309 *Type:* Private *Accred.:* 1991 (ACCSCT) *CEO:* Dir. Carol Ruiz
(619) 582-1319

ELDORADO COLLEGE
2204 El Camino Real, Ste. 104, Oceanside 92054 *Type:* Private business *Accred.:* 1980/1986 (ACICS) *Calendar:* Qtr. plan *Degrees:* C *CEO:* Dir. Lisa Halco
(619) 433-3660

ESCONDIDO CAMPUS
385 N. Escondido Blvd., Escondido 92025 *Accred.:* 1989 (ACICS)
(619) 743-2100

SAN DIEGO CAMPUS
2255 Camino Del Rio, Ste. 200, San Diego 92108-3605 *Accred.:* 1992 (ACICS)
(619) 294-9256

ELDORADO COLLEGE
1901 Pacific Ave., West Covina 91790 *Type:* Private business *Accred.:* 1985 (ACICS) *Calendar:* Qtr. plan *Degrees:* C *CEO:* Dir. Delores Moran Coe
(818) 960-5173

ELEGANCE INTERNATIONAL
4929 Wilshire Blvd., Los Angeles 90010-1734 *Type:* Private *Accred.:* 1978/1989 (ACCSCT) *Calendar:* Sem. plan *Degrees:* C *CEO:* Pres. Wynna Miller
(213) 937-4838

ELITE PROGRESSIVE SCHOOL
5522 Garfield Ave., Sacramento 95841 *Type:* Private *Accred.:* 1993 (ACCSCT) *Degrees:* C *CEO:* Owner Manhal Mansour
(916) 338-1885

FRESNO INSTITUTE OF TECHNOLOGY
1545 N. Fulton St., Fresno 93720 *Type:* Private *Accred.:* 1991 (ACCSCT) *Degrees:* C *CEO:* Dir. Fred Freedman
(209) 442-3574

GALEN COLLEGE OF MEDICAL AND DENTAL ASSISTANTS
1325 N. Wishon Ave., Fresno 93728-2381 *Type:* Private *Accred.:* 1974/1988 (ACC-SCT) *Degrees:* C *CEO:* Pres. Stella Mesple
(209) 264-9726

MODESTO CAMPUS
1604 Ford Ave., Ste. 10, Modesto 95350-4665 *Accred.:* 1988 (ACCSCT)
(209) 527-5084

VISALIA CAMPUS
3746 W. Mineral King Ave., Ste. C, Visalia 93291-5510 *Accred.:* 1988 (ACCSCT)
(209) 264-9726

GEMOLOGICAL INSTITUTE OF AMERICA
1660 Stewart St., Santa Monica 90404-4088 *Type:* Private technical and distance education *Accred.:* 1973/1986 (ACCSCT); 1965/

1991 (DETC) *Degrees:* C *CEO:* Pres. William A. Boyajian
(310) 829-2991

NEW YORK CAMPUS
580 Fifth Ave., New York, NY 10036-4794 *Accred.:* 1986 (ACCSCT)
(212) 944-5900

HACIENDA LA PUENTE ADULT EDUCATION
15540 E. Fairgrove Ave., La Puente 91744 *Type:* Public *Degrees:* C *Prof. Accred.:* Respiratory Therapy Technology *CEO:* Dir. Sidney Coffin
(818) 855-3138

HEALTH STAFF TRAINING INSTITUTE
1505 E. 17th St., No. 122, Santa Ana 92701 *Type:* Private *Accred.:* 1988/1994 (ABHES) *Degrees:* C *CEO:* Pres. Dianna Standoff
(714) 543-9828

HELICOPTER ADVENTURES
81 John Glenn Dr., Concorde 94520 *Accred.:* 1994 (ACCSCT) *Degrees:* C *CEO:* Pres. Patrick Corr
(510) 686-2917

HEMPHILL SCHOOLS
2562 E. Colorado Blvd., Pasadena 91107-3744 *Type:* Private distance education *Accred.:* 1966/1992 (DETC) *Degrees:* C *CEO:* Vice Pres. Yolanda Jimenez-Agheli
(818) 568-8146

HOSPITALITY MANAGEMENT TRAINING INSTITUTE
814 Mission St., Ste. 500, San Francisco 94103 *Type:* Private business *Accred.:* 1995 (ACICS) *Degrees:* C *CEO:* Pres. Sherris Goodwin
Enroll: 78   (415) 896-0370

HUNTINGTON COLLEGE OF DENTAL TECHNOLOGY
7466 Edinger Ave., Huntington Beach 92647-3510 *Type:* Private *Accred.:* 1987 (ACCSCT) *Degrees:* C *CEO:* Pres. Edward M. Beram
(714) 841-9500

HYPNOSIS MOTIVATION INSTITUTE
18607 Ventura Blvd., Ste. 310, Tarzana 91356 *Type:* Private distance education *Accred.:* 1989/1995 (DETC) *Degrees:* C *CEO:* Dir. George J. Kappas
(800) 6000-HMI

INSTITUTE FOR BUSINESS & TECHNOLOGY
2550 Scott Blvd., Santa Clara 95050-9998 *Type:* Private *Accred.:* 1979/1986 (ACC-SCT) *Degrees:* C *Prof. Accred.:* Medical Assisting *CEO:* Pres. M.A. Mikhail
(408) 727-1060

NATIONAL CAREER EDUCATION
6060 Sunrise Vista Dr., Ste. 3000, Citrus Heights 95610-7053 *Accred.:* 1986 (ACC-SCT) *Prof. Accred.:* Medical Assisting
(916) 969-4900

INTERNATIONAL DEALERS SCHOOL
6329 E. Washington Blvd., Commerce 90040 *Type:* Private *Accred.:* 1985/1990 (ACCSCT) *Degrees:* C *CEO:* Admin. Candetta Simone
(213) 890-0030

IRVINE COLLEGE OF BUSINESS
16591 Noyes Ave., Irvine 92714 *Type:* Private business *Accred.:* 1977/1995 (ACICS) *Degrees:* C *CEO:* Pres. William D. Polick, Sr.
(714) 863-1145

JOHN TRACY CLINIC
806 W. Adams Blvd., Los Angeles 90007 *Type:* Private distance education *Accred.:* 1965/1992 (DETC) *Degrees:* C *CEO:* Dir. Sandra Meyer
(800) 522-4582

LEARNING TREE UNIVERSITY
20916 Knapp St., Chatsworth 91311 *Type:* Private *Calendar:* Qtr. plan *Degrees:* C *Prof. Accred.:* Art (A) *CEO:* Dir. Christy Wilson
(818) 882-5685

LEDERWOLFF CULINARY ACADEMY
3300 Stockton Blvd., Sacramento 95820-1450 *Type:* Private *Accred.:* 1987 (ACC-SCT) *Degrees:* C *CEO:* Owner Kristine Wolff
(916) 456-7002

LEICESTER SCHOOL
1106 W. Olympic Blvd., Los Angeles 90015 *Type:* Private *Accred.:* 1992 (ACCSCT) *Degrees:* C *CEO:* Dir. Victor Weintraub
(213) 746-7666

LOS ANGELES ORT TECHNICAL INSTITUTE
635 S. Harvard Blvd., Los Angeles 90005-2586 *Type:* Private *Accred.:* 1988 (ACC-SCT) *Degrees:* C *CEO:* Dir. Joseph Neman
(213) 387-4244

VALLEY CAMPUS
15130 Ventura Blvd., No. 250, Sherman Oaks 91403-3301 *Accred.:* 1988 (ACCSCT)
(818) 788-7222

MANAGEMENT COLLEGE OF SAN FRANCISCO
1255 Post St., No. 450, San Francisco 94109 *Type:* Private *Accred.:* 1993 (ACCSCT) *Degrees:* C *CEO:* Owner Marilyn Mayer
(405) 776-7244

MARIC COLLEGE OF MEDICAL CAREERS
3666 Kearny Villa Rd., San Diego 92123 *Type:* Private *Accred.:* 1982/1988 (ACC-SCT) *Degrees:* C *Prof. Accred.:* Medical Assisting *CEO:* Campus Dir. Ken Humphrey
(619) 583-8232

MARIC COLLEGE OF MEDICAL CAREERS
1300 Rancheros Dr., San Marcos 92069-3033 *Type:* Private *Accred.:* 1984/1990 (ACCSCT) *Degrees:* C *Prof. Accred.:* Medical Assisting *CEO:* Campus Dir. Diane Heath
(619) 747-1555

VISTA CAMPUS BRANCH
1593-C E. Vista Way, Vista 92084-3577 *Accred.:* 1990 (ABHES); 1990 (ACCSCT)
(619) 758-8640

MICROCOMPUTER EDUCATION CENTER
2212 M Winery, No. 122, Fresno 93703 *Accred.:* 1994 (ACCSCT) *CEO:* Admin. Rick Trevino
Enroll: 150 (209) 456-0623

MODERN TECHNOLOGY SCHOOL OF X-RAY
1232 E. Katella Ave., Anaheim 92805-6623 *Type:* Private *Accred.:* 1988 (ACCSCT)

Degrees: C *CEO:* Admin. Dir. Harvey S. Caplan

(714) 978-7702

MODERN TECHNOLOGY SCHOOL OF X-RAY
6180 Laurel Canyon Blvd., North Hollywood 91606 *Type:* Private *Accred.:* 1987/1993 (ACCSCT) *Degrees:* C *CEO:* Exec. Dir. Beverly Yourstone

(818) 763-2563

MOLER BARBER COLLEGE
3500 Broadway St., Oakland 94611-5729 *Type:* Private *Accred.:* 1980/1988 (ACCSCT) *Degrees:* C *CEO:* Owner Willie C. McHenry

(510) 652-4177

MOLER BARBER COLLEGE
727 J St., Sacramento 95814-2501 *Type:* Private *Accred.:* 1980/1993 (ACCSCT) *Degrees:* C *CEO:* Dir. James A. Murray, Jr.

(916) 441-0072

BRANCH CAMPUS
2645 El Camino Ave., Sacramento 95821-2901 *Accred.:* 1991/1993 (ACCSCT)

(916) 482-0871

STOCKTON CAMPUS
410 E. Weber Ave., Stockton 95202-3025 *Accred.:* 1991 (ACCSCT)

(916) 465-3218

MOLER BARBER COLLEGE
50 Mason St., San Francisco 94102-2890 *Type:* Private *Accred.:* 1980/1987 (ACCSCT) *Degrees:* C *CEO:* Dir. Donald A. Forfang, II

(415) 362-5885

MONTEREY PARK COLLEGE
583 Monterey Pass Rd., Monterey Park 91754 *Type:* Private Business *Accred.:* 1994 (ACICS) *Degrees:* C *CEO:* Pres. Henry H. Hua

(818) 576-2444

MTI BUSINESS COLLEGE OF STOCKTON INC.
6006 N. El Dorado St., Stockton 95207-4349 *Type:* Private *Accred.:* 1987 (ACCSCT) *Degrees:* C *CEO:* Dir. Felix G. Brenner

(209) 957-3030

MTI COLLEGE
2011 W. Chapman Ave., Ste. 100, Orange 92668-2632 *Type:* Private *Accred.:* 1987 (ACCSCT) *Calendar:* Qtr. plan *Degrees:* C *CEO:* Dir. Ton Bui

(714) 385-1132

COLTON CAMPUS
760 Via Lata, No. 300, Colton 92324-3916 *Accred.:* 1988 (ACCSCT)

(714) 424-0123

MUSICIANS INSTITUTE
1655 N. McCadden Place, Hollywood 90028 *Type:* Private *Degrees:* C *Prof. Accred.:* Music *CEO:* Pres. Naho Shibuya

(213) 462-1384

NATIONAL EDUCATION CENTER—BRYMAN CAMPUS
1120 N. Brookhurst St., Anaheim 92801-1702 *Type:* Private *Accred.:* 1973 (ACCSCT) *Degrees:* C *CEO:* Dir. Pam Burns

(714) 953-6500

NATIONAL EDUCATION CENTER—BRYMAN CAMPUS
5350 Atlantic Ave., Long Beach 90805-6020 *Type:* Private *Accred.:* 1968/1989 (ACCSCT) *Degrees:* C *Prof. Accred.:* Medical Assisting (AMA) *CEO:* Exec. Dir. Roger Gugelmeyer

(310) 422-6007

NATIONAL EDUCATION CENTER—BRYMAN CAMPUS
1017 Wilshire Blvd., Los Angeles 90017-2493 *Type:* Private *Accred.:* 1973/1990 (ACCSCT) *Degrees:* C *CEO:* Dir. Dick Whitaker

(213) 481-1640

NATIONAL EDUCATION CENTER—BRYMAN CAMPUS
3505 N. Hart Ave., Rosemead 91770-2096 *Type:* Private *Accred.:* 1968/1990 (ACCSCT) *Degrees:* C *Prof. Accred.:* Medical Assisting (AMA) *CEO:* Dir. George Ballew

(818) 573-5470

NATIONAL EDUCATION CENTER—BRYMAN
CAMPUS
731 Market St., San Francisco 94103-9946
Type: Private *Accred.:* 1972/1990 (ACCSCT)
Degrees: C *Prof. Accred.:* Medical Assisting
(AMA) *CEO:* Dir. Vicki L. Wallace
(415) 777-2500

NATIONAL EDUCATION CENTER—BRYMAN
CAMPUS
2015 Naglee Ave., San Jose 95128-4801
Type: Private *Accred.:* 1973/1986 (ACCSCT)
Degrees: C *Prof. Accred.:* Medical Assisting
(AMA) *CEO:* Exec. Dir. Sandra Pella
(408) 275-8800

NEW ORLEANS CAMPUS
2322 Canal St., New Orleans, LA 70119-
6504 *Accred.:* 1991 (ACCSCT)
(504) 822-4500

NATIONAL EDUCATION CENTER—BRYMAN
CAMPUS
4212 W. Artesia Blvd., Torrance 90504-3198
Type: Private *Accred.:* 1973/1990 (ACCSCT)
Degrees: C *Prof. Accred.:* Medical Assisting
(AMA) *CEO:* Dir. Judy Kavenaugh
(310) 542-6951

NATIONAL EDUCATION CENTER—BRYMAN
CAMPUS
20835 Sherman Way, Winnetka 91306-2795
Type: Private *Accred.:* 1974/1987 (ACC-
SCT) *Degrees:* C *Prof. Accred.:* Medical
Assisting *CEO:* Dir. Tapas Ghosh
(818) 887-7911

NATIONAL EDUCATION CENTER—SAWYER
CAMPUS
8475 Jackson Rd., Sacramento 95826 *Type:*
Private business *Accred.:* 1973/1991 (AC-
ICS) *Degrees:* C *CEO:* Dir. Maryanne
Racette
(916) 383-1909

NAVAL EXPEDITIONARY WARFARE TRAINING
GROUP, PACIFIC
3423 Guadalcanal Rd., Bldg. 401, San Diego
92155-5099 *Type:* Public (federal) technical
Accred.: 1979/1989 (COE) *Degrees:* C
CEO: Cmnd. Ofcr. T. M. Hayes
FTE Enroll: 304 (619) 437-3726

NAVAL CONSTRUCTION TRAINING CENTER
363 Whitehouse Way, Port Hueneme 93043-
4303 *Type:* Public (federal) technical
Accred.: 1979/1991 (COE) *Degrees:* C
CEO: Cmnd. Ofcr. M. B. Samuels
FTE Enroll: 309 (805) 982-4153

NAVAL FLEET ANTI-SUBMARINE WARFARE
TRAINING CENTER—PACIFIC
32444 Echo Ln., Ste. 100, San Diego 92147-
5199 *Type:* Public (federal) technical *Accred.:*
1991 (COE) *Degrees:* C *CEO:* Commandant
Bruce Linder
FTE Enroll: 645 (619) 524-1664

NAVAL SERVICE SCHOOL COMMAND
32224 Roosevelt Rd. No. 220-B, Naval
Trainig Ctr., San Diego 92133-1368 *Type:*
Public (federal) technical *Accred.:* 1985/
1989 (COE) *Degrees:* C *CEO:* Cmnd. Ofcr.
C. R. Rondestvedt
FTE Enroll: 888 (619) 524-4857

NAVAL FLEET TRAINING CENTER DETACHMENT
Treasure Island, 1070 M Ave., San Francisco
94130-1070 *Type:* Public (federal) technical
Accred.: 1987/1992 (COE) *Degrees:* C
CEO: Cmnd. Ofcr. Deane K. Gibson
FTE Enroll: 153 (415) 395-3073

NAVAL TRANSPORTATION MANAGEMENT SCHOOL
Oakland Army Base, Bldg. 790, Oakland
94626-5790 *Type:* Public (federal) technical
Accred.: 1986/1991 (COE) *Degrees:* C
CEO: Cmnd. Ofcr. Richard Elgin
FTE Enroll: 68 (510) 466-2155

NEWBRIDGE COLLEGE
700 El Camino Real, Tustin 92680 *Type:* Private *Accred.:* 1988 (ACCSCT) *Degrees:* C
CEO: Owner J. Ramon Villanueva
(714) 573-8787

NEWSCHOOL OF ARCHITECTURE
1249 F St., San Diego 92101 *Type:* Private
senior *Accred.:* 1994 (ACICS) *CEO:* Pres.
C. Gordon Bishop
(619) 235-4100

NORTH PARK COLLEGE
3956 30th St., San Diego 92104-3005 *Type:* Private *Accred.:* 1989 (ACCSCT) *Degrees:* C *CEO:* Pres. Ross Lipsker
(619) 297-3333

BRANCH CAMPUS
4718 Clairemont Mesa Blvd., San Diego 92117 *Accred.:* 1993 (ACCSCT)
(619) 483-3088

NORTHWEST COLLEGE OF MEDICAL AND DENTAL ASSISTANTS
530 E. Union Ave., Pasadena 91101-1744 *Type:* Private *Accred.:* 1983/1988 (ACCSCT) *Degrees:* C *CEO:* Exec. Dir. Marla Mittskys
(818) 796-5815

NORTHWEST COLLEGE OF MEDICAL AND DENTAL ASSISTANTS
134 W. Holt Ave., Pomona 91768-3199 *Type:* Private *Accred.:* 1976/1988 (ACCSCT) *Degrees:* C *CEO:* Exec. Dir. Susan Hutchison
(909) 623-1552

NORTHWEST COLLEGE OF MEDICAL AND DENTAL ASSISTANTS
2121 W. Garvey Ave., West Covina 91790-2097 *Type:* Private *Accred.:* 1973/1990 (ACCSCT) *Degrees:* C *CEO:* Exec. Dir. Jacky Ford
(818) 962-3495

GLENDALE CAMPUS
124 S. Glendale Ave., Glendale 91205-1109 *Accred.:* 1986 (ACCSCT)
(818) 242-0205

NOVA INSTITUTE OF HEALTH TECHNOLOGY
3000 S. Robertson Blvd., Ste. 300, Los Angeles 90034 *Type:* Private *Accred.:* 1987 (ACCSCT) *Degrees:* C *CEO:* Dir. Rashed B. Elyas
(310) 840-5777

NOVA INSTITUTE OF HEALTH TECHNOLOGY
520 N. Euclid Ave., Ontario 91762-3591 *Type:* Private *Accred.:* 1986 (ACCSCT) *Degrees:* C *CEO:* Dir. Martha L. Escobar
(909) 984-5027

NOVA INSTITUTE OF HEALTH TECHNOLOGY
11416 Whittier Blvd., Whittier 90601-3198 *Type:* Private *Accred.:* 1991 (ACCSCT) *Degrees:* C *CEO:* Dir. Nagui Elyas
(310) 695-0771

ORANGE COUNTY BUSINESS COLLEGE
2035 E. Ball Rd., Anaheim 92806 *Type:* Private business *Accred.:* 1973/1990 (ACICS) *Degrees:* C *CEO:* Dir. Susan A. Fechtman
(714) 772-6941

PACIFIC GATEWAY COLLEGE
3018 Carmel St., Los Angeles 90065-1401 *Type:* Private *Accred.:* 1988 (ACCSCT) *Degrees:* C *CEO:* Pres. John R. Phalen
(818) 247-9544

PACIFIC TRAVEL SCHOOL
2515 N. Main St., Santa Ana 92701-1300 *Type:* Private *Accred.:* 1968/1990 (ACCSCT) *Degrees:* C *CEO:* Dir. Celia Sifry
(714) 543-9495

PLATT COLLEGE
7470 N. Figueroa St., Los Angeles 90041-1717 *Type:* Private *Accred.:* 1987/1993 (ACCSCT) *Degrees:* C *CEO:* Dir. William W. Lockwood
(213) 258-8050

PLATT COLLEGE
3901 MacArthur Blvd., Newport Beach 92600 *Accred.:* 1985 (ACCSCT) *Calendar:* Tri. plan *Degrees:* C *CEO:* Dir. Kerry Sousse
Enroll: 180   (714) 833-2300

PLATT COLLEGE
9521 Business Center Dr., Rancho Cucam 91730 *Type:* Private *Accred.:* 1987 (ACCSCT) *Degrees:* C *CEO:* Pres. Jan E. Hartz
(909) 989-1187

PLATT COLLEGE
301 Mission St., No. 450, San Francisco 94105-2243 *Type:* Private *Accred.:* 1988 (ACCSCT) *Degrees:* C *CEO:* Dir. Carel R. Thomas
(415) 495-4000

PLATT COLLEGE SAN DIEGO
6250 El Cajon Blvd., San Diego 92115-3919
Type: Private *Accred.:* 1985/1990 (ACC-SCT) *Degrees:* C *CEO:* Pres. Robert D. Leiker
(619) 265-0107

PRACTICAL SCHOOLS
900 E. Ball Rd., Anaheim 92805-5915 *Type:* Private *Accred.:* 1973/1990 (ACCSCT) *Degrees:* C *CEO:* Pres. Marlyn B. Sheehan
(714) 535-6000

PREMIER CAREER COLLEGE
12901 Ramona Blvd., Ste. D, Irwindale 91706 *Type:* Private business *Accred.:* 1995 (ACICS) *CEO:* Pres. Fe Ludovico-Aragon
Enroll: 85　　　　　　　(818) 814-2080

ROSSTON SCHOOL OF HAIR DESIGN
673 W. Fifth St., San Bernardino 92410-3201 *Type:* Private *Accred.:* 1976/1988 (ACCSCT) *Degrees:* C *CEO:* Pres. John Olivas
(909) 884-2719

SAN FRANCISCO BARBER COLLEGE
64 Sixth St., San Francisco 94103-1608 *Type:* Private *Accred.:* 1984/1989 (ACC-SCT) *Degrees:* C *CEO:* Pres. Frank Yorkis
(415) 621-6802

SANTA BARBARA BUSINESS COLLEGE
211 S. Real Rd., Bakersfield 93301 *Type:* Private business *Accred.:* 1983/1991 (ACICS) *Calendar:* Qtr. plan *Degrees:* C *Prof. Accred.:* Medical Assisting *CEO:* Dir. Kathy Gibson
(805) 322-3006

SANTA BARBARA BUSINESS COLLEGE
4333 Hansen Ave., Freemont 94536 *Type:* Private business *Accred.:* 1976/1986 (AC-ICS) *Calendar:* Qtr. plan *Degrees:* C *Prof. Accred.:* Medical Assisting *CEO:* Dir. Susan Rocha
(510) 793-4342

SANTA BARBARA BUSINESS COLLEGE
5266 Hollister Ave., Santa Barbara 93111 *Type:* Private business *Accred.:* 1976/1990 (ACICS) *Calendar:* Qtr. plan *Degrees:* C

Prof. Accred.: Medical Assisting *CEO:* Dir. Susan Corvino
(805) 967-9677

SANTA BARBARA BUSINESS COLLEGE
303 E. Plaza Dr., Santa Maria 93454 *Type:* Private business *Accred.:* 1983/1991 (AC-ICS) *Calendar:* Qtr. plan *Degrees:* C *Prof. Accred.:* Medical Assisting *CEO:* Dir. Carol Gastiger
(805) 922-8256

SAWYER COLLEGE
441 W. Trimble Rd., San Jose 95131 *Type:* Private business *Accred.:* 1973/1990 (AC-ICS) *Degrees:* C *CEO:* Dir. Beverly Yourstone
(408) 954-8200

SAWYER COLLEGE AT VENTURA
2101 E. Gonzales Rd., Oxnard 93030 *Type:* Private business *Accred.:* 1969/1996 (AC-ICS) *Degrees:* C *CEO:* Pres. Doreen E. Adamache
(805) 485-6000

SCHOOL OF COMMUNICATION ELECTRONICS
184 Second St., San Francisco 94105-3809 *Type:* Private *Accred.:* 1985 (ACCSCT) *Degrees:* C *CEO:* Owner Robert W. Lew
(415) 896-0858

SEQUOIA INSTITUTE
420 Whitney Pl., Fremont 94539-7663 *Type:* Private *Accred.:* 1977/1989 (ACCSCT) *Degrees:* C *CEO:* Pres. Timothy T. Schutz
(510) 490-6900

SIERRA ACADEMY OF AERONAUTICS TECHNICAL INSTITUTE
Oakland International Airport, P.O. Box 2429, Oakland 94614-0429 *Type:* Private *Accred.:* 1987 (ACCSCT) *Degrees:* C *CEO:* Pres. Norris N. Everett
(510) 568-6100

SIERRA VALLEY BUSINESS COLLEGE
4747 N. First St., Bldg. D, Fresno 93726 *Type:* Private business *Accred.:* 1981/1987 (ACICS) *Degrees:* C *CEO:* Pres. Donald D. Goodpaster
(209) 222-0947

SILICON VALLEY COLLEGE
41350 Christy St., Fremont 94538 *Type:* Private *Accred.:* 1991 (ACCSCT) *Degrees:* C *CEO:* Chrmn. Ellis C. Gedney
(510) 623-9966

SIMI VALLEY ADULT SCHOOL
3192 Los Angeles Ave., Simi Valley 93065 *Type:* Private *Degrees:* C *Prof. Accred.:* Respiratory Therapy Technology, Surgical Technology *CEO:* Dir. Sondra Jones
(805) 527-4840

SOUTH COAST COLLEGE OF COURT REPORTING
1380 S. Sanderson Ave., Anaheim 92806 *Type:* Private business *Accred.:* 1984/1996 (ACICS) *Degrees:* C *CEO:* Pres. Jean Gonzalez
(714) 635-6464

FOUNTAIN VALLEY CAMPUS
17911 Bushard St., Fountain Valley 92708
(714) 378-4510

SOUTHERN CALIFORNIA COLLEGE OF COURT REPORTING
1100 S. Claudina Pl., Anaheim 92805 *Type:* Private business *Accred.:* 1991/1994 (ACICS) *Degrees:* C *CEO:* Pres. Gene Lee
(714) 758-1500

SOUTHERN CALIFORNIA INSTITUTE OF TECHNOLOGY
1900 W. Crescent Ave., Anaheim 92801 *Accred.:* 1994 (ACCSCT) *CEO:* Dir. Parviz Shams
Enroll: 200   (714) 520-5552

SUTECH SCHOOL OF VOCATIONAL-TECHNICAL TRAINING
3427 E. Olympic Blvd., Los Angeles 90023-3076 *Type:* Private *Accred.:* 1989 (ACCSCT) *Degrees:* C *CEO:* Pres. Oswaldo Forero
(213) 262-3210

ANAHEIM CAMPUS
1855 S. Santa Cruz St., Anaheim 92805 *Accred.:* 1993 (ACCSCT)
(714) 939-7860

SYSTEMS PROGRAMMING DEVELOPMENT INSTITUTE
4900 Triggs St., City of Commerce 90022-4832 *Type:* Private *Accred.:* 1984/1989 (ACCSCT) *Degrees:* C *CEO:* Pres. Jose Luis Segura
(213) 261-8181

TRAVEL AND TRADE CAREER INSTITUTE
3635 Atlantic Ave., Long Beach 90807 *Type:* Private *Accred.:* 1972/1989 (ACCSCT) *Degrees:* C *CEO:* Pres. Rodger Erickson
(310) 426-8841

GARDEN GROVE CAMPUS
12541 Brookhurst St., Ste. 100, Garden Grove 92640-9802 *Accred.:* 1972/1989 (ACCSCT)
(714) 636-2611

TRAVEL UNIVERSITY INTERNATIONAL
3655 Ruffin Rd. N., Ste. 225, San Diego 92123-1853 *Type:* Private *Accred.:* 1987 (ACCSCT) *Degrees:* C *CEO:* Pres. Nancy Chappie
(619) 292-9755

HONOLULU CAMPUS
1441 Kapiolani Blvd., Ste. 1414, Honolulu, HI 96814-4401 *Accred.:* 1988 (ACCSCT)
(808) 946-3535

TRUCK DRIVING ACADEMY
5711 Florin-Perkins Rd., Sacramento 95828-1002 *Type:* Private *Accred.:* 1988 (ACCSCT) *Degrees:* C *CEO:* Owner Charles J. Grant
(916) 381-2285

FRESNO CAMPUS
5168 N. Blythe Ave., No. 102, Fresno 93722-6429 *Accred.:* 1991 (ACCSCT) *Degrees:* C
(209) 276-5708

TRUCK MARKETING INSTITUTE
1090 Eugenia Pl., P.O. Box 5000, Carpinteria 93014-5000 *Type:* Private distance education *Accred.:* 1968/1994 (DETC) *Degrees:* C *CEO:* Dir. Robert Godfrey
(805) 684-4558

WATTERSON COLLEGE
150 S. Los Robles Ave., Ste. 100, Pasadena 91101 *Type:* Private business *Accred.:* 1953/ 1996 (ACICS) *Calendar:* Qtr. plan *Degrees:* C *CEO:* Dir. Rita A. Totten
(818) 449-3990

WATTERSON COLLEGE
1422 S. Azusa Ave., West Covina 91791 *Type:* Private business *Accred.:* 1988/1994 (ACICS) *Calendar:* Qtr. plan *Degrees:* C *CEO:* Dir. Rita Totten
(818) 919-8701

WESTECH COLLEGE
500 W. Mission Blvd., Pomona 91766-1532 *Type:* Private *Accred.:* 1991 (ACCSCT) *Degrees:* C *CEO:* Exec. Dir. Barry Maleki
(714) 622-6486

WESTERN CAREER COLLEGE
8909 Folsom Blvd., Sacramento 95826 *Type:* Private *Accred.:* 1970/1987 (ACC-SCT) *Degrees:* C *Prof. Accred.:* Medical Assisting *CEO:* Pres. Richard G. Nathanson
(916) 361-1660

WESTERN CAREER COLLEGE
170 Bayfair Mall, San Leandro 94578-3711 *Type:* Private *Accred.:* 1986 (ACCSCT) *Degrees:* C *Prof. Accred.:* Medical Assisting *CEO:* Dir. Jay Harris
(510) 278-2888

WESTERN TRUCK SCHOOL
4565 N. Golden State Blvd., Fresno 93722-3829 *Type:* Private *Accred.:* 1988 (ACC-SCT) *Degrees:* C *CEO:* Dir. Gerald Payne
(209) 276-1220

WESTERN TRUCK SCHOOL
4521 W. Capitol Ave., West Sacramento 95691-2121 *Type:* Private *Accred.:* 1980/ 1993 (ACC-SCT) *Degrees:* C *CEO:* Pres. Everett G. Nord
(916) 372-6500

BAKERSFIELD CAMPUS
5800 State Rd., Bakersfield 93308
(805) 399-0701

PHOENIX CAMPUS
3201 E. Broadway Rd., Phoenix, AZ 85040
(602) 437-5303

SAN DIEGO CAMPUS
8775 Aero Dr., San Diego 92123
(619) 514-8902

STOCKTON CAMPUS
1053 N. Broadway, Stockton 95205-3924 *Accred.:* 1989 (ACCSCT)
(209) 465-1191

WESTLAKE INSTITUTE OF TECHNOLOGY
31826A Village Center Rd., Westlake Village 91361 *Type:* Private *Accred.:* 1991 (ACCSCT) *Degrees:* C *CEO:* Owner Bruce H. Dotson
(818) 991-9992

COLORADO

ACADEMY OF FLORAL DESIGN
837 Acoma St., Denver 80204 *Type:* Private business *Accred.:* 1983/1987 (ACICS) *Degrees:* C *CEO:* Pres./Dir. Noel S. Valnes
(303) 623-8855

BOULDER SCHOOL OF MASSAGE THERAPY
3285 30th St., Boulder 80301-1451 *Type:* Private *Accred.:* 1991 (ACCSCT) *Degrees:* C *CEO:* Dir. Lorraine M. Zinn
(303) 443-5131

BOULDER VALLEY AREA VOCATIONAL-
TECHNICAL CENTER
6600 E. Arapahoe Ave., Boulder 80303 *Type:* Private *Degrees:* C *Prof. Accred.:* Medical Assisting (AMA) *CEO:* Exec. Dir. Lonnie M. Hart
Enroll: 36   (303) 447-5247

COLLEGEAMERICA—DENVER
720 S. Colorado Blvd., Ste. 260, Denver 80222-1912 *Type:* Private *Accred.:* 1993 (AC-CSCT) *Degrees:* C *CEO:* Dir. Kathy A. Metcalf
(303) 691-9756

COLORADO SCHOOL OF TRAVEL
608 Garrison St., Unit J, Lakewood 80215-5881 *Type:* Private *Accred.:* 1991 (ACCSCT) *Degrees:* C *CEO:* Pres. Paula E. Wagner
(303) 233-8654

CONCORDE CAREER INSTITUTE
770 Grant St., Denver 80203-3517 *Type:* Private *Accred.:* 1991 (ACCSCT) *Degrees:* C *Prof. Accred.:* Surgical Technology *CEO:* Dir. Richard K. Shepard
(303) 861-1151

DENVER AUTOMOTIVE AND DIESEL COLLEGE
405 S. Platte River Dr., Denver 80223-9960 *Type:* Private *Accred.:* 1968/1988 (ACCSCT) *Degrees:* C *CEO:* Dir. Joseph R. Chalupa
(303) 722-5724

DENVER PARALEGAL INSTITUTE
1401 19th St., Denver 80202-1213 *Type:* Private *Accred.:* 1979/1990 (ACCSCT) *Degrees:* C *CEO:* Dir. Betsy O'Neil Covington
(800) 848-0550

COLORADO SPRINGS CAMPUS
105 E. Vermijo Ave., Ste. 415, Colorado Springs 80903 *Accred.:* 1992 (ACCSCT)
(719) 444-0190

DURANGO AIR SERVICE
1300 County Rd. 309, Durango 81301 *Type:* Private *Accred.:* 1993 (ACCSCT) *Degrees:* C *CEO:* Pres. Donley E. Watkins
(303) 247-5535

EMILY GRIFFITH OPPORTUNITY SCHOOL
1250 Welton St., Denver 80204 *Type:* Private *Degrees:* C *Prof. Accred.:* Dental Assisting, Medical Assisting (AMA) *CEO:* Princ. Mary Ann Parthum
(303) 572-8218

HERITAGE COLLEGE OF HEALTH CAREERS
12 Lakeside Ln., Denver 80212-7413 *Type:* Private *Accred.:* 1991 (ACCSCT) *Degrees:* C *CEO:* Pres. Richard Herold
(303) 477-7240

INSTITUTE OF BUSINESS AND MEDICAL
CAREERS, INC
1609 Oakridge Dr., Ste 102, Fort Collins 80525 *Type:* Private *Accred.:* 1990 (AB-HES) *Degrees:* C *CEO:* Pres. Richard B. Laub
(303) 223-2669

PPI HEALTH CAREERS SCHOOL
2345 N. Academy Blvd., Colorado Springs 80909 *Type:* Private *Accred.:* 1983/1990 (ABHES) *Degrees:* C *Prof. Accred.:* Medical Assisting, Medical Laboratory Technology *CEO:* Pres. Thomas J. Twardowski
(719) 596-7400

PRESBYTERIAN-ST. LUKE CENTER FOR HEALTH
SCIENCE EDUCATION
1719 E. 19th Ave., Denver 80218 *Type:* Private *Degrees:* C *Prof. Accred.:* Clinical Lab Scientist, Radiography *CEO:* Pres. Thomas Petty
(303) 839-6740

T.H. PICKENS TECHNICAL CENTER
500 Buckley Rd., Aurora 80011 *Type:* Private *Degrees:* C *Prof. Accred.:* Clinical Lab Technology (C), Dental Assisting, Medical Assisting (AMA), Respiratory Therapy Technology *CEO:* Exec. Dir. Dale McCall
(303) 344-4910

CONNECTICUT

ALBERT I. PRINCE REGIONAL VOCATIONAL-
TECHNICAL SCHOOL
500 Bookfield St., Hartford 06106 *Type:* Private *Degrees:* C *Prof. Accred.:* Dental Assisting *CEO:* Dir. Silas Shannon
(203) 246-8594

ALLSTATE TRACTOR TRAILER TRAINING SCHOOL
870 Housatonic Ave., Bridgeport 06004-2720 *Type:* Private *Accred.:* 1989 (ACCSCT) *Degrees:* C *CEO:* Pres. Vincent Mariano
(203) 336-9567

BARAN INSTITUTE OF TECHNOLOGY
611 Day Hill Rd., Windsor 06095 *Type:* Private *Accred.:* 1993 (ACCSCT) *Degrees:* C *CEO:* Owner Bradley R. Baran
(203) 688-3353

BRANFORD HALL CAREER INSTITUTE
9 Business Park Dr., Branford 06405 *Type:* Private business *Accred.:* 1977/1994 (ACICS) *Degrees:* C *CEO:* Pres. Michael Bouman
(203) 488-2525

BUTLER BUSINESS SCHOOL
2710 North Ave., Bridgeport 06604 *Type:* Private business *Accred.:* 1979/1991 (ACICS) *Degrees:* C *CEO:* Pres. Robert M. Butler
(203) 333-3601

CONNECTICUT BUSINESS INSTITUTE
605 Broad St., Stratford 06497 *Type:* Private business *Accred.:* 1972/1988 (ACICS) *Calendar:* Tri. plan *Degrees:* C *CEO:* Dir. Edward Schwartz
(203) 377-1775

EAST HARTFORD CAMPUS
809 Main St., East Hartford 06108 *Accred.:* 1993 (ACICS)
(203) 291-2880

NORTH HAVEN CAMPUS
447 Washington Ave., North Haven 06473 *Accred.:* 1972/1988 (ACICS)
(203) 239-7660

CONNECTICUT CENTER FOR MASSAGE THERAPY
75 Kitts Ln., Newington 06111-3954 *Type:* Private *Accred.:* 1985/1990 (ACCSCT) *Degrees:* C *CEO:* Dir. Stephen Kitts
(203) 667-1886

WESTPORT CAMPUS
25 Sylvan Rd. S., Westport 06880 *Accred.:* 1993 (ACCSCT)
(203) 221-7325

CONNECTICUT INSTITUTE OF ART
230 Farmington Ave., US 1, Farmington 06032 *Accred.:* 1994 (ACCSCT) *Degrees:* C *CEO:* Pres. David Tine
(203) 677-7869

CONNECTICUT INSTITUTE OF ART
581 W. Putnam Ave., Greenwich 06830-6005 *Type:* Private *Accred.:* 1980/1990 (ACCSCT) *Calendar:* Sem. plan *Degrees:* C *CEO:* Pres. August J. Propersi
(203) 869-4430

CONNECTICUT INSTITUTE OF HAIR DESIGN
1681 Meriden Rd., Wolcott 06716-3322 *Type:* Private *Accred.:* 1980/1987 (ACCSCT) *Degrees:* C *CEO:* Dir. John A. Varanelli
(203) 879-4247

CONNECTICUT SCHOOL OF ELECTRONICS
586 Ella T. Grasso Blvd., New Haven 06519-0308 *Type:* Private *Accred.:* 1968/1989 (ACCSCT) *Calendar:* Sem. plan *Degrees:* C *CEO:* Vice Pres. Karen George
(203) 624-2121

DATA INSTITUTE
745 Burnside Ave., East Hartford 06108 *Type:* Private business *Accred.:* 1983/1987 (ACICS) *Degrees:* C *Prof. Accred.:* Medical Assisting *CEO:* Pres. Mark Scheinberg
(203) 528-4111

WATERBURY CAMPUS
101 Pierpont Rd., Waterbury 06705 *Accred.:* 1993 (ACICS)
(203) 756-5500

ELI WHITNEY REGIONAL VOCATIONAL-
TECHNICAL SCHOOL
71 Jones Rd., Hamden 06514 *Type:* Private
Degrees: C *Prof. Accred.:* Dental Assisting
(conditional) *CEO:* Dir. Cecil Robinson
(203) 397-4031

FOX INSTITUTE OF BUSINESS
765 Asylum Ave., Hartford 06105 *Type:* Private business *Accred.:* 1979/1990 (ACICS)
Calendar: Qtr. plan *Degrees:* C *CEO:* Pres.
Patrick J. Fox
(203) 522-2888

HARTFORD CAMERATA CONSERVATORY
834 Asylum Ave., Hartford 06105 *Type:* Private professional *Accred.:* 1979/1995 (NE-ASC-CTCI) *Calendar:* Sem. plan *Degrees:*
C *CEO:* Dir. Claudia Bell
FTE Enroll: 42   (203) 246-2588

HUNTINGTON INSTITUTE
193 Broadway, Norwich 06360 *Type:* Private business *Accred.:* 1980/1986 (ACICS)
Degrees: C *CEO:* Dir. Thomas Haggerty
(203) 886-0507

INDUSTRIAL MANAGEMENT AND TRAINING, INC.
233 Mill St., Waterbury 06706 *Type:* Private
Accred.: 1993 (ACCSCT) *Degrees:* C *CEO:*
Owner Marcel Veronneau
(203) 753-7910

LYME ACADEMY OF FINE ARTS
84 Lyme St., Old Lyme 06371 *Type:* Private
Degrees: C *Prof. Accred.:* Art (A) *CEO:*
Acad. Dean Sharon Hunter
(203) 434-5232

MORSE SCHOOL OF BUSINESS
275 Asylum St., Hartford 06103 *Type:* Private business *Accred.:* 1953/1996 (ACICS)
Degrees: C *Prof. Accred.:* Medical Assisting
(AMA) *CEO:* Pres. Michael S. Taub
(203) 522-2261

NAVAL SUBMARINE SCHOOL
Box 700, Bldg. 84, Code 01A, Groton
06340-5700 *Type:* Public (federal) *Accred.:*
1993/1994 (NEASC-CTCI) *Degrees:* C
CEO: Cmnd. Ofcr. W. A. Peters
(203) 449-4369

NEW ENGLAND TECHNICAL INSTITUTE OF
CONNECTICUT
200 John Downey Dr., New Britain 06051-0651 *Type:* Private *Accred.:* 1983/1988 (AC-CSCT) *Degrees:* C *CEO:* Dir. Paul S. Taub
(203) 225-8641

NEW ENGLAND TRACTOR TRAILER TRAINING
SCHOOL OF CONNECTICUT
32 Field Rd., Somers 06071-0326 *Type:* Private *Accred.:* 1982/1988 (ACCSCT) *Degrees:* C *CEO:* Dir. Arlan Greenberg
(203) 749-0711

PORTER AND CHESTER INSTITUTE
P.O. Box 364, Stratford 06497-0364 *Type:*
Private *Accred.:* 1972/1990 (ACCSCT)
Calendar: Qtr. plan *Degrees:* C *CEO:* Dir.
Raymond R. Clark
(203) 375-4463

ENFIELD CAMPUS
138 Weymouth St., Enfield 06082-6028
Accred.: 1980/1990 (ACCSCT) *Prof.
Accred.:* Medical Assisting
(800) 870-6789

WATERTOWN CAMPUS
320 Sylvan Lake Rd., Watertown 06779-1400 *Accred.:* 1972/1987 (ACCSCT)
Prof. Accred.: Medical Assisting
(203) 274-9294

WETHERSFIELD CAMPUS
125 Silas Deane Hwy., Wethersfield
06109-1238 *Accred.:* 1979/1990 (ACC-SCT) *Prof. Accred.:* Medical Assisting
(203) 529-2519

RIDLEY-LOWELL BUSINESS AND TECHNICAL
INSTITUTE
470 Bank St., New London 06320 *Type:* Private business *Accred.:* 1979/1995 (ACICS)
Degrees: C *CEO:* Dir. W. T. Weymouth
(203) 443-7441

ROFFLER ACADEMY FOR HAIRSTYLISTS
454 Park St., Hartford 06106-1525 *Type:*
Private *Accred.:* 1974/1990 (ACCSCT) *Degrees:* C *CEO:* Dir. Carlos J. Vigo
(203) 522-2359

SOUTHINGTON CAMPUS
709 Queen St., Southington 06489 *Accred.:* 1990 (ACCSCT)
(203) 620-9260

SCHOOL OF THE HARTFORD BALLET
Hartford Courant Arts Ctr., 224 Farmington Ave., Hartford 06105 *Type:* Private *Degrees:* C *Prof. Accred.:* Dance *CEO:* Dir. Enid Lynn
(203) 525-9396

STONE ACADEMY
1315 Dixwell Ave., Hamden 06514 *Type:* Private business *Accred.:* 1974/1995 (ACICS) *Degrees:* C *Prof. Accred.:* Medical Assisting (AMA) *CEO:* Pres. Janet S. Arena
(203) 288-7474

TECHNICAL CAREERS INSTITUTE
11 Kimberly Ave., West Haven 06516-4499 *Type:* Private *Accred.:* 1974/1987 (ACCSCT) *Degrees:* C *CEO:* Dir. Ronald G. Anderson
(203) 932-2282

TECHNICAL CAREERS INSTITUTE
605 Day Hill Rd., Windsor 06095-0126 *Type:* Private *Accred.:* 1986 (ACCSCT) *CEO:* Dir. Linda Perkins
(203) 688-8351

WESTLAWN INSTITUTE OF MARINE TECHNOLOGY
733 Summer St., Stamford 06901 *Type:* Private distance education *Accred.:* 1971/1992 (DETC) *Degrees:* C *CEO:* Dir. Norman Nudelman
(203) 359-0500

WINDHAM REGIONAL VOCATIONAL-TECHNICAL SCHOOL
210 Birch St., Willimantic 06226 *Type:* Private *Degrees:* C *Prof. Accred.:* Dental Assisting *CEO:* Dir. Charles Wilt
(203) 456-3879

DELAWARE

DAWN TRAINING INSTITUTE
New Castle County Airport, 120 Old
Churchmans Rd., New Castle 19720-3116
Type: Private *Accred.:* 1991 (ACCSCT)
Degrees: C *CEO:* Pres. Hollis Anglin
(302) 328-9695

STAR TECHNICAL INSTITUTE
Graystone Plaza, 631 W. Newport Pike,
Wilmington 19804 *Type:* Private *Accred.:*
1988/1993 (ACCSCT) *Degrees:* C *CEO:*
Dir. Edward Webber
(302) 999-7827

ALLENTOWN CAMPUS
2101 Union Blvd., Allentown, PA 18103
Accred.: 1988 (ACCSCT)
(610) 434-9963

DISTRICT OF COLUMBIA

HANNAH HARRISON CAREER SCHOOL
4470 MacArthur Blvd., N.W., Washington
20007 *Type:* Private *Degrees:* C *Prof. Accred.:* Practical Nursing *CEO:* Dir. Jane
Town
(202) 333-3500

LEVINE SCHOOL OF MUSIC
1690 36th St., N.W., Washington 20007
Type: Private *Degrees:* C *Prof. Accred.:*
Music *CEO:* Dir. William Reeder
(202) 337-2227

MARGARET MURRAY WASHINGTON VOCATIONAL
SCHOOL
27 O St., N.W., Washington 20001 *Type:*
Public *Degrees:* C *Prof. Accred.:* Dental
Assisting, Practical Nursing (warning) *CEO:*
Princ. Alethia Spraggins
(202) 673-7224

MARINE CORPS INSTITUTE
Marine Barracks, 8th and Eye Sts., S.E.,
Washington 20390-5000 *Type:* Public (federal) distance education *Accred.:* 1977/
1992 (DETC) *Degrees:* C *CEO:* Dir. D. G.
Dotterrer
(202) 433-2728

MCGRAW-HILL CONTINUING EDUCATION
CENTER
4401 Connecticut Ave., N.W., Washington
20008 *Type:* Private distance education
Accred.: 1956/1992 (DETC) *Degrees:* C
CEO: Pres. Harold B. Reeb
(202) 244-1600

NRI SCHOOLS
4401 Connecticut Ave., N.W., Washington
20008 *Accred.:* 1992 (DETC)
(202) 244-1600

NATIONAL CONSERVATORY OF DRAMATIC ARTS
1556 Wisconsin Ave., N.W., Washington
20007-2758 *Type:* Private *Accred.:* 1980/
1987 (ACCSCT) *Degrees:* C *CEO:* Pres. C.
Wayne Rudisill
(202) 333-2202

WASHINGTON CONSERVATORY OF MUSIC, INC.
5144 Massachusetts Ave., N.W., P.O. Box
5758, Washington 20816 *Type:* Private professional *Degrees:* C *Prof. Accred.:* Music
(A) *CEO:* Admin. Joan T. Willoughby
(301) 320-2770

FLORIDA

ACADEMY OF CREATIVE HAIR DESIGN
2911 Jacksonville Rd., Ocala 34470-4973
Type: Private *Accred.:* 1993 (COE) *Degrees:*
C *CEO:* Dir. Dale Fuller
FTE Enroll: 46   (904) 351-5900

ACADEMY OF HEALING ARTS, MASSAGE AND
FACIAL SKIN CARE
3141 S. Military Trail, Lake Worth 33463-
2113 *Type:* Private *Accred.:* 1992 (ACC-
SCT) *Degrees:* C *CEO:* CEO M. J. Artemik
                                          (407) 965-5550

AMERICAN FLYERS COLLEGE
5400 N.W. 21st Terr., Fort Lauderdale
33309 *Type:* Private *Accred.:* 1993 (ACC-
SCT) *Degrees:* C *CEO:* Exec. Dir. Edward
C. Hertberg
                                          (305) 772-7500

ATI CAREER TRAINING CENTER
3501 N.W. 9th Ave., Oakland Park 33309-
5900 *Type:* Private *Accred.:* 1984/1989
(ACCSCT) *Calendar:* Qtr. plan *Degrees:* C
CEO: Dir. Donald Neman
                                          (305) 563-5899

MIAMI CAMPUS
One N.E. 19th St., Miami 33132 *Accred.:*
1991 (ACCSCT)
                                          (305) 573-1600

ATI HEALTH EDUCATION CENTER
1395 N.W. 167th St., Ste. 200, Miami
33169-5745 *Type:* Private *Accred.:* 1991
(ACCSCT) *Calendar:* Qtr. plan *Degrees:* C
Prof. Accred.: Respiratory Therapy, Respiratory Therapy Technology *CEO:* Dir. Barbara
Monk
                                          (305) 628-1000

ATLANTIC VOCATIONAL-TECHNICAL CENTER
4700 Coconut Creek Pkwy., Coconut Creek
33063 *Type:* Public (state) technical *Accred.:* 1978/1994 (COE) *Degrees:* C *Prof.
Accred.:* Practical Nursing *CEO:* Dir.
Robert Crawford
FTE Enroll: 3,578   (305) 977-2000

POMPANO BEACH CAMPUS
1400 N.E. 6th St., Pompano Beach 33060
                                          (305) 786-7600

AVANTI HAIR TECH
905 E. Memorial Blvd., Lakeland 33801-
1919 *Type:* Private *Accred.:* 1987 (ACC-
SCT) *Degrees:* C *CEO:* Dir. Joan Ogden
                                          (813) 686-2224

AVANTI HAIR TECH
8803 N. Florida Ave., Ste. B, Tampa 33604
Type: Private *Accred.:* 1988 (ACCSCT)
Degrees: C *CEO:* Pres. Stewart A. Smith
                                          (813) 933-6603

AVANTI HAIR TECH
8803 N. Florida Ave., Ste. C, Tampa 33604
Type: Private *Accred.:* 1981/1988 (ACC-
SCT) *Degrees:* C *CEO:* Dir. Dwayne Adams
                                          (813) 931-8500

WINTER PARK CAMPUS
5433 Lake Howell Rd., Winter Park
32792-1033 *Accred.:* 1991 (ACCSCT)
                                          (305) 657-0700

AVIATION CAREER ACADEMY
2945 Medulla Rd., Lakeland *Accred.:* 1991
(ACCSCT) *Degrees:* C *CEO:* Dir. William
Aitkenhed
Enroll: 140   (813) 648-2004

BEACON CAREER INSTITUTE
2900 N.W. 183rd St., Miami 33056 *Type:*
Private technical *Accred.:* 1992 (COE)
Degrees: C *CEO:* Dir. Eddie Pabon
FTE Enroll: 450   (305) 620-4637

BEAUTY SCHOOLS OF AMERICA
1305 W. 49th St., Hialeah 33012 *Type:* Private *Accred.:* 1989/1992 (COE) *Degrees:* C
CEO: Dir. John Rebstock
FTE Enroll: 482   (305) 362-9003

MIAMI CAMPUS
1176 S.W. 67th Ave., Miami 33144
                                          (305) 267-6604

BUSINESS AND TECHNOLOGY INSTITUTE
8991 S.W. 107 Ave., 200, Ste. 323, Miami 33176 *Type:* Private *Accred.:* 1991/1994 (COE) *Degrees:* C *CEO:* Dir. Fernando N. Llerena
FTE Enroll: 117   (305) 273-4499

BUSINESS TRAINING INSTITUTE
1270 Wickham Rd., Ste. 26, Melbourne 32935 Type: Private business Accred: 1988/1996 (ACICS) Degrees: C CEO: Darlene Wohl
(407) 255-9232

CHARLOTTE VOCATIONAL-TECHNICAL CENTER
18300 Toledo Blade Blvd., Port Charlotte 33948-3399 *Type:* Public (state) technical *Accred.:* 1983/1993 (COE) *Degrees:* C *Prof. Accred.:* Dental Assisting *CEO:* Director Judith R. Willis
FTE Enroll: 634   (941) 629-6819

CONCORDE CAREER INSTITUTE
7960 Arlington Expy., Jacksonville 32211-7429 *Type:* Private *Accred.:* 1991 (ACCSCT) *Degrees:* C *CEO:* Dir. Sonnie Willingham
(904) 725-0525

CONCORDE CAREER INSTITUTE
4000 N. State Rd. 7, Lauderdale Lakes 33319 *Type:* Private *Accred.:* 1991 (ACCSCT) *Degrees:* C *CEO:* Dir. Patricia Trax
(305) 731-8880

CONCORDE CAREER INSTITUTE
4202 W. Spruce St., Tampa 33607-4127 *Type:* Private *Accred.:* 1991 (ACCSCT) *Degrees:* C *CEO:* Dir. Thomas L. Buck
(813) 874-0094

MIAMI CAMPUS
285 N.W. 199th St., Miami 33169-2920 *Accred.:* 1992 (ACCSCT)
(305) 652-0055

DAVID G. ERWIN TECHNICAL CENTER
2010 E. Hillsborough Ave., Tampa 33610 *Type:* Public (state) technical *Accred.:* 1981/1991 (COE) *Degrees:* C *Prof. Accred.:* Clinical Lab Technology (C), Dental Assisting (conditional), Medical Assisting (AMA),

Respiratory Therapy Technology, Surgical Technology *CEO:* Dir. Michael Donohue
FTE Enroll: 904   (813) 231-1800

DEFENSE EQUAL OPPORTUNITY MANAGEMENT INSTITUTE
740 O'Malley Rd., Patrick Air Force Base 32925-3399 *Type:* Public (federal) *Accred.:* 1983/1993 (COE) *Degrees:* C *CEO:* Dir. Ronald M. Joe
FTE Enroll: 251   (407) 494-6976

EURO HAIR DESIGN INSTITUTE
1964 W. Tennessee St., No. 14, Tallahassee 32304-3238 *Type:* Private *Accred.:* 1983/1988 (ACCSCT) *Degrees:* C *CEO:* Pres. Stewart A. Smith
(904) 576-2174

FAA CENTER FOR MANAGEMENT DEVELOPMENT
4500 Palm Coast Pkwy., S.E., Palm Coast 32137 *Type:* Private *Accred.:* 1989/1994 (COE) *Degrees:* C *CEO:* Dir. Woodie Woodward
FTE Enroll: 144   (904) 446-7136

FEDERAL CORRECTIONAL INSTITUTION
501 Capital Cir., N.E., Tallahassee 32301-3572 *Type:* Public (federal) *Accred.:* 1985/1990 (COE) *Degrees:* C *CEO:* Dir. Lewis James
FTE Enroll: 313   (904) 878-2173

FLIGHTSAFETY INTERNATIONAL
Vero Beach Airport, P.O. Box 2708, Vero Beach 32961-2708 *Type:* Private *Accred.:* 1975/1988 (ACCSCT) *Degrees:* C *CEO:* Admin. Jeffrey Krell
(407) 567-5178

FLORIDA INSTITUTE OF MASSAGE THERAPY AND ESTHETICS
5453 N. University Dr., Lauderhill 33351 *Type:* Private *Accred.:* 1991 (ACCSCT) *Degrees:* C *CEO:* Dir. Neal R. Heller
(305) 742-8399

MIAMI CAMPUS
7925 NW 12th St., Ste. 201, Miami 33126 *Accred.:* 1994 (ACCSCT)
Enroll: 200   (305) 597-9599

FLORIDA INSTITUTE OF TRADITIONAL CHINESE
MEDICINE
5335 66th Street N, St. Petersburg 33709
Type: Private *Prof. Accred.:* Acupuncture
Calendar: 12-mos. program *Degrees:* C
CEO: Dir. Su Liang Ku
FTE Enroll: 75   (813) 546-6565

FLORIDA INSTITUTE OF ULTRASOUND, INC.
8800 University Pkwy., Bldg. A, No. 4, Pensacola 32514 *Type:* Private technical *Accred.:* 1985/1992 (ABHES) *Degrees:* C *CEO:*
Dir. J. Jay Crittenden
      (904) 478-7300

FLORIDA SCHOOL OF BUSINESS
2990 N.W. 81st Terr., Miami 33147 *Type:*
Private business *Accred.:* 1986/1996
(ACICS) *Calendar:* Qtr. plan *Degrees:* C
CEO: Pres. Hugh B. Alpeter
      (305) 696-6312

FLORIDA SCHOOL OF BUSINESS
4817 N. Florida Ave., Tampa 33603 *Type:*
Private business *Accred.:* 1986/1996 (AC-
ICS) *Calendar:* Qtr. plan *Degrees:* C *CEO:*
Dir. Richard Doebler
      (813) 239-3334

GARCES COMMERCIAL COLLEGE
1301 S.W. First St., Miami 33135 *Type:* Private *Accred.:* 1990/1992 (COE) *Degrees:* C
CEO: Dir. Elena Nespereira
FTE Enroll: 389   (305) 643-1044

MIAMI SPRINGS CAMPUS
5385 N.W. 36th St., Miami Springs 33166
      (305) 871-6535

GEORGE STONE VOCATIONAL-TECHNICAL
CENTER
2400 Longleaf Dr., Pensacola 32526-8922
Type: Public (state) *Accred.:* 1981/1991
(COE) *Degrees:* C *CEO:* Dir. Robert Lindner
FTE Enroll: 856   (904) 944-1424

GEORGE T. BAKER AVIATION SCHOOL
3275 N.W. 42nd Ave., Miami 33142 *Type:*
Private technical *Accred.:* 1978/1993 (COE)
Degrees: C *CEO:* Dir. Doris Southern
FTE Enroll: 362   (305) 871-3143

THE HAIR DESIGN SCHOOL
5110 University Blvd., Bldg. C, Jacksonville
32216-5940 *Type:* Private *Accred.:* 1979/
1986 (ACCSCT) *Degrees:* C *CEO:* Exec.
Vice Pres. Stewart A. Smith
      (904) 731-7500

HENRY W. BREWSTER TECHNICAL CENTER
2222 N. Tampa St., Tampa 33602 *Type:* Public (state) *Accred.:* 1989/1990 (COE) *Degrees:* C *CEO:* Dir. Joe Kolinsky
FTE Enroll: 622   (813) 276-5448

HI-TECH SCHOOL OF MIAMI
10350 W. Flagler St., Miami 33174 *Type:*
Private *Accred.:* 1993 (ACCSCT) *Degrees:*
C *CEO:* Pres. Eric Arencibia
      (305) 221-3423

HIALEAH TECHNICAL CENTER
1780 E. 4th Ave., Hialeah 33012-3122 *Type:*
Private *Accred.:* 1991 (ACCSCT) *Degrees:*
C *CEO:* Dir. Roberto Luna
      (305) 884-4387

HUMANITIES CENTER INSTITUTE OF ALLIED
HEALTH/SCHOOL OF MASSAGE
4045 Park Blvd., Pinellas Park 34665-3634
Type: Private *Accred.:* 1984/1989 (ACC-
SCT) *Degrees:* C *CEO:* Dir. Sherry L. Fears
      (813) 541-5200

JAMES L. WALKER VOCATIONAL-TECHNICAL
CENTER
3702 Estey Ave., Naples 33942-4498 *Type:*
Public (state) *Accred.:* 1980/1990 (COE)
Degrees: C *Prof. Accred.:* Dental Assisting
CEO: Dir. Charlotte Gore
FTE Enroll: 1,295   (941) 643-0919

LAKE COUNTY AREA VOCATIONAL-TECHNICAL
CENTER
2001 Kurt St., Eustis 32726 *Type:* Public
(state) *Accred.:* 1974/1994 (COE) *Degrees:*
C *Prof. Accred.:* EMT-Paramedic *CEO:* Dir.
Steve Hand
FTE Enroll: 1,013   (904) 742-6486

LEE COUNTY VOCATIONAL HIGH TECH CENTER-
CENTRAL
3800 Michigan Ave., Fort Myers 33916
Type: Public (state) *Accred.:* 1978/1993

(COE) *Degrees:* C *CEO:* Dir. Ronald E. Pentiuk
FTE Enroll: 994   (941) 334-4544

LINDSEY HOPKINS TECHNICAL EDUCATION CENTER
750 N.W. 20th St., Miami 33127 *Type:* Public (state) *Accred.:* 1972/1992 (COE) *Degrees:* C *Prof. Accred.:* Dental Assisting, Dental Laboratory Technology, Practical Nursing, Surgical Technology *CEO:* Dir. John Leyva
FTE Enroll: 2,418   (305) 324-6070

LIVELY AREA VOCATIONAL-TECHNICAL CENTER
500 N. Appleyard Dr., Tallahassee 32304-2895 *Type:* Public (state) *Accred.:* 1977/1992 (COE) *Degrees:* C *CEO:* Dir. Robert J. Gill
FTE Enroll: 1,221   (904) 487-7401

FLORIDA STATE HOSPITAL CAMPUS
HRS, Dist. 2, Chattahoochee 32324
                                     (904) 663-7202

LIVELY AVIATION CENTER
3290 Capital Cir., S.W., Tallahassee 32310
                                     (904) 488-4161

LIVELY CRIMINAL JUSTICE TRAINING ACADEMY
Rte. 1, Box 3250, Havana 32333
                                     (904) 487-2258

MANATEE AREA VOCATIONAL-TECHNICAL CENTER
5603 34th St., W., Bradenton 34210 *Type:* Public (state) *Accred.:* 1980/1990 (COE) *Degrees:* C *Prof. Accred.:* Dental Assisting, EMT-Paramedic *CEO:* Dir. Napoleon Mills
FTE Enroll: 526   (941) 751-7904

MARION COUNTY SCHOOL OF RADIOLOGIC TECHNOLOGY
438 S.W. Third St., Ocala 32674 *Type:* Private *Calendar:* 24-mos. program *Degrees:* C *Prof. Accred.:* Radiography *CEO:* Admin. Sam Lauff, Jr.
Enroll: 36   (904) 629-7545

MASTER SCHOOLS
824 S.W. 24th St., Fort Lauderdale 33315-2644 *Type:* Private *Accred.:* 1983 (ACCSCT) *Calendar:* Sem. plan *Degrees:* C *CEO:* Dir. Marta Alvarez
                                     (305) 541-8140

MEDICAL ARTS TRAINING CENTER, INC.
441 S. State Rd. 7, Margate 33068-1934 *Type:* Private technical *Degrees:* C *Prof. Accred.:* EMT-Paramedic *CEO:* Chrmn. Lauren Hemedinger
                                     (305) 968-3500

MEDICAL CAREER CENTER
4700 Bayou Blvd., Pensacola 32503 *Type:* Private *Accred.:* 1994 (ABHES) *Degrees:* C *CEO:* Dir. Ann M. Roundry
                                     (904) 494-9784

MIAMI INSTITUTE OF TECHNOLOGY
1001 S.W. First St., Miami 33130-1008 *Type:* Private *Accred.:* 1980/1987 (ACCSCT) *Degrees:* C *CEO:* Dir. Octavio Gutierrez
                                     (305) 324-6781

MIAMI JOB CORPS CENTER
3050 NW 183rd St., Miami 33056-3536 *Type:* Public *Accred.:* 1986/1991 (COE) *Degrees:* C *CEO:* Dir. Luis Cerezo
FTE Enroll: 572   (305) 325-1276

MIAMI LAKES TECHNICAL EDUCATION CENTER
5780 N.W. 158th St., Miami 33014 *Type:* Public (state) *Accred.:* 1983/1993 (COE) *Degrees:* C *Prof. Accred.:* Practical Nursing *CEO:* Dir. Noward Dean
FTE Enroll: 1,194   (305) 557-1100

MIAMI TECHNICAL INSTITUTE
14701 N.W. 7th Ave., North Miami 33168-3103 *Type:* Private *Accred.:* 1987 (ACCSCT) *Degrees:* C *CEO:* Pres. Robert Piacenti
                                     (305) 688-8811

MIAMI CAMPUS
7061 W. Flagler St., Miami 33144-2453 *Accred.:* 1991 (ACCSCT)
                                     (305) 263-9832

NATIONAL AVIATION ACADEMY
5770 Roosevelt Blvd., No. 105, Clearwater 34620 *Type:* Private technical *Accred.:* 1991 (COE) *Degrees:* C *CEO:* Pres. Joe Fisher
FTE Enroll: 282   (813) 531-2080

NATIONAL SCHOOL OF TECHNOLOGY
16150 N.E. 17th Ave., North Miami Beach 33162-4799 *Type:* Private *Accred.:* 1983/ 1988 (ACCSCT) *Degrees:* C *Prof. Accred.:* Medical Assisting *CEO:* Dir. Arthur Ortiz
(305) 949-9500

HIALEAH CAMPUS
4410 W. 16th Ave., Hialeah 33012-7628 *Accred.:* 1988 (ACCSCT) *Prof. Accred.:* Medical Assisting
(305) 558-9500

NATIONAL TRAINING, INC.
188 College Dr., P.O. Box 1899, Orange Park 32067-1899 *Type:* Private distance education *Accred.:* 1982/1992 (DETC) *Degrees:* C *CEO:* Pres. Frank Lark
(904) 272-4000

NAVAL DIVING AND SALVAGE TRAINING CENTER
Panama City 32407-5002 *Type:* Public (federal) *Accred.:* 1983/1994 (COE) *Degrees:* C *CEO:* Commandant M.C. Herb
FTE Enroll: 124   (904) 235-5207

NAVAL SERVICE SCHOOL COMMAND
2200 Leahy Ave., Orlando 32813-5800 *Type:* Public (federal) technical *Accred.:* 1976/1991 (COE) *Degrees:* C *CEO:* Commandant Johnnie M. Boynton
FTE Enroll: 152   (407) 646-4315

NAVAL TECHNICAL TRAINING CENTER
Corry Sta., 640 Roberts Ave., Rm. 112, Pensacola 32511-5138 *Type:* Public (federal) technical *Accred.:* 1975/1990 (COE) *Degrees:* C *CEO:* Commandant George Schu
FTE Enroll: 1,201   (904) 452-6516

NEW ENGLAND INSTITUTE OF TECHNOLOGY AT PALM BEACH
1126 53rd Ct., West Palm Beach 33407-2384 *Type:* Private *Accred.:* 1992/1994 (COE candidate) *Calendar:* Qtr. plan *Degrees:* C *CEO:* Pres. William Bennett
FTE Enroll: 878   (407) 842-8324

WEST PALM BEACH CAMPUS
2400 Metro Center Blvd., West Palm Beach 33407
(407) 842-8324

NORTH TECHNICAL EDUCATION CENTER
7071 Garden Rd., Riviera Beach 33404 *Type:* Public (state) *Accred.:* 1976/1991 (COE) *Degrees:* C *CEO:* Dir. Patricia I. Nugent
FTE Enroll: 801   (407) 881-4639

OKALOOSA APPLIED TECHNOLOGY
1976 Lewis Turner Blvd., Fort Walton Beach 32547 *Type:* Public (state) technical *Accred.:* 1979/1994 (COE) *Degrees:* C *CEO:* Dir. Mary Jo Sisson
FTE Enroll: 564   (904) 833-3500

OMNI TECHNICAL SCHOOL
2242 W. Broward Blvd., Fort Lauderdale 33312-1460 *Type:* Private *Accred.:* 1992 (ACCSCT) *Degrees:* C *CEO:* Pres. Stewart A. Smith
(305) 584-4730

OMNI TECHNICAL SCHOOL
1710 N.W. Seventh St., Miami 33125-3502 *Type:* Private *Accred.:* 1992 (ACCSCT) *Degrees:* C *CEO:* Dir. Hipolito Ramos
(305) 541-6200

ORANGE TECHNICAL EDUCATION CENTER-MID FLORIDA TECH
2900 W. Oak Ridge Rd., Orlando 32809-3799 *Type:* Public (state) *Accred.:* 1974/ 1994 (COE) *Degrees:* C *CEO:* Dir. Robert J. Clark
FTE Enroll: 3,714   (407) 855-5880

ORANGE TECHNICAL EDUCATION CENTER-ORLANDO TECH
301 W. Amelia St., Orlando 32801 *Type:* Public (state) *Accred.:* 1983/1993 (COE) *Degrees:* C *Prof. Accred.:* Dental Assisting *CEO:* Director Kaye Chastain
FTE Enroll: 1,884   (407) 425-2756

ORANGE TECHNICAL EDUCATION CENTER-
WESTSIDE TECH
955 E. Story Rd., Winter Garden 34787
Type: Public (state) *Accred.:* 1981/1991
(COE) *Degrees:* C *CEO:* Dir. Walt Cobb
FTE Enroll: 2,335   (407) 656-2851

EDGEWOOD RANCH CAMPUS
Edgewood Ranch, 2499 Edgewood Ranch
Rd., Orlando 32811
(407) 295-2464

TECHNOLOGY INFORMATION CENTER CAMPUS
Technology Information Ctr., 6628 Old
Winter Garden Rd., Orlando 32811
(407) 292-8696

ORANGE TECHNICAL EDUCATION CENTER
WINTER PARK TECH
901 Webster Ave., Winter Park 32789 *Type:*
Public (state) *Accred.:* 1986/1993 (COE)
Degrees: C *Prof. Accred.:* Medical Assisting
(AMA) *CEO:* Dir. Joseph A. McCoy
FTE Enroll: 979   (407) 647-6366

PALM BEACH BEAUTY AND BARBER SCHOOL
4645 Gun Club Rd., West Palm Beach
33415-2882 *Type:* Private *Accred.:* 1982/
1991 (ACCSCT) *Degrees:* C *CEO:* Dir. Rex
Anderson
(407) 683-1238

PARALEGAL CAREERS
1211 N. Westshore Blvd., Ste. 100, Tampa
33607 *Type:* Private *Accred.:* 1988 (COE)
Degrees: C *CEO:* Dir. Charles Sweet
FTE Enroll: 50   (813) 289-6025

PHD HAIR ACADEMY
27380 U.S. Hwy. 19 N., Clearwater 34621-
2953 *Type:* Private *Accred.:* 1984/1988
(ACCSCT) *Degrees:* C *CEO:* Dir. Gayl E.
McCanless
(813) 791-7438

PINELLAS TECHNICAL EDUCATION CENTER-
CLEARWATER CAMPUS
6100 154th Ave., N., Clearwater 34620
Type: Public (state) *Accred.:* 1970/1990
(COE) *Degrees:* C *CEO:* Dir. Clide Cassity
FTE Enroll: 1,866   (813) 538-7167

BRANCH CAMPUS
14400 49th St., N., Clearwater 34620
(813) 531-3531

BRANCH CAMPUS
2375 Whitney Rd., Clearwater 34620
(813) 530-0617

PINELLAS TECHNICAL EDUCATION CENTER—ST.
PETERSBURG CAMPUS
910 34th St., St. Petersburg 33711-2298 *Type:*
Public (state) *Accred.:* 1975/1995 (COE)
Degrees: C *Prof. Accred.:* Dental Assisting,
Medical Assisting (AMA), Respiratory Ther-
apy Technology *CEO:* Dir. Warren Laux
FTE Enroll: 1,262   (813) 893-2500

POLITECHNICAL INSTITUTE
1321 S.W. 107th Avenue, No. 202-B, Miami
33174 *Type:* Private *Accred.:* 1989/1994
(COE) *Degrees:* C *CEO:* Dir. Ivan Curiel
FTE Enroll: 490   (305) 226-8099

POMPANO ACADEMY OF AERONAUTICS
1006 N.E. 10th St., Pompano Beach 33060-
5722 *Type:* Private *Accred.:* 1991 (ACC-
SCT) *Degrees:* C *CEO:* Dir. Gardner H.
Craft
(800) 545-7262

THE POYNTER INSTITUTE FOR MEDIA STUDIES
801 Third St., S., St. Petersburg 33701 *Type:*
Private *Accred.:* 1983/1993 (COE) *Degrees:*
C *CEO:* Pres. Robert J. Haiman
FTE Enroll: 1,484   (813) 821-9494

QUALTEC INSTITUTE FOR COMPETITIVE
ADVANTAGE
11760 U.S. Hwy. 1, No. 500, North Palm
Beach 33408 *Type:* Private *Accred.:* 1990
(COE) *Degrees:* C *CEO:* Dir. Ben Fowke, III
FTE Enroll: 243   (407) 775-8300

RADFORD M. LOCKLIN TECHNICAL CENTER
5330 Berryhill Rd., Milton 32570 *Type:* Public (state) *Accred.:* 1988/1993 (COE) *Degrees:* C *CEO:* Dir. Jane Allen
FTE Enroll: 417   (904) 983-5700

RECREATIONAL VEHICLE SERVICE ACADEMY
1127 Ellenton Gillette Rd., Ellenton 34222
Type: Private *Accred.:* 1989/1991 (ACCSCT)
Degrees: C *CEO:* Dir. Thomas J. Santoro
(813) 722-7244

RIDGE VOCATIONAL-TECHNICAL CENTER
7700 State Rd. 544, Winter Haven 33881
Type: Public (state) *Accred.:* 1982/1992
(COE) *Degrees:* C *CEO:* Dir. Carl Ray
FTE Enroll: 852   (941) 422-6402

ROBERT MORGAN VOCATIONAL-TECHNICAL
INSTITUTE
18180 S.W. 122nd Ave., Miami 33177 *Type:*
Public (state) *Accred.:* 1983/1994 (COE)
Degrees: C *Prof. Accred.:* Dental Assisting
CEO: Dir. Frederick Reed
FTE Enroll: 175   (305) 253-9920

ROMAR BEAUTY ACADEMY
1608 S. Federal Hwy., Boynton Beach
33435 *Type:* Private *Accred.:* 1990 (COE)
Degrees: C *CEO:* Dir. Patricia Teofani
FTE Enroll: 127   (407) 737-3430

RTI TECHNICAL INSTITUTE
Fairfield Plaza, 1412 W. Fairfield Dr., Pensacola 32501-1105 *Type:* Private *Accred.:*
1985/1990 (ACCSCT) *Degrees:* C *CEO:*
Dir. Larry Bryant
(904) 433-6547

ST. AUGUSTINE TECHNICAL CENTER
2980 Collins Ave., St. Augustine 32095-
1919 *Type:* Public (state) *Accred.:* 1980/
1990 (COE) *Degrees:* C *Prof. Accred.:*
EMT-Paramedic *CEO:* Dir. Earnie Matthews
FTE Enroll: 1,764   (904) 824-4401

EAST PALATKA CAMPUS
113 Putnam County Blvd., East Palatka
32131
(914) 329-2550

SARASOTA COUNTY TECHNICAL INSTITUTE
4748 Beneva Rd., Sarasota 34235 *Type:*
Public (state) *Accred.:* 1971/1991 (COE)
Degrees: C *Prof. Accred.:* EMT-Paramedic,
Medical Assisting (AMA), Practical Nursing
CEO: Dir. Steve Harvey
FTE Enroll: 2,291   (941) 924-1365

SEGAL INSTITUTE
18850 U.S. Hwy. 19, N., No. 565, Clearwater 34624 *Type:* Private *Accred.:* 1991
(COE) *Degrees:* C *CEO:* Dir. Susan Segal
FTE Enroll: 82   (813) 535-0608

SER-IBM BUSINESS INSTITUTE
42 N.W. 27th Ave., No. 421, Miami 33125
Type: Private *Accred.:* 1985/1990 (COE warning) *Degrees:* C *CEO:* Dir. Melvin Chaves
FTE Enroll: 105   (305) 649-7500

SHERIDAN VOCATIONAL-TECHNICAL CENTER
5400 Sheridan St., Hollywood 33021 *Type:*
Public (state) *Accred.:* 1974/1994 (COE)
Degrees: C *Prof. Accred.:* Clinical Lab Tech-
nology (C), Practical Nursing
FTE Enroll: 2,075   (305) 985-3220

SOUTH TECHNICAL EDUCATION CENTER
1300 S.W. 30th Ave., Boynton Beach 33426
Type: Public (state) *Accred.:* 1980/1990
(COE) *Degrees:* C *CEO:* Dir. James L. Rasco
FTE Enroll: 1,259   (407) 369-7000

SOUTHEASTERN ACADEMY, INC.
233 Academy Dr., P.O. Box 421768, Kissimmee 32742-1768 *Type:* Private distance education *Accred.:* 1986 (ACCSCT); 1977/1992
(DETC) *Degrees:* C *CEO:* Pres. David L.
Peoples
(407) 847-4444

PEOPLES COLLEGE OF INDEPENDENT STUDIES
233 Academy Dr., P.O. Box 421768,
Kissimmee 34742-1768 *Accred.:* 1992
(DETC)
(407) 847-4444

SOUTHERN TECHNICAL CENTER
19151 S. Dixie Hwy., Miami 33157 *Type:*
Private *Accred.:* 1988 (ACCSCT) *Degrees:*
C *CEO:* Dir. Joaquin Bassolles
(305) 254-0995

STENOTYPE INSTITUTE OF JACKSONVILLE
500 Ninth Ave., N., Jacksonville Beach
32250 *Type:* Private distance education *Accred.:* 1968/1995 (ACICS); 1987/1992
(DETC) *Degrees:* C *CEO:* Pres. Milton
Archer
(904) 246-7466

SUNCOAST CENTER FOR NATURAL HEALTH/
SUNCOAST SCHOOL
4910 Cypress St., Tampa 33607-3802 *Type:*
Private *Accred.:* 1986 (ACCSCT) *Degrees:*
C *CEO:* Dir. Daniel A. Ulrich
(813) 287-1099

SUNSTATE ACADEMY OF HAIR DESIGN
2418 Colonial Blvd., Fort Myers 33907-
1491 *Type:* Private *Accred.:* 1988/1990 (AC-
CSCT) *Degrees:* C *CEO:* Dir. Kenneth F.
Stone
(813) 278-1311

SUNSTATE ACADEMY OF HAIR DESIGN
1825 Tamiami Trail., No. E6, Port Charlotte
33948 *Type:* Private *Accred.:* 1983/1986
(ACCSCT) *Degrees:* C *CEO:* Dir. Kenneth
F. Stone
(813) 255-1366

SUNSTATE ACADEMY OF HAIR DESIGN
4424 Bee Ridge Rd., Sarasota 34233-2502
Type: Private *Accred.:* 1983/1989 (ACC-
SCT) *Degrees:* C *CEO:* Dir. James A. Stone
(813) 377-4880

SUWANEE-HAMILTON AREA VOCATIONAL-
TECHNICAL AND ADULT EDUCATION CENTER
415 Pinewood Dr., S.W., Live Oak 32060
Type: Public (state) *Accred.:* 1973/1990 (COE)
Degrees: C *CEO:* Dir. Walter Boatright, Jr.
FTE Enroll: 404   (904) 364-2750

TAYLOR TECHNICAL INSTITUTE
3233 Hwy. 19, S., Perry 32347 *Type:* Public
Accred.: 1993 (COE) *Degrees:* C *CEO:* Dir.
Ken Olson
FTE Enroll: 147   (904) 838-2545

TECHNICAL CAREER INSTITUTE
720 N.W. 27th Ave., Miami 33125 *Type:* Private *Accred.:* 1991/1995 (COE) *Degrees:* C
CEO: Dir. Greg Reger
FTE Enroll: 157   (305) 642-2200

TOM P. HANEY TECHNICAL CENTER
3016 Hwy. 77, Panama City 32405 *Type:*
Public (state) *Accred.:* 1977/1992 (COE)
Degrees: C *CEO:* Dir. Marion Riviere
FTE Enroll: 704   (904) 747-5565

TRAVISS TECHNICAL CENTER
3225 Winter Lake Rd., Lakeland 33813
Type: Public (state) *Accred.:* 1978/1994
(COE) *Degrees:* C *CEO:* Dir. Charles Paulk
FTE Enroll: 1,445   (813) 449-2700

U.S. SCHOOLS
100 N. Plaza, Miami 33147 *Type:* Private
Accred.: 1989/1992 (COE) *Degrees:* C
CEO: Dir. Hugh Alpeter
FTE Enroll: 182   (305) 836-7424

WASHINGTON-HOLMES AREA VOCATIONAL-
TECHNICAL CENTER
757 Hoyt St., Chipley 32428 *Type:* Public
(state) *Accred.:* 1976/1991 (COE) *Degrees:*
C *CEO:* Dir. Raymond Norris
FTE Enroll: 597   (904) 638-1180

WEBSTER INSTITUTE OF TECHNOLOGY
3910 US Hwy. 301 N., Ste. 200, Tampa
33619-1259 *Type:* Private *Accred.:* 1985
(ACCSCT) *Calendar:* Qtr. plan *Degrees:* C
CEO: Exec. Dir. Samuel L. Warren
Enroll: 130   (813) 620-1446

WEST TECHNICAL EDUCATION CENTER
2625 State Rd. 715, Belle Glade 33430 *Type:*
Public (state) *Accred.:* 1984/1994 (COE)
Degrees: C *CEO:* Dir. Shirley W. Maxson
FTE Enroll: 529   (407) 996-4930

WILLIAM T. MCFATTER VOCATIONAL-
TECHNICAL CENTER
6500 Nova Dr., Davie 33317 *Type:* Public
(state) *Accred.:* 1989/1994 (COE) *Degrees:*
C *Prof. Accred.:* Dental Laboratory Technol-
ogy, Practical Nursing *CEO:* Director Robert
Boegli
FTE Enroll: 1,938   (305) 370-8324

BROWARD FIRE ACADEMY CAMPUS
Broward Fire Acad., 2600 S.W. 71 Terr.,
Davie 33314
(305) 370-8324

CRIMINAL JUSTICE INSTITUE CAMPUS
Criminal Justice Inst., 3501 S.W. Davie
Rd., Davie 33317
(305) 370-8324

WITHLACOOCHEE TECHNICAL INSTITUTE
1201 W. Main St., Inverness 34450 *Type:*
Public (state) *Accred.:* 1984/1994 (COE)
Degrees: C *CEO:* Dir. Steven S. Kinard
FTE Enroll: 583   (904) 726-2430

GEORGIA

ALBANY TECHNICAL INSTITUTE
1021 Lowe Rd., Albany 31708-2301 *Type:*
Public (state) *Accred.:* 1974/1994 (COE)
Degrees: C *Prof. Accred.:* Dental Assisting,
Radiography, Surgical Technology *CEO:*
Pres. Anthony O. Parker
FTE Enroll: 1,037   (912) 430-3500

ALLIANCE TRACTOR TRAILER TRAINING CENTER
333 Industrial Blvd., P.O. Box 1008, McDo-
nough 30253-1008 *Type:* Private *Accred.:*
1987/1993 (ACCSCT) *Degrees:* C *CEO:*
Dir. Scott McElrath
                              (404) 957-6401

ALTAMAHA TECHNICAL INSTITUTE
1777 W. Cherry St., Jesup 31545 *Type:* Public (state) *Accred.:* 1992 (COE) *Degrees:* C
CEO: Pres. C. Paul Scott
FTE Enroll: 551   (912) 427-5800

HAZLEHURST CAMPUS
Cromartie St., Hazlehurst 31539
                              (912) 375-6740

ARMY SIGNAL CENTER AND SCHOOL
Fort Gordon 30905-5080 *Type:* Public (fed-
eral) technical *Accred.:* 1976/1991 (COE)
Degrees: C *CEO:* Commandant Douglas D.
Buchholz
FTE Enroll: 9,285   (706) 791-6208

ARTISTIC BEAUTY COLLEGE
1820 Hwy. 20, Ste. 200, Conyers 30208
Type: Private *Accred.:* 1990/1995 (COE)
Degrees: C *CEO:* Dir. Diane Holder
FTE Enroll: 124   (404) 922-7653

ASHER SCHOOL OF BUSINESS
100 Pinnacle Way, Ste. 110, Norcross 30071
Type: Private *Accred.:* 1989/1994 (COE)
Degrees: C *CEO:* Dir. Joe Voyles
FTE Enroll: 172   (770) 368-0800

ATLANTA AREA TECHNICAL SCHOOL
1560 Stewart Ave., S.W., Atlanta 30310
Type: Public (state) *Accred.:* 1971/1991
(COE) *Degrees:* C *Prof. Accred.:* Clinical
Lab Technology (C), Dental Laboratory

Technology, Medical Assisting (AMA)
CEO: Dir. Jerry L. Adams
FTE Enroll: 5,629   (404) 756-3703

BRANCH CAMPUS
4191 Northside Dr., N.W., Atlanta 30342
                              (404) 842-8117

ATLANTA INSTITUTE OF MUSIC
6145-D Northbelt Pkwy., Norcross 30071
Type: Private *Accred.:* 1994 (COE) *Calendar:* Qtr. plan *Degrees:* C *CEO:* Pres. Harvey Driscoll
FTE Enroll: 152   (770) 242-7717

ATLANTA JOB CORPS CENTER
239 W. Lake Ave., N.W., Atlanta 30314
Type: Public (district) *Accred.:* 1985/1995
(COE) *Degrees:* C *CEO:* Dir. Lonnie Hall
FTE Enroll: 579   (404) 794-9512

ATLANTA SCHOOL OF MASSAGE
2300 Peachford Rd., Ste. 3200, Atlanta
30338-5820 *Type:* Private *Accred.:* 1988
(ACCSCT) *Degrees:* C *CEO:* Dir. Beth
Geno
                              (404) 454-7167

BEN HILL-IRWIN TECHNICAL INSTITUTE
667 Perry House Rd., Fitzgerald 31750
Type: Public (state) *Accred.:* 1973/1994
(COE) *Degrees:* C *CEO:* Dir. Edgar B.
Greene
FTE Enroll: 543   (912) 468-7487

DOUGLAS CAMPUS
210 W. Jackson St., Douglas 31533
                              (912) 384-7520

BROWN COLLEGE OF COURT REPORTING AND
MEDICAL TRANSCRIPTION
1100 Spring St., N.W., No. 200, Atlanta
30376 *Type:* Private *Accred.:* 1984/1995
(COE) *Degrees:* C *CEO:* Dir. Lorie A.
Brown
FTE Enroll: 206   (404) 876-1227

LONGVIEW CAMPUS
501 Spur 63, Ste. B-3, Longview, TX
75601
(903) 757-4338

BUSINESS TRAVEL INSTITUTE
5555 Oakbrook Pkwy., Ste. 645, Norcross
30093 *Type:* Private *Accred.:* 1994 (ACC-
SCT) *Degrees:* C *CEO:* Pres. Luis Celorio
Enroll: 142 (770) 662-3090

COBB BEAUTY COLLEGE
3096 Cherokee St., Kennesaw 30144 *Type:*
Private *Accred.:* 1993 (COE) *Degrees:* C
CEO: Dir. Gail Little
FTE Enroll: 36 (770) 424-6915

COOSA VALLEY TECHNICAL INSTITUTE
785 Cedar Ave., Rome 30161 *Type:* Public
(state) *Accred.:* 1972/1992 (COE) *Degrees:*
C *Prof. Accred.:* Radiography, Respiratory
Therapy Technology *CEO:* Dir. Ronald E.
Swanson
FTE Enroll: 400 (770) 295-6927

THE CREATIVE CIRCUS
1935 Cliff Valley Way, No. 210, Atlanta
30329 *Type:* Private *Accred.:* 1983/1994
(COE warning) *Degrees:* C *CEO:* Dir.
Rochelle A. Moore
FTE Enroll: 63 (404) 633-1990

DALTON VOCATIONAL SCHOOL OF HEALTH
OCCUPATIONS
1221 Elkwood Dr., Dalton 30720 *Type:* Pub-
lic (state) technical *Accred.:* 1975/1990
(COE) *Degrees:* C *CEO:* Dir. Rubye P. Sane
FTE Enroll: 60 (770) 278-8922

DEKALB BEAUTY COLLEGE
6254 Memorial Dr., No. M, Stone Mountain
30083 *Type:* Private *Accred.:* 1987/1992
(COE) *Degrees:* C *CEO:* Dir. Betty Lyon
FTE Enroll: 224 (404) 879-6673

DERMA CLINIC ACADEMY
5600 Roswell Rd., No. 110, Atlanta 30066
Type: Private *Accred.:* 1987/1993 (COE)
Degrees: C *CEO:* Dir. Margaret A. Ruffin
FTE Enroll: 31 (404) 250-9600

DRAUGHONS COLLEGE
1430 W. Peachtree St., Ste. 101, Atlanta
30309 *Type:* Private business *Accred.:* 1990/
1995 (ACICS) *Degrees:* C *CEO:* Exec. Dir.
Ann H. Gibson
(404) 892-0814

EXECUTIVE TRAVEL INSTITUTE
5775 Peachtree Dunwoody Rd., Ste. 300-E,
Atlanta 30342-1505 *Type:* Private *Accred.:*
1991 (ACCSCT) *Degrees:* C *CEO:* Dir.
Joseph M. Brown
(404) 303-2929

FLINT RIVER TECHNICAL INSTITUTE
1533 Hwy. 19, S., Thomaston 30286 *Type:*
Public (state) *Accred.:* 1973/1990 (COE)
Degrees: C *CEO:* Dir. Carlos Schmitt
FTE Enroll: 272 (706) 647-9616

GEORGIA INSTITUTE OF COSMETOLOGY
3341 Lexington Hwy., Athens 30605 *Type:*
Private *Accred.:* 1993 (COE) *Degrees:* C
CEO: Dir. Fiesel Elkabanni
FTE Enroll: 62 (706) 549-6400

GEORGIA MEDICAL INSTITUTE
40 Marietta St., Fls. 5 and 13, Atlanta 30303
Type: Private *Accred.:* 1985/1993 (ABHES)
Degrees: C *CEO:* Pres. Dominic J. Dean
(404) 525-3272

ATLANTA CAMPUS
1895 Phoenix Blvd., Ste. 310, Atlanta
30349 *Accred.:* 1993 (ABHES) *Degrees:* C
(404) 994-1900

MARIETTA CAMPUS
1395 S Marietta Pkwy, Bldg 500, Ste. 202,
Marietta 30067 *Accred.:* 1993 (ABHES)
Degrees: C
Enroll: 218 (404) 428-6303

GRIFFIN TECHNICAL INSTITUTE
501 Varsity Rd., Griffin 30223 *Type:* Public
(state) *Accred.:* 1971/1991 (COE); 1995
(SACS-CC candidate) *Calendar:* Qtr. plan
Degrees: C *Prof. Accred.:* Radiography
CEO: Dir. Coy L. Hodges
FTE Enroll: 928 (770) 228-7366

GWINNETT COLLEGE
4230 Hwy. 29, Ste. 11, Liburn 30247 *Type:* Private business *Accred.:* 1988/1992 (ACICS) *Calendar:* Qtr. plan *Degrees:* C *CEO:* Pres. Michael Davis
(770) 381-7200

HEART OF GEORGIA TECHNICAL INSTITUTE
560 Pinehill Rd., Dublin 31021 *Type:* Public (state) *Accred.:* 1986/1991 (COE) *Degrees:* C *CEO:* Pres. Ron Henderson
FTE Enroll: 335   (912) 275-6590

EASTMAN CAMPUS
109 Airport Rd., Eastman 31023
(912) 374-6980

INTERACTIVE COLLEGE OF TECHNOLOGY
5600 Roswell Rd., N.E., Atlanta 30342 *Type:* Private *Accred.:* 1989/1994 (COE) *Degrees:* C *CEO:* Pres. Elmer Smith
FTE Enroll: 218   (404) 250-9000

COLLEGE PARK CAMPUS
4814 Old National Hwy., College Park 30337
(404) 765-9777

DAY RIDGE CAMPUS
11 S. Main St., Day Ridge, KY 41035
(606) 824-3573

FLORENCE CAMPUS
6612 Dixie Hwy., Ste. 2, Florence, KY 41042
(606) 282-8989

MARIETTA CAMPUS
2759 Delk Rd., Ste. 101, Marietta 30067
(404) 951-2367

TUCKER CAMPUS
2171 Northlake Pkwy., Ste. 100, Tucker 30084
(404) 939-6008

INTERACTIVE LEARNING SYSTEMS
200 Cleveland Rd. No. 6, Bogart 30622 *Type:* Private business *Accred.:* 1989/1994 (COE) *Degrees:* C *CEO:* Dir. Don Reed
FTE Enroll: 27   (706) 548-9800

INTERNATIONAL SCHOOL OF SKIN AND NAILCARE
5600 Roswell Rd., N.E., Atlanta 30342 *Type:* Private *Accred.:* 1987/1992 (COE) *Degrees:* C *CEO:* Dir. Sissy McQuinn-Boulus
FTE Enroll: 124   (404) 843-1005

KERR BUSINESS COLLEGE
P.O. Box 1986, 2623 Washington Rd., Bldg. B, Augusta 30903 *Type:* Private *Accred.:* 1984/1990 (ACICS) *Degrees:* C *CEO:* Dir. Darryl H. Kerr
(404) 738-5046

LAGRANGE CAMPUS
P.O. Box 976, 3011 Hogansville Rd., LaGrange 30241 business *Accred.:* 1976/1995 (ACICS)
(706) 884-1751

LAGRANGE COSMETOLOGY SCHOOL
1008 Colquitt St., LaGrange 30240 *Type:* Private *Accred.:* 1994 (COE) *Degrees:* C *CEO:* Dir. Winston A. Dahl
FTE Enroll: 40   (706) 884-5750

LANIER TECHNICAL INSTITUTE
2990 Landrum Education Dr., Oakwood 30566 *Type:* Public (state) *Accred.:* 1972/1992 (COE) *Degrees:* C *Prof. Accred.:* Clinical Lab Technology (C), Dental Assisting, Dental Hygiene *CEO:* Pres. Joe E. Hill
FTE Enroll: 713   (404) 531-6304

MABLE BAILEY FASHION COLLEGE SCHOOL OF MODELING AND COSMETOLOGY
3121 Cross Country Hill, Columbus 31906-1714 *Type:* Private *Accred.:* 1983/1994 (COE) *Degrees:* C *CEO:* Dir. Richard M. Leukhardt
FTE Enroll: 90   (706) 563-0606

MACON BEAUTY SCHOOL
630-J North Ave., Macon 31211 *Type:* Private *Accred.:* 1990/1995 (COE) *Degrees:* C *CEO:* Dir. Barry Broadnax
FTE Enroll: 124   (912) 746-3243

MACON TECHNICAL INSTITUTE
3300 Macon Tech Dr., Macon 31206 *Type:* Public (state) *Accred.:* 1973/1993 (COE)

Degrees: C *Prof. Accred.:* Clinical Lab Technology (C) *CEO:* Pres. Melton Palmer
FTE Enroll: 1,164   (912) 757-3501

BRANCH CAMPUS
940 Forsyth St., Macon 31206
(912) 744-4812

METROPOLITAN COLLEGE OF BUSINESS
4319 Covington Hwy., No. 300, Decatur 30032 *Type:* Private *Accred.:* 1990 (COE)
Degrees: C *CEO:* Pres. Bernard Clay
FTE Enroll: 38   (404) 288-6241

METROPOLITAN SCHOOL OF HAIR DESIGN
5244 Memorial Dr., No. 1002, Stone Mountain 30083 *Type:* Private *Accred.:* 1989/1991 (COE) *Degrees:* C *CEO:* Dir. Jerry Vaughn
FTE Enroll: 67   (404) 294-5697

MIDDLE GEORGIA TECHNICAL INSTITUTE
1311 Corder Rd., Warner Robins 31088 *Type:* Public (state) *Accred.:* 1978/1993 (COE)
Degrees: C *CEO:* Pres. Billy G. Edenfield
FTE Enroll: 602   (912) 929-6800

ROBBINS AIR FORCE BASE CAMPUS
Robbins Air Force Museum, Robbins Air Force Base 31099
(912) 929-6849

MOULTRIE AREA TECHNICAL INSTITUTE
361 Industrial Dr., Moultrie 31768 *Type:* Public (state) *Accred.:* 1974/1995 (COE)
Degrees: C *CEO:* Pres. Michael Moye
FTE Enroll: 367   (912) 891-7000

TIFTON CAMPUS
314 E. 14th St., Tifton 31794
(912) 891-7000

THE NATIONAL BUSINESS INSTITUTE
243 W. Ponce de Leon Ave., Decatur 30030
Type: Private *Accred.:* 1990/1995 (COE)
Degrees: C *CEO:* Pres. Mark Lavinsky
FTE Enroll: 151   (404) 377-0500

THE NATIONAL CENTER FOR PARALEGAL TRAINING
3414 Peachtree Rd., NE, Ste. 528, Atlanta 30326 *Type:* Private business *Accred.:* 1995

(ACICS) *Degrees:* C *CEO:* Dir. V. Toni French
(404) 266-1060

NATIONAL EDUCATION CENTER—BRYMAN CAMPUS
40 Marietta St., 8th Fl., Atlanta 30303-2816
Type: Private *Accred.:* 1973/1986 (ACC-SCT) *Degrees:* C *Prof. Accred.:* Medical Assisting (AMA) *CEO:* Dir. John Mathias
(404) 524-8800

NAVY SUPPLY CORPS SCHOOL
1425 Prince Ave., Athens 30606-2205 *Type:* Public (federal) technical *Accred.:* 1981/1991 (COE) *Degrees:* C *CEO:* Cmnd. Ofcr. George Hudan
FTE Enroll: 246   (706) 354-7200

NORTH FULTON BEAUTY COLLEGE
10930 Crabapple Rd., No. 4 A&B, Roswell 30075 *Type:* Private *Accred.:* 1992 (COE)
Degrees: C *CEO:* Dir. Jane Champion
FTE Enroll: 22   (404) 552-9570

NORTH GEORGIA TECHNICAL INSTITUTE
Hwy. 197, N., Clarkesville 30523 *Type:* Public (state) *Accred.:* 1972/1992 (COE)
Degrees: C *Prof. Accred.:* Clinical Lab Technology (C) *CEO:* Dir. Judy Hulsey
FTE Enroll: 613   (706) 754-7700

NORTH METRO TECHNICAL INSTITUTE
5198 Ross Rd., Acworth 30080 *Type:* Public (state) *Accred.:* 1991 (COE) *Degrees:* C
CEO: Pres. Kenneth Allen
FTE Enroll: 429   (770) 975-4052

OCCUPATIONAL EDUCATION CENTER—CENTRAL
3075 Alton Rd., Chamblee 30341 *Type:* Public (state) *Accred.:* 1988/1993 (SACS-CC)
Degrees: C *CEO:* Dir. Robert Burns
FTE Enroll: 122   (404) 457-3393

OCCUPATIONAL EDUCATION CENTER—NORTH
1995 Womack Rd., Dunwoody 30338 *Type:* Public (state) *Accred.:* 1988/1993 (SACS-CC) *Degrees:* C *CEO:* Dir. Frank Hall
FTE Enroll: 296   (404) 394-0321

OCCUPATIONAL EDUCATION CENTER—SOUTH
3303 Pantherville Rd., Decatur 30034 *Type:*
Public (state) *Accred.:* 1988/1993 (SACS-
CC) *Degrees:* C *CEO:* Dir. Larry Ladner
FTE Enroll: 192   (404) 241-9400

OGEECHEE TECHNICAL INSTITUTE
One Joe Kennedy Blvd., Statesboro 30458-
8049 *Type:* Public (state) *Accred.:* 1992
(COE) *Degrees:* C *CEO:* Pres. Stephen A.
Deraney
FTE Enroll: 1,870   (912) 681-5500

OKEFENOKEE TECHNICAL INSTITUTE
1701 Carswell Ave., Waycross 31503 *Type:*
Public (state) *Accred.:* 1972/1992 (COE)
Degrees: C *Prof. Accred.:* Clinical Lab Technology (C), Radiography, Surgical Technology *CEO:* Dir. Joseph Ray Miller
FTE Enroll: 521   (912) 287-6854

PICKENS TECHNICAL INSTITUTE
100 Pickens Tech Dr., Jasper 30143 *Type:*
Public (state) *Accred.:* 1971/1991 (COE)
Degrees: C *CEO:* Dir. Tom Harrison
FTE Enroll: 527   (706) 692-3411

PORTFOLIO CENTER
125 Bennett St., N.W., Atlanta 30309 *Type:*
Private professional *Accred.:* 1982/1992
(COE) *Degrees:* C *CEO:* Dir. Gemma Gatt
FTE Enroll: 212   (404) 351-5055

PRO-WAY HAIR SCHOOL
8649 Tara Blvd., Jonesboro 30236 *Type:* Private *Accred.:* 1983/1990 (COE) *Degrees:* C
CEO: Dir. Francis Sullivan
FTE Enroll: 88   (404) 477-2651

MEMPHIS CAMPUS
3099 S. Perkins Rd., Memphis, TN 38118-
3239
                             (901) 363-3553

PROFESSIONAL CAREER DEVELOPMENT
INSTITUTE
3597 Parkway Ln., Ste. 100, Norcross 30092
Type: Private distance education *Accred.:*
1993 (DETC) *Degrees:* C *CEO:* Pres.
Richard A. Kruger
                             (770) 729-8400

ROFFLER MOLER HAIRSTYLING COLLEGE
P.O. Box 518, Forest Park 30050-0518 *Type:*
Private *Accred.:* 1985/1990 (ACCSCT) *De-
grees:* C *CEO:* Dir. Ruby Sheffield
                             (404) 366-2838

MARIETTA CAMPUS
1311 Roswell Rd., Marietta 30062
Accred.: 1988 (ACCSCT)
                             (404) 565-3285

SAMVERLY COLLEGE
210 Edgewood Ave., N.E., Atlanta 30303-
2322 *Type:* Private *Accred.:* 1990/1992
(ACCSCT) *Degrees:* C *CEO:* Dir. Beverly
Purdie
                             (404) 522-4370

SOUTH GEORGIA TECHNICAL INSTITUTE
728 Southerfield Rd., Americus 31709-9691
Type: Public (state) *Accred.:* 1973/1993
(COE) *Degrees:* C *CEO:* Dir. Dea Pounders
FTE Enroll: 357   (912) 931-2150

SOUTHEASTERN SCHOOL OF AERONAUTICS
Herbert Smart Downtown Airport, Macon
31201 *Type:* Private *Accred.:* 1992 (COE
warning) *Degrees:* C *CEO:* Pres. Cheryl
Miresse
FTE Enroll: 71   (912) 745-0964

SOUTHEASTERN TECHNICAL INSTITUTE
3001 E. First St., Vidalia 30474 *Type:* Private *Accred.:* 1992 (COE) *Degrees:* C *CEO:*
Dir. Larry Siefferman
FTE Enroll: 1,335   (912) 537-0386

SWAINSBORO TECHNICAL INSTITUTE
346 Kite Rd., Swainsboro 30401 *Type:* Public (state) *Accred.:* 1973/1993 (COE)
Degrees: C *CEO:* Dir. Donald Speir
FTE Enroll: 754   (912) 237-6465

THOMAS TECHNICAL INSTITUTE
Hwy. 319 at 19, Thomasville 31792 *Type:*
Public (state) *Accred.:* 1973/1993 (COE)
Degrees: C *Prof. Accred.:* Clinical Lab Tech-
nology (A), Clinical Lab Technology (C),
Medical Assisting (AMA), Physical Therapy
Assisting, Radiation Therapy Technology,
Radiography, Respiratory Therapy Technol-

ogy, Surgical Technology *CEO:* Dir. Charles R. DeMott
FTE Enroll: 563   (912) 225-4096

TRIDENT TRAINING FACILITY
1040 USS Georgia Ave., Kings Bay 31547-6300 *Type:* Public (federal) *Accred.:* 1993 (COE) *Degrees:* C *CEO:* Commandant M. G. Duncan
FTE Enroll: 401   (912) 673-3472

TURNER JOB CORPS CENTER
2000 Schilling Ave., Albany 31705-1524 *Type:* Public (district) *Accred.:* 1984/1994 (COE) *Degrees:* C *CEO:* Dir. Martin Reyna
FTE Enroll: 676   (912) 431-1821

VALDOSTA TECHNICAL INSTITUTE
4089 Val-Tech Rd., Valdosta 31603-0928 *Type:* Public (state) *Accred.:* 1974/1990

(COE) *Degrees:* C *Prof. Accred.:* Medical Assisting (AMA), Radiography *CEO:* Dir. James Bridges
FTE Enroll: 731   (912) 333-2100

WALKER TECHNICAL INSTITUTE
265 Bicentennial Trail., Rock Spring 30739 *Type:* Public (state) *Accred.:* 1972/1992 (COE); 1995 (SACS-CC candidate) *Calendar:* Qtr. plan *Degrees:* C *CEO:* Dir. Ray Brooks
FTE Enroll: 793   (706) 764-3530

WEST GEORGIA TECHNICAL INSTITUTE
303 Fort Dr., LaGrange 30240 *Type:* Public (state) *Accred.:* 1973/1993 (COE) *Degrees:* C *Prof. Accred.:* Radiography *CEO:* Dir. Roger Slater
FTE Enroll: 433   (706) 883-8324

HAWAII

ELECTRONIC INSTITUTE
1270 Queen Emma St., Rm. 107, Honolulu 96813 *Type:* Private *Accred.:* 1993 (ACC-SCT) *Degrees:* C *CEO:* Acting Princ. Herbert Yamada
(808) 521-5290

HAWAII BUSINESS COLLEGE
33 S. King St, Fourth Fl, Honolulu 96813-4316 *Type:* Private business *Accred.:* 1976/1994 (ACICS) *Degrees:* C *CEO:* Exec. Vice Pres. Anne Omori
(808) 524-4014

HAWAII INSTITUTE OF HAIR DESIGN
71 S. Hotel St., Honolulu 96813-3112 *Type:* Private *Accred.:* 1978/1990 (ACCSCT) *Degrees:* C *CEO:* Pres. Margaret Williams
(808) 533-6596

MED-ASSIST SCHOOL OF HAWAII
1149 Bethel St., Ste. 605, Honolulu 96813 *Type:* Private *Accred.:* 1984/1990 (ABHES) *Degrees:* C *Prof. Accred.:* Medical Assisting *CEO:* Pres. James Takemoto
(808) 524-3363

NEW YORK TECHNICAL INSTITUTE OF HAWAII
1375 Dillingham Blvd., Honolulu 96817-4415 *Type:* Private *Accred.:* 1990 (ACC-SCT) *Degrees:* C *CEO:* Owner Tracy Hamilton
(808) 841-5827

TRAVEL INSTITUTE OF THE PACIFIC
1314 S. King St., Ste. 1164, Honolulu 96814-2004 *Type:* Private *Accred.:* 1990 (ACCSCT) *Degrees:* C *CEO:* Dir. James Hughes
(808) 591-2708

IDAHO

AMERICAN INSTITUTE OF HEALTH TECHNOLOGY, INC.

6600 Emerald St., Boise 83704 *Type:* Private *Accred.:* 1982/1994 (ABHES) *Degrees:* C *Prof. Accred.:* Occupational Therapy Assisting *CEO:* Pres. Judy L. Groothuis
(208) 377-8080

ILLINOIS

AMERICAN CAREER TRAINING
237 S. State St., Chicago 60604 *Type:* Private *Accred.:* 1985/1991 (ACCSCT) *Degrees:* C *CEO:* Exec. Dir. David C. Kujawa
(312) 461-0700

AMERICAN COLLEGE OF TECHNOLOGY
1300 W. Washington St., Bloomington 61701-4712 *Type:* Private *Accred.:* 1983/1988 (ACCSCT) *Degrees:* C *CEO:* Vice Pres. Douglas E. Minter
(309) 828-5151

AMERICAN HEALTH INFORMATION MANAGEMENT ASSOCIATION
919 N. Michigan Ave., Ste. 1400, Chicago 60611-1683 *Type:* Private distance education *Accred.:* 1970/1995 (DETC) *Degrees:* C *CEO:* Dir. Barbara A. Glondys
(312) 787-2672

BELLEVILLE BARBER COLLEGE
329 N. Illinois St., Belleville 62220-1291 *Type:* Private *Accred.:* 1985/1990 (ACCSCT) *Degrees:* C *CEO:* Owner Betty Boeving
(618) 234-4424

CAIN'S BARBER COLLEGE
365 E. 51st St., Chicago 60615 *Type:* Private *Accred.:* 1993 (ACCSCT) *Degrees:* C *CEO:* Dir. Leroy Cain
(312) 536-4623

CAPITAL AREA VOCATIONAL CENTER
12201 Toronto Rd., Springfield 62707 *Type:* Private *Degrees:* C *Prof. Accred.:* Practical Nursing *CEO:* Dir. Shirley McConnaughay
(217) 529-5431

CAVE TECHNICAL INSTITUTE
2842 S. State St., Lockport 60441-4915 *Type:* Private *Accred.:* 1988 (ACCSCT) *Degrees:* C *CEO:* Dir. Harold C. Jones
(815) 727-1576

COMPUTER LEARNING CENTER
200 S. Michigan Ave., 3rd Fl., Chicago 60604-2404 *Type:* Private business *Accred.:*

1985/1991 (ACICS) *Degrees:* C *CEO:* Dir. Deloris Reynolds
(312) 427-2700

CONNECTICUT SCHOOL OF BROADCASTING
200 W. 22nd St., Ste. 202, Lombard 60148 *Type:* Private *Accred.:* 1993 (ACCSCT) *Degrees:* C *CEO:* Pres. Robert Mills
(708) 916-1700

COOKING AND HOSPITALITY INSTITUTE OF CHICAGO
361 W. Chestnut St., Chicago 60610-3050 *Type:* Private *Accred.:* 1986 (ACCSCT) *Degrees:* C *CEO:* Pres. Linda Calafiore
(312) 944-2725

COYNE AMERICAN INSTITUTE
1235 W. Fullerton Ave., Chicago 60614-2102 *Type:* Private *Accred.:* 1968/1993 (ACCSCT) *Calendar:* Qtr. plan *Degrees:* C *CEO:* Pres. John J. Freeman
(312) 935-2520

ENVIRONMENTAL TECHNICAL INSTITUTE
1101 W. Thorndale Ave., Itasca 60143-1334 *Type:* Private *Accred.:* 1988 (ACCSCT) *Degrees:* C *CEO:* Dir. Lynn Tortorello
(708) 285-9100

BLUE ISLAND CAMPUS
13010 S. Division St., Blue Island 60406-2606 *Accred.:* 1988 (ACCSCT)
(708) 385-0707

FOX SECRETARIAL COLLEGE
4201 W. 93rd St., Oak Lawn 60453 *Type:* Private business *Accred.:* 1987/1992 (ACICS) *Calendar:* Qtr. plan *Degrees:* C *CEO:* Pres. Edward L. Kapelinski
(708) 636-7700

THE HADLEY SCHOOL FOR THE BLIND
700 Elm St., Winnetka 60093 *Type:* Private distance education *Accred.:* 1958/1995 (DETC) *Degrees:* C *CEO:* Pres. Robert J. Winn
(708) 446-8111

HEARTLAND SCHOOL OF BUSINESS
211 W. State St., Ste. 204, Jacksonville 62650 *Type:* Private business *Accred.:* 1993/1995 (ACICS) *Degrees:* C *CEO:* Dir. Mark G. Woodworth
(217) 243-9001

ILLINOIS SCHOOL OF HEALTH CAREERS
1607 W. Howard St., Ste. 305, Chicago 60626 *Type:* Private *Accred.:* 1993 (ABHES) *Degrees:* C *CEO:* Dir. Karen Genander
Enroll: 25   (312) 973-0299

LINCOLN TECHNICAL INSTITUTE
7320 W. Agatite Ave., Norridge 60656-9975 *Type:* Private *Accred.:* 1971/1985 (ACCSCT) *Degrees:* C *CEO:* Exec. Dir. James O. Yeaman
(312) 625-1535

LINCOLN TECHNICAL INSTITUTE
8920 S. Cicero Ave., Oak Lawn 60453-1315 *Type:* Private *Accred.:* 1984 (ACCSCT) *Degrees:* C *CEO:* Dir. Kenneth R. Ruff
(708) 423-9000

M G INSTITUTE
40 E. Delaware Pl., Chicago 60611 *Type:* Private *Accred.:* 1993 (ACCSCT) *Degrees:* C *CEO:* Pres. Mary Ghorbanian
(312) 943-4190

MEDICAL CAREERS INSTITUTE
116 S. Michigan Ave., 2nd Fl., Chicago 60603 *Type:* Private *Accred.:* 1986/1994 (ABHES) *Degrees:* C *CEO:* Dir. William Zane
(312) 782-9804

MIDWEST INSTITUTE OF TECHNOLOGY
3712 W. Montrose, Chicago 60618 *Type:* Private *Accred.:* 1994 (ACCSCT) *Degrees:* C *CEO:* Owner Buten Kowalski
Enroll: 8   (312) 478-0119

MOLER HAIRSTYLING COLLEGE
5840 W. Madison St., Chicago 60644-3839 *Type:* Private *Accred.:* 1982/1988 (ACCSCT) *Degrees:* C *CEO:* Dir. Kenneth M. Edwards
(312) 287-2552

MUSIC CENTER OF THE NORTH SHORE
300 Green Bay Rd., Winnetka 60093 *Type:* Private *Degrees:* C *Prof. Accred.:* Music *CEO:* Exec. Dir. Frank Little
(708) 446-3822

PATHFINDER TRAINING INSTITUTE
19 E. 21st St., Chicago 60616-1701 *Type:* Private *Accred.:* 1992 (ACCSCT) *Degrees:* C *CEO:* Pres. Melvyn R. May
(312) 842-7272

QUINCY TECHNICAL SCHOOLS
501 N. Third St., Quincy 62301-9990 *Type:* Private *Accred.:* 1977/1988 (ACCSCT) *Calendar:* Qtr. plan *Degrees:* C *CEO:* Dir. William G. Dubuque, Jr.
(800) 438-5621

ROCKFORD SCHOOL OF PRACTICAL NURSING
978 Haskell Ave., Rockford 61103 *Type:* Private *Degrees:* C *Prof. Accred.:* Practical Nursing *CEO:* Dir. Shirley Asher
(815) 966-3716

SPANISH COALITION FOR JOBS, INC.
2011 W. Pershing Rd., Chicago 60609 *Type:* Private business *Accred.:* 1994 (ACICS) *Degrees:* C *CEO:* Exec. Dir. Kathleen S. Peterfish
(312) 247-0707

SPARKS COLLEGE
131 S. Morgan St., Shelbyville 62565 *Type:* Private business *Accred.:* 1954/1995 (ACICS) *Degrees:* C *CEO:* Dir. Jack Allen
(217) 774-5112

TYLER SCHOOL OF SECRETARIAL SCIENCES
8030 S. Kedzie Ave., Chicago 60652 *Type:* Private business *Accred.:* 1984/1988 (ACICS) *Degrees:* C *CEO:* Pres. Michael Franzak
(312) 436-5050

WORSHAM COLLEGE OF MORTUARY SCIENCE
495 Northgate Pkwy., Wheeling 60090 *Type:* Private professional *Calendar:* 12-mos. program *Degrees:* C *Prof. Accred.:* Funeral Service Education (Mortuary Science) *CEO:* Chief Admin. Frederick C. Cappetta
(708) 808-8444

INDIANA

ACADEMY OF HAIR DESIGN
2150 Lafayette Rd., Indianapolis 46222-2394
Type: Private *Accred.:* 1982/1988 (ACCSCT)
Degrees: C *CEO:* Owner Jack Hale
(317) 637-7227

DEFENSE INFORMATION SCHOOL
Bldg. 400, Fort Benjamin Harrison 46216-6200 *Type:* Public (federal) *Accred.:* 1979/1990 (NCA) *Degrees:* C *CEO:* Commandant Ronald A. Grubb
(317) 542-4046

HORIZON CAREER COLLEGE
8315 Virginia St., Ste. A, Merrillville 46307
Type: Private *Accred.:* 1995 (ABHES) *Degrees:* C *CEO:* Pres. Renee Kimberling
Enroll: 350   (219) 756-6811

INDIANA BARBER/STYLIST COLLEGE
121 S. Ridgeview Dr., Irving Plaza Shopping Ctr., Indianapolis 46219-6426 *Type:* Private *Accred.:* 1973/1988 (ACCSCT) *Degrees:* C *CEO:* Pres. Rachel Merritt
(317) 356-8222

PROFESSIONAL CAREERS INSTITUTE
2611 Waterfront Pkwy., East Dr., Indianapolis 46214-2028 *Type:* Private *Accred.:* 1970/1990 (ACCSCT) *Degrees:* C *Prof. Accred.:* Dental Assisting, Medical Assisting (AMA) *CEO:* Dir. Richard H. Weiss
(317) 299-6001

IOWA

AMERICAN COLLEGE OF HAIRSTYLING—CEDAR
RAPIDS
   1531 First Ave., S.E., Cedar Rapids 52402-
   5123 *Type:* Private *Accred.:* 1977/1991 (AC-
   CSCT) *Degrees:* C *CEO:* Pres. T. L. Millis
                                        (319) 362-1488

AMERICAN COLLEGE OF HAIRSTYLING—DES
MOINES
   603 E. Sixth St., Des Moines 50309-5478
   Type: Private *Accred.:* 1975/1986 (ACC-
   SCT) *Degrees:* C *CEO:* Pres. T. L. Millis
                                        (515) 244-0971

CAPRI COLLEGE
   315 2nd Ave., S.E., Cedar Rapids *Type:* Private *Accred.:* 1994 (ACCSCT) *Degrees:* C
   CEO: Dir. Melissa Sheetz
   Enroll: 60   (319) 364-1541

CAPRI COLLEGE
   1815 E. Kimberly Rd., Davenport 52807
   Type: Private *Accred.:* 1994 (ACCSCT)
   Degrees: C *CEO:* Dir. Kelly Mussell
   Enroll: 70   (319) 359-1306

CAPRI COLLEGE
   395 Main St., P.O. Box 873, Dubuque
   52004-0873 *Type:* Private *Accred.:* 1991
   (ACCSCT) *Degrees:* C *CEO:* Dir. Lois
   Leytem
                                        (319) 588-4545

COLLEGE OF HAIR DESIGN
   810 LaPorte Rd., Waterloo 50702-1834
   Type: Private *Accred.:* 1991 (ACCSCT) *Degrees:* C *CEO:* Pres. Joe O. Squires
                                        (319) 232-9995

KANSAS

ADVANCED HAIR TECH
4323 State Ave., Kansas City 66101 *Type:* Private *Accred.:* 1987/1992 (ACCSCT) *Degrees:* C *CEO:* Dir. Douglas Rushing
(913) 321-0214

AMTECH INSTITUTE
4011 E. 31st St. S., Wichita 67210-1588 *Type:* Private *Accred.:* 1971/1986 (ACCSCT) *Degrees:* C *CEO:* Dir. Rex Spaulding
(316) 682-6548

BRYAN INSTITUTE
1004 S. Oliver St., Wichita 67214 *Type:* Private *Accred.:* 1971/1988 (ACCSCT) *Degrees:* C *Prof. Accred.:* Medical Assisting *CEO:* Pres. Larry Prather
(316) 685-2284

ARLINGTON CAMPUS
1719 W. Pioneer Pkwy., Arlington, TX 76013-4799 *Accred.:* 1982/1992 (ACCSCT) *Prof. Accred.:* Medical Assisting
(817) 265-5588

BRIDGETON CAMPUS
12184 Natural Bridge Rd., Bridgeton, MO 63044-2078 *Accred.:* 1979/1989 (ACCSCT) *Calendar:* Sem. plan *Degrees:* C *Prof. Accred.:* Medical Assisting
(314) 291-0241

TULSA CAMPUS
2843 E. 51st St., Tulsa, OK 74105-6247 *Accred.:* 1974/1989 (ACCSCT) *Degrees:* C *Prof. Accred.:* Medical Assisting
(918) 749-6891

BRYAN TRAVEL COLLEGE
1527 Fairlawn Rd., Topeka 66604 *Type:* Private business *Accred.:* 1990/1994 (ACICS) *Degrees:* C *CEO:* Admin. William Garlic
(913) 272-7511

CAPITOL CITY BARBER COLLEGE
812 N. Kansas Ave., Topeka 66608-1211 *Type:* Private *Accred.:* 1994 (ACCSCT) *Degrees:* C *CEO:* Pres. Douglas Rushing *Enroll:* 11   (913) 234-5401

CENTER FOR TRAINING IN BUSINESS AND INDUSTRY
2211 Silicon Ave., Lawrence 66046 *Type:* Private business *Accred.:* 1989 (ACICS) *Degrees:* C *CEO:* Pres. Patricia M. Anderson
(913) 841-9640

CLIMATE CONTROL INSTITUTE
3030 N. Hillside St., Wichita 67219-3902 *Type:* Private *Accred.:* 1976/1985 (ACCSCT) *Degrees:* C *CEO:* Dir. Susan Hampton
(316) 686-7355

TRAVEL CAREERS DIVISION CAMPUS
150 Collins St., Memphis, TN 37601-1710 *Accred.:* 1992 (ACCSCT)
(901) 761-5730

FLINT HILLS TECHNICAL SCHOOL
3301 W. 18th Ave., Emporia 66801 *Type:* Private *Degrees:* C *Prof. Accred.:* Dental Assisting *CEO:* Dir. Keith Stover
(316) 342-6404

KANSAS SCHOOL OF HAIRSTYLING
1207 E. Douglas Ave., Wichita 67211-1693 *Type:* Private *Accred.:* 1985/1990 (ACCSCT) *Degrees:* C *CEO:* Owner John Jewell
(316) 264-4891

NORTH CENTRAL KANSAS AREA VOCATIONAL-TECHNICAL SCHOOL
P.O. Box 507, Beloit 67420 *Type:* Public professional *Accred.:* 1981/1992 (NCA) *Calendar:* Qtr. plan *Degrees:* C *Prof. Accred.:* Practical Nursing *CEO:* Dir. D. William Reeves
Enroll: 1,223   (913) 738-2276

HAYS CAMPUS
2205 Wheatland, Hays 67601
(913) 625-2437

REMINGTON COLLEGE
2443 S. Meridian, Wichita 67213-1993 *Type:* Private *Accred.:* 1981 (ACCSCT) *Degrees:* C *CEO:* Dir. Patty Evans
(316) 681-6700

TOPEKA TECHNICAL COLLEGE
1620 N.W. Gage Blvd., Topeka 66618-2830 *Type:* Private *Accred.:* 1968/1987 (ACC-SCT) *Calendar:* Qtr. plan *Degrees:* C *CEO:* Pres. Ann K. Colgan
(913) 232-5858

WICHITA AREA VOCATIONAL-TECHNICAL SCHOOL
324 N. Emporia St., Wichita 67202 *Type:* Private *Degrees:* C *Prof. Accred.:* Clinical Lab Technology (C), Practical Nursing, Surgical Technology *CEO:* Dir. Rosemary A. Kirby
(316) 833-4664

WICHITA TECHNICAL INSTITUTE
942 S. West St., Wichita 67213-1681 *Type:* Private *Accred.:* 1971/1988 (ACCSCT) *Degrees:* C *Prof. Accred.:* Dental Assisting *CEO:* Pres. Paul D. Moore
(316) 943-2241

WRIGHT BUSINESS SCHOOL
9500 Marshall Dr., Lenexa 66215 *Type:* Private business *Accred.:* 1984/1994 (ACICS) *Degrees:* C *CEO:* Dir. Lisa Grigg
(913) 492-2888

KANSAS CITY CAMPUS
5528 N.E. Antioch Rd., Kansas City, MO 64119 *Accred.:* 1989/1994 (ACICS)
(816) 452-4411

OKLAHOMA CITY CAMPUS
2219 S.W. 74th St., Ste. 122, Oklahoma City, OK 73159 business *Accred.:* 1986/1994 (ACICS)
(405) 681-2300

KENTUCKY

ASHLAND REGIONAL TECHNOLOGY CENTER
4818 Roberts Dr., Ashland 41102-9046
Type: Public (state) technical *System:* Kentucky Tech Northeast Region *Accred.:* 1971/1995 (COE) *Degrees:* C *CEO:* Dir. Richard Kendall
(606) 928-6427

BALLARD COUNTY AREA VOCATIONAL CENTER
Rte. 1, U.S. Hwy. 60, Box 214, Barlow 42024 *Type:* Public (state) technical *Accred.:* 1975/1990 (SACS-CC) *Degrees:* C *CEO:* Dir. Donald G. Wells
FTE Enroll: 80   (502) 665-5112

BARREN COUNTY AREA TECHNOLOGY CENTER
491 Trojan Trail, Glasgow 42141 *Type:* Public (state) technical *System:* Kentucky Tech Southern Region *Accred.:* 1972/1992 (COE) *Degrees:* C *CEO:* Princ. Max Doty
(502) 651-2196

BARRETT AND COMPANY SCHOOL OF HAIR DESIGN
973 Kimberly Square, Nicholasville 40356 *Type:* Private *Accred.:* 1987/1992 (COE) *Degrees:* C *CEO:* Dir. James Barrett
FTE Enroll: 44   (606) 885-9135

BELFRY AREA TECHNOLOGY CENTER
P.O. Box 280, Belfry 41514 *Type:* Public (state) technical *System:* Kentucky Tech Northeast Region *Accred.:* 1974/1995 (COE) *Degrees:* C *CEO:* Princ. Danny O'Neal
(606) 353-4951

BELL COUNTY AREA TECHNOLOGY CENTER
Box 199-A, Rte. 7, Pineville 40977 *Type:* Public (state) technical *System:* Kentucky Tech Southeast Region *Accred.:* 1975/1995 (COE) *Degrees:* C *CEO:* Princ. Ron Mason
(606) 337-3094

BOONE COUNTY AREA TECHNOLOGY CENTER
3320 Cougar Path, Hebron 41048 *Type:* Public (state) technical *System:* Kentucky Tech North Central Region *Accred.:* 1973/1993 (COE) *Degrees:* C *CEO:* Princ. Stephanie Rottman
(606) 689-7855

BOWLING GREEN REGIONAL TECHNOLOGY CENTER
1845 Loop Dr., Bowling Green 42101 *Type:* Public (state) technical *System:* Kentucky Tech Southern Region *Accred.:* 1972/1992 (COE) *Degrees:* C *Prof. Accred.:* Dental Assisting, Radiography, Respiratory Therapy Technology, Surgical Technology *CEO:* Dir. Donald R. Williams
(502) 746-7461

BREATHITT COUNTY AREA TECHNOLOGY CENTER
P.O. Box 786, Jackson 41339 *Type:* Public (state) technical *System:* Kentucky Tech Southeast Region *Accred.:* 1973/1994 (COE) *Degrees:* C *CEO:* Princ. Fred Deaton
(606) 666-5153

BULLITT COUNTY AREA TECHNOLOGY CENTER
395 High School Dr., Shepherdsville 40165 *Type:* Public (state) technical *System:* Kentucky Tech Northwest Region *Accred.:* 1973/1993 (COE) *Degrees:* C *CEO:* Princ. Beverly Dennis
(502) 543-7018

CALDWELL COUNTY AREA TECHNOLOGY CENTER
P.O. Box 350, Voc. School Rd., Princeton 42445 *Type:* Public (state) technical *System:* Kentucky Tech West Region *Accred.:* 1971/1991 (COE) *Degrees:* C *CEO:* Coord. Arthur Dunn
(502) 365-5563

CARL D. PERKINS JOB CORPS CENTER
363 Meadows Branch Rd., Prestonsburg 41653 *Type:* Private *Accred.:* 1985/1995 (COE) *Degrees:* C *CEO:* Dir. Edna Higginbotham
FTE Enroll: 287   (606) 886-1037

CARROLL COUNTY AREA TECHNOLOGY CENTER
1704 Highland Ave., Carrollton 41008 *Type:* Public (state) technical *System:* Kentucky Tech North Central Region *Accred.:* 1973/1993 (COE) *Degrees:* C *CEO:* Princ. Carolyn Barnes
(502) 732-4479

CASEY COUNTY AREA TECHNOLOGY CENTER
Rte. 4, Hwy 70 E., Box 49, Liberty 42539
Type: Public (state) technical *System:* Kentucky Tech Southern Region *Accred.:* 1974/1995 (COE) *Degrees:* C *CEO:* Princ. J. D. Shugars
(606) 787-6241

CE MCCORMICK AREA TECHNOLOGY CENTER
50 Orchard Ln., Alexandria 41001 *Type:* Public (state) technical *System:* Kentucky Tech North Central Region *Accred.:* 1973/ 1993 (COE) *Degrees:* C *CEO:* Princ. Kenneth McCormick
(606) 635-4101

CLAY COUNTY AREA TECHNOLOGY CENTER
Rte. 2, Box 256, Manchester 40962 *Type:* Public (state) technical *System:* Kentucky Tech Southeast Region *Accred.:* 1975/1995 (COE) *Degrees:* C *CEO:* Princ. Charles McWhorter
(606) 598-2194

CLINTON COUNTY AREA TECHNOLOGY CENTER
Rte. 5, Box 5023, Albany 42602 *Type:* Public (state) technical *System:* Kentucky Tech Southern Region *Accred.:* 1974/1995 (COE) *Degrees:* C *CEO:* Acting Princ. Harold Van Hook
(606) 387-6448

COMPUTER EDUCATION SERVICES
981 S. Third St., Ste. 106, Louisville 40203 *Type:* Private *Accred.:* 1992 (COE) *Degrees:* C *CEO:* Pres. Linda Crowe
FTE Enroll: 51   (502) 583-2860

THE COMPUTER SCHOOL
820 Lane Allen Rd., Lexington 40504-3615 *Type:* Private *Accred.:* 1991 (ACCSCT) *Degrees:* C *CEO:* Pres. John J. Weikel
(606) 276-1929

CORBIN AREA TECHNOLOGY CENTER
1909 S. Snyder Ave., Corbin 40701 *Type:* Public (state) technical *System:* Kentucky Tech Southeast Region *Accred.:* 1975/1995 (COE) *Degrees:* C *CEO:* Dir. Ronnie Partin
(606) 528-5338

CUMBERLAND VALLEY HEALTH TECHNOLOGY CENTER
U.S. 25E, P.O. Box 187, Pineville 40977 *Type:* Public (state) technical *System:* Kentucky Tech Southeast Region *Accred.:* 1975/1995 (COE) *Degrees:* C *Prof. Accred.:* Radiography, Respiratory Therapy Technology, Surgical Technology *CEO:* Dir. Denise Sharpe
(606) 337-3106

DANVILLE HEALTH TECHNOLOGY CENTER
340 S. Third St., Danville 40423 *Type:* Public (state) technical *System:* Kentucky Tech North Central Region *Accred.:* 1972/1992 (COE) *Degrees:* C *CEO:* Dir. Sandra Houston
(606) 236-2053

EARLE C. CLEMENTS JOB CORPS CENTER
2302 U.S. Highway 60 East, Morganfield 42437 *Type:* Private *Accred.:* 1983/1993 (COE) *Degrees:* C *CEO:* Dir. Jack Carson
FTE Enroll: 959   (502) 389-2419

GARRARD COUNTY AREA TECHNOLOGY CENTER
306 W. Maple Ave., Lancaster 40444 *Type:* Public (state) technical *System:* Kentucky Tech North Central Region *Accred.:* 1972/1992 (COE) *Degrees:* C *CEO:* Princ. James Spurlin
(606) 792-2144

GARTH AREA TECHNOLOGY CENTER
HC 79, Box 205, Martin 41649 *Type:* Public (state) technical *System:* Kentucky Tech Northeast Region *Accred.:* 1974/1995 (COE) *Degrees:* C *CEO:* Princ. Ronald Turner
(606) 285-3088

GREEN COUNTY AREA TECHNOLOGY CENTER
Carlisle Ave., P.O. Box 167, Greensburg 42743 *Type:* Public (state) technical *System:* Kentucky Tech Southern Region *Accred.:* 1974/1995 (COE) *Degrees:* C *CEO:* Princ. Rick Atwell
(502) 932-4263

GREENUP COUNTY AREA TECHNOLOGY CENTER
Box 4009, Ohio River Rd., Greenup 41144 *Type:* Public (state) technical *System:* Kentucky Tech Northeast Region *Accred.:*

1971/1995 (COE) *Degrees:* C *CEO:* Princ. Helen Spears

(606) 473-9344

HARLAN REGIONAL TECHNOLOGY CENTER
21 Ballpark Rd., Harlan 40831 *Type:* Public (state) technical *System:* Kentucky Tech Southeast Region *Accred.:* 1975/1995 (COE) *Degrees:* C *CEO:* Acting Dir. Kenny Boggs

(606) 573-1506

HARRISON COUNTY AREA TECHNOLOGY CENTER
551 Webster Ave., Cynthiana 41031 *Type:* Public (state) technical *System:* Kentucky Tech North Central Region *Accred.:* 1972/1992 (COE) *Degrees:* C *CEO:* Princ. John Hodge

(606) 234-5286

HARRODSBURG AREA TECHNOLOGY CENTER
661 Tapp Rd., P.O. Box 628, Harrodsburg 40330 *Type:* Public (state) technical *System:* Kentucky Tech North Central Region *Accred.:* 1972/1992 (COE) *Degrees:* C *CEO:* Princ. L. Hughes Jones

(606) 734-9329

HAZARD REGIONAL TECHNOLOGY CENTER
101 Vo-Tech Dr., Hazard 41701 *Type:* Public (state) technical *System:* Kentucky Tech Southeast Region *Accred.:* 1973/1994 (COE) *Degrees:* C *CEO:* Dir. Connie W. Johnson
FTE Enroll: 1,076   (606) 435-6101

THE HEALTH INSTITUTE OF LOUISVILLE
612 S. Fourth St., No. 400, Louisville 40202 *Type:* Private *Accred.:* 1983/1995 (COE warning) *Degrees:* C *Prof. Accred.:* Practical Nursing *CEO:* Director Michael Hendricks
FTE Enroll: 463   (502) 583-6525

ST. PETERSBURG CAMPUS
9549 Koger Blvd., Gadsden Bldg. No. 100, St. Petersburg, FL 33716

(813) 577-1497

SAN ANTONIO CAMPUS
6800 Park Ten Blvd., Ste. 160, S., San Antonio, TX 78213

(210) 733-3056

HEALTH TECHNOLOGY CENTER
1215 N. Race St., Glasgow 42141 *Type:* Public (state) technical *System:* Kentucky Tech Southern Region *Accred.:* 1972/1992 (COE) *Degrees:* C *CEO:* Dir. Rebecca Forrest

(502) 651-5673

HENDERSON COUNTY AREA TECHNOLOGY CENTER
2440 Zion Rd., Henderson 42420 *Type:* Public (state) technical *System:* Kentucky Tech West Region *Accred.:* 1973/1994 (COE) *Degrees:* C *CEO:* Princ. Dennis Harrell

(502) 827-3810

J.D. PATTON AREA TECHNOLOGY CENTER
3234 Turkeyfoot Rd., Fort Mitchell 41017 *Type:* Public (state) technical *System:* Kentucky Tech North Central Region *Accred.:* 1973/1993 (COE) *Degrees:* C *CEO:* Princ. Eugene Penn

(606) 341-2266

KENTUCKY ADVANCED TECHNOLOGY CENTER
1127 Morgantown Rd., Bowling Green 42101-9202 *Type:* Public (state) technical *Accred.:* 1972/1992 (COE) *Degrees:* C *CEO:* Dir. Jack Thomas
FTE Enroll: 187   (502) 746-7807

KENTUCKY COLLEGE OF BARBERING AND HAIRSTYLING
1230 S. Third St., Louisville 40203-2906 *Type:* Private *Accred.:* 1983/1988 (ACC-SCT) *Degrees:* C *CEO:* Dir. David Durbin

(502) 634-0521

KENTUCKY TECH—BRECKINRIDGE COUNTY AREA TECHNOLOGY CENTER
P.O. Box 68, Hwy. 60, Harned 40144 *Type:* Public (state) technical *System:* Kentucky Tech Northwest Region *Accred.:* 1974/1992 (COE) *Degrees:* C *CEO:* Princ. Wayne A. Spencer

(502) 756-2138

KENTUCKY TECH—CENTRAL CAMPUS
104 Vo-Tech Rd., Lexington 40510 *Type:* Public (state) technical *System:* Kentucky Tech North Central Region *Accred.:* 1972/1992 (COE) *Degrees:* C *Prof. Accred.:* Dental Assisting (conditional), Radiography,

Respiratory Therapy Technology, Surgical Technology *CEO:* Dir. Ron Baugh
FTE Enroll: 1,156   (606) 255-8501

KENTUCKY TECH—CHRISTIAN COUNTY AREA TECHNOLOGY CENTER
705 North Elm St., Hopkinsville 42240 *Type:* Public (state) technical *System:* Kentucky Tech West Region *Accred.:* 1971/ 1991 (COE) *Degrees:* C *CEO:* Coord. Ann Claxton
                                       (502) 886-3734

KENTUCKY TECH—CLARK COUNTY AREA TECHNOLOGY CENTER
650 Boone Ave., Winchester 40391 *Type:* Public (state) technical *System:* Kentucky Tech North Central Region *Accred.:* 1972/ 1992 (COE) *Degrees:* C *CEO:* Princ. William Lockhart
                                       (606) 744-1250

KENTUCKY TECH—DAVIESS COUNTY CAMPUS
1901 Southeastern Pkwy., Owensboro 42303-1677 *Type:* Public (state) technical *System:* Kentucky Tech West Region *Accred.:* 1973/1994 (COE) *Degrees:* C *CEO:* Princ. Ray Gillaspie
                                       (502) 687-7620

KENTUCKY TECH—ELIZABETHTOWN
505 University Dr., Elizabethtown 42701 *Type:* Public (state) technical *System:* Kentucky Tech Northwest Region *Accred.:* 1974/1992 (COE) *Degrees:* C *CEO:* Dir. Neil Ramer
                                       (502) 766-5137

KENTUCKY TECH—FULTON COUNTY AREA TECHNOLOGY CENTER
2720 Moscow, Hickman 42050 *Type:* Public (state) technical *System:* Kentucky Tech West Region *Accred.:* 1975/1990 (COE) *Degrees:* C *CEO:* Coord. Larry Lynch
                                       (502) 236-2517

KENTUCKY TECH—JEFFERSON CAMPUS
727 W. Chestnut St., Louisville 40203 *Type:* Public (state) technical *System:* Kentucky Tech Northwest Region *Accred.:* 1973/1993 (COE) *Degrees:* C *Prof. Accred.:* Medical

Assisting (AMA) *CEO:* Acting Director Marvin Copes
FTE Enroll: 798   (502) 595-4136

KENTUCKY TECH—LAUREL COUNTY CAMPUS
235 S. Laurel Rd., London 40741 *Type:* Public (state) technical *System:* Kentucky Tech Southeast Region *Accred.:* 1975/1995 (COE) *Degrees:* C *CEO:* Dir. Ronnie Partin
FTE Enroll: 1,259   (606) 864-7311

KENTUCKY TECH—OWENSBORO CAMPUS
1501 Frederica St., Owensboro 42301 *Type:* Public (state) technical *System:* Kentucky Tech West Region *Accred.:* 1973/1988 (COE) *Degrees:* C *CEO:* Princ. Mike Wright
FTE Enroll: 786   (502) 825-6546

KENTUCKY TECH—PHELPS AREA TECHNOLOGY CENTER
11500 Phelps, 632 Rd., Phelps 41553 *Type:* Public (state) technical *System:* Kentucky Tech Northeast Region *Accred.:* 1974/1995 (COE) *Degrees:* C *CEO:* Princ. Curtis Akers
                                       (606) 456-8136

KENTUCKY TECH—SOMERSET REGIONAL TECHNOLOGY CENTER
230 Airport Rd., Somerset 42501 *Type:* Public (state) technical *System:* Kentucky Tech Southern Region *Accred.:* 1974/1989 (COE) *Degrees:* C *CEO:* Dir. Carol Ann Van Hook
FTE Enroll: 1,042   (606) 677-4049

KNOTT COUNTY AREA TECHNOLOGY CENTER
HCR 60, Box 1100, Hindman 41822 *Type:* Public (state) technical *System:* Kentucky Tech Southeast Region *Accred.:* 1973/1994 (COE) *Degrees:* C *CEO:* Princ. Willa Dean Williams
                                       (606) 785-5350

KNOX COUNTY AREA TECHNOLOGY CENTER
210 Wall St., Barbourville 40906 *Type:* Public (state) technical *System:* Kentucky Tech Southeast Region *Accred.:* 1975/1995 (COE) *Degrees:* C *CEO:* Princ. Charles Frazier
                                       (606) 546-5320

LEE COUNTY AREA TECHNOLOGY CENTER
P.O. Box B, Beattyville 41311 *Type:* Public (state) technical *System:* Kentucky Tech

Southeast Region *Accred.:* 1973/1994 (COE) *Degrees:* C *CEO:* Princ. Fred Kincaid

(606) 464-5018

LESLIE COUNTY AREA TECHNOLOGY CENTER
P.O. Box 902, Hyden 41749 *Type:* Public (state) technical *System:* Kentucky Tech Southeast Region *Accred.:* 1973/1994 (COE) *Degrees:* C *CEO:* Princ. Betty Huff

(606) 672-2859

LETCHER COUNTY AREA TECHNOLOGY CENTER
610 Circle Dr., Whitesburg 41858 *Type:* Public (state) technical *System:* Kentucky Tech Southeast Region *Accred.:* 1973/1994 (COE) *Degrees:* C *CEO:* Princ. Barbara Frazier

(606) 633-5053

MADISON COUNTY AREA TECHNOLOGY CENTER
703 N. 2nd St., P.O. Box 809, Richmond 40475 *Type:* Public (state) technical *System:* Kentucky Tech North Central Region *Accred.:* 1972/1992 (COE) *Degrees:* C *CEO:* Princ. Evelyn Watson

(606) 624-4520

MADISONVILLE HEALTH TECHNOLOGY CENTER
P.O. Box 608, Madisonville 42431 *Type:* Private *Degrees:* C *Prof. Accred.:* Clinical Lab Technology (C), Radiography, Respiratory Therapy Technology, Surgical Technology *CEO:* Dir. Bill M. Hatley

(502) 825-6546

MADISONVILLE HEALTH TECHNOLOGY CENTER
750 N. Laffoon, Madisonville 42431 *Type:* Public (state) technical *System:* Kentucky Tech West Region *Accred.:* 1971/1991 (COE) *Degrees:* C *CEO:* Coord. Mary Stanley

(502) 824-7552

MADISONVILLE REGIONAL TECHNOLOGY CENTER
150 School Ave., Madisonville 42431 *Type:* Public (state) technical *System:* Kentucky Tech West Region *Accred.:* 1971/1991 (COE) *Degrees:* C *CEO:* Princ. James Pfeffer, Jr. *FTE Enroll:* 716 (502) 824-7544

MARION COUNTY AREA TECHNOLOGY CENTER
721 E. Main, Lebanon 40033 *Type:* Public (state) technical *System:* Kentucky Tech Northwest Region *Accred.:* 1974/1992 (COE) *Degrees:* C *CEO:* Princ. Howard Carey

(502) 692-3155

MARTIN COUNTY AREA TECHNOLOGY CENTER
HC 68, Box 2177, Inez 41224 *Type:* Public (state) technical *System:* Kentucky Tech Northeast Region *Accred.:* 1974/1995 (COE) *Degrees:* C *CEO:* Princ. Charlie Six

(606) 298-3879

MASON COUNTY AREA TECHNOLOGY CENTER
646 Kenton Station Rd., Maysville 41056 *Type:* Public (state) technical *System:* Kentucky Tech Northeast Region *Accred.:* 1975/1995 (COE) *Degrees:* C *CEO:* Princ. Clifford Wells

(606) 759-7101

MAYFIELD-GRAVES COUNTY AREA TECHNOLOGY CENTER
710 Douthitt St., Mayfield 42066 *Type:* Public (state) technical *System:* Kentucky Tech West Region *Accred.:* 1975/1990 (COE) *Degrees:* C *CEO:* Coordinator Teresa Harper

(502) 247-4710

MAYO REGIONAL TECHNOLOGY CENTER
513 Third St., Paintsville 41240 *Type:* Public (state) technical *System:* Kentucky Tech Northeast Region *Accred.:* 1974/1995 (COE) *Degrees:* C *Prof. Accred.:* Respiratory Therapy Technology *CEO:* Dir. Gary Coleman
FTE Enroll: 492 (606) 789-5321

MEADE COUNTY AREA TECHNOLOGY CENTER
110 Greer St., Brandenburg 40108 *Type:* Public (state) technical *System:* Kentucky Tech Northwest Region *Accred.:* 1974/1992 (COE) *Degrees:* C *CEO:* Princ. Faye Campbell

(502) 422-3955

MILLARD AREA TECHNOLOGY CENTER
7925 Millard Hwy., Pikeville 41501 *Type:* Public (state) technical *System:* Kentucky Tech Northeast Region *Accred.:* 1974/1995

(COE) *Degrees:* C *CEO:* Princ. William Justice

(606) 437-6059

MONROE COUNTY AREA TECHNOLOGY CENTER
309 Emberton St., Tompkinsville 42167 *Type:* Public (state) technical *System:* Kentucky Tech Southern Region *Accred.:* 1972/ 1992 (COE) *Degrees:* C *CEO:* Princ. Bill Polland

(502) 487-8261

MONTGOMERY COUNTY AREA TECHNOLOGY CENTER
682 Woodford Dr., Mount Sterling 40353 *Type:* Public (state) technical *System:* Kentucky Tech Northeast Region *Accred.:* 1975/ 1995 (COE) *Degrees:* C *CEO:* Princ. Charlie Williams

(606) 498-1103

MORGAN COUNTY AREA TECHNOLOGY CENTER
P.O. Box 249, Rd. 191, West Liberty 41472 *Type:* Public (state) technical *System:* Kentucky Tech Northeast Region *Accred.:* 1975/ 1995 (COE) *Degrees:* C *CEO:* Princ. Ron Woods

(606) 743-4321

MUHLENBERG COUNTY AREA TECHNOLOGY CENTER
201 Airport Rd., Greenville 42345 *Type:* Public (state) technical *System:* Kentucky Tech West Region *Accred.:* 1971/1991 (COE) *Degrees:* C *CEO:* Coord. Andrew Swansey

(502) 338-1271

MURRAY-CALLOWAY COUNTY AREA TECHNOLOGY CENTER
1800 Sycamore St., Murray 42071 *Type:* Public (state) technical *System:* Kentucky Tech West Region *Accred.:* 1975/1990 (COE) *Degrees:* C *CEO:* Princ. Sandra Parks

(502) 753-1870

NELSON COUNTY AREA TECHNOLOGY CENTER
1060 Bloomfield Rd., Bardstown 40004 *Type:* Public (state) technical *System:* Kentucky Tech Northwest Region *Accred.:*

1974/1992 (COE) *Degrees:* C *CEO:* Princ. Myra Wilson

(502) 348-9096

NEW IMAGE CAREERS
109 E. Sixth St., Corbin 40701 *Type:* Private *Degrees:* C *CEO:* Dir. Wanda Powers
FTE Enroll: 60   (606) 528-1490

NORTHERN CAMPBELL TECH
90 Campbell Dr., Highland Heights 41076 *Type:* Public (state) technical *System:* Kentucky Tech North Central Region *Accred.:* 1973/1993 (COE) *Degrees:* C *CEO:* Dir. Earl Wittenrock

(606) 441-2010

NORTHERN KENTUCKY HEALTH TECHNOLOGY CENTER
790 Thomas More Pkwy., Edgewood 41017 *Type:* Public (state) technical *System:* Kentucky Tech North Central Region *Accred.:* 1973/1993 (COE) *Degrees:* C *CEO:* Dir. Wade Halsey

(606) 341-5200

NORTHERN KENTUCKY TECH
1025 Amsterdam Rd., Covington 41011-2098 *Type:* Public (state) technical *System:* Kentucky Tech North Central Region *Accred.:* 1973/1993 (COE) *Degrees:* C *CEO:* Dir. Edward Burton
FTE Enroll: 668   (606) 292-3930

NU-TEK ACADEMY OF BEAUTY
Maysville Rd., Mount Sterling 40391 *Type:* Private *Accred.:* 1990/1993 (COE) *Degrees:* C *CEO:* Dir. Rebecca Taylor
FTE Enroll: 45   (606) 498-4460

OHIO COUNTY AREA TECHNOLOGY CENTER
1406 S. Main St., Hartford 42347 *Type:* Public (state) technical *System:* Kentucky Tech West Region *Accred.:* 1973/1994 (COE) *Degrees:* C *CEO:* Coord. Ray Price

(502) 274-9612

OLDHAM COUNTY AREA TECHNOLOGY CENTER
P.O. Box 127, Hwy. 393, Buckner 40010 *Type:* Public (state) technical *System:* Kentucky Tech Northwest Region *Accred.:*

1973/1993 (COE) *Degrees:* C *CEO:* Princ.
Bob Hazelrigg

(502) 222-0131

PADUCAH AREA TECHNOLOGY CENTER
2400 Adams St., Paducah 42001 *Type:* Public (state) technical *System:* Kentucky Tech
West Region *Accred.:* 1975/1990 (COE)
Degrees: C *CEO:* Princ. Robert Rouff

(502) 443-6592

PJ'S COLLEGE OF COSMETOLOGY
1901 Russellville Rd., No. 10, Bowling
Green 42101 *Type:* Private *Accred.:* 1986/
1991 (COE) *Degrees:* C *CEO:* Dir. Elnora
Wade
FTE Enroll: 105   (502) 842-8149

PJ'S COLLEGE OF COSMETOLOGY
124 S. Public Square, Glasgow 42141 *Type:*
Private *Accred.:* 1987/1992 (COE) *Degrees:*
C *CEO:* Dir. Odilla Garner
FTE Enroll: 11   (502) 651-6553

ROCKCASTLE COUNTY AREA TECHNOLOGY
CENTER
West Main, Mount Vernon 40456 *Type:* Pub-
lic (state) technical *System:* Kentucky Tech
Southeast Region *Accred.:* 1975/1995
(COE) *Degrees:* C *Prof. Accred.:* Respirato-
ry Therapy Technology *CEO:* Princ. Donna
Hopkins

(606) 256-4346

ROWAN REGIONAL TECHNOLOGY CENTER
609 Viking Dr., Morehead 40351 *Type:* Pub-
lic (state) technical *System:* Kentucky Tech
Northeast Region *Accred.:* 1975/1995
(COE) *Degrees:* C *Prof. Accred.:* Respirato-
ry Therapy Technology *CEO:* Dir. Kenneth
Brown
FTE Enroll: 333   (606) 783-1538

ROY'S OF LOUISVILLE BEAUTY ACADEMY
151 Chenoweth Ln., Louisville 40207 *Type:*
Private *Accred.:* 1989/1994 (COE probational) *Degrees:* C *CEO:* Dir. Thomas Esrey
FTE Enroll: 91   (502) 897-9401

BRANCH CAMPUS
5200 Dixie Hwy., Louisville 40216

(502) 448-1016

RUSSELL AREA TECHNOLOGY CENTER
705 Red Devil Ln., Russell 41169 *Type:*
Public (state) technical *System:* Kentucky
Tech Northeast Region *Accred.:* 1971/1989
(COE) *Degrees:* C *CEO:* Princ. Michael
Chapman

(606) 836-1256

RUSSELL COUNTY TECHNOLOGY CENTER
P.O. Box 599, Russell Springs 42642 *Type:*
Public (state) technical *System:* Kentucky
Tech Southern Region *Accred.:* 1974/1989
(COE) *Degrees:* C *CEO:* Princ. Chester
Taylor

(502) 866-6175

RUSSELLVILLE AREA TECHNOLOGY CENTER
1103 W. 9th St., Russellville 42276 *Type:*
Public (state) technical *System:* Kentucky
Tech Southern Region *Accred.:* 1972/1992
(COE) *Degrees:* C *CEO:* Princ. Keith Dick-
inson

(502) 726-8432

SCHOOL OF BUSINESS AND BANKING
5045 Preston Hwy., Louisville 40213-2213
Type: Private *Accred.:* 1991 (COE) *Degrees:*
C *CEO:* Pres. J. Martin Gossman
FTE Enroll: 57   (502) 969-2004

SHELBY COUNTY AREA TECHNOLOGY CENTER
230 Rocket Ln., Shelbyville 40065 *Type:*
Public (state) technical *System:* Kentucky
Tech Northwest Region *Accred.:* 1973/1993
(COE) *Degrees:* C *CEO:* Princ. Mary A.
Stratton

(502) 633-6554

TRI-STATE BEAUTY ACADEMY
219 W. Main St., Morehead 40351 *Type:* Private *Accred.:* 1983/1993 (COE) *Degrees:* C
CEO: Dir. Betty Stucky
FTE Enroll: 50   (606) 784-6725

WAYNE COUNTY AREA TECHNOLOGY CENTER
150 Cardinal Way, Monticello 42633 *Type:*
Public (state) technical *System:* Kentucky
Tech Southern Region *Accred.:* 1974/1989
(COE) *Degrees:* C *CEO:* Princ. Anita Hopper

(606) 348-8424

WEBSTER COUNTY AREA VOCATIONAL EDU-CATION CENTER
325 State Rd., Dixon 42409 *Type:* Public (state) technical *System:* Kentucky Tech West Region *Accred.:* 1971/1991 (COE) *Degrees:* C *CEO:* Coord. Terry Turner
(502) 639-5035

WEST KENTUCKY TECHNICAL
5200 Blandville Rd., Paducah 42002 *Type:* Public (state) technical *Accred.:* 1975/1990 (COE) *Degrees:* C *Prof. Accred.:* Dental Assisting, Diagnostic Medical Sonography, Medical Assisting (AMA), Radiography, Respiratory Therapy Technology, Surgical Technology *CEO:* Dir. Lee Hicklin
FTE Enroll: 1,238   (502) 554-9754

CRAWFORDSVILLE CAMPUS
113 N. Washington St., Crawfordsville, IN 47933
(800) 627-2566

GREENFIELD CAMPUS
1400 W. Main St., Greenfield, IN 46140
(800) 627-2566

INDIANAPOLIS CAMPUS
5539 S. Madison Ave., Indianapolis, IN 46227
(800) 627-2566

KOKOMO CAMPUS
3023 S. Lafountain St., Kokomo, IN 46902
(800) 627-2566

MUNCIE CAMPUS
2006 N. Walnut St., Muncie, IN 47303
(800) 627-2566

PLAINFIELD CAMPUS
2026 Stafford Rd., Plainfield, IN 46168
(800) 627-2566

LOUISIANA

ABBEVILLE BEAUTY ACADEMY
1828 Veterans Memorial Dr., Abbeville 70510 *Type:* Private *Accred.:* 1991 (COE) *Degrees:* C *CEO:* Dir. Hazel Doucet
FTE Enroll: 22   (318) 893-1228

AMERICAN SCHOOL OF BUSINESS
702 Professional Dr. N., Shreveport 71105 *Type:* Private business *Accred.:* 1988 (ACICS) *Degrees:* C *CEO:* Dir. Judith Killough
(318) 798-3333

ASCENSION COLLEGE
320 E. Ascension St., Gonzales 70737 *Type:* Private technical *Accred.:* 1991 (COE) *Degrees:* C *CEO:* Dir. Midge Jacobsen
FTE Enroll: 197   (504) 647-6609

AYERS INSTITUTE
2924 Knight St., Ste. 318, Shreveport 71133-3941 *Type:* Private business *Accred.:* 1995 (COE) *Degrees:* C *CEO:* Dir. J. Pat Furlong
FTE Enroll: 62   (318) 868-3000

J.M. FRAZIER VOCATIONAL-TECHNICAL SCHOOL
555 Julia St., Baton Rouge 70802
(504) 359-9204

CAMBRIDGE EDUCATION CENTER
4528 Bennington Ave., No. 100, Baton Rouge 70808-3109 *Type:* Private *Accred.:* 1991 (COE) *Degrees:* C *CEO:* Dir. Chris Miteff
FTE Enroll: 21   (504) 923-0017

CAMELOT CAREER COLLEGE
2618 Wooddale Blvd., Ste. A, Baton Rouge 70805 *Type:* Private business *Accred.:* 1990/1995 (ACICS) *Degrees:* C *CEO:* Pres. Ronnie Williams
(504) 928-3005

CAREER TRAINING SPECIALISTS
1611 Louisville Ave., Monroe 71201 *Type:* Private *Accred.:* 1995 (COE) *Degrees:* C *CEO:* Dir. Lloydelle Hopkins
FTE Enroll: 354   (318) 323-2889

CLOYD'S BEAUTY SCHOOL NO. 2
1311 Winnsboro Rd., Monroe 71202 *Type:* Private *Accred.:* 1991 (COE) *Degrees:* C *CEO:* Dir. Bill DeLoach
FTE Enroll: 144   (318) 323-2138

CLOYD'S BEAUTY SCHOOL NO. 3
2514 Ferrand St., Monroe 71201 *Type:* Private *Accred.:* 1995 (COE) *Degrees:* C *CEO:* Dir. J. Rhett Mathieu
FTE Enroll: 106   (318) 388-3710

COMMERCIAL COLLEGE OF BATON ROUGE
5677 Florida Blvd., Baton Rouge 70806 *Type:* Private business *Accred.:* 1972/1995 (ACICS) *Degrees:* C *CEO:* Dir. Glenna McCollister
(504) 927-3470

COMMERCIAL COLLEGE OF SHREVEPORT
2640 Youree Dr., Shreveport 71104 *Type:* Private business *Accred.:* 1971/1995 (ACICS) *Degrees:* C *CEO:* Dir. John Kelsall
(318) 865-6571

CULINARY ARTS INSTITUTE OF LOUISIANA
427 Lafayette St., Baton Rouge 70802 *Type:* Private *Accred.:* 1991 (ACCSCT) *Degrees:* C *CEO:* Pres. Violet Harrington
(504) 343-6233

DENHAM SPRINGS BEAUTY COLLEGE
923 Florida Ave., S.E., Denham Springs 70726 *Type:* Private *Accred.:* 1994 (COE) *Degrees:* C *CEO:* Dir. Frances Hand
FTE Enroll: 101   (504) 665-6188

DIESEL DRIVING ACADEMY
8136 Airline Hwy., Baton Rouge 70815 *Type:* Private *Accred.:* 1990/1992 (COE) *Degrees:* C *CEO:* Dir. Ed Mathes
FTE Enroll: 59   (504) 929-9990

DIESEL DRIVING ACADEMY
4709 Greenwood Rd., Shreveport 71133-6949 *Type:* Private *Accred.:* 1982/1993 (COE) *Degrees:* C *CEO:* Dir. Philip O. Johnson, Jr.
FTE Enroll: 48   (318) 636-6300

DOMESTIC HEALTH CARE INSTITUTE
4826 Jamestown Ave., Baton Rouge 70808
Type: Private *Accred.:* 1990 (ABHES)
Degrees: C *CEO:* Pres. Dan Chavis
(504) 925-5312

EASTERN COLLEGE OF HEALTH VOCATIONS
3540 I-10 Service Rd., S., Metairie 70001
Type: Private *Accred.:* 1986/1992 (ABHES)
Degrees: C *CEO:* Pres. Susan Dalto
(504) 834-8644

FRANKLIN COLLEGE OF COURT REPORTING
1200 S. Clearview Pkwy., New Orleans
70123 *Type:* Private *Accred.:* 1995 (COE)
Degrees: C *CEO:* Pres. Mary Franklin
FTE Enroll: 74　　　　(504) 734-1000

LOUISIANA ART INSTITUTE
7380 Exchange Pl., Baton Rouge 70806-
3851 *Type:* Private *Accred.:* 1987 (ACC-
SCT) *Degrees:* C *CEO:* Owner David W.
Clark
(504) 928-7770

LOUISIANA HAIR DESIGN COLLEGE
7909 Airline Hwy., Metairie 70003-6438
Type: Private *Accred.:* 1987/1991 (ACCSCT)
Degrees: C *CEO:* Dir. Shirley Whitaker
(504) 737-2376

LOUISIANA INSTITUTE OF TECHNOLOGY
6666 Colisieum Blvd., Alexandria 71303
Type: Private *Accred.:* 1991 (COE) *Degrees:*
C *CEO:* Pres. Darryll Augurson
FTE Enroll: 104　　　　(318) 442-1864

LAFAYETTE CAMPUS
115 Henderson Rd., Lafayette 70508
(318) 233-0776

LOUISIANA TECHNICAL COLLEGE-ACADIAN
CAMPUS
1933 W. Hutchinson Ave., Crowley 70526
Type: Public (state) *Accred.:* 1976/1991
(COE) *Degrees:* C *CEO:* Dir. Richard A.
Arnaud
FTE Enroll: 207　　　　(318) 788-7520

LOUISIANA TECHNICAL COLLEGE-ALEXANDRIA
CAMPUS
4311 S. MacArthur Dr., Alexandria 71307-
5698 *Type:* Public (state) *Accred.:* 1976/
1991 (COE) *Degrees:* C *CEO:* Dir. Patricia
F. Juneau
FTE Enroll: 337　　　　(318) 487-5443

LOUISIANA TECHNICAL COLLEGE-ASCENSION
CAMPUS
9697 Airline Hwy., Sorrento 70778 *Type:* Pub-
lic (state) *Accred.:* 1982/1992 (COE) *Degrees:*
C *CEO:* Dir. Cleveland Marchand, Jr.
FTE Enroll: 135　　　　(504) 675-5397

LOUISIANA TECHNICAL COLLEGE-AVOYELLES
CAMPUS
508 Choupique St., Cottonport 71327 *Type:*
Public (state) *Accred.:* 1979/1991 (COE)
Degrees: C *CEO:* Dir. Ward Nash
FTE Enroll: 261　　　　(318) 876-2401

LOUISIANA TECHNICAL COLLEGE-BASTROP
CAMPUS
Kammell St., Bastrop 71221 *Type:* Public
(state) *Accred.:* 1981/1994 (COE) *Degrees:*
C *CEO:* Dir. Norene Smith
FTE Enroll: 169　　　　(318) 283-0836

LOUISIANA TECHNICAL COLLEGE-BATON ROUGE
CAMPUS
3250 N. Acadian Thruway, Baton Rouge
70805 *Type:* Public (state) *Accred.:* 1973/
1992 (COE) *Degrees:* C *CEO:* Dir. Robert
R. Buck
FTE Enroll: 476　　　　(504) 359-9204

LOUISIANA TECHNICAL COLLEGE-CHARLES B.
COREIL CAMPUS
One Vocational Dr., Ville Platte 70586-0296
Type: Public (state) *Accred.:* 1981/1992
(COE) *Degrees:* C *CEO:* Dir. Danny Lemoine
FTE Enroll: 171　　　　(318) 363-2197

LOUISIANA TECHNICAL COLLEGE-CLAIBORNE
CAMPUS
3001 Minden Rd., Homer 71040-0509 *Type:*
Public (state) *Accred.:* 1989/1992 (COE)
Degrees: C *CEO:* Dir. Thomas Ragland
FTE Enroll: 144　　　　(318) 927-2034

LOUISIANA TECHNICAL COLLEGE-DELTA
OUACHITA CAMPUS
609 Vocational Pkwy., West Monroe 71292-
9064 *Type:* Public (state) *Accred.:* 1976/
1991 (COE) *Degrees:* C *CEO:* Dir. Irving D.
Adkins
FTE Enroll: 394   (318) 396-7431

LOUISIANA TECHNICAL COLLEGE-EVANGELINE
CAMPUS
600 S. Martin Luther King, Jr. Dr., Mart-
inville 70582 *Type:* Public (state) *Accred.:*
1974/1994 (COE) *Degrees:* C *CEO:* Dir.
Prosper Chretien
FTE Enroll: 464   (318) 394-6108

LOUISIANA TECHNICAL COLLEGE-FLORIDA
PARRSHES CAMPSU
100 College Dr., Greensburg 70441 *Type:*
Public (state) *Accred.:* 1977/1995 (COE) *De-
grees:* C *CEO:* Dir. Herman B. Landreneau
FTE Enroll: 85   (504) 222-4251

LOUISIANA TECHNICAL COLLEGE-FOLKES
CAMPUS
3337 Hwy. 10, E., Jackson 70748 *Type:* Public (state) *Accred.:* 1981/1992 (COE) *Degrees:* C *CEO:* Dir. Faith B. Rohner
FTE Enroll: 154   (504) 634-2636

BRANCH CAMPUS
Dixon Correctional Inst., Hwy. 68, Jackson 70748
                        (504) 634-2636

LOUISIANA TECHNICAL COLLEGE-GULF AREA
CAMPUS
1115 Clover St., Abbeville 70510 *Type:* Public (state) *Accred.:* 1975/1990 (COE) *Degrees:* C *CEO:* Dir. Ray Lavergne
FTE Enroll: 369   (318) 893-4984

LOUISIANA TECHNICAL COLLEGE-HAMMOND
AREA CAMPUS
111 Pride Ave., Hammond 70404 *Type:* Public (state) *Accred.:* 1975/1990 (COE) *Degrees:* C *CEO:* Dir. Francis N. Bickham
FTE Enroll: 139   (504) 543-4120

LOUISIANA TECHNICAL COLLEGE-HUEY P. LONG
CAMPUS
303 S. Jones St., Winnfield 71483 *Type:*
Public (state) *Accred.:* 1977/1993 (COE)
Degrees: C *CEO:* Dir. Larry Williams
FTE Enroll: 426   (318) 628-4342

JENA CAMPUS
117 East Bradford St., Jena 71342
                        (318) 628-4342

LOUISIANA TECHNICAL COLLEGE-JEFFERSON
CAMPUS
5200 Blair Dr., Metairie 70001 *Type:* Public
(state) *Accred.:* 1975/1994 (COE) *Degrees:*
C *CEO:* Dir. Justin LeMaitre
FTE Enroll: 267   (504) 736-7076

LOUISIANA TECHNICAL COLLEGE-JEFFERSON
DAVIS CAMPUS
1230 N. Main St., Jennings 70546-1327
Type: Public (state) *Accred.:* 1976/1991
(COE) *Degrees:* C *CEO:* Dir. Johnnie Smith
FTE Enroll: 79   (318) 824-4811

LOUISANA TECHNICAL COLLEGE-JUMONVILLE
MEMORIAL CAMPUS
Hwy. 3131, Hospital Rd., New Roads 70760
Type: Public (state) *Accred.:* 1976/1991 (COE)
Degrees: C *CEO:* Dir. Tommy Ganthier
FTE Enroll: 523   (504) 638-8613

ANGOLA CAMPUS
Loiusiana State Penitentiary, General
Delivery, Angola 70712
                        (504) 688-8613

HUNT CORRECTIONAL CENTER CAMPUS
Hunt Correctional Center., P.O. Box 40,
St. Gabriel 70776
                        (504) 642-3306

LOUISIANA CORRECTIONAL INSTITUTE
CAMPUS
Louisiana Correctional Institute, P.O. Box
40, St. Gabriel 70776
                        (504) 642-5529

LOUISIANA TECHNICAL COLLEGE-LAFAYETTE
CAMPUS
1101 Bertrand Dr., Lafayette 70502 *Type:*
Public (state) technical *Accred.:* 1981/1991

(COE) *Degrees:* C *Prof. Accred.:* Clinical Lab Technology (C) *CEO:* Dir. Ted Ardoin
FTE Enroll: 501   (318) 265-5962

LOUISIANA TECHNICAL COLLEGE-LAFOURCHE CAMPUS
1425 Tiger Dr., Thibodaux 70302-1831 *Type:* Public (state) *Accred.:* 1988/1994 (COE) *Degrees:* C *CEO:* Dir. Kenneth Callahan
FTE Enroll: 134   (504) 447-0924

LOUISIANA TECHNICAL COLLEGE-LAMAR SALTER CAMPUS
15014 Lake Charles Hwy., Leesville 71446 *Type:* Public (state) *Accred.:* 1983/1993 (COE) *Degrees:* C *CEO:* Dir. Tommy Cordova
FTE Enroll: 206   (318) 537-3135

LOUISIANA TECHNICAL COLLEGE-MANSFIELD CAMPUS
943 Oxford Rd., Mansfield 71052 *Type:* Public (state) *Accred.:* 1993 (COE) *Degrees:* C *CEO:* Director Jill Frazier
FTE Enroll: 137   (318) 872-2243

LOUISIANA TECHNICAL COLLEGE-NATCHITOCHES CAMPUS
6587 Hwy. 1 Bypass, S. Bypass, Natchitoches 71458-0657 *Type:* Public (state) *Accred.:* 1982/1992 (COE) *Degrees:* C *CEO:* Dir. Dolores H. Tucker
FTE Enroll: 195   (318) 357-3162

LOUISIANA TECHNICAL COLLEGE-NEW ORLEANS CAMPUS
980 Navarre Ave., New Orleans 70124 *Type:* Public (state) *Accred.:* 1988/1993 (COE) *Degrees:* C *CEO:* Dir. Simone Charbonnet
FTE Enroll: 297   (504) 483-4666

LOUISIANA TECHNICAL COLLEGE-NORTH CENTRAL CAMPUS
605 N. Boundary, Farmerville 71241 *Type:* Public (state) *Accred.:* 1979/1993 (COE) *Degrees:* C *CEO:* Dir. Johnny Bridges
FTE Enroll: 86   (318) 368-3179

LOUISIANA TECHNICAL COLLEGE-NORTHEAST LOUISIANA CAMPUS
1710 Warren St., Winnsboro 71295 *Type:* Public (state) *Accred.:* 1976/1992 (COE) *Degrees:* C *CEO:* Dir. John Pinckard
FTE Enroll: 109   (318) 435-2163

LOUISIANA TECHNICAL COLLEGE-NORTHWEST LOUISIANA CAMPUS
814 Constable St., Minden 71058-0835 *Type:* Public (state) *Accred.:* 1975/1995 (COE) *Degrees:* C *CEO:* Dir. Charles T. Strong
FTE Enroll: 244   (318) 371-3035

LOUISIANA TECHNICAL COLLEGE-OAKDALE CAMPUS
Old Pelican Hwy., Oakdale 71463 *Type:* Public (state) *Accred.:* 1983/1991 (COE) *Degrees:* C *CEO:* Dir. Darrell Rodriguez
FTE Enroll: 82   (318) 335-3944

LOUISIANA TECHNICAL COLLEGE-RIVER PARISHES CAMPUS
251 Regala Park Rd., Reserve 70084 *Type:* Public (state) *Accred.:* 1984/1995 (COE) *Degrees:* C *CEO:* Dir. Dennis R. Murphy
FTE Enroll: 364   (504) 536-4418

LOUISIANA TECHNICAL COLLEGE-RUSTON CAMPUS
1010 James St., Ruston 71270 *Type:* Public (state) *Accred.:* 1982/1994 (COE) *Degrees:* C *CEO:* Dir. Donald Walsworth
FTE Enroll: 129   (318) 251-4145

LOUISIANA TECHNICAL COLLEGE-SABINE VALLEY CAMPUS
Hwy. 171, S., Many 71449 *Type:* Public (state) *Accred.:* 1977/1993 (COE) *Degrees:* C *CEO:* Dir. David B. Crittenden
FTE Enroll: 79   (318) 256-4101

LOUISIANA TECHNICAL COLLEGE-SHELBY M. JACKSON CAMPUS
2100 N. E.E. Wallace Blvd., Ferriday 71334-0152 *Type:* Public (state) *Accred.:* 1980/1995 (COE) *Degrees:* C *CEO:* Dir. Ray King
FTE Enroll: 125   (318) 757-6501

LOUISIANA TECHNICAL COLLEGE-SHREVEPORT-
BOSSIER CAMPUS
2010 N. Market St., Shreveport 71137-8527
Type: Public (state) *Accred.:* 1976/1991
(COE) *Degrees:* C *CEO:* Dir. Sam Merritt
FTE Enroll: 456   (318) 676-7811

LOUISIANA TECHNICAL COLLEGE-SIDNEY N.
COLLIER CAMPUS
3727 Louisa St., New Orleans 70126 *Type:*
Public (state) *Accred.:* 1977/1993 (COE)
Degrees: C *CEO:* Dir. Levi Lewis, Sr.
FTE Enroll: 273   (504) 942-8333

LOUISIANA TECHNICAL COLLEGE-SLIDELL
CAMPUS
1000 Canulette Rd., Slidell 70458 *Type:*
Public (state) *Accred.:* 1974/1994 (COE)
Degrees: C *CEO:* Dir. Gerald J. Ayo
FTE Enroll: 164   (504) 646-6430

LOUISIANA TECHNICAL COLLEGE-SOUTH
LOUISIANA CAMPUS
201 St. Charles St., Houma 70361-5033 *Type:*
Public (state) *Accred.:* 1975/1990 (COE)
Degrees: C *CEO:* Dir. Kenneth Callahan
FTE Enroll: 233   (504) 857-3655

HOUMA CAMPUS
Louisiana Marine and Petroleum I, Sta. 1,
Box 10251, Houma 70361
                              (504) 857-3698

LOUISIANA TECHNICAL COLLEGE-SOWELA
CAMPUS
3820 Legion St., Lake Charles 70616 *Type:*
Public (state) *Accred.:* 1971/1992 (COE)
Degrees: A *CEO:* Dir. W. Stanley Leger
FTE Enroll: 907   (318) 491-2698

DEQUINCY CAMPUS
Louisiana Correctional and Indus, P.O.
Box 1056, DeQuincy 70633
                              (318) 491-2698

LOUISIANA TECHNICAL COLLEGE-SULLIVAN
CAMPUS
1710 Sullivan Dr., Bogalusa 70427 *Type:*
Public (state) *Accred.:* 1970/1993 (COE)
Degrees: C *CEO:* Dir. M. J. Murphy
FTE Enroll: 305   (504) 732-6640

ANGIE CAMPUS
Washington Correctional Inst., Rte. 2, Box
500, Angie 70426
                              (504) 732-6640

LOUISIANA TECHNICAL COLLEGE-TALLULAH
CAMPUS
Old Hwy. 65 S., Tallulah 71284-1740 *Type:*
Public (state) *Accred.:* 1980/1995 (COE)
Degrees: C *CEO:* Dir. Patrick T. Murphy
FTE Enroll: 183   (318) 574-4820

LAKE PROVIDENCE CAMPUS
Hwy. 803-1, Lake Providence 71254
                              (318) 559-0864

LOUISIANA TECHNICAL COLLEGE-TECHE AREA
CAMPUS
609 Ember Dr., Acadiana Airport, New
Iberia 70562-1057 *Type:* Public (state) *Ac-
cred.:* 1976/1991 (COE) *Degrees:* C *CEO:*
Dir. Paul Fair
FTE Enroll: 254   (318) 373-0011

LOUISIANA TECHNICAL COLLEGE-T.H. HARRIS
CAMPUS
337 E. South St., Opelousas 70570 *Type:*
Public (state) *Accred.:* 1970/1990 (COE)
Degrees: C *CEO:* Dir. Raymond Lalonde
FTE Enroll: 468   (318) 948-0239

LOUISIANA TECHNICAL COLLEGE-WEST
JEFFERSON CAMPUS
475 Manhattan Blvd., Harvey 70058 *Type:*
Public (state) *Accred.:* 1982/1993 (COE)
Degrees: C *Prof. Accred.:* Respiratory Ther-
apy Technology *CEO:* Dir. Donna H. Wilson
FTE Enroll: 173   (504) 361-6464

LOUISIANA TECHNICAL COLLEGE-WESTSIDE
CAMPUS
59125 Bayou Rd., Plaquemine 70765 *Type:*
Public (state) *Accred.:* 1974/1992 (COE)
Degrees: C *CEO:* Dir. Alfred S. Bell
FTE Enroll: 257   (504) 687-6392

LOUISIANA TECHNICAL COLLEGE-YOUNG
MEMORIAL CAMPUS
900 Youngs Rd., Morgan City 70380 *Type:*
Public (state) *Accred.:* 1976/1991 (COE)
Degrees: C *CEO:* Dir. Greg Garrett
FTE Enroll: 241   (504) 380-2436

LOUISIANA TRAINING CENTER
942-A Arizona St., Sulphur 70663 *Type:* Private *Accred.:* 1992/1995 (COE) *Degrees:* C
CEO: Pres. Danny Bedford
FTE Enroll: 77   (318) 625-9469

MEDICAL CAREER ACADEMY
3333 Drusilla Ln., Baton Rouge 70809 *Type:* Private *Accred.:* 1995 (ABHES) *Calendar:* Qtr. plan *Degrees:* C *CEO:* Pres. Beau Hutchinson
Enroll: 35   (504) 929-7041

NICK RANDAZZO VOCATIONAL TRAINING INSTITUTE
125 Lafayette St., Gretna 70053-5835 *Type:* Private *Accred.:* 1993 (ACCSCT) *Degrees:* C *CEO:* Pres. Nick Randazzo
          (504) 366-5409

OCHSNER SCHOOL OF ALLIED HEALTH SCIENCES
880 Commerce Rd., W., New Orleans 70123-3335 *Type:* Private technical *Accred.:* 1978/1993 (COE) *Degrees:* C *Prof. Accred.:* Blood Bank Technology, Clinical Lab Scientist, Diagnostic Medical Sonography, Nuclear Medicine Technology, Perfusion, Radiation Therapy Technology, Radiography, Respiratory Therapy, Respiratory Therapy Technology, Surgical Technology *CEO:* Dir. Edward D. Frohlich
FTE Enroll: 118   (504) 842-3700

REFRIGERATION SCHOOL OF NEW ORLEANS
1201 Mazant St., New Orleans 70117-9909 *Type:* Private *Accred.:* 1991 (ACCSCT) *Degrees:* C *CEO:* Pres. Earl J. Martin, Jr.
          (504) 949-2712

SOUTH LOUISIANA BEAUTY COLLEGE
300 Howard Ave., Houma 70363 *Type:* Private *Accred.:* 1987/1992 (COE) *Degrees:* C *CEO:* Dir. Catherine A. Nagy
FTE Enroll: 102   (504) 873-8978

MAINE

AIR-TECH INCORPORATION
West Ramp, Sanford Municipal Airport, Sanford 04073 *Type:* Private *Accred.:* 1993 (ACCSCT) *Degrees:* C *CEO:* Treas. Patricia B. Smith
(207) 324-8404

THE LANDING SCHOOL OF BOAT BUILDING AND DESIGN
P.O. Box 1490, Kennebunkport 04046-1490 *Type:* Private *Accred.:* 1987 (ACCSCT) *Degrees:* C *CEO:* Dir. David Van Cleef
(207) 985-7976

NEW ENGLAND SCHOOL OF BROADCASTING
One College Cir., Bangor 04401-2999 *Type:* Private *Accred.:* 1986 (ACCSCT) *Degrees:* C *CEO:* Pres. George E. Wildey
(207) 947-6083

MARYLAND

ABBIE BUSINESS INSTITUTE
5310 Spectrum Dr., Frederick 21701 *Type:*
Private business *Accred.:* 1981/1994 (AC-
ICS) *Degrees:* C *CEO:* Pres. Allan R. Short
(301) 694-0211

ACUPUNTURE SCHOOL OF MARYLAND
4400 East-West Hwy., Ste. 128, Bethesda
20814 *Type:* Private *Calendar:* Sem. plan
Prof. Accred.: Acupuncture *CEO:* Pres.
Ralph E. Coan
(301) 907-8986

ARMY ORDNANCE CENTER AND SCHOOL
Bldg. 3072, Room 217-C, Aberdeen Prov-
ing Ground 21005-5201 *Type:* Public (fed-
eral) technical *Accred.:* 1978/1993 (COE)
Degrees: C *CEO:* Commandant Russell
Childress, Jr.
FTE Enroll: 3,052   (410) 278-2994

ARUNDEL INSTITUTE OF TECHNOLOGY
1808 Edison Hwy., Baltimore 21213-1549
Type: Private *Accred.:* 1971/1988 (ACC-
SCT) *Calendar:* Qtr. plan *Degrees:* C *CEO:*
Dir. R. Wayne Moore
(410) 327-6640

BROADCASTING INSTITUTE OF MARYLAND
7200 Harford Rd., Baltimore 21234-7765
Type: Private *Accred.:* 1980/1990 (ACC-
SCT) *Calendar:* Sem. plan *Degrees:* C
CEO: Pres. John C. Jeppi, Sr.
(410) 254-2770

BUREAU OF MEDICINE & SURGERY (U.S. NAVY)
2300 E. St., Bldg. 2, Washington 20372-
5300 *Type:* Public (federal) technical *Accred.:* 1984/1990 (COE) *Degrees:* C *Prof.
Accred.:* Psychology Internship, Radiography *CEO:* Cmnd. Ofcr. David G. Kemp
FTE Enroll: 3,935   (202) 762-3370

FIELD MEDICAL SERVICE SCHOOL
Camp Pendleton, CA 92055-5031
(619) 725-2672

FIELD MEDICAL SERVICE SCHOOL
Camp Lejuene, NC 28542-0042
(910) 451-0929

NAVAL AEROSPACE MEDICAL INSTITUTE
Pensacola, FL 32508-5600
(904) 452-4554

NAVAL DENTAL SCHOOL—MAXILLOFACIAL
Bethesda, MD 20889-5602 *Prof. Accred.:*
Combined Prosthodontics, Endodontics,
General Dentistry, Maxillofacial Prostho-
dontics, Oral Pathology, Periodontics
(301) 295-0064

NAVAL HOSPITAL CORPS SCHOOL
Great Lakes, IL 60088-5257
(708) 688-5680

NAVAL SCHOOL OF DENTAL ASSISTING
Naval Sta., San Diego, CA 92136-5567
(619) 556-7640

NAVAL SCHOOL OF HEALTH SCIENCE
Medical Ctr., Bethesda, MD 20889-5611
Prof. Accred.: Clinical Lab Technology
(C), Cytotechnology, Electroneurodiag-
nostic Technology, Nuclear Medicine
Technology, Nurse Anesthesia Education
(M), Surgical Technology
(301) 295-1204

NAVAL SCHOOL OF HEALTH SCIENCE
Portsmouth, VA 23708-5200 *Prof.
Accred.:* Surgical Technology
(804) 398-5032

NAVAL SCHOOL OF HEALTH SCIENCE
San Diego, CA 92134-5291 *Prof. Accred.:*
Clinical Lab Technology (C), Physician
Assisting/Surgeon Assisting, Surgical
Technology
(619) 532-7700

NAVAL UNDERSEA MEDICAL INSTITUTE
Groton, CT 06349-5159
(860) 449-2874

OPTHALMIS SUPPORT AND TRAINING
Yorktown, VA 23691-5071
(804) 887-7611

DIESEL INSTITUTE OF AMERICA
Rte. 40, P.O. Box 69, Grantsville 21536-0069 *Type:* Private *Accred.:* 1988 (ACCSCT) *Degrees:* C *CEO:* Dir. F. C. Bud Poland
(301) 895-5139

EMERGENCY MANAGEMENT INSTITUTE
16825 S. Seton Ave., Emmitsburg 21727 *Type:* Public (federal) distance education *Accred.:* 1988/1992 (DETC) *Degrees:* C *CEO:* Prgm. Mgr. Susan Hernandez
(301) 447-1240

FLEET BUSINESS SCHOOL
2530 Riva Rd., Ste. 201, Annapolis 21401 *Type:* Private business *Accred.:* 1971/1995 (ACICS) *Calendar:* Qtr. plan *Degrees:* C *CEO:* Pres. Carole Nicholson
(410) 266-8500

JOHNSTON SCHOOL OF PRACTICAL NURSING
201 E. University Pkwy., Baltimore 21218 *Type:* Private professional *Degrees:* C *Prof. Accred.:* Practical Nursing *CEO:* Dir. Judith Feustle
(410) 554-2327

LINCOLN TECHNICAL INSTITUTE
3200 Wilkens Ave., Baltimore 21229-4289 *Type:* Private *Accred.:* 1968/1989 (ACCSCT) *Degrees:* C *CEO:* Dir. Joseph Buechner
(410) 646-5480

LINCOLN TECHNICAL INSTITUTE
7800 Central Ave., Landover 20785-4807 *Type:* Private *Accred.:* 1968/1988 (ACCSCT) *Degrees:* C *CEO:* Dir. Steven Buchenot
(301) 336-7250

MARYLAND DRAFTING INSTITUTE
2045 University Blvd. E., Langley Park 20783-4137 *Type:* Private *Accred.:* 1974/1989 (ACCSCT) *Degrees:* C *CEO:* Dir. Carol B. Sawyer
(301) 439-7776

SPRINGFIELD CAMPUS
8001 Forbes Pl., North Springfield, VA 22151-2205 *Accred.:* 1985/1990 (ACCSCT)
(703) 321-9777

THE MEDIX SCHOOL
1017 York Rd., Towson 21204-2511 *Type:* Private *Accred.:* 1971/1988 (ACCSCT) *Degrees:* C *Prof. Accred.:* Dental Assisting (conditional), Medical Assisting (AMA) *CEO:* Dir. Ben E. Wilke
(410) 337-5155

MARIETTA CAMPUS
2480 Windy Hill Rd., Marietta, GA 30067-9744 *Accred.:* 1988 (ACCSCT) *Prof. Accred.:* Dental Assisting, Medical Assisting (AMA)
(404) 980-0002

NATIONAL CRYPTOLOGIC SCHOOL
9800 Savage Rd., Fort Meade 20755-6000 *Type:* Public (federal) *Accred.:* 1990 (COE) *Degrees:* C *CEO:* Commandant Julia B. Wetzel
FTE Enroll: 1,821   (410) 859-6266

NEW ENGLAND TRACTOR TRAILER TRAINING SCHOOL
1410 Bush St., Baltimore 21230-9910 *Type:* Private *Accred.:* 1989/1991 (ACCSCT) *Degrees:* C *CEO:* Dir. Henry Holder, III
(410) 783-0100

TESST ELECTRONICS AND COMPUTER INSTITUTE
5122 Baltimore Ave., Hyattsville 20781-2080 *Type:* Private *Accred.:* 1975/1993 (ACCSCT) *Degrees:* C *CEO:* Vice Pres. Richard J. Armbruster
(301) 864-5750

MASSACHUSETTS

BANCROFT SCHOOL OF MASSAGE THERAPY
50 Franklin St., Worcester 01608-1996 *Type:* Private *Accred.:* 1986 (ACCSCT) *Degrees:* C *CEO:* Pres. Steven Tankanow
(508) 757-7923

BAY STATE SCHOOL OF APPLIANCES
225 Turnpike St., Rte. 138, Canton 02021 *Type:* Private *Accred.:* 1986 (ACCSCT) *Degrees:* C *CEO:* Dir. Robert Mason
(617) 828-3434

BUTERA SCHOOL OF ART
111 Beacon St., Boston 02116-1597 *Type:* Private *Accred.:* 1977/1989 (ACCSCT) *Calendar:* Sem. plan *Degrees:* C *CEO:* Pres. Joseph L. Butera
(617) 536-4623

THE CAMBRIDGE SCHOOL OF CULINARY ARTS
2020 Massachusetts Ave., Cambridge 02140-2124 *Type:* Private *Accred.:* 1989/1992 (ACCSCT) *Degrees:* C *CEO:* Dir. Roberta Dowling
(617) 354-3836

CATHERINE E. HINDS INSTITUTE OF ESTHETICS
65 Riverside Pl., Woburn 02155-4604 *Type:* Private *Accred.:* 1983/1987 (ACCSCT) *Degrees:* C *CEO:* Dir. Karen S. Clickner
(617) 391-3733

BRANCH CAMPUS
82 Olympia Ave., Woburn 01801
(617) 933-2501

CHARLES H. MCCANN TECHNICAL SCHOOL
Hodges Crossroad, North Adams 01247 *Type:* Private *Degrees:* C *Prof. Accred.:* Dental Assisting (conditional) *CEO:* Supt. Howard Brookner
(413) 663-5383

COMPUTER LEARNING CENTER
5 Middlesex Ave., Somerville 02145 *Type:* Private business *Accred.:* 1982/1991 (ACICS) *Degrees:* C *CEO:* Exec. Dir. Mark Dugan
(617) 776-3500

METHUEN CAMPUS
436 Broadway, Methuen 01844
(508) 794-0233

COMPUTER PROCESSING INSTITUTE
615 Massachusetts Ave., Cambridge 02139 *Type:* Private business *Accred.:* 1982/1988 (ACICS) *Degrees:* C *CEO:* Dir. William D. John Almond
(617) 354-6900

EAST COAST AERO TECHNICAL SCHOOL
696 Virginia Rd., Concord 01742 *Type:* Private *Accred.:* 1970/1986 (ACCSCT) *Degrees:* C *CEO:* Dir. Robert McTique
(508) 371-9977

FORSYTH SCHOOL FOR DENTAL HYGIENISTS
140 The Fenway, Boston 02115 *Type:* Private *Degrees:* C *Prof. Accred.:* Dental Hygiene *CEO:* Dir. John W. Hein
(617) 262-5200

HALLMARK INSTITUTE OF PHOTOGRAPHY
P.O. Box 308, Turners Falls 01376-0308 *Type:* Private *Accred.:* 1982/1993 (ACCSCT) *Degrees:* C *CEO:* Pres. George J. Rosa, III
(413) 863-2478

HICKOX SCHOOL
200 Tremont St., Boston 02116 *Type:* Private business *Accred.:* 1968/1986 (ACICS) *Degrees:* C *CEO:* Pres. S. Arthur Verenis
(617) 482-7655

KINYON-CAMPBELL BUSINESS SCHOOL
59 Linden St., New Bedford 02740 *Type:* Private business *Accred.:* 1971/1994 (ACICS) *Calendar:* Qtr. plan *Degrees:* C *CEO:* Dir. Dennis Saccoia
(508) 992-5448

BROCKTON CAMPUS
1041 Pearl St., Brockton 02401
(508) 584-6869

LONGY SCHOOL OF MUSIC, INC.
One Follen St., Cambridge 02138 *Type:* Private *Accred.:* 1995 (NEASC-CIHE) *De-*

grees: C *Prof. Accred.:* Music *CEO:* Dir. Victor Rosenbaum

(617) 876-0956

MASSACHUSETTS SCHOOL OF BARBERING AND MEN'S HAIRSTYLING
152 Parkingway St., Quincy 02169-5058 *Type:* Private *Accred.:* 1978/1990 (ACC-SCT) *Calendar:* Sem. plan *Degrees:* C *CEO:* Gen. Mgr. Richard Conragan

(617) 770-4444

NATIONAL EDUCATION CENTER—BRYMAN CAMPUS
323 Boylston St., Brookline 02146-7685 *Type:* Private *Accred.:* 1973/1990 (ACCSCT) *Degrees:* C *CEO:* Exec. Dir. Paul Flaherty

(617) 232-6035

NEW ENGLAND HAIR ACADEMY
492-500 Main St., Malden 02148-5105 *Type:* Private *Accred.:* 1979/1989 (ACCSCT) *Degrees:* C *CEO:* Dir. Anthony Clemente

(617) 324-6799

HAVERHILL CAMPUS
80 Merrimack St., Haverhill 01830

(508) 521-6200

NEW ENGLAND SCHOOL OF ACCOUNTING
155 Ararat St., Worcester 01606 *Type:* Private business *Accred.:* 1969/1987 (ACICS) *Calendar:* Sem. plan *Degrees:* C *CEO:* Dir. Kevin Albano

(508) 853-8972

NEW ENGLAND SCHOOL OF ACUPUNCTURE
30 Common St., Watertown 02172 *Type:* Private professional *Calendar:* Sem. plan *Degrees:* C *Prof. Accred.:* Acupuncture *CEO:* Pres. Daniel Seitz
FTE Enroll: 120   (617) 926-1788

NEW ENGLAND SCHOOL OF ART AND DESIGN
28 Newbury St., Boston 02116-3276 *Type:* Private *Accred.:* 1968 (ACCSCT) *Degrees:* C *CEO:* Dir. Anne Mary Blevins

(617) 536-00383

NEW ENGLAND SCHOOL OF PHOTOGRAPHY
537 Commonwealth Ave., Boston 02215-2005 *Type:* Private *Accred.:* 1981/1986 (AC-

CSCT) *Degrees:* C *CEO:* Pres. William R. Carruthers

(617) 437-1868

NEW ENGLAND TRACTOR TRAILER TRAINING SCHOOL OF MASSACHUSETTS
1093 N. Montello St., Brockton 02401-1642 *Type:* Private *Accred.:* 1982/1992 (ACCSCT) *Degrees:* C *CEO:* Dir. John Henry

(508) 587-1100

NORTH BENNET STREET SCHOOL
39 N. Bennet St., Boston 02113-1998 *Type:* Private *Accred.:* 1982/1987 (ACCSCT) *Degrees:* C *CEO:* Exec. Dir. Cynthia Stone

(617) 227-0155

NORTHEAST BROADCASTING SCHOOL
142 Berkeley St., Boston 02116-5100 *Type:* Private *Accred.:* 1972/1987 (ACCSCT) *Calendar:* Sem. plan *Degrees:* C *CEO:* Pres. Howard E. Horton

(617) 267-7910

NORTHEAST INSTITUTE OF INDUSTRIAL TECHNOLOGY
41 Phillips St., Boston 02114-3699 *Type:* Private *Accred.:* 1971/1987 (ACCSCT) *Calendar:* Sem. plan *Degrees:* C *CEO:* Assoc. Dir. Richard Riman

(617) 523-2869

PEDIGREE CAREER INSTITUTE
Harbor Mall, Rte. 1A, Lynnway, Lynn 01901-1797 *Type:* Private *Accred.:* 1982/1987 (ACCSCT) *Degrees:* C *CEO:* Owner Kevin Hallinan

(617) 592-3647

RETS ELECTRONIC SCHOOLS
965 Commonwealth Ave., Boston 02215-1397 *Type:* Private *Accred.:* 1974/1989 (AC-CSCT) *Degrees:* C *CEO:* Dir. Don Harris

(617) 783-1197

ST. JOHN'S SCHOOL OF BUSINESS
P.O. Box 1190, West Springfield 01090-1190 *Type:* Private business *Accred.:* 1981/1994 (ACICS) *Calendar:* Qtr. plan *Degrees:* C *CEO:* Dir. Kenneth C. Ballard

(413) 781-0390

THE SALTER SCHOOL
155 Ararat St., Worcester 01606 *Type:* Private business *Accred.:* 1953/1988 (ACICS) *Calendar:* Sem. plan *Degrees:* C *CEO:* Dir. John F. Albano
(508) 853-1074

SPRINGFIELD CAMPUS
458 Bridge St., Springfield 01103
(413) 731-7353

SOUTHEASTERN TECHNICAL INSTITUTE
250 Foundry St., South Easton 02375 *Type:* Private *Degrees:* C *Prof. Accred.:* Clinical Lab Technology (C), Dental Assisting, Medical Assisting (AMA) *CEO:* Supt. Paul K. O'Leary
(508) 238-4374

TAD TECHNICAL INSTITUTE
45 Spruce St., Chelsea 02150-2397 *Type:* Private *Accred.:* 1968/1991 (ACCSCT) *Degrees:* C *CEO:* Pres. Rod Kruse
(617) 889-3600

TRAVEL EDUCATION CENTER
100 Cambridge Park Dr., Cambridge 02140 *Type:* Private *Accred.:* 1979/1990 (ACC-SCT) *Degrees:* C *CEO:* Pres. Linda Paresky
(617) 547-7750

NASHUA CAMPUS
402 Amherst St., Nashua, NH 03063-1278
(603) 880-7200

TRAVEL SCHOOL OF AMERICA
1047 Commonwealth Ave., Boston 02215-1099 *Type:* Private *Accred.:* 1978/1988 (ACC-SCT) *Degrees:* C *CEO:* Pres. Bernard Garber
(617) 787-1214

WORCESTER TECHNICAL INSTITUTE
251 Belmont St., Worcester 01605 *Type:* Public (state) technical *Accred.:* 1982/1992 (NE-ASC-CTCI) *Calendar:* Sem. plan *Degrees:* C *Prof. Accred.:* Dental Assisting, Surgical Technology *CEO:* Dir. Janet M. Doe
FTE Enroll: 268   (508) 799-1945

MICHIGAN

ACADEMY OF HEALTH CAREERS
27301 Dequindre Rd., Ste. 200, Madison Heights 48071 *Type:* Private *Accred.:* 1988/ 1991 (ACCSCT) *Degrees:* C *CEO:* Pres. Dale Saham
(810) 547-8400

AMERICAN EDUCATION CENTER
26075 Woodward Ave., Huntington Woods 48070 *Type:* Private *Accred.:* 1988 (ACC-SCT) *Degrees:* C *CEO:* Dir. Susan Lefever
(810) 399-5522

ANN ARBOR SCHOOL OF BUSINESS
3810 Packard Rd., Ste. 270, Ann Arbor 48108 *Type:* Private business *Accred.:* 1994 (ACICS) *Calendar:* Qtr. plan *Degrees:* C *CEO:* Mgr. of Business Ed. Rosalie England *Enroll:* 24   (313) 973-9530

BLACK FOREST HALL
2787 Quick Rd., P.O. Box 140, Harbor Springs 49740-0140 *Type:* Private *Accred.:* 1987/1993 (ACCSCT) *Degrees:* C *CEO:* Pres. Ceejay Heckenberg
(616) 526-7066

CARNEGIE INSTITUTE
550 Stephenson Hwy., Ste. 100, Troy 48083-1159 *Type:* Private *Accred.:* 1968/1993 (ACCSCT) *Calendar:* Qtr. plan *Degrees:* C *Prof. Accred.:* Medical Assisting (AMA) *CEO:* Pres. Gloria J. McEachern
(313) 589-1078

CENTER FOR CREATIVE STUDIES—INSTITUTE OF MUSIC AND DANCE
201 E. Kirby St., Detroit 48202 *Type:* Private *Degrees:* C *Prof. Accred.:* Music *CEO:* Chrmn. Michael Stockdale
(313) 872-3118

DETROIT BUSINESS INSTITUTE
1249 Washington Blvd., Ste. 1200, Detroit 48226 *Type:* Private business *Accred.:* 1961/ 1987 (ACICS) *Calendar:* Qtr. plan *Degrees:* C *CEO:* Dir. Gertha Dodson
(313) 962-6534

DETROIT BUSINESS INSTITUTE—DOWNRIVER
19100 Fort St., Riverview 48192 *Type:* Private business *Accred.:* 1983/1995 (ACICS) *Calendar:* Qtr. plan *Degrees:* C *Prof. Accred.:* Medical Assisting *CEO:* Pres. Leon Gust
(313) 479-0660

DETROIT INSTITUTE OF OPHTHALMOLOGY
15415 E. Jefferson Ave., Grosse Pointe Park 48230 *Type:* Private *Degrees:* C *Prof. Accred.:* Ophthalmic Medical Technology *CEO:* Pres. Philip C. Hessburg
Enroll: 16   (313) 824-4800

DORSEY BUSINESS SCHOOL
30821 Barrington Ave., Madison Heights 48071 *Type:* Private business *Accred.:* 1984/ 1996 (ACICS) *Degrees:* C *CEO:* Dir. Mary Byrnes
(313) 585-9200

DORSEY BUSINESS SCHOOL
31542 Gratiot Ave., Roseville 48066 *Type:* Private business *Accred.:* 1961/1996 (AC-ICS) *Calendar:* Qtr. plan *Degrees:* C *CEO:* Dir. Kim Flynn
(313) 296-3225

DORSEY BUSINESS SCHOOL
15755 Northline Rd., Southgate 48195 *Type:* Private business *Accred.:* 1972/1996 (AC-ICS) *Calendar:* Qtr. plan *Degrees:* C *CEO:* Managing Dir. Sara Calupina
(313) 285-5400

DORSEY BUSINESS SCHOOL
34841 Veteran's Plaza, Wayne 48184 *Type:* Private business *Accred.:* 1984/1996 (AC-ICS) *Degrees:* C *CEO:* Dir. Sara Calupina
(313) 595-1540

EDUCATIONAL INSTITUTE OF THE AMERICAN HOTEL AND MOTEL ASSOCIATION
1407 S. Harrison Rd., P.O. Box 1240, East Lansing 48826 *Type:* Private distance education *Accred.:* 1963/1993 (DETC) *Degrees:* C *CEO:* Pres. E. Ray Swan
(517) 353-5500

FLINT INSTITUTE OF BARBERING
3214 Flushing Rd., Flint 48504-4395 *Type:* Private *Accred.:* 1972/1988 (ACCSCT) *Degrees:* C *CEO:* Pres. John L. Ayre
(313) 232-4711

GRAND RAPIDS EDUCATIONAL CENTER
1750 Woodworth St., N.E., Grand Rapids 49505 *Type:* Private *Accred.:* 1978/1989 (ACCSCT) *Degrees:* C *Prof. Accred.:* Medical Assisting *CEO:* Pres. Robert J. Malone
(616) 364-8464

KALAMAZOO CAMPUS
Golf Ridge Ctr., 5349 W. Main St., Kalamazoo 49009-1083
(616) 381-9616

HAWES CAREER INSTITUTE
Willow Run Airport, 47884 D St., Belleville 48111-1278 *Type:* Private *Accred.:* 1976/1991 (ACCSCT) *Degrees:* C *CEO:* Pres. Charles Hawes
(800) 447-1310

ITT TECHNICAL INSTITUTE
4020 Sparks Dr., S.E., Grand Rapids 49546 *Type:* Private *Accred.:* 1972/1989 (ACCSCT) *Degrees:* C *CEO:* Dir. Dennis Hormel
(616) 956-1060

MATTESON CAMPUS
600 Holiday Plaza Dr., Matteson, IL 60443
(708) 747-2571

LANSING COMPUTER INSTITUTE
501 N. Marshall St., Ste. 101, Lansing 48912-2300 *Type:* Private *Accred.:* 1985/ 1990 (ACCSCT) *Degrees:* C *CEO:* Dir. Virginia Hilbert
(517) 482-8896

LAWTON SCHOOL
21800 Greenfield, Oak Park 48237 *Type:* Private *Accred.:* 1988/1991 (ACCSCT) *Degrees:* C *CEO:* Exec. Dir. Audrey Gaylor
(313) 968-2421

MICHIGAN BARBER SCHOOL INC.
8988-90 Grand River Ave., Detroit 48204-2244 *Type:* Private *Accred.:* 1986 (ACC-

SCT) *Degrees:* C *CEO:* Dir. Forrest F. Green, Jr.
(313) 894-2300

MICHIGAN CAREER INSTITUTE
14520 Gratiot Ave., Detroit 48205-2395 *Type:* Private *Accred.:* 1968/1989 (ACCSCT) *Degrees:* C *CEO:* Dir. Andrew G. Vignone
(313) 526-6600

MICHIGAN SCHOOL OF CANINE COSMETOLOGY
3022 S. Ceder, Lansing 48910 *Type:* Private *Accred.:* 1994 (ACCSCT) *CEO:* Dir. Sandy Cook
Enroll: 20   (517) 393-6311

MOTECH EDUCATION CENTER
35155 Industrial Rd., Livonia 48150-1238 *Type:* Private *Accred.:* 1976/1990 (ACCSCT) *Calendar:* Sem. plan *Degrees:* C *CEO:* Dir. Paul Alberts
(313) 522-9510

NATIONAL EDUCATION CENTER—NATIONAL INSTITUTE OF TECHNOLOGY CAMPUS
18000 Newburgh Rd., Livonia 48152-2695 *Type:* Private *Accred.:* 1970/1990 (ACCSCT) *Calendar:* Qtr. plan *Degrees:* C *CEO:* Dir. Harry Strong
(313) 464-7387

NATIONAL EDUCATION CENTER—NATIONAL INSTITUTE OF TECHNOLOGY CAMPUS
2620/2630 Remico St., S.W., Wyoming 49509-9990 *Type:* Private *Accred.:* 1973/ 1990 (ACCSCT) *Calendar:* Qtr. plan *Degrees:* C *CEO:* Dir. Jenell L. McKinney
(616) 538-3170

PAYNE-PULLIAM SCHOOL OF TRADE AND COMMERCE
2345 Cass Ave., Detroit 48201 *Type:* Private business *Accred.:* 1978/1996 (ACICS) *Degrees:* C *CEO:* Pres. Betty E. Pulliam
(313) 963-4710

ROSS BUSINESS INSTITUTE
22293 Eureka Rd., Taylor 48180 *Type:* Private business *Accred.:* 1983/1995 (ACICS) *Calendar:* Qtr. plan *Degrees:* C *Prof.*

Accred.: Medical Assisting *CEO:* Dir. Judith Sierota

(313) 374-2135

CLINTON TOWNSHIP CAMPUS
37065 Gratoit, Clinton Township 48036
Prof. Accred.: Medical Assisting

(313) 954-3083

MONROE CAMPUS
1285 N. Telegraph Rd., Monroe 48162
Prof. Accred.: Medical Assisting

(313) 243-5456

ROSS MEDICAL EDUCATION CENTER
1036 Gilbert Rd., Flint 48532-3527 *Type:* Private *Accred.:* 1978/1987 (ACCSCT) *Degrees:* C *Prof. Accred.:* Medical Assisting *CEO:* Dir. Sharon McCaughrin

(313) 230-1100

JACKSON CAMPUS
1188 N. West Ave., Jackson 49202 *Prof. Accred.:* Medical Assisting

(517) 782-7677

ROOSEVELT PARK CAMPUS
950 W. Norton Ave., Roosevelt Park 48441-4156 *Prof. Accred.:* Medical Assisting

(616) 739-1531

SAGINAW CAMPUS
4054 Bay Rd., Saginaw 48603-1201 *Prof. Accred.:* Medical Assisting

(517) 793-9800

ROSS MEDICAL EDUCATION CENTER
913 W. Holmes Rd., Ste. 260, Lansing 48910-4490 *Type:* Private *Accred.:* 1982/1987 (ACCSCT) *Degrees:* C *Prof. Accred.:* Medical Assisting *CEO:* Dir. Laura Shultz

(517) 887-0180

GRAND RAPIDS CAMPUS
2035 28th St., S.E., Ste. 0, Grand Rapids 49508-1539 *Prof. Accred.:* Medical Assisting

(616) 243-3070

ROSS MEDICAL EDUCATION CENTER
26417 Hoover Rd., Warren 48089-1190
Type: Private *Accred.:* 1981/1986 (ACCSCT) *Degrees:* C *Prof. Accred.:* Medical Assisting *CEO:* Dir. Dolores Jurko

(313) 758-7200

DETROIT CAMPUS
15670 E. Eight Mile Rd., Detroit 48205-1496

(313) 371-2131

WATERFORD CAMPUS
253 Summit Dr., Waterford 48328-3364
Prof. Accred.: Medical Assisting

(313) 683-1166

ROSS TECHNICAL INSTITUTE
1490 S. Military Trail, Ste. 11, West Palm Beach, FL 33415-9141 *Accred.:* 1991 (ACCSCT) *Prof. Accred.:* Medical Assisting

(407) 433-1288

ROSS TECHNICAL INSTITUTE
5757 Whitmore Lake Rd., Ste. 800, Brighton 48116 *Type:* Private *Accred.:* 1986/1993 (ACCSCT) *Degrees:* C *Prof. Accred.:* Medical Assisting *CEO:* Dir. Sharon Treumuth

(810) 227-0160

ANN ARBOR CAMPUS
4703 Washtenaw Ave., Ann Arbor 48108-1411 *Prof. Accred.:* Medical Assisting

(313) 434-7320

ROSS TECHNICAL INSTITUTE
1553 Woodward Ave., Ste. 650, Detroit 48226-1695 *Type:* Private *Accred.:* 1979/1989 (ACCSCT) *Degrees:* C *Prof. Accred.:* Medical Assisting *CEO:* Dir. Aimee B. Davis

(313) 965-7451

OAK PARK CAMPUS
20820 Greenfield Rd., 1st Fl., Oak Park 48237-3011 *Prof. Accred.:* Medical Assisting

(810) 967-3100

SAGINAW BEAUTY ACADEMY
P.O. Box 423, Saginaw 48601-0423 *Type:*
Private *Accred.:* 1992 (ACCSCT) *Degrees:*
C *CEO:* Dir. Carlean Gill
(517) 752-9261

SER BUSINESS AND TECHNICAL INSTITUTE
9301 Michigan Ave., Detroit 48210 *Type:*
Private business *Accred.:* 1989/1993 (AC-
ICS) *Degrees:* C *CEO:* Educ. Dir. Eva G.
Dewaelsche
(313) 846-2240

CHICAGO CAMPUS
5150 W. Roosevelt, Chicago, IL 60650
(312) 379-1152

SHARP'S ACADEMY OF HAIRSTYLING
115 Main St., Flushing 48433 *Type:* Private
Accred.: 1993 (ACCSCT) *Degrees:* C *CEO:*
Owner Patricia Sharp
(313) 659-3348

GRAND BLANC CAMPUS
8166 Holly Rd., Grand Blanc 48499
(313) 695-6742

SPECS HOWARD SCHOOL OF BROADCAST ARTS
INC.
19900 W. Nine Mile Rd., Ste. 115, Southfield 48075-5273 *Type:* Private *Accred.:*
1978/1990 (ACCSCT) *Degrees:* C *CEO:*
Exec. Dir. Specs Howard
(810) 569-0101

TRAVEL EDUCATION INSTITUTE
24901 Northwestern Hwy., Ste. 110, South-
field 48075 *Type:* Private *Accred.:* 1992
(ACCSCT) *Degrees:* C *CEO:* Pres. Patricia
Klein
Enroll: 250   (810) 352-4875

WARREN CAMPUS
30100 Van Dyke, Ste. 200, Warren 48093
Enroll: 150   (810) 751-5634

TRAVEL TRAINING CENTER
5003-05 Schaefer Rd., Dearborn 48126-
3539 *Type:* Private *Accred.:* 1990 (ACC-
SCT) *Degrees:* C *CEO:* Dir. M. R. Younis
(313) 584-5000

MINNESOTA

ART INSTRUCTION SCHOOLS
3309 Northeast Broadway., Minneapolis 55413 *Type:* Private distance education *Accred.:* 1956/1991 (DETC) *Degrees:* C *CEO:* Pres. Thomas R. Stuart
(612) 339-6656

AVANTE SCHOOL OF COSMETOLOGY
1650 White Bear Ave., St. Paul 55106-1610 *Type:* Private *Accred.:* 1987 (ACCSCT) *Degrees:* C *CEO:* Dir. James Turner
(612) 772-1417

HUBERT H. HUMPHREY JOB CORPS CENTER
1480 Snelling Ave., St. Paul 55108 *Type:* Public *Accred.:* 1983/1994 (NCA) *Degrees:* C *CEO:* Dir. Ralph DiBattista
Enroll: 293   (612) 642-1133

LAKELAND MEDICAL-DENTAL ACADEMY
1402 W. Lake St., Minneapolis 55408-2682 *Type:* Private *Accred.:* 1968/1989 (ACCSCT) *Calendar:* Qtr. plan *Degrees:* C *Prof. Accred.:* Clinical Lab Technology (C), Dental Assisting, Medical Assisting (AMA) *CEO:* Dir. Lorrie Laurin
(612) 827-5656

THE MCCONNELL SCHOOL
831 Second Ave. S., Minneapolis 55402-2861 *Type:* Private *Accred.:* 1967/1989 (ACCSCT) *Degrees:* C *CEO:* Dir. William McKay
(612) 332-4238

MEDICAL INSTITUTE OF MINNESOTA
5503 Green Valley Dr., Bloomington 55437 *Type:* Private *Accred.:* 1985/1995 (ABHES) *Degrees:* C *Prof. Accred.:* Clinical Lab Technology (A), Medical Assisting (AMA), Veterinary Technology *CEO:* Pres. Phillip Miller
(612) 844-0064

MINNEAPOLIS DRAFTING SCHOOL
5700 W. Broadway, Minneapolis 55428-3548 *Type:* Private *Accred.:* 1972/1988 (ACCSCT) *Calendar:* Qtr. plan *Degrees:* C *CEO:* Pres. Robert X. Casserly
(612) 535-8843

MINNEAPOLIS TECHNICAL COLLEGE
1415 Hennepin Ave. S., Rm. 446, Minneapolis 55403 *Type:* Public *Degrees:* C *Prof. Accred.:* Dental Assisting, Practical Nursing *CEO:* Pres. Joe King, Jr.
(612) 370-9400

MINNESOTA INSTITUTE OF ACUPUNCTURE AND HERBAL STUDIES
5251 Chicago Ave., S., Minneapolis 55417-1731 *Type:* Private non-profit *Calendar:* Qtr. plan *Degrees:* C *Prof. Accred.:* Acupuncture *CEO:* Pres. Edith Davis
(612) 823-6235

MINNESOTA SCHOOL OF BARBERING
3615 E. Lake St., Minneapolis 55406 *Type:* Private *Accred.:* 1983/1988 (ACCSCT) *Degrees:* C *CEO:* Dir. Margaret Schmidt
(612) 722-1996

MOLER BARBER SCHOOL OF HAIRSTYLING
1411 Nicollet Ave., Minneapolis 55403-2666 *Type:* Private *Accred.:* 1983/1988 (ACCSCT) *Degrees:* C *CEO:* Owner Delano Martinson
(612) 871-3754

MUSIC TECH
304 N. Washington Ave., Minneapolis 55401 *Type:* Private *Degrees:* C *Prof. Accred.:* Music *CEO:* Educ. Dir. Douglas W. Smith
(612) 338-0175

NEI COLLEGE OF TECHNOLOGY
825 41st Ave., N.E., Columbia Heights 55421-2974 *Type:* Private *Accred.:* 1968/1988 (ACCSCT) *Calendar:* Qtr. plan *Degrees:* C *CEO:* Pres. Charles R. Dettmann
(612) 781-4881

SCHOOL OF COMMUNICATION ARTS
2526 27th Ave. S., Minneapolis 55406-1310 *Type:* Private *Accred.:* 1980/1990 (ACCSCT) *Calendar:* Sem. plan *Degrees:* C *CEO:* Pres. Roger Klietz
(612) 721-5357

MISSISSIPPI

AMHERST CAREER CENTER
201 W. Park Ave., Greenwood 38930 *Type:*
Private *Accred.:* 1991 (COE warning) *Degrees:* C *CEO:* Dir. Gladys Flaggs
FTE Enroll: 116   (601) 453-0480

JACKSON CAMPUS
330 N. Mart Plaza, Jackson 37206
(601) 336-0392

BATESVILLE JOB CORPS CENTER
Hwy. 51, S., Batesville 38606 *Type:* Public
(state) *Accred.:* 1989/1994 (COE) *Degrees:*
C *CEO:* Dir. Laura Bruton
FTE Enroll: 480   (601) 563-4656

DELTA TECHNICAL INSTITUTE
323 Central Ave., Cleveland 38732-2647
Type: Private *Accred.:* 1987 (ACCSCT) *Degrees:* C *CEO:* Pres. Van P. Carmicle
(601) 843-6063

GULFPORT JOB CORPS CENTER
3300 20th St., Gulfport 39501 *Type:* Public
(state) *Accred.:* 1985/1992 (COE) *Degrees:*
C *CEO:* Dir. Karen Kennedy
FTE Enroll: 350   (601) 864-9691

JACKSON ACADEMY OF BEAUTY
2525 Robinson Rd., Jackson 39209 *Type:*
Private *Accred.:* 1990 (COE) *Degrees:* C
CEO: Dir. Jim Bailey
FTE Enroll: 123   (601) 352-3003

MISSISSIPPI JOB CORPS CENTER
400 Harmony Rd., Crystal Springs 39059
Type: Public (state) *Accred.:* 1984/1994
(COE) *Degrees:* C *CEO:* Dir. Debbie Zeiger
FTE Enroll: 507   (601) 892-3348

MOORE CAREER COLLEGE
2460 Terry Rd., Jackson 39204 *Type:* Private
Accred.: 1985/1990 (COE) *Degrees:* C
CEO: Dir. Acka Dolloff
FTE Enroll: 340   (601) 371-2900

HATTIESBURG CAMPUS
1500 N. 31st Ave., Hattiesburg 39401
(601) 583-4100

MERIDIAN CAMPUS
1500 Hwy. 19, N., Meridian 39307
(601) 693-2900

TUPELO CAMPUS
880 Cliff Gookin Blvd., Tupelo 38801
(601) 842-7600

NAVAL CONSTRUCTION TRAINING CENTER
5510 CBC 8th St., Gulfport 39501-5003
Type: Public (federal) technical *Accred.:*
1975/1990 (COE) *Degrees:* C *CEO:* Commandant G. R. Henderson
FTE Enroll: 298   (601) 871-2531

NAVAL TECHNICAL TRAINING CENTER
740 Fletcher Rd., Ste. 100, Meridian 39309-
5040 *Type:* Public (federal) technical *Accred.:* 1976/1991 (COE) *Degrees:* C *CEO:*
Commandant Corey Whitehead
FTE Enroll: 721   (601) 679-2161

NORTH MISSISSIPPI EMS AUTHORITY
308 Troy St., P.O. Box 377, Tupelo 38802
Type: Public *Degrees:* C *Prof. Accred.:*
EMT-Paramedic *CEO:* Exec. Dir. John
Charles Morris, Jr.
Enroll: 6,000   (601) 844-5870

SOUTHERN DRIVER'S ACADEMY
3906 I-55, S., Jackson 39284 *Type:* Private
Accred.: 1990 (COE) *Degrees:* C *CEO:* Dir.
Johnnie E. Twiner
FTE Enroll: 54   (601) 371-1371

SOUTHERN VOCATIONAL-TECHNICAL INSTITUTE
905 Hardy St., Hattiesburg 39401 *Type:*
Private *Accred.:* 1991 (COE) *Degrees:* C
CEO: Dir. N. Bryan Saliba
FTE Enroll: 85   (601) 583-2523

MISSOURI

AERO MECHANICS SCHOOL
200 Northwest Pkwy., Riverside 64150 *Type:* Private *Accred.:* 1991 (ACCSCT) *Degrees:* C *CEO:* Exec. Dir. Robert J. Andrist, Jr.
(816) 741-7700

AL-MED ACADEMY
10963 St. Charles Rock Rd., St. Louis 63074 *Type:* Private *Accred.:* 1985/1991 (ABHES) *Degrees:* C *Prof. Accred.:* Medical Assisting *CEO:* Pres. C. Larkin Hicks
(314) 739-4450

BASIC INSTITUTE OF TECHNOLOGY
4455 Chippewa Ave., St. Louis 63116-9990 *Type:* Private *Accred.:* 1974/1989 (ACCSCT) *Calendar:* Qtr. plan *Degrees:* C *CEO:* Dir. J. A. Zoeller
(314) 771-1200

BRYAN CAREER COLLEGE
520 W. University St., Ste. B, Springfield 65807 *Type:* Private business *Accred.:* 1991/1994 (ACICS) *Degrees:* C *CEO:* Dir. Debra Lee
(417) 862-5700

GRANDVIEW CAMPUS
12220 S. Blue Ridge Blvd, Ste. F, Grandview 64138
Enroll: 20   (816) 763-1000

CAPE GIRARDEAU AREA VOCATIONAL-TECHNICAL SCHOOL
301 N. Clark St., Cape Girardeau 63701 *Type:* Private *Degrees:* C *Prof. Accred.:* Respiratory Therapy Technology *CEO:* Dir. Harold C. Tilley
(314) 334-3358

CONCORDE CAREER INSTITUTE
3239 Broadway, Kansas City 64111-2407 *Type:* Private *Accred.:* 1986/1990 (ACCSCT) *Calendar:* Qtr. plan *Degrees:* C *Prof. Accred.:* Medical Assisting (AMA) *CEO:* Dir. Peggy Ammons
(816) 531-5223

DIAMOND COUNCIL OF AMERICA
9140 Ward Pkwy., Kansas City 64114 *Type:* Private distance education *Accred.:* 1984/1993 (DETC) *Degrees:* C *CEO:* Exec. Dir. Jerry Fogel
(816) 444-3500

DICK HILL INTERNATIONAL FLIGHT SCHOOL
P.O. Box 10603, Springfield 65808-0603 *Type:* Private *Accred.:* 1987 (ACCSCT) *Degrees:* C *CEO:* Dir. Marlene J. Hill
(417) 485-3474

EASTERN JACKSON COUNTY COLLEGE OF ALLIED HEALTH
808 S. 15th St., Blue Springs 64015 *Type:* Private *Accred.:* 1984/1991 (ABHES) *Degrees:* C *CEO:* Pres. Kathryn L. Harmon
(816) 229-4720

FLORISSANT UPHOLSTERY SCHOOL
1420 N. Vandeventer St., St. Louis 63113-3416 *Type:* Private *Accred.:* 1987/1993 (ACCSCT) *Degrees:* C *CEO:* Dir. Charles S. Davis
(314) 534-1886

HANNIBAL AREA VOCATIONAL-TECHNICAL SCHOOL
4500 McMasters Ave., Hannibal 63401 *Type:* Private *Degrees:* C *Prof. Accred.:* Respiratory Therapy Technology *CEO:* Dir. Harold D. Ward
(314) 221-4430

IHM HEALTH STUDIES CENTER
2500 Abbott Pl., St. Louis 63143 *Type:* Private *Accred.:* 1992 (ABHES) *Degrees:* C *CEO:* Dir. Tina Stumpf
(314) 768-1234

LEONARD'S BARBER COLLEGE
4974 Natural Bridge Rd., St. Louis 63115 *Type:* Private *Accred.:* 1992 (ACCSCT) *Degrees:* C *CEO:* Dir. Leonard Hall
Enroll: 18   (314) 382-3000

MIDWEST INSTITUTE FOR MEDICAL ASSISTANTS
10910 Manchester Rd, Kirkwood 63122
Type: Private *Accred.:* 1978/1990 (ABHES)
Degrees: C *CEO:* Dir. Elizabeth Shreffler
(314) 965-8363

MISSOURI SCHOOL OF BARBERING AND
HAIRSTYLING
1125 N. Hwy. 67, Florissant 63031 *Type:*
Private *Accred.:* 1992 (ACCSCT) *Degrees:*
C *CEO:* Pres. T. L. Millis
(314) 839-0310

MISSOURI SCHOOL OF BARBERING AND
HAIRSTYLING
3740 Noland Rd., Independence 64055-3343
Type: Private *Accred.:* 1987 (ACCSCT) *De-grees:* C *CEO:* Dir. Lana Jones
(816) 836-4118

NICHOLS CAREER CENTER
609 Union St., Jefferson City 65101 *Type:*
Private *Degrees:* C *Prof. Accred.:* Dental
Assisting, Practical Nursing, Radiography
CEO: Dir. Harold Lynch
(314) 659-3000

ROLLA TECHNICAL INSTITUTE
1304 E. Tenth St., Rolla 65401-3699 *Type:*
Public *Calendar:* Sem. plan *Degrees:* C *Prof.
Accred.:* Radiography, Respiratory Therapy
Technology *CEO:* Dir. Bob Chapman
(314) 364-3726

ST. LOUIS COLLEGE OF HEALTH CAREERS
4484 W. Pine Blvd., St. Louis 63108 *Type:*
Private *Accred.:* 1986/1992 (ABHES) *De-grees:* C *CEO:* Pres. Rush L. Robinson
(314) 652-0300

SOUTH COUNTY CAMPUS
4044 Butler Hill Rd, St. Louis 63129
(314) 845-6100

ST. LOUIS SYMPHONY COMMUNITY MUSIC
SCHOOL
560 Trinity Ave. at Delmar Blvd., St. Louis
63130 *Type:* Private *Degrees:* C *Prof.
Accred.:* Music *CEO:* Dean Shirley Bartzen
(314) 863-3033

ST. LOUIS TECH
9741 St. Charles Rock Rd., St. Louis 63114
Type: Private *Accred.:* 1977/1988 (ACC-SCT) *Degrees:* C *CEO:* Pres. Ted M. Petry
(314) 427-3600

STE. GENEVIEVE BEAUTY COLLEGE
755 Market St., Ste. Genevieve 63670-1525
Type: Private *Accred.:* 1991 (ACCSCT)
Degrees: C *CEO:* Mgr. Vicky Fithian
(314) 883-5550

SOUTHWEST SCHOOL OF BROADCASTING
1031 E. Battlefield Rd., Ste. 212B, Spring-field 65807-5083 *Type:* Private *Accred.:*
1988 (ACCSCT) *Degrees:* C *CEO:* Vice
Pres. Johnie F. Jones
(417) 883-4060

TAD TECHNICAL INSTITUTE
7910 Troost Ave., Kansas City 64131-1920
Type: Private *Accred.:* 1977/1989 (ACC-SCT) *Calendar:* Qtr. plan *Degrees:* C *CEO:*
Pres. Waunda Thomas
(816) 361-5140

TRANS WORLD TRAVEL ACADEMY
Lindbergh Training Ctr., 11495 Natural
Bridge Rd., St. Louis 63044-9842 *Type:* Pri-vate distance education *Accred.:* 1981/1993
(DETC) *Degrees:* C *CEO:* Exec. Dir. Frank
A. Bugler
(314) 895-6754

THE VANDERSCHMIDT SCHOOL
4625 Lindell Blvd., St. Louis 63108 *Type:*
Private business *Accred.:* 1985/1995 (AC-ICS) *Degrees:* C *CEO:* Exec. Dir. Nancy S.
Rendleman
(314) 361-6000

VATTEROTT EDUCATIONAL CENTERS
3854 Washington Ave., St. Louis 63108-3406 *Type:* Private *Accred.:* 1976/1986
(ACCSCT) *Degrees:* C *CEO:* Pres. John C.
Vatterott
(314) 534-2586

MONTANA

BIG SKY COLLEGE OF BARBER STYLING
750 Kensington Ave., Missoula 59801-5720
Type: Private *Accred.:* 1988 (ACCSCT) *De-grees:* C *CEO:* Pres. Gary T. Lucht
(406) 721-5588

BILLINGS SCHOOL OF BARBERING AND
HAIRSTYLING
206 N. 13th St., Billings 59101 *Type:* Private
Accred.: 1985/1990 (ACCSCT) *Degrees:* C
CEO: Dir. Monte Krause
(406) 259-9369

MAY TECHNICAL COLLEGE
1306 Central Ave., Billings 59102-5531
Type: Private *Accred.:* 1983/1988 (ACC-SCT) *Degrees:* C *CEO:* Pres. Michael May
(406) 259-7000

GREAT FALLS CAMPUS
1807 Third St., N.W., Great Falls 59404-1922 *Accred.:* 1988 (ACCSCT)
(406) 761-4000

SAGE TECHNICAL SERVICES
1148 16th St. W., Billings 59102 *Type:*
Private *Accred.:* 1994 (ACCSCT) *Degrees:*
C *CEO:* Dir. Lewis Grill
Enroll: 40   (406) 652-3030

NEBRASKA

COLLEGE OF HAIR DESIGN
304 S. 11th St., Lincoln 68508-2199 *Type:*
Private *Accred.:* 1977/1987 (ACCSCT)
Calendar: Qtr. plan *Degrees:* C *CEO:* Pres.
Alyce Howard
(402) 474-4244

DR. WELBES COLLEGE OF MASSAGE THERAPY
2602 J St., Omaha 68107-1643 *Type:* Private
Accred.: 1991 (ACCSCT) *Degrees:* C *CEO:*
Owner John Welbes
(402) 731-6768

OMAHA COLLEGE OF HEALTH CAREERS
10845 Harney St., Omaha 68154 *Type:*
Private *Accred.:* 1986 (ACCSCT) *Degrees:*
C *Prof. Accred.:* Dental Assisting, Medical
Assisting (AMA), Veterinary Technology
CEO: Pres. William J. Stuckey
(402) 333-1400

OMAHA OPPORTUNITIES INDUSTRIALIZATION
CENTER
2724 N. 24th St., Omaha 68110-2100 *Type:*
Private *Accred.:* 1986 (ACCSCT) *Degrees:*
C *CEO:* Exec. Dir. Bernice Dodd
(402) 457-4222

UNIVERSAL TECHNICAL INSTITUTE
902 Capitol Ave., Omaha 68102-9954 *Type:*
Private *Accred.:* 1967/1987 (ACCSCT) *Degrees:* C *CEO:* Owner Ivan Abdouch
(402) 345-2422

NEVADA

ACADEMY OF MEDICAL CAREERS
5243 W. Charleston Blvd., No. 11, Las Vegas
89102 *Type:* Private *Accred.:* 1993 (ACC-SCT) *Degrees:* C *CEO:* Pres. William M. Paul
(818) 896-2272

INTERIOR DESIGN INSTITUTE
4225 S. Eastern Ave., No. 4, Las Vegas 89119-5427 *Type:* Private *Accred.:* 1992 (ACCSCT)
Degrees: C *CEO:* Pres. Nancy Wolff
(702) 369-9944

INTERNATIONAL DEALERS SCHOOL
503 E. Fremont St., Las Vegas 89101 *Type:*
Private *Accred.:* 1983/1988 (ACCSCT)
Degrees: C *CEO:* Dir. Karen Reilly
(702) 385-7665

NATIONAL ACADEMY FOR CASINO DEALERS
557 S. Sahara Ave., Ste. 108, Las Vegas
89104 *Type:* Private *Accred.:* 1984/1989
(ACCSCT) *Degrees:* C *CEO:* Pres. Al
Rodrigues
(702) 735-4884

NEVADA JEWELRY MANUFACTURING
953 E. Sahara, Ste. B-27, Las Vegas 89104
Type: Private *Accred.:* 1994 (ACCSCT)
Degrees: C *CEO:* Dir. Egardo Mazzola
(702) 735-4191

PCI DEALERS SCHOOL
920 S. Valley View Blvd., Las Vegas 89107-4416 *Type:* Private *Accred.:* 1991 (ACC-SCT) *Degrees:* C *CEO:* Pres. Joel Lauer
(702) 877-4724

PROFESSIONAL CAREERS
3305 Spring Mountain Rd., Ste. 7, Las Vegas
89193-6895 *Type:* Private *Accred.:* 1991
(ACCSCT) *Degrees:* C *CEO:* Pres. Mathew
Klabacka
(702) 368-2338

RENO TAHOE GAMING ACADEMY
One First St., Ste. 1405, Reno 89501 *Type:*
Private *Accred.:* 1994 (ACCSCT) *CEO:*
Pres. William C. Thorton
(702) 348-7700

VEGAS CAREER SCHOOL
3333 S. Maryland Pkwy., Ste. 12, Las Vegas
89102 *Type:* Private *Accred.:* 1990 (ACC-SCT) *Degrees:* C *CEO:* Owner John Rosich
(702) 792-6299

NEW HAMPSHIRE

NORTHEAST CAREER SCHOOLS
749 E. Industrial Park Dr., Manchester
03109 *Type:* Private *Accred.:* 1986 (ACC-
SCT) *Degrees:* C *CEO:* Pres. Chris Liponis
(603) 622-2866

NEW JERSEY

ACADEMY OF PROFESSIONAL DEVELOPMENT
98 Mayfield Ave., Edison 08837 *Type:* Private business *Accred.:* 1986 (ACICS) *Degrees:* C *CEO:* Pres. A. Roy Kirkley, Jr.
(908) 417-9100

EWING CAMPUS
934 Parkway Ave., Ewing 08618
(609) 538-0400

AMERICAN BUSINESS ACADEMY
66 Moore St., Hackensack 07601 *Type:* Private business *Accred.:* 1976/1994 (ACICS) *Calendar:* Qtr. plan *Degrees:* C *CEO:* Pres. Theodore S. Takvorian
(201) 488-9400

BERDAN INSTITUTE
265 Rte. 46 W., Totowa 07512-1819 *Type:* Private *Accred.:* 1980/1990 (ACCSCT) *Degrees:* C *Prof. Accred.:* Dental Assisting, Medical Assisting (AMA) *CEO:* Dir. E. Lynn Thacker
(201) 256-3444

BOARDWALK AND MARINA CASINO DEALERS SCHOOL
1923 Bacharach Blvd., Atlantic City 08401-6401 *Type:* Private *Accred.:* 1989 (ACCSCT) *Degrees:* C *CEO:* Pres. Arnold Hasson
(609) 344-1986

BRICK COMPUTER SCIENCE INSTITUTE
515 Hwy. 70, Brick 08723-4043 *Type:* Private *Accred.:* 1974/1990 (ACCSCT) *Degrees:* C *CEO:* Dir. Robert H. Forshee, Jr.
(908) 477-0975

BUSINESS TRAINING INSTITUTE
4 Forest Ave., Paramus 07652 *Type:* Private business *Accred.:* 1985/1990 (ACICS) *Degrees:* C *CEO:* Pres. James P. Mellett, Jr.
(201) 845-9300

CAPE MAY COUNTY TECHNICAL INSTITUTE
188 Crest Haven Rd., Cape May Courthouse 08210 *Type:* Public *Calendar:* Sem. plan *Degrees:* C *Prof. Accred.:* Dental Assisting

(conditional) *CEO:* Supt. Wilber J. Kistler, Jr.
Enroll: 600   (609) 465-3064

THE CHUBB INSTITUTE
8 Sylvan Way, Parsippany 07054-0342 *Type:* Private *Accred.:* 1972/1987 (ACCSCT) *Degrees:* C *CEO:* Dir. Todd A. Brown
(201) 682-4900

JERSEY CITY CAMPUS
40 Journal Sq., Jersey City 07306-4009
(201) 656-0330

CITTONE INSTITUTE
1697 Oak Tree Rd., Edison 08820-2896 *Type:* Private business *Accred.:* 1975/1994 (ACICS) *Degrees:* C *CEO:* Exec. Dir. John J. Willie
(908) 548-8798

MOUNT LAUREL CAMPUS
523 Fellowship Rd., Ste. 625, Mount Laurel 08054-3414
(609) 722-9333

PRINCETON CAMPUS
100 Canal Pointe Blvd., Princeton 08540
(609) 520-8798

COMPUTER LEARNING CENTER
160 E. Rte. 4, Paramus 07652 *Type:* Private business *Accred.:* 1984/1991 (ACICS) *Degrees:* C *CEO:* Dir. Christopher Coutts
(201) 845-6868

DIVERS ACADEMY OF THE EASTERN SEABOARD
2500 S. Broadway, Camden 08104-2431 *Type:* Private *Accred.:* 1981/1986 (ACCSCT) *Degrees:* C *CEO:* Dir. Tamara M. Brown
(800) 238-3483

DOVER BUSINESS COLLEGE
15 E. Blackwell St., Dover 07801 *Type:* Private business *Accred.:* 1974/1986 (ACICS) *Calendar:* Qtr. plan *Degrees:* C *CEO:* Dir. Susan Baumstein
(201) 366-6700

PARAMUS CAMPUS
E. 81 Rte. 4 W., Paramus 07652
(201) 712-0107

DRAKE COLLEGE OF BUSINESS
125 Broad St, Elizabeth 07201 *Type:* Private business *Accred.:* 1982/1994 (ACICS) *Calendar:* Sem. plan *Degrees:* C *CEO:* Pres. Frieda Kay
(201) 352-5509

EAST ORANGE CAMPUS
60 Evergreen Pl., East Orange 07018
(201) 673-6009

DU CRET SCHOOL OF THE ARTS
1030 Central Ave., Plainfield 07060-2898 *Type:* Private *Accred.:* 1979/1989 (ACCSCT) *Calendar:* Sem. plan *Degrees:* C *CEO:* Dir. Frank J. Falotico
(908) 757-7171

EMPIRE TECHNICAL SCHOOLS OF NEW JERSEY
576 Central Ave., East Orange 07018-1983 *Type:* Private *Accred.:* 1969/1990 (ACCSCT) *Degrees:* C *CEO:* Dir. Timothy M. Rodgers
(201) 675-0565

ENGINE CITY TECHNICAL INSTITUTE
Rte. 22 W., Box 3116, Union 07083-8517 *Type:* Private *Accred.:* 1984/1989 (ACCSCT) *Degrees:* C *CEO:* Dir. Larry L. Berlin
(201) 964-1450

GENERAL TECHNICAL INSTITUTE WELDING TRADE SCHOOL
1118 Baltimore Ave., Linden 07036-1899 *Type:* Private *Accred.:* 1967/1987 (ACCSCT) *Degrees:* C *CEO:* Pres. Gregory G. Sytch
(201) 486-9353

HARRIS SCHOOL OF BUSINESS
654 Longwood Ave., Cherry Hill 08002 *Type:* Private business *Accred.:* 1978/1994 (ACICS) *Degrees:* C *CEO:* Dir. Alan Harris
(609) 662-5300

HOHOKUS SCHOOL
50 South Franklin Turnpike, Ramsey 07446 *Type:* Private business *Accred.:* 1976/1991

(ACICS) *Degrees:* C *CEO:* Pres. Thomas M. Eastwick
(201) 327-8877

JOE KUBERT SCHOOL OF CARTOON AND GRAPHIC ART
37 Myrtle Ave., Dover 07801-4054 *Type:* Private *Accred.:* 1980/1990 (ACCSCT) *Calendar:* Sem. plan *Degrees:* C *CEO:* Owner Joseph Kubert
(201) 361-1327

KANE BUSINESS INSTITUTE
206 Haddonfield Rd., Cherry Hill 08002 *Type:* Private business *Accred.:* 1985/1994 (ACICS) *Degrees:* C *CEO:* Dir. Frances Granville
(609) 488-1166

LINCOLN TECHNICAL INSTITUTE
Haddonfield Rd. at Rte. 130N, Pennsauken 08110-1208 *Type:* Private *Accred.:* 1967/1988 (ACCSCT) *Degrees:* C *CEO:* Exec. Dir. Deborah M. Ramentol
(609) 665-3010

LINCOLN TECHNICAL INSTITUTE
2299 Vauxhall Rd., Union 07083-5032 *Type:* Private *Accred.:* 1967/1988 (ACCSCT) *Degrees:* C *CEO:* Exec. Dir. Robert P. Gioella
(908) 964-7800

MAHWAH CAMPUS
70 McKee Dr., Mahwah 07430 *Accred.:* 1994 (ACCSCT) *Calendar:* 12-mos. program
(201) 529-1414

METROPOLITAN TECHNICAL INSTITUTE
11 Daniel Rd., Fairfield 07004-2506 *Type:* Private *Accred.:* 1983/1988 (ACCSCT) *Degrees:* C *CEO:* Dir. Frank Gergelyi
(201) 227-8191

NATIONAL EDUCATION CENTER—RETS CAMPUS
103 Park Ave., Nutley 07110-3505 *Type:* Private *Accred.:* 1977/1988 (ACCSCT) *Calendar:* Qtr. plan *Degrees:* C *CEO:* Dir. Martin Klangasky
(201) 661-0600

OMEGA INSTITUTE
7050 Rte. 38 E., Pennsauken 08109 *Type:* Private business *Accred.:* 1982/1996 (ACICS) *Degrees:* C *Prof. Accred.:* Medical Assisting *CEO:* Exec. Dir. Lee Cobleigh
(609) 663-4299

PENNCO TECH
P.O. Box 1427, Blackwood 08012-9961 *Type:* Private *Accred.:* 1980/1993 (ACCSCT) *Degrees:* C *CEO:* Dir. Donald S. Van-Demark, Jr.
(609) 232-0310

THE PLAZA SCHOOL
The Bergen Mall, Paramus 07652-9948 *Type:* Private *Accred.:* 1972/1988 (ACCSCT) *Degrees:* C *CEO:* Pres. Leslie Balter
(201) 843-0344

STAR TECHNICAL INSTITUTE
Deptwood Ctr., 251 N. Delsea Dr., Deptford 08096 *Type:* Private *Accred.:* 1982/1991 (ACCSCT) *Degrees:* C *CEO:* Dir. B. J. Torres
(609) 384-2888

STAR TECHNICAL INSTITUTE
2224 U.S. Hwy., 130 Park Pl., Edgewater Park 08010-3105 *Type:* Private *Accred.:* 1987/1992 (ACCSCT) *Degrees:* C *CEO:* Dir. Barbara Torres
(609) 877-2727

KINGSTON CAMPUS
212 Wyoming Ave., Kingston, PA 18704
(717) 287-9777

SCRANTON CAMPUS
1600 Nay Aug Ave., Greenridge Plaza, Scranton, PA 18509
(717) 963-0144

STAR TECHNICAL INSTITUTE
Somerdale Sq., Ste. 2, Somerdale 08083-1345 *Type:* Private *Accred.:* 1985/1992 (ACCSCT) *Degrees:* C *CEO:* Dir. Marcie Evans
(609) 435-7827

LAKEWOOD CAMPUS
1255 Rte. 70, Ste. 12N, Lakewood 08701-5947
(908) 901-0001

STAR TECHNICAL INSTITUTE
1386 S. Delsea Dr., Vineland 08360-6210 *Type:* Private *Accred.:* 1985/1992 (ACCSCT) *Degrees:* C *CEO:* Dir. Niles Commisso
(609) 696-0500

TOWNSHIP CAMPUS
2105 Hwy. 35, Ocean Township 07712-7201
(908) 493-1660

STUART SCHOOL OF BUSINESS ADMINISTRATION
2400 Belmar Blvd., Wall 07719 *Type:* Private business *Accred.:* 1967/1991 (ACICS) *Calendar:* Sem. plan *Degrees:* C *CEO:* Dir. Letitia M. Cooper
(908) 681-7200

TECHNICAL INSTITUTE OF CAMDEN COUNTY
343 Berlin-Cross Keys Rd., Sicklerville 08081-9709 *Type:* Private *Degrees:* C *Prof. Accred.:* Dental Assisting, Medical Assisting (AMA) *CEO:* Supt. R. Sanders Haldeman
(609) 767-7000

TETERBORO SCHOOL OF AERONAUTICS
80 Moonachie Ave., Teterboro Airport, Teterboro 07608-1083 *Type:* Private *Accred.:* 1973/1993 (ACCSCT) *Degrees:* C *CEO:* Dir. Edward Chudzik
(201) 288-6300

TITAN HELICOPTER ACADEMY
Bldg. 90, Easterwood St., Millville 08332-4810 *Type:* Private *Accred.:* 1992 (ACCSCT) *Degrees:* C *CEO:* Pres. Peter Amico
(609) 327-5203

NEW MEXICO

ALBUQUERQUE BARBER COLLEGE
525 San Pedro Dr., N.E., Ste. 104, Albuquerque 87108-1847 *Type:* Private *Accred.:* 1987 (ACCSCT) *Degrees:* C *CEO:* Owner Gene J. Varoz
(505) 266-4900

ALBUQUERQUE JOB CORPS CENTER
1500 Indian School Rd. NW, Albuquerque 87104 *Type:* Public *Accred.:* 1986/1995 (NCA) *Degrees:* C *CEO:* Dir. Barbara Calderon
Enroll: 410   (505) 842-6500

INTERNATIONAL BUSINESS COLLEGE
650 E. Montana Ave., Ste. F, Las Cruces 88001 *Type:* Private business *Accred.:* 1981/1987 (ACICS) *Degrees:* C *CEO:* Pres. Larry Madrid
(505) 526-5579

METROPOLITAN COLLEGE OF COURT REPORTING
2201 San Pedro St., N.E., Bldg. 1, No. 1300, Albuquerque 87110 *Type:* Private *Accred.:* 1993 (ACCSCT) *Degrees:* C *CEO:* Dir. Bob Evans
(505) 888-3400

THE ROSWELL JOB CORPS CENTER
P.O. Box 5970, Roswell 88202 *Type:* Public *Accred.:* 1985/1995 (NCA) *Degrees:* C *CEO:* Dir. Greg Redmon
Enroll: 224   (505) 347-5414

WESTERN BUSINESS INSTITUTE
3200 N. White Sands Blvd., Alamogordo 88310 *Type:* Private business *Accred.:* 1982/1987 (ACICS) *Degrees:* C *CEO:* Dir. Linda Wallace
(505) 437-1854

NEW YORK

ACADEMY FOR CAREER EDUCATION
55-05 Myrtle Ave., Ridgewood 11385 *Type:*
Private business *Accred.:* 1990/1994 (ACICS)
Degrees: C *CEO:* Pres. Chana Schachner
(718) 497-4900

THE ALVIN AILEY AMERICAN DANCE CENTER
211 W. 61st St., 3rd Fl., New York 10023
Type: Private *Degrees:* C *Prof. Accred.:*
Dance *CEO:* Dance Exec. Denise Jefferson
(212) 767-0940

AMERICAN BALLET CENTER/JOFFREY BALLEY
SCHOOL
434 Ave. of the Americas, New York 10011
Type: Private *Degrees:* C *Prof. Accred.:*
Dance *CEO:* Exec. Dir. Edith D'Addario
(212) 254-8520

THE AMERICAN MUSICAL AND DRAMATIC
ACADEMY
2109 Broadway, New York 10023 *Type:* Private *Degrees:* C *Prof. Accred.:* Theatre
CEO: Exec. Dir. Jan Martin
(212) 787-5300

APEX TECHNICAL SCHOOL
635 Ave. of the Americas, New York 10011
Type: Private *Accred.:* 1968/1989 (ACC-
SCT) *Degrees:* C *CEO:* Pres. Bill Cann
(212) 645-3300

ASA INSTITUTE OF BUSINESS AND COMPUTER
TECHNOLOGY
151 Lawrence St., 2nd Fl., Brooklyn 11201
Type: Private business *Accred.:* 1991 (AC-
ICS) *Degrees:* C *CEO:* Dir. Alex Schegol
(718) 522-9073

BERK TRADE AND BUSINESS SCHOOL
312 W. 36th St., New York 10018 *Type:* Private *Accred.:* 1973/1988 (ACCSCT) *Degrees:* C *CEO:* Dir. Irving Berk
(212) 629-3736

BLAKE BUSINESS SCHOOL
P.O. Box 1052, 20 Cooper Sq., New York
10276 *Type:* Private business *Accred.:* 1974/

1986 (ACICS) *Degrees:* C *CEO:* Pres. Barbara
Marion
(212) 254-1233

BRANCH CAMPUS
145 A Fourth Ave, New York 10003
(212) 995-1711

BUSINESS INFORMATICS CENTER
134 S. Central Ave., Valley Stream 11580-
5431 *Type:* Private *Accred.:* 1988/1991 (AC-
CSCT) *Degrees:* C *CEO:* Dir. Joseph Brown
(516) 561-0050

CASHIER TRAINING INSTITUTE
500 Eighth Ave., New York 10018-6504
Type: Private *Accred.:* 1985 (ACCSCT) *Degrees:* C *CEO:* Pres. Harry Lokos
(212) 564-0500

CHARLES STUART SCHOOL OF DIAMOND
SETTING
1420 Kings Hwy., Brooklyn 11229 *Type:*
Private *Accred.:* 1993 (ACCSCT) *Degrees:*
C *CEO:* Dir. Charles Wechsler
(718) 339-2640

CHAUFFEURS TRAINING SCHOOL
12 Railroad Ave., Albany 12205-5727 *Type:*
Private *Accred.:* 1980/1990 (ACCSCT) *Degrees:* C *CEO:* Dir. Albert V. Hanley
(518) 482-8601

CHERYL FELL'S SCHOOL OF BUSINESS
2541 Military Rd., Niagara Falls 14304
Type: Private business *Accred.:* 1981/1996
(ACICS) *Degrees:* C *CEO:* Dir. Cheryl Anne
Fell

(716) 297-2750

CIRCLE IN THE SQUARE THEATRE SCHOOL
1633 Broadway, New York 10019 *Type:* Private *Degrees:* C *Prof. Accred.:* Theatre
CEO: Exec. Dir. E. Colin O'Leary
(212) 307-3732

COMMERCIAL DRIVER TRAINING
600 Patton Ave., West Babylon 11704-1421 *Type:* Private *Accred.:* 1984/1989 (ACC-SCT) *Degrees:* C *CEO:* Pres. John B. Rayne
(516) 249-1330

COMPUTER CAREER CENTER
474 Fulton Ave., Hempstead 11550 *Type:* Private *Accred.:* 1993/1995 (ACICS) *Degrees:* C *CEO:* Pres. Kenneth G. Barrett
(516) 486-2526

CONTINENTAL DENTAL ASSISTANT SCHOOL
633 Jefferson Rd., Rochester 14623 *Type:* Private *Accred.:* 1983/1990 (ABHES) *Degrees:* C *CEO:* Pres. Arthur J. Resso
(716) 272-8060

COPE INSTITUTE
84 Williams St., 4th Flr., New York 10038 *Type:* Private business *Accred.:* 1981/1996 (ACICS) *Calendar:* Qtr. plan *Degrees:* C *CEO:* Dir. Yerachmiel Barash
(718) 809-5935

DANCE THEATRE OF HARLEM, INC.
466 W. 152nd St., New York 10031 *Type:* Private *Degrees:* C *Prof. Accred.:* Dance *CEO:* Dir. Walter R. Raines
(212) 690-2800

DRAKE BUSINESS SCHOOL
2122 White Plains Rd, Bronx 10462 *Type:* Private business *Accred.:* 1974/1986 (ACICS) *Degrees:* C *CEO:* Dir. Thomas Hull
(718) 822-8080

DRAKE BUSINESS SCHOOL
36-09 Main St., 6th Fl., Flushing 11354 *Type:* Private business *Accred.:* 1974/1986 (ACICS) *Degrees:* C *CEO:* Dir. Muriel Adler
(718) 353-3535

DRAKE BUSINESS SCHOOL
225 Broadway, New York 10007 *Type:* Private business *Accred.:* 1974/1986 (ACICS) *Degrees:* C *CEO:* Dir. Phyllis Haimson
(212) 349-7900

DRAKE BUSINESS SCHOOL
25 Victory Blvd., Staten Island 10301 *Type:* Private business *Accred.:* 1974/1986 (ACICS) *Degrees:* C *CEO:* Dir. Richard De Crescenzo
(718) 447-1515

ELMIRA BUSINESS INSTITUTE
180 Clemens Center Pkwy., Elmira 14901 *Type:* Private business *Accred.:* 1969/1986 (ACICS) *Calendar:* Sem. plan *Degrees:* C *CEO:* Pres. Brad C. Phillips
(607) 733-7177

FEGS TRADES AND BUSINESS SCHOOL
17 Battery Pl., Ste. 6 N., New York 10004 *Type:* Private *Accred.:* 1986 (ACCSCT) *Degrees:* C *CEO:* Vice Pres. Virginia Cruickshank
(212) 440-8130

BROOKLYN CAMPUS
199 Jay St., Brooklyn 11201
(718) 448-0120

FOLK ART INSTITUTE OF THE MUSEUM OF AMERICAN FOLK ART
61 W. 62nd St., New York 10023-7015 *Type:* Private *Calendar:* 24-mos. program *Degrees:* C *Prof. Accred.:* Art (A) *CEO:* Dir. Barbara Kaufman-Cate
(212) 977-7170

FRENCH CULINARY INSTITUTE
462 Broadway, New York 10013 *Type:* Private *Accred.:* 1985/1990 (ACCSCT) *Degrees:* C *CEO:* Pres. Dorothy Cann Hamilton
(212) 219-8890

GLOBAL BUSINESS INSTITUTE
1931 Mott Ave., Far Rockaway 11691 *Type:* Private business *Accred.:* 1984/1988 (ACICS) *Degrees:* C *CEO:* Dir. Sandy Basso
(718) 327-2220

NEW YORK CAMPUS
209 W. 125th St., New York 10027
(212) 663-1500

GLOBE INSTITUTE OF TECHNOLOGY
291 Broadway, 4th Fl, New York 10007 *Type:* Private business *Accred.:* 1987/1991 (ACICS) *Degrees:* C *CEO:* Dir. Leon Rabinovch
(212) 349-4330

BRANCH CAMPUS
Five Beekman St, Ste 501, New York 10038)
(212) 349-9768

HUNTER BUSINESS SCHOOL
3601 Hempstead Tpke., Levittown 11756 *Type:* Private business *Accred.:* 1982/1986 (ACICS) *Degrees:* C *CEO:* Pres. Florence Kruman
(516) 796-1000

INSTITUTE OF ALLIED MEDICAL PROFESSIONS
106 Central Park S., No. 23D, New York 10019 *Type:* Private *Degrees:* C *Prof. Accred.:* Nuclear Medicine Technology *CEO:* Pres. Eugene Vinciguerra
(212) 757-0520

INSTITUTE OF AUDIO RESEARCH
64 University Pl., New York 10003-4595 *Type:* Private *Accred.:* 1985/1990 (ACCSCT) *Degrees:* C *CEO:* Dir. Miriam Friedman
(212) 677-7580

ISABELLA G. HART SCHOOL OF PRACTICAL NURSING
1425 Portland Ave., Rochester 14621 *Type:* Private professional *Degrees:* C *Prof. Accred.:* Practical Nursing *CEO:* Dir. Judith Sawyer
(716) 338-4784

ISLAND DRAFTING AND TECHNICAL INSTITUTE
128 Broadway, Amityville 11701-2789 *Type:* Private *Accred.:* 1967/1987 (ACCSCT) *Degrees:* C *CEO:* Pres. Joseph P. DiLiberto
(516) 691-8733

KRISSLER BUSINESS INSTITUTE
166 Mansion Sq. Park, Poughkeepsie 12601 *Type:* Private business *Accred.:* 1975/1996 (ACICS) *Degrees:* C *CEO:* Dir. Jean Theobald
(914) 471-0330

LABAN/BARTENIEFF INSTITUTE OF MOVEMENT STUDIES, INC.
11 E. 4th St., New York 10003-6902 *Type:* Private *Degrees:* C *Prof. Accred.:* Dance *CEO:* Exec. Dir. Amy Schwartzman
(212) 477-4299

LEWIS A. WILSON TECHNICAL CENTER
17 Westminster Ave., Dix Hills 11746 *Type:* Private *Degrees:* C *Prof. Accred.:* Practical Nursing *CEO:* Coord. Margaret A. Shields
(516) 667-6000

LONG ISLAND BUSINESS INSTITUTE
6500 Jericho Turnpike., Commack 11725 *Type:* Private business *Accred.:* 1978/1996 (ACICS) *Calendar:* Qtr. plan *Degrees:* C *CEO:* Dir. Genevieve Baron
(516) 499-7100

MANDL SCHOOL
254 W. 54th St., New York 10019-5516 *Type:* Private *Accred.:* 1987/1993 (ABHES); 1967/1987 (ACCSCT) *Degrees:* C *CEO:* Pres. Melvyn P. Weiner
(212) 247-3434

MARION S. WHELAN SCHOOL OF PRACTICAL NURSING
196-198 North St., Geneva 14456 *Type:* Private professional *Degrees:* C *Prof. Accred.:* Practical Nursing *CEO:* Dir. Ann McGuane
(315) 789-4222

MARTHA GRAHAM SCHOOL OF CONTEMPORARY DANCE, INC.
316 E. 63rd St., New York 10021 *Type:* Private *Degrees:* C *Prof. Accred.:* Dance *CEO:* Dir. Diane Gray
(212) 838-5886

MERCE CUNNINGHAM STUDIO
55 Bethune St., New York 10014 *Type:* Private *Degrees:* C *Prof. Accred.:* Dance *CEO:* Artistic Dir. Merce Cunningham
(212) 255-3130

MILDRED ELLEY BUSINESS SCHOOL
2 Computer Dr. S., Albany 12205 *Type:* Private business *Accred.:* 1982/1988 (ACICS)

Calendar: Sem. plan *Degrees:* C *CEO:* Pres. Faith Ann Takes

(518) 446-0595

PITTSFIELD CAMPUS
400 Columbus Ave., Pittsfield, MA 01201
(413) 499-8618

MODERN WELDING SCHOOL
1740 Broadway, Schenectady 12306-4998 *Type:* Private *Accred.:* 1984/1989 (ACC-SCT) *Degrees:* C *CEO:* Dir. Dana J. Gillenwalters

(518) 374-1216

MUNSON-WILLIAMS-PROCTOR INSTITUTE
310 Genesee St., Utica 13502 *Type:* Private *Calendar:* 24-mos. program *Degrees:* C *Prof. Accred.:* Art *CEO:* Dir. Clyde E. McCulley

(315) 797-8260

NATIONAL SHAKESPEARE CONSERVATORY
591 Broadway, New York 10012 *Type:* Private *Degrees:* C *Prof. Accred.:* Theatre *CEO:* Dir. Albert Schoemann

(212) 219-9874

NATIONAL TAX TRAINING SCHOOL
4 Melnick Dr., P.O. Box 382, Monsey 10952 *Type:* Private distance education *Accred.:* 1965/1996 (DETC) *Degrees:* C *CEO:* Dir. Ben D. Eisenberg

(914) 352-3634

NATIONAL TRACTOR TRAILER SCHOOL
P.O. Box 208, Liverpool 13088-0208 *Type:* Private *Accred.:* 1984/1989 (ACCSCT) *Degrees:* C *CEO:* Pres. Harry Kowalchyk, Jr.

(315) 451-2430

BUFFALO CAMPUS
175 Katherine St., Buffalo 14210-2007
(716) 849-6887

NEIGHBORHOOD PLAYHOUSE SCHOOL OF THEATRE
340 E. 54th St., New York 10022-5017 *Type:* Private *Degrees:* C *Prof. Accred.:* Theatre *CEO:* Dir. Harold G. Baldridge
Enroll: 87   (212) 688-3770

NEW SCHOOL OF CONTEMPORARY RADIO
50 Colvin Ave., Albany 12206-1106 *Type:* Private *Accred.:* 1981/1993 (ACCSCT) *Degrees:* C *CEO:* Dir. Thomas Brownlie, III
(518) 438-7682

NEW YORK FOOD AND HOTEL MANAGEMENT SCHOOL
154 W. 14th St., New York 10011-7307 *Type:* Private *Accred.:* 1973/1989 (ACC-SCT) *Calendar:* Sem. plan *Degrees:* C *CEO:* Dir. Joseph S. Monaco
(212) 675-6655

NEW YORK INSTITUTE OF BUSINESS TECHNOLOGY
401 Park Ave. S., 2nd Fl., New York 10016 *Type:* Private business *Accred.:* 1974/1991 (ACICS) *Degrees:* C *CEO:* Dir. Leith E. Yetman
(212) 725-9400

NEW YORK PARALEGAL SCHOOL
299 Broadway, Ste. 200, New York 10007 *Type:* Private business *Accred.:* 1994 (ACICS) *Degrees:* C *CEO:* Dir. William P. Jenkins
Enroll: 400   (212) 349-8800

NEW YORK RESTAURANT SCHOOL
75 Varwick St., 16th Fl., New York 10013 *Type:* Private *Accred.:* 1994 (ACCSCT) *Degrees:* C *CEO:* Pres. James Devaney
(212) 226-5500

NEW YORK SCHOOL FOR MEDICAL/DENTAL ASSISTANTS
116-16 Queens Blvd., Forest Hills 11375-2330 *Type:* Private *Accred.:* 1973/1988 (ACCSCT) *Degrees:* C *CEO:* Pres. Clinton Arnaboldi
(718) 793-2330

NEW YORK SCHOOL OF DOG GROOMING
248 E. 34th St., New York 10016-4873 *Type:* Private *Accred.:* 1973/1989 (ACCSCT) *Degrees:* C *CEO:* Dir. Sam Kohl
(212) 685-3776

NEW HYDE PARK CAMPUS
265-17 Union Tpke., New Hyde Park 11040-1425
(718) 343-3130

NIKOLAIS AND LOUIS DANCE LAB
375 W. Broadway, 5th Fl., New York 10012 *Type:* Private *Degrees:* C *Prof. Accred.:* Dance *CEO:* Dir. Lynn Lesniak Needle
(212) 226-7000

PROFESSIONAL BUSINESS INSTITUTE
125 Canal St., New York 10002 *Type:* Private business *Accred.:* 1985/1994 (ACICS) *Degrees:* C *CEO:* Dir. Elayne S. Zinbarg
(212) 226-7300

RIDLEY-LOWELL BUSINESS AND TECHNICAL INSTITUTE
116 Front St., Binghamton 13905 *Type:* Private business *Accred.:* 1977/1987 (ACICS) *Degrees:* C *CEO:* Dir. Carol Zindle
(607) 724-2941

ROYAL BARBER AND BEAUTY SCHOOL
108-112 Broadway, Schenectady 12305-2592 *Type:* Private *Accred.:* 1987 (ACCSCT) *Degrees:* C *CEO:* Dir. Sondra Kaczmarek
(518) 346-2288

ST. FRANCIS SCHOOL OF PRACTICAL NURSING
2221 W. State St., Olean 14760 *Type:* Private professional *Degrees:* C *Prof. Accred.:* Practical Nursing *CEO:* Dir. Redempta Grawunder
(716) 375-7316

THE SONIA MOORE STUDIO OF THE THEATRE
485 Park Ave., No. 6A, New York 10022 *Type:* Private *Degrees:* C *Prof. Accred.:* Theatre (A) *CEO:* Pres. Sonia Moore
(212) 755-5120

SOTHEBY'S EDUCATIONAL STUDIES
1334 York Ave., New York 10021 *Type:* Private *Degrees:* C *Prof. Accred.:* Art *CEO:* Vice Pres. Elisabeth D. Garrett
(212) 606-7822

SPANISH-AMERICAN INSTITUTE
215 W. 43rd St., New York 10036-3913 *Type:* Private business *Accred.:* 1986/1995 (ACICS) *Degrees:* C *CEO:* Exec. Dir. Dante V. Ferraro
(212) 840-7111

SPENCER BUSINESS AND TECHNICAL INSTITUTE
200 State St., Schenectady 12305 *Type:* Private business *Accred.:* 1981/1987 (ACICS) *Degrees:* C *CEO:* Dir. David G. Sampson
(518) 374-7619

STELLA ADLER CONSERVATORY OF ACTING
419 Lafayette St., 6th Fl., New York 10003 *Type:* Private *Calendar:* Sem. plan *Degrees:* C *Prof. Accred.:* Theatre *CEO:* Exec. Dir. Hossein Fassa
(212) 260-0525

STENOTOPIA, THE WORLD OF COURT REPORTING
45 S. Service Rd., Plainview 11803 *Type:* Private business *Accred.:* 1990/1996 (ACICS) *Degrees:* C *CEO:* Pres. Randy Scheff Gordon
(516) 777-1117

SUBURBAN TECHNICAL SCHOOL
175 Fulton Ave., Hempstead 11550-3771 *Type:* Private *Accred.:* 1972/1987 (ACCSCT) *Degrees:* C *CEO:* Pres. Randy S. Proto
(516) 481-6660

EAST ISLIP CAMPUS
2650 Sunrise Hwy., East Islip 11730-1017
(516) 224-5001

SUPERIOR CAREER INSTITUTE
116 W. 14th St., New York 10011-7395 *Type:* Private *Accred.:* 1983/1988 (ACCSCT) *Degrees:* C *CEO:* Dir. Carolyn Moffett
(212) 675-2140

THE SWEDISH INSTITUTE
226 W. 26th St., 5th Fl., New York 10001-6700 *Type:* Private *Accred.:* 1981/1986 (ACCSCT) *Calendar:* Sem. plan *Degrees:* C *CEO:* Pres. Patricia J. Eckardt
(212) 924-5900

SYRIT COMPUTER SCHOOL SYSTEMS
1760 53rd St., Brooklyn 11204-9004 *Type:* Private *Accred.:* 1981/1986 (ACCSCT) *Degrees:* C *CEO:* Dir. Elliot Amsel
(718) 853-1212

TECHNO-DENT TRAINING CENTER
101 W. 31st St., 4th Fl., New York 10001-3507 *Type:* Private *Accred.:* 1983/1988

(ACCSCT) *Calendar:* Tri. plan *Degrees:* C
CEO: Pres. George A. Nossa
(212) 695-1818

TRAVEL INSTITUTE
15 Park Row, No. 617, New York 10038-
2301 *Type:* Private *Accred.:* 1990 (ACC-
SCT) *Degrees:* C *CEO:* Owner/Dir. Robert
Berger
(212) 349-3331

TRI-STATE INSTITUTE OF TRADITIONAL CHINESE
ACUPUNCTURE
80 8th Avenue, 4th Floor, New York 10011
Type: Private professional *Calendar:* Sem.
plan *Degrees:* C *Prof. Accred.:* Acupuncture
CEO: Pres. Mark Seem
FTE Enroll: 95 (212) 242-2255

ULTRASOUND DIAGNOSTIC SCHOOL
121 W. 27th St., Ste. 504, New York 10001
Type: Private *Accred.:* 1984/1990 (ABHES)
Degrees: C *CEO:* Exec. Dir. William Spier
(212) 645-9116

ATLANTA CAMPUS
One Corporate Square Blvd, Ste. 216,
Atlanta, GA 30329
(404) 248-9070

BELLAIRE CAMPUS
6575 W. Loop S., Ste. 200, Bellaire, TX
77401
(713) 664-9632

CARLE PLACE CAMPUS
One Old Country Rd., Carle Place 11514
(516) 248-6060

ELMSFORD CAMPUS
2269 Saw Mill River Rd., Elmsford 10523
(914) 347-6817

INDEPENDENCE CAMPUS
4700 Rockside Rd., Summit One, No.
610, Independence, OH 44131
(216) 573-5833

IRVING CAMPUS
580 Decker Dr., Ste 211, Irving, TX 75062
(214) 791-1120

ISELIN CAMPUS
Plaza One at Gill Ln., Ste. 6B, 675 Rte. 1,
Iselin, NJ 08830
(908) 634-1131

JACKSONVILLE CAMPUS
10199 Southside Blvd., Ste. 106, Jacksonville, FL 32256
(904) 363-6221

MARLBOROUGH CAMPUS
33 Boston Post Rd. W., Ste. 140, Marlborough, MA 01752
(508) 485-1213

PITTSBURGH CAMPUS
5830 Ellsworth Ave., Ste 102, Pittsburgh,
PA 15232
(412) 362-9404

POMPANO CAMPUS
2760 E. Atlantic Blvd., Pompano Beach,
FL 33062
(305) 942-6551

SILVER SPRING CAMPUS
1320 Fenwick Ln., Silver Spring, MD
20910
(301) 588-0786

TAMPA CAMPUS
9950 Princess Palm Pkwy., Registry II,
Ste. 234, Tampa, FL 33619
(813) 621-0072

TREVOSE CAMPUS
3 Neshaminy Interplex, Ste. 117, Trevose,
PA 19053
(215) 244-4906

UNIVERSAL BUSINESS AND MEDIA SCHOOL
220 E. 106th St., New York 10029 *Type:* Private business *Accred.:* 1991 (ACICS) *Degrees:* C *CEO:* Pres. Georgina Falu
(212) 360-1210

WESTCHESTER CONSERVATORY OF MUSIC
20 Soundview Ave., White Plains 10606
Type: Private *Degrees:* C *Prof. Accred.:*
Music *CEO:* Exec. Dir. Laura Calzolari
(914) 761-3715

NORTH CAROLINA

ACADEMY OF ARTISTIC HAIR DESIGN
314 Tenth St., North Wilkesboro 28659
Type: Private *Accred.:* 1987/1992 (COE)
Degrees: C *CEO:* Dir. Sabrina Franklin
FTE Enroll: 56   (919) 838-4571

ALLIANCE TRACTOR TRAILER TRAINING CENTER
P.O. Box 883, Arden 28704-0883 *Type:*
Private *Accred.:* 1986 (ACCSCT) *Degrees:*
C *CEO:* Vice Pres. Brenda Rice
           (704) 684-4454

AMERICAN BUSINESS AND FASHION INSTITUTE
1515 Mockingbird Ln., Ste. 600, Charlotte
28209-3236 *Type:* Private business *Accred.:*
1978/1987 (ACICS) *Degrees:* C *CEO:* Pres.
Elizabeth M. Guinan
           (704) 523-3738

AMERICAN EDUCATION INSTITUTE OF
COSMETOLOGY
415 Seventh Ave., S.W., Hickory 29601
Type: Private *Accred.:* 1990 (COE warning)
Degrees: C *CEO:* Dir. C. Roger Harris
FTE Enroll: 79   (704) 327-2887

ARNOLD'S BEAUTY COLLEGE
3117 Shannon Rd., Durham 27707 *Type:*
Private *Accred.:* 1989/1991 (COE) *Degrees:*
C *CEO:* Dir. Arnold Braun
FTE Enroll: 217   (919) 493-9557

BLACK WORLD COLLEGE OF HAIR DESIGN
P.O. Box 669403, Charlotte 28266-9403
Type: Private *Accred.:* 1985 (ACCSCT)
Degrees: C *CEO:* Vice Pres. Luther Gore
           (704) 372-8172

BROOKSTONE COLLEGE OF BUSINESS
8307 University. Executive Park Dr., Ste.
240, Charlotte 28262 *Type:* Private business
Accred.: 1984/1996 (ACICS); 1993 (COE)
Calendar: Qtr. plan *Degrees:* C *CEO:* Dir.
Jack Henderson, III
FTE Enroll: 486   (704) 547-8600

GREENSBORO CAMPUS
7815 National Service Rd., Greensboro
27409
           (919) 668-2627

BURKE ACADEMY OF COSMETIC ART
304 W. Union St., Morganton 28655 *Type:*
Private *Degrees:* C *CEO:* Dir. Emily Lowe
FTE Enroll: 60   (704) 437-1028

NEWTON CAMPUS
609 W. 29th St., Newton 28658
           (704) 465-7281

CAROLINA BEAUTY COLLEGE
801 English Rd., High Point 27262 *Type:*
Private *Accred.:* 1984/1995 (COE) *Degrees:*
C *CEO:* Pres. Marion Fields
FTE Enroll: 925   (910) 886-4712

CHARLOTTE CAMPUS
5430-0 N. Tryon St., Charlotte 28213
           (704) 597-5641

DURHAM CAMPUS
5106 N. Roxboro Rd., Durham 22704
           (919) 477-4014

GREENSBORO CAMPUS
2001 E. Wendover Ave., Greensboro
27405
           (910) 272-2966

MONROE CAMPUS
1201 Stafford St., Ste. 12, Monroe 28110
           (704) 283-2514

SALISBURY CAMPUS
19012 S. Main St., Salisbury 28144
           (704) 639-0382

WINSTON-SALEM CAMPUS
7736-C Northpoint Blvd., Winston-Salem
27127
           (910) 759-7969

FAYETTEVILLE BEAUTY COLLEGE
2018 Ft. Bragg Rd., Fayetteville 28303
Type: Private *Accred.:* 1989/1993 (COE)
Degrees: C *CEO:* Dir. Bonnie Henry
FTE Enroll: 206   (910) 484-9370

HAIRSTYLING INSTITUTE OF CHARLOTTE
209-B S. Kings Dr., Charlotte 28204-2621
Type: Private *Accred.:* 1983/1988 (ACC-

SCT) *Degrees:* C *CEO:* Owner. Costas Melissaris

(704) 334-5511

KING'S COLLEGE
322 Lamar Ave., Charlotte 28204 *Type:* Private business *Accred.:* 1954/1986 (AC-ICS) *Calendar:* Qtr. plan *Degrees:* C *Prof. Accred.:* Medical Assisting (AMA) *CEO:* Pres. Gary L. Pritchett

(704) 372-0266

LYNDON B. JOHNSON CIVILIAN CONSERVATION CENTER
466 Job Corps Dr., Franklin 28734 *Type:* Public (state) *Accred.:* 1991 (COE) *Degrees:* C *CEO:* Dir. Edward Washington
FTE Enroll: 211   (704) 369-7338

MARIA PARHAM HOSPITAL, INC.
Ruin Creek Rd. at I-85, P.O. Drawer 59, Henderson 27536 *Type:* Private *Degrees:* C *Prof. Accred.:* Medical Laboratory Technology *CEO:* Admin. Winn Clayton

(919) 438-4143

MR. DAVID'S SCHOOL OF HAIR DESIGN
4348 Market St., Wilmington 28403 *Type:* Private *Accred.:* 1989/1992 (COE) *Degrees:* C *CEO:* Dir. David Atkinson
FTE Enroll: 191   (910) 763-4418

NORTH CAROLINA ACADEMY OF COSMETIC ART
131 Sixth Ave. E., Hendersonville 28792 *Type:* Private *Accred.:* 1994 (COE) *Degrees:* C *CEO:* Dir. Paula Jennings
FTE Enroll: 51   (910) 692-5211

NORTHERN HOSPITAL OF SURRY COUNTY SCHOOL OF MEDICAL TECHNOLOGY
P.O. Box 1101, 830 Rockford St., Mount Airy 27030 *Type:* Private *Degrees:* C *Prof. Accred.:* Medical Laboratory Technology *CEO:* Tech. Dir. David A. McCullough

(910) 719-7124

OCONALUFTEE JOB CORPS CIVILIAN CONSERVATION CENTER
200 Park Cir., Cherokee 28719-9702 *Type:* Public (federal) *Accred.:* 1984/1994 (COE) *Degrees:* C *CEO:* Dir. Gary Trickles
FTE Enroll: 280   (704) 497-5411

SALISBURY BUSINESS COLLEGE
1400 Jake Alexander Blvd. W., Salisbury 28147-9912 *Type:* Private business *Accred.:* 1975/1986 (ACICS) *Calendar:* Qtr. plan *Degrees:* C *CEO:* Pres. Bill Hensley

(704) 636-4071

SCHENCK CIVILIAN CONSERVATION CENTER
98 Schenck Dr., Pisgah Forest 28768 *Type:* Public (federal) *Accred.:* 1985/1990 (COE) *Degrees:* C *CEO:* Dir. Roger Mullins
FTE Enroll: 237   (704) 877-3291

SKYLAND ACADEMY
170 Rosscraggon Rd., Skyland 28776 *Type:* Private *Accred.:* 1988/1994 (COE) *Degrees:* C *CEO:* Dir. Luci Ratliff
FTE Enroll: 63   (704) 687-1643

WINSTON-SALEM BARBER SCHOOL
1531 Silas Creek Pkwy., Winston-Salem 27127-3757 *Type:* Private *Accred.:* 1990 (AC-CSCT) *Degrees:* C *CEO:* Pres. Joseph Long

(910) 724-1459

NORTH DAKOTA

MEYER VOCATIONAL TECHNICAL SCHOOL
P.O. Box 2126, Minot 58702-2126 *Type:*
Private *Accred.:* 1989 (ACCSCT) *Degrees:*
C *CEO:* Dir. Scott Meyer
(701) 852-0427

MINOT SCHOOL FOR ALLIED HEALTH
110 Burdick Expressway W., Minot 58701
Type: Private *Degrees:* C *Prof. Accred.:*
Radiography *CEO:* Acting Pres. Terry Hoff
(701) 857-5620

MOLER BARBER COLLEGE OF HAIRSTYLING
16 S. Eighth St., Fargo 58103 *Type:* Private
Accred.: 1992 (ACCSCT) *Degrees:* C *CEO:*
Pres. Joel K. Cannon
(701) 232-6773

TRAVEL CAREER INSTITUTE
218 N. 4th St., Bismarck 58504-9967 *Type:*
Private *Accred.:* 1988 (ACCSCT) *Degrees:*
C *CEO:* Dir. Pam Wentz-Baccus
(701) 258-9419

OHIO

ACADEMY OF HAIR DESIGN
1440 Whipple Ave., Canton 44708 *Type:* Private *Accred.:* 1987/1991 (ACCSCT) *Degrees:* C *CEO:* Dir. Franklin D. Ferren
(216) 477-6695

AKRON BARBER COLLEGE
3200 S. Arlington Rd., Ste. 2, Akron 44312-5269 *Type:* Private *Accred.:* 1986 (ACCSCT) *Degrees:* C *CEO:* Dir. Mary Jane Sabotin
(216) 644-9114

AKRON MACHINING INSTITUTE INC.
2959 Barber Rd., Barberton 44203-1005 *Type:* Private *Accred.:* 1986 (ACCSCT) *Degrees:* C *CEO:* Dir. Joan Cook
(216) 745-1111

CLEVELAND MACHINING INSTITUTE
2500 Brookpark Rd., Cleveland 44134-1407
(216) 741-1100

AKRON MEDICAL-DENTAL INSTITUTE
733 W. Market St., Akron 44303-1078 *Type:* Private *Accred.:* 1977/1987 (ACCSCT) *Calendar:* Qtr. plan *Degrees:* C *Prof. Accred.:* Medical Assisting (AMA) *CEO:* Dir. Elizabeth Husk
(216) 762-9788

AKRON SCHOOL OF PRACTICAL NURSING
619 Sumner St., Akron 44311 *Type:* Private professional *Degrees:* C *Prof. Accred.:* Practical Nursing *CEO:* Dir. Dottie Stiles
(216) 376-4129

ALLSTATE HAIRSTYLING AND BARBER COLLEGE
2546 Lorain Ave., Cleveland 44113-3413 *Type:* Private *Accred.:* 1985/1990 (ACCSCT) *Degrees:* C *CEO:* Dir. Phil D'Amico
(216) 241-6684

AMERICAN SCHOOL OF NAIL TECHNIQUES AND COSMETOLOGY
924 E. Tallmadge Ave., Akron 44310 *Type:* Private *Accred.:* 1992 (ACCSCT) *Degrees:* C *CEO:* Dir. Nancy L. Kolson
(216) 633-9427

AMERICAN SCHOOL OF TECHNOLOGY
2100 Morse Rd., Bldg. 4599, Columbus 43229-6665 *Type:* Private *Accred.:* 1985/1991 (ACCSCT) *Degrees:* C *CEO:* Dir. Susan R. Stella
(614) 436-4820

CENTRAL SCHOOL OF PRACTICAL NURSING
3300 Chester Ave., Cleveland 44114 *Type:* Private professional *Degrees:* C *Prof. Accred.:* Practical Nursing *CEO:* Dir. Pat Turk
(216) 391-8434

CHOFFIN CAREER CENTER
200 E. Wood St., Youngtown 44503 *Type:* Private *Degrees:* C *Prof. Accred.:* Dental Assisting, Practical Nursing, Surgical Technology *CEO:* Princ. Raymond Brown
(216) 744-8700

CLEVELAND INSTITUTE OF DENTAL-MEDICAL ASSISTANTS, INC.
1836 Euclid Ave., Rm. 401, Cleveland 44115-2285 *Type:* Private *Accred.:* 1982/1995 (ABHES); 1979/1989 (ACCSCT) *Degrees:* C *Prof. Accred.:* Medical Assisting *CEO:* Pres. Beverly A. Davis
(216) 241-2930

LYNDHURST CAMPUS
5564 Mayfield Rd., Lyndhurst 44124-2928
(216) 473-6273

MENTOR CAMPUS
5733 Hopkins Rd., Mentor 44060-2035
(216) 946-9530

COLUMBUS PARA-PROFESSIONAL INSTITUTE
1077 Lexington Ave., Columbus 43201 *Type:* Private *Accred.:* 1985/1990 (ACCSCT) *Calendar:* Qtr. plan *Degrees:* C *CEO:* Dir. Sandra Moomaw
(614) 299-0200

CONNECTICUT SCHOOL OF BROADCASTING
4790 Red Bank Expressway, No. 102, Cincinnati 45227-1509 *Type:* Private *Ac-*

cred.: 1992 (ACCSCT) *Degrees:* C *CEO:* Pres. Robert Mills

(216) 271-6060

CONNECTICUT SCHOOL OF BROADCASTING
6701 Rockside Rd., Ste. 204, Independence 44131-2316 *Type:* Private *Accred.:* 1991 (ACCSCT) *Degrees:* C *CEO:* Pres. Robert Mills

(216) 447-9117

FAIRFIELD CAREER CENTER
4000 Columbus-Lancaster Rd., Carroll 43112 *Type:* Public *Accred.:* 1988 (NCA) *Calendar:* Qtr. plan *Degrees:* C *Prof. Accred.:* Medical Assisting (AMA) *CEO:* Supt. Claude Graves

(614) 837-9443

HAMRICK TRUCK DRIVING SCHOOL
1156 Medina Rd., Medina 44256-9615 *Type:* Private *Accred.:* 1987/1993 (ACCSCT) *Degrees:* C *CEO:* Pres. Denver Hamrick

(216) 239-2229

HANNAH E. MULLINS SCHOOL OF PRACTICAL NURSING
2094 E. State St., Salem 44460 *Type:* Private professional *Degrees:* C *Prof. Accred.:* Practical Nursing *CEO:* Coord. Donna J. Lynn

(216) 332-8940

HOBART INSTITUTE OF WELDING TECHNOLOGY
Trade Sq. E., Troy 45373-9989 *Type:* Private *Accred.:* 1972/1991 (ACCSCT) *Degrees:* C *CEO:* Registrar Ruth E. Ogletree

(513) 332-5214

HOSPITALITY TRAINING CENTER
220 N. Main St., Hudson 44236 *Type:* Private distance education *Accred.:* 1986/1996 (DETC) *Degrees:* C *CEO:* Pres. Duane R. Hills

(216) 653-9151

INSTITUTE OF MEDICAL AND DENTAL TECHNOLOGY
375 Glensprings Dr., Ste. 201, Cincinnati 45246 *Type:* Private *Accred.:* 1983/1995 (ABHES) *Degrees:* C *CEO:* Pres. Vincent J. Sofia

(513) 851-8500

BRANCH CAMPUS
4452 Eastgate Blvd., Ste. 209, Cincinnati 45244

(513) 753-5030

INTERNATIONAL COLLEGE OF BROADCASTING
6 S. Smithville Rd., Dayton 45431-1833 *Type:* Private *Accred.:* 1976/1986 (ACCSCT) *Degrees:* C *CEO:* Pres. Michael LeMaster

(513) 258-8251

KNOX COUNTY CAREER CENTER
306 Martinsburg Rd., Mount Vernon 43050 *Type:* Private *Degrees:* C *Prof. Accred.:* Medical Assisting (AMA) *CEO:* Supt. Ray Richardson

(614) 397-5820

MARYMOUNT SCHOOL OF PRACTICAL NURSING
12300 McCracken Rd., Garfield Heights 44125 *Type:* Private professional *Degrees:* C *Prof. Accred.:* Practical Nursing *CEO:* Dir. Louise Evans

(216) 587-8160

MEDINA COUNTY CAREER CENTER
1101 W. Liberty St., Medina 44256-9969 *Type:* Private *Degrees:* C *Prof. Accred.:* Medical Assisting (AMA) *CEO:* Supt. Thomas Horwedel

(216) 953-7118

NATIONAL EDUCATION CENTER—NATIONAL INSTITUTE OF TECHNOLOGY CAMPUS
1225 Orlen Ave., Cuyahoga Falls 44221-2955 *Type:* Private *Accred.:* 1969/1990 (ACCSCT) *Calendar:* Qtr. plan *Degrees:* C *CEO:* Dir. Donald Miller

(216) 923-9959

NHRAW HOME STUDY INSTITUTE
1389 Dublin Rd., P.O. Box 16790, Columbus 43216 *Type:* Private distance education *Accred.:* 1969/1995 (DETC) *Degrees:* C *CEO:* Dir. James H. Healy

(614) 488-1835

OHIO AUTO-DIESEL TECHNICAL INSTITUTE
1421 E. 49th St., Cleveland 44103-1269
Type: Private *Accred.:* 1973/1988 (ACCSCT)
Degrees: C *CEO:* Pres. Marc L. Brenner
(216) 881-1700

OHIO COLLEGE OF MASSOTHERAPY
1018 Kenmore Blvd., Akron 44314 *Type:*
Private *Accred.:* 1994 (ACCSCT) *Degrees:*
C *CEO:* Pres. Ann Morrow
(216) 745-6170

OHIO STATE COLLEGE OF BARBER STYLING
4614 E. Broad St., Columbus 43223 *Type:*
Private *Accred.:* 1977/19989 (ACCSCT)
Degrees: C *CEO:* Dir. Robert D. Glenn
(614) 868-1015

OHIO STATE COLLEGE OF BARBER STYLING
329 Superior St., Toledo 43604-1421 *Type:*
Private *Accred.:* 1983/1988 (ACCSCT)
Degrees: C *CEO:* Pres. Roger Bradley
(419) 241-5618

CAREER TRAINING INSTITUTES
101 W. Main St., Leesburg, FL 34748-5173
(904) 326-5134

CAREER TRAINING INSTITUTE
2120 W. Colonial Dr., Orlando, FL 32804-
6948
(407) 843-3984

PROFESSIONAL SKILLS INSTITUTE
20 Arco Dr, Toledo 43607 *Type:* Private
Accred.: 1986/1992 (ABHES) *Degrees:* C
Prof. Accred.: Physical Therapy Assisting
CEO: Dir. Thomas Howard
(419) 531-9610

SANTA BARBARA CAMPUS
4213 State St., Ste. 302, Santa Barbara,
CA 93110
(805) 683-1902

RAEDEL COLLEGE AND INDUSTRIAL WELDING
SCHOOL
137 Sixth St., N.E., Canton 44702 *Type:* Private business *Accred.:* 1986 (ACICS) *Degrees:* C *CEO:* Dir. Fred G. Holloway
(216) 454-9006

SCHOOL OF ADVERTISING ART
2900 Acosta St., Kettering 45420-3467
Type: Private *Accred.:* 1988 (ACCSCT) *Degrees:* C *CEO:* Mgr. Terry Wilson
(513) 294-0592

TDDS
1688 N. Princetown Rd., Diamond 44412-
9608 *Type:* Private *Accred.:* 1987 (ACC-
SCT) *Degrees:* C *CEO:* Pres. Richard
Rathburn
(216) 538-2216

TECHNOLOGY EDUCATION COLLEGE
288 S. Hamilton Rd., Columbus 43213-2087
Type: Private *Accred.:* 1980/1991 (ACC-
SCT) *Degrees:* C *CEO:* Dir. Thomas D.
Greenhouse
(614) 759-7700

TOTAL TECHNICAL INSTITUTE
6500 Pearl Rd., Parma Heights 44130 *Type:*
Private *Accred.:* 1984/1990 (ACCSCT) *Degrees:* C *CEO:* Dir. David Mondi
(216) 843-2323

OKLAHOMA

ADVANCE BARBER COLLEGE
5301 S. Penn, Oklahoma City *Type:* Private *Accred.:* 1994 (ACCSCT) *Degrees:* C *CEO:* Owner Johni Warren
Enroll: 12   (405) 685-0172

CENTRAL OKLAHOMA AREA VOCATIONAL-
TECHNICAL CENTER
3 CVT Cir., Drumright 74030 *Type:* Private *Degrees:* C *Prof. Accred.:* Practical Nursing *CEO:* Supt. John Hopper
                                          (918) 352-2551

CLIMATE CONTROL INSTITUTE
708 S. Sheridan Rd., Tulsa 74112-3140 *Type:* Private *Accred.:* 1978/1988 (ACCSCT) *Calendar:* Qtr. plan *Degrees:* C *CEO:* Pres. Sue Kloehr
                                          (918) 836-6656

FRANCIS TUTTLE VOCATIONAL-TECHNICAL
CENTER
12777 N. Rockwell Ave., Oklahoma City 73142 *Type:* Private *Degrees:* C *Prof. Accred.:* Practical Nursing, Respiratory Therapy Technology *CEO:* Supt. Bruce Gray
                                          (405) 722-7799

GREAT PLAINS AREA VOCATIONAL-TECHNICAL
CENTER
4500 W. Lee Blvd., Lawton 73505 *Type:* Private *Degrees:* C *Prof. Accred.:* Practical Nursing, Radiography, Respiratory Therapy Technology, Surgical Technology *CEO:* Supt. Kenneth Bridges
                                          (405) 355-6371

HOLLYWOOD COSMETOLOGY CENTER
P.O. Box 890488, Oklahoma City 73189 *Type:* Private *Accred.:* 1991 (ACCSCT) *Degrees:* C *CEO:* Dir. Crystal Burgess
                                          (405) 364-3375

MERIDIAN TECHNOLOGY CENTER
1312 S. Sangre St., Stillwater 74074 *Type:* Private *Degrees:* C *Prof. Accred.:* Radiography *CEO:* Supt. Fred A. Shultz
                                          (405) 377-3333

METROPOLITAN COLLEGE OF COURT REPORTING
2525 Northwest Expressway, No. 215, Oklahoma City 73112 *Type:* Private *Accred.:* 1992 (ACCSCT) *Degrees:* C *CEO:* Pres. David L. Stephenson
                                          (405) 840-2181

METROPOLITAN COLLEGE OF LEGAL STUDIES
2865 E. Skelly Dr., Tulsa 74105 *Type:* Private *Accred.:* 1991 (ACCSCT) *Degrees:* C *CEO:* Pres. David L. Stephenson
                                          (918) 745-9946

MID-DEL COLLEGE
3420 S. Sunny Ln., Del City 73115-3535 *Type:* Private *Accred.:* 1981/1986 (ACCSCT) *Degrees:* C *CEO:* Dir. Sidney Carey
                                          (405) 677-8311

MISS SHIRLEY'S BEAUTY COLLEGE
309 S.W. 59th St., Ste. 305, Oklahoma City 73109 *Type:* Private *Accred.:* 1991 (ACCSCT) *Degrees:* C *CEO:* Owner Glynn Mize
                                          (405) 631-0055

OKLAHOMA FARRIER'S COLLEGE
Rte. 2, Box 88, Sperry 74073-9446 *Type:* Private *Accred.:* 1980/1993 (ACCSCT) *Degrees:* C *CEO:* Pres. Bud Beaston
                                          (918) 288-7221

OKLAHOMA STATE HORSESHOEING SCHOOL
Rte. 1, Box 28-B, Ardmore 73401-9707 *Type:* Private *Accred.:* 1990 (ACCSCT) *Degrees:* C *CEO:* Owner Reggie Kester
                                          (405) 223-0064

O.T. AUTRY AREA VOCATIONAL-TECHNICAL
CENTER
1201 W. Willow St., Enid 73703 *Type:* Private *Degrees:* C *Prof. Accred.:* Radiography, Surgical Technology *CEO:* Supt. James Strate
                                          (405) 242-2750

PLATT COLLEGE
4821 S. 72nd E. Ave., Tulsa 74145-6502 *Type:* Private *Accred.:* 1985/1990 (ACCSCT) *Degrees:* C *CEO:* Pres. George Gillard
                                          (918) 663-9000

OKLAHOMA CITY CAMPUS
3737 N. Portland Ave., Oklahoma City
73112
(405) 942-8683

STATE BARBER AND HAIR DESIGN COLLEGE INC.
2514 S. Agnew Ave., Oklahoma City 73108-
6220 *Type:* Private *Accred.:* 1987 (ACC-
SCT) *Degrees:* C *CEO:* Owner Bobby
Lewis
(405) 631-8621

TULSA TECHNOLOGY CENTER
3420 S. Memorial Dr., Tulsa 74145-1390
Type: Private *Degrees:* C *Prof. Accred.:* Practical Nursing, Radiography, Surgical Technology *CEO:* Supt. Gene Callahan
(918) 627-7200

TULSA WELDING SCHOOL
3038 Southwest Blvd., Tulsa 74107-3818
Type: Private *Accred.:* 1970/1990 (ACC-
SCT) *Degrees:* C *CEO:* Pres. Roger Hess
(918) 587-6789

UNITED STATES COAST GUARD INSTITUTE
5900 S.W. 64th St., Rm. 235, Oklahoma City
73169-6990 *Type:* Public (federal) distance
education *Accred.:* 1981/1996 (DETC) *Degrees:* C *CEO:* Cmnd. Ofcr. William B. Baker
(405) 680-4262

OREGON

AIRMAN PROFICIENCY CENTER
3565 N.E. Cornell Rd., Hillsboro 97124
Type: Private *Accred.:* 1992 (ACCSCT)
Degrees: C *CEO:* Dir. Gail Young
(503) 648-2831

APOLLO COLLEGE OF MEDICAL-DENTAL
CAREERS
2600 S.E. 98th St., Portland 97266-1302
Type: Private *Accred.:* 1985/1990 (ABHES)
Degrees: C *CEO:* Pres. Margaret M. Carlson
(503) 761-6100

BROADCAST PROFESSIONALS COMPLETE SCHOOL
OF RADIO BROADCASTING
11507-D S.W. Pacific Hwy., Portland 97223-
8628 *Type:* Private *Accred.:* 1989 (ACC-
SCT) *Degrees:* C *CEO:* Exec. Dir. Keith
Allen Glutsch
(503) 244-5113

COLLEGE OF LEGAL ARTS
527 S.W. Hall St., Ste. 308, Portland 97201
Type: Private business *Accred.:* 1978/1996
(ACICS) *Degrees:* C *CEO:* Pres./Dir. Billy
P. Ellis
(503) 223-5100

COLLEGEAMERICA
921 S.W. Washington St., Ste. 200, Portland
97205-2820 *Type:* Private *Accred.:* 1982/
1987 (ACCSCT) *Degrees:* C *Prof. Accred.:*
Dental Assisting, Medical Assisting (AMA)
CEO: Dir. Floyd W. King
(503) 242-9000

COMMERCIAL TRAINING SERVICES
2416 N. Marine Dr., Portland 97217-7741
Type: Private *Accred.:* 1973/1990 (ACC-
SCT) *Degrees:* C *CEO:* Pres. Clifford
Georgioff
(503) 285-7542

CONCORDE CAREER INSTITUTE
1827 N.E. 44th Ave., Portland 97213 *Type:*
Private *Accred.:* 1969/1991 (ACCSCT)
Degrees: C *CEO:* Dir. Larry W. Cartmill
(503) 281-4181

DIESEL TRUCK DRIVER TRAINING SCHOOL
90801 Hwy. 99 N., Eugene 97402-9624
Type: Private *Accred.:* 1991 (ACCSCT)
Degrees: C *CEO:* Dir. John Klabacka
(800) 888-7075

MOLER BARBER COLLEGE
517 S.W. Fourth St., Portland 97204-2118
Type: Private *Accred.:* 1987 (ACCSCT)
Degrees: C *CEO:* Pres. Gordon Scarbrough
(503) 223-9818

OREGON SCHOOL OF ARTS AND CRAFTS
8245 S.W. Barnes Rd., Portland 97225 *Type:*
Private professional *Degrees:* C *Prof.
Accred.:* Art (A) *CEO:* Pres. Paul C.
Magnusson
Enroll: 65   (503) 297-5544

PARAMEDIC TRAINING INSTITUTE
P.O. Box 1878, Beaverton 97075 *Type:*
Private *Degrees:* C *Prof. Accred.:* EMT-
Paramedic *CEO:* Dir. Louise A. Evans
(503) 297-5592

PIONEER PACIFIC COLLEGE
25195 S.W. Parkway Ave., Wilsonville
97070 *Type:* Private business *Accred.:* 1995
(ACICS) *Degrees:* C *CEO:* Pres. Raymond
C. Gauthier
Enroll: 200   (503) 682-3903

TARA LARA ACADEMY OF K-9 HAIR DESIGN
16307 S.E. McLoughlin Blvd., Portland
97267-5134 *Type:* Private *Accred.:* 1988/
1991 (ACCSCT) *Degrees:* C *CEO:* Dir.
Arlene F. Steinle
(503) 653-7134

WEST COAST TRAINING
11919 N. Jensen Ave., Ste. 292, Portland
97217 *Type:* Private *Accred.:* 1986 (ACC-
SCT) *Degrees:* C *CEO:* Dir. William Myer
(503) 289-8661

MILWAUKIE CAMPUS
2525 S.E. Stubb St., Milwaukie 97222-
7323
(503) 659-5181

WESTERN CULINARY INSTITUTE
1316 S.W. 13th Ave., Portland 97201-3355 *Type:* Private *Accred.:* 1990 (ACCSCT) *Degrees:* C *CEO:* Dir. Nick Fluge
(503) 223-2245

WESTERN TRUCK SCHOOL
10510 S.W. Industrial Way, Bldg. 1, Bay 1, Tualatin 97062-0826 *Type:* Private *Accred.:* 1988/1993 (ACCSCT) *Degrees:* C *CEO:* Dir. Art Hadduck
(503) 691-0113

PENNSYLVANIA

ACADEMY OF MEDICAL ARTS AND BUSINESS
279 Boas St., Harrisburg 17102-2944 *Type:*
Private *Accred.:* 1983/1988 (ACCSCT) *Degrees:* C *Prof. Accred.:* Medical Assisting
CEO: Pres. Gary Kay
(717) 233-2172

ALL-STATE CAREER SCHOOL
501 Seminole St., Lester 19029-1825 *Type:*
Private *Accred.:* 1987 (ACCSCT) *Degrees:*
C *CEO:* Pres. Joseph W. Marino
(215) 521-1818

BALTIMORE CAMPUS
201 S. Arlington Ave., Baltimore, MD
21223
(410) 566-7111

ALLEGHENY BUSINESS INSTITUTE
239 Fourth Ave., Ste. 617 Investment Bldg.,
Pittsburgh 15222 *Type:* Private business
Accred.: 1990/1995 (ACICS) *Degrees:* C
CEO: Pres. James Rudolph
(412) 456-7100

ALLIED MEDICAL CAREERS
104 Woodward Hill Rd., Edwardsville
18704 *Type:* Private *Degrees:* C *Prof. Accred.:* Medical Assisting *CEO:* Pres. Damon
A. Young
(717) 288-8400

SCRANTON CAMPUS
2901 Pittston Ave., Scranton 18505 *Prof.
Accred.:* Medical Assisting
(717) 342-8000

ANTONELLI MEDICAL AND PROFESSIONAL
INSTITUTE
1700 Industrial Hwy., Pottstown 19464-
9250 *Type:* Private *Accred.:* 1989/1993
(ACCSCT) *Degrees:* C *CEO:* Dir. G.
Michael Orthaus
(215) 323-7270

AUTOMOTIVE TRAINING CENTER
114 Pickering Way, Exton 19341-1310 *Type:*
Private *Accred.:* 1973/1993 (ACCSCT) *Degrees:* C *CEO:* Dir. Steven C. Hiscox
(215) 363-6716

BARBER STYLING INSTITUTE
3433 Simpson Ferry Rd., Camp Hill 17011-
6485 *Type:* Private *Accred.:* 1983/1988 (ACCSCT) *Degrees:* C *CEO:* Dir. Gregory
Mekulski
(717) 763-4787

BERKS TECHNICAL INSTITUTE
832 N. Park Rd., 4 Park Plaza, Wyomissing
19610-1341 *Type:* Private *Accred.:* 1984/
1993 (ACCSCT) *Degrees:* C *Prof. Accred.:*
Medical Assisting (AMA) *CEO:* Pres.
Kenneth S. Snyder
(215) 372-1722

BETA TRAINING SERVICES
225 S. Chester Rd., Ste. 5, Swarthmore
19081 *Type:* Private *Accred.:* 1994 (ACCSCT) *Degrees:* C *CEO:* Pres. Barbara Ekdahl
Enroll: 187   (61) 543-5000

BIDWELL TRAINING CENTER
1815 Metropolitan St., Pittsburgh 15233
Type: Private *Accred.:* 1993 (ACCSCT) *Degrees:* C *CEO:* Exec. Dir. William E.
Strickland
(412) 323-4000

THE CAREER INSTITUTE
1825 John F. Kennedy Blvd., Philadelphia
19103 *Type:* Private business *Accred.:* 1984/
1988 (ACICS) *Calendar:* Qtr. plan *Degrees:*
C *CEO:* Exec. Dir. Eve M. Corey
(215) 561-7600

WILMINGTON CAMPUS
711 Market St. Mall, Wilmington, DE
19801
(302) 575-1400

CAREER TRAINING ACADEMY
703 Fifth Ave., New Kensington 15068-6301
Type: Private *Accred.:* 1987/1992 (ACCSCT) *Degrees:* C *Prof. Accred.:* Medical
Assisting (AMA) *CEO:* CEO John M. Reddy
(412) 337-1000

MONROEVILLE CAMPUS
244 Center Rd., Monroeville 15146
(412) 372-3900

COMPUTER LEARNING CENTER
3600 Market St., Philadelphia 19104-2684
Type: Private business *Accred.:* 1981/1991
(ACICS) *Degrees:* C *CEO:* Dir. Richard
Dormuth
(215) 222-6450

COMPUTER LEARNING NETWORK
1110 Fernwood Ave., Camp Hill 17011-6996
Type: Private *Accred.:* 1985/1990 (ACC-
SCT) *Degrees:* C *CEO:* Pres. Kenneth E.
Whittington
(717) 761-1481

ALTOONA CAMPUS
2900 Fairway Dr., Altoona 16602-4457
(814) 944-5643

DELAWARE COUNTY INSTITUTE OF TRAINING
615 Ave. of the States, Chester 19013-6022
Type: Private *Accred.:* 1984/1989 (ACC-
SCT) *Degrees:* C *CEO:* Dir. Howard K.
Kauff
(215) 874-1888

DELAWARE VALLEY ACADEMY OF MEDICAL AND
DENTAL ASSISTANTS
3330 Grant Ave., Philadelphia 19114 *Type:*
Private *Accred.:* 1986/1992 (ABHES)
Degrees: C *CEO:* Dir. David M. Goldsmith
(215) 676-1200

FRANKLIN ACADEMY
324 N. Centre St., Pottsville 17901 *Type:*
Private *Accred.:* 1992 (ACCSCT) *Degrees:*
C *CEO:* Pres. Franklin K. Schoeneman
(717) 622-8370

GARFIELD BUSINESS INSTITUTE
709 Third Ave., New Brighton 15066 *Type:*
Private business *Accred.:* 1988/1991 (AC-
ICS) *Degrees:* C *CEO:* Dir. Richard Miller
(412) 728-4050

GATEWAY TECHNICAL INSTITUTE
100 Seventh St., Pittsburgh 15222-3404
Type: Private *Accred.:* 1969/1993 (ACC-
SCT) *Calendar:* Tri. plan *Degrees:* C *CEO:*
Dir. Wayne D. Smith
(412) 281-4111

GLEIM TECHNICAL INSTITUTE
200 S. Spring Garden St., Carlisle 17013
Type: Private *Accred.:* 1992 (ACCSCT)
Degrees: C *CEO:* Dir. Karen L. Gleim
(800) 922-8399

GREATER JOHNSTOWN AREA VOCATIONAL-
TECHNICAL SCHOOL
445 Schoolhouse Rd., Johnstown 15904-
2998 *Type:* Private *Degrees:* C *Prof. Accred.:* Respiratory Therapy Technology
CEO: Admin. Dir. Barry Dallara
(814) 266-6073

JAMES MARTIN ADULT HEALTH OCCUPATIONS
Alvin A. Swenson Skills Ctr., 2600 Red Lion
Rd., Philadelphia 19114-1020 *Type:* Public
(city) *Degrees:* C *Prof. Accred.:* Respiratory
Therapy Technology *CEO:* Supervisor
Corrine Kurzen
(215) 961-2131

J.H. THOMPSON ACADEMIES
2908 State St., Erie 16508-1832 *Type:*
Private *Accred.:* 1979/1989 (ACCSCT) *Degrees:* C *CEO:* Dir. Jack Thompson
(814) 456-6217

JNA MARKETING
1212 S. Broad St., Philadelphia 19146 *Type:*
Private *Accred.:* 1994 (ACCSCT) *Degrees:*
C *CEO:* Pres. Joseph DiGironimo
(215) 468-8838

JOSEPH DONAHUE INTERNATIONAL SCHOOL OF
HAIRSTYLING
2485 Grant Ave., Philadelphia 19114-1004
Type: Private *Accred.:* 1984/1989 (ACC-
SCT) *Degrees:* C *CEO:* Owner Nancy L.
Johnson
(215) 969-1313

LEARNING AND EVALUATION CENTER
420 West 5th St., P.O. Box 616, Bloomsburg
17815 *Type:* Private distance education
Accred.: 1985/1995 (DETC) *Degrees:* C
CEO: Pres. Gerald E. Burns
(717) 784-5220

LIFETIME CAREER SCHOOLS
101 Harrison St., Archbald 18403 *Type:*
Private distance education *Accred.:* 1957/

1995 (DETC) *Degrees:* C *CEO:* Pres. Michael J. Zadarosni

(717) 876-6340

LINCOLN TECHNICAL INSTITUTE
9191 Torresdale Ave., Philadelphia 19136 *Type:* Private *Accred.:* 1969/1993 (ACC-SCT) *Degrees:* C *CEO:* Dir. Douglas M. Johnson

(215) 335-0800

NAVAL DAMAGE CONTROL TRAINING CENTER
Naval Base, Philadelphia 19112-5089 *Type:* Public (federal) *Accred.:* 1985/1990 (COE) *Degrees:* C *CEO:* Cmnd. Ofcr. W.A. Smart *FTE Enroll:* 178   (215) 897-5677

NEW ENGLAND TRACTOR TRAILER TRAINING SCHOOL
3715 E. Thompson St., Philadelphia 19137-1483 *Type:* Private *Accred.:* 1987/1991 (AC-CSCT) *Degrees:* C *CEO:* Dir. Diane M. Pelli

(215) 288-7800

NORTH HILLS SCHOOL OF HEALTH OCCUPATIONS
1500 Northway Mall, Pittsburgh 15237-3013 *Type:* Private *Accred.:* 1987/1993 (AB-HES) *Degrees:* C *CEO:* Exec. Dir. R. Gary Drent

(412) 367-8003

OAKBRIDGE ACADEMY OF ARTS
401 Ninth St., New Kensington 15068-6470 *Type:* Private *Accred.:* 1980/1990 (ACC-SCT) *Degrees:* C *CEO:* Dir. William H. Breyak

(412) 335-5336

ORLEANS TECHNICAL INSTITUTE
1330 Rhawn St., Philadelphia 19111-2899 *Type:* Private *Accred.:* 1981/1986 (ACC-SCT) *Degrees:* C *CEO:* Dir. Jayne Siniari

(215) 728-4700

THE COURT REPORTING INSTITUTE
1845 Walnut St., Ste. 700, Philadelphia 19103-4707

(215) 854-1823

PENNSYLVANIA GUNSMITH SCHOOL
812 Ohio River Blvd., Pittsburgh 15202-2699 *Type:* Private *Accred.:* 1985 (ACC-SCT) *Degrees:* C *CEO:* Dir. George Thacker

(412) 766-1812

PENNSYLVANIA INSTITUTE OF CULINARY ARTS
717 Liberty Ave., Pittsburgh 15222-3500 *Type:* Private *Accred.:* 1990 (ACCSCT) *Degrees:* C *CEO:* Pres. Nicholas Hoban

(412) 566-2433

PENNSYLVANIA INSTITUTE OF TAXIDERMY
Rural Rte. 3, Box 188, Ebensburg 15931-8947 *Type:* Private *Accred.:* 1988/1991 (AC-CSCT) *Degrees:* C *CEO:* Pres. Dan A. Bantley

(814) 472-4510

PENNSYLVANIA SCHOOL OF ART AND DESIGN
204 N. Prince St., Lancaster 17603 *Type:* Private professional *Degrees:* C *Prof. Accred.:* Art *CEO:* Pres. Mary C. Heil

(717) 396-7833

PHILADELPHIA WIRELESS TECHNICAL INSTITUTE
1533 Pine St., Philadelphia 19102-4693 *Type:* Private *Accred.:* 1985/1990 (ACC-SCT) *Degrees:* C *CEO:* Dir. Peter Honczar

(215) 546-0745

THE PJA SCHOOL
7900 W. Chester Pike, Upper Darby 19082-1926 *Type:* Private *Accred.:* 1985/1990 (ACCSCT) *Degrees:* C *CEO:* Dir. David M. Hudiak

(610) 789-6700

QUAKER CITY INSTITUTE OF AVIATION
2565 Grays Ferry Ave., Philadelphia 19146 *Type:* Private *Accred.:* 1994 (ACCSCT) *Degrees:* C *CEO:* Pres. Robert Levitt

(215) 545-7518

RALPH AMODEI INTERNATIONAL INSTITUTE OF HAIR DESIGN AND TECHNOLOGY
4451 Frankford Ave., Philadelphia 19124-3636 *Type:* Private *Accred.:* 1986 (ACC-SCT) *Degrees:* C *CEO:* Pres. Ralph Amodei

(215) 289-4433

ROSEDALE TECHNICAL INSTITUTE
4634 Browns Hill Rd., Pittsburgh 15217-2919 *Type:* Private *Accred.:* 1974/1989 (ACCSCT) *Calendar:* Qtr. plan *Degrees:* C *CEO:* Exec. Vice Pres. David N. McCormick
(412) 521-6200

SETTLEMENT MUSIC SCHOOL
416 Queen St., Philadelphia 19147 *Type:* Private professional *Degrees:* C *Prof. Accred.:* Music *CEO:* Exec. Dir. Robert Capanna
(215) 336-0400

THE SHIRLEY ROCK SCHOOL OF THE PENNSYLVANIA BALLET
1101 S. Broad St., Philadelphia 19147 *Type:* Private *Degrees:* C *Prof. Accred.:* Dance (A) *CEO:* Dir. Bojan Spassoff
(215) 551-7000

STAR TECHNICAL INSTITUTE
2101 Union Blvd., Allentown 18103 *Type:* Private *Accred.:* 1994 (ACCSCT) *Degrees:* C *CEO:* Pres. Harry Commisso
(610) 434-9663

STAR TECHNICAL INSTITUTE
9149 Roosevelt Blvd., Philadelphia 19114 *Type:* Private *Accred.:* 1994 (ACCSCT) *Degrees:* C *CEO:* Pres. Harry Commisso
(610) 969-5877

STAR TECHNICAL INSTITUTE
Greenridge Plaza, Nay Aug Ave., Scranton 18509 *Type:* Private *Accred.:* 1994 (ACCSCT) *Degrees:* C *CEO:* Pres. Harry Commisso
(717) 963-0144

STAR TECHNICAL INSTITUTE
1570 Garrett Rd., Upper Darby 19082 *Type:* Private *Accred.:* 1994 (ACCSCT) *Degrees:* C *CEO:* Pres. Harry Commisso
(610) 626-2700

STAR TECHNICAL INSTITUTE
34 S. Main St.,Ste. 22, Wilkes Barre 18701 *Type:* Private *Accred.:* 1994 (ACCSCT) *Degrees:* C *CEO:* Pres. Harry Commisso
(717) 829-6960

SWANSON'S DRIVING SCHOOLS INC.
9915 Frankstown Rd., Pittsburgh 15235-1646 *Type:* Private *Accred.:* 1992 (ACCSCT) *Degrees:* C *CEO:* Vice Pres. Gene Swanson
(412) 241-6963

TRI-CITY BARBER SCHOOL
128 E. Main St., Norristown 19401-4917 *Type:* Private *Accred.:* 1987 (ACCSCT) *Degrees:* C *CEO:* Dir. Peggy Porche
(215) 279-4432

TRI-CITY BARBER SCHOOL
5901 N. Broad St., Philadelphia 19141-1801 *Type:* Private *Accred.:* 1986 (ACCSCT) *Degrees:* C *CEO:* Exec. Dir. Marc S. Jacobs
(215) 927-3232

WELDER TRAINING AND TESTING INSTITUTE
100 Pennsylvania Ave., Selinsgrove 17870-9339 *Type:* Private *Accred.:* 1981/1990 (ACCSCT) *Degrees:* C *CEO:* Exec. Dir. Ted S. Zenzinger
(800) 326-9306

WESTERN SCHOOL OF HEALTH AND BUSINESS CAREERS
327 5th Ave., 2nd Fl., Pittsburgh 15222 *Type:* Private *Accred.:* 1986 (ACCSCT) *Degrees:* C *Prof. Accred.:* Histologic Technology, Medical Assisting, Radiography, Respiratory Therapy *CEO:* Pres. Ross M. Perilman
(412) 281-2600

MONROEVILLE CAMPUS
One Monroeville Ctr., Rte. 22 and 3824 Northern Pike, Monroeville 15146-2142 *Prof. Accred.:* Medical Assisting
(412) 373-6400

YORK TECHNICAL INSTITUTE
3351 Whiteford Rd., York 17402-9017 *Type:* Private *Accred.:* 1979/1989 (ACCSCT) *Degrees:* C *CEO:* Dir. Harold L. Maley
(717) 757-1100

PUERTO RICO

ABBYNELL BEAUTY AND TECHNICAL INSTITUTE
Box 7216, Caguas 00626-7216 *Type:* Private
Accred.: 1989 (ACCSCT) *Degrees:* C *CEO:*
Pres. Magdalena Reyes Ortiz
(809) 743-3339

ACADEMIA SINGER DEALER AUTORIZADO INC.
101 Comercio St., Ponce 00731 *Type:* Private *Accred.:* 1990 (ACCSCT) *Degrees:* C
CEO: Owner Anabel Santiago Rivera
(809) 848-4949

AMERICAN EDUCATIONAL COLLEGE
P.O. Box 62, Carretera No. 2, KM 11 HM 8,
Edificio Federal, Bayamon 00960 *Type:* Private business *Accred.:* 1985/1991 (ACICS)
Degrees: C *CEO:* Pres. Joaquin E. Gonzalez
Pinto
(809) 798-1199

ANTILLES SCHOOL OF TECHNICAL CAREERS
Calle Domenech No. 107, Hato Rey 00917
Type: Private *Accred.:* 1985/1992 (ABHES)
Degrees: C *Prof. Accred.:* Practical Nursing
CEO: Dir. Carmaen Ramirez
(809) 764-7576

ARROYO TECHNICAL SCHOOL
Calle Morse No. 75, Arroyo 00714 *Type:*
Private *Accred.:* 1994 (ACCSCT) *CEO:*
Pres. Paulino Mariani
(809) 839-3518

CENTRO DE ESTUDIOS MULTIDISCIPLINARIOS
602 Barbosa Ave., 2nd Fl., Hato Rey 00917-
4387 *Type:* Private *Accred.:* 1981/1986 (AC-
CSCT) *Degrees:* C *Prof. Accred.:* Practical
Nursing *CEO:* Dir. Juan F. Pagani
(809) 765-4210

HUMACAO CAMPUS
6 Dr. Vidal St., Humacao 00791
(809) 852-5530

COLEGIO MAYOR DE TECNOLOGIA
Calle Morse No. 151, Arroyo 00714 *Type:*
Private *Accred.:* 1988 (ACCSCT) *Degrees:*
C *CEO:* Pres. Mancio Vicente
(809) 839-5266

COLEGIO TECNICO DE ELECTRICIDAD
1251 Franklin D. Roosevelt Ave., Puerto
Nuevo 00920 *Type:* Private *Accred.:* 1992
(ACCSCT) *Degrees:* C *CEO:* Vice Pres.
Jorge A. Melecio Rivera
(809) 782-5126

COLEGIO TECNOLOGICO Y COMERCIAL DE
PUERTO RICO
Calle Paz 165 Altos, Aguada 00602 *Type:*
Private business *Accred.:* 1990/1996 (AC-
ICS) *Degrees:* C *CEO:* Dir. Roberto Davila
Martinez
(809) 868-2688

D'MART INSTITUTE
Jose de Diego No. 150 Altos, Box 2337,
Cayey 00737-2337 *Type:* Private *Accred.:*
1991 (ACCSCT) *Degrees:* C *CEO:* Owner
Marta L. Rivera Luna
(809) 738-5474

ESCUELA DE PERITOS ELECTRICISTAS DE ISABEL
P.O. Box 457, Ave. Aguadilla No. 242, Isabel
00662 *Type:* Private *Accred.:* 1993 (ACC-
SCT) *Degrees:* C *CEO:* Dir. Maria M. Santiago Maldonado
(809) 872-1747

FASHION DESIGN COLLEGE
Calle Degetau No. 5, Esq. Betances, Bayamon 00961-6208 *Type:* Private *Accred.:*
1988 (ACCSCT) *Degrees:* C *CEO:* Pres.
Arturo Auiles
(809) 785-2388

RIO PEDRAS CAMPUS
210 Arzuage St., Rio Piedras 00925
(809) 765-0001

FASHION MERCHANDISING AND TECHNICAL
INSTITUTE
P.O. Box 2206, Bayamon 00621 *Type:* Private *Accred.:* 1986 (ACCSCT) *Degrees:* C
CEO: Pres. Ralph James
(809) 798-8870

INSTITUTO CHAVIANO DE MAYAGUEZ
Calle Ramos Antonini, No. 116 Este,
Mayaguez 00608-5045 *Type:* Private *Ac-*

cred.: 1987 (ACCSCT) *Degrees:* C *CEO:* Vice Pres. Blanca Llantin

(809) 833-2474

INSTITUTO DE BANCA Y COMERCIO
996 Munoz Rivera Ave., Rio Piedras 00925 *Type:* Private business *Accred.:* 1978/1995 (ACICS) *Degrees:* C *CEO:* Dir. Rafael Jimenez

(809) 765-8687

CAYEY CAMPUS
Box 37-2710, 164 Jose de Diego, Cayey 00634

(809) 738-5555

FAJARDO CAMPUS
250 (Altos) Munoz Rivera, Fajardo 00738

(809) 860-6262

GUAYAMA CAMPUS
Box 6092, RR-1, Guayama 00784-9601

(809) 864-3220

MANATI CAMPUS
56 Carrera No 2, Manati 00674

(809) 854-6709

MAYAGUEZ CAMPUS
Calle Post No. 154 N., Mayaguez 00708

(809) 833-4647

PONCE CAMPUS
Box 7623, Ponce 00732

(809) 840-6119

INSTITUTO DE COSMETOLOGIA Y ESTETICA "LA REINE"
Ave. Colon No. 8A, Manati 00674 *Type:* Private *Accred.:* 1991 (ACCSCT) *Degrees:* C *CEO:* Owner Carmen Ocasio

(809) 854-1119

INSTITUTO DE EDUCACION UNIVERSAL
P.O. Box 1027, Sabana Seca 00947-1027 *Type:* Private *Accred.:* 1984/1989 (ACCSCT) *Degrees:* C *CEO:* Pres. Juan Jimenez

(809) 798-5000

CAGUAS CAMPUS
52 Ruiz Belvis St., Caguas 00626

(809) 798-5000

CAROLINA CAMPUS
Aptdo. 209, Carolina 00986

(809) 757-5000

HATO REY CAMPUS
404 Ave. Barbosa, Hato Rey 00917-4302

(809) 767-2000

INSTITUTO DEL ARTE MODERNO
Ave. Monserrate FR-5, Villa Fontana, Carolina 00938-3912 *Type:* Private *Accred.:* 1985 (ACCSCT) *Degrees:* C *CEO:* Dir. Myriam Aponte

(809) 768-2532

INSTITUTO FONTECHA
Calle 3 PDA, 8 Altos Cara 7 deTierra St., San Juan 00906 *Type:* Private *Accred.:* 1994 (ACCSCT) *Degrees:* C *CEO:* Exec. Dir. Carlos Alfonso

(809) 723-8193

INSTITUTO TECNICO DE LAS ARTES MANUALES
P.O. Box 2911, Marina Sta., Mayaguez 00681 *Type:* Private *Accred.:* 1992 (ACCSCT) *Degrees:* C *CEO:* Owner Kelmy Morales

(809) 851-1658

INSTITUTO VOCACIONAL CURELZA
P.O. Box 617, Corozal 00643 *Type:* Private *Accred.:* 1992 (ACCSCT) *Degrees:* C *CEO:* Owner Monserrate Rivera Rosado

(809) 859-1274

INSTITUTO VOCATIONAL Y COMERCIAL, EDIC
Calle 8, Equina 5 Urb., P.O. Box 9120, Caguas 00625 *Type:* Private business *Accred.:* 1990 (ACICS) *Degrees:* C *CEO:* Pres. Jose Cartagena

(809) 743-4346

INTERNATIONAL TECHNICAL COLLEGE
1302 Central Ave., Puerto Nuevo, Rio Piedras 00921 *Type:* Private *Accred.:* 1988 (ACCSCT) *Degrees:* C *CEO:* Pres. Roberto Rios Rivera

(809) 792-5620

JOHN DEWEY COLLEGE
P.O. Box 19538, Fernandez Juncos Station 00910 *Type:* Private business *Accred.:* 1994

(ACICS) *Degrees:* C *CEO:* Pres. Carlos Quinones

(809) 753-0039

LICEO DE ARTE Y DISENOS
Calle Acosta No. 47, P.O. Box 1889, Caguas 00626-1889 *Type:* Private *Accred.:* 1990 (ACCSCT) *Degrees:* C *CEO:* Exec. Dir. Sylvia Rodriguez Aponte

(809) 743-7447

LICEO DE ARTE Y TECNOLOGIA
P.O. Box 2346, Hato Rey 00918-2346 *Type:* Private *Accred.:* 1978/1988 (ACCSCT) *Degrees:* C *CEO:* Dir. Carlos M. Valencia

(809) 754-9800

MBTI BUSINESS TRAINING INSTITUTE
1256 Ponce de Leon Ave., Santurce 00907 *Type:* Private business *Accred.:* 1974/1996 (ACICS) *Degrees:* C *CEO:* Pres. Michael Bartels

(809) 723-9402

MERLIX PROFESSIONAL & TECHNICAL INSTITUTE
Calle Betances No. 24, Box 6241, Sta. 1, Bayamon 00961-9998 *Type:* Private *Accred.:* 1989 (ACCSCT) *Degrees:* C *CEO:* Admin. Dir. Felix M. Vargas

(809) 786-7035

METRO COLLEGE, INC.
1126 Ponce de Leon Ave., Rio Piedras 00928 *Type:* Private business *Accred.:* 1989/1996 (ACICS) *Degrees:* C *CEO:* Pres. Luis E. Vazquez

(809) 754-7120

PONCE CAMPUS
Villa 144, Ponce 00731

(809) 259-7272

NATIONAL COMPUTER COLLEGE
P.O. Box 1009, Fajardo 00648 *Type:* Private business *Accred.:* 1986/1994 (ACICS) *Degrees:* C *CEO:* Pres. Antonio Caban

(809) 863-0593

PONCE PARAMEDICAL COLLEGE
L-15 Acacia St., Villa Flores Urbanization, Ponce 00731 *Type:* Private *Accred.:* 1987 (ACCSCT) *Degrees:* C *Prof. Accred.:* Respi-

ratory Therapy Technology *CEO:* Exec. Dir. Alberto Aristizabal

(809) 848-1589

PONCE TECHNICAL SCHOOL, INC.
16 Salud St., Ponce 00731 *Type:* Private *Accred.:* 1985/1992 (ABHES) *Degrees:* C *Prof. Accred.:* Practical Nursing *CEO:* Pres. Fernando Torres

(809) 844-7940

PROFESSIONAL ELECTRICAL SCHOOL
Ramos Velez No. 3, P.O. Box 1797, Manati 00704 *Type:* Private *Accred.:* 1993 (ACCSCT) *Degrees:* C *CEO:* Dir. Paulino Delgado

(809) 854-4776

PROFESSIONAL TECHNICAL INSTITUTION
Betances Mail Sta., Ave. Betances No. 73, Ste. 491, Bayamon 00959-5200 *Type:* Private *Accred.:* 1992 (ACCSCT) *Degrees:* C *CEO:* Pres. Luis L. Montero

(809) 740-6810

PUERTO RICO BARBER COLLEGE
2018 Borinquen Ave., Box 14215, B.O. Obrero Sta., Santurce 00916-4215 *Type:* Private *Accred.:* 1986 (ACCSCT) *Degrees:* C *CEO:* Pres. Sergio Cardona

(809) 727-1961

FAJARDO CAMPUS
E52 Garrido Morales St., Fajardo 00648

(809) 863-2970

PUERTO RICO HOTEL SCHOOL
P.O. Box 37879, International Airport Sta., Carolina 00937 *Type:* Private business *Accred.:* 1993/1995 (ACICS) *Degrees:* C *CEO:* Dir. Luz Rosario

(809) 791-6210

SAN JUAN CITY COLLEGE
501 Roberto H. Todd Ave., Call Box 9300, Santurce Sta., Santurce 00908-9998 *Type:* Private *Accred.:* 1984/1990 (ACCSCT) *Degrees:* C *CEO:* Pres. Americo Reyes Morales

(809) 724-5050

JUANA DIAZ CAMPUS
P.O. Box 1821, Juana Diaz 00665-1821

(809) 837-5050

TRINITY COLLEGE OF PUERTO RICO
  Box 213 Playa Sta., Playa de Ponce 00734
  Type: Private business *Accred.:* 1994
  (ACICS) *Calendar:* Qtr. plan *Degrees:* C
  CEO: Exec. Dir. Agustin Echevarria
  Enroll: 178   (809) 842-0000

RHODE ISLAND

NASSON INSTITUTE
286 Main St., Pawtucket 02860 *Type:* Private business *Accred.:* 1980/1996 (AC-ICS) *Degrees:* C *CEO:* Exec. Dir. Florence Tate
(401) 728-1570

WARWICK CAMPUS
1276 Bald Hill Rd., Warwick 02886
(401) 823-3773

WOONSOCKET CAMPUS
191 Social St., Woonsocket 02895
(401) 769-2066

NEW ENGLAND TECHNICAL COLLEGE
2500 Post Rd., Warwick 02886 *Type:* Private *Accred.:* 1991 (ACCSCT) *CEO:* Pres. Richard I. Gouse
(401) 739-5000

NEW ENGLAND TRACTOR TRAILER TRAINING SCHOOL OF RHODE ISLAND
10 Dunnell Ln., Pawtucket 02860-5801 *Type:* Private *Accred.:* 1985/1993 (ACC-SCT) *Degrees:* C *CEO:* Dir. Fred Hazard
(401) 725-1220

OCEAN STATE BUSINESS INSTITUTE
Mariner Sq., Boxes 1 and 2, 140 Point Judith Rd., Unit 3A, Narragansett 02882 *Type:* Private business *Accred.:* 1979/1994 (AC-ICS) *Degrees:* C *CEO:* Dir. Donald Cotham
(401) 789-0287

SAWYER SCHOOL
101 Main St., Pawtucket 02860 *Type:* Private business *Accred.:* 1973/1991 (AC-ICS) *Degrees:* C *CEO:* Pres. Paul T. Kelly
(401) 272-8400

HAMDEN CAMPUS
1125 Dixwell Ave., Hamden, CT 06514
(203) 239-6200

WARWICK CAMPUS
1222 Warwick Ave., Warwick 02888
(401) 463-3555

SCHOOL OF MEDICAL AND LEGAL SECRETARIAL SCIENCES
60 S. Angell St., Providence 02906-5208 *Type:* Private *Accred.:* 1981/1986 (ACC-SCT) *Degrees:* C *CEO:* Pres. Norma M. Casale
(401) 331-1711

SOUTH CAROLINA

ALPHA BEAUTY SCHOOL
10 Liberty Ln., Greenville 29607-2315 *Type:*
Private *Accred.:* 1986/1991 (COE) *Degrees:*
C *CEO:* Dir. Kenneth W. Lochridge
FTE Enroll: 139   (803) 370-0693

ANDERSON CAMPUS
2619 S. Main St., Anderson 29624
(803) 224-8338

ASHEVILLE CAMPUS
85 Tunnel Rd., Innsbruck Mall, Asheville,
NC 28805
(704) 253-2875

BAMBERG JOB CORPS CENTER
200 S. Carlisle St., Bamberg 29003 *Type:*
Public *Accred.:* 1994 (COE) *Degrees:* C
CEO: Dir. Doris Hall-James
FTE Enroll: 264
(803) 245-5101

CHARLESTON COSMETOLOGY INSTITUTE
8484 Dorchester Rd., Charleston 29420
Type: Private *Accred.:* 1986/1991 (COE)
Degrees: C *CEO:* Dir. Jerry R. Poer, Jr.
FTE Enroll: 205   (803) 552-3670

CHARZANNE BEAUTY COLLEGE
1549 Hwy. 72, E., Greenwood 29649 *Type:*
Private *Accred.:* 1986/1995 (COE) *Degrees:*
C *CEO:* Dir. Martha Roberts
FTE Enroll: 21   (803) 223-7321

CHRIS LOGAN CAREER CENTER
505 Seventh Ave., N., Myrtle Beach 29577-
0261 *Type:* Private *Accred.:* 1988/1993
(COE) *Degrees:* C *CEO:* Dir. Chris Logan
FTE Enroll: 1,645   (803) 665-4602

BENNETTSVILLE CAMPUS
1125 15-401 By-pass, Ste. A, Bennettsville
29512
(803) 479-4076

COLUMBIA CAMPUS
6405-B Two Notch Rd., Columbia 29223
(803) 641-1100

FLORENCE CAMPUS
1810-B Second Loop Rd., Florence 29501
(803) 665-4602

GREENVILLE CAMPUS
1235 S. Pleasantburg Dr., Ste. A, Greenville 29605
(803) 299-0000

NORTH AUGUSTA CAMPUS
Martintown Plaza, North Augusta 29841
(803) 328-1838

ROCK HILL CAMPUS
1930 N. Cherry Rd., Rock Hill 29730
(803) 328-1838

SUMTER CAMPUS
256 S. Pike Rd., Sumter 29150
(803) 773-8481

FARAH'S BEAUTY SCHOOL
520 Bush River Rd., Columbia 29210 *Type:*
Private *Accred.:* 1987/1992 (COE) *Degrees:*
C *CEO:* Dir. Rebecca Farah
FTE Enroll: 92   (803) 772-0101

NORTH AMERICAN INSTITUTE OF AVIATION
Conway-Horry County Airport, P.O. Box
680, Conway 29526-0680 *Type:* Private *Accred.:* 1981/1986 (ACCSCT) *Degrees:* C
CEO: Pres. Douglas W. Beckner
(803) 397-9111

PROFESSIONAL HAIR DESIGN ACADEMY
1540 Wade Hampton Blvd., Greenville
29607-5063 *Type:* Private *Accred.:* 1987
(ACCSCT) *Degrees:* C *CEO:* Owner Stewart
A. Smith
(803) 232-2676

SOUTH CAROLINA CRIMINAL JUSTICE ACADEMY
5400 Broad River Rd., Columbia 29210
Type: Public (state) professional *Accred.:*
1991 (COE) *Degrees:* C *CEO:* Dir. William
C. Gibson
FTE Enroll: 574   (803) 996-7779

SUMTER BEAUTY COLLEGE
  921 Carolina Ave., Sumter 29150 *Type:* Private *Accred.:* 1988/1993 (COE) *Degrees:* C
  CEO: Dir. Faye Smith
  FTE Enroll: 63   (803) 773-7311

TENNESSEE

ARNOLD'S BEAUTY SCHOOL
1179 S. Second St., Milan 38358 *Type:* Private *Accred.:* 1983/1993 (COE) *Degrees:* C *CEO:* Dir. Norma Arnold
FTE Enroll: 35   (901) 686-7351

ARTISTE SCHOOL OF COSMETOLOGY
129 Springbrook Dr., Johnson City 37601-1711 *Type:* Private *Accred.:* 1988 (ACC-SCT) *Degrees:* C *CEO:* Owner Phyllis Blair
(615) 282-2279

BOBBIE'S SCHOOL OF BEAUTY ARTS
108 Decatur Pike, Athens 37371 *Type:* Private *Accred.:* 1992 (COE) *Degrees:* C *CEO:* Dir. Wanda Reed
FTE Enroll: 26   (615) 745-8929

CHATTANOOGA BARBER COLLEGE
405 Market St., Chattanooga 37402-1204 *Type:* Private *Accred.:* 1987 (ACCSCT) *Degrees:* C *CEO:* Owner Judy E. Griggs
(615) 266-7013

CONCORDE CAREER INSTITUTE
5100 Poplar Ave., Ste. 132, Memphis 38137 *Type:* Private *Accred.:* 1980/1990 (COE warning) *Degrees:* C *Prof. Accred.:* Dental Assisting (prelim. provisional) *CEO:* Dir. Tommy Stewart
FTE Enroll: 453   (901) 761-9494

CUMBERLAND SCHOOL OF TECHNOLOGY
1065 E. Tenth St., Cookeville 38501 *Type:* Private 2-year *Accred.:* 1988/1993 (COE) *Degrees:* C *Prof. Accred.:* Clinical Lab Technology (C) *CEO:* Dir. Patty Bowman
FTE Enroll: 136   (615) 526-3660

BATON ROUGE CAMPUS
4173 Government St., Baton Rouge, LA 70806
(504) 338-9085

JETT COLLEGE OF COSMETOLOGY AND BARBERING
3740 N. Watkins St., Memphis 38127 *Type:* Private *Accred.:* 1989/1991 (COE) *Degrees:* C *CEO:* Dir. Esther Kelly
FTE Enroll: 58   (901) 357-0388

JETT COLLEGE OF COSMETOLOGY AND BARBERING
524 S. Cooper St., Memphis 38104 *Type:* Private *Accred.:* 1989/1991 (COE) *Degrees:* C *CEO:* Dir. Sharon Taylor
FTE Enroll: 27   (901) 358-5121

JETT COLLEGE OF COSMETOLOGY AND BARBERING
1286 Southbrook Mall, Memphis 38116 *Type:* Private *Accred.:* 1989/1991 (COE) *Degrees:* C *CEO:* Dir. Delores Dunlap
FTE Enroll: 31   (901) 332-7330

KNOXVILLE INSTITUTE OF HAIR DESIGN
1221 N. Central St., Knoxville 37917-6366 *Type:* Private *Accred.:* 1979/1993 (ACC-SCT) *Degrees:* C *CEO:* Dir. Jack W. Rogers
(615) 971-1529

MEDICAL CAREER COLLEGE
537 Main St., Nashville 37206 *Type:* Private *Calendar:* Qtr. plan *Degrees:* C *CEO:* Pres. Nollie Long
FTE Enroll: 88   (615) 255-7531

MID-STATE BARBER STYLING COLLEGE INC.
510 Jefferson St., Nashville 37208-2626 *Type:* Private *Accred.:* 1989/1991 (ACC-SCT) *Degrees:* C *CEO:* Dir. James Oldham
(615) 242-9300

MISTER WAYNE'S SCHOOL OF UNISEX HAIR DESIGN
170 S. Willow Ave., Cookeville 38501 *Type:* Private *Accred.:* 1984/1990 (ACCSCT) *Degrees:* C *CEO:* Owner Charles W. Fletcher
(615) 526-1478

NASHVILLE CAREER SCHOOL
51 Century Blvd., Ste. 350, Nashville 37214-3609 *Type:* Private *Accred.:* 1989 (ACC-SCT) *Degrees:* C *CEO:* Vice Pres. Tom Vecchio
(615) 885-9770

NATIONAL SCHOOL OF HAIR DESIGN
3641 Brainerd Rd., Chattanooga 37411-3604 *Type:* Private *Accred.:* 1986 (ACC-SCT) *CEO:* Dir. Steve Barnett
(615) 624-6451

NAVAL AIR TECHNICAL TRAINING CENTER
7800 Third Ave., Millington 38054-5059 *Type:* Public (federal) *Accred.:* 1976/1991 (COE) *Degrees:* C *CEO:* Cmnd. J. W. Parker, Jr.
FTE Enroll: 2,888   (901) 873-5106

LAKEHURST CAMPUS
Detachment, Lakehurst, NJ 08733-5001
FTE Enroll: 151   (908) 323-7433

NORTH CENTRAL INSTITUTE
2469 Fort Campbell Blvd., Clarksville 37042 *Type:* Private *Accred.:* 1992 (COE) *Degrees:* C *CEO:* Pres. Tami Taliento
FTE Enroll: 15   (615) 552-6200

O'MORE COLLEGE OF DESIGN
423 S. Margin St., P.O. Box 908, Franklin 37065-0908 *Type:* Private professional *Accred.:* 1994 (ACCSCT) *Calendar:* Sem. plan *Degrees:* C *Prof. Accred.:* Interior Design *CEO:* Pres. Randall N. Yearwood
Enroll: 150   (615) 794-4254

QUEEN CITY COLLEGE
1594 Fort Campbell Blvd., Clarksville 37042 *Type:* Private *Accred.:* 1987/1992 (COE) *Degrees:* C *CEO:* Dir. Greg Ross
FTE Enroll: 261   (615) 645-2361

GREENVILLE CAMPUS
800 Hwy. One, S., Greenville, MS 38701
(601) 334-9120

RICE COLLEGE
2485 Union Ave., Memphis 38112 *Type:* Private business *Accred.:* 1990 (COE) *Degrees:* C *CEO:* Pres. William McGuire
FTE Enroll: 343   (901) 324-7423

JACKSON CAMPUS
2525 Robinson Rd., Jackson, MS 39209
(601) 355-8100

JACKSONVILLE CAMPUS
5430 Norwood Ave., Jacksonville, FL 32208
(904) 765-7300

KNOXVILLE CAMPUS
1515 Magnolia Ave., Knoxville 37917
(615) 637-9899

SEMINARY EXTENSION INDEPENDENT STUDY INSTITUTE
901 Commerce St., Ste. 500, Nashville 37203-3631 *Type:* Private distance education *Accred.:* 1972/1992 (DETC) *Degrees:* C *CEO:* Dir. Doran C. McCarty
(615) 242-2453

SOUTHEASTERN PARALEGAL INSTITUTE
2416 21st Ave., S., Ste. 300, Nashville 37212 *Type:* Private *Accred.:* 1985/1990 (COE) *Degrees:* C *CEO:* Dir. Bruce Mallard
FTE Enroll: 29   (615) 269-9900

TENNESSEE TECHNOLOGY CENTER AT ATHENS
1635 Vo-Tech Dr., Athens 37303 *Type:* Public (state) technical *Accred.:* 1971/1992 (COE) *Degrees:* C *CEO:* Dir. Margaret H. Mahery
FTE Enroll: 164   (615) 744-2814

TENNESSEE TECHNOLOGY CENTER AT COVINGTON
1600 Hwy. 51 S., Covington 38019 *Type:* Public (state) technical *Accred.:* 1972/1992 (COE) *Degrees:* C *CEO:* Dir. Joe D. Martin
FTE Enroll: 91   (901) 475-2526

TENNESSEE TECHNOLOGY CENTER AT CROSSVILLE
715 N. Miller Ave., Crossville 38555 *Type:* Public (state) technical *Accred.:* 1971/1992 (COE) *Degrees:* C *CEO:* Dir. James G. Purcell
FTE Enroll: 192   (615) 484-7502

TENNESSEE TECHNOLOGY CENTER AT CRUMP
Hwy. 64, W., Crump 38327 *Type:* Public (state) technical *Accred.:* 1974/1992 (COE) *Degrees:* C
FTE Enroll: 148   (901) 632-3393

TENNESSEE TECHNOLOGY CENTER AT DICKSON
740 Hwy. 46, Dickson 37055 *Type:* Public
(state) technical *Accred.:* 1974/1994 (COE)
Degrees: C *CEO:* Dir. Bobby Sullivan
FTE Enroll: 187   (615) 441-6220

TENNESSEE TECHNOLOGY CENTER AT
ELIZABETHTON
1500 Arney St., Elizabethton 37643 *Type:*
Public (state) technical *Accred.:* 1973/1993
(COE) *Degrees:* C *CEO:* Dir. Kelly C. Yates
FTE Enroll: 113   (423) 542-4174

TENNESSEE TECHNOLOGY CENTER AT
HARRIMAN
1745 Harriman Hwy., Harriman 37748-1109
Type: Public (state) technical *Accred.:* 1973/
1993 (COE) *Degrees:* C *CEO:* Dir. Farrell
W. Kennedy
FTE Enroll: 146   (423) 882-6703

TENNESSEE TECHNOLOGY CENTER AT
HARTSVILLE
716 McMurry Blvd., Hartsville 37074 *Type:*
Public (state) technical *Accred.:* 1971/1992
(COE) *Degrees:* C *CEO:* Dir. H. Dean Ward
FTE Enroll: 72   (615) 374-2147

TENNESSEE TECHNOLOGY CENTER AT
HOHENWALD
813 W. Main St., Hohenwald 38462-2201
Type: Public (state) technical *Accred.:* 1972/
1992 (COE) *Degrees:* C *CEO:* Dir. Rick
Brewer
FTE Enroll: 139   (615) 796-5351

TENNESSEE TECHNOLOGY CENTER AT
JACKSBORO
Elkins Rd., Jacksboro 37757 *Type:* Public
(state) technical *Accred.:* 1972/1992 (COE)
Degrees: C *CEO:* Dir. Coy Gibson
FTE Enroll: 136   (423) 566-9629

TENNESSEE TECHNOLOGY CENTER AT JACKSON
2468 Westover Rd., Jackson 38301 *Type:*
Public (state) technical *Accred.:* 1972/1992
(COE) *Degrees:* C *CEO:* Dir. Jo Evelyn
Alred
FTE Enroll: 251   (901) 424-0691

TENNESSEE TECHNOLOGY CENTER AT
KNOXVILLE
1100 Liberty St., Knoxville 37919 *Type:*
Public (state) technical *Accred.:* 1971/1992
(COE) *Degrees:* C *Prof. Accred.:* Dental
Assisting *CEO:* Dir. Phillip W. Johnston
FTE Enroll: 405   (423) 546-5567

TENNESSEE TECHNOLOGY CENTER AT
LIVINGSTON
740 Airport Rd., Livingston 38570 *Type:*
Public (state) technical *Accred.:* 1971/1992
(COE) *Degrees:* C *CEO:* Dir. Ralph E.
Robbins
FTE Enroll: 240   (615) 823-5525

TENNESSEE TECHNOLOGY CENTER AT
MCKENZIE
16940 Highland Dr., McKenzie 38201 *Type:*
Public (state) technical *Accred.:* 1971/1992
(COE) *Degrees:* C *CEO:* Pres. Brad Hurley
FTE Enroll: 105   (901) 352-5364

TENNESSEE TECHNOLOGY CENTER AT
MCMINNVILLE
241 Vo-Tech Dr., McMinnville 37110 *Type:*
Public (state) technical *Accred.:* 1971/1992
(COE) *Degrees:* C *CEO:* Dir. Charles
Nunley
FTE Enroll: 114   (615) 473-5587

TENNESSEE TECHNOLOGY CENTER AT MEMPHIS
550 Alabama Ave., Memphis 38105-3799
Type: Public (state) technical *Accred.:* 1970/
1990 (COE) *Degrees:* C *Prof. Accred.:* Dental
Assisting, Respiratory Therapy Technology,
Surgical Technology *CEO:* Dir. James King
FTE Enroll: 454   (901) 543-6100

BRANCH CAMPUS
2752 Winchester Rd., Memphis 38116
     (901) 345-1995

TENNESSEE TECHNOLOGY CENTER AT
MORRISTOWN
821 W. Louise Ave., Morristown 37813
Type: Public (state) technical *Accred.:* 1971/
1993 (COE) *Degrees:* C *CEO:* Dir. Lynn
Elkins
FTE Enroll: 460   (423) 586-5771

ROGERSVILLE CAMPUS
316 E. Main St., Rogersville 37857
(615) 272-2100

TENNESSEE TECHNOLOGY CENTER AT
MURFREESBORO
1303 Old Fort Pkwy., Murfreesboro 37129-
3312 *Type:* Public (state) technical *Accred.:*
1980/1995 (COE) *Degrees:* C *CEO:* Dir.
Wallace E. Burke
FTE Enroll: 133   (615) 898-8010

TENNESSEE TECHNOLOGY CENTER AT
NASHVILLE
100 White Bridge Rd., Nashville 37209
Type: Public (state) technical *Accred.:* 1972/
1992 (COE) *Degrees:* C *CEO:* Dir. Charles
F. Malin
FTE Enroll: 406   (615) 741-1241

BRANCH CAMPUS
7204 Cockrill Bend Rd., Nashville 37209
(615) 350-6224

TENNESSEE TECHNOLOGY CENTER AT NEWBERN
340 Washington St., Newbern 38059 *Type:*
Public (state) technical *Accred.:* 1972/1992
(COE) *Degrees:* C *CEO:* Dir. Wallace E.
Sexton
FTE Enroll: 117   (901) 627-2511

TENNESSEE TECHNOLOGY CENTER AT ONEIDA
120 Eli Ln., Oneida 37841 *Type:* Public
(state) technical *Accred.:* 1973/1993 (COE)
Degrees: C *CEO:* Dir. Arvis Blakley
FTE Enroll: 107   (423) 569-8338

TENNESSEE TECHNOLOGY CENTER AT PARIS
312 S. Wilson St., Paris 38242 *Type:* Public
(state) technical *Accred.:* 1974/1992 (COE)
Degrees: C *CEO:* Dir. Jimmie R. Pritchard
FTE Enroll: 178   (901) 644-7365

TENNESSEE TECHNOLOGY CENTER AT PULASKI
1233 E. College St., Pulaski 38478-0614
Type: Public (state) technical *Accred.:* 1973/
1993 (COE) *Degrees:* C *CEO:* Dir. Henry H.
Sims
FTE Enroll: 113   (615) 424-4014

TENNESSEE TECHNOLOGY CENTER AT RIPLEY
S. Industrial Park, Ripley 38063 *Type:*
Public (state) technical *Accred.:* 1973/1993
(COE) *Degrees:* C *CEO:* Dir. Jerry W. Little
FTE Enroll: 56   (901) 635-3368

TENNESSEE TECHNOLOGY CENTER AT
SHELBYVILLE
1405 Madison St., Shelbyville 37160 *Type:*
Public (state) technical *Accred.:* 1972/1992
(COE) *Degrees:* C *CEO:* Dir. Ronald
Adcock
FTE Enroll: 206   (615) 685-5013

TENNESSEE TECHNOLOGY CENTER AT
WHITEVILLE
330 Hwy. 100, Whiteville 30875 *Type:*
Public (state) technical *Accred.:* 1980/1990
(COE) *Degrees:* C *CEO:* Dir. Russell
Shelton
FTE Enroll: 124   (901) 254-8521

UNIVERSITY OF BEAUTY
5798-A Brainerd Rd., Chattanooga 37411
Type: Private *Accred.:* 1988/1992 (COE)
Degrees: C *CEO:* Dir. M. Crocker
(615) 899-0246

UNIVERSITY OF BEAUTY
1701-G S. Lee Plaza, Cleveland 37311-1701
Type: Private *Accred.:* 1988/1992 (COE)
Degrees: C *CEO:* Dir. Dan Miller
FTE Enroll: 342   (615) 472-1702

WEST TENNESSEE BUSINESS COLLEGE
1186 Hwy. 45 By-Pass, Jackson 38301-1668
Type: Private business *Accred.:* 1953/1991
(ACICS) *Calendar:* Tri. plan *Degrees:* C
CEO: Exec. Dir. Vicki Burch
(901) 668-7240

WILLIAM R. MOORE SCHOOL OF TECHNOLOGY
1200 Poplar Ave., Memphis 38104 *Type:*
Private *Accred.:* 1971/1991 (COE) *Degrees:*
C *CEO:* Dir. Gaylon S. Hall
FTE Enroll: 87   (901) 726-1977

TEXAS

A-PROFESSIONAL
9225 Katy Frwy. No. 114, Houston 77024
Type: Private *Accred.:* 1994 (ACCSCT)
Degrees: C *CEO:* Owner Cheryl Polker
(713) 468-4600

ACADEMY OF ORIENTAL MEDICINE
4105 S. First St., Austin 78745 *Type:* Private
Degrees: C *Prof. Accred.:* Acupuncture
CEO: Exec. Dir. Stuart Watts
(512) 444-6744

ACTION CAREER TRAINING
Rte. 3, Box 41, Merkel 79536 *Type:* Private
Accred.: 1989 (COE warning) *Degrees:* C
CEO: Dir. Gilbert Balch
FTE Enroll: 156   (915) 676-3136

ADVANCED CAREER TRAINING
8800 N. Central Expressway., Ste. 120,
Dallas 75231-6416 *Type:* Private *Accred.:*
1989 (ACCSCT) *Degrees:* C *CEO:* Dir.
Chris Padgett
(214) 692-5400

AIMS ACADEMY
1106 N. Hwy. 360, Ste. 305, Grand Prairie
75050 *Type:* Private technical *Accred.:* 1990/
1993 (COE) *Degrees:* C *CEO:* Dir. Crystal
Hackling
FTE Enroll: 76   (214) 988-3202

DALLAS CAMPUS
6510 Abrams Rd., Dallas 75232
(214) 988-3202

ALLIED HEALTH CAREERS
5424 Hwy. 290, W., No. 105, Austin 78735
Type: Private *Accred.:* 1991/1994 (COE)
Degrees: C *CEO:* Pres. Raymond Perrilloux
FTE Enroll: 78   (512) 892-5210

AMERICAN COMMERCIAL COLLEGE
402 Butternut St., Abilene 79602 *Type:*
Private business *Accred.:* 1970 (ACICS)
Degrees: C *CEO:* Dir. Michael J. Otto
(915) 672-8495

AMERICAN COMMERCIAL COLLEGE
2007 34th St., Lubbock 79411 *Type:* Private
business *Accred.:* 1982/1987 (ACICS) *Degrees:* C *CEO:* Dir. Brent Sheets
(806) 747-4339

AMERICAN COMMERCIAL COLLEGE
2115 E. Eighth St., Odessa 79761 *Type:*
Private business *Accred.:* 1970/1994 (AC-
ICS) *Degrees:* C *CEO:* Dir. Scot Shaw
(915) 332-0768

AMERICAN COMMERCIAL COLLEGE
3177 Executive Dr., San Angelo 76904 *Type:*
Private business *Accred.:* 1990/1994 (AC-
ICS) *Degrees:* C *CEO:* Dir. B.A. Reed
(915) 942-6797

AMERICAN INSTITUTE OF COMMERCE
9330 LBJ Frwy., Ste. 350, Dallas 75243
Type: Private business *Accred.:* 1989/1995
(ACICS) *Degrees:* C *CEO:* Dir. Skip Walls
(214) 690-1978

AMERICAN WELD TESTING SCHOOL
921 Broadway, Pasadena 77506 *Type:*
Private *Accred.:* 1994 (ACCSCT) *Calendar:*
9-mos. program *Degrees:* C *CEO:* Dir. Dan
Strain
Enroll: 61   (713) 475-2300

ARLINGTON COURT REPORTING COLLEGE
901 Ave. K., Grand Prairie 75050 *Type:*
Private *Accred.:* 1987 (ACCSCT) *Degrees:*
C *CEO:* Dir. Ronda Vecchio
(214) 647-1607

ARMY ACADEMY OF HEALTH SCIENCES
2250 Stanley Rd., Bldg. 2840, San Antonio
78234-6100 *Type:* Public (federal) professional *Accred.:* 1983/1993 (COE) *Degrees:*
C *Prof. Accred.:* Dental Laboratory Technology, Occupational Therapy Assisting,
Physician Assisting/Surgeon Assisting,
Radiography, Respiratory Therapy Technology *CEO:* Commandant. C. E. Maxwell
FTE Enroll: 5,379   (512) 221-8542

ARMY MEDICAL EQUIPMENT AND OPTICIAN
SCHOOL
Aurora, CO 80045-7040
(303) 943-4107

SCHOOL OF AVIATION MEDICINE
Fort Rucker, AL 36362-5377
(205) 558-7409

ATI—AMERICAN TRADES INSTITUTES
6627 Maple Ave., Dallas 75235-4623 *Type:*
Private *Accred.:* 1975/1990 (ACCSCT)
Degrees: C *CEO:* Dir. Mike Thayer
(214) 352-2222

ATI CAREER TRAINING CENTER
2351 W. Northwest Hwy., Ste 1301, Dallas
75229 *Type:* Private *Degrees:* C *Prof. Accred.:* Medical Assisting *CEO:* Dir. Joseph P.
Mehlmann
(214) 688-0467

ATI CAREER TRAINING CENTER
235 N.E. Loop 820, Ste. 110, Hurst 76053-
7396 *Type:* Private *Accred.:* 1986/1993
(ACCSCT) *Degrees:* C *Prof. Accred.:* Medical Assisting *CEO:* Dir. Gerald E. Parr
(817) 589-1994

BELLAIRE BEAUTY COLLEGE
5014 Bellaire Blvd., Bellaire 77401 *Type:*
Private *Accred.:* 1992/1995 (COE warning)
Degrees: C *CEO:* Dir. Howard Conlon
FTE Enroll: 86   (713) 666-2318

BRADFORD SCHOOL OF BUSINESS
4669 Southwest Frwy., Ste. 300, Houston
77027 *Type:* Private business *Accred.:* 1980/
1986 (ACICS) *Degrees:* C *CEO:* Pres. Julie
Hayes
(713) 629-8940

BUSINESS SKILLS TRAINING CENTER
616 Fort Worth Dr., Ste. B, Denton 76201-
7170 *Type:* Private *Accred.:* 1991 (ACC-
SCT) *Degrees:* C *CEO:* Pres. Jane M.
Hadley
(817) 382-7922

CAPITOL CITY CAREERS
4630 Westgate Blvd., Austin 78745 *Type:*
Private *Accred.:* 1989/1992 (COE) *Degrees:*
C *CEO:* Dir. Sherie Sadlier
FTE Enroll: 93   (512) 892-4270

CAPITOL CITY TRADE AND TECHNICAL SCHOOL
205 E. Riverside Dr., Austin 78704 *Type:*
Private *Accred.:* 1979/1994 (COE) *Degrees:*
C *CEO:* Pres. Nancy H. Ellis
FTE Enroll: 115   (512) 444-3257

CAREER ACADEMY
32 Oaklawn Village, Texarkana 75501 *Type:*
Private *Accred.:* 1988/1995 (COE) *Degrees:*
C *CEO:* Dir. Monet Lasater
FTE Enroll: 105   (903) 832-1021

CAREER CENTERS OF TEXAS—EL PASO
8375 Burnham Rd., El Paso 79907 *Type:*
Private *Accred.:* 1988/1989 (COE) *Degrees:*
C *Prof. Accred.:* Medical Assisting *CEO:*
Dir. Rose Duenez
FTE Enroll: 342   (915) 595-1935

CAREER DEVELOPMENT CENTER
413 S. Chestnut St., Lufkin 75901-4967
Type: Private *Degrees:* C *CEO:* Dir. Linda
Amadon
FTE Enroll: 94   (409) 637-1740

CAREER POINT BUSINESS SCHOOL
485 Spencer Ln., San Antonio 78201 *Type:*
Private business *Accred.:* 1984/1989 (AC-
ICS) *Degrees:* C *CEO:* Dir. Norma Bramlett
(512) 732-3000

TULSA CAMPUS
3138 S. Garnett Rd., Tulsa, OK 74146-
1933 *Accred.:* 1987 (ACICS)
(918) 622-4100

CAREERS UNLIMITED
335 S. Bonner St., Tyler 75702 *Type:* Private
Accred.: 1993 (ACCSCT) *Degrees:* C *CEO:*
Pres. Jim Craddock
(903) 593-4424

CAREERS UNLIMITED BEAUTY SCHOOL
1225 Lone Star St., Henderson 75652
Accred.: 1994 (ACCSCT) *Degrees:* C *CEO:*
Schl. Dir. Betty Powell
Enroll: 24   (903) 657-0048

CENTRAL TEXAS COMMERCIAL COLLEGE
P.O. Box 1324, 315 N. Center St., Brownwood 76801 *Type:* Private business *Accred.:*
1971/1995 (ACICS) *Calendar:* Qtr. plan
Degrees: C *CEO:* Dir. Kathy Day
                              (915) 646-0521

DALLAS CAMPUS
9400 N. Central Expressway., Ste. 200,
Dallas 75231 *Accred.:* 1987/1995 (ACICS)
                              (214) 368-3680

CHENIER
6300 Richmond Ave., Ste. 300, Houston
77057 *Type:* Private *Accred.:* 1979/1989
(COE warning) *Degrees:* C *CEO:* Dir.
Timothy Connolly
FTE Enroll: 382   (713) 886-3102

CHENIER
2819 Loop 306, San Angelo 76904
FTE Enroll: 62   (915) 944-4404

COMPUTER CAREER CENTER
6101 Montana Ave., El Paso 79925 *Type:*
Private *Accred.:* 1989/1994 (COE) *Degrees:*
C *CEO:* Pres. Janine Young
FTE Enroll: 258   (915) 779-8031

ALBUQUERQUE CAMPUS
4121 Wyoming Blvd., N.E., Albuquerque,
NM 87111
                              (505) 271-8200

DALFORT AIRCRAFT TECH
7701 Lemmon Ave., Dallas 75209-3091
Type: Private *Accred.:* 1990 (ACCSCT)
Degrees: C *CEO:* Exec. Dir. David Evans
                              (214) 358-7820

ATLANTA CAMPUS
990 Toffie Terr., Atlanta, GA 30320
Accred.: 1993 (ACCSCT)
                              (404) 428-9056

DALLAS INSTITUTE OF FUNERAL SERVICES
3909 S. Buckner Blvd., Dallas 75227 *Type:*
Private professional *Calendar:* Qtr. plan
Degrees: C *Prof. Accred.:* Funeral Service
Education (Mortuary Science) *CEO:* Pres.
James Shoemake
FTE Enroll: 181   (214) 388-5466

DAVID L. CARRASCO JOB CORPS CENTER
11155 Gateway W., El Paso 79935 *Accred.:*
1986/1994 (COE) *Degrees:* C *CEO:* Dir.
Mary Young
FTE Enroll: 451   (915) 594-0022

DELTA CAREER INSTITUTE
1310 Pennsylvania Ave., Beaumont 77701
Type: Private business *Accred.:* 1988
(ACICS); 1992 (COE) *Calendar:* Qtr. plan
Degrees: C *CEO:* Dir. Kenneth A. Webb
FTE Enroll: 184   (409) 833-6161

EURO HAIR SCHOOL
2301-A Morgan Ave., Corpus Christi 78405
Type: Private *Accred.:* 1993 (ACCSCT)
Degrees: C *CEO:* Owner Stewart A. Smith
                              (512) 887-8494

EUROPEAN HEALTH AND SCIENCES INSTITUTE
1201 Airway A-2, El Paso 79925 *Type:*
Private *Accred.:* 1993 (ACCSCT) *Degrees:*
C *CEO:* Owner Florencia M. Zelonis
                              (915) 772-4243

GARY JOB CORPS CENTER
Hwy. 21, San Marcos 78667 (Federal)
Accred.: 1985/1992 (COE) *Degrees:* C
CEO: Dir. Modesto Gloria
FTE Enroll: 1,924   (512) 396-6652

GULF COAST TRADES CENTER
FM 1375 W., New Waverly 77358 *Type:*
Private Non-Profit *Accred.:* 1984/1994
(COE) *Degrees:* C *CEO:* Dir. Thomas M.
Buzbee
FTE Enroll: 248   (409) 344-6677

HOUSTON ALLIED HEALTH CAREERS, INC.
2800 San Jacinto St., Houston 77004 *Type:*
Private *Accred.:* 1994 (ABHES) *Calendar:*
Qtr. plan *Degrees:* C *CEO:* Dir. Evelyn Scott
                              (713) 650-6155

HOUSTON BALLET ACADEMY
1921 W. Bell St., P.O. Box 130487, Houston 77219-0487 *Type:* Private *Degrees:* C *Prof. Accred.:* Dance *CEO:* Admin. Lisa Morton
(713) 523-6300 x201

HOUSTON TRAINING SCHOOL
704 Shotwell, Houston 77020 *Type:* Private *Accred.:* 1979/1993 (COE) *Degrees:* C *CEO:* Dir. I.H. Perry
FTE Enroll: 183   (713) 675-4300

BRANCH CAMPUS
1260 Blalock, No. 200, Houston 77055
(713) 464-1659

BRANCH CAMPUS
6969 Gulf Frwy., Ste. 200, Houston 77087
(713) 649-5050

INTERACTIVE LEARNING SYSTEMS
8585 N. Stemmons Frwy., No. M-50, Dallas 75247 *Type:* Private *Accred.:* 1989/1994 (COE) *Degrees:* C *CEO:* Dir. Martha Gonzalez
FTE Enroll: 72   (214) 637-3377

HOUSTON CAMPUS
10200 Richmond Ave., Houston 77042
(713) 782-5161

INTERNATIONAL AVIATION AND TRAVEL ACADEMY
4846 S. Collins, Arlington 76018 *Type:* Private *Accred.:* 1979/1994 (COE); 1988/ 1992 (DETC) *Degrees:* C *CEO:* Pres. DeWayne Weeks
FTE Enroll: 425   (817) 784-7000

INTERNATIONAL AVIATION AND TRAVEL ACADEMY
17340 Chanute Rd., Houston 77032 *Type:* Private *Accred.:* 1991 (COE) *Degrees:* C *CEO:* Dir. Dewayne Weeks
FTE Enroll: 211   (800) 627-4379

INTERNATIONAL BUSINESS COLLEGE
4121 Montana Ave., El Paso 79903 *Type:* Private business *Accred.:* 1969/1999 (AC-ICS) *Degrees:* C *CEO:* Dir. Margie Aguilar
(915) 566-8644

EL PASO CAMPUS
1030 N. Zaragosa Rd., El Paso 79907
(915) 859-3986

INTERNATIONAL BUSINESS COLLEGE
4630 50th St., Ste 200, Lubbock 79414 *Type:* Private business *Accred.:* 1985/1995 (AC-ICS) *Degrees:* C *CEO:* Pres. Kirk Williams
(806) 797-1933

DENTON CAMPUS
3801 I-35 N., Ste. 138, Denton 76205 *Accred.:* 1993 (ACICS)
(817) 380-0024

SHERMAN CAMPUS
4107 N. Texoma Pkwy., Sherman 75090 *Accred.:* 1991 (ACICS)
(806) 893-6604

IVERSON INSTITUTE OF COURT REPORTING
1200 Copeland Rd., Ste. 305, Arlington 76011 *Type:* Private *Accred.:* 1988/1993 (COE) *Degrees:* C *CEO:* Dir. Audrey Iverson
FTE Enroll: 97   (817) 274-6465

LE HAIR DESIGN COLLEGE
505 Golden Triangle Shopping C, Polk St. at Marvin D. Love Frwy, Dallas 75224-4425 *Type:* Private *Accred.:* 1988/1991 (ACC-SCT) *Degrees:* C *CEO:* Dir. Lori Ruidant
(214) 375-0592

LE HAIR DESIGN COLLEGE
217 Pleasant Grove Shopping Ct, Dallas 75217-1700 *Type:* Private *Accred.:* 1988/ 1991 (ACCSCT) *Degrees:* C *CEO:* Dir. Daniel Ruidant
(214) 398-5905

LE HAIR DESIGN COLLEGE
1125 E. Seminary Dr., Fort Worth 76115-2829 *Type:* Private *Accred.:* 1986 (ACC-SCT) *Degrees:* C *CEO:* Dir. Thomas L. Campo
(817) 926-7555

LE HAIR DESIGN COLLEGE
2410 W. Walnut St., Garland 75042-6623 *Type:* Private *Accred.:* 1988/1991 (ACC-SCT) *Degrees:* C *CEO:* Dir. Daniel Ruidant
(214) 272-8283

LE HAIR DESIGN COLLEGE
5201 E. Belknap, Haltom City 76117 *Type:* Private *Accred.:* 1988/1991 (ACCSCT) *Degrees:* C *CEO:* Dir. Thomas L. Campo
(817) 831-7261

LECHEF COLLEGE OF HOSPITALITY CAREERS
6020 Dillard Cir., Austin 78752 *Type:* Private Non-Profit *Accred.:* 1990/1995 (COE) *Degrees:* C *CEO:* Dir. Ronald Boston
FTE Enroll: 110   (512) 323-2511

LINCOLN TECHNICAL INSTITUTE
2501 E. Arkansas Ln., Grand Prairie 75051-9990 *Type:* Private *Accred.:* 1968/1988 (ACCSCT) *Degrees:* C *CEO:* Dir. Paul R. McGuirk
(214) 660-5701

M AND M WORD PROCESSING INSTITUTE
5050 Westheimer Rd., Ste. 300, Houston 77056 *Type:* Private *Accred.:* 1990 (ACC-SCT) *Degrees:* C *CEO:* Owner Olgha Isid
(713) 961-0500

M. WEEKS WELDING LABORATORY TESTING AND SCHOOL
4405 Hwy. 347, Nederland 77627 *Type:* Private *Accred.:* 1991 (COE) *Degrees:* C *CEO:* Pres. Morris Weeks
FTE Enroll: 12   (409) 727-7640

MID-CITIES BARBER COLLEGE
411 Marshall Plaza, Grand Prairie 75050 *Type:* Private *Accred.:* 1994 (ACCSCT) *Degrees:* C *CEO:* Dir. Nachita Cano
Enroll: 15   (214) 642-1892

NATIONAL EDUCATION CENTER—NATIONAL INSTITUTE OF TECHNOLOGY CAMPUS
3622 Fredericksburg Rd., San Antonio 78201-3841 *Type:* Private *Accred.:* 1981/1990 (ACCSCT) *Calendar:* Qtr. plan *Degrees:* C *CEO:* Dir. Ed Howard
(210) 733-6000

THE NELL INSTITUTE
2101 IH 35 S., 3rd Fl., Austin 78741 *Type:* Private business *Accred.:* 1978/1996 (AC-ICS) *Degrees:* C *CEO:* Dir. Jackie Ward
(512) 447-9415

OCCUPATIONAL SAFETY TRAINING INSTITUTE
8415 W. Bellfort St., Ste. 300, Houston 77031 *Type:* Private *Accred.:* 1991 (COE) *Degrees:* C *CEO:* Dir. Eva Bonilla
FTE Enroll: 169   (713) 270-6882

THE OCEAN CORPORATION
10840 Rockley Rd., Houston 77099-3416 *Type:* Private *Accred.:* 1989 (ACCSCT) *Degrees:* C *CEO:* Pres. Les Joiner
(713) 530-0202

THE OFFICE CAREERS CENTRE
7001 Grapevine Hwy., No. 202, Fort Worth 76180-8812 *Type:* Private *Accred.:* 1988/1994 (COE) *Degrees:* C *CEO:* Dir. Helen Johnston
FTE Enroll: 26   (817) 284-8107

PCI HEALTH TRAINING CENTER
8101 John Carpenter Frwy., Dallas 75247-4720 *Type:* Private *Accred.:* 1986/1991 (AC-CSCT) *Degrees:* C *CEO:* Dir. Bobby Prince
(214) 630-0568

POLYTECHNIC INSTITUTE
4625 North Frwy., Ste. 109, Houston 77022-2929 *Type:* Private *Accred.:* 1990 (ACC-SCT) *Degrees:* C *CEO:* Pres. Luis R. Cano
(713) 694-6027

PROFESSIONAL COURT REPORTING SCHOOL
1401 N. Central Expressway., Richardson 75080 *Type:* Private *Accred.:* 1987 (ACC-SCT) *Degrees:* C *CEO:* Pres. Ardith Spies
Enroll: 147   (214) 231-9502

R/S INSTITUTE
7122 Lawndale Ave., Houston 77023 *Type:* Private *Accred.:* 1984/1991 (COE) *Degrees:* C *CEO:* Dir. Rhonda Morris
FTE Enroll: 31   (713) 923-6968

RHDC HAIR DESIGN COLLEGE
3209 N. Main St., Fort Worth 76106 *Type:*
Private *Accred.:* 1993 (ACCSCT) *Degrees:*
C *CEO:* Pres. Pat Collins
(817) 624-0871

RICE AVIATION, A DIVISION OF A AND J
ENTERPRISES
8880 Telephone Rd., Houston 77061 *Type:*
Private *Accred.:* 1988/1991 (COE) *Degrees:*
C *CEO:* Dir. James W. Rice
FTE Enroll: 712   (713) 644-6616

PHOENIX CAMPUS
3201 E. Broadway Rd., Phoenix, AZ
85040
(602) 243-6611

INGLEWOOD CAMPUS
8911 Aviation Blvd., Inglewood, CA
90301-2904
(310) 337-4444

BALTIMORE CAMPUS
701 Wilson Point Rd., D-4, Baltimore,
MD 21220
(410) 682-2226

HOUSTON CAMPUS
7811 N. Shepherd, No. 100, Houston 77088
(713) 591-2908

CHESAPEAKE CAMPUS
5202 W. Military Hwy., Hangar 7,
Chesapeake, VA 23321
(804) 465-2813

SAN ANTONIO COLLEGE OF MEDICAL AND
DENTAL ASSISTANTS
4205 San Pedro Ave., San Antonio 78212-
1899 *Type:* Private *Accred.:* 1970/1985
(ACCSCT); 1984/1989 (COE) *Degrees:* C
Prof. Accred.: Medical Assisting *CEO:* Pres.
Comer M. Alden, Jr.
FTE Enroll: 849   (512) 733-0777

MCALLEN CAMPUS
3900 N. 23rd St., McAllen 78501-6053
Accred.: 1990 (ACCSCT) *Prof. Accred.:*
Medical Assisting
(210) 360-1499

BRANCH CAMPUS
5280 Medical Dr., Ste. 100, San Antonio
78229-9944 *Accred.:* 1990 (ACCSCT)
Prof. Accred.: Surgical Technology
(210) 692-3829

SAN ANTONIO TRADE SCHOOL
120 Playmoor St., San Antonio 78210 *Type:*
Private *Accred.:* 1982/1992 (COE) *Degrees:*
C *CEO:* Dir. Charles Lee
FTE Enroll: 381   (512) 533-9126

DEL RIO CAMPUS
117 W. Martin, Del Rio 78840
(512) 774-5646

SAN ANTONIO TRAINING DIVISION
9350 S. Presa, San Antonio 78223-4799
Type: Public *Accred.:* 1984/1994 (COE)
Degrees: C *CEO:* Dir. Jackie Gorman
FTE Enroll: 161   (210) 633-1000

BRANCH CAMPUS
Bldg. 210 and 308, Kelly AFB, San
Antonio 78241-5000
(210) 633-2893

BRANCH CAMPUS
Hemisfair Park, Bldg. 277, P.O. Box 40,
San Antonio 78291-0040
(210) 633-1000

SCHOOL OF AUTOMOTIVE MACHINISTS
1911 Antoine Dr., Houston 77055-1803
Type: Private *Accred.:* 1991 (ACCSCT) *Degrees:* C *CEO:* Dir. Linda Massingill
FTE Enroll: 67   (713) 683-3817

SCHOOL OF HEALTH CARE SCIENCES
917 Missile Rd., Air Force Base, Sheppard
76311-2246 *Type:* Private *Degrees:* C *Prof.
Accred.:* Dental Assisting, Dental Laboratory Technology *CEO:* Cmnd. Gary Wasem
(817) 676-4033

SEBRING CAREER SCHOOLS
2212 Ave. I, Huntsville 77340 *Type:* Private
Accred.: 1985/1990 (COE) *Degrees:* C
CEO: Dir. Reese Moore
FTE Enroll: 294   (409) 291-6299

SEGUIN BEAUTY SCHOOL
102 E. Court St., Seguin 78155 *Type:* Private
Accred.: 1987/1992 (COE) *Degrees:* C
CEO: Dir. Joseph P. Evans
FTE Enroll: 43   (210) 372-0935

NEW BRAUNFELS CAMPUS
214 W. San Antonio St., New Braunfels
78130
                                    (512) 620-1301

SOUTH TEXAS VO-TECH INSTITUTE
2255 N. Coria, Brownsville 78520 *Type:*
Private *Accred.:* 1982/1994 (COE) *Degrees:*
C *CEO:* Dir. Ray Garcia
FTE Enroll: 109   (512) 546-0353

SOUTH TEXAS VO-TECH INSTITUTE
2901 N. 23rd St., Ste. B, McAllen 78501-6148
Type: Private *Accred.:* 1982/1992 (COE)
Degrees: C *CEO:* Dir. Rolando Rodriquez
FTE Enroll: 292   (210) 631-1107

SOUTH TEXAS VO-TECH INSTITUTE
2419 E. Haggar Ave., Weslaco 78596 *Type:*
Private *Accred.:* 1982/1992 (COE) *Degrees:*
C *CEO:* Dir. Carlos Rodriguez
FTE Enroll: 170   (210) 969-1564

SOUTHEASTERN PARALEGAL INSTITUTE
5440 Harvest Hill Rd., No. 200, Dallas
75230 *Type:* Private *Accred.:* 1989/1990
(COE) *Degrees:* C *CEO:* Dir. Janice Bailey
FTE Enroll: 72   (214) 385-1446

SOUTHERN CAREERS INSTITUTE
2301 S. Congress Ave., No. 27, Austin 78704
Type: Private *Accred.:* 1991 (COE) *Degrees:*
C *CEO:* Dir. Joel Meck
FTE Enroll: 409   (512) 326-1415

CORPUS CHRISTI CAMPUS
5333 Everhart Rd., Bldg. C, Corpus
Christi 78415
                                    (512) 857-5700

PHARR CAMPUS
1414 N. Jackson Rd., Pharr 78577
                                    (210) 687-1415

SAN ANTONIO CAMPUS
1405 N. Main No. 100, San Antonio 78212
                                    (210) 271-0096

S.W. SCHOOL OF BUSINESS AND TECHNICAL
CAREERS
272 Commercial St., Eagle Pass 78852 *Type:*
Private *Accred.:* 1989/1995 (COE) *Degrees:*
C *CEO:* Dir. Jesus Dela Garza
FTE Enroll: 68   (512) 773-1373

S.W. SCHOOL OF BUSINESS AND TECHNICAL
CAREERS
505 E. Travis, San Antonio 78205 *Type:*
Private *Accred.:* 1992 (COE) *Degrees:* C
CEO: Dir. Angelita Delgado
FTE Enroll: 33   (210) 225-7287

S.W. SCHOOL OF BUSINESS AND TECHNICAL
CAREERS
602 W. Southcross Blvd., San Antonio
78221 *Type:* Private *Accred.:* 1982/1992
(COE) *Degrees:* C *CEO:* Dir. Al Salazar
FTE Enroll: 318   (210) 921-0951

UVALDE CAMPUS
122 W. North St., Uvalde 78801
                                    (210) 228-4103

TAYLOR'S INSTITUTE OF COSMETOLOGY
842C W. 7th Ave., Corsicana 75110 *Type:*
Private *Accred.:* 1992/1994 (COE) *Degrees:*
C *CEO:* Dir. Robb Taylor
FTE Enroll: 21   (903) 874-7312

TEMPLE ACADEMY OF COSMETOLOGY
5 S. First St., Temple 76501 *Type:* Private
Accred.: 1986/1991 (COE) *Degrees:* C
CEO: Dir. Lenda Tuck
FTE Enroll: 43   (817) 778-2221

LONGVIEW CAMPUS
1408 W. Marshall Ave., Longview 76504
                                    (903) 753-4717

TEXAS BARBER COLLEGE
531 W. Jefferson Blvd., Dallas 75208 *Type:*
Private *Accred.:* 1988/1993 (COE) *Degrees:*
C *CEO:* Dir. Helen Spears
FTE Enroll: 142   (214) 943-7255

BRANCH CAMPUS
2406 Gus Thomason Rd., Dallas 75228
(214) 324-2851

RICHARDSON CAMPUS
525 West Arapaho, Richardson 75080
(214) 644-4106

TEXAS INSTITUTE OF TRADITIONAL CHINESE
MEDICINE
4005 Manchaca Rd., Ste. 200, Austin 78704
Type: Private *Prof. Accred.:* Acupuncture
Calendar: Sem. plan *Degrees:* C *CEO:* Dir.
Paul Lin
FTE Enroll: 22   (512) 444-8082

TEXAS SCHOOL OF BUSINESS
711 Airtex Blvd., Houston 77073 *Type:*
Private business *Accred.:* 1985/1991 (AC-
ICS) *Degrees:* C *CEO:* Dir. Dale Spradling
(713) 876-2888

TEXAS SCHOOL OF BUSINESS—SOUTHWEST
10250 Bissonnet St., Houston 77036 *Type:*
Private business *Accred.:* 1989/1996 (AC-
ICS) *Degrees:* C *CEO:* Dir. Jody Hawk
(713) 771-1177

TEXAS VOCATIONAL SCHOOL
3107 N. Sugar Rd., Pharr 78577 *Type:*
Private *Accred.:* 1982/1993 (COE) *Degrees:*
C *CEO:* Dir. Gene Calhoun
FTE Enroll: 182   (512) 533-0150

TEXAS VOCATIONAL SCHOOL
1913 S. Flores St., San Antonio 78204-1934
Type: Private *Accred.:* 1982/1993 (COE)
Degrees: C *CEO:* Dir. Melvin Heitkamp
FTE Enroll: 241   (210) 225-3253

TEXAS VOCATIONAL SCHOOLS
1921 E. Red River, Victoria 77901 *Type:*
Private *Accred.:* 1983/1993 (COE) *Degrees:*
C *CEO:* Dir. Angie S. Boone
FTE Enroll: 191   (512) 575-4768

BRANCH CAMPUS
201 E. Rio Grande, Victoria 77901
(512) 575-4768

VANGUARD INSTITUTE OF TECHNOLOGY
221 North 8th Street, Edinburg 78539 *Type:*
Private *Accred.:* 1990/1995 (COE) *Degrees:*
C *CEO:* Dir. Domingo Lopez, Jr.
FTE Enroll: 280   (210) 380-3264

HARLINGEN CAMPUS
603 Ed Carey Dr., Harlingen 78550
(210) 428-4999

UTAH

AMERICAN INSTITUTE OF MEDICAL-DENTAL
TECHNOLOGY
    1675 N. Freedom Blvd., Bldg. 4, Provo
84604 *Type:* Private *Accred.:* 1984/1990
(ABHES) *Degrees:* C *Prof. Accred.:* Dental
Assisting, Medical Assisting (AMA) *CEO:*
Admin. Keith T. Van Soest
                        (801) 377-2900
ST. GEORGE CAMPUS
    640 E. 700 S. St. George 84770 *Accred.:*
1995 (ABHES)
                        (801) 652-0900

THE BRYMAN SCHOOL
    1144 W. 3300 S., Salt Lake City 84119-3330
Type: Private *Accred.:* 1973/1989 (ACC-
SCT) *Degrees:* C *Prof. Accred.:* Medical
Assisting (AMA) *CEO:* Pres. John S. Cowan
                        (801) 975-7000

INTERMOUNTAIN COLLEGE OF COURT REPORTING
    5980 S. 300 E., Murray 84107 *Type:* Private
business *Accred.:* 1981/1988 (ACICS)
Calendar: Qtr. plan *Degrees:* C *CEO:* Pres.
Linda J. Smurthwaite
                        (801) 268-9271

MYOTHERAPY INSTITUTE OF UTAH
    3350 S. 2300 E., Salt Lake City 84109 *Type:*
Private *Accred.:* 1992 (ACCSCT) *Degrees:*
C *CEO:* Owner Shirley Foster
                        (801) 484-7624

PROVO COLLEGE
    1450 W. 820 N., Provo 84601 *Type:* Private
Accred.: 1986 (ACCSCT) *Degrees:* C *Prof.
Accred.:* Dental Assisting *CEO:* Pres. Keith
Poelman
                        (801) 375-1861

VERMONT

FANNY ALLEN MEMORIAL SCHOOL OF
PRACTICAL NURSING
  125 College Pkwy., Colchester 05446 *Type:*
Private professional *Degrees:* C *Prof. Accred.:* Practical Nursing *CEO:* Dir. Phyllis
Iorlano
                                   (802) 655-2540

THOMPSON SCHOOL OF PRACTICAL NURSING
  30 Maple St., Brattleboro 05301 *Type:*
Private professional *Degrees:* C *Prof. Accred.:* Practical Nursing *CEO:* Interim Dir.
Rosemary Tarbell
                                   (802) 254-5570

VIRGINIA

ALLIANCE TRACTOR TRAILER TRAINING
CENTERS II
100 Nye Rd., P.O. Box 804, Wytheville
24382-0804 *Type:* Private *Accred.:* 1987/
1993 (ACCSCT) *Degrees:* C *CEO:* Dir.
Mark Pressley
(703) 228-6101

TRAINING CENTER V CAMPUS
P.O. Box 579, Benson, NC 27504-0579
Accred.: 1990 (ACCSCT)
(910) 892-8370

ANTHONY'S BARBER STYLING COLLEGE
1307 Jefferson Ave., Newport News 23607-
5617 *Type:* Private *Accred.:* 1989 (ACC-
SCT) *Degrees:* C *CEO:* Dir. Irene Anthony
(804) 244-2311

APPLIED CAREER TRAINING INC.
1100 Wilson Blvd., Mall Level, Arlington
22209 *Type:* Private *Accred.:* 1993 (COE)
Degrees: C *CEO:* Dir. Levi McGlothlin
FTE Enroll: 267   (703) 527-6660

APPRENTICE SCHOOL—NEWPORT NEWS
SHIPBUILDING
4101 Washington Ave., Newport News
23607 *Type:* Private *Accred.:* 1982/1992
(SACS-CC) *Degrees:* C *CEO:* Dir. James
H. Hughes
FTE Enroll: 597   (804) 380-2682

THE ARMY INSTITUTE FOR PROFESSIONAL
DEVELOPMENT
U.S. Army Training Support Ctr, Fort Eustis
23604-5121 *Type:* Public (federal) distance
education *Accred.:* 1978/1995 (DETC)
Degrees: C *CEO:* Dir. Ned C. Motter
(804) 878-4774

ARMY QUARTERMASTER CENTER AND SCHOOL
Fort Lee 23801-5034 *Type:* Public (federal)
technical *Accred.:* 1975/1990 (COE) *Degrees:* C *CEO:* Cmnd. Ofcr. Robert K. Guest
FTE Enroll: 3,011   (804) 734-3683

ARMY TRANSPORTATION AND AVIATION
LOGISTICS SCHOOL
ATSD-BD-S, Fort Eustis 23604-5450 *Type:*
Public (federal) technical *Accred.:* 1975/
1992 (COE) *Degrees:* C *CEO:* Command-
ant Kenneth Wykle
FTE Enroll: 3,294   (804) 878-4802

ATI CAREER INSTITUTE
7777 Leesburg Pike, No. 100, Falls Church
22043 *Type:* Private *Accred.:* 1992/1995
(COE) *Degrees:* C *CEO:* Pres. Richard
Shurtz
FTE Enroll: 320   (703) 821-8570

QUANTICO CAMPUS
Quantico High School, Quantico 22134-
5023
(703) 640-0738

ATI—HOLLYWOOD
3024 Trinkle Ave., Roanoke 24012 *Type:*
Private *Accred.:* 1989/1992 (COE) *Degrees:*
C *CEO:* Pres. Todd Rothrock
FTE Enroll: 60   (540) 362-9338

BRANCH CAMPUS
1108 Brandon Ave., S.W., Roanoke 24015
(540) 343-0153

SALEM CAMPUS
109 E. Main St., Salem 24153
(540) 389-1500

THE BRAXTON SCHOOL
4917 Augusta Ave., Richmond 23230-3601
Type: Private business *Accred.:* 1988
(ACICS) *Degrees:* C *CEO:* Dir. Emily
Swelnis
(804) 353-4458

CAREER TRAINING CENTER
4000 W. Broad St., Richmond 23230 *Type:*
Private *Accred.:* 1991 (COE) *Degrees:* C
CEO: Dir. Joe Dillard
FTE Enroll: 261   (804) 342-1190

LYNCHBURG CAMPUS
2600 Memorial Ave., No. 201, Lynchburg
24501
(804) 845-7949

ROANOKE CAMPUS
3223 Brandon Ave., S.W., Roanoke 24018
(703) 981-0925

THE CATHOLIC HOME STUDY INSTITUTE
781 Catoctin Ridge, Paeonian Springs 22129
Type: Private distance education *Accred.:*
1986/1991 (DETC) *Degrees:* C *CEO:* Exec.
Dir. Marianne E. Mount
(540) 883-3737

CENTRAL SCHOOL OF PRACTICAL NURSING
1330 N. Military Hwy., Norfolk 23502
Type: Private professional *Degrees:* C *Prof.
Accred.:* Practical Nursing *CEO:* Dir. Gloria
Rudibaugh
(804) 441-5625

COMPUTER DYNAMICS INSTITUTE
5361 Virginia Beach Blvd., Virginia Beach
23462 *Type:* Private *Accred.:* 1990 (COE)
Degrees: C *CEO:* Dir. Christine Carroll
FTE Enroll: 252   (804) 499-4900

COMPUTER LEARNING CENTER
6295 Edsall Rd., Ste. 210, Alexandria
22312-2617 *Type:* Private business *Accred.:*
1979/1997(ACICS); 1984/1989 (COE) *Degrees:* C *CEO:* Dir. Daniel J. Tokarski
FTE Enroll: 955   (703) 823-0300

LOMBARD CAMPUS
1919 S. Highland Ave, Ste 325-A, Lombard, IL 60148 business *Accred.:* 1979/
1991 (ACICS)
(708) 889-0252

DEFENSE MAPPING SCHOOL
5825 21st St., Ste 106, Fort Belvoir 22060-
5921 *Type:* Public (federal) *Accred.:* 1975/
1990 (SACS-CC) *Degrees:* C *CEO:* Commandant James R. Nichols
FTE Enroll: 210   (703) 805-2557

DOMINION BUSINESS SCHOOL
933 Reservoir St., Harrisonburg 22801
Type: Private business *Accred.:* 1986/1996

(ACICS) *Degrees:* C *CEO:* Dir. Dianne
Phipps
(540) 433-6977

DOMINION BUSINESS SCHOOL
4142-1 Melrose Ave., N.W., No. 1, Roanoke
24017 *Type:* Private business *Accred.:*
1972/1996 (ACICS) *Degrees:* C *CEO:*
Interim Dir. Kathy Duncan
(703) 362-7738

DOMINION BUSINESS SCHOOL
825 Richmond Rd., Staunton 24401 *Type:*
Private business *Accred.:* 1986/1996
(ACICS) *Degrees:* C *CEO:* Dir. Dianne
Phipps
(540) 886-3596

FLATWOODS CIVILIAN CONSERVATION CENTER
Rte. 1, Box 211, Coeburn 24230 Job Corps
Accred.: 1989/1994 (COE) *Degrees:* C
CEO: Dir. Al Lavergne
FTE Enroll: 196   (540) 395-3384

MEDICAL CAREERS INSTITUTE
605 Thimble Shoals Blvd., Ste. 209,
Newport News 23606 *Type:* Private *Ac-
cred.:* 1983/1993 (COE) *Degrees:* C *CEO:*
Pres. Patricia Ettus
FTE Enroll: 185   (804) 873-2423

MICROCOMPUTER TECHNOLOGY CENTER
14904 Jefferson Davis Hwy., Ste. 411,
Woodbridge 22190 *Type:* Private distance
education *Accred.:* 1992/1996 (DETC)
Degrees: C *CEO:* Dir. Kathy Oliver
(703) 491-0393

NATIONAL EDUCATION CENTER—KEE BUSINESS
COLLEGE
803 Dilligence Dr., Newport News 23606
Type: Private business *Accred.:* 1955/1994
(ACICS) *Calendar:* Qtr. plan *Degrees:* C
CEO: Exec. Dir. Zoe Thompson
(804) 873-1111

NAVAL GUIDED MISSILES SCHOOL
2025 Tartar Ave., Virginia Beach 23461-
1996 *Type:* Public (federal) technical
Accred.: 1983/1988 (COE) *Degrees:* C
CEO: Commandant. T. L. Parry, Jr.
FTE Enroll: 210   (804) 433-6628

NAVY AND MARINE CORPS INTELLIGENCE
TRAINING CENTER
Bldg. 420, 2088 Regulus Ave., Virginia
Beach 23461-2099 *Type:* Public (federal)
Accred.: 1987/1992 (SACS-CC) *Degrees:* C
CEO: Commandant. Frank Notz
FTE Enroll: 280   (804) 433-8001

NAVAL SURFACE WARFARE TRAINING CENTER
5395 First St., Dahlgren 22448-5190 *Type:*
Public (federal) *Accred.:* 1993 (COE) *Degrees:* C *CEO:* Dir. E. B. Hontz
FTE Enroll: 276   (540) 653-1023

NORFOLK SKILLS CENTER
922 W. 21st St., Norfolk 23517-1516 *Type:*
Public *Accred.:* 1988/1992 (COE) *Degrees:*
C *CEO:* Dir. Raymond L. Murray
FTE Enroll: 145   (804) 441-2665

OMEGA TRAVEL SCHOOL
3102 Omega Office Park, Fairfax 22031
Type: Private *Accred.:* 1993 (ACCSCT)
Degrees: C *CEO:* Pres. Gloria Bohan
(703) 359-8830

PHILLIPS BUSINESS COLLEGE
P.O. Box 169, 1912 Memorial Ave.,
Lynchburg 24501 *Type:* Private business
Accred.: 1953/1996 (ACICS) *Calendar:* Qtr.
plan *Degrees:* C *CEO:* Dir. J. Dean Hall
(804) 847-7701

PORTSMOUTH GENERAL HEALTH CAREER
CENTER
1000 Leckie St., Portsmouth 23704 *Type:*
Private *Accred.:* 1994 (ACCSCT) *Degrees:*
CEO: Dir. Shirley Schuyler
(804) 398-4646

POTOMAC ACADEMY OF HAIR DESIGN
9101 Center St., Manassas 22110-5405
Type: Private *Accred.:* 1990 (ACCSCT)
Degrees: C *CEO:* Pres. Gail O. Donaway
(703) 361-7775

REPORTING ACADEMY OF VIRGINIA
Pembrook One, Ste. 600, Virginia Beach
23462 *Type:* Private business *Accred.:* 1986
(ACICS) *Calendar:* Qtr. plan *Degrees:* C
CEO: Pres. Jane F. Braithwaite
(804) 499-5447

RICHMOND CAMPUS
1001 Boulders Pkwy., Ste. 305, Richmond
23225 *Accred.:* 1988 (ACICS)
(804) 323-1020

SPRINGFIELD CAMPUS
5501 Backlick Rd., Ste. 250, Springfield
22151 *Accred.:* 1990 (ACICS)
(703) 658-0588

RICHARD M. MILBURN HIGH SCHOOL
14416 Jefferson Davis Hwy., Ste. 12,
Woodbridge 22191 *Type:* Private *Accred.:*
1994 (DETC) *Degrees:* C *CEO:* Pres. Robert
H. Crosby
(703) 494-0147

SOUTHSIDE TRAINING SKILLS CENTER
Hwy. 460, E., Crewe 23930-0258 *Type:*
Public *Accred.:* 1988/1991 (COE) *Degrees:*
C *CEO:* Dir. Gary Groneweg
FTE Enroll: 37   (804) 645-7471

TESST ELECTRONICS AND COMPUTER
INSTITUTE
1400 Duke St., Alexandria 22314-3403
Type: Private *Accred.:* 1986/1993 (ACC-
SCT) *Degrees:* C *CEO:* Dir. Clete
Mehringer
(703) 548-4800

TIDEWATER TECH
2697 Dean Dr., Ste. 100, Virginia Beach
23452 *Type:* Private *Accred.:* 1986 (ACC-
SCT) *Degrees:* C *CEO:* Dir. Carolyn Lake
(804) 340-2121

CHESAPEAKE CAMPUS
932 B Ventures Way, Ste. 310, Chesapeake 23320 *Accred.:* 1993 (ACCSCT)
(804) 548-2828

NEWPORT NEWS CAMPUS
616 Denbigh Blvd., Newport News 23402
Accred.: 1991 (ACCSCT)
(804) 874-2121

NORFOLK CAMPUS
1760 E. Little Creek Rd., Norfolk 23518-
4202 *Accred.:* 1990 (ACCSCT)
(804) 588-2121

VIRGINIA HAIR ACADEMY
3312 Williamson Rd., N.W., Roanoke
24012-4049 *Type:* Private *Accred.:* 1981/
1986 (ACCSCT) *Degrees:* C *CEO:* Pres.
Linwood Locklear

(703) 563-2015

VIRGINIA SCHOOL OF COSMETOLOGY
1516 Willow Lawn Dr., Richmond 23226
Type: Private *Accred.:* 1987/1992 (COE)
Degrees: C *CEO:* Dir. Francis Michael
FTE Enroll: 88   (804) 288-7923

WASHINGTON BUSINESS SCHOOL OF NORTHERN
VIRGINIA
1980 Gallows Rd., Vienna 22182 *Type:*
Private business *Accred.:* 1969/1996 (AC-
ICS) *Calendar:* Qtr. plan *Degrees:* C *CEO:*
Dir. Katherine C. Embrey

(703) 556-8888

WASHINGTON COUNTY ADULT SKILL CENTER
848 Thompson Dr., Abingdon 24210 *Type:*
Public (state) *Accred.:* 1990 (COE) *Degrees:* C *CEO:* Dir. Jerry Crabtree
FTE Enroll: 136   (540) 676-1948

WENTWORTH TECHNICAL SCHOOL
696 Virginia Rd., Concord 01742 *Type:*
Private *Accred.:* 1973/1988 (ACCSCT)
Degrees: C *CEO:* Dir. Dorothy G. Pesek

(508) 371-9977

WOODROW WILSON REHABILITATION CENTER
P.O. Box W-81, Fishersville 22939 *Type:*
Public *Accred.:* 1983/1993 (COE) *Degrees:*
C *CEO:* Dir. Judith Kibler
FTE Enroll: 232   (540) 332-7265

WASHINGTON

BATES TECHNICAL COLLEGE
1101 S. Yakima Ave., Tacoma 98405 *Type:*
Public (district) *System:* Washington State
Board for Community and Technical Colleges *Accred.:* 1988/1995 (NASC) *Calendar:* Sem. plan *Degrees:* C *Prof. Accred.:*
Dental Assisting, Dental Laboratory Technology *CEO:* Pres. William P. Mohler
Enroll: 7,071　　　　　(206) 596-1500

BELLINGHAM TECHNICAL COLLEGE
3028 Lindbergh Ave., Bellingham 98225-
1599 *Type:* Public (district) *System:* Washington State Board for Community and
Technical Colleges *Accred.:* 1995 (NASC
candidate) *Degrees:* C *Prof. Accred.:* Dental
Assisting, EMT-Paramedic *CEO:* Pres.
Desmond McArdle
　　　　　(360) 738-0221

CAREER FLORAL DESIGN INSTITUTE
14350 N.E. 21st, Ste. 1, Bellevue 98005-
2004 *Type:* Private *Accred.:* 1989/1992 (AC-
CSCT) *Degrees:* C *CEO:* Owner Katherine
Salvog
　　　　　(206) 746-8340

CLOVER PARK TECHNICAL COLLEGE
4500 Steilacoom Blvd., S.W., Tacoma
98499-4098 *Type:* Public (district) *System:*
Washington State Board for Community and
Technical Colleges *Accred.:* 1995/1995
(NASC candidate) *Degrees:* C *Prof. Accred.:*
Clinical Lab Technology (C), Dental Assist-
ing (conditional) *CEO:* Admin. Alson E.
Green, Jr.
　　　　　(206) 589-5800

COMMERCIAL TRAINING SERVICES
24325 Pacific Hwy. S., Des Moines 98198-
4026 *Type:* Private *Accred.:* 1978/1990
(ACCSCT) *Degrees:* C *CEO:* Dir. David F.
Minear
　　　　　(206) 824-3970

COURT REPORTING INSTITUTE
929 N. 130th St., Ste. 2, Seattle 98133 *Type:*
Private business *Accred.:* 1991/1994 (AC-
ICS) *Degrees:* C *CEO:* Pres. Alen Janisch
　　　　　(206) 363-8300

SAN DIEGO CAMPUS
1333 Camino del Rio S., San Diego, CA
92108 *Accred.:* 1991/1994 (ACICS)
　　　　　(619) 294-5700

CROWN ACADEMY
8739 S. Hosmer St., Tacoma 98444 *Type:*
Private *Accred.:* 1979/1989 (ACCSCT) *Degrees:* C *CEO:* Pres. John M. Wabel
　　　　　(206) 531-3123

DIVERS INSTITUTE OF TECHNOLOGY
P.O. Box 70667, 4315 11th Ave., N.W., Seattle 98107-0667 *Type:* Private *Accred.:* 1973/
1988 (ACCSCT) *Degrees:* C *CEO:* Dir. John
L. Ritter
　　　　　(206) 783-5542

EMIL FRIES PIANO AND TRAINING CENTER
2510 E. Evergreen Blvd., Vancouver 98661
Type: Private *Accred.:* 1993 (ACCSCT)
Degrees: C *CEO:* Dir. Diane Dees
　　　　　(206) 693-1511

ETON TECHNICAL INSTITUTE
3649 Frontage Rd., Port Orchard 98366
Type: Private business *Accred.:* 1979/1994
(ACICS) *Degrees:* C *Prof. Accred.:* Medical
Assisting *CEO:* Pres. Andy Jones
　　　　　(206) 479-3866

EVERETT CAMPUS
209 E. Casino Rd., Everett 98208 *Accred.:*
1988/1994 (ACICS) *Prof. Accred.:* Medical Assisting
　　　　　(206) 353-4888

FEDERAL WAY CAMPUS
31919 Sixth Ave. S., Federal Way 98003
Accred.: 1987/1994 (ACICS) *Prof. Accred.:* Medical Assisting
　　　　　(206) 941-5800

FOX TRAVEL INSTITUTE
520 Pike St., Ste. 2800, Seattle 98101-4000
Type: Private *Accred.:* 1990 (ACCSCT) *Degrees:* C *CEO:* Vice Pres. Robert Veeder
　　　　　(206) 224-7800

INTERNATIONAL AIR ACADEMY
2901 E. Mill Plain Blvd., Vancouver 98661-4899 *Type:* Private *Accred.:* 1983/1988 (AC-CSCT) *Degrees:* C *CEO:* Pres. Arch Miller
(206) 695-2500

ONTARIO CAMPUS
2980 Inland Empire Blvd., Ontario, CA 91764-4804 *Accred.:* 1991 (ACCSCT)
(714) 989-5222

NORTHWEST SCHOOL OF WOODEN BOATBUILDING
251 Otto St., Port Townsend 98368 *Type:* Private *Accred.:* 1993 (ACCSCT) *Degrees:* C *CEO:* Dir. Andrew L. Patten
(360) 385-4948

PACIFIC NORTHWEST BALLET SCHOOL
4649 Sunnyside Ave. N., Seattle 98103 *Type:* Private *Degrees:* C *Prof. Accred.:* Dance *CEO:* Dir. Francia Russell
(206) 547-5910

PERRY TECHNICAL INSTITUTE
2011 W. Washington Ave., Yakima 98903-1296 *Type:* Private *Accred.:* 1969/1990 (AC-CSCT) *Degrees:* C *CEO:* Dir. J. Tuman
(509) 453-0374

TRIDENT TRAINING FACILITY
Silverdale 98315-5400 *Type:* Public (federal) *Accred.:* 1991 (NASC) *Degrees:* C *CEO:* Cmnd. Ofcr. Jimmy Lee Ellis
Enroll: 5,302   (206) 396-4068

VOCATIONAL TRAINING INSTITUTE
6400M N.E. Hwy. 99, Vancouver 98665 *Type:* Private *Accred.:* 1992 (ACCSCT) *Degrees:* C *CEO:* Pres. Charles Kroninger
(206) 695-5186

WEST VIRGINIA

B.M. SPURR SCHOOL OF PRACTICAL NURSING
800 Wheeling Ave., Glen Dale 26038 *Type:* Public *Degrees:* C *Prof. Accred.:* Practical Nursing *CEO:* Dir. Dorothy McCulley
(304) 845-3211

BOONE COUNTY CAREER CENTER
Box 50 B, Danville 25053 *Type:* Private *Degrees:* C *Prof. Accred.:* Medical Laboratory Technology *CEO:* Dir. Rodney Smith
(304) 369-4585

CARVER CAREER AND TECHNICAL EDUCATION CENTER
4799 Midland Dr., Charleston 25306 *Type:* Private *Degrees:* C *Prof. Accred.:* Respiratory Therapy Technology *CEO:* Princ. Norma Miller
(304) 348-1965

CLARKSBURG SKILLS TRAINING CENTER
120 Linden Ave., Clarksburg 26301 *Accred.:* 1994 (ACCSCT) *Calendar:* 12-mos. program *Degrees:* C *CEO:* Proj. Dir. Homer Kincaid
Enroll: 34
(304) 623-6036

MONONGALIA COUNTY TECHNICAL EDUCATION CENTER
1000 Mississippi St., Morgantown 26505 *Type:* Public *Degrees:* C *Prof. Accred.:* Surgical Technology *CEO:* Dir. Donald R. Riley
(304) 291-9240

MORGANTOWN SKILLS TRAINING CENTER
1644 Mileground, Morgantown 26505 *Type:* Private *Accred.:* 1994 (ACCSCT) *Degrees:* C *CEO:* Proj. Dir. Homer Kincaid
Enroll: 60
(304) 296-3548

WOOD COUNTY VOCATIONAL SCHOOL
1511 Blizzard Dr., Parkersburg 26101 *Type:* Public *Degrees:* C *Prof. Accred.:* Practical Nursing *CEO:* Dir. William Gainer
(304) 420-9501

WISCONSIN

ACME INSTITUTE OF TECHNOLOGY
102 Revere Dr., Manitowoc 54220 *Type:* Private *Accred.:* 1967/1989 (ACCSCT) *Degrees:* C *CEO:* Dir. Barbara A. Pitrowski
(414) 682-6144

ACME INSTITUTE OF TECHNOLOGY
819 S. 60th St., West Allis 53214-3365 *Type:* Private *Accred.:* 1967/1989 (ACCSCT) *Degrees:* C *CEO:* Dir. Shirle A. Miick
(414) 257-1011

CAPRI COLLEGE
6414 Odana Rd., Madison 53719 *Type:* Private *Accred.:* 1994 (ACCSCT) *Calendar:* Qtr. plan *Degrees:* C *CEO:* Dir. Brenda Gavinski *Enroll:* 92
(608) 274-5390

DIESEL TRUCK DRIVER TRAINING SCHOOL
Hwy. 151 and Elder Ln., Rte. 2, Sun Prairie 53590-0047 *Type:* Private *Accred.:* 1973/1988 (ACCSCT) *Degrees:* C *CEO:* Pres. Mark Klabacka
(608) 837-7800

MBTI BUSINESS TRAINING INSTITUTE
606 W. Wisconsin Ave., Milwaukee 53203 *Type:* Private business *Accred.:* 1969/1987 (ACICS) *Degrees:* C *CEO:* Pres. Sandra C. Suzuki
(414) 272-2192

WAUKESHA CAMPUS
237 South St., Waukesha 53186 *Accred.:* 1993 (ACICS)
(414) 527-3221

MIDWEST CENTER FOR THE STUDY OF ORIENTAL MEDICINE
6226 Bankers Rd., Stes. 5 and 6, Racine 53403 *Type:* Private professional *Calendar:* Qtr. plan *Degrees:* C *Prof. Accred.:* Acupuncture (C) *CEO:* Pres. William Dunbar
FTE Enroll: 57   (414) 554-2010

TRANS AMERICAN SCHOOL OF BROADCASTING
600 Williamson St., Madison 53703-3588 *Type:* Private *Accred.:* 1972/1987 (ACCSCT) *Calendar:* Sem. plan *Degrees:* C *CEO:* Dir. Chris Hutchings
(608) 257-4600

WISCONSIN CONSERVATORY OF MUSIC, INC.
1584 N. Prospect Ave., Milwaukee 53202 *Type:* Private *Degrees:* C *Prof. Accred.:* Music *CEO:* Exec. Dir. Joyce Altman
(414) 276-5760

WISCONSIN SCHOOL OF PROFESSIONAL PET GROOMING
34197 Wisconsin Ave., Okauchee 53069 *Type:* Private *Accred.:* 1991 (ACCSCT) *Degrees:* C *CEO:* Admin. Delores Lillge
(414) 569-9492

WYOMING

CHEYENNE AERO TECH
1204 Airport Pkwy., Cheyenne 82001-1552 *Type:* Private *Accred.:* 1985/1988 (ACC-SCT) *Degrees:* C *CEO:* Exec. Dir. Michael A. Smith
(307) 632-1090

SAGE TECHNICAL SERVICES
190 Pronghorn St., Casper 82604 *Type:* Private *Accred.:* 1994 (ACCSCT) *Degrees:* C *CEO:* Dir. Brent Boettiger
Enroll: 100   (307) 234-0242

WYOMING TECHNICAL INSTITUTE
4373 N. Third St., Laramie 82070 *Type:* Private *Accred.:* 1969/1989 (ACCSCT) *Degrees:* C *CEO:* Vice Pres. Jim Mathis
(307) 742-3776

OUTSIDE THE UNITED STATES

BAHAMAS

BAHAMAS HOTEL TRAINING COLLEGE
  College Ave., Oakes Field, Nassau *Type:*
  Public technical *Accred.:* 1977/1990 (COE)
  Degrees: C *CEO:* Dir. Kendal C. Johnson
  FTE Enroll: 66   (809) 323-8175

FREEPORT CAMPUS
  P.O. Box F-1679, Freeport
                              (809) 352-2896

CANADA

DAWSON COLLEGE
  2120 Sherbrooke St. E., Montreal H2K 1C1
  Type: Private *Calendar:* Sem. plan *Degrees:*
  C *Prof. Accred.:* Interior Design *CEO:*
  Chrmn. Eugene Zamorski
                              (514) 931-8371

LAKELAND COLLEGE
  Bag 5100, Vermillion T0B 4M0 *Type:* Private
  Calendar: Sem. plan *Degrees:* C *Prof. Ac-
  cred.:* Interior Design *CEO:* Pres. D. Schmit
                              (403) 853-8400

MOUNT ROYAL COLLEGE
  4825 Richard Rd., S.W., Calgary T3E 6K6
  Type: Private *Calendar:* Sem. plan *Degrees:*
  C *Prof. Accred.:* Interior Design *CEO:*
  Chairperson Janice Smith
                              (403) 240-6100

SWITZERLAND

HOTEL MANAGEMENT SCHOOL, "LES ROCHES"
  Bluche Crans-Montana, Valais CH-3975
  Type: Private *Accred.:* 1991 (NEASC-CTCI)
  Degrees: C *CEO:* Dir. Peter Schlatter
  FTE Enroll: 966   [41] (27) 41-1223

MAJOR CHANGES

ALABAMA

C.A. Fredd State Technical College *and* Shelton State Community College merged to become Shelton State Community College (summer 1994)

Coastal Training Institute closed (winter 1995)

Jefferson Davis State Junior College *and* Atmore State Technical College merged to become Jefferson Davis Community College (summer 1994)

J. F. Ingram State Community Technical College changes its name to Ingram State Community College (fall 1993)

Livingston University changed its name to The University of West Alabama (spring 1995)

Meadows College of Business closed (spring 1995)

Mobile College changed its name to University of Mobile (summer 1993)

National Career College closed (summer 1994)

New World College of Business closed (summer 1994)

Phillips Junior College (Birmingham) closed (fall 1995)

Phillips Junior College (Mobile) closed (fall 1995)

Shoals Community College *and* Northwest Alabama Community College merged to become Northwest Shoals Community College (summer 1994)

Southern Union State Junior College *and* Opelika Technical College merged to become Southern Union State Community College (summer 1994)

Walker College *and* University of Alabama–Birmingham merged to become University of Alabama Birmingham–Walker College (summer 1994)

ALASKA

Alaska Junior College closed (fall 1995)

The Travel Academy changed its name to The Career Academy (summer 1995)

ARIZONA

American Indian Bible College changed its name to American Indian College of the Assemblies of God (summer 1994)

American Tellers Schools *and* Arizona Institute of Technology merged to become Arizona Institute of Technology (summer 1995)

Apollo College—Westridge closed (winter 1995)

Arizona School of Pharmacy Technology changed its name to Arizona College of Allied Health (winter 1995)

Institute of Business and Medical Technology closed (summer 1995)

Lamson Business College changed its name to Interstate Career College (summer 1995)

Lamson Junior College closed (summer 1994)

Laural School changed its name to Distance Learning International and moved to Southdale, TX (winter 1995)

Modern Schools of America moved to Southdale, TX (winter 1995)

Northern Arizona Institute of Technology closed (fall 1995)

Pedigree Career Institute (Phoenix) closed (winter 1995)

Southwestern Assemblies of God College changes its name to Southwestern Assemblies of God University (summer 1995)

Sterling School changed its name to Arizona Paralegal Training Program (fall 1995)

ARKANSAS

Arkansas College changed its name to Lyon College (summer 1994)

Major Changes

South Central Career College closed (summer 1994)

CALIFORNIA
California School of Court Reporting (Santa Ana) closed (fall 1995)
California Family Study Center changed its name to Phillips Graduate Institute (spring 1995)
Catherine College closed (fall 1995)
Christ College changed its name to Concordia University (summer 1993)
Cogswell College changed its name to Cogswell Polytechnical College (spring 1994)
Computer Learning Center (Riverside) closed (summer 1994)
ConCorde Career Institute (Van Nuys) closed (summer 1994)
Institute of Business and Medical Technology closed (fall 1995)
Med-Help Training School closed (spring 1994)
Merit College closed (fall 1995)
National Education Center—Bryman Campus (Oakland) closed (summer 1994)
National Education Center—Sawyer Campus (Commerce) closed (fall 1995)
National Hispanic University (Oakland) closed (spring 1995)
Oakland College of Court Reporting closed (summer 1994)
Phillips Junior College (Fresno) closed (fall 1995)
Sawyer College at Pomona closed (fall 1995)
St. Joseph's College closed (fall 1993)
Technical Health Careers School closed (spring 1994)
Watterson College Pacific (Oxnard and Vista) closed (winter 1995)
Western State University College of Law of San Diego changed its name to Thomas Jefferson
School of Law (summer 1995)

COLORADO
American Diesel and Auto College closed (summer 1995)
Columbine College closed (summer 1995)
Denver Academy of Court Reporting (Colorado Springs) closed (fall 1995)
Medical Careers Training Center changed its name to Institute of Business and Medical Careers
(summer 1995)
Mile Hi College, Inc. closed (summer 1994)
St. Thomas Theological Seminary closed (summer 1995)

CONNECTICUT
Bridgeport Engineering Institute *and* Fairfield University merged to become Fairfield University
(summer 1994)
Hartford Secretarial School changed its name to Fox Institute of Business (summer 1994)
St. Vincent's College of Nursing changed its name to St. Vincent's College (spring 1995)
The Salter School closed (summer 1994)

DELAWARE
Delaware State College changed its name to Delaware State University (summer 1993)

DISTRICT OF COLUMBIA
Defense Intelligence College changed its name to Joint Military Intelligence College (summer
1994)
National Education Center Capitol Hill Campus closed (summer 1994)

FLORIDA
Atlantic Coast Institute closed (summer 1994)
Bay Area Legal Academy closed (summer 1994)
Branell Institute closed (summer 1994)
Briarcliff College closed (summer 1994)
Business Training Institute (Clearwater) closed (summer 1994)
Career City College changed its name to City College (summer 1994)
Crown Business Institute closed (fall 1995)
Florida Career Institute changed its name to Southwest Florida College of Business (summer 1994)
Legal Career Institute changed its name to Atlantic Coast Institute (summer 1994)
Miami Christian College changed its name to Trinity College at Miami (summer 1994)
National Education Center—Tampa Technical Institute changed its name to Education America
    (summer 1995)
North Florida Junior College changed its name to North Florida Community College (summer 1995)
Phillips Junior College closed (fall 1995)
West Virginia Career College (Daytona Beach) closed (fall 1995)
Wilma Boyd Career Schools (West Palm Beach) closed (summer 1994)

GEORGIA
American College of the Applied Arts changed its name to American College (summer 1994)
Atlanta College of Medical and Dental Careers closed (winter 1994)
Branell Institute closed (summer 1994)
Brenau College changed its name to Brenau University (winter 1993)
Massey Institute closed (fall 1995)
Meadows College of Business closed (summer 1994)
Quality Plus Office Skills and Motivational Training Center closed (fall 1995)

GUAM
International Business College of Guam closed (summer 1994)

HAWAII
Cannon's International Business College closed (summer 1994)

ILLINOIS
Brown's Business College closed (summer 1994)
Catherine College closed (summer 1994)
Chicago College of Osteopathic Medicine changed its name to Midwestern University (summer 1993)
Lexington Institute of Hospitality Careers changed its name to Lexington College (winter 1995)
Marycrest College (Kankakee) closed (summer 1994)
Montay College closed (summer 1995)
Phillips College of Chicago closed (summer 1994)
Quincy College changed its name to Quincy University (spring 1993)
Sangamon State University changed its name to University of Illinois—Springfield (summer 1995)
Spertus College of Judaica changed its name to Spertus Institute of Jewish Studies (summer 1994)
The University of Health Sciences/The Chicago Medical School changed its name to The Herman
    M. Finch University of Health Sciences/The Chicago Medical School (winter 1994)
Trinity College at Miami changed its name to Trinity International University—South Florida
    (winter 1994)
Woodbridge Business Institute closed (summer 1993)

Major Changes

INDIANA

Aristotle College of Medical and Dental Technology (Indianapolis) closed (fall 1994)

Aristotle College of Medical and Dental Technology (Hammond) closed (fall 1994)

Goshen Biblical Seminary and Mennonite Biblical Seminary merged to become Associated Mennonite Biblical Seminary (summer 1993)

Indiana Vocational Technical Colleges changed their names to Ivy Tech State Colleges (summer 1994)

Teikyo Westmar University changed its name to Westmar University (spring 1995)

IOWA

Buena Vista College changed its name to Buena Vista University(summer 1995)

Cedar Rapids School of Hairstyling changed its name to American College of Hairstyling — Cedar Rapids (winter 1995)

Hawkeye Institute of Technology changed its name to Hawkeye Community College (summer 1993)

Iowa School of Barbering and Hairstyling changed its name to American College of Hairstyling— Des Moines (winter 1995)

Maharishi International University changed its name to Maharishi University of Management (summer 1995)

Spencer School of Business changed its name to Spencer College (summer 1994)

KANSAS

Wichita Business College closed (fall 1995)

KENTUCKY

CareerCom Junior College of Business closed (fall 1995)

Humana Health Institute changed its name to The Health Institute of Louisville (summer 1994)

Kentucky School of Financial Education changed its name to School of Business and Banking (summer 1994)

LOUISIANA

Delta Career College closed (summer 1994)

Delta College (Houma) closed (fall 1995)

Delta Junior College (Baton Rouge) closed (fall 1995)

Delta Junior College (Covington) closed (fall 1995)

Delta Schools closed (fall 1995)

Elaine P. Nunez Community College changed its name to Nunez Community College (summer 1994)

Louisiana State Colleges and Universities changed its name to University of Louisiana System (summer 1995)

Our Lady of the Lake College of Nursing and Allied Health changed its name to Our Lady of the Lake College (summer 1995)

Phillips Junior College closed (fall 1995)

Southern Technical College changed its name to Remington College (summer 1994)

MAINE

Washington County Vocational-Technical Institute changed its name to Washington County Technical College (summer 1993)

MARYLAND
National Education Center Temple School Campus closed (summer 1994)
Woodridge Business Institute closed (winter 1995)

MASSACHUSETTS
Dean Junior College changed its name to Dean College (summer 1993)
Weston School of Theology changed its name to Weston Jesuit School of Theology (summer 1995)

MICHIGAN
Detroit Business Institute (Southfield) closed (summer 1994)
Dorsey Business School (Southfield) closed (summer 1994)
Grand Rapids Baptist College and Seminary changed its name to Cornerstone College and Grand
    Rapids Baptist Seminary (summer 1994)
Pontiac Business Institute closed (fall 1995)
Sawyer School of Business closed (winter 1995)

MINNESOTA
College of Associated Arts changed its name to College of Visual Arts (summer 1995)
ConCorde Career Institute closed (fall 1995)
Luther Northwestern Theological Seminary changed its name to Luther Seminary (summer 1994)
St. Mary's College of Minnesota changed its name to St. Mary's University of Minnesota
    (Fall 1994)

MISSISSIPPI
Moore Career College (Meridian) closed (fall 1994)
Phillips Junior College closed (fall 1995)
Queen City College (Greenville) closed (spring 1995)
Wood Junior College changed its name to Wood College (winter 1993)

MISSOURI
Berean College changed its name to Berean University (winter 1995)
Bryan Travel College changed its name to Bryan Career College (fall 1995)
Heart of the Ozarks Technical Community College changed its name to Ozarks Technical
    Community College (summer 1994)
Missouri School for Doctors' Assistants changed its name to Missouri College (summer 1995)
National Career Institute closed (fall 1995)
Omaha College of Business closed (summer 1994)
Rolla Area Vocational-Technical School changed its name to Rolla Technical Institute (Winter 1993)
St. Louis Conservatory and School for the Arts changed its name to St. Louis Symphony
    Community Music School (summer 1994)
Watterson College closed (summer 1994)
William Woods College changed its name to William Woods University (spring 1993)

MONTANA
Billings Vocational-Technical Center changed its name to Montana State
    University–Billings/College of Technology (summer 1994)
Butte Vocational-Technical Center changed its name to Montana Tech of The University of
    Montana–Division of Technology (summer 1994)
College of Great Falls changed its name to University of Great Falls (summer 1995)

Major Changes

Eastern Montana College changed its name to Montana State University–Billings (summer 1994)
Great Falls Vocational-Technical Center changed its name to Montana State University College of Technology–Great Falls (summer 1994)
Helena Vocational-Technical Center changed its name to Helena College of Technology of The University of Montana (summer 1994)
Missoula Vocational-Technical Center changed its name to The University of Montana–Missoula/College of Technology (summer 1994)
Montana College of Mineral Science changed its name to Montana Tech of The University of Montana (summer 1994)
Montana State University changed its name to Montana State University–Bozeman (summer 1994)
The University of Montana changed its name to The University of Montana–Missoula (summer 1994)
Western Montana College changed its name to Western Montana College of The University of Montana (summer 1994)

NEBRASKA

Bellevue College changed its name to Bellevue University (summer 1994)
Gateway Electronics Institute changed its name to Gateway College (summer 1995)
Grace College of the Bible has changed its name to Grace University (summer 1995)
Institute of Computer Science closed (summer 1995)
Omaha College of Business closed (summer 1994)

NEVADA

Northern Nevada Community College changed its name to Great Basin College (summer 1995)
Phillips Junior College changed its name to Phillips College (fall 1995)

NEW HAMPSHIRE

School for Lifelong Learning changed its name to College for Lifelong Learning (summer 1993)

NEW JERSEY

Bilingual Institute closed (fall 1995)
Drake College of Business (East Orange) closed (fall 1995)
Global Business Institute closed (summer 1994)
Sawyer School closed (summer 1994)
SCS Business and Technical Institute closed (summer 1994)
The Richard Stockton College of New Jersey changed its name to Stockton College of New Jersey (summer 1994)
Upsala College closed (fall 1995)
Westminster Choir College–Rider College changed its name to Westminster Choir College of Rider University (summer 1994)

NEW MEXICO

AzTech College closed (winter 1995)
International Business College changed its name to Western Business Institute (summer 1994)
Lajuc Business College closed (summer 1994)

NEW YORK

Advanced Software Analysis (Brooklyn) changed its name to ASA Institute of Business and Computer Technology (fall 1995)

Advanced Software Analysis (Broadway) changed its name to Globe Institute of Technology
(summer 1994)
American Business Institute closed (summer 1994)
Maryknoll School of Theology closed (fall 1995)
Mercy College (Peekskill Campus) closed (spring 1993)
Pace Business School (Bronx and Yonkers locations) closed (summer 1994)
SCS Business and Technical Institute closed (summer 1994)
The Berkeley School of New York changed its name to Berkeley College of New York City
(fall 1995)
The King's College closed (winter 1994)
Union College (Poughkeepsie Branch Campus) closed (summer 1994)

NORTH CAROLINA
Carolina Beauty College (Gastonia) closed (winter 1995)
Carolina Beauty College (Kannapolis) closed (Fall 1994)
Carolina Beauty College (Mt. Airy) closed (winter 1995)
Carolina Beauty College (Statesville) closed (winter 1995)
Cecils Junior College of Business changed its name to Cecils College (summer 1994)
Gardner-Webb College changed its name to Gardner-Webb University (summer 1993)
Skyline Academy of Cosmetic Arts changed its name to American Education Institute of
Cosmetology (summer 1994)
Wingate College changed its name to Wingate University (summer 1995)

NORTH DAKOTA
Turtle Mountain School of Paramedical Technique closed (summer 1994)

OHIO
Antonelli Institute of Art and Photography changed its name to Antonelli College
(summer 1995)
Cincinnati School of Court Reporting and Business closed (winter 1995)
Cincinnati Technical College changed its name to Cincinnati State Technical and Community
College (summer 1994)
Clermont College changed its name to University of Cincinnati–Clermont College
(summer 1994)
Dyke College changed its name to David Myers College (summer 1995)
Hammel College closed (summer 1994)
Jefferson Technical College changed its name to Jefferson Community College (summer 1995)
Marycrest College (Toledo) closed (summer 1994)
Miami-Jacobs Junior College of Business changed its name to Miami-Jacobs College (summer 1994)
Owens Technical College changed its name to Owens Community College (summer 1994)
Penn-Ohio College closed (fall 1995)
Raymond Walters College changed its name to University of Cincinnati–Raymond Walters
College (summer 1994)
Southern Ohio College (Fairfield) closed (fall 1995)
Stautzenberger College–South closed (summer 1994)
Technology Education Center changed its name to Technology Education College (Spring 1994)
Terra Technical College changed its name to Terra State Community College (summer 1994)
Walsh College changed its name to Walsh University (winter 1993)

Major Changes

OKLAHOMA
Draughon's College (Tulsa) closed (winter 1994)
Indian Meridian Vocational-Technical Center changed its name to Meridian Technology Center (winter 1994)
Oklahoma Junior College closed (fall 1995)
Phillips Graduate Seminary changed its name to Phillips Theological Seminary (summer 1995)

OREGON
Concordia College changed its name to Concordia University (summer 1995)
La Grande College of Business closed (fall 1995)
Marylhurst College for Lifelong Learning changed its name to Marylhurst College (winter 1993)
Multnomah School of the Bible changed its name to Multnomah Bible College (fall 1993)
Oklahoma Junior College closed (summer 1994)
Trend College closed (summer 1994)
Western Medical College of Allied Health Careers closed (summer 1994)

PENNSYLVANIA
Hahnemann University *and* Medical College of Pennsylvania merged to become Medical College of Pennsylvania and Hahnemann University (summer 1994)
Harcum Junior College changed its name to Harcum College (winter 1993)
Keystone Junior College changed its name to Keystone College (Winter 1995)
Lehigh County Community College changed its name to Lehigh Carbon Community College (winter 1994)
Liberty Academy of Business closed (winter 1995)
New Kensington Commercial School changed its name to Newport Business Institute (fall 1995)
Palmer Business Institute closed (summer 1994)
Pennsylvania Business Institute (Pottstown) closed (fall 1995)
Pennsylvania Business Institute (Nesquehoning) closed (fall 1995)
SCS Business and Technical Institute (Philadelphia) closed (summer 1994)
Shenango Valley School of Business changed its name to Business Institute of Pennsylvania (fall 1995)
Valley Forge Military Junior College changed its name to Valley Forge Military College (summer 1993)
Washington Institute of Technology closed (summer 1994)

PUERTO RICO
Allied Schools of Puerto Rico closed (fall 1995)
Bayamon Technical & Commercial Inc. closed (summer 1994)
Benedict School of Languages and Commerce closed (summer 1994)
Columbia College (Rio Grande) closed (fall 1995)
Coastal Training Institute closed (winter 1995)
Humacao Community College (Fajardo) closed (fall 1995)
Institute of Multiple Technology closed (summer 1994)
International College of Business and Technology changed its name to International Junior College (summer 1994)
San Juan City College (Arecibo) closed (winter 1994)

SOUTH CAROLINA
Central Wesleyan College changed its name to Southern Wesleyan University (fall 1995)

Columbia Bible College and Seminary changed its name to Columbia International University (winter 1993)

Navy Fleet and Mine Warfare Training Center closed (fall 1995)

University of South Carolina–Coastal Carolina changed its name to Coastal Carolina University (summer 1993)

SOUTH DAKOTA

Mitchell Vocational-Technical Institute changed its name to Mitchell Technical Institute (summer 1993)

Sioux Falls College changed its name to University ofSioux Falls (winter 1995)

Western Dakota Vocational-Technical Institute changed its name to Western Dakota Technical Institute (summer 1993)

TENNESSEE

Bobbie's School of Beauty Arts changed its name to Academy of Beauty Arts (summer 1994)

Branell Institute closed (summer 1994)

Court Reporting Institute of Tennessee changed its name to Nashville Career School (winter 1994)

Draughon's College (Memphis) closed (summer 1994)

International Barber and Style College (Chattanooga) changes its name to National School of Hair Design (spring 1994)

International Barber and Style College (Madison) closed (spring 1994)

Memphis Aero Tech closed (winter 1995)

Memphis State University changed its name to University of Memphis (summer 1994)

Miller-Hawkins Business College closed (summer 1994)

Nashville College closed (spring 1994)

State Area Vocational-Technical School—Knoxville changed its name to Tennessee Technology Center—Knoxville (summer 1995)

State Area Vocational-Technical School—Memphis changed its name to Tennessee Technology Center—Memphis(summer 1995)

University of Beauty (Cleveland) closed (winter 1995)

William Jennings Bryan College changed its name to Bryan College (summer 1993)

TEXAS

Ambassador College changed its name to Ambassador University (fall 1994)

ATI—Graphic Arts Institute closed (summer 1994)

Bauder Fashion College—Arlington closed (fall 1995)

Bish Mathis Institute closed (summer 1994)

Branell Institute closed (summer 1994)

Brazos Business College closed (summer 1994)

Concordia Lutheran College changed its name to Concordia University at Austin (summer 1995)

Cooke County College changed its name to North Central Texas College (summer 1994)

Draughon's College (Ft. Worth) closed (summer 1994)

Four-C College closed (summer 1994)

International Aviation and Travel Academy (Dallas) closed (winter 1995)

Keith's Metro Hair Academy closed (summer 1995)

Lamar University System closed (summer 1995)

Laredo State University changed its name to Texas A&M International University (summer 1993)

Massey Business College closed (summer 1994)

Metro Business Academy closed (summer 1995)

National Education Center—Fort Worth Campus changed its name to Education America (summer 1995)

Major Changes

National Education Center Bryman Campus (Houston) closed (summer 1994)

Old Texas College of Osteopathic Medicine changed its name to University of North Texas Health
    Science Center at Fort Worth (fall 1995)

Phillips School of Business and Technology closed (summer 1994)

Sebring Career Schools (Corsicana, TX) changed its name to Taylor's Institute of Cosmetology
    (summer 1994)

Texas State Technical College—Amarillo is now a branch of Amarillo College and changed its
    name to Amarillo College—Amarillo Technical Center (Summer 1995)

Tyler School of Business closed (summer 1994)

West Texas State University changed its name to West Texas A&M University (summer 1993)

Utah

Utah Valley Community College changed its name to Utah Valley State College (summer 1993)

Virginia

Commonwealth College closed (spring 1995)

National Education Center Kee Business College (Norfolk, Richmond, and Portsmouth locations)
    closed (summer 1994)

Southern Virginia College for Women changed its name to Southern Virginia College
    (summer 1994)

Woodbridge Business Institute closed (summer 1994)

Washington

Bastyr College changed its name to Bastyr University (winter 1993)

Capitol Business College closed (summer 1994)

Cogswell College North changed its name to Henry Cogswell College (summer 1995)

Griffin College closed (summer 1993)

Trend College closed (summer 1994)

West Virginia

South West Virginia Community College changed its name to South West Virginia Community
    and Technical College (summer 1995)

Wisconsin

Northwestern College merged with Martin Luther College in New Ulm, MN and closed the
    Wisconsin campus (summer 1995)

OUTSIDE THE UNITED STATES

Micronesia

Community College of Micronesia changed its name to College of Micronesia (summer 1993)

Micronesian Occupational College changed its name to Palau Community College (summer 1993)

Switzerland

Hotel Institute for Management closed (winter 1995)

Candidates

Candidates for Accreditation

Candidate for Accreditation is a status of affiliation with a recognized accrediting commission which indicates that an institution has achieved initial recognition and is progressing toward, but has not been assured, accreditation.

The Candidate for Accreditation classification is designed for postsecondary institutions which may or may not be fully operative. In either case, the institution must provide evidence of sound planning, the resources to implement these plans, and appear to have the potential for attaining its goals within a reasonable time.

To be considered for Candidate for Accreditation status, the applicant organization must be a postsecondary education institution with the following characteristics:

(1) Have a charter and/or formal authority from an appropriate governmental agency to award a certificate, diploma, or degree.
(2) Have a governing board which includes representation reflecting the public interest.
(3) Have employed a chief administrative officer.
(4) Offer, or plan to offer, one or more educational programs of at least one academic year in length, or the equivalent at the postsecondary level, with clearly defined and published educational objectives, as well as a clear statement of the means for achieving them.
(5) Include general education at the postsecondary level as a prerequisite to or as an essential element in its principal educational programs.
(6) Have admission policies compatible with its stated objectives.
(7) Have developed a preliminary survey or evidence of basic planning for the development of the institution.
(8) Have established an adequate financial base of funding commitments and have available a summary of its latest audited financial statement.

DEGREE GRANTING CANDIDATE INSTITUTIONS

ARIZONA

COCONINO COUNTY COMMUNITY COLLEGE
3000 N. 4th St. Ste.17, Flaggstaff 86004
Type: Public *Accred.:* 1994/1996 (NCA candidate) *Calendar:* Sem. plan *Degrees:* A
CEO: Pres. Phillip Tullar
Enroll: 3,527   (602) 527-1222

ARKANSAS

COSSATOT TECHNICAL COLLEGE
PO Box 960, DeQueen 71832 *Type:* Public
System: Arkansas Department of Higher
Education *Accred.:* 1994 (NCA candidate)
Calendar: Sem. plan *Degrees:* A *CEO:* Pres.
Frank G. Adams
Enroll: 462   (501) 584-4471

MID-SOUTH COMMUNITY COLLEGE
PO Box 2067, West Memphis 72301 *Type:*
Public *System:* Arkansas Department of
Higher Education *Accred.:* 1995 (NCA candidate) *Degrees:* A *CEO:* Pres. Glen Fenter
Enroll: 508   (501) 773-6700

OUACHITA TECHNICAL COLLEGE
One College Dr., Malvern 72104 *Type:* Public *System:* Arkansas Department of Higher
Education *Accred.:* 1994 (NCA candidate)
Calendar: Sem. plan *Degrees:* A *CEO:* Pres.
Ken Martin
Enroll: 482   (501) 332-3658

OZARKA TECHNICAL COLLEGE
P.O. Box 10, Melbourne 72556 *Type:* Public
technical *System:* Arkansas Department of
Higher Education *Accred.:* 1993/1995 (NCA
candidate) *Calendar:* Sem. plan *Degrees:* A,
C *CEO:* Pres. Douglas Rush
Enroll: 371   (501) 368-7371

PETIT JEAN TECHNICAL COLLEGE
Hwy. 9 N., P.O. Box 586, Morrilton 72110
Type: Public technical *System:* Arkansas
Department of Higher Education *Accred.:*
1993/1995 (NCA candidate) *Calendar:* Sem.

plan *Degrees:* A, C *CEO:* Pres. Nathan
Crook
Enroll: 617   (501) 354-2465

PINES TECHNICAL COLLEGE
1900 Hazel St., Pine Bluff 71603 *Type:* Public *System:* Arkansas Department of Higher
Education *Accred.:* 1994 (NCA candidate)
Calendar: Sem. plan *Degrees:* A *CEO:* Pres.
Terry Puckett
Enroll: 806   (501) 543-5900

CALIFORNIA

FIVE BRANCHES INSTITUTE COLLEGE OF
TRADITIONAL CHINESE MEDICINE
200 7th Ave., Ste. 115, Santa Cruz 95062
Type: Private professional *Calendar:* Sem.
plan *Degrees:* M *Prof. Accred.:* Acupuncture
(M-candidate) *CEO:* Dean Ron Zaidman
FTE Enroll: 75   (408) 476-9424

INSTITUTE OF TRANSPERSONAL PSYCHOLOGY
744 San Antonio Rd., Ste. 15, Palo Alto
94303-4613   *Type:*   Private   *Accred.:*
1992/1995 (WASC-Sr. candidate) *Calendar:*
Qtr. plan *Degrees:* M, D *CEO:* Pres. Ben A.
Mancini
FTE Enroll: 294   (415) 493-4430

PACIFICA GRADUATE INSTITUTE
249 Lambert Rd., Carpinteria 93013 *Type:*
Private *Accred.:* 1994 (WASC-Sr. candidate)
Calendar: Qtr. plan *Degrees:* M, D *CEO:*
Pres. Stephen Aizenstat
FTE Enroll: 363   (805) 969-3626

FLORIDA

FLORIDA HOSPITAL COLLEGE OF HEALTH
SCIENCES
800 Lake Estelle Dr., Orlando 32803 *Type:*
Private *Accred.:* 1994 (SACS-CC candidate)
Calendar: Sem. plan *Degrees:* A *CEO:* Pres.
David E. Greenlaw
FTE Enroll: 248   (407) 895-7747

FLORIDA NATIONAL COLLEGE
4206 W. 12th Ave., Hialeah 33012 *Type:* Private *Accred.:* 1993 (SACS-CC candidate) *Degrees:* A *CEO:* Dir. Jose Regueiro
FTE Enroll: 834   (305) 821-3333

MIAMI CAMPUS
11373 W. Flagler St., Miami 33172
(305) 226-9999

MIAMI CAMPUS
5761 S.W. Bird Rd., Miami 33155
(305) 663-6464

TRINITY COLLEGE OF FLORIDA
2430 Trinity Oaks Blvd., New Port Richey 34655 *Type:* Private (nondenominational) *Accred.:* 1990 (AABC candidate) *Calendar:* Sem. plan *Degrees:* A, B, C *CEO:* Pres. Glenn Speed, Jr.
FTE Enroll: 74   (813) 376-6911

WORSLEY INSTITUTE OF CLASSICAL ACUPUNCTURE
6175 N.W. 153rd St., Ste. 324, Miami Lakes 33014 *Type:* Private professional *Calendar:* Tri. plan *Degrees:* M *Prof. Accred.:* Acupuncture *CEO:* Pres. J. R. Worsley
FTE Enroll: 40   (305) 823-7270

ILLINOIS

HEBREW THEOLOGICAL COLLEGE
7135 Carpenter Rd., Skokie 60077 *Type:* Private *Accred.:* 1995 (NCA candidate) *Calendar:* Sem. plan *Degrees:* B *CEO:* Chanc. Jerold Isenberg
Enroll: 105   (847) 674-7750

ST. JOHN'S COLLEGE
421 N. Ninth St., Springfield 62702 *Type:* Private professional *Accred.:* 1993 (NCA candidate) *Calendar:* Sem. plan *Degrees:* B *CEO:* Chanc. Jane Schachtsiek
Enroll: 129   (217) 525-5628

MARYLAND

CAPITAL BIBLE SEMINARY
6511 Princess Garden Pkwy., Lanham 20706 *Type:* Private Nondenominational *Accred.:*

1995 (ATS candidate) *Degrees:* M *CEO:* Pres. Homer Heater, Jr.
Enroll: 144   (301) 552-1400

CARROLL COMMUNITY COLLEGE
1601 Washington Rd., Westminster 21157-6913 *Type:* Public (local) two-year *System:* Maryland Higher Education Commission *Accred.:* 1993 (MSA candidate) *Calendar:* Sem. plan *Degrees:* A, C *Prof. Accred.:* Physical Therapy Assisting *CEO:* Pres. Joseph F. Shields
Enroll: 2,527   (410) 876-3880

MASSACHUSETTS

BOSTON GRADUATE CENTER OF PSYCHOANALYTIC STUDIES
1583 Beacon St., Brookline 02146 *Type:* Private *Accred.:* 1995 (NEASC-CIHE candidate) *Degrees:* M *CEO:* Pres. Phyllis W. Meadow
Enroll: 59   (617) 277-3915

MICHIGAN

S.S. CYRIL AND METHODIUS SEMINARY
Orchard Lake 48324 *Type:* Private (Roman Catholic) graduate only *Accred.:* 1991/1995 (ATS candidate) *Calendar:* Sem. plan *Degrees:* M *CEO:* Rector Francis B. Koper
Enroll: 94   (313) 683-0311

MINNESOTA

THE GRADUATE SCHOOL OF AMERICA
121 S. Eighth St., Minneapolis 55402 *Type:* Private profit *Accred.:* 1995 (NCA candidate) *Degrees:* M, D *CEO:* Pres. Harold Abel
Enroll: 59   (612) 339-8650

PILLSBURY BAPTIST BIBLE COLLEGE
315 S. Grove St., Owatonna 55060 *Type:* Private *Accred.:* 1990/1994 (NCA candidate) *Calendar:* Sem. plan *Degrees:* A, B, C *CEO:* Interim Pres. Earle Mattson
Enroll: 238   (507) 451-2710

RANGE TECHNICAL COLLEGE—EVELETH
1100 Industrial Park Dr., Eveleth 55734 *Type:* Public *System:* Minnesota State Col-

leges and Universities *Accred.:* 1995 (NCA candidate) *Calendar:* Qtr. plan *Degrees:* A, C *CEO:* Pres. Joe Dennie
Enroll: 944 (218) 744-3302

MISSOURI

SANFORD-BROWN COLLEGE
1655 Des Peres Rd., Ste. 150, St. Louis 63131 *Type:* Private *Accred.:* 1991/1995 (NCA candidate) *Calendar:* Sem. plan *Degrees:* A *CEO:* Pres. Brett Combs
Enroll: 1,410 (800) 456-7222

MONTANA

DULL KNIFE MEMORIAL COLLEGE
P.O. Box 98, Lame Deer 59043 *Type:* Private (tribal) junior *Accred.:* 1990/1995 (NASC candidate) *Calendar:* Sem. plan *Degrees:* A *CEO:* Pres. Alonzo Spang
Enroll: 378 (406) 477-6215

NEW HAMPSHIRE

THE THOMAS MORE COLLEGE OF LIBERAL ARTS
6 Manchester St., Merrimack 03054-3805 *Type:* Private *Accred.:* 1990 (NEASC-CIHE candidate) *Calendar:* Sem. plan *Degrees:* B *CEO:* Pres. Peter V. Sampo
Enroll: 70 (603) 880-8308

NEW JERSEY

RABBI JACOB JOSEPH SCHOOL
One Plainfield Ave., Edison 08817 *Type:* Private professional *Accred.:* 1991 (AARTS candidate) *Calendar:* Sem. plan *Degrees:* Talmudic (1st and Advanced) *CEO:* Pres. M. Schick
Enroll: 49 (908) 985-6533

NEW MEXICO

SOUTHWESTERN COLLEGE
P.O. Box 4788, Santa Fe 87502 *Type:* Private *Accred.:* 1992/1994 (NCA candidate) *Calendar:* Sem. plan *Degrees:* M *CEO:* Pres. Robert Waterman
Enroll: 109 (505) 471-5756

NEW YORK

KOL YAAKOV TORAH CENTER
29 W. Maple Ave., P.O. Box 402, Monsey 10952 *Type:* Private professional *Accred.:* 1984/1995 (AARTS candidate) *Calendar:* Sem. plan *Degrees:* Rabbinic (1st) *CEO:* Pres. Leib Tropper
Enroll: 31 (914) 425-3863

RABBINICAL COLLEGE OF OHR SHIMON YISROEL
215-217 Hewes St., Brooklyn 11211 *Type:* Private professional *Accred.:* 1992 (AARTS candidate) *Calendar:* Sem. plan *Degrees:* Talmudic (1st) *CEO:* Pres. Shulem Walter
Enroll: 50 (718) 387-5588

TALMUDICAL INSTITUTE OF UPSTATE NEW YORK
769 Park Ave., Rochester 14607 *Type:* Private professional *Accred.:* 1984/1993 (AARTS candidate) *Calendar:* Sem. plan *Degrees:* Talmudic (1st and 2nd) *CEO:* Pres. M. Davidowitz
Enroll: 50 (716) 473-2810

UNIFICATION THEOLOGICAL SEMINARY
10 Dock Rd., Barrytown 12507 *Type:* Private United Church of Christ *Accred.:* 1988 (MSA candidate) *Calendar:* Sem. plan *Degrees:* M, P *CEO:* Pres. Theodore T. Shimmyo
Enroll: 172 (914) 758-6881

YESHIVA AND KOLEL BAIS MEDRASH ELYON
73 Main St., Monsey 10952 *Type:* Private professional *Accred.:* 1989 (AARTS candidate) *Calendar:* Sem. plan *Degrees:* Talmudic (1st and 2nd) *CEO:* Pres. I. Falk
Enroll: 70 (914) 356-7064

YESHIVA AND KOLLEL HARBOTZAS TORAH
1049 E. 15th St., Brooklyn 11230 *Type:* Private professional *Accred.:* 1985/1991 (AARTS candidate) *Calendar:* Sem. plan *Degrees:* Talmudic (1st and 2nd) *CEO:* Pres. Y. Bittersfeld
Enroll: 36 (718) 692-0208

YESHIVA GEDOLAH IMREI YOSEF D'SPINKA
1460 56th St., Brooklyn 11219 *Type:* Private professional *Accred.:* 1989 (AARTS candi-

date) *Calendar:* Sem. plan *Degrees:* Talmudic (1st) *CEO:* Pres. Mordechai Majerowitz
Enroll: 63   (718) 851-1600

NORTH CAROLINA

HOOD THEOLOGICAL SEMINARY
800 West Thomas St., Salisbury 28144 *Type:* Private African Methodist Episcopal Zion *Accred.:* 1995 (ATS candidate) *Degrees:* M *CEO:* Interim Pres. Roy D. Hudson
Enroll: 59   (704) 638-5644

OKLAHOMA

SPARTAN SCHOOL OF AERONAUTICS
Tulsa International Airport, 8820 E. Pine St., Tulsa 74115 *Type:* Private *Accred.:* 1991/1995 (NCA candidate) *Calendar:* Sem. plan *Degrees:* A, C *CEO:* Pres. Ross L. Alloway
Enroll: 1,277   (800) 331-1204

PUERTO RICO

ESCUELA DE ARTES PLASTICAS DE PUERTO RICO
Apartado 1112, San Juan 00902-1112 *Type:* Public (state) *Accred.:* 1988 (MSA candidate) *Calendar:* Sem. plan *Degrees:* B *CEO:* Chanc. Marimar Benitez
Enroll: 192   (809) 725-8120

SOUTH DAKOTA

CENTRAL INDIAN BIBLE COLLEGE
Riverfront Dr., Mobridge 57601 *Type:* Private (Assemblies of God) *Accred.:* 1992 (AABC candidate) *Calendar:* Sem. plan *Degrees:* A, C *CEO:* Pres. M. George Kallappa
FTE Enroll: 17   (605) 845-7801

TENNESSEE

HARDING UNIVERSITY GRADUATE SCHOOL OF RELIGION
1000 Cherry Rd., Memphis 38117 *Type:* Private *Accred.:* 1995 (ATS candidate) *Calendar:* Sem. plan *Degrees:* M, D *CEO:* Dean Bill Flatt
FTE Enroll: 86   (901) 761-1358

VIRGINIA

BAPTIST THEOLOGICAL SEMINARY AT RICHMOND
1204 Palmyra Ave., PO Box 9157, Richmond 23227 *Type:* Private Cooperative Baptist Fellowship *Accred.:* 1995 (ATS candidate) *Degrees:* M *CEO:* Pres. Thomas H. Graves
Enroll: 125   (804) 355-8135S

DEGREE GRANTING CANDIDATE INSTITUTIONS OUTSIDE THE UNITED STATES

CANADA

CENTRAL PENTECOSTAL COLLEGE
1303 Jackson Ave., Saskatoon S7H 2M9
Type: Private (Pentecostal Assemblies of Canada) *Accred.:* 1992 (AABC candidate) *Calendar:* Sem. plan *Degrees:* B *CEO:* Pres. Ronald Kadyschuk
FTE Enroll: 79   (306) 374-6655

EDMONTON BAPTIST SEMINARY
11525-23 Ave., Edmonton AB T6J 4T3
Type: Private Baptist *Accred.:* 1994 (ATS candidate) *Calendar:* Sem. plan *Degrees:* M *CEO:* Pres. Paul Siewert
Enroll: 77   (403) 437-1960

HERITAGE BAPTIST COLLEGE
30 Grand Ave., London N6C 1K8 *Type:* Private (Baptist) *Accred.:* 1991 (AABC candidate) *Calendar:* Sem. plan *Degrees:* B, C *CEO:* Pres. Marvin Brubacher
FTE Enroll: 132   (519) 434-6801

PRAIRIE BIBLE COLLEGE
319 5th Ave. N., P.O. Box 4000, Three Hills AB T0M2N0 *Type:* Private *Accred.:* 1994 (AABC candidate) *Calendar:* Sem. plan *Degrees:* A, B, C *CEO:* Pres. Paul Ferris, Jr.
FTE Enroll: 415   (403) 443-5511

SAINT ANDREW'S COLLEGE
1121 College Dr., Saskatoon S7N0N3 *Type:* Public *Accred.:* 1994 (ATS candidate) *Calendar:* Sem. plan *Degrees:* B, M *CEO:* Co-Pres. Michael Bourgeois
CEO: Co-Pres. Charlotte A. Caron
Enroll: 49   (306) 966-8970

TRINITY WESTERN UNIVERSITY
Fosmark Ctr., 7600 Glover Rd., Langley V3A 6H4 *Type:* Private *Accred.:* 1994 (ATS candidate) *Calendar:* Sem. plan *Degrees:* B, M *CEO:* Pres. Neil Snider
Enroll: 2,128   (604) 888-7511

GREECE

AMERICAN COLLEGE OF HIGHER STUDIES OF ANATOLIA COLLEGE
P.O. Box 21021, Pylea, Thessaloniki 555 10 *Type:* Private *Accred.:* 1994 (NEASC-CIHE candidate) *Degrees:* B *CEO:* Pres. William W. McGrew
Enroll: 418   [30] (31) 301071

NON-DEGREE GRANTING CANDIDATE INSTITUTION

ALASKA

ALASKA VOCATIONAL-TECHNICAL CENTER
889 Second Ave., Seward 99664 *Accred.:* 1995
(COE candidate) *CEO:* Pres. Mark Ganser
FTE Enroll: 194   (907) 224-3322

FLORIDA

AMERICA DURAN SKIN CARE, MASSAGE AND
NAIL SCHOOL
3400 Coral Way, Ste. 105, Miami 33145
Type: Private *Accred.:* 1992 (COE candi-
date) *Degrees:* C *CEO:* Pres. America Duran
FTE Enroll: 8   (305) 642-4104

BRADFORD-UNION AREA VOCATIONAL-
TECHNICAL CENTER
609 N. Orange St., Starke 32091 *Accred.:*
1995 (COE candidate) *CEO:* Dir. James E.
Ward
FTE Enroll: 156   (904) 964-6800

CORAL RIDGE NURSE'S ASSISTANT TRAINING
SCHOOL
2740 East Oakland Park Blvd., Ft. Laud-
erdale 33306 *Accred.:* 1995 (COE candidate)
CEO: Dir. Ethline Mais
FTE Enroll: 60   (305) 561-2022

FLORIDA STATE FIRE COLLEGE
11655 N.W. Gainesville Rd., Ocala 32675-
1330 *Type:* Public *Accred.:* 1993 (COE candidate) *Degrees:* C *CEO:* Supt. Donn Manno
FTE Enroll: 3,000   (904) 732-1330

INSTITUTE OF SPECIALIZED TRAINING & MAN-
AGEMENT
853 East Hwy. 436, No. 200, Casselberry
32707 *Type:* Private *Accred.:* 1994 (COE
candidate) *Degrees:* C *CEO:* Admin. Ofcr.
Linda Hart
FTE Enroll: 61   (407) 831-8466

LEE COUNTY HIGH TECH CENTER
360 Juanita Blvd. Ext., Cape Coral 33909
Accred.: 1995 (COE candidate) *CEO:* Dir.
Susan Kasper
FTE Enroll: 464   (941) 574-4440

NEW ENGLAND INSTITUTE OF TECHNOLOGY AT
PALM BEACH
1126 53rd Ct., West Palm Beach 33407-2384
Type: Private *Accred.:* 1992/1994 (COE can-
didate) *Calendar:* Qtr. plan *Degrees:* C
CEO: Pres. William Bennett
FTE Enroll: 878   (407) 842-8324

BRANCH CAMPUS
2400 Metro Center Blvd., West Palm
Beach 33407
       (407) 842-8324

SARASOTA SCHOOL OF MASSAGE THERAPY
1970 Main St., Sarasota 34236 *Type:* Private
Accred.: 1994 (COE candidate) *Degrees:* C
CEO: Dir. Michael Rosen-Pyros
FTE Enroll: 39   (941) 957-0577

TECHNICAL EDUCATION CENTER-OSCEOLA
501 Simpson Rd., Kissimmee 34744 *Accred.:* 1995 (COE candidate) *CEO:* Dir. Barry
Linville
FTE Enroll: 400   (407) 344-5080

BRANCH CAMPUS
2300 S. Poinciana Blvd., Kissimmee
34758

BRANCH CAMPUS
93 Panther Paws Trail, Kissimmee 34744

BRANCH CAMPUS
420 S. Thacker Avenue, Kissimmee 34741

YOUTH CO-OP TRAINING INSTITUTE
801 NW 37th Ave., No. 212, Miami 33125
Accred.: 1995 (COE candidate) *CEO:* Dir.
Maria Rodriguez
FTE Enroll: 13   (305) 643-6730

GEORGIA

ARMY INFANTRY SCHOOL
Ft. Benning 31905-5593 *Accred.:* 1994 (COE
candidate) *CEO:* Dir. Michael McKean
FTE Enroll: 6,779   (706) 545-5717

UNITED STATES ARMY INFANTRY SCHOOL
Ft. Benning 31905-5593 *Type:* Public *Accred.:* 1994 (SACS-CC candidate) *De-grees:* C *CEO:* Commandant Howard Crawford
(706) 545-5717

KENTUCKY

TOYOTA MANUFACTURING USA
1001 Cherryt Blossom Way HR/TC, George-town 40324 *Accred.:* 1995 (COE candidate) *CEO:* Dir. Dewey Crawford
FTE Enroll: 107   (502) 868-2901

MISSISSIPPI

AMERICAN CAREER COLLEGE
2200 25th Ave., Gulfport 39501 *Type:* Private *Accred.:* 1994 (COE candidate) *Calendar:* Sem. plan *Degrees:* C *CEO:* Chief Executive Officer Berinda Logan
FTE Enroll: 193   (601) 864-3866

OCEAN SPRINGS CAMPUS
1531 Bienville Rd., Ocean Springs 39564
(601) 872-9772

WAVELAND CAMPUS
703 A Hwy 90, Waveland 38576
(601) 466-4475

NEW YORK

NEW CENTER FOR WHOLISTIC HEALTH EDUCATION AND RESEARCH
6801 Jericho Tpke., Syosset 11791-4465 *Type:* Private professional *Calendar:* Tri. plan *Degrees:* C *Prof. Accred.:* Acupuncture (C-candidate) *CEO:* Pres. Steven Schenkman
FTE Enroll: 19   (516) 364-0808

NORTH CAROLINA

SCHOOL OF COMMUNICATION ARTS
3220 Spring Forest Rd., Raleigh 27604 *Type:* Private *Accred.:* 1994 (COE candidate) *Degrees:* C *CEO:* Dir. Deborah Hooper
FTE Enroll: 97   (919) 981-0972

TENNESSEE

ACADEMY OF BEAUTY ARTS
303 Keith St. Cleveland 37320 *Type:* Private *Accred.:* 1992 (COE candidate) *Degrees:* C *CEO:* Dir. Chris Duncan
FTE Enroll: 33   (615) 476-3742

LACARM SCHOOL OF COSMETOLOGY
228-A McMinnville Shopping Pl., McMinnville 37110 *Type:* Private *Accred.:* 1992/1993 (COE candidate) *Degrees:* C
FTE Enroll: 14   (615) 473-2615

MIDDLE TENNESSEE SCHOOL OF COSMETOLOGY
46 E. Broad St., Cookeville 38501 *Type:* Private *Accred.:* 1993 (COE candidate) *Degrees:* C *CEO:* Dir. Lisa Burchfield
FTE Enroll: 28   (615) 526-4515

VOLUNTEER FLIGHT TRAINING
200 Airport Rd., Bldg. 1, Outlaw Field, Clarksville 37042 *Accred.:* 1994 (COE candidate) *CEO:* Dir. Robert Anderson
FTE Enroll: 10   (615) 431-4170

TEXAS

AMERICAN ACADEMY OF ACUPUNCTURE AND TRADITIONAL CHINESE MEDICINE
9100 Park West Dr., Houston 77063 *Type:* Private professional *Calendar:* Sem. plan *Degrees:* C *Prof. Accred.:* Acupuncture (D-Candidate) *CEO:* Pres. Shen Ping Liang
FTE Enroll: 14   (713) 780-9777

G AND M BEAUTY COLLEGE
215 Earl Garrett, Kerrville 78028 *Type:* Private *Accred.:* 1993/1994 (COE candidate) *Degrees:* C *CEO:* Dir. Loretta Guthrie
FTE Enroll: 29   (210) 792-4008

ICC TECHNICAL INSTITUTE
3333 Fannin St., No. 203, Houston 77004 *Type:* Private Non-Profit *Accred.:* 1991/1995 (COE candidate) *Degrees:* C *CEO:* Dir. Chi Do
FTE Enroll: 377

INTERNATIONAL BIBLE COLLEGE
2369 Benrus Blvd, San Antonia 78228 *Type:* Private Nondenominational *Accred.:* 1995

(AABC candidate) *Calendar:* Sem. plan *Degrees:* C *CEO:* Pres. Troy Parker
FTE Enroll: 147   (210) 434-5541

KING BEAUTY CAREERS
4714 F.M. 1960 W., Ste. 104, Houston 77069
Type: Private *Accred.:* 1993/1994 (COE candidate) *Degrees:* C *CEO:* Dir. Brian King
FTE Enroll: 105   (713) 580-2554

LAREDO JOB CORPS CENTER
701 Island, Laredo 78041 *Type:* Public
Accred.: 1993 (COE candidate) *Degrees:* C
CEO: Dir. John M. Bruce
FTE Enroll: 300   (210) 727-5147

RIO GRANDE BIBLE INSTITUTE
4300 S. Business 281, Edinburg 78539 *Type:*
Private *Accred.:* 1994 (AABC candidate)
Degrees: C *CEO:* Pres. Gordon Johnson
Enroll: 109   (210) 380-8100

SAVANT TRAINING AND TECHNOLOGY
626 S. Zarzamora, San Antonio 78207 *Type:*
Private *Accred.:* 1993/1994 (COE candidate)
Degrees: C *CEO:* Dir. Maria Pantoja
FTE Enroll: 88   (210) 435-1132

TEXAS COLLEGE OF COSMETOLOGY
918 N. Chadbourne St., San Angelo 76903
Type: Private *Accred.:* 1993/1994 (COE candidate) *Degrees:* C *CEO:* Dir. Tom Adams
FTE Enroll: 77   (915) 659-2622

TRANSWORLD ACADEMY
6220 Westpark, No. 110, Houston 77057
Accred.: 1995 (COE candidate) *CEO:* Dir.
Michael Chung
FTE Enroll: 61   (713) 266-6594

VIRGINIA

BLUE RIDGE JOB CORPS CENTER
245 W. Main St., Marion 24354 *Accred.:*
1995 (COE candidate) *CEO:* Dir. Wayne E.
Tapp
FTE Enroll: 269   (540) 783-7221

DEFENSE COMMISSARY AGENCY
38th and E. Ave., Fort Lee 23801-6300 *Type:*
Public Dept. of Defense *Accred.:* 1995 (COE
candidate) *Degrees:* C *CEO:* Commandant
W.L. Hasty, III
FTE Enroll: 13   (804) 734-8164

EASTECH
293 Independence Blvd., Pembroke Five,
No. 128, Virginia Beach 23462 *Accred.:*
1995 (COE candidate) *CEO:* Dir. Herbert
Smith
FTE Enroll: 34   (804) 499-6633

SUBMARINE TRAINING FACILITY
1915 C Ave., Norfolk 23511 *Type:* Public
(federal) *Accred.:* 1994 (COE candidate)
Degrees: C *CEO:* Dir. R.E. Harris
FTE Enroll: 139   (804) 445-1900

Public Systems of Higher Education

ALABAMA

Alabama Commission on Higher Education
P.O. Box 302000, Montgomery 36130-2000
Exec. Dir. Henry J. Hector
(334) 242-1998

Alabama Agricultural and Mechanical University
4900 Meridian Ave., Normal 35762
Interim Pres. Virginia Caples
(205) 851-5000

Alabama State University
915 S. Jackson St., Montgomery 36101-0271
Pres. William H. Harris
(334) 293-4100

Auburn University System
Auburn University 36849-5113
Pres. William V. Muse
(334) 844-4650

Auburn University
Auburn University 36849-5206
Pres. William V. Muse
(334) 844-4000

Auburn University at Montgomery
7300 University Dr., Montgomery 36117-3596
Chanc. Roy H. Saigo
(334) 244-3000

Jacksonville State University
700 N. Pelham Rd., Jacksonville 36265-9982
Pres. Harold J. McGee
(205) 782-5781

The Troy State University System
University Ave., Troy 36082
Chanc. Jack Hawkins, Jr.
(334) 670-3200

Troy State University
University Ave., Troy 36082
Chanc. Jack Hawkins, Jr.
(334) 670-3200

Troy State University at Dothan
P.O. Box 8368, 3601 U.S. Hwy. 231 N., Dothan 36304-0368
Interim Pres. Doug Patterson
(334) 983-6556

Troy State University in Montgomery
231 Montgomery St., P.O. Drawer 4419, Montgomery 36103-4419
Pres. Glenda S. McGaha-Curry
(334) 834-1400

The University of Alabama System
401 Queen City Ave., Tuscaloosa 35401-1551
Chanc. Philip E. Austin
(205) 348-5861

The University of Alabama
P.O. Box 870166, Tuscaloosa 35487-0166
Pres. E. Roger Sayers
(205) 348-6300

The University of Alabama at Birmingham
701 S. 20th St., Birmingham 35294-0111
Pres. J. Claude Bennett
(205) 934-4011

The University of Alabama in Huntsville
301 Sparkman Dr., Huntsville 35899
Pres. Frank A. Franz
(205) 895-6120

University of Montevallo
Sta. 6001, Montevallo 35115-6001
Pres. Robert M. McChesney
(205) 665-6000

University of North Alabama
601 N. Pine St., Florence 35632-0001
Pres. Robert L. Potts
(205) 760-4100

University of South Alabama
307 University Blvd., Mobile 36688
Pres. Frederick P. Whiddon
(334) 460-6101

The University of West Alabama
Sta. 4, Livingston 35470
Pres. Donald C. Hines
(205) 652-3400

**State of Alabama Department of
Postsecondary Education**
401 Adams Ave., Montgomery 36130
Chanc. Fred J. Gainous
(334) 242-2900

Alabama Aviation and Technical College
P.O. Box 1209, S. Union Ave.,
Ozark 36361-1209
Pres. Shirley H. Woodie
(205) 774-5113

Alabama Southern Community College
P.O. Box 2000, Monroeville 36461
Pres. John A. Johnson
(334) 575-3156

Athens State College
300 N. Beaty St., Athens 35611
Pres. Jerry Bartlett
(205) 233-8100

Bessemer State Technical College
1100 Ninth Ave., S.W., Bessemer
35021
Pres. W. Michael Bailey
(205) 428-6391

Bevill State Community College
P.O. Box 800, 101 State St.,
Sumiton 35148
Pres. Harold Wade
(205) 648-3271

Bishop State Community College
351 N. Broad St., Mobile 36603-
5898
Pres. Yvonne Kennedy
(334) 690-6416

Central Alabama Community College
908 Cherokee Rd., P.O. Box 699,
Alexander City 35010
Pres. James H. Cornell
(205) 234-6346

*Chattahoochee Valley State Community
College*
2602 College Dr., Phenix City
36869
Pres. Richard J. Federinko
(205) 291-4900

Chauncey Sparks State Technical College
Hwy. 431, S., P.O. Drawer 580,
Eufaula 36072-0580
Pres. Linda C. Young
(205) 687-3543

*Douglas MacArthur State Technical
College*
1708 N. Main St., P.O. Box 649,
Opp 36467
Pres. Raymond V. Chisum
(334) 493-6631

Enterprise State Junior College
600 Plaza Dr., P.O. Box 1300,
Enterprise 36331
Interim Pres. Stafford L. Thompson
(334) 347-2623

Gadsden State Community College
P.O. Box 227, Gadsden 35902-0227
Pres. Victor B. Ficker
(205) 549-8200

*George C. Wallace State Community
College*
Rte. 6, Box 62, Dothan 36303-9234
Pres. Larry Beaty
(334) 983-3521

*George Corley Wallace State Community
College*
P.O. Drawer 1049, 3000 Range Line
Rd., Selma 36702-1049
Pres. Julius R. Brown
(334) 875-2634

Harry M. Ayers State Technical College
1801 Coleman Rd., P.O. Box 1647,
Anniston 36202
Interim Pres. Don Jarrells
(205) 835-5400

J.F. Drake State Technical College
3421 Meridian St., N., Huntsville
35811
Pres. Johnny L. Harris
(205) 539-8161

J.F. Ingram Community College
P.O. Box 209, 5375 Ingram Rd.,
Deatsville 36022
Interim Pres. James Selman
(334) 285-5177

*James H. Faulkner State Community
College*
1900 Hwy. 31 S., Bay Minette 36507
Pres. Gary L. Branch
(334) 580-2100

Jefferson Davis Community College
220 Alco Dr., Brewton 36426
Pres. Sandra K. McLeod
(334) 867-4832

Jefferson State Community College
2601 Carson Rd., Birmingham
35215-3098
Pres. Judy M. Merritt
(205) 856-1200

*John C. Calhoun State Community
College*
P.O. Box 2216, Decatur 35609-2216
Pres. Richard G. Carpenter
(205) 306-2500

*John M. Patterson State Technical
College*
3920 Troy Hwy., Montgomery 36116
Pres. J. Larry Taunton
(334) 200-1080

Lawson State Community College
3060 Wilson Rd., S.W., Birmingham
35221
Pres. Perry W. Ward
(205) 929-2515

Lurleen B. Wallace State Junior College
P.O. Drawer 1418, Andalusia 36420
Pres. Seth Hammett
(334) 222-6591

*Northeast Alabama State Community
College*
P.O. Box 159, Hwy. 35, Rainsville
35986
Pres. Charles M. Pendley
(205) 228-6001

Northwest Shoals Community College
P.O. Box 2545, George Wallace
Blvd., Muscle Shoals 35662
Pres. Larry McCoy
(205) 331-5200

Reid State Technical College
I-65 at Hwy. 83, P.O. Box 588,
Evergreen 36401
Pres. Ullysses McBride
(334) 578-1313

Shelton State Community College
202 Skyland Blvd., Tuscaloosa 35405
Pres. Thomas E. Umphrey
(205) 759-1541

Snead State Community College
P.O. Drawer D, 220 N. Walnut St.,
Boaz 35957
Pres. William H. Osborn
(205) 593-5120

Southern Union State Community College
P.O. Box 1000, Roberts St., Wadley
36276
Pres. Roy W. Johnson
(205) 395-2211

Trenholm State Technical College
1225 Air Base Blvd., P.O. Box
9039, Montgomery 36108
Interim Pres. Leroy Bell, Jr.
(334) 832-9000

Wallace State Community College
801 Main St., N.W., P.O. Box 2000,
Hanceville 35077-2000
Pres. James C. Bailey
(205) 352-8000

ALASKA

University of Alaska System
Butrovich Bldg., Ste. 202, 910 Yukon
Dr., Fairbanks 99775
Pres. Jerome Komisar
(907) 474-7311

*Prince William Sound Community
College*
P.O. Box 97, Valdez 99686
Pres. Jo Ann C. McDowell
(907) 835-2421

University of Alaska Anchorage
3211 Providence Dr., Anchorage
99508
Chanc. Edward Lee Gorsuch
(907) 786-1437

University of Alaska Fairbanks
320 Signers' Hall, Fairbanks 99775
Chanc. Joan K. Wadlow
(907) 474-7112

University of Alaska Southeast
11120 Glacier Hwy., Juneau 99801
Chanc. Marshall L. Lind
(907) 465-6509

ARIZONA

Arizona Board of Regents
2020 N. Central Ave., Ste. 230, Phoenix
85004
Exec. Dir. Frank H. Besnette
(602) 229-2500

Arizona State University
Tempe 85287-2203
Pres. Lattie F. Coor
(602) 965-9011

Arizona State University East
6001 S. Power Rd., Bldg. 314, Mesa
85206-0903
Interim Pres. Ben R. Forsyth
(602) 965-3278

Arizona State University West
4701 W. Thunderbird Rd., P.O. Box
37100, Phoenix 85069-7100
Vice Pres. Ben R. Forsyth
(602) 543-5500

Northern Arizona University
Box 4092, Flagstaff 86011-4092
Pres. Clara Lovett
(602) 523-3232

University of Arizona
712 Admin. Bldg., Tucson 85721
Pres. Manuel T. Pacheco
(602) 621-5511

**State Board of Directors for Community
Colleges of Arizona**
3225 N. Central Ave., Century Plaza, Ste.
1220, Phoenix 85012
Exec. Dir. Donald E. Puyear
(602) 255-4037

Arizona Western College
P.O. Box 929, Yuma 85366
Pres. James Carruthers
(602) 726-1000

Central Arizona College
8470 N. Overfield Rd., Coolidge
85228
Pres. John J. Klein
(602) 426-4444

Cochise College
4190 W. Hwy. 80, Box 100, Douglas
85607
Pres. Walter S. Patton
(800)966-7943

Eastern Arizona College
600 Church St., Thatcher 85552-
0769
Pres. Gherald L. Hoopes, Jr.
(602) 428-8233

**Maricopa County Community College
District**
2411 W. 14th St., Tempe 85281-
6941
Chanc. Paul A. Elsner
(602) 731-8000

*Chandler-Gilbert Community
College*
2626 E. Pecos Rd., Chandler
85225-2499
Chanc. Arnette S. Ward
(602) 732-7000

Gateway Community College
108 N. 40th St., Phoenix 85034
Pres. Phil D. Randolph
(602) 392-5000

Glendale Community College
6000 W. Olive Ave., Glendale
85302
Pres. Tessa Martinez Pollack
(602) 435-3000

Mesa Community College
1833 W. Southern Ave., Mesa
85202
Pres. Larry K. Christiansen
(602) 461-7000

Paradise Valley Community College
18401 N. 32nd St., Phoenix
85032
Pres. Raul Cardenas
(602) 493-2600

Phoenix College
  1202 W. Thomas Rd., Phoenix
    85013
  Pres. Marie Pepicello
  (602) 264-2492

Rio Salado Community College
  640 N. First Ave., Phoenix
    85003
  Pres. Linda M. Thor
  (602) 223-4000

Scottsdale Community College
  9000 E. Chaparral Rd.,
    Scottsdale 85250-2699
  Pres. Arthur W. DeCabooter
  (602) 423-6000

South Mountain Community College
  7050 S. 24th St., Phoenix
    85040
  Pres. John A. Cordova
  (602) 243-8000

Mohave Community College
  1971 Jagerson Ave., Kingman 86401
  Pres. Charles W. Hall
  (520) 757-4331

Northland Pioneer College
  103 First Ave. at Hopi Dr., P.O. Box
    610, Holbrook 86025
  Pres. John H. Anderson
  (602) 524-1993

Pima County Community College District
  4905 E. Broadway Blvd., Tucson
    85709-1010
  Chanc. Robert D. Jensen
  (520) 748-4666

Yavapai College
  1100 E. Sheldon St., Prescott 86301
  Pres. Doreen B. Dailey
  (520) 445-7300

ARKANSAS

Arkansas Department of Higher Education
114 E. Capitol Ave., Little Rock 72201-
3818
Dir. Diane S. Gilleland
(501) 324-9300

Arkansas State University
P.O. Box 10, State University 72467
Pres. Leslie Wyatt, III
(501) 972-2100

Arkansas Tech University
Russellville 72801-2222
Pres. Robert C. Brown
(501) 968-0389

Black River Technical College
Hwy. 304 E., P.O. Box 468,
Pocahontas 72455
Dir. Richard Gaines
(501) 892-4565

East Arkansas Community College
Newcastle Rd., Forrest City 72335-
9598
Pres. George McCormick
(501) 633-4480

Garland County Community College
101 College Dr., Hot Springs 71913
Pres. Tom Spencer
(501) 767-9371

Henderson State University
1100 Henderson St., Arkadelphia
71999-0001
Pres. Charles D. Dunn
(501) 230-5000

Mississippi County Community College
P.O Drawer 1109, Blytheville 72316
Pres. John P. Sullins
(501) 762-1020

*North Arkansas Community/Technical
College*
Pioneer Ridge, Harrison 72601
Pres. William Bert Baker
(501) 743-3000

NorthWest Arkansas Community College
P.O. Box 1408, 1 College Dr.,
Bentonville 72712
Pres. Bob C. Burns
(501) 636-9222

Phillips County Community College
Box 785, Helena 72342-0785
Pres. Steven W. Jones
(501) 338-6474

Pulaski Technical College
3000 W. Scenic Rd., North Little
Rock 72118-3399
Pres. Benjamin Wyatt
(501) 771-1000

Red River Technical College
Hwy. 29 S., P.O. Box 140, Hope
71801
Dir. Johnny Rapert
(501) 777-5722

Rich Mountain Community College
1100 Bush St., Mena 71953
Pres. Bill Abernathy
(501) 394-5012

South Arkansas Community College
P.O. Box 7010, 300 S.W. Ave., El
Dorado 71731-7010
Pres. Ben T. Whitfield
(501) 862-8131

Southern Arkansas University
SAU Box 1402, Magnolia 71753
Pres. Steven G. Gamble
(501) 235-4001

**University of Arkansas System
Administration**
Univ. Tower Bldg., Ste. 601, 1123 S.
University Ave., Little Rock 72204
Pres. B. Alan Sugg
(501) 686-2500

University of Arkansas at Fayetteville
Administration Bldg. 425,
Fayetteville 72701
Chanc. Daniel E. Ferritor
(501) 575-2000

University of Arkansas at Little Rock
2801 S. University Ave., Little
Rock 72204
Chanc. Charles E. Hathaway
(501) 569-3200

University of Arkansas at Monticello
P.O. Box 3596, Monticello
71655-3596
Chanc. Fred J. Taylor
(501) 367-6811

University of Arkansas at Pine Bluff
1200 N. Univ. Dr., Pine Bluff
71601
Chanc. Lawrence A. Davis, Jr
(501) 543-8000

University of Arkansas for Medical Sciences
4301 W. Markham St., Little
Rock 72205
Chanc. Harry P. Ward
(501) 686-5000

University of Central Arkansas
Conway 72035-0001
Pres. Winfred L. Thompson
(501) 450-5000

Westark Community College
P.O. Box 3649, Fort Smith 72913-
3649
Pres. Joel Stubblefield
(501) 788-7000

CALIFORNIA

California Community Colleges
1107 Ninth St., 6th Fl., Sacramento
95814
Chanc. David Mertes
(916) 322-4005

Allan Hancock Joint Community College District
800 S. College Dr., Santa Maria
93454
Supt. Ann Foxworthy Stephenson
(805) 922-6966

Allan Hancock College
800 S. College Dr., Santa
Maria 93454-6399
Supt./Pres. Ann Foxworthy
Stephenson
(805) 922-6966

Antelope Valley Community College District
3041 W. Ave. K, Lancaster 93536-
5426
Supt. Allan W. Kurki
(805) 943-3241

Antelope Valley College
3041 W. Ave. K, Lancaster
93536
Pres. Allan W. Kurki
(805) 943-3241

Barstow Community College District
2700 Barstow Rd., Barstow 92311-
6699
Supt. Judith A. Strattan
(619) 252-2411

Barstow College
2700 Barstow Rd., Barstow
92311
Supt./Pres. Joseph A. Clark, Jr.
Pres. Judith A. Strattan
(619) 252-2411

Butte Community College District
3536 Butte Campus Dr., Oroville
95965-8399
Supt. Betty M. Dean
(916) 895-2511

Butte College
3536 Butte Campus Dr.,
Oroville 95965
Pres. Betty M. Dean
(916) 895-2511

Cabrillo Community College District
6500 Soquel Dr., Aptos 95003
Supt. John D. Hurd
(408) 479-6100

Cabrillo College
6500 Soquel Dr., Aptos 95003
Pres. John D. Hurd
(408) 479-6100

Cerritos Community College District
11110 Alondra Blvd., Norwalk
90650-6298
Supt. Fred Gaskin
(310) 860-2451

Cerritos College
11110 Alondra Blvd., Norwalk
90650-6298
Pres. Fred Gaskin
(310) 860-2451

Chabot-Las Positas Community College District
5673 Gibraltar Dr., Ste. 100,
Pleasanton 94588
Chanc. Ronald A. Kong
(510) 460-5334

Chabot College
25555 Hesperian Blvd.,
Hayward 94545-5001
Pres. Raul Cardoza
(510) 786-6600

Las Positas College
3033 Collier Canyon Rd.,
Livermore 94550-9797
Pres. Susan A. Cota
(510) 373-5800

Chaffey Community College District
5885 Haven Ave., Rancho
Cucamonga 91737-3002
Supt. Jerry W. Young
(909) 987-1737

Chaffey College
5885 Haven Ave., Rancho
Cucamonga 91701
Pres. Jerry W. Young
(909) 987-1737

Citrus Community College District
1000 W. Foothill Blvd., Glendora
91741-1899
Supt. Louis E. Zellers
(818) 914-8821

Citrus College
1000 W. Foothill Blvd.,
Glendora 91741-1899
Pres. Louis E. Zellers
(818) 963-0323

Coast Community College District
1370 Adams Ave., Costa Mesa
92626
Chanc. William M. Vega
(714) 432-5813

Coastline Community College
11460 Warner Ave., Fountain
Valley 92708
Pres. Leslie N. Purdy
(714) 546-7600

Golden West College
15744 Golden West St.,
Huntington Beach 92647-
0592
Interim Pres. Kenneth D.
Yglesias
(714) 892-7711

Orange Coast College
2701 Fairview Rd., P.O. Box
5005, Costa Mesa 92628-
5005
Interim Pres. James L.
McIlwain
(714) 432-0202

Compton Community College District
1111 E. Artesia Blvd., Compton
90221-5392
Pres./Supt. Byron R. Skinner
(310) 637-2660

Compton Community College
1111 E. Artesia Blvd., Compton
90221
Pres. Byron R. Skinner
(310) 637-2660

Contra Costa Community College District
500 Court St., Martinez 94553
Interim Chanc. Jack Miyamoto
(510) 229-1000

Contra Costa College
2600 Mission Bell Dr., San
Pablo 94806
Pres. D. Candy Rose
(510) 235-7800

Diablo Valley College
321 Golf Club Rd., Pleasant
Hill 94523
Pres. Phyllis L. Peterson
(510) 685-1230

Los Medanos College
2700 E. Leland Rd., Pittsburg
94565
Interim Pres. Helen Spencer
(510) 439-2181

Desert Community College District
43-500 Monterey Ave., Palm Desert
92260
Supt. David A. George
(619) 346-8041

College of the Desert
43-500 Monterey Ave., Palm
Desert 92260
Pres. David A. George
(619) 346-8041

El Camino Community College District
16007 Crenshaw Blvd., Torrance
90506
Supt. Thomas Fallo
(310) 532-3670

El Camino College
16007 Crenshaw Blvd.,
Torrance 90506
Pres. Thomas Fallo
(310) 532-3670

Feather River Community College District
570 Golden Eagle Ave., P.O. Box
11110, Quincy 95971-6023
Supt./Pres. Donald J. Donato
(916) 283-0202

Feather River College
P.O. Box 11110, Quincy 95971
Pres. Donald J. Donato
(916) 283-0202

Foothill-DeAnza Community College District
12345 El Monte Rd., Los Altos Hills
94022-4599
Pres. Leo Chavez
(415) 949-6100

De Anza College
21250 Stevens Creek Blvd.,
Cupertino 95014
Pres. Martha J. Kanter
(408) 864-5678

Foothill College
12345 El Monte Rd., Los Altos
Hills 94022
Pres. Bernadine Chuck Fong
(415) 949-7200

Fremont-Newark Community College District
43600 Mission Blvd., P.O. Box
3909, Fremont 94539-5884
Supt. Floyd M. Hogue
(510) 659-6000

Ohlone College
43600 Mission Blvd., Fremont
94539
Pres./Supt. Floyd Hogue
(510) 659-6000

Gavilan Joint Community College District
5055 Santa Teresa Blvd., Gilroy
95020
Supt. Glenn E. Mayle
(408) 847-1400

Gavilan College
5055 Santa Teresa Blvd.,
Gilroy 95020
Pres. Glenn E. Mayle
(408) 848-4712

Glendale Community College District
1500 N. Verdugo Rd., Glendale
91208
Supt. John A. Davitt
(818) 240-1000

Glendale Community College
1500 N. Verdugo Rd., Glendale
91208
Pres. John A. Davitt
(818) 240-1000

Grossmont-Cuyamaca Community College District
8800 Grossmont College Dr., El
Cajon 92020-1799
Chanc. Jeanne L. Atherton
(619) 697-9090

Cuyamaca College
2950 Jamacha Rd., El Cajon
92019-4304
Pres. Sherrill L. Amador
(619) 670-5425

Grossmont College
8800 Grossmont College Dr.,
El Cajon 92020
Pres. Richard Sanchez
(619) 465-1700

Hartnell Community College District
156 Homestead Ave., Salinas 93901
Pres. Ed Valeau
(408) 755-6900

Hartnell College
   156 Homestead Ave., Salinas
   93901
   Pres. Edward J. Valeau
   (408) 755-6900

Imperial Community College District
   P.O. Box 158, Imperial 92251-0158
   Interim Supt. Gilbert Dominguez
   (619) 352-8320

Imperial Valley College
   P.O. Box 158, Imperial 92251
   Interim Pres. Gilbert
   Dominguez
   (619) 352-8320

Kern Community College District
   2100 Chester Ave., Bakersfield
   93301
   Chanc. James C. Young
   (805) 395-4100

Bakersfield College
   1801 Panorama Dr.,
     Bakersfield 93305
   Pres. Richard L. Wright
   (805) 395-4011

Cerro Coso Community College
   3000 College Heights Blvd.,
     Ridgecrest 93555
   Pres. Raymond A. McCue
   (619) 375-5001

Porterville College
   100 E. College Ave., Porterville
   93257
   Pres. Bonnie Rogers
   (209) 781-3130

Lake Tahoe Community College District
   One College Dr., South Lake Tahoe
   96150
   Supt. Guy F. Lease
   (916) 541-4660

Lake Tahoe Community College
   One College Dr., South Lake
     Tahoe 96150
   Pres. Guy F. Lease
   (916) 541-4660

Lassen Community College District
   Hwy. 139, P.O. Box 3000,
   Susanville 96130
   Supt. Dennis P. Adams
   (916) 257-6181

Lassen College
   P.O. Box 3000, Susanville
   96130
   Pres. Dennis Adams
   (916) 257-6181

Long Beach Community College District
   4901 E. Carson St., Long Beach
   90808
   Supt. Barbara A. Adams
   (310) 420-4111

Long Beach City College
   4901 E. Carson St., Long
     Beach 90808
   Pres. Barbara A. Adams
   (310) 420-4111

Los Angeles Community College District
   770 Wilshire Blvd., Los Angeles
   90017-3896
   Chanc. Neil Yoneji
   (213) 891-2000

East Los Angeles College
   1301 Cesar Chavez Ave.,
     Monterey Park 91754
   Pres. Ernest H. Moreno
   (213) 265-8650

Los Angeles City College
   855 N. Vermont Ave., Los
     Angeles 90029-3590
   Pres. Jose Robledo
   (213) 953-4000

Los Angeles Harbor College
   1111 Figueroa Pl., Wilmington
   90744
   Pres. James L. Heinselman
   (310) 522-8200

Los Angeles Mission College
13356 Eldridge Ave., Sylmar
91342-3244
Acting Pres. William E.
Norland
(818) 364-7600

Los Angeles Pierce College
6201 Winnetka Ave., Woodland
Hills 91371
Pres. Mary E. Lee
(818) 347-0551

Los Angeles Southwest College
1600 W. Imperial Hwy., Los
Angeles 90047
Pres. Carolyn G. Williams
(213) 241-5225

*Los Angeles Trade-Technical
College*
400 W. Washington Blvd., Los
Angeles 90015
Interim Pres. Betty Hartwig
(213) 744-9000

Los Angeles Valley College
5800 Fulton Ave., Van Nuys
91401
Pres. Tyree O. Wieder
(818) 781-1200

West Los Angeles College
4800 Freshman Dr., Culver
City 90230
Pres. Evelyn C. Wong
(310) 287-4200

Los Rios Community College District
1919 Spanos Ct., Sacramento
95825-3981
Pres. Queen F. Randall
(916) 568-3021

American River College
4700 College Oak Dr.,
Sacramento 95841
Pres. Marie B. Smith
(916) 484-8011

Cosumnes River College
8401 Center Pkwy.,
Sacramento 95823
Pres. Merrilee Lewis
(916) 688-7451

Sacramento City College
3835 Freeport Blvd.,
Sacramento 95822
Pres. Robert M. Harris
(916) 558-2100

Marin Community College District
885 College Ave., Kentfield 94904
Supt. James E. Middleton
(415) 485-9500

College of Marin
835 College Ave., Kentfield
94904
Pres. James E. Middleton
(415) 457-8811

**Mendocino-Lake Community College
District**
1000 Hensley Creek Rd., Ukiah
95482
Supt. Carl J. Ehmann
(707) 468-3002

Mendocino College
P.O. Box 3000, Ukiah 95482
Pres. Carl J. Ehmann
(707) 468-3100

Merced Community College District
3600 M St., Merced 95348-2898
Supt. E. Jan Moser
(209) 384-6000

Merced College
3600 M St., Merced 95348
Pres. E. Jan Moser
(209) 384-6000

MiraCosta Community College District
One Barnard Dr., Oceanside 92056
Supt. H. Deon Holt
(619) 757-2121

Mira Costa College
One Barnard Dr., Oceanside
92056
Pres. Tim Dong
(619) 757-2121

**Monterey Peninsula Community
College District**
980 Fremont St., Monterey 93940
Supt. Edward O. Gould
(408) 646-4000

Monterey Peninsula College
980 Fremont St., Monterey
93940
Pres. Edward O. Gould
(408) 646-4000

**Mount San Antonio Community
College District**
1100 N. Grand Ave., Walnut 91789
Supt. William H. Feddersen
(909) 594-5611

Mount San Antonio College
1100 N. Grand Ave., Walnut
91789
Pres. William H. Feddersen
(909) 594-5611

**Mount San Jacinto Community College
District**
1499 N. State St., San Jacinto 92583
Supt. Roy B. Mason, II
(909) 487-6752

Mount San Jacinto College
1499 N. State St., San Jacinto
92583
Pres. Roy B. Mason, II
(909) 672-6752

Napa Valley Community College District
2277 Napa-Vallejo Hwy., Napa
94558
Supt. Diane E. Carey
(707) 253-3360

Napa Valley College
2277 Napa-Vallejo Hwy., Napa
94558
Pres. Diane E. Carey
(707) 253-3000

**North Orange County Community
College District**
1000 N. Lemon St., Fullerton 92634
Chanc. Tom K. Harris, Jr.
(714) 871-4030

Cypress College
9200 Valley View St., Cypress
90630
Pres. Christine Johnson
(714) 527-8238

Fullerton College
321 E. Chapman Ave.,
Fullerton 92632
Pres. Vera Martinez
(714) 992-7000

Palo Verde Community College District
811 W. Chanslor Way, Blythe 92225
Supt. Robert L. Wilmoth
(619) 922-6168

Palo Verde College
811 W. Chanslorway, Blythe
92225
Pres. Robert L. Wilmoth
(619) 922-6168

Palomar Community College District
1140 W. Mission Rd., San Marcos
92069-1487
Supt./Pres. George R. Boggs
(619) 744-1150

Palomar College
1140 W. Mission Rd., San
Marcos 92069
Pres. George R. Boggs
(619) 744-1150

**Pasadena Area Community College
District**
1570 E. Colorado Blvd., Pasadena
91106
Supt. James Kossler
(818) 585-7123

Pasadena City College
1570 E. Colorado Blvd.,
Pasadena 91106
Pres. James P. Kossler
(818) 585-7123

Peralta Community College District
333 E. Eighth St., Oakland 94606
Chanc. Al Harrison, II
(510) 466-7200

College of Alameda
555 Atlantic Ave., Alameda
94501
Pres. George Herring
(510) 522-7221

Laney College
900 Fallon St., Oakland 94607
Pres. Odell Johnson
(510) 834-5740

Merritt College
12500 Campus Dr., Oakland
94619
Pres. Wise E. Allen
(510) 531-4911

Vista College
2020 Milvia St., Berkeley
94704
Pres. Barbara A. Beno
(510) 841-8431

Rancho Santiago Community College District
1530 W. 17th St., Santa Ana 92706
Chanc. Vivian B. Blevins
(714) 564-6000

Rancho Santiago College—Santa Ana
17th and Bristol Sts., Santa Ana
92706
Chanc. Vivian B. Blevins
(714) 564-6000

Redwoods Community College District
7351 Tompkins Hill Rd., Eureka
95501
Supt. Cedric A. Sampson
(707) 445-6700

College of the Redwoods
7351 Tompkins Hill Rd.,
Eureka 95501
Pres. Cedric A. Sampson
(707) 445-6700

Rio Hondo Community College District
3600 Workman Mill Rd., Whittier
90608
Supt. Jess Carreon
(310) 692-0921

Rio Hondo College
3600 Workman Mill Rd.,
Whittier 90608
Pres. Jesus Carreon
(310) 692-0921

Riverside Community College District
4800 Magnolia Ave., Riverside
92506-1299
Pres. Salvatore G. Rotella
(909) 222-8000

Riverside Community College
4800 Magnolia Ave., Riverside
92506-1299
Pres. Salvatore G. Rotella
(909) 222-8000

Saddleback Community College District
28000 Marguerite Pkwy., Mission
Viejo 92692
Pres. Robert A. Lombardi
(714) 582-4840

Irvine Valley College
5500 Irvine Center Dr., Irvine
92720
Pres. Daniel Larios
(714) 559-9300

Saddleback College
28000 Marguerite Pkwy.,
Mission Viejo 92692
Pres. Ned Doffoney, Jr.
(714) 582-4500

San Bernardino Community College District
441 W. 8th St., San Bernardino
92401-1007
Chanc. Stuart M. Bundy
(909) 888-6511

Crafton Hills College
11711 Sand Canyon Rd.,
Yucaipa 92399
Pres. Luis S. Gomez
(714) 794-2161

San Bernardino Valley College
701 S. Mt. Vernon Ave., San
Bernardino 92410
Pres. Donald L. Singer
(909) 888-6511

San Diego Community College District
3375 Camino del Rio S., San Diego
92108
Chanc. Augustine P. Gallego
(619) 584-6957

San Diego City College
1313 Twelfth Ave., San Diego
92101
Pres. Jerome Hunter
(619) 230-2400

San Diego Mesa College
7250 Mesa College Dr., San
Diego 92111
Pres. Constance M. Carroll
(619) 627-2600

San Diego Miramar College
10440 Black Mountain Rd.,
San Diego 92126
Pres. Louis C. Murillo
(619) 536-7800

**San Francisco Community College
District**
50 Phelan Ave., E201, San Francisco
94112
Chanc. Dell M. Anderson
(415) 239-3000

City College of San Francisco
50 Phelan Ave., E201, San
Francisco 94112
Chanc. Dell M. Anderson
(415) 239-3000

**San Joaquin Delta Community College
District**
5151 Pacific Ave., Stockton 95207-
6370
Supt. L.H. Horton, Jr.
(209) 474-5151

San Joaquin Delta College
5151 Pacific Ave., Stockton
95207
Pres. L.H. Horton, Jr.
(209) 474-5151

**San Jose-Evergreen Community
College District**
4750 San Felipe Rd., San Jose
95135-1599
Acting Chanc. Michael Hill
(408) 270-6402

Evergreen Valley College
3095 Yerba Buena Rd., San.
Jose 95135
Pres. Noelia Vela
(408) 274-7900

San Jose City College
2100 Moorpark Ave., San Jose
95128
Interim Pres. Raul Rodriguez
(408) 289-2181

**San Luis Obispo Community College
District**
P.O. Box 8106, San Luis Obispo
93403-8106
Supt. Grace N. Mitchell
(805) 546-3100

Cuesta College
P.O. Box 8106, San Luis
Obispo 93403
Pres. Grace N. Mitchell
(805) 546-3100

**San Mateo County Community College
District**
3401 CSM Dr., San Mateo 94402-
3699
Chanc./Supt. Lois A. Callahan
(415) 574-6550

Canada College
4200 Farm Hill Blvd.,
Redwood City 94061
Pres. Marie E. Rosenwasser
(415) 306-3100

College of San Mateo
1700 W. Hillsdale Blvd., San
Mateo 94402
Pres. Peter J. Landsberger
(415) 574-6161

Skyline College
3300 College Dr., San Bruno
94066
Pres. Linda Graef Salter
(415) 355-7000

**Santa Barbara Community College
District**
721 Cliff Dr., Santa Barbara 93109
Supt. Peter R. MacDougall
(805) 965-0581

Santa Barbara City College
721 Cliff Dr., Santa Barbara
93109
Pres. Peter R. MacDougall
(805) 965-0581

**Santa Clarita Community College
District**
26455 N. Rockwell Canyon Rd.,
Santa Clarita 91355
Supt. Dianne G. Van Hook
(805) 259-7800

College of the Canyons
26455 N. Rockwell Canyon
Rd., Santa Clarita 91355
Pres. Dianne G. Van Hook
(805) 259-7800

**Santa Monica Community College
District**
1900 Pico Blvd., Santa Monica
90405
Supt. Piedad F. Robertson
(310) 452-9200

Santa Monica College
1900 Pico Blvd., Santa Monica
90405-1628
Pres./Supt. Piedad F. Robertson
(310) 450-5150

Sequoias Community College District
915 S. Mooney Blvd., Visalia 93277
Pres. M. Douglas Kechter
(209) 730-3700

College of the Sequoias
915 S. Mooney Blvd., Visalia
93277
Pres. M. Douglas Kechter
(209) 730-3700

**Shasta-Tehama-Trinity Joint
Community College District**
11555 Old Oregon Tr., Redding
96049
Supt. Douglas Treadway
(916) 225-4600

Shasta College
P.O. Box 496006, Redding
96049
Pres. Douglas M. Treadway
(916) 225-4600

**Sierra Joint Community College
District**
5000 Rocklin Rd., Rocklin 95677
Supt. Kevin M. Ramirez
(916) 624-3333

Sierra College
5000 Rocklin Rd., Rocklin
95677
Pres. Kevin M. Ramirez
(916) 624-3333

**Siskiyou Joint Community College
District**
800 College Ave., Weed 96094
Supt. Martha G. Romero
(916) 938-4462

College of the Siskiyous
800 College Ave., Weed 96094
Pres. Martha G. Romero
(916) 938-4462

Solano County Community College District
4000 Suisun Valley Rd., Suisun 94585
Pres. Stan R. Arterberry
(707) 864-7112

Solano Community College
4000 Suisun Valley Rd., Suisun 94585
Pres./Supt. Stan Arterbery
(707) 864-7000

Sonoma County Junior College District
1501 Mendocino Ave., Santa Rosa 95401
Pres./Supt. Robert F. Agrella
(707) 527-4411

Santa Rosa Junior College
1501 Mendocino Ave., Santa Rosa 95401
Pres. Robert F. Agrella
(707) 527-4011

Southwestern Community College District
900 Otay Lakes Rd., Chula Vista 91910-7299
Supt. Joseph M. Conte
(619) 482-6301

Southwestern College
900 Otay Lakes Rd., Chula Vista 91910
Pres. Joseph M. Conte
(619) 421-6700

State Center Community College District
1525 E. Weldon Ave., Fresno 93704
Chanc. Bill F. Stewart
(209) 226-0720

Fresno City College
1101 E. University Ave., Fresno 93741
Pres. Brice W. Harris
(209) 442-4600

Kings River Community College
995 N. Reed Ave., Reedley 93654
Pres. Richard J. Giese
(209) 638-3641

Ventura County Community College District
71 Day Rd., Ventura 93003
Chanc. Philip Westin
(805) 654-6412

Moorpark College
7075 Campus Rd., Moorpark 93021
Pres. James W. Walker
(805) 378-1400

Oxnard College
4000 S. Rose Ave., Oxnard 93033
Pres. Elise D. Schneider
(805) 986-5800

Ventura College
4667 Telegraph Rd., Ventura 93003
Interim Pres. Larry Calderon
(805) 654-6460

Victor Valley Community College District
18422 Bear Valley Rd., Victorville 92392
Interim Supt. Nicholas Halisky
(619) 245-4271

Victor Valley College
18422 Bear Valley Rd., Victorville 92392
Interim Pres. Nicholas Halisky
(619) 245-4271

West Hills Community College District
300 Cherry Ln., Coalinga 93210
Supt. Francis P. Gornick
(209) 935-0801

West Hills Community College
300 Cherry Ln., Coalinga
93210
Pres. Francis P. Gornick
(209) 935-0801

West Kern Community College District
29 Emmons Park Dr., Taft 93268
Supt. David Cothrun
(805) 763-4282

Taft College
29 Emmons Park Dr., Taft
93268
Pres. David Cothrun
(805) 763-4282

West Valley-Mission College District
14000 Fruitvale Ave., Saratoga
95070
Chanc. Rose Tseng
(408) 867-2200

Mission College
3000 Mission College Blvd.,
Santa Clara 95054
Pres. Michael Rao
(408) 988-2200

West Valley College
14000 Fruitvale Ave., Saratoga
95070
Interim Pres. Sam Schauerman
(408) 867-2200

Yosemite Community College District
P.O. Box 4065, Modesto 95352-
4065
Chanc. Pamila J. Fisher
(209) 575-6508

Columbia College
P.O. Box 1849, Columbia
95310
Pres. Kenneth B. White
(209) 533-5100

Modesto Junior College
435 College Ave., Modesto
95350
Pres. Maria Sheehan
(209) 575-6067

Yuba Community College District
2088 N. Beale Rd., Marysville
95901
Supt. Stephen M. Epler
(916) 741-6700

Yuba College
2088 N. Beale Rd., Marysville
95901
Pres. Stephen M. Epler
(916) 741-6700

California School of Professional Psychology
2749 Hyde St., San Francisco 94109
Pres. John R. O'Neil
(415) 346-4500

*California School of Professional
Psychology—Almeda*
1005 Atlantic Ave., Alameda 94501
Chanc. Katsuyuki Sakamoto
(510) 523-2300

*California School of Professional
Psychology—Fresno*
1350 M St., Fresno 93721
Chanc. Mary Beth Kenkel
(209) 486-8420

*California School of Professional
Psychology—Los Angeles*
1000 S. Fremont Ave., Alhambra
91803-1360
Chanc. Lisa M. Porche-Burke
(818) 284-2777

*California School of Professional
Psychology—San Diego*
6160 Cornerstone Ct. E., San Diego
92121-3275
Chanc. Raymond J. Trybus
(619) 452-1664

The California State University System
400 Golden Shore, Long Beach 90802-
4275
Chanc. Barry Munitz
(310) 985-2500

California Maritime Academy
200 Maritime Academy Dr., P.O.
Box 1392, Vallejo 94590-0644
Pres. Mary E. Lyons
(707) 648-4200

California Polytechnic State University—
San Luis Obispo
San Luis Obispo 93407
Pres. Warren J. Baker
(805) 756-1111

California State Polytechnic University—
Pomona
3801 W. Temple Ave., Pomona
91768
Pres. Bob H. Suzuki
(909) 869-7659

California State University—Bakersfield
9001 Stockdale Hwy., Bakersfield
93311-1099
Pres. Tomas A. Arciniega
(805) 664-2011

California State University—Chico
First and Normal Sts., Chico 95929-
0110
Pres. Manuel A. Esteban
(916) 898-6116

California State University—Dominguez
Hills
1000 E. Victoria St., Carson 90747
Pres. Robert C. Detweiler
(310) 516-3300

California State University—Fresno
5241 N. Maple Ave., Fresno 93740-
0054
Pres. John D. Welty
(209) 278-4240

California State University—Fullerton
800 N. State College Blvd., P.O.
Box 34080, Fullerton 92634
Pres. Milton A. Gordon
(714) 773-2011

California State University—Hayward
25800 Carlos Bee Blvd., Hayward
94542-3011
Pres. Norma S. Rees
(510) 881-3000

California State University—Long Beach
1250 Bellflower Blvd., Long Beach
90840
Pres. Robert C. Maxson
(310) 985-4111

California State University—Los Angeles
5151 State University Dr., Los
Angeles 90032
Pres. James M. Rosser
(213) 343-3000

California State University—Northridge
18111 Nordhoff St., Northridge
91330
Pres. Blenda J. Wilson
(818) 885-1200

California State University—Sacramento
6000 J St., Sacramento 95819-2694
Pres. Donald R. Gerth
(916) 278-6011

California State University—San
Bernardino
5500 State University Pkwy., San
Bernardino 92407-2397
Pres. Anthony H. Evans
(909) 880-5000

California State University—San Marcos
San Marcos 92096-0001
Pres. Bill W. Stacy
(619) 750-4000

California State University—Stanislaus
801 W. Monte Vista Ave., Turlock
95380
Pres. Marvalene Hughes
(209) 667-3122

Humboldt State University
Arcata 95521
Pres. Alistair W. McCrone
(707) 826-3011

San Diego State University
5500 Campanile Dr., San Diego
92182-0763
Pres. Thomas B. Day
(619) 594-5000

San Francisco State University
1600 Holloway Ave., San Francisco
94132
Pres. Robert A. Corrigan
(415) 338-1111

San Jose State University
One Washington Sq., San Jose
95192-0002
Pres. Robert L. Caret
(408) 924-1000

Sonoma State University
1801 E. Cotati Ave., Rohnert Park
94928
Pres. Ruben Arminana
(707) 664-2880

Claremont University Center
Harper Hall 122, 150 East 10th St.,
Claremont 91711-6160
Exec. Vice Pres. John M. Dorger
(909) 621-8026

The Claremont Graduate School
160 E. 10th St., Claremont 91711
Pres. John D. Maguire
(909) 621-8000

Claremont McKenna College
850 Columbia Ave., Claremont
91711
Pres. Jack L. Stark
(909) 621-8111

Harvey Mudd College
301 E. 12th St., Claremont 91711
Pres. Henry E. Riggs
(909) 621-8000

Pitzer College
1050 N. Mills Ave., Claremont
91711-6110
Pres. Marilyn Chapin Massey
(909) 621-8000

Pomona College
550 N. College Ave., Claremont
91711
Pres. Peter W. Stanley
(909) 621-8000

Scripps College
1030 N. Columbia Ave., Claremont
91711
Pres. Nancy Y. Bekavac
(909) 621-8148

Heald Colleges
1453 Mission St., 4th Fl., San Francisco
94103
Pres. Scott R. Loring
(415) 864-5060

Heald Business College—Concord
2150 John Glenn Dr., Concord
94520
Dir. Steven M. Kinzer
(510) 827-1300

Heald Business College—Fresno
255 W. Bullard Ave., Fresno 93704
Dir. Alex Babigan
(209) 438-4222

Heald Business College—Hayward
777 Southland Dr., Hayward 94545
Dir. Barbara Gordon
(510) 784-7000

Heald Business College—Honolulu HI
1500 Kapiolani Rd., Honolulu, HI
96814
Dir. Evelyn Schemmel
(808) 955-1500

Heald Business College—Oakland
1000 Broadway, Oakland 94607
Dir. Carolyn Greenleaf
(510) 444-0201

Heald Business College—Sacramento
2910 Prospect Park Dr., Rancho
Cordova 95670
Dir. Donald E. Hardenbrook
(916) 638-1616

Heald Business College—Salinas
 1333 Schilling Pl., P.O. Box 3167,
  Salinas 93901
 Dir. Chris Tilley
 (408) 757-1700

Heald Business College—San Francisco
 1453 Mission St., San Francisco
  94103
 Dir. Linda Sempliner
 (415) 673-5500

Heald Business College—San Jose
 2665 N. First St., Ste. 110, San Jose
  95134
 Dir. Peter Lee
 (408) 955-9555

Heald Business College—Santa Rosa
 2425 Mendocino Ave., Santa Rosa
  95403
 Dir. Gordon Kent
 (707) 525-1300

Heald Business College—Stockton
 1776 W. March Ln., 3rd Fl.,
  Stockton 95207
 Dir. Michael Mallory
 (209) 477-1114

Heald Institute of Technology—Hayward
 24301 Southland Dr., Ste. 500,
  Hayward 94545
 Dir. Michael Bennett
 (510) 783-2100

Heald Institute of Technology—Martinez
 2860 Howe Rd., Martinez 94553
 Dir. Douglas Cole
 (510) 228-9000

Heald Institute of Technology—
Sacramento
 3737 Marconi Ave., Sacramento
  95821
 Dir. William Johnson
 (916) 972-0999

Heald Institute of Technology—San
Francisco
 250 Executive Park Blvd., Ste.
  1000, San Francisco 94134
 Dir. Timothy Cassady
 (415) 822-2900

Heald Institute of Technology—San Jose
 341-A Great Mall Pkwy., Milpitas
  95035-8008
 Dir. Kenneth Heinemann
 (408) 295-8000

San Joaquin Valley College System
 8400 W. Mineral King Ave., Visalia
  93291-9283
 Pres. Mark Perry
 (209) 651-2500

San Joaquin Valley College—Bakersfield
 201 New Stine Rd., Bakersfield
  93309-2606
 Dir. Jane Parker
 (805) 834-0126

San Joaquin Valley College—Fresno
 3333 N. Bond St., Fresno 93726-
  9941
 Dir. Richard Muella
 (209) 229-7800

San Joaquin Valley College—Fresno
 4985 E. Andersen Ave., Fresno
  93727-1501
 Dir. Bob Loogman
 (209) 453-0380

San Joaquin Valley College—Visalia
 8400 W. Mineral King Ave., Visalia
  93291-9283
 Dir. Steve Perry
 (209) 651-2500

University of California Office of the
President
 300 Lakeside Dr., Oakland 94612-3550
 Pres. Richard C. Atkinson
 (510) 987-0700

San Francisco Art Institute
800 Chestnut St., San Francisco
94133
Pres. Ella King Torrey
(415) 771-7020

University of California, Berkeley
Berkeley 94720
Chanc. Chang-Lin Tien
(510) 642-6000

University of California, Davis
Davis 95616
Chanc. Larry N. Vanderhoef
(916) 752-1011

University of California, Hastings
College of the Law
200 McAllister St., San Francisco
94102
Dean Mary Kay Kane
(415) 565-4600

University of California, Irvine
Campus Dr., Irvine 92717
Chanc. Laurel L. Wilkening
(714) 824-5011

University of California, Los Angeles
405 Hilgard Ave., Los Angeles
90024
Chanc. Charles E. Young
(310) 825-4321

University of California, Riverside
Riverside 92521
Chanc. Raymond L. Orbach
(909) 787-1012

University of California, San Diego
9500 Gilman Dr., Mail Code 0056,
La Jolla 92093
Interim Chanc. Marjorie C. Caserio
(619) 534-2230

University of California, San Francisco
513 Parnassus Ave., San Francisco
94143
Chanc. Joseph B. Martin
(415) 476-9000

University of California, Santa Barbara
Santa Barbara 93106-2030
Chanc. Henry T. Yang
(805) 893-8000

University of California, Santa Cruz
1156 High St., Santa Cruz 95064
Chanc. Karl S. Pister
(408) 459-0111

COLORADO

Colorado Commission on Higher Education
1300 Broadway, 2nd Fl., Denver 80203
Chanc. Dwayne C. Nuzum
(303) 866-2723

**Colorado Community College and
Occupational Education System**
1391 N. Speer Blvd., Ste. 600,
Denver 80204-2554
Pres. Jerome F. Wartgow
(303) 620-4000

Arapahoe Community College
2500 W. College Dr., P.O. Box
9002, Littleton 80160-9002
Pres. James F. Weber
(303) 794-1550

Community College of Aurora
16000 E. Centretech Pkwy.,
Aurora 80011
Pres. Larry D. Carter
(303) 360-4700

Community College of Denver
Campus Box 250, P.O. Box
173363, Denver 80217-3363
Pres. Byron N. McClenney
(303) 556-2600

Front Range Community College
3645 W. 112th Ave.,
Westminster 80030
Pres. Thomas Gonzales
(303) 466-8811

Lamar Community College
2401 S. Main St., Lamar 81052
Pres. Marvin E. Lane
(719) 336-2248

Morgan Community College
17800 Rd. 20, Fort Morgan
80701
Pres. Richard Bond
(800) 622-0216

Otero Junior College
1802 Colorado Ave., La Junta
81050
Pres. Joe M. Treece
(719) 384-8721

Pikes Peak Community College
5675 S. Academy Blvd.,
Colorado Springs 80906
Pres. Marijane A. Paulsen
(800) 456-6847

Pueblo Community College
900 W. Orman Ave., Pueblo
81004
Pres. Joe D. May
(719) 549-3200

Red Rocks Community College
13300 W. Sixth Ave.,
Lakewood 80401-5398
Pres. Dorothy Horrell
(303) 988-6160

Trinidad State Junior College
600 Prospect St., Trinidad
81082
Pres. Harold Deselms
(719) 846-5011

Colorado School of Mines
1500 Illinois St., Golden 80401
Pres. George S. Ansell
(303) 273-3280

Colorado State University
102 Administration Bldg., Fort
Collins 80523
Pres. Albert C. Yates
(303) 491-1101

Fort Lewis College
1000 Rim Dr., Durango 81301-3999
Pres. Joel M. Jones
(970) 247-7100

The State Colleges in Colorado
1580 Lincoln St., Ste. 750, Denver
80203
(303) 874-2700

Adams State College
208 Edgemont, Alamosa 81101
Pres. J. Thomas Gilmore
(719) 589-7011

Mesa State College
P.O. Box 2647, Grand Junction
81502
Pres. Raymond N. Kieft
(970) 248-1020

Metropolitan State College of
Denver
Campus Box 48, P.O. Box
173362, Denver 80217-3362
Pres. Sheila Kaplan
(303) 556-3022

Western State College
214 Taylor Hall, Gunnison
81231
Interim Pres. William M.
Fulkerson, Jr.
(800) 876-5309

University of Colorado Central
Administration
914 Broadway, Boulder 80309
Interim Pres. John C. Buechner
(303) 492-6201

University of Colorado Health
Sciences Center
Campus Box A095, 4200 E. 9th
Ave., Denver 80262
Chanc. Vincent A. Fulginiti
(303) 399-1211

University of Colorado at Boulder
Campus Box B-17, Boulder
80309
Chanc. Roderic Park
(303) 492-1411

University of Colorado at Colorado
Springs
P.O. Box 7150, Colorado
Springs 80933-7150
Chanc. Linda Bunnell Shade
(719) 593-3000

University of Colorado at Denver
P.O. Box 173364, Denver
80217-3364
Chanc. John C. Buechner
(303) 556-3279

University of Northern Colorado
Greeley 80639
Pres. Herman D. Lujan
(970) 351-1890

University of Southern Colorado
2200 Bonforte Blvd., Pueblo 81001-
4901
Pres. Robert C. Shirley
(719) 549-2100

CONNECTICUT

State of Connecticut Department of Higher Education
61 Woodland St., Hartford 06105-2391
Commiss. Andrew G. De Rocco
(860) 566-5766

Charter Oak State College
66 Cedar St., Ste. 301, Newington 06111-2646
Acting Pres. Richard J. Hamilton
(860) 666-4595

Connecticut State University Central Office
P.O. Box 2008, New Britain 06050
Pres. William J. Cibes, Jr.
(860) 832-0011

Central Connecticut State University
1615 Stanley St., New Britain 06050
Interim Pres. Merle W. Harris
(860) 832-3200

Eastern Connecticut State University
83 Windham St., Willimantic 06226-2295
Pres. David G. Carter
(860) 465-5000

Southern Connecticut State University
501 Crescent St., New Haven 06515-0901
Pres. Michael J. Adanti
(203) 392-5200

Western Connecticut State University
181 White St., Danbury 06810
Pres. James R. Roach
(203) 837-8200

State of Connecticut Board of Trustees of Community-Technical Colleges
61 Woodland St., Hartford 06105-2392
Exec. Dir. Andrew C. McKirdy
(860) 566-8760

Asnuntuck Community-Technical College
170 Elm St., Enfield 06082
Pres. Harvey S. Irlen
(860) 253-3000

Capital Community-Technical College Woodland Campus
61 Woodland St., Hartford 06105
Pres. Conrad L. Mallett
(860) 520-7800

Gateway Community-Technical College—Long Wharf Campus
60 Sargent Dr., New Haven 06511
Interim Pres. Leila Gonzalez-Sullivan
(203) 789-7071

Housatonic Community-Technical College
510 Barnum Ave., Bridgeport 06608
Pres. Vincent S. Darnowski
(203) 579-6400

Manchester Community-Technical College
60 Bidwell St., Manchester 06040
Pres. Jonathan M. Daube
(860) 647-6000

Middlesex Community-Technical College
100 Training Hill Rd., Middletown 06457
Interim Pres. Robert E. Miller
(860) 343-5800

Naugatuck Valley Community-Technical College
750 Chase Pkwy., Waterbury 06708
Pres. Richard L. Sanders
(203) 575-8040

*Northwestern Connecticut
  Community-Technical College*
    Park Pl., Winsted 06098
    Pres. R. Eileen Baccus
    (860) 738-6300

*Norwalk Community-Technical
  College*
    188 Richards Ave., Norwalk
      06854
    Pres. William H. Schwab
    (203) 857-7000

*Quinebaug Valley Community-
  Technical College*
    742 Upper Maple St.,
      Danielson 06239
    Pres. Dianne E. Williams
    (860) 774-1130

*Three Rivers Community-Technical
  College Mohegan Campus*
    P.O. Box 629, Mahan Dr.,
      Norwich 06360
    Pres. Booker T. DeVaughn, Jr.
    (860) 886-1931

*Tunxis Community-Technical
  College*
    271 Scott Swamp Rd.,
      Farmington 06032
    Pres. Cathryn L. Addy
    (860) 677-7701

The University of Connecticut
    Route 195, Storrs 06269
    Pres. Harry J. Hartley
    (860) 486-2000

*The University of Connecticut Health
  Center*
    263 Farmington Ave., Farmington
      06032
    Exec. Dir. Leslie S. Cutler
    (860) 679-2000

DELAWARE

Delaware Higher Education Commission
Carvel State Office Bldg., 820 N. French
St., Wilmington 19801
Exec. Dir. Marliyn B. Quinn
(302) 577-3240

Delaware State University
1200 N. Dupont Hwy., Dover 19901
Pres. William B. DeLauder
(302) 739-4901

**Delaware Technical & Community
College Office of the President**
P.O. Box 897, Dover 19903
Pres. Orlando J. George, Jr.
(302) 739-4053

*Delaware Technical & Community
College Stanton/Wilmington
Campus*
400 Stanton Christiana Rd.,
Newark 19713
Vice Pres./Campus Dir.
Lawrence Miller
(302) 454-3917

*Delaware Technical & Community
College/Southern Campus*
P.O. Box 610, Georgetown
19947
Vice Pres./Campus Dir. G.
Timothy Kavel
(302) 856-5400

*Delaware Technical & Community
College/Terry Campus*
1832 N. Dupont Pkwy., Dover
19901
Vice Pres./Campus Dir.
Marguerite M. Johnson
(302) 739-5321

University of Delaware
104 Hullihen Hall, Newark 19716
Pres. David P. Roselle
(302) 831-2000

FLORIDA

Florida Metropolitan University System
Office of The Chancellor, 5421 Diplomat
Cir., Orlando 32810
Interim Chanc. Ronald Kimberling
(407) 628-5870

Florida Metropolitan University System-
Fort Lauderdale College
1040 Bayview Dr., Fort Lauderdale
33304
Dir. Joel D. Boyd
(305) 568-1600

Florida Metropolitan University System-
Orlando College—North Campus
5421 Diplomat Cir., Orlando 32810
Pres. Ouida B. Kirby
(407) 628-5870

Florida Metropolitan University System-
Tampa College—Pinellas Campus
2471 McMullen Booth Rd, Ste. 200,
Clearwater 34619
Pres. Mark Page
(813) 539-8404

Florida Metropolitan University System-
Tampa College—W. Hillsborough Cty
Camp
3319 W. Hillsborough Ave., Tampa
33614
Pres. Joyce Meadows
(813) 879-6000

Florida State Board of Community Colleges
1314 Florida Educ. Ctr., 325 W. Gaines
St., Tallahassee 32399-0400
Exec. Dir. Clark Maxwell, Jr.
(904) 488-1721

Brevard Community College
1519 Clearlake Rd., Cocoa 32922-
6597
Pres. Maxwell C. King
(407) 632-1111

Broward Community College
225 E. Las Olas Blvd., Fort
Lauderdale 33301
Pres. Willis N. Holcombe
(305) 475-6500

Central Florida Community College
P.O. Box 1388, 3001 S.W. College
Rd., Ocala 34478-1388
Pres. William J. Campion
(904) 237-2111

Chipola Junior College
3094 Indian Cir., Marianna 32446-
2053
Pres. H. Dale O'Daniel
(904) 526-2761

Daytona Beach Community College
P.O. Box 2811, Daytona Beach
32120-2811
Pres. Philip R. Day, Jr.
(904) 255-8131

Edison Community College
8099 College Pkwy., S.W., P.O. Box
60210, Fort Myers 33906-6210
Pres. Kenneth P. Walker
(941) 489-9300

Florida Community College at
Jacksonville
501 W. State St., Jacksonville
32202-4030
Pres. Charles C. Spence
(904) 632-3000

Florida Keys Community College
5901 W. College Rd., Key West
33040-4397
Pres. William A. Seeker
(305) 296-9081

Gulf Coast Community College
5230 W. U.S. Hwy. 98, Panama City
32401-1044
Pres. Robert L. McSpadden
(904) 769-1551

Hillsborough Community College
39 Columbia Dr., Tampa 33631-
3127
Pres. Andreas A. Paloumpis
(813) 253-7000

Indian River Community College
3209 Virginia Ave., Fort Pierce
34981-5599
Pres. Edwin R. Massey
(407) 462-4700

Lake City Community College
Rte. 19, Box 1030, Lake City 32305
Pres. Muriel Kay Heimer
(904) 752-1822

Lake-Sumter Community College
9501 U.S. Hwy. 441 S., Leesburg
34788-8751
Pres. Robert W. Westrick
(904) 787-3747

Manatee Community College
5840 26th St. W., P.O. Box 1849,
Bradenton 34207-1849
Pres. Stephen J. Korcheck
(813) 755-1511

Miami-Dade Community College
300 N.E. Second Ave., Miami 33132
Pres. Eduardo J. Padron
(305) 237-3366

North Florida Community College
1000 Turner Davis Dr., Madison
32340-1698
Pres. Beverly M. Grissom
(904) 973-2288

Okaloosa-Walton Community College
100 College Blvd., Niceville 32578
Pres. James R. Richburg
(904) 678-5111

Palm Beach Community College
4200 Congress Ave., Lake Worth
33461-4796
Pres. Edward M. Eissey
(407) 439-8004

Pasco-Hernando Community College
36727 Blanton Rd., Dade City
33525-7599
Pres. Robert W. Judson, Jr.
(904) 567-6701

Pensacola Junior College
1000 College Blvd., Pensacola
32504-8998
Pres. Horace E. Hartsell
(904) 484-1000

Polk Community College
999 Ave. H, N.E., Winter Haven
33881-4299
Pres. Maryly VanLeer Peck
(941) 297-1000

Santa Fe Community College
3000 N.W. 83rd St., Gainesville
32606-6200
Pres. Lawrence W. Tyree
(904) 395-5000

Seminole Community College
100 Weldon Blvd., Sanford 32773-
6199
Pres. E. Ann McGee
(407) 328-4722

South Florida Community College
600 W. College Dr., Avon Park
33825-9399
Pres. Catherine P. Cornelius
(813) 453-6661

St. Johns River Community College
5001 St. Johns Ave., Palatka 32177-
3897
Pres. Robert L. McLendon, Jr.
(904) 328-1571

St. Petersburg Junior College
P.O. Box 13489, St. Petersburg
33733-3489
Pres. Carl M. Kuttler, Jr.
(813) 341-3600

Tallahassee Community College
444 Appleyard Dr., Tallahassee
32304-2895
Pres. T.K. Wetherell
(904) 488-9200

Valencia Community College
P.O. Box 3028, Orlando 32802-3028
Pres. Paul C. Gianini, Jr.
(407) 299-5000

State University System of Florida
325 W. Gaines St., Tallahassee 32399-
1950
Chanc. Charles B. Reed
(904) 488-4234

*Florida Agricultural and Mechanical
University*
S. Martin Luther King Blvd., 400
Lee Hall, Tallahassee 32307
Pres. Frederick S. Humphries
(904) 599-3000

Florida Atlantic University
777 Glades Rd., Boca Raton 33431-
0991
Pres. Anthony J. Catanese
(407) 367-3000

Florida International University
Univ. Park and Tamiami Trail,
Miami 33199
Pres. Modesto A. Maidique
(305) 348-2000

Florida State University
Tallahassee 32306
Pres. Talbot D'Alemberte
(904) 644-2525

University of Central Florida
4000 Central Florida Blvd., Orlando
32816
Pres. John C. Hitt
(407) 823-2000

University of Florida
226 Tigert Hall, Gainesville 32611
Pres. John V. Lombardi
(904) 392-3261

University of North Florida
4567 St. Johns Bluff Rd., S.,
Jacksonville 32224-2645
Pres. Adam W. Herbert, Jr.
(904) 646-2666

University of South Florida
4202 E. Flower Avenue, Tampa
33620-6100
Pres. Betty Castor
(813) 974-2154

University of West Florida
11000 University Pkwy., Pensacola
32514-5750
Pres. Morris L. Marx
(904) 474-2200

GEORGIA

Board of Regents of the University System of Georgia
244 Washington St., S.W., Atlanta 30334
Chanc. Stephen R. Portch
(404) 656-2202

Abraham Baldwin Agricultural College
ABAC 1,2802 Moore Hwy., Tifton
31794-2601
Pres. Harold J. Loyd
(912) 386-3230

Albany State College
504 College Dr., Albany 31705-
2794
Pres. Billy C. Black
(912) 430-4604

Armstrong State College
11935 Abercorn Ext., Savannah
31419-1997
Pres. Robert A. Burnett
(912) 927-5258

Atlanta Metropolitan College
1630 Stewart Ave., S.W., Atlanta
30310
Pres. Harold E. Wade
(404) 756-4000

Augusta College
Augusta 30910
Pres. William A. Bloodworth
(706) 737-1440

Bainbridge College
Hwy. 84 E., Bainbridge 31717
Pres. Edward D. Mobley
(912) 248-2510

Brunswick College
3700 Altama Ave., Brunswick
31520-3644
Pres. Dorothy L. Lord
(912) 264-7201

Clayton State College
5900 N. Lee St., Morrow 30260
Pres. Richard Skinner
(770) 961-3403

Columbus College
4225 Univ. Ave., Columbus 31907-
5645
Pres. Frank D. Brown
(770) 568-2211

Dalton College
213 N. College Dr., Dalton 30720
Pres. James A. Burran
(706) 272-4438

Darton College
2400 Gillionville Rd., Albany
31707-3098
Pres. Peter J. Sireno
(912) 430-6000

DeKalb College
3251 Panthersville Rd., Decatur
30034
Pres. Jacquelyn M. Belcher
(404) 244-2364

East Georgia College
131 Coll. Circle, Swainsboro 30401
Pres. Jeremiah J. Ashcroft
(912) 237-7831

Floyd College
P.O. Box 1864, Rome 30162-1864
Pres. H. Lynn Cundiff
(706) 295-6328

Fort Valley State College
1005 State College Dr., Fort Valley
31030-3298
Pres. Oscar L. Prater
(912) 825-6211

Gainesville College
Mundy Mill Rd., P.O. Box 1358,
Gainesville 30503-1358
Pres. J. Foster Watkins
(770) 535-6239

Georgia College
C.B.X. Box 020, Milledgeville
31061-0490
Pres. Edwin G. Speir, Jr.
(912) 453-5004

Georgia Institute of Technology
225 North Ave., N.W., Atlanta
30332-0325
Pres. Wayne G. Clough
(404) 894-5051

Georgia Southern University
Landrum Box 8033, Statesboro
30460-8033
Pres. Nicholas L. Henry
(912) 681-5211

Georgia Southwestern College
800 Wheatley St., Americus 31709-
4693
Pres. Joan Eliason
(912) 928-1279

Georgia State University
University Plaza, Atlanta 30303-
3083
Pres. Carl V. Patton
(404) 651-2560

Gordon College
419 College Dr., Barnesville 30204
Pres. Jerry M. Williamson
(770) 358-5000

Kennesaw State College
1000 Chastain Rd., Kennesaw
30144-5591
Pres. Betty L. Siegel
(770) 423-6033

Macon College
100 College Sta. Dr., Macon 31297
Pres. S. Aaron Hyatt
(912) 471-2800

Medical College of Georgia
1120 15th St., Augusta 30912
Pres. Francis J. Tedesco
(706) 721-0211

Middle Georgia College
1100 Second St., S.E., Cochran
31014
Pres. Joe Ben Welch
(912) 934-3011

North Georgia College
College Ave., Dahlonega 30597
Pres. Delmas J. Allen
(706) 864-1993

Savannah State College
State College Br., P.O. Box 20419,
Savannah 31404
Pres. John T. Wolfe, Jr.
(912) 356-2187

South Georgia College
100 W. College Park Dr., Douglas
31533-5098
Pres. Edward D. Jackson, Jr.
(912) 383-4380

Southern College of Technology
1100 S. Marietta Pkwy., Marietta
30060-2896
Pres. Stephen R. Cheshier
(770) 528-7281

The University of Georgia
456 E. Broad St., Athens 30602-1661
Pres. Charles B. Knapp
(404) 542-3000

Valdosta State University
1500 N. Patterson St., Valdosta
31602
Pres. Hugh C. Bailey
(912) 333-5952

Waycross College
2001 Francis St., Waycross 31503-
9248
Pres. James M. Dye
(912) 285-6130

West Georgia College
1600 Maple St., Carrollton 30118-
0001
Pres. Beheruz N. Sethna
(770) 836-6449

HAWAII

University of Hawaii Office of the President
2444 Dole St., Honolulu 96822
Pres. Kenneth P. Mortimer
(808) 956-8207

University of Hawaii Office of the Chancellor for Community Colleges
2327 Dole St., Honolulu 96822
Sr. V.P. & Chanc., Comm. Colleges
Joyce S. Tsunoda
(808) 956-7313

Hawaii Community College
200 W. Kawili St., Hilo 96720-4091
Provost Sandra T. Sakaguchi
(808) 933-3311

Honolulu Community College
874 Dillingham Blvd., Honolulu 96817
Provost Peter R. Kessinger
(808) 845-9211

Kapiolani Community College
4303 Diamond Head Rd., Honolulu 96816
Provost John E. Morton
(808) 734-9111

Kauai Community College
3-1901 Kaumualii Hwy., Lihue 96766
Campus Pres. David Iha
(808) 245-8311

Leeward Community College
96-045 Ala Ike, Pearl City 96782
Provost Barbara B. Polk
(808) 455-0011

Maui Community College
310 Kaahumanu Ave., Kahului 96732
Provost Clyde M. Sakamoto
(808) 244-9181

Windward Community College
45-720 Keaahala Rd., Kaneohe 96744
Provost Peter T. Dyer
(808) 235-0077

University of Hawaii at Hilo
Hilo 96720-4091
Chanc. Kenneth L. Perrin
(808) 933-3445

University of Hawaii at Manoa
2444 Dole St., Honolulu 96822
Chanc. Kenneth P. Mortimer
(808) 956-8207

University of Hawaii at West Oahu
96-043 Ala Ike, Pearl City 96782
Chanc. Kenneth L. Perrin
(808) 453-6565

IDAHO

State Board of Education and Board of Regents of the University of Idaho
L.B. Jordan Bldg., Rm. 307, 650 W. State St., P.O. 83720, Boise 83720-0037
Exec. Dir. Rayburn Barton
(208) 334-2270

Boise State University
1910 Univ. Dr., Boise 83725
Pres. Charles P. Ruch
(208) 385-1491

College of Southern Idaho
315 Falls Ave., P.O. Box 1238, Twin Falls 83301
Pres. Gerald R. Meyerhoeffer
(208) 733-9554

Idaho State University
Pocatello 83209-0009
Pres. Richard L. Bowen
(208) 236-3340

Lewis-Clark State College
500 8th Ave., Lewiston 83501
Pres. James W. Hottois
(208) 799-5272

North Idaho College
Coeur d'Alene 83814
Pres. C. Robert Bennett
(208) 769-3300

University of Idaho
Moscow 83843
Interim Pres. Thomas O. Bell
(208) 885-6111

ILLINOIS

DeVry Institutes
One Tower Ln., Oak Brook Terrace
60181
Pres. Ronald Taylor
(708) 571-7700

DeVry Institute of Technology—Addison
1221 N. Swift Rd., Addison 60101-
6106
Pres. Jerry R. Dill
(708) 953-1300

DeVry Institute of Technology—Chicago
3300 N. Campbell Ave., Chicago
60618-5994
Pres. E. Arthur Stunard
(312) 929-8500

DeVry Institute of Technology—Columbus
1350 Alum Creek Dr., Columbus,
OH 43209-2705
Pres. Richard A. Czerniak
(614) 253-7291

DeVry Institute of Technology—Decatur
250 N. Arcadia Ave., Decatur, GA
30030
Pres. Ronald W. Bush
(404) 292-7900

DeVry Institute of Technology—Irving
4801 Regent Blvd., Irving, TX
75063-2440
Pres. Francis V. Cannon
(214) 929-6777

DeVry Institute of Technology—Kansas City
11224 Holmes Rd., Kansas City,
MO 64131
Pres. Charles Robert Levalley
(816) 941-0430

DeVry Institute of Technology—Phoenix
2149 W. Dunlap Ave., Phoenix, AZ
85021-2995
Pres. James A. Dugan
(602) 870-9222

DeVry Institute of Technology—Pomona
901 Corporate Center Dr., Pomona,
CA 91768-2642
Pres. RoseMarie Dishman
(909) 622-8866

DeVry Technical Institute—Woodbridge
479 Green St., Woodbridge, NJ
07095
Pres. Robert M. Bocchino
(908) 634-3460

Illinois Board of Governors Universities
700 E. Adams St., Ste. 200, Springfield
62701
Acting Chanc. Jack Bleicher
(217) 782-6392

Chicago State University
9501 S. King Dr., Chicago 60628-
1598
Pres. Dolores E. Cross
(312) 995-2000

Eastern Illinois University
600 Lincoln Ave., Charleston 61920
Pres. David L. Jorns
(217) 581-5000

Governors State University
University Park 60466
Pres. Paula Wolff
(708) 534-5000

Northeastern Illinois University
5500 N. St. Louis Ave., Chicago
60625
Pres. Salme H. Steinberg
(312) 583-4050

Western Illinois University
1 Univ. Cir., Macomb 61455-1390
Pres. Donald S. Spencer
(309) 295-1414

Illinois Community College Board
509 S. Sixth St., Ste. 400, Springfield
62701-1874
Exec. Dir. Geraldine A. Evans
(217) 785-0123

Belleville Area College
2500 Carlyle Rd., Belleville 62221
Pres. Joseph J. Cipfl
(618) 235-2700

Black Hawk College
6600 34th Ave., Moline 61265
Pres. Judith A. Redwine
(309) 796-1311

Carl Sandburg College
2232 S. Lake Storey Rd., Galesburg
61401
Pres. Donald G. Crist
(309) 344-2518

City Colleges of Chicago
226 W. Jackson Blvd., Chicago
60606-6998
Chanc. Ronald J. Temple
(312) 641-0808

Harold Washington College
30 E. Lake St., Chicago 60601
Pres. Nancy C. DeSombre
(312) 553-5600

Harry S Truman College
1145 W. Wilson Ave., Chicago
60640
Interim Pres. Donald B. Smith
(312) 878-1700

Kennedy-King College
6800 S. Wentworth Ave.,
Chicago 60621
Pres. Wayne D. Watson
(312) 602-5000

Malcolm X College
1900 W. Van Buren St.,
Chicago 60612
Pres. Zerrie D. Campbell
(312) 850-7000

Olive-Harvey College
10001 S. Woodlawn Ave.,
Chicago 60628
Pres. Lawrence Cox
(312) 291-6100

Richard J. Daley College
7500 S. Pulaski Rd., Chicago
60652
Pres. Ted Martinez, Jr.
(312) 838-7500

Wilbur Wright College
4300 N. Narragansett Ave.,
Chicago 60634
Pres. Raymond F. Le Fevour
(312) 777-7900

College of DuPage
22nd St. and Lambert Rd., Glen
Ellyn 60137
Pres. Michael T. Murphy
(708) 858-2800

College of Lake County
19351 W. Washington St., Grayslake
60030
Interim Pres. Gretchen J. Naff
(708) 223-6601

Danville Area Community College
2000 E. Main St., Danville 61832
Pres. Harry J. Braun
(217) 443-1811

Elgin Community College
1700 Spartan Dr., Elgin 60123
Pres. Roy Flores
(708) 697-1000

Heartland Community College
1226 Towanda Ave., Bloomington
61701
Pres. Jonathan M. Astroth
(309) 827-0500

Highland Community College
2998 Pearl City Rd., Freeport
61032-9341
Pres. Ruth Mercedes Smith
(815) 235-6121

Illinois Central College
One College Dr., East Peoria 61635
Pres. Thomas K. Thomas
(309) 694-5011

Illinois Eastern Community Colleges System
233 E. Chestnut St., Olney 62450-2298
Chanc. Ronald M. Hutkin
(618) 393-2982

Frontier Community College
Lot No. 2 Frontier Dr., Fairfield 62837
Pres. Richard L. Mason
(618) 842-3711

Lincoln Trail College
11220 State Hwy. 1, Robinson 62454
Interim Pres. John Arabatgis
(618) 544-8657

Olney Central College
305 N. West St., Olney 62450
Pres. Edward J. Covey
(618) 395-4351

Wabash Valley College
2200 College Dr., Mount Carmel 62863
Pres. Harry K. Benson
(618) 262-8641

Illinois Valley Community College
815 N. Orlando Smith Ave., Oglesby 61348
Pres. Alfred E. Wisgoski
(815) 224-2720

John A. Logan College
Rural Rte. 2, Carterville 62918
Pres. J. Ray Hancock
(618) 985-3741

John Wood Community College
150 S. 48th St., Quincy 62301
Pres. Robert C. Keys
(217) 224-6500

Joliet Junior College
1215 Houbolt Rd., Joliet 60431-8938
Pres. Thomas E. Gamble
(815) 729-9020 x2207

Kankakee Community College
P.O. Box 888, Kankakee 60901
Pres. Lawrence D. Huffman
(815) 933-0345

Kaskaskia College
27210 College Rd., Centralia 62801
Pres. Alice M. Mumaw
(800) 642-0859

Kishwaukee College
21193 Malta Rd., Malta 60150
Pres. Norman L. Jenkins
(815) 825-2086

Lake Land College
5001 Lake Land Blvd., Mattoon 61938
Pres. Robert K. Luther
(217) 234-5253

Lewis and Clark Community College
5800 Godfrey Rd., Godfrey 62035
Pres. Dale T. Chapman
(618) 466-3411

Lincoln Land Community College
Shepherd Rd., Springfield 62794
Pres. Norman L. Stephens
(217) 786-2200

McHenry County College
8900 U.S. Hwy. 14, Crystal Lake 60012-2761
Pres. Robert C. Bartlett
(815) 455-3700

Moraine Valley Community College
10900 S. 88th Ave., Palos Hills 60465
Pres. Vernon O. Crawley
(708) 974-4300

Morton College
3801 S. Central Ave., Cicero 60650
Pres. John Neuhaus
(708) 656-8000

Oakton Community College
1600 E. Golf Rd., Des Plaines 60016
Pres. Margaret Lee
(708) 635-1600

Parkland College
2400 W. Bradley Ave., Champaign
61821
Pres. Zelema M. Harris
(217) 351-2200

Prairie State College
202 S. Halsted St., Chicago Heights
60411
Pres. E. Timothy Lightfield
(708) 756-3110

Rend Lake College
Rural Rte. 1, Ina 62846
Pres. Mark S. Kern
(618) 437-5321

Richland Community College
One College Park, Decatur 62521
Pres. Charles R. Novak
(217) 875-7200

Rock Valley College
3301 N. Mulford Rd., Rockford
61114
Pres. Karl J. Jacobs
(815) 654-4250

Sauk Valley Community College
173 Illinois Rte. 2, Dixon 61021
Pres. Richard L. Behrendt
(815) 288-5511

Shawnee Community College
Shawnee College Rd., Ullin 62992-
9725
Pres. Jack D. Hill
(618) 634-2242

South Suburban College of Cook County
15800 S. State St., South Holland
60473
Pres. Richard W. Fonte
(708) 596-2000

Southeastern Illinois College
3575 College Rd., Harrisburg 62946
Interim Pres. Ben Cullers
(618) 252-6376

Spoon River College
Rural Rte. 1, Canton 61520
Pres. Felix T. Haynes, Jr.
(309) 647-4645

*State Community College of East St.
Louis*
601 James R. Thompson Blvd., East
St. Louis 62201
Interim Pres. Janet Finch
(618) 583-2500

Triton College
2000 Fifth Ave., River Grove 60171
Pres. George T. Jorndt
(708) 456-0300

Waubonsee Community College
Illinois Rte. 47 at Harter Rd., Sugar
Grove 60554
Pres. John J. Swalec
(708) 466-4811

William Rainey Harper College
1200 W. Algonquin Rd., Palatine
60067-7398
Pres. Paul N. Thompson
(708) 397-3000

Southern Illinois University System
Colyer Hall, Mail Code 6801,
Carbondale 62901-6801
Pres. Ted Sanders
(618) 536-3331

*Southern Illinois University at
Carbondale*
Carbondale 62901-4333
Pres. John C. Guyon
(618) 453-2121

*Southern Illinois University at
Edwardsville*
Edwardsville 62026
Pres. Nancy Belck
(618) 692-2000

Trinity International University
2065 Half Day Rd., Deerfield 60015
Pres. Gregory L. Waybright
(847) 945-8800

Trinity College
2065 Half Day Rd., Deerfield 60015
Pres. Gregory L. Waybright
(847) 945-8800

Trinity Evangelical Divinity School
2065 Half Day Rd., Deerfield 60015
Pres. Greg Waybright
(847) 945-8800

University of Illinois Central Office
506 S. Wright St., Rm. 364, Urbana
61801
Pres. James J. Stukel
(217) 333-3070

University of Illinois at Chicago
P.O. Box 4348, Chicago 60680
Pres. James G. Stukel
(312) 996-3000

*University of Illinois at Urbana-
Champaign*
601 E. John St., Champaign 61820
Chanc. Michael Aiken
(217) 333-6290

INDIANA

Indiana Commission for Higher Education
101 W. Ohio St., Ste. 550, Indianapolis
46204
Commiss. Stanley G. Jones
(317) 464-4400

Ball State University
2000 University Ave., Muncie 47306
Pres. John E. Worthen
(317) 289-1241

Indiana State University
217 N. Sixth St., Terre Haute 47809
Pres. John W. Moore
(812) 237-6311

Indiana University System
Bloomington 47405
Pres. Myles Brand
(812) 332-0211

Indiana University Bloomington
Indiana and Kirkwood Ave.,
Bloomington 47405
Pres. Myles Brand
(812) 332-0211

Indiana University East
2325 N. Chester Blvd.,
Richmond 47374
Chanc. David J. Fulton
(317) 973-8200

Indiana University Northwest
3400 Broadway, Gary 46408
Chanc. Hilda Richards
(219) 980-6500

Indiana University Southeast
4201 Grant Line Rd., New
Albany 47150
Chanc. Leon Rand
(812) 941-2200

Indiana University at Kokomo
P.O. Box 9003, 2300 S.
Washington St., Kokomo
46904-9003
Chanc. Emita B. Hill
(317) 455-9200

Indiana University at South Bend
1700 Mishawaka Ave., P.O.
Box 7111, South Bend 46634
Acting Chanc. Lester C. Lamon
(219) 237-4111

*Indiana University-Purdue
University at Fort Wayne*
2101 Coliseum Blvd. E., Fort
Wayne 46805-1499
Chanc. Michael A. Wartell
(219) 481-6100

*Indiana University-Purdue
University at Indianapolis*
355 N. Lansing St.,
Indianapolis 46202
Chanc. Gerald L. Bepko
(317) 274-5555

Purdue University System
West Lafayette 47907-1031
Pres. Steven C. Beering
(317) 494-9708

Purdue University
Frederick L. Hovde Hall, Room
200, West Lafayette 47907-
1031
Pres. Steven C. Beering
(317) 494-4600

Purdue University Calumet
Hammond 46323
Chanc. James W. Yackel
(219) 989-2993

Purdue University North Central
1401 S. U.S. Hwy. 421,
Westville 46391-9528
Chanc. Dale W. Alspaugh
(219) 785-5200

University of Southern Indiana
8600 University Blvd., Evansville
47712
Pres. H. Ray Hoops
(812) 464-8600

Vincennes University
   1002 N. First St., Vincennes 47591-
   5201
   Pres. Phillip M. Summers
   (812) 885-4208

**Ivy Tech State College Office of the
President**
   One W. 26th St., P.O. Box 1763,
   Indianapolis 46206
   Pres. Gerald I. Lamkin
   (317) 921-4860

   **Ivy Tech State College—Central
   Indiana Region**
      One W. 26th St., Indianapolis
      46206-1763
      Vice Pres./Chanc. Meredith L.
      Carter
      (317) 921-4750

      Ivy Tech State College—Indianapolis
         One W. 26th St., P.O. Box
         1763, Indianapolis 46206-
         1763
         Vice Pres./Chanc. Meredith L.
         Carter
         (317) 921-4882

   **Ivy Tech State College—Columbus
   Region**
      8204 Hwy. 311, Sellersburg 47172-
      1897
      Vice Pres./Chanc. Homer B. Smith
      (812) 246-3301

      *Ivy Tech State College—
      Bloomington*
         3116 Canterbury Ct.,
         Bloomington 47401-0393
         Exec. Dean Thomas S. Jordan
         (812) 332-1559

      Ivy Tech State College—Columbus
         4475 Central Ave., Columbus
         47203
         Exec. Dean Gregory K. Flood
         (800) 922-4838

Ivy Tech State College—East Chicago
   410 Columbus Dr., East Chicago
   46312-2714
   Exec. Dean J. Robert Jeffs
   (219) 392-3600

**Ivy Tech State College—EastCentral
Region**
   2325 Chester Blvd., Richmond
   47374-1298
   Exec. Dean James L. Steck
   (317) 966-2656

   Ivy Tech State College—Anderson
      104 W. 53rd St., Anderson
      46013-1502
      Exec. Dean Jack Voelz
      (317) 643-7133

   Ivy Tech State College—Marion
      2983 W. 38th St., Marion
      46953-9370
      Dir. James Luttrull
      (317) 662-9843

   Ivy Tech State College—Muncie
      4301 S. Cowan Rd., P.O. Box
      3100, Muncie 47302-9448
      Interim Exec. Dean James D.
      Luttrull
      (317) 289-2291

**Ivy Tech State College—Kokomo
Region**
   1534 West Sample St., South Bend
   46619-3892
   Vice Pres./Chanc. Carl F. Lutz
   (219) 289-7001

   Ivy Tech State College—Kokomo
      1815 E. Morgan St., Kokomo
      46903-1373
      Exec. Dean Shanon L.
      Christiansen
      (317) 459-0561

   Ivy Tech State College—Logansport
      3001 E Market St., Ste. 7,
      Logansport 46947-2152
      Dir. Rebecca Nickoli
      (219) 753-5101

Ivy Tech State College—Lafayette Region
3101 S. Creasy Ln., Lafayette 47905-6266
Exec. Dean Elizabeth J. Doversberger
(317) 772-9100

Ivy Tech State College—Lafayette
P.O. Box 6299, Lafayette 46903-6299
Exec. Dean Elizabeth J. Doversberger
(317) 772-9100

Ivy Tech State College—Northcentral Region
1534 West Sample St., South Bend 44619-3892
Vice Pres./Chanc. Carl F. Lutz
(219) 289-7001

Ivy Tech State College—Elkhart
2521 Industrial Pkwy., Elkhart 46516-5430
Dir. Jane Perez
(219) 293-4657

Ivy Tech State College—South Bend
1534 W. Sample St., South Bend 46619-3892
Exec. Dean Gene Bruce
(219) 289-7001

Ivy Tech State College—Warsaw
850 E. Smith St., Warsaw 46580-4546
Dir. Stephen A. Grill
(219) 267-5428

Ivy Tech State College—Northeast Region
3800 N. Anthony Blvd., Ft. Wayne 46805-1489
Vice Pres./Chanc. Jon L. Rupright
(219) 482-9171

Ivy Tech State College—Ft. Wayne
3800 N. Anthony Blvd., Fort Wayne 46805-1489
Vice Pres./Chanc. Jon L. Rupright
(219) 482-9171

Ivy Tech State College—Northwest Region
1440 E. 35th Ave., Gary 46409-1499
Vice Pres./Chanc. Darnell E. Cole
(219) 981-1111

Ivy Tech State College—Northwest Technical Institute
1440 E. 35th Ave., Gary 46409-1499
Exec. Dean Darnell E. Cole
(219) 981-1111

Ivy Tech State College—Valparaiso
2401 Valley Dr., Valparaiso 46383-2520
Acting Exec. Dir. Jerry Huddleston
(219) 464-8514

Ivy Tech State College—Southcentral Region
8204 Hwy. 311, Sellersburg 47172-1897
Vice Pres./Chanc. Homer B. Smith
(812) 246-3301

Ivy Tech State College—Sellersburg
8204 Hwy 311, Sellersburg 47172
Exec. Dean James R. Wells
(812) 246-3301

Ivy Tech State College—Southeast Region
8204 Hwy. 311, Sellersburg 47172-1897
Vice Pres./Chanc. Homer B. Smith
(812) 246-3301

Ivy Tech State College—
Lawrenceburg
575 Main St., Lawrenceburg
47205-1661
Site Dir. Gwen Wright
(812) 537-4010

Ivy Tech State College—Madison
590 Ivy Tech Dr., Madison
47250-1881
Exec. Dean Jonathan W.
Thomas
(812) 265-2580

Ivy Tech State College—Southwest
Region
3101 S. Creasy Ln, Lafayette
47905-5266
Exec. Dean Elizabeth Doversberger
(317) 477-9138

Ivy Tech State College—Evansville
3501 First Ave., Evansville
47710-3398
Exec. Dean Daniel J. Schenk
(812) 426-2865

Ivy Tech State College—Wabash Valley
Region
501 S. Airport St., Terre Haute
47803
Vice Pres./Chanc. Sam E. Borden
(812) 877-3616

Ivy Tech State College—Terre Haute
7999 U.S. Hwy. 41, Terre
Haute 47802-4898
Exec. Dean Scott Knapp
(812) 299-1121

Ivy Tech State College—Whitewater
Region
2325 Chester Blvd., Richmond
47374-1298
Vice Pres./Chanc.
(317) 966-2656

Ivy Tech State College—Richmond
2325 Chester Blvd., Richmond
47374
Exec. Dean James L. Steck
(317) 966-2656

IOWA

Iowa Department of Education Division of Community Colleges
Grimes State Office Bldg., Des Moines
50319-0146
Admin. Harriet Howell Custer
(515) 281-8260

Des Moines Area Community College
2006 S. Ankeny Blvd., Ankeny
50021
Pres. Joseph A. Borgen
(515) 964-6200

Eastern Iowa Community College District
306 W. River Dr., Davenport 52801
Chanc. John T. Blong
(319) 322-5015

Clinton Community College
1000 Lincoln Blvd., Clinton
52732
Dean Karen J. Vickers
(319) 242-6841

Muscatine Community College
152 Colorado St., Muscatine
52761
Pres. Victor G. McAvoy
(319) 263-8250

Scott Community College
500 Belmont Rd., Bettendorf
52722
Pres. Lenny E. Stone
(319) 359-7531

Hawkeye Community College
1501 E. Orange Rd., Box 8015,
Waterloo 50704
Pres. Phillip O. Barry
(319) 296-2320

Indian Hills Community College
525 Grandview Ave., Ottumwa
52501
Pres. Lyle Adrian Hellyer
(515) 683-5111

Iowa Central Community College
330 Ave. M, Fort Dodge 50501
Pres. Bob Paxton
(515) 576-7201

Iowa Lakes Community College
19 S. 7th St., Estherville 51334
Pres. James E. Billings
(800) 242-5106

Iowa Valley Community College District
3702 S Center St., Marshalltown
50158
Pres. Paul A. Tambrino
(515) 752-4643

Ellsworth Community College
1100 College Ave., Iowa Falls
50126
Dean Duane R. Lloyd
(515) 648-4611

Marshalltown Community College
3700 S. Center St.,
Marshalltown 50158
Dean William M. Simpson
(515) 752-7106

Iowa Western Community College
2700 College Rd., Box 4-C, Council
Bluffs 51501
Pres. Dan D. Kinney
(712) 325-3200

Kirkwood Community College
6301 Kirkwood Blvd., S.W., P.O.
Box 2068, Cedar Rapids 52406-
2068
Pres. Norman R. Nielsen
(319) 398-5411

North Iowa Area Community College
500 College Dr., Mason City 50401
Pres. David L. Buettner
(515) 423-1264

Northeast Iowa Community College
　　Box 400, Hwy. 150, Calmar 52132
　　Pres. Don Roby
　　(800) 728-2256

Northwest Iowa Community College
　　603 W. Park St., Sheldon 51201
　　Pres. Carl H. Rolf
　　(800) 352-4907

Southeastern Community College
　　Drawer F, 1015 S. Gear Ave., West
　　　　Burlington 52655
　　Pres. R. Gene Gardner
　　(319) 752-2731

Southwestern Community College
　　1501 Townline St., P.O. Box 458,
　　　　Creston 50801
　　Pres. Richard L. Byerly
　　(515) 782-7081

Western Iowa Tech Community College
　　4647 Stone Ave., P.O. Box 265,
　　　　Sioux City 51102-0265
　　Pres. Robert E. Dunker
　　(712) 274-6400

Iowa State Board of Regents
　　Old Historical Bldg., Des Moines 50319
　　Exec. Dir. R. Wayne Richey
　　(515) 281-3934

Iowa State University
　　117 Beardshear Hall, Ames 50011-
　　　　2035
　　Pres. Martin Charles Jischke
　　(515) 294-2042

University of Iowa
　　101 Jessup Hall, Iowa City 52242-
　　　　1316
　　Pres. Mary Sue Coleman
　　(319) 335-3500

University of Northern Iowa
　　Cedar Falls 50614
　　Pres. Robert D. Koob
　　(319) 273-2311

Palmer Chiropractic University System
　　3543 E. Kimberly Rd., Davenport 52807
　　Chanc. Michael Crawford
　　(319) 355-4730

Palmer College of Chiropractic
　　1000 Brady St., Davenport 52803
　　Interim Pres. Virgil V. Strang
　　(800) 722-2586

Palmer College of Chiropractic-West
　　90 E. Tasman Dr., San Jose, CA
　　　　95134
　　Pres. Peter A. Martin
　　(408) 944-6000

KANSAS

Kansas Board of Regents
700 S.W. Harrison St., Ste. 1410, Topeka
66603-3760
Exec. Dir. Stephen M. Jordan
(913) 296-3421

Emporia State University
1200 Commercial St., Emporia
66801-5087
Pres. Robert E. Glennen, Jr.
(316) 343-1200

Fort Hays State University
600 Park St., Hays 67601
Pres. Edward H. Hammond
(913) 628-4000

Kansas State University
Anderson Hall 110, Manhattan
66506-0113
Pres. Jon Wefald
(913) 532-6011

Pittsburg State University
1701 S. Broadway, Pittsburg 66762
Pres. John R. Darling
(316) 231-7000

University of Kansas
203 Strong Hall, Lawrence 66045
Chanc. Robert E. Hemenway
(913) 864-2700

Wichita State University
1845 Fairmont St., Wichita 67260
Pres. Eugene M. Hughes
(800) 362-2594

Kansas State Board of Education
120 S.E. Tenth Ave., Topeka 66612-1182
Int. Commis. Dale M. Dennis
(913) 296-3201

Allen County Community College
1801 North Central, Iola 66749
Pres. John Masterson
(316) 365-5116

Barton County Community College
Rural Rte. 3, Box 136Z, Great Bend
67530
Pres. Jimmie L. Downing
(800) 748-7594

Butler County Community College
901 S. Haverhill Rd., El Dorado
67042
Pres. Jacqueline A. Vietti
(316) 312-2222

Cloud County Community College
2221 Campus Dr., P.O. Box 1002,
Concordia 66901-1002
Pres. James P. Ihrig
(800) 729-5101

Coffeyville Community College
400 W. 11th St., Coffeyville 67337
Pres. Ronald Thomas
(316) 251-7700

Colby Community College
1255 S. Range, Colby 67701
Pres. Mikel V. Ary
(913) 462-3984

Cowley County Community College
125 S. Second St., P.O. Box 1147,
Arkansas City 67005
Pres. Patrick J. McAtee
(800) 593-2222

Dodge City Community College
2501 N. 14th St., Dodge City 67801
Interim Pres. Carl L. Heinrich
(800) 262-4565

Fort Scott Community College
2108 S. Horton St., Fort Scott 66701
Pres. Laura Meeks
(316) 223-2700

Garden City Community College
801 Campus Dr., Garden City 67846
Pres. James H. Tangeman
(800) 658-1696

Highland Community College
  Box 68, Highland 66035
  Pres. Betty Stevens
  (913) 442-3236

Hutchinson Community College
  1300 N. Plum St., Hutchinson
  67501
  Pres. Edward E. Berger
  (800) 289-3501

Independence Community College
  College Ave. and Brookside Dr.,
  P.O. Box 708, Independence
  67301
  Pres. Don Schoening
  (316) 331-4100

Johnson County Community College
  12345 College Blvd., Overland Park
  66210
  Pres. Charles J. Carlsen
  (913) 469-8500

Kansas City Kansas Community College
  7250 State Ave., Kansas City 66112
  Pres. Thomas R. Burke
  (913) 334-1100

Labette Community College
  200 S. 14th St., Parsons 67357
  Pres. Joe Birmingham
  (316) 421-6700

Neosho County Community College
  1000 S. Allen, Chanute 66720
  Pres. Theodore W. Wischropp
  (316) 431-2820

Pratt Community College
  348 N.E. SR 61, Pratt 67124
  Pres. William A. Wojciechowski
  (316) 672-5641

Seward County Community College
  1801 N. Kansas St., Box 1137,
  Liberal 67901
  Pres. James R. Grote
  (316) 624-1951

KENTUCKY

Kentucky Council on Higher Education
1050 U.S. 127 S., Ste. 101, W. Frankfort
Office Complex, Frankfort 40601-4395
Exec. Dir. Gary S. Cox
(502) 564-3553

Eastern Kentucky University
Lancaster Ave., Richmond 40475-3101
Pres. H. Hanly Funderburk, Jr.
(606) 622-1000

Kentucky State University
400 E. Main St., Frankfort 40601
Pres. Mary L. Smith
(502) 227-6000

Morehead State University
University Blvd., Morehead 40351
Pres. Ronald G. Eaglin
(606) 783-2221

Murray State University
One Murray St., Murray 42071-3305
Pres. Kern Alexander
(502) 762-3011

Northern Kentucky University
Nunn Dr., Highland Heights 41099
Pres. Leon E. Boothe
(606) 572-5100

University of Kentucky
206 Administration Bldg., Lexington
40506-0032
Pres. Charles T. Wethington, Jr.
(606) 257-9000

University of Kentucky Community College System
Breckinridge Hall, Lexington
40506-0056
Chanc. Ben W. Carr, Jr.
(606) 257-8607

Ashland Community College
1400 College Dr., Ashland
41101-3683
Pres. Charles R. Dassance
(606) 329-2999

Elizabethtown Community College
600 College Street Rd.,
Elizabethtown 42701-3053
Pres. Charles E. Stebbins
(502) 769-2371

Hazard Community College
One Community College Dr.,
Hazard 41701
Pres. G. Edward Hughes
(606) 436-5721

Henderson Community College
2660 S. Green St., Henderson
42420
Pres. Patrick R. Lake
(502) 827-1867

Hopkinsville Community College
P.O. Box 2100, Hopkinsville
42241-2100
Pres. A. James Kerley
(502) 886-3921

Jefferson Community College
109 E. Broadway, Louisville
40202
Pres. Richard Green
(502) 584-0181

Lexington Community College
Oswald Bldg., Cooper Dr.,
Lexington 40506-0235
Pres. Janice Friedd
(606) 257-4831

Madisonville Community College
2000 College Dr., Madisonville
42431
Pres. Arthur D. Stumpf
(502) 821-2250

Maysville Community College
1755 U.S. 68, Maysville 41056
Pres. James C. Shires
(606) 759-7141

Owensboro Community College
4800 New Hartford Rd.,
Owensboro 42303
Pres. John M. McGuire
(502) 686-4400

Paducah Community College
P.O. Box 7380, Paducah
42002-7380
Pres. Leonard F. O'Hara
(502) 554-9200

Prestonsburg Community College
One Bert T. Combs Dr.,
Prestonsburg 41653
Pres. Deborah Lee Floyd
(606) 886-3863

Somerset Community College
808 Monticello Rd., Somerset
42501
Pres. Rollin J. Watson
(606) 679-8501

Southeast Community College
300 College Rd., Cumberland
40823-1099
Pres. W. Bruce Ayers
(606) 589-2145

University of Louisville
2301 S. Third St., Louisville 40292-
0001
Pres. John W. Shumaker
(502) 852-5555

Western Kentucky University
1526 Bid Red Way, Bowling Green
42101
Pres. Thomas C. Meredith
(502) 745-0111

Kentucky Tech North Central Region
150 Vo-Tech Rd., Lexington 40510-1001
Regl. Exec. Dir. Louis Reed
(606) 233-3002

Boone County Area Technology Center
3320 Cougar Path, Hebron 41048
Princ. Stephanie Rottman
(606) 689-7855

CE McCormick Area Technology Center
50 Orchard Ln., Alexandria 41001
Princ. Kenneth McCormick
(606) 635-4101

Carroll County Area Technology Center
1704 Highland Ave., Carrollton
41008
Princ. Carolyn Barnes
(502) 732-4479

Danville Health Technology Center
340 South Third St., Danville 40423
Dir. Sandra Houston
(606) 236-2053

Garrard County Area Technology Center
306 W. Maple Ave., Lancaster
40444
Princ. James Spurlin
(606) 792-2144

Harrison County Area Technology Center
551 Webster Ave., Cynthiana 41031
Princ. John Hodge
(606) 234-5286

Harrodsburg Area Technology Center
661 Tapp Rd., P.O. Box 628,
Harrodsburg 40330
Princ. L. Hughes Jones
(606) 734-9329

J.D. Patton Area Technology Center
3234 Turkeyfoot Rd., Fort Mitchell
41017
Princ. Eugene Penn
(606) 341-2266

Kentucky Tech—Central Campus
104 Vo-Tech Rd., Lexington 40510
Dir. Ron Baugh
(606) 255-8501

Madison County Area Technology Center
703 N. 2nd St., P.O. Box 809,
  Richmond 40475
Princ. Evelyn Watson
(606) 624-4520

Northern Campbell Tech.
90 Campbell Dr., Highland Heights
  41076
Dir. Earl Wittenrock
(606) 441-2010

Northern Kentcuky Tech
1025 Amsterdam Rd., Covington
  41011-2098
Dir. Edward Burton
(606) 292-3930

Northern Kentucky Health Technology
Center
790 Thomas More Pkwy.,
  Edgewood 41017
Dir. Wade Halsey
(606) 341-5200

Kentucky Tech—Clark County Area
Technology Center
650 Boone Ave., Winchester 40391
Princ. William Lockhart
(606) 744-1250

Kentucky Tech Northeast Region
4818 Roberts Dr., Ashland 41102-9046
Reg. Exec. Dir. Howard W. Moore
(606) 928-6427

Ashland Regional Technology Center
4818 Roberts Dr., Ashland 41102-
  9046
Schl. Dir. Richard Kendall
(606) 928-6427

Belfry Area Technology Center
P.O. Box 280, Belfry 41514
Princ. Danny O'Neal
(606) 353-4951

Garth Area Technology Center
HC 79, Box 205, Martin 41649
Princ. Ronald Turner
(606) 285-3088

Greenup County Area Technology Center
Box 4009, Ohio River Rd., Greenup
  41144
Princ. Helen Spears
(606) 473-9344

Kentucky Tech—Phelps Area Technology
Center
11500 Phelps, 632 Rd., Phelps
  41553
Princ. Curtis Akers
(606) 456-8136

Martin County Area Technology Center
HC 68, Box 2177, Inez 41224
Princ. Charlie Six
(606) 298-3879

Mason County Area Technology Center
646 Kenton Station Rd., Maysville
  41056
Princ. Clifford Wells
(606) 759-7101

Mayo Regional Technology Center
513 Third St., Paintsville 41240
Schl. Dir. Gary Coleman
(606) 789-5321

Millard Area Technology Center
7925 Millard Hwy., Pikeville 41501
Princ. William Justice
(606) 437-6059

Montgomery County Area Technology
Center
682 Woodford Dr., Mount Sterling
  40353
Princ. Charlie Williams
(606) 498-1103

Morgan County Area Technology Center
P.O. Box 249, Rd. No. 191, West
  Liberty 41472
Princ. Ron Woods
(606) 743-4321

Rowan Regional Technology Center
609 Viking Dr., Morehead 40351
Schl. Director Kenneth Brown
(606) 783-1538

Russell Area Technology Center
705 Red Devil Ln., Russell 41169
Princ. Michael Chapman
(606) 836-1256

Kentucky Tech Northwest Region
505 University Dr., Elizabethtown 42701
Reg. Exec. Dir. Roye S. Wilson
(502) 766-5137

Bullitt County Area Technology Center
395 High School Dr., Shepherdsville
40165
Princ. Beverly Dennis
(502) 543-7018

*Kentucky Tech—Breckinridge County
Area Technology Center*
P.O. Box 68, Hwy. 60, Harned
40144
Princ. Wayne A. Spencer
(502) 756-2138

Kentucky Tech—Elizabethtown
505 University Dr., Elizabethtown
42701
Dir. Neil Ramer
(502) 766-5137

Kentucky Tech—Jefferson Campus
727 W. Chestnut St., Louisville
40203
Acting Director Marvin Copes
(502) 595-4136

Marion County Area Technology Center
721 E. Main, Lebanon 40033
Princ. Howard Carey
(502) 692-3155

Meade County Area Technology Center
110 Greer St., Brandenburg 40108
Princ. Faye Campbell
(502) 422-3955

Nelson County Area Technology Center
1060 Bloomfield Rd., Bardstown
40004
Princ. Myra Wilson
(502) 348-9096

Oldham County Area Technology Center
P.O. Box 127, Hwy. 393, Buckner
40010
Princ. Bob Hazelrigg
(502) 222-0131

Shelby County Area Technology Center
230 Rocket Ln., Shelbyville 40065
Princ. Mary A. Stratton
(502) 633-6554

Kentucky Tech Southeast Region
101 Vo-Tech Dr., Hazard 41701
Regional Exec. Dir. Finley Begley
(606) 439-2500

Bell County Area Technology Center
Box 199-A, Rte. 7, Pineville 40977
Princ. Ron Mason
(606) 337-3094

Breathitt County Area Technology Center
P.O. Box 786, Jackson 41339
Princ. Fred Deaton
(606) 666-5153

Clay County Area Technology Center
Rte. 2, Box 256, Manchester 40962
Princ. Charles McWhorter
(606) 598-2194

Corbin Area Technology Center
1909 S. Snyder Ave., Corbin 40701
Dir. Ronnie Partin
(606) 528-5338

*Cumberland Valley Health Technology
Center*
U.S. 25E, P.O. Box 187, Pineville
40977
Dir. Denise Sharpe
(606) 337-3106

Harlan Regional Technology Center
21 Ballpark Rd., Harlan 40831
Acting Dir. Kenny Boggs
(606) 573-1506

Hazard Regional Technology Center
101 Vo-Tech Dr., Hazard 41701
Dir. Connie W. Johnson
(606) 435-6101

Kentucky Tech—Laurel County Campus
235 S. Laurel Rd., London 40741
Dir. Ronnie Partin
(606) 864-7311

Knott County Area Technology Center
HCR 60, Box 1100, Hindman 41822
Princ. Willa Dean Williams
(606) 785-5350

Knox County Area Technology Center
210 Wall St., Barbourville 40906
Princ. Charles Frazier
(606) 546-5320

Lee County Area Technology Center
P.O. Box B, Beattyville 41311
Princ. Fred Kincaid
(606) 464-5018

Leslie County Area Technology Center
P.O. Box 902, Hyden 41749
Princ. Betty Huff
(606) 672-2859

Letcher County Area Technology Center
610 Circle Dr., Whitesburg 41858
Princ. Barbara Frazier
(606) 633-5053

*Rockcastle County Area Technology
Center*
West Main, Mount Vernon 40456
Princ. Donna Hopkins
(606) 256-4346

Kentucky Tech Southern Region
1845 Loop Dr., Bowling Green 42101-
3601
Regional Exec. Dir. Ann W. Cline
(502) 746-7467

Barren County Area Technology Center
491 Trojan Tr., Glasgow 42141
Princ. Max Doty
(502) 651-2196

*Bowling Green Regional Technology
Center*
1845 Loop Dr., Bowling Green 42101
Schl. Dir. Donald R. Williams
(502) 746-7461

Casey County Area Technology Center
Rte. 4, Hwy 70 E., Box 49, Liberty
42539
Schl. Prin. J. D. Shugars
(606) 787-6241

Clinton County Area Technology Center
Rte. 5, Box 5023, Albany 42602
Acting Schl. Princ. Harold Van
Hook
(606) 387-6448

Green County Area Technology Center
Carlisle Ave., P.O. Box 167,
Greensburg 42743
Schl. Princ. Rick Atwell
(502) 932-4263

Health Technology Center
1215 N. Race St., Glasgow 42141
Schl. Dir. Rebecca Forrest
(502) 651-5673

*Kentucky Tech—Somerset Regional
Technology Center*
230 Airport Rd., Somerset 42501
Schl. Dir. Carol Ann Van Hook
(606) 677-4049

Monroe County Area Technology Center
309 Emberton St., Tompkinsville
42167
Schl. Prin. Bill Polland
(502) 487-8261

Russell County Technology Center
P.O. Box 599, Russell Springs
42642
Princ. Chester Taylor
(502) 866-6175

Russellville Area Technology Center
1103 W. 9th St., Russellville 42276
Schl. Princ. Keith Dickinson
(502) 726-8432

Wayne County Area Technology Center
150 Cardinal Way, Monticello
42633
Schl. Princ. Anita Hopper
(606) 348-8424

Kentucky Tech West Region
100 School Ave., Madisonville 42431
Reg. Exec. Dir. Bill M. Hatley
(502) 825-6546

Caldwell County Area Technology Center
P.O. Box 350, Voc. School Rd.,
Princeton 42445
Coord. Arthur Dunn
(502) 365-5563

*Henderson County Area Technology
Center*
2440 Zion Rd., Henderson 42420
Princ. Dennis Harrell
(502) 827-3810

*Kentucky Tech—Christian County Area
Technology Center*
705 N. Elm St., Hopkinsville 42240
Coord. Ann Claxton
(502) 886-3734

Kentucky Tech—Daviess County Campus
1901 Southeastern Pkwy.,
Owensboro 42303-1677
Princ. Ray Gillaspie
(502) 687-7620

*Kentucky Tech—Fulton County Area
Technology Center*
2720 Moscow, Hickman 42050
Coord. Larry Lynch
(502) 236-2517

Kentucky Tech—Owensboro Campus
1501 Frederica St., Owensboro
42301
Principal Mike Wright
(502) 825-6546

Madisonville Health Technology Center
750 N. Laffoon, Madisonville 42431
Coord. Mary Stanley
(502) 824-7552

Madisonville Regional Technology Center
150 School Ave., Madisonville
42431
Princ. James Pfeffer, Jr.
(502) 824-7544

*Mayfield-Graves County Area Technology
Center*
710 Douthitt St., Mayfield 42066
Coordinator Teresa Harper
(502) 247-4710

*Muhlenberg County Area Technology
Center*
201 Airport Rd., Greenville 42345
Coord. Andrew Swansey
(502) 338-1271

*Murray-Calloway County Area
Technology Center*
1800 Sycamore St., Murray 42071
Principal Sandra Parks
(502) 753-1870

Ohio County Area Technology Center
1406 S. Main St., Hartford 42347
Coord. Ray Price
(502) 274-9612

Paducah Area Technology Center
2400 Adams St., Paducah 42001
Princ. Robert Rouff
(502) 443-6592

*Webster County Area Vocational
Education Center*
325 State Rd., Dixon 42409
Coord. Terry Turner
(502) 639-5035

LOUISIANA

Louisiana State University System
3810 W. Lakeshore Dr., Baton Rouge
70808
Pres. Allen A. Copping
(504) 388-2111

*Louisiana State University Medical
Center*
433 Bolivar St., New Orleans
70112-2223
Chanc. Mervin L. Trail
(504) 568-4808

*Louisiana State University and
Agricultural and Mechanical College*
Baton Rouge 70803
Chanc. William E. Davis
(504) 388-3202

Louisiana State University at Alexandria
8100 Hwy. 71 S., Alexandria 71302-
9121
Chanc. Robert Cavanaugh
(318) 445-3672

Louisiana State University at Eunice
P.O. Box 1129, Eunice 70535
Chanc. Michael Smith
(318) 457-7311

Louisiana State University in Shreveport
One University Plaza, Shreveport
71115-2399
Chanc. Vince Marsala
(318) 797-5000

University of New Orleans
Lakefront, New Orleans 70148
Chanc. Gregory M. St. L. O'Brien
(504) 286-6000

**Southern University and Agricultural and
Mechanical College System**
Baton Rouge 70813
Pres. Dolores R. Spikes
(504) 771-4680

*Southern University and Agricultural and
Mechanical College at Baton Rouge*
P.O. Box 9374, Baton Rouge 70813
Chanc. Marvin L. Yates
(504) 771-4500

Southern University at New Orleans
6400 Press Dr., New Orleans 70126
Chanc. Robert B. Gex
(504) 286-5000

Southern University in Shreveport
3050 Martin Luther King, Jr. Dr.,
Shreveport 71107
Chanc. Jerome Greene, Jr.
(318) 674-3300

University of Louisiana System
State Office Bldg., Third F, 150 Third St.,
Baton Rouge 70801
Pres. James A. Caillier
(504) 342-6950

Delgado Community College
501 City Park Ave., New Orleans
70119-4399
Pres. Ione H. Elioff
(504) 483-4114

Grambling State University
P.O. Drawer 607, Grambling 71245
Pres. Raymond A. Hicks
(318) 274-2000

Louisiana Tech University
P.O. Box 3168, Tech Sta., Ruston
71272
Pres. Daniel D. Reneau
(318) 257-0211

McNeese State University
P.O. Box 93300, Lake Charles
70609-3300
Pres. Robert D. Hebert
(318) 446-8111

Nicholls State University
P.O. Box 2001, Thibodaux 70310
Pres. Donald J. Ayo
(504) 448-8111

Northeast Louisiana University
700 University Ave., Monroe 71209
Pres. Lawson L. Swearingen, Jr.
(318) 342-1000

Northwestern State University
College Ave., Natchitoches 71497
Pres. Robert A. Alost
(318) 357-6361

Nunez Community College
3700 LaFontaine St., Chalmette
70043
Pres. Carol F. Hopson
(504) 278-7440

Southeastern Louisiana University
SLU 784, Hammond 70402
Pres. Sally Clausen
(504) 549-2000

University of Southwestern Louisiana
E. University Ave., Lafayette 70504
Pres. Ray P. Authement
(318) 482-1000

MAINE

University of Maine System
107 Maine Ave., Bangor 04401-1805
Chanc. Terrence MacTaggart
(207) 947-0336

University of Maine
Orono 04469-0102
Pres. Frederick E. Hutchinson
(207) 581-1512

University of Maine at Augusta
Augusta 04330
Acting Pres. Charles MacRoy
(207) 621-3403

University of Maine at Farmington
86 Main St., Farmington 04938
Pres. Theodora J. Kalikow
(207) 778-7000

University of Maine at Fort Kent
Pleasant St., Fort Kent 04743
Pres. Richard G. Dumont
(207) 834-3162

University of Maine at Machias
Machias 04654
Pres. Paul E. Nordstrom
(207) 255-3313

University of Maine at Presque Isle
181 Main St., Presque Isle 04769
Pres. W. Michael Easton
(207) 764-0311

University of Southern Maine
96 Falmouth St., Portland 04103
Pres. Richard L. Pattenaude
(207) 780-4141

MARYLAND

Maryland Higher Education Commission
The Jeffrey Bldg., 16 Francis St.,
Annapolis 21401-1781
Secy. of Educ. Patricia S. Florestano
(410) 974-2971

Allegany Community College
Willowbrook Rd., Cumberland
21502
Pres. Donald L. Alexander
(301) 724-7700

Anne Arundel Community College
101 College Pkwy., Arnold 21012
Pres. Martha A. Smith
(410) 647-7100

Baltimore City Community College
2901 Liberty Heights Ave.,
Baltimore 21215
Pres. James D. Tschechtelin
(410) 333-5555

Cecil Community College
1000 North East Rd., North East
21901-1999
Pres. Robert L. Gell
(410) 287-6060

Charles County Community College
Mitchell Rd., P.O. Box 910, La Plata
20646-0910
Pres. John M. Sine
(301) 934-2251

Chesapeake College
P.O. Box 8, Wye Mills 21679-0008
Pres. John R. Kotula
(410) 822-5400

Community Colleges of Baltimore County
401 Washington Ave., Ste. 1010,
Towson 21204
Chanc. Daniel J. LaVista
(410) 825-9180

Catonsville Community College
800 S. Rolling Rd., Catonsville
21228
Pres. Frederick J. Walsh
(410) 455-6050

Dundalk Community College
7200 Sollers Point Rd.,
Dundalk 21222-4692
Pres. Harold D. McAninch
(410) 282-6700

Essex Community College
7201 Rossville Blvd.,
Baltimore 21237-3899
Pres. Donald J. Slowinski
(410) 682-6000

Frederick Community College
7932 Oppossumtown Pike,
Frederick 21702-2097
Pres. Lee John Betts
(301) 846-2400

Garrett Community College
P.O. Box 151, Mosser Rd.,
McHenry 21541
Pres. Stephen J. Herman
(301) 387-3000

Hagerstown Junior College
11400 Robinwood Dr., Hagerstown
21740-6590
Pres. Norman P. Shea
(301) 790-2800

Harford Community College
401 Thomas Run Rd., Bel Air
21015-1698
Pres. Claudia E. Chiesi
(410) 836-4000

Howard Community College
10901 Little Patuxent Pkwy.,
Columbia 21044
Pres. Dwight A. Burrill
(410) 992-4800

Montgomery College Central Administration
900 Hungerford Dr., Rockville 20850
Pres. Robert E. Parilla
(301) 279-5000

Montgomery College—Germantown Campus
20200 Observation Dr., Germantown 20876
Provost Noreen A. Lyne
(301) 353-7700

Montgomery College—Rockville Campus
51 Mannakee St., Rockville 20850
Provost Floyd Cumberbatch
(301) 279-5000

Montgomery College—Takoma Park Campus
Takoma Ave. and Fenton St., Takoma Park 20912
Provost Heijia L. Wheeler
(301) 650-1300

Morgan State University
Hillen Rd. and Cold Spring Ln., Baltimore 21239
Pres. Earl S. Richardson
(410) 319-3333

Prince George's Community College
301 Largo Rd., Largo 20772-2199
Pres. Robert I. Bickford
(301) 336-6000

St. Mary's College of Maryland
St. Mary's City 20686
Pres. Edward T. Lewis
(301) 862-0200

University of Maryland System
3330 Metzerott Rd., Adelphi 20783-1690
Chanc. Donald N. Langenberg
(301) 445-1901

Bowie State University
14000 Jericho Park Rd., Bowie 20715-9465
Pres. Nathanael Pollard, Jr.
(301) 464-3000

Coppin State College
2500 W. North Ave., Baltimore 21216-3698
Pres. Calvin W. Burnett
(410) 383-5585

Frostburg State University
Frostburg 21532-1099
Pres. Catherine R. Gira
(301) 687-4000

Salisbury State University
1101 Camden Ave., Salisbury 21801-6837
Interim Pres. K. Nelson Butler
(410) 543-6000

Towson State University
Towson 21204-7097
Pres. Hoke L. Smith
(410) 830-2000

University of Baltimore
1420 N. Charles St., Baltimore 21201-5779
Pres. H. Mebane Turner
(410) 837-4200

University of Maryland Baltimore County
5401 Wilkens Ave., Baltimore 21228-5398
Pres. Freeman A. Hrabowski, III
(410) 455-1000

University of Maryland College Park
Rte. 1, Balt. Blvd., College Park 20742
Pres. William E. Kirwan
(301) 405-1000

University of Maryland Eastern Shore
Princess Anne 21853-1299
Pres. William P. Hytche
(410) 651-2200

*University of Maryland University
  College*
    University Blvd. at Adelphi
      Rd., College Park 20742-
      1600
    Pres. T. Benjamin Massey
    (301) 985-7000

University of Maryland at Baltimore
    520 W. Lombard St., Baltimore
      21201-1627
    Pres. David J. Ramsay
    (410) 706-3100

Wor-Wic Community College
    32000 Campus Dr., Salisbury 21801
    Pres. Arnold H. Maner
    (410) 334-2800

MASSACHUSETTS

The Commonwealth of Massachusetts
Higher Education Coordinating Council
McCormack Bldg., Rm. 1401, One
Ashburton Pl., Boston 02108-1696
Chanc. Stanley Z. Koplik
(617) 727-7785

Berkshire Community College
West St., Pittsfield 01201
Pres. Barbara A. Viniar
(413) 499-4660

Bridgewater State College
Bridgewater 02324
Pres. Adrian Tinsley
(508) 697-1200

Bristol Community College
777 Elsbree St., Fall River 02720-
7395
Pres. Eileen T. Farley
(508) 678-2811

Bunker Hill Community College
Rutherford Ave., Boston 02129
Interim Pres. Maurice O'Shea
(617) 228-2000

Cape Cod Community College
Rte. 132, West Barnstable 02668
Pres. Richard A. Kraus
(508) 362-2131

Fitchburg State College
160 Pearl St., Fitchburg 01420
Pres. Michael P. Riccards
(508) 345-2151

Framingham State College
100 State St., Framingham 01701-
9101
Interim Pres. Helen Heineman
(508) 626-1220

Greenfield Community College
One College Dr., Greenfield 01301
Pres. Charles Wall
(413) 774-3131

Holyoke Community College
303 Homestead Ave., Holyoke
01040
Pres. David M. Bartley
(413) 538-7000

Massachusetts Bay Community College
50 Oakland St., Wellesley Hills
02181-5399
Pres. Roger A. Van Winkle
(617) 237-1100

Massachusetts College of Art
621 Huntington Ave., Boston 02115
Pres. William F. O'Neil
(617) 232-1555

Massachusetts Maritime Academy
101 Academy Dr., Buzzards Bay
02532
Pres. Peter M. Mitchell
(508) 830-5000

Massasoit Community College
One Massasoit Blvd., Brockton
02402
Pres. Gerard F. Burke
(508) 588-9100

Middlesex Community College
Springs Rd., Bedford 01730
Pres. Carole A. Cowan
(617) 280-3200

Mount Wachusett Community College
444 Green St., Gardner 01440
Pres. Daniel M. Asquino
(508) 632-6600

North Adams State College
North Adams 01247
Pres. Thomas D. Aceto
(413) 664-4511

North Shore Community College
1 Ferncroft Rd., Danvers 01923-4093
Pres. George Traicoff
(508) 762-4000

Northern Essex Community College
100 Elliott Way, Haverhill 01830-2399
Pres. David Hartled
(508) 374-3900

Quinsigamond Community College
670 W. Boylston St., Worcester 01606
Pres. Sandra L. Kurtinitus
(508) 853-2300

Roxbury Community College
1234 Columbus Ave., Roxbury Crossing 02120-3400
Pres. Grace Carolyn Brown
(617) 427-0060

Salem State College
352 Lafayette St., Salem 01970-4589
Pres. Nancy D. Harrington
(508) 741-6000

Springfield Technical Community College
One Armory Sq., Springfield 01105
Pres. Andrew M. Scibelli
(413) 781-7822

**University of Massachusetts
President's Office**
18 Tremont St., Ste. 800, Boston 02108
Pres. William Bulger
(617) 287-7000

University of Massachusetts Boston
Harbor Campus, 100 Morrisey Blvd., Boston 02125-3393
Chanc. Sherry H. Penney
(617) 287-6800

University of Massachusetts Dartmouth
North Dartmouth 02747
Chanc. Peter Cressy
(508) 999-8004

University of Massachusetts Lowell
One University Ave., Lowell 01854
Chanc. William T. Hogan
(508) 934-4000

University of Massachusetts Medical Center at Worcester
55 Lake Ave., N., Worcester 01605
Chanc. Aaron Lazare
(508) 856-8100

University of Massachusetts at Amherst
Amherst 01003
Chanc. David K. Scott
(413) 545-0111

Westfield State College
Western Ave., Westfield 01086
Pres. Ronald L. Applbaum
(413) 568-3311

Worcester State College
486 Chandler St., Worcester 01602-2597
Pres. Kalyan K. Ghosh
(508) 793-8000

MICHIGAN

Baker College System
1050 W. Bristol Rd., Flint 48507-5508
Pres. Edward J. Kurtz
(810) 767-7600

Baker College Center for Graduate
Studies
1050 W. Bristol Rd., Flint 48507-
5508
Dir. Steven L. Williams
(810) 766-4390

Baker College Corporate Services
1050 W. Bristol Rd., Flint 48507-
5508
Co-Dir. Pamela L. Baker
Co-Dir. James Kullman
(810) 766-4242

Baker College of Auburn Hills
1500 University Dr., Auburn Hills
48326-2642
Campus Dir./Dean Sandra Kay Krug
(810) 340-0600

Baker College of Cadillac
9600 E. 13th St., Cadillac 49601-
9600
Campus Dir./Dean Maynard W.
Thompson
(616) 775-8458

Baker College of Flint
1050 W. Bristol Rd., Flint 48507-
5508
Pres. Julianne T. Princinsky
(810) 767-7600

Baker College of Jackson
2800 Springport Rd., Jackson
49202-1299
Pres. Jack D. Bunce
(517) 789-6123

Baker College of Mount Clemens
34950 Little Mack Ave., Clinton
Township 48035-6611
Campus Dir./Dean Rodolfo Morales,
Jr.
(810) 791-6610

Baker College of Muskegon
123 E. Apple Ave., Muskegon
49442-3497
Pres. Rick E. Amidon
(616) 726-4904

Baker College of Owosso
1020 S. Washington St., Owosso
48867-4400
Pres. Denise A. Bannan
(517) 723-5251

Baker College of Port Huron
3403 Lapeer Rd., Port Huron 48060-
2597
Campus Dir./Dean Donald R. Torline
(810) 985-7000

Michigan Department of Education
Comm. Coll. Services Unit, P.O. Box
30008, Lansing 48909
Pres. Clark Durant
(517) 373-3900

Alpena Community College
666 Johnson St., Alpena 49707
Pres. Donald L. Newport
(517) 356-9021

Bay de Noc Community College
2001 N. Lincoln Rd., Escanaba
49829
Pres. Dwight E. Link
(800) 221-2001

Central Michigan University
Warriner 165, Mount Pleasant 48859
Pres. Leonard E. Plachta
(517) 774-4000

Charles Stewart Mott Community College
1401 E. Court St., Flint 48502-2394
Pres. Allen D. Arnold
(810) 762-0200

Delta College
Delta and Mackinow Rds.,
University Center 48710
Pres. Peter D. Boyse
(517) 686-9000

Eastern Michigan University
202 Welch Hall, Ypsilanti 48197
Pres. William E. Shelton
(313) 487-1849

Ferris State University
Big Rapids 49307
Pres. William A. Sederburg
(616) 592-2100

Glen Oaks Community College
62249 Shimmel Rd., Centreville
49032
Pres. Philip G. Ward
(616) 467-9945

Gogebic Community College
E-4946 Jackson Rd., Ironwood
49938
Pres. Donald J. Foster
(906) 932-4231

Grand Rapids Community College
143 Bostwick St., N.E., Grand
Rapids 49503
Pres. Richard W. Calkins
(616) 771-4000

Grand Valley State University
One Campus Dr., Allendale 49401
Pres. Arend D. Lubbers
(616) 895-6611

Henry Ford Community College
5101 Evergreen Rd., Dearborn
48128
Pres. Andrew A. Mazzara
(313) 271-2750

Highland Park Community College
Glendale Ave. at Third St., Highland
Park 48203
Pres. Thomas Lloyd
(313) 252-0475

Jackson Community College
2111 Emmons Rd., Jackson 49201
Pres. E. Lee Howser
(517) 787-0800

Kalamazoo Valley Community College
P.O. Box 4070, Kalamazoo 49003-
4070
Pres. Marilyn J. Schlack
(616) 372-5000

Kellogg Community College
450 North Ave., Battle Creek 49017-
3397
Pres. Paul R. Ohm
(616) 965-3931

Kirtland Community College
10775 N. St. Helen Rd.,
Roscommon 48653
Pres. Dorothy N. Franke
(517) 275-5121

Lake Michigan College
2755 E. Napier St., Benton Harbor
49022
Pres. Richard J. Pappas
(616) 927-3571

Lake Superior State University
1000 College Dr., Sault Ste. Marie
49783
Pres. Robert D. Arbuckle
(906) 632-6841

Lansing Community College
521 N. Washington Sq., Box 40010,
Lansing OA901-7210
Pres. Abel B. Sykes, Jr.
(517) 483-1851

Macomb Community College
14500 E. Twelve Mile Rd., Warren
48093-3896
Pres. Albert L. Lorenzo
(810) 445-7999

Michigan State University
450 Admin. Bldg., East Lansing 48824
Pres. M. Peter McPherson
(517) 355-1855

Michigan Technological University
1400 Townsend Dr., Houghton
49931
Pres. Curtis J. Tompkins
(906) 487-1885

Mid Michigan Community College
   1375 S. Clare Ave., Harrison 48625
   Pres. Charles J. Corrigan
   (517) 386-6622

Monroe County Community College
   1555 S. Raisinville Rd., Monroe
      48161
   Pres. Gerald D. Welch
   (313) 242-7300

Montcalm Community College
   2800 College Dr., S.W., P.O. Box
      300, Sidney 48885-0300
   Pres. Donald C. Burns
   (517) 328-2111

Muskegon Community College
   221 S. Quarterline Rd., Muskegon
      49442
   Pres. Frank Marczak
   (616) 777-0311

North Central Michigan College
   1515 Howard St., Petoskey 49770
   Pres. Robert B. Graham
   (616) 348-6600

Northern Michigan University
   1401 Presque Isle Ave., Marquette
      49855
   Pres. William E. Vandament
   (906) 227-1000

Northwestern Michigan College
   1701 E. Front St., Traverse City
      49686-3061
   Pres. Timothy G. Quinn
   (616) 922-1010

Oakland Community College
   2480 Opdyke Rd., Bloomfield Hills
      48304-2266
   Interim Chanc. Anthony D. Jarson
   (810) 540-1500

Oakland University
   Rochester 48309
   Interim Pres. Gary D. Russi
   (810) 370-2100

Saginaw Valley State University
   7400 Bay Rd., University Center
      48710
   Pres. Eric R. Gilbertson
   (517) 790-4000

Schoolcraft College
   18600 Haggerty Rd., Livonia
      48152-2696
   Pres. Richard W. McDowell
   (313) 462-4400

Southwestern Michigan College
   58900 Cherry Grove Rd., Dowagiac
      49047-9793
   Pres. David C. Briegel
   (616) 782-5113

St. Clair County Community College
   323 Erie St., P.O. Box 5015, Port
      Huron 48061-5015
   Pres. R. Ernest Dear
   (810) 984-3881

Washtenaw Community College
   4800 E. Huron River Dr., P.O. Box
      D-1, Ann Arbor 48106-0978
   Pres. Gunder A. Myran
   (313) 973-3300

Wayne County Community College
   801 W. Fort St., Detroit 48226-3010
   Pres. Curtis L. Ivery
   (313) 496-2510

Wayne State University
   4200 Admin. Bldg., Detroit 48202
   Pres. David W. Adamany
   (313) 577-2424

West Shore Community College
   3000 N. Stiles Rd., P.O. Box 277,
      Scottville 49454
   Pres. William M. Anderson
   (616) 845-6211

Western Michigan University
   Kalamazoo 49008
   Pres. Diether H. Haenicke
   (616) 387-1000

The University of Michigan System
Ann Arbor 48109
Pres. James J. Duderstadt
(313) 764-1817

University of Michigan
2068 Admin. Bldg., Ann Arbor
48109
Pres. James J. Duderstadt
(313) 764-1817

University of Michigan—Dearborn
4901 Evergreen Rd., Dearborn
48128-1491
Chanc. James C. Renick
(313) 593-5000

University of Michigan—Flint
Flint 48502-2186
Chanc. Charlie Nelms
(810) 762-3000

MINNESOTA

Minnesota State Colleges and Universities
550 Cedar St., St. Paul 55101
Chanc. Judith S. Eaton
(612) 296-8012

*Akita Campus of Minnesota State
Colleges and Universities*
193-2 Oku-Tsubakidai, Yuwa-
Machi, Akita, Japan 010-12
Provost John Norris
(612) 296-5284

Anoka-Ramsey Community College
11200 Mississippi Blvd. N.W., Coon
Rapids 55433-3499
Pres. Patrick M. Johns
(612) 427-2600

Arrowhead Community College
1855 E. Hwy. 169, Grand Rapids
55744-3361
Interim Pres. Mary E. Retterer
(218) 327-4380

*Fond Du Lac Tribal and Community
College*
2101 14th St., Cloquet 55720
Pres. Lester J. Briggs
(218) 879-0800

Hibbing Community College
1515 E. 25th St., Hibbing
55746-3354
Pres. Anthony J. Kuznik
(218) 262-6700

Itasca Community College
1851 E. Hwy. 169, Grand
Rapids 55744-3361
Exec. Dean James Clarke
(218) 327-4461

Mesabi Community College
1001 W. Chestnut St., Virginia
55792
Pres. Jon Harris
(218) 749-7700

Rainy River Community College
1501 Hwy. 71, International
Falls 56649-2160
Pres. Allen Rasmussen
(218) 285-7722

Vermilion Community College
1900 E. Camp St., Ely 55731-
1918
Pres. Jon Harris
(218) 365-7200

Austin Community College
1600 8th Ave., N.W., Austin 55912-
1407
Pres. Vicky R. Smith
(800) 747-6941

Bemidji State University
1500 Birchmont Dr., N.E., Bemidji
56601-2699
Pres. M. James Bensen
(218) 755-2000

Central Lakes College
501 W. College Dr., Brainerd
56401-3900
Pres. Sally Jane Ihne
(218) 828-2525

Fergus Falls Community College
1414 College Way, Fergus Falls
56537-1009
Pres. Daniel F. True
(218) 739-7500

Hennepin Technical College
9000 Brooklyn Blvd., Brooklyn
Park 55455
Pres. Sharon Grossbach
(612) 425-3800

Inver Hills Community College
2500 80th St. E., Inver Grove
Heights 55076-3224
Pres. Steven R. Wallace
(612) 450-8500

Lake Superior College
2101 Trinity Rd., Duluth 55811-
3399
Pres. Harold P. Erickson
(218) 722-2801

Lakewood Community College
3401 Century Ave., White Bear
Lake 55110-5655
Pres. James Meznek
(612) 779-3200

Mankato State University
PO Box 8400, Mankato 56002-8400
Pres. Richard R. Rush
(800) 722-0544

Metropolitan State University
700 E. 7th St., 2nd Fl. New Main,
St. Paul 55106-5000
Pres. Susan A. Cole
(612) 772-7777

Minneapolis Community College
1501 Hennepin Ave., Minneapolis
55403-1779
Pres. Diann Schindler
(612) 341-7000

Minnesota Riverland Technical College
1225 S.W. Third St., Faribault
55021
Interim Pres. Donald T. Olson
(507) 334-3965

Moorhead State University
1104 7th Ave. S., Moorhead 56563
Pres. Roland E. Barden
(218) 236-2011

Normandale Community College
9700 France Ave. S., Bloomington
55431-4309
Pres. Thomas A. Horak
(612) 832-6000

North Hennepin Community College
7411 85th Ave. N., Brooklyn Park
55445-2231
Pres. Katherine H. Sloan
(612) 424-0811

*Northland Community and Technical
College*
1301 Hwy. 1 E., Thief River Falls
56701-2598
Pres. Orley Gunderson
(218) 681-0701

Northwest Technical College
1103 Roosevelt Rd., S.E., Bemidji
56601
Pres. Ray Goss
(218) 755-4292

Pine Technical College
1100 Fourth St., Pine City 55063
Pres. Eugene Biever
(612) 629-6764

Range Technical College—Hibbing
2900 E. Beltline, Hibbing 55746
Pres. Joe Sertich
(218) 262-7200

Red Wing/Winona Technical College
308 Pioneer Rd. and Hwy. 58, Red
Wing 55066
Vice Pres. Ron Matuska
(612) 388-8271

Red Wing/Winona Technical College
308 Pioneer Rd. and Hwy.58, Red
Wing 55066
Pres. Jim Johnson
(612) 388-8271

Rochester Community College
851 30th Ave., S.E., Rochester
55904-4915
Pres. Karen E. Nagle
(507) 285-7210

South Central Technical College
1920 Lee Blvd., North Mankato
56003
Pres. Ken Mills
(507) 389-7200

Southwest State University
1501 State St., Marshall 56258
Pres. Douglas Sweetland
(800) 642-0684

Southwestern Technical College
Highway 212 W., Granite Falls
56241
Pres. Ralph Knapp
(612) 564-4511

Southwestern Technical College—
Granite Falls
1593 11th Ave., Granite Falls
56241
Pres. Richard Pooley
(800) 658-2522

St. Cloud State University
720 Fourth Ave. S., St. Cloud
56301-4498
Pres. Bruce F. Grube
(612) 255-0121

Willmar Community College
County Rd., P.O. Box 797, Willmar
56201-0797
Pres. Mary E. Retterer
(612) 231-5102

Winona State University
Winona 55987
Pres. Darrell W. Krueger
(800) 342-5978

Worthington Community College
1450 College Way, Worthington
56187-3024
Pres. C.W. Burchill
(507) 372-2107

University of Minnesota System
100 Church St., S.E., Minneapolis
55455-0110
Pres. Nils Hasselmo
(612) 625-5000

University of Minnesota—Crookston
Hwys. 2 and 75 N., Crookston 56716
Chanc. Donald G. Sargeant
(218) 281-6510

University of Minnesota—Duluth
515 Darland Admin. Bldg., 10
University Dr., Duluth 55812
Chanc. Kathryn A. Martin
(218) 726-8000

University of Minnesota—Morris
600 E. Fourth St., Morris 56267
Chanc. David C. Johnson
(612) 589-2211

University of Minnesota—Twin Cities
202 Morrill Hall, 100 Church St.,
S.E., Minneapolis 55455
Pres. Nils Hasselmo
(612) 625-5000

MISSISSIPPI

Mississippi Board of Trustees of State Institutions of Higher Learning
3825 Ridgewood Rd., Jackson 39211
Commissioner. Thomas D. Layzell
(601) 982-6611

Alcorn State University
1000 Oakland Cir., Lorman 39096-9402
Pres. Clinton Bristow, Jr.
(601) 877-6100

Delta State University
Hwy. 8 W., Cleveland 38733
Pres. F. Kent Wyatt
(601) 846-3000

Jackson State University
1400 J. R. Lynch St., Jackson 39217
Pres. James E. Lyons, Sr.
(601) 968-2121

Mississippi State University
Mississippi State 39762
Pres. Donald W. Zacharias
(601) 325-3920

Mississippi University for Women
P.O. Box W-1602, Columbus 39701
Pres. Clyda S. Rent
(601) 329-4750

Mississippi Valley State University
14000 Hwy. 82 W., Itta Bena 38941-1400
Pres. William W. Sutton
(601) 254-3997

University of Mississippi
109 Lyceum Bldg., University 38677
Chanc. Robert C. Khayat
(601) 232-7211

University of Mississippi Medical Center
2500 N. State St., Jackson 39216-4505
Vice Chanc. A. Wallace Conerly
(601) 984-1000

The University of Southern Mississippi
Southern Sta., Box 5001,
Hattiesburg 39406-5001
Pres. Aubrey K. Lucas
(601) 266-4111

Mississippi State Board for Community and Junior Colleges
3825 Ridgewood Rd., Jackson 39211
Exec. Dir. Olon E. Ray
(601) 982-6518

Coahoma Community College
3240 Friars Pt. Rd., Clarksdale 38614
Pres. Vivian M. Presley
(601) 627-2571

Copiah-Lincoln Community College
P.O. Box 457, Wesson 39191
Pres. Billy B. Thames
(601) 643-5101

East Central Community College
P.O. Box 129, Decatur 39327-0129
Pres. Eddie M. Smith
(601) 635-2111

East Mississippi Community College
P.O. Box 158, Scooba 39358
Pres. Thomas L. Davis, Jr.
(601) 476-8442

Hinds Community College
505 E. Main St., Raymond 39154-9799
Pres. V. Clyde Muse
(601) 857-5261

Holmes Community College
P.O. Box 369, Goodman 39079
Pres. Starkey A. Morgan, Sr.
(601) 472-2312

Itawamba Community College
602 W. Hill St., Fulton 38843-1099
Pres. David Cole
(601) 862-3101

Jones County Junior College
900 Court St., Ellisville 39437
Pres. T. Terrell Tisdale
(601) 477-4000

Meridian Community College
910 Hwy. 19 N., Meridian 39307
Pres. William F. Scaggs
(601) 483-8241

Mississippi Delta Community College
P.O. Box 668, Moorhead 38761
Pres. Bobby S. Garvin
(601) 246-6322

*Mississippi Gulf Coast Community
College*
P.O. Box 67, Perkinston 39573
Pres. Barry L. Mellinger
(601) 928-5211

*Northeast Mississippi Community
College*
101 Cunningham Blvd., Booneville
38829
Pres. Joe M. Childers
(601) 728-7751

*Northwest Mississippi Community
College*
510 N. Panola, Senatobia 38668
Pres. David M. Haraway
(601) 562-3200

Pearl River Community College
101 Hwy. 11 N., Sta. A, Poplarville
39470-2298
Pres. Ted J. Alexander
(601) 795-6801

*Southwest Mississippi Community
College*
Summit 39666-9704
Pres. Horace C. Holmes
(601) 276-2000

MISSOURI

Missouri Coordinating Board for Higher Education
3515 Amazonas Dr., Jefferson City 65109-5717
Commissioner Kala M. Stroup
(314) 751-2361

Central Missouri State University
Warrensburg 64093
Pres. Ed M. Elliott
(816) 543-4111

Crowder College
601 Laclede, Neosho 64850
Pres. Kent Farnsworth
(417) 451-3223

East Central College
P.O. Box 529, Union 63084
Pres. Dale L. Gibson
(314) 583-5193

Harris-Stowe State College
3026 Laclede Ave., St. Louis 63103
Pres. Henry Givens, Jr.
(314) 340-3366

Jefferson College
1000 Viking Dr., Hillsboro 63050-1000
Pres. Gregory D. Adkins
(314) 789-3951

Lincoln University
820 Chestnut St., Jefferson City 65102-0029
Pres. Wendell G. Rayburn, Sr.
(314) 681-5000

The Metropolitan Community College District
3200 Broadway, Kansas City 64111-2429
Chanc. Wayne E. Giles
(816) 759-1011

Longview Community College
500 Longview Rd., Lee's Summit 64081
Pres. Aldo W. Leker
(816) 672-2000

Maple Woods Community College
2601 N.E. Barry Rd., Kansas City 64156
Pres. Stephen R. Brainard
(816) 437-3000

Penn Valley Community College
3201 S.W. Trafficway, Kansas City 64111
Pres. E. Paul Williams
(816) 759-4000

Mineral Area College
P.O. Box 1000, Hwy. 67 and 32, Park Hills 63601
Pres. Dixie A. Kohn
(314) 431-4593

Missouri Southern State College
3950 E. Newman Rd., Joplin 64801-1595
Pres. Julio S. Leon
(417)624-9300

Missouri Western State College
4525 Downs Dr., St. Joseph 64507
Pres. Janet G. Murphy
(816) 271-4200

Moberly Area Community College
College and Rollins Sts., Moberly 65270
Pres. Andrew Komar, Jr.
(816) 263-4110

North Central Missouri College
1301 Main St., Trenton 64683
Pres. James E. Selby
(816) 359-3948

Northeast Missouri State University
200 McClain Hall, Kirksville
63501-9980
Interim Pres. W. Jack Magruder
(816) 785-4000

Northwest Missouri State University
800 University Dr., Maryville
64468-6001
Pres. Dean L. Hubbard
(816) 562-1212

Ozarks Technical Community College
1417 N. Jefferson Ave., Springfield
65802
Pres. Norman K. Myers
(417) 895-7000

Southeast Missouri State University
One University Plaza, Cape
Girardeau 63701
Pres. William L. Atchley
(314) 651-2000

Southwest Missouri State University
901 S. National Ave., Springfield
65804
Pres. John H. Keiser
(800) 492-7900

St. Charles County Community College
4601 Mid Rivers Mall Dr., P.O. Box
76975, St. Peters 63376
Pres. Donald D. Shook
(314) 922-8000

St. Louis Community College District
300 S. Broadway, St. Louis 63102-
1708
Chanc. Gwendolyn W. Stephenson
(314) 539-5150

*St. Louis Community College at
Florissant Valley*
3400 Pershall Rd., Ferguson
63135
Pres. Irving P. McPhail
(314) 595-4200

*St. Louis Community College at
Forest Park*
5600 Oakland Ave., St. Louis
63110
Pres. Henry D. Shannon
(314) 644-9100

*St. Louis Community College at
Meramec*
11333 Big Bend Blvd.,
Kirkwood 63122
Pres. Richard A. Black
(314) 984-7500

State Fair Community College
3201 W. 16th St., Sedalia 65301
Pres. Marvin R. Fielding
(816) 530-5800

Three Rivers Community College
2080 Three Rivers Blvd., Poplar
Bluff 63901
Pres. Stephen M. Poort
(314) 840-9600

University of Missouri System
321 University Hall, Columbia
65211
Pres. George A. Russell
(314) 882-2011

University of Missouri—Columbia
105 Jesse Hall, Columbia 65211
Chanc. Charles A. Kiesler
(314) 882-2121

University of Missouri—Kansas City
5100 Rockhill Rd., Kansas City
64110
Chanc. Eleanor B. Schwartz
(816) 235-1000

University of Missouri—Rolla
206 Parker Hall, Rolla 65401
Chanc. John T. Park
(314) 341-4114

University of Missouri—St. Louis
8001 Natural Bridge Rd., St.
Louis 63121
Chanc. Blanche M. Touhill
(314) 516-5000

MONTANA

Montana University System
2500 Broadway, Helena 59620
Commissioner of Higher Educ. Jeffrey D.
Baker
(406) 444-6570

Dawson Community College
Box 421, Glendive 59330
Pres. Donald H. Kettner
(406) 365-3396

Flathead Valley Community College
777 Grandview Dr., Kalispell 59901
Pres. David Beyer
(406) 756-3822

Helena College of Technology of The
University of Montana
1115 N. Roberts St., Helena 59601
Dean Alex Capdeville
(406) 444-6800

Miles Community College
2715 Dickinson, Miles City 59301
Pres. Frank Williams
(406) 232-3031

Montana State University College of
Technology—Great Falls
2100 16th Ave., S., Great Falls 59405
Dean Willard R. Weaver
(406) 771-1240

Montana State University—Billings
1500 N. 30th St., Billings 59101
Chanc. Ronald Sexton
(406) 657-2011

Montana State University—Bozeman
Bozeman 59717
Pres. Michael P. Malone
(406) 994-0211

Montana State University—Northern
P.O. Box 7751, Havre 59501
Chanc. William Daehling
(406) 265-3700

Montana Tech of The University of
Montana
1300 W. Park St., Butte 59701-8997
Chanc. Lindsay D. Norman
(406) 496-4101

The University of Montana—Missoula
Missoula 59812
Pres. George M. Dennison
(406) 243-0211

Western Montana College of The
University of Montana
710 S. Atlantic St., Dillon 59725-
3511
Chanc. Sheila M. Stearns
(406) 683-7151

NEBRASKA

Nebraska Coordinating Commission for Postsecondary Education
140 N. 8th St., Ste. 300, P.O. Box 95005, Lincoln 68509-5005
Exec. Dir. David R. Powers
(402) 471-2847

Central Community College
P.O. Box 4903, Grand Island 68802-4903
Pres. Joseph W. Preusser
(308) 384-5220

Chadron State College
1000 Main St., Chadron 69337
Pres. Samuel H. Rankin, Jr.
(308) 432-6000

Metropolitan Community College
P.O. Box 3777, Omaha 68103
Pres. J. Richard Gilliland
(800) 228-9553

Mid-Plains Community College Area
416 N. Jeffers, North Platte 69101
Area Pres. Gregory G. Fitch
(308) 534-9265

McCook Community College
1205 E. Third St., McCook 69001
Pres. Robert G. Smallfoot
(308) 345-6303

Mid-Plains Community College
601 W. State Farm Rd., North Platte 69101
Chanc. Gregory G. Fitch
(308) 532-8980

Northeast Community College
801 E. Benjamin Ave., P.O. Box 469, Norfolk 68702-0469
Pres. James C. Underwood
(402) 371-2020

Peru State College
Peru 68421
Pres. Robert Burns
(402) 872-3815

Southeast Community College
8800 O St., Lincoln 68520
Chanc. Jack Huck
(402) 437-2500

University of Nebraska
3835 Holdrege St., Lincoln 68583
Pres. L. Dennis Smith
(402) 472-2111

University of Nebraska Medical Center
600 S. 42nd St., Omaha 68198-6605
Chanc. Carol A. Aschenbrener
(402) 559-4200

University of Nebraska at Kearney
905 W. 25th St., Kearney 68849
Chanc. Gladys Styles Johnston
(308) 236-8441

University of Nebraska at Omaha
60th and Dodge, Omaha 68182-0108
Chanc. Delbert D. Weber
(402) 554-2200

University of Nebraska—Lincoln
14th and R Sts., Lincoln 68588-0419
Chanc. James C. Moeser
(402) 472-7211

Wayne State College
1111 Main St., Wayne 68787
Pres. Donald J. Mash
(402) 375-7000

Western Nebraska Community College
1601 E. 27th St., Scottsbluff 69361
Pres. John N. Harms
(308) 635-3606

NEVADA

University and Community College System of Nevada
2601 Enterprise Rd., Reno 89512
Chanc. Richard S. Jarvis
(702) 784-4901

Community College of Southern Nevada
3200 E. Cheyenne Ave., North Las Vegas 89106
Pres. Richard Moore
(702) 651-4491

Great Basin College
1500 College Pkwy., Elko 89801
Pres. Ronald K. Remington
(702) 738-8493

Truckee Meadows Community College
7000 Dandini Blvd., Reno 89512
Pres. Kenneth E. Wright
(702) 673-7000

University of Nevada, Las Vegas
4505 Maryland Pkwy., Las Vegas 89154
Pres. Carol C. Harter
(702) 895-3011

University of Nevada, Reno
Reno 89557
Pres. Joseph N. Crowley
(702) 784-1105

Western Nevada Community College
2201 W. College Pkwy., Carson City 89703
Pres. James R. Randolph
(702) 887-3000

NEW HAMPSHIRE

University System of New Hampshire
Dunlap Ctr., 25 Concord Rd., Durham
03824-3545
Chanc. William J. Farrell
(603) 868-1800

College for Lifelong Learning
125 N. State St., Concord 03301-
6430
Dean Victor B. Montana
(603) 228-3000

Keene State College
229 Main St., Keene 03435-1502
Pres. Stanley J. Yarosewick
(603) 352-1909

Plymouth State College
Plymouth 03264-1567
Pres. Donald P. Wharton
(603) 535-5000

University of New Hampshire
Durham 03824-3547
Interim Pres. Walter R. Peterson
(603) 862-1234

NEW JERSEY

New Jersey Commission on Higher Education
20 W. State St., CN 542, Trenton 08625
Exec. Dir. Martine Hammond-Paludan
(609) 292-4310

Atlantic Community College
5100 Black Horse Pike, Mays
Landing 08330-2699
Pres. John T. May
(609) 343-4900

Bergen Community College
400 Paramus Rd., Paramus 07652
Pres. Judith K. Winn
(201) 447-7100

Brookdale Community College
765 Newman Springs Rd., Lincroft
07738
Pres. Peter F. Burnham
(908) 842-1900

Burlington County College
County Rte. 530, Pemberton 08068-
1599
Pres. Robert C. Messina, Jr.
(609) 894-9311

Camden County College
P.O. Box 200, Blackwood 08012
Pres. Phyllis Della Vecchia
(609) 227-7200

County College of Morris
Rte. 10 and Center Grove Rd.,
Randolph 07869
Pres. Edward J. Yaw
(201) 328-5000

Cumberland County College
College Dr., P.O. Box 517, Vineland
08360
Pres. Roland J. Chapdelaine
(609) 691-8600

Essex County College
303 University Ave., Newark 07102
Pres. A. Zachary Yamba
(201) 877-3000

Gloucester County College
Tanyard and Salisnas Rds., Sewell
08080
Pres. Richard H. Jones
(609) 468-5000

Hudson County Community College
168 Sip Ave., Jersey City 07306
Pres. Glen Gabert
(201) 656-2020

Jersey City State College
2039 Kennedy Blvd., Jersey City
07305-1597
Pres. Carlos Hernandez
(201) 200-2000

Kean College of New Jersey
1000 Morris Ave., Union 07083
Interim Pres. Henry J. Ross
(908) 527-2000

Mercer County Community College
1200 Old Trenton Rd., Trenton
08690-0182
Pres. Thomas D. Sepe
(609) 586-4800

Middlesex County College
155 Mill Rd., P.O. Box 3050,
Edison 08818-3050
Interim Pres. John Bakum
(908) 548-6000

Montclair State University
Valley Rd. and Normal Ave., Upper
Montclair 07043-1624
Pres. Irvin D. Reid
(201) 655-4000

New Jersey Institute of Technology
27 Eberhardt Hall, University
Heights, Newark 07102-1982
Pres. Saul K. Fenster
(201) 596-3000

Ocean County College
  College Dr., P.O. Box 2001, Toms
    River 08754-2001
  Pres. Milton Shaw
  (908) 255-4000

Passaic County Community College
  College Blvd., Paterson 07509
  Pres. Elliott Collins
  (201) 684-6800

Ramapo College of New Jersey
  505 Ramapo Valley Rd., Mahwah
    07430-1680
  Pres. Robert A. Scott
  (201) 529-7500

Raritan Valley Community College
  P.O. Box 3300, Somerville 08876
  Pres. Cary A. Israel
  (908) 526-1200

Richard Stockton College of New Jersey
  Jim Leeds Rd., Pomona 08240
  Pres. Vera King Farris
  (609) 652-1776

Rowan College of New Jersey
  201 Mullica Hill Rd., Glassboro
    08028-1701
  Pres. Herman D. James
  (609) 256-4100

**Rutgers, The State University of New
Jersey Central Office**
  George and Somerset Sts., New
    Brunswick 08903
  Pres. Francis L. Lawrence
  (908) 932-1766

  *Rutgers, The State University of New
  Jersey Camden Campus*
    Armitage Hall, Camden 08102
    Provost Walter K. Gordon
    (609) 225-6095

  *Rutgers, The State University of New
  Jersey New Brunswick Campus*
    18 Bishop Pl., New Brunswick
      08903
    Provost Joseph A. Potenza
    (908) 932-7461

*Rutgers, The State University of New
Jersey Newark Campus*
  15 Washington St., Newark
    07102
  Provost Norman Samuels
  (201) 648-1766

Salem Community College
  460 Hollywood Ave., Carneys Point
    08069-2799
  Pres. Linda C. Jolly
  (609) 299-2100

Sussex County Community College
  College Hill, Newton 07860
  Pres. William A. Connor
  (201) 300-2100

Thomas A. Edison State College
  101 W. State St., Trenton 08608-
    1176
  Pres. George A. Pruitt
  (609) 984-1100

Trenton State College
  Hillwood Lakes, P.O. Box 4700,
    Trenton 08650-4700
  Pres. Harold W. Eickhoff
  (609) 771-1855

Union County College
  1033 Springfield Ave., Cranford
    07016
  Pres. Thomas H. Brown
  (908) 709-7000

*University of Medicine and Dentistry of
New Jersey*
  30 Bergen St., Newark 07107-3007
  Pres. Stanley S. Bergen, Jr.
  (201) 982-4300

Warren County Community College
  Box 55A, Rte. 57 W., R.D. 1,
    Washington 07882
  Pres. Vincent De Sanctis
  (908) 689-1090

William Paterson College of New Jersey
  300 Pompton Rd., Wayne 07470
  Pres. Arnold Speert
  (201) 595-2000

NEW MEXICO

New Mexico Commission on Higher Education
1068 Cerrillos Rd., Santa Fe 87501-4295
Exec. Dir. Bruce D. Hamlett
(505) 827-7383

Albuquerque Technical Vocational Institute
525 Buena Vista Dr., S.E.,
Albuquerque 87106
Pres. Alex A. Sanchez
(505) 224-3000

Clovis Community College
417 Schepps Blvd., Clovis 88101
Pres. Jay Gurley
(505) 769-2811

Eastern New Mexico University
Campus Sta. No. 1, Portales 88130
Pres. Everett L. Frost
(505) 562-2121

Luna Vocational Technical Institute
P.O. Drawer K, Las Vegas 87701
Pres. Samuel F. Vigil
(505) 454-2500

New Mexico Highlands University
National Ave., Las Vegas 87701
Pres. Selimo Rael
(505) 454-3229

New Mexico Institute of Mining and Technology
Brown Hall, Socorro 87801
Pres. Daniel H. Lopez
(505) 835-5500

New Mexico Junior College
5317 Lovington Hwy., Hobbs 88240
Pres. Charles D. Hays, Jr.
(505) 392-4510

New Mexico Military Institute
100 W. College Blvd., Roswell
88201
Supt. Winfield W. Scott, Jr.
(800) 421-5376

New Mexico State University
Box 30001, Dept. 3Z, Las Cruces
88003
Pres. J. Michael Orenduff
(505) 646-0111

Northern New Mexico Community College
1002 N. Onate St., Espanola 87532
Pres. Connie A. Valdez
(505) 747-2100

San Juan College
4601 College Blvd., Farmington
87402
Pres. James C. Henderson
(800) 241-6327

Santa Fe Community College
P.O. Box 4187, Santa Fe 87502-
4187
Pres. Leonardo de la Garza
(505) 471-8200

The University of New Mexico
Scholes Hall 160, Albuquerque
87131
Pres. Richard E. Peck
(505) 277-0111

Western New Mexico University
P.O. Box 680, 1000 W. College
Ave., Silver City 88062
Pres. John E. Counts
(800) 222-9668

NEW YORK

The City University of New York Office of the Chancellor
535 E. 80th St., New York 10021
Chanc. W. Ann Reynolds
(212) 794-5555

Bernard M. Baruch College
17 Lexington Ave., New York 10010
Pres. Matthew Goldstein
(212) 802-2000

Borough of Manhattan Community College
199 Chambers St., New York 10007
Pres. Antonio Perez
(212) 346-8000

Bronx Community College
W. 181st St. and University Ave., Bronx 10453
Acting Pres. Leo A. Corbie
(718) 220-6920

Brooklyn College
2900 Bedford Ave., Brooklyn 11210-2889
Pres. Vernon E. Lattin
(718) 951-5000

The City College
Convent Ave. at 138th St., New York 10031
Pres. Yolanda T. Moses
(212) 650-7000

City University School of Law at Queens College
65-21 Main St., Flushing 11367
Dean Kristin Booth Glen
(718) 575-4200

College of Staten Island
2800 Victory Blvd., Staten Island 10314
Pres. Marlene Springer
(718) 982-2000

Graduate School and University Center
33 W. 42nd St., New York 10036
Pres. Frances Degen Horowitz
(212) 642-2000

Herbert H. Lehman College
Bedford Park Blvd. W., Bronx 10468
Pres. Ricardo R. Fernandez
(718) 960-8000

Hostos Community College
475 Grand Concourse, Bronx 10451
Pres. Isaura Santiago
(718) 518-4246

Hunter College
695 Park Ave., New York 10021
Pres. David A. Caputo
(212) 772-4000

John Jay College of Criminal Justice
899 10th Ave., New York 10019
Pres. Gerald W. Lynch
(212) 237-8000

Kingsborough Community College
2001 Oriental Blvd., Manhattan Beach, Brooklyn 11235
Pres. Leon M. Goldstein
(718) 368-5000

La Guardia Community College
31-10 Thomson Ave., Long Island City 11101
Pres. Raymond C. Bowen
(718) 482-7200

Medgar Evers College
1650 Bedford Ave., Brooklyn 11225
Pres. Edison O. Jackson
(718) 270-4900

Mount Sinai School of Medicine
One Gustave L. Levy Pl., New York 10029
Pres. John W. Rowe
(212) 241-8888

New York City Technical College
300 Jay St., Brooklyn 11201
Pres. Charles W. Merideth
(718) 260-5000

Queens College
65-40 Kissena Blvd., Flushing 11367
Pres. Allen L. Sessoms
(718) 997-5000

Queensborough Community College
222-05 56th Ave., Bayside 11364-
1497
Pres. Kurt R. Schmeller
(718) 631-6262

York College
94-20 Guy R. Brewer Blvd.,
Jamaica 11451
Acting Pres. Thomas K. Minter
(718) 262-2000

State University of New York System Office
State University Plaza, Albany 12246
Chanc. Thomas A. Bartlett
(518) 443-5355

*State University of New York College at
Brockport*
350 New Campus Dr., Brockport
14420
Pres. John E. Van de Wetering
(716) 395-2211

*State University of New York College at
Buffalo*
1300 Elmwood Ave., Buffalo 14222
Interim Pres. Muriel A. Moore
(716) 878-4000

*State University of New York College at
Cortland*
P.O. Box 2000, Cortland 13045
Pres. Judson H. Taylor
(607) 753-2201

*State University of New York College at
Fredonia*
Fredonia 14063
Pres. Donald A. MacPhee
(716) 673-3111

*State University of New York College at
Geneseo*
Geneseo 14454
Pres. Christopher C. Dahl
(716) 245-5501

*State University of New York College at
New Paltz*
New Paltz 12561
Pres. Alice Chandler
(914) 257-2121

*State University of New York College at
Old Westbury*
P.O. Box 210, Old Westbury 11568
Pres. L. Eudora Pettigrew
(516) 876-3000

*State University of New York College at
Oneonta*
Oneonta 13820-4015
Pres. Alan B. Donovan
(607) 436-2500

*State University of New York College at
Oswego*
Oswego 13126
Acting Pres. Deborah F. Stanley
(315) 341-2500

*State University of New York College at
Plattsburg*
Plattsburgh 12901
Pres. Horace A. Judson
(518) 564-2000

*State University of New York College at
Purchase*
735 Anderson Hill Rd., Purchase
10577-1400
Pres. Bill Lacy
(914) 251-6000

*State University of New York College of
Agriculture and Technology at
Cobleski*
Cobleskill 12043
Pres. Kenneth E. Wing
(518) 234-5111

State University of New York College of Agriculture and Technology at Morrisvi
Morrisville 13408
Pres. Frederick W. Woodward
(315) 684-6000

State University of New York College of Environmental Science and Forestry
Syracuse 13210
Pres. Ross S. Whaley
(315) 470-5000

State University of New York College of Optometry
100 E. 24th St., New York 10010
Pres. Alden N. Haffner
(212) 780-4900

State University of New York College of Technology at Alfred
Huntington Bldg., Alfred 14802
Pres. William D. Rezak
(607) 587-4111

State University of New York College of Technology at Canton
Cornell Dr., Canton 13617
Pres. Joseph L. Kennedy
(315) 386-7204

State University of New York College of Technology at Delhi
Delhi 13753
Pres. Mary Ellen Duncan
(607) 746-4111

State University of New York College of Technology at Farmingdale
Melville Rd., Farmingdale 11735
Pres. Frank A. Cipriani
(516) 420-2000

State University of New York Empire State College
One Union Ave., Saratoga Springs 12866
Pres. James W. Hall
(518) 587-2100

State University of New York Health Science Center at Brooklyn
450 Clarkson Ave., Brooklyn 11203
Pres. Russell L. Miller
(718) 270-1000

State University of New York Health Science Center at Syracuse
750 E. Adams St., Syracuse 13210
Pres. Gregory L. Eastwood
(315) 464-5540

State University of New York Institute of Technology at Utica/Rome
P.O. Box 3050, Utica 13504-3050
Pres. Peter J. Cayan
(315) 792-7400

State University of New York Maritime College
Fort Schuyler, Throggs Neck 10465
Pres. David C. Brown
(212) 409-7200

State University of New York Office of Community Colleges
State University Plaza, Rm. T-705, Albany 12246
Dir. Comm. Colls. Educ. Serv.
Glenn DuBois
(518) 443-5134

Adirondack Community College
Bay Rd., Queensbury 12804
Pres. Roger C. Andersen
(518) 743-2200

Broome Community College
Upper Front St., P.O. Box 1017, Binghamton 13902
Pres. Donald A. Dellow
(607) 778-5000

Cayuga County Community College
Franklin St., Auburn 13021
Pres. Lawrence H. Poole
(315) 255-1743

Clinton Community College
136 Clinton Point Dr., Box 8A,
Plattsburgh 12901-9573
Pres. Jay L. Fennell
(518) 562-4200

*Columbia-Greene Community
College*
P.O. Box 1000, Hudson 12534
Pres. Terry A. Cline
(518) 828-4181

Corning Community College
Spencer Hill, Corning 14830
Pres. Eduardo J. Marti
(607) 962-9011

Dutchess Community College
53 Pendell Rd., Poughkeepsie
12601-1595
Pres. D. David Conklin
(914) 431-8000

*Erie Community College City
Campus*
121 Ellicott St., Buffalo 14203
Pres. Louis M. Ricci
(716) 851-1001

Fashion Institute of Technology
Seventh Ave. at 27th St., New
York 10001-5992
Pres. Allan F. Hershfield
(212) 760-7700

Finger Lakes Community College
4355 Lake Shore Dr.,
Canandaigua 14424
Pres. Daniel T. Hayes
(716) 394-3500

*Fulton-Montgomery Community
College*
2805 State Hwy. 67, Johnstown
12095
Pres. Priscilla J. Bell
(518) 762-4651

Genesee Community College
One College Rd., Batavia 14020
Pres. Stuart Steiner
(716) 343-0055

*Herkimer County Community
College*
Reservoir Rd., Herkimer 13350
Pres. Ronald F. Williams
(315) 866-0300

Hudson Valley Community College
80 Vandenburgh Ave., Troy
12180
Pres. Joseph J. Bulmer
(518) 283-1100

Jamestown Community College
525 Falconer St., Jamestown
14701
Pres. Gregory T. DeCinque
(716) 665-5220

Jefferson Community College
Outer Coffeen St., Watertown
13601
Pres. John W. Deans
(315) 786-2230

Mohawk Valley Community College
1101 Sherman Dr., Utica 13501
Pres. Michael I. Schafer
(315) 792-5400

Monroe Community College
1000 E. Henrietta Rd.,
Rochester 14623
Pres. Peter A. Spina
(716) 292-2100

Nassau Community College
One Education Dr., Garden
City 11530
Pres. Sean A. Fanelli
(516) 572-7205

Niagara County Community College
3111 Saunders Settlement Rd.,
Sanborn 14132
Pres. Gerald L. Miller
(716) 731-3271

North Country Community College
20 Winona Ave., P.O. Box 89,
Saranac Lake 12983
Pres. Gail Rogers Rice
(518) 891-2915

Onondaga Community College
Rte. 173, Syracuse 13215
Pres. Bruce H. Leslie
(315) 469-7741

Orange County Community College
115 South St., Middletown
10940
Pres. William F. Messner
(914) 341-4701

Rockland Community College
145 College Rd., Suffern 10901
Pres. Neal A. Raisman
(914) 574-4000

*Schenectady County Community
College*
78 Washington Ave.,
Schenectady 12305
Pres. Gabriel J. Basil
(518) 346-6211

**Suffolk County Community
College Central Administration**
533 College Rd., Selden 11784
Pres. John F. Cooper
(516) 451-4111

**Suffolk County Community
College Ammerman Campus**
533 College Rd., Selden
11784
Provost N. Patricia
Yarborough
(516) 451-4110

**Suffolk County Community
College Eastern Campus**
Speonk-Riverhead Rd.,
Riverhead 11901
Provost Elizabeth Blake
(516) 548-2500

**Suffolk County Community
College Western Campus**
Crooked Hill Rd.,
Brentwood 11717
Provost Salvatore La Lima
(516) 434-6789

Sullivan County Community College
P.O. Box 4002, Loch Sheldrake
12759-4002
Pres. Jeffrey B. Willens
(914) 434-5750

*Tompkins Cortland Community
College*
P.O. Box 139, 170 North St.,
Dryden 13053
Pres. Carl E. Haynes
(607) 844-8211

Ulster County Community College
Stone Ridge 12484
Pres. Robert T. Brown
(914) 687-5000

Westchester Community College
75 Grasslands Rd., Valhalla
10595
Pres. Joseph N. Hankin
(914) 785-6600

State University of New York at Albany
1400 Washington Ave., Albany 12222
Interim Pres. Karen R. Hitchcock
(518) 442-3300

*State University of New York at
Binghamton*
P.O. Box 6000, Binghamton 13902-
6000
Pres. Lois B. DeFleur
(607) 777-2000

State University of New York at Buffalo
Capen Hall, Buffalo 14260
Pres. William R. Greiner
(716) 645-2000

*State University of New York at Stony
Brook*
Nicolls Rd., Stony Brook 11794-0701
Pres. Shirley Strum Kenny
(516) 689-6000

*State Universityn of New York College at
Postdam*
Pierrepont Ave., Potsdam 13676
Pres. William C. Merwin
(315) 267-2000

NORTH CAROLINA

North Carolina Community College System
200 W. Jones St., The Caswell Bldg.,
   Raleigh 27603-1337
Pres. Lloyd V. Hackley
(919) 733-7051

Alamance Community College
P.O. Box 8000, Graham 27253-8000
Pres. W. Ronald McCarter
(910) 578-2002

Anson Community College
P.O. Box 126, Polkton 28135
Pres. Donald P. Altieri
(704) 272-7635

*Asheville-Buncombe Technical
   Community College*
340 Victoria Rd., Asheville 28801
Pres. K. Ray Bailey
(704) 254-1921

Beaufort County Community College
P.O. Box 1069, Washington 27889
Pres. U. Ronald Champion
(919) 946-6194

Bladen Community College
P.O. Box 266, Dublin 28332-0266
Pres. Lynn G. King
(910) 862-2164

Blue Ridge Community College
College Dr., Box 133A, Flat Rock
   28731-9624
Pres. David W. Sink, Jr.
(704) 692-3572

Brunswick Community College
P.O. Box 30, Supply 28462-0030
Pres. W. Michael Reaves
(910) 754-6900

*Caldwell Community College and
   Technical Institute*
100 Hickory Blvd., Lenoir 28645
Pres. Kenneth A. Boham
(704) 726-2200

Cape Fear Community College
411 N. Front St., Wilmington
   28401-3993
Pres. Eric B. McKeithan
(910) 251-5100

Carteret Community College
3505 Arendell St., Morehead City
   28557
Pres. Donald W. Bryant
(919) 247-6000

Catawba Valley Community College
2550 Hwy. 70 SE., Hickory 28602-
   9699
Pres. Cuyler A. Dunbar
(704) 327-7000

Central Carolina Community College
1105 Kelly Dr., Sanford 27330
Pres. Marvin R. Joyner
(919) 775-5401

Central Piedmont Community College
P.O. Box 35009, Charlotte 28235
Pres. Paul Anthony Zeiss
(704) 342-6633

Cleveland Community College
137 S. Post Rd., Shelby 28150
Pres. L. Steve Thornburg
(704) 484-4000

Coastal Carolina Community College
444 Western Blvd., Jacksonville
   28546-6877
Pres. Ronald K. Lingle
(910) 455-1221

College of The Albemarle
P.O. Box 2327, Elizabeth City
   27906-2327
Pres. Larry R. Donnithorne
(919) 335-0821

Craven Community College
800 College Court, New Bern 28562
Pres. Lewis S. Redd
(919) 638-4131

Davidson County Community College
P.O. Box 1287, Lexington 27293-
1287
Pres. J. Bryan Brooks
(704) 249-8186

Durham Technical Community College
1637 Lawson St., Durham 27703
Pres. Phail Wynn, Jr.
(919) 598-9222

Edgecombe Community College
2009 W. Wilson St., Tarboro 27886
Pres. Hartwell Fuller, Jr.
(919) 823-5166

Fayetteville Technical Community College
P.O. Box 35236, 2201 Hull Rd.,
Fayetteville 28303-0236
Pres. Robert Craig Allen
(910) 678-8400

Forsyth Technical Community College
2100 Silas Creek Pkwy., Winston-
Salem 27103-5150
Pres. Desna L. Wallin
(910) 723-0371

Gaston College
201 Hwy. 321 S., Dallas 28034-1499
Pres. Patricia Skinner
(704) 922-6200

Guilford Technical Community College
P.O. Box 309, Jamestown 27282
Pres. Donald W. Cameron
(910) 334-4822

Halifax Community College
P.O. Drawer 809, Weldon 27890
Pres. Elton L. Newbern, Jr.
(919) 536-2551

Haywood Community College
1 Freedlander Dr., Clyde 28721
Pres. Dan W. Moore
(704) 627-2821

Isothermal Community College
P.O. Box 804, Spindale 28160
Pres. Willard L. Lewis, III
(704) 286-3636

James Sprunt Community College
P.O. Box 398, Kenansville 28349-
0398
Pres. Donald L. Reichard
(910) 296-2400

Johnston Community College
P.O. Box 2350, Smithfield 27577
Pres. John L. Tart
(919) 934-3051

Lenoir Community College
P.O. Box 188, Kinston 28501
Pres. Lonnie H. Blizzard
(919) 527-6223

Martin Community College
1161 Kehukee Park Rd.,
Williamston 27892
Pres. Martin H. Nadelman
(919) 792-1521

Mayland Community College
P.O. Box 547, Spruce Pine 28777
Pres. Nathan L. Hodges
(704) 765-7351

McDowell Technical Community College
Rte. 1, Box 170, Marion 28752
Pres. Robert M. Boggs
(704) 652-6021

Mitchell Community College
500 W. Broad St., Statesville 28677
Pres. Douglas O. Eason
(704) 878-3200

Montgomery Community College
P.O. Box 787, Troy 27371
Pres. Theodore H. Gasper, Jr.
(910) 576-6222

Nash Community College
P.O. Box 7488, Rocky Mount 27804
Pres. J. Reid Parrott, Jr.
(919) 443-4011

Pamlico Community College
P.O. Box 185, Hwy. 306 S.,
Grantsboro 28529
Pres. E. Douglas Kearney, Jr.
(919) 249-1851

Piedmont Community College
P.O. Box 1197, Roxboro 27573
Pres. H. James Owen
(910) 599-1181

Pitt Community College
P.O. Drawer 7007, Greenville 27835
Pres. Charles E. Russell
(919) 321-4200

Randolph Community College
P.O. Box 1009, Asheboro 27204-
1009
Pres. Larry K. Linker
(910) 629-1471

Richmond Community College
P.O. Box 1189, Hamlet 28345
Pres. Joseph W. Grimsley
(910) 582-7000

Roanoke-Chowan Community College
Rte. 2, Box 46-A, Ahoskie 27910
Pres. Harold E. Mitchell
(919) 332-5921

Robeson Community College
P.O. Box 1420, Lumberton 28359
Pres. Frederick G. Williams, Jr.
(919) 738-7101

Rockingham Community College
P.O. Box 38, Wentworth 27375-
0038
Pres. N. Jerry Owens, Jr.
(910) 342-4261

Rowan-Cabarrus Community College
P.O. Box 1595, Salisbury 28145-
1595
Pres. Richard L. Brownell
(704) 637-0760

Sampson Community College
P.O. Drawer 318, Clinton 28328
Pres. Clifton W. Paderick
(910) 592-8081

Sandhills Community College
2200 Airport Rd., Pinehurst 28374
Pres. John R. Dempsey
(910) 692-6185

Southeastern Community College
P.O. Box 151, Whiteville 28472
Pres. Stephen C. Scott
(910) 642-7141

Southwestern Community College
275 Webster Rd., Sylva 28779
Pres. Barry W. Russell
(704) 586-4091

Stanly Community College
141 College Dr., Albemarle 28001
Pres. Jan J. Crawford
(704) 982-0121

Surry Community College
S. Maine St., Dobson 27017
Pres. James M. Reeves
(910) 386-8121

Tri-County Community College
2300 Hwy. 64 E., Murphy 28906
Interim Pres. Frank D. Slagle
(704) 847-6810

Vance-Granville Community College
P.O. Box 917, Henderson 27536
Pres. Benjamin F. Currin
(919) 492-2061

Wake Technical Community College
9101 Fayetteville Rd., Raleigh 27603
Pres. Bruce I. Howell
(919) 662-3400

Wayne Community College
Caller Box 8002, Goldsboro 27533-
8002
Pres. Edward H. Wilson, Jr.
(919) 735-5151

Western Piedmont Community College
1001 Burkemont Ave., Morganton
28655-9978
Pres. James A. Richardson
(704) 438-6000

Wilkes Community College
P.O. Box 120, Collegiate Dr.,
Wilkesboro 28697-0120
Interim Pres. Swanson Richards
(910) 651-8600

Wilson Technical Community College
P.O. Box 4305, 902 Herring Ave.
  Woodard Sta., Wilson 27893
Pres. Frank L. Eagles
(919) 291-1195

The University of North Carolina General Administration
P.O. Box 2688, Chapel Hill 27515-2688
Pres. C. D. Spangler, Jr.
(919) 962-1000

Appalachian State University
Boone 28608
Chanc. Francis T. Borkowski
(704) 262-2000

East Carolina University
E. Fifth St., Greenville 27858-4353
Chanc. Richard R. Eakin
(919) 328-6131

Elizabeth City State University
1704 Weeksville Rd., Elizabeth City
  27909
Interim Chanc. Mickey L. Burnim
(919) 335-3400

Fayetteville State University
1200 Murchison Rd., Newbold Sta.,
  Fayetteville 28301-4298
Chanc. Willis B. McLeod
(910) 486-1111

*North Carolina Agricultural and
Technical State University*
1601 E. Market St., Greensboro
  27411
Chanc. Edward B. Fort
(910) 334-7500

North Carolina Central University
1801 Fayetteville St., Durham 27707
Chanc. Julius L. Chambers
(919) 560-6100

North Carolina School of the Arts
200 Waughtown St., P.O. Box
  12189, Winston-Salem 27117-
  2189
Chanc. Alexander C. Ewing
(910) 770-3399

North Carolina State University
P.O. Box 7001, Raleigh 27695-7001
Chanc. Larry K. Monteith
(919) 515-2011

Pembroke State University
P.O. Box 1510, One University Dr.,
  Pembroke 28372-1510
Chanc. Joseph B. Oxendine
(910) 521-6000

*The University of North Carolina at
Asheville*
One University Heights, Asheville
  28804-3299
Chanc. Patsy B. Reed
(704) 251-6600

*The University of North Carolina at
Chapel Hill*
CB 9100, 103 S. Bldg., Chapel Hill
  27599-9100
Chanc. Michael K. Hooker
(919) 962-2211

*The University of North Carolina at
Charlotte*
University City Blvd., Charlotte
  28223
Chanc. James H. Woodward, Jr.
(704) 547-2000

*The University of North Carolina at
Greensboro*
1000 Spring Garden St., Greensboro
  27412
Chanc. Patricia A. Sullivan
(910) 334-5000

*The University of North Carolina at
Wilmington*
601 S. College Rd., Wilmington
  28403-3297
Chanc. James R. Leutze
(910) 395-3000

Western Carolina University
Cullowhee 28723
Chanc. John W. Bardo
(704) 227-7211

Winston-Salem State University
  601 Martin Luther King, Jr. Dr,
    Winston-Salem 27110
  Chanc. Alvin J. Schexnider
  (910) 750-2000

NORTH DAKOTA

North Dakota University System
State Capitol, 600 E. Blvd. Ave.,
Bismarck 58505-0230
Chanc. Larry Isaak
(701) 328-2960

Bismarck State College
1500 Edwards Ave., Bismarck
58501-1299
Pres. Donna S. Thigpen
(701) 224-5400

Dickinson State University
291 Campus Dr., Dickinson 58601-
4896
Pres. Philip W. Conn
(800) 227-2507

Mayville State University
330 3rd St., N.E., Mayville 58257-
1299
Pres. Ellen E. Chaffee
(701) 786-2301

Minot State University
500 University Ave., W., Minot
58707-0001
Pres. H. Erik Shaar
(701) 858-3000

North Dakota State College of Science
800 N. 6th St., Wahpeton 58076-
0001
Pres. Jerry C. Olson
(701) 671-2221

North Dakota State University
State University Sta., Fargo 58105
Pres. Thomas R. Plough
(701) 231-8011

North Dakota State University—
Bottineau
First and Simrall Blvd., Bottineau
58318-1198
Exec. Dean J.W. Smith
(701) 228-2277

University of North Dakota
Box 8193, University Sta., Grand
Forks 58202-8193
Pres. Kendall L. Baker
(701) 777-2011

University of North Dakota—Lake Region
1801 N. College Dr., Devils Lake
58301-1598
Exec. Dean Sharon L. Etemad
(701) 662-1600

University of North Dakota—Williston
P.O. Box 1326, Williston 58802-
1326
Exec. Dean Garvin L. Stevens
(701) 774-4200

Valley City State University
101 College St. S.E., Valley City
58072-4195
Pres. Ellen E. Chaffee
(701) 845-7122

OHIO

Ohio Board of Regents
30 E. Broad St., 36th Fl., Columbus
43266-0417
Chanc. Elaine H. Hairston
(614) 466-6000

Belmont Technical College
120 Fox-Shannon Pl., St. Clairsville
43950
Pres. Wesley R. Channell
(614) 695-9500

Bowling Green State University
Bowling Green 43403
Pres. Sidney A. Ribeau
(419) 372-2531

Central Ohio Technical College
1179 University Dr., Newark 43055-
1767
Pres. Rafael L. Cortada
(614) 366-1351

Central State University
1400 Brush Row Rd., Wilberforce
45384
Pres. Herman B. Smith, Jr.
(513) 376-6011

*Cincinnati State Technical and
Community College*
3520 Central Pkwy., Cincinnati
45223
Pres. James P. Long
(513) 569-1500

Clark State Community College
570 E. Leffels Ln., P.O. Box 570,
Springfield 45505
Pres. Albert A. Salerno
(513) 325-0691

Cleveland State University
Euclid Ave. at E. 24th St., Cleveland
44115
Pres. Claire A. Van Ummersen
(216) 687-2000

Columbus State Community College
550 E. Spring St., P.O. Box 1609,
Columbus 43215-1722
Pres. Marvin G. Gutter
(800) 621-6407

Cuyahoga Community College
700 Carnegie Ave., Cleveland 44115
Pres. Jerry Sue Thornton
(216) 987-6000

Edison State Community College
1973 Edison Dr., Piqua 45356
Pres. Kenneth A. Yowell
(800) 922-3722

Hocking Technical College
3301 Hocking Pkwy., Nelsonville
45764
Pres. John J. Light
(614) 753-3591

Jefferson Community College
4000 Sunset Blvd., Steubenville
43952
Pres. Edward L. Florak
(614) 264-5591

Kent State University
P.O. Box 5190, Kent 44242
Pres. Carol A. Cartwright
(216) 672-3000

Lakeland Community College
7700 Clocktower Dr., Kirkland
44094-5198
Pres. Ralph R. Doty
(800) 589-8520

Lima Technical College
4240 Campus Dr., Lima 45804
Pres. James J. Countryman
(419) 221-1112

Lorain County Community College
1005 N. Abbe Rd., Elyria 44035
Pres. Roy A. Church
(800) 955-5222

Marion Technical College
1467 Mt. Vernon Ave., Marion
43302-5694
Pres. John Richard Bryson
(614) 389-4636

Medical College of Ohio
3000 Arlington, P.O. Box 10008,
Toledo 43699-0008
Pres. Roger C. Bone
(419) 381-4267

Miami University
201 Roudebush Hall, Oxford 45056
Acting Pres. Anne H. Hopkins
(513) 529-1809

Muskingum Area Technical College
1555 Newark Rd., Zanesville 43701
Pres. Lynn H. Willett
(800) 686-8324

North Central Technical College
P.O. Box 698, Mansfield 44901-0698
Pres. Byron E. Kee
(419) 755-4800

Northeastern Ohio Universities College of Medicine
4209 State Rte. 44, P.O. Box 95,
Rootstown 44272-0095
Pres./Dean Robert S. Blacklow
(216) 325-2511

Northwest State Community College
22-600 State Rte. 34, Archbold
43502
Pres. Larry G. McDougle
(419) 267-5511

The Ohio State University
205 Bricker Hall, 190 N. Oval Dr.,
Columbus 43210
Pres. E. Gordon Gee
(614) 292-6446

Ohio University
Athens 45701
Pres. Robert Glidden
(614) 593-1000

Owens Community College
P.O. Box 10000, Toledo 43699
Pres. Daniel H. Brown
(419) 661-7000

Shawnee State University
940 Second St., Portsmouth 45662
Pres. Clive C. Veri
(614) 354-3205

Sinclair Community College
444 W. Third St., Dayton 45402
Pres. David H. Ponitz
(513) 226-2500

Southern State Community College
200 Hobart Dr., Hillsboro 45133
Pres. Lawrence N. Dukes
(513) 393-3431

Stark Technical College
6200 Frank Ave., N.W., Canton
44720
Pres. John J. McGrath, Jr.
(216) 494-6170

Terra State Community College
2830 Napoleon Rd., Fremont 43420
Pres. Charlotte J. Lee
(419) 334-8400

The University of Akron
302 Buchtel Common, Akron 44325
Pres. Peggy Gordon Elliott
(216) 972-7111

University of Akron—Wayne College
1901 Smucker Rd., Orrville 44667
Dean Tyrone M. Turning
(800) 221-8308

University of Cincinnati
P.O. Box 210063, Cincinnati 45221-
0063
Pres. Joseph A. Steger
(513) 556-2201

University of Cincinnati - Raymond Walters College
9555 Plainfield Rd., Cincinnati 45236
Dean Barbara A. Bardes
(513) 745-5600

*University of Cincinnati— Clermont
    College*
    725 College Dr., Batavia 45103
    Dean Roger J. Barry
    (513) 732-5200

University of Toledo
    2801 W. Bancroft St., Toledo 43606
    Pres. Frank E. Horton
    (419) 537-2072

Washington State Community College
    710 Colegate Dr., Marietta 45750
    Pres. Carson K. Miller
    (614) 374-8716

Wright State University
    3640 Colonel Glenn Hwy., Dayton
    45435
    Pres. Harley E. Flack
    (513) 873-3333

Youngstown State University
    410 Wick Ave., Youngstown 44555
    Pres. Leslie H. Cochran
    (216) 742-3000

OKLAHOMA

Oklahoma State Regents for Higher Education
500 Education Bldg., State Capitol
   Complex, Oklahoma City 73105-4503
Chanc. Hans Brisch
(405) 524-9120

Cameron University
2800 Gore Blvd., Lawton 73505-
   6377
Pres. Don Davis
(405) 581-2200

Carl Albert State College
1507 S. McKenna, Poteau 74953-
   5208
Pres. Joe E. White
(918) 647-1200

Connors State College
Rte. 1, Box 1000, Warner 74469-9700
Pres. Ron Garner
(918) 463-2931

East Central University
Ada 74820-6899
Pres. Bill S. Cole
(405) 332-8000

Eastern Oklahoma State College
1301 W. Main St., Wilburton 74578-
   4999
Pres. Bill H. Hill
(918) 465-2361

Langston University
P.O. Box 907, Langston 73050-0907
Pres. Ernest L. Holloway
(405) 466-2231

Murray State College
1100 S. Murray, Tishomingo 73460-
   3130
Pres. Glen Pedersen
(405) 371-2371

Northeastern Oklahoma A&M College
200 I St. N.E., Miami 74354-6497
Pres. Jerry D. Carroll
(918) 542-8441

Northeastern State University
Tahlequah 74464-7099
Pres. W. Roger Webb
(918) 456-5511

Northern Oklahoma College
P.O. Box 310, Tonkawa 74653-0310
Pres. Joe M. Kinzer, Jr.
(405) 628-6200

Northwestern Oklahoma State University
709 Oklahoma Blvd., Alva 73717-
   9848
Pres. Joe J. Struckle
(405) 327-1700

Oklahoma City Community College
7777 S. May Ave., Oklahoma City
   73159-4444
Pres. Robert P. Todd
(405) 682-1611

Oklahoma Panhandle State University
Box 430, Goodwell 73939-9728
Pres. John W. Goodwin
(405) 349-2611

Redlands Community College
1300 S. Country Club Rd., El Reno
   73036-5304
Pres. Larry F. Devane
(405) 262-2552

Rogers State College
Will Rogers and College Hill,
   Claremore 74017-2099
Acting Pres. Danette McNamara-
   Boyle
(918) 343-7500

Rose State College
6420 S.E. 15th St., Midwest City
   73110-2799
Pres. Larry Nutter
(405) 733-7311

Seminole Junior College
P.O. Box 351, Seminole 74868-0351
Pres. James J. Cook
(405) 382-9950

Southeastern Oklahoma State University
 Sta. A, Durant 74701-0609
 Pres. Larry Williams
 (405) 924-0121

Southwestern Oklahoma State University
 100 Campus Dr., Weatherford
 73096-3098
 Pres. Joe Anna Hibler
 (405) 772-6611

Tulsa Junior College
 6111 E. Skelly Dr., Rm. 200, Tulsa
 74135-6198
 Pres. Dean P. Van Trease
 (918) 595-7000

University of Central Oklahoma
 100 N. University Dr., Edmond
 73060-0170
 Pres. George Nigh
 (405) 341-2980

**University of Oklahoma President's
Office**
 660 Parrington Oval, Rm. 110,
 Norman 73019
 Pres. Richard L. Van Horn
 (405) 325-3916

University of Oklahoma
 660 Parrington Oval, Ste. 110,
 Norman 73019-0390
 Pres. David L. Boren
 (405) 325-0311

*University of Oklahoma Health
Sciences Center*
 P.O. Box 26901, Oklahoma
 City 73126-0901
 Interim Provost Joseph Ferretti
 (405) 271-4000

*University of Science and Arts of
Oklahoma*
 P.O. Box 82345, Chickasha 73018-
 0001
 Pres. Roy Troutt
 (405) 224-3140

Western Oklahoma State College
 2801 N. Main St., Altus 73521-1397
 Pres. M. Ray Brown
 (405) 477-2000

OREGON

Oregon Office of Community College
Services
255 Capitol St., N.E., Salem 97310-0203
Commissioner Roger J. Bassett
(503) 378-8648

Blue Mountain Community College
P.O. Box 100, Pendleton 97801
Pres. Ronald L. Daniels
(541) 276-1260

Central Oregon Community College
Bend 97701-5998
Pres. Robert L. Barber
(541) 383-7700

Chemeketa Community College
P.O. Box 14007, Salem 97309
Pres. Gerard J. Berger
(503) 399-5000

Clackamas Community College
19600 S. Molalla Ave., Oregon City
97045
Pres. John S. Keyser
(503) 657-6958

Clatsop Community College
1653 Jerome Ave., Astoria 97103
Pres. John W. Wubben
(503) 325-0910

Lane Community College
4000 E. 30th Ave., Eugene 97405
Pres. Jerry Moskus
(541) 747-4501

Linn-Benton Community College
Albany 97321
Pres. Jon Carnahan
(541) 917-4999

Mount Hood Community College
26000 S.E. Stark St., Gresham
97030
Pres. Paul E. Kreider
(503) 667-6422

Portland Community College
P.O. Box 19000, Portland 97219-
0990
Pres. Daniel F. Moriarty
(503) 244-6111

Rogue Community College
3345 Redwood Hwy., Grants Pass
97527
Pres. Harvey Bennett
(541) 479-5541

Southwestern Oregon Community College
1988 Newmark, Coos Bay 97420
Pres. Stephen Kridelbaugh
(541) 888-2525

Treasure Valley Community College
Ontario 97914
Pres. Berton Glandon
(541) 889-6493

Umpqua Community College
Roseburg 97470
Pres. James M. Kraby
(541) 440-4600

Oregon State System of Higher Education
P.O. Box 3175, Eugene 97403-0175
Chanc. Joseph W. Cox
(541) 346-5700

Eastern Oregon State College
La Grande 97850
Pres. David E. Gilbert
(541) 962-3512

Oregon Health Sciences University
3181 S.W. Sam Jackson Park Rd.,
Portland 97201
Pres. Peter O. Kohler
(503) 494-8252

Oregon Institute of Technology
Klamath Falls 97601-8801
Pres. Lawrence J. Wolf
(541) 885-1103

Oregon State University
Corvallis 97331
Pres. Paul G. Risser
(541) 737-2565

Portland State University
P.O. Box 751, Portland 97207
Pres. Judith A. Ramaley
(503) 725-4419

Southern Oregon State College
Ashland 97520
Pres. Stephen J. Reno
(541) 552-6111

University of Oregon
Eugene 97403-1226
Pres. David B. Frohnmayer
(541) 346-3036

Western Oregon State College
345 N. Monmouth Ave., Monmouth
97361
Pres. Betty J. Youngblood
(503) 838-8215

PENNSYLVANIA

**Community College of Allegheny County
College Office**
800 Allegheny Ave., Pittsburgh 15233
Pres. John M. Kingsmore
(412) 323-2323

*Community College of Allegheny County
Allegheny Campus*
808 Ridge Ave., Pittsburgh 15212
Exec. Dean/Vice Pres. J. David
Griffin
(412) 237-2525

*Community College of Allegheny County
Boyce Campus*
595 Beatty Rd., Monroeville 15146
Vice Pres./Exec. Dean Jacqueline D.
Taylor
(412) 371-8651

*Community College of Allegheny County
North Campus*
8701 Perry Hwy., Pittsburgh 15237
Vice Pres./Exec. Dean Patricia A.
McDonald
(412) 366-7000

*Community College of Allegheny County
South Campus*
1750 Clairton Rd., Rte. 885, West
Mifflin 15122
Exec. Dean/Vice Pres. Thomas A.
Juravich
(412) 469-1100

**Pennsylvania State System of Higher
Education**
Dixon University Ctr., 2986 North
Second St., Harrisburg 17110
Chanc. James H. McCormick
(717) 720-4000

Bloomsburg University of Pennsylvania
400 E. 2nd St., Bloomsburg 17815
Pres. Jessica S. Kozloff
(717) 389-4000

California University of Pennsylvania
250 University Ave., California
15419-1934
Pres. Angelo Armenti, Jr.
(412) 938-4000

Cheyney University of Pennsylvania
Cheyney and Creek Rds., Cheyney
19319
Interim Pres. Donald L. Mullett
(610) 399-2000

Clarion University of Pennsylvania
Clarion 16214
Pres. Diane L. Reinhard
(814) 226-2000

*East Stroudsburg University of
Pennsylvania*
200 Prospect St., East Stroudsburg
18301
Pres. James E. Gilbert
(717) 422-3211

Edinboro University of Pennsylvania
Edinboro 16444
Pres. Foster F. Diebold
(814) 732-2000

Indiana University of Pennsylvania
Indiana 15705
Pres. Lawrence K. Pettit
(412) 357-2100

Kutztown University of Pennsylvania
Kutztown 19530
Pres. David E. McFarland
(610) 683-4000

Lock Haven University of Pennsylvania
Lock Haven 17745
Pres. Craig D. Willis
(717) 893-2011

Mansfield University of Pennsylvania
Academy St., Mansfield 16933
Pres. Rodney C. Kelchner
(717) 662-4000

Millersville University of Pennsylvania
  P.O. Box 1002, Millersville 17551-
    1002
  Pres. Joseph A. Caputo
  (717) 872-3024

Shippensburg University of Pennsylvania
  Shippensburg 17257
  Pres. Anthony F. Ceddia
  (717) 532-9121

Slippery Rock University of Pennsylvania
  Slippery Rock 16057
  Pres. Robert N. Aebersold
  (412) 738-0512

West Chester University of Pennsylvania
  S. High St., West Chester 19383
  Pres. Madeleine Wing Adler
  (610) 436-1000

PUERTO RICO

**Inter American University of Puerto Rico
Central Administration**
P.O. Box 363255, San Juan 00936-3255
Pres. Jose R. Gonzalez
(809) 766-1912

*Inter American University of Puerto Rico
Aguadilla Campus*
P.O. Box 20000, Aguadilla 00605-
2000
Chanc. Hilda M. Baco
(809) 891-0925

*Inter American University of Puerto Rico
Arecibo Campus*
P.O. Box 4050, Arecibo 00614-4050
Chanc. Zaida Vega-Lugo
(809) 878-5475

*Inter American University of Puerto Rico
Barranquitas Campus*
P.O. Box 517, Barranquitas 00794
Chanc. Irene Fernandez
(809) 857-2585

*Inter American University of Puerto Rico
Bayamon Campus*
Urb. Industrial Minillas, Carr. 174
No. 172, Bayamon 00959-1911
Chanc. Felix Torres-Leon
(809) 780-4040

*Inter American University of Puerto Rico
Fajardo Campus*
P.O. Box 1029, Fajardo 00738-1029
Chanc. Yolanda Robles-Garcia
(809) 863-2390

*Inter American University of Puerto Rico
Guayama Campus*
P.O. Box 10004, Guayama 00785
Chanc. Samuel F. Febres
(809) 864-2222

*Inter American University of Puerto Rico
Metropolitan Campus*
P.O. Box 191293, San Juan 00919-
1293
Chanc. Manuel J. Fernos
(809) 250-1912

*Inter American University of Puerto Rico
Ponce Campus*
Bo. Sabanetas, Carr. 1, Mercedita
00715
Chanc. Marilina L. Wayland
(809) 284-1912

*Inter American University of Puerto Rico
San German Campus*
P.O. Box 5100, San German 00683-
9801
Chanc. Agnes Mojica
(809) 264-1912

*Inter American University of Puerto Rico
School of Law*
P.O. Box 70351, San Juan 00936-
8351
Dean Carlos E. Ramos-Gonzalez
(809) 751-1912

*Inter American University of Puerto Rico
School of Optometry*
P.O. Box 191049, San Juan 00919-
1049
Dean Arthur J. Afanador
(809) 765-1915

**Sistema Universitario Ana G. Mendez
Central Office**
P.O. Box 21345, San Juan 00928-1345
Pres. Jose F. Mendez
(809) 751-0178

Colegio Universitario del Este
P.O. Box 2010, Carolina 00983-2010
Chanc. Alberto Maldonado Ruiz
(809) 257-7373

Universidad Metropolitana
Box 21150, Rio Piedras 00928
Chanc. Rene L. Labarca Bonnet
(809) 766-1717

Universidad del Turabo
Box 3030, Gurabo 00778
Rector Dennis Aliceo Rodriguez
(809) 743-7979

University of Puerto Rico Central Administration
P.O. Box 363255, San Juan 00936-4984
Pres. Norman I. Maldonado
(809) 250-0000

University of Puerto Rico Regional Colleges Administration
P.O. Box 21876, San Juan 00931-1876
Chanc. Juan J. Adrover-Santiago
(809) 758-3454

University of Puerto Rico—Aguadilla Regional College
P.O. Box 250160, Aguadilla 00604-0160
Dir. Juana Segarra-Jaramillo
(809) 890-2681

University of Puerto Rico—Arecibo Technological University College
P.O. Box 1806, Arecibo 00613
Dir. Juan Ramirez
(809) 828-2830

University of Puerto Rico—Bayamon Technological University College
Bayamon Gardens Sta., Bayamon 00959-1919
Dir. Carmen Ana Rivera
(809) 786-6840

University of Puerto Rico—Carolina Regional College
P.O. Box 4800, Carolina 00984-4800
Acting Dean/Dir. Myrna Mayol
(809) 257-0000

University of Puerto Rico—La Montana Regional College
P.O. Box 2500, Utuado 00641
Acting Dean/Dir. Ramon Colon Murphy
(809) 894-2828

University of Puerto Rico—Ponce Technological University College
P.O. Box 7186, Ponce 00732
Dir. Antonia Lopez
(809) 844-8181

University of Puerto Rico—Cayey Campus
Antonio R. Barcelo Ave., Cayey 00633
Chanc. Jose Luis Monserrate
(809) 738-2161

University of Puerto Rico—Humacao Campus
CUH Sta., Humacao 00661
Chanc. Roberto Marrero-Corletto
(809) 850-0000

University of Puerto Rico—Mayaguez Campus
P.O. Box 5000, College Sta., Mayaguez 00681
Chanc. Stuart Ramos
(809) 834-4040

University of Puerto Rico—Medical Sciences Campus
P.O. Box 365067, San Juan 00936-5067
Chanc. Jorge L. Sanchez-Colon
(809) 758-2525

University of Puerto Rico—Rio Piedras Campus
Ponce de Leon Ave., Stop 38, San Juan 00931
Chanc. Efrain Gonzalez Tejera
(809) 764-0000

RHODE ISLAND

State of Rhode Island Office of Higher Education
  301 Promenade St., Providence 02908-5089
  Commissioner Americo W. Petrocelli
  (401) 277-6560

Community College of Rhode Island
  400 East Ave., Warwick 02886-1805
  Pres. Edward J. Liston
  (401) 825-2188

Rhode Island College
  Providence 02908
  Pres. John Nazarian
  (401) 456-8100

University of Rhode Island
  Kingston 02881-0806
  Pres. Robert L. Carothers
  (401) 792-2444

SOUTH CAROLINA

South Carolina Commission on Higher Education
1333 Main St., Ste. 200, Columbia 29201
Commissioner Fred R. Sheheen
(803) 253-6260

The Citadel
Citadel Sta., 171 Moultrie St.,
Charleston 29409-0205
Pres. Claudius E. Watts, III
(803) 353-5000

Clemson University
201 Sikes Hall, Clemson 29634
Pres. Constantine W. Curris
(803) 656-3311

Coastal Carolina University
P.O. Box 1954, Myrtle Beach 29526
Chanc. Ronald R. Ingle
(803) 347-3161

College of Charleston
66 George St., Charleston 29424
Pres. Alexander M. Sanders, Jr.
(803) 953-5507

Francis Marion University
P.O. Box 100547, Florence 29501-
0547
Pres. Lee A. Vickers
(803) 661-1362

Lander University
320 Stanley Ave., Greenwood
29649-2099
Pres. William C. Moran
(803) 229-8200

Medical University of South Carolina
171 Ashley Ave., Charleston 29425
Pres. James B. Edwards
(803) 792-2211

South Carolina State University
300 College Ave. N.E., Orangeburg
29117
Interim Pres. Leroy Davis
(803) 536-7000

University of South Carolina Central Office
Columbia 29208
Pres. John M. Palms
(803) 777-2001

University of South Carolina—Aiken
171 University Pkwy., Aiken
29801
Chanc. Robert E. Alexander
(803) 648-6851

University of South Carolina—Columbia
Columbia 29208
Pres. John M. Palms
(803) 777-7000

University of South Carolina—Spartanburg
800 University Way,
Spartanburg 29303
Chanc. John C. Stockwell
(803) 599-2000

Winthrop University
701 Oakland Ave., Rock Hill 29733
Pres. Anthony J. DiGiorgio
(803) 323-2211

South Carolina State Board for Technical and Comprehensive Education
111 Executive Center Dr., Columbia
29210
Exec. Dir. Michael B. McCall
(803) 737-9320

Aiken Technical College
P.O. Box 696, Aiken 29802-0696
Pres. Kathleen A. Noble
(803) 593-9231

Central Carolina Technical College
506 N. Guignard Dr., Sumter 29150-
2499
Pres. Herbert C. Robbins
(803) 778-1961

Chesterfield-Marlboro Technical College
1201 Chesterfield Hwy., Cheraw
29520-1007
Pres. Ronald W. Hampton
(803) 921-6900

Denmark Technical College
P.O. Box 327, Denmark 29042-0327
Pres. Joann R. G. Boyd-Scotland
(803) 793-3301

Florence-Darlington Technical College
P.O. Box 100548, Florence 29501-0548
Pres. Charles W. Gould
(803) 661-8324

Greenville Technical College
P.O. Box 5616, Sta. B, Greenville
29606-5616
Pres. Thomas E. Barton, Jr.
(803) 250-8000

Horry-Georgetown Technical College
P.O. Box 1966, Conway 29526-1966
Pres. D. Kent Sharples
(803) 347-3186

Midlands Technical College
P.O. Box 2408, Columbia 29202-2408
Pres. James L. Hudgins
(803) 738-1400

Orangeburg-Calhoun Technical College
3250 St. Matthews Rd., N.E.,
Orangeburg 29118
Pres. Jeffery R. Olson
(803) 536-0311

Piedmont Technical College
P.O. Drawer 1467, Greenwood
29648-1467
Pres. Lex D. Walters
(803) 941-8324

Spartanburg Technical College
P.O. Drawer 4386, Spartanburg
29305-4386
Pres. Jack A. Powers
(803) 591-3600

Technical College of the Lowcountry
921 S. Ribaut Rd., P.O. Box 1288,
Beaufort 29901-1288
Pres. Anne S. McNutt
(803) 525-8324

Tri-County Technical College
P.O. Box 587, Hwy. 76, Pendleton
29670-0587
Pres. Don C. Garrison
(803) 646-8361

Trident Technical College
P.O. Box 118067, Charleston 29423-8067
Pres. Mary Dellamura Thornley
(803) 572-6111

Williamsburg Technical College
601 MLK Jr. Ave., Kingstree 29556-4197
Pres. Norman Scott
(803) 354-2021

York Technical College
452 S. Anderson Rd., Rock Hill
29730-3395
Pres. Dennis F. Merrell
(803) 327-8000

SOUTH DAKOTA

South Dakota Board of Regents
207 E. Capitol Ave., Pierre 57501-3159
Exec. Dir. Robert T. Tad Perry
(605) 773-3455

Black Hills State University
1200 University Ave., Spearfish
57799-9500
Pres. Thomas O. Flickema
(605) 642-6011

Dakota State University
820 N. Washington St., Madison
57042
Pres. Jerald A. Tunheim
(605) 256-5111

Northern State University
1200 S. Jay St., Aberdeen 57401
Pres. John Hutchinson
(605) 626-2521

*South Dakota School of Mines and
Technology*
501 E. St. Joseph St., Rapid City
57701
Pres. Richard J. Gowen
(605) 394-2511

South Dakota State University
Box 2201, University Sta.,
Brookings 57007
Pres. Robert T. Wagner
(605) 688-4151

The University of South Dakota
414 E. Clark St., Vermillion 57069-
2390
Pres. Betty Turner Asher
(605) 677-5276

TENNESSEE

Tennessee Board of Regents
1415 Murfreesboro Rd., Ste. 350,
Nashville 37217-2833
Chanc. Charles E. Smith
(615) 366-4400

Austin Peay State University
601 College St., Clarksville 37044
Pres. Sal D. Rinella
(615) 648-7011

*Chattanooga State Technical Community
College*
4501 Amnicola Hwy., Chattanooga
37406
Pres. James L. Catanzaro
(423) 697-4400

Cleveland State Community College
P.O. Box 3570, Cleveland 37320-
3570
Pres. Owen F. Cargol
(423) 472-7141

Columbia State Community College
P.O. Box 1315, 1665 Hampshire
Pike, Columbia 38402-1315
Pres. L. Paul Sands
(615) 540-2722

Dyersburg State Community College
1510 Lake Rd., Dyersburg 38024
Pres. Karen A. Bowyer
(901) 286-3200

East Tennessee State University
P.O. Box 70734, Johnson City
37614-0734
Pres. Roy S. Nicks
(423) 929-4112

Jackson State Community College
2046 North Pkwy., Jackson 38301-
3797
Pres. Walter L. Nelms
(901) 424-3520

Middle Tennessee State University
1301 E. Main St., Murfreesboro
37132
Pres. James E. Walker
(615) 898-2300

Motlow State Community College
P.O. Box 88100, Ledford Mill Rd.,
Tullahoma 37388-8100
Pres. A. Frank Glass
(615) 393-1500

Nashville State Technical Institute
120 White Bridge Rd., Nashville
37209-4515
Pres. George H. Van Allen
(615) 353-3333

*Northeast State Technical Community
College*
P.O. Box 246, 2425 Hwy. 75,
Blountville 37617-0246
Pres. R. Wade Powers
(423) 323-3191

*Pellissippi State Technical Community
College*
10915 Hardin Valley Rd., P.O. Box
22990, Knoxville 37933-0990
Pres. Allen G. Edwards
(423) 694-6400

Roane State Community College
276 Patton Ln., Harriman 37748
Pres. Sherry L. Hoppe
(423) 354-3000

Shelby State Community College
P.O. Box 40568, Memphis 38174-
0568
Interim Pres. Mark L. Stansbury
(901) 544-5000

State Technical Institute at Memphis
5983 Macon Cove, Memphis 38134-
7693
Pres. Doug Call
(901) 383-4111

Tennessee State University
  3500 John Merritt Blvd., Nashville
    37209-1561
  Pres. James A. Hefner
  (615) 963-5000

Tennessee Technological University
  N. Dixie Ave., Campus Box 5007,
    Cookeville 38505
  Pres. Angelo A. Volpe
  (615) 372-3101

The University of Memphis
  Memphis 38152
  Pres. V. Lane Rawlins
  (901) 678-2000

Volunteer State Community College
  1360 Nashville Pike, Gallatin 37066
  Pres. Hal R. Ramer
  (615) 452-8600

Walters State Community College
  500 S. Davy Crockett Pkwy.,
    Morristown 37813-6899
  Pres. Jack E. Campbell
  (615) 585-2600

The University of Tennessee System
  Knoxville 37996
  Pres. Joseph E. Johnson
  (615) 974-2241

*The University of Tennessee at
  Chattanooga*
    615 McCallie Ave., Chattanooga
      37403-2598
    Chanc. Frederick W. Obear
    (423) 744-4111

The University of Tennessee at Martin
  University St., Martin 38238
  Chanc. Margaret N. Perry
  (901) 587-7000

The University of Tennessee, Knoxville
  527 Andy Holt Tower, Knoxville
    37996-0150
  Chanc. William T. Snyder
  (615) 974-1000

The University of Tennessee, Memphis
  800 Madison Ave., Memphis 38163
  Chanc. William R. Rice
  (901) 448-5500

TEXAS

Texas Higher Education Coordinating Board
P.O. Box 12788, Capitol Sta., Austin 78711
Commissioner Kenneth H. Ashworth
(512) 483-6100

Alamo Community College District
811 W. Houston St., San Antonio 78207-3033
Chanc. Robert W. Ramsay
(210) 220-1520

Palo Alto College
1400 W. Villaret Blvd., San Antonio 78224-2499
Pres. Joel E. Vela
(210) 921-5260

San Antonio College
1300 San Pedro Ave., San Antonio 78284
Pres. Ruth Burgos-Sasscer
(210) 733-2000

St. Philip's College
211 Nevada St., San Antonio 78203
Pres. Charles A. Taylor
(210) 531-3500

Alvin Community College
3110 Mustang Rd., Alvin 77511-4898
Pres. A. Rodney Allbright
(713) 331-6111

Amarillo College
P.O. Box 447, Amarillo 79178
Pres. Luther Bud Joyner
(806) 371-5000

Angelina College
P.O. Box 1768, Lufkin 75902
Pres. Larry M. Phillips
(409) 639-1301

Austin Community College
5930 Middle Fiskville Rd., Austin 78752-4390
Pres. William E. Segura
(512) 483-7598

Bee County College
3800 Charco Rd., Beeville 78102
Pres. Norman E. Wallace
(512) 358-3130

Blinn College
902 College Ave., Brenham 77833
Pres. Donald Voelter
(409) 830-4000

Brazosport College
500 College Dr., Lake Jackson 77566
Pres. John R. Grable
(409) 266-3000

Central Texas College
P.O. Box 1800, Killeen 76540-9990
Chanc. James R. Anderson
(817) 526-7161

Cisco Junior College
Rte. 3, Box 3, Cisco 76437
Pres. Roger C. Schustereit
(817) 442-2567

Clarendon College
P.O. Box 968, Clarendon 79226
Pres. Scott Elliott
(806) 874-3571

College of the Mainland
1200 Amburn Rd., Texas City 77591
Pres. Larry L. Stanley
(409) 938-1211

Collin County Community College
2200 W. University Dr., McKinney 75070-8001
Pres. John H. Anthony
(214) 548-6790

Dallas County Community College District
701 Elm St., Dallas 75202-3299
Chanc. J. William Wenrich
(214) 746-2125

Brookhaven College
3939 Valley View Ln., Farmers
Branch 75244-4997
Pres. Walter G. Bumphus
(214) 620-4700

Cedar Valley College
3030 N. Dallas Ave., Lancaster
75134
Pres. Carol J. Spencer
(214) 372-8200

Eastfield College
3737 Motley Dr., Mesquite
75150-2099
Pres. Robert Aguero
(214) 324-7100

El Centro College
Main and Lamar Sts., Dallas
75202-3604
Pres. Wright L. Lassiter, Jr.
(214) 746-2010

Mountain View College
4849 W. Illinois Ave., Dallas
75211-6599
Pres. Monique Amerman
(214) 333-8700

North Lake College
5001 N. MacArthur Blvd.,
Irving 75038-3899
Pres. James F. Horton, Jr.
(214) 659-5229

Richland College
12800 Abrams Rd., Dallas
75243-2199
Pres. Stephen K. Mittelstet
(214) 238-6194

Del Mar College
Baldwin and Ayers, Corpus Christi
78404-3897
Pres. Terry L. Dicianna
(512) 886-1200

East Texas State University
ETSU Sta., Commerce 75429-3011
Pres. Jerry D. Morris
(903) 886-5102

East Texas State University at Texarkana
P.O. Box 5518, Texarkana 75505-
0518
Pres. Stephen R. Hensley
(903) 838-6514

El Paso Community College
P.O. Box 20500, El Paso 79998
Pres. Adriana D. Barrera
(915) 594-2000

Frank Phillips College
P.O. Box 5118, Borger 79008-5118
Pres. William A. Griffin, Jr.
(806) 274-5311

Galveston College
4015 Ave. Q, Galveston 77550
Pres. Carlisle B. Rathburn, III
(409) 763-6551

Grayson County College
6101 Grayson Dr., Denison 75020
Pres. James M. Williams, Jr.
(903) 465-6030

Hill College
112 Lamar Dr., Hillsboro 76645
Pres. William R. Auvenshine
(817) 582-2555

Houston Community College System
P.O. Box 7849, Houston 77270-7849
Interim Chanc. James Harding
(713) 869-5021

Howard County Junior College District
1001 Birdwell Ln., Big Spring 79720
Pres. Cheryl T. Sparks
(915) 267-6311

Howard College
1001 Birdwell Ln., Big Spring
79720
Pres. Cheryl T. Sparks
(915) 264-5000

Kilgore College
1100 Broadway, Kilgore 75662-
3299
Pres. J. Frank Thornton
(903) 984-8531

Laredo Community College
W. End Washington St., Laredo
78040-4395
Pres. Ramon H. Dovalina
(210) 722-0521

Lee College
P.O. Box 818, Baytown 77522-0818
Pres. Jackson N. Sasser
(713) 427-5611

McLennan Community College
1400 College Dr., Waco 76708
Pres. Dennis F. Michaelis
(817) 756-0934

Midland College
3600 N. Garfield St., Midland
79705
Pres. David E. Daniel
(915) 685-4500

Midwestern State University
3410 Taft Blvd., Wichita Falls
76308-2099
Pres. Louis J. Rodriguez
(817) 689-4000

Navarro College
3200 W. Seventh Ave., Corsicana
75110
Pres. Gerald E. Burson
(903) 874-6501

North Central Texas Community College
1525 W. California St., Gainesville
76240-4699
Pres. Ronnie Glasscock
(817) 668-7731

*North Harris Montgomery Community
College District*
250 N. Sam Houston Pkwy., East
Houston 77060
Chanc. John E. Pickelman
(713) 591-3500

Northeast Texas Community College
P.O. Drawer 1307, Mount Pleasant
75456-1307
Pres. Charles Florio
(903) 572-1911

Odessa College
201 W. University Blvd., Odessa
79764
Pres. Vance Gipson
(915) 335-6400

Panola College
1109 W. Panola St., Carthage 75633
Pres. William Edmonson
(903) 693-2022

Paris Junior College
2400 Clarksville St., Paris 75460
Pres. Bobby R. Walters
(903) 784-9370

Ranger College
College Cir., Ranger 76470-3298
Pres. Joe Mills
(817) 647-3234

San Jacinto College District
4624 Fairmont Pwy., Ste. 200,
Pasadena 77504
Chanc. J.B. Whiteley
(713) 998-6100

South Plains College
1401 College Ave., Levelland 79336
Pres. Gary D. McDaniel
(806) 894-9611

Southwest Texas Junior College
2401 Garner Field Rd., Uvalde
78801-6297
Pres. Billy Word
(210) 278-4401

Stephen F. Austin State University
P.O. Box 6078, SFA Sta.,
Nacogdoches 75962
Pres. Daniel D. Angel
(409) 468-2201

Tarrant County Junior College
1500 Houston St., Fort Worth
76102-6599
Chanc. C. A. Roberson
(817) 336-7851

Temple Junior College
2600 S. First St., Temple 76504-
7435
Pres. Marc A. Nigliazzo
(817) 773-9961

Texarkana College
2500 N. Robinson Rd., Texarkana
75501
Pres. Carl M. Nelson
(903) 838-4541

The Texas A&M University System
State Headquarters Bldg., 301
Tarrow, 7th Fl., College Station
77843-1122
Chanc. Barry B. Thompson
(409) 845-3211

Prairie View A&M University
P.O. Box 188, Prairie View
77429
Pres. Charles A. Hines
(409) 857-3311

Tarleton State University
1333 W. Washington St.,
Tarleton Sta., Stephenville
76402
Pres. Dennis P. McCabe
(817) 968-9100

Texas A&M International University
5201 University Blvd., Laredo
78041
Interim Pres. Hose Garcia
(210) 326-2001

Texas A&M University
College Sta. 77843
Pres. Ray M. Bowen
(409) 845-3211

Texas A&M University at Galveston
P.O. Box 1675, Galveston
77553
Pres. Robert A. Duce
(409) 740-4400

*Texas A&M University—Corpus
Christi*
6300 Ocean Dr., Corpus Christi
78412
Pres. Robert R. Furgason
(512) 991-5700

Texas A&M University—Kingsville
Campus Box 101, Kingsville
78363
Pres. Manuel L. Ibanez
(512) 595-2111

West Texas A&M University
2501 Fourth Ave., P.O. Box
997, W.T. Station, Canyon
79016
Pres. Russell C. Long
(806) 656-2100

Texas Southern University
3100 Cleburne St., Houston 77004
Pres. James M. Douglas
(713) 527-7011

Texas Southmost College
80 Fort Brown St., Brownsville
78520
District Exec. Dir. Michael Putegnat
(210) 544-8200

Texas State Technical College System
3801 Campus Dr., Waco 76705
Chanc. Cecil L. Groves
(817) 799-3611

Texas State Technical College—
Harlingen
  2424 Boxwood St., Harlingen
  78550
  Pres. J. Gilbert Leal
  (210) 425-4922

Texas State Technical College—
Sweetwater
  Rte. 3, Box 18, Sweetwater
  79556
  Pres. Clay G. Johnson
  (915) 235-7300

Texas State Technical College—
Waco
  3801 Campus Dr., Waco 76705
  Pres. Fred L. Williams
  (817) 799-3611

The Texas State University System
  333 Guadalupe St., Tower III, Ste.
  810, Austin 78701-3942
  Chanc. Lamar Urbanovsky
  (512) 463-1808

Angelo State University
  2601 West Ave. N., San Angelo
  76909
  Pres. James Hindman
  (915) 942-2073

Lamar University
  P.O. Box 10001, Beaumont
  77710
  Pres. Rex L. Cottle
  (409) 880-7011

Lamar University—Institute of
Technology
  P.O. Box 10001, Beaumont
  77710
  Pres. Robert Krienke
  (409) 880-8185

Lamar University—Orange
  410 W. Front St., Orange
  77630
  Pres. J. Michael Shahan
  (409) 883-7750

Lamar University—Port Arthur
  P.O. Box 310, Port Arthur
  77641-0310
  Pres. W. Sam Monroe
  (409) 983-4921

Sam Houston State University
  Huntsville 77341
  Interim Pres. B. K. Marks
  (409) 294-1111

Southwest Texas State University
  P.O. Box 1002, SWTSU
  Station, San Marcos 78666-
  4616
  Pres. Jerome H. Supple
  (512) 245-2121

Sul Ross State University
  Hwy. 90, Alpine 79832
  Pres. R. Victor Morgan
  (915) 837-8011

Texas Tech University
  P.O. Box 4349, Lubbock 79409
  Pres. Robert W. Lawless
  (806) 742-2011

Texas Tech University Health Sciences
Center
  3601 Fourth St., Lubbock 79430
  Pres. Robert W. Lawless
  (806) 743-3111

Texas Woman's University
  P.O. Box 425587, Denton 76204-
  3587
  Pres. Carol D. Surles
  (817) 898-3201

Trinity Valley Community College
  500 S. Prairieville, Athens 75751
  Pres. Ronald C. Baugh
  (903) 677-8822

Tyler Junior College
  P.O. Box 9020, Tyler 75711
  Interim Pres. William R. Crowe
  (903) 510-2200

University of Houston System
1600 Smith St., Ste. 3400, Houston
77002
Chanc. William P. Hobby
(713) 754-7404

University of Houston
4800 Calhoun Blvd., Houston
77004
Pres. Glenn A. Goerke
(713) 749-1000

University of Houston—Clear Lake
2700 Bay Area Blvd., Houston
77058
Pres. William A. Staples
(713) 488-7170

University of Houston—Downtown
One Main St., Houston 77002
Pres. Max Castillo
(713) 221-8000

University of Houston—Victoria
2506 E. Red River, Victoria
77901-4450
Interim Pres. Karen Haynes
(512) 576-3151

University of North Texas
P.O. Box 13737, Denton 76203
Chanc. Alfred F. Hurley
(817) 565-2000

*University of North Texas Health Science
Center at Fort Worth*
3500 Camp Bowie Blvd., Fort
Worth 76107-2970
Pres. David M. Richards
(817) 735-2000

University of North Texas
P.O. Box 13737, Denton 76203
Chanc. Alfred F. Hurley
(817) 565-2000

*University of North Texas Health Science
Center at Fort Worth*
3500 Camp Bowie Blvd., Fort
Worth 76107-2970
Pres. David M. Richards
(817) 735-2000

The University of Texas System
601 Colorado St., Austin 78701
Chanc. William H. Cunningham
(512) 499-4201

*The University of Texas Health
Science Center at Houston*
P.O. Box 20036, Houston 77225
Pres. M. David Low
(713) 792-2121

*The University of Texas Health
Science Center at San Antonio*
7703 Floyd Curl Dr., San
Antonio 78284-7834
Pres. John P. Howe, III
(210) 567-7000

*The University of Texas Medical
Branch at Galveston*
301 University Blvd., Ste. 604,
Galveston 77550
Pres. Thomas N. James
(409) 761-1011

*The University of Texas
Southwestern Medical Center at
Dallas*
5323 Harry Hines Blvd., Dallas
75235-9002
Pres. C. Kern Wildenthal
(214) 648-3111

The University of Texas at Arlington
701 S. Nedderman, Arlington
76019
Pres. Robert E. Witt
(817) 273-3365

The University of Texas at Austin
University Sta., Austin 78712
Pres. Robert M. Berdahl
(512) 471-3434

*The University of Texas at
Brownsville/Texas Southmost
College Partnership*
80 Fort Brown, Brownsville
78520
Pres. Juliet V. Garcia
(210) 544-8200

The University of Texas at Dallas
P.O. Box 830688, Richardson
75083-0688
Pres. Franklyn G. Jenifer
(214) 883-2111

The University of Texas at El Paso
500 W. University Ave., El
Paso 79968-0500
Pres. Diana S. Natalicio
(915) 747-5000

The University of Texas at San Antonio
6900 N. Loop 1604 W., San
Antonio 78249-0617
Pres. Samuel A. Kirkpatrick
(210) 691-4100

The University of Texas at Tyler
3900 University Blvd., Tyler
75799
Pres. George F. Hamm
(903) 566-7000

The University of Texas of the Permian Basin
4901 E. University Blvd.,
Odessa 79762
Pres. Charles A. Sorber
(915) 552-2020

The University of Texas—Pan American
1201 W. University Dr.,
Edinburg 78539-2999
Pres. Miguel A. Nevarez
(210) 381-2011

Vernon Regional Junior College
4400 College Dr., Vernon 76384-4092
Pres. R. Wade Kirk
(817) 552-6291

The Victoria College
2200 E. Red River St., Victoria
77901-4494
Pres. Jimmy L. Goodson
(512) 573-3291

Weatherford College
308 E. Park Ave., Weatherford
76086
Pres. James Boyd
(817) 594-5471

Western Texas College
6200 S. College Ave., Snyder 79549
Pres. Harry L. Krenek
(915) 573-8511

Wharton County Junior College
911 Boling Hwy., Wharton 77488
Pres. Frank R. Vivelo
(409) 532-4560

UTAH

Utah System of Higher Education
355 W. North Temple, 3 Triad Ctr., Ste.
550, Salt Lake City 84180-1205
Commissioner Cecelia H. Foxley
(801) 321-7103

College of Eastern Utah
Price 84501
Pres. Michael A. Petersen
(801) 637-2120

Dixie College
St. George 84770
Pres. Robert C. Huddleston
(801) 652-7501

Salt Lake Community College
P.O. Box 30808, Salt Lake City
84130
Pres. Frank W. Budd
(801) 957-4227

Snow College
Ephraim 84627
Pres. Gerald J. Day
(801) 283-4021

Southern Utah University
Cedar City 84720
Pres. Gerald R. Sherratt
(801) 586-7701

University of Utah
Salt Lake City 84112
Pres. Arthur K. Smith
(801) 581-5701

Utah State University
Logan 84322-1400
Pres. George H. Emert
(801) 797-1157

Utah Valley State College
800 W. 1200 S., Orem 84058
Pres. Kerry D. Romesburg
(801) 222-8133

Weber State University
3750 Harrison Blvd., Ogden 84408-
1004
Pres. Paul H. Thompson
(801) 626-6001

VERMONT

Vermont State Colleges
P.O. Box 359, Waterbury 05676-0359
Chanc. Charles I. Bunting
(802) 241-2520

Castleton State College
Castleton 05735
Pres. Martha K. Farmer
(802) 468-5611

Community College of Vermont
Waterbury 05676
Pres. Barbara E. Murphy
(802) 241-3535

Johnson State College
Johnson 05656
Pres. Robert T. Hahn
(802) 635-2356

Lyndon State College
Vail Hill, Lyndonville 05851
Pres. Margaret R. (Peggy) Williams
(802) 626-9371

Vermont Technical College
Randolph Center 05061
Pres. Robert G. Clarke
(802) 728-3391

VIRGINIA

**Commonwealth of Virginia Council of
Higher Education**
James Monroe Bldg., 101 N. 14th St.,
Richmond 23219
Dir. Gordon K. Davies
(804) 225-2600

Christopher Newport University
50 Shoe Ln., Newport News 23606-
2998
Pres. Paul S. Trible, Jr.
(804) 594-7000

**The College of William and Mary
Central Office**
Williamsburg 23187-8795
Pres. Timothy J. Sullivan
(804) 221-4000

The College of William and Mary
P.O. Box 8795, Williamsburg
23187-8795
Pres. Timothy J. Sullivan
(804) 221-4000

Richard Bland College
11301 Johnson Rd., Petersburg
23805
Pres. Clarence Maze, Jr.
(804) 862-6213

George Mason University
4400 University Dr., Fairfax 22030-
4444
Pres. George W. Johnson
(703) 993-1000

James Madison University
Harrisonburg 22807
Pres. Ronald E. Carrier
(703) 568-6211

Longwood College
201 High St., Farmville 23909
Pres. William F. Dorrill
(804) 395-2000

Mary Washington College
1301 College Ave., Fredericksburg
22401
Pres. William M. Anderson, Jr.
(703) 898-4100

Norfolk State University
2401 Corprew Ave., Norfolk 23504
Pres. Harrison B. Wilson
(804) 683-8600

Old Dominion University
5215 Hampton Blvd., Norfolk
23529
Pres. James V. Koch
(804) 683-3000

Radford University
Box 6890, Radford 24142
Pres. H. Douglas Covington
(703) 831-5000

University of Virginia Central Office
Charlottesville 22906-9011
Pres. John T. Casteen, III
(804) 924-3337

*Clinch Valley College of the
University of Virginia*
College Ave., Wise 24293
Chanc. L. Jay Lemons
(703) 328-0100

University of Virginia
P.O. Box 9011, Charlottesville
22906
Pres. John T. Casteen, III
(804) 924-3337

Virginia Commonwealth University
910 W. Franklin St., VCU Box
842520, Richmond 23284-2525
Pres. Eugene P. Trani
(804) 828-0100

Virginia Community College System
James Monroe Bldg., 101 N. 14th
St., Richmond 23219
Chanc. Arnold R. Oliver
(804) 225-2117

Blue Ridge Community College
P.O. Box 80, Weyers Cave
24486
Pres. James R. Perkins
(703) 234-9261

Central Virginia Community College
3506 Wards Rd., Lynchburg
24502-2498
Pres. Belle S. Whelan
(804) 386-4500

*Dabney S. Lancaster Community
College*
P.O. Box 1000, Clifton Forge
24422-1000
Pres. Richard R. Teaff
(540) 862-4246

Danville Community College
1008 S. Main St., Danville
24541
Pres. B. Carlyle Ramsey
(804) 797-2222

Eastern Shore Community College
29300 Lankford Hwy., Melfa
23410
Pres. John C. Fiege
(804) 787-5900

Germanna Community College
P.O. Box 339, Locust Grove
22508
Pres. Francis S. Turnage
(540) 423-1333

*J. Sargeant Reynolds Community
College*
P.O. Box 85622, Richmond
23285-5622
Pres. S.A. Burnette
(804) 371-3200

John Tyler Community College
13101 Jefferson Davis Hwy.,
Chester 23831-5399
Pres. Marshall W. Smith
(804) 796-4000

Lord Fairfax Community College
P.O. Box 47, Middletown
22645
Pres. Marilyn C. Beck
(703) 869-1120

*Mountain Empire Community
College*
P.O. Drawer 700, Big Stone
Gap 24219
Pres. Robert H. Sandel
(703) 523-2400

New River Community College
P.O. Drawer 1127, Dublin
24084
Pres. Edwin L. Barnes
(703) 674-3600

*Northern Virginia Community
College*
4001 Wakefield Chapel Rd.,
Annandale 22003-3723
Pres. Richard J. Ernst
(703) 323-3000

Patrick Henry Community College
P.O. Drawer 5311, Martinsville
24114
Pres. Max F. Wingett
(703) 638-8777

Paul D. Camp Community College
100 N. College Rd., P.O. Box
737, Franklin 23851
Pres. Jerome J. Friga
(804) 569-6700

*Piedmont Virginia Community
College*
501 College Dr., Charlottesville
22902-7589
Pres. Deborah M. DiCroce
(804) 977-3900

Rappahannock Community College
P.O. Box 287, Glenns 23149
Pres. John H. Upton
(804) 758-6700

*Southside Virginia Community
College*
109 Campus Dr., Alberta 23821
Pres. John J. Cavan
(804) 949-1000

*Southwest Virginia Community
College*
P.O. Box SVCC, Richlands
24641
Pres. Charles R. King
(703) 964-2555

Thomas Nelson Community College
P.O. Box 9407, Hampton
23670
Pres. Shirley Robinson Pippins
(804) 825-2700

Tidewater Community College
7000 College Dr., Portsmouth
23703
Pres. Larry L. Whitworth
(804) 484-2121

*Virginia Highlands Community
College*
P.O. Box 828, State Rte. 372
off Rte. 140, Abingdon
24212-0828
Pres. F. David Wilkin
(703) 628-6094

Virginia Western Community College
3095 Colonial Ave., S.W., P.O.
Box 14045, Roanoke 24038
Pres. Charles L. Downs
(703) 857-7311

Wytheville Community College
1000 E. Main St., Wytheville
24382
Pres. William F. Snyder
(703) 228-5541

Virginia Military Institute
Smith Hall, Lexington 24450
Superint. Josiah Bunting, III
(703) 464-7000

*Virginia Polytechnic Institute and State
University*
210 Burruss Hall, Blacksburg
24061-0131
Pres. Paul E. Torgersen
(703) 231-6000

Virginia State University
1 Hayden Pl., Box 9001, Petersburg
23806
Pres. Eddie N. Moore, Jr.
(804) 524-5000

WASHINGTON

Washington Higher Education Coordinating Board
917 Lakeridge Way, P.O. Box 43430, Olympia 98504-3430
Exec. Dir. Elson S. Floyd
(206) 753-3241

Central Washington University
208 Bouillon, Ellensburg 98926
Pres. Ivory V. Nelson
(509) 963-1111

Eastern Washington University
Cheney 99004
Pres. Marshall E. Drummond
(509) 359-6200

Evergreen State College
Olympia 98505
Pres. Jane L. Jervis
(206) 866-6000

University of Washington
Seattle 98195
Pres. Richard L. McCormick
(206) 543-2100

Washington State University
Pullman 99164-1046
Pres. Samuel H. Smith
(509) 335-3564

Western Washington University
Bellingham 98225
Pres. Karen W. Morse
(360) 650-3000

Washington State Board for Community and Technical Colleges
319 Seventh Ave., P.O. Box 42495, Olympia 98504-2495
Exec. Dir. Earl Hale
(206) 753-7412

Bates Technical College
1101 S. Yakima Ave., Tacoma 98405
Pres. William P. Mohler
(206) 596-1500

Bellevue Community College
3000 Landerholm Cir., S.E., Bellevue 98007-6484
Pres. B. Jean Floten
(206) 641-0111

Bellingham Technical College
3028 Lindbergh Ave., Bellingham 98225-1599
Pres. Desmond McArdle
(360) 738-0221

Big Bend Community College
7662 Chanute St., Moses Lake 98837-3299
Pres. William C. Bonaudi
(509) 762-5351

Centralia College
600 W. Locust, Centralia 98531
Pres. Henry P. Kirk
(360) 736-9391

Clark College
1800 E. McLoughlin Blvd., Vancouver 98663
Pres. Earl P. Johnson
(360) 992-2000

Clover Park Technical College
4500 Steilacoom Blvd., S.W., Tacoma 98499-4098
Admin. Alson E. Green, Jr.
(206) 589-5800

Columbia Basin College
2600 N. 20th Ave., Pasco 99301-3397
Pres. Lee R. Thornton
(509) 547-0511

Community Colleges of Spokane
N2000 Greene St., Spokane 99207-5499
CEO Terrance R. Brown
(509) 533-7401

Spokane Community College
N. 1810 Greene St., Spokane
99207
Pres. James Williams
(509) 533-7000

Spokane Falls Community College
W. 3410 Fort George Wright
Dr., Spokane 99204
Pres. Vern Jerome Loland
(509) 533-3500

Edmonds Community College
20000 68th Ave. W., Lynnwood
98036
Pres. Carleton M. Opgaard
(206) 640-1500

Everett Community College
801 Wetmore Ave., Everett 98201-
1327
Pres. Susan C. Carroll
(206) 388-9100

Grays Harbor College
1620 Edward P. Smith Dr.,
Aberdeen 98520
Pres. Jewell C. Manspeaker
(360) 538-4000

Green River Community College
12401 S.E. 320th St., Auburn 98002
Pres. Richard A. Rutkowski
(206) 833-9111

Highline Community College
P.O. Box 98000, Des Moines 98198-
9800
Pres. Edward M. Command
(206) 878-3710

Lake Washington Technical College
11605 132nd Ave., N.E., Kirkland
98034
Pres. Donald W. Fowler
(206) 828-5600

Lower Columbia College
1600 Maple, Longview 98632-0310
Pres. Vernon R. Pickett
(360) 577-2300

Olympic College
1600 Chester Ave., Bremerton
98310
Interim Pres. Donna Allen
(360) 478-4544

Peninsula College
1502 E. Lauridsen Blvd., Port
Angeles 98362
Pres. Wallace H. Sigmar
(360) 417-6500

Pierce College
9401 Farwest Dr., S.W., Tacoma
98498
Pres. George A. Delaney
(206) 964-6500

Renton Technical College
3000 Fourth St., N.E., Renton 98056
Pres. Robert C. Roberts
(206) 235-2352

Seattle Community College District
1500 Harvard St., Seattle 98122
Chanc. Charles A. Kane
(206) 587-3872

North Seattle Community College
9600 College Way N., Seattle
98103
Pres. Constance W. Rice
(206) 527-3600

Seattle Central Community College
1701 Broadway, Seattle 98122
Pres. Charles H. Mitchell
(206) 587-3800

South Seattle Community College
6000 16th Ave., S.W., Seattle
98106
Pres. Peter C. Ku
(206) 764-5300

Shoreline Community College
16101 Greenwood Ave. N., Seattle
98133
Pres. Gary L. Oertli
(206) 546-4101

Skagit Valley College
2405 College Way, Mount Vernon
98273
Pres. Lydia Ledesma
(360) 428-1261

South Puget Sound Community College
2011 Mottman Rd., S.W., Olympia
98512
Pres. Kenneth J. Minnaert
(360) 754-7711

Tacoma Community College
5900 S. 12th St., Tacoma 98465
Pres. Raymond J. Needham
(206) 566-5000

Walla Walla Community College
500 Tausick Way, Walla Walla
99362
Pres. Steven L. Van Ausdle
(509) 522-2500

Wenatchee Valley College
1300 Fifth St., Wenatchee 98801
Interim Pres. Woody Ahn
(509) 662-1651

Whatcom Community College
237 W. Kellogg Rd., Bellingham
98226
Pres. Harold G. Heiner
(360) 676-2170

Yakima Valley Community College
P.O. Box 1647, Yakima 98907
Pres. Linda Kaminski
(509) 575-2350

WEST VIRGINIA

State College System of West Virginia
1018 Kanawha Blvd., E., Charleston
25301
Chanc. Clifford M. Trump
(304) 558-0699

Bluefield State College
219 Rock St., Bluefield 24701
Pres. Robert E. Moore
(800) 344-8892

Concord College
P.O. Box 1000, Athens 24712
Pres. Jerry L. Beasley
(304) 384-3115

Fairmont State College
Locust Ave., Fairmont 26554
Pres. Robert J. Dillman
(800) 641-5678

Glenville State College
200 High St., Glenville 26351
Pres. William K. Simmons
(800) 344-4407

Shepherd College
Shepherdstown 25443
Interim Pres. John P. Watkins
(304) 876-2511

*Southern West Virginia Community and
Technical College*
P.O. Box 2900, Mount Gay 25637
Pres. Travis P. Kirkland
(304) 792-7098

West Liberty State College
West Liberty 26074
Interim Pres. Donald C. Danton
(304) 336-5000

West Virginia Institute of Technology
405 Fayette Pike, Montgomery
25136
Pres. John P. Carrier
(304) 442-3071

*West Virginia Northern Community
College*
1704 Market St., Wheeling 26003
Pres. Linda S. Dunn
(304) 233-5900

West Virginia State College
P.O. Box 399, Institute 25112
Pres. Hazo W. Carter, Jr.
(304) 766-3000

University System of West Virginia
1018 Kanawha Blvd., E., Ste. 700,
Charleston 25301
Chanc. Charles W. Manning
(304) 558-0267

Marshall University
400 Hal Greer Blvd., Huntington
25755
Pres. J. Wade Gilley
(800) 642-3463

*Potomac State College of West Virginia
University*
Fort Ave., Keyser 26726
Pres. Kathrine Brailer
(800) 262-7332

West Virginia Graduate College
100 Angus E. Peyton Dr., South
Charleston 25303-1600
Pres. Dennis P. Prisk
(800) 642-9842

*West Virginia School of Osteopathic
Medicine*
400 N. Lee St., Lewisburg 24901
Pres. Olen E. Jones, Jr.
(304) 645-6270

West Virginia University
Box 6201, Morgantown 26506-6201
Pres. David C. Hardesty, Jr.
(304) 293-0111

West Virginia University at Parkersburg
Rte. 5, Box 167-A, Parkersburg 26101
Pres. Eldon L. Miller
(304) 424-8000

WISCONSIN

The University of Wisconsin System
1220 Linden Dr., Madison 53706
Pres. Katharine C. Lyall
(608) 262-2321

University of Wisconsin Centers
780 Regent St., P.O. Box 8680,
Madison 53708-8680
Chanc. Lee E. Grugel
(608) 262-1783

University of Wisconsin—Eau Claire
P.O. Box 4004, Eau Claire 54701
Chanc. Larry G. Schnack
(715) 836-2637

University of Wisconsin—Green Bay
2420 Nicolet Dr., Green Bay 54311-
7001
Chanc. Mark Perkins
(414) 465-2000

University of Wisconsin—La Crosse
1725 State St., La Crosse 54601
Chanc. Judith L. Kuipers
(608) 785-8000

University of Wisconsin—Madison
500 Lincoln Dr., Madison 53706
Chanc. David Ward
(608) 262-1234

University of Wisconsin—Milwaukee
P.O. Box 413, Milwaukee 53201
Chanc. John H. Schroeder
(414) 229-4331

University of Wisconsin—Oshkosh
800 Algoma Blvd., Oshkosh 54901
Chanc. John E. Kerrigan
(414) 424-1234

University of Wisconsin—Parkside
Box 2000, Kenosha 53141-2000
Chanc. Eleanor J. Smith
(414) 595-2345

University of Wisconsin—Platteville
One University Plaza, Platteville
53818-3099
Chanc. Robert G. Culbertson
(608) 342-1234

University of Wisconsin—River Falls
410 S. 3rd St., River Falls 54022
Chanc. Gary A. Thibodeau
(715) 425-3201

University of Wisconsin—Stevens Point
2100 Main St., Stevens Point 54481
Interim Chanc. Howard Thoyre
(715) 346-0123

University of Wisconsin—Stout
328 Administration Bldg., P.O. Box
790, Menomonie 54751-0790
Chanc. Charles W. Sorensen
(800) 447-8688

University of Wisconsin—Superior
1800 Grand Ave., Superior 54880
Acting Chanc. Jan G. Womack
(715) 394-8101

University of Wisconsin—Whitewater
800 W. Main St., Whitewater 53190
Chanc. H. Gaylon Greenhill
(414) 472-1918

WYOMING

Wyoming Community College Commission
2020 Carey Avenue, 8th Fl., Cheyenne
82002
Exec. Dir. Thomas C. Henry
(307) 777-7763

Casper College
125 College Dr., Casper 82601
Pres. Leroy Strausner
(307) 268-2547

Central Wyoming College
2660 Peck Ave., Riverton 82501
Pres. Jo Anne McFarland
(307) 856-9291

Eastern Wyoming College
3200 W. C St., Torrington 82240
Pres. Jack Bottenfield
(307) 532-8200

Laramie County Community College
1400 E. College Dr., Cheyenne
82007
Pres. Charles H. Bohlen
(307) 778-5222

Northwest College
231 W. Sixth St., Powell 82435
Pres. John P. Hanna
(307) 754-6111

Sheridan College
P.O. Box 1500, Sheridan 82801
Pres. Stephen J. Maier
(307) 674-6446

Western Wyoming Community College
P.O. Box 428, Rock Springs 82902-
0428
Pres. Tex Boggs
(307) 382-1600

Appendices

A. The Accrediting Process

Accreditation is a system for recognizing education institutions and professional programs affiliated with those institutions for a level of performance, integrity, and quality which entitles them to the confidence of the education community and the public they serve. In the United States, this recognition is extended primarily through nongovernmental, voluntary institutional or professional associations. These groups establish criteria for accreditation, arrange site visits, evaluate those institutions and professional programs which desire accredited status, and publicly designate those which meet their criteria.

In most other countries, the establishment and maintenance of education standards are the responsibilities of a central government bureau. In the United States, however, public authority in education is constitutionally reserved to the states. The system of voluntary nongovernmental evaluation, called accreditation, has evolved to promote both regional and national approaches to the determination of educational quality. While accreditation is basically a private, voluntary process, accrediting decisions are used as a consideration in many formal actions—by governmental funding agencies, scholarship commissions, foundations, employers, counselors, and potential students. Accrediting bodies therefore have come to be viewed as quasi-public entities with certain responsibilities to the many groups which interact with the education community.

In America, accreditation at the postsecondary level performs a number of important functions, including the encouragement of efforts toward maximum educational effectiveness. The accrediting process requires institutions and programs to examine their goals, activities, and achievements; to consider the expert criticism and suggestions of a visiting team; and to determine internal procedures for action on recommendations from the accrediting body. Because accreditation status is reviewed on a periodic basis, recognized institutions and professional programs are encouraged to maintain continuous self-study and improvement mechanisms.

Types of Accreditation

Institutional accreditation is granted by the regional and national accrediting commissions of schools and colleges, which collectively serve most of the institutions chartered or licensed in the United States and its possessions. These commissions and associations accredit total operating units only.

Specialized accreditation of professional or occupational schools and programs is granted by national professional organizations in such fields as business, dentistry, engineering, and law. Each of these groups has its distinctive definitions of eligibility, criteria for accreditation, and operating procedures, but all have undertaken accreditation activities primarily to provide quality assurances concerning the educational preparation of members of the profession or occupation. Many of the specialized accrediting bodies will consider requests for accreditation reviews only from programs affiliated with institutions holding comprehensive accreditation. Some specialized agencies, however, accredit professional programs at institutions not otherwise accredited. These generally are independent institutions which offer only the particular specified discipline or course of study in question.

Procedures in Accreditation

The accrediting process is continuously evolving. The trend has been toward reliance on qualitative criteria, from the early days of simple checklists to an increasing interest in and emphasis on measuring the outcomes of educational experiences.

The process begins with the institutional or programmatic self-study, a comprehensive effort to measure progress according to previously accepted objectives. The self-study considers the interests of a broad cross-section of constituencies—students, faculty, administrators, alumni, trustees, and, in some circumstances, the local community.

The resulting report is reviewed by the appropriate commission and serves as the basis for evaluation by a site-visit team from the accrediting group. The site-visit team normally consists of professional educators (faculty and administrators), specialists selected according to the nature of the institution, and members representing specific interests. The visiting team assesses the institution or program in light of the self-study and adds judgments based on its own expertise and its external perspective. The team prepares an evaluation report, which is reviewed by the institution or program for factual accuracy.

The original self-study, the team report, and any response the institution or program may wish to make are forwarded to the accreditation commission. The review body uses these materials as the basis for action regarding the accreditation status of the institution or program. Negative actions may be appealed according to established procedures of the accrediting body.

Although accreditation generally is granted for a specific term (e.g., five or ten years), accrediting bodies reserve the right to review member institutions or programs for cause at any time. They also reserve the right to review any substantive change, such as an expansion from undergraduate to graduate offerings. Such changes may require prior approval and/or review upon implementation. In this way, accrediting bodies hold their member institutions and programs continually responsible to their educational peers, to the constituents they serve, and to the public.

Accreditation's Purposes
Throughout the evolution of its procedures, postsecondary accreditation's aims have been and are to:
- foster excellence in postsecondary education through the development of uniform national criteria and guidelines for assessing educational effectiveness;
- encourage improvement through continuous self-study and review;
- assure the educational community, the general public, and other agencies or organizations that an institution or program has clearly defined and appropriate objectives, maintains conditions under which their achievement can reasonably be expected, is in fact accomplishing them substantially, and can be expected to continue to do so;
- provide counsel and assistance to established and developing institutions and programs; and
- endeavor to protect institutions against encroachments which might jeopardize their educational effectiveness or academic freedom.

Postsecondary education in the United States derives its strength and excellence from the unique and diverse character of its many individual institutions. Such qualities are best sustained and extended by the freedom of these institutions to determine their own objectives and to experiment in the ways and means of education within the framework of their respective authority and responsibilities.

Public as well as educational needs must be served simultaneously in determining and fostering standards of quality and integrity in postsecondary education institutions and in such specialized programs as they offer. Accreditation, through nongovernmental institutional and specialized agencies, provides a major means for meeting those needs.

Role of the Commission on Recognition of Postsecondary Accreditation
The Commission on Recognition of Postsecondary Accreditation (CORPA) is a voluntary, nongovernmental organization that works to foster and facilitate the role of accrediting bodies in promoting and ensuring the quality and diversity of American postsecondary education. The accrediting bodies, while established and supported by their membership, are intended to serve the broader interests of society as well. To promote these ends, CORPA recognizes, coordinates, and periodically reviews the work of its recognized accrediting bodies and the appropriateness of existing or proposed accrediting bodies and their activities through its granting of recognition and performance of other related functions.

B. Accrediting Groups Recognized by CORPA

CORPA periodically evaluates the accrediting activities of institutional and professional associations. Upon determining that those activities meet or exceed CORPA provisions, the accrediting organizations are publicly recognized through this listing. Groups that are regional in nature are identified with their geographic areas; all others are national in their activities.

NATIONAL INSTITUTIONAL ACCREDITING BODIES

AMERICAN ASSOCIATION OF BIBLE COLLEGES
Commission on Accrediting
Colleges that offer certificates, diplomas, associate and/or baccalaureate degrees aimed at preparing students for Christian ministries through biblical, church/vocational, and general studies
Randall E. Bell, Executive Director
P.O. Box 1523
(130 F North College Avenue)
Fayetteville, AR 72702 (72701)
(501) 521-8164, Fax: (501) 521-9202

ACCREDITING BUREAU OF HEALTH EDUCATION SCHOOLS
Board of Commissioners
The accreditation of programs for Medical Laboratory Technicians and Medical Assistants leading to certificates or the Associate of Applied Science or the Associate of Occupational Science degrees and private institutions which offer exclusively programs in allied health leading to certificates or the Associate of Applied Science or the Associate of Occupational Science degrees
Carol Moneymaker, Executive Director
2700 South Quincy Street, Suite 210
Arlington, VA 22206
(703) 998-1200, Fax: (703) 998-2550

ACCREDITING COMMISSION FOR CAREER SCHOOLS/COLLEGES OF TECHNOLOGY
Private trade and technical schools
Thomas A. Kube, Executive Director
2101 Wilson Boulevard, Suite 302
Arlington, VA 22201
(703) 247-4212, Fax: (703) 247-4533

ACCREDITING COUNCIL FOR INDEPENDENT COLLEGES AND SCHOOLS
Private junior and senior colleges of business offering associates, bachelor',s and master's degrees, and private business schools offering certificates, diplomas, and specialized associate degrees
Stephen D. Parker, Executive Director
750 First Street, NE, Suite 980
Washington, DC 20002-4241
(202) 336-6780, Fax: (202) 842-2593

ASSOCIATION OF ADVANCED RABBINICAL AND TALMUDIC SCHOOLS
Accreditation Commission
Rabbinical and Talmudic schools which offer rabbinical degrees, ordination, and appropriate undergraduate and graduate degrees in the field of rabbinical and talmudic education
Bernard Fryshman, Executive Vice President
175 Fifth Avenue, Suite 711
New York, NY 10010
(212) 477-0950, Fax: (212) 533-5335

THE ASSOCIATION OF THEOLOGICAL SCHOOLS IN THE UNITED STATES AND CANADA
Commission on Accrediting
Graduate professional schools of theology, theological seminaries, and graduate programs in theology
James L. Waits, Executive Director
10 Summit Park Drive
Pittsburgh, PA 15275-1103
(412) 788-6505, Fax: (412) 788-6510

COUNCIL ON OCCUPATIONAL EDUCATION
(formerly SACS-COEI)
Postsecondary, pre-baccalaureate, educational institutions that are exclusively occupational/vocational in mission and are either non-degree granting or, if degree granting, offer only an Associate of Applied Science or the Associate of Occupational Science degrees in specific occupational/vocational fields
Harry L. Bowman, Executive Director
41 Perimeter Center East, NE, Suite 640
Atlanta, GA 30346
(770) 396-3898, Fax: (412) 788-6510

DISTANCE EDUCATION AND TRAINING COUNCIL
(formerly NATIONAL HOME STUDY COUNCIL-NHSC)
Accrediting Commission
Postsecondary distance or home study education institutions offering non-degree and degree courses and programs through the master's degree level
Michael P. Lambert, Executive Director
1601 18th Street, NW
Washington, DC 20009
(202) 234-5100, Fax: (202) 332-1386

Appendices

REGIONAL INSTITUTIONAL ACCREDITING BODIES

MIDDLE STATES ASSOCIATION OF COLLEGES
AND SCHOOLS
Commission on Higher Education
*Degree granting institutions which offer one
or more postsecondary educational programs
of at least one academic year in length in
Delaware, District of Columbia, Maryland,
New Jersey, New York, Pennsylvania, Puerto
Rico, Virgin Islands, and other geographic
areas in which the commission now conducts
accrediting activities*
Jean Avnet Morse, Executive Director
3624 Market Street
Philadelphia, PA 19104
(215) 662-5606, Fax: (215) 662-5950

NEW ENGLAND ASSOCIATION OF SCHOOLS
AND COLLEGES
**Commission on Institutions of Higher
Education**
*Institutions that award bachelor's, master's,
or doctoral degrees; and two-year institutions which include in their offerings degrees
in liberal arts and general studies; Connecticut, Maine, Massachusetts, New Hampshire,
Rhode Island, Vermont, and other geographic areas in which the commission now
conducts accrediting activities*
Charles M. Cook, Director
209 Burlington Road
Bedford, MA 01730-1433
(617) 271-0022, Fax: (617) 271-0950

**Commission on Technical and Career
Institutions**
*Non-profit and privately owned one- or two-
year degree and non-degree granting institutions, and three- and/or four-year non-degree
granting institutions which offer general or
specialized programs which lead to career
opportunities; Connecticut, Maine, Massachusetts, New Hampshire, Rhode Island, Vermont, and other geographic areas in which
the commission now conducts accrediting
activities*
Richard E. Mandeville, Director
209 Burlington Road
Bedford, MA 01730-1433
(617) 271-0022, Fax: (617) 271-0950

NORTH CENTRAL ASSOCIATION OF COLLEGES
AND SCHOOLS
**Commission on Institutions of Higher
Education**
*Institutions which offer one or more under-
graduate educational programs at least two
academic years in length, or one or more*

*graduate programs at least one academic
year in length if only graduate programs are
offered; Arizona, Arkansas, Colorado, Illinois, Indiana, Iowa, Kansas, Michigan, Minnesota, Missouri, Nebraska, New Mexico,
North Dakota, Ohio, Oklahoma, South
Dakota, West Virginia, Wisconsin, Wyoming,
and other geographic areas in which the commission now conducts accrediting activities*
Patricia A. Thrash, Executive Director
30 North LaSalle Street, Suite 2400
Chicago, IL 60602
(312) 263-0456, Fax: (312) 263-7462

THE NORTHWEST ASSOCIATION OF SCHOOLS
AND COLLEGES
Commission on Colleges
*Postsecondary institutions with programs of
at least one academic year in length in
Alaska, Idaho, Montana, Nevada, Oregon,
Utah, Washington, and other geographic
areas in which the commission now conducts
accrediting activities*
Joseph A. Malik, Executive Director
3700-B University Way, NE
Seattle, WA 98105
(206) 543-0195, Fax: (206) 685-4621

SOUTHERN ASSOCIATION OF COLLEGES AND
SCHOOLS
Commission on Colleges
*Postsecondary degree granting institutions in
Alabama, Florida, Georgia, Kentucky,
Louisiana, Mississippi, North Carolina, South
Carolina, Tennessee, Texas, Virginia, and
other geographic areas in which the commis-
sion now conducts accrediting activities*
James T. Rogers, Executive Director
1866 Southern Lane
Decatur, GA 30033-4097
(404) 679-4500, Fax: (404) 679-4558

WESTERN ASSOCIATION OF SCHOOLS
AND COLLEGES
**Accrediting Commission for Community
and Junior Colleges**
*Institutions which offer one or more educa-
tional programs of two academic years in
length and award the associate degree; California, Hawaii, Guam, and other geographic
areas in which the commission now conducts
accrediting activities*
John C. Petersen, Executive Director
P.O. Box 70, 3060 Valencia Avenue
Aptos, CA 95003
(408) 688-7575, Fax: (408) 688-1841

Accrediting Commission for Senior Colleges and Universities
Institutions which offer one or more educational programs leading to the baccalaureate or higher degree in California, Hawaii, Guam, and other geographic areas in which the commission now conducts accrediting activities
Ralph A. Wolff, Executive Director
P.O. Box 9990, Mills College
Oakland, CA 94613-0990
(510) 632-5000, Fax: (510) 632-8361

SPECIALIZED ACCREDITING BODIES

ACCREDITATION BOARD FOR ENGINEERING
AND TECHNOLOGY*
Engineering Accreditation Commission
Technology Accreditation Commission
Professional engineering programs at the
baccalaureate and master's levels preparing
for entry into the engineering profession;
baccalaureate and two-year programs
(including those leading to the associate
degree) in engineering technology; programs
in industrial hygiene at the master's level;
programs in occupational health and safety
at the baccalaureate and master's level; and
programs in surveying or surveying and
mapping at the baccalaureate level
George D. Peterson, Executive Director
111 Market Place, Suite 1050
Baltimore, MD 21202
(410) 347-7700, Fax: (410) 625-2238

ACCREDITING COMMISSION ON EDUCATION
FOR HEALTH SERVICES ADMINISTRATION
Graduate programs at the master's degree
level or the equivalent in health services
administration, health planning, and health
policy analysis
Patrick M. Sobczak, President
1911 North Fort Myer Drive, Suite 503
Arlington, VA 22209
(703) 524-0511, Fax: (703) 525-4791

ACCREDITING COUNCIL ON EDUCATION
IN JOURNALISM AND MASS COMMUNICATIONS
Units within institutions, a major part of the
unit's activities being to offer professional
programs preparing students at the bache-
lor's and master's levels for careers in jour-
nalism and mass communications
Susanne Shaw, Executive Director
Stauffer-Flint Hall
University of Kansas
Lawrence, KS 66045
(913) 864-3986, Fax: (913) 864-5225

AMERICAN ASSOCIATION FOR MARRIAGE
AND FAMILY THERAPY
Commission on Accreditation
for Marriage and Family Therapy
Education
Master's degree, doctoral degree, and post-
graduate degree clinical training programs
in marriage and family therapy
Colleen Peterson, Executive Director
1133 15th Street, NW, Suite 300
Washington, DC 20005
(202) 452-0109, Fax: (202) 223-2329

AMERICAN ASSOCIATION OF FAMILY
AND CONSUMER SCIENCES
Council for Accreditation
Baccalaureate programs in home economics
Ann Collins Chadwick, Acting Executive
Director
1555 King Street
Alexandria, VA 22314
(703) 706-4600, Fax: (703) 706-4663

AMERICAN BAR ASSOCIATION
Council of the Section of Legal Education
and Admissions to the Bar
Programs leading to the first professional
degree and advanced degrees in law
James P. White, Consultant on Legal Education
550 West North Street
Indianapolis, IN 46202
(317) 264-8340, Fax: (317) 264-8355

AMERICAN BOARD OF FUNERAL SERVICE
EDUCATION
Committee on Accreditation
Institutions and programs offering diplomas
and/or associate and baccalaureate degrees
in funeral service education and mortuary
science education
Gordon S. Bigelow, Executive Director
P.O. Box 1305, #316
Brunswick, ME 04011
(207) 798-5801, Fax: (207) 798-5988

AMERICAN COUNCIL FOR CONSTRUCTION EDUCATION
Board of Trustees
Associate degree programs in construction
and baccalaureate programs in construction,
construction science, construction manage-
ment, and construction technology
Daniel E. Dupree, Executive Vice President
901 Hudson Lane
Monroe, LA 71201
(318) 328-2413, Fax: (318) 323-2413

AMERICAN COUNSELING ASSOCIATION
Council for Accreditation of Counseling
and Related Educational Programs
Master's degree programs designed to prepare
individuals for community counseling, mental
health counseling, marriage and family counsel-
ing, school counseling, student affairs practice
in higher education, and doctoral-level pro-
grams in counselor education and supervision
Carol L. Bobby, Executive Director
5999 Stevenson Avenue
Alexandria, VA 22304
(703) 823-9800, Fax: (703) 823-0252

* Agency relinquished CORPA recognition, February 1996.

AMERICAN DENTAL ASSOCIATION
Commission on Dental Accreditation
First professional degree programs in dental education; degree, certificate, and diploma programs in allied dental education (dental assisting, dental hygiene, and dental laboratory technology); and advanced degrees and certificate programs in dental education (dental public health, endodontics, oral pathology, oral and maxillofacial surgery, orthodontics, pediatric dentistry, periodontics, prosthodontics, general practice residency and general dentistry)
Karen M. Hart, Interim Director, Division of Education
211 East Chicago Avenue
Chicago, IL 60611
(312) 440-2703, Fax: (312) 440-2915

AMERICAN DIETETIC ASSOCIATION
Commission on Accreditation/Approval for Dietetics Education
Associate degree dietetic technician programs, coordinated bachelor's degree programs, post-baccalaureate dietetic internship programs, and coordinated master's degree programs in dietetics
Beverly E. Mitchell, Administrator
216 West Jackson Boulevard, Suite 800
Chicago, IL 60606-6995
(312) 899-4872, Fax: (312) 899-1758

AMERICAN LIBRARY ASSOCIATION
Committee on Accreditation
First professional degree programs at the master's level in library and information studies
Prudence W. Dalrymple, Director
50 East Huron Street
Chicago, IL 60611-2795
(312) 280-2432, Fax: (312) 280-2433

COMMISSION ON ACCREDITATION OF ALLIED HEALTH EDUCATION PROGRAMS
CORPA recognizes the Commission on Accreditation of Allied Health Education Programs (CAAHEP) as an umbrella agency for 16 review committees representing professional organizations collaborating in the accreditation of programs in the following areas of allied health. All questions concerning accreditation of these programs should be directed to CAAHEP at the address given. The review committees are:

- Accreditation Review Committee on Education for the *Anesthesiologist Assistant*;
- Committee on Accreditation (AABB), *Specialist in Blood Bank Technology* Schools;
- Joint Review Committee on Education in *Cardiovascular Technology*;
- *Cytotechnology* Programs Review Committee;
- Joint Review Committee on Education in *Diagnostic Medical Sonography;*
- Joint Review Committee on Education in *Electroneurodiagnostic Technology*;
- Joint Review Committee on Educational Programs for the *EMT-Paramedic;*
- Joint Review Committee on Educational Programs in *Athletic Training;*
- National Commission on *Orthotic* and *Prosthetic* Education (NCOPE)
- Curriculum Review Board (AAMA), *Medical Assistant;*
- Accreditation Review Committee for the *Medical Illustrator;*
- Council on Accreditation, American Health Information Management Association (AHIMA), *Medical Record Technician, Medical Record Administrator;*
- Joint Review Committee for the *Ophthalmic Medical Technician/Technologist;*
- Accreditation Committee for *Perfusion Education;*
- Accreditation Review Committee of Education for *Physician Assistants, Surgeon's Assistants;*
- Joint Review Committee for *Respiratory Therapy Education, Respiratory Therapist, Respiratory Therapy Technician;*
- Accreditation Review Committee on Education in *Surgical Technology.*

Lawrence M. Detmer, Executive Director
515 North State Street, Suite 7530
Chicago, IL 60610-4377
(312) 464-4660, Fax: (312) 464-5830

AMERICAN OCCUPATIONAL THERAPY ASSOCIATION
Accreditation Council for Occupational Therapy Education
Occupational therapist and occupational therapy assistant
Martha S. O'Connor, Director
4720 Montgomery Lane
Bethesda, MD 20824-1220
(301) 652-2682, Fax: (301) 652-7711

AMERICAN OPTOMETRIC ASSOCIATION
Council on Optometric Education
Optometric technician associate degree programs, professional optometric doctoral degree programs, and optometric post-doctoral residency programs
Joyce Urbek, Administrative Director
243 North Lindbergh Boulevard
St. Louis, MO 63141
(314) 991-4100, Fax: (314) 991-4101

AMERICAN OSTEOPATHIC ASSOCIATION
Council on Predoctoral Education
Programs leading to the Doctor of Osteopathy degree
W. Douglas Ward, Associate Executive Director
142 East Ontario Street
Chicago, IL 60611-2864
(312) 280-5840, Fax: (312) 280-5893

AMERICAN PHYSICAL THERAPY ASSOCIATION
Commission on Accreditation in Physical Therapy Education
Physical therapist assistant programs at the associate degree level and physical therapist programs at the baccalaureate, post-baccalaureate certificate, and master's degree levels
Virginia M. Nieland, Director
Transpotomac Plaza
1111 North Fairfax Street
Alexandria, VA 22314-1488
(703) 706-3245, Fax: (703) 684-7343

AMERICAN PODIATRIC MEDICAL ASSOCIATION
Council on Podiatric Medical Education
Programs leading to the degree of Doctor of Podiatric Medicine
Jay Levrio, Director
9312 Old Georgetown Road
Bethesda, MD 20814-1621
(301) 571-9200, Fax: (301) 530-2752

AMERICAN PSYCHOLOGICAL ASSOCIATION
Committee on Accreditation
Doctoral programs in professional specialties of psychology and pre-doctoral internship training programs in professional psychology
Paul D. Nelson, Director, Office of Program Consultation and Accreditation
750 First Street, NE
Washington, DC 20002-4242
(202) 336-5979, Fax: (202) 336-5978

AMERICAN SOCIETY OF LANDSCAPE ARCHITECTS
Landscape Architectural Accreditation Board
First professional programs at the bachelor's or master's level
Ronald C. Leighton, Accreditation Manager
4401 Connecticut Avenue, NW, 5th Floor
Washington, DC 20008-2302
(202) 686-2752, Fax: (202) 686-1001

AMERICAN SPEECH-LANGUAGE-HEARING ASSOCIATION
Educational Standards Board
Graduate educational programs that provide entry-level professional preparation with a major emphasis in speech-language pathology and/or audiology
Sharon Goldsmith, Director
10801 Rockville Pike
Rockville, MD 20852
(301) 897-5700, Fax: (301) 571-0457

AMERICAN VETERINARY MEDICAL ASSOCIATION
Council on Education
First professional degree programs in veterinary medicine at the doctoral level
Janet D. Donlin, Assistant Director
1931 North Meacham Road, Suite 100
Schaumburg, IL 60173-4360
(708) 925-8070, Fax: (708) 925-1329

ASSOCIATION OF AMERICAN LAW SCHOOLS
Accreditation Committee
Programs leading to the first professional degree in law
Carl C. Monk, Executive Vice President
1201 Connecticut Avenue, NW, Suite 800
Washington, DC 20036-2605
(202) 296-8851, Fax: (202) 296-8869

ASSOCIATION OF COLLEGIATE SCHOOLS OF PLANNING
Planning Accreditation Board
Programs in planning at the baccalaureate and master's levels
Beatrice Clupper, Director
Iowa State University, Research Park
2501 North Loop Drive, Suite 800
Ames, IA 50010
(515) 296-7030, Fax: (515) 296-9910

COMPUTING SCIENCES ACCREDITATION BOARD
Computer Science Accreditation Commission
Baccalaureate degree programs designated as computer science programs which prepare students for entry into the computer science profession
Patrick M. LaMalva, Executive Director
Two Landmark Square, Suite 209
Stamford, CT 06901
(203) 975-1117, Fax: (203) 975-1222

COUNCIL ON ACCREDITATION OF NURSE
ANESTHESIA EDUCATIONAL PROGRAMS
*Nurse anesthesia programs that prepare
graduates for entry level practice at the certificate, baccalaureate, master's, or doctoral
degree levels*
Betty J. Horton, Director of Accreditation
222 South Prospect Avenue, Suite 304
Park Ridge, IL 60068-4010
(708) 692-7050, Fax: (708) 692-7137

THE COUNCIL ON CHIROPRACTIC EDUCATION
Commission on Accreditation
*Institutions and programs offering the doctor
of chiropractic degree*
Paul D. Walker, Executive Vice President
7975 North Hayden Road, Suite A-210
Scottsdale, AZ 85258
(602) 443-8877, Fax: (602) 483-7333

COUNCIL ON REHABILITATION EDUCATION
**Commission on Standards
and Accreditation**
*Master's degree programs in rehabilitation
counselor education*
Jeanne Boland Patterson, Ph.D., Executive
Director
1835 Rohlwing Road, Suite E
Rolling Meadows, IL 60008
(708) 394-1785, Fax: (708) 394-2108

COUNCIL ON SOCIAL WORK EDUCATION
Division of Standards and Accreditation
*Baccalaureate and master's degree pro-
grams in social work education*
Nancy Randolph, Director
1600 Duke Street, Suite 300
Alexandria, VA 22314-3421
(703) 683-8080, Fax: (703) 683-8099

FOUNDATION FOR INTERIOR DESIGN EDUCATION
RESEARCH
*Programs from the junior college through the
graduate level in interior design*
Kayem Dunn, Executive Director
60 Monroe Center, NW, Suite 300
Grand Rapids, MI 49503-2920
(616) 458-0400, Fax: (616) 458-0460

JOINT REVIEW COMMITTEE ON EDUCATION PRO-
GRAMS IN NUCLEAR MEDICINE TECHNOLOGY
Nuclear medicine technologist
Elaine Cuklanz, Executive Director
1144 West 3300 South
Salt Lake City, UT 84119-3330
(801) 975-1144, Fax: (801) 975-7872

NATIONAL ACCREDITATION COMMISSION FOR
SCHOOLS AND COLLEGES OF ACUPUNCTURE
AND ORIENTAL MEDICINE
*First professional master's degree and pro-
fessional master's level certificate and
diploma programs in acupuncture and first
professional master's degree and professional master's level certificate and diploma
programs in Oriental medicine with a con-
centration in both acupuncture and herbal
therapies*
Dolores Llanso, Director of Administrative
Services
8403 Colesville Road, Suite 370
Silver Spring, MD 20910
(301) 608-9680, Fax: (301) 608-9576

NATIONAL ASSOCIATION OF SCHOOLS OF ART
AND DESIGN*
Commission on Accreditation
*Institutions and units within institutions
which offer associate, baccalaureate, and/or
graduate degree programs in art, design and
art/design-related disciplines; also non-
degree granting institutions having programs
in these areas*
Samuel Hope, Executive Director
11250 Roger Bacon Drive, Suite 21
Reston, VA 22090
(703) 437-0700, Fax: (703) 437-6312

NATIONAL ASSOCIATION OF SCHOOLS OF
DANCE*
Commission on Accreditation
*Institutions and units within institutions
which offer associate, baccalaureate, and/or
graduate degree programs in dance and
dance-related disciplines; and non-degree
granting institutions having programs in
these areas*
Samuel Hope, Executive Director
11250 Roger Bacon Drive, Suite 21
Reston, VA 22090
(703) 437-0700, Fax: (703) 437-6312

NATIONAL ASSOCIATION OF SCHOOLS OF MUSIC*
Commission on Accreditation
*Institutions and units within institutions
which offer associate, baccalaureate, and/or
graduate degree programs in music and/or
music-related disciplines and non-degree-
granting institutions having programs in
these areas*
Samuel Hope, Executive Director
11250 Roger Bacon Drive, Suite 21
Reston, VA 22090
(703) 437-0700, Fax: (703) 437-6312

* Agency relinquished CORPA recognition, February 1996.

NATIONAL ASSOCIATION OF SCHOOLS OF PUBLIC
AFFAIRS AND ADMINISTRATION
**Commission on Peer Review
and Accreditation**
*Master's degree programs in public affairs
and administration*
Alfred M. Zuck, Executive Director
1120 G Street, NW, Suite 730
Washington, DC 20005
(202) 628-8965, Fax: (202) 626-4978

NATIONAL ASSOCIATION OF SCHOOLS
OF THEATRE*
Commission on Accreditation
*Institutions and units within institutions
which offer associate, baccalaureate, and/or
graduate degree programs in theatre and
theatre-related disciplines; and non-degree
granting institutions having programs in
these areas*
Samuel Hope, Executive Director
11250 Roger Bacon Drive, Suite 21
Reston, VA 22090
(703) 437-0700, Fax: (703) 437-6312

NATIONAL COUNCIL FOR ACCREDITATION
OF TEACHER EDUCATION
*Units within institutions offering professional
education programs at the basic and
advanced levels*
Arthur E. Wise, President
2010 Massachusetts Avenue, NW, Suite 200
Washington, DC 20036-1023
(202) 466-7496, Fax: (202) 296-6620

NATIONAL LEAGUE FOR NURSING
Division of Education and Accreditation
*Practical nurse, diploma, associate, bac-
calaureate, and higher degree programs*
Sue Abbe, Associate Director of Accreditation
350 Hudson Street
New York, NY 10014
(212) 989-9393, (800) NOW-1-NLN
Fax: (212) 989-3710

NATIONAL RECREATION AND PARK ASSOCIATION
Council on Accreditation
*Programs in recreation, park resources, and
leisure services at the baccalaureate degree
level*
Michelle Park, Professional Services Director
2775 South Quincy Street, Suite 300
Arlington, VA 22206-2204
(703) 820-4940, Fax: (703) 671-6772

SOCIETY OF AMERICAN FORESTERS
Committee on Accreditation
*First professional degree programs, bac-
calaureate or graduate, in forestry education*
P. Gregory Smith, Director, Science and
Education
5400 Grosvenor Lane
Bethesda, MD 20814
(301) 897-8720, Fax: (301) 897-3690

* Agency relinquished CORPA recognition, February 1996.

C. Joint Statement on Transfer and Award of Academic Credit

The following set of guidelines originally was developed by three national associations in higher education whose member institutions are directly involved in the transfer and award of academic credit. In 1990, a fourth national association joined the original three by officially approving the statement. It is one in a series of policy guidelines developed through the American Council on Education to respond to issues in higher education by means of voluntary self-regulation. Each statement is developed through a process of wide review among representatives of different types of institutions and professional responsibilities in higher education. They are intended to summarize general principles of good practice that can be adapted to the specific circumstances of each college and university.

Transfer of credit is a concept that now involves transfer between dissimilar institutions and curricula and recognition of extra-institutional learning, as well as transfer between institutions and curricula of similar characteristics. As their personal circumstances and educational objectives change, students seek to have their learning, wherever and however attained, recognized by educational institutions where they enroll for further study. It is important for reasons of social equity and educational effectiveness, as well as the wide use of resources, for all institutions to develop reasonable and definitive policies and procedures for acceptance of transfer credit. Such policies and procedures should provide maximum consideration for the individual student who has changed institutions or objectives. It is the receiving institution's responsibility to provide reasonable and definitive policies and procedures for determining a student's knowledge in required subject areas. All institutions have a responsibility to furnish transcripts and other documents necessary for a receiving institution to judge the quality and quantity of the work. Institutions also have a responsibility to advise the students that the work *reflected* on the transcript *may or may not* be accepted by a receiving institution.

Inter-Institutional Transfer of Credit

Transfer of credit from one institution to another involves at least three considerations:

(1) the educational quality of the institution from which the student transfers;
(2) the comparability of the nature, content, and level of credit earned to that offered by the receiving institution; and
(3) the appropriateness and applicability of the credit earned to the programs offered by the receiving institution in light of the student's educational goals.

Accredited Institutions

Accreditation speaks primarily to the first of these considerations, serving as the basic indicator that an institution meets certain minimum standards. Users of accreditation are urged to give careful attention to the accreditation conferred by accrediting bodies recognized by the Commission on Recognition of Postsecondary Accreditation (CORPA). CORPA has a formal process of recognition which requires that any accrediting body so recognized must meet the same standards. Under these standards, CORPA has recognized a number of accrediting bodies, including:

(1) regional accrediting commissions (which historically accredited the more traditional colleges and universities but which now accredit proprietary, vocational-technical, and single-purpose institutions as well);
(2) national accrediting bodies that accredit various kinds of specialized institutions; and
(3) certain professional organizations that accredit free-standing professional schools, in addition to programs within multi-purpose institutions. (CORPA annually publishes a list of recognized accrediting bodies, and the American Council on Education publishes for CORPA this directory of institutions accredited by these organizations.)

Although accrediting agencies vary in the ways in which they are organized and in their statements of scope and mission, all accrediting bodies that meet CORPA's provisions for recognition function to ensure that the institutions or programs they accredit have met generally accepted minimum standards for accreditation.

Accreditation affords reason for confidence in an institution's or a program's purposes, in the appropriateness of its resources and plans for carrying out these purposes, and in its effectiveness in accomplishing its goals, insofar as these things can be judged. Accreditation speaks to the probability, but does not guarantee, that students have met acceptable standards of educational accomplishment.

Appendices

Comparability and Applicability

Comparability of the nature, content, and level of transfer credit and the appropriateness and applicability of the credit earned to programs offered by the receiving institution are as important in the evaluation process as the accreditation status of the institution at which the transfer credit was awarded. Because accreditation does not address these questions, this information must be obtained from catalogues and other materials and from direct contact between knowledgeable and experienced faculty and staff at both the receiving and sending institutions. When such considerations as comparability and appropriateness of credit are satisfied, however, the receiving institution should have reasonable confidence that students from accredited institutions are qualified to undertake the receiving institution's educational program.

Admissions and Degree Purposes

At some institutions, there may be differences between the acceptance of credit for admission purposes and applicability of credit for degree purposes. A receiving institution may accept previous work, place a credit value on it, and enter it on the transcript. However, that previous work, because of its nature and not its inherent quality, may be determined to have no applicability to a specific degree to be pursued by the student.

Institutions have a responsibility to make this distinction and its implications clear to students before they decide to enroll. This should be a matter of full disclosure, with the best interests of the student in mind. Institutions also should make every reasonable effort to reduce the gap between the number of credits accepted and credits applied toward an educational credential.

Unaccredited Institutions

Institutions of postsecondary education that are not accredited by CORPA-recognized accrediting bodies may lack that status for reasons unrelated to questions of quality. Such institutions, however, cannot provide a reliable, third-party assurance that they meet or exceed minimum standards. That being the case, students transferring from such institutions may encounter special problems in gaining acceptance and transferring credits to accredited institutions. Institutions admitting students from unaccredited institutions should take steps to validate credits previously earned.

Foreign Institutions

In most cases, foreign institutions are chartered and authorized by their national governments, usually through a ministry of education. Although this provides for a standardization within a country, it does not produce useful information about comparability from one country to another. No other nation has a system comparable to voluntary accreditation. At the operational level, three organizations—the National Council on the Evaluation of Foreign Student Credentials (CEC), the National Association for Foreign Student Affairs (NAFSA), and the National Liaison Committee on Foreign Student Admissions (NLC)—often can assist institutions by distributing general or specific guidelines on admission and placement of foreign students. Equivalency or placement recommendations are to be evaluated in terms of the programs and policies of the individual receiving institution.

Validation of Extra-Institutional and Experiential Learning for Transfer Purposes

Transfer-of-credit policies should encompass educational accomplishment attained in extra-institutional settings as well as at accredited postsecondary institutions. In deciding on the award of credit for extra-institutional learning, institutions will find the service of the American Council on Education's Center for Adult Learning and Educational Credentials helpful. One of the center's functions is to operate and foster programs to determine credit equivalencies for various modes of extra-institutional learning. The center maintains evaluation programs for formally structured courses offered by the military and by civilian noncollegiate sponsors such as businesses, corporations, government agencies, and labor unions. Evaluation services also are available for examination programs, for occupations with validated job proficiency evaluation systems, and for correspondence courses offered by schools accredited by the Distance Education and Training Council. The results are published in a *Guide* series. Another resource is the General Educational Development (GED) Testing Program, which provides a means for assessing high school equivalency.

For learning that has not been validated through the ACE formal credit recommendation process or through credit-by-examination programs, institutions are urged to explore the Council for Adult and

Experiential Learning (CAEL) procedures and processes. CAEL publications designed for this purpose are available from CAEL National Headquarters, 223 West Jackson Boulevard, Suite 510, Chicago, IL 60606.

Uses of This Statement

This statement has been endorsed by the four national associations most concerned with practices in the area of transfer and awarding of credit—the American Association of Collegiate Registrars and Admissions Officers, the American Council on Education/Commission on Educational Credit and Credentials, the Commission on Recognition of Postsecondary Accreditation, and the American Association of Community Colleges.

Institutions are encouraged to use this statement as a basis for discussions in developing or reviewing institutional policies with regard to transfer. If the statement reflects an institution's policies, that institution might want to use this publication to inform faculty, staff, and students.

It is recommended that accrediting bodies reflect the essential precepts of this statement in their criteria.

Approved by the COPA Board
October 10, 1978; Reaffirmed April 25, 1990/Reaffirmed by CORPA January 1994

Approved by the American Council on Education/Commission on Educational Credit
December 5, 1978; Reaffirmed by the Commission on Educational Credit and Credentials September 26, 1990

Approved by the Executive Committee, American Association of Collegiate Registrars and Admission Officers
November 21, 1978; Reaffirmed February 1989

Approved by the Board of Directors, American Association of Community and Junior Colleges April 1990

Institutional Index

A

A-Professional 513
Abbeville Beauty Acad. 454
Abbie Business Inst. 461
Abbynell Beauty & Technical Inst. 502
Abilene Christian Univ. 339
Abilene Intercollegiate Sch. of Nursing 339
Abraham Baldwin Agricultural Coll. 83, 586
ACA Coll. of Design 267
Academia Singer Dealer Autorizado Inc. 502
Acad. Educ. Ctr. 180
Acad. for Career Educ. 482
Acad. of Art Coll. 24
Acad. of Artistic Hair Design 488
Acad. of Beauty Arts 551
Acad. of Business Coll. 13
Acad. of Chinese Culture and Health Sciences 24
Acad. of Court Reporting 267
Acad. of Creative Hair Design 423
Acad. of Floral Design 416
Acad. of Hair Design 442 (IN), 491 (OH)
Acad. of Healing Arts, Massage & Facial Skin Care 423
Acad. of Health Careers 466
Acad. of Medical Arts and Business 498
Acad. of Medical Careers 476
Acad. of Oriental Medicine 513
Acad. of Professional Development 478
Acad. of the New Church 293
Acad. Pacific Business and Travel Coll. 405
Acadia Divinity Coll. 390
Acme Inst. of Technology 530
Action Career Training 513
Acupuncture Sch. of Maryland 461
Adams State Coll. 56, 579
Adelphi Univ. 226
Adirondack Comm. Coll. 226, 637
Adler Inst. of Minnesota (see: Alfred Adler Inst. of Minnesota)
Adler Sch. of Professional Psychology 97
Adolphus Coll. (see: Gustavus Adolphus Coll.)
Adrian Coll. 169
Advance Barber Coll. 494
Advanced Career Training 513
Advanced Hair Tech 444
Advanced Legal Studies Ctr. (see: Ctr. for Advanced Legal Studies)
Advanced Software Analysis (see: Globe Inst. of Technology)
Advanced Software Analysis 538
Advertising Art Sch. (see: Sch. of Advertising Art)
Advertising Arts Coll. 24
Aero Mechanics Sch. 472
Aeronautics Coll. (see: Coll. of Aeronautics)
Agnes Scott Coll. 83
Aiken Technical Coll. 322, 658
Ailey American Dance Ctr. (see: Alvin Ailey American Dance Ctr.)
AIMS Acad. 513
Aims Comm. Coll. 56
Air Force Acad. (see: United States Air Force Acad.)
Air Force Comm. Coll. (see: Comm. Coll. of the Air Force)
Air Force Inst. of Technology 267
Air-Tech Incorporation 460
Airman Proficiency Ctr. 496
Akita Campus of Minnesota State Colls. and Universities 395, 621
Akron Barber Coll. 491
Akron Machining Inst. Inc. 491
Akron Medical-Dental Inst. 491
Akron Sch. of Practical Nursing 491
Al Collins Graphic Design Sch. 13
Al-Med Acad. 472
Alabama Agricultural and Mechanical Univ. 3, 555
Alabama Aviation and Technical Coll. 3, 556
Alabama Commission on Higher Educ. 555
Alabama Southern Comm. Coll. 3, 556
Alabama State Coll. of Barber Styling 399
Alabama State Univ. 3, 555
Alamance Comm. Coll. 253, 640
Alameda Coll. (see: Coll. of Alameda)
Alamo Comm. Coll. District 4, 663
Alaska Bible Coll. 11
Alaska Junior Coll. 533
Alaska Pacific Univ. 11
Alaska Vocational-Technical Ctr., 550
Albany Coll. of Pharmacy of Union Univ. 226
Albany Medical Coll. of Union Univ. 226
Albany State Coll. 83, 586
Albany State Univ. (see: State Univ. of New York at Albany)
Albany Technical Inst. 432
Albemarle Coll. (see: Coll. of The Albemarle)
Albert I. Prince Regional Vocational-Technical Sch. 418
Albert State Coll. (see: Carl Albert State Coll.)
Albertson Coll. of Idah0 95
Albertus Magnus Coll. 63
Albion Coll. 169
Albright Coll. 293
Albuquerque Barber Coll. 481
Albuquerque Job Corps Ctr., 481
Albuquerque Technical Vocational Inst. 223, 634
Alcorn State Univ. 190, 624
Alderson-Broaddus Coll. 378
Alexandria Technical Coll. 180
Alfred Adler Inst. of Minnesota 180
Alfred Univ. 226
Alice Lloyd Coll. 137
All-State Career Sch. 498
Allan Hancock Coll. 24, 563
Allan Hancock Joint Comm. Coll. District 563
Allegany Comm. Coll. 151, 612
Allegheny Business Inst. 498
Allegheny Coll. 293
Allegheny Cty. Comm. Coll. Allegheny Campus (see: Comm. Coll. of Allegheny Cty. Allegheny Campus)
Allegheny Cty. Comm. Coll. Boyce Campus (see: Comm. Coll. of Allegheny Cty. Boyce Campus)
Allegheny Cty. Comm. Coll. North Campus (see: Comm. Coll. of Allegheny Cty. North Campus)
Allegheny Cty. Comm. Coll. South Campus (see: Comm. Coll. of Allegheny Cty. South Campus)
Allen Coll. of Nursing 124
Allen Cty. Comm. Coll. 131, 601
Allen Memorial Sch. of Practical Nursing (see: Fanny Allen Memorial Sch. of Practical Nursing)
Allen Univ. 322
Allentown Coll. of St. Francis De Sales 293
Alliance Tractor Trailer Training Ctr., 432, 488
Alliance Tractor Trailer Training Ctrs. II, 523
Allied Health Careers 513
Allied Medical Careers 498
Allied Schs. of Puerto Rico 540
Allstate Hairstyling and Barber Coll. 491
Allstate Inst. of Technology 157
Allstate Tractor Trailer Training Sch. 418
Alma Coll. 169
Alpena Comm. Coll. 169, 617

Accredited Institutions of Postsecondary Education I 1995–96

C

C.A. Fredd State Technical Coll.
533
Cabot Coll. 405
Cabrillo Coll. 25, 563
Cabrillo Comm. Coll. District 563
Cabrini Coll. 294
CAD Inst. 14
Cain's Barber Coll. 440
Caldwell Coll. 216
Caldwell Comm. Coll. and
Technical Inst. 254, 640
Caldwell Cty. Area Technology
Ctr. 446, 608
Caldwell Cty. Area Vocational
Educ. Ctr. (see: Caldwell Cty.
Area Technology Ctr.)
Calhoun State Comm. Coll. (see:
John C. Calhoun State Comm.
Coll.)
California Acad. of Merchandising
Art & Design 405
California Baptist Coll. 26
California Career Schs. 405
California Coll. for Health
Sciences 26
California Coll. of Arts and Crafts
26
California Coll. of Podiatric
Medicine 26
California Comm. Colls. 563
California Culinary Acad. 26
California Design Coll. 26
California Family Study Ctr. 534,
(see: Phillips Graduate Inst.)
California Inst. of Integral Studies
26
California Inst. of Locksmithing
406
California Inst. of Technology 26
California Inst. of the Arts 26
California Lutheran Univ. 26
California Maritime Acad. 26, 574
California Nannie Coll. 406
California Paramedical &
Technical Coll. 405-406
California Polytechnic State
Univ.—San Luis Obispo 26, 574
California Sch. of Court Reporting
406, 534
California Sch. of Professional
Psychology 573
California Sch. of Professional
Psychology—Almeda 573
California Sch. of Professional
Psychology—Fresno 573
California Sch. of Professional
Psychology—Los Angeles 573
California Sch. of Professional
Psychology—San Diego 573

California State Polytechnic
Univ.—Pomona 574
California State Univ. System 573
California State Univ.—Bakers-
field 27, 574
California State Univ.—Chico 27,
574
California State Univ.—
Dominguez Hill 27, 574
California State Univ.—Fresno 27-
28, 574
California State Univ.—Fullerton
28, 574
California State Univ.—Hayward
28, 574
California State Univ.—Long
Beach 28, 574
California State Univ.—Los
Angeles 28, 574
California State Univ.—Northridge
28, 574
California State Univ.—
Sacramento 28, 574
California State Univ.—San
Bernardino 29, 574
California State Univ.—San
Marcos 29, 574
California State Univ.—Stanislaus
29, 574
California Univ. of Pennsylvania
295, 653
California Western Sch. of Law 29
Calumet Coll. of St. Joseph 114
Calvary Bible Coll. 195
Calvin Coll. 170
Calvin Theological Seminary 170
Cambria-Rowe Business Coll. 295
Cambridge Coll. 159
Cambridge Educ. Ctr. 454
Cambridge Sch. of Culinary Arts
463
Camden Cty. Coll. 216 632
Camelot Career Coll. 454
Cameron Univ. 283, 649
Camp Comm. Coll. (see: Paul D.
Camp Comm. Coll.)
Campbell Univ. 254
Campbellsville Coll. 137
Canada Coll. 29, 571
Canadian Bible Coll. 390
Canisius Coll. 228
Cannon's International Business
Coll. 535
Canyons Coll. (see: Coll. of the
Canyons)
Cape Cod Comm. Coll. 159, 615
Cape Fear Comm. Coll. 254, 640
Cape Girardeau Area Vocational-
Technical Sch. 472
Cape May Cty. Technical Inst. 478
Capital Area Vocational Ctr. 440

Capital Bible Seminary 546
Capital Comm.-Technical Coll.
Woodland Campus 63, 580
Capital Univ. 269
Capitol Business Coll. 542
Capitol City Barber Coll. 444
Capitol City Careers 514
Capitol City Trade & Technical
Sch. 514
Capitol Coll. 151
Capps Coll. 399
Capri Coll. 443, 530
Cardinal Stritch Coll. 382
Career Acad. 401 (AK), 514 (TX)
Career Ctr. 71
Career Ctr.s of Texas—El Paso 514
Career City Coll. 535
Career Coll. of Northern Nevada
211
Career Development Inst. 399, 436
Career Educ. Acad. (see: Acad. for
Career Educ.)
Career Floral Design Inst. 527
Career Inst. 498
Career Management Inst. 406
Career Point Business Sch. 514
Career Training Acad. 498
Career Training Ctr. 423, 514, 523
Career Training Specialists 454
Career West Acad. 406
CareerCom Junior Coll. of
Business 536
Careers Unlimited Beauty Sch. 515
Careers Unlimited 514
Carey Coll. (see: William Carey
Coll.)
Caribbean Ctr. for Advanced
Studies 314
Caribbean Univ. 314
Carl Albert State Coll. 649, 283
Carl D. Perkins Job Corps Ctr. 446
Carl Sandburg Coll. 98, 591
Carleton Coll. 181
Carlow Coll. 295
Carnegie Inst. 466
Carnegie Mellon Univ. 295
Carolina Beauty Coll. 539
Carrasco Job Corps Ctr. (see: David
L. Carrasco Job Corps Ctr.)
Carroll Coll. 205, 382
Carroll Comm. Coll. 546
Carroll Cty. Area Technology Ctr.
446, 604
Carroll Cty. Area Vocational Educ.
Ctr. (see: Carroll Cty. Area
Technology Ctr.)
Carroll Technical Inst. 84
Carroll Univ. (see: John Carroll
Univ.)
Carson-Newman Coll. 331
Carteret Comm. Coll. 254, 640

Accredited Institutions of Postsecondary Education | 1995–96

Coll. at New Paltz (see: State Univ. of New York Coll. at New Paltz)

Coll. at Old Westbury (see: State Univ. of New York Coll. at Old Westbury)

Coll. at Oneonta (see: State Univ. of New York Coll. at Oneonta)

Coll. at Oswego (see: State Univ. of New York Coll. at Oswego)

Coll. at Plattsburgh (see: State Univ. of New York Coll. at Plattsburg)

Coll. at Potsdam (see: State Univ.n of New York Coll. at Postdam)

Coll. at Purchase (see: State Univ. of New York Coll. at Purchase)

Coll. for Financial Planning 56

Coll. for Lifelong Learning 213, 631

Coll. for Recording Arts 406

Coll. Misericordia 296

Coll. of Aeronautics 229

Coll. of Agriculture and Technology at Cobleskill (see: State Univ. of New York Coll. of Agriculture and Technology at Cobleskill)

Coll. of Agriculture and Technology at Morrisville (see: State Univ. of New York Coll. of Agriculture and Technology at Morrisville)

Coll. of Alameda 31, 569

Coll. of Associated Arts 537 (see: Coll. of Visual Arts)

Coll. of Charleston 323, 658

Coll. of Court Reporting 16, 114

Coll. of DuPage 99, 591

Coll. of Eastern Utah 358, 670

Coll. of Environmental Science and Forestry at Syracuse (see: State Univ. of New York Coll. of Environmental Science and Forestry)

Coll. of Great Falls 537 (see: Univ. of Great Falls)

Coll. of Hair Design 443 (IA), 475 (NE)

Coll. of Insurance 229

Coll. of Lake Cty. 99, 591

Coll. of Legal Arts 496

Coll. of Marin 31, 567

Coll. of Micronesia 395

Coll. of Mount St. Joseph 270

Coll. of Mount St. Vincent 229

Coll. of New Rochelle 229

Coll. of Notre Dame of Maryland 152

Coll. of Notre Dame 31

Coll. of Oceaneering 31

Coll. of Office Technology 99

Coll. of Osteopathic Medicine of the Pacific 31

Coll. of Our Lady of the Elms 159

Coll. of San Mateo 31, 571

Coll. of Santa Fe 223

Coll. of Southeastern Europe 394

Coll. of Southern Idaho 95, 589

Coll. of St. Benedict 181

Coll. of St. Catherine 181

Coll. of St. Elizabeth 217

Coll. of St. Francis 99, 293

Coll. of St. Joseph 114, 360

Coll. of St. Mary 207

Coll. of St. Rose 230

Coll. of St. Scholastica 181

Coll. of St. Thomas Moore 341

Coll. of Staten Island 230, 635

Coll. of Technology at Alfred (see: State Univ. of New York Coll. of Technology at Alfred)

Coll. of Technology at Canton (see: State Univ. of New York Coll. of Technology at Canton)

Coll. of Technology at Delhi (see: State Univ. of New York Coll. of Technology at Delhi)

Coll. of Technology at Farmingdale (see: State Univ. of New York Coll. of Technology at Farmingdale)

Coll. of The Albemarle 255, 640

Coll. of the Atlantic 148

Coll. of the Canyons 31, 571

Coll. of the Desert 31, 564

Coll. of the Holy Cross 159

Coll. of the Mainland 341, 663

Coll. of the Marshall Islands 395

Coll. of the Ozarks 196

Coll. of the Redwoods 31, 569

Coll. of the Sequoias 31, 571

Coll. of the Siskiyous 32, 571

Coll. of the Southwest 223

Coll. of Visual Arts 181

Coll. of West Virginia 378-379

Coll. of William and Mary Central Office 672

Coll. of William and Mary 363, 672

Coll. of Wooster 270

Coll.America 496

Coll.America—Denver 416

Coll.America—San Francisco 406

Collier Technical Inst. (see: Louisiana Technical Coll.-Sidney N. Collier Campus)

Collin Cty. Comm. Coll. 341, 663

Collins Graphic Design Sch. (see: Al Collins Graphic Design Sch.)

Colorado Aero Tech 56

Colorado Christian Univ. 56

Colorado Coll. 56

Colorado Commission on Higher Educ. 578

Colorado Comm. Coll. and Occupational Educ. System 578

Colorado Inst. of Art 56

Colorado Mountain Coll. 56

Colorado Northwestern Comm. Coll. 57

Colorado Sch. of Mines 57, 578

Colorado Sch. of Trades 57

Colorado Sch. of Travel 416

Colorado State Univ. 57, 578

Colorado Technical Univ. 57

Columbia Basin Coll. 372, 675

Columbia Bible Coll. and Seminary 541

Columbia Bible Coll. 390

Columbia Coll. Hollywood 32

Columbia Coll. of Nursing 382

Columbia Coll. 32 (CA), 99 (IL), 196 (MO), 314 (PR), 323 (SC), 573, 676

Columbia International Univ. 323

Columbia Junior Coll. of Business 323

Columbia State Comm. Coll. 332, 661

Columbia Theological Seminary 85

Columbia Union Coll. 152

Columbia Univ. 230

Columbia-Greene Comm. Coll., 230 638

Columbine Coll. 534

Columbus Coll. of Art and Design 270

Columbus Coll. 85, 586

Columbus Para-Professional Inst. 491

Columbus State Comm. Coll. 270, 646

Columbus Technical Inst. 85 (see: Ivy Tech State Coll.—Columbus)

Combat Systems Technical Schs. Command 406

Commercial Coll. of Baton Rouge 454

Commercial Coll. of Shreveport 454

Commercial Driver Training 483

Commercial Inst. of Puerto Rico (see: Instituto Comercial de Puerto Rico Junior Coll.)

Commercial Training Services 496, 527

Commonwealth Business Coll. 114

Commonwealth Coll.

Commonwealth Coll. 363

Commonwealth Inst. of Funeral Service 341

Accredited Institutions of Postsecondary Education I 1995–96

Accredited Institutions of Postsecondary Education | 1995–96

Accredited Institutions of Postsecondary Education | 1995–96

I

Accredited Institutions of Postsecondary Education | 1995–96

Louisiana Technical Coll.-Teche
Area Campus 458
Louisiana Technical Coll.-West
Jefferson Campus 458
Louisiana Technical Coll.-Westside
Campus 458
Louisiana Technical Coll.-Young
Memorial Campus 458
Louisiana Training Ctr. 459
Louisville Presbyterian
Theological Seminary 139
Louisville Technical Inst. 140
Lourdes Coll. 274
Lowcountry Technical Coll. (see:
Technical Coll. of the
Lowcountry)
Lower Columbia Coll. 374, 676
Lowthian Coll. 183
Loyola Coll. in Maryland, 153
Loyola Marymount Univ. 41
Loyola Univ. of Chicago, 105
Loyola Univ. 1144
Lubbock Christian Univ. 346
Luna Vocational Technical Inst.
223, 634
Lurleen B. Wallace State Junior
Coll. 6, 557
Luther Coll. 127, 184
Luther Northwestern Theological
Seminary , 537
Luther Seminary 183
Lutheran Bible Inst. of Seattle, 374
Lutheran Coll. of Health
Professions 120
Lutheran Sch. of Theology at
Chicago, 105
Lutheran Theological Seminary at
Gettysburg 302
Lutheran Theological Seminary at
Philadelphia 302
Lutheran Theological Seminary 391
Lutheran Theological Southern
Seminary 324
Luzerne Cty. Comm. Coll. 302
Lycoming Coll. 303
Lyme Acad. of Fine Arts 419
Lynchburg Coll. 366
Lyndon B. Johnson Civilian
Conservation Ctr. 489
Lyndon State Coll. 360, 671
Lynn Univ. 77
Lyon Coll. 21

M

M & M Word Processing Inst. 517
M G Inst. 441
M. Weeks Welding Laboratory
Testing & Sch. 517
Mable Bailey Fashion Coll. Sch.

of Modeling and Cosmetology
434
Macalester Coll. 183
MacArthur State Technical Coll.
(see: Douglas MacArthur State
Technical Coll.)
MacCormac Junior Coll. 105
Machzikei Hadath Rabbinical Coll.
236
MacMurray Coll. 105
Macomb Comm. Coll. 174, 618
Macon Beauty Sch. 434
Macon Coll. 88, 587
Macon Technical Inst. 434
Madison Area Technical Coll. 383
Madison Cty. Area Technology
Ctr. 450 605
Madison Cty. Area Vocational
Education Ctr. (see: Madison
Cty. Area Technology Ctr.)
Madison Junior Coll. of Business
383
Madison Univ. (see: James
Madison Univ.)
Madisonville Comm. Coll. 140, 603
Madisonville Health Occupations
Sch. (see: Madisonville Health
Technology Ctr.)
Madisonville Health Technology
Ctr. 450, 608
Madisonville Regional Technology
Ctr. 450, 608
Madisonville State Vocational-
Technical Sch. (see: Madison-
ville Regional Technology Ctr.)
Madonna Univ. 174
Magnolia Bible Coll. 191
Magnus Coll. (see: Albertus
Magnus Coll.)
Maharishi International Univ. 542
(see: Maharishi Univ. of
Management)
Maharishi Univ. of Management
127
Maine Coll. of Art 149
Maine Maritime Acad. 149
Mainland Coll. (see: Coll. of the
Mainland)
Malcolm X Coll. 105, 591
Malone Coll. 274
Management Coll. of San
Francisco 409
Manatee Area Vocational-
Technical Ctr. 426
Manatee Comm. Coll. 77, 584
Manchester Coll. 120
Manchester Comm.-Technical
Coll. 64, 580
Mandl Sch. 484
Manhattan Christian Coll. 134
Manhattan Coll. 236

Manhattan Comm. Coll. (see:
Borough of Manhattan Comm.
Coll.)
Manhattan Sch. of Music, 236
Manhattanville Coll. 236
Mankato State Univ. 183, 622
Manor Junior Coll. 303
Mansfield Univ. of Pennsylvania
303, 653
Maple Woods Comm. Coll. 198, 626
Marantha Baptist Bible Coll. 383
Margaret Murray Washington
Vocational Sch. 422
Maria Coll. of Albany 236
Maria Parham Hospital, Inc. 489
Marian Coll. of Fond du Lac, 383
Marian Coll. 121, 383
Marian Court Junior Coll. 162
Maric Coll. of Medical Careers 409
Maricopa Cty. Comm. Coll.
District 559
Marietta Coll. 274
Marin Coll. (see: Coll. of Marin)
Marin Comm. Coll. District 567
Marine Corps Inst. 422
Marion Cty. Area Technology Ctr.
450, 606
Marion Cty. Sch. of Radiologic
Technology 426
Marion Military Inst. 6
Marion S. Whelan Sch. of
Practical Nursing 484
Marion Technical Coll. 274, 647
Marion Univ. (see: Francis Marion
Univ.)
Marist Coll. 236
Maritime Coll. (see: State Univ. of
New York Maritime Coll.)
Marlboro Coll. 360
Marquette Univ. 384
Mars Hill Coll. 258
Marshall Islands Coll. (see: Coll.
of the Marshall Islands)
Marshall Law Sch. (see: John
Marshall Law Sch.)
Marshall Univ. 379, 678
Marshalltown Comm. Coll. 127, 599
Martha Graham Sch. of Contemp-
orary Dance Inc. 484
Marti Coll. of Fashion and Art
(see: Virginia Marti Coll. of
Fashion and Art)
Martin Adult Health Occupations
(see: James Martin Adult Health
Occupations)
Martin Coll. 77
Martin Comm. Coll. 258, 641
Martin Cty. Area Technology Ctr.
450, 605
Martin Luther Coll. 184
Martin Methodist Coll. 334

Accredited Institutions of Postsecondary Education | 1995–96

Ozarks Coll. (see: Coll. of the Ozarks)
Ozarks Technical Comm. Coll. 200, 627

P

Pace Business Sch. 539
Pace Inst. 305
Pace Univ. 240
Pacific Christian Coll. 43
Pacific Coll. of Oriental Medicine 43
Pacific Gateway Coll. 412
Pacific Graduate Sch. of Psychology 44
Pacific Lutheran Theological Seminary 44
Pacific Lutheran Univ. 374
Pacific Northwest Ballet Sch. 528
Pacific Northwest Coll. of Art 290
Pacific Oaks Coll. 44
Pacific Sch. of Religion 44
Pacific Travel Sch. 412
Pacific Union Coll. 44
Pacific Univ. 290
Pacifica Graduate Inst. 545
Paducah Area Technology Ctr. 452, 608
Paducah Area Vocational Education Ctr. (see: Paducah Area Technology Ctr.)
Paducah Comm. Coll. 141, 604
Paier Coll. of Art 65
Paine Coll. 89
Palau Comm. Coll. 395
Palm Beach Atlantic Coll. 78
Palm Beach Beauty & Barber Sch. 428
Palm Beach Comm. Coll. 78, 584
Palmer Business Inst. 540
Palmer Chiropractic Univ. System, 600
Palmer Coll. of Chiropractic, 128, 600
Palmer Coll. of Chiropractic—West 44, 600
Palo Alto Coll. 348, 663
Palo Verde Coll. 44, 568
Palo Verde Comm. Coll. District 568
Palomar Coll. 44, 568
Palomar Comm. Coll. District 568
Pamlico Comm. Coll. 260, 641
Pan American Univ. (see: Univ. of Texas—Pan American)
Panama Canal Coll. 395
Panola Comm. Coll. 348, 665
Paper Science and Technology Inst. (see: Inst. of Paper Science and Technology)

Paradise Valley Comm. Coll. 16, 559
Paralegal Careers 428
Paralegal Inst. Inc. 16
Paramedic Training Inst. 496
Parham Hospital (see: Maria Parham Hospital Inc.)
Paris Junior Coll. 348, 665
Park Coll. 200
Parker Coll. of Chiropractic, 348
Parkland Coll. 108, 593
Parks Coll. 202 (MO), 224 (NM)
Parks Junior Coll. 60
Pasadena Area Comm. Coll. District 568
Pasadena City Coll. 44, 568
Pasco-Hernando Comm. Coll. 78, 584
Passaic Cty. Comm. Coll. 219, 633
Paterson Coll. of New Jersey (see: William Paterson Coll. of New Jersey)
Pathfinder Training Inst. 441
Patricia Stevens Coll. 200
Patrick Henry Comm. Coll. 368, 673
Patten Coll. 44
Patterson State Technical Coll. (see: John M. Patterson State Technical Coll.)
Patton Area Vocational Education Ctr. (see: J.D. Patton Area Technology Ctr.)
Paul D. Camp Comm. Coll. 368, 673
Paul Quinn Coll. 348
Paul Smith's Coll. 241
Payne Theological Seminary 278
Payne Univ. (see: Howard Payne Univ.)
Payne-Pulliam Sch. of Trade and Commerce 467
PCI Dealers Sch. 476
PCI Health Training Ctr. 517
Peace Coll. 260
Pearl River Comm. Coll. 192, 625
Pedigree Career Inst. 464, 533
Peirce Coll. 305
Pellissippi State Technical Comm. Coll. 335, 661
Pembroke State Univ. 260, 643
Peninsula Coll. 374, 676
Penn Coll. (see: William Penn Coll.)
Penn Commercial Coll. 305
Penn Technical Inst. 305
Penn Valley Comm. Coll. 200, 626
Penn-Ohio Coll. 539
Pennco Tech 305, 480
Pennsylvania Acad. of the Fine Arts 305
Pennsylvania Ballet Sch. (see: Shirley Rock Sch. of the Pennsylvania Ballet)

Pennsylvania Business Inst. 540
Pennsylvania Coll. of Optometry 305
Pennsylvania Coll. of Podiatric Medicine 305
Pennsylvania Coll. of Technology 305
Pennsylvania Gunsmith Sch. 500
Pennsylvania Inst. of Culinary Arts 500
Pennsylvania Inst. of Taxidermy 500
Pennsylvania Inst. of Technology 306
Pennsylvania Sch. of Art and Design 500
Pennsylvania State System of Higher Education 653
Pennsylvania State Univ. 306
Pensacola Junior Coll. 78, 584
Pepperdine Univ. 44
Peralta Comm. Coll. District 569
Perkins Job Corps Ctr. (see: Carl D. Perkins Job Corps Ctr.)
Perry Technical Inst. 528
Peru State Coll. 209, 629
Petit Jean Technical Coll. 545
Pfeiffer Coll. 260
PHD Hair Acad. 428
Philadelphia Art Inst. (see: Art Inst. of Philadelphia)
Philadelphia Coll. of Bible 307
Philadelphia Coll. of Osteopathic Medicine 307
Philadelphia Coll. of Pharmacy and Science 307
Philadelphia Coll. of Textiles and Science 307
Philadelphia Comm. Coll. (see: Comm. Coll. of Philadelphia)
Philadelphia Wireless Technical Inst. 500
Philander Smith Coll. 21
Phillips Beth Israel Sch. of Nursing 241
Phillips Business Coll. 525
Phillips Coll. (see: Frank Phillips Coll.)
Phillips Coll. Inland Empire Campus 45
Phillips Coll. of Chicago 535
Phillips Coll. 211
Phillips Cty. Comm. Coll. 21, 561
Phillips Graduate Inst. 45
Phillips Graduate Seminary 540 (see: Phillips Theological Seminary)
Phillips Junior Coll. 45 (CA), 201 (MO, 358 (UT), 535 (AL), 534 (CA), 535 (FL), 536 (LA), 537 (MS), 538 (NV)

Quinn Coll. (see: Paul Quinn Coll.)
Quinnipiac Coll. 65
Quinsigamond Comm. Coll. 165, 616

R

R/S Inst. 517
Rabbi Jacob Joseph Sch. 547
Rabbinical Acad. Mesivta Rabbi Chaim Berlin 241
Rabbinical Coll. Beth Shraga 241
Rabbinical Coll. Bobover Yeshiva B'nei Zion 241
Rabbinical Coll. Ch'san Sofer 242
Rabbinical Coll. of America 219
Rabbinical Coll. of Long Island 242
Rabbinical Coll. of Ohr Shimon Yisroel 547
Rabbinical Coll. of Telshe 278
Rabbinical Seminary Adas Yereim, 242
Rabbinical Seminary M'kor Chaim 242
Rabbinical Seminary of America 242
Radcliffe Coll. 165
Radford M. Locklin Technical Ctr. 428
Radford Univ. 368, 672
Raedel Coll. and Industrial Welding Sch. 493
Rainy River Comm. Coll. 186 621
Ralph Amodei International Inst. of Hair Design & Technology 500
Ramapo Coll. of New Jersey 220, 633
Ramirez Coll. of Business and Technology 317
Rancho Santiago Coll.—Santa Ana 45, 569
Rancho Santiago Comm. Coll. District 569
Rand Graduate Sch. of Policy Studies 45
Randazzo Vocational Training Inst. (see: Nick Randazzo Vocational Training Inst.)
Randolph Comm. Coll. 260, 642
Randolph-Macon Coll. 368
Randolph-Macon Woman's Coll. 368
Range Technical Coll.—Eveleth 546
Range Technical Coll.—Hibbing 186, 622
Ranger Coll. 348, 665
Ranken Technical Coll. 201

Rappahannock Comm. Coll. 369 673
Raritan Valley Comm. Coll. 220, 633
Rasmussen Coll. Eagan 186
Rasmussen Coll. Mankato 186
Rasmussen Coll. Minnetonka 186
Rasmussen Coll. St. Cloud 186
Ray Coll. of Design 109
Raymond Walters Coll.. 539
Reading Area Comm. Coll. 308
Reconstructionist Rabbinical Coll. 308
Recording Arts & Sciences Conservatory (see: Conservatory of Recording Arts & Sciences)
Recording Arts Coll. (see: Coll. for Recording Arts)
Recreational Vehicle Service Acad. 429
Red River Technical Coll. 22, 561
Red Rocks Comm. Coll. 60, 578
Red Wing/Winona Technical Coll. 186, 622
Redlands Comm. Coll. 285, 649
Redwoods Coll. (see: Coll. of the Redwoods)
Redwoods Comm. Coll. District 569
Reed Coll. 290
Reformed Bible Coll. 176
Reformed Presbyterian Theological Seminary 308
Reformed Theological Seminary 192
Refrigeration Sch. of New Orleans 459
Refrigeration Sch. 17
Regent Coll. 392
Regent Univ. 369
Regents Coll. of the Univ. of the State of New York, 242
Regis Coll. 165 (MA), 392 (CN)
Regis Univ. 60
Reid State Technical Coll. 7, 557
Reinhardt Coll. 89
Remington Coll. 145 (LA), 404 (AR), 444 (KS)
Rend Lake Coll. 109, 593
Reno Tahoe Gaming Acad. 476
Rensselaer Polytechnic Inst. 242
Renton Technical Coll. 375, 676
Reporting Acad. of Virginia 525
Research Coll. of Nursing 201
Resource Ctr. for the Handicapped 375
Restaurant Sch. 308
RETS Education Ctr. 308
RETS Electronic Inst. 141
RETS Electronic Schs. 464
RETS Tech Ctr. 278
RETS Technical Training Ctr. 154

RETS Training Ctr. 145
Reynolds Comm. Coll. (see: J. Sargeant Reynolds Comm. Coll.)
RHDC Hair Design Coll. 517-518
Rhode Island Coll. 320, 657
Rhode Island Comm. Coll. (see: Comm. Coll. of Rhode Island)
Rhode Island Sch. of Design 321
Rhodes Coll. 336
Rice Aviation A Division of A&J Enterprises 518
Rice Coll. 400, 510
Rice Univ. (see: William Marsh Rice Univ.)
Rich Mountain Comm. Coll. 22, 561
Richard Bland Coll. 369, 672
Richard J. Daley Coll. 109, 591
Richard M. Milburn High Sch. 525
Richard Stockton Coll. of New Jersey 220, 633
Richland Coll. 349, 664
Richland Comm. Coll. 109, 593
Richmond Coll. The American International Univ. in London 396
Richmond Comm. Coll. 261, 642
Ricks Coll. 96
Rider Univ. 220
Ridge Vocational-Technical Ctr. 429
Ridley-Lowell Business and Technical Inst. 419 ((CT), 486 (NY)486
Ringling Sch. of Art and Design 78
Rio Grande Bible Inst. 552
Rio Hondo Coll. 45, 569
Rio Hondo Comm. Coll. District 569
Rio Salado Comm. Coll. 17, 560
Ripon Coll. 385
Riverside Comm. Coll. District 569
Riverside Comm. Coll. 46, 569
Rivier Coll. 214
Roane State Comm. Coll. 336, 661
Roanoke Bible Coll. 261
Roanoke Coll. 369
Roanoke Valley Comm. Hospital Coll. of Health Sciences (see: Comm. Hospital of Roanoke Valley Coll. of Health Sciences)
Roanoke-Chowan Comm. Coll. 261, 642
Robert Morgan Vocational-Technical Inst. 429
Robert Morris Coll. 109 (IL), 308 (PA)
Roberto-Venn Sch. of Luthiery 403
Roberts Univ. (see: Oral Roberts Univ.)
Roberts Wesleyan Coll. 242

Accredited Institutions of Postsecondary Education I 1995–96

Univ. of Southern Maine 150, 611
Univ. of Southern Mississippi, 193, 624
Univ. of Southwestern Louisiana 146, 610
Univ. of St. Mary of the Lake Mundelein Seminary 113
Univ. of St. Michael's Coll. 393
Univ. of St. Thomas 188, 355
Univ. of Tampa 81
Univ. of Tennessee at Chattanooga 337, 662
Univ. of Tennessee at Martin 337, 662
Univ. of Tennessee System 662
Univ. of Tennessee Knoxville 337, 662
Univ. of Tennessee Memphis 338, 662
Univ. of Texas at Arlington 355, 668
Univ. of Texas at Austin 355, 668
Univ. of Texas at Brownsville/Texas Southmost Coll. Partnership, 355
Univ. of Texas at Dallas 355, 669
Univ. of Texas at El Paso 355, 669
Univ. of Texas at San Antonio 355, 669
Univ. of Texas at Tyler 356, 669
Univ. of Texas Health Science Ctr. at Houston 356, 668
Univ. of Texas Health Science Ctr. at San Antonio 356, 668
Univ. of Texas Medical Branch at Galveston 356, 668
Univ. of Texas of the Permian Basin 356, 669
Univ. of Texas Southwestern Medical Ctr. at Dallas 356, 668
Univ. of Texas System 668
Univ. of Texas—Pan American 356, 669
Univ. of the Arts 311
Univ. of the District of Columbia 70
Univ. of the Ozarks 23
Univ. of the Pacific 53
Univ. of the Sacred Heart 319
Univ. of the South 338
Univ. of the Virgin Islands 362
Univ. of Toledo 281, 648
Univ. of Toronto 393
Univ. of Tulsa 287
Univ. of Utah 359, 670
Univ. of Vermont 361
Univ. of Victoria 393
Univ. of Virginia Central Office 672
Univ. of Virginia 370, 672
Univ. of Washington 376, 675
Univ. of Waterloo 393
Univ. of West Alabama 10, 556
Univ. of West Florida 82, 585

Univ. of West Los Angeles 53
Univ. of Western Ontario 393
Univ. of Windsor 394
Univ. of Wisconsin Ctr.s 386, 679
Univ. of Wisconsin System 679
Univ. of Wisconsin—Eau Claire 386, 679
Univ. of Wisconsin—Green Bay 386, 679
Univ. of Wisconsin—La Crosse 386, 679
Univ. of Wisconsin—Madison 386, 679
Univ. of Wisconsin—Milwaukee 387, 679
Univ. of Wisconsin—Oshkosh 387, 679
Univ. of Wisconsin—Parkside 387, 679
Univ. of Wisconsin—Platteville 387, 679
Univ. of Wisconsin—River Falls 387 679
Univ. of Wisconsin—Stevens Point 387, 679
Univ. of Wisconsin—Stout 387, 679
Univ. of Wisconsin—Superior 388, 679
Univ. of Wisconsin—Whitewater 388, 679
Univ. of Wyoming 389
Univ. System of New Hampshire 631
Univ. System of West Virginia 678
Upper Iowa Univ. 129
Upsala Coll. 538
Urbana Univ. 281
Ursinus Coll. 311
Ursuline Coll. 281
Utah State Univ. 359, 670
Utah System of Higher Education 670
Utah Valley Comm. Coll. 542
Utah Valley State Coll. 359, 670
Utica Coll. of Syracuse Univ. 250
Utica Sch. of Commerce 250
UUniv. of California Office of the President 576
Univ. of Missouri System 627

V

Valdosta State Univ. 90, 587
Valdosta Technical Inst. 437
Vale Technical Inst. (see: National Education Ctr.—Vale Technical Inst. Campus)
Valencia Comm. Coll. 82, 585
Valley City State Univ. 266, 645
Valley Commercial Coll. 53

Valley Forge Christian Coll. 311
Valley Forge Military Coll. 312
Valley Forge Military Junior Coll. 540
Valparaiso Univ. 123
Van Dyck Inst. of Tourism 82
Vance-Granville Comm. Coll. 263, 642
Vancouver Sch. of Theology 394
Vanderbilt Univ. 338
VanderCook Coll. of Music 113
Vanderschmidt Sch. 473
Vanguard Inst. of Technology 520
Vassar Coll. 250
Vatterott Coll. 204
Vatterott Educational Ctrs. 473
Vegas Career Sch. 476
Vennard Coll. 129
Ventura Coll. 53
Ventura Coll. 572
Ventura Cty. Comm. Coll. District 572
Vermilion Comm. Coll. 188, 621
Vermont Coll. 361
Vermont Comm. Coll. (see: Comm. Coll. of Vermont)
Vermont Law Sch. 361
Vermont State Colls. 671
Vermont Technical Coll. 361, 671
Vernon Regional Junior Coll. 357, 669
Victor Valley Coll. 53, 572
Victor Valley Comm. Coll. District 572
Victoria Coll. 357, 669
Villa Julie Coll. 156
Villa Maria Coll. of Buffalo 250
Villanova Univ. 312
Vincennes Univ. 123, 596
Virgin Islands Univ. (see: Univ. of the Virgin Islands)
Virginia Coll. 10
Virginia Commonwealth Univ. 370, 672
Virginia Comm. Coll. System 672
Virginia Episcopal Theological Seminary (see: Protestant Episcopal Theological Seminary in Virginia)
Virginia Hair Acad. 526
Virginia Highlands Comm. Coll. 370, 674
Virginia Intermont Coll. 370
Virginia Marti Coll. of Fashion and Art 281
Virginia Military Inst. 370, 674
Virginia Polytechnic Inst. and State Univ. 370, 674
Virginia Sch. of Cosmetology 526
Virginia State Univ. 371, 674
Virginia Union Univ. 371

Williamson Free Sch. of
Mechanical Trades 313
Williamsport Sch. of Commerce 313
Willmar Comm. Coll. 189, 623
Wilma Boyd Career Schs. 313, 535
Wilmington Coll. 68 (DE), 282 (OH)
Wilson Coll. (see: Warren Wilson
Coll.)
Wilson Coll. 139 (see: Lindsey
Wilson Coll.)
Wilson Rehabilitation Ctr. (see:
Woodrow Wilson Rehabilitation
Ctr.)
Wilson Technical Ctr. (see: Lewis
A. Wilson Technical Ctr.)
Wilson Technical Comm. Coll.
264, 643
Windham Regional Vocational-
Technical Sch. 420
Windward Comm. Coll. 94, 588
Winebrenner Theological
Seminary 282
Wingate Coll. (see: Wingate Univ.)
Wingate Univ. 264
Winona State Univ. 189, 623
Winston Cty. Technical Ctr. 400
Winston-Salem Barber Sch. 489
Winston-Salem State Univ. 264, 644
Winthrop Univ. 327, 658
Wisconsin Conservatory of Music
Inc. 530
Wisconsin Indianhead Technical
Coll. 388
Wisconsin Lutheran Coll. 388
Wisconsin Sch. of Electronics 388
Wisconsin Sch. of Professional Pet
Grooming 530
Wisconsin Sch. of Professional
Psychology 388
Withlacoochee Technical Inst. 431
Wittenberg Univ. 282
Wofford Coll. 327
Wood Coll. 194
Wood Comm. Coll. (see: John
Wood Comm. Coll.)

Wood Cty. Vocational Sch. 529
Wood Junior Coll. (see:Wood Coll.)
Woodbridge Business Inst. 535, 537
Woodbury Coll. 361
Woodbury Univ. 54
Woodrow Wilson Rehabilitation
Ctr. 526
Woods Univ. (see: William Woods
Univ.)
Wooster Coll. (see: Coll. of Wooster)
Wor-Wic Comm. Coll. 156, 614
Worcester Polytechnic Inst. 168
Worcester State Coll. 168, 616
Worcester Technical Inst. 465
Worsham Coll. of Mortuary
Science 441
Worsley Inst. of Classical
Acupuncture 546
Worthington Comm. Coll. 189, 623
Wright Business Sch. 445
Wright Coll. (see: Wilbur Wright
Coll.)
Wright Inst. 54
Wright Sch. of Architecture (see:
Frank Lloyd Wright Sch. of
Architecture)
Wright State Univ. 282, 648
Wycliffe Coll. 394
Wyoming Comm. Coll.
Commission 680
Wyoming Technical Inst. 531
Wytheville Comm. Coll. 371, 674

X

Xavier Univ. of Louisiana 147
Xavier Univ. 282

Y

Yakima Valley Comm. Coll. 377,
677
Yale Univ. 67

Yavapai Coll. 19, 560
Yeshiva and Kolel Bais Medrash
Elyon 547
Yeshiva and Kollel Harbotzas
Torah 547
Yeshiva Beth Moshe 313
Yeshiva Beth Yehuda-Yeshiva
Gedolah of Greater Detroit 179
Yeshiva Derech Chaim 251
Yeshiva Gedolah Imrei Yosef
D'Spinka 547
Yeshiva Karlin Stolin Beth Aaron
V'Israel Rabbinical Inst. 251
Yeshiva Mikdash Melech 251
Yeshiva of Nitra—Rabbinical Coll.
Yeshiva Farm Settlement 251
Yeshiva Ohr Elchonon-
Chabad/West Coast Talmudic
Seminary 54
Yeshiva Shaar HaTorah Talmudic
Research Inst. 251
Yeshiva Toras Chaim Talmudic
Seminary 62
Yeshiva Univ. 251
Yeshivas Novominsk 252
Yeshivath Viznitz, 252
Yesivath Zichron Moshe 252
Yo San Univ. of Traditional
Chinese Medicine 54
York Coll. of Pennsylvania 313
York Coll. 210 (NE), 252 (NY),
636
York Technical Coll. 327, 659
York Technical Inst. 01
Yorktowne Business Inst. 313
Yosemite Comm. Coll. District
573
Young Harris Coll. 91
Youngstown State Univ. 282, 648
Youth Co-op Training Inst. 550
Yuba Coll. 55, 573
Yuba Comm. Coll. District 573

AMERICAN COUNCIL ON EDUCATION

BOARD OF DIRECTORS 1996

STEVEN S. KOBLIK, PRESIDENT
Reed College
3203 S.E. Woodstock
Boulevard
Portland, OR 97202-8199
(503) 771-7500

MICHELE TOLELA MYERS,
PRESIDENT
Denison University
Granville, OH 43023
(614) 587-6281

EDUARDO J. PADRÓN,
PRESIDENT
Miami-Dade Community
College
300 N.E. Second Avenue
Miami, FL 33132
(305) 237-3316

ELISABETH ZINSER,
CHANCELLOR
University of Kentucky
111 Administration Building
Lexington, KY 40506-0032
(606) 257-2911

ELECTED OFFICERS OF
ASSOCIATIONS—
EX OFFICIO FOR
THREE-YEAR TERMS:

*Association of American
Colleges & Universities*
HAROLD W. EICKHOFF,
PRESIDENT
Trenton State College
Hillwood Lakes, CN 4700
Trenton, NJ 08650-4700
(609) 771-1855

*American Association of
Community Colleges*
DANIEL F. MORIARTY,
PRESIDENT
Portland Community College
PO Box 19000
Portland, OR 97280
(503) 977-4916

*American Association of
State Colleges &
Universities*
(To be appointed)

*Association of American
Universities*
F. PATRICK ELLIS, FSC,
PRESIDENT
The Catholic University of
America
620 Michigan Avenue, NE
Washington, DC 20064
(202) 319-5100

*Association of Catholic
Colleges & Universities*
(To be appointed)

*Association of Jesuit
Colleges & Universities*
JOHN P. SCHLEGEL, SJ,
PRESIDENT
University of San Francisco
2130 Fulton Street
San Francisco, CA 94117
(415) 666-6762

*Council of Independent
Colleges*
JOHN L. HENDERSON,
PRESIDENT
Wilberforce University
Wilberforce, OH 45384
(513) 376-2911 x704

*National Association for
Equal Opportunity in Higher
Education*
EARL S. RICHARDSON,
PRESIDENT
Morgan State University
Hillen Road & Cold
Spring Lane
Baltimore, MD 21239
(410) 319-3200

*National Association of
Independent Colleges &
Universities*
MICHAEL F. ADAMS, PRESIDENT
Centre College
600 West Walnut St.
Danville, KY 40422
(606) 238-5220

*National Association of
State Universities & Land-
Grant Colleges*
FREDERICK E. HUTCHINSON,
PRESIDENT
University of Maine
Orono, ME 04469-5703
(207) 581-1512

ELECTED OFFICERS OF
ASSOCIATIONS—
EX OFFICIO FOR
ONE-YEAR TERMS:

*National Association of
Student Financial Aid
Administrators*
DALLAS MARTIN, PRESIDENT
National Association of
Student Financial Aid
Administrators
1920 L Street, NW
Washington, D.C. 20036-
5020
(202) 785-0453

*Association of American
Medical Colleges*
PAUL J. FRIEDMAN, M.D.
PROFESSOR OF RADIOLOGY
University of California
Medical Center–8756
200 West Arbor Drive
San Diego, CA 92103-8756
(619) 543-6633

*Washington Higher
Education Secretariat*
MARY BURGAN, GENERAL
SECRETARY
American Association of
University Professors
1012 14th Street, NW,
Suite 500
Washington, DC 20005
(202) 737-5900 x3019

EXECUTIVE SECRETARY IRENE
L. GOMBERG
American Council on
Education
One Dupont Circle, NW
Washington, DC 20036
(202) 939-9315

NOTES